S0-BAU-229

A HISTORY OF
WORLD SOCIETIES

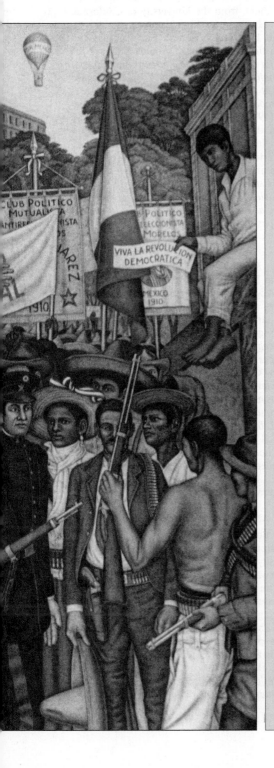

A HISTORY OF WORLD SOCIETIES

SECOND EDITION

VOLUME II:
SINCE 1500

JOHN P. McKAY

BENNETT D. HILL

JOHN BUCKLER

University of Illinois at Urbana-Champaign

HOUGHTON MIFFLIN COMPANY   BOSTON

Dallas   Geneva, Illinois   Palo Alto   Princeton

Text Credits Excerpts from "Richard II," Act II, Scene 1, and "Hamlet," Act III, Scene 1, from *The Complete Plays and Poems of William Shakespeare,* eds., William A. Neilson and C. J. Hill. Copyright © 1942 by Houghton Mifflin Company. Copyright renewed 1969. Reprinted by permission of the publisher. Tabular data from Philip D. Curtin, *Economic Change in Precolonial Africa: Senegambia in the Era of Slave Trade* (Madison: University of Wisconsin Press, 1975). Used by permission of the publisher. Tabular data from James A. Rawley, *The Transatlantic Slave Trade: A History* (New York: W. W. Norton, 1981). Used by permission of the publisher. Excerpts from Robert Edgar Conrad, *Children of God's Fire: A Documentary History of Black Slavery in Brazil,* pp. 20–23. Copyright © 1983 by Princeton University Press. Reprinted by permission of the publisher.

Chapter opener credits appear on page C-1.

Cover: Jose Sabogal, *Young Girl from Ayacucho,* 1937. The Museum of Modern Art, New York.

Copyright © 1988 by Houghton Mifflin Company. All rights reserved.

No part of this work may be reproduced or transmitted in any form or by any means, electronic or mechanical, including photocopying and recording, or by any information storage or retrieval system without the prior written permission of Houghton Mifflin Company unless such copying is expressly permitted by federal copyright law. Address inquiries to Permissions, Houghton Mifflin Company, One Beacon Street, Boston, MA 02108.

Printed in the U.S.A.

Library of Congress Catalog Card Number: 87–81266

ISBN: 0-395-36915-0

CDEFGHIJ–RM–9543210/898

About the Authors

John P. McKay Born in St. Louis, Missouri, John P. McKay received his B.A. from Wesleyan University (1961), his M.A. from the Fletcher School of Law and Diplomacy (1962), and his Ph.D. from the University of California, Berkeley (1968). He began teaching history at the University of Illinois in 1966 and became a professor there in 1976. John won the Herbert Baxter Adams Prize for his book *Pioneers for Profit: Foreign Entrepreneurship and Russian Industrialization, 1885–1913* (1970). He has also written *Tramways and Trolleys: The Rise of Urban Mass Transport in Europe* (1976) and has translated Jules Michelet's *The People* (1973). His research has been supported by fellowships from the Ford Foundation, the Guggenheim Foundation, the National Endowment for the Humanities, and IREX. His articles and reviews have appeared in numerous journals, including *The American Historical Review, Business History Review, The Journal of Economic History,* and *Slavic Review.* He edits *Industrial Development and the Social Fabric: An International Series of Historical Monographs.*

Bennett D. Hill A native of Philadelphia, Bennett D. Hill earned an A.B. at Princeton (1956) and advanced degrees from Harvard (A.M., 1958) and Princeton (Ph.D., 1963). He taught history at the University of Illinois at Urbana, where he was department chairman from 1978 to 1981. He has published *English Cistercian Monasteries and Their Patrons in the Twelfth Century* (1968) and *Church and State in the Middle Ages* (1970); and articles in *Analecta Cisterciensia, The New Catholic Encyclopaedia, The American Benedictine Review,* and *The Dictionary of the Middle Ages.* His reviews have appeared in *The American Historical Review, Speculum, The Historian, The Catholic Historical Review,* and *Library Journal.* He has been a fellow of the American Council of Learned Societies and has served on committees for the National Endowment for the Humanities. Now a Benedictine monk at St. Anselm's Abbey, Washington, D.C., he is also a Lecturer at Georgetown University, Washington, D.C.

John Buckler Born in Louisville, Ky., John Buckler received his B.A. from the University of Louisville in 1967. Harvard University awarded him the Ph.D. in 1973. From 1984 to 1986 he was the Alexander von Humboldt Fellow at Institut für Alte Geschichte, University of Munich. He is currently an associate professor at the University of Illinois, and is serving on the Subcommittee on Cartography of the American Philological Association. In 1980 Harvard University Press published his *The Theban Hegemony, 371–362 B.C.* His articles have appeared in journals both here and abroad, like the *American Journal of Ancient History, Classical Philology, Rheinisches Museum für Philologie, Classical Quarterly, Wiener Studien,* and *Symbolae Osloenses.*

CONTENTS

MAPS

PREFACE

A HISTORY OF WORLD SOCIETIES grew out of the authors' desire to infuse new life into the study of world civilizations. We knew full well that historians were using imaginative questions and innovative research to open up vast new areas of historical interest and knowledge. We also recognized that these advances had dramatically affected the subject of economic, intellectual, and, especially, social history, while new research and fresh interpretations were also revitalizing the study of the traditional mainstream of political, diplomatic, and religious development. Despite history's vitality as a discipline, however, it seemed to us that both the broad public and the intelligentsia were generally losing interest in the past. The mathematical economist of our acquaintance who smugly quipped "What's new in history?"—confident that the answer was nothing and that historians were as dead as the events they examine—was not alone.

It was our conviction, based on considerable experience introducing large numbers of students to the broad sweep of civilization, that a book reflecting current trends could excite readers and inspire a renewed interest in history and the human experience. Our strategy was twofold. First, we made social history the core element of our work. Not only did we incorporate recent research by social historians, but also we sought to re-create the life of ordinary people in appealing human terms. A strong social element seemed to us especially appropriate in a world history, for identification with ordinary people of the past allows today's reader to reach an empathetic understanding of different cultures and civilizations. At the same time we were determined to give great economic, political, intellectual, and cultural developments the attention they unquestionably deserve. We wanted to give individual readers and instructors a balanced, integrated perspective, so that they could pursue on their own or in the classroom those themes and questions that they found particularly exciting and significant.

Second, we made a determined effort to strike an effective global balance. We were acutely aware of the great drama of our times — the passing of the European era and the simultaneous rise of Asian and African peoples in world affairs. Increasingly, the whole world interacts, and to understand that interaction and what it means for today's citizens we must study the whole world's history. Thus we adopted a comprehensive yet realistic global perspective. We studied all geographical areas and the world's main civilizations, conscious of their separate identities and unique contributions. Yet we also stressed the links between civilizations, for these links eventually transformed multicentered world history into a complex interactive process of different continents, peoples, and civilizations in recent times. Finally, it was our place neither to praise nor to vilify our own civilization's major role in the growth of global integration, accepting it rather as part of our world heritage and seeking to understand it and the consequences for all concerned.

Changes in the Second Edition

In an effort to realize fully the potential of our fresh approach and balanced perspective, we have made many changes, large and small, in the second edition. First, we have worked hard to keep our book up-to-date, and every chapter has been carefully revised to incorporate recent scholarship. Many of our revisions relate to the ongoing explosion in social history, and once again important findings on such subjects as class relations, population, women, and the family have been integrated into the text. New scholarship also led to substantial revisions on many other questions, such as the Neolithic agricultural revolution and the first river civilizations, the Aryans in India, political and economic growth in ancient Greece, the rise and spread of Christianity, the dynastic cycle in China, the Germanic nobility, medieval feudalism, Muslim attitudes toward medieval Europe, the origins of the Renaissance, colonial administration in Latin America, Louis XIV and the French nobility, eighteenth-century absolutism, the French Revolution and Napoleon, nationalism in Asia, global inequality in the nineteenth century, and agricultural development in contemporary China. We believe that the incorporation of newer interpretations of the main European political developments in the medieval, early modern, and French revolutionary periods is a particularly noteworthy improvement in this edition. Recent developments around the world have also been systematically updated in Chapters 37–40 on the basis of considerable research.

Second, we have examined the entire book and each section in it for organization, clarity, and balance. Several medieval and early modern chapters, in particular, have been reorganized substantially to achieve a more logical presentation of material and a clearer chronological sequence. We have also taken special care to explain terms and concepts as soon as they are introduced. Above all, the treatment of non-European societies has been expanded and enriched, while the discussion of European developments has been reorganized and condensed. The most important changes in this regard may be noted.

The early development of Islam now receives a full chapter, based carefully on recent scholarship. More extensive discussion of Islamic areas continues throughout the book, most obviously in Chapter 23, where early modern Africa, the Ottoman Empire, and India are all treated in greater depth and with greater thematic unity. Similar treatment is accorded China and Japan in a separate and considerably revised Chapter 24. Other major non-European additions include new sections on early river civilizations in Chapter 1; early African societies, southern Africa, and Ethiopia in Chapter 16; the global consequences of industrialization in Chapter 30; and the development of Canada in Chapter 31. Our tightening up of European material has been painstaking and judicious. It includes a combination of two previous chapters into a single new one on three occasions: separate chapters on early and high medieval Europe have been restructured as Chapter 12, while the Renaissance and Reformation have been treated together in Chapter 17. Eighteenth-century European social and economic developments have been effectively integrated in Chapter 22. With these changes and other less noticeable modifications in the rest of the text, we feel we have succeeded in improving the geographical and cultural balance that we achieved in our first effort at world history.

Third, we have added or expanded material on previously neglected topics to help keep our work fresh and appealing. Coverage of religious developments, with special emphasis on their popular and social aspects, now extends from ancient to modern times. New sections address Islam in sub-Saharan Africa, heresies in medieval Europe, and popular religion in eighteenth-century Europe. The reader will also find new or expanded material on many other topics, notably ancient Israel, Theravada and Mahayana Buddhism, the Minoans, Greek and Roman wars, medieval Germany and the Hanseatic League, the Mongol conquest of China, the African slave trade, the Mayas, Hume and d'Holbach, the pre-revolutionary French elite, Mill, imperialism in Egypt, Palestine, neocolonialism, and Asian nationalism.

Finally, the illustrative component of our work has been completely revised. There are many new illustrations, including a tripling of the color plates that let both great art and earlier times come alive. Twenty-two new maps containing social as well as political material have also been added, while maps from the first edition have been re-edited and placed in a more effective format. As in the first edition, all illustrations have been carefully selected to complement the text, and all carry captions that enhance their value. Artwork remains an integral part of our book, for the past can speak in pictures as well as words.

Distinctive Features

Distinctive features from the first edition remain in the second. To help guide the reader toward historical understanding we have posed specific historical questions at the beginning of each chapter. These questions are then answered in the course of the chapter, each of which concludes with a concise summary of the chapter's findings. The timelines of the first edition have proved useful, and still more are found in this edition, including six double-page timelines that allow students to compare simultaneous developments within different world areas.

We have also tried to suggest how historians actually work and think. We have quoted extensively from a wide variety of primary sources and have demonstrated in our use of these quotations how historians sift and weigh evidence. We want the reader to realize that history is neither a list of cut-and-dried facts nor a senseless jumble of conflicting opinions. It is our further hope that the primary quotations, so carefully fitted into their historical context, will give the reader a sense that even in the earliest and most remote periods of human experience history has been shaped by individual men and women, some of them great aristocrats, others ordinary folk.

Each chapter concludes with carefully selected suggestions for further reading. These suggestions are briefly described in order to help readers know where to turn to continue thinking and learning about world history. The chapter bibliographies have been revised and expanded in order to keep them current with the vast and complex new work being done in many fields.

World civilization courses differ widely in chronological structure from one campus to another. To accommodate the various divisions of historical time into intervals that fit a two-quarter or two-semester period, *A History of World Societies* is being published in three versions, each set embracing the complete work:

One-volume hardcover edition, A HISTORY OF WORLD SOCIETIES; and a two-volume paperback, A HISTORY OF WORLD SOCIETIES *Volume I: To 1715* (Chapters 1–20), *Volume II: Since 1500* (Chapters 18–40); and a three-volume paperback, A HISTORY OF WORLD SOCIETIES *Volume A: From Antiquity Through the Middle Ages* (Chapters 1–16), *Volume B: From 1300 Through the French Revolution* (Chapters 15–25), *Volume C: From the French Revolution to the Present* (Chapters 25–40).

Note that overlapping chapters in the two- and three-volume sets permit still wider flexibility in matching the appropriate volume with the opening and closing dates of a course term.

Ancillaries

Learning and teaching ancillaries, including a *Study Guide, MicroStudy Plus, Instructor's Manual, Test Items, MicroTest,* and *Map Transparencies,* also contribute to the usefulness of the text. The excellent *Study Guide* has been revised by Professor James Schmiechen of Central Michigan University. Professor Schmiechen has continued to give us many valuable suggestions and his warmly appreciated support. His *Study Guide* contains chapter summaries, chapter outlines, review questions, extensive multiple-choice and geography exercises, self-check lists of important concepts and events, and a variety of study aids and suggestions. One innovation in the *Study Guide* that has proved useful to the student is the step-by-step Reading with Understanding exercises, which take the reader by ostensive example through reading and studying activities like underlining, summarizing, identifying main points, classifying information according to sequence, and making historical comparisons. To enable both students and instructors to use the *Study Guide* with the greatest possible flexibility, the guide is available in two volumes, with considerable overlapping of chapters. Instructors and students who use only Volumes A and B of the text have all the pertinent study materials in a single volume, *Study Guide, Volume 1* (Chapters 1–25); likewise, those who use only Volumes B and C of the text also have all the necessary materials in one volume, *Study Guide, Volume 2* (Chapters 15–40). The multiple-choice sections of the *Study Guide* are also available in a computerized version, *MicroStudy Plus,* which provides the student with tutorial instruction.

The *Instructor's Manual,* prepared by Professor Philip Adler of East Carolina University, contains learning objectives, chapter synopses, suggestions for lectures and discussion, paper and class activity topics, and lists of audio-visual resources. Also provided for class exercises are outline maps of the major world areas. The accompanying *Test Items,* also by Professor Adler, offers more than 1400 multiple-choice and essay questions and approximately 600 identification terms. *MicroTest* offers the test items to adopters on computer tape and disk. In addition, a set of fifty color map transparencies is available on adoption.

ACKNOWLEDGMENTS

It is a pleasure to thank the many instructors who have read and critiqued the manuscript through its development: Philip J. Adler, East Carolina University; Norman Beck, Lansing Community College; Dan Binkley, Hawaii Pacific College; Robert Brown, Sonoma State University; Arden K. Bucholz, State University of New York at Brockport; Thomas Callahan, Jr., Rider College; Dennis M. Castelli and his colleagues at Shippensburg State University: Paul Adams, James Coolsen, Paul Gill, Richard McLeod, Jack Morrison, and George Snow; Edward Colbert, Eastern Illinois University; Ronald Davis, Western Michigan University; Marc Gilbert, North Georgia College; Robert J. Gowen, East Carolina University; Joseph Kirklighter, Auburn University; Gary G. Kuhn, University of Wisconsin at La Crosse; Robert B. Luehrs, Fort Hays State University; David Northrup, Boston College; Vicente L. Rafael, University of Hawaii, Manoa; John D. Ruedy, Georgetown University; Steven Topik, University of California at Irvine; Richard H. Wilde, California State University at Long Beach; and Madeline C. Zilfi, University of Maryland.

Many of our colleagues at the University of Illinois kindly provided information and stimulation for our book, often without even knowing it. N. Frederick Nash, Rare Book Librarian, gave freely of his time and made many helpful suggestions for illustrations. The World Heritage Museum at the University continued to allow us complete access to its sizable holdings. James Dengate kindly supplied information on objects from the museum's collection. Caroline Buckler took many excellent photographs of the museum's objects and generously helped us at crucial moments in production. Such wide-ranging expertise was a great asset for which we are very appreciative. Bennett Hill wishes to express his sincere appreciation to Ramón de la Fuente of Washington, D.C., for his support, encouragement, and research assistance in the preparation of this second edition. John Buckler extends his thanks to Elke Bernlocher.

Each of us has benefited from the generous criticism of his co-authors, although each of us assumes responsibility for what he has written. John Buckler has written Chapters 1–8 and 11; Bennett Hill has continued the narrative in Chapters 9–10, 12–19, 23–24, and 31; and John McKay has written Chapters 20–22, 25–30, and 32–40. Finally, we continue to welcome from our readers comments and suggestions for improvements, for they have helped us greatly in this ongoing endeavor.

JOHN P. MCKAY
BENNETT D. HILL
JOHN BUCKLER

INTRODUCTION

THE ORIGINS OF MODERN WORLD SOCIETIES

THE ORIGINS of modern world societies lie in the ancient and medieval past. Scholars trace the roots of world civilizations to the ancient Middle East, India, and China. Geographical factors, especially four great rivers, conditioned the development of those civilizations. Early Egyptian society relied on the 4,000-mile-long Nile River. To the east, successive civilizations flourished in Mesopotamia, the area between the Tigris and the Euphrates rivers. The Indus River in northwestern India, which flows about 1,980 miles before reaching the ocean, nourished ancient Indian civilization. In China the Yellow River, 2,700 miles long, facilitated the birth of Chinese civilization. These rivers helped enrich the soil, allowing steadily expanding amounts of land to be cultivated and increasing amounts of food to be produced. Increased food production led to population growth and wealth, ingredients essential in the evolution of sophisticated social structures. The achievements of each society became the legacies that were absorbed and used by later cultures. History, the study of change over time, reveals that each age has reinterpreted the cultural legacy of its predecessors in the effort to meet its own needs. The modern world exists as the product of all that has gone before.

THE ANCIENT WORLD

The ancient world provided numerous cultural elements that the modern world has inherited. In the West first came the beliefs of the Hebrews (Jewish forebears) in one God and in a chosen people with whom God had made a covenant. The book known as the Scriptures, or "sacred writings," embodied Hebraic law, history, and culture. Second, Greek architectural, philosophical, and scientific ideas have exercised a profound influence on Western thought. Rome subsequently gave the West language and law. The Latin language became the instrument of verbal and written communication for over a thousand years; Roman concepts of law and government molded Western ideas of political organization. Finally, Christianity, the spiritual faith and ecclesiastical organization that derived from the Palestinian Jew, Jesus of Nazareth (ca 3 B.C.–A.D. 29), also conditioned Western religious, social, and moral values and systems.

The ancient Eastern world witnessed the appearance of religions and philosophies that have continued to influence modern societies. In South Asia before 250 B.C., Indians developed many views about the nature of life and the afterlife that affected all later generations. From India, Buddhism spread to China and other parts of Asia. Hinduism, a collection of religious beliefs that encompasses a sacred division of society, emerged to prove itself the dominant feature of India's cultural heritage. In China mastery of the land and evolution of a systematic method of agriculture that would support a large population led to a sophisticated intellectual life. The period before A.D. 200 witnessed the birth of three powerful forms of Chinese thought: Confucianism, Taoism, and Legalism.

THE HEBREWS

The Hebrews probably originated in northern Mesopotamia. Nomads who tended flocks of sheep, they were forced by drought to follow their patriarch Abraham into the Nile Delta in Egypt. The Egyptians enslaved them and put them to work on various agricultural and building projects. In the crucial event in early Jewish history, the lawgiver Moses, in response to God's command, led the Hebrews out of Egypt into the promised land (Palestine) in the thirteenth century B.C. At that time, the Hebrews consisted of twelve disunited tribes made up of families. They all believed themselves descendants of a common ancestor, Abraham. The family was their primary social institution, and most families engaged in agricultural or pastoral pursuits. Under the pressure of a series of wars for the control of Palestine, the twelve independent Hebrew tribes were united into a centralized political force under one king. Kings Saul, David, and especially Solomon (ca 965–925 B.C.) built the Hebrew nation with its religious center at Jerusalem, the symbol of Jewish unity.

The Hebrews developed their religious ideas in the Scriptures, also known as the Old Testament. In their migrations, the Jews had come in contact with many peoples, such as the Mesopotamians and the Egyp-

tians, who had many gods. The Jews, however, were monotheistic: their God was the one and only God, he had created all things, his presence filled the universe, and he took a strong personal interest in the individual. During the Exodus from Egypt, God had made a covenant with the Jews. He promised to protect them as his chosen people and to give them the land; in return, they must worship only him and obey the Ten Commandments that he had given Moses. The Ten Commandments comprise an ethical code of behavior, forbidding the Jews to steal, lie, murder, or commit adultery. This covenant was to prove a constant force in Jewish life. The Old Testament also contains detailed legal proscriptions, books of history, concepts of social and familial structure, wisdom literature, and prophecies of a Messiah to come. Parts of the Old Testament show the Hebraic debt to other cultures. For example, the Books of Proverbs and Sirach reflect strong Egyptian influences. The Jews developed an emotionally satisfying religion whose ideals shaped not only later faiths, such as Christianity and Islam, but also the modern world.

THE GREEKS

While ancient Middle Eastern peoples like the Hebrews interpreted the origins, nature, and end of man in religious terms, the Greeks treated these issues in terms of reason. In the fifth century B.C., small independent city-states (poleis) dotted the Greek peninsula. Athens, especially, created a brilliant culture that greatly influenced Western civilization. Athens developed a magnificent architecture whose grace, beauty, and quiet intensity still speak to humankind. In their comedies and tragedies, the Athenians Aeschylus, Sophocles, and Euripedes were the first playwrights to treat eternal problems of the human condition. Athens also experimented with the political system we call democracy. All free adult males participated directly in the making of laws and in the government of the polis. Since a large part of the population—women and slaves—were not allowed to share in the activity of the Assembly, and since aristocrats held most important offices in the polis, Athenian democracy must not be confused with modern democratic practices. The modern form of democracy, moreover, is representative rather than direct: citizens express their views and wishes through elected representatives. Nevertheless, in their noble experiment in which the people were the government, and in their view that the state existed for the good of the citizen, Athenians served to create a powerful political ideal.

Classical Greece of the fifth and fourth centuries B.C. also witnessed an incredible flowering of philosophical ideas. Though not the first people to speculate about the nature of man and the universe, Greeks were original in treating these questions in rational instead of religious terms. Hippocrates, the "father of medicine," taught that natural means—not magical or religious ones—could be found to fight disease. He based his opinions on observation and experimentation. Hippocrates also insisted that medicine was a branch of knowledge separate from philosophy. This distinction between natural science and philosophy was supported by the sophists, who traveled the Greek world teaching young men that human beings were the proper subject for study. They laid great emphasis on logic and the meaning of words and criticized traditional beliefs, religion, even the law of the polis.

Building on the approach of the sophists, Socrates (ca 470–399 B.C.) spent his life questioning and investigating. Socrates held that human beings and their environments represent the essential subject for philosophical inquiry. He taught that excellence could be learned and, by seeing excellence through knowledge, human beings could find the highest good and ultimately true happiness. Socrates' pupil, Plato (427–347 B.C.), continued his teacher's work. Plato wrote down his thoughts, which survive in the form of dialogues. He founded a school, the Academy, where he developed the theory that visible, tangible things are unreal, archetypes of "ideas" or "forms" that are constant and indestructible. In *The Republic,* the first literary description of a utopian society, Plato discusses the nature of justice in the ideal state. In *The Symposium,* he treats the nature and end of love.

Aristotle (384–322 B.C.), Plato's student, continued the philosophical tradition in the next generation. The range of his subjects of investigation is vast. He explores the nature of government in *Politics,* ideas of matter and motion in *Physics* and *Metaphysics,* outer space in *On the Heavens,* conduct in the *Nichomachian Ethics,* and language and literature in *Rhetoric.* In all his works, Aristotle emphasizes the importance of the direct observation of nature; he in-

sists that theory must follow fact. Led by thinkers such as Aristotle, the Greeks originated medicine, science, philosophy, and other branches of knowledge.

These phenomenal intellectual advances took place against a background of constant warfare. The long and bitter struggle between the cities of Athens and Sparta called the Peloponnesian War (459–404 B.C.) ended in Athens' defeat. Shortly afterward, Sparta, Athens, and Thebes contested for hegemony in Greece, but no single state was strong enough to dominate the others. Taking advantage of the situation, Philip II (359–336 B.C.) of Macedon, a small kingdom comprising part of modern Greece and Yugoslavia, defeated a combined Theban-Athenian army in 338 B.C. Unable to resolve their domestic quarrels, the Greeks lost their freedom to the Macedonian invader.

In 323 B.C. Philip's son, Alexander of Macedonia, died at the ripe age of 32. During the twelve short years of his reign, Alexander had conquered an empire stretching from Macedonia in the present-day Balkans across the Middle East into Asia as far as India. Because none of the generals who succeeded him could hold together such a vast territory, it disintegrated into separate kingdoms. Scholars label the period from ca 800 B.C. to 323 B.C., in which the polis predominated, the Hellenic Age. The time span from 323 B.C. to the collapse of Egypt to Rome in 30 B.C., which was characterized by independent kingdoms, is commonly called the Hellenistic Age. The Hellenistic period witnessed two profoundly significant developments: the diffusion of Greek culture through Asia Minor, and the further advance of science, medicine, and philosophy.

ROME

The city of Rome, situated near the center of the boot-shaped peninsula of modern Italy, conquered all of what it considered the civilized world. Rome's great achievement, however, rested in its ability not only to conquer peoples but to incorporate them into the Roman way of life. Rome created an empire that embraced the entire Mediterranean basin. It bequeathed to the Middle Ages and the modern world three great legacies: Roman law, the Latin language, and flexible administrative practices.

Scholars customarily divide Roman history into two stages: the Republic (ca 509–31 B.C.), during which Rome grew from a small city-state to an empire, and the Empire, the period when the old republican constitution fell to a constitutional monarchy. Between 509 and 290 B.C. Rome subdued all of Italy, and between 282 and 146 B.C. slowly acquired an overseas empire. The dominant feature of the social history of the early Republic was the clash between patrician aristocrats and plebeian commoners.

Whereas the Greeks speculated about the ideal state, the Romans pragmatically developed methods of governing themselves and their empire. Their real genius lay in government and law. Because the Romans continually faced concrete challenges, change was a constant feature of their political life. The senate acted as the most important institution of the Republic. Composed of aristocratic elders, it initially served to advise the other governing group, the magistrates. As the senate's prestige increased, its advice came to have the force of law. Roman law, called the *ius civilis* or "civil law," consisted of statutes, customs, and forms of procedure. The goal of the *ius civilis* was to protect citizens' lives, property, and reputations. As Rome expanded, first throughout Italy, then the Mediterranean basin, legal devices had to be found to deal with disputes among foreigners or between foreigners and Romans. Sometimes, magistrates adopted parts of other (foreign) legal systems. On other occasions, they used the law of equity: with no precedent to guide them, they made decisions on the basis of what seemed fair to all parties. Thus with flexibility the keynote in dealing with specific cases and circumstances, a new body of law, the *ius gentium* or "law of the peoples," evolved. This law was applicable to both Romans and foreigners.

Law was not the only facet of Hellenistic culture to influence the Romans. The Roman conquest of the Hellenistic East led to the wholesale confiscation of Greek sculpture and paintings to adorn Roman temples. Greek literary and historical classics were translated into Latin; Greek philosophy was studied in the Roman schools; Greek plays were adapted to the Roman stage; educated people learned Greek as a matter of course. Rome assimilated the Greek achievement, and Hellenism became an enduring feature of Roman life.

With territorial conquests Rome also acquired serious problems, which surfaced by the late second century B.C. Characteristically, the Romans responded practically with a system of provincial administration that placed at the head of local governments appointed state officials, who were formally incorporated into the Republic's constitution. The Romans devised an efficient system of tax collection as well. Overseas warfare required armies of huge numbers of men for long periods of time. A few officers gained fabulous wealth, but most soldiers did not and returned home to find their farms in ruins. Those with cash to invest bought up small farms, creating vast estates called *latifundia*. Since the law forbade landless men to serve in the army, most veterans migrated to Rome seeking work. Victorious armies had already sent tens of thousands of slaves to Rome, and veterans could not compete in the labor market with slaves. A huge unemployed urban proletariat resulted. Its demands for work and political reform were bitterly resisted by the aristocratic senate, and civil war characterized the first century B.C.

The reign of Augustus (31 B.C.–A.D. 14) marked the end of the Republic and the beginning of what historians call the "Empire." By fashioning a means of cooperation in government among the people, magistrates, senate, and army, Augustus established a constitutional monarchy that replaced the Republic. His own power derived from the various magistracies he held and the power granted him by the senate. Thus, as commander of the Roman army, he held the title of *imperator,* which later came to mean "emperor" in the modern sense of sovereign power. Augustus ended domestic turmoil and secured the provinces. He found new colonies, mainly in the western Mediterranean basis, which promoted the spread of Greco-Roman culture and the Latin language to the West. Colonists with latifundia exercised authority in the regions as representatives of Rome. (Later, after the Empire disintegrated, they continued to exercise local power.) Augustus extended Roman citizenship to all freemen. A system of Roman roads and sea lanes united the empire. For two hundred years the Mediterranean world experienced the *pax Romana* —a period of peace, order, harmony, and flourishing culture.

In the third century this harmony collapsed. Rival generals backed by their troops contested the imperial throne. In the disorder caused by the civil war that ensued, the frontiers were left unmanned, and Germanic invaders poured across the borders.

Throughout the Empire, civil war and barbarian invasions devastated towns and farms, causing severe economic depression. The emperors Diocletian (A.D. 285–305) and Constantine (A.D. 306–337) tried to halt the general disintegration by reorganizing the Empire, expanding the state of bureaucracy, and imposing heavier taxation. For administrative purposes, Diocletian divided the Empire into a western half and an eastern half. Constantine established the new capital city of Constantinople in Byzantium. The two parts drifted further apart in the fourth century, when the division became permanent. Diocletian's unrealistic attempt to curb inflation by arbitrarily freezing wages and prices failed. In the early fifth century the borders collapsed entirely, and various Germanic tribes completely overran the western provinces. In 410 and again in 455, Rome itself was sacked by the barbarians.

After the Roman Empire's decline, the rich legacy of Greco-Roman culture was absorbed by the medieval world and ultimately the modern world. The Latin language remained the basic medium of communication among educated people for the next thousand years; for almost two thousand years, Latin literature formed the core of all Western education. Roman roads, buildings, and aqueducts remained in use. Roman law left its mark on the legal and political systems of most European countries. Rome had preserved the best of ancient cultures for later times.

Roman military expansion to the east coincided with Chinese expansion to the west. The remarkable result was a period when the major civilizations of the ancient world were in touch with one another. In spite of constant warfare between the Roman emperors and the Persian kings in western Asia, important commercial contacts by land and maritime routes developed, linking the Roman world, China, and India. Over the famous Silk Road, named for the shipments of silk that passed from China through Parthia to the Roman Empire, were transported volumes of luxury goods, as well as ideas, artistic inspiration, and religious lore. Established in the second century A.D., this web of communication linking East and West was never entirely broken.

CHRISTIANITY

The ancient Western world also left behind a powerful religious legacy, Christianity. Christianity derives from the life, teachings, death, and resurrection of the Galilean Jew, Jesus of Nazareth (ca 3 B.C.–A.D. 29). Thoroughly Jewish in his teaching, Jesus preached the coming of the kingdom of God, a "kingdom not of this world," but one of eternal peace and happiness. He urged his followers and listeners to reform their lives according to the commandments, especially that stating, "You shall love the Lord your God with your whole heart, your whole mind, and your whole soul, and your neighbor as yourself." Thus, the heart of Christian teaching is love of God and love of neighbor. Some Jews believed that Jesus was the long-awaited Messiah. Others, to whom Jesus represented a threat to ancient traditions, hated and feared him. Though Jesus did not preach rebellion against the Roman governors, the Roman prefect of Judea, Pontius Pilate, feared that the popular agitation surrounding Jesus could lead to revolt against Rome. When Jewish leaders subsequently delivered Jesus to the Roman authorities, to avert violence Pilate sentenced him to death by crucifixion—the usual method for common criminals. Jesus' followers maintained that he rose from the dead three days later.

Those followers might have remained a small Jewish sect but for the preaching of the Hellenized Jew, Paul of Tarsus (ca A.D. 5–67), who traveled between and wrote letters to the Christian communities at Corinth, Ephesus, Thessalonica, and other cities. As the Roman Empire declined, Christianity spread throughout the Roman world. Because it welcomed people of all social classes, offered a message of divine forgiveness and salvation, and taught that every individual has a role to play in the building of the kingdom of God, thereby fostering a deep sense of community in many of its followers, Christianity won thousands of adherents. Roman efforts to crush Christianity failed. The emperor Constantine legalized Christianity, and in 392 the emperor Theodosius made it the state religion of the Empire. Carried by settlers, missionaries, and merchants to Gaul, Spain, North Africa, and Britain, Christianity formed a fundamental element of Western civilization.

INDIA

The vast subcontinent of India, protected from outsiders by the towering Himalayan Mountains to the north and by oceans on its three remaining borders, witnessed the development of several early civilizations, primarily in the richly cultivated Indus Valley. Only in the northwest—the area between modern Afghanistan and Pakistan—was India accessible to invasion. Through this region, by way of the Khyber Pass, the Aryans, a nomadic Indo-European people, penetrated India ca 1500 B.C. By 500 B.C. the Aryans ruled a number of large kingdoms in which cities were the centers of culture. The period of Aryan rule saw the evolution of a caste system designed to distinguish Aryan from non-Aryan and to denote birth or descent. The four groups that emerged—the Brahman (priest), the Kshatriya (warrior), the Vaishya (peasant), and the Shudra (serf)—became the permanent classes of Indian society. Those persons without a place in this division, or who lost their caste system by some ritual violation, were *outcastes.*

Through the Khyber Pass in 513 B.C. the Persian King Darius I entered India and conquered the Indus Valley. The Persians introduced techniques for political administration and for coin minting, and they brought India into commercial and cultural contact with the sophisticated ancient Middle East. From the Persians the Indians adopted the Aramaic language and script and adapted that script to their needs and languages. In 326 B.C. the Macedonian king, Alexander the Great, invaded the subcontinent, but his conquests had no lasting effect. Under Ashoka (269–232 B.C.), ancient India's greatest ruler, India enjoyed a high degree of peace and stability, but from 180 B.C. to A.D. 200 it suffered repeated foreign invasions.

India's most enduring legacies are the three great religions that flowered in the sixth and fifth centuries B.C.: Hinduism, Jainism, and Buddhism. One of the modern world's largest religions, Hinduism holds that the *Vedas,* or hymns in praise of the Aryan gods, are sacred revelations, and that these revelations prescribe the caste system. Religiously and philosophically diverse, Hinduism assures that there are many legitimate ways to worship Brahma, the supreme principle of life. India's best-loved hymn, the *Bhagavad Gita,* guides the Hindu in a pattern of life in the world and of release from it.

Jainism derives from the great thinker Vardhamana Mahavira (ca 540–468 B.C.), who held that only an ascetic life leads to bliss and that all life is too sacred to be destroyed. Nonviolence is a cardinal principle of Jainism. Thus, a Jain who wishes to do the least violence to life turns to vegetarianism.

Mahavira's contemporary, Siddhartha Gautama (ca 563–483 B.C.), better known as "Buddha," was so deeply distressed by human suffering that he abandoned his Hindu beliefs in a search for ultimate enlightenment. Meditation alone, he maintained, brought that total enlightenment in which everything is understood. Buddha developed the "Eightfold Path," a series of steps of meditation that could lead to *nirvana,* a state of happiness attained by the extinction of self and human desires. Buddha opposed all religious dogmatism and insisted that anyone, regardless of sex or class, could achieve enlightenment. He attracted many followers, and although Buddism split into two branches after his death, Buddhist teachings spread throughout India to China, Japan, Korea, and Vietnam. Buddhism remains one of the great Asian religions, and in recent times has attracted adherents in the West.

CHINA

Whereas Indian mystics discussed the goals and meaning of life in theological terms, Chinese thinkers were more secular than religious in outlook. Interested primarily in social and economic problems, they sought universal rules of human conduct. Ancient China witnessed the development of Confucianism, Taoism, and Legalism, philosophies that profoundly influenced subsequent Chinese society and culture.

K'ung Fu-tzu (551–479 B.C.), known in the West as "Confucius," was interested in orderly and stable human relationships, and his thought focused on the proper duties and behavior of the individual in society. Confucius considered the family the basic unit within society. Within the family male was superior to female, age to youth. If order is to exist in society, he taught, order must begin in the family. Only gentlemanly conduct, which involved a virtuous and ethical life, would lead to well-run government and peaceful conditions in society at large. Discipline of the self, courtesy to others, punctiliousness in service to the state, justice to the people—these virtues characterize the obligations and behavior of the Confucian gentleman. Confucius minimized the importance of class distinctions, and even men of humble birth, through education and self-discipline, could achieve a high level of conduct. The fundamental ingredient in the evolution of the Chinese civil service,

Confucianism continued to shape Chinese government up to the twentieth century.

Taoism treated the problems of government very differently. A school of thought ascribed to Lao-tzu, of whom little is known, Taoism maintained that people would find true happiness only if they abandoned the world and reverted to nature. Taoists insisted that the best government was the least active government. Public works and government services require higher taxes, which lead to unhappiness and popular resistance. According to the Taoists, the people should be materially satisfied and kept uneducated. A philosophy of consolation, Taoism enjoyed popularity with Chinese rulers and their governing ministers.

"Legalism" is the name given to a number of related political theories originating in the third century B.C. The founders of Legalism proposed pragmatic solutions to the problems of government, exalted the power of the state, and favored an authoritarian ruler who rooted out dissent. Though Legalism proposed an effective, if harsh, solution to the problems of Chinese society, it was too narrow in conception to compete successfully with Confucianism and Taoism.

In 256 B.C. the leader of the state of Ch'in deposed the ruling king and within thirty-five years won control of China. The new dynasty was called *Ch'in,* from which the Western term "China" derives. Under the Ch'in Dynasty and its successor, the Han, China achieved a high degree of political and social stability and economic prosperity. Though sometimes threatened by internal disorder and foreign invasion, China's cultural heritage remained strong. By the end of the Han Dynasty (ca A.D. 200), writing, Confucianism, and the strong political organization of a vast region had left an enduring mark on the Chinese people.

THE MIDDLE AGES IN EUROPE, CA 400–1400

Fourteenth-century European writers coined the term "Middle Ages," meaning a middle period of Gothic barbarism between two ages of enormous cultural brilliance—the Roman world of the first and second centuries, and their own age, the fourteenth century, which these writers thought had recaptured the true spirit of classical antiquity. Recent scholars have demonstrated that the thousand-year period between roughly the fourth and fourteenth centuries witnessed incredible developments: social, political, intellectual, economic, and religious. The men and women of the Middle Ages built on their cultural heritage and made phenomenal advances in their own right.

THE EARLY MIDDLE AGES

The time period that historians mark off as the early Middle Ages, extending from about the fifth to the tenth century, saw the emergence of a distinctly Western society and culture. The geographical center of that society shifted northward from the Mediterranean basin to western Europe. Whereas a rich urban life and flourishing trade had characterized the ancient world, the Germanic invasions led to the decline of cities and the destruction of commerce. Early medieval society was rural and local, with the farm or latifundium serving as the characteristic social unit. Several ingredients went into the making of European culture. First, Europe became Christian. Christian missionary activity led to the slow, imperfect Christianization of the Germanic peoples who had overrun the Roman Empire. Christianity introduced these peoples to a universal code of morality and behavior and served as the integrating principle of medieval society. Christian writers played a powerful role in the conservation of Greco-Roman thought. They used Latin as their medium of communication, thereby preserving it. They copied and transmitted classical texts. Writers such as St. Augustine of Hippo (354–430) used Roman rhetoric and Roman history to defend Christian theology. In so doing, they assimilated classical culture with Christian teaching.

Second, as the Germanic tribes overran the Roman Empire, they intermarried with the old Gallo-Roman aristocracy. The elite class that emerged held the dominant political, social, and economic power in early—and later—medieval Europe. Germanic custom and tradition, such as ideals of military prowess and bravery in battle, became part of the mental furniture of Europeans.

Third, in the eight century the Carolingian dynasty, named after its most illustrious member, Charles the Great, or Charlemagne (768–814), gradually acquired a broad hegemony over much of modern France, Germany, and northern Italy. Charlemagne's coronation by the pope at Rome in a ceremony filled with Latin anthems represented a fusion of classical, Christian, and Germanic elements. This Germanic warrior-king supported Christian missionary efforts and encouraged both classical and Christian scholarship. For the first time since the decay of the Roman Empire, Western Europe had achieved a degree of political unity. Similarly, the culture of Carolingian Europe blended Germanic, Christian, and Greco-Roman elements.

Its enormous size proved to be the undoing of the Carolingian empire, and Charlemagne's descendants could not govern it. Attacks by Viking (early Scandinavian), Muslim, and Magyar (early Hungarian) marauders led to the collapse of centralized power. Real authority passed into the hands of local strongmen. Scholars describe the society that emerged as feudal and manorial: a small group of military leaders held public political power. They gave such protection as they could to the people living on their estates. They held courts, coined money, and negotiated with outside powers. The manor or local estate was the basic community unit. Serfs on the manor engaged in agriculture, the dominant form of economy throughout Europe. Since no feudal lord could exercise authority or provide peace over a very wide area, political instability, violence, and chronic disorder characterized Western society.

The High and Later Middle Ages

By the beginning of the eleventh century, the European world showed distinct signs of recovery, vitality, and creativity. Over the next two centuries, that recovery and creativity manifested itself in every facet of culture—economic, social, political, intellectual, and artistic. A greater degree of peace paved the way for these achievements.

The Viking and Magyar invasions gradually ended. Warring knights supported ecclesiastical pressure against violence, and disorder declined. Improvements in farming technology, such as the use of the horse collar, led to an agricultural revolution. Farm land was better used and new land brought under cultivation. Agricultural productivity increased tremendously, leading to considerable population growth.

Increased population contributed to some remarkable economic and social developments. A salient manifestation of the recovery of Europe and of the vitality of the High Middle Ages was the rise of towns and concurrent growth of a new commercial class. Surplus population and the search for new economic opportunities led to the expansion of old towns, such as London and Cologne, and the foundation of completely new ones, such as Munich and Berlin. A new artisan and merchant class, frequently called the "middle class," appeared. In medieval sociology, only three classes existed: the clergy, who prayed; the nobility, who fought; and the peasantry, who tilled the land. The middle class, engaging in manufacturing and trade, seeking freedom from the jurisdiction of feudal lords, and pursuing wealth with a fiercely competitive spirit, fit none of the standard categories. Townspeople represented a radical force for change.

The twelfth and thirteenth centuries witnessed an enormous increase in the volume of local and international trade. For example, Italian merchants traveled to the regional fairs of France and Flanders to exchange silk from China and slaves from the Crimea for English woolens, French wines, and Flemish textiles. Strongly capitalistic, merchants adopted new business techniques to make more money. These developments added up to what scholars have termed a commercial revolution, a major turning point in the economic and social life of the West. The High Middle Ages saw the transformation of Europe from a rural and agrarian society into an urban and industrial one.

The High Middle Ages also saw the birth of the modern centralized state. Rome had bequeathed to Western civilization the concepts of the state and the law, but for centuries after the disintegration of the Roman Empire the state as a reality did not exist. Beginning in the twelfth century, kings worked to establish means of communication with all their peoples, to weaken the influence of feudal lords and thus to strengthen their own authority, and to build efficient bureaucracies. Drawing on the Roman *ius civilis,* kings often created courts of law, which served not only to punish criminals and reduce violence but also to increase royal income. Thus the law courts strengthened royal influence. People began to extend their primary loyalty to the king rather than to the "international" church or the local feudal lord. By the end of the thirteenth century, the kings of France and England had achieved a high degree of unity and laid the foundations of modern centralized states. In Italy, Germany, and Spain, however, strong independent local authorities continued to predominate.

In the realm of government and law, the Middle Ages made other powerful contributions to the modern world. The use of law to weaken feudal barons and to strengthen royal authority worked to increase respect for the law itself. Following a bitter dispute with his barons, King John of England (1199–1216) was forced to sign the document known as Magna Carta. Magna Carta contains the principle that there is an authority higher than the king to which even he is responsible: the law. The idea of the "rule of law" became embedded in the Western political consciousness. English kings following John recognized this common law, a law that their judges applied throughout the country. Exercise of common law often involved juries of local people to answer questions of fact. The common law and jury system of the Middle Ages have become integral features of Anglo-American jurisprudence. In the fourteenth century, kings also summoned meetings of the leading classes in their kingdoms, and thus were born representative assemblies, most notably the English parliament.

In their work of consolidation and centralization, kings increasingly used the knowledge of university-trained officials. Universities first emerged in western Europe in the thirteenth century. Medieval universities were educational guilds that produced educated and trained officials for the new bureaucratic states. The universities at Bologna in Italy and Montpellier in France, for example, were centers for the study of Roman law. After Aristotle's works had been translated from Arabic into Latin, Paris became the leading university for the study of philosophy and theology. Medieval scholastics (as philosophers and theologians were called because they belonged to schools) such as Thomas Aquinas (1225–1274) sought to harmonize Greek philosophy with Christian teaching. They wanted to use reason to deepen the understanding of what was believed on faith. Medieval universities developed the basic structures familiar to modern students: colleges, universities, examinations, and degrees. Colleges and universities represent a major legacy of the Middle Ages to the modern world.

Under the leadership of the Christian church, Christian ideals permeated all aspects of medieval culture. The village priest blessed the fields before the spring planting and the fall harvesting. Guilds of merchants sought the protection of patron saints. University lectures and meetings of parliaments began with prayers. Kings relied on the services of bishops and abbots in the work of the government. Around the parish church not only the religious life but the social, political, and often economic life of the community centered. The twelfth and thirteenth centuries witnessed a remarkable outburst of Christian piety, as the crusades (or "holy wars" waged against the Muslims for control of Jerusalem) and Gothic cathedrals reveal. More stone was quarried for churches in medieval France than had been mined in ancient Egypt, where the Great Pyramid alone consumed 40.5 million cubic feet of stone. Churches and cathedrals were visible manifestations of community civic pride. But ideals can rarely be achieved. As centuries passed, abuses in the church multiplied; so did cries for reform.

The high level of energy and creativity that characterized the twelfth and thirteenth centuries could not be sustained indefinitely. In the fourteenth century, every conceivable disaster struck western Europe. Drought or excessive rain destroyed harvests, causing widespread famine. The bubonic plague (or Black Death) swept across the continent, taking a terrible toll on population. England and France became deadlocked in a long and bitter struggle known as the Hundred Years' Year (1337–1453). Schism in the Catholic church resulted in the simultaneous claim by two popes of jurisdiction. Many parts of Europe experienced a resurgence of feudal violence and petty warfare. Out of this misery, disorder, and confusion, a new society gradually emerged.

THE ISLAMIC WORLD, CA 600–1400

One of the most important developments in world history and one whose consequences redound to our own day was the rise and remarkable expansion of the faith of Islam in the early Middle Ages. Inspired by Muhammad (ca 570–632), a devout merchant of Mecca in present-day Saudi Arabia, Islam united the many pagan tribes of Arabia before Muhammad's death. Within two centuries his followers controlled Syria, Palestine, Egypt, Iraq, Iran, northern India, Spain, and southern France, and his beliefs had been carried eastward across central Asia to the borders of China. In the ninth, tenth, and eleventh centuries the Muslims created a brilliant civilization centered at Baghdad in Iraq, a culture that has profoundly influenced Eastern and Western civilizations.

Muhammad believed that God sent him messages or revelations. These were later collected and published as the *Qur'an,* from an Arabic word meaning "reading" or "recitation." On the basis of God's revelations to him, Muhammad preached a strictly monotheistic faith based on the principle of the absolute unity and omnipotence of Allah, God. Since Allah is all-powerful, believers must submit to him. Thus, Islam means "submission to God," and the community of Muslims consists of those who have submitted to Allah by accepting the final revelation of his message as given by Muhammad. (Earlier revelations of Allah, held by Muslims to be the same God worshiped by Jews and Christians, had come from the prophets Abraham, Moses, and Jesus, whose work Muslims believe Muhammad completed.)

Driven by the religious zeal of the *jihad,* the obligation to expand their faith, Muslims carried their religion to the east and west by military conquest. Their own economic needs, the political weaknesses of their enemies, a strong military organization, and the practice of establishing army camps in newly conquered territories account for their rapid expansion.

The assassination of one of the caliphs, or successors of Muhammad, led to a division within the Islamic community. When the caliph Ali (656–661) was murdered, his followers claimed that because Ali (Muhammad's cousin and son-in-law) was related by blood to Muhammad, who in addition had designated him leader of the community prayer, Ali had been Muhammad's prescribed successor. These supporters of Ali were called *Shi'ites,* or *Shi'a,* partisans of Ali; they claimed to possess special divine knowledge that Muhammad had given his heirs. Other Muslims adhered to traditional beliefs and practices of the community based on the precedents set by Muhammad. They were called *Sunnis,* a term derived from the Arabic *Sunna,* a collection of Muhammad's sayings and conduct in particular situations. This schism within Islam continues today.

Long-distance trade and commerce, which permitted further expansion of the Muslim faith, played a prominent role in the Islamic world, in contrast to the limited position it held in the heavily agricultural medieval West. The Black and Caspian seas, the Volga River giving access deep into Russia, the Arabian Sea and the Indian Ocean, and to a lesser extent the Mediterranean Sea—these were the great commercial waterways of the Islamic world. Goods circulated freely over them. Muslim commercial techniques such as the bill of exchange, the check, and the joint stock company were borrowed by Westerners. Likewise, such financial and business terms as "check," "coffer," "cipher," "risk," and "zero" entered the English language from Arabic.

Long-distance trade brought the wealth that supported a gracious and sophisticated culture in the cities of the Muslim world. Baghdad in Iraq and Cordoba in Spain, whose streets were thronged with a kaleidoscope of races, creeds, customs, and cultures and whose many shops offered goods from all over the world, stand out as superb examples of cosmopolitan Muslim civilization. Baghdad and Cordoba were also great intellectual centers where Muslim scholars made advances in mathematics, medicine, and philosophy. The Arabs translated many ancient Greek texts by writers such as Plato and Aristotle. When, beginning in the ninth century, those texts were translated from Arabic into Latin, they came to play an important part in the formation of medieval European scientific, medical, and philosophical thought. Modern scholars consider Muslim civilization in the period from about 900 to 1200 among the most brilliant in the world's history.

TRADITION AND CHANGE IN ASIA, CA 320–1400

Between about 320 and 1400 the various societies of Asia continued to evolve their own distinct social, political, and religious institutions. These years also saw momentous changes sweep across Asia. Arab conquerors and their Muslim faith reached the Indian subcontinent. The Turks, moving westward from the Chinese border, converted to Islam. China, under the T'ang and Sung dynasties, experienced a "golden age." Japan emerged into the light of written history. These centuries witnessed cultural developments that have molded and influenced later Asian societies.

INDIA

Under the Gupta kings, who ruled from ca 320 to 500, India enjoyed a great cultural flowering. Interest in Sanskrit literature, the literature of the Aryans, led to the preservation of much Sanskrit poetry. A distinctly Indian drama appeared, and India's greatest poet Kalidasa (ca 380–450), like Shakespeare, blended poetry and drama. Mathematicians arrived at the concept of zero, essential for higher mathematics, and scientific thinkers wrestled with the concept of gravitation.

The Gupta kings succeeded in uniting much of the subcontinent. They also succeeded in repulsing an invasion of the Huns, but the effort exhausted the dynasty. After 600 India reverted to the pattern of strong local kingdoms in frequent conflict. Then, between 600 and 1400, India suffered repeated invasion as waves of Arabs, Turks, and Mongols swept down through the northwest corridor. By ca 1400 India was as politically splintered as it had been before Gupta rule. The most lasting impact of the invaders was the victory of Islam over Hinduism and Buddhism in the Indus Valley (modern Pakistan). Elsewhere Hinduism resisted Islam.

One other development had a lasting effect on Indian society: the proliferation and hardening of the caste system. Early Indian society had been divided into four major groups (see page xxii). After the fall of the Guptas, further subdivisions arose, reflecting differences of profession, trade, tribal or racial affiliation, religious belief, even place of residence. By 800 India had more than 3,000 castes, each with its own rules and governing body. As India was politically divided, so castes served to fragment it socially.

CHINA

Scholars consider the period between 580 and 1400, which saw the rule of the T'ang and Sung dynasties, as China's golden age. In religion, political administration, agricultural productivity, and art, Chinese society attained a remarkable level of achievement.

Merchants and travelers from India introduced Buddhism to China. Scholars, rulers, the middle classes, and the poor all found appealing concepts in Buddhist teachings, and the new faith won many adherents. China distilled Buddhism to meet its own needs, and Buddhism gained a place next to Confucianism in Chinese life.

The T'ang Dynasty, which some historians consider the greatest in Chinese history, built a state bureaucracy unequaled until recent times for its political sophistication. T'ang emperors subdivided the imperial administration into departments of military organization, maintenance and supply of the army, foreign affairs, justice, education, finance, building, and transportation. To staff this vast administration, an imperial civil service developed in which education, talent, and merit could lead to high office, wealth, and prestige. So effective was the T'ang civil service and so deep-rooted did it become in Chinese society that it lasted until the twentieth century.

Under the Sung Dynasty (960–1279), greatly expanded agricultural productivity, combined with advances in the technology of coal and iron and efficient water transport, supported a population of 100 million. (By contrast, Europe did not reach this figure before the late eighteenth century.) Greater urbanization followed in China. Political stability and economic growth fostered technological innovation, the greatest being the invention of printing. T'ang craftsmen invented the art of carving words and pictures into wooden blocks, inking them, and then pressing the blocks onto paper. The invention of movable type followed in the eleventh century. As happened in Europe in the fifteenth century, the invention of printing in China lowered the price and increased the availability of books and contributed to the spread of literacy. Printing led to the use of paper money, replacing the bulky copper coinage, and to developments in banking. The highly creative T'ang and Sung periods also witnessed the inventions of gunpowder, originally used for fireworks, and the abacus, which permitted the quick computation of complicated sums. Finally, in the creation of a large collection of fine poetry and prose, and in the manufacture of porcelain of superb quality and delicate balance, the T'ang and Sung periods revealed an extraordinary literary and artistic efflorescence.

Between 1127 and 1279 the Sung emperors built a large merchant marine fleet. Trade expanded as Japan and Korea eagerly imported Chinese silks and porcelains. The Muslims shipped Chinese goods across the Indian Ocean to East African and Middle Eastern markets. Southern China participated in a commercial network that stretched from Japan to the Mediterranean. The Mongol conquest of China (ca 1279) under Jenghiz Khan and his grandson Kublai Khan ended a glorious era in Chinese history and brought the country under foreign rule. In 1368 Hung Wu, the first emperor of the Ming Dynasty, restored Chinese rule.

JAPAN

The chain of islands that constitutes Japan entered the light of written history only in sporadic references in Chinese writings, the most reliable set down in A.D. 297. Because the land of Japan is rugged, lacking navigable waterways, and only perhaps 20 percent of it is arable, political unification by land proved difficult until modern times. The Inland Sea served both as the readiest means of communication and as a rich source of food; the Japanese have traditionally been fishermen and mariners.

Early Japan was divided into numerous political units, each under the control of a particular *clan,* a large group of families claiming descent from a common ancestor and worshipping a common diety. In the third century A.D. the Yamato clan gained control of the fertile area south of modern Kyoto near Osaka Bay and subordinated many other clans to it. The Yamato chieftain proclaimed himself emperor and assigned specific duties and functions to subordinate chieftains. The Yamato established their chief shrine in the eastern part (where the sun-goddess could catch the first rays of the rising sun) of Honshu, the largest of Japan's four main islands. Around this shrine local clan cults sprang up, giving rise to a native religion that the Japanese called *Shinto,* the "Way of the Gods." Shinto became a unifying force and the protectress of the nation. Through Korea two significant Chinese influences entered Japan and profoundly influenced Japanese culture: the Chinese system of writing and record keeping, and Buddhism. Under Prince Shotoku (574–622), talented young Japanese were sent to T'ang China to learn Chinese methods of administration and Chinese Buddhism. They returned to Japan to share and enforce what they had learned. The Nara era of Japanese history (710–794), so-called from Japan's first capital city north of modern Osaka, was characterized by the steady importation of Chinese ideas and methods. Buddhist monasteries became both religious and political centers, supporting Yamato rule.

In response to the attempt of a Buddhist monk at Nara to usurp the throne, in 770 the imperial family removed the capital to Heian (modern Kyoto), where it remained until 1867. A strong reaction against Buddhism and Chinese influences followed, symbolized by the severance of relations with China in 838. The eclipse of Chinese influences liberated Japanese artistic and cultural forces. A new Japanese style of art and architecture appeared. In writing, Japanese scholars modified the Chinese script. They produced two *syllabaries,* sets of phonetic signs that stand for syllables instead of whole words or letters. Unshackled from Chinese forms, Japanese writers created their own literary style and mode of expression. The writing of history and poetry flowered, and the Japanese produced their first novel, *The Tale of Genji,* a classic of court life by the court lady Murasaki Shikibu (978–ca 1016).

The later Heian period witnessed the breakdown of central authority as aristocrats struggled to free themselves from imperial control. In 1156 civil war among the leaders of the great clans erupted. By 1192 the Minamato clan had defeated all opposition. Their leader Yoritomo (1147–1199) became *shogun,* or general-in-chief. Thus began the Kamakura Shogunate, which lasted until 1333.

In addition to the powerful shogun, a dominant figure in the new society was the *samurai,* the warrior who by the twelfth century exercised civil, judicial, and military power over the peasants who worked the land. The samurai held his land in return for the promise to fight for a stronger lord. In a violent society strikingly similar to that of western Europe in the early Middle Ages, the Japanese samurai, like the French knight, constituted the ruling class at the local level. Civil war among the emperor, the leading families, and the samurai erupted again in 1331. In 1338 one of the most important military leaders, Ashikaga Takauji, defeated the emperor and established the Ashikaga Shogunate, which lasted until 1573. Meanwhile, the samurai remained the significant social figure.

AFRICA AND THE AMERICAS BEFORE EUROPEAN INTRUSION, CA 400–1500

Between approximately 400 and 1500, Africa and the Americas witnessed the development of highly sophisticated civilizations alongside a spectrum of more simply organized societies. Only recently have Asians, Europeans, and Americans learned very much about Africa and the Americas before the arrival of Columbus. The more that scholars have learned about these early civilizations, the more they have appreciated their richness, diversity, and dynamism.

EARLY AFRICAN SOCIETIES

Africa, the world's second largest continent (after Asia), covers 20 percent of the earth's land surface. Africa is diverse in both typography and peoples. Five geographical zones divide the continent, and geography has shaped the economic development of the peoples of Africa. The native Berbers of North Africa have intermingled with Phoenicians, Greeks, Italians, Muslim Arabs, and Spanish Jews, who over the centuries settled there. Egyptians are a cultural rather than a racial group, and black Africans live south of the 3.5 million–square mile desert, the Sahara.

A settled method of agriculture, expanding southward from the Atlantic in the west to the Nile in the east, reached the borders of the equatorial rain forest several millenia before Christ. Likewise, between 1000 B.C. and A.D. 200 the peoples of the Western Sudan shifted from nomadic hunting to settled agriculture. The village was the basic social unit, comprising families and clans affiliated by blood kinship. Extended families made up villages that collectively formed small kingdoms. The arrival of the camel ca A.D. 200 spurred the development of long-distance trade, which in turn fostered the expanded control of small kingdoms over sizable territories.

Between 200 and 700, a network of caravan routes running south from the Mediterranean coast across the terrible Sahara to the Sudan developed. Arab-Berber merchants exchanged manufactured goods for African gold, ivory, gum, and slaves from the West African savanna. This trade stimulated the mining of gold in parts of present-day Senegal, Nigeria, and Ghana, as well as the search for slaves for the Middle Eastern and European markets. In addition, the trans-Saharan trade encouraged the growth of urban centers in West Africa. Sizable concentrations of people grew at Jenne, Gao, Timbuktu, and Kumbi, each a center of the export-import trade and each ruled by black merchant dynasties. These cities played a dynamic role in the commercial life of West Africa and became centers of intellectual creativity. Perhaps the most far-reaching consequence of the trans-Saharan trade was the introduction of Islam to West Africa. Conversion led to the involvement of Muslims in African governments, bringing efficient techniques of statecraft and advanced scientific knowledge and engineering skills. Between the ninth and fifteenth centuries, Islam greatly accelerated the development of the African kingdoms.

The period from 800 to 1450 witnessed the flowering of several powerful African states. In the western Sudan, the large empires of Ghana (ca 900–1100) and Mali (ca 1200–1450) arose. Each had an elaborate royal court, massive state bureaucracy, sizable army, sophisticated judicial system, and strong gold industry. Indeed, the fame of Ghana rested on gold, and when the fabulously rich Mali king Mansa Musa (ca 1312–1327), a devout Muslim, made a pilgrimage to Mecca, his entourage included one hundred elephants, each carrying one hundred pounds of gold.

Meanwhile, the east African coast gave rise to powerful city-states such as Kilwa, Mombassa, and Mogadishu, which maintained a rich maritime trade with India, China, and the Muslim cities of the Middle East; like the Western Sudan, the east African cities were much affected by Muslim influences. In southern Africa the empire of Great Zimbabwe, built on the gold trade with the east coast, flourished between the eleventh and fifteenth centuries.

THE GEOGRAPHY AND PEOPLES OF THE AMERICAS

Across the Atlantic, several great Amerindian cultures flourished between 400 and 1500. The Americas, named for the Florentine explorer Amerigo Vespucci (1451–1512), who in 1502 sailed down the western coast of South America to Brazil, extend 11,000 miles from the Bering Strait to the tip of South America. Like Africa, Mexico and South America are geographically highly varied. Mexico is dominated by high plateaus bounded by coastal plains; thickly jungled lowlands run along the Caribbean coast of Central America, whose western uplands have a more temperate climate and fertile agricultural lands. South America contains the high Andes Mountains, plains around the continent's periphery, and tropical rain forests.

Asian peoples crossing the Bering Sea from Russian Siberia some 20,000 years ago migrated southward, and by 2300 B.C. settled in central Mexico and the area of modern Peru. They raised corn, beans, squash, and, in Peru, white potatoes. Careful cultivation of the land produced bumper crops, which contributed to a high fertility rate and in turn to a population boom. Amerindian civilizations used their large labor forces to construct religious and political buildings and standing armies.

Population growth facilitated the growth of successive Mesoamerican (the area of present-day Mexico and Central America) civilizations: the Olmec, Teotihuacán, and Toltec. Each of these societies was based on an agricultural economy, and each contained ceremonial centers to which pilgrims thronged. Each civilization collapsed before successive waves of new invaders, who absorbed the cultural legacy of their predecessors.

The last peoples to arrive in central Mexico were the Aztecs, who—building on Toltec antecedents—created the last unified civilization before the arrival of Europeans. Aztec society included a strong mercantile class, a nobility of soldiers and imperial officials, and a large population of agricultural and manual workers—all presided over by the fabulously rich court of the emperor. The Aztecs controlled a large confederation of city-states by sacrificing to their gods prisoners seized in battle and by demanding from subject states an annual tribute of people to be sacrificed. The sophistication of the Aztec cities astounded the Spanish, who subsequently conquered them. The capital city of Tenochitilán numbered perhaps 500,000 people, who thronged the flower-decked public squares and marketplaces where all varieties of goods were available. Aqueducts reflecting complicated engineering skills supplied the city with fresh water. In sculpture, architecture, and engineering, the Aztecs created a remarkably dynamic civilization.

So too did the Maya of Central America. They invented an original system of writing, a calendar considered more accurate than the European Gregorian calendar, and attained a level of mathematical knowledge not equaled by Europeans for centuries. Recent decipherment of Maya hieroglyphics reveals that their stele are actually historical documents providing enormous information about the Maya royal dynasties. The Maya proved themselves masters of abstract knowledge and of the recording of history.

Like the Aztecs, the Incas of Peru were a small militaristic group who vanquished surrounding peoples and established a strong empire. Whereas the Aztecs controlled subject peoples through terror, the Incas governed by cultural unification. They imposed their language and religion on newly conquered peoples, whom they transferred to areas that had long been under Inca rule. A remarkable system of roads, bridges, and tunnels linked the Inca Empire. Highly gifted organizers, the Incas created a state that was virtually unique for its time in assuming responsibility for the social welfare of all its people.

EARLY MODERN EUROPE, CA 1400–1600

The period frequently labeled early modern Europe was an age of great change in European society. Men and women of the Renaissance and the Reformation laid the foundations of a new Europe. But Europe remained very different from our modern contemporary world. The industrial and the French revolutions, the growth of nationalism, and the profound secularization of culture occurred in the eighteenth and nineteenth centuries; these forces unleashed what we mean when we speak of the "modern world." By late twentieth-century standards, fifteenth- and sixteenth-century Europe remained—in its class structure, economic life, technology, and methods of communication—closer to imperial Rome than to present-day Europe and America.[1] Our emphasis, therefore rests on *early* modern Europe, which nevertheless saw phenomenal development. The Renaissance, the Reformation, and the expansion of Europe overseas drastically altered European attitudes, values, and lifestyles.

THE RENAISSANCE

While war, famine, disease, and death swept across northern Europe in the fourteenth century, a new culture was emerging in Italy. Italian society underwent great changes. In the fifteenth century, these phenomena spread beyond Italy and gradually influenced northern Europe. These cultural changes have collectively been called the Renaissance. The

[1] Eugene F. Rice, *The Foundations of Early Modern Europe, 1460–1559,* W. W. Norton & Co., New York, 1970, p. x.

Italian Renaissance evolved in two broad and overlapping stages. In the first period, ca 1050 to 1300, a new economy emerged, based on Venetian and Florentine banking and cloth manufacturing. At the end of the thirteenth century, Florentine bankers gained control of the papal banking. From this position as tax collectors for the papacy, Florentine mercantile families began to dominate. The wealth so produced brought into existence a new urban and aristocratic class.

In the industrial cities of Venice and Florence, this new aristocratic class governed as oligarchs: they maintained the façade of republican government in which political power theoretically resides in the people and is exercised by their chosen representatives, but, in fact, they ruled. In cities with strong agricultural bases, such as Verona, Mantua, and Ferrara, despots predominated. In the fifteenth century, political power and elite culture centered at the princely courts of oligarchs and despots. At his court the Renaissance prince displayed his patronage of the arts and learning.

The second stage of the Italian Renaissance, which lasted from about 1300 to 1600, was characterized by extraordinary manifestations of intellectual and artistic energies. Scholars commonly use the French term *renaissance* ("rebirth") to describe the cultural achievements of the fourteenth through sixteenth centuries. As an intellectual movement the Renaissance possed certain hallmarks that held profound significance for the evolution of the modern world.

Fourteenth- and fifteenth-century Italians had the self-conscious awareness that they were living in new times. They believed that theirs was a golden age of creativity, an age of rebirth of classical antiquity. They identified with early Greek and Roman philosophers and artists, copied the lifestyles of the ancients, and expressed contempt for their immediate medieval past. Second, the Renaissance manifested a new attitude toward men, women, and the world, an attitude often described as individualism. Individualism stressed personality, uniqueness, genius, the fullest possible development of human potential. Artist, athlete, sculptor, scholar, whatever—a person's potential should be stretched until fully realized. The thirst for fame, the burning quest for glory was a central component of Renaissance individualism.

Closely connected with individualism was a deep interest in the Latin classics. This feature of the Renaissance became known as "the new learning," or simply "humanism." The terms "humanism" and "humanist" derive from the Latin *humanitas,* which refers to the literary culture needed by anyone who would be considered educated or civilized. Humanists studied the Latin classics to discover past insights into human nature.

A new secular spirit constitutes another basic feature of the Italian Renaissance. Secularism involves a greater regard for, and interest in, the things of this world, rather than in otherworldly concerns. Medieval people certainly pursued financial profits ruthlessly, and Renaissance men and women had deep spiritual concerns. In the Middle Ages, however, the dominant ideals focused on life after death. The fourteenth and fifteenth centuries witnessed the slow and steady growth of secularism in Italy. Economic changes, preoccupation with money-making, and the rising prosperity of the Italian cities precipitated a fundamental change in the attitudes and values of the urban aristocracy and bourgeoisie.

The age also saw profound social changes that have enormously influenced the modern West. The invention of the printing press in the mid-fifteenth century revolutionized communication. Printing made governmental propaganda possible, bridged the gap between the oral and written cultures, and stimulated the literacy of lay people. Whereas women in the Middle Ages often had great responsibilities, in the Renaissance their purpose came merely to be decorative—to grace the courts of princes and aristocrats. As servants and slaves, black people entered Europe during the Renaissance in sizable numbers for the first time since the collapse of the Roman Empire. In northern Europe urban merchants and rural gentry allied with rising monarchies. With the newly levied taxes paid by businesspeople, kings provided a greater degree of domestic peace and order. In Spain, France, and England, rulers also emphasized royal dignity and authority; they used the tough ideas of the Italian political theorist Machiavelli to ensure the preservation and continuation of their governments. Feudal monarchies gradually evolved in the direction of nation-states.

As the intellectual features of the Renaissance spread outside Italy, they affected the culture of all Europe. A secular attitude toward life has become one of the dominant features of modern Western societies. Its germ was planted in the attitudes and approaches of the Italian humanists. Those humanists studied classical literature to understand human nature and to strengthen their interest in the world around them. Similarly, a strong belief in the complete realization of individual potential has become an abiding component of the Western world-view.

THE REFORMATION

The idea of reform is as old as Christianity itself. Jesus had preached the coming of the kingdom of God through the reform of the individual, and through the centuries his cry has been repeated. The need for the reform of the individual Christian and of the institutional church is central to the Christian faith. Christian humanists of the fifteenth and sixteenth centuries urged the reform of the church on the pattern of the early Christian communities.

In 1517 Martin Luther (1483–1546), a professor of Scripture at a minor German university, launched an attack on certain church practices. Asked to recant, Luther rejected church authority itself. The newly invented printing press swept Luther's prolific ideas across Germany and Europe. He and other reformers soon won the support of northern German princes who embraced Luther's reforming or "Protestant" ideas. Some of the princes coveted church lands and revenues. Others resented the authority of the strongly Catholic Holy Roman Emperor, Charles V. By accepting Luther's religious ideas—and thereby denying orthodox Catholic doctrine—the princes also rejected the emperor's political authority. In a world that insisted on the necessity on religious unity for political order and social stability, the adoption of the new faith implied political opposition. In England, largely because the papacy would not approve his request for a divorce, King Henry VIII (1509–1547) broke with Rome and established the English Church. Kings and princes, political and economic issues played the decisive role in the advance of the Reformation.

In the first half of the sixteenth century, perhaps a fourth of the population of Western Europe accepted some version of Protestantism. Besides northern Germany, all of Scandinavia, England, Scotland, and the cities of Geneva and Zurich in Switzerland and Strasbourg in Germany rejected the religious authority of the Roman church and adopted new faiths. The number of Protestant sects proliferated, but the core of Protestant doctrine remained. First, Protestants believe that salvation comes by faith alone, not from faith and good works, as Catholic teaching asserts. Second, authority in the Christian church resides in the Scriptures, not in tradition or papal authority (which all Protestants rejected). The church itself consists of the community of all believers; medieval churchmen had tended to identify the church with the clergy.

In the later sixteenth century, the Roman church worked to clean up its house. The Council of Trent, meeting intermittently from 1545 to 1563, suppressed pluralism and the sale of church offices, redefined doctrine, made provision for the education of all the clergy, and laid the basis for general spiritual renewal. New religious orders, such as the Society of Jesus (or Jesuits), sought to re-convert Protestants. A new church department, the Holy Office, tried to impose doctrinal uniformity everywhere.

The break with Rome and the rise of Lutheran, Anglican, Calvinist, and other faiths shattered the unity of Europe as an organic Christian society. On the other hand, religious belief remained exceedingly strong. In fact, the strength of religious convictions caused political fragmentation. In the later sixteenth and throughout most of the seventeenth centuries, religion and religious issues continued to play a major role in the lives of individuals and in the policies and actions of governments. Religion, whether Protestant or Catholic, decisively influenced the evolution of national states. Though most reformers rejected religious toleration, they helped pave the way for the toleration and pluralism that characterize the modern world.

BENNETT D. HILL

18

NE.NOSE

**THE AGE OF EUROPEAN
EXPANSION AND
RELIGIOUS WARS**

*B*ETWEEN 1450 AND 1650 two developments dramatically altered the world in which Europeans lived: overseas expansion and the reformations of the Christian churches. Overseas expansion broadened Europeans' geographical horizons and brought them into confrontation with ancient civilizations in Africa, Asia, and the Americas. These confrontations led first to conquest, then to exploitation, and finally to profound social changes in both Europe and the conquered territories. Likewise, the Renaissance and the reformations drastically changed intellectual, political, religious, and social life in Europe. War and religious issues dominated the politics of European states. Though religion was commonly used to rationalize international conflict, wars were fought for power and territorial expansion.

Meanwhile, Europeans carried their political, religious, and social attitudes to the territories they subdued. Why, in the sixteenth and seventeenth centuries, did a relatively small number of people living on the edge of the Eurasian land mass gain control of the major sea lanes of the world and establish political and economic hegemony on distant continents? How were a few Spaniards, fighting far from home, able to overcome the powerful Aztec and Inca empires in America? What effect did overseas expansion have on Europe and on conquered societies? What were the causes and consequences of the religious wars in France, the Netherlands, and Germany? How did the religious crises of this period affect the status of women? How and why did African slave labor become the dominant form of labor organization in the New World? What religious and intellectual developments led to the growth of skepticism? What literary masterpieces of the English-speaking world did this period produce? This chapter will address these questions.

DISCOVERY, RECONNAISSANCE, AND EXPANSION

Historians have variously called the period from 1450 to 1650 the "Age of Discovery," "Age of Reconnaissance," and "Age of Expansion." All three labels are appropriate. *Age of Discovery* refers to the

World Map of Vesconte Maggioli, 1511 Renaissance geographers still accepted the Greco-Egyptian Ptolemy's theory (second century A.D.) that the earth was one continuous land mass. Cartographers could not subscribe to the idea of a new, separate continent. Thus, this map, inaccurate when it was drawn, shows America as an extension of Asia. *(John Carter Brown Library, Brown University, Providence)*

era's phenomenal advances in geographical knowledge and technology, often achieved through trial and error. In 1350 it took as long to sail from the eastern end of the Mediterranean to the western end as it had taken a thousand years earlier. Even in the fifteenth century, Europeans knew little more about the earth's surface than the Romans had. By 1650, however, Europeans had made an extensive reconnaissance—or preliminary exploration—and had sketched fairly accurately the physical outline of the whole earth. Much of the geographical information they had gathered was tentative and not fully understood—hence the appropriateness of the term *Age of Reconnaissance.*

Age of Expansion refers to the migration of Europeans to other parts of the world. This colonization resulted in political control of much of South and North America; of coastal regions of Africa, India, China, and Japan; and of many Pacific islands. Political hegemony was accompanied by economic exploitation, religious domination, and the introduction of European patterns of social and intellectual life. The sixteenth-century expansion of European society launched a new age in world history.

OVERSEAS EXPLORATION AND CONQUEST

The outward expansion of Europe began with the Viking voyages across the Atlantic in the ninth and tenth centuries. Under Eric the Red and Leif Ericson, the Vikings discovered Greenland and the eastern coast of North America. The Crusades of the eleventh through thirteenth centuries were another phase in Europe's attempt to explore, Christianize, and exploit peoples on the periphery of the Continent. But these early thrusts outward resulted in no permanent settlements. The Vikings made only quick raids in search of booty. Lacking stable political institutions

in Scandinavia, they had no workable forms of government to impose on distant continents. In the twelfth and thirteenth centuries, the lack of a strong territorial base, weak support from the West, and sheer misrule combined to make the medieval Crusader kingdoms short-lived. Even in the mid-fifteenth century, Europe seemed ill prepared for international ventures. By 1450 a grave new threat had appeared in the East—the Ottoman Turks.

Combining excellent military strategy with efficient administration of their conquered territories, the Turks had subdued most of Asia Minor and begun to settle on the western side of the Bosporus. The Ottoman Turks under Sultan Muhammad II (1451–1481) captured Constantinople in 1453, pressed into the Balkans, and by the early sixteenth century controlled the eastern Mediterranean. The Turkish menace badly frightened Europeans. In France in the fifteenth and sixteenth centuries, twice as many books were printed about the Turkish threat as about the American discoveries. The Turks imposed a military blockade on eastern Europe, thus forcing Europeans' attention westward. Yet the fifteenth and sixteenth centuries witnessed a fantastic continuation, on a global scale, of European expansion.

Portugal, situated on the extreme southwestern edge of the European continent, got the start on the rest of Europe. Its taking of Ceuta, an Arab city in northern Morocco, in 1415 marked the beginning of European exploration and control of overseas territory. The objectives of Portuguese policy included the Christianization of Muslims and the search for gold, for an overseas route to the spice markets of India, and for the mythical Christian ruler of Ethiopia, Prester John.

In the early phases of Portuguese exploration, Prince Henry (1394–1460), called "the Navigator" because of the annual expeditions he sent down the western coast of Africa, played the leading role. In the fifteenth century, most of the gold that reached Europe came from the Sudan in West Africa and from Ashanti blacks living near the area of present-day Ghana. Muslim caravans brought the gold from the African cities of Niani and Timbuktu and carried it north across the Sahara to Mediterranean ports. Then the Portuguese muscled in on this commerce in gold. Prince Henry's carefully planned expeditions succeeded in reaching Guinea, and, under King John

II (1481–1495), the Portuguese established trading posts and forts on the Guinea coast and penetrated into the continent all the way to Timbuktu (Map 18.1). Portuguese ships transported gold to Lisbon, the Portugese capital, and by 1500 Portugal controlled the flow of gold to Europe. The golden century of Portuguese prosperity had begun.

Still the Portuguese pushed farther south down the west coast of Africa. In 1487 Bartholomew Diaz rounded the Cape of Good Hope at the southern tip, but storms and a threatened mutiny forced him to turn back. On a second expedition (1497–1499), the Portuguese mariner Vasco da Gama reached India and returned to Lisbon loaded with samples of Indian wares. King Manuel (1495–1521) promptly dispatched thirteen ships under the command of Pedro Alvares Cabral, assisted by Diaz, to set up trading posts in India. On April 22, 1500, the coast of Brazil in South America was sighted and claimed for the crown of Portugal. Cabral then proceeded south and east around the Cape of Good Hope and reached India. Half the fleet was lost on the return voyage, but the six spice-laden vessels that dropped anchor in Lisbon harbor in July 1501 more than paid for the entire expedition. Thereafter, convoys were sent out every March. Lisbon became the entrance port for Asian goods into Europe—but not without a fight.

For centuries the Muslims had controlled the rich spice trade of the Indian Ocean, and they did not surrender it willingly. Portuguese commercial activities were accompanied by the destruction or seizure of strategic Muslim coastal forts, which later served Portugal as both trading posts and military bases. Alfonso de Albuquerque, whom the Portuguese crown appointed as governor of India (1509–1515), decided that these bases and not inland territories should control the Indian Ocean. Accordingly, his cannon blasted open the ports of Calicut, Ormuz, Goa, and Malacca, the vital centers of Arab domination of south Asian trade. This bombardment laid the foundation for Portuguese imperialism in the sixteenth and seventeenth centuries — a strange way to bring Christianity to "those who were in darkness." As one scholar wrote about the opening of China to the West, "while Buddha came to China on white elephants, Christ was borne on cannon balls."[1]

Political centralization in Spain helps to explain that country's outward push. In the fifteenth century, Isabella and Ferdinand had consolidated their several kingdoms to achieve a more united Spain. The Catholic rulers reduced the powers of the nobility, revamped the Spanish bureaucracy, and humbled dissident elements, notably the Muslims and the Jews. The Spanish monarchy was stronger than ever before and in a position to support foreign ventures; it could bear the costs and dangers of exploration.

In March 1493, Spanish ships entered Lisbon harbor bearing a triumphant Italian explorer in the service of the Spanish monarchy. Christopher Columbus (1451–1506), a Genoese mariner, had secured Spanish support for an expedition to the East. He sailed from Palos, Spain, to the Canary Islands and crossed the Atlantic to the Bahamas, landing in October 1492 on an island that he named "San Salvador" and believed to be off the coast of India. Like most people of his day, Columbus was deeply religious. The crew of his flagship, *Santa Maria,* recited vespers every night and sang a hymn to the Virgin before going to bed. Nevertheless, the Spanish fleet, sailing westward to find the East, sought wealth as well as souls to convert.

Between 1492 and 1502, Columbus made four voyages to America, discovering all the major islands of the Caribbean—Haiti (which he called "Dominica" and the Spanish named "Hispaniola"), San Salvador, Puerto Rico, Jamaica, Cuba, Trinidad—and Honduras in Central America. Columbus believed until he died that the islands he found were off the coast of India. In fact, he had opened up for the rulers of Spain a whole new world. The Caribbean islands —the West Indies—represented to Spanish missionary zeal millions of Indian natives for conversion to Christianity. Hispaniola, Puerto Rico, and Cuba also offered gold.

The search for precious metals determined the direction of Spanish exploration and expansion into South America. When it became apparent that placer mining (in which ore is separated from soil by panning) in the Caribbean islands was slow and the rewards slim, new routes to the East and new sources of gold and silver were sought.

In 1519 the Spanish ruler Charles V commissioned Ferdinand Magellan (1480–1521) to find a direct route to the Moluccan Islands off the southeast coast of Asia. Magellan sailed southwest across the Atlantic to Brazil and proceeded south around Cape Horn into the Pacific Ocean (see Map 18.1). He crossed the Pacific, sailing west, to the Malay Archipelago, which

Columbus Lands on San Salvador The printed page and illustrations, such as this German woodcut, spread reports of Columbus's voyage all over Europe. According to Columbus, a group of naked Indians greeted the Spaniards' arrival. Pictures of the Indians as "primitive" and "uncivilized" instilled prejudices that centureis have not erased. *(New York Public Library)*

he called the "Western Isles." (These islands were conquered in the 1560s and named the "Philippines" for Philip II of Spain.)

Though Magellan was killed, the expedition continued, returning to Spain in 1522 from the east by way of the Indian Ocean, the Cape of Good Hope, and the Atlantic. Terrible storms, mutiny, starvation, and disease haunted this voyage. Nevertheless, it verified Columbus's theory that the earth was round and brought information about the vastness of the Pacific. Magellan also proved that the earth was much larger than Columbus and others had believed.

In the West Indies, the slow recovery of gold, the shortage of a healthy labor force, and sheer restlessness speeded up Spain's search for wealth. In 1519,

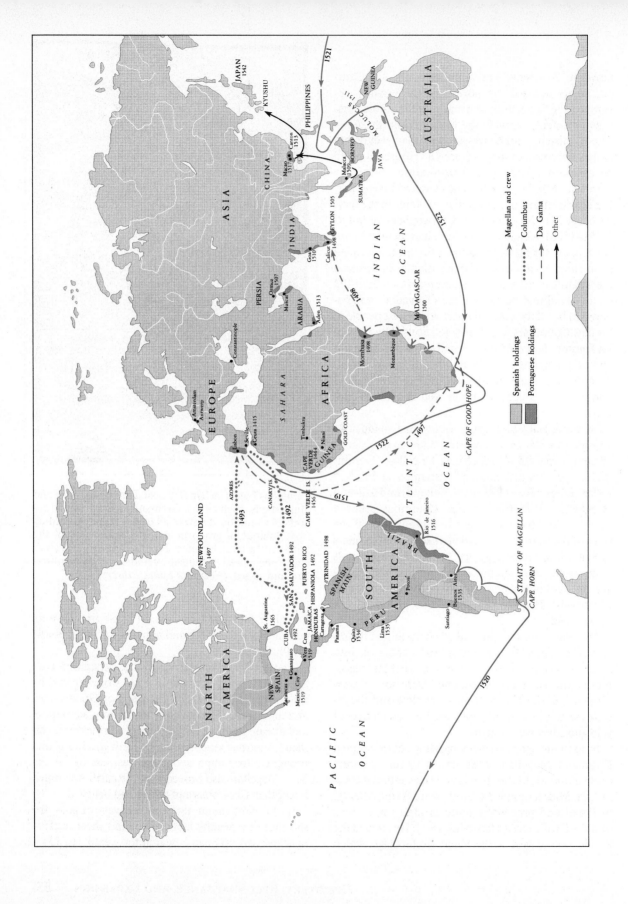

Map 18.1 Overseas Exploration and Conquest, Fifteenth and Sixteenth Centuries The voyages of discovery marked another phase in the centuries-old migrations of European peoples. Consider the major contemporary significance of each of the voyages depicted on the map.

the year Magellan departed on his worldwide expedition, a brash and determined Spanish adventurer, Hernando Cortés (1485–1547), crossed from Hispaniola to mainland Mexico with six hundred men, seventeen horses, and ten cannon. Within three years, Cortés had conquered the fabulously rich Aztec Empire, taken captive the Aztec emperor Montezuma, and founded Mexico City as the capital of New Spain. The subjugation of northern Mexico took longer, but between 1531 and 1550 the Spanish gained control of Zacatecas and Guanajuato, where rich silver veins were soon tapped.

Another Spanish conquistador (explorer), Francisco Pizarro (1470–1541), repeated Cortés's feat in Peru. Between 1531 and 1536, with even fewer resources, Pizarro crushed the Inca Empire in northern South America and established the Spanish viceroyalty of Peru with its center at Lima. In 1545 Pizarro opened at Potosí in the Peruvian highlands what became the richest silver mines in the New World.

Between 1525 and 1575, the riches of the Americas poured into Lisbon and the Spanish port of Seville. For all their new wealth, however, Lisbon and Seville did not become important trading centers. It was the Flemish city of Antwerp, controlled by the Spanish Habsburgs, that developed into the great entrepôt for overseas bullion and Portuguese spices and served as the commercial and financial capital of the entire European world.

Since the time of the great medieval fairs, cities of the Low Countries had been important sites for the exchange of products from the Baltic and Italy. Antwerp, ideally situated on the Scheldt River at the intersection of many trading routes, steadily expanded as the chief intermediary for international commerce and finance. English woolens; Baltic wheat, fur, and timber; Portuguese spices; German iron and copper; Spanish fruit; French wines and dyestuffs; Italian silks, marbles, and mirrors; together with vast amounts of cash—all were exchanged at Antwerp.

The city's harbor could dock 2,500 vessels at once, and 5,000 merchants from many nations gathered daily in the *bourse* (exchange).

By the end of the sixteenth century, Amsterdam had overtaken Antwerp as the financial capital of Europe (see page 610). The Dutch had also embarked on foreign exploration and conquest. The Dutch East India Company, founded in 1602, became the major organ of Dutch imperialism and within a few decades expelled the Portuguese from Ceylon and other East Indian islands. By 1650 the Dutch West India Company had successfully intruded on the Spanish possessions in America and gained control of much of the African and American trade.

English and French explorations lacked the immediate, sensational results of the Spanish and Portuguese. In 1497 John Cabot, a Genoese merchant living in London, sailed for Brazil but discovered Newfoundland. The next year he returned and explored the New England coast and perhaps as far south as Delaware. Since these expeditions found no spices or gold, King Henry VII lost interest in exploration. Between 1534 and 1541, the Frenchman Jacques Cartier made several voyages and explored the Saint Lawrence region of Canada, but the first permanent French settlement, at Quebec, was not founded until 1608.

The Explorers' Motives

The expansion of Europe was not motivated by demographic pressures. The Black Death had caused serious population losses from which Europe had not recovered in 1500. Few Europeans immigrated to North or South America in the sixteenth century. Half of those who did sail to begin a new life in the Americas died en route; half of those who reached the New World eventually returned to their homeland. Why, then, did explorers brave the Atlantic and Pacific oceans, risking their lives to discover new continents and spread European culture?

The reasons are varied and complex. People of the sixteenth century were still basically medieval in the sense that their attitudes and values were shaped by religion and expressed in religious terms. In the late fifteenth century, crusading fervor remained a basic part of the Portuguese and Spanish national ideal. The desire to Christianize Muslims and pagan peoples played a central role in European expansion, as evidenced by Columbus's explanation of his first voyage:

And Your Highnesses, as Catholic Christians and Princes devoted to the Holy Christian Faith and the propagators thereof, and enemies of the sect of Mahomet and of all idolatries and heresies, resolved to send me . . . to the said regions of India, to see the said princes and peoples and lands and [to observe] the disposition of them and of all, and the manner in which may be undertaken their conversion to our Holy Faith, and ordained that I should not go by land (the usual way) to the Orient, but by the route of the Occident, by which no one to this day knows for sure that anyone has gone.[2]

Queen Isabella of Spain showed a fanatical zeal for converting the Muslims to Christianity, but she concentrated her efforts on the Arabs in Granada. After the abortive crusading attempts of the thirteenth century, Isabella and other rulers realized full well that they lacked the material resources to mount the full-scale assault on Islam necessary for victory. Crusading impulses thus shifted from the Muslims to the pagan peoples of India, Africa, and the Americas.

Moreover, after the reconquista, enterprising young men of the Spanish upper classes found economic and political opportunities severely limited. As a recent study of the Castilian city of Ciudad Real shows, the ancient aristocracy controlled the best agricultural land and monopolized urban administrative posts. Great merchants and a few nobles (surprisingly, since Spanish law forbade noble participation in commercial ventures) dominated the textile and leather glove manufacturing industries. Consequently, many ambitious men immigrated to the Americas to seek their fortunes.[3]

Government sponsorship and encouragement of exploration also help to account for the results of the various voyages. Mariners and explorers could not afford, as private individuals, the massive sums needed to explore mysterious oceans and to control remote continents. The strong financial support of Prince Henry the Navigator led to Portugal's phenomenal success in the spice trade. Even the grudging and modest assistance of Isabella and Ferdinand eventually brought untold riches—and complicated problems—to Spain. The Dutch in the seventeenth century, through the Dutch East India Company and other government-sponsored trading companies,

reaped enormous wealth. Although the Netherlands was a small country in size, it dominated the European economy in 1650. In England, by contrast, Henry VII's lack of interest in exploration delayed English expansion for a century.

Scholars have frequently described the European discoveries as a manifestation of Renaissance curiosity about the physical universe, the desire to know more about the geography and peoples of the world. There is truth to this explanation. Cosmography, natural history, and geography aroused enormous interest among educated people in the fifteenth and sixteenth centuries. Just as science fiction and speculation about life on other planets excite readers today, quasi-scientific literature about Africa, Asia, and the Americas captured the imaginations of literate Europeans. Spanish chronicler Oviedo's *General History of the Indies* (1547), a detailed eyewitness account of plants, animals, and peoples, was widely read.

Spices were another important incentive to voyages of discovery. Introduced into western Europe by the Crusaders in the twelfth century, nutmeg, mace, ginger, cinnamon, and pepper added flavor and variety to the monotonous diet of Europeans. Spices were also used in the preparation of medicinal drugs and incense for religious ceremonies. In the late thirteenth century, the Venetian Marco Polo (ca 1254–1324) had visited the court of the Chinese emperor. The widely publicized account of his travels in the *Book of Various Experiences* stimulated a rich trade in spices between Asia and Italy. The Venetians came to hold a monopoly on the spice trade in western Europe.

Spices were grown in India and China, shipped across the Indian Ocean to ports on the Persian Gulf, and then transported by Arabs across the Arabian Desert to Mediterranean ports. But the rise of the Ming Dynasty in China in the late fourteenth century resulted in the expulsion of foreigners. And the steady penetration of the Ottoman Turks into the eastern Mediterranean and of hostile Muslims across North Africa forced Europeans to seek a new route to the Asian spice markets.

The basic reason for European exploration and expansion, however, was the quest for material profit. Mariners and explorers frankly admitted this. As Bartholomew Diaz put it, his motives were "to serve God and His Majesty, to give light to those who were

Market at Cartagena Founded in 1533 as a port on the Caribbean Sea, Cartagena (modern Colombia) became the storage depot for precious metals waiting shipment to Spain. In this fanciful woodcut, male Indians wearing tunics composed of overlapping feathers and nude females sell golden necklaces, fish, fruit, and grain. *(New York Public Library)*

in darkness and to grow rich as all men desire to do." When Vasco da Gama reached the port of Calicut, India, in 1498, a native asked what the Portuguese wanted. Da Gama replied, "Christians and spices."[4] The bluntest of the Spanish conquistadors, Hernando Cortés, announced as he prepared to conquer Mexico, "I have come to win gold, not to plow the fields like a peasant."[5]

Portuguese and Spanish explorers carried the fervent Catholicism and missionary zeal of the Iberian Peninsula to the New World, and once in America they urged home governments to send clerics. At bottom, however, wealth was the driving motivation. A sixteenth-century diplomat, Ogier Gheselin de Busbecq, summed up this paradoxical attitude well: in expeditions to the Indies and the Antipodes, he said, "religion supplies the pretext and gold the motive."[6] The mariners and explorers were religious and "medieval" in justifying their actions, while remaining materialistic and "modern" in their behavior.

TECHNOLOGICAL STIMULI TO EXPLORATION

Technological developments were the key to Europe's remarkable outreach. By 1350 cannon had been fully developed in western Europe. These pieces of artillery emitted frightening noises and great flashes of fire and could batter down fortresses and even city walls. Sultan Muhammad II's siege of Constantinople in 1453 provides a classic illustration of the effectiveness of cannon fire.

Constantinople had very strong walled fortifications. The sultan secured the services of a Western technician who built fifty-six small cannon and a gigantic gun that could hurl stone balls weighing about eight hundred pounds. The gun could be moved only by several hundred oxen and loaded and fired only by about a hundred men working together. Reloading took two hours. This awkward but powerful weapon breached the walls of Constantinople before it cracked on the second day of the bombardment. Lesser cannon finished the job.

Early cannon posed serious technical difficulties. Iron cannon were cheaper than bronze to construct, but they were difficult to cast effectively and were liable to crack and injure the artillerymen. Bronze guns, made of copper and tin, were less subject than iron to corrosion, but they were very expensive. All cannon were extraordinarily difficult to move, required considerable time for reloading, and were highly inaccurate. They thus proved inefficient for land warfare. However, they could be used at sea.

The mounting of cannon on ships and improved techniques of shipbuilding gave impetus to European expansion. Since ancient times, most seagoing vessels had been narrow, open galleys, propelled by manpower. Slaves or convicts who had been sentenced to the galleys manned the oars of the ships that sailed the Mediterranean, and both cargo and warships carried soldiers for defense. Though well suited to the placid and thoroughly explored waters of the Mediterranean, galleys could not withstand the rough winds and uncharted shoals of the Atlantic. The need for sturdier craft, as well as population losses caused by the Black Death, forced the development of a new style of ship that would not require soldiers for defense.

In the course of the fifteenth century, the Portuguese developed the *caravel,* a small, light, three-masted sailing ship. Though somewhat slower than the galley, the caravel held more cargo and was highly maneuverable. When fitted with cannon, it could dominate larger vessels, such as the round ships commonly used as merchantmen. The substitution of wind power for manpower, and artillery fire for soldiers, signaled a great technological advance and gave Europeans navigational and military ascendancy over the rest of the world.[7]

Other fifteenth-century developments in navigation helped make possible the conquest of the Atlantic. The magnetic compass, brought to Europe from China by the Muslims, enabled sailors to determine their direction and position at sea. The astrolabe, an instrument developed by Muslim navigators in the twelfth century and used to determine the altitude of the sun and other celestial bodies, permitted mariners to plot their latitude (position north or south of the equator). Steadily improved maps and sea charts provided information about distance, sea depths, and general geography.

THE CONQUEST OF AZTEC MEXICO AND INCA PERU

Technological development also helps to explain the Spanish conquest of Aztec Mexico and Inca Peru. The strange end of the Aztec nation remains one of the most fascinating events in the annals of human societies. The Spanish adventurer Hernando Cortés landed at Vera Cruz in February 1519. In November he entered Tenochtitlán (Mexico City) and soon had the emperor Montezuma II in custody. In less than two years he had destroyed the monarchy, gained complete control of the Mexican capital, and extended his jurisdiction over much of the Aztec Empire. Why did a strong people defending its own territory succumb so quickly to a handful of Spaniards fighting in dangerous and completely unfamiliar circumstances? How indeed, since Montezuma's scouts sent him detailed reports of the Spaniards' movements? The answer lies in the Spaniards' boldness and timing, and in the Aztecs' psychology, political structure, attitude toward war, and technology.

The Spaniards arrived in late summer, when the Aztecs were preoccupied with harvesting their crops and not thinking of war. From the Spaniards' perspective, their timing was ideal. Then, a series of natural phenomena, signs, and portents seemed to augur disaster. A comet was seen in daytime, a column of fire appeared every midnight for a year, and two temples were suddenly destroyed, one by lightning unaccompanied by thunder. These and other apparently inexplicable events raised the specter of the return of Quetzalcoatl (page 476), and had a pervasively unnerving effect on the Aztecs. They looked on the Europeans riding "wild beasts" as extraterrestrial forces coming to establish a new social order. Defeatism swept the nation and paralyzed its will.

The Aztecs had never developed an effective method of governing subject peoples. The empire was actually a group of subject communities lacking legal or governmental ties to what today is called the "state." The Aztecs controlled them through terror, requiring from each clan an annual tribute of humans to be sacrificed to the gods. Tributary peoples seethed with revolt. When the Spaniards appeared, the Totonacs greeted them as liberators, and other subject groups joined them in battle against the Aztecs.

Montezuma refrained from attacking the Spaniards as they advanced toward his capital, and welcomed Cortés and his men into Tenochtitlán. Historians have often condemned the Aztec ruler for vacillation and weakness. Is this a fair assessment? Montezuma relied on the advice of his state council, itself divided, and on the dubious loyalty of tributary communities. When Cortés—with incredible boldness—took Montezuma hostage, the emperor's influence over his people crumbled.

But the major explanation for the collapse of the Aztec Empire to 600 Spaniards lies in the Aztec notion of warfare and level of technology. Forced to leave Tenochtitlán to settle a conflict elsewhere, Cortés placed his lieutenant, Alvarado, in charge. Alvarado's harsh rule drove the Aztecs to revolt, and they almost succeeded in destroying the Spanish garrison. When Cortés returned just in time, the Aztecs allowed his reinforcements to join Alvarado's besieged force. No threatened European or Oriental state would have conceived of doing such a thing: dividing an enemy's army and destroying the separate parts was basic to European and Asian military tactics. But for the Aztecs warfare was a ceremonial act, in which "divide and conquer" had no place.

Having allowed the Spanish forces to reunite, the entire population of Tenochtitlán attacked the invaders. The Aztecs killed many Spaniards, who in retaliation executed Montezuma. The Spaniards escaped from the city and inflicted a crushing defeat on the Aztec army at Otumba near Lake Texcoco on July 7, 1520. The Spaniards won because "the simple Indian methods of mass warfare were of little avail against the manoeuvring of a well-drilled force."[8] Aztec weapons proved no match for the terrifyingly noisy and lethal Spanish cannon, muskets, crossbows, and steel swords. European technology decided the battle. Cortés began the systematic conquest of Mexico.

In 1527 the Inca ruled as a benevolent despot. His power was limited only by custom. His millions of subjects looked on him as a god, firm but just to his people, merciless to his enemies. ("Looked on" is figurative. Only a few of the Inca's closest relatives dared look at his divine face: nobles approached him on their knees, and the masses kissed the dirt as he rode by in his litter.) The borders of his vast empire were well fortified, threatened by no foreign invaders. No sedition or civil disobedience disturbed the domestic tranquillity. Grain was plentiful, and apart from an outbreak of smallpox in a distant province —introduced by the Spaniards—no natural disaster upset the general peace. An army of 50,000 loyal troops stood at the Inca's instant disposal. Why, then, did this powerful empire fall so easily to Francisco Pizarro and his band of 175 men armed with one small ineffective cannon? This question has troubled students for centuries. There can be no definitive answers, but several explanations have been offered.

First, the Incas were totally isolated. They had no contact with other Amerindian cultures and knew nothing at all of Aztec civilization or its collapse to the Spaniards in 1521. Since about 1500 Inca scouts had reported "floating houses" on the seas, manned by white men with beards. Tradesmen told of strange large animals with feet of silver (as horseshoes appeared in the brilliant sunshine). Having observed a border skirmish between Indians and white men, intelligence sources advised the Inca that the Europeans' swords were as harmless as women's weaving battens. A coastal chieftain had poured chicha, the native beer, down the barrel of a gun to appease the god of thunder. These incidents suggest that Inca culture provided no basis for understanding the Spaniards and the significance of their arrival. Moreover, if the strange pale men planned war, there were very few of them, and the Incas believed that they could not be reinforced from the sea.[9]

At first the Incas did not think that the strangers intended trouble. They believed the old Inca legend that the creator-god Virocha—who had brought civilization to them, become displeased, and sailed away promising to return someday—had indeed returned. Like the Aztecs, belief in a legend prevented the Incas from taking prompt action.

A political situation may also have lain at the root of their difficulty. The Incas apparently had no definite principle for the succession of the emperor. The reigning emperor, with the advice of his council, chose his successor—usually the most capable son of his chief wife. In 1527, however, the Inca Huayna Capac died without naming his heir. The council chose Huascar, son of his chief wife, who was accordingly crowned at Cuzco with the imperial *borla*, the fringed headband symbolizing the imperial office. The people and the generals, however, supported Atahualpa, son of a secondary wife and clearly Huayna's favorite son. A bitter civil war ensued. Atahualpa emerged victorious, but the five-year struggle may have exhausted him and damaged his judgment.

Soon after Pizarro landed at Tumbes on May 13, 1532—the very day Atahualpa won the decisive battle against his brother—he learned of all these events. As Pizarro advanced across the steep Andes toward the capital at Cuzco, Atahualpa—simultaneously proceeding to the capital for his coronation—stopped at the provincial town of Cajamarca. He, like Montezuma, was kept fully informed of the Spaniards' movements. The Inca's strategy was to lure the Spaniards into a trap, seize their horses and ablest men for his army, and execute the rest. What had the Inca, surrounded by his thousands of troops, to fear? Atahualpa thus accepted Pizarro's invitation to come with his bodyguards "unarmed so as not to give offense" into the central plaza of Cajamarca. He rode right into the Spaniard's trap. Pizarro knew that if he could capture the person of the Inca, from whom all power devolved, he would have the "Kingdom of Gold" for which he had come to the New World. The Inca's litter arrived in the ominously quiet town square. One cannon blast terrified the Indians. The

Spaniards rushed out from hiding and ruthlessly slaughtered the Indians. Atahualpa's headband was instantly torn from his head. He offered to purchase his freedom with a roomful of gold. Pizarro agreed to this ransom, and an appropriate document was drawn up and signed. After the gold had been gathered from all parts of the empire to fill the room—17 feet by 22 feet by 9 feet—the Spaniards trumped up charges against the Inca and strangled him. The Inca Empire lay at Pizarro's feet.

THE SOUTH AMERICAN HOLOCAUST

In the sixteenth century, about 200,000 Spaniards immigrated to the New World. Soldiers demobilized from the Spanish and Italian campaigns, adventurers and drifters unable to find work in Spain, they did not intend to work in the New World either. After having assisted in the conquest of the Aztecs and the subjugation of the Incas, these drifters wanted to settle down and become a ruling class. In temperate grazing areas they carved out vast estates and imported Spanish sheep, cattle, and horses for the kinds of ranching with which they were familiar. In the coastal tropics, unsuited for grazing, the Spanish erected huge sugar plantations. Columbus had introduced sugar into the West Indies; Cortés, into Mexico. Sugar was a great luxury in Europe, and demand for it was high. Around 1550 the discovery of silver at Zacatecas and Guanajuato in Mexico and Potosí in present-day Bolivia stimulated silver rushes. How were the cattle ranches, sugar plantations, and silver mines to be worked? Obviously, by the Indians.

The Spanish quickly established the *encomiendas* system, whereby the Crown granted the conquerors the right to employ groups of Indians in a town or area as agricultural or mining laborers or as tribute-payers. Theoretically, the Spanish were forbidden to enslave the Indian natives; in actuality, the encomiendas were a legalized form of slavery. The European demand for sugar, tobacco, and silver prompted the colonists to exploit the Indians mercilessly. Unaccustomed to forced labor, especially in the blistering heat of tropical cane fields or the dark, dank, and dangerous mines, Indians died like flies. Recently scholars have tried to reckon the death rate of the Amerinds in the sixteenth century. Some historians maintain that when Columbus landed at Hispaniola in 1492, the island's population stood at 100,000; in 1570, 300 people survived. The Indian population of Peru is estimated to have fallen from 1.3 million in 1570 to 600,000 in 1620; central Mexico had 25.3 million Indians in 1519 and 1 million in 1605.[10] Some demographers dispute these figures, but all agree that the decline of the native Indian population in all of Spanish-occupied America amounted to a catastrophe greater in scale than any that has occurred even in the twentieth century.

What were the causes of this devastating slump in population? Students of the history of medicine have suggested the best explanation: disease. The major cause of widespread epidemics is migration, and those peoples isolated longest from other societies suffer most. Contact with disease builds up bodily resistance. At the beginning of the sixteenth century, American Indians probably had the unfortunate distinction of longer isolation from the rest of humankind than any other people on earth. Crowded concentrations of laborers in the mining camps bred infection, which was then carried by the miners back to their home villages. With little or no resistance to diseases brought from the Old World, the inhabitants of the highlands of Mexico and Peru, especially, fell victim to smallpox. According to one expert, smallpox caused "in all likelihood the most severe single loss of aboriginal population that ever occurred."[11]

Disease was the prime cause of the Indian holocaust, but the Spaniards contributed heavily to the Indians' death rate.[12] According to the Franciscan missionary Bartolomé de Las Casas (1474–1566), the Spanish maliciously murdered thousands:

This infinite multitude of people [the Indians] was . . . without fraud, without subtilty or malice . . . [toward] the Spaniards *whom they serve, patient, meek and peaceful. . . .*

To these quiet Lambs . . . came the Spaniards *like most c(r)uel Tygres, Wolves and Lions, enrag'd with a sharp and tedious hunger; for these forty years past, minding nothing else but the slaughter of these unfortunate wretches, whom with divers kinds of torments neither seen nor heard of before, they have so cruelly and inhumanely butchered, that of three millions of people which* Hispaniola *it self did contain, there are left remaining alive scarce three hundred persons. And for the Island of* Cuba *. . . it lies wholly desert, until'd and ruin'd. The Islands of St. John and Jamaica lie waste*

and desolate. The Lucayan Islands . . . are now totally unpeopled and destroyed; the inhabitants thereof amounting to above 5,000,000 souls, partly killed, and partly forced away to work in other places.[13]

Las Casas's remarks concentrate on the tropical lowlands, but the death rate in the highlands was also staggering.

The Christian missionaries who accompanied the conquistadors and settlers—Franciscans, Dominicans, and Jesuits—played an important role in converting the Indians to Christianity, teaching them European methods of agriculture, and inculcating loyalty to the Spanish crown. In terms of numbers of people baptized, missionaries enjoyed phenomenal success, though the depth of the Indians' understanding of Christianity remains debatable. Missionaries, especially Las Casas, asserted that the Indians had human rights, and through Las Casas's persistent pressure the emperor Charles V abolished the worst abuses of the encomiendas system.

Some scholars offer a psychological explanation for the colossal death rate of the Indians: they simply lost the will to survive. Their gods appeared to have abandoned them to a world over which they had no control. Hopelessness, combined with abusive treatment and overwork, pushed many men to suicide, many women to abortion or infanticide. Whatever its precise causes, the astronomically high death rate created a severe labor shortage in Spanish America. As early as 1511, King Ferdinand of Spain observed that the Indians seemed to be "very frail" and that "one black could do the work of four Indians."[14] Thus was born an absurd myth and the massive importation of black slaves from Africa (pages 579–582).

COLONIAL ADMINISTRATION

Having seized the great Indian ceremonial centers in Mexico and Peru, the Spanish conquistadors proceeded to subdue the main areas of native American civilization in the New World. Columbus, Cortés, and Pizarro claimed the lands they had "discovered" for the crown of Spain. How were they to be governed?

According to the Spanish theory of absolutism, the crown was entitled to exercise full authority over all imperial lands. In the sixteenth century the crown divided its New World territories into four vice royalties or administrative divisions: New Spain, which consisted of Mexico, Central America, and present-day California, Arizona, New Mexico, and Texas, with the capital at Mexico City; Peru, originally all the lands in continental South America, later reduced to the territory of modern Peru, Chile, Bolivia, and Ecuador, with the viceregal seat at Lima; New Granada, including present-day Venezuela, Colombia, Panama, and after 1739 Ecuador, with Bogotá as its administrative center; and La Plata, consisting of Argentina, Uruguay, and Paraguay, with Buenos Aires as the capital. Within each territory, the viceroy or imperial governor exercised broad military and civil authority as the direct representative of the sovereign in Madrid. The viceroy presided over the *audiencia,* a board of twelve to fifteen judges, which served as his advisory council and the highest judicial body.

From the early sixteenth century to the beginning of the nineteenth, the Spanish monarchy acted on the mercantilist principle that the colonies existed for the financial benefit of the mother country. The mining of gold and silver was always the most important industry in the colonies. The crown claimed the *quinto,* one-fifth of all precious metals mined in the Americas. Gold and silver yielded the Spanish monarchy 25 percent of its total income. In return, it shipped manufactured goods to the New World and discouraged the development of native industries.

The Portuguese governed their colony of Brazil in a similar manner. After the union of the crowns of Portugal and Spain in 1580, Spanish administrative forms were introduced. Local officials called *corregidores* held judicial and military powers. Mercantilist policies placed severe restrictions on Brazilian industries that might compete with those of Portugal. In the seventeenth century the use of black slave labor made possible the cultivation of coffee, cotton, and sugar; and in the eighteenth century Brazil led the world in the production of sugar. The unique feature of colonial Brazil's culture and society was its thoroughgoing mixture of Indians, whites, and blacks.

The Economic Effects of Spain's Discoveries in the New World

The sixteenth century has often been called the "Golden Century" of Spain. The influence of Spanish armies, Spanish Catholicism, and Spanish wealth was felt all over Europe. This greatness rested largely on the influx of precious metals from the New World.

The mines at Zacatecas and Guanajuato in Mexico and Potosí in Peru poured out huge quantities of precious metals. To protect this treasure from French and English pirates, armed convoys transported it each year to Spain. Between 1503 and 1650, 16 million kilograms of silver and 185,000 kilograms of gold entered the port of Seville. Spanish predominance, however, proved temporary.

In the sixteenth century, Spain experienced a steady population increase, creating a sharp rise in the demand for food and goods. Spanish colonies in the Americas also represented a demand for products. Since Spain had expelled some of the best farmers and businessmen, the Muslims and the conversos, in the fifteenth century, the Spanish economy was suffering and could not meet the new demands. Prices rose. Because the costs of manufacturing cloth and other goods increased, Spanish products could not compete in the international market with cheaper products made elsewhere. The textile industry was badly hurt. Prices spiraled upward, faster than the government could levy taxes to dampen the economy. (Higher taxes would have cut the public's buying power; with fewer goods sold, prices would have come down.)

Did the flood of American silver bullion cause the inflation? Prices rose most steeply before 1565, but bullion imports reached their peak between 1580 and 1620. Thus there is no direct correlation between silver imports and the inflation rate. Did the substantial population growth accelerate the inflation rate? Perhaps, since when the population pressure declined after 1600, prices gradually stabilized. One fact is certain: the price revolution severely strained governmental budgets. Several times between 1557 and 1647, Philip II and his successors were forced to repudiate the state debt, which in turn undermined confidence in the government. By the seventeenth century, the Spanish economy was a shambles.

As Philip II paid his armies and foreign debts with silver bullion, the Spanish inflation was transmitted to the rest of Europe. Between 1560 and 1600, much of Europe experienced large price increases. Prices doubled and in some cases quadrupled. Spain suffered most severely, but all European countries were affected. People who lived on fixed incomes, such as the continental nobles, were badly hurt because their money bought less. Those who owed fixed sums of money, such as the middle class, prospered: in a time of rising prices, debts had less value each year. Food costs rose most sharply, and the poor fared worst of all.

Seaborne Trading Empires

By 1550, European overseas reconnaissance had led to the first global seaborne trade. For centuries the Muslims had conducted sophisticated commercial activities that spanned continents. Although they controlled the rich spice trade of the Indian Ocean, most Muslim expeditions had been across Asian and African land routes. The Europeans' discovery of the Americas and their exploration of the Pacific for the first time linked the entire world by intercontinental seaborne trade. That trade brought into being three successive commercial empires: the Portuguese, the Spanish, and the Dutch.

In the sixteenth century, naval power and ship-borne artillery gave the Portuguese hegemony over the sea route to India. Their fleet brought spices to Lisbon, which the Portuguese paid for with textiles produced at Gujarat and Coromandel in India and with gold and ivory from East Africa. From their fortified bases at Goa on the Arabian Sea and at Malacca in the Malay Peninsula, ships of Malabar teak carried goods to the Portuguese settlement at Macao on the South China Sea. From Macao, loaded with Chinese silks and porcelains, Portuguese ships sailed to the Japanese port of Nagasaki and to the Philippine port of Manila where Chinese goods were exchanged for Spanish (that is, Latin American) silver. Throughout Asia, the Portuguese traded in slaves—blacks from Africa, Chinese, and Japanese. The Portuguese imported to India horses from Mesopotamia and copper from Arabia; they exported from India hawks and peacocks for the Chinese and Japanese markets. Across the Atlantic, Portuguese Brazil provided most of the sugar consumed in Europe in the sixteenth and early seventeenth centuries. African slave labor produced the sugar on the plantations of Brazil, and Portuguese merchants, many of them Jewish, controlled both the slave trade between West Africa and Brazil (pages 717–722) and the commerce in sugar between Brazil and Portugal. The Portuguese were the first worldwide traders, and Portuguese was the language of the Asian maritime trade (see Map 18.2).

Spanish possessions in the New World constituted basically a land empire and, as described on page 560, in the sixteenth century the Spaniards devised a method of governing it. But the Spaniards also built a seaborne empire across the Pacific centered at Manila in the Philippines. Discovered by Magellan, in 1563 the Spanish navigator Miguel Lopez de Legazpi sailed from Mexico and through a swift and almost bloodless conquest took over the Philippine Islands between 1564 and 1571. Legazpi founded Manila, which served as the trans-Pacific bridge between Spanish America and the extreme Eastern trade. Chinese silk, sold by the Portuguese in Manila for American silver, was transported to Acapulco in Mexico, from which it was carried overland to Vera Cruz for re-export to Spain. Because hostile Pacific winds prohibited direct passage from the Philippines to Peru, large shipments also went south from Acapulco to Peru. Spanish merchants could never satisfy the European demand for silk, which meant that huge amounts of bullion went from Acapulco to Manila. For example, in 1597, 12 million pesos of silver, almost the total value of the transatlantic trade, crossed the Pacific. After about 1640, the Spanish silk trade declined because it could not compete with Dutch imports.

In the latter half of the seventeenth century, the worldwide Dutch seaborne trade predominated. The Dutch Empire was built on spices. In 1599 a Dutch fleet returned to Amsterdam carrying 600,000 pounds of pepper and 250,000 pounds of cloves and nutmeg. Those who had invested in the expedition received a 100 percent profit. The voyage led to the establishment in 1602 of the Dutch East India Company, founded with the stated intention of capturing the spice trade from the Portuguese. The Dutch fleet, sailing from the Cape of Good Hope and avoiding the Portuguese forts in India, steered directly for the Straits of Sunda in Indonesia. The Dutch wanted direct access to and control of the Indonesian sources of spices. In return for assisting Indonesian princes in local squabbles and disputes with the Portuguese, the Dutch won broad commercial concessions. Through agreements, seizures, and outright war, they gained control of the western access to the Indonesian archipelago. Gradually, they acquired political domination over the archipelago itself. Exchanging European manufactured goods—armor, firearms, linens, and toys—the Dutch soon had a monopoly on the very lucrative spice trade.[15]

The seaborne empires profited from the geographical reconnaissance and technological developments

MAP 18.2 Seaborne Trading Empires, Sixteenth and Seventeenth Centuries In the sixteenth century, for the first time the entire globe was linked by seaborne trade. In the seventeenth century American silver paid for Asian silks and spices; African slaves in Latin America produced sugar for the tables of Europe.

of the sixteenth century. The empires of Portugal, Spain, and Holland had strong commercial ambitions. They also paved the way for the eighteenth-century mercantilist empires of France and Great Britain (see page 808).

POLITICS, RELIGION, AND WAR

In 1559 France and Spain signed the Treaty of Cateau-Cambrésis, which ended the Habsburg-Valois Wars. This event marks a decisive watershed in early modern European history. Spain was the victor. France, exhausted by the struggle, had to acknowledge Spanish dominance in Italy, where much of the war had been fought. Spanish governors ruled in Sicily, Naples, and Milan, and Spanish influence was strong in the Papal States and Tuscany.

Emperor Charles V had divided his attention between the Holy Roman Empire and Spain. Under his son Philip II (1556–1598), however, the center of the Habsburg Empire and the political center of gravity for all of Europe shifted westward to Spain. Before 1559, Spain and France had fought bitterly for control of Italy; after 1559, the two Catholic powers aimed their guns at Protestantism. The Treaty of Cateau-Cambrésis ended an era of strictly dynastic wars and initiated a period of conflicts in which politics and religion played the dominant roles.

Because a variety of issues were stewing, it is not easy to generalize about the wars of the late sixteenth century. Some were continuations of struggles between the centralizing goals of monarchies and the feudal reactions of nobilities. Some were crusading battles between Catholics and Protestants. Some were struggles for national independence or for international expansion.

These wars differed considerably from earlier wars. Sixteenth- and seventeenth-century armies were bigger than medieval ones; some forces numbered as many as fifty thousand men. Because large armies were expensive, governments had to reorganize their administrations to finance them. The use of gunpowder altered both the nature of war and popular attitudes toward it. Guns and cannon killed and wounded from a distance, indiscriminately. Gunpowder weakened the notion, common during the Hundred Years' War, that warfare was an ennobling experience. Governments had to utilize propaganda, pulpits, and the printing press to arouse public opinion to support war.[16]

Late-sixteenth-century conflicts fundamentally tested the medieval ideal of a unified Christian society governed by one political ruler, the emperor, to whom all rulers were theoretically subordinate, and one church, to which all people belonged. The Protestant Reformation had killed this ideal, but few people recognized it as dead. Catholics continued to believe that Calvinists and Lutherans could be reconverted; Protestants persisted in thinking that the Roman church should be destroyed. Most people believed that a state could survive only if its members shared the same faith. Catholics and Protestants alike feared people of the other faith living in their midst. The settlement finally achieved in 1648, known as the Peace of Westphalia, signaled acknowledgment of the end of the medieval ideal.

THE ORIGINS OF DIFFICULTIES IN FRANCE (1515–1559)

In the first half of the sixteenth century, France continued the recovery begun under Louis XI (see page 513). The population losses caused by the plague and the disorders accompanying the Hundred Years' War had created such a labor shortage that serfdom virtually disappeared. Cash rents replaced feudal rents and servile obligations. This development clearly benefited the peasantry. Meanwhile, the declining buying power of money hurt the nobility. The steadily increasing French population brought new lands under cultivation, but the division of property among sons meant that most peasant holdings were very small. Domestic and foreign trade picked up; mercantile centers such as Rouen and Lyons expanded; and in 1517 a new port city was founded at Le Havre.

The charming and cultivated Francis I (1515–1547) and his athletic, emotional son Henry II (1547–1559) governed through a small, efficient

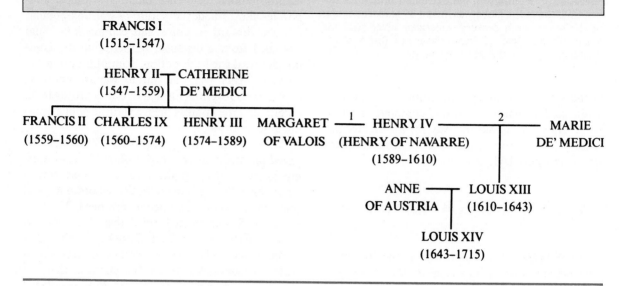

THE FRENCH BOURBON SUCCESSION, 1515–1715

FRANCIS I
(1515–1547)

HENRY II — CATHERINE
(1547–1559)   DE' MEDICI

FRANCIS II   CHARLES IX   HENRY III   MARGARET — 1 — HENRY IV — 2 — MARIE
(1559–1560)   (1560–1574)   (1574–1589)   OF VALOIS   (HENRY OF NAVARRE)   DE' MEDICI
                                                                              (1589–1610)

ANNE — LOUIS XIII
OF AUSTRIA   (1610–1643)

LOUIS XIV
(1643–1715)

council. Great nobles held titular authority in the provinces as governors, but Paris-appointed baillis and seneschals continued to exercise actual fiscal and judicial responsibility (page 392). In 1539 Francis issued an ordinance that placed the whole of France under the jurisdiction of the royal law courts and made French the language of those courts. This act had a powerful centralizing impact. The taille land tax provided what strength the monarchy had and supported a strong standing army. Unfortunately, the tax base was too narrow for France's extravagant promotion of the arts and ambitious foreign policy.

Deliberately imitating the Italian Renaissance princes, the Valois monarchs lavished money on a magnificent court, a vast building program, and Italian artists. Francis I commissioned the Paris architect Pierre Lescot to rebuild the palace of the Louvre. Francis secured the services of Michelangelo's star pupil, Il Rosso, who decorated the wing of the Fontainebleau chateau, subsequently called the "Gallery Francis I," with rich scenes of classical and mythological literature. After acquiring Leonardo da Vinci's Mona Lisa, Francis brought Leonardo himself to France, where he soon died. Henry II built a castle at Dreux for his mistress, Diana de Poitiers, and a palace in Paris, the Tuileries, for his wife, Catherine de' Medici. Art historians credit Francis I and Henry II

with importing Italian Renaissance art and architecture to France. Whatever praise these monarchs deserve for their cultural achievement, they spent far more than they could afford.

The Habsburg-Valois Wars, waged intermittently through the first half of the sixteenth century, also cost more than the government could afford. Financing the war posed problems. In addition to the time-honored practices of increasing taxes and heavy borrowing, Francis I tried two new devices to raise revenue: the sale of public offices and a treaty with the papacy. The former proved to be only a temporary source of money. The offices sold tended to become hereditary within a family, and once a man bought an office he and his heirs were tax-exempt. The sale of public offices thus created a tax-exempt class called the "nobility of the robe," whose members held positions beyond the jurisdiction of the crown.

The treaty with the papacy was the Concordat of Bologna (1516), which in effect rescinded the Pragmatic Sanction of Bourges (page 513). In it Francis agreed to recognize the supremacy of the papacy over a universal council. In return, the French crown gained the right to appoint all French bishops and abbots. This understanding gave the monarchy a rich supplement of money and offices and a power over

Rosso and Primaticcio: The Gallery of Frances I Flat paintings alternating with rich sculpture provide a rhythm that directs the eye down the long gallery at Fontainebleau, constructed between 1530 and 1540. Francis I sought to re-create in France the elegant Renaissance lifestyle found in Italy. *(Giraudon/Art Resource)*

the church that lasted until the Revolution of 1789. The Concordat of Bologna helps to explain why France did not later become Protestant: in effect, it established Catholicism as the state religion. Because they possessed control over appointments and had a vested financial interest in Catholicism, French rulers had no need to revolt from Rome.

However, the Concordat of Bologna perpetuated disorders within the French church. Ecclesiastical offices were used primarily to pay and reward civil servants. Churchmen in France, as elsewhere, were promoted to the hierarchy not for any special spiritual

qualifications but because of their services to the state. Such bishops were unlikely to work to elevate the intellectual and moral standards of the parish clergy. Few of the many priests in France devoted scrupulous attention to the needs of their parishioners. The teachings of Luther and Calvin found a receptive audience.

Luther's tracts first appeared in France in 1518, and his ideas attracted some attention. After the publication of Calvin's *Institutes* in 1536, sizable numbers of French people were attracted to the "reformed religion," as Calvinism was called. Because

Calvin wrote in French rather than Latin, his ideas gained wide circulation. Initially, Calvinism drew converts from among reform-minded members of the Catholic clergy, the industrious middle classes, and artisan groups. Most Calvinists lived in major cities, such as Paris, Lyons, Meaux, and Grenoble.

In spite of condemnation by the universities, government bans, and massive burnings at the stake, the numbers of Protestants grew steadily. When Henry II died in 1559, there were 40 well-organized and 2,150 mission churches in France. Perhaps one-tenth of the population had become Calvinist (see Map 17.4).

RELIGIOUS RIOTS AND CIVIL WAR IN FRANCE (1559–1589)

For thirty years, from 1559 to 1589, violence and civil war divided and shattered France. The feebleness of the monarchy was the seed from which the weeds of civil violence germinated. The three weak sons of Henry II who occupied the throne could not provide the necessary leadership. Francis II (1559–1560) died after seventeen months. Charles IX (1560–1574) succeeded at the age of ten and was thoroughly dominated by his opportunistic mother, Catherine de' Medici, who would support any party or position to maintain her influence. The intelligent and cultivated Henry III (1574–1589) divided his attention between debaucheries with his male lovers and frantic acts of repentance.

The French nobility took advantage of this monarchial weakness. In the second half of the sixteenth century, between two-fifths and one-half of the nobility at one time or another became Calvinist. Just as German princes in the Holy Roman Empire had adopted Lutheranism as a means of opposition to the emperor Charles V, so French nobles frequently adopted the "reformed religion" as a religious cloak for their independence. No one believed that peoples of different faiths could coexist peacefully within the same territory. The Reformation thus led to a resurgence of feudal disorder. Armed clashes between Calvinist antimonarchial lords and Catholic royalist lords occurred in many parts of France.

Among the upper classes the Calvinist-Catholic conflict was the surface issue, but the fundamental object of the struggle was power. Working-class crowds composed of skilled craftsmen and the poor wreaked terrible violence on people and property.

Both Calvinists and Catholics believed that the others' books, services, and ministers polluted the community. Preachers incited violence, and ceremonies (baptisms, marriages, funerals) triggered it. Protestant pastors encouraged their followers to destroy statues and liturgical objects in Catholic churches. Catholic priests urged their flocks to shed the blood of the Calvinist heretics.

In 1561 in the Paris church of Saint-Médard, a Protestant crowd cornered a baker guarding a box containing the consecrated Eucharistic bread. Taunting "Does your God of paste protect you now from the pains of death?" the mob proceeded to kill the poor man.[17] Calvinists believed that the Catholics' emphasis on symbols in their ritual desecrated what was truly sacred and promoted the worship of images. In scores of attacks on Catholic churches, religious statues were knocked down, stained-glass windows smashed, and sacred vestments, vessels, and Eucharistic elements defiled. In 1561 a Catholic crowd charged a group of just-released Protestant prisoners, killed them, and burned their bodies in the street. Hundreds of Huguenots, as French Calvinists were called, were tortured, had their tongues or throats slit, were maimed or murdered.

In the fourteenth and fifteenth centuries, crowd action—attacks on great nobles and rich prelates—had expressed economic grievances. Religious rioters of the sixteenth century believed that they could assume the power of public magistrates and rid the community of corruption. Municipal officials criticized the crowds' actions, but the participation of pastors and priests in these riots lent them some legitimacy.[18]

A savage Catholic attack on Calvinists in Paris on August 24 (Saint Bartholomew's Day), 1572, followed the usual pattern. The occasion was a religious ceremony, the marriage of the king's sister Margaret of Valois to the Protestant Henry of Navarre, which was intended to help reconcile Catholics and Huguenots. Among the many Calvinists present for the wedding festivities was the admiral of Coligny, head of one of the great noble families of France and leader of the Huguenot party. Coligny had recently replaced Catherine in influence over the young king Charles IX. When, the night before the wedding, the leader of the Catholic aristocracy, Henry of Guise, had Coligny murdered, rioting and slaughter followed. The Huguenot gentry in Paris were massacred, and religious violence spread to the provinces. Between August 25 and October 3, perhaps twelve thousand Huguenots perished at Meaux, Lyons, Orléans, and Paris. The contradictory orders of the unstable Charles IX worsened the situation.

The Saint Bartholomew's Day massacre led to fighting that launched the War of the Three Henrys, a civil conflict among factions led by the Catholic Henry of Guise, the Protestant Henry of Navarre, and King Henry III, who succeeded the tubercular Charles IX. Though he remained Catholic, King Henry realized that the Catholic Guise group represented his greatest danger. The Guises wanted, through an alliance of Catholic nobles called the "Holy League," not only to destroy Calvinism but to replace Henry III with a member of the Guise family. France suffered fifteen more years of religious rioting and domestic anarchy. Agriculture in many areas was destroyed; commercial life declined severely; starvation and death haunted the land.

What ultimately saved France was a small group of Catholic moderates called *politiques* who believed that only the restoration of strong monarchy could reverse the trend toward collapse. No religious creed was worth the incessant disorder and destruction. Therefore the politiques supported religious toleration. The death of Catherine de' Medici, followed by the assassinations of Henry of Guise and King Henry III, paved the way for the accession of Henry of Navarre, a politique who became Henry IV (1589–1610).

This glamorous prince, "who knew how to fight, to make love, and to drink," as a contemporary remarked, wanted above all a strong and united France. He knew, too, that the majority of the French were Roman Catholics. Declaring "Paris is worth a Mass," Henry knelt before the archbishop of Bourges and was received into the Roman Catholic church. Henry's willingness to sacrifice religious principles to political necessity saved France. The Edict of Nantes, which Henry published in 1598, granted to Huguenots liberty of conscience and liberty of public worship in two hundred fortified towns, such as La Rochelle. The reign of Henry IV and the Edict of Nantes prepared the way for French absolutism in the seventeenth century by helping to restore internal peace in France.

THE NETHERLANDS UNDER CHARLES V

In the last quarter of the sixteenth century, the political stability of England, the international prestige of Spain, and the moral influence of the Roman papacy all became mixed up with the religious crisis in the Low Countries. The Netherlands was the pivot around which European money, diplomacy, and war revolved. What began as a movement for the reformation of the church developed into a struggle for Dutch independence.

The emperor Charles V (1519–1556) had inherited the seventeen provinces that compose present-day Belgium and Holland (see Map 17.3). Ideally situated for commerce between the Rhine and Scheldt rivers, the great towns of Bruges, Ghent, Brussels, Arras, and Amsterdam made their living by trade and industry. The French-speaking southern towns produced fine linens and woolens, while the wealth of the Dutch-speaking northern cities rested on fishing, shipping, and international banking. The city of Antwerp was the largest port and the greatest money market in Europe. In the cities of the Low Countries, trade and commerce had produced a vibrant cosmopolitan atmosphere, which was well personified by the urbane Erasmus of Rotterdam (page 510).

Each of the seventeen provinces of the Netherlands possessed historical liberties: each was self-governing and enjoyed the right to make its own laws and collect its own taxes. Only the recognition of a common ruler in the person of the emperor Charles V united the provinces. Delegates from each province met together in the Estates General, but important decisions had to be referred back to each province for approval. In the middle of the sixteenth century, the provinces of the Netherlands had a limited sense of federation.

In the Low Countries, as elsewhere, corruption in the Roman church and the critical spirit of the Renaissance provoked pressure for reform. Lutheran tracts and Dutch translations of the Bible flooded the seventeen provinces in the 1520s and 1530s, attracting many people to Protestantism. Charles V's government responded with condemnation and mild repression. This policy was not particularly effective, however, because ideas circulated freely in the cosmopolitan atmosphere of the commercial centers. But Charles's Flemish loyalty checked the spread of Lutheranism. Charles had been born in Ghent and raised in the Netherlands; he was Flemish in language and culture. He identified with the Flemish and they with him.

In 1556, however, Charles V abdicated, dividing his territories between his brother Ferdinand, who received Austria and the Holy Roman Empire, and his son Philip, who inherited Spain, the Low Countries, Milan and the kingdom of Sicily, and the Spanish possessions in America. Charles delivered his abdication speech before the Estates General at Brussels. The emperor was then fifty-five years old, white haired, and so crippled in the legs that he had to lean for support on the young Prince William of Orange. According to one contemporary account of the emperor's appearance:

His under lip, a Burgundian inheritance, as faithfully transmitted as the duchy and county, was heavy and hanging, the lower jaw protruding so far beyond the upper that it was impossible for him to bring together the few fragments of teeth which still remained, or to speak a whole sentence in an intelligible voice.[19]

Charles spoke in Flemish. His small, shy, and sepulchral son Philip responded in Spanish; he could speak neither French nor Flemish. The Netherlanders had always felt Charles one of themselves. They were never to forget that Philip was a Spaniard.

THE REVOLT OF THE NETHERLANDS (1566–1587)

By the 1560s, there was a strong, militant minority of Calvinists in most of the cities of the Netherlands. The seventeen provinces possessed a large middle-class population, and the "reformed religion," as a contemporary remarked, had a powerful appeal "to those who had grown rich by trade and were therefore ready for revolution."[20] Calvinism appealed to the middle classes because of its intellectual seriousness, moral gravity, and emphasis on any form of labor well done. It took deep root among the merchants and financiers in Amsterdam and the northern provinces. Working-class people were also converted, partly because their employers would hire only fellow Calvinists. Well organized and with the backing of rich merchants, Calvinists quickly gained a wide following. Lutherans taught respect for the powers that be. The reformed religion, however, tended to encourage opposition to "illegal" civil authorities.

In 1559 Philip II appointed his half-sister Margaret as regent of the Netherlands (1559–1567). A proud, energetic, and strong-willed woman, who once had Ignatius Loyola as her confessor, Margaret pushed Philip's orders to wipe out Protestantism. She introduced the Inquisition. Her more immediate problem, however, was revenue to finance the government of the provinces. Charles V had steadily increased taxes in the Low Countries. When Margaret appealed to the Estates General, they claimed that the Low Countries were more heavily taxed than Spain. Nevertheless, Margaret raised taxes. In so doing, she quickly succeeded in uniting the opposition to the government's fiscal policy with the opposition to official repression of Calvinism.

In August 1566, a year of very high grain prices, fanatical Calvinists, primarily of the poorest classes, embarked on a rampage of frightful destruction. As in France, Calvinist destruction in the Low Countries was incited by popular preaching, and attacks were aimed at religious images as symbols of false doctrines, not at people. The cathedral of Notre Dame at Antwerp was the first target. Begun in 1124 and finished only in 1518, this church stood as a monument to the commercial prosperity of Flanders, the piety of the business classes, and the artistic genius of centuries. On six successive summer evenings, crowds swept through the nave. While the town harlots held tapers to the greatest concentration of art works in northern Europe, people armed with axes and sledgehammers smashed altars, statues, paintings, books, tombs, ecclesiastical vestments, missals, manuscripts, ornaments, stained-glass windows, and sculptures. Before the havoc was over, thirty more churches had been sacked and irreplaceable libraries burned. From Antwerp the destruction spread to Brussels and Ghent and north to the provinces of Holland and Zeeland.

From Madrid, Philip II sent twenty thousand Spanish troops under the duke of Alva to pacify the Low Countries. Alva interpreted *pacification* to mean the ruthless extermination of religious and political dissidents. On top of the Inquisition he opened his own tribunal, soon called the "Council of Blood." On March 3, 1568, fifteen hundred men were executed. Alva resolved the financial crisis by levying a 10 percent sales tax on every transaction, which in a commercial society caused widespread hardship and confusion.

For ten years, between 1568 and 1578, civil war raged in the Netherlands between Catholics and Protestants and between the seventeen provinces and Spain. A series of Spanish generals could not halt the

To Purify the Church The destruction of pictures and statues representing biblical events, Christian doctrine, or sacred figures was a central feature of the Protestant Reformation. Here Dutch Protestant soldiers destroy what they consider idols in the belief that they are purifying the church. *(Freeman & Co., London)*

fighting. In 1576 the seventeen provinces united under the leadership of Prince William of Orange, called "the Silent" because of his remarkable discretion. In 1578 Philip II sent his nephew Alexander Farnese, duke of Parma, to crush the revolt once and for all. A general with a superb sense of timing, an excellent knowledge of the geography of the Low Countries, and a perfect plan, Farnese arrived with an army of German mercenaries. Avoiding pitched battles, he fought by patient sieges. One by one the cities of the south fell—Maastricht, Tournai, Bruges, Ghent, and finally the financial capital of northern Europe, Antwerp. Calvinism was forbidden in these territories, and Protestants were compelled to convert or leave. The collapse of Antwerp marked the farthest extent of Spanish jurisdiction and ultimately the religious division of the Netherlands.

The ten southern provinces, the Spanish Netherlands (the future Belgium), remained under the control of the Spanish Habsburgs. The seven northern provinces, led by Holland, formed the Union of Utrecht and in 1581 declared their independence from Spain. Thus was born the United Provinces of the Netherlands (Map 18.3).

Geography and sociopolitical structure differentiated the two countries. The northern provinces

MAP 18.3 The Netherlands, 1578–1609 Though small in geographical size, the Netherlands held a strategic position in the religious struggles of the sixteenth century. Why?

Elizabeth survived a massive uprising by the Catholic north in 1569 to 1570. She survived two serious plots against her life. In the 1570s the presence in England of Mary, Queen of Scots, a Roman Catholic and the legal heir to the English throne, produced a very embarrassing situation. Mary was the rallying point of all opposition to Elizabeth, yet the English sovereign hesitated to set the terrible example of regicide by ordering Mary executed.

Elizabeth faced a grave dilemma. If she responded favorably to Dutch pleas for military support against the Spanish, she would antagonize Philip II. The Spanish king had the steady flow of silver from the Americas at his disposal, and Elizabeth, lacking such treasure, wanted to avoid war. But if she did not help the Protestant Netherlands and they were crushed by Farnese, the likelihood was that the Spanish would invade England.

Three developments forced Elizabeth's hand. First, the wars in the Low Countries—the chief market for English woolens—badly hurt the English economy. When wool was not exported, the crown lost valuable customs revenues. Second, the murder of William the Silent in July 1584 eliminated not only a great Protestant leader but the chief military check on the Farnese advance. Third, the collapse of Antwerp appeared to signal a Catholic sweep through the Netherlands. The next step, the English feared, would be a Spanish invasion of their island. For these reasons, Elizabeth pumped £250,000 and two thousand troops into the Protestant cause in the Low Countries between 1585 and 1587. Increasingly fearful of the plots of Mary, Queen of Scots, Elizabeth finally signed her death warrant. Mary was beheaded on February 18, 1587. Sometime between March 24 and 30, the news of Mary's death reached Philip II.

PHILIP II AND THE SPANISH ARMADA

Philip pondered the Dutch and English developments at the Escorial northwest of Madrid. Begun in 1563 and completed under the king's personal supervision in 1584, the monastery of Saint Lawrence of the Escorial served as a monastery for Jeromite monks, a tomb for the king's Habsburg ancestors, and a royal palace for Philip and his family. The vast buildings resemble a gridiron, the instrument on which Saint Lawrence (d. 258) had supposedly been roasted alive. The royal apartments were in the center of the Italian Renaissance building complex.

were ribboned with sluices and canals and therefore were highly defensible. Several times the Dutch had broken the dikes and flooded the countryside to halt the advancing Farnese. In the Southern provinces the Ardennes Mountains interrupt the otherwise flat terrain. In the north the commercial aristocracy possessed the predominant power; in the south the landed nobility had the greater influence. The north was Protestant; the south remained Catholic.

Philip II and Alexander Farnese did not accept this geographical division, and the struggle continued after 1581. The United Provinces repeatedly begged the Protestant queen Elizabeth of England for assistance.

The crown on the head of Elizabeth I did not rest easily. She had steered a moderately Protestant course between the Puritans, who sought the total elimination of Roman Catholic elements in the English church, and the Roman Catholics, who wanted full restoration of the old religion (see page 533).

King Philip's tiny bedchamber possessed a concealed sliding window that opened directly onto the high altar of the monastery church so he could watch the services and pray along with the monks. In this somber atmosphere, surrounded by a community of monks and close to the bones of his ancestors, the Catholic ruler of Spain and much of the globe passed his days.

Philip of Spain considered himself the international defender of Catholicism and the heir to the medieval imperial power. Hoping to keep England within the Catholic church when his wife Mary Tudor died, Philip had asked Elizabeth to marry him; she had emphatically refused. Several popes had urged him to move against England. When Pope Sixtus V (1585–1590) heard of the death of the queen of Scots, he promised to pay Philip one million gold ducats the moment Spanish troops landed in England. Alexander Farnese had repeatedly warned that to subdue the Dutch, he would have to conquer England and cut off the source of Dutch support. Philip worried that the vast amounts of South American silver he was pouring into the conquest of the Netherlands seemed to be going down a bottomless pit. Two plans for an expedition were considered. Philip's naval adviser recommended that a fleet of 150 ships sail from Lisbon, attack the English navy in the Channel, and invade England. Another proposal had been to assemble a collection of barges and troops in Flanders to stage a cross-Channel assault. With the expected support of English Catholics, Spain would achieve a great victory. Parma opposed this plan as militarily unsound.

Philip compromised. He prepared a vast armada to sail from Lisbon to Flanders, fight off Elizabeth's navy if it attacked, rendezvous with Farnese, and escort his barges across the English Channel. The expedition's purpose was to transport the Flemish army.

On May 9, 1588, *la felicissima armada*—"the most fortunate fleet," as it was ironically called in official documents—sailed from Lisbon harbor on the last medieval crusade. The Spanish fleet of 130 vessels carried 123,790 cannon balls and perhaps 30,000 men, every one of whom had confessed his sins and received the Eucharist. An English fleet of about 150 ships met the Spanish in the Channel. It was composed of smaller, faster, more maneuverable ships, many of which had greater firing power. A combination of storms and squalls, spoiled food and rank water, inadequate Spanish ammunition, and to a lesser extent, English fire ships that caused the Spanish to panic and scatter gave England the victory. Many Spanish ships went to the bottom of the ocean; perhaps 65 managed to crawl home by way of the North Sea.

The battle in the Channel has frequently been described as one of the decisive battles in the history of the world. In fact, it had mixed consequences. Spain soon rebuilt its navy, and the quality of the Spanish fleet improved. The destruction of the armada did not halt the flow of silver from the New World. More silver reached Spain between 1588 and 1603 than in any other fifteen-year period. The war between England and Spain dragged on for years.

The defeat of the Spanish Armada was decisive, however, in the sense that it prevented Philip II from reimposing unity on western Europe by force. He did not conquer England, and Elizabeth continued her financial and military support of the Dutch. In the Netherlands, however, neither side gained significant territory. The borders of 1581 tended to become permanent. In 1609 Philip III of Spain (1598–1621) agreed to a truce, in effect recognizing the independence of the United Provinces. In seventeenth-century Spain memory of the defeat of the armada contributed to a spirit of defeatism.

THE THIRTY YEARS' WAR (1618–1648)

While Philip II dreamed of building a second armada and Henry IV began the reconstruction of France, the political-religious situation in central Europe deteriorated. An uneasy truce had prevailed in the Holy Roman Empire since the Peace of Augsburg of 1555 (page 527). The Augsburg settlement, in recognizing the independent power of the German princes, had destroyed the authority of the central government. The Habsburg ruler in Vienna enjoyed the title of emperor but had no power.

According to the Augsburg settlement, the faith of the prince determined the religion of his subjects. Later in the century, though, Catholics grew alarmed because Lutherans, in violation of the Peace of Augsburg, were steadily acquiring north German bishoprics. The spread of Calvinism further confused the issue. The Augsburg settlement had pertained only to Lutheranism and Catholicism, but Calvinists ignored it and converted several princes. Lutherans

Defeat of the Spanish Armada The crescent-shaped Spanish formation was designed to force the English to fight at close quarters—by ramming and boarding. When the English sent burning ships against the Spaniards, the crescent broke up, the English pounced on individual ships, and an Atlantic gale swept the Spaniards into the North Sea, finishing the work of destruction. *(National Maritime Museum, London)*

feared that the Augsburg principles would be totally undermined by Catholic and Calvinist gains. Also, the militantly active Jesuits had reconverted several Lutheran princes to Catholicism. In an increasingly tense situation, Lutheran princes formed the Protestant Union (1608) and Catholics retaliated with the Catholic League (1609). Each alliance was determined that the other should make no religious (that is, territorial) advance. The empire was composed of two armed camps.

Dynastic interests were also involved in the German situation. When Charles V abdicated in 1556, he had divided his possessions between his son Philip II and his brother Ferdinand I. This partition began the Austrian and Spanish branches of the Habsburg family. Ferdinand inherited the imperial title and the Habsburg lands in central Europe, including Austria. Ferdinand's grandson Matthias had no direct heirs and promoted the candidacy of his fiercely Catholic cousin, Ferdinand of Styria. The Spanish Habsburgs strongly supported the goals of their Austrian relatives: the unity of the empire and the preservation of Catholicism within it.

In 1617 Ferdinand of Styria secured election as king of Bohemia, a title that gave him jurisdiction over Silesia and Moravia as well as Bohemia. The Bohemians were Czech and German in nationality, and Lutheran, Calvinist, Catholic, and Hussite in religion; all these faiths enjoyed a fair degree of religious freedom. When Ferdinand proceeded to close some Protestant churches, the heavily Protestant Estates of Bohemia protested. On May 23, 1618, Protestants hurled two of Ferdinand's officials from a castle window in Prague. They fell seventy feet but survived: Catholics claimed that angels had caught them; Protestants said the officials fell on a heap of soft horse manure. Called the "defenestration of Prague," this event marked the beginning of the Thirty Years' War (1618–1648).

Historians traditionally divide the war into four phases. The first, or Bohemian, phase (1618–1625) was characterized by civil war in Bohemia between the Catholic League, led by Ferdinand, and the Protestant Union, headed by Prince Frederick of the Palatinate. The Bohemians fought for religious liberty and independence from Habsburg rule. In 1618 the

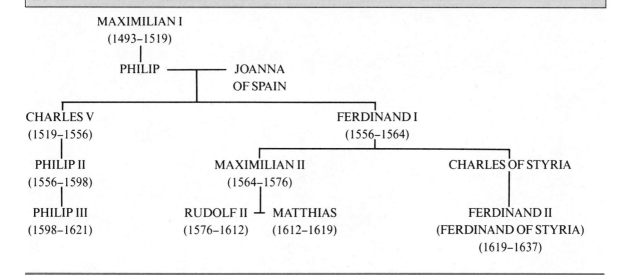

```
                    MAXIMILIAN I
                    (1493–1519)
                         │
                    PHILIP ──────────── JOANNA
                                        OF SPAIN

   CHARLES V                        FERDINAND I
   (1519–1556)                      (1556–1564)

   PHILIP II           MAXIMILIAN II              CHARLES OF STYRIA
   (1556–1598)         (1564–1576)

   PHILIP III      RUDOLF II ─ MATTHIAS           FERDINAND II
   (1598–1621)     (1576–1612)  (1612–1619)       (FERDINAND OF STYRIA)
                                                  (1619–1637)
```

Bohemian Estates deposed Ferdinand and gave the crown of Bohemia to Frederick, thus uniting the interests of German Protestants with those of the international enemies of the Habsburgs. Frederick wore his crown only a few months. In 1620 he was totally defeated by Catholic forces at the Battle of the White Mountain. Ferdinand, who had recently been elected Holy Roman emperor as Ferdinand II, followed up his victories by wiping out Protestantism in Bohemia through forcible conversions and the activities of militant Jesuit missionaries. Within ten years, Bohemia was completely Catholic.

The second, or Danish, phase of the war (1625–1629)—so called because of the participation of King Christian IV of Denmark (1588–1648), the ineffective leader of the Protestant cause—witnessed additional Catholic victories. The Catholic imperial army led by Albert of Wallenstein scored smashing victories. It swept through Silesia, north through Schleswig and Jutland to the Baltic, and east into Pomerania. Wallenstein had made himself indispensable to the emperor Ferdinand, but he was an unscrupulous opportunist who used his vast riches to build an army loyal only to himself. The general seemed interested more in carving out an empire for himself than in aiding the Catholic cause. He quarreled with the league, and soon the Catholic forces were divided. Religion was eclipsed as a basic issue of the war.

The year 1629 marked the peak of Habsburg power. The Jesuits persuaded the emperor to issue the Edict of Restitution, whereby all Catholic properties lost to Protestantism since 1552 were to be restored and only Catholics and Lutherans (not Calvinists, Hussites, or other sects) were to be allowed to practice their faiths. Ferdinand appeared to be embarked on a policy to unify the empire. When Wallenstein began ruthless enforcement of the edict, Protestants throughout Europe feared collapse of the balance of power in the north-central region.

The third, or Swedish, phase of the war (1630–1635) began with the arrival in Germany of the Swedish king Gustavus Adolphus (1594–1632). The ablest administrator of his day and a devout Lutheran, Gustavus Adolphus intervened to support the oppressed Protestants within the empire and to assist his relatives, the exiled dukes of Mecklenburg. Cardinal Richelieu, the chief minister of King Louis XIII of France (1610–1643), subsidized the Swedes, hoping to weaken Habsburg power in Europe. In 1631, with a small but well-disciplined army equipped with superior muskets and warm uniforms, Gustavus Adolphus won a brilliant victory at Breitenfeld. Again in 1632 he was victorious at Lützen, though he was fatally wounded in the battle.

The participation of the Swedes in the Thirty Years' War proved decisive for the future of Protes-

Soldiers Pillage a Farmhouse Billeting troops on civilian populations caused untold hardships. In this late seventeenth-century Dutch illustration, brawling soldiers take over a peasant's home, eat his food, steal his possessions, and insult his family. Peasant retaliation sometimes proved swift and bloody. *(Rijksmuseum, Amsterdam)*

tantism and later German history. When Gustavus Adolphus landed on German soil, he had already brought Denmark, Poland, Finland, and the smaller Baltic States under Swedish influence. The Swedish victories ended the Habsburg ambition of uniting all the German states under imperial authority.

The death of Gustavus Adolphus, followed by the defeat of the Swedes at the Battle of Nördlingen in 1634, prompted the French to enter the war on the side of the Protestants. Thus began the French, or international, phase (1635–1648) of the Thirty Years' War. For almost a century, French foreign policy had been based on opposition to the Habsburgs, because a weak empire divided into scores of independent principalities enhanced France's international stature. In 1622, when the Dutch had resumed the war against Spain, the French had supported Holland. Now, in 1635, Cardinal Richelieu declared war on Spain and again sent financial and military assistance to the Swedes and the German Protestant princes. The war dragged on. French, Dutch, and Swedes, supported by Scots, Finns, and German mercenaries, burned, looted, and destroyed German agriculture

and commerce. The Thirty Years' War lasted so long because neither side had the resources to win a quick, decisive victory. Finally, in October 1648, peace was achieved.

The treaties signed at Münster and Osnabrück, commonly called the "Peace of Westphalia," mark a turning point in European political, religious, and social history. The treaties recognized the sovereign, independent authority of the German princes. Each ruler could govern his particular territory and make war and peace as well. With power in the hands of more than three hundred princes, with no central government, courts, or means of controlling unruly princes, the Holy Roman Empire as a real state was effectively destroyed (Map 18.4).

The independence of the United Provinces of the Netherlands was acknowledged. The international

MAP 18.4 Europe in 1648 Which country emerged from the Thirty Years' War as the strongest European power? What dynastic house was that country's major rival in the early modern period?

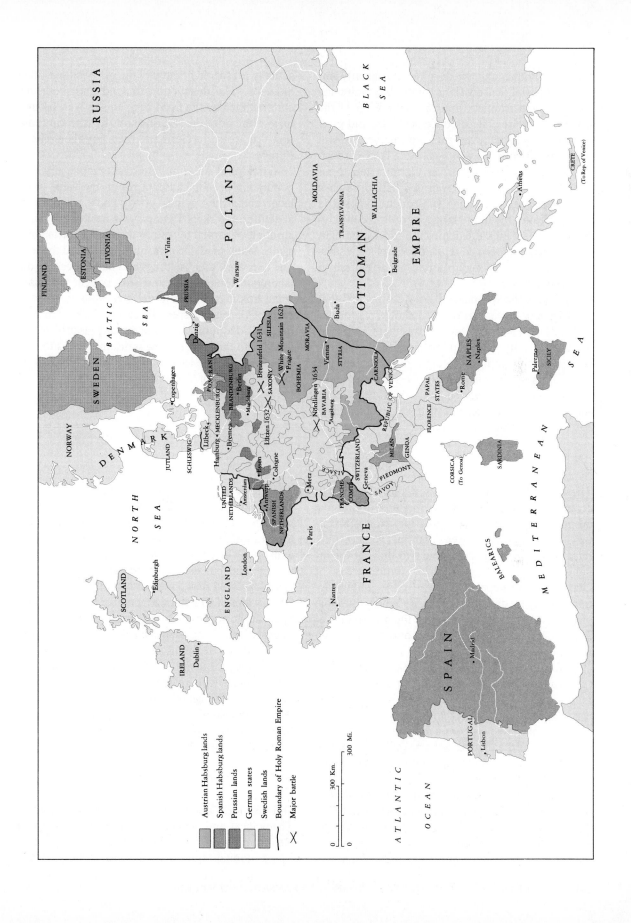

RUSSIA

BLACK SEA

FINLAND

ESTONIA

LIVONIA

POLAND

MOLDAVIA

•Vilna

WALLACHIA

TRANSYLVANIA

OTTOMAN EMPIRE

SWEDEN

BALTIC SEA

•Warsaw

•Belgrade

PRUSSIA

•Danzig

SILESIA

Buda•

NORWAY

DENMARK

•Copenhagen

POMERANA

MECKLENBURG

BRANDENBURG

Berlin•

•Magdeburg

Breitenfeld 1631

White Mountain 1620

Prague•

MORAVIA

Vienna•

STYRIA

CARNIOLA

NAPLES

Naples

•Palermo

SICILY

SEA

JUTLAND

SCHLESWIG

Lübeck•

Hamburg•

Bremen•

SAXONY

Lützen 1632

Nördlingen 1634

BOHEMIA

REPUBLIC OF VENICE

PAPAL STATES

•Rome

PAPAL STATES

NORTH SEA

UNITED NETHERLANDS

Amsterdam•

Hesse•

Cologne•

BAVARIA

Augsburg•

FLORENCE

SARDINIA

SCOTLAND

•Edinburgh

ENGLAND

London•

Antwerp•

SPANISH NETHERLANDS

•Metz

ALSACE

SWITZERLAND

Geneva•

FRANCHE COMTÉ

MILAN

PIEDMONT

SAVOY

GENOA

CORSICA

(To Genoa)

CRETE

(To Rep. of Venice)

Athens•

IRELAND

Dublin•

•Paris

FRANCE

BALEARICS

MEDITERRANEAN SEA

ATLANTIC OCEAN

Nantes•

SPAIN

Madrid•

PORTUGAL

Lisbon•

Austrian Habsburg lands

Spanish Habsburg lands

Prussian lands

German states

Swedish lands

Boundary of Holy Roman Empire

Major battle

300 Km.

300 Mi.

stature of France and Sweden was also greatly improved. The political divisions within the empire, the weak German frontiers, and the acquisition of the province of Alsace increased France's size and prestige. The treaties allowed France to intervene at will in German affairs. Sweden received a large cash indemnity and jurisdiction over German territories along the Baltic Sea. The powerful Swedish presence in northeastern Germany subsequently posed a major threat to the future kingdom of Brandenburg-Prussia. The treaties also denied the papacy the right to participate in German religious affairs—a restriction symbolizing the reduced role of the church in European politics.

In religion, the Westphalian treaties stipulated that the Augsburg agreement of 1555 should stand permanently. The sole modification was that Calvinism, along with Catholicism and Lutheranism, would become a legally permissible creed. In practice, the north German states remained Protestant, the south German states Catholic. The war settled little. Both sides had wanted peace, and with remarkable illogic they fought for thirty years to get it.

Germany After the Thirty Years' War

The Thirty Years' War was a disaster for the German economy and society, probably the most destructive event in German history before the twentieth century. Population losses were frightful. Perhaps one-third of the urban residents and two-fifths of the inhabitants of rural areas died. Entire areas of Germany were depopulated, partly by military actions, partly by disease—typhus, dysentery, bubonic plague, and syphilis accompanied the movements of armies—and partly by the thousands of refugees who fled to safer areas.

In the late sixteenth and early seventeenth centuries, all Europe experienced an economic crisis primarily caused by the influx of silver from the Americas. Because the Thirty Years' War was fought on German soil, these economic difficulties were badly aggravated in the empire. Scholars still cannot estimate the value of losses in agricultural land and livestock, in trade and commerce. The trade of southern cities like Augsburg, already hard hit by the shift in transportation routes from the Mediterranean to the Atlantic, was virtually destroyed by the fighting in the south. Meanwhile, towns like Lübeck, Hamburg, and Bremen in the north and Essen in the Ruhr area

actually prospered because of the many refugees they attracted. The destruction of land and foodstuffs, compounded by the flood of Spanish silver, brought on a severe price rise. During and after the war, inflation was worse in Germany than anywhere else in Europe.

Agricultural areas suffered catastrophically. The population decline caused a rise in the value of the labor, and owners of great estates had to pay more for agricultural workers. Farmers who needed only small amounts of capital to restore their lands started over again. Many small farmers, however, lacked the revenue to rework their holdings and had to become day laborers. Nobles and landlords bought up many small holdings and acquired great estates. In some parts of Germany, especially east of the Elbe in areas like Mecklenburg and Pomerania, peasants' loss of land led to the rise of a new serfdom.[21] Thus the war contributed to the legal and economic decline of the largest segment of German society.

CHANGING ATTITUDES

The age of religious wars revealed extreme and violent contrasts. While Europeans indulged in gross sensuality, the social status of women declined. The exploration of new continents reflects deep curiosity and broad intelligence, yet Europeans believed in witches and burned thousands at the stake. Europeans explored new continents, partly with the missionary aim of Christianizing native peoples. Yet the Spanish, Portuguese, Dutch, and English proceeded to enslave the Indians and blacks they encountered. It was a deeply religious period in which men fought passionately for their beliefs; 70 percent of the books printed dealt with religious subjects. Yet the times saw the beginnings of religious skepticism. Sexism, racism, and skepticism had all originated in ancient times. But late in the sixteenth century they began to take on their familiar modern forms.

The Status of Women

Did new ideas about women appear in this period? Theological and popular literature on marriage in Reformation Europe helps to answer this question. These manuals emphasize the qualities expected of each partner. A husband was obliged to provide for the material welfare of his wife and children, to protect his family while remaining steady and self-controlled. He was to rule his household firmly but justly; he was not to behave like a tyrant, a guideline counselors repeated frequently. A wife was to be mature, a good household manager, and subservient and faithful to her spouse. The husband also owed fidelity. Both Protestant and Catholic moralists rejected the double standard of sexual morality as a threat to family unity. Counselors believed that marriage should be based on mutual respect and trust. While they discouraged impersonal unions arranged by parents, they did not think romantic attachments—based on physical attraction and emotional love—a sound basis for an enduring relationship.

Moralists held that the household was a woman's first priority. She might assist in her own or her husband's business and do charitable work. Involvement in social or public activities, however, was inappropriate because it distracted the wife from her primary responsibility, her household. If women suffered under their husbands' yoke, writers explained that submission was their punishment inherited from Eve, penance for man's fall, like the pain of childbearing. Moreover, they said, a woman's lot was no worse than a man's: he must earn the family's bread by the sweat of his brow. [22]

Catholics viewed marriage as a sacramental union, which, validly entered into, could not be dissolved. Protestants stressed the contractual form of marriage, whereby each partner promised the other support, companionship, and the sharing of mutual goods. Protestants recognized a mutual right to divorce and remarriage for various reasons, including adultery and irreparable breakdown. [23] Society in the early modern period was patriarchal. While women neither lost their identity nor lacked meaningful work, the all-pervasive assumption was that men ruled. Leading students of the Lutherans, Catholics, French Calvinists, and English Puritans tend to concur that there was no amelioration in women's definitely subordinate status.

There are some remarkable success stories, however. Elizabeth Hardwick, the orphaned daughter of an obscure English country squire, made four careful marriages, each of which brought her more property and carried her higher up the social ladder. She managed her estates, amounting to more than a hundred thousand acres, with a degree of business sense rare in any age. The two great mansions she built, Chatsworth and Hardwick, stand today as monuments to her acumen. As countess of Shrewsbury, "Bess of Hardwick" so thoroughly enjoyed the trust of Queen Elizabeth that Elizabeth appointed her jailer of Mary, Queen of Scots. Having established several aristocratic dynasties, the countess of Shrewsbury died in 1608, past her eightieth year, one of the richest people in England. [24]

Artists' drawings of plump, voluptuous women and massive, muscular men reveal the contemporary standards of physical beauty. It was a sensual age that gloried in the delights of the flesh. Some people found sexual satisfaction with both sexes. Reformers and public officials simultaneously condemned and condoned sexual "sins." The oldest profession had many practitioners, and, when in 1566 Pope Pius IV expelled all the prostitutes from Rome, so many people left and the city suffered such a loss of revenue that in less than a month the pope was forced to rescind the order. Scholars debated Saint Augustine's notion that whores serve a useful social function by preventing worse sins. Prostitution was common because desperate poverty forced women and young men into it. The general public took it for granted. Consequently, civil authorities in both Catholic and Protestant countries licensed houses of public prostitution. These establishments were intended for the convenience of single men, and some Protestant cities, such as Geneva and Zurich, installed officials in the brothels with the express purpose of preventing married men from patronizing them. Moralists naturally railed against prostitution. For example, Melchior Ambach, the Lutheran editor of many tracts against adultery and whoring, wrote in 1543 that if "houses of women" for single and married men were allowed, why not provide a "house of boys" for womenfolk who lack a husband to service them? "Would whoring be any worse for the poor, needy female sex?"[25] Ambach, of course, was not being serious: by treating infidelity from the perspective of female rather than male customers, he was still insisting that prostitution destroyed the family and society.

What became of the thousands of women who left their convents and nunneries during the Reformation? The question concerns primarily women of the upper classes, who formed the dominant social group in the religious houses of late medieval Europe. (Single women of the middle and working classes in the sixteenth and seventeenth centuries worked in many

Veronese: Mars and Venus United by Love Taking a theme from classical mythology, the Venetian painter Veronese celebrates in clothing, architecture, and landscape the luxurious wealth of the aristocracy (painted ca 1580). The curvaceous Venus and the muscular Mars reflect the frank sensuality of the age. *(Metropolitan Museum of Art, New York, John Stewart Kennedy Fund, 1910)*

occupations and professions—as butchers, shopkeepers, nurses, goldsmiths, and midwives and in the weaving and printing industries. Those who were married normally assisted in their husbands' businesses.) Luther and the Protestant reformers believed that the monastic cloister symbolized antifeminism, that young girls were forced by their parents into convents and once there were bullied by men into staying. Therefore reformers favored the suppression of women's religious houses and encouraged ex-nuns to marry. Marriage, the reformers maintained, not only gave women emotional and sexual satisfaction, it freed them from clerical domination, cultural deprivation, and sexual repression.[26] It would appear, consequently, that women passed from clerical domination to subservience to husbands.

If some nuns in the Middle Ages lacked a genuine religious vocation and if some religious houses witnessed financial mismanagement and moral laxness, convents nevertheless provided women of the upper classes with scope for their literary, artistic, medical, or administrative talents if they could not or would not marry. Marriage became virtually the only occupation for Protestant women. This helps explain why Anglicans, Calvinists, and Lutherans established communities of religious women, such as the Lutheran one at Kaiserwerth in the Rhineland, in the eighteenth and nineteenth centuries.[27]

THE GREAT EUROPEAN WITCH HUNT

The great European witch scare reveals something about contemporary attitudes toward women. The period of the religious wars witnessed a startling increase in the phenomenon of witch-hunting, whose prior history was long but sporadic. "A witch," according to Chief Justice Coke of England, "was a person who hath conference with the Devil to consult with him or to do some act." This definition by the highest legal authority in England demonstrates that educated people, as well as the ignorant, believed in witches. Belief in *witches*—individuals who could mysteriously injure other people, for instance by causing them to become blind or impotent, and who could harm animals, for example, by preventing cows from giving milk—dates back to the dawn of time. For centuries, tales had circulated about old women who made nocturnal travels on greased broomsticks to *sabbats,* or assemblies of witches, where they participated in sexual orgies and feasted on the flesh of infants. In the popular imagination witches had definite characteristics. The vast majority were married women or widows between fifty and seventy years old, crippled or bent with age, with pockmarked skin. They often practiced midwifery or folk medicine, and most had sharp tongues.

In the sixteenth century, religious reformers' extreme notions of the Devil's powers and the insecurity created by the religious wars contributed to the growth of belief in witches. The idea developed that witches made pacts with the Devil in return for the power to work mischief on their enemies. Since pacts with the Devil meant the renunciation of God, witchcraft was considered heresy, and all religions persecuted it.

Fear of witches took a terrible toll of innocent lives in parts of Europe. In southwestern Germany, 3,229 witches were executed between 1561 and 1670, most by burning. The communities of the Swiss Confederation tried 8,888 persons between 1470 and 1700 and executed 5,417 of them as witches. In all the centuries before 1500, witches in England had been suspected of causing perhaps "three deaths, a broken leg, several destructive storms and some bewitched genitals." Yet between 1559 and 1736, witches were thought to have caused thousands of deaths, and almost 1,000 witches were executed in England.[28]

Historians and anthropologists have offered a variety of explanations for the great European witch hunt. Some scholars maintain that charges of witchcraft were a means of accounting for inexplicable misfortunes. Just as the English in the fifteenth century had blamed their military failures in France on Joan of Arc's sorcery, so in the seventeenth century the English Royal College of Physicians attributed undiagnosable illnesses to witchcraft. Some scholars hold that in small communities, which typically insisted on strict social conformity, charges of witchcraft were a means of attacking and eliminating the nonconformist; witches, in other words, served the collective need for scapegoats. The evidence of witches' trials, some writers suggest, shows that women were not accused because they harmed or threatened their neighbors; rather, their communities believed such women worshiped the Devil, engaged in wild sexual activities with him, and ate infants. Other scholars argue the exact opposite: that people were tried and executed as witches because their neighbors feared their evil powers. Finally, there is the theory that the unbridled sexuality attributed to witches was a psychological projection on the part of their accusers, resulting from Christianity's repression of sexuality.

The reasons for the persecution of women as witches probably varied from place to place. Though several hypotheses exist, scholars still cannot fully understand the phenomenon. Nevertheless, given the broad strand of misogyny (hatred of women) in Western religion, the ancient belief in the susceptibility of women (so-called weaker vessels) to the Devil's allurements, and the pervasive seventeenth-century belief about women's multiple and demanding orgasms and thus their sexual insatiability, it is not difficult to understand why women were accused of all sorts of mischief and witchcraft. Charges of witchcraft provided a legal basis for the execution of tens of thousands of women. As the most important capital crime for women in early modern times, witchcraft has considerable significance for the history and status of women.[29]

EUROPEAN SLAVERY AND THE ORIGINS OF AMERICAN RACISM

Almost all peoples in the world have engaged in the enslavement of other human beings at some time in their histories. Since ancient times, victors in battle have enslaved conquered peoples. In the later Middle Ages slavery was deeply entrenched in southern Italy, Sicily, Crete, and Mediterranean Spain. The bubonic plague, famines, and other epidemics created a severe shortage of agricultural and domestic workers in parts of northern Europe, encouraging Italian merchants to buy slaves from the Balkans, Thrace, southern Russia, and central Anatolia for sale in the West. In 1364 the Florentine government allowed the unlimited importation of slaves, so long as they were not Roman Catholics. Between 1414 and 1423, at least ten thousand slaves were sold in Venice alone. Where profits were lucrative, papal threats of excommunication completely failed to stop Genoese slave traders. The Genoese set up colonial stations in the Crimea and along the Black Sea. According to an international authority on slavery, these outposts were "virtual laboratories" for the development of slave plantation agriculture in the New World.[30] This form of slavery had nothing to do with race; almost all slaves were white. How, then, did black African slavery enter the European picture and take root in the New World?

In 1453 the Ottoman capture of Constantinople halted the flow of white slaves from the Black Sea region and the Balkans. Mediterranean Europe, cut off from its traditional source of slaves, had no alternative source for slave labor but sub-Saharan Africa. The centuries-old trans-Saharan trade was greatly stimulated by finding a ready market in the vineyards and sugar plantations of Sicily and Majorca. By the later fifteenth century, the Mediterranean had developed an "American" form of slavery before the discovery of America.

Meanwhile, the Genoese and other Italians had colonized the Canary Islands off the western coast of Africa. Prince Henry the Navigator's sailors discovered the Madeira Islands and made settlements there. In this stage of European expansion, "the history of slavery became inextricably tied up with the history

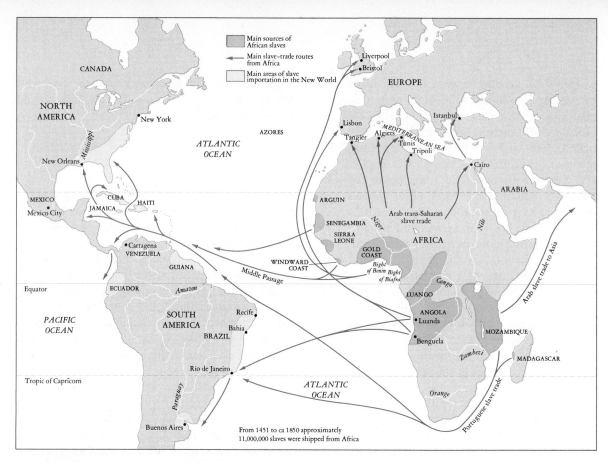

MAP 18.5 The African Slave Trade Decades before the discovery of America, Greek, Russian, Bulgarian, Armenian, and then black slaves worked the plantation economies of southern Italy, Sicily, Portugal, and Mediterranean Spain—thereby serving as models for the American form of slavery.

of sugar." Though an expensive luxury that only the affluent could afford, population increases and monetary expansion in the fifteenth century led to a growing demand for sugar. Resourceful Italians provided the capital, cane, and technology for sugar cultivation on plantations in southern Portugal, Madeira, and the Canary Islands. In Portugal between 1490 and 1530, between 300 and 2,000 black slaves were annually imported into the port of Lisbon (Map 18.5). From Lisbon, where African slaves performed most of the manual labor and constituted about 10 percent of the city's population, slaves were transported to the sugar plantations of Madeira, the Azores, the Cape Verdes, and then Brazil. Sugar and the small Atlantic islands gave New World slavery its distinctive shape.[31]

As already discussed, European expansion across the Atlantic led to the economic exploitation of the Americas. In the New World the major problem

settlers faced was a shortage of labor. As early as 1495 the Spanish solved the problem by enslaving the native Indians. In the next two centuries, the Portuguese, Dutch, and English followed suit.

Unaccustomed to any form of forced labor, certainly not to panning gold for more than twelve hours a day in the broiling sun, the Amerinds died "like fish in a bucket."[32] In 1517 Las Casas urged King Charles V to end Indian slavery in his American dominions (page 559). Las Casas recommended the importation of blacks from Africa, both because church law did not strictly forbid black slavery and because blacks could better survive under South American conditions. The king agreed, and in 1518 the African slave trade began. Columbus's introduction of sugar plants, moreover, stimulated the need for black slaves; and the experience and model of plantation slavery in Portugal and the Atlantic islands encouraged a like agricultural pattern in the New World.

Several European nations participated in the African slave trade. Portugal brought the first slaves to Brazil; by 1600, about 4,000 were being imported annually. After its founding in 1621, the Dutch West India Company, with the full support of the government of the United Provinces, transported thousands of Africans to Brazil and the Caribbean. Only in the late seventeenth century, with the chartering of the Royal African Company, did the English get involved. Thereafter, large numbers of African blacks poured into the West Indies and North America (see Map 18.5). In 1790 there were 757,181 blacks in a total U.S. population of 3,929,625. When the first census was taken in Brazil in 1798, blacks numbered about 2 million in a total population of 3.25 million.

Settlers brought to the Americas the racial attitudes they had absorbed in Europe. Their beliefs about and attitudes toward blacks derived from two basic sources: Christian theological speculation (see page 509) and Muslim ideas. In the sixteenth and seventeenth centuries, the English, for example, were extremely curious about Africans' lives and customs, and slavers' accounts were extraordinarily popular. Travel literature depicted Africans as savages because of their eating habits, morals, clothing, and social customs; as barbarians because of their language and methods of war; and as heathens because they were not Christian. English people saw similarities between apes and Africans; thus the terms *bestial* and *beastly* were frequently applied to Africans. Africans were believed to possess a potent sexuality. One seventeenth-century observer considered African men "very lustful and impudent . . . their [members'] extraordinary greatness . . . is a token of their lust." African women were considered sexually aggressive with a "temper hot and lascivious."[33]

"At the time when Columbus sailed to the New World, Islam was the largest world religion, and the only world religion that showed itself capable of expanding rapidly in areas as far apart and as different from each other as Senegal [in northwest Africa], Bosnia [in the Balkans], Java, and the Philippines."[34] Medieval Arabic literature characterized blacks as physically repulsive, mentally inferior, and primitive. In contrast to civilized peoples from the Mediterranean to China, Muslim writers claimed, sub-Saharan blacks were the only peoples who had produced no sciences or stable states. The fourteenth-century Arab historian Ibn Khaldun wrote that the "only people who accept slavery are the Negroes,

African Slave and Indian Woman A black slave approaches an Indian prostitute. Unable to explain what he wants, he point with his finger; she eagerly grasps for the coin. The Spanish caption above moralizes on the black man using stolen money—yet the Spaniards ruthlessly expropriated all South American mineral wealth. *(New York Public Library)*

owing to their low degree of humanity and their proximity to the animal stage." Though black kings, Ibn Khaldun alleged, sold their subjects without even a pretext of crime or war, the victims bore no resentment because they gave no thought to the future and have "by nature few cares and worries; dancing and rhythm are for them inborn."[35] It is easy to see how such absurd images would develop into the classic stereotypes used to justify black slavery in South and North America in the seventeenth, eighteenth, and nineteenth centuries. Medieval Christians and Muslims had similar notions of blacks as inferior and primitive people ideally suited to enslavement. Perhaps centuries of commercial contacts between Muslim and Mediterranean peoples had familiarized the latter with Muslim racial attitudes.

The racial attitudes of fourteenth- and fifteenth-century European and Muslim intellectuals, however, did not automatically become the views of the general populace in eighteenth-century America. It was the institutionalization of slavery, as manifested by slave plantation society in the Americas, that served as the laboratory of modern racism.[36]

THE ORIGIN OF MODERN SKEPTICISM: MICHEL DE MONTAIGNE

The decades of religious fanaticism, bringing in their wake death, famine, and civil anarchy, caused both Catholics and Protestants to doubt that any one faith contained absolute truth. The late sixteenth and early seventeenth centuries witnessed the beginnings of modern skepticism. *Skepticism* is a school of thought founded on doubt that total certainty or definitive knowledge is ever attainable. The skeptic is cautious and critical and suspends judgment. Perhaps the finest representative of early modern skepticism is the Frenchman Michel de Montaigne (1533–1592).

Montaigne came from a bourgeois family that had made a fortune selling salted herring and in 1477 had purchased the title and property of Montaigne in Gascony. Montaigne received a classical education before studying law and securing a judicial appointment in 1554. Though a member of the nobility, in embarking on a judicial career he identified with the new nobility of the robe. He condemned the ancient nobility of the sword for being more concerned with war and sports than with the cultivation of the mind.

At the age of thirty-eight, Montaigne resigned his judicial post, retired to his estate, and devoted the rest of his life to study, contemplation, and the effort to understand himself. Like the Greeks, he believed that the object of life was to "know thyself," for self-knowledge teaches men and women how to live in accordance with nature and God. Montaigne developed a new literary genre, the essay—from the French *essayer,* meaning "to test" or "to try"—to express his thoughts and ideas.

Montaigne's *Essays* provide insight into the mind of a remarkably humane, tolerant, and civilized man. He was a humanist; he loved the Greek and Roman writers and was always eager to learn from them. In his essay "On Solitude," he quoted the Roman poet Horace:

Reason and sense remove anxiety,
Not villas that look out upon the sea

Some said to Socrates that a certain man had grown no better by his travels. "I should think not," he said; "he took himself along with him. . . ."
We should have wife, children, goods, and above all health, if we can; but we must not bind ourselves to them so strongly that our happiness depends on them. We must reserve a back shop all our own, entirely free, in which to establish our real liberty and our principal retreat and solitude.[37]

From the ancient authors, especially the Roman Stoics, Montaigne acquired a sense of calm, inner peace, and patience. The ancient authors also inculcated in him a tolerance and broad-mindedness. Montaigne had come of age during the French civil wars, perhaps the worst kind of war. He wrote:

In this controversy . . . France is at present agitated by civil wars, the best and soundest side is undoubtedly that which maintains both the old religion and the old government of the country. However, among the good men who follow that side . . . we see many whom passion drives outside the bounds of reason, and makes them sometimes adopt unjust, violent, and even reckless courses.[38]

Though he remained a Catholic, Montaigne possessed a detachment, an independence, and a willingness to look at all sides of a question: "I listen with attention to the judgment of all men; but so far as I can remember, I have followed none but my own. Though I set little value upon my own opinion, I set no more on the opinions of others."

In the book-lined tower where Montaigne passed his days, he became a deeply learned man. Yet he was not ignorant of world affairs, and he criticized scholars and bookworms who ignored the life around them. Montaigne's essay "On Cannibals" reflects the impact of overseas discoveries on Europeans' consciousness. His tolerant mind rejected the notion that one culture is superior to another:

I long had a man in my house that lived ten or twelve years in the New World . . . in . . . [Brazil]. . . .

I find that there is nothing barbarous and savage in [that] nation, by anything that I can gather, excepting, that every one gives the title of barbarism to everything that is not in use in his own country. As, indeed, we have no other level of truth and reason, than the example and idea of the opinions and customs of the place wherein we live. [39]

In his belief in the nobility of human beings in the state of nature, uncorrupted by organized society, and in his cosmopolitan attitude toward different civilizations, Montaigne anticipated many eighteenth-century thinkers.

The thought of Michel de Montaigne marks a sharp break with the past. Faith and religious certainty had characterized the intellectual attitudes of Western society for a millennium. Montaigne's rejection of any kind of dogmatism, his secularism, and his skepticism represented a basic change. In his own time and throughout the seventeenth century, few would have agreed with him. The publication of his ideas, however, anticipated a basic shift in attitudes. Montaigne inaugurated an era of doubt. "Wonder," he said, "is the foundation of all philosophy, research is the means of all learning, and ignorance is the end." [40]

ELIZABETHAN AND JACOBEAN LITERATURE

The age of the religious wars and European expansion also experienced an extraordinary degree of intellectual ferment. In addition to the development of the essay as a distinct literary genre, the late sixteenth and early seventeenth centuries fostered remarkable creativity in other branches of literature. England, especially in the latter part of Elizabeth's reign and the first years of that of her successor, James I (1603–1625), witnessed unparalleled brilliance. The terms *Elizabethan* and *Jacobean* (referring to the reign of James) are used to designate the English music, poetry, prose, and drama of this period. The poems of Sir Philip Sidney (1554–1586), such as *Astrophel and Stella,* strongly influenced later poetic writing. *The Faerie Queene* of Edmund Spenser (1552–1599) endures as one of the greatest moral epics in any language. The rare poetic beauty of the plays of Christopher Marlowe (1564–1593), such as *Tamburlaine*

and *The Jew of Malta,* paved the way for the work of Shakespeare. Above all, the immortal dramas of Shakespeare and stately prose of the Authorized or King James Bible mark the Elizabethan and Jacobean periods as the golden age of English literature.

William Shakespeare (1564–1616), the son of a successful glove manufacturer who rose to the highest municipal office in the Warwickshire town of Stratford-on-Avon, chose a career on the London stage. By 1592 he had gained recognition as an actor and playwright. Between 1599 and 1603, Shakespeare performed in the Lord Chamberlain's Company and became co-owner of the Globe Theatre, which after 1603 presented his plays.

Shakespeare's genius lies in the originality of his characterizations, the diversity of his plots, his understanding of human psychology, and his unexcelled gift for language. Shakespeare was a Renaissance man in his deep appreciation for classical culture, individualism, and humanism. Such plays as *Julius Caesar, Pericles,* and *Antony and Cleopatra* deal with classical subjects and figures. Several of his comedies have Italian Renaissance settings. The nine history plays, including *Richard II, Richard III,* and *Henry IV,* enjoyed the greatest popularity among Shakespeare's contemporaries. Written during the decade after the defeat of the Spanish Armada, the history plays express English national consciousness. Lines such as these from *Richard II* reflect this sense of national greatness with unparalleled eloquence:

This royal Throne of Kings, this sceptre'd Isle,
This earth of Majesty, this seat of Mars,
This other Eden, demi-paradise,
This fortress built by Nature for herself,
Against infection and the hand of war:
This happy breed of men, this little world,
This precious stone, set in the silver sea,
Which serves it in the office of a wall,
Or as a moat defensive to a house,
Against the envy of less happier Lands,
This blessed plot, this earth, this Realm, this England.

Shakespeare's later plays, above all the tragedies *Othello, Macbeth,* and *Hamlet,* explore an enormous range of human problems and are open to an almost infinite variety of interpretations. *Othello,* which the nineteenth-century historian Thomas Macaulay called "perhaps the greatest work in the world," portrays an honorable man destroyed by a flaw in his

Velazquez: Juan de Pareja This portrait (1650) of the Spanish painter Velazquez's one-time assistant, a black man of obvious intellectual and sensual power and himself a renowned religious painter, suggests the integration of some blacks in seventeenth-century society. The elegant lace collar attests to his middle-class status. *(Metropolitan Museum of Art, purchased with purchase funds and special contributions bequeathed or given by friends of the museum)*

own character and the satanic evil of his supposed friend Iago. *Macbeth*'s central theme is exorbitant ambition. Shakespeare analyzes the psychology of sin in the figures of Macbeth and Lady Macbeth, whose mutual love under the pressure of ambition leads to their destruction. The central figure in *Hamlet,* a play suffused with individuality, wrestles with moral problems connected with revenge and with man's relationship to life and death. The soliloquy in which Hamlet debates suicide is perhaps the most widely quoted passage in English literature:

To be, or not to be: that is the question:
Whether 'tis nobler in the mind to suffer
The slings and arrows of outrageous fortune,
Or to take arms against a sea of troubles,
And by opposing end them? . . .

Hamlet's sad cry, "There is nothing either good or bad but thinking makes it so," expresses the anguish and uncertainty of modern man. *Hamlet* has always enjoyed great popularity, because in his many faceted personality people have seen an aspect of themselves.

Shakespeare's dynamic language bespeaks his extreme sensitivity to the sounds and meanings of words. Perhaps no phrase better summarizes the reason for his immortality than this line, slightly modified, from *Antony and Cleopatra*: "Age cannot wither [him], nor custom stale/ [his] infinite variety."

The other great masterpiece of the Jacobean period was the Authorized Bible. At a theological conference in 1604, a group of Puritans urged James I to support a new translation of the Bible. The king in turn assigned the task to a committee of scholars, who published their efforts in 1611. Based on the best scriptural research of the time and divided into chapters and verses, the "Authorized Version," so called because it was produced under royal sponsorship—it had no official ecclesiastical endorsement—is actually a revision of earlier Bibles more than an original work. Yet it provides a superb expression of the mature English vernacular in the early seventeenth century. Thus Psalm 37:

Fret not thy selfe because of evill doers, neither bee thou
envious against the workers of iniquitie.
For they shall soone be cut downe like the grasse; and
wither as the greene herbe.
Trust in the Lord, and do good, so shalt thou dwell in the
land, and verely thou shalt be fed.
Delight thy selfe also in the Lord; and he shall give thee
the desires of thine heart.
Commit thy way unto the Lord: trust also in him, and he
shall bring it to passe.
And he shall bring forth thy righteousness as the light,
and thy judgement as the noone day.

The Authorized Version represented the Anglican and Puritan desire to encourage lay people to read the Scriptures. It quickly achieved great popularity and displaced all earlier versions. British settlers carried this Bible to the North American colonies, where it became known as the "King James Bible." For centuries the King James Bible has had a profound influence on the language and lives of English-speaking peoples.

In the sixteenth and seventeenth centuries, Europeans for the first time gained access to large parts of the globe. European peoples had the intellectual curiosity, driving ambition, and scientific technology to attempt feats that were as difficult and expensive then as going to the moon is today. Exploration and exploitation contributed to a more sophisticated standard of living, in the form of spices and Asian luxury goods, and to a terrible international inflation resulting from the influx of South American silver and gold. Governments, the upper classes, and especially the peasantry were badly hurt by the inflation. Meanwhile the middle class of bankers, shippers, financiers, and manufacturers prospered for much of the seventeenth century.

Europeans' technological development contributed to their conquest of Aztec Mexico and Inca Peru. Along with technology, Europeans brought disease to the New World, which caused a terrible holocaust among the Indians. Overseas reconnaissance led to the first global seaborne commercial empires of the Portuguese, the Spanish, and the Dutch.

European expansion and colonization took place against a background of religious conflict and rising national consciousness. The sixteenth and seventeenth centuries were by no means a secular period. Though the medieval religious framework had broken down, people still thought largely in religious terms. Europeans explained what they did politically and economically in terms of religious doctrine. Religious ideology served as a justification for a variety of conflicts: the French nobles' opposition to the crown, the Dutch struggle for political and economic independence from Spain. In Germany, religious pluralism and foreign ambitions added to political difficulties. After 1648 the divisions between Protestant and Catholic tended to become permanent. Sexism, racism, and religious skepticism were harbingers of developments to come.

NOTES

1. Quoted in C. M. Cipolla, *Guns, Sails, and Empires: Technological Innovation and the Early Phases of European Expansion, 1400–1700* (New York: Minerva Press, 1965), pp. 115–116.
2. Quoted in S. E. Morison, *Admiral of the Ocean Sea: A Life of Christopher Columbus* (Boston: Little, Brown, 1946), p. 154.
3. See C. R. Phillips, *Ciudad Real, 1500–1750: Growth, Crisis, and Readjustment in the Spanish Economy* (Cambridge, Mass.: Harvard University Press, 1979), pp. 103–104, 115.
4. Quoted in Cipolla, *Guns, Sails, and Empires,* p. 132.
5. Quoted in F. H. Littell, *The Macmillan Atlas History of Christianity* (New York: Macmillan, 1976), p. 75.
6. Quoted in Cipolla, *Guns, Sails, and Empires,* p. 133.
7. J. H. Parry, *The Age of Reconnaissance. Discovery, Exploration and Settlement, 1450–1650* (Berkeley, Calif: University of California Press, 1981), chaps. 3, 5.
8. G. C. Vaillant, *Aztecs of Mexico* (New York: Penguin Books, 1979), p. 241. Chapter 15, on which this section leans, is fascinating.
9. V. W. Von Hagen, *Realm of the Incas* (New York: New American Library, 1961), pp. 204–207.
10. N. Sanchez-Albornoz, *The Population of Latin America: A History,* trans. W. A. R. Richardson (Berkeley, Calif: University of California Press, 1974), p. 41.
11. Quoted in A. W. Crosby, *The Columbian Exchange: Biological and Cultural Consequences of 1492* (Westport, Conn.: Greenwood Publishing, 1972), p. 39.
12. Ibid., chap. 2, pp. 35–59.
13. Quoted in C. Gibson, ed., *The Black Legend: Anti-Spanish Attitudes in the Old World and the New* (New York: Alfred Knopf, 1971), pp. 74–75.
14. Quoted in L. B. Rout, Jr., *The African Experience in Spanish America* (New York: Cambridge University Press, 1976), p. 23.
15. See Parry, *Age of Reconnaissance,* chaps. 12, 14, 15.
16. See J. Hale, "War and Public Opinion in the Fifteenth and Sixteenth Centuries," *Past and Present* 22 (July 1962):18–32.
17. Quoted in N. Z. Davis, "The Rites of Violence: Religious Riots in Sixteenth Century France," *Past and Present* 59 (May 1973):59.
18. See ibid., pp. 51–91.
19. Quoted in J. L. Motley, *The Rise of the Dutch Republic,* vol. 1 (Philadelphia: David McKay, 1898), p.109.
20. Quoted in P. Smith, *The Age of the Reformation* (New York: Henry Holt, 1951), p. 248.

21. H. Kamen, "The Economic and Social Consequences of the Thirty Years' War," *Past and Present* 39 (April 1968): 44–61.

22. Based heavily on S. Ozment, *When Fathers Ruled: Family Life in Reformation Europe* (Cambridge, Mass.: Harvard University Press, 1983), pp. 50–99.

23. Ibid., pp. 85–92.

24. See D. Durant, *Bess of Hardwick: Portrait of an Elizabethan Dynast* (London: Weidenfeld & Nicolson, 1977).

25. Quoted in Ozment, *When Fathers Ruled,* p. 56.

26. Ibid., pp. 9–14.

27. See F. Biot, *The Rise of Protestant Monasticism* (Baltimore: Helicon Press, 1968), pp. 74–78.

28. N. Cohn, *Europe's Inner Demons: An Enquiry Inspired by the Great Witch-hunt* (New York: Basic Books, 1975), pp. 253–254; K. Thomas, *Religion and the Decline of Magic* (New York: Scribner's, 1971), pp. 450–455.

29. See E. W. Monter, "The Pedestal and the Stake: Courtly Love and Witchcraft," in *Becoming Visible: Women in European History,* ed. R. Bridenthal and C. Koonz (Boston: Houghton Mifflin, 1977), pp. 132–135, and A. Fraser, *The Weaker Vessel* (New York: Random House, 1985), pp. 100–103.

30. See C. Verlinden, *The Beginnings of Modern Colonization,* trans. Y. Freccero (Ithaca, N.Y.: Cornell University Press, 1970), pp. 5–6, 80–97.

31. This section leans heavily on D. B. Davis, *Slavery and Human Progress* (New York: Oxford University Press, 1984), pp. 54–62.

32. Quoted in D. P. Mannix with M. Cordley, *Black Cargoes: A History of the Atlantic Slave Trade* (New York: Viking, 1968), p. 5.

33. Ibid., p. 19.

34. Quoted in Davis, *Slavery and Human Progress,* p. 40.

35. Ibid., pp. 43–44.

36. W. Rodney, "Africa, Europe and the Americas," in R. Gray, ed., *Cambridge History of Africa* (Cambridge: Cambridge University Press, 1975), vol. 4, pp. 580–581, 590.

37. Quoted in D. M. Frame, trans., *The Complete Works of Montaigne* (Stanford, Calif.: Stanford University Press, 1958), pp. 175–176.

38. Ibid., p. 177.

39. Quoted in C. Cotton, trans., *The Essays of Michel de Montaigne* (New York: A. L. Burt, 1893), pp. 207, 210.

40. Ibid., p. 523.

SUGGESTED READING

Perhaps the best starting point for the study of European society in the age of exploration is Parry's *Age of Reconnaissance,* cited in the Notes, which treats the causes and consequences of the voyages of discovery. Parry's splendidly illustrated *The Discovery of South America* (1979) examines Europeans' reactions to the maritime discoveries and treats the entire concept of new *discoveries.* The urbane studies of C. M. Cipolla present fascinating material on technological and sociological developments written in a lucid style: In addition to the title cited in the Notes, see *Clocks and Culture, 1300–1700* (1967); *Cristofano and the Plague: A Study in the History of Public Health in the Age of Galileo* (1973); and *Public Health and the Medical Profession in the Renaissance* (1976). Morison's *Admiral of the Ocean Sea,* also listed in the Notes, is the standard biography of the great discoverer. The advanced student should consult F. Braudel, *Civilization and Capitalism, 15th–18th Century,* trans. S. Reynolds, vol. 1, *The Structures of Everyday Life* (1981); vol. 2, *The Wheels of Commerce* (1982); and vol. 3, *The Perspective of the World* (1984). These three fat volumes combine vast erudition, a global perspective, and remarkable illustrations.

For the religious wars, in addition to the references in the Suggested Reading for Chapter 17 and the Notes to this chapter, see J. H. M. Salmon, *Society in Crisis: France in the Sixteenth Century* (1975), which traces the fate of French institutions during the civil wars. A. N. Galpern, *The Religions of the People in Sixteenth-century Champagne* (1976), is a useful case study in religious anthropology, and W. A. Christian, Jr., *Local Religion in Sixteenth Century Spain* (1981), traces the attitudes and practices of ordinary people.

A cleverly illustrated introduction to the Low Countries is K. H. D. Kaley, *The Dutch in the Seventeenth Century* (1972). The old study of J. L. Motley cited in the Notes still provides a good comprehensive treatment and makes fascinating reading. For Spanish military operations in the Low Countries, see G. Parker, *The Army of Flanders and the Spanish Road, 1567–1659: The Logistics of Spanish Victory and Defeat in the Low Countries' Wars* (1972). The same author's *Spain and the Netherlands, 1559–1659: Ten Studies* (1979) contains useful essays, of which students may especially want to consult "Why Did the Dutch Revolt Last So Long?" For the later phases of the Dutch-Spanish conflict, see J. I. Israel, *The Dutch Republic and the Hispanic World, 1606–1661* (1982), which treats the struggle in global perspective.

Of the many biographies of Elizabeth of England, W. T. MacCaffrey, *Queen Elizabeth and the Making of Policy, 1572–1588* (1981), examines the problems posed by the Reformation and how Elizabeth solved them. J. E. Neale, *Queen Elizabeth I* (1957), remains valuable, and L. B. Smith, *The Elizabethan Epic* (1966), is a splendid evocation of the age of Shakespeare with Elizabeth at the center. The best recent biography is C. Erickson, *The First Elizabeth* (1983), a fine, psychologically resonant portrait.

Nineteenth- and early twentieth-century historians described the defeat of the Spanish Armada as a great victory for Protestantism, democracy, and capitalism, which those scholars tended to link together. Recent historians have treated the event in terms of its contemporary significance. For a sympathetic but judicious portrait of the man who launched the armada, see G. Parker, *Philip II* (1978). D. Howarth, *The Voyage of the Armada* (1982), discusses the expedition largely in terms of the individuals involved, while G. Mattingly, *The Armada* (1959), gives the diplomatic and political background; both Howarth and Mattingly tell very exciting tales. M. Lewis, *The Spanish Armada* (1972), also tells a good story, but strictly from the English perspective. Significant aspects of Portuguese culture are treated in A. Hower and R. Preto-Rodas, eds., *Empire in Transition. The Portuguese World in the Time of Camões* (1985).

C. V. Wedgwood, *The Thirty Years' War* (1961), must be qualified in light of recent research on the social and economic effects of the war, but it is still a good (if detailed) starting point on a difficult period. A variety of opinions on the causes and results of the war are given in T. K. Rabb's anthology, *The Thirty Years' War* (1981). In addition to the articles by Hale and Kamen cited in the Notes, the following articles, both of which appear in the scholarly journal *Past and Present,* provide some of the latest important findings: J. V. Polišenský, "The Thirty Years' War and the Crises and Revolutions of Sixteenth Century Europe," 39 (1968), and, for the overall significance of Sweden, M. Roberts, "Queen Christina and the General Crisis of the Seventeenth Century," 22 (1962).

As background to the intellectual changes instigated by the Reformation, D. C. Wilcox, *In Search of God and Self: Renaissance and Reformation Thought* (1975), contains a perceptive analysis, and T. Ashton, ed., *Crisis in Europe, 1560–1660* (1967), is fundamental. For women, marriage, and the family, see L. Stone, *The Family, Sex, and Marriage in England, 1500–1800* (1977), an important but controversial work; D. Underdown, "The Taming of the Scold," and S. Amussen, "Gender, Family, and the Social Order," in A. Fletcher and J. Stevenson, eds., *Order and Disorder in Early Modern England* (1985); A. Macfarlane, *Marriage and Love in England. Modes of Reproduction, 1300–1848* (1986); C. R. Boxer, *Women in Iberian Expansion Overseas, 1415–1815* (1975), an invaluable study of women's role in overseas immigration; and S. M. Wyntjes, "Women in the Reformation Era," in Bridenthal and Koonz's *Becoming Visible* (see the Notes), a quick survey of conditions in different countries. Ozment's *When Fathers Ruled,* cited in the Notes, is a seminal study concentrating on Germany and Switzerland.

On witches and witchcraft see, in addition to the titles by Cohn and Thomas in the Notes, J. B. Russell, *Witchcraft in the Middle Ages* (1976) and *Lucifer: The Devil in the Middle Ages* (1984); M. Summers, *The History of Witchcraft and Demonology* (1973); and H. R. Trevor-Roper, *The European Witch-craze of the Sixteenth and Seventeenth Centuries* (1967), an important collection of essays.

As background to slavery and racism in North and South America, students should see J. L. Watson, ed., *Asian and African Systems of Slavery* (1980), a valuable collection of essays. Davis's *Slavery and Human Progress,* cited in the Notes, shows how slavery was viewed as a progressive force in the expansion of the Western world. For North American conditions, interested students should consult W. D. Jordan, *The White Man's Burden: Historical Origins of Racism in the United States* (1974), and the title by Mannix listed in the Notes, a hideously fascinating account. For Caribbean and South American developments, see F. P. Bowser, *The African Slave in Colonial Peru* (1974); J. S. Handler and F. W. Lange, *Plantation Slavery in Barbados: An Archeological and Historical Investigation* (1978); and R. E. Conrad, *Children of God's Fire: A Documentary History of Black Slavery in Brazil* (1983).

The leading authority on Montaigne is D. M. Frame. In addition to his translation of Montaigne's works cited in the Notes, see his *Montaigne's Discovery of Man* (1955).

19

ABSOLUTISM AND CONSTITUTIONALISM IN WESTERN EUROPE (CA 1589–1715)

*T*HE SEVENTEENTH century was a period of revolutionary transformation. Some of its most profound developments were political: it has been called the "century when government became modern." The sixteenth century had witnessed the emergence of the nation-state. The long series of wars fought in the name of religion—actually contests between royal authority and aristocratic power—brought social dislocation and agricultural and commercial disaster. Increasingly, strong national monarchy seemed the only solution. Spanish and French monarchs gained control of the major competing institution in their domains, the Roman Catholic church. Rulers of England and some of the German principalities, who could not completely regulate the church, set up national churches. In the German empire, the Treaty of Westphalia placed territorial sovereignty in the princes' hands. The kings of France, England, and Spain claimed the basic loyalty of their subjects. Monarchs made laws, to which everyone within their borders was subject. These powers added up to something close to sovereignty.

A state may be termed *sovereign* when it possesses a monopoly over the instruments of justice and the use of force within clearly defined boundaries. In a sovereign state no system of courts, such as ecclesiastical tribunals, competes with state courts in the dispensation of justice; and private armies, such as those of feudal lords, present no threat to royal authority because the state's army is stronger. Royal law touches all persons within the country. Sovereignty had been evolving during the late sixteenth century. Seventeenth-century governments now needed to address the problem of *which* authority within the state would possess sovereignty—the crown or the nobility.

In the period between roughly 1589 and 1715, two basic patterns of government emerged in Europe: absolute monarchy and the constitutional state. Almost all subsequent governments have been modeled on one of these patterns. In what sense were they "modern"? How did these forms of government differ from the feudal and dynastic monarchies of earlier centuries? Which Western countries most clearly illustrate the new patterns of political organization? This chapter will focus on these political questions.

ABSOLUTISM

In the *absolutist* state, sovereignty is embodied in the person of the ruler. The ruler is not restrained by legal authority. Absolute kings claim to rule by divine right, meaning they are responsible to God alone. (Medieval kings governed "by the grace of God," but invariably they acknowledged that they had to respect and obey the law.) Absolute monarchs in the seventeenth and eighteenth centuries had to respect the divine law and the fundamental laws of the land. But they were not checked by national assemblies. Estates general and parliaments met at the wish and in response to kings' needs. Because these meetings provided opportunities for opposition to the crown to coalesce, absolute monarchs eventually stopped summoning them.

Absolute rulers effectively controlled all competing jurisdictions, institutions, and interest groups in their territories. They regulated religious sects. They abolished the liberties long held by certain areas, groups, and provinces. Absolute kings also secured mastery over the one class that historically had posed the greatest threat to monarchy, the nobility. Medieval governments, restrained by church leaders, powerful feudal nobles, and their own financial limitations, had been denied all of these characteristics.

In some respects, the key to the power and success of absolute monarchs lay in how they solved their financial problems. Kings frequently found temporary financial support through bargains with the nobility: the nobility agreed to an ad hoc grant in return for freedom from future taxation. The absolutist solution was the creation of new state bureaucracies, which directed the economic life of the country in the interests of the king, either increasing taxes ever higher or devising alternative methods of raising revenue.

Bureaucracies were composed of career officials, appointed by and solely accountable to the king. The backgrounds of these civil servants varied. Absolute monarchs sometimes drew on the middle class, as in France, or utilized members of the nobility, as in Spain. Where there was no middle class or an insignificant one, as in Austria, Prussia, Spain, and Russia, the government of the absolutist state consisted of an interlocking elite of monarchy, aristocracy, and bureaucracy.

The most striking difference between seventeenth-century bureaucracies and their medieval predecessors was that seventeenth-century civil servants served the state as represented by the king. Bureaucrats recognized that the offices they held were public, or state, positions. The state paid them salaries to handle revenues that belonged to the crown, and they were not supposed to use their positions for private gain. Bureaucrats gradually came to distinguish between public duties and private property.

Absolute monarchs also maintained permanent standing armies. Medieval armies had been raised by feudal lords for particular wars or campaigns, after which the troops were disbanded. In the seventeenth century, monarchs alone recruited and maintained armies—in peacetime as well as during war. Kings deployed their troops both inside and outside the country in the interests of the monarchy. Armies became basic features of absolutist, and modern, states. Absolute rulers also invented new methods of compulsion. They concerned themselves with the private lives of potentially troublesome subjects, often through the use of secret police.

Rule of absolute monarchs was not all-embracing, because they lacked the financial and military resources and the technology to make it so. Thus the absolutist state was not the same as a totalitarian state. *Totalitarianism* is a twentieth-century phenomenon; it seeks to direct all facets of a state's culture—art, education, religion, the economy, and politics—in the interests of the state. By definition totalitarian rule is total regulation. By twentieth-century standards, the ambitions of an absolute monarch were quite limited: he sought the exaltation of himself as the embodiment of the state. Whether or not Louis XIV of France actually said, "L'état, c'est moi!" ("I am the state!"), the remark expresses his belief that he personified the French nation. Yet the absolutist state did foreshadow recent totalitarian regimes in two fundamental respects: in the glorification of the state over all other aspects of the state's culture, and in the use of war and an expansionist foreign policy to divert attention from domestic ills.

All of this is best illustrated by the experience of France, aptly known as the model of absolute monarchy.

THE CORNERSTONE OF FRENCH ABSOLUTISM: LOUIS XIII AND RICHELIEU

Early in the seventeenth century, the queen-regent Marie de' Medici led the government for the child-king Louis XIII (1610–1643), but in fact feudal nobles and princes of the blood dominated the political scene. In 1624 Marie de' Medici secured the appointment of Armand Jean du Plessis—Cardinal Richelieu (1585–1642)—to the council of ministers. It was a remarkable appointment. The next year Richelieu became president of the council, and after 1628 he was first minister of the French crown. Richelieu used his strong influence over King Louis XIII to exalt the French monarchy as the embodiment of the French state. One of the greatest servants of the French state, Richelieu set in place the cornerstone of French absolutism, and his work served as the basis for France's cultural domination of Europe in the later seventeenth century.

Richelieu's policy was the total subordination of all groups and institutions to the French monarchy. The French nobility, with its selfish and independent interests, had long constituted the foremost threat to the centralizing goals of the crown and to a strong national state. Therefore, Richelieu tried to break the power of the nobility. He leveled castles, long the symbol of feudal independence. He crushed aristocratic conspiracies with quick executions.

The constructive genius of Cardinal Richelieu is best reflected in the administrative system he established. He extended the use of the royal commissioners called *intendants*. France was divided into thirty-two *généralités* (districts), in each of which a royal intendant had extensive responsibility for justice, the police, and finances. The intendants were authorized "to decide, order and execute all that they see good to do." Usually members of the upper middle class or minor nobility, the intendants were appointed directly by the monarch, to whom they were solely responsible. The intendants recruited men for the army, supervised the collection of taxes, presided over the administration of local law, checked up on the local nobility, and regulated economic activities —commerce, trade, the guilds, marketplaces—in their districts. They were to use their power for two related purposes: to enforce royal orders and to weaken the power of the regional nobility.

Philippe de Champaigne: Cardinal Richelieu This portrait, with its penetrating eyes, expression of haughty and imperturable cynicism, and dramatic sweep of red robes, suggests the authority, grandeur, and power that Richelieu wished to convey as first minister of France. *(Reproduced by courtesy of the Trustees, The National Gallery, London)*

France lacked a sound system of taxation, a method of raising sufficient revenue to meet the needs of the state. Richelieu reverted to the old device of selling offices. He increased the number of sinecures, tax exemptions, and benefices that were purchasable and inheritable. In 1624 this device brought in almost 40 percent of royal revenues.

The rising cost of foreign and domestic policies led to the auctioning of *tax farms,* a system whereby a man bought the right to collect taxes. Tax farmers kept a very large part of the receipts they collected. The sale of offices and this antiquated system of tax collection were improvisations that promoted confusion and corruption. Even worse, state offices, once purchased, were passed on to heirs, which meant that a family that held a state office was eternally exempt from taxation. Richelieu's inadequate and temporary solutions created grave financial problems for the future.

The cardinal perceived that Protestantism all too often served as a cloak for the political intrigues of ambitious lords. When the Huguenots revolted in 1625, under the duke of Rohan, Richelieu personally supervised the siege of their walled city, La Rochelle, and forced it to surrender. Thereafter, fortified places of security were abolished. Huguenots were allowed to practice their faith, but they no longer possessed armed strongholds or the means to be an independent party in the state. Another aristocratic prop was knocked down.

French foreign policy under Richelieu was aimed at the destruction of the fence of Habsburg territories that surrounded France. Consequently Richelieu supported the Habsburgs' enemies. In 1631 he signed a treaty with the Lutheran king Gustavus Adolphus, promising French support against the Catholic Habsburgs in the Thirty Years' War (pages 571–576). When the war was over, France had acquired extensive rights in Alsace in the east and Arras in the north, as well as the right to intervene in German affairs.

Richelieu personified the increasingly secular spirit of the seventeenth century. Though a bishop of the Roman Catholic church, he gave his first loyalty to the French state. Though a Roman Catholic cardinal, he gave strong support to the Protestant Lutherans of Germany.

Richelieu had persuaded Louis XIII to appoint his protégé Jules Mazarin (1602–1661) as his successor. An Italian diplomat of great charm, Mazarin served on the council of state under Richelieu, acquiring considerable political experience. He became a cardinal in 1641 and a French citizen in 1643. When Louis XIII followed Richelieu to the grave in 1643 and a regency headed by Queen Anne of Austria governed for the child-king Louis XIV, Mazarin became the dominant power in the government. He continued the antifeudal and centralizing policies of Richelieu, but his attempts to increase royal revenues led to the civil wars known as the "Fronde."

The word *fronde* means "slingshot" or "catapult," and a *frondeur* was originally a street urchin who threw mud at the passing carriages of the rich. The term came to be used for anyone who opposed the policies of the government. Richelieu had stirred up the bitter resentment of the aristocracy, who felt its constitutional status and ancient privileges threatened. He also bequeathed to the crown a staggering debt, and when Mazarin tried to impose financial reforms, the monarchy incurred the enmity of the middle classes. Both groups plotted against Anne and Mazarin. Most historians see the Fronde as the last serious effort by the French nobility to oppose the monarchy by force. When in 1648 Mazarin proposed new methods for raising income, bitter civil war ensued between the monarchy on the one side and the frondeurs (the nobility and the upper middle classes) on the other. Riots and public turmoil wracked Paris and the nation. The violence continued intermittently for almost twelve years. Factional disputes among the nobles led to their ultimate defeat.

The conflicts of the Fronde had two significant results for the future: a badly disruptive effect on the French economy and a traumatic impact on the young Louis XIV. The king and his mother were frequently threatened and sometimes treated as prisoners by aristocratic factions. On one occasion a mob broke into the royal bedchamber to make sure the king was actually there; it succeeded in giving him a bad fright. Louis never forgot such humiliations. The period of the Fronde formed the cornerstone of his political education and of his conviction that the sole alternative to anarchy was absolute monarchy.

THE ABSOLUTE MONARCHY OF LOUIS XIV

According to the court theologian Bossuet, the clergy at the coronation of Louis XIV in Reims Cathedral asked God to cause the splendors of the French court to fill all who beheld it with awe. God subsequently granted that prayer. In the reign of Louis XIV (1643–1715), the longest in European history, the French monarchy reached the peak of absolutist development. In the magnificence of his court, in his absolute power, in the brilliance of the culture over which he presided and that permeated all of Europe, and in

Coysevox: Louis XIV (1687–1689) The French court envisioned a new classical age with the Sun King as emperor and his court a new Rome. This statue depicts Louis in a classical pose, clothed (escept for the wig) as for a Roman military triumph. *(Caisse Nationale des Monuments Historiques et des Sites, Paris ©ARS, NY SPADEM 1987)*

his remarkably long life, the "Sun King" dominated his age. No wonder scholars have characterized the second half of the seventeenth century as the "Grand Century," the "Age of Magnificence," and, echoing the eighteenth-century philosopher Voltaire, the "Age of Louis XIV."

Recent scholarship indicates that Louis XIV introduced important governmental innovations: the most significant was his acquisition of absolute control over the French nobility. Indeed it is often said that Louis achieved complete "domestication of the nobility." In doing so, Louis XIV turned the royal court into a fixed institution. In the past, the king of

France and the royal court had traveled constantly, visiting the great noblemen, the king's properties, and his *bonnes villes* or "good towns." Since the time of Louis IX, or even Charlemagne, rulers had traveled to maintain order in distant parts of the realm, to impress humbler subjects with the royal dignity and magnificence, and to bind the country together through loyalty to the king. Since the early Middle Ages, the king's court had consisted of his family, trusted advisers and councilors, a few favorites, and servants. Except for the very highest state officials, members of the council had changed constantly.

Louis XIV installed the court at Versailles, a small town ten miles from Paris. He required all the great nobles of France, at the peril of social, political, and sometimes economic disaster, to come live at Versailles for at least part of the year. Today Versailles stands as the best surviving museum on earth of a vanished society. In the seventeenth century, it became a model of rational order, the center of France and thus the center of Western civilization, the perfect symbol of the king's absolute power.

Louis XIII began Versailles as a hunting lodge, a retreat from a queen he did not like. His son's architects, Le Nôtre and Le Vau, turned what the courtier Saint-Simon called "the most dismal and thankless of sights" into a veritable paradise. Wings were added to the original building to make the palace U-shaped. Everywhere at Versailles the viewer had a sense of grandeur, vastness, and elegance. Enormous state rooms became display galleries for inlaid tables, Italian marble statuary, Gobelin tapestries woven at the state factory in Paris, silver ewers, and beautiful (if uncomfortable) furniture. If genius means attention to detail, Louis XIV and his designers had it: the décor was perfected down to the last doorknob and keyhole. In the gigantic Hall of Mirrors, later to reflect so much of German as well as French history, hundreds of candles illuminated the domed ceiling, where allegorical paintings celebrated the king's victories.

The Ambassador's Staircase was of brilliantly colored marble, with part of the railing gold plated. The staircase was dominated by a great bust of the king, which, when completed, so overwhelmed a courtier that he exclaimed to the sculptor Bernini, "Don't do anything more to it, it's so good I'm afraid you might spoil it." The statue, like the staircase—and the entire palace—succeeded from the start in its purpose: it awed.

The formal, carefully ordered, and perfectly landscaped gardens at Versailles express at a glance the spirit of the age of Louis XIV. Every tree, every bush, every foot of grass, every fountain, pool, and piece of statuary within three miles is perfectly laid out. The vista is of the world made rational and absolutely controlled. Nature itself was subdued to enhance the greatness of the king.

The art and architecture of Versailles served as fundamental tools of state policy under Louis XIV, used to awe subjects and foreign visitors. Versailles was seen as a reflection of French genius. Thus the Russian tsar Peter the Great imitated Versailles in the construction of his palace, Peterhof, in St. Petersburg, as did the Prussian king Frederick the Great in his palace at Potsdam outside Berlin.

As in art and architecture, so too in language. Beginning in the reign of Louis XIV, French became the language of polite society and the vehicle of diplomatic exchange. French also gradually replaced Latin as the language of international scholarship and learning. The wish of other kings to ape the courtly style of Louis XIV and the imitation of French intellectuals and artists spread the language all over Europe. The royal courts of Sweden, Russia, Poland, and Germany all spoke French. In the eighteenth century, the great Russian aristocrats were more fluent in French than in Russian. In England, the first Hanoverian king, George I, spoke fluent French, halting English. France, in the person of its king, inspired a cosmopolitan European culture in the late seventeenth century. That is why the French today revere Louis XIV as a great national heroe.

Against this background of magnificent splendor, as Saint-Simon describes him, Louis XIV

reduced everyone to subjection, and brought to his court those very persons he cared least about. Whoever was old enough to serve did not dare demur. It was still another device to ruin the nobles by accustoming them to equality and forcing them to mingle with everyone indiscriminately. . . .

To keep everyone . . . attentive, the King personally named the guests for each festivity. . . . These were his rewards and punishments. . . . He substituted idle rewards for real ones and these operated through jealousy, the petty preferences he showed many times a day, and his artfulness in showing them. . . .

Upon rising, at bedtime, during meals, in his apartments, in the gardens of Versailles, everywhere the court-

iers had a right to follow, he would glance right and left to see who was there; he saw and noted everyone; he missed no one, even those who were hoping they would not be seen. . . .

Louis XIV took great pains to inform himself on what was happening everywhere, in public places, private homes, and even on the international scene. . . . Spies and informers of all kinds were numberless. . . .

But the King's most vicious method of securing information was opening letters. [1]

Though this passage was written by one of Louis' severest critics, all agree that the king used court ceremonial to undermine the power of the great nobility. By excluding the highest nobles from his councils, he destroyed their ancient right to advise the king and to participate in government; they became mere instruments of royal policy. Operas, fetes, balls, gossip, and trivia occupied the nobles' time and attention. Through painstaking attention to detail and precisely calculated showmanship, Louis XIV emasculated the major threat to his absolute power. He separated status and grandeur from power: the nobility enjoyed the status and grandeur in which they lived; the king alone held the power.

Louis dominated the court, and, in his scheme of things, the court was more significant than the government. In government Louis utilized several councils of state, which he personally attended, and the intendants, who acted for the councils throughout France. A stream of questions and instructions flowed between local districts and Versailles, and under Louis XIV a uniform and centralized administration was imposed on the country. In 1685 France was the strongest and most highly centralized state in Europe.

Councilors of state and intendants came from the recently ennobled or the upper middle class. Royal service provided a means of social mobility. These professional bureaucrats served the state in the person of the king, but they did not share power with him. Louis stated that he chose bourgeois officials because he wanted "people to know by the rank of the men who served him that he had no intention of sharing power with them."[2] If great ones were the king's advisers, they would seem to share the royal authority; professional administrators from the middle class would not.

Throughout his long reign and despite increasing financial problems, he never called a meeting of the Estates General. The nobility, therefore, had no means of united expression or action. Nor did Louis have a first minister, freeing him from worry about the inordinate power of a Richelieu. Louis' use of terror—a secret police force, a system of informers, and the practice of opening private letters—foreshadowed some of the devices of the modern state. French government remained highly structured, bureaucratic, centered at Versailles, and responsible to Louis XIV.

FINANCIAL AND ECONOMIC MANAGEMENT UNDER LOUIS XIV: COLBERT

Finance was the grave weakness of Louis XIV's absolutism. An expanding professional bureaucracy, the court of Versailles, and extensive military reforms (page 597) cost a great amount of money. The French method of collecting taxes consistently failed to produce enough revenue. Tax farmers pocketed the difference between what they raked in and what they handed over to the state. Consequently, the tax farmers profited, while the government got far less than the people paid. Then, by an old agreement between the crown and the nobility, the king could freely tax the common people, provided he did not tax the nobles. Nobles thereby relinquished a role in government: since they did not pay taxes, they could not legitimately claim a say in how taxes were spent. Louis, however, lost enormous potential revenue. The middle classes, moreover, secured many tax exemptions. With the rich and prosperous classes exempt, the tax burden fell heavily on those least able to pay, the poor peasants.

The king named Jean-Baptiste Colbert (1619–1683), the son of a wealthy merchant-financier of Reims, as controller-general of finances. Colbert came to manage the entire royal administration and proved himself a financial genius. Colbert's central principle was that the wealth and the economy of France should serve the state. He did not invent the system called "mercantilism," but he rigorously applied it to France.

Mercantilism is a collection of governmental policies for the regulation of economic activities, especially commercial activities, by and for the state. In seventeenth- and eighteenth-century economic theory, a nation's international power was thought to be based on its wealth, specifically its gold supply. To accumulate gold, a country should always sell abroad more than it buys. Colbert believed that a successful economic policy meant more than a favorable balance of trade. He insisted that the French sell abroad and buy nothing back. If France was self-sufficient, able to produce within its borders everything the subjects of the French king needed, the outflow of gold would be halted. As debtor states paid in bullion, the wealth of the nation would increase and its power and prestige would be enhanced.

Colbert attempted to accomplish self-sufficiency through state support for both old industries and newly created ones. He subsidized the established cloth industries at Abbeville, Saint-Quentin, and Carcassonne. He granted special royal privileges to the rug and tapestry industries at Paris and Beauvais. New factories at Saint-Antoine in Paris manufactured mirrors to replace Venetian imports. Looms at Chantilly and Alençon competed with English lacemaking, and foundries at Saint-Etienne made steel and firearms that cut Swedish imports. To ensure a high-quality finished product, Colbert set up a system of state inspection and regulation. To ensure order within every industry, he compelled all craftsmen to organize into guilds, and within every guild he gave the masters absolute power over their workers. Colbert encouraged skilled foreign craftsmen and manufacturers to immigrate to France, and he gave them special privileges. To improve communications, he built roads and canals, the most famous linking the Mediterranean and the Bay of Biscay. To protect French goods, he abolished many domestic tariffs and enacted high foreign tariffs, which prevented foreign products from competing with French ones.

Colbert's most important work was the creation of a powerful merchant marine to transport French goods. He gave bonuses to French ship owners and builders and established a method of maritime conscription, arsenals, and academies for the training of sailors. In 1661 France possessed 18 unseaworthy vessels; by 1681 it had 276 frigates, galleys, and ships of the line. Colbert tried to organize and regulate the entire French economy for the glory of the French state as embodied in the king.

Colbert hoped to make Canada—rich in untapped minerals and some of the best agricultural land in the world—part of a vast French Empire. He gathered four thousand peasants from western France and shipped them to Canada, where they peopled the province of Quebec. (In 1608, one year after the Eng-

lish arrived at Jamestown, Virginia, Sully had established the city of Quebec, which became the capital of French Canada.) Subsequently, the Jesuit Marquette and the merchant Joliet sailed down the Mississippi River and took possession of the land on both sides, as far south as present-day Arkansas. In 1684 the French explorer La Salle continued down the Mississippi to its mouth and claimed vast territories and the rich Delta for Louis XIV. The area was called, naturally, "Louisiana."

How successful were Colbert's policies? His achievement in the development of manufacturing was prodigious. The textile industry, especially in woolens, expanded enormously, and "France . . . had become in 1683 the leading nation of the world in industrial productivity."[3] The commercial classes prospered, and between 1660 and 1700 their position steadily improved. The national economy, however, rested on agriculture. Although French peasants did not become serfs, as did the peasants of eastern Europe, they were mercilessly taxed. After 1685 other hardships afflicted them: poor harvests, continuing deflation of the currency, and fluctuation in the price of grain. Many peasants emigrated. With the decline in population and thus in the number of taxable people (the poorest), the state's resources fell. A totally inadequate tax base and heavy expenditure for war in the later years of the reign nullified Colbert's achievements.

THE REVOCATION OF THE EDICT OF NANTES

We now see with the proper gratitude what we owe to God . . . for the best and largest part of our subjects of the so-called reformed religion have embraced Catholicism, and now that, to the extent that the execution of the Edict of Nantes remains useless, we have judged that we can do nothing better to wipe out the memory of the troubles, of the confusion, of the evils that the progress of this false religion has caused our kingdom . . . than to revoke entirely the said Edict.[4]

Thus in 1685, Louis XIV revoked the Edict of Nantes, by which his grandfather Henry IV had granted liberty of conscience to French Huguenots. The new law ordered the destruction of churches, the closing of schools, the Catholic baptism of Huguenots, and the exile of Huguenot pastors who refused to renounce their faith. Why? There had been so many mass conversions during previous years (many of them forced) that Madame de Maintenon, Louis' second wife, could say that "nearly all the Huguenots were converted." Some Huguenots had emigrated. Richelieu had already deprived French Calvinists of political rights. Why, then, did Louis, by revoking the edict, persecute some of his most loyal and industrially skilled subjects, force others to flee abroad, and provoke the outrage of Protestant Europe?

Recent scholarship has convincingly shown that Louis XIV was basically tolerant. He insisted on religious unity not for religious but for political reasons. His goal was "one king, one law, one faith." He hated division within the realm and insisted that religious unity was essential to his royal dignity and to the security of the state. The seventeenth century, moreover, was not a tolerant one. While France in the early years of Louis' reign permitted religious liberty, it was not a popular policy. Revocation was solely the king's decision, and it won him enormous praise. "If the flood of congratulation means anything, it . . . was probably the one act of his reign that, at the time, was popular with the majority of his subjects."[5]

While contemporaries applauded Louis XIV, scholars since the eighteenth century damned him for the adverse impact that revocation had on the economy and foreign affairs. Tens of thousands of Huguenot craftsmen, soldiers, and business people emigrated, depriving France of their skills and tax revenues and carrying their bitterness to Holland, England, and Prussia. Modern scholarship has greatly modified this picture. While Huguenot settlers in northern Europe aggravated Protestant hatred for Louis, the revocation of the Edict of Nantes had only minor and scattered effects on French economic development.[6]

LOUIS XIV'S WARS

Just as the architecture and court life at Versailles served to reflect the king's glory, and as the economy of the state under Colbert was managed to advance the king's prestige, so did Louis XIV use war to exalt himself above the other rulers and nations of Europe. He visualized himself as a great military hero. "The character of a conqueror," he remarked, "is regarded as the noblest and highest of titles." Military glory was his aim. In 1666 Louis appointed François le Tellier (later marquis of Louvois) as secretary of war.

The Spider and the Fly In reference to the insect symbolism (upper left), the caption on the lower left side of this illustration states, "The noble is the spider, the peasant the fly." The other caption (upper right) notes, "The more people have, the more they want. The poor man brings everything—wheat, fruit, money, vegetables. The greedy lord sitting there ready to take everything will not even give him the favor of a glance." This satirical print summarizes peasant grievances. *(New York Public Library)*

Louvois created a professional army, which was modern in the sense that the French state, rather than private nobles, employed the soldiers. The king himself took personal command of the army and directly supervised all aspects and details of military affairs.

A commissariat was established to feed the troops, in place of their ancient practice of living off the countryside. An ambulance corps was designed to look after the wounded. Uniforms and weapons were standardized. Finally, a rational system of recruitment, training, discipline, and promotion was imposed. With this new military machine, for the first time in Europe's history one national state, France, was able to dominate the politics of Europe.

Louis continued on a broader scale the expansionist policy begun by Cardinal Richelieu. In 1667, using a dynastic excuse, he invaded Flanders, part of the Spanish Netherlands, and Franche-Comté in the east. In consequence he acquired twelve towns, including the important commercial centers of Lille and Tournai (Map 19.1). Five years later, Louis personally led an army of over a hundred thousand men into Holland. The Dutch ultimately saved themselves only by opening the dikes and flooding the countryside. This war, which lasted six years and eventually involved the Holy Roman Empire and Spain, was concluded by the Treaty of Nijmegen (1678). Louis gained additional Flemish towns and the whole of Franche-Comté.

Encouraged by his successes, by the weakness of the German empire, and by divisions among the other European powers, Louis continued his aggression. In 1681 he seized the city of Strasbourg and three years later sent his armies into the province of Lorraine. At that moment the king seemed invincible. In fact, Louis had reached the limit of his expansion at Nijmegen. The wars of the 1680s and 1690s brought him no additional territories. In 1689 the Dutch prince William of Orange, a bitter foe of Louis XIV, became king of England. William joined the League of Augsburg—which included the Habsburg emperor, the kings of Spain and Sweden, and the electors of Bavaria, Saxony, and the Palatinate—adding British resources and men to the alliance. Neither the French nor the league won any decisive victories. The alliance served instead as preparation for the long-expected conflict known as the "War of the Spanish Succession" (1701–1713).

This struggle, provoked by the territorial disputes of the past century, also involved the dynastic question of the succession to the Spanish throne. It was an open secret in Europe that the king of Spain, Charles II (1665–1700), was mentally defective and sexually impotent. In 1698 the European powers, including France, agreed by treaty to partition, or divide, the vast Spanish possessions between the king of France and the Holy Roman emperor, who were Charles II's brothers-in-law. When Charles died in 1700, however, his will left the Spanish crown and the worldwide Spanish Empire to Philip of Anjou, Louis XIV's grandson. While the will specifically rejected the union of the French and Spanish crowns, Louis was obviously the power in France, not his seventeen-year-old grandson. Louis reneged on the treaty and accepted the will.

The Dutch and the English would not accept French acquisition of the Spanish Netherlands and of the rich trade with the Spanish colonies. The union of the Spanish and French crowns, moreover, would have totally upset the European balance of power. The Versailles declaration that "the Pyrenees no longer exist" provoked the long-anticipated crisis. In 1701 the English, Dutch, Austrians, and Prussians formed the Grand Alliance against Louis XIV. They claimed that they were fighting to prevent France from becoming too strong in Europe, but during the previous half century, overseas maritime rivalry among France, Holland, and England had created serious international tension. The secondary motive of the allied powers was to check France's expanding commercial power in North America, Asia, and Africa. In the ensuing series of conflicts, two great soldiers dominated the alliance against France: Eugene, prince of Savoy, representing the Holy Roman Empire, and the Englishman John Churchill, subsequently duke of Marlborough. Eugene and Churchill inflicted a severe defeat on Louis in 1704 at Blenheim in Bavaria. Marlborough followed with another victory at Ramillies near Namur in Brabant.

The war was finally concluded at Utrecht in 1713, where the principle of partition was applied. Louis' grandson Philip remained the first Bourbon king of Spain on the understanding that the French and Spanish crowns would never be united. France surrendered Newfoundland, Nova Scotia, and the Hudson Bay territory to England, which also acquired Gibraltar and Minorca, and control of the African slave trade from Spain. The Dutch gained little because Austria received the former Spanish Netherlands.

The Peace of Utrecht had important international consequences. It represented the balance-of-power principle in operation, setting limits on the extent to which any one power, in this case France, could expand. The treaty completed the decline of Spain as a great power. It vastly expanded the British Empire. Finally, Utrecht gave European powers experience in international cooperation, thus preparing them for the alliances formed against France at the end of the century.

The Peace of Utrecht marked the end of French expansionist policy. In Louis' thirty-five-year quest for military glory, his main territorial acquisition was Strasbourg. Even revisionist historians, who portray the aging monarch as responsible in negotiation and

MAP 19.1 The Acquisitions of Louis XIV, 1668–1713 The desire for glory and the weakness of his German neighbors encouraged Louis XIV's expansionist policy. But he paid a high price for his acquisitions.

moderate in his demands, acknowledge "that the widespread misery in France during the period was in part due to royal policies, especially the incessant wars."[7] To raise revenue for the wars, forty thousand additional offices had been sold, thus increasing the number of families exempt from future taxation. Constant war had disrupted trade, which meant the state could not tax the profits of trade. Widespread starvation in the provinces provoked peasant revolts, especially in Brittany. In 1714 France hovered on the brink of financial bankruptcy. Louis had exhausted the country without much compensation. It is no wonder that when he died on September 1, 1715, Saint-Simon wrote, "Those . . . wearied by the heavy and oppressive rule of the King and his ministers, felt a delighted freedom. . . . Paris . . . found relief in the hope of liberation. . . . The provinces . . . quivered with delight . . . [and] the people, ruined, abused, despairing, now thanked God for a deliverance which answered their most ardent desires."[8]

THE DECLINE OF ABSOLUTIST SPAIN IN THE SEVENTEENTH CENTURY

Spanish absolutism and greatness had preceded that of the French. In the sixteenth century, Spain (or, more precisely, the kingdom of Castile) had developed the standard features of absolute monarchy: a permanent bureaucracy staffed by professionals employed in the various councils of state, a standing army, and national taxes, the *servicios,* which fell most heavily on the poor.

France depended on financial and administrative unification within its borders; Spain had developed an international absolutism on the basis of silver bullion from Mesoamerica and Peru. Spanish gold and silver, armies, and glory had dominated the Continent for most of the sixteenth century, but by the 1590s the seeds of disaster were sprouting. While France in the seventeenth century represented the classic model of the modern absolute state, Spain was experiencing steady decline. Fiscal disorder, political incompetence, population decline, intellectual isolation, and psychological malaise—all combined to reduce Spain, by 1715, to the rank of a second-rate power.

The fabulous and seemingly inexhaustible flow of silver from Mexico and Peru had led Philip II to assume the role of defender of Roman Catholicism in Europe (page 571). In order to humble the Protestant Dutch and to control the Spanish Netherlands, Philip believed that England, the Netherlands' greatest supporter, had to be crushed. He poured millions of Spanish ducats and all of Spanish hopes into the vast fleet that sailed in 1588. When the "Invincible Armada" went down in the North Sea, a century of Spanish pride and power went with it. After 1590 a spirit of defeatism and disillusionment crippled almost all efforts at reform.

Philip II's Catholic crusade had been financed by the revenues of the Spanish-Atlantic economy. These included, in addition to silver and gold bullion, profits from the sale of cloth, grain, oil, and wine to the colonies. In the early seventeenth century, the Dutch and English began to trade with the Spanish colonies, cutting into the revenues that had gone to Spain. Mexico and Peru themselves developed local industries, further lessening their need to buy from Spain. Between 1610 and 1650, Spanish trade with the colonies fell 60 percent.

At the same time, the native Indians and African slaves who worked the American silver mines suffered staggering death rates from abuse and disease (pages 558–559). Moreover, the lodes started to run dry. Consequently, the quantity of metal produced for Spain steadily declined. Nevertheless, in Madrid royal expenditures constantly exceeded income. The remedies applied in the face of a mountainous state debt and declining revenues were devaluation of the coinage and declarations of bankruptcy. In 1596, 1607, 1627, 1647, and 1680, Spanish kings found no solution to the problem of an empty treasury other than to cancel the national debt. Given the frequency of cancellation, naturally public confidence in the state deteriorated.

Spain, in contrast to the other countries of western Europe, had only a tiny middle class. Disdain for money, in a century of increasing commercialism and bourgeois attitudes, reveals a significant facet of the Spanish national character. Public opinion, taking its cue from the aristocracy, condemned money-making as vulgar and undignified. Those with influence or connections sought titles of nobility and social prestige. Thousands entered economically unproductive professions and became priests, monks, and nuns: there were said to be nine thousand monasteries in the kingdom of Castile alone. The flood of gold and silver had produced severe inflation, pushing the costs of production in the textile industry higher and higher, to the point that Castilian cloth could not compete in colonial and international markets. Many manufacturers and businessmen found so many obstacles in the way of profitable enterprise that they simply gave up.[9]

Spanish aristocrats, attempting to maintain an extravagant lifestyle they could no longer afford, increased the rents on their estates. High rents and heavy taxes in turn drove the peasants from the land. Agricultural production suffered, and the peasants departed for the large cities, where they swelled the ranks of unemployed beggars.

Their most Catholic majesties, the kings of Spain, had no solutions to these dire problems. If one can discern personality from pictures, the portraits of Philip III (1598–1621), Philip IV (1621–1665), and Charles II hanging in the Prado, the Spanish national museum in Madrid, reflect the increasing weakness of the dynasty. Their faces—the small, beady eyes, the long noses, the jutting Habsburg jaws, the pathetically stupid expressions—tell a story of excessive inbreeding and decaying monarchy. The Spanish kings all lacked force of character. Philip III, a pallid, melancholy, and deeply pious man "whose only virtue appeared to reside in a total absence of vice," handed the government over to the lazy duke of Lerma, who used it to advance his personal and familial wealth. Philip IV left the management of his several kingdoms to Count Olivares.

Olivares was an able administrator. He did not lack energy and ideas; he devised new sources of revenue. But he clung to the grandiose belief that the solution to Spain's difficulties rested in a return to the

Velazquez: The Maids of Honor The Infanta Margarita painted in 1656 with her maids and playmates has invaded the artist's studio, while her parents' image is reflected in the mirror on the back wall. Velazquez (extreme left), who powerfully influenced nineteenth-century impressionist painters, imbued all of his subjects, including the pathetic dwarf (right, in black) with a sense of dignity. *(Giraudon/Art Resource)*

imperial tradition. Unfortunately, the imperial tradition demanded the revival of war with the Dutch, at the expiration of a thirteen-year truce in 1622, and a long war with France over Mantua (1628–1659). Spain thus became embroiled in the Thirty Years' War. These conflicts, on top of an empty treasury, brought disaster.

In 1640 Spain faced serious revolts in Naples and Portugal, and in 1643 the French inflicted a crushing defeat on a Spanish army in Belgium. By the Treaty of the Pyrenees of 1659, which ended the French-Spanish wars, Spain was compelled to surrender extensive territories to France. This treaty marked the end of Spain as a great power.

Seventeenth-century Spain was the victim of its past. It could not forget the grandeur of the sixteenth century and look to the future. The bureaucratic councils of state continued to function as symbols of the absolute Spanish monarchy. But because those councils were staffed by aristocrats, it was the aristocracy that held the real power. Spanish absolutism had been built largely on slave-produced gold and silver.

When the supply of bullion decreased, the power and standing of the Spanish state declined.

The most cherished Spanish ideals were military glory and strong Roman Catholic faith. In the seventeenth century, Spain lacked the finances and the manpower to fight the expensive wars in which it foolishly got involved. Spain also ignored the new mercantile ideas and scientific methods, because they came from heretical nations, Holland and England. The incredible wealth of South America destroyed the tiny Spanish middle class and created contempt for business and manual labor.

The decadence of the Habsburg dynasty and the lack of effective royal councilors also contributed to Spanish failure. Spanish leaders seemed to lack the will to reform. Pessimism and fatalism permeated national life. In the reign of Philip IV, a royal council was appointed to plan the construction of a canal linking the Tagus and Manzanares rivers in Spain. After interminable debate, the committee decided that "if God had intended the rivers to be navigable, He would have made them so."

In the brilliant novel *Don Quixote,* the Spanish writer Cervantes (1547–1616) produced one of the great masterpieces of world literature. *Don Quixote* —on which the modern play *The Man of La Mancha* is based—delineates the whole fabric of sixteenth-century Spanish society. The main character, Don Quixote, lives in a world of dreams, traveling about the countryside seeking military glory. From the title of the book, the English language has borrowed the word *quixotic.* Meaning "idealistic but impractical," the term characterizes seventeenth-century Spain. As a leading scholar has written, "The Spaniard convinced himself that reality was what he felt, believed, imagined. He filled the world with heroic reverberations. Don Quixote was born and grew."[10]

CONSTITUTIONALISM

The seventeenth century, which witnessed the development of absolute monarchy, also saw the appearance of the constitutional state. While France and later Austria, Prussia, and Russia solved the question of sovereignty with the absolutist state, England and Holland evolved toward the constitutional state. What is constitutionalism? Is it identical to democracy?

Constitutionalism is the limitation of government by law. Constitutionalism also implies a balance between the authority and power of the government on the one hand and the rights and liberties of the subjects on the other. The balance is often very delicate.

A nation's constitution may be written or unwritten. It may be embodied in one basic document, occasionally revised by amendment or judicial decision, like the Constitution of the United States. Or a constitution may be partly written and partly unwritten and include parliamentary statutes, judicial decisions, and a body of traditional procedures and practices, like the English and Canadian constitutions. Whether written or unwritten, a constitution gets its binding force from the government's acknowledgment that it must respect that constitution—that is, that the state must govern according to the laws. Likewise, in a constitutional state, the people look on the law and the constitution as the protectors of their rights, liberties, and property.

Modern constitutional governments may take either a republican or a monarchial form. In a constitutional republic, the sovereign power resides in the electorate and is exercised by the electorate's representatives. In a constitutional monarchy, a king or queen serves as the head of state and possesses some residual political authority, but again the ultimate or sovereign power rests in the electorate.

A constitutional government is not, however, quite the same as a democratic government. In a complete democracy, *all* the people have the right to participate either directly, or indirectly through their elected representatives, in the government of the state. Democratic government, therefore, is intimately tied up with the *franchise* (the vote). Most men could not vote until the late nineteenth century. Even then, women—probably the majority in Western societies —lacked the franchise; they gained the right to vote only in the twentieth century. Consequently, although constitutionalism developed in the seventeenth century, full democracy was achieved only in very recent times.

THE DECLINE OF ROYAL ABSOLUTISM IN ENGLAND (1603–1649)

In the late sixteenth century the French monarchy was powerless; a century later, the king's power was absolute. In 1588 Queen Elizabeth I of England exercised very great personal power; by 1689 the English monarchy was severely circumscribed. Change in England was anything but orderly. The nation experienced a bloody civil war, executed one king, experimented with military dictatorship, then restored the son of the murdered king, and finally, after a bloodless revolution, established constitutional monarchy. Political stability came only in the 1690s. How do scholars account for the fact that, after such a violent and tumultuous century, England laid the foundations for constitutional monarchy? What combination of political, socioeconomic, and religious factors brought on a civil war in 1642 to 1649 and then the constitutional settlement of 1688 and 1689?

The extraordinary success of Elizabeth I had rested on her political shrewdness and flexibility, her careful management of finances, her wise selection of ministers, her clever manipulation of Parliament, and her sense of royal dignity and devotion to hard work. After her Scottish cousin James Stuart succeeded her as James I (1603–1625), Elizabeth's strengths seemed even greater than they actually had been. The Stuarts lacked every quality Elizabeth had possessed.

Abysmally ignorant of English law and of the English Parliament, but sublimely arrogant, James was devoted to the theory of the divine right of kings. He expressed his ideas about divine right in his essay "The Trew Law of Free Monarchy." According to James I, a monarch has a divine (or God-given) right to his authority and is responsible only to God. Rebellion is the worst of political crimes. If a king orders something evil, the subject should respond with passive disobedience but should be prepared to accept any penalty for noncompliance.

James substituted political theorizing and talk for real work. He lectured the House of Commons: "There are no privileges and immunities which can stand against a divinely appointed King." This notion, implying total royal jurisdiction over the liberties, persons, and properties of English men and women, formed the basis of the Stuart concept of absolutism. Such a view ran directly counter to the long-standing English idea that a person's property could not be taken away without due process of law. James's expression of such views before the English House of Commons constituted a grave political mistake.

The House of Commons guarded the state's pocketbook, and James and later Stuart kings badly needed to open that pocketbook. Elizabeth had bequeathed to James a sizable royal debt. Through prudent management the debt could have been gradually reduced, but James I looked on all revenues as a happy windfall to be squandered on a lavish court and favorite courtiers. In reality, the extravagance displayed in James's court, as well as the public flaunting of his male lovers, weakened respect for the monarchy.

Elizabeth had also left to her Stuart successors a House of Commons that appreciated its own financial strength and intended to use that strength to acquire a greater say in the government of the state. The knights and burgesses who sat at Westminster in the early seventeenth century wanted to discuss royal expenditures, religious reform, and foreign affairs. In short, the Commons wanted what amounted to sovereignty.

Profound social changes had occurred since the sixteenth century. The English House of Commons during the reigns of James I and his son Charles I (1625–1649) was very different from the assembly Henry VIII had terrorized into passing his Reformation legislation. A social revolution had brought about the change. The dissolution of the monasteries and the sale of monastic land had enriched many people. Agricultural techniques like the draining of wasteland and the application of fertilizers improved the land and its yield. Old manorial common land had been enclosed and turned into sheep runs; breeding was carefully supervised, and the size of the flocks increased. In these activities, as well as in renting and leasing parcels of land, precise accounts were kept.

Many men invested in commercial ventures at home, such as the expanding cloth industry, and in partnerships and joint stock companies engaged in foreign enterprises. They made prudent marriages. All these developments led to a great deal of social mobility. Both in agriculture and in commerce, the English in the late sixteenth and early seventeenth centuries were capitalists, investing their profits to make more money. Though the international inflation of the period hit everywhere, in England agricultural and commercial income rose faster than prices. Wealthy country gentry, rich city merchants, and financiers invested abroad.

The typical pattern was for the commercially successful to set themselves up as country gentry, thus creating an elite group that possessed a far greater proportion of land and of the national wealth in 1640 than had been the case in 1540. Small wonder that in

THE
LAMENTABLE
COMPLAINTS
OF
Nick Froth the Tapſter, and Rvlerost the Cooke.

Concerning the reſtraint lately ſet forth,
againſt drinking, potting, and piping on the Sab-
bath day, and againſt ſelling meate.

Printed in the yeare, 1 6 4 1.

Puritan Ideals Opposed The Puritans preached sober living and abstention from alcoholic drink, rich food, and dancing. This pamphlet reflects the common man's hostility to such restraints. "Potting" refers to tankards of beer; "piping" means making music. *(The British Library)*

1640 someone could declare in the House of Commons, probably accurately, "We could buy the House of Lords three times over." Increased wealth had also produced a better-educated and more articulate House of Commons. Many members had acquired at least a smattering of legal knowledge, and they used that knowledge to search for medieval precedents from which to argue against the king. The class that dominated the Commons wanted political power corresponding to its economic strength.

In England, unlike France, there was no social stigma attached to paying taxes. Members of the House of Commons were willing to tax themselves provided they had some say in the expenditure of those taxes and in the formulation of state policies. The Stuart kings, however, considered such ambitions intolerable presumption and a threat to their divine-right prerogative. Consequently, at every parliament between 1603 and 1629, bitter squabbles erupted between the crown and the wealthy, articulate, and legal-minded Commons. Charles I's attempt to govern without Parliament (1629–1640), to finance his government by arbitrary nonparliamentary levies, brought the country to a crisis.

An issue graver than royal extravagance and Parliament's desire to make law also disturbed the English and embittered relations between the king and the House of Commons. That problem was religion. In the early seventeenth century, increasing numbers of English people felt dissatisfied with the Church of England established by Henry VIII and reformed by Elizabeth (pages 531–533). Many Puritans believed that Reformation had not gone far enough. They wanted to "purify" the Anglican church of Roman Catholic elements—elaborate vestments and ceremonial, the position of the altar in the church, even the giving and wearing of wedding rings.

It is very difficult to establish what proportion of the English population was Puritan. According to the present scholarly consensus, the dominant religious groups in the early seventeenth century were Calvinist and Protestant; their more zealous members were Puritans. It also seems clear that many English men and women were attracted by the socioeconomic implications of John Calvin's theology. Calvinism emphasized hard work, sobriety, thrift, competition, and postponement of pleasure, and tended to link sin and poverty with weakness and moral corruption. These attitudes fit in precisely with the economic approaches and practices of many (successful) businessmen and farmers. These values have frequently been called the "Protestant," "middle class," or "capitalist ethic." Although it is hazardous to identify capitalism and progress with Protestantism—there were many successful Catholic capitalists—the "Protestant virtues" represented the prevailing values of members of the House of Commons.

James I and Charles I both gave the impression of being highly sympathetic to Roman Catholicism. Charles supported the policies of William Laud, archbishop of Canterbury (1573–1645), who tried to impose elaborate ritual and rich ceremonial on all churches. Laud insisted on complete uniformity of church services and enforced that uniformity through an ecclesiastical court called the "Court of High Commission." People believed the country was being led back to Roman Catholicism. When in 1637 Laud attempted to impose a new prayer book, modeled on the Anglican Book of Common Prayer, on the Presbyterian Scots, the Scots revolted. In order to finance an army to put down the Scots, King Charles was compelled to summon Parliament in November 1640.

For eleven years Charles I had ruled without Parliament, financing his government through extraordinary stopgap levies, considered illegal by most English people. For example, the king revived a medieval law requiring coastal districts to help pay the cost of ships for defense, but levied the tax, called "ship money," on inland as well as coastal counties. When the issue was tested in the courts, the judges, having been suborned, decided in the king's favor.

Most members of Parliament believed that such taxation without consent amounted to arbitrary and absolute despotism. Consequently, they were not willing to trust the king with an army. Accordingly, this parliament, commonly called the "Long Parliament" because it sat from 1640 to 1660, proceeded to enact legislation that limited the power of the monarch and made arbitrary government impossible.

In 1641 the Commons passed the Triennial Act, which compelled the king to summon Parliament every three years. The Commons impeached Archbishop Laud and abolished the House of Lords and the Court of High Commission. It went further and threatened to abolish the institution of episcopacy. King Charles, fearful of a Scottish invasion—the original reason for summoning Parliament—accepted these measures. Understanding and peace were not achieved, however, partly because radical members of the Commons pushed increasingly revolutionary propositions, partly because Charles maneuvered to rescind those he had already approved. An uprising in Ireland precipitated civil war.

Ever since Henry II had conquered Ireland in 1171, English governors had mercilessly ruled the Irish, and English landlords had ruthlessly exploited them. The English Reformation had made a bad situation worse: because the Irish remained Catholic, religious differences became united with economic and political oppression. Without an army, Charles I could neither come to terms with the Scots nor put down the Irish rebellion, and the Long Parliament remained unwilling to place an army under a king it did not trust. Charles thus instigated military action against parliamentary forces. He recruited an army drawn from the nobles and their cavalry staff, the rural gentry, and mercenaries. The parliamentary army was composed of the militia of the city of London, country squires with business connections, and men with a firm belief in the spiritual importance of serving.

The English civil war (1642–1646) tested whether sovereignty in England was to reside in the king or in Parliament. The civil war did not resolve that problem, although it ended with the execution of King Charles in 1649 on the charge of high treason—a severe blow to the theory of divine-right monarchy. The period between 1649 and 1660, called the "Interregnum" because it separated two monarchial periods, witnessed England's solitary experience of military dictatorship.

The problem of sovereignty was vigorously debated in the middle years of the seventeenth century. In *Leviathan,* the English philosopher and political theorist Thomas Hobbes (1588–1679) maintained that sovereignty is ultimately derived from the people, who transfer it to the monarchy by implicit contract. The power of the ruler is absolute, but kings do not hold their power by divine right. This view pleased no one in the seventeenth century.

When Charles I was beheaded on January 30, 1649, the kingship was abolished. A *commonwealth,* or republican form of government, was proclaimed. Theoretically, legislative power rested in the surviving members of Parliament and executive power in a council of state. In fact, the army that had defeated the royal forces controlled the government, and Oliver Cromwell controlled the army. Though called the "Protectorate," the rule of Cromwell (1653–1658) constituted military dictatorship.

Absolute government collapsed when Cromwell died in 1658 because the English got fed up with military rule. They longed for a return to civilian government, restoration of the common law, and social stability. Moreover, the strain of creating a community of puritanical saints proved too psychologically exhausting. Government by military dictatorship was an unfortunate experiment that the English never forgot nor repeated. By 1660 they were ready to restore the monarchy.

The House of Commons This seal of the Commonwealth shows the small House of Commons in session with the speaker presiding: the legend "in the third year of freedom" refers to 1651, three years after the abolition of the monarchy. In 1653, however, Cromwell abolished this "Rump Parliament"—so-called because it consisted of the few surviving members elected before the civil war. *(The British Library)*

THE RESTORATION OF THE ENGLISH MONARCHY

The Restoration of 1660 re-established the monarchy in the person of Charles II (1660–1685), eldest son of Charles I. At the same time both houses of Parliament were restored, together with the established Anglican church, the courts of law, and the system of local government through justices of the peace. The Restoration failed to resolve two serious problems. What was to be the attitude of the state toward Puritans, Catholics, and dissenters from the established church? And what was to be the constitutional position of the king—that is, what was to be the relationship between the king and Parliament?

About the first of these issues, Charles II, a relaxed, easygoing, and sensual man, was basically indifferent. He was not interested in doctrinal issues. Parliamentarians were, and they proceeded to enact a body of laws that sought to compel religious uniformity. Those who refused to receive the sacrament of the Church of England could not vote, hold public office, preach, teach, attend the universities, or even assemble for meetings, according to the Test Act of 1673. These restrictions could not be enforced. When the Quaker William Penn held a meeting of his Friends and was arrested, the jury refused to convict him.

In politics, Charles II was determined "not to set out in his travels again," which meant that he intended to get along with Parliament. Charles II's solution to the problem of the relationship between the king and the House of Commons had profound importance for later constitutional development. Generally good rapport existed between the king and the strongly royalist Parliament that had restored him. This rapport was due largely to the king's appointment of a council of five men who served both as his major advisers and as members of Parliament, thus acting as liaisons between the executive and the legislature. This body—known as the "Cabal" from the names of its five members (Clifford, Arlington, Buckingham, Ashley-Cooper, and Lauderdale)—was an ancestor of the later cabinet system (page 609). It gradually came to be accepted that the Cabal was answerable in Parliament for the decisions of the king. This development gave rise to the concept of ministerial responsibility: royal ministers must answer to the Commons.

Harmony between the crown and Parliament rested on the understanding that Charles would summon frequent parliaments and that Parliament would vote him sufficient revenues. However, although Parliament believed Charles had a virtual divine right to govern, it did not grant him an adequate income. Accordingly, in 1670 Charles entered into the Treaty of Dover, a secret agreement with Louis XIV. The French king would give Charles £200,000 annually; in return Charles would relax the laws against Catholics, gradually re-Catholicize England, and support French policy against the Dutch.

When the details of this secret treaty leaked out, a great wave of anti-Catholic fear swept England. This fear was compounded by a crucial fact: although Charles had produced several bastards, he had no legitimate children. It therefore appeared that his brother and heir, James, duke of York, who had publicly acknowledged his Catholicism, would inaugurate a Catholic dynasty. The combination of hatred for the French absolutism embodied in Louis XIV, hostility to Roman Catholicism, and fear of a permanent Catholic dynasty produced virtual hysteria. The Commons passed an exclusion bill denying the succession to a Roman Catholic, but Charles quickly dissolved Parliament and the bill never became law.

James II (1685–1688) did succeed his brother. Almost at once the worst English anti-Catholic fears, already aroused by Louis XIV's revocation of the Edict of Nantes, were realized. In direct violation of the Test Act, James appointed Roman Catholics to positions in the army, the universities, and local government. When these actions were tested in the courts, the judges, whom James had appointed, decided for the king. The king was suspending the law at will and appeared to be reviving the absolutism of his father and grandfather. He went further. Attempting to broaden his base of support with Protestant dissenters and nonconformists, James issued a declaration of indulgence granting religious freedom to all.

Two events gave the signals for revolution. First, seven bishops of the Church of England petitioned the king that they not be forced to read the declaration of indulgence because of their belief that it was an illegal act. They were imprisoned in the Tower of London but subsequently acquitted amid great public enthusiasm. Second, in June 1688 James's second wife produced a male heir. A Catholic dynasty seemed assured. The fear of a Roman Catholic monarchy, supported by France and ruling outside the law, prompted a group of eminent persons to offer the English throne to James's Protestant daughter, Mary, and her Dutch husband, Prince William of Orange. In November 1688 James II, his queen, and their infant son fled to France and became pensioners of Louis XIV.

The Triumph of England's Parliament: Constitutional Monarchy and Cabinet Government

The English call the events of 1688 the "Glorious Revolution." The revolution was indeed glorious in the sense that it replaced one monarchy with another with a minimum of bloodshed. It also represented the destruction, once and for all, of the idea of divine-right monarchy. William and Mary accepted the English throne from Parliament and in so doing explicitly recognized the supremacy of Parliament. The revolution of 1688 established the principle that sovereignty, the ultimate power in the state, rested in

Parliament and that the king ruled with the consent of the governed.

The men who brought about the revolution quickly framed their intentions in the Bill of Rights, the cornerstone of the modern British constitution. The basic principles of the Bill of Rights were formulated in direct response to Stuart absolutism. Law was to be made in Parliament; once made, it could not be suspended by the crown. Parliament had to be called at least every three years. Both elections to and debate in Parliament were to be free, in the sense that the Crown was not to interfere in them; this aspect of the bill was widely disregarded in the eighteenth century. Judges would hold their offices "during good behavior," which assured the independence of the judiciary. No longer could the crown get the judicial decisions it wanted by threats of removal. There was to be no standing army in peacetime—a limitation designed to prevent the repetition of either Stuart or Cromwellian military government. The Bill of Rights granted "that the subjects which are Protestants may have arms for their defense suitable to their conditions and as allowed by law," meaning that Catholics could not possess firearms because the Protestant majority feared them.[11] Additional legislation granted freedom of worship to Protestant dissenters and nonconformists and required that the English monarch always be Protestant.

The Glorious Revolution found its best defense in the political philosopher John Locke's "Second Treatise on Civil Government" (1690). Locke (1632–1704) maintained that men set up civil governments in order to protect their property. The purpose of government, therefore, is to protect life, liberty, and property. A government that oversteps its proper function—protecting the natural rights of life, liberty, and property—becomes a tyranny. (By "natural" rights, Locke meant rights basic to all men because all have the ability to reason.) Under a tyrannical government, the people have the natural right to rebellion. Rebellion can be avoided if the government carefully respects the rights of citizens and if the people zealously defend their liberty. Recognizing the close relationship between economic and political freedom, Locke linked economic liberty and private property with political freedom. Locke served as the great spokesman for the liberal English revolution of 1688 and for representative government. His idea, inherited from the Stoics of ancient Greece (page 155), that there are natural or universal

The Rise of Western Absolutism and Constitutionalism

1581	Formation of the United Provinces of the Netherlands
1588	Defeat of the Spanish Armada
1589–1610	Reign of Henry IV of France; economic reforms help to restore public order, lay foundation for absolutist rule
1598	Edict of Nantes: Henry IV ends the French wars of religion
1608	France establishes its first Canadian settlement, at Quebec
1609	Philip III of Spain recognizes Dutch independence
1610–1650	Spanish trade with the New World falls by 60 percent
1618–1648	Thirty Years' War
1624–1643	Richelieu dominates French government
1625	Huguenot revolt in France; siege of La Rochelle
1629–1640	Eleven Years' Tyranny: Charles I attempts to rule England without the aid of Parliament
1640–1660	Long Parliament in England
1642–1646	English civil war
1643–1661	Mazarin dominates France's regency government
1643–1715	Reign of Louis XIV
1648–1660	The Fronde: French nobility opposes centralizing efforts of monarchy
1648	Peace of Westphalia confirms Dutch independence from Spain
1649	Execution of Charles I; beginning of the Interregnum in England
1653–1658	The Protectorate: Cromwell heads military rule of England
1659	Treaty of the Pyrenees forces Spain to cede extensive territories to France, marks end of Spain as a great power
1660	Restoration of the English monarchy: Charles II returns from exile
1661	Louis XIV enters into independent rule
ca 1663–1683	Colbert directs Louis XIV's mercantilist economic policy
1670	Treaty of Dover: Charles II secretly agrees with Louis XIV to re-Catholicize England
1673	Test Act excludes Roman Catholics from public office in England
	France invades Holland
1678	Treaty of Nijmegen: Louis XIV acquires Franche-Comté
1681	France acquires Strasbourg
1685	Louis XIV revokes the Edict of Nantes
1685–1688	James II rules England, attempts to restore Roman Catholicism as state religion
1688	The Glorious Revolution establishes a constitutional monarchy in England under Mary and William III
1689	Enactment of the Bill of Rights
1701–1713	War of the Spanish Succession
1713	Peace of Utrecht ends French territorial acquisitions, expands the British Empire

rights, equally valid for all peoples and societies, played a powerful role in eighteenth-century Enlightenment thought. His ideas on liberty and tyranny were especially popular in colonial America.

The events of 1688 and 1689 did not constitute a *democratic* revolution. The revolution placed sovereignty in Parliament, and Parliament represented the upper classes. The great majority of English people acquired no say in their government. The English revolution established a constitutional monarchy; it also inaugurated an age of aristocratic government that lasted until at least 1832 and probably 1914.

In the course of the eighteenth century, the cabinet system of government evolved. The term *cabinet* refers to the small private room in which English rulers consulted their chief ministers. In a cabinet system, the leading ministers, who must have seats in and the support of a majority of the House of Commons, formulate common policy and conduct the business of the country. During the administration of one royal minister, Sir Robert Walpole (1721–1742), the idea developed that the cabinet was responsible to the House of Commons. The Hanoverian king George I (1714–1727) normally presided at cabinet meetings throughout his reign, but his son and heir George II (1727–1760) discontinued the practice. The influence of the crown in decision making accordingly declined. Walpole enjoyed the favor of the monarchy and of the House of Commons and came to be called the king's first, or "prime," minister. In the English cabinet system, both legislative and executive power are held by the leading ministers, who form the government.

THE DUTCH REPUBLIC IN THE SEVENTEENTH CENTURY

The seventeenth century witnessed an unparalleled flowering of Dutch scientific, artistic, and literary achievement. In this period, often called the "golden age of the Netherlands," Dutch ideas and attitudes played a profound role in shaping a new and modern world-view. At the same time, the republic of the United Provinces of the Netherlands represents another model of the development of the modern state.

In the late sixteenth century, the seven northern provinces of the Netherlands, of which Holland and Zeeland were the most prosperous, succeeded in throwing off Spanish domination. This success was based on their geographical lines of defense, the wealth of their cities, the brilliant military strategy of William the Silent, the preoccupation of Philip II of Spain with so many other concerns, and the northern provinces' vigorous Calvinism. In 1581 the seven provinces of the Union of Utrecht had formed the United Provinces (page 569). Philip II continued to try to crush the Dutch with the armada, but in 1609 his son Philip III agreed to a truce that implicitly recognized the independence of the United Provinces. At the time neither side expected the peace to be permanent. The Peace of Westphalia in 1648, however, confirmed the Dutch republic's independence.

Within each province an oligarchy of wealthy merchants called "regents" handled domestic affairs in the local Estates. The provincial Estates held virtually all the power. A federal assembly, or States General, handled matters of foreign affairs, such as war. But the States General did not possess sovereign authority, since all issues had to be referred back to the local Estates for approval. The States General appointed a representative, the *stadholder,* in each province. As the highest executive there, the stadholder carried out ceremonial functions and was responsible for defense and good order. The sons of William the Silent, Maurice and William Louis, held the office of stadholder in all seven provinces. As members of the House of Orange, they were closely identified with the struggle against Spain and Dutch patriotism. The regents in each province jealously guarded local independence and resisted efforts at centralization. Nevertheless, Holland, which had the largest navy and the most wealth, dominated the republic and the States General. Significantly, the Estates assembled at Holland's capital, The Hague.

The government of the United Provinces fits none of the standard categories of seventeenth-century political organization. The Dutch were not monarchial, but fiercely republican. The government was controlled by wealthy merchants and financiers. Though rich, their values were not aristocratic but strongly middle class, emphasizing thrift, hard work, and simplicity in living. The Dutch republic was not a strong federation but a confederation—that is, a weak union of strong provinces. The provinces were a temptation to powerful neighbors, yet the Dutch resisted the long Spanish effort at reconquest and withstood both French and English attacks in the second half of the century. Louis XIV's hatred of the Dutch was proverbial. They represented all that he despised—middle-class values, religious toleration, and political independence.

The political success of the Dutch rested on the phenomenal commercial prosperity of the Netherlands. The moral and ethical bases of that commercial wealth were thrift, frugality, and religious toleration. John Calvin had written, "From where do the merchant's profits come except from his own diligence and industry." This attitude undoubtedly encouraged a sturdy people who had waged a centuries-old struggle against the sea.

Alone of all European peoples in the seventeenth century, the Dutch practiced religious toleration.

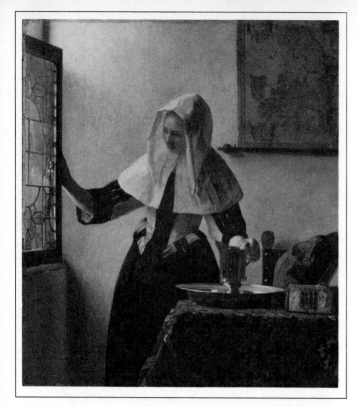

Vermeer: Young Woman with a Water Jug The mystery of light fascinated seventeenth-century scientists and artists, perhaps the Dutch painter Vermeer most of all. His calm quiet scenes of ordinary people performing everyday tasks in rooms suffused with light has given him the title "poet of domesticity." The map on the wall suggests curiosity about the wider world. *(Metropolitan Museum of Art, Gift of Henry G. Marquand, 1889)*

Peoples of all faiths were welcome within their borders. It is a striking testimony to the urbanity of Dutch society that in a century when patriotism was closely identified with religious uniformity, the Calvinist province of Holland allowed its highest official, Jan van Oldenbarneveldt, to continue to practice his Roman Catholic faith. As long as a businessman conducted his religion in private, the government did not interfere with him.

Toleration also paid off: it attracted a great deal of foreign capital and investment. Deposits at the Bank of Amsterdam were guaranteed by the city council, and in the middle years of the century the bank became Europe's best source of cheap credit and commercial intelligence and the main clearing-house for bills of exchange. Men of all races and creeds traded in Amsterdam, at whose docks on the Amstel River five thousand ships, half the merchant marine of the

United Provinces, were berthed. Joost van den Vondel, the poet of Dutch imperialism, exulted:

God, God, the Lord of Amstel cried, hold every conscience free;
And Liberty ride, on Holland's tide, with billowing sails to sea,
And run our Amstel out and in; let freedom gird the bold,
And merchant in his counting house stand elbow deep in gold.[12]

The fishing industry was the cornerstone of the Dutch economy. For half the year, from June to December, fishing fleets combed the dangerous English coast and the North Sea, raking in tiny herring. Profits from herring stimulated shipbuilding, and even before 1600 the Dutch were offering the lowest shipping rates in Europe. Although Dutch cities became famous for their exports—diamonds from Amsterdam, linen from Haarlem, pottery from Delft—Dutch wealth depended less on exports than on transport. The merchant marine was the largest in Europe.

In 1602 a group of the regents of Holland formed the Dutch East India Company, a joint stock company. Each investor received a percentage of the profits proportional to the amount of money he had put in. Within half a century, the Dutch East India Company had cut heavily into Portuguese trading in East Asia (page 561). The Dutch seized and established trading posts in the Cape of Good Hope, Ceylon, and Malacca. In the 1630s the Dutch East India Company was paying its investors about a 35 percent annual return on their investments. The Dutch West India Company, founded in 1621, traded extensively with Latin America and Africa.

Although the initial purpose of both companies was commercial—the import of spices and silks to Europe—the Dutch found themselves involved in the imperialistic exploitation of large parts of the Pacific and Latin America. Amsterdam, the center of a worldwide Dutch Empire, became the commercial and financial capital of Europe. During the seventeenth century, the Dutch translated their commercial acumen and flexibility into political and imperialist terms with striking success. But war with France and England in the 1670s hurt the United Provinces. The long War of the Spanish Succession, in which the Dutch supported England against France, was a costly drain on Dutch manpower and financial re-

Amsterdam Harbor, 1663 Amsterdam's great wealth depended on the presence of a relatively large number of people with capital for overseas investment *and* on its fleet, which brought goods from all over the world. As shown here, because the inner docks were often jammed to capacity, many ships had to be moored outside the city. *(Scheepvaart Museum, Amsterdam)*

sources. The peace signed in 1713 to end the war marked the beginning of Dutch economic decline.

According to Thomas Hobbes, the central drive in every man is "a perpetual and restless desire of Power, after Power, that ceaseth only in Death." The seventeenth century solved the problem of sovereign power in two fundamental ways: absolutism and constitutionalism. The France of Louis XIV witnessed the emergence of the fully absolutist state. The king commanded all the powers of the state: judicial, military, political, and, to a great extent, ecclesiastical. France developed a centralized bureaucracy, a state-directed economy, a professional army, all of which Louis personally supervised. For the first time in history all the institutions and powers of the national state were effectively controlled by a single person. The king saw himself as the representative of God on earth, and "to the seventeenth century imagination God was a sort of image of Louis XIV."[13]

As Louis XIV personifies absolutism, so Stuart England exemplifies the evolution of the first modern constitutional state. The conflicts between Parliament and the first two Stuart rulers, James I and Charles I, tested where sovereign power would rest in the state. The resulting civil war did not solve the problem. The Instrument of Government, the document produced in 1653 by the victorious parliamentary army, provided for a balance of governmental authority and recognition of popular rights; as such, the instrument has been called the first modern constitution. Unfortunately, it lacked public support. James II's absolutist tendencies brought on the revolution of 1688, and the people who made that revolution settled three basic issues. Sovereign power was divided between king and Parliament, with Parliament enjoying the greater share. Government was to be based on the rule of law. And the liberties of English people were made explicit in written form, in the Bill of Rights. The framers of the English constitution left to later generations the task of making constitutional government work.

The models of governmental power established by seventeenth-century France and England strongly influenced other states then and ever since. As the American novelist William Faulkner wrote, "The past isn't dead; it's not even past."

NOTES

1. S. de Gramont, ed., *The Age of Magnificence: Memoirs of the Court of Louis XIV by the Duc de Saint-Simon* (New York: Capricorn Books, 1964), pp. 141–145.
2. Quoted in J. Wolf, *Louis XIV* (New York: Norton, 1968), p. 146.
3. Quoted in A. Trout, *Jean-Baptiste Colbert* (Boston: Twayne Publishers, 1978), p. 128.
4. Quoted in Wolf, *Louis XIV*, p. 394.
5. Ibid.
6. See W. C. Scoville, *The Persecution of the Huguenots and French Economic Development: 1680–1720* (Berkeley, Calif.: University of California Press, 1960).
7. W. F. Church, *Louis XIV in Historical Thought: From Voltaire to the Annales School* (New York: Norton, 1976), p. 92.
8. De Gramont, *Age of Magnificence*, p. 183.
9. J. H. Elliott, *Imperial Spain, 1469–1716* (New York: Mentor Books, 1963), pp. 306–308.
10. See B. Bennassar, *The Spanish Character: Attitudes and Mentalities from the Sixteenth to the Nineteenth Century*, trans. B. Keen (Berkeley, Calif.: University of California Press, 1979), p. 125.
11. C. Stephenson and G. F. Marcham, *Sources of English Constitutional History* (New York: Harper & Row, 1937), p. 601.
12. Quoted in D. Maland, *Europe in the Seventeenth Century* (New York: Macmillan, 1967), pp. 198–199.
13. Quoted in C. J. Friedrich and C. Blitzer, *The Age of Power* (Ithaca, N.Y.: Cornell University Press, 1957), p. 112.

SUGGESTED READING

Students who wish to explore the problems presented in this chapter in greater depth will easily find a rich and exciting literature, with many titles available in paperback editions. The following surveys all provide good background material. G. Parker, *Europe in Crisis, 1598–1618* (1980), provides a sound introduction to the social, economic, and religious tensions of the period. R. S. Dunn, *The Age of Religious Wars, 1559–1715*, 2d ed. (1979), examines the period from the perspective of the confessional strife between Protestants and Catholics, but also includes stimulating material on absolutism and constitutionalism. T. Aston, ed., *Crisis in Europe, 1560–1660* (1967), contains essays by leading historians. P. Anderson, *Lineages of the Absolutist State* (1974), is a Marxist interpretation of absolutism in western and eastern Europe. M. Beloff, *The Age of Absolutism* (1967), concentrates on the social forces that underlay administrative change. H. Rosenberg, "Absolute Monarchy and Its Legacy," in N. F. Cantor and S. Werthman, eds., *Early Modern Europe, 1450–1650* (1967), is a seminal study. The classic treatment of constitutionalism remains that of C. H. McIlwain, *Constitutionalism: Ancient and Modern* (1940), written by a great scholar during the rise of German fascism. S. B. Crimes, *English Constitutional History* (1967), is an excellent survey with useful chapters on the sixteenth and seventeenth centuries.

Louis XIV and his age have predictably attracted the attention of many scholars. The title by Wolf in the Notes remains the best available biography. Two works of W. H. Lewis, *The Splendid Century* (1957) and *The Sunset of the Splendid Century* (1963), make delightful light reading, especially for the beginning student. The advanced student will want to consult the work by Church listed in the Notes, an excellent historiographical analysis. Perhaps the best work of the Annales school on the period is P. Goubert, *Louis XIV and Twenty Million Frenchmen* (1972), and his heavily detailed *The Ancien Régime: French Society, 1600–1750*, 2 vols. (1969–1973), which contains invaluable material on the lives and work of ordinary people. For the French economy and financial conditions, the old study of C. W. Cole, *Colbert and a Century of French Mercantilism*, 2 vols. (1939), is still valuable but should be supplemented by R. Bonney, *The King's Debts: Finance and Politics in France, 1589–1661* (1981). Also see the Trout and, especially, the Scoville titles cited in the Notes; the latter is a significant book in revisionist history. For Louis XIV's foreign policy and wars, see R. Hatton, "Louis XIV: Recent Gains in Historical Knowledge," *Journal of Modern History* 45 (1973), and her edited work *Louis XIV and Europe* (1976), an important collection of essays. Hatton's *Europe in the Age of Louis XIV* (1979) is a splendidly illustrated survey of many aspects of seventeenth-century European culture. O. Ranum, *Paris in the Age of Absolutism* (1968), describes the geographical, political, economic, and architectural significance of the cultural capital of Europe, while V. L. Tapie, *The Age of Grandeur: Baroque Art and Architecture* (1960), also emphasizes the relationship between art and politics with excellent illustrations.

For Spain and Portugal, see J. H. Elliott, *Imperial Spain, 1469–1716,* rev. ed. (1977), a sensitively written and authoritative study. The Bennassar title in the Notes and M. Defourneaux, *Daily Life in Spain in the Golden Age* (1976), are highly useful for an understanding of ordinary people and of Spanish society. C. R. Phillips, *Ciudad Real, 1570–1750: Growth, Crisis, and Readjustment in the Spanish Economy* (1979), is a significant case study.

The following works all offer solid material on English political and social issues of the seventeenth century: M. Ashley, *England in the Seventeenth Century,* rev. ed. (1980), and *The House of Stuart: Its Rise and Fall* (1980); C. Hill, *A Century of Revolution* (1961); J. P. Kenyon, *Stuart England* (1978); and K. Wrightson, *English Society, 1580–1680* (1982). Perhaps the most comprehensive treatment of Parliament is C. Russell, *Crisis of Parliaments, 1509–1660* (1971) and *Parliaments and English Politics, 1621–1629* (1979). On the background of the English civil war, L. Stone's *The Crisis of the Aristocracy* (1965) and *The Causes of the English Revolution* (1972) are standard works, while both B. Manning, *The English People and the English Revolution* (1976), and D. Underdown, *Revel, Riot, and Rebellion* (1985), discuss the extent of popular involvement; Underdown's is the more sophisticated treatment. For English intellectual currents, see J. O. Appleby, *Economic Thought and Ideology in Seventeenth Century England* (1978); and C. Hill, *Intellectual Origins of the English Revolution* (1966) and *Society and Puritanism in Pre-Revolutionary England* (1964).

For the several shades of Protestant sentiment in the early seventeenth century, see P. Collinson, *The Religion of Protestants* (1982). C. M. Hibbard, *Charles I and the Popish Plot* (1983), treats Roman Catholic influence; like Collinson's work, it is an excellent, fundamental reference for religious issues, though the older work of W. Haller, *The Rise of Puritanism* (1957), is still valuable. For women, see R. Thompson, *Women in Stuart England and America* (1974), and A. Fraser, *The Weaker Vessel* (1985). For Cromwell and the Interregnum, C. Firth, *Oliver Cromwell and the Rule of the Puri-*

tans in England (1956), C. Hill, *God's Englishman* (1972), and A. Fraser, *Cromwell, The Lord Protector* (1973), are all valuable. J. Morrill, *The Revolt of the Provinces,* 2d ed. (1980), is the best study of neutralism, while C. Hill, *The World Turned Upside Down* (1972), discusses radical thought during the period.

For the Restoration and the Glorious Revolution, see A. Fraser, *Royal Charles: Charles II and the Restoration* (1979), a highly readable biography; R. Ollard, *The Image of the King: Charles I and Charles II* (1980), which examines the nature of monarchy; J. Miller, *James II: A Study in Kingship* (1977); J. Childs, *The Army, James II, and the Glorious Revolution* (1980); J. R. Jones, *The Revolution of 1688 in England* (1972); and L. G. Schwoerer, *The Declaration of Rights, 1689* (1981), a fine assessment of the English Bill of Rights. The ideas of John Locke are analyzed by J. P. Kenyon, *Revolution Principles: The Politics of Party, 1689–1720* (1977). R. Hutton, *The Restoration, 1658–1667* (1985), is a thorough if somewhat difficult narrative.

On Holland, K. H. D. Haley, *The Dutch Republic in the Seventeenth Century* (1972), is a splendidly illustrated appreciation of Dutch commercial and artistic achievements, while J. L. Price, *Culture and Society in the Dutch Republic During the Seventeenth Century* (1974), is a sound scholarly work. R. Boxer, *The Dutch Seaborne Empire* (1980), and the appropriate chapters of the Maland work listed in the Notes are useful for Dutch overseas expansion and the reasons for Dutch prosperity. The following works focus on the economic and cultural life of the leading Dutch city: V. Barbour, *Capitalism in Amsterdam in the Seventeenth Century* (1950), and D. Regin, *Traders, Artists, Burghers: A Cultural History of Amsterdam in the Seventeenth Century* (1977). J. M. Montias, *Artists and Artisans in Delft: A Socio-Economic Study of the Seventeenth Century* (1982), examines another major city. The leading statesmen of the period may be studied in these biographies: H. H. Rowen, *John de Witt, Grand Pensionary of Holland, 1625–1672* (1978); S. B. Baxter, *William the III and the Defense of European Liberty, 1650–1702* (1966); and J. den Tex, *Oldenbarnevelt,* 2 vols. (1973).

Many facets of the lives of ordinary French, Spanish, English, and Dutch people are discussed by P. Burke, *Popular Culture in Early Modern Europe* (1978), an important and provocative study.

20

ABSOLUTISM IN EASTERN EUROPE TO 1740

*T*HE SEVENTEENTH century witnessed a struggle between constitutionalism and absolutism in eastern Europe. With the notable exception of the kingdom of Poland, monarchial absolutism was everywhere triumphant in eastern Europe; constitutionalism was decisively defeated. Absolute monarchies emerged in Austria, Prussia, and Russia. This was a development of great significance: these three monarchies exercised enormous influence until 1918, and they created a strong authoritarian tradition that is still dominant in eastern Europe.

Although the monarchs of eastern Europe were greatly impressed by Louis XIV and his model of royal absolutism, their states differed in several important ways from their French counterpart. Louis XIV built French absolutism on the heritage of a well-developed medieval monarchy and a strong royal bureaucracy. And when Louis XIV came to the throne, the powers of the nobility were already somewhat limited, the French middle class was relatively strong, and the peasants were generally free from serfdom. Eastern absolutism rested on a very different social reality: a powerful nobility, a weak middle class, and an oppressed peasantry composed of serfs.

These differences in social conditions raise three major questions. First, why did the basic structure of society in eastern Europe move away from that of western Europe in the early modern period? Second, how and why, in their different social environments, did the rulers of Austria, Prussia, and Russia manage to build powerful absolute monarchies, which proved more durable than that of Louis XIV? Finally, how did the absolute monarchs' interaction with artists and architects contribute to the splendid achievements of baroque culture? These are the questions that will be explored in this chapter.

LORDS AND PEASANTS IN EASTERN EUROPE

When absolute monarchy took shape in eastern Europe in the seventeenth century, it built on social and economic foundations laid between roughly 1400 and 1650. In those years, the princes and the landed nobility of eastern Europe rolled back the gains made by the peasantry during the High Middle Ages and reimposed a harsh serfdom on the rural masses. The nobility also reduced the importance of the towns and the middle classes. This process differed profoundly from developments in western Europe at the same time. In the west, peasants won greater freedom and the urban capitalistic middle class continued its rise. Thus, the east that emerged contrasted sharply with the west—another aspect of the shattered unity of medieval Latin Christendom.

THE MEDIEVAL BACKGROUND

Between roughly 1400 and 1650, nobles and rulers re-established serfdom in the eastern lands of Bohemia, Silesia, Hungary, eastern Germany, Poland, Lithuania, and Russia. The east—the land east of the Elbe River in Germany, which historians often call "East Elbia"—gained a certain social and economic unity in the process. But eastern peasants lost their rights and freedoms. They became bound first to the land they worked and then, by degrading obligations, to the lords they served.

This development was a tragic reversal of trends in the High Middle Ages. The period from roughly 1050 to 1300 had been a time of general economic expansion characterized by the growth of trade, towns, and population. Expansion also meant clearing the forests and colonizing the frontier beyond the Elbe River. Anxious to attract German settlers to their sparsely populated lands, the rulers and nobles of eastern Europe had offered potential newcomers attractive economic and legal incentives. Large numbers of incoming settlers obtained land on excellent terms and gained much greater personal freedom. These benefits were also gradually extended to the local Slavic populations, even those of central Russia. Thus by 1300 there had occurred a very general improvement in peasant conditions in eastern Europe. Serfdom all but disappeared. Peasants bargained freely with their landlords and moved about as they pleased. Opportunities and improvements east of the Elbe had a positive impact on western Europe, where the weight of serfdom was also reduced between 1100 and 1300.

After about 1300, however, as Europe's population and economy both declined grievously, mainly because of the Black Death, the east and the west went in different directions. In both east and west there occurred a many-sided landlord reaction, as lords sought to solve their tough economic problems by more heavily exploiting the peasantry. Yet this reaction generally failed in the west. In many western areas by 1500 almost all of the peasants were completely free, and in the rest of western Europe serf obligations had declined greatly. East of the Elbe, however, the landlords won. By 1500 eastern peasants were well on their way to becoming serfs again.

Throughout eastern Europe, as in western Europe, the drop in population and prices in the fourteenth and fifteenth centuries caused severe labor shortages and hard times for the nobles. Yet rather than offer better economic and legal terms to keep old peasants and attract new ones, eastern landlords used their political and police power to turn the tables on the peasants. They did this in two ways.

First, the lords made their kings and princes issue laws that restricted or eliminated the peasants' precious, time-honored right of free movement. Thus, a peasant could no longer leave to take advantage of better opportunities elsewhere without the lord's permission, and the lord had no reason to make such concessions. In Prussian territories by 1500, the law required that runaway peasants be hunted down and returned to their lords; a runaway servant was to be nailed to a post by one ear and given a knife to cut himself loose. Until the middle of the fifteenth century, medieval Russian peasants had been free to move wherever they wished and seek the best landlord. Thereafter this freedom was gradually curtailed, so that by 1497 a Russian peasant had the right to move only during a two-week period after the fall harvest. Eastern peasants were losing their status as free and independent men and women.

Second, lords steadily took more and more of their peasants' land and imposed heavier and heavier labor obligations. Instead of being independent farmers paying reasonable, freely negotiated rents, peasants tended to become forced laborers on the lords' estates. By the early 1500s, lords in many territories could command their peasants to work for them without pay as many as six days a week. A German writer of the mid-sixteenth century described peasants in eastern Prussia who "do not possess the heritage of their holdings and have to serve their master whenever he wants them."[1]

The gradual erosion of the peasantry's economic position was bound up with manipulation of the legal system. The local lord was also the local prosecutor, judge, and jailer. As a matter of course, he ruled in his own favor in disputes with his peasants. There were no independent royal officials to provide justice or uphold the common law.

THE CONSOLIDATION OF SERFDOM

Between 1500 and 1650, the social, legal, and economic conditions of peasants in eastern Europe continued to decline. Free peasants lost their freedom and became serfs. In Poland, for example, nobles gained complete control over their peasants in 1574, after which they could legally inflict the death penalty on their serfs whenever they wished. In Prussia a long series of oppressive measures reached their culmination in 1653. Not only were all the old privileges of the lords reaffirmed, but peasants were assumed to be in "hereditary subjugation" to their lords unless they could prove the contrary in the lords' courts, which was practically impossible. Prussian peasants were serfs tied to their lords as well as to the land.

In Russia the right of peasants to move from a given estate was "temporarily" suspended in the 1590s and permanently abolished in 1603. In 1649 a new law code spelled out the enserfment of the peasants that had been taking place. At the insistence of the lower nobility, the Russian tsar lifted the nine-year time limit on the recovery of runaways. Henceforth runaway peasants were to be returned to their lords whenever they were caught, as long as they lived. The last small hope of escaping serfdom was gone. Control of serfs was strictly the lords' own business, for the new law code set no limits on the lords' authority over their peasants. Although the political development of the various eastern states differed, the legal re-establishment of permanent hereditary serfdom was the common fate of peasants in the east by the middle of the seventeenth century.

The consolidation of serfdom between 1500 and 1650 was accompanied by the growth of estate agriculture, particularly in Poland and eastern Germany. In the sixteenth century, European economic expansion and population growth resumed after the great declines of the late Middle Ages. Prices for agricultural commodities also rose sharply as gold and silver flowed in from the New World. Thus Polish and German lords had powerful economic incentives to increase the production of their estates. And they did.

Lords seized more and more peasant land for their own estates and then demanded and received ever more unpaid serf labor on those enlarged estates.

Punishing Serfs This seventeenth-century illustration from Olearius's famous *Travels to Moscovy* suggests what eastern serfdom really meant. The scene is set in eastern Poland. There, according to Olearius, a common command of the lord was, "Beat him till the skin falls from the flesh." *(University of Illinois, Champaign)*

Even when the estates were inefficient and technically backward, as they generally were, the great Polish nobles and middle-rank German lords squeezed sizable, cheap, and thus very profitable surpluses out of their impoverished peasants. These surpluses in wheat and timber were easily sold to big foreign merchants, who exported them to the growing cities of the west. The poor east helped feed the much wealthier west.

The re-emergence of serfdom in eastern Europe in the early modern period was clearly a momentous human development, and historians have advanced a variety of explanations for it. As always, some scholars have stressed the economic interpretation. Agricultural depression and population decline in the fourteenth and fifteenth centuries led to a severe labor shortage, they have argued, and thus eastern landlords naturally tied their precious peasants to the land. With the return of prosperity and the development of export markets in the sixteenth century, the landlords finished the job, grabbing the peasants' land and making them work as unpaid serfs on the enlarged estates. This argument by itself is not very convincing, for almost identical economic developments "caused" the opposite result in the west. Indeed, some historians have maintained that labor shortage and subsequent expansion were key factors in the virtual disappearance of western serfdom.

It seems fairly clear, therefore, that political rather than economic factors were crucial in the simultaneous rise of serfdom in the east and decline of serfdom in the west. Specifically, eastern lords enjoyed much greater political power than their western counterparts. In the late Middle Ages, when much of eastern

Europe experienced innumerable wars and general political chaos, the noble landlord class greatly increased its political power at the expense of the ruling monarchs. There were, for example, many disputed royal successions, so that weak kings were forced to grant political favors to win the support of the nobility. Thus while strong "new monarchs" were rising in Spain, France, and England and providing effective central government, kings were generally losing power in the east. Such weak kings could not resist the demands of the lords regarding their peasants.

Moreover, most eastern monarchs did not want to resist even if they could. The typical king was only first among equals in the noble class. He, too, thought mainly in private rather than public terms. He, too, wanted to squeeze as much as he could out of his peasants and enlarge his estates. The western concept and reality of sovereignty, as embodied in a king who protected the interests of all his people, was not well developed in eastern Europe before 1650.

The political power of the peasants was also weaker in eastern Europe and declined steadily after about 1400. Although there were occasional bloody peasant uprisings against the oppression of the landlords, they never succeeded. Nor did eastern peasants effectively resist day-by-day infringements on their liberties by their landlords. Part of the reason was that the lords, rather than the kings, ran the courts—one of the important concessions nobles extorted from weak monarchs. It has also been suggested that peasant solidarity was weaker in the east, possibly reflecting the lack of long-established village communities.

Finally, with the approval of weak kings, the landlords systematically undermined the medieval privileges of the towns and the power of the urban classes. Instead of selling their products to local merchants in the towns, as required in the Middle Ages, the landlords sold directly to big foreign capitalists. For example, Dutch ships sailed up the rivers of Poland and eastern Germany to the loading docks of the great estates, completely by-passing the local towns. Moreover, "town air" no longer "made people free," for the eastern towns lost their medieval right of refuge and were compelled to return runaways to their lords. The population of the towns and the importance of the urban middle classes declined greatly. This development both reflected and promoted the supremacy of noble landlords in most of eastern Europe in the sixteenth century.

THE RISE OF AUSTRIA AND PRUSSIA

Despite the strength of the nobility and the weakness of many monarchs before 1600, strong kings did begin to emerge in many lands in the course of the seventeenth century. War and the threat of war aided rulers greatly in their attempts to build absolute monarchies. There was an endless struggle for power, as eastern rulers not only fought one another but also battled with hordes of Asiatic invaders. In this atmosphere of continuous wartime emergency, monarchs reduced the political power of the landlord nobility. Cautiously leaving the nobles the unchallenged masters of their peasants, the absolutist monarchs of eastern Europe gradually gained and monopolized political power in three key areas. They imposed and collected permanent taxes without consent. They maintained permanent standing armies, which policed their subjects in addition to fighting abroad. And they conducted relations with other states as they pleased.

As with all general historical developments, there were important variations on the absolutist theme in eastern Europe. The royal absolutism created in Prussia was stronger and more effective than that established in Austria. This advantage gave Prussia a thin edge over Austria in the struggle for power in east-central Europe in the eighteenth century. That edge had enormous long-term political significance, for it was a rising Prussia that unified the German people in the nineteenth century and imposed on them a fateful Prussian stamp.

AUSTRIA AND THE OTTOMAN TURKS

Like all the peoples and rulers of central Europe, the Habsburgs of Austria emerged from the Thirty Years' War impoverished and exhausted (see pages 571–576). The effort to root out Protestantism in the German lands had failed utterly, and the authority of the Holy Roman Empire and its Habsburg emperors had declined almost to the vanishing point. Yet defeat in central Europe also opened new vistas. The Habsburg monarchs were forced to turn inward and eastward in the attempt to fuse their diverse collection of territories and peoples into a strong unified state.

An important step in this direction had actually been taken in Bohemia during the Thirty Years' War. Protestantism had been strong among the Czechs, a Slavic people concentrated in Bohemia. In 1618 the Czech nobles who controlled the Bohemian Estates had risen up against their Habsburg king. Not only was this revolt crushed, but the old Czech nobility was wiped out as well. Those Czech nobles who did not die in 1620 at the Battle of the White Mountain (see page 573), a momentous turning point in Czech history, had their estates confiscated. The Habsburg king, Ferdinand II (1619–1637), then redistributed the Czech lands to a motley band of aristocratic soldiers of fortune, who had nothing in common with the Czech-speaking peasants.

In fact, after 1650, 80 to 90 percent of the nobility in Bohemia was of recent foreign origin and owed everything to the Habsburgs. With the help of this new nobility, the Habsburgs established strong direct rule over reconquered Bohemia. The condition of the enserfed peasantry worsened: three days per week of unpaid labor—the *robot*—became the norm, and a quarter of the serfs worked for their lords every day but Sundays and religious holidays. Serfs also paid the taxes, which further strengthened the alliance between the Habsburg monarch and the Bohemian nobility. Protestantism was also stamped out, in the course of which a growing unity of religion was brought about. The reorganization of Bohemia was a giant step toward absolutism.

After the Thirty Years' War, Ferdinand III centralized the government in the old hereditary German-speaking provinces of Austria proper, the second part of the Habsburg holdings. For the first time, under Ferdinand was created a permanent standing army, which stood ready to put down any internal opposition. The Habsburg monarchy was then ready to turn toward the vast plains of Hungary, which it claimed as the third and largest part of its dominion, in opposition to the Ottoman Turks.

The Ottomans came out of Anatolia, in present-day Turkey, to create one of history's greatest military empires. At their peak in the middle of the sixteenth century under Suleiman the Magnificent (1520–1566), they ruled the most powerful empire in the world. Their possessions stretched from western Persia across North Africa and up into the heart of central Europe (see Map 23.2). Apostles of Islam, the Ottomans were old and determined foes of the Catholic Habsburgs. Their armies had almost captured Vienna in 1529, and for more than 150 years thereafter the Ottomans ruled all of the Balkan territories, almost all of Hungary, and part of southern Russia.

In the late seventeenth century, under vigorous reforming leadership, the Ottoman Empire succeeded in marshaling its forces for one last mighty blow at Christian Europe. After wresting territory from Poland, fighting a long inconclusive war with Russia, and establishing an alliance with Louis XIV of France, the Turks turned again on Austria. A huge Turkish army surrounded Vienna and laid siege to it in 1683. But after holding out against great odds for two months, the city was relieved by a mixed force of Habsburg, Saxon, Bavarian, and Polish troops, and the Ottomans were forced to retreat. Soon the retreat became a rout. As their Russian and Venetian allies attacked on other fronts, the Habsburgs conquered all of Hungary and Transylvania (part of present-day Rumania) by 1699 (Map 20.1).

The Turkish wars and this great expansion strengthened the Habsburg army and promoted some sense of unity in the Habsburg lands. The Habsburgs moved to centralize their power and make it as absolute as possible. These efforts to create a fully developed, highly centralized, absolutist state were only partly successful.

The Habsburg state was composed of three separate and distinct territories—the kingdom of Bohemia, the old "hereditary provinces" of Austria, and the kingdom of Hungary. These three parts were tied together primarily by their common ruler—the Habsburg monarch. Each part had its own laws and political life, for the three noble-dominated Estates continued to exist, though with reduced powers. The Habsburgs themselves were well aware of the fragility of the union they had forged. In 1713 Charles VI (1711–1740) proclaimed the so-called Pragmatic Sanction, which stated that the Habsburg possessions were never to be divided and were always to be passed intact to a single heir, who might be female since Charles had no sons. Charles spent much of his reign trying to get this principle accepted by the various branches of the Habsburg family, by the three different Estates of the realm, and by the states of Europe. His fears turned out to be well founded.

The Hungarian nobility, despite its reduced strength, effectively thwarted the full development of Habsburg absolutism. Time and again throughout the seventeenth century, Hungarian nobles—the

The Siege of Vienna, 1683 The Turks dreamed of establishing a western Muslim Empire in the heart of Europe. But their army of nearly 300,000 men failed to pierce the elaborate fortifications that protected the old city walls from cannon fire and underground mines. *(The Mansell Collection)*

most numerous in Europe, making up 5 to 7 percent of the Hungarian population—rose in revolt against the attempts of Vienna to impose absolute rule. They never triumphed decisively, but neither were they ever crushed and replaced, as the Czech nobility had been in 1620.

Hungarians resisted because many of them were Protestants, especially in the area long ruled by the more tolerant Turks, and they hated the heavy-handed attempts of the conquering Habsburgs to re-Catholicize everyone. Moreover, the lords of Hungary often found a powerful military ally in Turkey. Finally, the Hungarian nobility, and even part of the Hungarian peasantry, had become attached to a national ideal long before most of the peoples of eastern Europe. They were determined to maintain as much independence and local control as possible. Thus when the Habsburgs were bogged down in the War of the Spanish Succession (see page 598), the Hungarians rose in one last patriotic rebellion under Prince

Francis Rakoczy in 1703. Rakoczy and his forces were eventually defeated, but this time the Habsburgs had to accept a definitive compromise. Charles VI restored many of the traditional privileges of the Hungarian aristocracy in return for Hungarian acceptance of hereditary Habsburg rule. Thus Hungary, unlike Austria or Bohemia, never came close to being fully integrated into a centralized, absolute Habsburg state.

PRUSSIA IN THE SEVENTEENTH CENTURY

After 1400 the status of east German peasants declined steadily; their serfdom was formally spelled out in the early seventeenth century. While the local princes lost political power and influence, a revitalized landed nobility became the undisputed ruling class. The Hohenzollern family, which ruled through its senior and junior branches as the electors of Brandenburg and the dukes of Prussia, had little real

MAP 20.1 The Growth of Austria and Brandenburg-Prussia to 1748 Austria expanded to the southwest into Hungary and Transylvania at the expense of the Ottoman Empire. It was unable to hold the rich German province of Silesia, however, which was conquered by Brandenburg-Prussia.

princely power. The Hohenzollern rulers were nothing more than the first among equals, the largest landowners in a landlord society.

Nothing suggested that the Hohenzollerns and their territories would ever play an important role in European or even German affairs. The elector of Brandenburg's right to help choose the Holy Roman emperor with six other electors was of little practical value, and the elector had no military strength whatsoever. The territory of his cousin, the duke of Prussia, was actually part of the kingdom of Poland. Moreover, geography conspired against the Hohenzollerns. Brandenburg, their power base, was completely cut off from the sea (see Map 20.1). A tiny part of the vast north European plain that stretches from France to Russia, Brandenburg lacked natural frontiers and lay open to attack from all directions. The land was poor, a combination of sand and swamp. Contemporaries contemptuously called Brandenburg the "sand-box of the Holy Roman Empire."[2]

Brandenburg was a helpless spectator in the Thirty Years' War, its territory alternately ravaged by Swedish and Habsburg armies. Population fell drastically, and many villages disappeared. The power of the Hohenzollerns reached its lowest point. Yet the devastation of the country prepared the way for Hohenzollern absolutism, because foreign armies dramatically weakened the political power of the Estates—the representative assemblies of the realm. This weakening of the Estates helped the very talented young elector Frederick William (1640–1688), later known as the "Great Elector," to ride roughshod over traditional parliamentary liberties and to take a giant step toward royal absolutism. This constitutional struggle, often unjustly neglected by historians, was the most crucial in Prussian history for hundreds of years, until that of the 1860s.

When he came to power in 1640, the twenty-year-old Great Elector was determined to unify his three quite separate provinces and to add to them by diplomacy and war. These provinces were historic Brandenburg, the area around Berlin; Prussia, inherited in 1618 when the junior branch of the Hohenzollern family died out; and completely separate, scattered holdings along the Rhine in western Germany, inherited in 1614 (see Map 20.1). Each of the three provinces was inhabited by Germans; but each had its own Estates, whose power had increased until about 1600 as the power of the rulers declined. Although the Estates had not met regularly during the chaotic Thirty Years' War, they still had the power of the purse in their respective provinces. Taxes could not be levied without their consent. The Estates of Brandenburg and Prussia were dominated by the nobility and the landowning classes, known as the "Junkers." But it must be remembered that this was also true of the English Parliament before and after the civil war. Had the Estates successfully resisted the absolutist demands of the Great Elector, they, too, might have evolved toward more broadly based constitutionalism.

The struggle between the Great Elector and the provincial Estates was long, complicated, and intense. After the Thirty Years' War, the representatives of the nobility zealously reasserted the right of the Estates to vote taxes, a right the Swedish armies of occupation had simply ignored. Yet first in Brandenburg in 1653 and then in Prussia between 1661 and 1663, the Great Elector eventually had his way.

To pay for the permanent standing army he first established in 1660, Frederick William forced the Estates to accept the introduction of permanent taxation without consent. Moreover, the soldiers doubled as tax collectors and policemen, becoming the core of the rapidly expanding state bureaucracy. The power of the Estates declined quickly thereafter, for the Great Elector had both financial independence and superior force. He turned the screws of taxation: the state's total revenue tripled during his reign. The size of the army leaped about tenfold. In 1688 a population of one million was supporting a peacetime standing army of thirty thousand. Many of the soldiers were French Huguenot immigrants, whom the Great Elector welcomed as the talented, hard-working citizens they were.

In accounting for the Great Elector's fateful triumph, two factors appear central. As in the formation of every absolutist state, war was a decisive factor. The ongoing struggle between Sweden and Poland for control of the Baltic after 1648 and the wars of Louis XIV in western Europe created an atmosphere of permanent crisis. The wild Tartars of southern Russia swept through Prussia in the winter of 1656 to 1657, killing and carrying off as slaves more than fifty thousand people, according to an old estimate. This invasion softened up the Estates and strengthened the urgency of the elector's demands for more money for more soldiers. It was no accident that, except for commercially minded Holland, constitutionalism won out only in England, the only major country to escape devastating foreign invasions in the seventeenth century.

Second, the nobility had long dominated the government through the Estates, but only for its own narrow self-interest. When the crunch came, the Prussian nobles proved unwilling to join the representatives of the towns in a consistent common front against royal pretensions. The nobility was all too concerned with its own rights and privileges, especially its freedom from taxation and its unlimited control over the peasants. When, therefore, the Great Elector reconfirmed these privileges in 1653 and after, even while reducing the political power of the Estates, the nobility growled but did not bite. It accepted a compromise whereby the bulk of the new taxes fell on towns, and royal authority stopped at the landlords' gates. The elector could and did use naked force to break the liberties of the towns. The main leader of the urban opposition in the key city of Königsberg, for example, was simply arrested and imprisoned for life without trial.

THE CONSOLIDATION OF PRUSSIAN ABSOLUTISM

By the time of his death in 1688, the Great Elector had created a single state out of scattered German-speaking principalities. But his new creation was still small and fragile. All the leading states of Europe had many more people—France with 20 million was fully twenty times as populous—and strong monarchy was still a novelty. Moreover, the Great Elector's successor, Elector Frederick III, "the Ostentatious" (1688–1713), was weak of body and mind.

Molding the Prussian Spirit Discipline was strict and punishment brutal in the Prussian army. This scene, from an eighteenth-century book used to teach school children, shows one soldier being flogged while another is being beaten with canes as he walks between rows of troops. The officer on horseback proudly commands. *(University of Illinois, Champaign)*

Like so many of the small princes of Germany and Italy at the time, Frederick III imitated Louis XIV in every possible way. He built his own very expensive version of Versailles. He surrounded himself with cultivated artists and musicians and basked in the praise of toadies and sycophants. His only real political accomplishment was to gain the title of king from the Holy Roman emperor, a Habsburg, in return for military aid in the War of the Spanish Succession, and in 1701 he was crowned King Frederick I.

This tendency toward luxury-loving, happy, and harmless petty tyranny was completely reversed by Frederick William I, "the Soldiers' King" (1713–1740). A crude, dangerous psychoneurotic, Frederick William I was nevertheless the most talented reformer ever produced by the Hohenzollern family. It was he who truly established Prussian absolutism and

gave it its unique character. It was he who created the the best army in Europe, for its size, and who infused military values into a whole society. In the words of a leading historian of Prussia:

For a whole generation, the Hohenzollern subjects were victimized by a royal bully, imbued with an obsessive bent for military organization and military scales of value. This left a deep mark upon the institutions of Prussiandom and upon the molding of the "Prussian spirit."[3]

Frederick William's passion for the army and military life was intensely emotional. He had, for example, a bizarre, almost pathological love for tall soldiers, whom he credited with superior strength and endurance. Austere and always faithful to his wife, he confided to the French ambassador: "The most beautiful girl or woman in the world would be a matter of indifference to me, but tall soldiers—they are my weakness." Like some fanatical modern-day basketball coach in search of a championship team, he sent his agents throughout Prussia and all of Europe, tricking, buying, and kidnapping top recruits. Neighboring princes sent him their giants as gifts to win his gratitude. Prussian mothers told their sons: "Stop growing or the recruiting agents will get you."[4]

Frederick William's love of the army was also based on a hardheaded conception of the struggle for power and a dog-eat-dog view of international politics. Even before ascending the throne, he bitterly criticized his father's ministers: "They say that they will obtain land and power for the king with the pen; but I say it can be done only with the sword." Years later he summed up his life's philosophy in his instructions to his son: "A formidable army and a war chest large enough to make this army mobile in times of need can create great respect for you in the world, so that you can speak a word like the other powers."[5] This unshakable belief that the welfare of king and state depended on the army above all else reinforced Frederick William's passion for playing soldier.

The cult of military power provided the rationale for a great expansion of royal absolutism. As the king himself put it with his characteristic ruthlessness: "I must be served with life and limb, with house and wealth, with honour and conscience, everything must be committed except eternal salvation—that belongs to God, but all else is mine."[6] To make good these extraordinary demands, Frederick William created a strong centralized bureaucracy. More commoners probably rose to top positions in the civil government than at any other time in Prussia's history. The last traces of the parliamentary Estates and local self-government vanished.

The king's grab for power brought him into considerable conflict with the noble landowners, the Junkers. In his early years, he even threatened to destroy them; yet in the end, the Prussian nobility was not destroyed but enlisted—into the army. Responding to a combination of threats and opportunities, the Junkers became the officer caste. By 1739 all but 5 of 245 officers with the rank of major or above were aristocrats, and most of them were native Prussians. A new compromise had been worked out, whereby the proud nobility imperiously commanded the peasantry in the army as well as on its estates.

Coarse and crude, penny-pinching and hard-working, Frederick William achieved results. Above all, he built a first-rate army on the basis of third-rate resources. The standing army increased from 38,000 to 83,000 during his reign. Prussia, twelfth in Europe in population, had the fourth largest army by 1740. Only the much more populous states of France, Russia, and Austria had larger forces, and even France's army was only twice as large as Prussia's. Moreover, soldier for soldier, the Prussian army became the best in Europe, astonishing foreign observers with its precision, skill, and discipline. For the next two hundred years, Prussia and then Prussianized Germany would almost always win the crucial military battles.

Frederick William and his ministers also built an exceptionally honest and conscientious bureaucracy, which not only administered the country but tried with some success to develop it economically. Finally, like the miser he was, living very frugally off the income of his own landholdings, the king loved his "blue boys" so much that he hated to "spend" them. This most militaristic of kings was, paradoxically, almost always at peace.

Nevertheless, the Prussian people paid a heavy and lasting price for the obsessions of the royal drillmaster. Civil society became rigid and highly disciplined. Prussia became the "Sparta of the North"; unquestioning obedience was the highest virtue. As a Prussian minister later summed up, "To keep quiet is the first civic duty."[7] Thus the policies of Frederick William I combined with harsh peasant bondage and Junker tyranny to lay the foundations for probably the most militaristic country of modern times.

THE DEVELOPMENT OF RUSSIA

One of the favorite parlor games of nineteenth-century Russian (and non-Russian) intellectuals was debating whether Russia was a western European or an Asian society. This question was particularly fascinating because it was unanswerable. To this day Russia differs fundamentally from the West in some basic ways, though Russian history has paralleled that of the West in other ways. A good case can be made for either position: thus the hypnotic attraction of Russian history.

The differences between Russia and the West were particularly striking before 1700, when Russia's overall development began to draw progressively closer to that of its western neighbors. These early differences and Russia's long isolation from Europe explain why little has so far been said here about Russia. Yet it is impossible to understand how Russia has increasingly influenced and been influenced by western European civilization since roughly the late seventeenth century without looking at the course of early Russian history. Such a brief survey will also help explain how, when absolute monarchy finally and decisively triumphed under the rough guidance of Peter the Great in the early eighteenth century, it was a quite different type of absolute monarchy from that of France or even Prussia.

THE VIKINGS AND THE KIEVAN PRINCIPALITY

In antiquity the Slavs lived as a single people in central Europe. With the start of the mass migrations of the late Roman Empire, the Slavs moved in different directions and split into three groups. Between the fifth and ninth centuries, the eastern Slavs, from whom the Ukrainians, the Russians, and the White Russians descend, moved into the vast and practically uninhabited area of present-day European Russia and the Ukraine (Map 20.2).

This enormous area consisted of an immense virgin forest to the north, where most of the eastern Slavs settled, and an endless prairie grassland to the south. Probably organized as tribal communities, the eastern Slavs, like many North American pioneers much later, lived off the great abundance of wild game and a crude "slash and burn" agriculture. After clearing a piece of the forest to build log cabins, they burned the stumps and brush. The ashes left a rich deposit of potash and lime, and the land gave several good crops before it was exhausted. The people then moved on to another untouched area and repeated the process.

In the ninth century, the Vikings, those fearless warriors from Scandinavia, appeared in the lands of the eastern Slavs. Called "Varangians" in the old Russian chronicles, the Vikings were interested primarily in international trade, and the opportunities were good, since the Muslim conquests of the eighth century had greatly reduced Christian trade in the Mediterranean. Moving up and down the rivers, the Vikings soon linked Scandinavia and northern Europe with the Black Sea and the Byzantine Empire

MAP 20.2 The Expansion of Russia to 1725 After the disintegration of the Kievan state and the Mongol conquest, the princes of Moscow and their heirs gradually extended their rule over an enormous territory.

with its capital at Constantinople. They built a few strategic forts along the rivers, from which they raided the neighboring Slavic tribes and collected tribute. Slaves were the most important article of tribute, and *Slav* even became the word for "slave" in several European languages.

In order to increase and protect their international commerce, the Vikings declared themselves the rulers of the eastern Slavs. According to tradition, the semilegendary chieftain Ruirik founded the princely dynasty about 860. In any event, the Varangian ruler Oleg (878–912) established his residence at Kiev. He and his successors ruled over a loosely united confederation of Slavic territories—the Kievan state—until 1054. The Viking prince and his clansmen quickly became assimilated into the Slavic population, taking local wives and emerging as the noble class.

Assimilation and loss of Scandinavian ethnic identity were speeded up by the conversion of the Vikings and local Slavs to Eastern Orthodox Christianity by missionaries from the Byzantine Empire. The written language of these missionaries, Slavic—church Slavonic—was subsequently used in all religious and nonreligious documents in the Kievan principality. Thus the rapidly Slavified Vikings left two important legacies for the future. They created a loose unification of Slavic territories under a single ruling prince and a single ruling dynasty. And they imposed a basic religious unity by accepting Orthodox Christianity, as opposed to Roman Catholicism, for themselves and the eastern Slavs.

Even at its height under Great Prince Iaroslav the Wise (1019–1054), the unity of the Kievan principality was extremely tenuous. Trade, rather than government, was the main concern of the rulers. Moreover, the Slavified Vikings failed to find a way of peacefully transferring power from one generation to the next. In medieval western Europe this fundamental problem of government was increasingly resolved by resort to the principle of primogeniture: the king's eldest son received the crown as his rightful inheritance when his father died. Civil war was thus averted; order was preserved. In early Kiev, however,

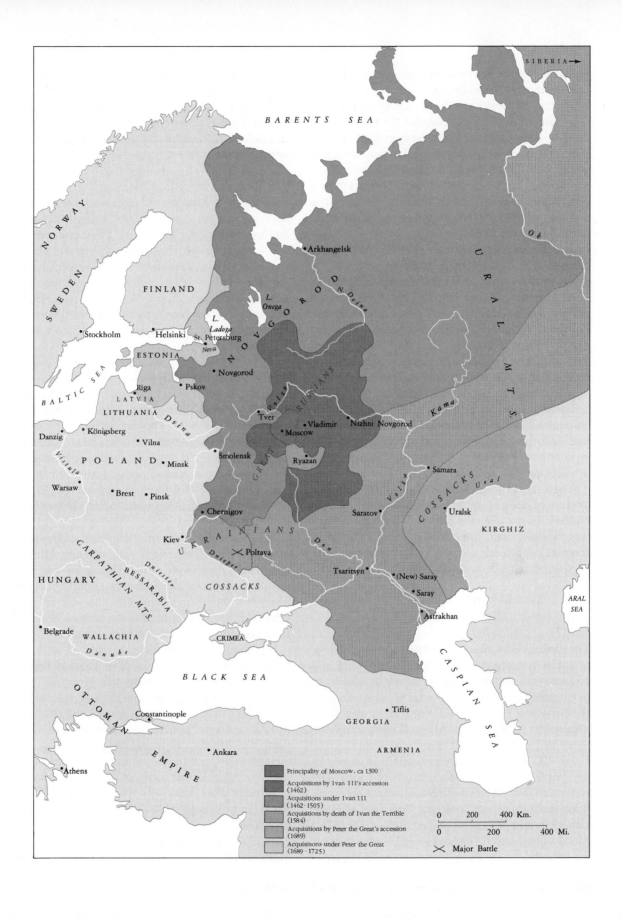

SIBERIA →

BARENTS SEA

NORWAY

SWEDEN

FINLAND

L. Onega

L. Ladoga

• Arkhangelsk

N. Dvina

Ob

U R A L

M T S.

Stockholm •

Helsinki •

St. Petersburg

Neva

ESTONIA

• Novgorod

N O V G O R O D

Kama

Riga •

• Pskov

BALTIC SEA

Volga

LATVIA

LITHUANIA

Dvina

• Tver

G R E A T   R U S S I A N S

• Vladimir

Nizhni Novgorod

Königsberg •

Danzig •

• Vilna

• Moscow

• Samara

Ural

POLAND

• Minsk

Smolensk •

Ryazan •

Volga

• Uralsk

C O S S A C K S

Warsaw •

• Brest

• Pinsk

Saratov •

KIRGHIZ

Chernigov •

U K R A I N I A N S

Dnieper

Don

Kiev •

× Poltava

CARPATHIAN MTS.

Dniester

BESSARABIA

Tsaritsyn •

(New) Saray

• Saray

HUNGARY

COSSACKS

• Astrakhan

ARAL SEA

• Belgrade

WALLACHIA

CRIMEA

Danube

B L A C K   S E A

C A S P I A N   S E A

O T T O M A N

• Constantinople

• Tiflis

GEORGIA

E M P I R E

• Ankara

ARMENIA

• Athens

Principality of Moscow, ca 1300

Acquisitions by Ivan III's accession (1462)

Acquisitions under Ivan III (1462-1505)

Acquisitions by death of Ivan the Terrible (1584)

Acquisitions by Peter the Great's accession (1689)

Acquisitions under Peter the Great (1689-1725)

| 0 | 200 | 400 Km. |

| 0 | 200 | 400 Mi. |

× Major Battle

there were apparently no fixed rules, and much strife accompanied each succession.

Possibly to avoid such chaos, before his death in 1054 Great Prince Iaroslav divided the Kievan principality among his five sons, who in turn divided their properties when they died. Between 1054 and 1237, Kiev disintegrated into more and more competing units, each ruled by a prince claiming to be a descendant of Ruirik. Even when only one prince was claiming to be the great prince, the whole situation was very unsettled.

The princes divided their land like private property because they thought of it as private property. A given prince owned a certain number of farms or landed estates and had them worked directly by his people, mainly slaves, called *kholops* in Russian. Outside of these estates, which constituted the princely domain, the prince exercised only very limited authority in his principality. Excluding the clergy, two kinds of people lived there: the noble *boyars* and the commoner peasants.

The boyars were the descendants of the original Viking warriors, and they also held their lands as free and clear private property. And although the boyars normally fought in princely armies, the customary law declared they could serve any prince they wished. The ordinary peasants were also truly free. The peasants could move at will wherever opportunities were greatest. In the touching phrase of the times, theirs was "a clean road, without boundaries."[8] In short, fragmented princely power, private property, and personal freedom all went together.

THE MONGOL YOKE AND THE RISE OF MOSCOW

The eastern Slavs, like the Germans and the Italians, might have emerged from the Middle Ages weak and politically divided had it not been for a development of extraordinary importance—the Mongol conquest of the Kievan state. Wild nomadic tribes from present-day Mongolia, the Mongols were temporarily unified in the thirteenth century by Jenghiz Khan (1162–1227), one of history's greatest conquerors. In five years his armies subdued much of China. His successors then wheeled westward, smashing everything in their path and reaching the plains of Hungary victorious before they pulled back in 1242. The Mongol army—the "Golden Horde"—was savage in the extreme, often slaughtering the entire popula-

tions of cities before burning them to the ground. En route to Mongolia, Archbishop John of Plano Carpini, the famous papal ambassador to Mongolia, passed through Kiev, which the Mongols had sacked in 1242, in 1245 and wrote an unforgettable eyewitness account:

The Mongols went against Russia and enacted a great massacre in the Russian land. They destroyed towns and fortresses and killed people. They besieged Kiev which had been the capital of Russia, and after a long siege they took it and killed the inhabitants of the city. For this reason, when we passed through that land, we found lying in the field countless heads and bones of dead people; for this city had been extremely large and very populous, whereas now it has been reduced to nothing: barely two hundred houses stand there, and those people are held in the harshest slavery.[9]

Having devastated and conquered, the Mongols ruled the eastern Slavs for more than two hundred years. They built their capital of Saray on the lower Volga (see Map 20.2). They forced all the bickering Slavic princes to submit to their rule and to give them tribute and slaves. If the conquered peoples rebelled, the Mongols were quick to punish with death and destruction. Thus, the Mongols unified the eastern Slavs, for the Mongol khan was acknowledged by all as the supreme ruler.

The Mongol unification completely changed the internal political situation. Although the Mongols conquered, they were quite willing to use local princes as their obedient servants and tax collectors. Therefore they did not abolish the title of great prince, bestowing it instead on the prince who served them best and paid them most handsomely.

Beginning with Alexander Nevsky in 1252, the previously insignificant princes of Moscow became particularly adept at serving the Mongols. They loyally put down popular uprisings and collected the khan's harsh taxes. By way of reward, the princes of Moscow emerged as hereditary great princes. Eventually the Muscovite princes were able to destroy their princely rivals and even to replace the khan as supreme ruler. In this complex process, two princes of Moscow after Alexander Nevsky—Ivan I (1328–1341) and Ivan III (1462–1505)—were especially noteworthy.

In 1327 the population of Tver revolted against Mongol oppression, and the prince of Tver, whom the Mongols at one point appointed as great prince, joined his people. Ivan I immediately went to Saray, where he was appointed commander of a large Russian-Mongol army, which then laid waste to Tver and its lands. For this proof of devotion, the Mongols made Ivan the general tax collector for all the Slavic lands they had subjugated and named him great prince. Ivan also convinced the metropolitan of Kiev, the leading churchman of all eastern Slavs, to settle in Moscow; Ivan I, popularly known as "Ivan the Moneybag," thus gained greater prestige, while the church gained a powerful advocate before the khan.

In the next hundred-odd years, in the course of innumerable wars and intrigues, the great princes of Moscow significantly increased their holdings. Then, in the reign of Ivan III (1462–1505), the long process was largely completed. After purchasing Rostov, Ivan conquered and annexed other principalities, of which Novgorod with its lands extending almost to the Baltic Sea was most crucial (see Map 20.2). Thus, more than four hundred years after Iaroslav the Wise had divided the embryonic Kievan state, the princes of Moscow defeated all the rival branches of the house of Ruirik to win complete princely authority.

Another dimension to princely power developed. Not only was the prince of Moscow the *unique* ruler, he was the *absolute* ruler, the autocrat, the *tsar*—the Slavic contraction for "caesar," with all its connotations. This imperious conception of absolute power is expressed in a famous letter from the aging Ivan III to the Holy Roman emperor Frederick III (1440–1493). Frederick had offered Ivan the title of king in conjunction with the marriage of his daughter to Ivan's nephew. Ivan proudly refused:

We by the grace of God have been sovereigns over our domains from the beginning, from our first forebears, and our right we hold from God, as did our forebears. . . . As in the past we have never needed appointment from anyone, so now do we not desire it.[10]

The Muscovite idea of absolute authority was powerfully reinforced by two developments. First, about 1480 Ivan III stopped acknowledging the khan as his supreme ruler. There is good evidence to suggest that Ivan and his successors saw themselves as khans. Certainly they assimilated the Mongol concept of kingship as the exercise of unrestrained and unpredictable power.

Second, after the fall of Constantinople to the Turks in 1453, the tsars saw themselves as the heirs of both the caesars and Orthodox Christianity, the one true faith. All the other kings of Europe were heretics: only the tsars were rightful and holy rulers. This idea was promoted by Orthodox churchmen, who spoke of "holy Russia" as the "Third Rome." As the monk Pilotheus stated: "Two Romes have fallen, but the third stands, and a fourth there will not be."[11] Ivan's marriage to the daughter of the last Byzantine emperor further enhanced the aura of an eastern imperial inheritance for Moscow. Worthy successor to the mighty khan and the true Christian emperor, the Muscovite tsar was a king above all others.

TSAR AND PEOPLE TO 1689

By 1505 the great prince of Moscow—the tsar—had emerged as the single hereditary ruler of "all the Russias"—all the lands of the eastern Slavs—and he was claiming unrestricted power as his God-given right. In effect, the tsar was demanding the same kind of total authority over all his subjects that the princely descendants of Ruirik had long exercised over their slaves on their own landed estates. This was an extremely radical demand.

While peasants had begun losing their freedom of movement in the fifteenth century, so had the noble boyars begun to lose power and influence. Ivan III pioneered in this regard, as in so many others. When Ivan conquered the principality of Novgorod in the 1480s, he confiscated fully 80 percent of the land, executing the previous owners or resettling them nearer Moscow. He then kept more than half of the confiscated land for himself and distributed the remainder to members of a newly emerging service nobility. The boyars had previously held their land as hereditary private property and been free to serve the prince of their choosing. The new service nobility held the tsar's land on the explicit condition that its members serve in the tsar's army. Moreover, Ivan III began to require boyars outside of Novgorod to serve him if they wished to retain their lands. Since there were no competing princes left to turn to, the boyars had to yield.

The rise of the new service nobility accelerated under Ivan IV (1533–1584), the famous Ivan the Terrible. Having ascended the throne at age three, Ivan had suffered insults and neglect at the hands of the haughty boyars after his mother mysteriously died,

St. Basil's Cathedral in Moscow, with its steeply sloping roofs and proliferation of multicolored onion-shaped domes, was a striking example of powerful Byzantine influences on Russian culture. According to tradition, an enchanted Ivan the Terrible blinded the cathedral's architects to ensure that they would never duplicate their fantastic achievement. *(The New York Public Library)*

possibly poisoned, when he was just eight. At age sixteen he suddenly pushed aside his hated boyar advisers. In an awe-inspiring ceremony, complete with gold coins pouring down on his head, he majestically crowned himself and officially took the august title of tsar for the first time.

Selecting the beautiful and kind Anastasia of the popular Romanov family for his wife and queen, the young tsar soon declared war on the remnants of Mongol power. He defeated the faltering khanates of Kazan and Astrakhan between 1552 and 1556, add-

ing vast new territories to Russia. In the course of these wars Ivan virtually abolished the old distinction between hereditary boyar private property and land granted temporarily for service. All nobles, old and new, had to serve the tsar in order to hold any land.

The process of transforming the entire nobility into a service nobility was completed in the second part of Ivan the Terrible's reign. In 1557 Ivan turned westward, and for the next twenty-five years Muscovy waged an exhausting, unsuccessful war primarily with the large Polish-Lithuanian state, which controlled not only Poland but much of the Ukraine in the sixteenth century. Quarreling with the boyars over the war and blaming them for the sudden death of his beloved Anastasia in 1560, the increasingly cruel and demented Ivan turned to strike down all who stood in his way.

Above all, he struck down the ancient Muscovite boyars with a reign of terror. Leading boyars, their relatives, and even their peasants and servants were executed en masse by a special corps of unquestioning servants. Dressed in black and riding black horses, they were forerunners of the modern dictator's secret police. Large estates were confiscated, broken up, and reapportioned to the lower service nobility. The great boyar families were severely reduced. The newer, poorer, more nearly equal service nobility, still less than .5 percent of the total population, was totally dependent on the autocrat.

Ivan also took giant strides toward making all commoners servants of the tsar. His endless wars and demonic purges left much of central Russia depopulated. It grew increasingly difficult for members of the lower service nobility to squeeze a living for themselves out of the peasants left on their landholdings. As the service nobles demanded more from the remaining peasants, more and more peasants fled toward the wild, recently conquered territories to the east and south. There they formed free groups and outlaw armies known as "Cossacks." The Cossacks maintained a precarious independence beyond the reach of the oppressive landholders and the tsar's hated officials. The solution to this problem was to tie the peasants to the land, effectively making them serfs bound to serve the noble landholders, who were bound in turn to serve the tsar.

In the time of Ivan the Terrible, urban traders and artisans were also bound to their towns and jobs, so that the tsar could tax them more heavily. Ivan assumed that the tsar owned Russia's trade and industry, just as he owned all the land. In the course of the sixteenth and seventeenth centuries, the tsars therefore took over the mines and industries and monopolized the country's important commercial activities. The urban classes had no security in their work or property, and even the wealthiest merchants were basically dependent agents of the tsar. If a new commercial activity became profitable, it was often taken over by the tsar and made a royal monopoly. This royal monopolization was in sharp contrast to developments in western Europe, where the capitalist middle classes were gaining strength and security in their private property. The tsar's service obligations checked the growth of the Russian middle classes, just as they led to decline of the boyars, rise of the lower nobility, and the final enserfment of the peasants.

As has so often occurred in Russia, the death of an iron-fisted tyrant—in this case, Ivan the Terrible in 1584—ushered in an era of confusion and violent struggles for power. Events were particularly chaotic after Ivan's son Theodore died in 1598 without an heir. The years 1598 to 1613 are aptly called the "Time of Troubles."

The close relatives of the deceased tsar intrigued against and murdered one another, alternately fighting and welcoming the invading Swedes and Poles, who even occupied Moscow. Most serious for the cause of autocracy, there was a great social upheaval as Cossack bands marched northward, rallying peasants and slaughtering nobles and officials. The mass of Cossacks and peasants called for the "true tsar," who would restore their freedom of movement and allow them to farm for whomever they pleased, who would reduce their heavy taxes and lighten the yoke imposed by the landlords.

This social explosion from below, which combined with a belated surge of patriotic opposition to Polish invaders, brought the nobles, big and small, to their senses. In 1613 they elected Ivan's sixteen-year-old grandnephew, Michael Romanov, the new hereditary tsar. Then they rallied around him in the face of common internal and external threats. Michael's election was a real restoration, and his reign saw the gradual re-establishment of tsarist autocracy. Michael was understandably more kindly disposed toward the supportive nobility than toward the sullen peasants. Thus, while peasants were completely enserfed by 1649, Ivan's heavy military obligations on the nobility were relaxed considerably. In the long reign of Michael's successor, the pious Alexis (1645–

1676), this asymmetry of obligations was accentuated. The nobility gained more exemptions from military service, while the peasants were further ground down.

The result was a second round of mass upheaval and protest. In the later seventeenth century, the unity of the Russian Orthodox church was torn apart by a great split. The surface question was the religious reforms introduced in 1652 by the patriarch Nikon, a dogmatic purist who wished to bring "corrupted" Russian practices of worship into line with the Greek Orthodox model. The self-serving church hierarchy quickly went along with the reforms, but the intensely religious common people resisted. They saw Nikon as the anti-Christ, who was stripping them of the only thing they had—the true religion of "holy Russia."

Great numbers left the church and formed illegal communities of Old Believers, who were hunted down and persecuted; as many as twenty thousand people burned themselves alive. After the great split, the Russian masses were alienated from the established church, which became totally dependent on the state for its authority.

Again the Cossacks revolted against the state, which was doggedly trying to catch up with them on the frontiers and reduce them to serfdom. Under Stenka Razin they moved up the Volga River in 1670 and 1671, attracting a great undisciplined army of peasants, murdering landlords and high church officials and proclaiming freedom from oppression. This rebellion to overthrow the established order was finally defeated by the government. In response, the thoroughly scared upper classes tightened the screws of serfdom even further. Holding down the peasants, and thereby maintaining the tsar, became almost the principal obligation of the nobility until 1689.

THE REFORMS OF PETER THE GREAT

It is now possible to understand the reforms of Peter the Great (1689–1725) and his kind of monarchial absolutism. Contrary to some historians' assertions, Peter was interested primarily in military power and not in some grandiose westernization plan. A giant for his time, at six feet seven inches, and possessing enormous energy and willpower, Peter was determined to redress the defeats the tsar's armies had occasionally suffered in their wars with Poland and Sweden since the time of Ivan the Terrible.

1050–1300	Increasing economic development in eastern Europe encourages decline in serfdom
1054	Death of Great Prince Iaroslav the Wise, under whom the Kievan principality reached its height of unity
1054–1237	Kiev is divided into numerous territories ruled by competing princes
1237–1242	Mongol invasion of Russia
1252	Alexander Nevsky, Prince of Moscow, recognizes Mongol overlordship
1327–1328	Suppression of the Tver revolt; Mongol khan recognizes Ivan I as great prince
1400–1650	The nobility reimposes serfdom in eastern Europe
ca 1480	Ivan III rejects Mongol overlordship and begins to use the title of tsar
1520–1566	Rule of Suleiman the Magnificent: Ottoman Empire reaches its height
1533–1584	Rule of Tsar Ivan IV (the Terrible): defeat of the khanates of Kazan and Astrakhan; subjugation of the boyar aristocracy
1574	Polish nobles receive the right to inflict the death penalty on their serfs
1598–1613	Time of Troubles in Russia
1613	Election of Michael Romanov as tsar: re-establishment of autocracy
1620	Battle of the White Mountain in Bohemia: Ferdinand II initiates Habsburg confiscation of Czech estates
1640–1688	Rule of Frederick William, the Great Elector, who unites Brandenburg, Prussia, and western German holdings into one state, Brandenburg-Prussia
1649	Tsar Alexis lifts the nine-year limit on the recovery of runaway serfs
1652	Patriarch Nikon's reforms split the Russian Orthodox church
1653	Principle of peasants' hereditary subjugation to their lords affirmed in Prussia
1670–1671	Cossack revolt of Stenka Razin in Russia
1683	Siege of Vienna by the Ottoman Turks
1683–1699	Habsburg conquest of Hungary and Transylvania
1689–1725	Rule of Tsar Peter the Great
1700–1721	Great Northern War between Russia and Sweden, resulting in Russian victory and territorial expansion
1701	Elector Frederick III crowned king of Prussia
1703	Founding of St. Petersburg
	Rebellion of Prince Francis Rakoczy in Hungary
1713	Pragmatic Sanction: Charles VII guarantees Maria Theresa's succession to the Austrian empire
1713–1740	Rule of King Frederick William I in Prussia

To be sure, these western foes had never seriously threatened the existence of the tsar's vast kingdom, except perhaps when they had added to the confusion of civil war and domestic social upheaval in the Time of Troubles. Russia had even gained a large mass of the Ukraine from the kingdom of Poland in 1667 (see Map 20.2). And tsarist forces had completed the conquest of the primitive tribes of all Siberia in the seventeenth century. Muscovy, which had been as large as all the rest of Europe combined in 1600, was three times as large as the rest of Europe in 1689 and by far

the largest kingdom on earth. But territorial expansion was the soul of tsardom, and it was natural that Peter would seek further gains. The thirty-six years of his reign knew only one year of peace.

When Peter came to the throne, the heart of his army still consisted of cavalry made up of boyars and service nobility. Foot soldiers played a secondary role, and the whole army served on a part-time basis. The Russian army lagged behind the professional standing armies being formed in Europe in the seventeenth century. The core of such armies was a highly disciplined infantry—an infantry that fired and re-fired rifles as it fearlessly advanced, until it charged with bayonets fixed. Such a large permanent army was enormously expensive and could be created only at great sacrifice. Given the desire to conquer more territory, Peter's military problem was serious.

Peter's solution was, in essence, to tighten up Muscovy's old service system and really make it work. He put the nobility back in harness with a vengeance. Every nobleman, great or small, was once again required to serve in the army or in the civil administration—for life. Since a more modern army and government required skilled technicians and experts, Peter created schools and even universities. One of his most hated reforms required five years of compulsory education away from home for every young nobleman. Peter established an interlocking military-civilian bureaucracy with fourteen ranks, and he decreed that all must start at the bottom and work toward the top. More people of nonnoble origins rose to high positions in the embryonic meritocracy. Peter searched out talented foreigners—twice in his reign he went abroad to study and observe—and placed them in his service. These measures combined to make the army and government more powerful and efficient.

Peter also greatly increased the service requirements of the commoners. He established a regular standing army of more than 200,000 soldiers, made up mainly of peasants commanded by officers from the nobility. In addition, special forces of Cossacks and foreigners numbered more than 100,000. The departure of a drafted peasant boy was celebrated by his family and village almost like a funeral, as indeed it was, since the recruit was drafted for life. The peasantry also served with its taxes, which increased threefold during Peter's reign, as people—"souls"—replaced land as the primary unit of taxation. Serfs were also arbitrarily assigned to work in the growing number of factories and mines. Most of these industrial enterprises were directly or indirectly owned by the state, and they were worked almost exclusively for the military. In general, Russian serfdom became more oppressive under the reforming tsar.

The constant warfare of Peter's reign consumed 80 to 85 percent of all revenues but brought only modest territorial expansion. Yet the Great Northern War with Sweden, which lasted from 1700 to 1721, was crowned in the end by Russian victory. After initial losses, Peter's new war machine crushed the smaller

"The Bronze Horseman" This equestrian masterpiece of Peter the Great, finished for Catherine the Great in 1783, dominates the center of St. Petersburg (modern Leningrad). The French sculptor Falconnet has captured the tsar's enormous energy, power, and determination. *(Conway Library, Courtauld Institute of Art)*

army of Sweden's Charles XII in the Ukraine at Poltava in 1709, one of the most significant battles in Russian history. Sweden never really regained the offensive, and Russia eventually annexed Estonia and much of present-day Latvia (see Map 20.2), lands that had never before been under Russian rule. Russia became the dominant power on the Baltic Sea and very much a European great power. If victory or defeat is the ultimate historical criterion, Peter's reforms were a success.

There were other important consequences of Peter's reign. Because of his feverish desire to use modern technology to strengthen the army, many westerners and western ideas flowed into Russia for the first time. A new class of educated Russians began to emerge. At the same time, vast numbers of Russians, especially among the poor and weak, hated Peter's massive changes. The split between the enserfed peasantry and the educated nobility thus widened, even though all were caught up in the endless demands of the sovereign.

A new idea of state interest, distinct from the tsar's personal interests, began to take hold. Peter himself fostered this conception of the public interest by claiming time and again to be serving the common good. For the first time a Russian tsar attached explanations to his decrees in an attempt to gain the confidence and enthusiastic support of the populace. Yet, as before, the tsar alone decided what the common good was. Here was a source of future tension between tsar and people.

In sum, Peter built on the service obligations of old Muscovy. His monarchial absolutism was truly the culmination of the long development of a unique Russian civilization. Yet the creation of a more modern army and state introduced much that was new and western to that civilization. This development paved the way for Russia to move much closer to the European mainstream in its thought and institutions during the Enlightenment, especially under that administrative and sexual lioness, Catherine the Great.

ABSOLUTISM AND THE BAROQUE

The rise of royal absolutism in eastern Europe had many consequences. Nobles served their powerful rulers in new ways, while the great inferiority of the urban middle classes and the peasants was reconfirmed. Armies became larger and more professional, while taxes rose and authoritarian traditions were strengthened. Nor was this all. Royal absolutism also interacted with baroque culture and art, baroque music and literature. Inspired in part by Louis XIV of France, the great and not-so-great rulers called on the artistic talent of the age to glorify their power and magnificence. This exaltation of despotic rule was particularly expressed through architecture.

BAROQUE ART AND MUSIC

Throughout European history, the cultural tastes of one age have often seemed quite unsatisfactory to the next. So it was with the baroque. The term *baroque* itself may have come from the Portuguese word for an "odd-shaped, imperfect pearl" and was commonly used by late-eighteenth-century art critics as an expression of scorn for what they considered an overblown, unbalanced style. The hostility of these critics, who also scorned the Gothic style of medieval cathedrals in favor of a classicism inspired by antiquity and the Renaissance, has long since passed.

Specialists agree that the triumphs of the baroque marked one of the high points in the history of Western culture.

The early development of the baroque is complex, but most scholars stress the influence of Rome and the revitalized Catholic church of the later sixteenth century. The papacy and the Jesuits encouraged the growth of an intensely emotional, exuberant art. These patrons wanted artists to go beyond the Renaissance focus on pleasing a small, wealthy cultural elite. They wanted artists to appeal to the senses and thereby touch the souls and kindle the faith of ordinary churchgoers, while proclaiming the power and confidence of the reformed Catholic church. In addition to this underlying religious emotionalism, the baroque drew its sense of drama, motion, and ceaseless striving from the Catholic Reformation. The interior of the famous Jesuit Church of Jesus in Rome —the Gesù—combined all these characteristics in its lavish, shimmering decorations and frescoes.

Taking definite shape in Italy after 1600, the baroque style in the visual arts developed with exceptional vigor in Catholic countries—in Spain and Latin America, Austria, southern Germany, and Poland. Yet baroque art was more than just "Catholic art" in the seventeenth century and the first half of the eighteenth. True, neither Protestant England nor the Netherlands ever came fully under the spell of the baroque, but neither did Catholic France. And Protestants accounted for some of the finest examples of baroque style, especially in music. The baroque style spread partly because its tension and bombast spoke to an agitated age, which was experiencing great violence and controversy in politics and religion.

In painting, the baroque reached maturity early with Peter Paul Rubens (1577–1640), the most outstanding and representative of baroque painters (see color insert IV). Studying in his native Flanders and in Italy, where he was influenced by masters of the High Renaissance, such as Michelangelo, Rubens developed his own rich, sensuous, colorful style, which was characterized by animated figures, melodramatic contrasts, and monumental size. Although Rubens excelled in glorifying monarchs such as Queen Mother Marie de' Medici of France, he was also a devout Catholic. Nearly half of his pictures treat Christian subjects. Yet one of Rubens's trademarks was fleshy, sensual nudes, who populate his canvases as Roman goddesses, water nymphs, and remarkably voluptuous saints and angels.

Rubens: The Education of Marie One of twenty-one pictures celebrating episodes from the life of Marie de' Medici, the influential widow of France's Henri IV, Rubens's painting is imbued with sensuous vitality. The three muses inspiring the studious young Marie dominate the canvas. *(Louvre/Giraudon/Art Resource)*

Rubens was enormously successful. To meet the demand for his work, he established a large studio and hired many assistants to execute his rough sketches and gigantic murals. Sometimes the master artist added only the finishing touches. Rubens's wealth and position—on occasion he was given special diplomatic assignments by the Habsburgs—attest that distinguished artists continued to enjoy the high social status they had won in the Renaissance.

In music, the baroque style reached its culmination almost a century later in the dynamic, soaring lines of the endlessly inventive Johann Sebastian Bach (1685–1750), one of the greatest composers the Western world has ever produced. Organist and choir master of several Lutheran churches across Germany, Bach was equally at home writing secular concertos and sublime religious cantatas. Bach's organ music, the greatest ever written, combined the baroque spirit of invention, tension, and emotion in an unforgettable striving toward the infinite. Bach was not fully appreciated in his lifetime, but since the early 1800s his reputation has grown steadily.

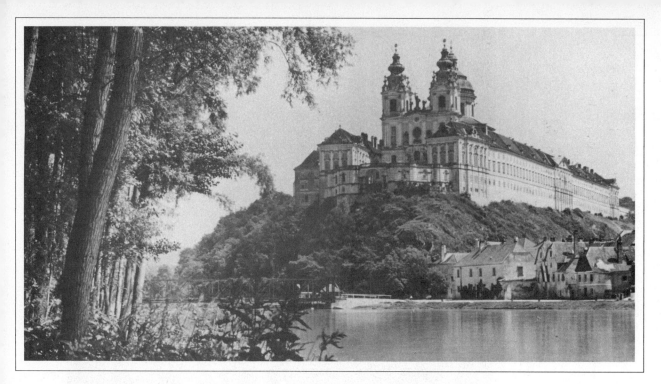

The Benedictine Abbey of Melk Rebuilt in the eighteenth century, this masterpiece of the Austrian baroque stands majestically on the heights above the Danube River. *(Archiv/Photo Researchers)*

PALACES AND POWER

As soaring Gothic cathedrals expressed the idealized spirit of the High Middle Ages, so dramatic baroque palaces symbolized the age of absolutist power. By 1700 palace building had become a veritable obsession for the rulers of central and eastern Europe. These baroque palaces were clearly intended to overawe the people with the monarch's strength. The great palaces were also visual declarations of equality with Louis XIV and were therefore modeled after Versailles to a greater or lesser extent. One such palace was Schönbrunn, an enormous Viennese Versailles, begun in 1695 by Emperor Leopold to celebrate Austrian military victories and Habsburg might. Charles XI of Sweden, having reduced the power of the aristocracy, ordered the construction in 1693 of his Royal Palace, which dominates the center of Stockholm to this day. Frederick I of Prussia began his imposing new royal residence in Berlin in 1701, the same year he attained the title of king.

Petty princes also contributed mightily to the palace-building mania. Frederick the Great of Prussia noted that every descendant of a princely family "imagines himself to be something like Louis XIV. He builds his Versailles, has his mistresses, and maintains his army."[12] The not-very-important elector-archbishop of Mainz, the ruling prince of that city, confessed apologetically that "building is a craze which costs much, but every fool likes his own hat."[13] The archbishop of Mainz's own "hat" was an architectural gem, like that of another churchly ruler, the prince-bishop of Würzburg.

In central and eastern Europe, the favorite noble servants of royalty became extremely rich and powerful, and they, too, built grandiose palaces in the capital cities. These palaces were in part an extension of the monarch, for they surpassed the buildings of less-favored nobles and showed all the high road to fame and fortune. Take, for example, the palaces of Prince Eugene of Savoy. A French nobleman by birth and education, Prince Eugene entered the service of Leopold I with the relief of the besieged Vienna in 1683, and he became Austria's most outstanding military hero. It was he who reorganized the Austrian army, smashed the Turks, fought Louis XIV to a standstill, and generally guided the triumph of absolutism in Austria. Rewarded with great wealth by his grateful royal employer, Eugene called on the leading architects of the day, J. B. Fischer von Erlach and Johann

Lukas von Hildebrandt, to consecrate his glory in stone and fresco. Fischer built Eugene's Winter (or Town) Palace in Vienna, and he and Hildebrandt collaborated on the prince's Summer Palace on the city's outskirts.

The Summer Palace is actually two enormous buildings, the Lower Belvedere and the Upper Belvedere, completed in 1713 and 1722 respectively and joined by one of the most exquisite gardens in Europe. The Upper Belvedere, Hildebrandt's masterpiece, stands gracefully, even playfully, behind a great sheet of water. One enters through magnificent iron gates into a hall where sculptured giants crouch as pillars and then moves on to a great staircase of dazzling whiteness and ornamentation. Even today the emotional impact of this building is great: here art and beauty create a sense of immense power and wealth.

Palaces like the Upper Belvedere are magnificent examples of the baroque style. They express the baroque delight in bold, sweeping statements, which were intended to provide a dramatic emotional experience. To create this experience, baroque masters dissolved the traditional artistic frontiers: the architect permitted the painter and the artisan to cover his undulating surfaces with wildly colorful paintings, graceful sculptures, and fanciful carvings. Space was used in a highly original way, to blend everything together in a total environment. These techniques shone in all their glory in the churches of southern Germany and in the colossal entrance halls of palaces like that in Würzburg. Artistic achievement and political statement reinforced each other.

Royal Cities

Absolute monarchs and baroque architects were not content with fashioning ostentatious palaces. They remodeled existing capital cities, or even built new ones, to reflect royal magnificence and the centralization of political power. Karlsruhe, founded in 1715 as the capital city of a small German principality, is one extreme example. There, broad, straight avenues radiated out from the palace, so that all roads—like all power—were focused on the ruler. More typically, the monarch's architects added new urban areas alongside the old city; these areas then became the real heart of the expanding capital.

The distinctive features of these new additions were their broad avenues, their imposing government buildings, and their rigorous mathematical layout. Along these major thoroughfares the nobles built elaborate baroque townhouses; stables and servants' quarters were built on the alleys behind. Wide avenues also facilitated the rapid movement of soldiers through the city to quell any disturbance (the king's planners had the needs of the military constantly in mind). Under the arcades along the avenues appeared smart and very expensive shops, the first department stores, with plate-glass windows and fancy displays.

The new avenues brought reckless speed to the European city. Whereas everyone had walked through the narrow, twisting streets of the medieval town, the high and mighty raced down the broad boulevards in their elegant carriages. A social gap opened between the wealthy riders and the gaping, dodging pedestrians. "Mind the carriages!" wrote one eighteenth-century observer in Paris:

Here comes the black-coated physician in his chariot, the dancing master in his coach, the fencing master in his surrey—and the Prince behind six horses at the gallop as if he were in the open country. . . . The threatening wheels of the overbearing rich drive as rapidly as ever over stones stained with the blood of their unhappy victims.[14]

Speeding carriages on broad avenues, an endless parade of power and position: here were the symbol and substance of the baroque city.

The Growth of St. Petersburg

No city illustrated better than St. Petersburg the close ties among politics, architecture, and urban development in this period. In 1700, when the Great Northern War between Russia and Sweden began, the city did not exist. There was only a small Swedish fortress on one of the water-logged islands at the mouth of the Neva River, where it flows into the Baltic Sea. In 1702 Peter the Great's armies seized this desolate outpost. Within a year the reforming tsar had decided to build a new city there and to make it, rather than ancient Moscow, his capital.

Since the first step was to secure the Baltic coast, military construction was the main concern for the next eight years. A mighty fortress was built on Peter Island, and a port and shipyards were built across the river on the mainland, as a Russian navy came into

St. Petersburg, ca 1760 Rastrelli's remodeled Winter Palace, which housed the royal family until the Russian Revolution of 1917, stands on the left along the Neva River, near the ministries of the tsar's government. The Navy Office with its famous golden spire is in the center. Russia became a naval power and St. Petersburg a great port. *(From G. H. Hamilton,* Art and Architecture in Russia, *Penguin Books, 1954)*

being. The land was swampy and uninhabited, the climate damp and unpleasant. But Peter cared not at all: for him, the inhospitable northern marshland was a future metropolis, gloriously bearing his name.

After the decisive Russian victory at Poltava in 1709 greatly reduced the threat of Swedish armies, Peter moved into high gear. In one imperious decree after another, he ordered his people to build a city that would equal any in the world. Such a city had to be western and baroque, just as Peter's army had to be western and permanent. From such a new city, his "window on Europe," Peter also believed it would be easier to reform the country militarily and administratively.

These general political goals matched Peter's architectural ideas, which had been influenced by his travels in western Europe. First, Peter wanted a comfortable, "modern" city. Modernity meant broad, straight, stone-paved avenues, houses built in a uniform line and not haphazardly set back from the street, large parks, canals for drainage, stone bridges, and street lighting. Second, all building had to con-

form strictly to detailed architectural regulations set down by the government. Finally, each social group —the nobility, the merchants, the artisans, and so on —was to live in a certain section of town. In short, the city and its population were to conform to a carefully defined urban plan of the baroque type.

Peter used the traditional but reinforced methods of Russian autocracy to build his modern capital. The creation of St. Petersburg was just one of the heavy obligations he dictatorially imposed on all social groups in Russia. The peasants bore the heaviest burdens. Just as the government drafted peasants for the army, it also drafted twenty-five to forty thousand men each summer to labor in St. Petersburg for three months, without pay. Every ten to fifteen peasant households had to furnish one such worker each summer and then pay a special tax in order to feed that worker in St. Petersburg.

Peasants hated this forced labor in the capital, and each year one-fourth to one-third of those sent risked brutal punishment and ran away. Many peasant construction workers died each summer from hunger, sickness, and accidents. Many also died because peasant villages tended to elect old men or young boys to labor in St. Petersburg, since strong and able-bodied men were desperately needed on the farm in the busy summer months. Thus beautiful St. Petersburg was built on the shoveling, carting, and paving of a mass of conscripted serfs.

Peter also drafted more privileged groups to his city, but on a permanent basis. Nobles were summarily ordered to build costly stone houses and palaces in St. Petersburg and to live in them most of the year. The more serfs a noble possessed, the bigger his dwelling had to be. Merchants and artisans were also commanded to build and settle in St. Petersburg. These nobles and merchants were then required to pay for the city's avenues, parks, canals, embankments, pilings, and bridges, all of which were very costly in terms of both money and lives because they were built on a swamp. The building of St. Petersburg was, in truth, an enormous direct tax levied on the wealthy, who in turn forced the peasantry to do most of the work. The only immediate beneficiaries were the foreign architects and urban planners. No wonder so many Russians hated Peter's new city.

Yet the tsar had his way. By the time of his death in 1725, there were at least six thousand houses and numerous impressive government buildings in St. Petersburg. Under the remarkable women who ruled Russia throughout most of the eighteenth century, St. Petersburg blossomed fully as a majestic and well-organized city, at least in its wealthy showpiece sections. Peter's youngest daughter, the quick-witted, sensual beauty, Elizabeth (1741–1762), named as her chief architect Bartolomeo Rastrelli, who had come to Russia from Italy as a boy of fifteen in 1715. Combining Italian and Russian traditions into a unique, wildly colorful St. Petersburg style, Rastrelli built many palaces for the nobility and all the larger government buildings erected during Elizabeth's reign. He also rebuilt the Winter Palace as an enormous, aqua-colored royal residence, now the Hermitage museum. There Elizabeth established a flashy, luxury-loving, and slightly crude court, which Catherine in turn made truly imperial. All the while St. Petersburg grew rapidly, and its almost 300,000 inhabitants in 1782 made it one of the world's largest cities. Peter and his successors had created out of nothing a magnificent and harmonious royal city, which unmistakably proclaimed the power of Russia's rulers and the creative potential of the absolutist state.

From about 1400 to 1650, social and economic developments in eastern Europe increasingly diverged from those in western Europe. In the east, peasants and townspeople lost precious freedoms, while the nobility increased its power and prestige. It was within this framework of resurgent serfdom and entrenched nobility that Austrian and Prussian monarchs fashioned absolutist states in the seventeenth and early eighteenth centuries. Thus monarchs won absolutist control over standing armies, permanent taxes, and legislative bodies. But they did not question the underlying social and economic relationships. Indeed, they enhanced the privileges of the nobility, which furnished the leading servitors for enlarged armies and growing state bureaucracies.

In Russia, the social and economic trends were similar, but the timing of political absolutism was different. Mongol conquest and rule was a crucial experience, and a harsh, indigenous tsarist autocracy was firmly in place by the reign of Ivan the Terrible in the sixteenth century. More than a century later, Peter the Great succeeded in tightening up Russia's traditional absolutism and modernizing it by reforming the army, the bureaucracy, and the defense industry. In Russia and throughout eastern Europe, war and the needs of the state in time of war weighed heavily in the triumph of absolutism.

Triumphant absolutism interacted spectacularly with the arts. Baroque art, which had grown out of the Catholic Reformation's desire to move the faithful and exalt the true faith, admirably suited the secular aspirations of eastern rulers. They built grandiose baroque palaces, monumental public squares, and even whole cities to glorify their power and majesty. Thus baroque art attained magnificent heights in eastern Europe, symbolizing the ideal and harmonizing with the reality of imperious royal absolutism.

NOTES

1. Quoted in F. L. Carsten, *The Origins of Prussia* (Oxford: Clarendon Press, 1954), p. 152.
2. Ibid., p. 175.
3. H. Rosenberg, *Bureaucracy, Aristocracy, and Autocracy: The Prussian Experience, 1660–1815* (Boston: Beacon Press, 1966), p. 38.

4. Quoted in R. Ergang, *The Potsdam Führer: Frederick William I, Father of Prussian Militarism* (New York: Octagon Books, 1972), pp. 85, 87.

5. Ibid., pp. 6–7, 43.

6. Quoted in R. A. Dorwart, *The Administrative Reforms of Frederick William I of Prussia* (Cambridge: Harvard University Press, 1953), p. 226.

7. Quoted in Rosenberg, *Bureaucracy*, p. 40.

8. Quoted in R. Pipes, *Russia Under the Old Regime* (New York: Scribner's, 1974), p. 48.

9. Quoted in N. V. Riasanovsky, *A History of Russia* (New York: Oxford University Press, 1963), p. 79.

10. Quoted in I. Grey, *Ivan III and the Unification of Russia* (New York: Collier Books, 1967), p. 39.

11. Quoted in ibid., p. 42.

12. Quoted in Ergang, *Potsdam Führer*, p. 13.

13. Quoted in A. Cobban, ed., *The Eighteenth Century: Europe in the Age of Enlightenment* (New York: McGraw-Hill, 1969), p. 80.

14. Quoted in L. Mumford, *The Culture of Cities* (New York: Harcourt Brace Jovanovich, 1938), p. 97.

SUGGESTED READING

All of the books cited in the Notes are highly recommended. Carsten's *Origin of Prussia* is the best study on early Prussian history, and Rosenberg's *Bureaucracy, Aristocracy, and Autocracy* is a masterful analysis of the social context of Prussian absolutism. In addition to Ergang's exciting and critical biography of ramrod Frederick William I, there is G. Ritter, *Frederick the Great* (1968), a more sympathetic study of the talented son by one of Germany's leading conservative historians. G. Craig, *The Politics of the Prussian Army, 1640–1945* (1964), expertly traces the great influence of the military on the Prussian state over three hundred years. R. J. Evans, *The Making of the Habsburg Empire, 1550–1770* (1979), and R. A. Kann, *A History of the Habsburg Empire, 1526–1918* (1974), analyze the development of absolutism in Austria, as does A. Wandruszka, *The House of Habsburg* (1964). J. Stoye, *The Siege of Vienna* (1964), is a fascinating account of the last great Ottoman offensive, which is also treated in the interesting study by P. Coles, *The Ottoman Impact on Europe, 1350–1699* (1968). The Austro-Ottoman conflict is also a theme of L. S. Stavrianos, *The Balkans Since 1453* (1958), and D. McKay's fine biography, *Prince Eugene of Savoy* (1978). A good general account is provided in D. McKay and H. Scott, *The Rise of the Great Powers, 1648–1815* (1983).

On eastern peasants and serfdom, J. Blum, "The Rise of Serfdom in Eastern Europe," *American Historical Review 62* (July 1957):807–836, is a good point of departure, while R. Mousnier, *Peasant Uprisings in Seventeenth-century France, Russia, and China* (1970), is an engrossing comparative study. J. Blum, *Lord and Peasant in Russia from the Ninth to the Nineteenth Century* (1961), provides a good look at conditions in rural Russia, and P. Avrich, *Russian Rebels, 1600–1800* (1972), treats some of the violent peasant upheavals those conditions produced. R. Hellie, *Enserfment and Military Change in Muscovy* (1971), is outstanding, as is A. Yanov's provocative *Origins of Autocracy: Ivan the Terrible in Russian History* (1981). In addition to the fine surveys by Pipes and Riasanovsky cited in the Notes, J. Billington, *The Icon and the Axe* (1970), is a stimulating history of early Russian intellectual and cultural developments, such as the great split in the church. M. Raeff, *Origins of the Russian Intelligentsia* (1966), skillfully probes the mind of the Russian nobility in the eighteenth century. B. H. Sumner, *Peter the Great and the Emergence of Russia* (1962), is a fine brief introduction, which may be compared with the brilliant biography by Russia's greatest prerevolutionary historian, V. Klyuchevsky, *Peter the Great* (trans. 1958), and with N. V. Riasanovsky, *The Image of Peter the Great in Russian History and Thought* (1985). G. Vernadsky and R. Fisher, eds., *A Source Book of Russian History from Early Times to 1917*, 3 vols. (1972), is an invaluable, highly recommended collection of documents and contemporary writings.

Three good books on art and architecture are E. Hempel, *Baroque Art and Architecture in Central Europe* (1965); G. Hamilton, *The Art and Architecture of Russia* (1954); and N. Pevsner, *An Outline of European Architecture,* 6th ed. (1960). Bach, Handel, and other composers are discussed intelligently by M. Bufkozer, *Music in the Baroque Era* (1947).

21

TOWARD A NEW
WORLD-VIEW
IN THE WEST

OST PEOPLE are not philosophers, but nevertheless they have a basic outlook on life, a more or less coherent world-view. At the risk of oversimplification, one may say that the world-view of medieval and early modern Europe was primarily religious and theological. Not only did Christian or Jewish teachings form the core of people's spiritual and philosophical beliefs, but religious teachings also permeated all the rest of human thought and activity. Political theory relied on the divine right of kings, for example, and activities ranging from marriage and divorce to eating habits and hours of business were regulated by churches and religious doctrines.

In the course of the eighteenth century, this religious and theological world-view of the educated classes of western Europe underwent a fundamental transformation. Many educated people came to see the world primarily in secular and scientific terms. And while few abandoned religious beliefs altogether, many became openly hostile toward established Christianity. The role of churches and religious thinking in earthly affairs and in the pursuit of knowledge was substantially reduced. Among many in the upper and middle classes, a new critical, scientific, and very "modern" world-view took shape. Why did this momentous change occur? How did this new outlook on life affect society and politics? This chapter will focus on these questions.

THE SCIENTIFIC REVOLUTION

The foremost cause of the change in world-view was the scientific revolution. Modern science—precise knowledge of the physical world based on the union of experimental observations with sophisticated mathematics—crystallized in the seventeenth century. Whereas science had been secondary and subordinate in medieval intellectual life, it became independent and even primary for many educated people in the eighteenth century.

The emergence of modern science was a development of tremendous long-term significance. A noted historian has even said that the scientific revolution of the late sixteenth and seventeenth centuries "outshines everything since the rise of Christianity and reduces the Renaissance and Reformation to the rank of mere episodes, mere internal displacements, within the system of medieval Christendom." The scientific revolution was "the real origin both of the modern world and the modern mentality."[1] This statement is an exaggeration, but not much of one. Of all the great civilizations, only that of the West developed modern science. It was with the scientific revolution that Western society began to acquire its most distinctive traits.

Though historians agree that the scientific revolution was enormously important, they approach it in quite different ways. Some scholars believe that the history of scientific achievement in this period had its own basic "internal" logic and that "nonscientific" factors had quite limited significance. These scholars write brilliant, often highly technical, intellectual studies, but they neglect the broader historical context. Other historians stress "external" economic, social, and religious factors, brushing over the scientific developments themselves. Historians of science now realize that these two approaches need to be brought together, but they are only beginning to do so. It is best, therefore, to examine the milestones on the fateful march toward modern science first and then to search for nonscientific influences along the route.

SCIENTIFIC THOUGHT IN 1500

Since developments in astronomy and physics were at the heart of the scientific revolution, one must begin with the traditional European conception of the universe and movement in it. In the early 1500s, traditional European ideas about the universe were still based primarily on the ideas of Aristotle, the great Greek philosopher of the fourth century B.C. These ideas had gradually been recovered during the Middle Ages and then brought into harmony with Christian doctrines by medieval theologians. According to this revised Aristotelian view, a motionless earth was fixed at the center of the universe. Around it moved ten separate, transparent, crystal spheres. In the first eight spheres were embedded, in turn, the moon, the sun, the five known planets, and the fixed stars. Then followed two spheres added during the Middle Ages to account for slight changes in the positions of the stars over the centuries. Beyond the tenth sphere was heaven, with the throne of God. Angels kept the spheres moving in perfect circles.

Aristotle's views, suitably revised by medieval philosophers, also dominated thinking about physics and motion on earth. Aristotle had distinguished sharply between the world of the celestial spheres and that of the earth—the sublunar world. The spheres consisted of a perfect, incorruptible "quintessence," or fifth essence. The sublunar world, however, was made up of four imperfect, changeable elements. The "light" elements—air and fire—naturally moved upward, while the "heavy" elements—water and earth—naturally moved downward. The natural directions of motion did not always prevail, however, for elements were often mixed together and could be affected by an outside force such as a human being. Aristotle and his followers also believed that a uniform force moved an object at a constant speed and that the object would stop as soon as that force was removed.

Aristotle's ideas about astronomy and physics were accepted with minor revisions for two thousand years, and with good reason. First, they offered an understandable, common-sense explanation for what the eye actually saw. Second, Aristotle's science, as interpreted by Christian theologians, fit neatly with Christian doctrines. It established a home for God and a place for Christian souls. It put human beings at the center of the universe and made them the critical link in a "great chain of being" that stretched from the throne of God to the most lowly insect on earth. Thus science was primarily a branch of theology, and it reinforced religious thought. At the same time, medieval "scientists" were already providing closely reasoned explanations of the universe, explanations they felt were worthy of God's perfect creation.

The Copernican Hypothesis

The desire to explain and thereby glorify God's handiwork led to the first great departure from the medieval system. This departure was the work of the Polish clergyman and astronomer Nicolaus Copernicus (1473–1543). As a young man, Copernicus studied church law and astronomy in various European universities. He saw how professional astronomers were still dependent for their most accurate calculations on the work of Ptolemy, the last great ancient astronomer, who had lived in Alexandria in the second century A.D. Ptolemy's achievement had been to work out complicated rules to explain the minor irregularities in the movement of the planets. These rules enabled stargazers and astrologers to track the planets

Ptolemy's System This 1543 drawing shows how the changing configurations of the planets moving around the earth form the twelve different constellations, or "signs," of the zodiac. The learned astronomer on the right is using his knowledge to predict the future for the king on the left. *(Mary Evans Picture Library)*

with greater precision. Many people then (and now) believed that the changing relationships between planets and stars influenced and even determined an individual's future.

The young Copernicus was uninterested in astrology and felt that Ptolemy's cumbersome and occasionally inaccurate rules detracted from the majesty of a perfect Creator. He preferred an old Greek idea being discussed in Renaissance Italy: that the sun rather than the earth was at the center of the universe. Finishing his university studies and returning to a church position in East Prussia, Copernicus worked on his hypothesis from 1506 to 1530. Never questioning the Aristotelian belief in crystal spheres or the idea that circular motion was most perfect and divine, Copernicus theorized that the stars and planets, including the earth, revolve around a fixed sun. Yet Copernicus was a cautious man. Fearing the ridicule of other astronomers, he did not publish his *On the Revolutions of the Heavenly Spheres* until 1543, the year of his death.

Copernicus's theory had enormous scientific and religious implications, many of which the conservative Copernicus did not anticipate. First, it put the stars at rest, their apparent nightly movement simply a result of the earth's rotation. Thus it destroyed the main reason for believing in crystal spheres capable of moving the stars around the earth. Second, Copernicus's theory suggested a universe of staggering size. If in the course of a year the earth moved around the sun and yet the stars appeared to remain in the same place, then the universe was unthinkably large or even infinite. Finally, by characterizing the earth as just another planet, Copernicus destroyed the basic idea of Aristotelian physics—that the earthly world was quite different from the heavenly one. Where, then, was the realm of perfection? Where were heaven and the throne of God?

The Copernican theory quickly brought sharp attacks from religious leaders, especially Protestants. Hearing of Copernicus's work even before it was published, Martin Luther spoke of him as the "new astrologer who wants to prove that the earth moves and goes round. . . . The fool wants to turn the whole art of astronomy upside down." Luther noted that "as the Holy Scripture tells us, so did Joshua bid the sun stand still and not the earth." Calvin also condemned Copernicus, citing as evidence the first verse of Psalm 93: "The world also is established that it cannot be moved." "Who," asked Calvin, "will venture to place the authority of Copernicus above that of the Holy Spirit?"[2] Catholic reaction was milder at first. The Catholic church had never been hypnotized by literal interpretations of the Bible, and not until 1616 did it officially declare the Copernican theory false.

This slow reaction also reflected the slow progress of Copernicus's theory for many years. Other events were almost as influential in creating doubts about traditional astronomical ideas. In 1572 a new star appeared and shone very brightly for almost two years.

The new star, which was actually a distant exploding star, made an enormous impression on people. It seemed to contradict the idea that the heavenly spheres were unchanging and therefore perfect. In 1577 a new comet suddenly moved through the sky, cutting a straight path across the supposedly impenetrable crystal spheres. It was time, as a typical scientific writer put it, for "the radical renovation of astronomy."[3]

FROM TYCHO BRAHE TO GALILEO

One astronomer who agreed was Tycho Brahe (1546–1601). Born into a leading Danish noble family and earmarked for a career in government, Brahe was at an early age tremendously impressed by a partial eclipse of the sun. It seemed to him "something divine that men could know the motions of the stars so accurately that they were able a long time beforehand to predict their places and relative positions."[4] Completing his studies abroad and returning to Denmark, Brahe established himself as Europe's leading astronomer with his detailed observations of the new star of 1572. Aided by generous grants from the king of Denmark, which made him one of the richest men in the country, Brahe built the most sophisticated observatory of his day. For twenty years he meticulously observed the stars and planets with the naked eye. An imposing man who had lost a piece of his nose in a duel and replaced it with a special bridge of gold and silver alloy, a noble who exploited his peasants arrogantly and approached the heavens humbly, Brahe's great contribution was his mass of data. His limited understanding of mathematics prevented him, however, from making much sense out of his data. Part Ptolemaic, part Copernican, he believed that all the planets revolved around the sun and that the entire group of sun and planets revolved in turn around the earth-moon system.

It was left to Brahe's brilliant young assistant, Johannes Kepler (1571–1630), to go much further. Kepler was a medieval figure in many ways. Coming from a minor German noble family and trained for the Lutheran ministry, he long believed that the universe was built on mystical mathematical relationships and a musical harmony of the heavenly bodies. Working and reworking Brahe's mountain of observations in a staggering sustained effort after the Dane's death, this brilliant mathematician eventually went beyond mystical intuitions.

Kepler formulated three famous laws of planetary motion. First, building on Copernican theory, he demonstrated in 1609 that the orbits of the planets around the sun are elliptical rather than circular. Second, he demonstrated that the planets do not move at a uniform speed in their orbits. Third, in 1619 he showed that the time a planet takes to make its complete orbit is precisely related to its distance from the sun. Kepler's contribution was monumental. Whereas Copernicus had speculated, Kepler proved mathematically the precise relations of a sun-centered (solar) system. His work demolished the old system of Aristotle and Ptolemy, and in his third law he came close to formulating the idea of universal gravitation.

While Kepler was unraveling planetary motion, a young Florentine named Galileo Galilei (1564–1642) was challenging all the old ideas about motion. Like so many early scientists, Galileo was a poor nobleman first marked for a religious career. However, he soon became fascinated by mathematics. A brilliant student, Galileo became a professor of mathematics in 1589 at age twenty-five. He proceeded to examine motion and mechanics in a new way. Indeed, his great achievement was the elaboration and consolidation of the modern experimental method. Rather than speculate about what might or should happen, Galileo conducted controlled experiments to find out what actually did happen.

In his famous acceleration experiment, he showed that a uniform force—in this case, gravity—produced a uniform acceleration. Here is how Galileo described his path-breaking method and conclusion in his *Two New Sciences:*

Tycho Brahe's Main Observatory Lavishly financed by the king of Denmark, Brahe built his magnificent observatory at Uraniborg between 1576 and 1580. For twenty years he studied the heavens and accumulated a mass of precise but undigested data. *(The British Library)*

A piece of wooden moulding . . . was taken; on its edge was cut a channel a little more than one finger in breadth. Having made this groove very straight, smooth and polished, and having lined it with parchment, also as smooth and polished as possible, we rolled along it a hard, smooth and very round bronze ball. . . . Noting . . . the time required to make the descent . . . we now rolled the ball only one-quarter the length of the channel; and having measured the time of its descent, we found it precisely one-half of the former. . . . In such experiments [over many distances], repeated a full hundred times, we always found that the spaces traversed were to each other as the squares of the times, and that this was true for all inclinations of the plane.[5]

With this and other experiments, Galileo also formulated the law of inertia. That is, rather than rest being the natural state of objects, an object continues in motion forever unless stopped by some external force. Aristotelian physics was in a shambles.

In the tradition of Brahe, Galileo also applied the experimental method to astronomy. His astronomical discoveries had a great impact on scientific development. On hearing of the invention of the telescope in Holland, Galileo made one for himself and trained it on the heavens. He quickly discovered the first four moons of Jupiter, which clearly suggested that Jupiter could not possibly be embedded in any impene-

Galileo Explains the two new sciences, astronomy and mechanics, to an eager young visitor to his observatory in this artist's reconstruction. After his trial for heresy by the papal Inquisition, Galileo spent the last eight years of his life under house arrest. *(The Mansell Collection)*

trable crystal sphere. This discovery provided new evidence for the Copernican theory, in which Galileo already believed.

Galileo then pointed his telescope at the moon. He wrote in 1610 in *Siderus Nuncius:*

I feel sure that the moon is not perfectly smooth, free from inequalities, and exactly spherical, as a large school of philosophers considers with regard to the moon and the other heavenly bodies. On the contrary, it is full of inequalities, uneven, full of hollows and protuberances, just like the surface of the earth itself, which is varied. . . . The next object which I have observed is the essence or substance of the Milky Way. By the aid of a telescope anyone may behold this in a manner which so distinctly appeals to the senses that all the disputes which have tormented philosophers through so many ages are exploded by the irrefutable evidence of our eyes, and we are freed from wordy disputes upon the subject. For the galaxy is nothing else but a mass of innumerable stars planted together in clusters. Upon whatever part of it you direct the telescope straightway a vast crowd of stars presents itself to view; many of them are tolerably large and extremely bright, but the number of small ones is quite beyond determination.[6]

Reading these famous lines, one feels that a crucial corner in Western civilization was being turned. The traditional religious and theological world-view, which rested on determining and then accepting the proper established authority, was beginning to give way in certain fields to a critical, "scientific" method. This new method of learning and investigating was the greatest accomplishment of the entire scientific revolution, for it has proved capable of great extension. A historian investigating documents of the past, for example, is not much different from a Galileo rolling balls and studying stars.

Galileo was employed in Florence by the Medici grand dukes of Tuscany, and his work eventually aroused the ire of some theologians. The issue was presented in 1624 to Pope Urban VIII, who permitted Galileo to write about different possible systems of the world as long as he did not presume to judge which one actually existed. After the publication in Italian of his widely read *Dialogue on the Two Chief Systems of the World* in 1632, which too openly lampooned the traditional views of Aristotle and Ptolemy and defended those of Copernicus, Galileo was tried for heresy by the papal Inquisition. Imprisoned and threatened with torture, the aging Galileo recanted, "renouncing and cursing" his Copernican errors. Of minor importance in the development of science, Galileo's trial later became for some writers the perfect symbol of the inevitable conflict between religious belief and scientific knowledge.

NEWTON'S SYNTHESIS

The accomplishments of Kepler, Galileo, and other scientists had taken effect by about 1640. The old astronomy and physics were in ruins, and several fundamental breakthroughs had been made. The new findings had not, however, been fused together in a new synthesis, a single explanatory system that would comprehend motion both on earth and in the skies. That synthesis, which prevailed until the twentieth century, was the work of Isaac Newton (1642–1727).

Newton was born into lower English gentry and attended Cambridge University. A great genius who spectacularly united the experimental and theoretical-mathematical sides of modern science, Newton was also fascinated by alchemy. He sought the elixir of life and a way to change base metals into gold and silver. Not without reason did the twentieth-century economist John Maynard Keynes call Newton the "last of the magicians." Newton was intensely religious. He had a highly suspicious nature, lacked all interest in women and sex, and in 1693 suffered a nervous breakdown from which he later recovered. He was far from being the perfect rationalist so endlessly eulogized by writers in the eighteenth and nineteenth centuries.

Of his intellectual genius and incredible powers of concentration there can be no doubt, however. Arriving at some of his most basic ideas about physics in 1666 at age twenty-four, but unable to prove these theories mathematically, he attained a professorship and studied optics for many years. In 1684 Newton returned to physics for eighteen extraordinarily intensive months. For weeks on end he seldom left his room except to read his lectures. His meals were sent up but he usually forgot to eat them, his mind fastened like a vise on the laws of the universe. Thus did Newton open the third book of his immortal *Mathematical Principles of Natural Philosophy,* published in Latin in 1687 and generally known as the *Principia,* with these lines:

In the preceding books I have laid down the principles of philosophy [that is, science]. . . . These principles are the laws of certain motions, and powers or forces, which chiefly have respect to philosophy. . . . It remains that from the same principles I now demonstrate the frame of the System of the World.

Newton made good his grandiose claim. His towering accomplishment was to integrate in a single explanatory system the astronomy of Copernicus, as corrected by Kepler's laws, with the physics of Galileo and his predecessors. Newton did this by means of a set of mathematical laws that explains motion and mechanics. These laws of dynamics are complex, and it took scientists and engineers two hundred years to work out all their implications. Nevertheless, the key feature of the Newtonian synthesis was the law of universal gravitation. According to this law, every body in the universe attracts every other body in the universe in a precise mathematical relationship, whereby the force of attraction is proportional to the quantity of matter of the objects and inversely proportional to the square of the distance between them. The whole universe—from Kepler's elliptical orbits to Galileo's rolling balls—was unified in one majestic system.

CAUSES OF THE SCIENTIFIC REVOLUTION

With a charming combination of modesty and self-congratulation, Newton once wrote: "If I have seen further [than others], it is by standing on the shoulders of Giants."[7] Surely the path from Copernicus to Newton confirms the "internal" view of the scientific revolution as a product of towering individual genius. The problems of science were inherently exciting, and solution of those problems was its own reward for inquisitive, high-powered minds. Yet there were certainly broader causes as well.

The long-term contribution of medieval intellectual life and medieval universities to the scientific revolution was much more considerable than historians unsympathetic to the Middle Ages once believed. By the thirteenth century, permanent universities with professors and large student bodies had been established in western Europe. The universities were supported by society because they trained the lawyers, doctors, and church leaders society required. By 1300 philosophy had taken its place alongside law, medicine, and theology. Medieval philosophers developed a limited but real independence from theologians and a sense of free inquiry. They nobly pursued a body of knowledge and tried to arrange it meaningfully by means of abstract theories.

Within this framework, science was able to emerge as a minor but distinct branch of philosophy. In the fourteenth and fifteenth centuries, first in Italy and then elsewhere in Europe, leading universities established new professorships of mathematics, astronomy, and physics (natural philosophy) within their faculties of philosophy. The prestige of the new fields was still low among both professors and students. Nevertheless, this pattern of academic science, which grew out of the medieval commitment to philosophy and did not change substantially until the late eighteenth century, undoubtedly promoted scientific development. Rational, critical thinking was applied to scientific problems by a permanent community of scholars. And an outlet existed for the talents of a Galileo or a Newton: all the great path breakers either studied or taught at universities.

The Renaissance also stimulated scientific progress. One of the great deficiencies of medieval science was its rather rudimentary mathematics. The recovery of the finest works of Greek mathematics—a byproduct of Renaissance humanism's ceaseless search for the knowledge of antiquity—greatly improved European mathematics well into the early seventeenth century. The recovery of more texts also showed that classical mathematicians had had their differences, and Europeans were forced to try to resolve these ancient controversies by means of their own efforts. Finally, the Renaissance pattern of patronage, especially in Italy, was often scientific as well as artistic and humanistic. Various rulers and wealthy businessmen supported scientific investigations, just as the Medici of Florence supported those of Galileo.

The navigational problems of long sea voyages in the age of overseas expansion were a third factor in the scientific revolution. Ship captains on distant shores needed to be able to chart their positions as accurately as possible, so that reliable maps could be drawn and the risks of international trade reduced. As early as 1484, the king of Portugal appointed a commission of mathematicians to perfect tables to help seamen find their latitude. This resulted in the first European navigation manual.

The problem of fixing longitude was much more difficult. In England, the government and the great capitalistic trading companies turned to science and scientific education in an attempt to solve this pressing practical problem. When the famous Elizabethan financier Sir Thomas Gresham (1519?–1579) bequeathed a large amount of money to establish Gresham College in London, he stipulated that three of the college's seven professors had to concern themselves exclusively with scientific subjects and the professor of astronomy was directed to teach courses on the science of navigation. At the college scientists had, for the first time in history, an honored role in society. They enjoyed close ties with the top officials of the Royal Navy and with leading merchants and shipbuilders. Gresham College became the main center of scientific activity in England in the first half of the seventeenth century. The close tie between practical men and scientists also led to the establishment in 1662 of the Royal Society of London, which published scientific papers and sponsored scientific meetings.

Navigational problems were also critical in the development of many new scientific instruments, such as the telescope, the barometer, the thermometer, the pendulum clock, the microscope, and the air pump. Better instruments, which permitted more accurate observations, often led to important new knowledge. Galileo with his telescope was by no means unique.

Better instruments were part of the fourth factor, the development of better ways of obtaining knowledge about the world. Two important thinkers, Francis Bacon (1561–1626) and René Descartes (1596–1650), represented key aspects of this improvement in scientific methodology.

State Support Governments supported scientific research because they thought it might be useful. Here Louis XIV visits the French Royal Academy of Sciences in 1671 and examines a plan for better military fortifications. The great interest in astronomy, anatomy, and geography is evident. *(Bibliothèque Nationale, Paris)*

The English politician and writer Francis Bacon was the greatest early propagandist for the new experimental method, as Galileo was its greatest early practitioner. Rejecting the Aristotelian and medieval method of using speculative reasoning to build general theories, Bacon argued that new knowledge had to be pursued through empirical, experimental research. That is, the researcher who wants to learn more about leaves or rocks should not speculate about the subject but rather collect a multitude of specimens and then compare and analyze them.

Thus freed from sterile medieval speculation, the facts will speak for themselves, and important general principles will then emerge. Knowledge will increase. Bacon's contribution was to formalize the empirical method, which had already been used by scientists like Brahe and Galileo, into the general theory of inductive reasoning known as "empiricism."

Bacon claimed that the empirical method would result not only in more knowledge, but in highly practical, useful knowledge. According to Bacon, sci-

René Descartes dismissed the scientific theories of Aristotle and his medieval disciples as outdated dogma. A brilliant philosopher and mathematician, he formulated rules for abstract, deductive reasoning and the search for comprehensive scientific laws. *(Royal Museum of Fine Arts, Copenhagen)*

entific discoveries like those so avidly sought at Gresham College would bring about much greater control over the physical environment and make people rich and nations powerful. Thus Bacon helped provide a radically new and effective justification for private and public support of scientific inquiry.

The French philosopher René Descartes was a true genius who made his first great discovery in mathematics. As a twenty-three-year-old soldier serving in the Thirty Years' War, he experienced on a single night in 1619 a life-changing intellectual vision. What Descartes saw was that there was a perfect correspondence between geometry and algebra and that geometrical, spatial figures could be expressed as algebraic equations and vice versa. A great step forward in the history of mathematics, Descartes' discovery of analytic geometry provided scientists with an important new tool. Descartes also made contributions to the science of optics, but his greatest achievement was to develop his initial vision into a whole philosophy of knowledge and science.

Like Bacon, Descartes scorned traditional science and had great faith in the powers of the human mind. Yet Descartes was much more systematic and mathematical than Bacon. He decided it was necessary to doubt everything that could reasonably be doubted and then, as in geometry, to use deductive reasoning from self-evident principles to ascertain scientific laws. Descartes' reasoning ultimately reduced all substances to "matter" and "mind"—that is, to the physical and the spiritual. His view of the world as consisting of two fundamental entities is known as "Cartesian dualism." Descartes was a profoundly original and extremely influential thinker.

It is important to realize that the modern scientific method, which began to crystallize in the late seventeenth century, combined Bacon's inductive experimentalism and Descartes' deductive, mathematical rationalism. Neither of these extreme approaches was sufficient by itself. Bacon's inability to appreciate the importance of mathematics and his obsession with practical results clearly showed the limitations of antitheoretical empiricism. Likewise, some of Descartes' positions—he believed, for example, that it was possible to deduce the whole science of medicine from first principles—aptly demonstrated the inadequacy of rigid, dogmatic rationalism. Significantly, Bacon faulted Galileo for his use of abstract formulas, while Descartes criticized the great Italian for being too experimental and insufficiently theoretical. Modern scientific method has joined precise observations and experimentalism with the search for general laws that can be expressed in rigorously logical, mathematical language.

Finally, there is the question of science and religion. Just as some historians have argued that Protestantism led to the rise of capitalism, others have concluded that Protestantism was a fundamental factor in the rise of modern science. Protestantism, particularly in its Calvinist varieties, supposedly made scientific inquiry a question of individual conscience and not of religious doctrine. The Catholic church, on the other hand, supposedly suppressed scientific theories that conflicted with its teachings and thus discouraged scientific progress.

The truth of the matter is more complicated. All religious authorities—Catholic, Protestant, and Jewish—opposed the Copernican system to a greater or lesser extent until about 1630, by which time the scientific revolution was definitely in progress. Catholic churchmen were initially less hostile than Protestant and Jewish leaders. This early Catholic toleration and the scientific interests of Renaissance Italy help account for the undeniable fact that Italian scientists played a crucial role in scientific progress right up to the trial of Galileo in 1633. Thereafter the Counter-Reformation church became more hostile to science, which explains in part the decline of science in Italy (but not in Catholic France) after 1640. At the same time, some Protestant countries became quite "pro-science," especially if they lacked a strong religious authority capable of imposing religious orthodoxy on scientific questions.

This was the case with England after 1630. English religious conflicts became so intense that it was impossible for the authorities to impose religious unity on anything, including science. It is significant that the forerunners of the Royal Society agreed to discuss only "neutral" scientific questions, so as not to come to blows over closely related religious and political disputes. The work of Bacon's many followers during Cromwell's commonwealth helped solidify the neutrality and independence of science. Bacon advocated the experimental approach precisely because it was open-minded and independent of any preconceived religious or philosophical ideas. Neutral and useful, science became an accepted part of life and developed rapidly in England after about 1640.

SOME CONSEQUENCES OF THE SCIENTIFIC REVOLUTION

The rise of modern science had many consequences, some of which are still unfolding. First, it went hand in hand with the rise of a new and expanding social group—the scientific community. Members of this community were linked together by learned societies, common interests, and shared values. Expansion of knowledge was the primary goal of this community, and scientists' material and psychological rewards depended on their success in this endeavor. Thus science became quite competitive, and even more scientific advance was inevitable.

Second, the scientific revolution introduced not only new knowledge about nature but also a new and revolutionary way of obtaining such knowledge—the modern scientific method. In addition to being both theoretical and experimental, this method was highly critical, and it differed profoundly from the old way of getting knowledge about nature. It refused to base its conclusions on tradition and established sources, on ancient authorities and sacred texts.

The scientific revolution had few consequences for economic life and the living standards of the masses until the late eighteenth century at the very earliest. True, improvements in the techniques of navigation facilitated overseas trade and helped enrich leading merchants. But science had relatively few practical economic applications, and the hopes of the early Baconians were frustrated. The close link between theoretical, or pure, science and applied technology, which we take for granted today, simply did not exist before the nineteenth century. Thus the scientific revolution of the seventeenth century was first and foremost an intellectual revolution. It is not surprising that for more than a hundred years its greatest impact was on how people thought and believed.

THE ENLIGHTENMENT

The scientific revolution was the single most important factor in the creation of the new world-view of the eighteenth-century Enlightenment. This world-view, which has played a large role in shaping the modern mind, was based on a rich mix of ideas, sometimes conflicting, for intellectuals delight in playing with ideas just as athletes delight in playing games. Despite this diversity, three central concepts stand out.

The most important and original idea of the Enlightenment was that the methods of natural science could and should be used to examine and understand all aspects of life. This was what intellectuals meant by *reason,* a favorite word of Enlightenment thinkers. Nothing was to be accepted on faith. Everything was to be submitted to the rational, critical, "scientific" way of thinking. This approach brought the Enlightenment into a head-on conflict with the established churches, which rested their beliefs on the special authority of the Bible and Christian theology. A second important Enlightenment concept was that the scientific method was capable of discovering the laws of human society as well as those of nature. Thus was social science born. Its birth led to the third key idea, that of progress. Armed with the proper method of discovering the laws of human existence, Enlightenment thinkers believed it was at least possible to

Popularizing Science The frontispiece illustration of Fontenelle's *Conversations on the Plurality of Worlds* invites the reader to share the pleasures of astronomy with an elegant lady and an entertaining teacher. *(University of Illinois)*

between the publication of Newton's masterpiece in 1687 and the death of Louis XIV in 1715 that tied the crucial knot between the scientific revolution and a new outlook on life.

Talented writers of that generation popularized hard-to-understand scientific achievements for the educated elite. The most famous and influential popularizer was a versatile Frenchman of letters, Bernard de Fontenelle (1657–1757). Fontenelle practically invented the technique of making highly complicated scientific findings understandable to a broad non-scientific audience. He set out to make science witty and entertaining, as easy to read as a novel. This was a tall order, but Fontenelle largely succeeded.

His most famous work, *Conversations on the Plurality of Worlds* (1686), begins with two elegant figures walking in the gathering shadows of a large park. One is a woman, a sophisticated aristocrat, and the other is her friend, perhaps her lover. They gaze at the stars, and their talk turns to a passionate discussion of . . . astronomy! He confides that "each star may well be a different world." She is intrigued by his novel idea: "Teach me about these stars of yours." And he does, gently but persistently stressing how error is giving way to truth. At one point he explains:

There came on the scene . . . Copernicus, who made short work of all those various circles, all those solid skies, which the ancients had pictured to themselves. The former he abolished; the latter he broke in pieces. Fired with the noble zeal of a true astronomer, he took the earth and spun it very far away from the center of the universe, where it had been installed, and in that center he put the sun, which had a far better title to the honor.[8]

Rather than tremble in despair in the face of these revelations, Fontenelle's lady rejoices in the advance of knowledge. Fontenelle thus went beyond entertainment to instruction, suggesting that the human mind was capable of making great progress.

This idea of progress was essentially a new idea of the later seventeenth century. Medieval and Reformation thinkers had been concerned primarily with sin and salvation. The humanists of the Renaissance had emphasized worldly matters, but they had looked backward. They had believed it might be possible to equal the magnificent accomplishments of the ancients, but they did not ask for more. Fontenelle and like-minded writers had come to believe that, at least in science and mathematics, their era had

create better societies and better people. Their belief was strengthened by some genuine improvements in economic and social life during the eighteenth century.

The Enlightenment was therefore profoundly secular. It revived and expanded the Renaissance concentration on worldly explanations. In the course of the eighteenth century, the Enlightenment had a profound impact on the thought and culture of the urban middle and upper classes. It did not have much appeal for the poor and the peasants.

THE EMERGENCE OF THE ENLIGHTENMENT

The Enlightenment did not reach its maturity until about 1750. Yet it was the generation that came of age gone far beyond antiquity. Progress, at least intellectual progress, was clearly possible. During the eighteenth century, this idea would sink deeply into the consciousness of the European elite.

Fontenelle and other literary figures of his generation were also instrumental in bringing science into conflict with religion. Contrary to what is often assumed, many seventeenth-century scientists, both Catholic and Protestant, believed that their work exalted God. They did not draw antireligious implications from their scientific findings. The greatest scientist of them all, Isaac Newton, was a devout if unorthodox Christian who saw all of his studies as directed toward explaining God's message. Newton devoted far more of his time to angels and biblical prophecies than to universal gravitation, and he was convinced that all of his inquiries were equally "scientific."

Fontenelle, on the other hand, was skeptical about absolute truth and cynical about the claims of organized religion. Since such unorthodox views could not be stated openly in Louis XIV's France, Fontenelle made his point through subtle editorializing about science. His depiction of the cautious Copernicus as a self-conscious revolutionary was typical. In his *Eulogies of Scientists,* Fontenelle exploited with endless variations the basic theme of rational, progressive scientists versus prejudiced, reactionary priests. Time and time again Fontenelle's fledgling scientists attended church and studied theology; then, at some crucial moment, each was converted from the obscurity of religion to the clarity of science.

The progressive and antireligious implications that writers like Fontenelle drew from the scientific revolution reflected a very real crisis in European thought at the end of the seventeenth century. This crisis had its roots in several intellectual uncertainties and dissatisfactions, of which the demolition of Aristotelian medieval science was only one.

A second uncertainty involved the whole question of religious truth. The destructive wars of religion had been fought, in part, because religious freedom was an intolerable idea in the early seventeenth century. Both Catholics and Protestants had believed that religious truth was absolute and therefore worth fighting and dying for. It was also generally believed that a strong state required unity in religious faith. Yet the disastrous results of the many attempts to impose such religious unity, such as Louis XIV's expulsion of the French Huguenots in 1685, led some people to ask if ideological conformity in religious matters was really necessary. Others skeptically asked if religious truth could ever be known with absolute certainty and concluded that it could not.

The most famous of these skeptics was Pierre Bayle (1647–1706), a French Huguenot who took refuge in Holland. A teacher by profession and a crusading journalist by inclination, Bayle critically examined the religious beliefs and persecutions of the past in his *Historical and Critical Dictionary,* published in 1697. Demonstrating that human beliefs had been extremely varied and very often mistaken, Bayle concluded that nothing can ever be known beyond all doubt. In religion as in philosophy, humanity's best hope was open-minded toleration. Bayle's skeptical views were very influential. Many eighteenth-century writers mined his inexhaustible vein of critical skepticism for ammunition in their attacks on superstition and theology. Bayle's four-volume *Dictionary* was found in more private libraries of eighteenth-century France than any other book.

The rapidly growing travel literature on non-European lands and cultures was a third cause of uncertainty. In the wake of the great discoveries, Europeans were learning that the peoples of China, India, Africa, and the Americas all had their own very different beliefs and customs. Europeans shaved their faces and let their hair grow. The Turks shaved their heads and let their beards grow. In Europe a man bowed before a woman to show respect. In Siam a man turned his back on a woman when he met her, because it was disrespectful to look directly at her. Countless similar examples discussed in the travel accounts helped change the perspective of educated Europeans. They began to look at truth and morality in relative rather than absolute terms. Anything was possible, and who could say what was right or wrong? As one Frenchman wrote: "There is nothing that opinion, prejudice, custom, hope, and a sense of honor cannot do." Another wrote disapprovingly of religious skeptics who were corrupted "by extensive travel and lose whatever shreds of religion that remained with them. Every day they see a new religion, new customs, new rites."[9]

A fourth cause and manifestation of European intellectual turmoil was John Locke's epoch-making "Essay Concerning Human Understanding." Published in 1690—the same year Locke published his famous "Second Treatise on Civil Government" (see page 607)—Locke's essay brilliantly set forth a new theory about how human beings learn and form their ideas. In doing so, he rejected the prevailing view of Descartes, who had held that all people are born with certain basic ideas and ways of thinking. Locke insisted that all ideas are derived from experience. The human mind is like a blank tablet (*tabula rasa*) at birth, a tablet on which environment writes the individual's understanding and beliefs. Human development is therefore determined by education and social institutions, for good or for evil. Locke's "Essay Concerning Human Understanding" passed through many editions and translations. It was, along with Newton's *Principia,* one of the dominant intellectual inspirations of the Enlightenment.

The Philosophes and Their Ideas

By the death of Louis XIV in 1715, many of the ideas that would soon coalesce into the new world-view had been assembled. Yet Christian Europe was still strongly attached to its traditional beliefs, as witnessed by the powerful revival of religious orthodoxy in the first half of the eighteenth century. By the outbreak of the American Revolution in 1775, however, a large portion of western Europe's educated elite had embraced many of the new ideas. This acceptance was the work of one of history's most influential groups of intellectuals, the philosophes. It was the philosophes who proudly and effectively proclaimed that they, at long last, were bringing the light of knowledge to their ignorant fellow creatures in a great Age of Enlightenment.

Philosophe is the French word for "philosopher," and it was in France that the Enlightenment reached its highest development. The French philosophes were indeed philosophers. They asked fundamental philosophical questions about the meaning of life, about God, human nature, good and evil, and cause and effect. But, in the tradition of Fontenelle and Bayle, they were not content with abstract arguments or ivory-tower speculations among a tiny minority of scholars and professors. They wanted to influence and convince a broad audience.

The philosophes were intensely committed to reforming society and humanity, yet they were not free to write as they wished, since it was illegal in France to criticize openly either church or state. Their most radical works had to circulate in France in manuscript form, very much as critical works are passed from hand to hand in unpublished form in dictator-

ships today. Knowing that direct attacks would probably be banned or burned, the philosophes wrote novels and plays, histories and philosophies, dictionaries and encyclopedias, all filled with satire and double meanings to spread their message.

One of the greatest philosophes, the baron de Montesquieu (1689–1755), brilliantly pioneered this approach in *The Persian Letters,* an extremely influential social satire published in 1721. Montesquieu's work consisted of amusing letters supposedly written by Persian travelers, who see European customs in unique ways and thereby cleverly criticize existing practices and beliefs.

Having gained fame using wit as a weapon against cruelty and superstition, Montesquieu settled down on his family estate to study history and politics. His interest was partly personal for, like many members of the high French nobility, he was dismayed that royal absolutism had triumphed in France under Louis XIV. But Montesquieu was also inspired by the example of the physical sciences, and he set out to apply the critical method to the problem of government in *The Spirit of Laws* (1748). The result was a complex comparative study of republics, monarchies, and despotisms—a great pioneering inquiry in the emerging social sciences.

Showing that forms of government were related to history, geography, and customs, Montesquieu focused on the conditions that would promote liberty and prevent tyranny. He argued that despotism could be avoided if political power was divided and shared by a diversity of classes and orders holding unequal rights and privileges. A strong, independent upper class was especially important, according to Montesquieu, because in order to prevent the abuse of power, "it is necessary that by the arrangement of things, power checks power." Admiring greatly the English balance of power among the king, the houses of Parliament, and the independent courts, Montesquieu believed that in France the thirteen high courts —the parlements—were front-line defenders of liberty against royal despotism. Clearly no democrat and apprehensive about the uneducated poor, Montesquieu's theory of separation of powers had a great impact on France's wealthy, well-educated elite. The constitutions of the young United States in 1789 and of France in 1791 were based in large part on this theory.

The most famous and in many ways most representative philosophe was François Marie Arouet,

Voltaire first gained fame as a poet and playwright, but today he is best remembered for the sparkling short stories he occasionally dashed off. A prodigious worker, this painting shows him dictating to his secretary from the very moment he hops out of bed. *(Bulloz)*

who was known by the pen name of Voltaire (1694–1778). In his long career, this son of a comfortable middle-class family wrote over seventy witty volumes, hobnobbed with kings and queens, and died a millionaire because of shrewd business speculations. His early career, however, was turbulent. In 1717 Voltaire was imprisoned for eleven months in the Bastille in Paris for insulting the regent of France. In 1726 a barb from his sharp tongue led a great French nobleman to have him beaten and arrested. This experience made a deep impression on Voltaire. All his life he struggled against legal injustice and class inequalities before the law.

Released from prison after promising to leave the country, Voltaire lived in England for three years. Sharing Montesquieu's enthusiasm for English institutions, Voltaire then wrote various works praising England and popularizing English scientific progress. Newton, he wrote, was history's greatest man, for he had used his genius for the benefit of humanity. "It is," wrote Voltaire, "the man who sways our minds by the prevalence of reason and the native force of truth, not they who reduce mankind to a state of slavery by force and downright violence . . . that claims our reverence and admiration."[10] In the true style of the Enlightenment, Voltaire mixed the glorification of science and reason with an appeal for better people and institutions.

Yet, like almost all of the philosophes, Voltaire was a reformer and not a revolutionary in social and political matters. Returning to France, he was eventually appointed royal historian in 1743, and his *Age of Louis XIV* portrayed Louis as the dignified leader of his age. Voltaire also began a long correspondence with Frederick the Great, and he accepted Frederick's flattering invitation to come brighten up the Prussian court in Berlin. The two men later quarreled, but Voltaire always admired Frederick as a free-thinker and an enlightened monarch.

Unlike Montesquieu, Voltaire pessimistically concluded that the best one could hope for in the way of government was a good monarch, since human beings "are very rarely worthy to govern themselves." Nor did he believe in social equality in human affairs. The idea of making servants equal to their masters was "absurd and impossible." The only realizable equality, Voltaire thought, was that "by which the citizen only depends on the laws which protect the freedom of the feeble against the ambitions of the strong."[11]

Voltaire's philosophical and religious positions were much more radical. In the tradition of Bayle, his voluminous writings challenged—often indirectly—the Catholic church and Christian theology at almost every point. Though he was considered by many devout Christians to be a shallow blasphemer, Voltaire's religious views were influential and quite typical of the mature Enlightenment. The essay on religion from his widely read *Philosophical Dictionary* sums up many of his criticisms and beliefs:

I meditated last night; I was absorbed in the contemplation of nature . . . the immensity, the course, the harmony of these infinite globes. . . .

I admired still more the intelligence which directs these vast forces. I said to myself: "One must be blind not to be dazzled by this spectacle; one must be stupid not to recognize its author; one must be mad not to worship the Supreme Being."

I was deep in these ideas when one of those genii who fill the intermundane spaces came down to me . . . and transported me into a desert all covered with piles of bones. . . . He began with the first pile. "These," he said, "are the twenty-three thousand Jews who danced before a calf, with the twenty-four thousand who were killed while lying with Midianitish women. The number of those massacred for such errors and offences amounts to nearly three hundred thousand.

"In the other piles are the bones of the Christians slaughtered by each other because of metaphysical disputes. . . ."

"What!" I cried, "brothers have treated their brothers like this, and I have the misfortune to be of this brotherhood! . . . Why assemble here all these abominable monuments to barbarism and fanaticism?"

"To instruct you. . . . Follow me now.". . .

I saw a man with a gentle, simple face, who seemed to me to be about thirty-five years old. From afar he looked with compassion upon those piles of whitened bones, through which I had been led to reach the sage's dwelling place. I was astonished to find his feet swollen and bleeding, his hands likewise, his side pierced, and his ribs laid

bare by the cut of the lash. "Good God!" I said to him, "is it possible for a just man, a sage, to be in this state? . . . Was it . . . by priests and judges that you were so cruelly assassinated?"

With great courtesy he answered, "Yes."

"And who were these monsters?"

"They were hypocrites."

"Ah! that says everything; I understand by that one word that they would have condemned you to the cruelest punishment. Had you then proved to them, as Socrates did, that the Moon was not a goddess, and that Mercury was not a god?"

"No, it was not a question of planets. My countrymen did not even know what a planet was; they were all arrant ignoramuses. Their superstitions were quite different from those of the Greeks."

"Then you wanted to teach them a new religion?"

"Not at all; I told them simply: 'Love God with all your heart and your neighbor as yourself, for that is the whole of mankind's duty.' Judge yourself if this precept is not as old as the universe; judge yourself if I brought them a new religion." . . .

"Did you not say once that you were come not to bring peace, but a sword?"

"It was a scribe's error; I told them that I brought peace and not a sword. I never wrote anything; what I said can have been changed without evil intention."

"You did not then contribute in any way by your teaching, either badly reported or badly interpreted, to those frightful piles of bones which I saw on my way to consult with you?"

"I have only looked with horror upon those who have made themselves guilty of all these murders." . . .

[Finally] I asked him to tell me in what true religion consisted.

"Have I not already told you? Love God and your neighbor as yourself." . . .

"Well, if that is so, I take you for my only master."[12]

This passage requires careful study, for it suggests many Enlightenment themes of religion and philosophy. As the opening paragraphs show, Voltaire clearly believed in a god. But the god of Voltaire and most philosophes was a distant, deistic god, a great Clockmaker who built an orderly universe and then stepped aside and let it run. Finally, the philosophes hated all forms of religious intolerance. They believed that people had to be wary of dogmatic certainty and religious disputes, which often led to fanaticism and savage, inhuman action. Simple piety

Canal with Locks The articles on science and the industrial arts in the *Encyclopedia* carried lavish explanatory illustrations. This typical engraving from the section on water and its uses shows advances in canal building and reflects the encyclopedists' faith in technical progress. *(University of Illinois)*

and human kindness—the love of God and the golden rule—were religion enough, even Christianity enough, as Voltaire's interpretation of Christ suggests.

The ultimate strength of the philosophes lay, however, in their numbers, dedication, and organization. The philosophes felt keenly that they were engaged in a common undertaking that transcended individuals. Their greatest and most representative intellectual achievement was, quite fittingly, a group effort —the seventeen-volume *Encyclopedia: The Rational Dictionary of the Sciences, the Arts, and the Crafts,* edited by Denis Diderot (1713–1774) and Jean le Rond d'Alembert (1717–1783). Diderot and d'Alembert made a curious pair. Diderot began his career as a hack writer, first attracting attention with a skeptical tract on religion that was quickly burned by the judges of Paris. D'Alembert was one of Europe's leading scientists and mathematicians, the orphaned and illegitimate son of celebrated aristocrats. Moving in different circles and with different inter-

ests, the two men set out to find coauthors who would examine the rapidly expanding whole of human knowledge. Even more fundamentally, they set out to teach people how to think critically and objectively about all matters. As Diderot said, he wanted the *Encyclopedia* to "change the general way of thinking."[13]

The editors of the *Encyclopedia* had to conquer innumerable obstacles. After the appearance in 1751 of the first volume, which dealt with such controversial subjects as atheism, the soul, and blind people—all words beginning with *a* in French—the government temporarily banned publication. The pope later placed it on the Index and pronounced excommunication on all who read or bought it. The timid publisher mutilated some of the articles in the last ten volumes without the editors' consent in an attempt to appease the authorities. Yet Diderot's unwavering belief in the importance of his mission held the encyclopedists together for fifteen years, and the enormous work was completed in 1765. Hundreds of thousands of articles by leading scientists and famous

Sugar Cane Mill Enlightenment thinkers were keenly interested in non-European societies and in the comparative study of human development. This engraving depicts an aspect of sugar production with slave labor in the Americas. *(Courtesy of the University of Minnesota Libraries)*

writers, skilled workers and progressive priests, treated every aspect of life and knowledge.

Not every article was daring or original, but the overall effect was little short of revolutionary. Science and the industrial arts were exalted, religion and immortality questioned. Intolerance, legal injustice, and out-of-date social institutions were openly criticized. More generally, the writers of the *Encyclopedia* showed that human beings could use the process of reasoning to expand human knowledge. Encyclopedists were convinced that greater knowledge would result in greater human happiness, for knowledge was useful and made possible economic, social, and political progress. The *Encyclopedia* was widely read and extremely influential in France and the rest of western Europe as well. It summed up the new world-view of the Enlightenment.

THE LATER ENLIGHTENMENT

After about 1770, the harmonious unity of the philosophes and their thought began to break down. As the new world-view became increasingly accepted by the educated public, some thinkers sought originality by exaggerating certain ideas of the Enlightenment to the exclusion of others. These latter-day philosophes often built rigid, dogmatic systems.

In his *System of Nature* (1770) and other works, the wealthy, aristocratic baron Paul d'Holbach (1723–1789) argued that human beings were machines completely determined by outside forces. Free will, God, and immortality of the soul were foolish myths. D'Holbach's aggressive atheism and determinism, which were coupled with deep hostility toward Christianity and all other religions, dealt the unity of the Enlightenment movement a severe blow. *Deists* such as Voltaire, who believed in God but not in established churches, were repelled by the inflexible atheism they found in the *System of Nature*. They saw in it the same dogmatic intolerance they had been fighting all their lives.

D'Holbach published his philosophically radical works anonymously to avoid possible prosecution, and in his lifetime he was best known to the public as the generous patron and witty host of writers and intellectuals. At his twice-weekly dinner parties, an inner circle of regulars who knew the baron's secret exchanged ideas with aspiring philosophes and distinguished visitors. One of the most important was the Scottish philosopher David Hume (1711–1776), whose carefully argued skepticism had a powerful long-term influence.

Building on John Locke's teachings on learning (see page 656), Hume argued that the human mind is really nothing but a bundle of impressions. These impressions originate only in sense experiences and people's habit of joining these experiences together. Since ideas ultimately reflect only sense experiences, reason cannot explain the origin of the universe, the existence of God, or other phenomena that cannot be verified by sense experience (in the form of controlled experiments or mathematics). Paradoxically, Hume's rationalistic inquiry ended up undermining the Enlightenment's faith in the very power of reason itself.

Other thinkers and writers began to attack the Enlightenment's faith in reason, progress, and moderation. The most famous of these was the Swiss Jean-Jacques Rousseau (1712–1778), a brilliant but difficult thinker, an appealing but neurotic individual. Born into a poor family of watchmakers in Geneva, Rousseau went to Paris and was greatly influenced by Diderot and Voltaire. Always extraordinarily sensitive and suspicious, Rousseau came to believe his philosophe friends were plotting against him. In the mid-1750s he broke with them personally and intellectually, living thereafter as a lonely outsider with his uneducated common-law wife and going in his own highly original direction.

Like other Enlightenment thinkers, Rousseau was passionately committed to individual freedom. Unlike them, however, he attacked rationalism and civilization as destroying rather than liberating the individual. Warm, spontaneous feeling had to complement and correct the cold intellect. Moreover, the individual's basic goodness had to be protected from the cruel refinements of civilization. These ideas greatly influenced the early romantic movement (see Chapter 27), which rebelled against the culture of the Enlightenment in the late eighteenth century.

Applying his heartfelt ideas to children, Rousseau had a powerful impact on the development of modern education. In his famous treatise *Emile* (1762), he argued that education must shield the naturally unspoiled child from the corrupting influences of civilization and too many books. According to Rousseau, children must develop naturally and spontaneously, at their own speed and in their own way. It is eloquent testimony to Rousseau's troubled life and complicated personality that he placed all five of his own children in orphanages.

Rousseau also made an important contribution to political theory in the *Social Contract* (1762). His fundamental ideas were the general will and popular sovereignty. According to Rousseau, the general will is sacred and absolute, reflecting the common interests of the people, who have displaced the monarch as the holder of the sovereign power. The general will is not necessarily the will of the majority, however, although minorities have to subordinate themselves to it without question. Little noticed before the French Revolution, Rousseau's concept of the general will appealed greatly to democrats and nationalists after 1789. The concept has also been used since 1789 by many dictators, who have claimed that they, rather than some momentary majority of the voters, represent the general will and thus the true interests of democracy and the sovereign masses.

THE SOCIAL SETTING OF THE ENLIGHTENMENT

The philosophes were splendid talkers as well as effective writers. Indeed, sparkling conversation in private homes spread Enlightenment ideas to Europe's upper middle class and aristocracy. Paris set the example, and other French cities and European capitals followed. In Paris a number of talented and often rich women presided over regular social gatherings of the great and near-great in their elegant drawing rooms, or *salons*. There a d'Alembert and a Fontenelle could exchange witty, uncensored observations on literature, science, and philosophy with great aristocrats, wealthy middle-class financiers, high-ranking officials, and noteworthy foreigners. These intellectual

Madame Geoffrin's Salon In this stylized group portrait a famous actor reads to a gathering of leading philosophes and aristocrats in 1755. Third from the right presiding over her gathering, is Madame Geoffrin, next to the sleepy ninety-eight-year-old Bernard de Fontenelle. *(Malmaison Chateau/Giraudon/Art Resource)*

salons practiced the equality the philosophes preached. They were open to all men and women with good manners, provided only that they were famous or talented, rich or important. More generally, the philosophes championed greater rights and expanded education for women, arguing that the subordination of females was an unreasonable prejudice and the sign of a barbaric society.

One of the most famous salons was that of Madame Geoffrin, the unofficial godmother of the *Encyclopedia.* Having lost her parents at an early age, the future Madame Geoffrin was married at fifteen by her well-meaning grandmother to a rich and boring businessman of forty-eight. It was the classic marriage of convenience—the poor young girl and the rich old man—and neither side ever pretended that love was a consideration. After dutifully raising her children, Madame Geoffrin sought to break out of her gilded cage as she entered middle age. The very proper businessman's wife became friendly with a neighbor, the marquise de Tencin. In her youth this aristocratic beauty had been rather infamous as the mistress of the regent of France, but she had settled down to run a salon that counted Fontenelle and the philosopher Montesquieu among its regular guests.

When the marquise died in 1749, Madame Geoffrin tactfully transferred these luminaries to her spacious mansion for regular dinners. At first Madame

Geoffrin's husband loudly protested the arrival of this horde of "parasites." But his wife's will was much stronger than his, and he soon opened his purse and even appeared at the twice-weekly dinners. "Who was that old man at the end of the table who never said anything?" an innocent newcomer asked one evening. "That," replied Madame Geoffrin without emotion, "was my husband. He's dead."[14]

When Monsieur Geoffrin's death became official, Madame Geoffrin put the large fortune and a spacious mansion she inherited to good use. She welcomed the encyclopedists—Diderot, d'Alembert, Fontenelle, and a host of others. She gave them generous financial aid and helped to save their enterprise from collapse, especially after the first eight volumes were burned by the authorities in 1759. She also corresponded with the king of Sweden and Catherine the Great of Russia. Madame Geoffrin was, however, her own woman. She remained a practicing Christian and would not tolerate attacks on the church in her house. It was said that distinguished foreigners felt they had not seen Paris unless they had been invited to one of her dinners. The plain and long-neglected Madame Geoffrin managed to become the most renowned hostess of the eighteenth century.

There were many other hostesses, but Madame Geoffrin's greatest rival, Madame du Deffand, was one of the most interesting. While Madame Geoffrin was middle class, pious, and chaste, Madame du Deffand was a skeptic from the nobility, who lived fast and easy, at least in the early years. Another difference was that women—mostly highly intelligent, worldly members of the nobility—were fully the equal of men in Madame du Deffand's intellectual salon. Forever pursuing fulfillment in love and life, Madame du Deffand was an accomplished and liberated woman. An exceptionally fine letter writer, she carried on a vast correspondence with leading men and women all across Europe. Voltaire was her most enduring friend.

Madame du Deffand's closest female friend was Julie de Lespinasse, a beautiful, talented young woman whom she befriended and made her protégée. The never-acknowledged illegitimate daughter of noble parents, de Lespinasse had a hard youth, but she flowered in Madame du Deffand's drawing room —so much so that she was eventually dismissed by her jealous patroness.

Once again de Lespinasse triumphed. Her friends gave her money so that she could form her own salon.

Her highly informal gatherings—she was not rich enough to supply more than tea and cake—attracted the keenest minds in France and Europe. As one philosophe wrote:

She could unite the different types, even the most antagonistic, sustaining the conversation by a well-aimed phrase, animating and guiding it at will. . . . Politics, religion, philosophy, news: nothing was excluded. Her circle met daily from five to nine. There one found men of all ranks in the State, the Church, and the Court, soldiers and foreigners, and the leading writers of the day.[15]

Thus in France the ideas of the Enlightenment thrived in a social setting that graciously united members of the intellectual, economic, and social elites. Never before and never again would intellectual and social life be so closely and so pleasantly joined. In such an atmosphere, the philosophes, the French nobility, and the upper middle class increasingly influenced one another. Critical thinking became fashionable and flourished alongside hopes for human progress through greater knowledge.

THE EVOLUTION OF ABSOLUTISM

How did the Enlightenment influence political developments? To this important question there is no easy answer. On the one hand, the philosophes were primarily interested in converting people to critical "scientific" thinking and were not particularly concerned with politics. On the other hand, such thinking naturally led to political criticism and interest in political reform. Educated people, who belonged mainly to the nobility and middle class, came to regard political change as both possible and desirable. A further problem is that Enlightenment thinkers had different views on politics. Some, led by the nobleman Montesquieu, argued for curbs on monarchial power in order to promote liberty, and some French judges applied such theories in practical questions.

Until the American Revolution, however, most Enlightenment thinkers believed that political change could best come from above—from the ruler —rather than from below, especially in central and eastern Europe. There were several reasons for this essentially moderate belief. First, royal absolutism was a fact of life, and the kings and queens of Europe's leading states clearly had no intention of giving up their great powers. Therefore the philosophes realistically concluded that a benevolent absolutism offered the best opportunities for improving society. Critical thinking was turning the art of good government into an exact science. It was necessary only to educate and "enlighten" the monarch, who could then make good laws and promote human happiness. Second, philosophes turned toward rulers because rulers seemed to be listening, treating them with respect, and seeking their advice. Finally, although the philosophes did not dwell on this fact, they distrusted the masses. Known simply as "the people" in the eighteenth century, the peasant masses and the urban poor were, according to the philosophes, still enchained by religious superstitions and violent passions. No doubt the people were maturing, but they were still children in need of firm parental guidance.

Encouraged and instructed by the philosophes, several absolutist rulers of the later eighteenth century tried to govern in an "enlightened" manner. Yet, because European monarchs had long been locked in an intense international competition, a more enlightened state often meant in practice a more effective state, a state capable of expanding its territory and defeating its enemies. Moreover, reforms from above had to be grafted onto previous historical developments and existing social structures. Little wonder, then, that the actual programs and accomplishments of these rulers varied greatly. It is important, therefore, to examine the evolution of monarchial absolutism at close range before trying to form any overall judgment regarding the meaning of what historians have often called the "enlightened absolutism" of the later eighteenth century.

THE "GREATS": FREDERICK OF PRUSSIA AND CATHERINE OF RUSSIA

Just as the French culture and absolutism of Louis XIV provided models for European rulers in the late seventeenth century, the Enlightenment teachings of the French philosophes inspired European monarchs in the second half of the eighteenth century. French was the international language of the educated classes, and the education of future kings and queens across Europe lay in the hands of French tutors espousing Enlightenment ideas. France's cultural leadership was reinforced by the fact that it was still the wealthiest and most populous country in Europe. Thus, absolutist monarchs in several west German and Italian states, as well as in Spain and Portugal, proclaimed themselves more enlightened. By far the most influential of the new-style monarchs were Frederick II of Prussia and Catherine II of Russia, both styled "the Great."

FREDERICK THE GREAT. Frederick II (1740–1786), also known as "Frederick the Great," built masterfully on his father's work. This was somewhat surprising for, like many children with tyrannical parents, he rebelled against his family's wishes in his early years. Rejecting the crude life of the barracks, Frederick embraced culture and literature, even writing poetry and fine prose in French, a language his father detested. He threw off his father's dour Calvinism and dabbled with atheism. After trying unsuccessfully to run away at age eighteen in 1730, he was virtually imprisoned and even compelled to watch his companion in flight beheaded at his father's command. Yet, like many other rebellious youths, Frederick eventually reached a reconciliation with his father, and by the time he came to the throne ten years later he was determined to use the splendid army his father had left him.

When, therefore, the emperor of Austria, Charles VI, also died in 1740 and his young and beautiful daughter, Maria Theresa, became ruler of the Habsburg dominions, Frederick suddenly and without warning invaded her rich, all-German province of Silesia. This action defied solemn Prussian promises to respect the Pragmatic Sanction, which guaranteed Maria Theresa's succession, but no matter. For Frederick, it was the opportunity of a lifetime to expand the size and power of Prussia. Although Maria Theresa succeeded in dramatically rallying the normally quarrelsome Hungarian nobility, her multinational army was no match for Prussian precision. In 1742, as other greedy powers were falling on her lands in the general European War of the Austrian Succession (1740–1748), she was forced to cede all of Silesia to Prussia. In one stroke, Prussia doubled its population to 6 million people. Now Prussia unquestionably towered above all the other German states and stood as a European great power.

Successful in 1742, Frederick had to spend much of his reign fighting against great odds to save Prussia from total destruction. Maria Theresa was deter-

Frederick the Great of Prussia Embracing the elegant, intellectual, and international culture of the Enlightenment, Frederick II was also a composer and accomplished musician. This painting shows Frederick playing the flute for family and friends with a chamber orchestra at his favorite retreat, the palace he called *Sans Souci* ("Free from Care"). *(The Mansell Collection)*

mined to regain Silesia, and when the ongoing competition between Britain and France for colonial empire brought renewed conflict in 1756, her able chief minister fashioned an aggressive alliance with France and Russia. The aim of the alliance was to conquer Prussia and divide up its territory, just as Frederick II and other monarchs had so recently sought to partition the Austrian Empire. Frederick led his army brilliantly, striking repeatedly at vastly superior forces invading from all sides. At times he believed all was lost, but he fought on with stoic courage. In the end, he was miraculously saved: Peter III came to the Russian throne in 1762 and called off the attack against Frederick, whom he greatly admired. The Seven Years' War (1756–1763) was over.

In the early years of his reign, Frederick II had kept his enthusiasm for Enlightenment culture strictly separated from a brutal concept of international politics. He wrote:

Of all States, from the smallest to the biggest, one can safely say that the fundamental rule of government is the principle of extending their territories. . . . The passions of rulers have no other curb but the limits of their power. Those are the fixed laws of European politics to which every politician submits.[16]

But the terrible struggle of the Seven Years' War tempered Frederick and brought him to consider how more humane policies for his subjects might also strengthen the state.

Thus Frederick went beyond a superficial commitment to Enlightenment culture for himself and his circle. He tolerantly allowed his subjects to believe as they wished in religious and philosophical matters. He promoted the advancement of knowledge, improving his country's schools and universities.

Second, Frederick tried to improve the lives of his subjects more directly. As he wrote his friend Voltaire, "I must enlighten my people, cultivate their manners and morals, and make them as happy as human beings can be, or as happy as the means at my disposal permit." The legal system and the bureaucracy were Frederick's primary tools. Prussia's laws were simplified, and judges decided cases quickly and impartially. Prussian officials became famous for their hard work and honesty. After the Seven Years' War ended in 1763, Frederick's government also energetically promoted the reconstruction of agriculture and industry in his war-torn country. In all this Frederick set a good example. He worked hard and lived modestly, claiming that he was "only the first servant of the state." Thus Frederick justified monarchy in terms of practical results and said nothing of the divine right of kings.

Frederick's dedication to high-minded principles went only so far, however. He never tried to change Prussia's existing social structure. True, he condemned serfdom in the abstract, but he accepted it in practice and did not even free the serfs on his own estates. He accepted and extended the privileges of the nobility, which he saw as his primary ally in the defense and extension of his realm. It became practically impossible for a middle-class person to gain a top position in the government. The Junker nobility remained the backbone of the army and the entire Prussian state.

CATHERINE THE GREAT. Catherine the Great of Russia (1762–1796) was one of the most remarkable rulers who ever lived, and the philosophes adored her. Catherine was a German princess from Anhalt-Zerbst, a totally insignificant principality sandwiched between Prussia and Saxony. Her father commanded a regiment of the Prussian army, but her mother was related to the Romanovs of Russia, and that proved to be her chance.

Peter the Great had abolished the hereditary succession of tsars so that he could name his successor and thus preserve his policies. This move opened a period of palace intrigue and a rapid turnover of rulers until Peter's youngest daughter Elizabeth came to the Russian throne in 1741. A crude, shrewd woman noted for her hard drinking and hard loving —one of her official lovers was an illiterate shepherd boy—Elizabeth named her nephew Peter heir to the throne and chose Catherine to be his wife in 1744. It was a mismatch from the beginning. The fifteen-year-old Catherine was intelligent and attractive; her husband was stupid and ugly, his face badly scarred by smallpox. Ignored by her childish husband, Catherine carefully studied Russian, endlessly read writers like Bayle and Voltaire, and made friends at court. Soon she knew what she wanted. "I did not care about Peter," she wrote in her *Memoirs,* "but I did care about the crown."[17]

As the old empress Elizabeth approached death, Catherine plotted against her unpopular husband. A dynamic, sensuous woman, Catherine used her sexuality to good political advantage. She selected as her new lover a tall, dashing young officer named Gregory Orlov, who with his four officer brothers commanded considerable support among the soldiers stationed in St. Petersburg. When Peter came to the throne in 1762, his decision to withdraw Russian troops from the coalition against Prussia alienated the army. Nor did Peter III's attempt to gain support from the Russian nobility by freeing it from compulsory state service succeed. At the end of six months, Catherine and the military conspirators deposed Peter III in a palace revolution. Then the Orlov brothers murdered him. The German princess became empress of Russia.

Catherine had drunk deeply at the Enlightenment well. Never questioning the common assumption that absolute monarchy was the best form of government, she set out to rule in an enlightened manner. One of her most enduring goals was to bring the sophisticated culture of western Europe to backward Russia. To do so, she imported Western architects, sculptors, musicians, and intellectuals. She bought masterpieces of Western art in wholesale lots and patronized the philosophes. An enthusiastic letter writer, she corresponded extensively with Voltaire and praised him as the "champion of the human race." When the French government banned the *Encyclopedia,* she offered to publish it in St. Petersburg. She discussed reform with Diderot in St. Petersburg; and when Diderot needed money, she purchased his library for a small fortune but allowed him to keep it during his lifetime. With these and countless similar

Catherine the Great Intelligent, pleasure-loving, and vain, Catherine succeeded in bringing Russia closer to western Europe than ever before. *(Freeman & Co., London)*

actions, Catherine skillfully won a good press for herself and for her country in the west. Moreover, this intellectual ruler, who wrote plays and loved good talk, set the tone for the entire Russian nobility. Peter the Great westernized Russian armies, but it was Catherine who westernized the thinking of the Russian nobility.

Catherine's second goal was domestic reform, and she began her reign with sincere and ambitious projects. Better laws were a major concern. In 1767 she drew up enlightened instructions for the special legislative commission she appointed to prepare a new law code. No new unified code was ever produced, but Catherine did restrict the practice of torture and allowed limited religious toleration. She also tried to improve education and strengthen local government. The philosophes applauded these measures and hoped more would follow.

Such was not the case. In 1773 a simple Cossack soldier named Emelian Pugachev sparked a gigantic uprising of serfs, very much as Stenka Razin had done a century earlier (see page 631). Proclaiming himself the true tsar, Pugachev issued "decrees" abolishing serfdom, taxes, and army service. Thousands joined his cause, slaughtering landlords and officials over a vast area of southwestern Russia. Pugachev's untrained hordes eventually proved no match for Catherine's noble-led regular army. Betrayed by his own company, Pugachev was captured and savagely executed.

Pugachev's rebellion was a decisive turning point in Catherine's domestic policy. On coming to the throne she had condemned serfdom in theory, but she was smart enough to realize that any changes would have to be very gradual or else she would quickly follow her departed husband. Pugachev's rebellion put an end to any illusions she might have had about reforming serfdom. The peasants were clearly dangerous, and her empire rested on the support of the nobility. After 1775 Catherine gave the nobles absolute control of their serfs. She extended serfdom into new areas, such as the Ukraine. In 1785 she formalized the nobility's privileged position, freeing its members forever from taxes and state service. She also confiscated the lands of the Russian Orthodox church and gave them to favorite officials. Under Catherine, the Russian nobility attained its most exalted position, and serfdom entered its most oppressive phase.

Catherine's third goal was territorial expansion, and in this respect she was extremely successful. Her armies subjugated the last descendants of the Mongols, the Crimean Tartars, and began the conquest of the Caucasus.

Her greatest coup by far was the partitioning of Poland. Poland showed the dangers of failing to build a strong absolutist state. For decades all important decisions had required the unanimous agreement of every Polish noble, which meant that nothing could ever be done. When between 1768 and 1772 Catherine's armies scored unprecedented victories against the Turks and thereby threatened to disturb the balance of power between Russia and Austria in eastern Europe, Frederick of Prussia obligingly came forward with a deal. He proposed that Turkey be let off easily, and that Prussia, Austria, and Russia each compensate itself by taking a gigantic slice of Polish territory. Catherine jumped at the chance. The first partition of Poland took place in 1772. Two more partitions, in

1793 and 1795, gave all three powers more Polish territory, and the kingdom of Poland simply vanished from the map (Map 21.1).

Expansion helped Catherine keep the nobility happy, for it provided her vast new lands to give to her faithful servants. Expansion also helped Catherine reward her lovers, of whom twenty-one have been definitely identified. On all these royal favorites she lavished large estates with many serfs, as if to make sure there were no hard feelings when her interest cooled. Until the end this remarkably talented woman—who always believed that, in spite of her domestic setbacks, she was slowly civilizing Russia—kept her zest for life. Fascinated by a new twenty-two-year-old flame when she was a roly-poly grandmother in her sixties, she happily reported her good fortune to a favorite former lover: "I have come back to life like a frozen fly; I am gay and well."[18]

ABSOLUTISM IN FRANCE AND AUSTRIA

The Enlightenment's influence on political developments in France and Austria was complex. In France, the monarchy maintained its absolutist claims, and some philosophes like Voltaire believed that the king was still the best source of needed reform. At the same time, discontented nobles and learned judges drew on thinkers such as Montesquieu for liberal arguments, and they sought with some success to limit the king's power. In Austria, two talented rulers did manage to introduce major reforms, although traditional power politics were more important than Enlightenment teachings.

LOUIS XV OF FRANCE. In building French absolutism, Louis XIV successfully drew on the middle class to curb the political power of the nobility. As long as the Grand Monarch lived, the nobility could only grumble and, like the duke of Saint-Simon in his *Memoirs,* scornfully lament the rise of "the vile bourgeoisie." But when Louis XIV finally died in 1715, to be succeeded by his five-year-old great-grandson, Louis XV (1715–1774), the Sun King's elaborate system of absolutist rule was challenged in a general reaction. Favored by the duke of Orléans, who governed as regent until 1723, the nobility made a strong comeback.

Most importantly, the duke restored to the high court of Paris—the Parlement—the right to "regis-

MAP 21.1 The Partition of Poland and Russia's Expansion, 1772–1795 Though all three of the great eastern absolutist states profited from the division of large but weak Poland, Catherine's Russia gained the most.

ter" and thereby approve the king's decrees. This was a fateful step. The judges of the Parlement of Paris had originally come from the middle class, and their high position reflected the way that Louis XIV (and earlier French monarchs) had chosen to use that class to build the royal bureaucracy so necessary for an absolutist state. By the eighteenth century, however, these "middle-class" judges had risen to become hereditary nobles for, although Louis XIV had curbed the political power of the nobility, he had never challenged its enormous social prestige. Thus, high position in the government continued to bestow the noble status that middle-class officials wanted, either immediately or after three generations of continuous service. The judges of Paris, like many high-ranking officials, actually owned their government jobs and freely passed them on as private property from father to son. By supporting the claim of this well-entrenched and increasingly aristocratic group to register the king's laws, the duke of Orléans sanctioned a counterweight to absolute power.

These implications became clear when the heavy expenses of the War of the Austrian Succession plunged France into financial crisis. In 1748 Louis XV appointed a finance minister who decreed a 5 percent income tax on every individual, regardless of social status. Exemption from most taxation had long been a hallowed privilege of the nobility, and other important groups—the clergy, the large towns, and some wealthy bourgeoisie—had also gained special tax advantages over time. The result was a vigorous protest from many sides, and the Parlement of Paris refused to ratify the tax law. The monarchy retreated; the new tax was dropped.

Following the disastrously expensive Seven Years' War, the conflict re-emerged. The government tried to maintain emergency taxes after the war ended. The Parlement of Paris protested and even challenged the basis of royal authority, claiming that the king's power must necessarily be limited to protect liberty. Once again the government caved in and withdrew the wartime taxes in 1764. Emboldened by its striking victory and widespread support from France's educated elite, the judicial opposition in Paris and the provinces pressed its demands. In a barrage of pamphlets and legal briefs, it asserted that the king could not levy taxes without the consent of the Parlement of Paris acting as the representative of the entire nation.

Indolent and sensual by nature, more interested in his many mistresses than in affairs of state, Louis XV finally roused himself for a determined defense of his absolutist inheritance. "The magistrates," he angrily told the Parlement of Paris in a famous face-to-face confrontation, "are my officers.... In my person only does the sovereign power rest."[19] In 1768 Louis appointed a tough career official named René de Maupeou as chancellor and ordered him to crush the judicial opposition.

Maupeou abolished the Parlement of Paris and exiled its members to isolated backwaters in the provinces. He created a new and docile parlement of royal officials, and he began once again to tax the privileged groups. A few philosophes like Voltaire applauded these measures: the sovereign was using his power to introduce badly needed reforms that had been blocked by a self-serving aristocratic elite. Most philosophes and educated public opinion as a whole sided with the old Parlement, however, and there was widespread dissatisfaction with royal despotism. Yet the monarchy's power was still great enough for Maupeou to simply ride over the opposition, and Louis XV would probably have prevailed—if he had lived to a very ripe old age.

But Louis XV died in 1774. The new king, Louis XVI (1774–1792), was a shy twenty-year-old with good intentions. Taking the throne, he is reported to have said: "What I should like most is to be loved."[20] The eager-to-please monarch decided to yield in the face of such strong criticism from so much of France's elite. He dismissed Maupeou and repudiated the strong-willed minister's work. The old Parlement of Paris was reinstated, as enlightened public opinion cheered and hoped for moves toward representative government. Such moves were not forthcoming. Instead, a weakened but unrepentant monarchy faced a judicial opposition that claimed to speak for the entire French nation. Increasingly locked in stalemate, the country was drifting toward renewed financial crisis and prolonged political upheaval.

THE AUSTRIAN HABSBURGS. Joseph II (1780–1790) was a fascinating individual. For an earlier generation of historians he was the "revolutionary emperor," a tragic hero whose lofty reforms were undone by the landowning nobility he dared to challenge. More recent scholarship has revised this romantic interpretation and stressed how Joseph II continued the state-building work of his mother, the empress Maria Theresa, a remarkable but old-fashioned absolutist.

Maria Theresa's long reign (1740–1780) began with her neighbors, led by Frederick II of Prussia, invading her lands and trying to dismember them (see page 664). Emerging from the long War of the Austrian Succession in 1748 with only the serious loss of Silesia, Maria Theresa and her closest ministers were determined to introduce reforms that would make the state stronger and more efficient. Three aspects were most important in these reforms. First, Maria Theresa introduced measures to bring relations between church and state under government control. Like some medieval rulers, the most devout and very Catholic Maria Theresa aimed at limiting the papacy's political influence in her realm. Second, a whole series of administrative reforms strengthened the central bureaucracy, smoothed out some provincial differences, and revamped the tax system, taxing even the lands of nobles without special exemptions. Finally, the government sought to improve the lot of the agricultural population, cautiously reducing the power of lords over both their hereditary serfs and partially free peasant tenants.

Coregent with his mother from 1765 onward and a strong supporter of change, Joseph II moved forward rapidly when he came to the throne in 1780. He controlled the established Catholic church even more closely, in an attempt to ensure that it produced better citizens. He granted religious toleration and civic rights to Protestants and Jews—a radical innovation that impressed his contemporaries. In even more spectacular peasant reforms, Joseph abolished serfdom in 1781, and in 1789 he decreed that all peasant labor obligations be converted into cash payments. This ill-conceived measure was violently rejected not only by the nobility but by the peasants it was intended to help, since their primitive barter economy was woefully lacking in money. When a disillusioned Joseph died prematurely at forty-nine, the entire Habsburg empire was in turmoil. His brother

Maria Theresa and her husband pose with eleven of their sixteen children at Schön-brunn palace. Joseph, the heir to the throne, stands at the center of the star pattern. Wealthy women often had very large families, in part because they seldom nursed their babies as poor women usually did. *(Kunsthistorisches Museum, Vienna)*

Leopold (1790–1792) was forced to cancel Joseph's radical edicts in order to re-establish order. Peasants lost most of their recent gains, and once again they were required to do forced labor for their lords, as in the 1770s under Maria Theresa.

An Overall Evaluation

Having examined the evolution of monarchial absolutism in four leading states, it is possible to look for meaningful generalizations and evaluate the overall

THE ENLIGHTENMENT

1686	Fontenelle, *Conversations on the Plurality of Worlds*
1687	Newton, *Principia*
1690	Locke, "Essay Concerning Human Understanding" and "Second Treatise on Civil Government"
1697	Bayle, *Historical and Critical Dictionary*
1715–1774	Rule of Louis XV in France
1721	Montesquieu, *The Persian Letters*
1740–1748	War of the Austrian Succession
1740–1780	Rule of Maria Theresa in Austria
1740–1786	Rule of Frederick II (the Great) in Prussia
1742	Austria cedes Silesia to Prussia
1743	Voltaire, *Age of Louis XIV*
1748	Montesquieu, *The Spirit of the Laws*
	Hume, *An Enquiry Concerning Human Understanding*
1751–1765	Publication of the *Encyclopedia,* edited by Diderot and d'Alembert
1756–1763	Seven Years' War
1762	Rousseau, *Social Contract*
1762–1796	Rule of Catherine II (the Great) in Russia
1767	Catherine the Great appoints commission to prepare a new law code
1770	D'Holbach, *The System of Nature*
1771	Maupeou, Louis XV's chancellor, abolishes Parlement of Paris
1772	First partition of Poland among Russia, Prussia, and Austria
1774	Ascension of Louis XVI in France; restoration of Parlement of Paris
1780–1790	Rule of Joseph II in Austria
1781	Abolition of serfdom in Austria
1785	Catherine the Great issues the Russian Charter of Nobility, which frees the nobles from taxes and state service
1790–1792	Rule of Leopold II in Austria; serfdom is re-established
1793	Second partition of Poland
1795	Third partition of Poland, which completes its absorption

influence of Enlightenment thought on politics. That thought, it will be remembered, was clustered in two distinct schools: the liberal critique of unregulated monarchy promoted by Montesquieu and the defenders of royal absolutism led by Voltaire.

It is clear that France diverged from its eastern neighbors in its political development in the eighteenth century. Thus, while neither the French monarchy nor the eastern rulers abandoned the absolutist claims and institutions they had inherited, the monarch's capacity to govern in a truly absolutist manner declined substantially in France, which was not the case in eastern Europe. The immediate cause of this divergence was the political resurgence of the French nobility after 1715 and the growth of judicial opposition, led by the Parlement of Paris. More fundamentally, however, the judicial and aristocratic opposition in France achieved its still rather modest successes because it received major support from educated public opinion, which increasingly made the liberal critique of unregulated royal authority its own. In France, then, the proponents of absolute monarchy were increasingly on the defense, as was the French monarchy itself.

The situation in eastern Europe was different. The liberal critique of absolute monarchy remained an intellectual curiosity, and proponents of reform from above held sway. Moreover, despite their differences, the leading eastern monarchs of the later eighteenth century all claimed that they were acting on the principles of the Enlightenment. The philosophes generally agreed with this assessment and cheered them on. Beginning in the mid-nineteenth century, historians developed the idea of a common "enlightened despotism" or "enlightened absolutism," and they canonized Frederick, Catherine, and Joseph as its most outstanding examples. More recent research has raised doubts about this old interpretation and has led to a fundamental re-evaluation.

First, there is general agreement that these absolutists, especially Frederick and Catherine, did encourage and spread the cultural values of the Enlightenment. Perhaps this was their greatest achievement. Skeptical in religion and intensely secular in basic orientation, they unabashedly accepted the here and now and sought their happiness in the enjoyment of it. At the same time, they were proud of their intellectual accomplishments and good taste, and they supported knowledge, education, and the arts. No wonder the philosophes felt the monarchs were kindred spirits.

Historians also agree that the absolutists believed in change from above and tried to enact needed reforms. Yet the results of these efforts brought only very modest improvements, and the life of the peasantry remained very hard in the eighteenth century. Thus some historians have concluded that these monarchs were not really sincere in their reform efforts. Others disagree, arguing that powerful nobilities determined to maintain their privileges blocked the absolutists' genuine commitment to reform. (The old interpretation of Joseph II as the tragic revolutionary emperor forms part of this argument.)

The emerging answer to this confusion is that the later eastern absolutists were indeed committed to reform, but that humanitarian objectives were of quite secondary importance. Above all, the absolutists wanted reforms that would strengthen the state and allow them to compete militarily with their neighbors. Modern scholarship has stressed, therefore, how Frederick, Catherine, and Joseph were in many ways simply continuing the state building of their predecessors, reorganizing their armies and expanding their bureaucracies to raise more taxes and troops. The reason for this continuation was simple. The international political struggle was brutal, and the stakes were high. First Austria under Maria Theresa, and then Prussia under Frederick the Great, had to engage in bitter fighting to escape dismemberment, while decentralized Poland was coldly divided and eventually liquidated.

Yet, in their drive for more state power, the later absolutists were also innovators, and the idea of an era of enlightened absolutism retains a certain validity. Sharing the Enlightenment faith in critical thinking and believing that knowledge meant power, these absolutists really were more enlightened because they put their state-building reforms in a new, broader perspective. Above all, they considered how more humane laws and practices could help their populations become more productive and satisfied, and thus able to contribute more substantially to the welfare of the state. It was from this perspective that they introduced many of their most progressive reforms, tolerating religious minorities, simplifying legal codes, and promoting practical education.

The primacy of state as opposed to individual interests—a concept foreign to North Americans long accustomed to easy dominion over a vast continent —also helps to explain some puzzling variations in social policies. For example, Frederick the Great basically favored the status quo, limiting only the counterproductive excesses of his trusted nobility against its peasants. Catherine the Great took measures that worsened the peasants' condition because she looked increasingly to the nobility as her natural ally and sought to strengthen it. On the other hand, Joseph II believed that greater freedom for peasants was the means to strengthen his realm, and he acted accordingly. Each enlightened absolutist sought greater state power, but each believed a different policy would attain that end.

In conclusion, the eastern absolutists of the later eighteenth century combined old-fashioned state building with the culture and critical thinking of the Enlightenment. In doing so, they succeeded in expanding the role of the state in the life of society. Unlike the successors of Louis XIV, they perfected bureaucratic machines that were to prove surprisingly adaptive and capable of enduring into the twentieth century.

This chapter has focused on the complex development of a new world-view in Western civilization. This new view of the world was essentially critical and secular, drawing its inspiration from the scientific revolution and crystallizing in the Enlightenment.

The decisive breakthroughs in astronomy and physics in the sixteenth and seventeenth centuries, which demolished the imposing medieval synthesis of Aristotelian philosophy and Christian theology, had only limited practical consequences despite the expectations of scientific enthusiasts like Bacon. Yet the impact of new scientific knowledge on intellectual life became great. Interpreting scientific findings and Newtonian laws in an antitraditional, antireligious manner, the French philosophes of the Enlightenment extolled the superiority of rational, critical thinking. This new method, they believed, promised not just increased knowledge but even the discovery of the fundamental laws of human society. Although they reached different conclusions when they turned to social and political realities, the philosophes nevertheless succeeded in spreading their radically new world view. That was a momentous accomplishment.

NOTES

1. H. Butterfield, *The Origins of Modern Science* (New York: Macmillan, 1951), p. viii.
2. Quoted in A. G. R. Smith, *Science and Society in the Sixteenth and Seventeenth Centuries* (New York: Harcourt Brace Jovanovich, 1972), p. 97.
3. Quoted in Butterfield, *Origins of Modern Science,* p. 47.
4. Quoted in Smith, *Science and Society,* p.100.
5. Ibid., pp. 115–116.
6. Ibid., p. 120.
7. Quoted in A. R. Hall, *From Galileo to Newton, 1630–1720* (New York: Harper & Row, 1963), p. 290.
8. Quoted in P. Hazard, *The European Mind, 1680–1715* (Cleveland: Meridian Books, 1963), pp. 304–305.
9. Ibid., pp.11–12.
10. Quoted in L. M. Marsak, ed., *The Enlightenment* (New York: Wiley, 1972), p. 56.
11. Quoted in G. L. Mosse et al., eds., *Europe in Review* (Chicago: Rand McNally, 1964), p. 156.
12. F. M. Arouet de Voltaire, *Oeuvres complètes,* vol. 8 (Paris: Firmin-Didot Frères, Fils et Cie, 1875), pp. 188–190.
13. Quoted in P. Gay, "The Unity of the Enlightenment," *History* 3 (1960): 25.
14. Quoted in G. P. Gooch, *Catherine the Great and Other Studies* (Hamden, Conn: Archon Books, 1966), p. 112.
15. Ibid., p. 149.
16. Quoted in L. Krieger, *Kings and Philosophers, 1689–1789* (New York: Norton, 1970), p. 257.
17. Ibid., p. 15.
18. Ibid., p. 53.
19. Quoted in R. R. Palmer, *The Age of Democratic Revolution* (Princeton, N. J.: Princeton University Press, 1959), 1.95–1.96.
20. Quoted in G. Wright, *France in Modern Times* (Chicago: Rand McNally, 1960), p. 42.

SUGGESTED READING

The first three authors cited in the Notes—Butterfield, Smith, and Hall—have written excellent general interpretations of the scientific revolution. Another good study is M. Boas, *The Scientific Renaissance, 1450–1630* (1966), which is especially insightful on the influence of magic on science and on Galileo's trial. T. Kuhn, *The Copernican Revolution* (1957), is the best treatment of the subject; his *The Structure of Scientific Revolutions* (1962) is a challenging, much-discussed attempt to understand major breakthroughs in scientific thought over time. Two stimulating books on the ties between science and society in history are R. K. Merton, *Science, Technology and Society in Seventeenth-century England,* rev. ed. (1970), and J. Ben-David, *The Scientist's Role in Society* (1971). E. Andrade, *Sir Isaac Newton* (1958), is a good short biography, which may be compared with F. Manuel, *The Religion of Isaac Newton* (1974).

The work by Hazard cited in the Notes is a classic study of the formative years of Enlightenment thought, and his *European Thought in the Eighteenth Century* (1954) is also recommended. A famous, controversial interpretation of the Enlightenment is that of C. Becker, *The Heavenly City of the Eighteenth Century Philosophes* (1932), which maintains that the world-view of medieval Christianity continued to influence the philosophes greatly. Becker's ideas are discussed interestingly in R. O. Rockwood, ed., *Carl Becker's Heavenly City Revisited* (1958). P. Gay has written several major studies on the Enlightenment: *Voltaire's Politics* (1959) and *The Party of Humanity* (1971) are two of the best. I. Wade, *The Structure and Form of the French Enlightenment* (1977), is a recent major synthesis. F. Baumer's *Religion and the Rise of Skepticism* (1969), H. Payne's *The Philosophes and the People* (1976), K. Rogers's *Feminism in Eighteenth-century England* (1982), and J. B. Bury's old but still exciting *The Idea of Progress* (1932) are stimulating studies of important aspects of Enlightenment thought. Above all, one should read some of the philosophes and let them speak for themselves. Two good anthologies are C. Brinton, ed., *The Portable Age of Reason* (1956), and F. Manuel, ed., *The Enlightenment* (1951). Voltaire's most famous and very amusing novel *Candide* is highly recommended, as are S. Gendzier, ed., *Denis Diderot: The Encyclopedia: Selections* (1967), and A. Wilson, *Diderot* (1972).

The culture of the time may be approached through A. Cobban, ed., *The Eighteenth Century* (1969), a richly illustrated work with excellent essays, and C. B. Behrens, *The Ancien Régime* (1967). C. Rosen, *The Classical Style: Haydn, Mozart, Beethoven* (1972), brilliantly synthesizes music and society, as did Mozart himself in his great opera *The Marriage of Figaro,* where the count is the buffoon and his servant the hero.

In addition to the works mentioned in the Suggested Reading for Chapters 19 and 20, the monarchies of Europe are carefully analyzed in C. Tilly, ed., *The Formation of National States in Western Europe* (1975), and in J. Gagliardo, *Enlightened Despotism* (1967), both of which have useful bibliographies. M. Anderson, *Historians and Eighteenth-century Europe* (1979), is a valuable introduction to recent scholarship. Other recommended studies on the struggle for power and reform in different countries are F. Ford, *Robe and Sword* (1953), which discusses the resurgence of the French nobility after the death of Louis XIV; R. Herr, *The Eighteenth-century Revolution in Spain* (1958), on the impact of Enlightenment thought in Spain; and P. Bernard, *Joseph II* (1968). In addition to I. de Madariaga's masterful *Russia in the Age of Catherine the Great* (1981) and D. Ransel's solid *Politics of Catherinean Russia* (1975), the ambitious reader should look at A. N. Radishchev, *A Journey from St. Petersburg to Moscow* (trans. 1958), a famous 1790 attack on Russian serfdom and an appeal to Catherine the Great to free the serfs, for which Radishchev was exiled to Siberia.

22

THE LIFE OF THE PEOPLE IN EUROPE

*T*HE WORLD of absolutism and aristocracy, a combination of raw power and elegant refinement, was a world apart from that of ordinary men and women. Weakness and uncertainty, poverty and pain—these were enduring realities that weighed heavily on the vast majority. Yet the common people were by no means helpless victims of fate, ignorance, and inequality. With courage and cunning, with hard work and family loyalties, ordinary men and women struggled and survived. There is a human dignity in the efforts of these people that is deeply moving.

This, then, is the story of those ordinary lives at a time when the idea of far-reaching scientific and material progress was only a sweet dream of a privileged elite in fashionable salons. How did the common people wring a living out of the land, still by far the most important source of employment? How with accumulated wisdom did they manage such basic things as marriage and children, food and diet, health and religion? How did everyday patterns change as new trends and developments appeared? How, in short, did the peasant masses and the urban poor really live before the age of revolution began at the end of the eighteenth century? This is the simple but profound question this chapter will seek to answer.

AGRICULTURE AND POPULATION

At the end of the seventeenth century, at least 80 percent of the people of all western European countries, with the possible exception of Holland, drew their livelihood from agriculture. In eastern Europe the percentage was considerably higher. Men and women lavished their attention on the land, and the land repaid their efforts, yielding up the food and most of the raw materials for industry that made life possible. Yet the land was stingy and capricious. Yields were low even in good years, and finding enough to eat was an endless challenge. If there were too many mouths to feed some would go hungry, or simply die from starvation or disease when harvests were bad or failed completely. As a result, peasant communities had generally learned to keep family size under control. If total population was to grow modestly, as it did in the eighteenth century, people had to find new sources of food and income.

The greatest accomplishment of medieval agriculture was the open-field system of village agriculture developed by European peasants (see page 362). That system divided the land to be cultivated by the peasants into a few large fields, which were in turn cut up into long narrow strips. The fields were open, and the strips were not enclosed into small plots by fences or hedges. An individual peasant family—if it was fortunate—held a number of strips scattered throughout the large fields. The land of those who owned but did not till, primarily the nobility, the clergy, and wealthy townsmen, was also in scattered strips. The peasants farmed each large field as a community, with each family following the same pattern of plowing, sowing, and harvesting in accordance with tradition and the village leaders.

The ever-present problem was exhaustion of soil. If the community planted wheat year after year in a field, the nitrogen in the soil was soon depleted. Crop failure and starvation were certain. Since the supply of manure for fertilizer was limited, the only way for the land to recover its life-giving fertility was for a field to lie fallow for a period of time. In the early Middle Ages, a year of fallow was alternated with a year of cropping, so that half the land stood idle in a given year. With time, three-year rotations were introduced, especially on more fertile lands. This system permitted a year of wheat or rye followed by a year of oats or beans or peas, and only then a year of fallow. Even so, results were modest. In a rich agricultural region like the Po Valley in northern Italy, every bushel of wheat sown yielded on average only five or six bushels of grain at harvest during the seventeenth century. The average French yield in the same period was somewhat less. Such yields were no more than those attained in fertile, well-watered areas in the thirteenth century or in ancient Greece. By modern standards, output in 1700 was distressingly low. (Today an American or French farmer with similar land can expect roughly fifty bushels of wheat for each bushel of wheat sown.) Only awareness of the tragic consequences of continuous cropping forced undernourished populations to let a third of their land lie constantly idle.

Traditional rights reinforced the traditional pattern of farming. In addition to rotating the field crops in a uniform way, villages held open meadows in common to provide animals with hay and natural

Farming the Land Agricultural methods in Europe changed very slowly from the Middle Ages to the early eighteenth century. This realistic picture from Diderot's *Encyclopedia* has striking similarities with agricultural scenes found in medieval manuscripts. *(University of Illinois)*

pasture. After the harvest, the people of the village also pastured their animals on the wheat or rye stubble. In many places such pasturing followed a brief period, also established by tradition, for the gleaning of grain. Poor women would go through the fields picking up the few single grains that had fallen to the ground in the course of the harvest. The subject of a great nineteenth-century painting, *The Gleaners* by Jean François Millet, this backbreaking labor by hard-working but impoverished women meant quite literally the slender margin of survival for some people in the winter months.

In the age of absolutism and nobility, state and landlord continued to levy heavy taxes and high rents as a matter of course. In so doing they stripped the peasants of much of their meager earnings. The level of exploitation varied. Conditions for the rural population were very different in different areas.

Millet: The Gleaners Poor French peasant women search for grains and stalks the harvesters (in the background) have missed. The open-field system seen here could still be found in parts of Europe in 1857, when this picture was painted. Millet is known for his great paintings expressing social themes. *(Cliché des Musées Nationaux, Paris)*

Generally speaking, the peasants of eastern Europe were worst off. As discussed in Chapter 20, they were still serfs, bound to their lords in hereditary service. Though serfdom in eastern Europe in the eighteenth century had much in common with medieval serfdom in central and western Europe, it was, if anything, harsher and more oppressive. In much of eastern Europe there were few limitations on the amount of forced labor the lord could require, and five or six days of unpaid work per week on the lord's land was not uncommon. Well into the nineteenth century, individual Russian serfs and serf families were regularly sold with and without land. Serfdom was often very close to slavery.

Social conditions were considerably better in western Europe. Peasants were generally free from serfdom. In France and western Germany, they owned land and could pass it on to their children. Yet life in the village was unquestionably hard, and poverty was the great reality for most people. For the Beauvais region of France at the beginning of the eighteenth century, it has been carefully estimated that in good years and bad only a tenth of the peasants could live satisfactorily off the fruits of their landholdings. Owning less than half of the land, the peasants had to pay heavy royal taxes, the church's tithe, and dues to the lord, as well as set aside seed for the next season. Left with only half of their crop for their own use, they had to toil and till for others and seek work far afield in a constant scramble for a meager living.

One possible way for European peasants to improve their difficult position was to take land from those who owned but did not labor. Yet the social and political conditions that squeezed the peasants were ancient and deep rooted, and powerful forces stood ready to crush any protest. Only with the coming of the French Revolution were European peasants, mainly in France, able to improve their position by means of radical mass action.

Technological progress offered another possibility. The great need was for new farming methods that would enable Europeans to produce more and eat more. The idle fields were the heart of the matter. If peasants could replace the fallow with crops, they could increase the land under cultivation by 50 percent. The secret was to eliminate the fallow by alternating grain with certain nitrogen-storing crops, such as turnips and potatoes, clovers and grasses. Such crops not only rejuvenate the soil better than fallowing, but give more produce as well. Technological progress had its price, though. The new rotations, based primarily on nitrogen-storing clovers and grasses, were scarcely possible within the traditional framework of open fields and common rights. A farmer who wanted to experiment with new methods would have to control the village's pattern of rotation. To wait for the entire village to agree might mean waiting forever. Therefore, the innovating agriculturalist sought to enclose and consolidate his scattered holdings into a compact, fenced-in field. In doing so, he would also seek to enclose his share of the natural pasture, the common. Yet the common rights, like gleaning, were precious to many rural people. When the small landholders and the poor could effectively oppose the enclosure of the open fields, they did so. Only powerful social and political pressures could overcome the traditionalism of rural communities.

Thus the old system of open fields held on tenaciously. Indeed, until the end of the eighteenth century, the promise of the new system was extensively realized only in the Low Countries and in England. Across the rest of Europe, technological progress was limited largely to the introduction of a single new but extremely important crop—the potato (see pages 683–684).

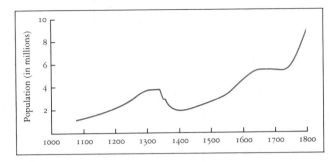

FIGURE 22.1 The Growth of Population in England 1000–1800 England is a good example of both the uneven increase of European population before 1700 and the third great surge of growth, which began in the eighteenth century. *(Source: E. A. Wrigley,* Population and History, *McGraw-Hill, New York, 1969)*

THE BALANCE OF NUMBERS

Many commonly held ideas about population in the past are wrong. One is that past societies were so ignorant that they could do nothing to control their numbers, that population was always growing too fast. On the contrary, until 1700 the total population of Europe grew slowly much of the time, and by no means constantly (Figure 22.1).

In seventeenth-century Europe, births and deaths, fertility and mortality, were in a crude but effective balance. The birthrate—annual births as a proportion of the population—was fairly high, but far lower than it would have been if all women between ages fifteen and forty-four had been having as many children as biologically possible. The death rate in normal years was also high, though somewhat lower than the birthrate. As a result, the population grew modestly in normal years at a rate of perhaps .5 to 1 percent. Yet even fairly modest population growth of 1 percent per year produces a very large increase over a long period—four times as many people in one hundred and fifty years, for example. Such gigantic increases simply did not occur in agrarian Europe before the eighteenth century. In certain abnormal years and tragic periods, many more people died than were born. Total population fell sharply, even catastrophically. A number of years of modest growth would then be necessary to make up for those who had died. Savage increases in deaths helped check

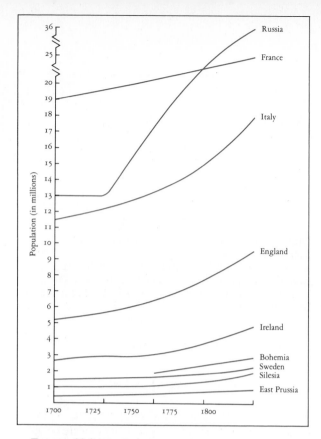

FIGURE 22.2 The Increase of Population in Europe in the Eighteenth Century France's large population continued to support French political and intellectual leadership. Russia emerged as Europe's most populous state because natural increase was complemented by growth from territorial expansion.

total numbers and kept the population from growing rapidly for long periods.

The grim reapers of demographic crisis were famine, epidemic disease, and war. Famine was the tragic result of low yields and periodic crop failures. In most regions of Europe in the sixteenth and seventeenth centuries, harvests were poor, or even failed completely, every eight or nine years. The rural population might survive a single bad harvest by eating less and drawing on its reserves of grain. But when the land combined with persistent bad weather—too much rain rotting the seed or drought withering the young stalks—the result was catastrophic. Meager grain reserves were soon exhausted, and the price of grain soared.

In these crisis years, which periodically stalked Europe even into the eighteenth century, a terrible tightening knot in the belly forced people to tragic substitutes— the 'famine foods" of a desperate population. They gathered chestnuts and stripped bark in the for-

ests; they cut dandelions and grass; and they ate these substitutes to escape starvation. Such unbalanced and inadequate food made people weak and extremely susceptible to illness and epidemics. Eating material unfit for human consumption, such as bark or grass, resulted in dysentery and intestinal ailments of every kind. Influenza and smallpox preyed with particular savagery on a population weakened by famine. With a brutal one-two punch, famine stunned and weakened the population and disease finished it off.

In years of famine and disease, the number of deaths soared far above normal. A third of a village's population might disappear in a year or two. The 1690s were as dismal as many of the worst periods of earlier times. One county in Finland, probably typical of the entire country, lost fully 28 percent of its inhabitants in 1696 and 1697. Certain well-studied villages in the Beauvais region of northern France suffered a similar fate.

Disease could also ravage independently, even in years of adequate harvests. Bubonic plague returned again and again in Europe for more than three hundred years after the onset of the Black Death in the fourteenth century. Not until the late 1500s did most countries have as many people as in the early 1300s. Epidemics of dysentery and smallpox could also operate independently of famine.

War was another scourge. The indirect effects were more harmful than the organized killing. War spread disease. Soldiers and camp followers passed venereal disease through the countryside to scar and kill. Armies requisitioned scarce food supplies for their own use and disrupted the agricultural cycle. The Thirty Years' War (see pages 571–576) witnessed all possible combinations of distress. In the German states, the number of inhabitants declined by more than two-thirds in some large areas and by at least one-third almost everywhere else. The Thirty Years' War reduced total German population by no less than 40 percent.

The brutal but effective balance considered here tipped decisively in favor of births in the eighteenth century. The population of Europe began to grow markedly, a development that had major consequences for millions of ordinary people. This increase in numbers occurred in all areas of Europe— western and eastern, northern and southern, dynamic and stagnant. Growth was especially dramatic after about 1750, as Figure 22.2 shows.

Although it is certain that Europe's population grew greatly, it is less clear why. Because population grew everywhere, it is best to look for general factors and not those limited to individual countries or areas. Whereas in some families women may have had more babies than before, the basic cause was a decline in mortality—fewer deaths.

Of great importance, the bubonic plague mysteriously disappeared. Following the Black Death in the fourteenth century, plagues had remained a part of the European experience, striking again and again with savage force, particularly in towns. As late as 1720, a ship from Syria and the eastern Mediterranean, where plague was ever-present, brought the monstrous disease to Marseilles. In a few weeks, forty thousand of the city's ninety thousand inhabitants died. The epidemic swept southern France, killing one-third, one-half, even three-fourths of those in the larger towns. Once again an awful fear swept across Europe. But the epidemic passed, and that was the last time plague fell on western and central Europe. The final disappearance of plague was due in part to stricter measures of quarantine in Mediterranean ports and along the Austrian border with Turkey. Human carriers of plague were carefully isolated. Chance and plain good luck were more important, however.

It is now understood that bubonic plague is, above all, a disease of rats. More precisely, it is the black rat that spreads major epidemics, for the black rat's flea is the principal carrier of the plague bacillus. After 1600, for reasons unknown, a new rat of Asiatic origin—the brown, or wander, rat—began to drive out and eventually eliminate its black competitor. In the words of a noted authority, "This revolution in the animal kingdom must have gone far to break the lethal link between rat and man."[1] Although the brown rat also carries the plague bacillus, another kind of flea is its main parasite. That flea carries the plague poorly and, for good measure, has little taste for human blood.

Advances in medical knowledge did not contribute much to reducing the death rate in the eighteenth century, as discussed on pages 696 through 701. But human beings were more successful in their efforts to safeguard the supply of food and protect against famine. The eighteenth century was a time of considerable canal and road building in western Europe. These advances in transportation, which were among the more positive aspects of strong absolutist states,

Doctor in Protective Clothing Most doctors believed, incorrectly, that poisonous smells carried the plague. This doctor has placed strong-smelling salts in his "beak" to protect himself against deadly plague vapors. *(Germanisches Nationalmuseum, Nurnberg)*

lessened the impact of local crop failure and famine. Emergency supplies could be brought in. The age-old spectacle of localized starvation became less frequent. War became more gentlemanly and less destructive than it had been in the seventeenth century and spread fewer epidemics. New foods, particularly the potato, were introduced. Potatoes served especially well when the grain crops were skimpy or failed. In short, population grew in the eighteenth century primarily because years of abnormal death rates were less catastrophic. Famines, epidemics, and wars continued to occur, but their severity moderated.

The Growth of Cottage Industry

The growth of population in the eighteenth century cannot be interpreted as a sign of human progress, however. Plague faded from memory, transport improved, people learned to eat potatoes; yet for the common people, life was still a great struggle. Indeed, it was often more of a struggle than ever, for in many areas increasing numbers led to overpopulation. There was only so much land available, and tradition slowed the adoption of better farming methods. Therefore agriculture could not provide enough work for the rapidly growing labor force, and poor people in the countryside had to look for new ways to make a living.

Making things at home for sale was one such way. Thus the growth of population contributed to the development of industry in rural areas. To be sure, peasant communities had always made some clothing, processed some food, and constructed some housing for their own use. But in the Middle Ages, peasants did not produce manufactured goods on a large scale for sale in a market. Industry was dominated and organized by urban craft guilds and urban merchants, who jealously regulated handicraft production and sought to maintain it as an urban monopoly. By the eighteenth century, however, the pressures of rural poverty and the need for employment in the countryside had proved too great, and a new system was expanding lustily. The new system had many names. Sometimes referred to as "cottage industry" or "domestic industry," it has often been called the "putting-out system."

The two main participants in the putting-out system were the merchant-capitalist and the rural worker. The merchant loaned or "put out" raw materials—raw wool, for example—to several cottage workers. Those workers processed the raw material in their own homes, spinning and weaving the wool into cloth in this case, and returned the finished product to the merchant. The merchant paid the "outworkers" for their work by the piece and proceeded to sell the finished product. There were endless variations on this basic relationship. Sometimes rural workers would buy their own materials and work as independent producers before they delivered to the merchant. The relative importance of earnings from the land and from industry varied greatly for handicraft workers. In all cases, however, the putting-out system was a kind of capitalism. Merchants needed large amounts of capital, which they held in the form of goods being worked up and sold in distant markets. They sought to make profits and increase their capital in their businesses. Rural workers were selling their labor, usually for considerably less than urban workers.

The growth of the putting-out system provided the poor with additional income. Since production in the countryside was unregulated, workers and merchants could change procedures and experiment as they saw fit. Because it did not need to meet rigid guild standards, which maintained quality but discouraged the development of new methods, cottage industry became capable of producing many kinds of goods. Textiles, all manner of knives, forks, and housewares, buttons and gloves, clocks and musical instruments could be produced quite satisfactorily in the countryside. The manufacture of luxury goods for the rich, such as exquisite tapestries and fine porcelain, demanded special training, close supervision, and centralized workshops. Yet such goods were as exceptional as those who used them. The skills of rural industry were sufficient for many everyday articles.

Rural manufacturing did not spread across Europe at an even rate. It appeared first in England and developed most successfully there, particularly for the spinning and weaving of woolen cloth. Continental countries developed rural industry more slowly. In France at the time of Louis XIV, Colbert had revived the urban guilds and used them as a means to control the cities and collect taxes (see page 596). But the pressure of rural poverty proved too great. In 1762 the special privileges of urban manufacturing were abolished in France, and the already-developing rural industries were given free rein from then on. Thus in France, as in Germany and other areas, the later part of the eighteenth century witnessed a remarkable expansion of rural industry in certain densely populated regions. The pattern established in England was spreading to the Continent.

Cottage industry, like peasant agriculture from which it evolved, was based on family enterprise. All the members of the family helped in the work, especially in textiles, the most important cottage industry.

Cottage Industry in Ireland Many steps went into making linen textiles. Here the women are beating away the coarse woody part of the flax plant so that the man can draw the soft part through a series of combs. The fine flax fibers will then be spun into thread and woven into cloth by this family enterprise. *(The Mansell Collection)*

While the women and children prepared the raw material and spun the thread, the man of the house wove the cloth. There was work for everyone, even the youngest. After the dirt was beaten out of the raw material, for example, it had to be thoroughly cleaned with strong soap in a tub, where tiny feet took the place of the agitator in a washing machine. A famous English textile inventor recalled that "soon after I was able to walk I was employed in the cotton manufacture. . . . My mother tucked up my petticoats about my waist, and put me into the tub to tread upon the cotton at the bottom."[2] Slightly older children and aged relatives carded and combed the cotton or wool, so that the mother and the older daughter she had taught could spin it into thread. Each member had a task, and family life overlapped with the work experience.

MARRIAGE AND THE FAMILY

The family is the basic unit of social organization. It is within the structure of the family that human beings love, mate, and reproduce themselves. It is primarily the family that teaches the child, imparting values and customs that condition an individual's behavior for a lifetime. The family is also an institution woven into the web of history. It evolves and changes, assuming different forms in different times and places.

EXTENDED AND NUCLEAR FAMILIES

In many traditional Asian and African societies, the typical family has often been an extended family. A newly married couple, instead of establishing their own home, go to live with either the bride's or the groom's family. The couple raise their children while living under the same roof with their own brothers and sisters, who may also be married. The family is a big, three- or four-generation clan, headed by a patriarch or perhaps a matriarch, and encompassing everyone from the youngest infant to the oldest grandparent.

Extended families, it is often said, provide security for adults and children in traditional agrarian peasant economies. Everyone has a place within the extended family, from cradle to grave. Sociologists frequently assume that the extended family gives way to the conjugal, or nuclear, family with the advent of industrialization and urbanization. Couples establish their own households and their own family identities when they marry. They live with the children they raise, apart from their parents. Something like this has indeed been happening in much of Asia and Africa in recent years. And since Europe was once agrarian and preindustrial, it has often been believed that the extended family must also have prevailed in Europe before being destroyed by the Industrial Revolution.

In fact, the situation was quite different in western and central Europe. By 1700 the extended three-generational family was a great rarity. Indeed, the extended family may never have been common in Europe, although it is hard to know about the Middle Ages because fewer records survive. When young European couples married, they normally established their own households and lived apart from their parents. When a three-generation household came into existence, it was usually a parent who moved in with a married child, rather than a newly married couple moving in with either set of parents. The married couple, and the children who were sure to follow, were on their own from the beginning.

Perhaps because European couples set up separate households when they married, people did not marry young in the seventeenth and early eighteenth centuries. Indeed, the average person, who was neither rich nor aristocratic, married surprisingly late, many years after reaching adulthood and many more after beginning to work. In one well-studied, typical English village, both men and women married for the first time at an average age of twenty-seven or older in the seventeenth and eighteenth centuries. A similar pattern existed in early-eighteenth-century France. Moreover, a substantial portion of men and women never married at all.

Between two-fifths and three-fifths of European women capable of bearing children—that is, women between fifteen and forty-four—were unmarried at any given time. The contrast with traditional non-Western societies is once again striking. In those societies, the pattern has very often been almost universal and very early marriage. The union of a teenage bride and her teenage groom has been the general rule.

The customs of late marriage and nuclear family were a distinctive characteristic of European society.

The consequences have been tremendous, though still only partially explored. It seems likely that the dynamism and creativity that have characterized European society were due in large part to the pattern of marriage and family. This pattern fostered and required self-reliance and independence. In preindustrial western Europe in the sixteenth through eighteenth centuries, marriage normally joined a mature man and a mature woman—two adults who had already experienced a great deal of life and could transmit self-reliance and real skills to the next generation.

Why was marriage delayed? The main reason was that couples normally could not marry until they could support themselves economically. The land remained the main source of income. The peasant son often needed to wait until his father's death to inherit the family farm and marry his sweetheart. Similarly, the peasant daughter and her family had to accumulate a small dowry to help her boyfriend buy land or build a house.

There were also laws and regulations to temper impetuous love and physical attraction. In some areas, couples needed the legal permission or tacit approval of the local lord or landowner in order to marry. In Austria and Germany, there were legal restrictions on marriage, and well into the nineteenth century poor couples had particular difficulty securing the approval of local officials. These officials believed that freedom to marry for the lower classes would mean more paupers, more abandoned children, and more money for welfare. Thus prudence, custom, and law combined to postpone the march to the altar. This pattern helped society maintain some kind of balance between the number of people and the available economic resources.

WORK AWAY FROM HOME

Many young people worked within their families until they could start their own households. Girls tended the cows and spun; boys plowed and wove. Many others left home to work elsewhere. In the towns, a lad might be apprenticed to a craftsman for seven or fourteen years to learn a trade. During that time he would not be permitted to marry. In most trades he earned little and worked hard, but if he were lucky he might eventually be admitted to a guild and establish his economic independence. More often, the young man would drift from one tough job to another: hired hand for a small farmer, laborer on a new road, water carrier in a nearby town. He was always subject to economic fluctuations, and unemployment was a constant threat.

Girls also left their families to work, at an early age and in large numbers. The range of opportunities open to them was more limited, however. Service in another family's household was by far the most common job. Even middle-class families often sent their daughters into service and hired others as servants in return. Thus, a few years away from home as a servant was a normal part of growing up. If all went well, the girl (or boy) would work hard and save some money for parents and marriage. At the least, there would be one less mouth to feed at home.

The legions of young servant girls worked hard but had little real independence. Sometimes the employer paid the girl's wages directly to her parents. Constantly under the eye of her mistress, her tasks were many—cleaning, shopping, cooking, caring for the baby—and often endless, for there were no laws to limit her exploitation. Few girls were so brutalized that they snapped under the strain, like the Russian servant girl Varka in Chekhov's chilling story, "Sleepy," who, driven beyond exhaustion, finally quieted her mistress's screaming child by strangling it in its cradle. But court records are full of complaints by servant girls of physical mistreatment by their mistresses. There were many others like the fifteen-year-old English girl in the early eighteenth century who told the judge that her mistress had not only called her "very opprobrious names, as Bitch, Whore and the like," but also "beat her without provocation and beyond measure."[3]

There was also the pressure of seducers and sexual attack. In theory, domestic service offered protection and security for a young girl leaving home. The girl had food, lodging, and a new family. She did not drift in a strange and often dangerous environment. But in practice, she was often the easy prey of a lecherous master, or his sons, or his friends. Indeed, "the evidence suggests that in all European countries, from Britain to Russia, the upper classes felt perfectly free to exploit sexually girls who were at their mercy."[4] If the girl became pregnant, she was quickly fired and thrown out in disgrace to make her own way. Prostitution and petty thievery were often the harsh alternatives that lay ahead. "What are we?" exclaimed a bitter Parisian prostitute. "Most of us are unfortunate women, without origins, without education, servants and maids for the most part."[5]

The Chimney Sweep Some boys and girls found work as chimney sweeps, especially if they were small. Climbing up into chimneys was dirty, dangerous work. Hot stones could set the sweep's clothing on fire. Such work for youngsters eventually died out in the nineteenth century, the period of this drawing. *(Photo: Caroline Buckler)*

PREMARITAL SEX AND BIRTH-CONTROL PRACTICES

Did the plight of some ex-servant girls mean that late marriage in preindustrial Europe went hand in hand with premarital sex and many illegitimate children? For most of western and central Europe, until at least 1750, the answer seems to be no. English parish registers, in which the clergy recorded the births and deaths of the population, seldom list more than one bastard out of every twenty children baptized. Some French parishes in the seventeenth century had extraordinarily low rates of illegitimacy, with less than 1 percent of the babies born out of wedlock. Illegitimate babies were apparently a rarity, at least as far as the official church records are concerned.

At the same time, premarital sex was clearly commonplace. In one well-studied English village, one-third of all first children were conceived before the couple was married, and many were born within three months of the marriage ceremony. No doubt many of these couples were already betrothed, or at least "going steady," before they entered into an intimate relationship. But the very low rates of illegitimate birth also reflect the powerful social controls of the traditional village, particularly the open-field village with its pattern of cooperation and common action. Irate parents and village elders, indignant priests and authoritative landlords, all combined to pressure any young people who wavered about marriage in the face of unexpected pregnancy. These controls meant that premarital sex was not entered into lightly. In the countryside it was generally limited to those contemplating marriage.

Once a woman was married, she generally had several children. This does not mean that birth control within marriage was unknown in western and central Europe before the nineteenth century. But it was primitive and quite undependable. The most common method was *coitus interruptus*—withdrawal by the male before ejaculation. The French, who were apparently early leaders in contraception, were using this method extensively to limit family size by the end of the eighteenth century. Withdrawal as a method of birth control was in keeping with the European pattern of nuclear family, in which the father bore the direct responsibility of supporting his children. Withdrawal—a male technique—was one way to meet that responsibility.

Mechanical and other means of contraception were not unknown in the eighteenth century, but they appear to have been used mainly by certain sectors of the urban population. The "fast set" of London used the "sheath" regularly, although primarily to protect against venereal disease, not pregnancy. Prostitutes used various contraceptive techniques to prevent pregnancy, and such information was probably available to anyone who really sought it. The second part of an indictment for adultery against a late-

sixteenth-century English vicar charged that the wayward minister was "also an instructor of young folks [in] how to commit the sin of adultery or fornication and not to beget or bring forth children."[6]

NEW PATTERNS OF MARRIAGE AND ILLEGITIMACY

In the second half of the eighteenth century, the pattern of late marriage and few illegitimate children began to break down. It is hard to say why. Certainly, changes in the economy had a gradual but profound impact. The growth of cottage industry created a way to earn a living that was not tied to limited and hard-to-get land. Because a scrap of ground for a garden and a cottage for the loom and spinning wheel could be quite enough for a modest living, young people had greater independence and did not need to wait for a good-sized farm. A contemporary observer of an area of rapidly growing cottage industry in Switzerland at the end of the eighteenth century described these changes: "The increased and sure income offered by the combination of cottage manufacture with farming hastened and multiplied marriages and encouraged the division of landholdings, while enhancing their value; it also promoted the expansion and embellishment of houses and villages."[7]

As a result, cottage workers married not only earlier but frequently for different reasons. Nothing could be so businesslike, so calculating, as a peasant marriage that was often dictated by the needs of the couple's families. After 1750, however, courtship became more extensive and freer as cottage industry grew. It was easier to yield to the attraction of the opposite sex and fall in love. Members of the older generation were often shocked by the lack of responsibility they saw in the early marriages of the poor, the union of "people with only two spinning wheels and not even a bed." But the laws and regulations they imposed, especially in Germany, were often disregarded. Unions based on love rather than on economic considerations were increasingly the pattern for cottage workers. Factory workers, numbers of whom first began to appear in England after about 1780, followed the path blazed by cottage workers.

Changes in the timing and motivation of marriage went hand in hand with a rapid increase in illegitimate births between about 1750 and 1850. Some historians even speak of an "illegitimacy explosion." In Frankfurt, Germany, for example, only about 2 percent of all births were illegitimate in the early 1700s; this figure rose to about 25 percent around 1850. In Bordeaux, France, illegitimate births rose steadily until by 1840 one out of every three babies was born out of wedlock. Small towns and villages less frequently experienced such startlingly high illegitimacy rates, but increases from a range of 1 to 3 percent initially to 10 to 20 percent between 1750 and 1850 were commonplace. A profound sexual and cultural transformation was taking place. Fewer girls were abstaining from premarital intercourse, and fewer boys were marrying the girls they got pregnant.

It is hard to know exactly why this change occurred and what it meant. The old idea of a safe, late, economically secure marriage did not reflect economic and social realities. The growing freedom of thought in the turbulent years beginning with the French Revolution in 1789 influenced sexual and marital behavior. Illegitimate births, particularly in Germany, were also the result of open rebellion against class laws limiting the right of the poor to marry. More fundamentally, the need to seek work outside farming and the village made young people more mobile. Mobility in turn encouraged new sexual and marital relationships, which were less subject to parental pressure and village tradition. As in the case of young servant girls who became pregnant and were then forced to fend for themselves, some of these relationships promoted loose living or prostitution. This resulted in more illegitimate births and strengthened an urban subculture of habitual illegitimacy.

It has been suggested that the increase in illegitimate births represented a stage in the emancipation of women. According to this view, new economic opportunities outside the home, in the city and later in the factory, revolutionized women's attitudes about themselves. Young working women became individualistic and rebelled against old restrictions like late marriage. They sought fulfillment in the pleasure of sexuality. Since there was little birth control, freer sex for single women meant more illegitimate babies.

No doubt single working women in towns and cities were of necessity more independent and self-reliant. Yet, until at least the late nineteenth century, it seems unlikely that such young women were motivated primarily by visions of emancipation and sexual liberation. Most women were servants or textile workers. These jobs paid poorly, and the possibility of a truly independent "liberated" life was correspondingly limited. Most women in the city probably

The Face of Poverty This woman and her children live by begging, which was widespread in eighteenth-century Europe. The missing father suggests that these children may well be products of the "illegitimacy explosion." *(Freeman & Co., London)*

looked to marriage and family life as an escape from hard, poorly paid work and as the foundation of a satisfying life.

Hopes and promises of marriage from men of the working girl's own class led naturally enough to sex.[8] In one medium-sized French city in 1787 to 1788, the great majority of unwed mothers stated that sexual intimacy had followed promises of marriage. Many soldiers, day laborers, and male servants were no doubt sincere in their proposals. But their lives were insecure, and many hesitated to take on the heavy economic burdens of wife and child. Nor were their backbones any longer stiffened by the traditional pressures of the village.

In a growing number of cases, therefore, the intended marriage did not take place. The romantic yet practical dreams and aspirations of many young working women and men were frustrated by low wages, inequality, and changing economic and social conditions. Old patterns of marriage and family were breaking down among the common people. Only in the late nineteenth century would more stable patterns reappear.

WOMEN AND CHILDREN

In the traditional framework of preindustrial Europe, women married late but then began bearing children rapidly. If a woman married before she was thirty, and if both she and her husband lived to forty-five, the chances were roughly one in two that she would give birth to six or more children. The newborn child entered a dangerous world. Infant mortality was high. One in five was sure to die and one in three was quite likely to, in the poorer areas. Newborn children were very likely to catch infectious diseases of the stomach and chest, which were not understood. Thus little could be done for an ailing child, even in rich families. Childhood itself was dangerous. Parents in preindustrial Europe could count themselves fortunate if half their children lived to adulthood.

CHILD CARE AND NURSING

Women of the lower classes generally breast-fed their infants, and for much longer periods than is customary today. Breast-feeding decreases the likelihood of pregnancy for the average woman by delaying the resumption of ovulation. Although women may have been only vaguely aware of the link between nursing and not getting pregnant, they were spacing their children—from two to three years apart—and limiting their fertility by nursing their babies. If a newborn baby died, nursing stopped and a new life could be created. Nursing also saved lives: the breast-fed infant was more likely to survive on its mother's milk than on any other foods.

In contrast to the laboring poor, the women of the aristocracy and upper middle class seldom nursed their own children. The upper-class woman felt that breast-feeding was crude, common, and well beneath her dignity. Instead she hired a wet nurse to suckle her child. The urban mother of more modest means —the wife of a shopkeeper or artisan—also com-

monly used a wet nurse, sending her baby to some poor woman in the country as soon as possible.

Wet-nursing was a very widespread and flourishing business in the eighteenth century, a dismal business within the framework of the putting-out system. The traffic was in babies rather than in wool and cloth, and two or three years often passed before the wet nurse finished her task. The great French historian Jules Michelet described with compassion the plight of the wet nurse, who was still plying her trade in early-nineteenth-century France:

People do not know how much these poor women are exploited and abused, first by the vehicles which transport them (often barely out of their confinement), and afterward by the employment offices which place them. Taken as nurses on the spot, they must send their own child away, and consequently it often dies. They have no contact with the family that hires them, and they may be dismissed at the first caprice of the mother or doctor. If the change of air and place should dry up their milk, they are discharged without any compensation. If they stay here [in the city] they pick up the habits of the easy life, and they suffer enormously when they are forced to return to their life of [rural] poverty. A good number become servants in order to stay in the town. They never rejoin their husbands, and the family is broken.[9]

Other observers noted the flaws of wet-nursing. It was a common belief that a nurse passed her bad traits to the baby with her milk. When a child turned out poorly, it was assumed that "the nurse changed it." Many observers charged that nurses were often negligent and greedy. They claimed that there were large numbers of "killing nurses" with whom no child every survived. The nurse let the child die quickly, so that she could take another child and another fee. No matter how the adults fared in the wet-nurse business, the child was a certain loser.

FOUNDLINGS AND INFANTICIDE

In the ancient world and in some Asian societies it was not uncommon to allow or force newborn babies, particularly girl babies, to die when there were too many mouths to feed. To its great and eternal credit, the early medieval church, strongly influenced by Jewish law, denounced infanticide as a pagan practice and insisted that every human life was sacred. The willful destruction of newborn children became a crime punishable by death. And yet, as the reference to killing nurses suggests, direct and indirect methods of eliminating unwanted babies did not disappear. There were, for example, many cases of "overlaying"—parents rolling over and suffocating the child placed between them in their bed. Such parents claimed they were drunk and had acted unintentionally. In Austria in 1784, suspicious authorities made it illegal for parents to take children under five into bed with them. Severe poverty on the one hand and increasing illegitimacy on the other conspired to force the very poor to thin their own ranks.

The young girl—very likely a servant—who could not provide for her child had few choices. If she would not resort to abortion or the services of a killing nurse, she could bundle up her baby and leave it on the doorstep of a church. In the late seventeenth century, Saint Vincent de Paul was so distressed by the number of babies brought to the steps of Notre Dame in Paris that he established a home for foundlings. Others followed his example. In England the government acted on a petition calling for a foundling hospital "to prevent the frequent murders of poor, miserable infants at birth" and "to suppress the inhuman custom of exposing newborn children to perish in the streets."

In much of Europe in the eighteenth century, foundling homes became a favorite charity of the rich and powerful. Great sums were spent on them. The foundling home in St. Petersburg, perhaps the most elaborate and lavish of its kind, occupied the former palaces of two members of the high nobility. In the early nineteenth century it had 25,000 children in its care and was receiving 5,000 new babies a year. At their best, the foundling homes of the eighteenth century were a good example of Christian charity and social concern in an age of tremendous poverty and inequality.

Yet the foundling home was no panacea. By the 1770s one-third of all babies born in Paris were immediately abandoned to the foundling home by their mothers. Fully a third of all those foundlings were abandoned by married couples, a powerful commentary on the standard of living among the working poor, for whom an additional mouth to feed often meant tragedy. In London competition for space in the foundling home soon became so great that it led "to the disgraceful scene of women scrambling and fighting to get to the door, that they might be of the fortunate few to reap the benefit of the Asylum."[10]

Furthermore, great numbers of babies entered, but few left. Even in the best of these homes half the babies normally died within a year. In the worst, fully 90 percent did not survive. They succumbed to long journeys over rough roads, the intentional and unintentional neglect of their wet nurses, and the customary childhood illnesses. So great was the carnage that some contemporaries called the foundling hospitals "legalized infanticide."

Certainly some parents and officials looked on the hospitals as dumps for unwanted babies. In the early 1760s, when the London Foundling Hospital was obliged to accept all babies offered, it was deluged with babies from the countryside. Many parish officers placed with the foundling home the abandoned children in their care in order to reduce the cost of welfare at the local level. Throughout the eighteenth century, millions of children of the poor continued to exit after the briefest of appearances on the earthly stage.

ATTITUDES TOWARD CHILDREN

What were the more typical circumstances of children's lives? Did the treatment of foundlings reflect the attitudes of all parents? Harsh as it may sound, young children were often of little concern to their parents and to society in the eighteenth century. This indifference toward children was found in all classes; rich children were by no means exempt. The practice of using wet nurses, who were casually selected and often negligent, is one example of how even the rich and the prosperous put children out of sight and out of mind. One French moralist, writing in 1756 about how to improve humanity, observed that "one blushes to think of loving one's children." It has been said that the English gentleman of the period "had more interest in the diseases of his horses than of his children."[11]

Parents believed that the world of the child was an uninteresting one. When parents did stop to notice their offspring, they often treated them as dolls or playthings—little puppies to fondle and cuddle in a moment of relaxation. The psychological distance between parent and child remained vast.

Much of the indifference was due to the terrible frequency, the terrible banality, of death among children of all classes. Parents simply could not afford to become too emotionally involved with their children, who were so unlikely to survive. The great

The Five Senses Published in 1774, J. B. Basedow's *Elementary Reader* helped spread new attitudes toward child development and education. Drawing heavily on the theories of Locke and Rousseau, the German educator advocated nature study and contact with everyday life. In this illustration for Basedow's reader, gentle teachers allow uncorrupted children to learn about the five senses through direct experience. *(Photo: Caroline Buckler)*

eighteenth-century English historian Edward Gibbon (1737–1794) wrote that "the death of a new born child before that of its parents may seem unnatural but it is a strictly probable event, since of any given number the greater part are extinguished before the ninth year, before they possess the faculties of the mind and the body." Gibbon's father named all his boys Edward, hoping that at least one of them would survive to carry his name. His prudence was not misplaced. Edward the future historian and eldest survived. Five brothers and sisters all died in infancy.

Doctors were seldom interested in the care of children. One contemporary observer quoted a famous doctor as saying that "he never wished to be called to a young child because he was really at a loss to know what to offer for it." There were "physicians of note who make no scruple to assert that there is nothing to be done for children when they are ill." Children were caught in a vicious circle: they were neglected because they were very likely to die and they were likely to die because they were neglected.

Indifference toward children often shaded off into brutality. When parents and other adults did turn toward children, it was normally to discipline and control them. The novelist Daniel Defoe (1660?–1731), always delighted when he saw very young children working hard in cottage industry, coined the axiom "Spare the rod and spoil the child." He meant it. So did Susannah Wesley, mother of John Wesley (1703–1791), the founder of Methodism. According to her, the first task of a parent toward her children was "to conquer the will, and bring them to an obedient temper." She reported that her babies were "taught to fear the rod, and to cry softly; by which means they escaped the abundance of correction they might otherwise have had, and that most odious noise of the crying of children was rarely heard in the house."[12]

It was hardly surprising that, when English parish officials dumped their paupers into the first factories late in the eighteenth century, the children were beaten and brutalized (see page 825). That was part of the child-rearing pattern—widespread indifference on the one hand and strict physical discipline on the other—that prevailed through most of the eighteenth century.

Late in the century, this pattern came under attack. Critics like Jean-Jacques Rousseau called for greater love, tenderness, and understanding toward children. In addition to supporting foundling homes to discourage infanticide and urging wealthy women to nurse their own babies, these new voices ridiculed the practice of swaddling. Wrapping youngsters in tight-fitting clothes and blankets was generally believed to form babies properly by "straightening them out." By the end of the century, small children were often dressed in simpler, more comfortable clothing, allowing much greater freedom of movement. More parents expressed a delight in the love of and intimacy with their children and found real pleasure in raising their offspring. These changes were part of the general growth of humanitarianism and optimism about human potential that characterized the eighteenth-century Enlightenment.

Schools and Education

The role of formal education outside the home, in those special institutions called "schools," was growing more important. The aristocracy and the rich had led the way in the sixteenth century with special colleges, often run by the Jesuits. But "little schools," charged with elementary education of the children of the masses, did not appear until the seventeenth century. Unlike medieval schools, which mingled all age groups, the little schools specialized in boys and girls from seven to twelve, who were instructed in basic literacy and religion.

Although large numbers of common people got no education at all in the eighteenth century, the beginnings of popular education were recognizable. France made a start in 1682 with the establishment of Christian schools, which taught the catechism and prayers as well as reading and writing. The Church of England and the dissenting congregations established "charity schools" to instruct the children of the poor. As early as 1717, Prussia made attendance at elementary schools compulsory. Inspired by the old Protestant idea that every believer should be able to read and study the Bible in the quest for personal salvation and by the new idea of a population capable of effectively serving the state, Prussia led the way in the development of universal education. Religious motives

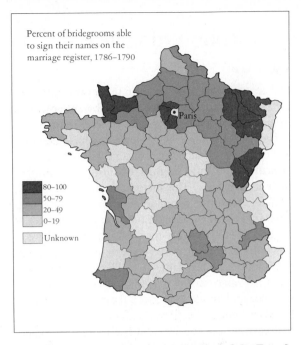

Percent of bridegrooms able to sign their names on the marriage register, 1786–1790

80–100
50–79
20–49
0–19
Unknown

Map 22.1 Literacy in France on the Eve of the French Revolution Literacy rates varied widely among and within states in eighteenth-century Europe. Northern France was clearly ahead of southern France.

were also extremely important elsewhere. From the middle of the seventeenth century, Presbyterian Scotland was convinced that the path to salvation lay in careful study of the Scriptures, and this belief led to an effective network of parish schools for rich and poor alike. The Enlightenment commitment to greater knowledge through critical thinking reinforced interest in education in the eighteenth century.

The result of these efforts was a remarkable growth of basic literacy between 1600 and 1800. Whereas in 1600 only one male in six was barely literate in France and Scotland, and one in four in England, by 1800 almost 90 percent of the Scottish male population was literate. At the same time, almost two out of three males were literate in France, and in advanced areas such as Normandy, literacy approached 90 percent (Map 22.1). More than half of English males were literate by 1800. In all three countries the bulk of the jump occurred in the eighteenth century. Women were also increasingly literate, although they probably lagged behind men somewhat in most countries. Some elementary education was becoming a reality for European peoples, and schools were of growing significance in everyday life.

FOOD AND MEDICINE

Plague, which recurred often in the seventeenth century, gradually disappeared in the eighteenth century. Also, a somewhat better supply of food reduced the danger of starvation. These developments, taken together, probably accounted in large part for the rapid growth in the total number of Europeans and for their longer lives. The increase in the average life span, allowing for regional variations, was remarkable. In 1700 the average European could expect at birth to live only twenty-five years. A century later, a newborn European could expect to live fully ten years longer, to age thirty-five. The doubling of the adult life span meant that there was more time to produce and create, and more reason for parents to stress learning and preparation for adulthood.

Precisely how and why did health and life expectancy improve? What was the role of diet and food in this improvement? And what were the differences between rich and poor? What was the contribution of doctors, hospitals, and medical science? To answer these questions, it is necessary first to follow the eighteenth-century family to the table.

DIETS AND NUTRITION

Although the accomplishments of doctors and hospitals are constantly in the limelight today, the greater, if less spectacular, part of medicine is preventive medicine. The great breakthrough of the second half of the nineteenth century was the development of public health techniques—proper sanitation and mass vaccinations—to prevent outbreaks of communicable diseases. Even before the nineteenth century, prevention was the key to longer life. Good clothing, warm dry housing, and plentiful food make for healthier populations, much more capable of battling off disease. Clothing and housing for the masses probably improved only modestly in the eighteenth century, but the limited modification of the three-field system and increased agricultural output had a beneficial effect. The average European ate more and better food and was healthier as a result in 1800 than in 1700. This pattern is apparent in the fare of the laboring poor.

At the beginning of the eighteenth century, ordinary men and women depended on grain as fully as they had in the past. Bread was quite literally the staff of life. Peasants in the Beauvais region of France ate two pounds of bread a day, washing it down with water, green wine, beer, or a little skimmed milk. Their dark bread was made from a mixture of rough-ground wheat and rye—the standard flour of the poor. The poor also ate grains in soup and gruel. In rocky northern Scotland, for example, people depended on oatmeal, which they often ate half-cooked so it would swell in their stomachs and make them feel full. No wonder, then, that the supply of grain and the price of bread were always critical questions for most of the population.

The poor, rural and urban, also ate a fair quantity of vegetables. Indeed, vegetables were considered "poor people's food." Peas and beans were probably the most common; grown as field crops in much of Europe since the Middle Ages, they were eaten fresh in late spring and summer. Dried, they became the basic ingredients in the soups and stews of the long winter months. In most regions, other vegetables, primarily cabbages, carrots, and wild greens, appeared in season on the tables of the poor. Fruit was uncommon and limited to the summer months.

The European poor loved meat and eggs, but they seldom ate their fill. Meat was too expensive. When the poor did eat meat—on a religious holiday or at a wedding or other special occasion—it was most likely lamb or mutton. Sheep could survive on rocky soils and did not compete directly with humans for the slender resources of grain.

Milk was rarely drunk. It was widely believed that milk caused sore eyes, headaches, and a variety of ills, except among the very young and very old. Milk was used primarily to make cheese and butter, which the poor liked but could afford only occasionally. Medical and popular opinion considered whey, the watery liquid left after milk was churned, "an excellent temperate drink."

The diet of the rich—aristocrats, officials, and the comfortable bourgeoisie—was traditionally quite different from that of the poor. The men and women of the upper classes were rapacious carnivores, and a person's standard of living and economic well-being were often judged by the amount of meat eaten. A truly elegant dinner among the great and powerful consisted of one rich meat after another—a chicken pie, a leg of lamb, a grilled steak, for example. Three separate meat courses might be followed by three fish courses, laced with piquant sauces and comple-

Le Nain: Peasant Family A little wine and a great deal of dark bread: the traditional food of the poor French peasantry accentuates the poetic dignity of this masterpiece, painted about 1640 by Louis Le Nain. *(Cliché des Musées Nationaux, Paris)*

mented with sweets, cheeses, and nuts of all kinds. Fruits and vegetables were not often found on the tables of the rich. The long-standing dominance of meat and fish in the diet of the upper classes continued throughout the eighteenth century. There was undoubtedly great overeating and gluttony.

There was also an enormous amount of overdrinking among the rich. The English squire, for example, who loved to ride with his hounds, loved drink with a similar passion. He became famous as the "four-bottle man." With his dinner he drank red wine from France or white wine from the Rhineland, and with his dessert he took sweet but strong port or Madiera from Portugal. Sometimes he ended the evening under the table in a drunken stupor.

The diet of small traders, master craftsmen, minor bureaucrats—the people of the towns and cities—was probably less monotonous than that of the peasantry. The markets, stocked by market gardens in the outskirts, provided a substantial variety of meats, vegetables, and fruits, although bread and beans still formed the bulk of the poor family's diet.

There were also regional dietary differences in 1700. Generally speaking, northern, Atlantic Europe ate better than southern, Mediterranean Europe. The poor of England probably ate best of all. Contemporaries on both sides of the Channel often contrasted the Englishman's consumption of meat with the French peasant's greater dependence on bread and vegetables. The Dutch were also considerably better fed than the average European, in large part because of their advanced agriculture and diversified gardens.

THE IMPACT OF DIET ON HEALTH

How were the poor and the rich served by their quite different diets? Good nutrition depends on a balanced supply of food as well as on an adequate number of calories. Modern research has shown that the chief determinant of nutritional balance is the relationship between carbohydrates (sugar and starch) and proteins. A diet consisting primarily of carbohydrates is seriously incomplete.

At first glance, the diet of the laboring poor, relying as it did on carbohydrates, seems unsatisfactory. Even when a peasant got his daily two or three pounds of bread, his supply of protein and essential vitamins would seem too low. A closer look reveals a brighter picture. Most bread was "brown" or "black," made from wheat or rye. The flour of the eighteenth century was a whole-meal flour, produced by stone grinding. It contained most of the bran—the ground-up husk—and the all-important wheat germ. The bran and germ contain higher proportions of some minerals, vitamins, and good-quality proteins than does the rest of the grain. Only when they are removed does bread become a foodstuff providing relatively more starch and less of the essential nutrients.

In addition, the field peas and beans eaten by poor people since Carolingian days contained protein that complemented the proteins in whole-meal bread. The proteins in whey, cheese, and eggs, which the poor ate at least occasionally, also supplemented the value of the protein in the bread and vegetables. Indeed, a leading authority concludes that if a pint of milk and some cheese and whey were eaten each day, the balance of the poor people's diet "was excellent, far better indeed than in many of our modern diets."[13]

The basic bread-and-vegetables diet of the poor in normal times was satisfactory. It protected effectively against most of the disorders associated with a deficiency of the vitamin B complex, for example. The lack of sugar meant that teeth were not so plagued by cavities. Constipation was almost unknown to peasants and laborers living on coarse cereal breads, which provided the roughage modern diets lack. The common diet of the poor also generally warded off anemia, although anemia among infants was not uncommon.

The key dietary problem was probably getting enough green vegetables (or milk), particularly in the late winter and early spring, to ensure adequate supplies of vitamins A and C. A severe deficiency of vitamin C produces scurvy, a disease that leads to rotting gums, swelling of the limbs, and great weakness. Before the season's first vegetables, many people had used up their bodily reserves of vitamin C and were suffering from mild cases of scurvy. Sailors on long voyages suffered most. By the end of the sixteenth century the exceptional antiscurvy properties of lemons and limes led to the practice of supplying some crews with a daily ration of lemon juice, which had highly beneficial effects.

The practice of gorging on meat, sweets, and spirits caused the rich their own nutritional problems. They, too, were very often deficient in vitamins A and C because of their great disdain for fresh vegetables. Gout was a common affliction of the overfed and underexercised rich. No wonder they were often caricatured dragging their flabby limbs and bulging bellies to the table, to stuff their swollen cheeks and poison their livers. People of moderate means, who could afford some meat and dairy products with fair regularity but who had not abandoned the bread and vegetables of the poor, were probably best off from a nutritional standpoint.

New Foods and New Knowledge

In nutrition and food consumption, Europe in the early eighteenth century had not gone beyond its medieval accomplishments. This situation began to change markedly as the century progressed. Although the introduction of new methods of farming was confined largely to the Low Countries and England, a new food—the potato—came to the aid of the poor everywhere.

Introduced into Europe from the Americas, along with corn, squash, tomatoes, chocolate, and many other useful plants, the humble potato is an excellent food. It contains a good supply of carbohydrates and calories, and is rich in vitamins A and C, especially if the skin is eaten and it is not overcooked. The lack of green vegetables that could lead to scurvy was one of the biggest deficiencies in the poor person's winter and early spring diet. The potato, which gave a much higher caloric yield than grain for a given piece of land, provided the needed vitamins and supplemented the bread-based diet. Doctors, increasingly aware of the dietary benefits of potatoes, prescribed them for the general public and in institutions such as schools and prisons.

For some poor people with little land the potato replaced grain as the primary food in the eighteenth century. This happened first in Ireland, where in the seventeenth century rebellion had led to English repression and the perfection of a savage system of exploitation. The foreign (and Protestant) English landlords took the best land, forcing large numbers of poor (and Catholic) peasants to live off tiny scraps of rented ground. By 1700 the poor in Ireland lived almost exclusively on the bountiful fruits of the potato plot.

Elsewhere in Europe, the potato took hold more slowly. Potatoes were first fed to pigs and livestock, and there was considerable debate over whether they were fit for humans. In Germany the severe famines caused by the Seven Years' War (1756–1763) settled the matter: potatoes were edible and not famine food. By the end of the century, the potato was an important dietary supplement in much of Europe.

There was also a general growth of market gardening and a greater variety of vegetables in towns and cities. Potatoes, cabbages, peas, beans, radishes, spinach, asparagus, lettuce, parsnips, carrots, and other vegetables were sold in central markets and streets. In the course of the eighteenth century, the large towns and cities of maritime Europe began to receive semitropical fruit, such as oranges, lemons, and limes, from Portugal and the West Indies, although they were not cheap.

The growing variety of food was matched by some improvement in knowledge about diet and nutrition. For the poor, such improvement was limited primarily to the insight that the potato and other root crops improved health in the winter and helped to prevent scurvy. The rich began to be aware of the harmful effects of their meat-laden, wine-drowned meals.

The waning influence of ancient medical teachings was another aspect of progress. The Roman synthesis of ancient medical doctrines held that the four basic elements—air, fire, water, and earth—combine to produce in each person a complexion and a corresponding temperament. Foods were grouped into four categories appropriate for each complexion. These notions dominated the dietary thinking of the seventeenth-century medical profession: "The flesh of a hare preventeth fatness, causeth sleep and cleanseth the blood," and so on for a thousand things.

The growth of scientific experimentation in the seventeenth century led to a generally beneficial questioning of the old views. Haphazardly, by trial and error, and influenced by advances in chemistry, saver ideas developed. Not all changes in the eighteenth century were for the better, however. Bread began to change, most noticeably in England. Rising incomes and new tastes led to a shift from whole-meal black or brown bread to white bread made from finely ground and sifted flour. On the Continent, such white bread was generally limited to the well-to-do. To the extent that the preferred wheaten flour was stone-ground and sifted for coarse particles only, white bread remained satisfactory. But the desire for "bread as white as snow" was already leading to a decline in nutritional value.

The coarser bran and at least some of the germ were already being sifted out to some extent. Bakers in English cities added the chemical alum to their white loaves to make them smoother, whiter, and larger. In the nineteenth century, "improvements" in milling were to lead to the removal of almost all the bran and germ from the flour, leaving it perfectly white and greatly reduced in nutritional value. The only saving grace in this sad deterioration was that people began to eat less bread and therefore to depend on it less.

Another sign of nutritional decline was the growing consumption of sweets in general and sugar in particular. Initially a luxury, sugar dropped rapidly in price as slave-based production increased in the Americas, and it was much more widely used in the eighteenth century. This development probably led to an increase in cavities and to other ailments as well. Overconsumption of refined sugar can produce, paradoxically, low blood sugar (hypoglycemia) and, for some individuals at least, a variety of physical and mental ailments. Of course the greater or lesser poverty of the laboring poor saved most of them from the problems of the rich and well-to-do.

THE MEDICAL PROFESSIONALS

Advances in medical science played a very small part in improving the health and lengthening the lives of people in the eighteenth century. Such seventeenth-century advances as William Harvey's discovery of the circulation of blood were not soon translated into better treatment. The sick had to await the medical revolution of the later nineteenth century for much help from doctors.

Yet developments in medicine reflected the general thrust of the Enlightenment. The prevailing focus on discovering the laws of nature and on human problems, rather than on God and the heavens, gave rise to a great deal of research and experimentation. The century saw a remarkable rise in the number of doctors, and a high value was placed on their services.

Thus when the great breakthroughs in knowledge came in the nineteenth century, they could be rapidly diffused and applied.

Care of the sick was the domain of several competing groups—faith healers, apothecaries, surgeons, and physicians. Since the great majority of common ailments have a tendency to cure themselves, each group could point to successes and win adherents. When the doctor's treatment made the patient worse, as it often did, the original medical problem could always be blamed.

Faith healers, who had been one of the most important kinds of physicians in medieval Europe, remained active. They and their patients believed that demons and evil spirits caused disease by lodging in people and that the proper treatment was to exorcise or drive out the offending devil. This demonic view of disease was strongest in the countryside, as was faith in the healing power of religious relics, prayer, and the laying on of hands. Faith healing was particularly effective in the treatment of mental disorders like hysteria and depression, where the link between attitude and illness is most direct.

Apothecaries, or pharmacists, sold a vast number of herbs, drugs, and patent medicines for every conceivable "temperament and distemper." Early pharmacists were seldom regulated, and they frequently diagnosed as freely as the doctors whose prescriptions they filled. Their prescriptions were incredibly complex—a hundred or more drugs might be included in a single prescription—and often very expensive. Some of the drugs undoubtedly worked: strong laxatives were routinely administered to the rich for their constipated bowels. Much purging was clearly harmful, and only bloodletting for the treatment of disease was more effective in speeding patients to their graves.

Drugs were prescribed and concocted in a helter-skelter way. With so many different drugs being combined, it was impossible to isolate cause and effect. Nor was there any standardization. A complicated prescription filled by ten different pharmacists would result in ten different preparations with different medical properties.

Surgeons competed vigorously with barbers and "bone benders," the forerunners of chiropractors. The eighteenth-century surgeon (and patient) labored in the face of incredible difficulties. Almost all operations were performed without any painkiller,

for anesthesia was believed too dangerous. The terrible screams of people whose limbs were being sawed off shattered hospitals and battlefields. Such operations were common, because a surgeon faced with an extensive wound sought to obtain a plain surface that he could cauterize with fire. Thus, if a person broke an arm or a leg and the bone stuck out, off came the limb. Many patients died from the agony and shock of these operations.

Surgery was also performed in the midst of filth and dirt. There simply was no knowledge of bacteriology and the nature of infection. The simplest wound treated by a surgeon festered, often fatally. In fact, surgeons encouraged wounds to fester in the belief that the pus was beneficially removing the base portions of the body.

Physicians, the fourth major group, were trained like surgeons. They were apprenticed in their teens to a practicing physician for several years of on-the-job training. This training was then rounded out with hospital work or some university courses. To their credit, physicians in the eighteenth century were increasingly willing to experiment with new methods, but tradition lay heavily on them. Bloodletting was still considered a medical cure-all. It was the way "bad blood," the cause of illness, was removed and the balance of humors necessary for good health restored. According to a physician practicing medicine in Philadelphia in 1799, bleeding was proper at the onset of all inflammatory fevers, in all inflammations, and for "asthma, sciatic pains, coughs, headaches, rheumatisms, the apoplexy, epilepsy, and bloody fluxes."[14] It was also necessary after all falls, blows, and bruises.

Physicians, like apothecaries, laid great stress on purging. They also generally believed that disease was caused by bad odors, and for this reason they carried canes whose heads contained ammonia salts. As they made their rounds in the filthy, stinking hospitals, physicians held their canes to their noses to protect themselves from illness.

While faith leaders were praying, apothecaries purging, surgeons sawing, and physicians bleeding, the growth of scientific experimentation from the seventeenth century onward led to a generally beneficial questioning of old views. In the eighteenth century, the leading medical thinkers attempted to pull together and assimilate all the accumulated information and misinformation, to systematize medicine around simple, basic principles, as Newton had done in physics. But the schools of thought resulting from such speculation and theorizing did little to improve medical care. Proponents of animism explained life and disease in terms of *anima,* the "sensitive soul," which they believed was present throughout the body and prevented its decay and self-destruction. Another school, *vitalism,* stressed "the vital principle," which inhabited all parts of the body. Vitalists tried to classify diseases systematically.

More interesting was the *homeopathic* system of Samuel Hahnemann of Leipzig. Hahnemann believed that very small doses of drugs that produce certain symptoms in a healthy person will cure a sick person with those symptoms. This theory was probably preferable to most eighteenth-century treatments, in that it was a harmless alternative to the extravagant and often fatal practices of bleeding, purging, drug taking, and induced vomiting. The patient gained confidence, and the body had at least a fighting chance of recovering.

HOSPITALS AND MENTAL ILLNESS

Hospitals were terrible throughout most of the eighteenth century. There was no isolation of patients. Operations were performed in the patient's bed. The nurses were old, ignorant, greedy, and often drunk women. Fresh air was considered harmful, and infections of every kind were rampant. Diderot's article in the *Encyclopedia* on the Hôtel-Dieu in Paris, the "richest and most terrifying of all French hospitals," vividly describes normal conditions of the 1770s:

Imagine a long series of communicating wards filled with sufferers of every kind of disease who are sometimes packed three, four, five or even six into a bed, the living alongside the dead and dying, the air polluted by this mass of unhealthy bodies, passing pestilential germs of their afflictions from one to the other, and the spectacle of suffering and agony on every hand. That is the Hôtel-Dieu.

The result is that many of these poor wretches come out with diseases they did not have when they went in, and often pass them on to the people they go back to live with. Others are half-cured and spend the rest of their days in an invalidism as hard to bear as the illness itself; and the rest perish, except for the fortunate few whose strong constitutions enable them to survive.[15]

Knives for Bloodletting In the eighteenth century doctors continued to use these diabolical instruments to treat almost every illness, with disastrous results. *(Courtesy, World Heritage Museum. Photo: Caroline Buckler)*

No wonder the poor of Paris hated hospitals and often saw confinement there as a plot to kill paupers.

In the last years of the century, the humanitarian concern already reflected in Diderot's description of the Hôtel-Dieu led to a movement for hospital reform throughout western Europe. Efforts were made to improve ventilation and eliminate filth, on the grounds that bad air caused disease. The theory was wrong, but the results were beneficial, since the spread of infection was somewhat reduced.

Mental hospitals, too, were incredibly savage institutions. The customary treatments for mental illness were bleeding and cold water, administered more to maintain discipline than to effect a cure. Violent persons were chained to the wall and forgotten. A breakthrough of sorts occurred in the 1790s, when William Tuke founded the first humane sanatorium in England. In Paris an innovative warden, Philippe Pinel, took the chains off the mentally disturbed in 1793

Hospital Life Patients crowded into hospitals like this one in Hamburg in 1746 had little chance of recovery. A priest by the window administers last rites, while in the center a surgeon coolly cuts off the leg of a man who has received no anesthesia. *(Germanisches Nationalmuseum, Nurnberg)*

and tried to treat them as patients rather than as prisoners.

In the eighteenth century, there were all sorts of wildly erroneous ideas about mental illness. One was that moonlight caused madness, a belief reflected in the word *lunatic*—someone harmed by lunar light. Another mid-eighteenth-century theory, which persisted until at least 1914, was that masturbation caused madness, not to mention acne, epilepsy, and premature ejaculation. Thus parents, religious institutions, and schools waged relentless war on masturbation by males, although they were curiously uninterested in female masturbation. In the nineteenth century, this misguided idea was to reach its greatest height, resulting in increasingly drastic medical treatment. Doctors ordered their "patients" to wear mittens, fitted them with wooden braces between the knees, or simply tied them up in straitjackets.

MEDICAL EXPERIMENTS AND RESEARCH

In the second half of the eighteenth century, medicine in general turned in a more practical and experimental direction. Some of the experimentation was creative quackery involving the recently discovered phenomenon of electricity. One magnificent quack, James Graham of London, opened a great hall filled with the walking sticks, crutches, eyeglasses, and ear trumpets of supposedly cured patients, which he kept as symbols of his victory over disease. Graham's principal treatment involved his Celestial Bed, which was lavishly decorated with electrical devices and which cost £100 for a single night—a great sum of money.

The rich could buy expensive treatments, but the prevalence of quacks and the general lack of knowledge meant they often got little for their money. Because so many treatments were harmful, the poor were probably much less deprived by their almost total lack of access to medical care than one might think.

Renewed experimentation and the intensified search for solutions to human problems also led to some real, if still modest, advances in medicine after 1750. The eighteenth century's greatest medical triumph was the conquest of smallpox.

With the progressive decline of bubonic plague, smallpox became the most terrible of the infectious diseases. In the words of the nineteenth-century historian Thomas Macaulay, "smallpox was always present, filling the churchyard with corpses, tormenting with constant fears all whom it had not stricken." It is estimated that 60 million Europeans died of it in the eighteenth century and that fully 80 percent of the population was stricken at some point in life. If ever a human problem cried out for solution, it was smallpox.

The first step in the conquest of this killer came in the early eighteenth century. An English aristocrat whose great beauty had been marred by the pox, Lady Mary Wortley Montague, learned about the practice of inoculation in the Ottoman Empire while her husband was serving as British ambassador there. She had her own son successfully inoculated in Constantinople and was instrumental in spreading the practice in England after her return in 1722.

Inoculation against smallpox had long been practiced in the Middle East. The skin was deliberately broken, and a small amount of matter taken from a pustule of a smallpox victim was applied. The person thus contracted a mild case of smallpox that gave lasting protection against further attack. Inoculation was risky, however, and about one person in fifty died from it. In addition, people who had been inoculated often spread the disease, so that the practice of inoculation against smallpox was widely condemned in the 1730s.

Success in overcoming this problem in British colonies led the British College of Physicians in 1754 to strongly advocate inoculation. Moreover, a successful search for cheaper methods led to something approaching mass inoculation in England in the 1760s. On the Continent, the well-to-do were also inoculated, beginning with royal families like those of Maria Theresa and Catherine the Great. The practice then spread to the middle classes. Smallpox inocula-tion played some part in the decline of the death rate in the late eighteenth century and the increase in population.

The final breakthrough against smallpox came at the end of the century. Edward Jenner (1749–1823), a talented country doctor, noted that in the English countryside there was a long-standing belief that dairy maids who had contracted cowpox did not get smallpox. Cowpox produces sores on the cow's udder and on the hands of the milker. The sores resemble those of smallpox, but the disease is mild and not contagious.

For eighteen years Jenner practiced a kind of Baconian science, carefully collecting data on protection against smallpox by cowpox. Finally, in 1796 he performed his first vaccination on a young boy, using matter taken from a milkmaid with cowpox. Two months later he inoculated the boy with smallpox pus, but the disease did not take. In the next two years, twenty-three successful vaccinations were performed, and in 1798 Jenner published his findings. There was some skepticism and hostility, but after Austrian medical authorities replicated Jenner's results, the new method of treatment spread rapidly. Smallpox soon declined to the point of disappearance in Europe and then throughout the world. Jenner eventually received prizes of £30,000 from the British government for his great discovery, a fitting recompense for a man who gave an enormous gift to humanity and helped lay the foundation for the science of immunology in the nineteenth century.

RELIGION AND CHRISTIAN CHURCHES

Though the critical spirit of the Enlightenment spread among the educated elite in the eighteenth century, the great mass of ordinary men and women remained firmly committed to the Christian religion, especially in rural areas. Religion offered answers to life's mysteries and gave comfort and courage in the face of sorrow and fear. Religion also remained strong because it was usually embedded in local traditions and everyday social experience.

Yet the popular religion of village Europe was everywhere enmeshed in a larger world of church hierarchies and state power. These powerful outside forces sought to regulate religious life at the local level. These efforts created tensions that helped set the scene for a vigorous religious revival in Germany and England.

THE INSTITUTIONAL CHURCH

As in the Middle Ages, the local parish church remained the basic religious unit all across Europe. Still largely coinciding with the agricultural village, the parish fulfilled many needs. The parish church was the focal point of religious devotion, which went far beyond sermons and Holy Communion. The parish church organized colorful processions and pilgrimages to local shrines. Even in Protestant countries, where such activities were severely restricted, congregations gossiped and swapped stories after services, and neighbors came together in church for baptisms, marriages, funerals, and special events. Thus the parish church was woven into the very fabric of community life.

Moreover, the local church had important administrative tasks. Priests and parsons were truly the bookkeepers of agrarian Europe, and it is because parish registers were so complete that historians have learned so much about population and family life. Parishes also normally distributed charity to the destitute, looked after orphans, and provided whatever primary education was available.

The many tasks of the local church were usually the responsibility of a resident priest or pastor, a full-time professional working with assistants and lay volunteers. Moreover, all clerics—whether Catholic, Protestant, or Orthodox—shared the fate of middlemen in a complicated institutional system. Charged most often with ministering to poor peasants, the priest or parson was the last link in a powerful church-state hierarchy that was everywhere determined to control religion down to the grassroots. However, the regulatory framework of belief, which went back at least to the fourth century, when Christianity became the official religion of the Roman Empire, had undergone important changes since 1500.

The Protestant Reformation had begun as a culmination of medieval religiosity and a desire to purify Christian belief. Martin Luther, the greatest of the reformers (see pages 520–528), preached that all men and women were saved from their sins and God's damnation only by personal faith in Jesus Christ.

The individual could reach God directly, without need of priestly intermediaries. This was the revolutionary meaning of Luther's "priesthood of all believers," which broke forever the monopoly of the priestly class over medieval Europe's most priceless treasure—eternal salvation.

As the Reformation gathered force, with peasant upheaval and doctrinal competition, Luther turned more conservative. The monkish professor called on willing German princes to put themselves at the head of official churches in their territories. Other monarchs in northern Europe followed suit. Protestant authorities, with generous assistance from state-certified theologians like Luther, then proceeded to regulate their "territorial churches" strictly, selecting personnel and imposing detailed rules. They joined with Catholics to crush the Anabaptists (see page 530), who with their belief in both freedom of conscience and separation of church and state had become the real revolutionaries. Thus the Reformation, initially so radical in its rejection of Rome and its stress on individual religious experience, eventually resulted in a bureaucratization of the church and local religious life in Protestant Europe.

The Reformation era also increased the practical power of Catholic rulers over "their" churches, but it was only in the eighteenth century that some Catholic monarchs began to impose striking reforms. These reforms, which had their counterparts in Orthodox Russia, had a very "Protestant" aspect. They increased state control over the Catholic church, making it less subject to papal influence.

Spain provides a graphic illustration of changing church-state relations in Catholic lands. A deeply Catholic country with devout rulers, Spain nevertheless took firm control of ecclesiastical appointments. Papal proclamations could not even be read in Spanish churches without prior approval from the government. Spain also asserted state control over the Spanish Inquisition (see page 516), which had been ruthlessly pursuing heretics as an independent agency under Rome's direction for two hundred years. In sum, Spain went far toward creating a "national" Catholic church, as France had done earlier.

A more striking indication of state power and papal weakness was the fate of the Society of Jesus. As the most successful of the Catholic Reformation's new religious orders (see page 540), the well-educated Jesuits were extraordinary teachers, missionaries, and agents of the papacy. In many Catholic countries, the Jesuits exercised tremendous political influence, since individual members held high government positions, and Jesuit colleges formed the minds of Europe's Catholic nobility. Yet, by playing politics so effectively, the Jesuits eventually raised a broad coalition of enemies, which destroyed their order. Especially bitter controversies over the Jesuits rocked the entire Catholic hierarchy in France. Following the earlier example of Portugal, Louis XV (1715–1774) ordered the Jesuits out of France in 1763 and confiscated their property. France and Spain then pressured Rome to dissolve the Jesuits completely. In 1773, reluctantly, Pope Clement XIV caved in, although the order was revived after the French Revolution.

Some Catholic rulers also turned their reforming efforts on monasteries and convents, believing that the large monastic clergy should make a more practical contribution to social and religious life. Austria, a leader in controlling the church (see page 670), showed how far the process could go. Whereas Maria Theresa sharply restricted entry into "unproductive" orders, Joseph II recalled the radical initiatives of the Protestant Reformation. In his *Edict on Idle Institutions,* Joseph abolished contemplative orders, henceforth permitting only orders engaged in teaching, nursing, or other practical work. The number of monks plunged from 65,000 to 27,000. The state also expropriated the dissolved monasteries and used their great wealth for charitable purposes and higher salaries for ordinary priests.

Catholic Piety

Catholic territorial churches also sought to purify religious practice somewhat. As might be expected, Joseph II went the furthest. Above all, he and his agents sought to root out what they considered to be idolatry and superstition. Yet pious peasants saw only an incomprehensible attack on the true faith and drew back in anger. Joseph's sledgehammer approach and the resulting reaction dramatized an underlying tension between Christian reform and popular piety after the Reformation.

Protestant reformers had taken very seriously the commandment that "Thou shalt not make any graven image" (Exodus 20:4), and their radical reforms had reordered church interiors. Relics and crucifixes had been permanently removed from crypt and altar, while stained-glass windows had been smashed and walls and murals covered with whitewash. Processions and pilgrimages, saints and shrines—all such nonessentials had been rigorously suppressed in the attempt to recapture the vital core of the Christian religion. Such revolutionary changes had often troubled ordinary churchgoers, but by the late seventeenth century, these reforms had been thoroughly routinized by official Protestant churches.

The situation was quite different in Catholic Europe around 1700. First of all, the visual contrast was striking; baroque art (see pages 634–635) had lavished rich and emotionally exhilarating figures and images on Catholic churches, just as Protestants had removed theirs. From almost every indication, people in Catholic Europe remained intensely religious. More than 95 percent of the population probably attended church for Easter Communion, the climax of the Catholic church year.

Much of the tremendous popular strength of religion in Catholic countries reflected that its practice went far beyond Sunday churchgoing and was an important part of community life. Thus, although Catholics reluctantly confessed their sins to the priest, they enthusiastically joined together in public processions to celebrate the passage of the liturgical year. In addition to the great processional days— such as Palm Sunday, the joyful re-enactment of Jesus' triumphal entry into Jerusalem, and Rogations, with its chanted supplications and penances three days before the bodily ascent of Jesus into heaven on Ascension Day—each parish had its own local processions. Led by its priest, a congregation might march around the village, or across the countryside to a local shrine or chapel. There were endless variations. In the southern French Alps, the people looked forward especially to "high-mountain" processions in late spring. Parishes came together from miles around on some high mountain. There the assembled priests asked God to bless the people with healthy flocks and pure waters, and then all joined together in an enormous picnic. Before each procession, the priest explained its religious significance to kindle group piety. But processions were also folklore and tradition, an escape from work and a form of recreation. A holiday atmosphere sometimes reigned on longer processions, with drinking and dancing and couples disappearing into the woods.

Devout Catholics held many religious beliefs that were marginal to the Christian faith, often of obscure or even pagan origin. On the Feast of Saint Anthony, priests were expected to bless salt and bread for farm animals to protect them from disease. One saint's relics could help cure a child of fear, and there were healing springs for many ailments. The ordinary person combined a strong Christian faith with a wealth of time-honored superstitions.

Parish priests and Catholic hierarchies were frequently troubled by the limitations of their parishioners' Christian understanding. One parish priest in France, who kept an invaluable daily diary, lamented that his parishioners were "more superstitious than devout . . . and sometimes appear as baptized idolators."[16]

Many parish priests in France, often acting on instructions from their bishops, made an effort to purify popular religious culture. For example, one priest tried to abolish pilgrimages to a local sacred spring of Our Lady, reputed to revive dead babies long enough for a proper baptism. French priests denounced particularly the "various remnants of paganism" found in popular bonfire ceremonies during Lent, in which young men, "yelling and screaming like madmen," tried to jump over the bonfires in order to help the crops grow and protect themselves from illness. One priest saw rational Christians turning back into pagan animals—"the triumph of Hell and the shame of Christianity."[17]

Yet, whereas Protestant reformers had already used the power of the territorial state to crush such practices, Catholic church leaders generally proceeded cautiously in the eighteenth century. They knew that old beliefs—such as the belief common throughout Europe that the priest's energetic ringing of church bells and his recitation of ritual prayers would protect the village from hail and thunderstorms—were an integral part of the people's religion. Thus Catholic priests and hierarchies generally preferred a compromise between theological purity and the people's piety, realizing perhaps that the line between divine truth and mere superstition is not easily drawn.

Protestant Revival

By the late seventeenth century, official Protestant churches had completed their vast reforms and had generally settled into complacency. In the Reformation heartland, one concerned German minister wrote that the Lutheran church "had become paralyzed in forms of dead doctrinal conformity" and badly needed a return to its original inspiration.[18] This voice was one of many that would prepare and then guide a powerful Protestant revival, a revival largely successful because it answered the intense but increasingly unsatisfied needs of common people.

The Protestant revival began in Germany. It was known as "Pietism," and three aspects helped explain its powerful appeal. First, Pietism called for warm emotional religion that everyone could experience. Enthusiasm—in prayer, in worship, in preaching, in life itself—was the key concept. "Just as a drunkard becomes full of wine, so must the congregation become filled with spirit," exclaimed one writer. Another stated simply, "The heart must burn."[19]

Second, Pietism reasserted the earlier radical stress on the "priesthood of all believers," thereby reducing the large gulf between the official clergy and the Lutheran laity, which had continued to exist after the Reformation. Bible reading and study were enthusiastically extended to all classes, which provided a powerful spur for popular education as well as individual religious development. Finally, Pietists believed in the practical power of Christian rebirth in everyday affairs. Reborn Christians were expected to lead good, moral lives and come from all walks of life.

Pietism had a major impact on John Wesley (1703–1791), who served as the catalyst for popular religious revival in England. Wesley came from a long line of ministers, and when he went to Oxford University to prepare for the clergy, he mapped a fanatically earnest "scheme of religion." Like some students during final exam period, he organized every waking moment. After becoming a teaching fellow at Oxford, he organized the Holy Club for similarly minded students, who were soon known contemptuously as "Methodists" because they were so methodical in their devotion. Yet, like the young Luther, Wesley remained intensely troubled about his own salvation, even after his ordination as an Anglican priest in 1728.

Wesley's anxieties related to grave problems of the faith in England. The Church of England was shamelessly used by the government to provide favorites with high-paying jobs and sinecures. Building of churches practically stopped while the population grew, and in many parishes there was a grave shortage of pews. Services and sermons had settled into an uninspiring routine. That the properly purified religion had been separated from local customs and social life

Open-air Preaching In an age when the established Church of England lacked religious fervor and smugly reinforced the social status quo, John Wesley carried the good news of salvation to common people across the land. Wesley sparked a powerful religious revival, symbolized by the joyful bell-ringing of the town crier in this illustration. *(Historical Pictures Service)*

was symbolized by church doors that were customarily locked on weekdays. Moreover, the skepticism of the Enlightenment was making inroads among the educated classes, and deism was becoming popular. Some bishops and church leaders acted as if they believed that doctrines like the Virgin Birth and the Ascension were little more than particularly elegant superstitions.

Living in an atmosphere of religious decline and uncertainty, Wesley became profoundly troubled by his lack of faith in his own salvation. Yet spiritual counseling from a sympathetic Pietist minister from Germany prepared Wesley for a mystical, emotional "conversion" in 1738. He described this critical turning point in his *Journal*:

In the evening I went to a [Christian] society in Aldersgate Street where one was reading Luther's preface to the Epistle to the Romans. *About a quarter before nine, while he was describing the change which God works in the heart through faith in Christ, I felt my heart strangely warmed. I felt I did trust in Christ, Christ alone for salvation; and an assurance was given me that he had taken away* my *sins, even* mine, *and saved* me *from the law of sin and death.*[20]

Wesley's emotional experience resolved his intellectual doubts. Moreover, he was convinced that any person, no matter how poor or simple, might have a similar heartfelt conversion and gain the same blessed assurance.

Wesley took the good news to the people. Since existing churches were often overcrowded and the church-state establishment was hostile, Wesley preached in open fields. People came in large numbers. Of critical importance, Wesley expanded on earlier Dutch theologians' views and emphatically rejected Calvinist predestination—the doctrine of salvation granted only to a select few (see page 528). Rather, all men and women who earnestly sought salvation might be saved. It was a message of hope and joy, of free will and universal salvation.

Traveling some 225,000 miles by horseback and preaching more than 40,000 sermons in fifty years, Wesley's ministry won converts, formed Methodist cells, and eventually resulted in a new denomination. Evangelicals in the Church of England and the old dissenting groups also followed Wesley's example, giving impetus to an even broader awakening among the lower classes. That result showed that in England, as throughout Europe despite different churches and different practices, religion remained a vital force in the lives of the people.

In recent years, imaginative research has greatly increased the specialist's understanding of ordinary life and social patterns in the past. The human experience, as recounted by historians, has become richer and more meaningful, and many mistaken ideas have fallen. This has been particularly true of eighteenth-century, preindustrial Europe. The world of everyday labor, the intimacies of family life, the contours of women's history and of childhood, and vital problems of medicine and religion are emerging from obscurity. Nor is this all. A deeper, truer understanding of the life of common people is shedding light on the great political and economic developments of the late eighteenth and early nineteenth centuries, developments considered in Chapters 25 and 26.

NOTES

1. Quoted in E. E. Rich and C. H. Wilson, eds., *Cambridge Economic History of Europe,* vol. 4 (Cambridge: Cambridge University Press, 1967), p. 85.
2. Quoted in S. Chapman, *The Lancashire Cotton Industry* (Manchester, England: Manchester University Press, 1903), p. 13.
3. Quoted in J. M. Beattie, "The Criminality of Women in Eighteenth-century England," *Journal of Social History 8* (Summer 1975):86.
4. W. L. Langer, "Infanticide: A Historical Survey," *History of Childhood Quarterly* 1 (Winter 1974): 357
5. Quoted in R. Cobb, *The Police and the People: French Popular Protest, 1789–1820* (Oxford: Clarendon Press, 1970), p. 238.
6. Quoted in E. A. Wrigley, *Population and History* (New York: McGraw-Hill, 1969), p. 127.
7. Quoted in D.S. Landes, ed., *The Rise of Capitalism* (New York: Macmillan, 1966), pp. 56–57.
8. See L. A. Tilly, J. W. Scott, and M. Cohen, "Women's Work and European Fertility Patterns," *Journal of Interdisciplinary History* 6 (Winter 1976):447–476.
9. J. Michelet, *The People,* trans. with an introduction by J. P. McKay (Urbana, Ill.: University of Illinois Press, 1973 [original publication 1846]), pp. 38–39.
10. J. Brownlow, *The History and Design of the Foundling Hospital* (London, 1868), p. 7.
11. Quoted in B. W. Lorence, "Parents and Children in Eighteenth-century Europe," *History of Childhood Quarterly* 2 (Summer 1974): 1–2.
12. Ibid., pp. 13, 16.
13. J. C. Drummond and A. Wilbraham, *The Englishman's Food: A History of Five Centuries of English Diet,* 2d ed. (London: Jonathan Cape, 1958), p. 75.
14. Quoted in L. S. King, *The Medical World of the Eighteenth Century* (Chicago: University of Chicago Press, 1958), p. 320.
15. Quoted in R. Sand, *The Advance to Social Medicine* (London: Staples Press, 1952), pp. 86–87.
16. Quoted in I. Woloch, *Eighteenth-century Europe: Tradition and Progress, 1715–1789* (New York: Norton, 1982), p. 292.
17. Quoted in T. Tackett, *Priest and Parish in Eighteenth-century France* (Princeton, N.J.: Princeton University Press, 1977), p. 214.
18. Quoted in K. Pinson, *Pietism as a Factor in the Rise of German Nationalism* (New York: Columbia University Press, 1934), p. 13.
19. Quoted in ibid., pp. 43–44.
20. Quoted in S. Andrews, *Methodism and Society* (London: Longmans, Green, 1970), p. 327.

SUGGESTED READING

Though often ignored in many general histories of the world, social topics of the kind considered in this chapter flourish in specialized journals today. The articles cited in the Notes are typical of the exciting work being done, and the reader is strongly advised to take time to look through recent volumes of some leading journals: *Journal of Social History, Past and Present, History of Childhood Quarterly,* and *Journal of Interdisciplinary History.* In addition, the number of book-length studies has begun to expand rapidly.

Two fine books on the growth of population are C. Cipolla's short and lively *The Economic History of World Population* (1962) and T. McKeown's scholarly *The Modern Rise of Population* (1977). W. McNeill, *Plagues and Peoples* (1976), is also noteworthy. B. H. Slicher van Bath, *The Agrarian History of Western Europe, A.D. 500–1850* (1963), is a wide-ranging general introduction to the gradual transformation of European agriculture, while J. Blum, *The End of the Old Order in Rural Europe* (1978), is an impressive comparative study. Two recommended and complementary studies on land-owning nobilities are R. Forster, *The Nobility of Toulouse in the Eighteenth Century* (1960), and G. E. Mingay, *English Landed Society in the Eighteenth Century* (1963). E. L. R. Ladurie, *The Peasants of Languedoc* (1976), a brilliant and challenging study of rural life in southern France for several centuries, complements J. Goody et al., eds., *Family and Inheritance: Rural Society in Western Europe, 1200–1800* (1976). Life in small-town preindustrial France comes alive in P. Higonnet, *Pont-de-Montvert: Social Structure and Politics in a French Villiage, 1700–1914* (1971), while O. Hufton deals vividly and sympathetically with rural migration, work, women and much more in *The Poor in Eighteenth-century France* (1974). F. Braudel, *Civilization and Capitalism, 15th–18th Century* (1981–1984), is a monumental and highly recommended three-volume synthesis of social and economic development. Another exciting work is J. Nef, *War and Human Progress* (1968), which examines the impact of war on economic and industrial development in European history between about 1500 and 1800 and may be compared with M. Gutmann, *War and Rural Life in the Early Modern Low Countries* (1980).

Among general introductions to the history of the family, women, and children, the work by Wrigley, cited in the Notes is excellent. It also covers the growth of population. P. Laslett, *The World We Have Lost* (1965), is an exciting, pioneering investigation of England before the Industrial Revolution, though some of his conclusions have been weakened by further research. L. Stone, *The Family, Sex and Marriage in England, 1500–1800* (1977), is a brilliant general interpretation, and L. Tilly and J. Scott, *Women, Work and Family* (1978), is excellent. P. Ariès, *Centuries of Childhood: A Social History of Family Life* (1962), is another stimu-lating study. E. Shorter, *The Making of the Modern Family* (1975), is an all-too-lively and rather controversial interpretation. All four works are highly recommended. T. Rabb and R. I. Rothberg, eds., *The Family in History* (1973), is a good collection of articles dealing with both Europe and the United States. A. MacFarlane, *The Family Life of Ralph Josselin* (1970), is a brilliant re-creation of the intimate family circle of a seventeenth-century English clergyman who kept a detailed diary; MacFarlane's *Origins of English Individualism: The Family, Property and Social Transition* (1978) is a major work. I. Pinchbeck and M. Hewitt, *Children in English Society* (1973), is a good introduction. E. Flexner has written a fine biography on the early feminist Mary Wollstonecraft (1972). Various aspects of sexual relationships are treated imaginatively by M. Foucault, *The History of Sexuality* (1981), and R. Wheaton and T. Hareven, eds., *Family and Sexuality in French History* (1980).

J. Burnett, *A History of the Cost of Living* (1969), has a great deal of interesting information about what people spent their money on in the past and complements the fascinating work of J. C. Drummond and A. Wilbraham, *The Englishman's Food: A History of Five Centuries of English Diet* (1958). Good introductions to the evolution of medical practices are B. Ingles, *History of Medicine* (1965); O. Bettmann, *A Pictorial History of Medicine* (1956); and H. Haggard's old but interesting *Devils, Drugs, and Doctors* (1929). W. Boyd, *History of Western Education* (1966), is a standard survey, which may be usefully supplemented by an important article by L. Stone, "Literacy and Education in England, 1640–1900," *Past and Present* 42 (February 1969): 69–139. M. D. George, *London Life in the Eighteenth Century* (1965), is a delightfully written book, while L. Chevalier, *Labouring Classes and Dangerous Classes* (1973), is a keen analysis of the poor people of Paris in a slightly later period. G. Rudé, *The Crowd in History, 1730–1848* (1964), is an innovative effort to see politics and popular protest from below. An important series edited by R. Forster and O. Ranuum considers neglected social questions such as diet, abandoned children, and deviants, as does P. Burke's excellent study, *Popular Culture in Early Modern Europe* (1978).

Good works on religious life include J. Delumeau, *Catholicism Between Luther and Voltaire: A New View of the Counter-Reformation* (1977); B. Semmel, *The Methodist Revolution* (1973); and J. Bettey, *Church and Community: The Parish Church in English Life* (1979). Also see the work by Tackett cited in the Notes.

AFRICA, THE MIDDLE EAST, AND INDIA, CA 1400–1800

*A*FRICAN STATES and societies of the fifteenth through seventeenth centuries represented a wide variety of languages, cultures, and kinds of economic and political development. European intrusion in Africa led to the transatlantic slave trade, one of the great forced migrations in world history. Africa helped substantially in building the West's industrial civilization. In the seventeenth century, an increasing desire for sugar in Europe resulted in an increasing demand for slave labor in South America and the West Indies. In the eighteenth century, Western technological changes, created a demand for cotton and other crops that required extensive human labor. As a result, the West's "need" for slaves from Africa increased dramatically.

Between 1450 and 1800, three powerful Muslim kingdoms reached the zenith of their territorial extension and of their intellectual and artistic vitality. With the conquest of Constantinople the Ottoman Turks gained an impregnable capital and the respect of all Islam. The Ottomans soon overran much of Anatolia, North Africa, and the Balkans. In Persia the Safavid dynasty created a theocracy and presided over a brilliant culture. A theological dispute between the Ottomans and the Safavids brought bitter division in the Islamic world and weakened both powers. Meanwhile, the Mughal leader Babur and his successors conquered the Indian subcontinent, and Mughal rule inaugurated a period of radical administrative reorganization in India and the flowering of intellectual and architectural creativity. In 1450 all the great highways of international trade were in Muslim hands, and the wealth of the Muslim states derived largely from commerce. By 1750 the Muslims had lost that control, and the Muslim states were declining economically, politically, and culturally.

What economic, political, and demographic effects did foreign trade, especially the slave trade, have on African kingdoms and societies? What features characterized the societies and governments of the Ottoman Empire and of Safavid Persia? What foreign and domestic difficulties caused their decline? How did Muslim governmental reform and artistic inspiration affect the dominant Hindu population in India? What political and social conditions in India enabled the British to expand their empire by gaining power there? These are the questions that this chapter will explore.

AFRICAN KINGDOMS AND SOCIETIES
(CA 1450—1800)

Africa's relationship with Asia, the Islamic world, and the West stretches back a very long time, but only recently have anthropologists, economists, and historians begun to ask critical questions about African societies in early modern times. What kinds of states and societies existed? How did the slave trade operate? What were the geographical and societal origins of the slaves shipped to the Americas and to Asia?

SENEGAMBIA AND BENIN

In the mid-fifteenth century, Africa consisted of a wide variety of kingdoms and states—political entities ruled by princes who governed defined areas through bureaucratic hierarchies—and of societies that lacked political structure but were held together by family or kinship ties.

A number of kingdoms flourished along the 2,000-mile west coast between Senegambia and modern Cameroon. Because much of the coastal region is covered by tropical rain forest, in contrast to the western Sudan, it is called the "West African Forest Region" (Map 23.1). The Senegambian states in the north possessed a homogeneous culture and a common history. For centuries Senegambia—named for its two rivers—had served as an important entrepôt for desert caravan contact with the Islamic civilizations of North Africa and the Middle East. Through the transatlantic slave trade, Senegambia contributed heavily to New World population in the early seventeenth century. That trade brought Senegambia into contact with Europe and the Americas. Thus Senegambia felt the impact of Islamic culture from the north and of European influences from the maritime West.

MAP 23.1 West African Kingdoms and Slave Trade, ca 1500–1800 Consider the role that rivers and other geographical factors played in the development of the West African slave trade. Why would Luanda and Benguela be the logical Portuguese source for slaves?

KANEM

BORNU

Lake Chad

HAUSALAND

Katsina

Kano

SAHARA DESERT

Niger

Gao

MALI

Timbuktu

Niani

FUTA JALON

SENEGAMBIA

Senegal

Gambia

WOLOF

SERER

Saint-Louis

Cape Verde

West African Forest line

ASHANTI

DAHOMEY

Whydah

BENIN

Benin City

Niger Delta

Brass

Bonny

SLAVE COAST

GOLD COAST

Cape Three Points

Cape Palmas

Volta

Bight of Benin

GULF OF GUINEA

Luanda

Benguela

400 Mi.

400 Km.

Major sources of slaves

The kingdoms of Ghana and Mali (pages 461–466) had incorporated parts of Senegambia, but by 1450 several northern states, such as Wolof, were completely independent; southern states like Kantora remained under Mali's hegemony. Mali's influence disintegrated after 1450, giving rise to a number of successor kingdoms that were independent but connected to one another through family ties. Stronger states rose and temporarily exercised power over weaker ones.

Scholars are still exploring the social and political structures of the various Senegambian states. The peoples of Senegambia spoke Wolof, Serer, and Pulaar, which are all members of the West African language group. Both the Wolof-speakers and Serer-speakers had clearly defined classes: royalty, nobility, warriors, peasants, low-caste artisans such as blacksmiths and leatherworkers, and slaves. Slaves consisted of those pawned for debt, house servants who could not be sold, and those acquired through war or purchase. Senegambian slavery, though it varied from society to society, generally was not a benign institution. In some places the harsh treatment of slaves resembled conditions later prevalent in the Western world. On the other hand, many slaves were not considered property that could be bought and sold, and some slaves served as royal advisers and enjoyed great power and prestige.[1]

Among the Wolof the nobility elected the king, who immediately acquired authority and a special religious charisma. He commanded contingents of soldier-slaves and appointed the village chiefs. Kings gained their revenues from the chiefs, from merchants, and from taxes on defeated peoples.[2] The Wolof had a well-defined governmental hierarchy. Among the stateless societies of Senegambia, where kinship and lineage groups tended to fragment communities, age-grade systems evolved. Age-grades were groups of men and women whom the society initiated into adulthood at the same time. Age-grades cut across family ties, created communitywide loyalties, and provided a means of local law enforcement, since the group was mutually responsible for the behavior of all its members.

The typical Senegambian community was a small self-supporting agricultural village of closely related families. Custom assigned a high value to cultivation of the land, the shared objective of the group; work was understood more in terms of social relationships than as labor in the abstract. Fields were cut from the surrounding forest, and the average farm of 6 or 8 acres supported a moderate-sized family. Often the family worked the land for a common harvest; sometimes individuals had their own private fields. Millet and sorghum were the staple grains in northern Senegambia; farther south, forest dwellers cultivated yams, often as big as a man's arm, as a staple. Senegambians supplemented their diet with plantain, beans, and bananas. Fish, oysters, and small game such as rabbits and monkeys provided protein. Along the Guinea coast rice was the basic cereal, and okra, onions, melons, and pepper spiced the regular diet. Frequent fairs in neighboring villages served as markets for the exchange of produce and opportunities for outside news and social diversion. As one scholar has put it, "Life was simple, government largely limited to the settlement of disputes by family heads or elders, the basic economy scarcely more than the production and consumption of food, social life centered on the ceremony accompanying birth, death, and family alliance, recreation preoccupied with the eternal round of visit and gossip which were the main pursuits of leisure time."[3]

The fifteenth and sixteenth centuries saw the emergence of the great forest kingdom of Benin in what is now southern Nigeria. Although scholars still know little about Benin's origins, its history seems to have been characterized by a power struggle between the king and the nobility that neither side ever completely won. An elaborate court ceremonial emerged exalting the position of the *oba*, or king, and lending stability to the state. In the later fifteenth century, the oba Ewuare played off his palace chiefs against the village chiefs and thereby maintained a balance of power. A great warrior, Ewuare strengthened his army and pushed Benin's borders as far as the Niger River on the east, westward into Yoruba country, and south to the Gulf of Guinea (see Map 23.1). During the late sixteenth and seventeenth centuries the office of the oba evolved from a warrior kingship to a position of spiritual leadership.

At its height in the late sixteenth century, Benin controlled a vast territory, and European visitors described sophisticated society. The capital, Benin City,

was a stronghold twenty-five miles in circumference, protected by walls and natural defenses, containing an elaborate royal palace and neatly laid-out houses with

ART: A MIRROR OF SOCIETIES

Art reveals the interests and values of societies and frequently gives intimate and unique glimpses of how people actually lived. In portraits and statues, whether of gods, ghanas, saints, samurai, maharanas, or merchants, it preserves the memory and fame of men and women who shaped societies. In paintings, drawings, and carvings it also shows how people worked, played, relaxed, suffered, and triumphed. Art, therefore, is extremely useful to the historian, especially for distant periods and remote cultures where written records are scarce or hard to understand.

Art also manifests the changes and continuity of societies; as values changed, so did major artistic themes. Europeans of the sixteenth and seventeenth centuries remained deeply religious and showed a new interest in the world around them; their middle-class attitudes and experiences and their appreciation of agricultural life replaced the activities and interests of a small, wealthy, cultural elite as the subject matter of art. The scenes of everyday life presented in seventeenth-century genre painting were considered interesting in themselves and worthy of high art.

In the later seventeenth century, the court baroque style, inspired by the rise of absolutism, spread throughout Europe. Art in Manchu China and Tokugawa Japan also reflected the power of emperors and the social distinction of nobles. Samurai displayed their wealth through elegant paintings and silk screens decorated with genre and erotic scenes, while all arts of the Ch'ing Dynasty were organized to exalt and glorify the Manchu emperor and state. As Plate IV-5 illustrates, the Ch'ing dealt harshly with art perceived as heretical; hence Manchu artists, discouraged from innovation, rarely displayed the brilliance of their predecessors.

Nonetheless, the Western enthusiasm for Manchu art inspired its abundant production, particularly in the medium of porcelain. The *famille verte* style of pottery, characterized by foliated edges and overglaze decorations of elegant court scenes and beautiful landscapes, was especially popular; the 4¼-inch bowl pictured below, painted with a full five-color palette, is an impressive example. (Ashmolean Museum, Oxford.) Its reception in Europe is just one instance of the impact of cultures on one another, as shown through art.

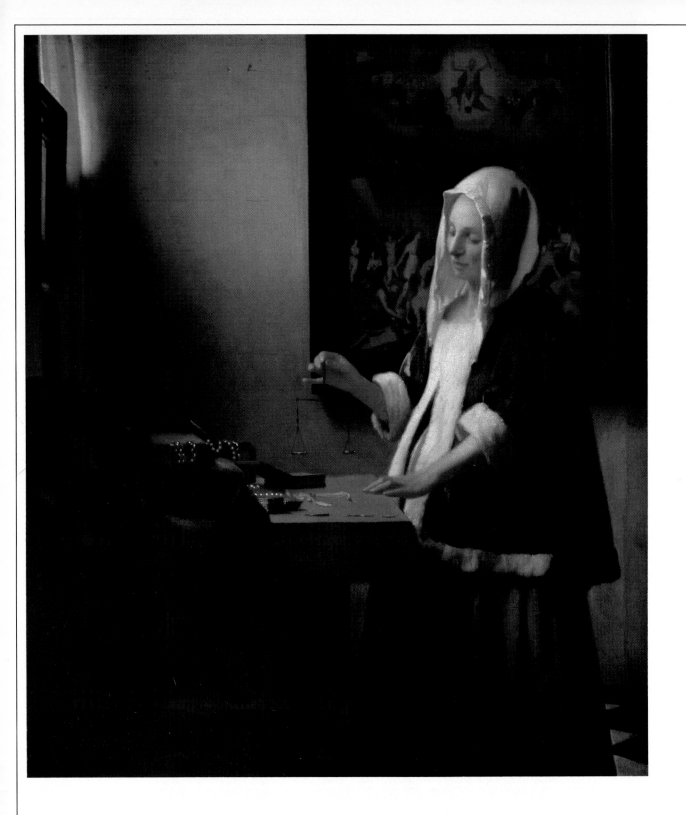

A Woman Weighing Gold Vermeer (ca 1657). Vermeer painted pictures of middle-class women involved in ordinary activities in the quiet interiors of their homes. Unrivaled among Dutch masters for his superb control of light, in this painting Vermeer illuminates the pregnant woman weighing gold on her scales, as Christ in the painting on the wall weighs the saved and the damned. *(National Gallery of Art, Washington, Widener Collection)*

Saint Mark's Square: Looking South-East Canaletto (1697–1768). The Venetian
Canaletto worked primarily for wealthy aristocrats. His most enthusiastic patrons were
English nobles, who became enamoured of his magnificent views of historic Venice
while making the continental "grand tour" that topped off the education of the English
upper class. This lively scene, showing much a visitor would wish to remember, features
Saint Mark's on the left, the Ducal Palace, ships in the lagoon, and market stalls.
(National Gallery of Art, Washington)

Japanese Combat Scene In the late eighteenth century, during the long Tokugawa peace, Japanese artists drew inspiration from the many legends of samurai warfare in earlier centuries. This six-leaf screen, which probably graced the home of a lord or wealthy merchant, provides useful information about armor and weapons: the shortage of iron in Japan meant that most armor consisted of layers of heavily padded cloth. *(Courtesy of Christie's, London/The Bridgeman Art Library)*

Burning of the Books (ca 1780) This vivid scene powerfully illustrates the royal absolutism of the Ch'ing period, which witnessed both the compilation of the great imperial manuscript collection, *The Four Treasuries,* and a literary inquisition that lasted for more than 15 years. From above the first emperor displays his domination of the Chinese learned world by ordering the burning of books considered anti-Ch'ing, a judgment that extended from rebellious tracts to works deemed merely unliterary. *(Bibliothèque Nationale, Paris/E. T. Archive)*

Ashanti Staff Top *(left)* In the early eighteenth century, the Ashanti of central Ghana expanded northward, subdued various peoples, and established a powerful successor state to the medieval African kingdoms of Ghana and Mali. The gold trade was the linchpin of its economic and political power. A splendid example of the Ashanti's superb skill in goldworking, this staff top reflects the region's proverbial wealth. *(Lee Boltin)*

The Spinners *(below)* Diego Velázquez (1599–1660). In the foreground of this complicated masterpiece, five sturdy women perform the menial task of transforming bundles of wool into yarn for weaving, while in the studio behind elegant ladies observe the mythological Arachne weave a tapestry (from a story in Ovid's *Metamorphoses,* Book VI). Velázquez intended to suggest the distinction between craft and art, between the worlds of myth and reality, and between the humble and aristocratic. *(Museo del Prado, Madrid)*

St. George in Ethiopian Art This image of a black St. George slaying a dragon from a seventeenth-century Ethiopian manuscript attests to the powerful and pervasive Christian influence in Ethiopian culture. *(The British Library)*

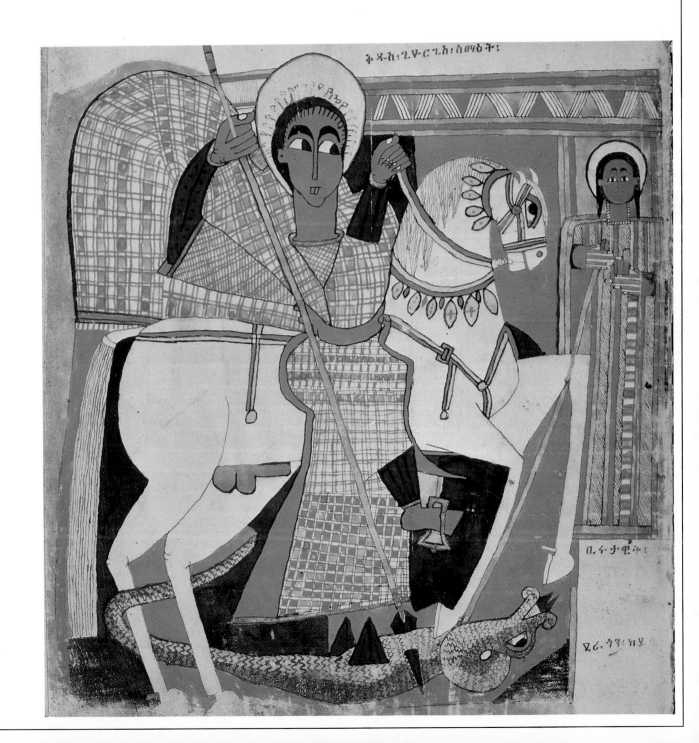

Woman with a Parrot The seventeenth century in India witnessed the tremendous expansion of Mughal power, which resulted in part from repression of all views alien to the Islamic faith. India's frequent civil uprisings during this period are belied by this charming scene, the imagery and formalized composition of which mark it as Islamic art. *(By courtesy of the Board of Trustees of the Victoria & Albert Museum/ E. T. Archive)*

The Oba of Benin The walls of the Oba's palace were decorated with bronze plaques that may date to the 16th–18th centuries. This plaque vividly conveys the Oba's power, majesty, and authority. The necklace (or choker) is his symbol of royalty. Attendants hold up his hands, while warriors raise shields over his head as sunshades. *(The Metropolitan Museum of Art, The Michael C. Rockefeller Memorial Collection, Gift of Nelson A. Rockefeller, 1965)*

verandas and balustrades, and divided by broad avenues and smaller intersecting streets. The power of the oba was apparent in his wealth, his divinity, his domination over commercial transactions, and his large and lavish court. In this prosperous society, the wealthier classes dressed and lived very well. Beef, mutton, chicken, and yams were staples, while the less well-to-do made do with yams, dried fish, beans and bananas.[4]

Visitors also noted that Benin City was kept scrupulously clean and had no beggars, and that public security was so effective that theft was unknown.

Beginning in 1485 the Portuguese and other Europeans appeared in Benin in pursuit of trade. A small exchange in pepper and slaves developed, but never acquired importance in the Benin economy. Nor did the Portuguese have much success in converting the staunchly animistic people to Christianity. Europe's impact on Benin was minimal. In the late seventeenth century, Benin's tributary states seceded, and stronger neighbors nibbled at its frontiers. The exact reasons for Benin's decline in the eighteenth and nineteenth centuries remain uncertain.

THE SUDAN: SONGHAY, KANEM-BORNU, AND HAUSALAND

The kingdom of Songhay, a successor state of Ghana and Mali, dominated the whole Niger region of the western and central Sudan (see Map 23.1). Muhammad Toure (1492–1528) completed the expansionist and administrative consolidation begun by his predecessors. A convert to Islam, Muhammad made a pilgrimage to Mecca; impressed by what he saw there, he tried to bring about greater centralization in his own territories. In addition to building a strong army and improving taxation procedures, he replaced local Songhay officials with more efficient Arab ones in an effort to substitute royal institutions for ancient kinship ties. Islamic institutions failed to take root in the countryside, however, and Muslim officials alienated the king from his people. His reforms were a failure. Nor was Muhammad able to ensure a peaceful succession. His death inaugurated a period of political instability that led to the slow disintegration of the Songhay kingdom.

Rice Ladle Known as a *Po* and possessed only by the wife or mother of a chief in the region of modern Sierra Leone and the Ivory Coast, this spoon was used by the woman to serve rice to villagers on ceremonial occasions. Rice symbolized prosperity and fertility. *(National Museum of African Art)*

Beginning in 1582 the sultanate of Morocco pressed southward in search of a greater share of the trans-Saharan trade. The people of Songhay, lacking effective leadership and believing the desert to be a sure protection against invasion, took no defensive precautions. In 1591 a Moroccan army of three thousand soldiers—many of whom were slaves of European origin—equipped with European muskets—crossed the Sahara and inflicted a crushing defeat on the Songhay at Tondibi. This battle spelled the end of the Songhay Empire. Although a moderate-sized kingdom lingered on in the south for a century or so, and weak political units arose, not until the eighteenth century did kingdoms able to exercise wide authority emerge again.

To the east of Songhay lay the kingdoms of Kanem-Bornu and Hausaland (see Map 23.1). Under the dynamic military leader Idris Alooma (1571–1603), Kanem-Bornu subdued weaker peoples and gained jurisdiction over an extensive area. Well drilled and equipped with firearms, camel-mounted cavalry and a standing army decimated warriors fighting with spears and arrows. Idris Alooma perpetuated the feudal pattern of government in which lands were granted to able fighters in return for loyalty and the promise of future military assistance. Meanwhile agriculture occupied most people, peasants and slaves alike. Kanem-Bornu shared in the trans-Saharan trade, shipping eunuchs and young girls to North Africa in return for horses and firearms. A devout Muslim, Idris Alooma elicited high praise from Ibn Fartura, who wrote a history of his reign called *The Kanem Wars:*

So he made the pilgrimage and visited [Medina] with delight. . . . He was enriched by visiting the tomb of the pious [Companions of the Prophet], the chosen, the perfect ones. . . .

Then he prepared to return to the kingdom of Bornu. When he reached the land called Barak [east of Lake Chad] he killed all the inhabitants who were warriors. They were strong but after this they became weak. . . . Among the benefits which God . . . conferred upon the Sultan [Idris Alooma] was the acquisition of Turkish musketeers and numerous household slaves who became skilled in firing muskets.

Hence the Sultan was able to kill the people of Amsaka with muskets, and there was no need for other weapons, so that God gave him great victory by reason of his superiority in arms.

Among the most surprising of his acts was the stand he took against obscenity and adultery, so that no such thing took place openly in his time. Formerly the people had been indifferent to such offences. . . . In fact he was a power among his people and from him came their strength.

The Sultan was intent on the clear path laid down by the Qur'an . . . in all his affairs and actions.[5]

Idris Alooma built mosques at his capital city of N'gazargamu and substituted Muslim courts and Islamic law for African tribunals and ancient customary law. His eighteenth-century successors lacked his vitality and military skills, however, and the empire declined.

Between Songhay and Kanem-Bornu were the lands of the Hausa. An agricultural people living in small villages, the Hausa grew millet, sorghum, barley, rice, cotton, and citrus fruit, and raised livestock. Some Hausa merchants carried on a heavy trade in slaves and kola nuts with North African communities across the Sahara. Obscure trading posts evolved into important Hausa city-states like Kano and Katsina, through which Islamic influences entered the region. Kano and Katsina became Muslim intellectual centers, and in the fifteenth century attracted scholars from distant Timbuktu. The Muslim chronicler of the reign of King Muhammad Rimfa of Kano (1463–1499) records that Muhammad introduced the Muslim practices of purdah, of the *idal-fitr* or festival after the fast of Ramadan, and of assigning eunuchs to the high offices of state.[6] As in Songhay and Kanem-Bornu, however, Islam made no strong imprint on the mass of the Hausa people, however, until the nineteenth century.

ETHIOPIA

At the beginning of the sixteenth century, the powerful East African Christian kingdom of Ethiopia extended from Massawa in the north to the tributary states of Fatajar, Doaro, and Bali in the south (see Map 16.1). The ruling Solomonid dynasty, however, faced serious troubles. Adal, a Muslim state along the southern base of the Red Sea, began incursions into Ethiopia, and in 1529 the Adal general Ahmad ibn-Ghazi inflicted a disastrous defeat on the Ethiopian emperor Lebna Dengel (1508–1540). Ahmad followed up his victory with systematic devastation of the land, destruction of many Ethiopian artistic and literary works, and the forced conversion of thousands to Islam. Lebna Dengel fled to the mountains and appealed to Portugal for assistance. The Portuguese, eager for a share in the wealth of the East African coast and interested in the conversion of Ethiopia to Roman Catholicism, responded with a force of musketeers. In 1541 they decisively defeated the Muslims near Lake Tana.

No sooner had the Muslim threat ended than Ethiopia encountered three more dangers. The Galla, Cushitic-speaking peoples, moved northward in great numbers, occupying portions of Harar, Shoa, and Amhara. The Ethiopians could not defeat them militarily, and the Galla were not interested in assimilation. For the next two centuries the two peoples lived together in an uneasy truce. Simultaneous with the Galla migrations, the Ottoman Turks seized Massawa and other coastal cities; the Ethiopian emperor could not dislodge them. Then the Jesuits arrived, anxious to capitalize on earlier Portuguese support, and attempted to force Roman Catholicism on a proud people whose form of Christianity long antedated the European version. The overzealous Jesuit missionary Alphonse Mendez tried to revamp the Ethiopian liturgy, rebaptize the people, and replace ancient Ethiopian customs and practices with Roman ones. Since Ethiopian national sentiment was closely tied up with Coptic Christianity, violent rebellion and anarchy ensued. In 1633 the Jesuit missionaries were expelled. For the next two centuries hostility to foreigners, weak political leadership, and regionalism characterized Ethiopia. Civil conflicts between the Galla and the Ethiopians erupted continually. The Coptic church, though lacking strong authority, survived as the cornerstone of Ethiopian national identity.

THE SWAHILI CITY-STATES

The Swahili city-states on the east coast of Africa enjoyed a worldwide reputation for commercial prosperity in the late fifteenth century. Mogadishu, Mombasa, Kilwa, and Sofala continued their ancient trade with the Arabian and Persian gulf ports, and also exchanged ivory, gold, and slaves for Indian beads and Chinese silks, textiles, and porcelains. Kilwa dominated the lesser states, including Sofala through which poured gold from the inland mines.

Dutch Colony, Cape of Good Hope Founded in 1657, by the mid-eighteenth century the Cape Colony had 15,000 inhabitants and may have been the largest European settlement on the African continent. Here crews took on fresh provisions, repaired their ships, and awaited favorable winds for crossing the Indian Ocean. *(BBC Hulton/The Bettmann Archive)*

The cities' culture was cosmopolitan and their standard of living, based on inland agriculture, was very high.

The arrival of the Portuguese explorer Vasco da Gama (see Map 18.1) in 1498 spelled the end of the Swahili cities' independence. Da Gama wanted to build a Portuguese maritime empire in the Indian Ocean, and between 1502 and 1507 the southern ports of Kilwa, Zanzibar, and Sofala fell before Portuguese guns and became Portuguese tributary states. The better-fortified northern cities, such as Mogadishu, survived as important entrepôts for goods to India. But the Portuguese victory in the south proved hollow: rather than accept Portuguese commercial restrictions, the residents deserted the towns and their economies crumbled. Large numbers of Kilwa's people, for example, immigrated to northern cities.

The flow of gold from inland mines to Sofala slowed to a trickle. Swahili passive resistance successfully prevented the Portuguese from gaining control of the local coastal trade.

Initially lured to the Indian Ocean by the spice trade, the Portuguese wanted a station on the East African coast. After the intermittent bombardment of several cities, Portugal finally won an administrative stronghold near Mombasa in 1589. Called Fort Jesus, it remained a Portuguese base for over a century. In the late seventeenth century, pressures from the northern European maritime powers—the Dutch, French, and English—aided greatly by the Arabs of Oman, combined with local African rebellions to bring about the collapse of Portuguese influence. A Portuguese presence remained only at Mozambique in the far south.

The Portuguese made no religious or cultural impact on the Swahili cities; their sole effect was the cities' economic decline.

AFRICA AND THE TRANSATLANTIC SLAVE TRADE

By the sixteenth century, slavery had a long history in Africa, and the transatlantic slave trade is properly understood against that background. "Slavery was already fundamental to the social, political, and economic order of parts of the northern savanna, Ethiopia and the East African coast. . . .Enslavement was an organized activity, sanctioned by law and custom. Slaves were a principal commodity in trade, including the export sector, and slaves were important in the domestic sphere" as concubines, servants, soldiers, and ordinary laborers (see Chapter 16). Islam had heavily conditioned African slavery, partly because before 1500 the major foreign market for slaves was North Africa and the Middle East, and partly because Islam had exerted a strong cultural influence in many of the states and societies of the northern savanna, the Ethiopian highlands, and the East African coast.[7] For example, African rulers justified enslavement with the Muslim argument that prisoners of war could be sold; and, since captured peoples were considered chattel, they could be used in the same roles practiced in the Muslim world. Between 650 and 1600, Muslims transported perhaps as many as 4.82 million black slaves across the trans-Saharan trade route.[8] When the transatlantic slave trade began, it represented little that was new.

Until recently scholars advanced two basic theories about the Atlantic slave trade. One school of thought, proposed by the defenders of African slavery, held that enslavement "freed" Africans from the "barbarism" of their own society, which was characterized by human sacrifice, cannibalism, and its own form of slavery. This thesis actually was a self-serving rationalization for economic exploitation. The other argument, begun by abolitionists, held that African kingdoms had had well-developed civilizations since the time of the Egyptian pharaohs, civilizations that the slave trade destroyed; moreover, the slave trade was itself a form of barbarism and the source of Africa's woes. This theory represents an oversimplification of very complicated issues, and it fails to address significant questions. What regions of Africa were the sources of slaves? How were the slaves treated? What goods and business procedures were involved in the exchange of slaves? What were the economic, social, political, and demographic effects of the slave trade on African societies?

As described in Chapter 18, the search for a sea route to India led the Portuguese in the fifteenth century to explore the West African coast. The transatlantic slave trade actually began when Christopher Columbus returned to Spain from the West Indies in 1493 with several hundred Indian slaves. The Portuguese, having "discovered" Brazil in 1500, founded a sugar colony at Bahia in 1551. Between 1551 and 1675, before the traffic to North America had gotten under way, the Portuguese delivered more African slaves to Brazil than would ever reach British North America (see Table 23.1). Portugal essentially monopolized the slave trade until 1600 and continued to play a large role in the seventeenth century, though increasingly threatened by the Dutch, French, and English. From 1690 until the House of Commons abolished the slave trade in 1807, England was the leading carrier of African slaves.

Population density and supply conditions along the African coast and the sailing time to New World markets determined the sources of slaves. As the demand for slaves rose, slavers moved down the West African coast from Senegambia to the more densely populated hinterlands of the Bights of Benin and Biafra. The abundant supply of slaves in Angola, the region south of the Congo River (see Map 18.5), however, and the quick passage from Angola to Brazil and the Caribbean established that region as the major coast for slavers. In the sixteenth and early seventeenth centuries, the Senegambian coast and the area near the mouth of the Congo River yielded the greatest numbers. By the late seventeenth century the British found the Ivory Coast region the most profitable territory; a century later the Bight of Benin and the Gold Coast had become the largest suppliers. The Portuguese acquired the bulk of their slaves from Angola. Transatlantic wind patterns partly determined the routes of exchange. Shippers naturally preferred the swiftest crossing—that is, from the African port nearest the latitude of the intended American destination. Thus, Portuguese shippers carried their cargoes from Angola to Brazil, and British merchants sailed from the Bight of Benin to the Caribbean. The

City of Luanda, Angola Founded by the Portuguese in 1575, Luanda was a center of the huge slave trade to Brazil. In this eighteenth-century print, offices and warehouses line the streets, while (right foreground) slaves are dragged to the ships for transportation to America. *(New York Public Library, Astor, Lenox, and Tilden Foundations)*

great majority of slaves were intended for the sugar and coffee plantations extending from the Caribbean islands to Brazil.[9]

Angola produced 26 percent of all African slaves and 70 percent of all Portuguese slaves. Trading networks extending deep into the interior culminated at two major ports on the Angolan coast, Luanda and Benguela. Between the 1730s and 1770s Luanda shipped between 8,000 and 10,000 slaves each year; at the end of the eighteenth century Benguela's numbers equaled those of Luanda. In 1820, the peak year, 18,957 blacks left Luanda. Although a few slaves were acquired through warfare, the Portuguese secured the vast majority through trade with African dealers; no whites participated in the inland markets. Almost all Portuguese shipments went to satisfy the virtually insatiable Brazilian demand for slaves.[10]

The slave trade lasted for almost four centuries and involved the terrible brutalization and exploitation of millions of human beings. Here is an excerpt from the report in 1793 of a Portuguese doctor with experience on the Middle Passage between Angola and Brazil:

When the slaves coming from many different parts of the interior reach the maritime ports of Africa, they are there once more traded for goods and merchandise. . . .

Here takes place the second round of hardships that these unlucky people are forced to suffer. . . .They are terribly handled and most scantily provided for . . . their human nature entirely overlooked. The dwelling place of the slave is simply the dirt floor of the compound, and he remains there exposed to harsh conditions and bad weather, and at night there are only a lean-to and some sheds . . . which they are herded into like cattle.

Their food continues scarce as before . . . limited at times to badly cooked beans, at other times to corn, also boiled, and at other times to beans mixed with corn to provide variety. They also add to the diet a small amount of salted fish, which abounds in Luanda and the kingdom of Angola. . . .

They suffer in other ways. When they are first traded, they are made to bear the brand mark of the backlander who enslaved them, so that they can be recognized in case they run away. And when they reach a port . . . they are branded on the right breast with the coat of arms of the king and nation, of whom they have become vas-

sals. . . . This mark is made with a hot silver instrument in the act of paying the king's duties, and this brand mark is called a carimbo.

They are made to bear one more brand mark. This one is ordered by their private master, under whose name they are transported to Brazil. . .

In this miserable and deprived condition the terrified slaves remain for weeks and months, and the great number of them who die is unspeakable. With some ten or twelve thousand arriving at Luanda each year, it often happens that only six or seven thousand are finally transported to Brazil. . . .

Shackled in the holds of ships, the black slaves . . . are far more deprived than when on land. First of all, with two or three hundred slaves placed under the deck, there is hardly room enough to draw a breath . . . . The captains, aware of their own (financial) interests, recognize the seriousness of the problem, and they try to remedy it to some extent. . . . Each day they order a certain number of slaves brought on deck in chains to get some fresh air, not allowing more because of their fear of rebellion. However, very little is accomplished in this way, because the slaves must go down again into the hold. . . .

Second, the slaves are afflicted with a very short ration of water, of poor quality and lukewarm because of the climate—hardly enough to water their mouths. The suffering that this causes is extraordinary, and their dryness and thirst cause epidemics which, beginning with one person, soon spread to many others. Thus, after only a few days at sea, they start to throw the slaves into the ocean.

Third, they are kept in a state of constant hunger. Their small ration of food, brought over from Brazil on the outward voyage, is spoiled and damaged. . . . They add to each ration a small portion of noxious fish from the Atlantic Ocean, which decays during the voyage.[11]

Unlike Great Britain, France, and the Netherlands, Portugal did not have a strong mercantile class involved in slaving in the eighteenth century. Instead the Portuguese colony of Brazil provided the ships, capital, and goods for the slave trade. Credit played a major role in the trade: Brazilian-controlled firms in Luanda extended credit to African operators, who had to make payments in slaves six or eight months later. Portuguese ironwares and wine, Brazilian tobacco and brandies, European and Asian textiles, firearms, and beads were the main goods exchanged for slaves. All commodities entered Angola from Brazil. Because the Luandan (or Benguelan) merchant determined the value of the goods in relation to a prime young slave, because the merchant undervalued the worth of the slave and overpriced the goods, and because sharp dealing was commonplace, the African operator frequently ended up in debt to the merchant. Although the demand was great, Portuguese merchants in Angola and Brazil sought to maintain only a steady trickle of slaves from the Afri-

Cross-section of a Slave Ship Packed, literally like sardines in a can, and forced to endure this method of transportation for weeks at sea (or until death): thus were thousands of blacks shipped from Angola to Brazil. *(Library of Congress)*

can interior to Luanda and across the ocean to Bahia and Rio de Janeiro: a flood of slaves would have depressed the American market. Rio, the port capital through which most slaves passed, commanded the Brazilian trade. Planters and mine operators from the provinces traveled to Rio to buy slaves. Between 1795 and 1808, approximately 10,000 Angolans per year stood in the Rio slave market. In 1810 the figure rose to 18,000; in 1828 it reached 32,000.[12]

The English ports of London, Bristol, and particularly Liverpool dominated the British slave trade. In the eighteenth century Liverpool was the world's greatest slave-trading port. In all three cities, small and cohesive merchant classes exercised great public influence. The cities also had huge stores of industrial products for export, growing shipping industries, and large amounts of ready cash for investment abroad. Merchants generally formed partnerships to raise capital and to share risks; each voyage was a separate business enterprise.

Slaving ships from Bristol searched the Gold Coast, the Bight of Benin, Bonny, and Calabar, while the ships of Liverpool drew slaves from Gambia, the Windward Coast, and the Gold Coast. To Africa, British ships carried textiles, gunpowder and flint, beer and spirits, British and Irish linens, and woolen cloth. African dealers wanted to trade their slaves for an equivalent value in consumer goods, while European traders wanted to sell their goods at a profit calculated in their own national currency. Thus a system based on both barter and monetary exchange developed. A collection of goods was grouped together into what was called the "sorting." An English sorting might include bolts of cloth, firearms, alcohol, tobacco, and hardware; this batch of goods would be traded for an individual slave or a quantity of gold, ivory, or dyewood. When Europeans added a markup for profit, Africans followed suit. Currency was not exchanged; instead it served as a standard of value and a method of keeping accounts.[13]

European traders had two systems for exchange. First, especially on the Gold Coast, they established factory-forts, fortified trading posts that were expensive to maintain but proved useful for fending off rival Europeans. In the second or shore method of trading, European ships sent boats into shore or invited African dealers to bring traders and slaves out to the ships. The English captain John Adams, who made ten voyages to Africa between 1786 and 1800, described the shore method of trading at Bonny:

This place is the wholesale market for slaves, as not fewer than 20,000 are annually sold here; 16,000 of whom are natives of one nation called Ibo. . . . Fairs where the slaves of the Ibo nation are obtained are held every five or six weeks at several villages, which are situated on the banks of the rivers and creeks in the interior, and to which the [African] traders of Bonny resort to purchase them.

The preparation necessary for going to these fairs generally occupies the Bonny people some days. Large canoes . . . are launched and stored for the voyage. The traders augment the quantity of their merchandise, by obtaining from their friends, the captains of the slave ships, a considerable quantity of goods on credit. . . . Evening is the period chosen for the time of departure, when they proceed in a body, accompanied by the noise of drums, horns, and gongs. At the expiration of the sixth day, they generally return bringing with them 1,500 or 2,000 slaves, who are sold to Europeans the evening after their arrival, and taken on board the ships. . . .

It is expected that every vessel, on her arrival [at Bonny], will fire a salute the instant the anchor is let go, as a compliment to the black monarch who soon afterwards makes his appearance in a large canoe, at which time, all those natives who happen to be alongside the vessel are compelled to proceed in their canoes to a respectful distance, and make way for his Majesty's barge. After a few compliments to the captain, he usually enquires after brother George [meaning the King of England, George III], and hopes he and his family are well. He is not pleased unless he is regaled with the best the ship affords. . . . His power is absolute; and the surrounding country, to a considerable distance, is subject to his dominion.[14]

The shore method of buying slaves allowed the ship to move easily from market to market. The final prices of the slaves depended on their ethnic origin, their availability when the shipper arrived, and their physical health when offered for sale in the West Indies or the North or South American colonies.

Meanwhile the northbound trade in slaves across the Sahara (page 458) "continued without serious disruption until the late nineteenth century, and in a clandestine way and on a much reduced scale it survived well into the twentieth century." Estimates of the numbers of slaves exported north to Algiers, Tripoli, and Cairo have ranged as high as 15 million for the sixteenth century alone, but that figure has been sharply disputed. The present scholarly consensus is that the trans-Saharan slave trade in the seventeenth and eighteenth centuries was never as important as the Atlantic trade. But it persisted.[15]

Supplying slaves for the foreign market either was in the hands of a small wealthy merchant class or was a state monopoly. Gathering a band of raiders and the capital for equipment, guides, and tolls, and maintaining raiders and captives before they reached the European or Muslim dealers—these involved considerable expense. By contemporary standards, slave raiding was a costly operation. Only black entrepreneurs with sizable capital and labor could afford to finance and direct raiding drives. They exported slaves because the profits on exports were greater than on using labor in the domestic economy:

The export price of slaves never rose to the point where it became cheaper for Europeans to turn to alternative sources of supply, and it never fell to the point where it caused more than a temporary check to the trade. Consequently, Africa was able consistently to undercut all other potential suppliers. . . . The remarkable expansion of the slave trade in the eighteenth century provides a horrific illustration of the rapid response of producers in an underdeveloped economy to price incentives.[16]

Europeans initiated the Atlantic slave trade, but its continuation was made possible through an alliance between European shippers and African suppliers.

What economic impact did European trade have on African societies? Africans possessed the technology needed to utilize their environment. Over the centuries they had cultivated a wide variety of plant foods, developed plant and animal husbandry techniques, and could mine, smelt, and smith a great variety of metals. Apart from firearms, American tobacco and rum, and the cheap brandy brought by the Portuguese, European goods presented no novelty to Africans. What made foreign products desirable to Africans was their price. Traders in Indian hand-woven cotton textiles, Venetian imitations of African beads, and iron bars from European smelteries could undersell African manufacturers. Africans exchanged slaves, ivory, gold, pepper, and animal skins for those goods; their earnings usually were not retained in Africa. African states eager to expand or to control commerce bought European firearms. The

difficulty of maintaining guns often gave their owners only marginal superiority over skilled bowmen.[17] Along the Gold Coast, the kingdom of Dahomey, however, built its power on the effective use of firearms.

Those African merchants who controlled the production of exports gained from foreign trade. The king of Dahomey, for example, had a gross income in 1750 of £250,000 from the overseas export of slaves. A portion of his profits was spent on goods that improved the living standards of his people. Slave-trading entrepôts, which provided opportunities for traders and for farmers who supplied foodstuffs to towns, caravans, and slave ships, prospered. But such economic returns did not spread very far.[18] International trade did not lead to the economic development of Africa. Neither technological growth nor the gradual spread of economic benefits occurred in Africa in early modern times.

The arrival of Europeans did cause basic social changes in some West African societies. In Senegambia, for example, chattel slavery seems to have been unknown before the growth of the transatlantic trade (page 712). By the late eighteenth century, however, chiefs were using the slave labor of craftsmen, sailors, and farm workers; if the price was right, they were sold off. Moreover, those who committed crimes had traditionally paid fines; with the urgent demand for slaves, many misdemeanors became punishable by sale to slave dealers. Europeans introduced corn, pineapple, cassava, and sweet potatoes to West Africa, which had important consequences for population growth. Finally, the intermarriage of French traders and Wolof women in Senegambia created a *métis* or mulatto class. In the emerging urban centers at Saint-Louis and Gorée, this small class adopted the French language, the Roman Catholic faith, and a French manner of life. The métis exercised considerable political and economic power. When granted French citizenship in the late eighteenth century, its members sent Senegalese grievances to the Estates General of 1789.[19] However, European cultural influences did not penetrate West African society beyond the seacoast.

The political consequences of the slave trade varied from place to place. In the kingdom of the Congo the perpetual Portuguese search for slaves undermined the monarchy, destroyed political unity, and led to constant disorder and warfare; power passed to the village chiefs. Likewise in Angola, which became

TABLE 23.1 ESTIMATED SLAVE IMPORTS BY DESTINATION, 1451–1870

Destination	Estimated Total Slave Imports
British North America	399,000
Spanish America	1,552,100
British Caribbean	1,665,000
French Caribbean	1,600,200
Dutch Caribbean	500,000
Danish Caribbean	28,000
Brazil	3,646,800
Old World	175,000
	9,566,100

Source: P. D. Curtin, *The Atlantic Slave Trade: A Census* (Madison, Wis.: University of Wisconsin Press, 1969), p. 268.

TABLE 23.2 THE TRANSATLANTIC SLAVE TRADE, 1450–1900

Period	Volume	Percent
1450–1600	367,000	3.1
1601–1700	1,868,000	16.0
1701–1800	6,133,000	52.4
1801–1900	3,330,000	28.5
Total	11,698,000	100.0

Source: P. E. Lovejoy, *Transformations in Slavery: A History of Slavery in Africa* (Cambridge, Cambridge University Press, 1983), p. 19.

a Portuguese proprietary colony, the slave trade decimated and scattered the population and destroyed the local economy. On the other hand, the military kingdom of Dahomey, which entered into the slave trade in the eighteenth century and made it a royal monopoly, prospered enormously from trading in slaves; the economic strength of the state rested on it. The royal army raided deep into the interior, and in the late eighteenth century Dahomey had become one of the major West African sources of slaves. When slaving expeditions failed to produce sizable catches, and when European demands declined, the resulting depression in the Dahomeyan economy caused serious political unrest. Iboland inland from the Niger Delta, from whose great port cities of Bonny and Brass the British drained tens of thousands of slaves, experienced minimal political effects and suffered no permanent population loss. A high birthrate kept pace with the incursions of the slave trade, and Ibo societies remained demographically and economically strong.

Finally, what of the overall demographic impact? Tables 23.1 and 23.2 report the somewhat divergent recent findings of two careful scholars.

The total number of slaves who left Africa over a four-hundred-year period seems to lie somewhere between 9 and 12 million. These numbers represent only the transatlantic slave trade; they do not include slaves exported from East Africa or across the Sahara. Furthermore, these are export figures; they do not include the approximately 10 to 15 percent who died during procurement or in transit. The demographic impact varied with time and place: the effect was obviously less severe in places where fewer blacks were enslaved, and African societies that raided the interior for slaves suffered less than did those that sold their own members. West Africa, a large supplier of slaves, lost an enormous labor supply, primarily of strong young men. The slaving coast of Angola suffered the greatest losses. Many African societies, particularly those organized in strong kingdoms, suffered no significant population loss.

The Atlantic slave trade was one of the great forced migrations of world history. Although it caused terrible human misery and individual degradation, the present scholarly consensus seems to be that the long-term effects of the slave trade on the course of African history were slight.

THE OTTOMAN AND SAFAVID EMPIRES

The spiritual descendants of Muhammad controlled three vast and powerful empires around 1450: the Ottoman Empire of Turkey, the Safavid Empire of Persia, and the Mughal Empire of India. From West Africa to central Asia, from the Balkans to Southeast Asia, Muslim arms pursued the religious ideal of the *jihad,* the holy war. The greatest of these empires, that of the Ottoman Turks, so severely threatened Italy and southeastern Europe that the aged Pope Pius II himself shouldered the cross of the crusader in

Ottoman Helmet Ottoman helmets resembled turbans: conical-shaped with swelling sides tapering toward the apex. This mid-sixteenth century jeweled and gold-inlaid steel helmet reflects the Ottomans' preoccupation with military regalia and their desire to display their wealth and power through weapons. *(Topkapi Saray Museum, Istanbul)*

1464. The Turks inspired such fear that even in distant Iceland the Lutheran Book of Common Prayer begged God for protection from "the cunning of the Pope and the terror of the Turk."

Who were the Ottomans and the Safavids, and what political and religious factors gave rise to their empires? What were their sources of power and how did they govern? What intellectual developments characterized the Ottoman and Safavid cultures?

THE OTTOMAN MILITARY STATE

The Ottomans took their name from Osman (1299–1326), the ruler of a Turkish-speaking people in western Anatolia who began expansionist moves in the fourteenth century. The Ottomans gradually absorbed other peoples in the peninsula, and the Ottoman state emerged as one of many small Turkish states during the breakup of the empire of the Seljuk Turks. The first Ottoman state thus occupied the border between Islam and Byzantine Christendom. The Ottoman ruler called himself "border chief" or leader of the *gazis,* frontier fighters in the holy war. The earliest Ottoman historical source, a fourteenth-century saga, defines the gazis as the "instrument of God's religion . . . God's scourge who cleanses the earth from the filth of polytheism . . . God's pure sword."[20] The principle of jihad was the cornerstone of Ottoman political theory and then of the Ottoman state. Europe was the frontier of the Muslim crusading mission. In 1389 in southern Yugoslavia the Ottomans defeated a combined force of Serbs and Bosnians, and in 1396 they crushed King Sigismund of Hungary supported by French, German, and English knights on the Danube in modern Bulgaria. The reign of Sultan Mehmed II (1451–1481) saw the end of all Turkish dynasties in Anatolia, and the Ottoman conquest of Constantinople, capital of the Byzantine Empire.

The six-week siege of Constantinople in 1453 remains one of the dramatic events in world history, because Constantinople had symbolized the continuation of imperial Rome. The Byzantine emperor Constantine IX Palaeologus with only about 10,000 men relied on the magnificent system of circular walls and stone fortifications that had protected the city for a thousand years. Mehmed II had over

Royal Ottoman Couple This scene from a palace court-yard appears in a five-volume illustrated history (1560) of the rulers of the Ottoman house. The man's ivory-handled dagger, the lady's embroidered cap, and the jeweled belts of both display their fabulous wealth. Islamic painting very rarely showed a mirror image. *(Courtesy of The Harvard University Art Museums [The Edward Binney 3rd Collection of Turkish Art])*

100,000 men and a large fleet, but iron chains spanning the harbor kept him out of the Golden Horn. Western technology eventually decided the battle: a renegade Hungarian working for the Ottomans cast huge bronze cannon on the spot, since it was easier to bring raw materials to the scene of military action than to move guns long distances.[21] When the thirty-inch bombard shattered a city gate, the Turks forced an entry. For three days the city suffered looting and rape. The Muslim historian Oruç described the conquest of the city:

Sultan Mehmed, the son of Sultan Murad, inspired by zeal, said "in the cause of God" and commanded plunder. The gazis, entering by force on every side, found a way in through the breaches in the fortress made by the guns and put the infidels in the fortress to the sword. The way was opened to the rest of the soldiers. They came through the trenches and set up ladders. They threw these against the walls of the towers and climbed up them. Mounting on the tower they destroyed the infidels who were inside and entered the city. They looted and plundered. They seized their money and possessions and made their sons and daughters slaves. Sultan Mehmed also gave orders to plunder the houses. In this way what could be taken was taken. The Muslims took so much booty that the wealth gathered in Istanbul [Constantinople] since it was built 2400 years before became the portion of the gazis. They plundered for three days, and after three days plunder was forbidden.[22]

The conquest of Constantinople inaugurated the imperial phase of the Ottoman military state. The Ottoman emperors considered themselves successors of the Byzantine emperor—as their title Sultan-i-Rum (Sultan of Rome) attests. From Constantinople, their new capital, the Ottomans pushed down the Aegean and up the Adriatic. In 1480 a fleet took the Italian port of Otranto; serious plans were laid for the conquest of all Italy. Only a disputed succession following the death of Mehmed II in 1481 caused the postponement—and, later, cancellation—of those plans. (The political vacuum in Italy in the late fifteenth century, and the ease with which the French conquered several Italian states after 1494, suggest that the history of Renaissance Italy and of all Europe would have been vastly different if the Turks had persisted.)

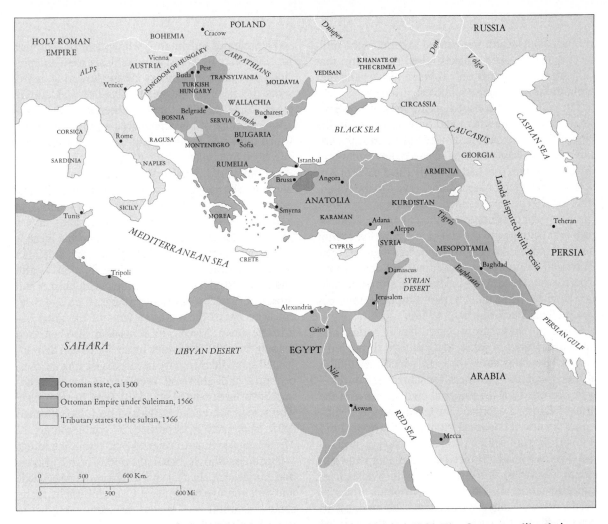

MAP 23.2 **The Ottoman Empire at Its Height, 1566** The Ottomans, like their great rivals the Habsburgs, rose to rule a vast dynastic empire encompassing many different peoples and ethnic groups. The army and the bureaucracy served to unite the disparate territories into a single state.

The Ottomans conquered Syria and Palestine (1516) and Egypt (1517), and extended their protection across North Africa to Algiers in Morocco. With Greece and the Balkans already under Ottoman domination, Suleiman II's army crushed the Hungarians in 1526, killing the king and thousands of his nobles. Three years later the Turks besieged the Habsburg capital at Vienna. Once again, only an accident—the army's insistence on returning home before winter—prevented Muslim control of all central Europe. In virtually every area, the Ottomans' success was due to the weakness and political disunity of

their enemies and to superior Turkish military organization and artillery. Gunpowder, invented by the Chinese and adapted to artillery use by the Europeans, played an influential role in the development of the Ottoman state.

Military organization also dominated the Ottoman social and administrative systems, which reached classic form under Suleiman I (1520–1566). The seventeenth-century Ottoman historian Mustafa Naima divided Muslim society into producers of wealth, Muslim and non-Muslim, and the military. Naima held that there could be no state without the military; that wealth was needed to support the military; that the state's subjects raised the wealth; that subjects could prosper only through justice; and that without the state there could be no justice.[23]

The ruling class consisted exclusively of Muslims, totally loyal to the sultan and fully immersed in the complex Islamic culture. Under Suleiman I, the Ottoman ruling class consisted in part of descendants of Turkish families that had formerly ruled parts of Anatolia. In return for bureaucratic service to the sultan, they held *trimars* (landed estates) on *sipahinek* (property) for the duration of their lifetimes. Since all property belonged to the sultan and reverted to him on the holder's death, Turkish nobles—unlike their European counterparts—could not put down roots. There was no security of landholding and no hereditary nobility. Thus the Ottoman Empire did not develop a feudal structure before 1600.

Slaves purchased from Spain, North Africa, and Venice, captured in battle, and acquired through the system known as *devshirme*—by which the sultan's agents swept the provinces for Christian youths—were recruited for the imperial civil service and the army. Islamic law forbade the enslavement of Muslims (but not of converts). Southern Europeans did not shrink from selling people into slavery, and, as the Ottoman jihad advanced in the fifteenth and sixteenth centuries, Albanian, Bosnian, Wallachian, and Hungarian slave boys filled Ottoman imperial needs. All were converted to Islam. The brightest 10 percent entered the palace school, where they learned to read and write Arabic, Ottoman Turkish, and Persian, received special religious instruction, and were trained for the civil service. Other boys were sent to Turkish farms where they acquired physical toughness in preparation for military service. Known as *janissaries* (Turkish for "recruits"), they formed the elite army corps. Thoroughly indoctrinated and absolutely loyal to the sultan, the janissary slave corps eliminated the influence of old Turkish families and played the central role in Ottoman military affairs in the sixteenth century. Some converts of Slavic origin rose to high positions in the Ottoman state as theologians, poets, jurists, and generals.

All authority theoretically emanated from the sultan and flowed from him to his state servants: police officers, provincial governors, heads of the treasury, generals. These men were frequently designated *pashas,* a title of distinction granted by the sultan.

The reign of Suleiman I, who extended Ottoman jurisdiction to its widest geographical extent and presided over an extraordinary artistic flowering, represents the peak of Ottoman influence and culture (Map 23.2). Muslims called Suleiman "the Lawgiver" because of his educational and legal reforms, which remained in effect until the 1800s. Europeans described Suleiman as "the Magnificent" because of the grandeur of his court. With annual state revenues of about $80 million, at a time when Elizabeth I of England could expect $150,000 and Francis I of France perhaps $1 million, with thousands of servants to cater to his every whim, and with a lifestyle no European monarch could begin to rival, Suleiman was indeed magnificent. He used his fabulous wealth and power to adorn Constantinople with palaces and mosques. Some of his undertakings, such as his reconstruction of the water systems of the great pilgrimage sites at Mecca and Jerusalem, also benefited his subjects. The Ottomans under Suleiman demonstrated splendid creativity in carpet weaving, textiles, ceramics, and, above all, architecture. In the buildings of Pasha Sinan (1491–1588), the Christian slave who rose to become imperial architect, the Ottoman spirit is powerfully expressed. A contemporary of Michelangelo, Sinan designed 312 public buildings —mosques, schools, hospitals, public baths, palaces, and burial chapels. His masterpieces, the Shehzade and Suleimaniye mosques at Constantinople, represented solutions to spatial problems unique to domed buildings, and expressed the discipline, the power, the devotion to Islam that characterized the Ottoman Empire under Suleiman the Magnificent. With pardonable exaggeration, Suleiman began a letter to the king of France, with whom he was allied against the Habsburgs after 1536, "I who am the sultan of sultans, the sovereign of sovereigns, the dispenser of crowns to the monarchs on the face of the earth . . . to thee who are Francis, King of the land of France."[24]

Following Suleiman's reign, repeated crises occurred over the succession. The sultan's oldest son was designated his heir, but to prevent threats of usurpation he was denied a role in governing and isolated in circumstances of lavish sensuality. When the prince succeeded his father, years of dissipation had often rendered him alcoholic or insane or exhausted from excessive sexual activity. An imperial councilor, the grand vizier, exercised the actual power.

In the seventeenth century a series of incompetent rulers enabled the janissaries to destroy the influence of the old Turkish families. Members of the elite army corps secured permanent military and administrative offices for their sons through bribery, making their positions hereditary. The janissaries thus became the powerful feudal class in Ottoman Turkey.

Under the grand vizier Muhammad Kuprili (ca 1570–1661) Ottoman fortunes revived. Kuprili abolished the corruption pervasive throughout the imperial administration, maintained domestic peace, and pursued a vigorous foreign policy. When Kurprili died his brother-in-law Kara Mustafa directed the empire's military operations. His object was an attack on the Habsburg capital, Vienna. When battle came on September 12, 1683, the combination of a strong allied Christian force (page 620) and Habsburg heavy artillery, which the Turks lacked, gave the Europeans the victory. The Ottomans rallied again, but defeat at Vienna and domestic disorders led to the decline of Ottoman power in the Balkans. "The Ottoman state was predicated upon, committed to, and organized for conquest .... An end to significant and sustained conquest rocked the entire state structure and sent aftershocks through all its institutions."[25]

THE PERSIAN THEOCRATIC STATE

Persia, after a long period of Arab and Mongol domination, emerged as a powerful Muslim state under the Safavid dynasty in the early sixteenth century. (Since 1935 Persia has been known as "Iran.") Between 1502 and 1510, Ismail (1502–1524), the founder of the dynasty, defeated petty Turkish leaders, united all of Persia under his sovereign rule, and proclaimed himself *shah,* or king. Shah Ismail declared the Shi'ite form of Islam the state religion. The Shi'ites claimed descent from Ali, Muhammad's cousin and son-in-law, and believed that leadership among Muslims rightfully belonged to the Prophet's descendants (pages 265–266). The Shi'ites also believed that they possessed a secret interpretation of the Qur'an transmitted from Muhammad to Ali, from whom it passed to his heirs. The guardians of this knowledge, the *ulema,* claimed infallible religious and political authority. The Safavids ruled a theocratic state. With its puritanical emphasis on the holy law and on self-flagellation in penance for any disloyalty to Ali, the Safavid state represented theocracy triumphant throughout the first half century of its existence.

Safavid power reached its height under Shah Abbas (1587–1629), whose military achievements, support for trade and commerce, and endowment for the arts earned him the epithet "the Great." The Persian army had hitherto consisted of tribal units under tribal leadership. Shah Abbas built a national army on the Ottoman model, composed of Armenian and Georgian recruits paid by and loyal to himself. Utilizing the engineering skills of the English adventurer Sir Anthony Sherley, who supplied the Persian artillery with cannon, Shah Abbas campaigned against the Turks and captured Baghdad, Mosul, and Diarbakr in Mesopotamia.

Military victories explain only part of Shah Abbas's claim to greatness. Determined to improve his country's export trade, he built the small cottage business of carpet weaving into a national industry. In the capital city of Isfahan alone, factories employed over 25,000 weavers who produced woolen carpets, brocades, and silks of brilliant color, design, and quality. Armenians controlled the carpet industry; the Safavids had brought them to Isfahan to protect them from Turkish persecution. Three hundred Chinese potters were imported to make glazed building tiles, which adorned the great Safavid buildings and captured much of the European tile market.

The jewel of the empire was Isfahan, whose prosperity and beauty rested on trade and industry. Shah Abbas himself supervised the reconstruction of the city. A seventeenth-century English visitor described Isfahan's bazaar as "the surprisingest piece of Greatness in Honour of commerce the world can boast of." Besides splendid rugs, stalls displayed pottery and fine china, metalwork of exceptionally high quality, silks and velvets of stunning weave and design. A city of perhaps 750,000 people, Isfahan boasted 162 mosques, 48 seminaries where future members of the ulema learned the sacred Muslim sciences, 273 public baths, and the vast imperial palace. Private houses had their own garden courts, and public gardens, pools, and parks adorned the wide streets. Tales of the beauty of Isfahan circulated worldwide, attracting thousands of tourists annually in the seventeenth and eighteenth centuries.

Shah Abbas was succeeded by inept rulers whose heavy indulgence in wine and the pleasures of the harem weakened the monarchy and fed the slow disintegration of the state. The harem dominated the court. Shi'ite theologians seized power. Internal weakness encouraged foreign aggression. In the eighteenth century the Turks, Afghans, and Russians invaded and divided Persia among themselves. Political anarchy and social chaos characterized Persian life.

INDIA: FROM MUGHAL DOMINATION TO BRITISH DOMINION (CA 1498–1805)

While African societies were experiencing their first large-scale contacts with Europeans, the Asian subcontinent of India achieved a remarkable culture under the domination of the Mughals. In 1504 Babur (1483–1530), ruler of the small Mughal territory in central Asia, captured Kabul and established a kingdom in Afghanistan. From Kabul he moved southward into India. In 1525 Babur launched a serious invasion; a year later, with a force of only twelve thousand men, he defeated the decrepit sultan of Delhi at the Battle of Panipat. Babur's capture of the cities of Agra and Delhi paved the way for further conquests in northern India (Map 23.3). Thus began Mughal rule, which lasted until the eighteenth century, when domestic disorder and incompetent government opened the door to lengthy European intervention. (Mughal refers to the Muslim empire of India. The name *Mughal,* however, a variant on *Mongol,* is technically inaccurate because the founders of the Mughal Empire were mainly Turks and Afghans, not Mongol descendants of Jenghiz Khan.)

THE RULE OF THE MUGHALS

At the start of the sixteenth century, India had already been the object of foreign conquest for almost a millennium. Muslims first invaded India in the seventh century (pages 295–296). The Turkish chieftain Mahmud conquered the Punjab in the tenth century, and in the thirteenth century the Turkish Muslim Qutb-ud-din established the sultanate of Delhi, which ruled northern India. In the next century, the sultanate of Delhi gained control over most of the subcontinent. In 1398, central Asian armies under Timur the Lame (Tamerlane) swept down through the northwest, looted Delhi, and seized tens of thousands of slaves as booty. Timur left Delhi completely destroyed with "not a bird moving" and all India politically fragmented. Although the vast majority of the people remained Hindu, Islam had a strong impact on the culture of India, especially in art and architecture.

The conquests of Babur, the great-grandson of Timur, laid the foundation for Mughal control of India. Babur's son Humayun reigned from 1530 to 1540 and from 1555 to 1556. When the Afghans of northern India rebelled, he lost most of the territories his father had acquired. Humayun went into temporary exile in Persia, where he developed a deep appreciation for Persian art and literature. This interest was to lead to a remarkable efflorescence of Mughal art under his son Akbar.

The reign of Akbar (1556–1605) may well have been the greatest in the history of India. Under his dynamic leadership the Mughal state took definite form. A boy of thirteen when he became *badshah,* or imperial ruler, Akbar was ably assisted during his early years by his father's friend Bairam Khan, a superb military leader. In 1555 Bairam Khan had defeated Hindu forces at Panipat and shortly afterward recaptured Delhi and Agra, the key fortresses of the north. Before falling from power in 1560, Bairam Khan took the great fortress of Gwalior, annexed the rich city of Jaunpur, and prepared for war against Malwa. Akbar continued this expansionist policy, gradually adding the territories of Malwa, Gondwana, and Gujarat (see Map 23.3). Because the Afghan tribesmen put up tremendous resistance, it took Akbar several years to acquire Bengal. The Mughal Empire under Akbar eventually included most of the subcontinent north of the Godavari River (see Map 23.3)

To govern this vast region Akbar developed an efficient bureaucracy staffed by able and well-trained officials, both Muslim and non-Muslim. As in the early modern nations of Europe (page 395), Mughal state solvency depended on the establishment of a careful system for recording income and expenditures. Under Akbar's finance minister Raja Todar Mal, a Hindu, a *diwan* (bureau of finance) and royal mint came into existence. Raja Todar Mal devised

MAP 23.3 **India, 1707–1805** In the eighteenth century Mughal power gradually yielded to the Hindu Marathas, the Sikhs, and the British East India Company.

Legend:
- —— Northern limit of Mughal Empire in 1707
- —— Muslim land in 1765
- Muslim land in 1805
- Area controlled by Hindus in 1805
- Land under British East India Company rule in 1805
- ✕ Site of important battle

methods for the assessment and collection of taxes that were applied throughout the entire empire. To administer the provinces, Akbar appointed about 800 *mansabdars,* or imperial officials, who performed a wide variety of financial, military, and judicial functions at the local level. The central government, however, rarely interfered in the life of village communities. Akbar's policies laid the basis for all later Mughal administration in India.

The cornerstone of Akbar's policies was religious toleration: he sought the peaceful mutual assimilation of Hindus and Muslims, especially in his government. Although this was not a radical innovation—a few Hindus had long been employed in the imperial army and in the administration—very deep prejudices divided the two peoples. When the refusal of many Hindus to serve under a Muslim ruler or to learn Persian, the court language, thwarted Akbar's goal, he took decisive steps to heal the breach. According to his principle of *sulahkul,* or universal tolerance, the *badshah* assumed responsibility for all the people, regardless of religion. In 1564 Akbar ended the pilgrim tax, which won him the gratitude of the many Hindus who traveled to various pilgrimage sites. Akbar's most widely acclaimed act was to abolish the *jizya,* a tax imposed on non-Muslim adult males. He immediately earned the support of the Hindu warrior class and the goodwill of the general Hindu population. Twice Akbar married Hindu princesses, one of whom became the mother of his heir Jahangir. Hindus eventually accounted for 30 percent of the imperial bureaucracy.

Scholars have heatedly debated Akbar's own religious beliefs. Although he considered himself an orthodox Muslim and demonstrated great devotion to the shrine of an Islamic mystic at Ajmer, he supported an eclectic assortment of theological ideas, a policy that caused serious domestic difficulties. In 1575 Akbar sponsored public theological debates among the Muslim ulema. When the discussions degenerated into mutual recriminations, Akbar declared himself the final interpreter of Islamic law. Orthodox Muslims became alarmed. After 1579 Akbar encouraged further debate, inviting Jains, Zoroastrians, Hindus, and Jesuits, as well as the Muslim ulema, to participate. From these discussions Akbar and his courtiers created the *Din-i-Ilahi* (literally, "divine discipleship"), which some advisers called a "syncretic religion" (a religion that reconciles different beliefs). The Din-i-Ilahi borrowed the concept of great respect for animal life from the Jains and reverence for the sun from the Zoroastrians, but it was primarily based on the rationalistic elements in the Islamic tradition and stressed the emperor as a Perfect Man. Some scholars interpret it as a reflection of Akbar's "cult of personality," intended to serve as a common bond for the court nobility. In any case, the Din-i-Ilahi antagonized all sects and provoked serious Muslim rebellions. Although misinterpreted by contemporaries and misunderstood later, the Din-i-Ilahi established Akbar's reputation as a philosopher-king.

The birth of his son Jahangir, which Akbar saw as fulfillment of a prophecy, inspired Akbar to build a new city, Fatehpur-Sikri. Akbar personally supervised the construction of the new city. It combined the Muslim tradition of domes, arches, and spacious

The Vizier at Work Sitting cross-legged on two beautiful Persian carpets, the vizier dictates to one scribe while another calculates on what appears to be abacus. The portrait suggests the importance of the office of vizier in Mughal India as throughout the Islamic world. *(Courtesy of The Harvard University Art Museums [Gift of John Goelet])* courts with the Hindu tradition of flat stone beams, ornate decoration, and solidity. According to Abu-l-Fazl, the historian of Akbar's reign, "His majesty plans splendid edifices, and dresses the work of his mind and heart in the garment of stone and clay."[26] Completed in 1578, the city included an imperial palace, a mosque, lavish gardens, and a hall of worship, as well as thousands of houses for ordinary people. Along with the ancient cities of Delhi and Agra, Fatehpur-Sikri served as an imperial capital and the center of Akbar's lavish court. Its construction reflects Akbar's desire to assimilate Hindus and Muslims and the vaunting power of his empire.

Akbar was gifted with a creative intellect and imagination. He enthusiastically supported artists who produced magnificent paintings and books in the Indo-Persian style. In Mughal India as throughout the Muslim world, books were regarded as precious objects. Time, talent, and expensive materials went into their production, and they were highly coveted because they reflected wealth, learning, and power. Akbar reportedly possessed 24,000 books when he died. Abu-l-Fazl described the library and Akbar's love of books:

His Majesty's library is divided into several parts. . . . Each part . . . is subdivided, according to the value of the books and the estimation in which the sciences are held of which the books treat. Prose works, poetical works, Hindi, Persian, Greek, Kashmirian, Arabic, are all separately placed. In this order they are also inspected. Experienced people bring them daily and read them before His Majesty, who hears every book from beginning to end. At whatever page the reader stops, His Majesty makes with his own pen a sign, according to the number of pages; and rewards the readers with presents of cash either in gold or silver, according to the number of leaves read out by them. Among books of renown there are few that are not read in His Majesty's assembly hall; and there are no historical facts of past ages, or curiosities of science, or interesting points of philosophy, with which His Majesty, a leader of impartial sages, is unacquainted.[27]

Official court biographies almost always exaggerate the achievements of their subjects, but Akbar's library attests to his sincere appreciation for learning. Akbar's son Jahangir (1605–1628) lacked his father's military abilities and administrative genius but did

Heavenly Joys Come to Earth for Akbar This is one of fifteen miniatures, each "as fragile as butterfly wings," produced in a manuscript in 1588 for Akbar. The emperor sits on cushions sipping wine from a gold goblet while beautiful women in diaphanous gowns entertain him with flutes, castenets, cymbals, and dance. Art historians believe this likeness captures Akbar's sensuality, as he stares into the servant girl's eyes. *(Courtesy of The Harvard University Art Museums [Gift of John Goelet])*

Sufism Triumphant Illuminated manuscript, ca 1615–1618. In this remarkable vignette, the emperor Jahangir celebrates the spiritual side of his reign while rejecting a merely worldly mode of government. The angels above bemoan his choice; the cherub on the left clutches a broken arrow symbolic of the power Jahangir has spurned. The ruler offers a book to the venerable Sufi sheik Husain to whom he owed his birth. The sheik had offered prayers on behalf of Jahangir's father Akbar the Great for a son and heir to the throne. Beneath Husain is a Turkish sultan, depicted in general rather than individual fashion. Next is James I of England, whose presence in the entourage underscores the inferior status given to monarchy untempered by the chastening force of piety. The royal portrait had reached India through the English merchant Thomas Roe, who had come to conclude a commercial treaty. According to Roe's memoirs, a picture of James I was displayed in the New Year's Durbar (state reception) of 1616. At the bottom the Hindu painter Bichitr advertises his respects with a placard of himself paying obeisance. Two further elements emphasize the glory of Jahangir's reign: the dazzling sun around his head and the pair of industrious angels writing a message on the hourglass throne pedestal: 'O, Shah, may the span of your life be a thousand years.' *(Courtesy of the Freer Gallery of Art, Smithsonian Institution)*

succeed in consolidating Mughal rule in Bengal. His patronage of the arts and lavish court have led scholars to characterize his reign as the "age of splendor."

Jahangir's son Shah Jahan (1628–1658) launched fresh territorial expansion. Faced with dangerous revolts by the Muslims in Ahmadnagar and the resistance of the newly arrived Portuguese in Bengal, Shah Jahan not only crushed them but strengthened his northwestern frontier. He reasserted Mughal authority in the Deccan and Golkunda.

The new capital that Shah Jahan founded at Delhi superseded Agra, Akbar's main capital. Situated on the rich land linking the Indus and Ganges valleys, Delhi eventually became one of the great cities of the Muslim world. The city boasted one of the finest mosques in Islam, the Juma Masjid, and magnificent boulevards. The Red Fort, named for its red sandstone walls, housed the imperial palace, the headquarters of the imperial administration, the imperial treasury, an arsenal, and a garrison. Subsequent Mughal rulers held their *durbar,* or court, at Delhi.

Shah Jahan also ordered the construction of the Peacock Throne. This famous device, actually a cot resting on golden legs, was encrusted with emeralds, diamonds, pearls, and rubies; took seven years to fashion; and cost the equivalent of $5 million. It served as the imperial throne of India until 1739, when the Persian warrior Nadir Shah seized it as plunder and carried it to Persia.

Shah Jahan's most enduring monument is the Taj Mahal, the supreme example of the garden tomb. The English word *paradise* derives from the old Persian *pairidaeza,* a walled garden. The Mughals sought to bring their vision of paradise alive in the walled garden tombs in which they buried their dead. Twenty thousand workers toiled eighteen years to build this memorial in Agra to Shah Jahan's favorite wife, Mumtaz Mahal, who died giving birth to their fifteenth child. One of the most beautiful structures in the world, the Taj Mahal is both an expression of love and a superb architectural blending of Islamic and Indian culture. It also asserted the power of the Mughal dynasty.

The Mughal state never developed a formal procedure for the imperial succession, and a crisis occurred toward the end of Shah Jahan's reign. Competition among his sons ended with the victory of Aurangzeb, who executed his elder brother and locked his father

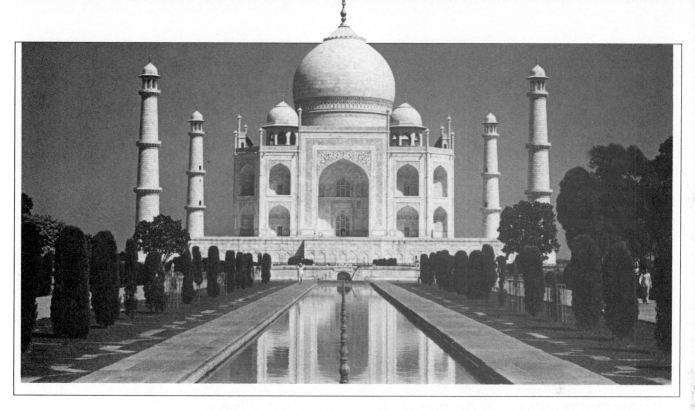

Taj Mahal at Agra The finest example of Muslim architecture in India. Its white marble exterior is inlaid with semi-precious stones in Arabic inscriptions and floral designs. The oblong pool reflects the building, which asserts the power of the Mughal dynasty. *(Ira Kirschenbaum/Stock, Boston)*

away until death in 1666. A puritanically devout and strictly orthodox Muslim, a skillful general and a clever diplomat, Aurangzeb ruled more of India than did any previous badshah. His reign witnessed the culmination of Mughal power and the beginning of its decline.

A combination of religious zeal and financial necessity seems to have prompted Aurangzeb to introduce a number of reforms. He appointed censors of public morals in important cities to enforce Islamic laws against gambling, prostitution, drinking, and the use of narcotics. He forbade the *sati*—the self-immolation of widows on their husbands' funeral pyres—and the castration of boys to sell them as eunuchs. He also abolished all taxes not authorized by Islamic law. This measure led to a serious loss of state revenues; to replace them, Aurangzeb in 1679 reimposed the jizya, the tax on non-Muslims. It fell most heavily on the Hindu majority.

Regulating Indian society according to Islamic law meant modifying the religious toleration and cultural cosmopolitanism instituted by Akbar. Aurangzeb or-

dered the destruction of some Hindu temples. He required Hindus to pay higher customs duties than Muslims. Out of fidelity to Islamic law, he even criticized his mother's tomb, the Taj Mahal: "The lawfulness of a solid construction over a grave is doubtful, and there can be no doubt about the extravagance involved."[28] On the other hand, Aurangzeb employed more Hindus in the imperial administration than any previous Mughal ruler. But his religious policy proved highly unpopular with the majority of his subjects. Although his indomitable military strength and persistent activity staved off difficulties and maintained the unity of the empire, Aurangzeb created problems weaker successors could not handle.

Aurangzeb's military ventures also had mixed results. A tireless general, he pushed the conquest of the south and succeeded in annexing the Golkunda and Bijapur sultanates. The stiffest opposition came from the Marathas, a militant Hindu group centered in the western Deccan. From 1681 until his death in 1707 at the age of ninety, Aurangzeb led repeated sorties through the Deccan. He took many forts and won several battles. Total destruction of the Maratha guerrilla bands eluded him, however, and after his death they played an important role in the collapse of the Mughal Empire.

Aurangzeb's eighteenth-century successors faced formidable problems. Repeated disputes over the succession contributed to the instability of the monarchy. Court intrigues replaced the battlefield as the testing ground for the nobility. Mughal provincial governors began to rule independently, giving only minimal allegiance to the badshahs at Delhi. The Marathas, who revolted and pressed steadily northward, constituted the gravest threat to Mughal authority. No ruler could defeat them.

In 1739 the Persian adventurer Nadir Shah invaded India, defeated the Mughal army, looted Delhi, and after a savage massacre carried off a huge amount of treasure, including the Peacock Throne. When Nadir Shah withdrew to Afghanistan, he took with him the prestige of the Mughal government. Constant skirmishes between the Afghans and the Marathas for control of the Punjab and northern India ended in 1761 at the Battle of Panipat, where the Marathas were crushingly defeated. India no longer had any power capable of imposing order on the subcontinent or of checking the rapacious penetration of the Europeans.

EUROPEAN RIVALRY FOR THE INDIAN TRADE

Shortly before Babur's invasion of India, the Portuguese under the navigator Pedro Alvares Cabral had opened the subcontinent to Portuguese trade. In 1510 they established the port of Goa on the Arabian Sea as their headquarters and through a policy of piracy and terrorism swept the Muslims off the Indian and Arabian oceans. Attempting to justify Portuguese seizure of commercial traffic that the Muslims had long dominated, the Portuguese historian Barroes wrote:

It is true that there does exist a common right to all to navigate the seas and in Europe we recognize the rights which others hold against us; but the right does not extend beyond Europe and therefore the Portuguese as Lords of the Sea are justified in confiscating the goods of all those who navigate the seas without their permission.[29]

For Europeans, in short, Western principles of international law did not apply in Asia. For almost a century the Portuguese controlled the spice trade over the Indian Ocean.

In 1602 the Dutch formed the Dutch East India Company with the stated goal of wresting the enormously lucrative spice trade from the Portuguese. The scent of fabulous profits also attracted the English. With a charter signed by Queen Elizabeth, eighty London merchants organized the British East India Company: their objective also was the Indian spice and cotton trade. Although the English initially had no luck, in 1619 Emperor Jahangir granted a British mission led by Sir Thomas Roe important commercial concessions at the port of Surat on the Gulf of Cambay. Gifts, medical services, and bribes to Indian rulers soon enabled the British to set up twenty-seven other forts along the coasts. Fort St. George on the eastern coast became the modern city of Madras. In 1668 the city of Bombay, given to England when the Portuguese princess Catherine of Braganza married King Charles II, was leased to the company. This event marks the virtually total British absorption of Portuguese power in India. Meanwhile the Dutch concentrated their efforts in Indonesia. In 1690 Job Charnock, a company official, established a fort that eventually became the city of Calcutta. Thus the three places that subsequently became centers of British economic and political imperialism—Madras, Bombay, and Calcutta—had already come into existence before 1700.

FACTORY-FORT SOCIETIES

The British called their trading post at Surat a "factory," and the word was later used for all European settlements in India. The term did not signify manufacturing; it designated the walled compound containing the residences, gardens, and offices of British East India Company officials and the warehouses where goods were stored before being shipped to Europe. The company president exercised political authority over all residents.

In exchange for English minerals—silver, copper, zinc, and lead—and fabrics, the company bought Indian cotton goods, silks, pepper and other spices, sugar, and opium. By the late seventeenth century the company was earning substantial profits; profitability increased even more after 1700 when it began

View of Goa The Portuguese admiral Albuquerque, attracted by the wealth of the Mughal Empire, seized Goa (on the Arabian Sea) in 1510. Notice the elegant dress and jewels of the veiled Muslim lady whose slave boy, imported from East Africa, holds a parasol as a sunshade. *(Courtesy The Oliveira Lima Library, The Catholic University of America. Photo: Paul McKane, OSB)*

to trade with China. Because the directors of the British East India Company in London discouraged all unnecessary expenses and financial risks, they opposed any interference in local Indian politics and even missionary activities. Indian conditions, however, brought about a fundamental change in the nature of the company's factories.

The violent disorders and political instability that wracked India during Aurangzeb's reign and in the early eighteenth century led to the evolution of the factories into forts and then into territorial settlements. In order to protect their trading interests, company officials transformed the factories into defensive installations manned by small garrisons of native troops. When warlords appeared or an uprising occurred, people from the surrounding country-side flocked into the fort. Because of the lack of a strong central government and because local princes were unable to provide security, the company factory-forts gradually came to exercise political authority over the territories around them.

Factory-forts existed to make profits from the Asian-European trade, and they evolved into flourishing centers of Indian economic profit. Some Indian merchants in Calcutta and Bombay made gigantic fortunes from the country trade—that is, trade within Asia.

In the European economies, Asian goods created serious problems. Indian and Chinese wares enjoyed great popularity in England and on the European continent in the late seventeenth and early eighteenth centuries. The middle classes wanted Indian textiles, which were colorful, durable, cheap, and washable. The upper classes desired Chinese wallpaper and porcelains, Indian silks and brocades. The import of these products into England threatened domestic goods. As early as 1695 English manufacturers called for an embargo on Indian cloth, while silk weavers picketed the House of Commons. Moreover, trade with Asia was one-way: Asians had little interest in European manufactured articles. The Dutch East India Company found the Siamese so oblivious to traditional Dutch goods that the company tried to interest them in collections of pornography. Europeans had to pay for everything they bought from Asia with precious metals. This circumstance gave rise to insistent pressure within England, France, and the Netherlands against the import of Asian goods. As one authority explains it:

The root of the argument from which grew a tree of many branches was the old fear of the drain of gold. When the English pamphleteers professed to be shocked by the transparency of Indian fabrics, their care for the modesty of English females was a disguise, not less transparent than muslin, for the objections of those who on general grounds deplored sending gold and silver abroad or on particular grounds were anxious to protect domestic industries.[30]

THE RISE OF THE BRITISH EAST INDIA COMPANY

The French were the last to arrive in India. Louis XIV's financial wizard Colbert (pages 595–596) planned the French East India Company for trade in the Eastern Hemisphere, and in the 1670s the company established factories at Chandernagore in Bengal, Pondicherry, and elsewhere. Joseph Dupleix (1697–1764), who was appointed governor general at Pondicherry in 1742, was the first European to appreciate fully the political as well as economic potential of India. He understood the instability of the Mughal Empire and realized that one European power would eventually govern India. Dupleix also knew that, since the French East India Company could expect no support from the government in Paris, it would have to be economically self-sufficient and acquire territory. He made allies with Indian princes and built an army of native troops, called *sepoys,* who were trained as infantrymen. The British likewise

built an army with Indian surrogates trained in Western military drill and tactics. War broke out at midcentury.

From 1740 to 1763 Britain and France were almost continually engaged in a tremendous global struggle. India, like North America in the Seven Years' War, became a battlefield and a prize. The French and the English both bid for the support of the rulers of the Deccan. In 1746 Dupleix captured Madras, and in 1751 the French gained control of the huge Deccan and Carnatic regions. But while the French won land battles, English seapower decided the first phase of the war. Then in 1757, the English commander Robert Clive, having bought up most of the officers of the French-supported *nawab* (Muslim governor) of Bengal, defeated him at Plassey. In a series of brilliant victories Clive went on to destroy French power in southern India. By preventing French reinforcements, British seapower again proved to be the determining factor, and Clive soon extended British jurisdiction over the important northern province of Bengal. The Treaty of Paris of 1763 recognized British control of much of India, and scholars acknowledge it as the beginning of the British Empire in India.

How was the vast subcontinent to be governed? Parliament believed that the British East India Company had too much power and considered the company largely responsible for the political disorders in India, which were bad for business. Parliament attempted to solve Indian problems with special legislation. The Regulating Act of 1773 deprived the company of some of its political power. The newly created office of governor general, with an advisory council, would exercise political authority over the territory controlled by the company. The India Act of 1784 required that the governor general be chosen from outside the company and made its directors subject to parliamentary supervision.

Implementation of these reforms fell to Warren Hastings, the governor of Bengal and first governor general (1774–1785) with jurisdiction over Bombay and Madras. Hastings tried to build an effective administrative system and to turn the British East India Company into a government. He laid the foundations for the first Indian civil service, abolished tolls to facilitate internal trade, placed the salt and opium trades under government control, and planned a codification of Muslim and Hindu laws. He sought allies among Indian princes and, in imitation of Dupleix, built an army of sepoy troops trained as infantrymen to support the British artillery. The biggest problem facing Hastings's administration was a coalition of the rulers of Mysore and the Marathas aimed at the expulsion of the British. Hastings's skillful diplomacy offset this alliance temporarily. In 1785, however, Hastings resigned his office and returned to England. Charges that he had interfered in provincial administrations, extorted money from Indian princes, and ordered the murder of an Indian merchant led to his impeachment; he was finally acquitted in 1795.

Hastings's successor Lord Charles Cornwallis (whom George Washington defeated at Yorktown) served as governor general of India from 1786 to 1794. Cornwallis continued the work of building a civil service and the war against Mysore. His introduction of the British style of property relations in effect converted a motley collection of ex-Mughal officers, tax collectors, and others into English-style landlords. A new land revenue system resulted. The third governor general, the marquess Richard Wellesley (1797–1805), defeated the Mysore in 1799 and four years later crushed the Marathas at the Battle of Assaye. Building on the work of his predecessors, he vastly extended British influence in India. Like most nineteenth-century British governors of India, Wellesley believed that British rule strongly benefited the Indians. With supreme condescension he wrote that British power should be established over the Indian princes in order "to deprive them of the means of prosecuting any measure or of forming any confederacy hazardous to the security of the British empire, and to enable us to preserve the tranquility of India by exercising a general control over the restless spirit of ambition and violence which is characteristic of every Asiatic government."[31]

At the beginning of the nineteenth century, the authority and power of the British East India Company had yielded to the government in London. Subsequent British rule of India rested on three foundations: the support of puppet Indian princes, who exercised the trappings but not the reality of power; a large army of sepoys of dubious loyalty; and an increasingly effective civil service, staffed largely by Englishmen with Hindus and Muslims in minor positions.

The period between 1450 and 1800 saw the rise of several different African societies. Although French culture influenced the coastal fringes of Senegambia, the English maintained factories along the Gold Coast, and the Portuguese held Angola as a colony and maintained an insecure grip on Mozambique in East Africa, European influence hardly penetrated the African interior. And despite the export of as many as 12 million slaves from Africa to meet the labor needs of South and North America, the overall impact of the slave trade on Africa was marginal. It appeared around 1810 that Africa's development would be entirely autonomous.

In the eighteenth century, the Ottoman Turks lived almost entirely within a closed Islamic environment. Very few knew European languages or had firsthand knowledge of Europe. Diplomatic relations with any European power did not exist before 1793. When the Ottomans thought of Europe at all, they believed it inferior to Islamic civilization, despite the plea in 1653 of Katib Chelebi, a renowned Ottoman historian, for greater Muslim knowledge of geography: "Sufficient and compelling proof of the necessity for [learning] this science is the fact that the unbelievers, by their application to and esteem for those branches of learning, have discovered the New World and have overrun the ports of India and the East Indies."[32] Everyone looked backward to the period of Suleiman the Magnificent, when the empire was at its height. There was no thought of innovation or experimentation. Some scholars believe that Islam's hostility to innovation is traceable to a saying of the Prophet's: "The worst things are those that are novelties, every novelty is an innovation, every innovation is an error, and every error leads to Hell-fire." After war with Russia (1736–1739), in which the Turks were largely successful, the Ottomans entered a long period of peace on their western frontier. Only with the reforms of Sultan Selim III (1761–1808), in which the imperial administration and the army were restructured, European languages studied, and relations established with European powers, did the Ottoman Empire begin to be transformed into a modern state.

The contemporary Indian writer V. S. Naipaul has called India "a wounded civilization." For centuries the economic prize of European commercial interests, in the 1700s the Indian subcontinent began to experience British political domination. Bitter hostility between Hindus and Muslims persisted as a dominant theme of Indian life.

NOTES

1. P. D. Curtin, *Economic Change in Precolonial Africa: Senegambia in the Era of the Slave Trade* (Madison, Wis.: University of Wisconsin Press, 1975), pp. 34–35; and J. A. Rawley, *The Transatlantic Slave Trade: A History* (New York: Norton, 1981), p. 12

2. R. W. July, *A History of the African People,* 3d ed. (New York: Scribner's, 1980), pp. 128–129.

3. R. W. July, *Precolonial Africa: An Economic and Social History* (New York: Scribner's, 1975), p. 99.

4. July, *History of the African People,* p. 141.

5. A. ibn Fartura, "The Kanem Wars," in *Nigerian Perspectives,* ed. T. Hodgkin (London: Oxford University Press, 1966), pp. 111–115.

6. "The Kano Chronicle," quoted in Hodgkin, *Nigerian Perspectives,* pp. 89–90.

7. I have leaned heavily here on P. E. Lovejoy, *Transformations in Slavery: A History of Slavery in Africa* (Cambridge: Cambridge University Press, 1983), p. 19.

8. See Table 2.1, "Trans-Saharan Slave Trade, 650–1600," in ibid., p. 25.

9. Rawley, *Transatlantic Slave Trade,* p. 45.

10. Ibid., pp. 41–47.

11. R. E. Conrad, *Children of God's Fire. A Documentary History of Black Slavery in Brazil* (Princeton, N.J.: Princeton University Press, 1983), pp. 20–23

12. Rawley, *Transatlantic Slave Trade,* pp. 45–47.

13. July, *History of the African People,* p. 208.

14. J. Adams, "Remarks on the Country Extending from Cape Palmas to the River Congo, " in Hodgkin, *Nigerian Perspectives,* pp. 178–180.

15. A. G. Hopkins, *An Economic History of West Africa* (New York: Columbia University Press, 1973), p. 83.

16. Ibid., p. 105.

17. July, *Precolonial Africa,* pp. 269–270.

18. Hopkins, *Economic History,* p. 119.

19. July, *History of the African People,* pp. 201–202.

20. Quoted in B. Lewis, *The Muslim Discovery of Europe* (New York: Norton, 1982), p. 29.

21. W. H. McNeill, *The Pursuit of Power: Technology, Armed Force, and Society Since A.D. 1000* (Chicago: University of Chicago Press, 1982), p. 87.

22. Quoted in Lewis, *Muslim Discovery,* p. 30.

23. F. Robinson, *Atlas of the Islamic World Since 1500* (New York: Facts on File, 1982), p. 72.

24. Quoted in P. K. Hitti, *The Near East in History* (Princeton, N.J.: Van Nostrand, 1961), p. 336.

25. N. Itzkowitz, *Ottoman Empire and Islamic Tradition* (Chicago: University of Chicago Press, 1980), p. 95.

26. Quoted in V. A. Smith, *The Oxford History of India* (Oxford: Oxford University Press, 1967), p. 398.

27. Quoted in M. C. Beach, *The Imperial Image: Paintings for the Mughal Court* (Washington, D. C.: Freer Gallery of Art, Smithsonian Institution, 1981), pp. 9–10.

28. Quoted in S. K. Ikram, *Muslim Civilization in India* (New York: Columbia University Press, 1964), p. 202.

29. Quoted in K. M. Panikkar, *Asia and Western Domination* (London: George Allen & Unwin, 1965), p. 35.

30. Quoted in ibid., p. 53.

31. Quoted in W. Bingham, H. Conroy, and F. W. Ikle, *A History of Asia,* vol. 2 (Boston: Allyn & Bacon, 1967), p. 74.

32. Quoted in ibid., p. 106.

SUGGESTED READING

Students should have little difficulty finding interesting and sound material on the topics raised in this chapter. For Africa in the era of the slave trade, in addition to the titles given in the Notes, see D. Gamble, *The Wolof of Senegambia* (1967), which discusses Wolof economy, political structure, and social organization; A. F. C. Ryder, *Benin and the Europeans, 1485–1897* (1969); R. E. Bradbury, *Benin Studies* (1973), which contains useful articles on government, art, and society; and E. Isichei, *The Ibo People and the Europeans* (1973), which treats internal migrations and the impact of the slave trade on society. L. W. Henderson, *Angola: Five Centuries of Conflict* (1979), provides a good survey of the

Portuguese in Angola, while G. J. Bender, *Angola Under the Portuguese: The Myth and the Reality* (1978), focuses on the nineteenth and twentieth centuries with some background sections. For the Swahili city-states, C. S. Nicholls, *The Swahili Coast* (1971), is an important work. W. Bascom and M. J. Herskovits, eds., *Continuity and Change in African Cultures* (1959), treats many facets of African cultures with emphasis on linguistics and ethnohistory. The standard reference works on African history are R. Oliver, ed., *The Cambridge History of Africa,* vol. 3, *ca 1050–1600* (1977), and R. Gray, ed., *The Cambridge History of Africa,* vol. 4, *ca 1600–ca 1870* (1975).

The best up-to-date accounts of Ottoman history are H. Inalcik, *The Ottoman Empire: The Classical Age, 1300–1600* (1973), and the work by Itzkowitz, cited in the Notes. O. G. de Busbecq, *Turkish Letters* (trans. E. S. Foster, 1967), is a firsthand report of the court of Suleiman the Magnificent. G. Goodwin, *A History of Ottoman Architecture* (1971), is probably the best available general study, and the famous architect has found his bi-ographer in A. Stratton, *Sinan* (1972). I. Andric, *The Bridge on the Drina* (trans. L. F. Edwards, 1959), is a brilliant novel evoking Balkan life under Turkish rule; it earned its author the Nobel Prize for literature. Islam's understanding of the West is studied in the excellent work by Lewis listed in the Notes; and R. W. Southern, *Western Views of Islam* (1962), is a fine summary of the Western viewpoint.

There is no up-to-date treatment of Mughal India, but the curious student might start with P. M. Holt et al., eds., *The Cambridge History of Islam,* 2 vols. (1970). M. Mujeeb, *The Indian Muslims* (1967), and I. Habib, *The Agrarian System of Mughal India, 1556–1707* (1963), are both useful. B. Gascoigne, *The Great Moghuls* (1971), and G. Hambly, *The Cities of Mughal India: Delhi, Agra, and Fatehpur Sikri* (1968), are well illustrated and highly readable. For the impact of Portuguese, Dutch, and English mercantile activities on India, see M. N. Pearson, *Merchants and Rulers in Gujarat: The Response to the Portuguese in the Sixteenth Century* (1976).

PERIOD (CA 1200–1700)	AFRICA AND THE MIDDLE EAST	THE AMERICAS	
1200	Kingdom of Mali, ca 1200–1450 Mongols conquer Baghdad, 1258; fall of Abbasid Dynasty	Maya civilization in Central America, ca 300–1500 Inca civilization in South America, ca 1000–1500 Toltec hegemony, ca 1000–1300	
1300	Rise of Yoruba states, West Africa, ca 1300 Height of Swahili (East African) city-states, ca 1300–1500 Mansa Musa rules Mali, 1312–1337	Tenochtitlán (Mexico City) founded by Aztecs, 1325	
1400	Zara Yakob rules Ethiopia, 1434–1468 Arrival of Portugese in Benin, ca 1440 Songhay Empire, West Africa, ca 1450–1591 Atlantic slave trade, ca 1450–1850 Ottoman Empire, 1453–1918 Da Gama arrives on East African coast, 1498	Height of Inca Empire, 1438–1493 Reign of Montezuma I, 1440–1468; height of Aztec culture Colombus reaches the Americas, 1492	
1500	Portugal dominates East Africa, ca 1500–1650 Peak of Ottoman power under Suleiman the Magnificent, 1520–1566 Height of Kanem-Bornu under Idris Alooma, 1571–1603 Portugese found Angola, 1571	South American holocaust, ca 1500–1600 First African slaves, ca 1510 Cortés arrives in Mexico, 1519; Aztec Empire falls, 1521 Pizarro reaches Peru, 1531; conquers Incas Spanish conquer the Philippines, 1571	
1600	Dutch West India Co. supplants Portugese in West Africa, ca 1630 Dutch settle Cape Town, 1651 Rise of Ashanti Empire, founded on Gold Coast trade, ca 1700–1750	British settle Jamestown, 1607 Champlain founds Quebec, 1608 Dutch found New Amsterdam, 1624 Slave labor allows tenfold increase in production of Virginian tobacco, ca 1700–1740 Silver production quadruples in Mexico and Peru, ca 1700–1800	

EAST ASIA	INDIA AND SOUTHEAST ASIA	EUROPE
Kamakura Shogunate, 1185–1333 Unsuccessful Mongol invasions of Japan, 1274, 1281 Yüan (Mongol) Dynasty, 1279–1368	Peak of Khmer Empire in southeast Asia, ca 1200 Turkish sultanate at Delhi, 1206–1526; Indian culture divided into Hindu and Muslim	Magna Carta, 1215 Thomas Aquinas, *Summa Theologica*, 1235 Prince Alexander Nevsky recognizes Mongol overlordship of Moscow, 1252
Marco Polo arrives at Kublai Khan's court, ca 1275 Ashikaga Shogunate, 1336–1408 Hung Wu drives Mongols from China, 1368; founds Ming Dynasty, 1368–1644	Turkish chieftain Timur conquers the Punjab, 1398	Babylonian Captivity of the papacy, 1309–1372 Tver revolt in Russia, 1327–1328 Hundred Years' War, 1337–1453 Bubonic plague, 1347–1352 Ottoman Turks invade Europe, 1356 Peasants' Revolt in England, 1381
Early Ming policy encourages foreign trade, ca 15th century Ming maritime expeditions to India, Middle East, Africa, 1405–1433	Sultan Mehmed II, 1451–1481 Pasha Sinon, Ottoman architect, 1491–1588 Da Gama reaches India, 1498	Italian Renaissance, ca 1400–1530 Voyages of discovery, ca 1450–1600 Ottomans capture Constantinople, 1453, signaling end of Byzantine Empire War of the Roses in England, 1455–1485 Unification of Spain completed, 1492
Portugese trade monopoly in East Asia, ca 16th century Christian missionaries active in China and Japan, ca 1550–1650 Unification of Japan, 1568–1600	Safavid Empire, 1501–1722 Barbur defeats Delhi sultanate, 1526–1527; founds Mughal Empire Akbar expands Mughal Empire, 1556–1605 Height of Safavid power under Shah Abbas, 1587–1629	Martin Luther, Ninety-five Theses, 1517 Charles V elected Holy Roman Emperor, 1519 Henry VIII leads English Reformation, 1534 Council of Trent, 1545–1563 Dutch United Provinces declare independence, 1581 Spanish Armada, 1588
Tokugawa Shogunate, 1600–1867 Japan expels all Europeans, 1637 Manchus establish Ch'ing Dynasty, 1644 Height of Manchu Dynasty under K'ang-hsi, 1662–1722 Height of Edo urban culture in Japan, ca 1700	Height of Mughal Empire under Shah Jahan, 1628–1658 British found Calcutta, 1690 Decline of Mughal Empire, ca 1700–1800 Persian invaders sack Delhi, 1739	Romanov Dynasty founded in Russia, 1613 Thirty Years' War, 1618–1648 Brandenburg-Prussia unified, 1640–1688 English Civil War, 1642–1646 Louis XIV, absolute king of France, 1643–1715 Ottoman Turks besiege Vienna, 1683 Revocation of Edict of Nantes, 1685 The Glorious Revolution in England, 1688 War of Spanish Succession, 1701–1713; Treaty of Utrecht, 1713

24

CHINA AND JAPAN,
CA 1400–1800

*T*HE PERIOD from about 1400 to 1800 witnessed growth and dynamic change in East Asia. In China the native Ming Dynasty had replaced the Yuan (page 309) and was in turn replaced by the foreign Ch'ing Dynasty. The early Ming period was a time of remarkable economic reconstruction and of the establishment of new and original social institutions. Over time, however, the bureaucracy prevented the changes necessary to meet new demands on the empire. The Ch'ing Dynasty inaugurated a long period of peace, relative prosperity, and population expansion. Under the Ch'ing, the Chinese Empire reached its greatest territorial extent, and literary and artistic creativity reached an unparalleled apogee.

The Japanese islands, united by Nobunaga and later the Tokugawa Shogunate, underwent further evolution of the feudal military aristocracy; although Japan developed in near-total isolation from outside influences, its sociopolitical system bore striking similarities to medieval European feudalism. The period of the Tokugawa Shogunate, like that of the Ming Dynasty in China, was marked by remarkable agricultural productivity and industrial growth.

What features characterized the governments of the Ming and Ch'ing in China and the Tokugawa Shogunate in Japan? How were Chinese and Japanese societies affected by agricultural and commercial developments? How did Chinese thinkers interpret and explain the shift from the Ming to the Ch'ing? What were the Chinese and Japanese attitudes toward Christian missionary efforts from the West? This chapter will explore these questions.

CHINA: FROM THE MING DYNASTY TO THE MID-MANCHU (CA 1368–1795)

A combination of Mongol repression, rapid inflation of the currency, disputes over succession among the khans, and the growth of peasant secret societies led to the decay of Mongol government in China (page 309). By 1368, Hung Wu, the leader of a secret society called the "Red Turbans," had pushed the Mongols out of China. Hung Wu (1368–1398), the founder of the Ming Dynasty, stands out in Chinese history along with Liu Pang, founder of the Han Dynasty, as the only peasants who founded major dynasties. The Ming Dynasty (1368–1644) is the only dynasty that originated south of the Yangtze River.

Under the Ming, China experienced remarkable change. Agricultural development and commercial reconstruction followed a long period of chaos and disorder. Hung Wu introduced far-reaching social and political institutions, intended to be hereditary, but by the middle of the fifteenth century his administrative framework had begun to decay. Ming government tended to be harshly autocratic. Externally, the Ming emperors strove to push back the Mongol borders in the north. Chinese defeats in Mongolia in the later fifteenth century led to a long period of steady Chinese withdrawal. Nevertheless, the Ming period stands out for its social and cultural achievements.

THE MING AGRICULTURAL AND COMMERCIAL REVOLUTIONS

Mongol exploitation and the civil disorders that accompanied the breakdown of Yuan rule had left China in economic chaos. Vast stretches of farm land were laid waste, some entirely abandoned. Damaged dikes and canals proved unusable, causing trade to decline.

A profound economic reconstruction occurred between 1370 and 1398. The agricultural revolution that China underwent in the Ming period was in part a gigantic effort at recovery after the disaster of Mongol rule, and in part a continuation of developments begun under the Sung (pages 301–303). This revolution involved radical improvement in methods of rice production. More than bread in Europe, rice supplied almost the total nourishment of the population. Terracing and irrigation of mountain slopes, introduced in the eleventh century, had led to larger rice harvests. The introduction of Indochinese, or Champa, rice proved an even greater boon. Champa rice was drought resistant, yielded larger harvests, and could be sown earlier in the year. Although Champa rice was of lower nutritional quality than traditional Chinese rice, it considerably increased the total output of food. Ming farmers experimented with Champa rice that required only sixty days from planting to harvesting, instead of the usual hundred days. Peasants soon reaped two harvests a year, an enormous increase in production.

Chinese Peasants at Work The Western artist who sketched this picture in the seventeenth century seems to be telling us that the use of human power in agriculture was as common in China as animal power. Coco palm trees (left) have many important uses, though they are not usually found as far north as China. The pigtailed men date the picture from the Manchu period. *(Photo: Caroline Buckler)*

Other innovations also had good results. Because the roots of rice plants require a rich supply of oxygen, the water in which rice grows must be kept in motion so that oxygenation can occur. Ming-era peasants introduced irrigation pumps worked by pedals. Farmers also began to stock the rice paddies with fish, which continuously fertilized the rice fields, destroyed malaria-bearing mosquitoes, and enriched the diet. Fish farming in the paddies eventually enabled large parts of southern China, previously uninhabitable, to be brought under cultivation. Farmers also discovered the possibilities of commercial cropping in cotton, sugar cane, and indigo. Finally, new methods of crop rotation allowed for continuous cultivation and more than one harvest per year from a single field.

The Ming rulers promoted the repopulation and colonization of devastated regions through massive transfers of people; immigrants received large plots and exemption from taxation for many years. Table 24.1, based on fourteenth-century records of newly tilled land, helps tell the story.[1]

Reforestation of the land was a dramatic aspect of the agricultural revolution. In 1391 the Ming government ordered 50 million trees planted in the Nanking area; the trees were intended for the construction of a maritime fleet. In 1392 each family holding colonized land in Anhwei province had to plant 200 mulberry trees, 200 jujube trees, and 200 persimmon trees. In 1396 peasants in the present-day provinces of Hunan and Hupei in the east planted 84 million fruit trees. Historians have estimated that 1 billion trees were planted during Hung Wu's reign.[2]

What were the social consequences of this agricultural development? Increased food production led to steady population growth. Demographers date the start of the Chinese population boom at about 1550, as a direct result of improved methods of rice production. Increases in total yields differed fundamentally, however, from comparable agricultural growth in

TABLE 24.1 LAND RECLAMATION IN EARLY MING CHINA

Year	Reclaimed Land (in hectares; 1 hectare = 2.5 acres)
1371	576,000
1373	1,912,000
1374	4,974,000
1379	1,486,000

Europe: Chinese grain harvests were improved through intensification of peasant labor. This meant lower income per capita.

Another outcome of population increase seems to have been the multiplication of towns and small cities. Urbanization in the Ming era (and, later, Ch'ing period) involved the proliferation of market centers and small towns, rather than the growth of "large" cities that characterized Europe in the High Middle Ages and China in the Sung period. Most people lived in tiny hamlets or villages, without markets. What distinguished a village from a town was that a town had a market. Towns held markets twice a week; in southern China, where a week was ten days long, markets were held three times a week. Town markets consisted of little open-air shops that sold essential goods—pins, matches, oil for lamps, candles, paper, incense, tobacco—to the country people who came in from surrounding hamlets. The market usually included a tearoom or tavern where tea and rice wine were sold, entertainers performed, and moneylenders and pawnshops sometimes did business. Because itinerant salesmen depended on the city market for their wares, town markets were not held on days when the nearest city had its market.

Tradesmen, who carried their wares on their backs, and craftsmen—carpenters, barbers, joiners, locksmiths—moved constantly from market to market. Large towns and cities became the focus for foodstuffs from the countryside and for rare and precious goods from distant places. Cities gradually became islands of sophistication in the highly localized Chinese economy. Nanking, for example, because of the residence of the imperial court and bureaucracy, spread out enormously. The concentration of people in turn created demand for goods and services. Industrial development was stimulated. Small busi-nesses manufactured textiles, paper, and luxury goods such as silks and porcelains. Nanking and Shanghai became centers for the production of cotton and silks, while Hsin-an specialized in the grain and salt trade and in silver. While small towns remained embedded in peasant culture, large towns and cities pursued contacts with the wider world.

THE GOVERNMENT OF HUNG WU

Hung Wu's governmental reforms rested on a few strong centralizing principles. He established China's capital at Nanking (literally, "southern capital"), his old base on the Yangtze River. He stripped many nobles of their estates and divided them among the peasantry. Although Hung Wu had been a monk, he confiscated many of the temples' tax-exempt lands, thereby increasing the proceeds of the state treasury. Unlike the Sung period, when commercial taxes fed the treasury, imperial revenues in the Ming (and, later, Ch'ing) period came mainly from agriculture. Farmers produced the state's resources.

Hung Wu ordered a general survey of all China's land and several censuses of the population; the data gathered were recorded in official registers. These registers provided valuable information about the taxes that landlords, temples, and peasants owed. According to the registers, the capital was owed 8 million *shih,* or 160,000 tons, of rice per year. Such thorough fiscal information contributed to the efficient operation of the state.

To secure soldiers for the army and personnel for his administration and to generate revenue, Hung Wu adopted the Yuan practice of requiring service to the state. He made all occupations hereditary. The entire Chinese population was classified into three hereditary categories: peasants, artisans, and soldiers. The state ministry with jurisdiction over a particular category designated the individual's obligations to the state. The ministry of finance oversaw the peasants, who provided the bulk of the taxes and performed public labor services. The ministry of public works supervised artisans and all people with special skills and crafts. The ministry of the army controlled the standing army of 2 million men. Every person entered a state category at birth, on the basis of his father's occupation; one's descendants belonged to the same category. When a soldier died or proved unable to fight, his family had to provide a replacement. Fi-

Chinese Marketplace This busy scene of commercial activity shows camels, horses, donkeys, and humans used to transport goods. The rich are carried in sedan chairs, while tea shops and restaurants provide a variety of refreshments. *(Werner Forman Archive)*

nally, each social category prevailed in a particular geographical region. Peasants lived in the countryside; craftsmen lived mainly in the neighborhoods of the cities for which they produced goods; and army families lived along the coasts and lengthy frontiers that they defended.

The Ming emperor wielded absolute and despotic power. Access to his personal favor was the only means of acquiring privilege or some limited derivative power. The complex ceremonial and court ritual surrounding any public appearance by the emperor, the vast imperial palace staffed only by servile women and eunuchs, and the precise procedures of the imperial bureaucracy—which blamed any diffi-

culties on the emperor's advisers—all lent the throne a rarefied aura and exalted the emperor's authority. Hung Wu also forced the military nobles (his old rebel comrades-in-arms) to live at his court in Nanking, where he could keep an eye on them. He raised many generals to the nobility, which carried honor and financial benefits but no political power whatsoever.

Late in his reign Hung Wu executed many nobles and divided China into principalities, putting one of his sons in charge of each. Suspicious even of his sons' loyalty, he carefully circumscribed their power. Positions in the imperial administration were filled in part by civil service examinations, whose re-estab-

The Emperor Hung Wu (1368–1398) Of peasant origin and with no resources or family connections, Hung Wu trusted no one and was known for his brutality. This portrait reveals a man of power, strength, and girth—suggesting his prosperity. The carefully manicured hands verify that he has risen far above his background and does not work with his hands. *(Cultural Relics Publishing House, Beijing)*

lishment proved to be Hung Wu's most enduring reform. The examination system later became the exclusive channel for official recruitment, lasting until the twentieth century. In the Ming period these examinations took on three inflexible characteristics: they required minute knowledge of the ancient Chinese classics, a formal and precise literary style, and they discouraged all originality. These features promoted conservatism and opposition to innovation in the bureaucracy.

After 1426 the eunuch-dominated secret police controlled the palace guards and the imperial workshops, infiltrated the civil service, and headed all foreign missions. Through blackmail, espionage, and corruption, the secret police exercised enormous do-mestic power. How did eunuchs acquire such power? Without heirs, they had no immediate family concerns. Drawn from the lowest classes of society, looked on with distaste by respectable people, eunuchs had no hope of gaining status except by satisfying every whim of the emperor. They were indifferent to public opinion. Because their submission to the emperor seemed total, the emperors believed them absolutely trustworthy. Several eunuchs—Wang Chih in the 1470s, Liu Chin in the 1500s, and Wei Chung-hsien in the 1620s—gained dictatorial power when their emperors lost interest in affairs of state.

Foreign affairs occupied much of Hung Wu's attention. He sought to control all Chinese contacts with the outside world and repeatedly invaded Mongolia, but the strengthening and extension of the Great Wall stands as Hung Wu's and his Ming successors' most visible achievement. According to one record, the defense system of the Great Wall throughout the Ming period "stretched 10,000 *li* [a *li* is about one-third of a mile] in an unbroken chain from the Yalu River in the east to Jiayuguan in the west."[3] The wall served as a protective girdle around the northern parts of the empire, sheltering towns, cities, and the inner countryside. The forts, beacon towers, and garrisons that pierced the wall at militarily strategic spots kept in close contact with the central government of the emperor. Because of the steady pressure of Mongol attacks in the fifteenth century, Hung Wu's successors continued the work of reinforcing the Great Wall.

Hung Wu forbade free commercial contacts along the coasts between Chinese and foreign merchants. He insisted that foreign states eager to trade with China acknowledge his suzerainty by offering tribute. The early Ming emperors displayed greater military and diplomatic efficiency than had any Chinese ruler for centuries. By the mid-fifteenth century, however, the emperors could not restrict the commercial demands of Chinese and foreign traders within tight commercial channels. Mongol raids by land and Japanese piracy at sea, often with the hidden cooperation of the local Chinese, were commonplace. Along the coasts of Kiangsu, Chekiang, and Fukien provinces, Japanese entered China disguised as merchants. If they were dissatisfied with the official rates of exchange, they robbed and destroyed. Neither fortresses and the transfer of coastal settlements inland, nor precautionary attacks on Japanese merchant raiders and their Chinese allies could suppress the problem. The imperial court came to regard foreigners arriving by ship as barbarians. When Europeans arrived in the sixteenth century, they too were commonly called "barbarians."

MARITIME EXPANSION

Another dramatic development of the Ming period was the series of naval expeditions sent out under Hung Wu's son, Yung Lo, and his successor between 1405 and 1433. China had a strong maritime history stretching back to the eleventh century, and these early fifteenth-century voyages represent the continuation of that tradition. The Ming expeditions established China as the greatest maritime power in the world, considerably ahead of Portugal whose major seafaring reconnaissances began a half century later. The expeditions revealed the scale of Chinese naval power in Asia and exalted the majesty and power of the Chinese emperor.

In contrast to Hung Wu's isolationist policy, which sought to close China to foreign trade, Yung Lo took a positive approach to foreign contacts and foreign trade: he favored overseas exploration and broader diplomatic and commercial contacts within the tribute system. Yung Lo had two basic motives for launching the voyages. First, he sent them in search of Chien Wen, a serious contender for the throne whom Yung Lo had actually defeated but whom legend claimed had escaped to Southeast Asia. Second, the expeditions were launched to explore, to expand trade, and to provide the imperial court with luxury objects. Led by the Muslim eunuch admiral Cheng Ho and navigated by compass, seven fleets sailed to East and South Asia. The first expedition (which carried, 27,800 men) involved 62 major ships, the largest 440 feet in length and 180 feet in the beam with 9 masts. The expeditions crossed the Indian Ocean to Ceylon, the Persian Gulf, and the east coast of Africa.

These voyages had important consequences. They extended the prestige of the Ming Dynasty throughout Asia. Trade, in the form of tribute from nineteen states including Java, Sumatra, Malacca, and even Cochin on the west coast of southern India, greatly increased. Diplomatic contacts made with the distant Middle East led to the arrival in Nanking of embassies from Egypt. These maritime expeditions also led to the publication of such geographical works as the *Treatise on the Barbarian Kingdoms on the Western Oceans* (1434) and *The Marvels Discovered by the Boat Bound for the Galaxy* (1436). The information acquired served as the basis of Chinese knowledge of the maritime world until the nineteenth century. Finally, these expeditions resulted in Chinese immigration to the countries of Southeast Asia and the ports of southern India. The voyages were terminated because Confucian court intellectuals persuaded the emperor that his quest for strange and exotic things signified the collapse of the dynasty.[4] After 1435, China returned to a policy of isolation.

DECLINE OF THE MING DYNASTY

A bitter struggle for the throne ensued when Hung Wu died. Eventually his fourth son prevailed, taking the regnal name Yung Lo (1403–1424). The bloody wars that brought Yung Lo to the throne devastated the territory between the Yellow River and the Yangtze, and he promoted a policy of resettlement there. Yung Lo continued his father's policies of requiring civil service examinations, controlling the nobility, and trying to restrain Japanese pirates. His most significant act, however, proved to be the transfer of the capital back to Peking. Yung Lo had served as governor *(wang)* of the north during his father's reign, and he felt greater support there than in the south. Peking was also closer to the northern frontier, and thus a better place for strategic defense against China's ancient enemies, the Mongols. This move pleased the military faction, but hurt the new gentry and mercantile groups whose economic interests centered around Nanking.

The extravagance of the imperial court also caused economic difficulties. Hung Wu had exercised fiscal restraint, but Yung Lo and his successors tried to outdo the splendor and magnificence of the Mongols. Yung Lo rebuilt his palaces and temples in a monumental style, whose grandeur surpassed that of Louis XIV's Versailles. The emperor and the court lived in the Forbidden City, a quarter-mile compound filled with palatial buildings, ceremonial halls, marbled terraces, and lengthy galleries. The Forbidden City was surrounded

by the Imperial City, an area of no less than three square miles, also closed to the public. Within the enclosure were numerous avenues and artificial lakes. In addition to imperial villas, temples, and residences of eunuch offi-

Imperial Palace at Peking Within the Imperial City stood the Forbidden City, filled with blocks of glazed tiled buildings at the heart of which was the Emperor's Palace. Later Ming emperors lived in great magnificence and oppressive, bureaucrat-ordered monotony. *(Photo: Caroline Buckler)*

cials inside the compound, there were also supply depots and material-processing plants. Among them was the court of Imperial Entertainments, which had the capacity to serve banquets for up to 15,000 men on short notice. Next to the bakery, distillery, and confectionery were the emperor's stable, armory, printing-office, and book depository. In sum, the palace was completely self-sufficient.[5]

A century and a half later, in the reign of the emperor Wan-li, everything required for the maintenance of the Imperial City was manufactured or deposited there. Approximately 20,000 eunuchs, some of whom held top positions in the imperial entourage, worked there. Some 3,000 female domestics performed household tasks. The emperor's immediate court—councilors, bodyguards, relatives, official wives, and concubines—numbered several thousand

people. Supporting so many people on so lavish a scale placed a terrible burden on the treasury, and financial difficulties played a major role in the decline of the Ming.

Yung Lo's successors lacked his drive and ability. The Mongols continued to press on the northern borders, and the Chinese had to yield some territory. In 1449 an ill-prepared and thoroughly inexperienced expedition launched by the eunuch Wang Zhen, with the participation of the young emperor Ying-tsung (1436–1450 and 1457–1464), met total disaster. The emperor himself was captured and remained a prisoner of the Mongols for seven years. He regained his throne only with great difficulty. In the south, a Chinese army of 200,000 had pressed into northern Vietnam in 1406. This imperialistic move led to temporary Chinese domination of the Red River basin and of much of central Vietnam. A Vietnamese liberation movement retaliated, and by 1427 had driven the occupiers out. In 1471 the Chinese also had to withdraw from the province of Annam in present-day Vietnam, which had been annexed in Yung Lo's reign. In the sixteenth century the Japanese accelerated their coastal raids and even sacked the cities of Ningpo and Yangchow. Difficulties in collecting taxes hindered the government's ability to strengthen the army. It was commonplace in the eleven hundred counties of Ming China for people to delay or simply refuse to pay their taxes, aware that no magistrate could prosecute thousands of delinquents. Their taxes were eventually written off. Without adequate revenues, the empire could not maintain a strong army to defend itself.

In spite of these foreign pressures, the empire did not fall apart. In fact, southern China enjoyed considerable prosperity in the late sixteenth and early seventeenth centuries. Why? Japanese, Portuguese, and Dutch merchants paid in silver for the Chinese silks and ceramics they bought. The steady flow of silver into China from the illicit trade with Japan—and, later, from the mines of Mexico and Peru via Spain—had momentous consequences. The value of Chinese paper currency, which had been in circulation since the eleventh century, drastically declined. Unable to control either the state economy or local commercial activity, the imperial government had to adopt a more liberal attitude and simply acquiesce in foreign trade. The emperor also had to recognize the triumph of silver as a medium of exchange.

Also merchants in the southern maritime provinces, where trade flourished with Japan, the Philippines, and Indonesia, invested surplus capital in new ventures in the towns. Peasants migrated to the towns seeking employment, and agriculture declined. Some businesses employed several hundred workers, many of them women. According to a French scholar, "Peasant women took jobs at Sung-chiang, southwest of Shanghai in the cotton mills. According to contemporary descriptions, in the big workshops the employees were already the anonymous labor force that we regard as characteristic of the industrial age."[6] Sung-chiang developed into a large cotton-weaving center, Soochow became famous for its luxury silks, and by the end of the sixteenth century paper factories in Kiangsi employed 50,000 workers.

By the late sixteenth century China was participating in the emerging global economy. Portuguese ships carried Chinese silks and ceramics to Nagasaki and returned with Japanese silver. The huge Ming merchant marine, built from the trees planted by Hung Wu and more technically proficient for long sea voyages than the Spanish and Portuguese fleets, transported textiles, porcelains, silk, and paper to Manila in the Philippines and brought back sweet potatoes, tobacco, firearms, and silver. From Manila the Spanish fleet carried Chinese goods to the markets of Barcelona, Antwerp, and Venice. The Dutch transported tea by the boatload from Fukien and Chekiang for the castles and drawing rooms of Europe.[7] Europeans paid for most of their imports with silver. Recent scholars argue that between one-third and one-half of all the silver mined in the Americas between 1527 and 1821 wound up in China. Spanish galleons carried it from Acapulco to Manila and thence to Chinese ports[8] (page 561).

In 1600 the Ming Dynasty faced grave political and economic problems. The Manchus, a Tungusic people from Manchuria, threatened from the north. Wars against the Japanese and Koreans had depleted the imperial treasury. As rich landowners bought up the lands assigned to farm families, the social structures set up by Hung Wu broke down. The government had to hire mercenaries; the military, considered a disreputable profession, drew the dregs of society. According to the Italian Jesuit missionary Matteo Ricci (1552–1610), "All those under arms lead a despicable life, for they have not embraced this profession out of love of their country or devotion to their king or love of honour and glory, but as men in the service of a provider of employment."[9]

Maintenance of the army placed a heavy burden on the state. The imperial court continued to squander vast sums on an ostentatious lifestyle and the allowances of the extended imperial family. Under the emperor Wan-li, forty-five princes of the first rank received annual incomes of 10,000 shih (the money equivalent of 10,000 tons of grain), while 21,000 lesser nobles also received large allowances. The emperors increased domestic sales taxes, established customs posts for export-import duties, and laid ever-more-crushing taxes on the peasants. New taxes provoked violent riots in the large commercial centers of Soochow, Hangchow, and Peking. Between 1619 and 1627 greedy court eunuchs helped precipitate a crisis. The eunuch Wei Chung-hsien (1568–1627) exercised a two-year reign of terror and sent hundreds of honest civil servants to their deaths as conspirators. The bureaucracy that the eunuchs controlled was so torn by factions that it could not function.

Finally, the emperors became victims of their training, and servants rather than masters of the bureaucracy. A Ming emperor was taught that his primary duties were to venerate Heaven (the Chinese deity) and to follow the precedents set by his ancestors. So long as the emperor performed certain time-honored rituals, he retained the Mandate of Heaven, the traditional legitimization of Chinese rulers. In a society lacking a strong army and effective bureaucratic institutions, it was imperial ritual that connected the ordinary person to the state by imbuing awe, respect, and loyalty. Thus the emperors spent a large part of each day in the performance of imperial ceremonies, which they came to resent.

The reign of Emperor Wan-li, who ruled longer than any other member of the dynasty, illustrates what happened when the emperor was at odds with the system. An intelligent man with some good ideas, Wan-li felt that the bureaucrats opposed everything he wanted to do. When he tried to increase the size of the army and to improve its effectiveness through drills and maneuvers, civil service officials sent him lengthy memorials calling for an end to such exercises. When he wanted to take personal command of the army at a time of foreign invasion, bureaucrats told him that precedent forbade his leaving the Imperial City. Wan-li gradually reached the conclusion that the monarchy had become no more than a set of stylized performances. Stymied in whatever he wanted to do, he simply refused to make state decisions. He devoted his time to his horses and, while still a young man, to the construction of his tomb. Imperial decisions were postponed. Factional strife among the court eunuchs and bureaucrats increased. The wheels of government ground to a halt.[10]

Meanwhile, the Manchus pressed against China's northeastern border. Under their leader Nurhachi (1559–1626), they built a powerful military and administrative organization and gained the allegiance of the Mongols and other tribes. As the Ming government in Peking floundered, public anger at bureaucratic corruption mounted. Ming troops, their pay in arrears, turned outlaw. Droughts led to crop failures, which in turn caused widespread famines. Starving peasants turned to banditry, and entire provinces re-

volted. The general decay paved the way for Manchu conquest.

This dynastic shift from the Ming to the Ch'ing (Manchu) seemed to fulfill the Han Confucian doctrine that history operates in a cyclical fashion. The Ming emperor apparently had so lived as to forfeit the Mandate of Heaven (page 97). A wise ruler satisfies Heaven's mandate by developing his own moral propriety. If the emperor observes the proper Confucian rites of social intercourse—is respectful to his parents, attentive to his ministers, and concerned for his subjects—then the empire and the civilized world will flourish. Because Chinese government lacked adequate checks on bureaucratic performance, imperial dynasties relied on Confucian modes of behavior —that is, officials' sense of self-restraint. The emperor was supposed to be a model. If he was virtuous, so were his officials. If he looked to his own self-interest, his civil servants would do likewise, to the cost of the general welfare. Then corruption would spread. Taxes would become oppressive, and peasants would revolt. Because in the popular understanding of the Mandate of Heaven the natural and political orders were closely linked, physical signs (droughts, earthquakes, floods, volcanic eruptions) verified Heaven's displeasure. Conditions were ripe for the appearance of a new dynasty.

Predictably, when it seemed that the mandate had been withdrawn and was about to redescend on someone worthy, ambitious generals, bandit warlords, and popular movements appeared. "The prospect of a new mandate feverishly excited rebellions, which seemed in turn to prove that the previous dynastic cycle had reached its term."[11] As such events accompanied the collapse of the Yuan and the rise of the Ming, so similar developments greeted the fall of the Ming and the emergence of the Ch'ing.

MANCHU RULE

The Manchus declared a new dynasty, the Ch'ing, in 1644, and went on to capture Peking and slowly gain control of all China. Their initial success was due more to the internal weaknesses of the Ming than to special strengths of their own. Other developments help explain their ultimate victory and rule. The gentry and business classes, centered in the south

MAP 24.1 China: Ch'ing Empire, 1759 The sheer size of the Ch'ing Empire in China almost inevitably led to its profound cultural influence on the rest of Asia. What geographical and political factors limited the extent of the Empire?

around Nanking, were alienated by the Ming court's fiscal mismanagement and demands for more taxes. Although various Ming princelings and local bandit groups rose against the Manchus, the Ming army lacked good equipment and staying power and gradually collapsed. The entry of the Manchus' imperial armies into Yunnan in 1681 marked their complete military triumph.

There remained the influential academic and intellectual classes. By purging the civil service of the old court eunuchs and troublesome factions, and by offering Chinese intellectuals positions in the bureaucracy, the Manchus gained the support of the academics. Chinese scholars flocked to Peking. The Manchu government, staffed by able and honest Chinese, became much more efficient than the Ming.

The Ch'ing Dynasty—the name adopted by the Manchus means "pure" or "unsullied"—ruled until 1912. In its heyday in the eighteenth century, the Ch'ing Empire covered much of Asia—China proper, Manchuria, Mongolia, Tibet, and Sinkiang —and enjoyed tribute from Burma, Nepal, Laos, Siam, Annam, and Korea (Map 24.1). China had the largest population on earth, and it achieved an unprecedented degree of prosperity.

How did 1 million Manchus govern 350 million Chinese? The Ch'ing Dynasty retained the basic structures of Ming and Confucian government. The emperor governed as supreme and autocratic ruler with the Mandate of Heaven. The bureaucracies continued as they had in Ming and earlier times: while the imperial household bureaucracy managed the

TABLE 24.2 POPULATION OF CHINA, 1578–1974

| Year | Government | Population (in millions) | |
		Families	Individuals
1578	Ming Dynasty	10.6	60.7
1662	Ch'ing Dynasty	19.2	100.0
1710		23.3	116.0
1729		25.5	127.0
1741			143.4
1754			184.5
1778			243.0
1796			275.7
1814			374.6
1850			414.5
1953	People's Republic		601.9
1974			800.0

emperor's palaces and households, the central bureaucracy administered his vast empire. Positions in the latter were mostly assigned on the basis of candidates' performances in the civil service examinations in the Confucian classics. The highest positions in Peking and in the provinces of China were open to Chinese as well as Manchus. These measures pacified the Chinese economic and intellectual elites. The Manchus, however, maintained a privileged status in society. They wore distinctive clothes, did not practice foot binding, retained their own language and alphabet, and maintained ethnic separatism by forbidding intermarriage with the Chinese. The Manchus required Chinese males to wear their hair in a pigtail as a sign of subjection to the Ch'ing.

The agricultural improvements begun in the Ming period had profound social effects in the eighteenth century. China experienced a population explosion, as the statistics in Table 24.2 illustrate.

Internal peace, relative prosperity, and engineering methods that prevented flooding of the countryside contributed to the steady growth of population. But that growth without increased agricultural output led, in the late eighteenth century, to rebellions and uprisings that would weaken the Ch'ing Dynasty.

The dynasty reached its zenith under the emperor K'ang-hsi (1662–1722). K'ang-hsi, a contemporary of the Indian ruler Aurangzeb, the French king Louis XIV, and the Russian tsar Peter the Great, demonstrated exceptional intelligence, energy, and concern for the welfare of his people. He also enjoyed much greater freedom of action than had the Ming emperor Wan-li a century earlier. Where Wan-li had been a captive of precedent, incapable of making changes, K'ang-hsi cut both court expenses and taxes, and traveled extensively throughout his domain. On these trips he investigated the conduct of local bureaucrats in an effort to prevent them from oppressing the people. Where Wan-li had vacillated in the face of domestic revolt and foreign invasion, K'ang-hsi squarely faced a massive rebellion in southern China in 1678 and thoroughly crushed it. He personally led an army into Mongolia and smashed the forces of the Mongol leader Galdan. This victory permanently eliminated the danger of a reinvigorated Mongolian Empire on China's borders.

K'ang-hsi also cultivated the arts of peace. He invited scholars to his court and subsidized the compilation of a huge encyclopedia and two monumental dictionaries. *The Complete Library of the Four Treasuries,* a collection of all of Chinese literature that required the work of 15,000 calligraphers and 361 editors, preserved the Chinese literary tradition. K'ang-hsi's contributions to literature hold a distinguished place in the long history of Chinese culture. Europe and America, however, appreciate the period primarily for its excellent porcelain. The word "china" entered the English language and became synonymous with fine pottery and tableware. An imperial factory at Kiangsi, directly controlled by K'ang-hsi's court, produced porcelain masterpieces: monochrome vases, bowls, and dishes in oxblood, pale green, and dark blue, and polychromes in blue and white enjoyed enormous popularity in Paris, London, and New York in the eighteenth century and ever since.

THE LIFE OF THE PEOPLE

The family is the fundamental unit of every society. In Ming and Ch'ing China, however, the family exercised greater social influence than it did anywhere else, and far more than in Western societies. The family directed the moral education of the child, the economic advancement and marriage of the young, and religious life through ceremonial rites honoring the family's ancestors. The Chinese family discharged many of the roles that the Christian church per-

Children Playing in a Garden Produced on silk, this charming scene of children (obviously upper class) playing reflects both the brilliance of Chinese manufacture and use of silk and the affection in which children were held. *(Courtesy of the Freer Gallery of Art, Smithsonian Institution)*

formed in Europe in the Middle Ages and that the state carries out today. It assumed total responsibility for the sick, the indigent, and the aged. The family expected and almost invariably received the full devotion and loyalty of its members. A person without a family had no material or psychological support.

Poor families tended to be nuclear: couples established their own households and raised their own children. The educated, middle class, and wealthy frequently resided in extended families: several generations of patrilineal relatives and their wives lived together in one large house or compound, individual families occupying different sections. In both kinds of families, the paternal head of the family held autocratic power over all members of the household. On his death, his authority passed to his eldest son. The father led the family in the ancient Confucian rites honoring its ancestors. If these ceremonies were not continued into the next generation, the family suffered social disgrace and the dead were believed to endure great misery. Thus marriage and childbearing were extremely important. Almost everyone mar-

ried. Reverence for one's parents, maintenance of the family, and perpetuation of the line required that sons marry shortly after reaching puberty. The father and family elders discussed the possibilities and employed a local go-between to negotiate with the prospective bride's family. The go-between drew up a marriage contract specifying the property, furniture, clothing, and gifts the two young people would bring to the union. As elsewhere, parents wanted to make the most economically and socially advantageous union for their children. The couple had no part in these arrangements; often they never even saw each other until the groom lifted the bride's veil on their wedding day. But they had been brought up to accept this.

A Chinese bride became part of her husband's family, subject to him and to her in-laws. Her first duty was to bear sons. If she did not, she might adopt one. Failure to give her husband heirs gave him grounds for divorce, which brought great disgrace on her family. A woman, however, could not divorce her husband for any reason. Divorce was extremely rare in

Chinese Scholars The civil service examinations, the chief means of access to governmental positions and social status, inculcated total submission to the autocratic state. The largest number of candidates took the examinations in general knowledge and literary ability. Here candidates stand at writing desks, composing essays. *(Bibliothèque Nationale, Paris)*

Chinese society, but a wealthy man with a "nonproductive" wife might take concubines who lived in the house with his wife. Because males performed the all-important ceremonies in honor of the family ancestors, they held a much higher position in society than did women. The desperately poor often killed girl babies or sold their daughters as concubines. Young brides came under the direct control of their mothers-in-law, whose severity and cruelty are a common theme in Chinese literature. A strong-willed woman, once she had sons, gained increasing respect as the years went by. The Chinese deeply respected age. Women of the wealthy classes, with servants to do the household chores, spent their days in semiseclusion nibbling dainties, smoking opium, and gambling. Poor women worked in the fields beside their husbands, in addition to bearing children and managing the household.

The educational system during the Ming and Ch'ing periods had both virtues and weaknesses. Most villages and all towns and cities operated schools that prepared boys for the all-important civil service examinations. Boys learned to write with a brush the approximately 3,000 commonly used characters of literary Chinese; they learned from memory the standard texts of Confucian philosophy, ethics, and history. The curriculum was very limited, and the instructional method stressed memorization and discouraged imagination. The successful civil service candidate received no practical training in the work of government. On the other hand, the system yielded a high percentage of literate men (relative to Europe at the same time), preserved the ethical values of Chinese culture; and gave Chinese society cohesion and stability. All educated Chinese shared the same basic literary culture, much as medieval Euro-

Chinese Fishermen The subtle and gentle lines of this ink and color drawing on paper reflect the traditional Chinese ethos that the life of the fisherman is one of peace and harmony with nature. *(Courtesy of the Freer Gallery of Art, Smithsonian Institution)*

peans were formed by Latin Christian culture. As in medieval Europe too, educational opportunities for girls were severely limited. Rich men occasionally hired tutors for their daughters, and a few women achieved exceptional knowledge. Most women of all classes received training that prepared them for roles as wives and mothers: courteous behavior, submission to their husbands, and the administration of a household.

In sharp contrast to the social structure of Europe, Chinese society had few hard-and-fast lines. The emperors fought the development of a hereditary aristocracy, which would have worked against the interest of absolute monarchy. Few titles of nobility were granted in perpetuity. Meanwhile the state bureaucracy provided opportunities and motivation for upward mobility. The entire family supported and encouraged intelligent sons to prepare for the civil

service examinations, and the work and self-sacrifice of the parents bore fruit in the sons. Positions in the bureaucracy brought salaries and gifts, which the family invariably invested in land. The competitive examinations—open, with few exceptions, to all classes—prevented the formation of a ruling caste. Since everyone accepted the Confucian principle that the nation should be led by the learned and civilized, scholars held the highest rank in the social order. They, along with Heaven, Earth, the emperor, and parents, deserved special veneration. With the possible exception of the Jewish people, no people has respected learning as much as the Chinese, who gave special deference to the teacher-scholar. Farmers merited esteem because they produced food; merchants less so because they supposedly lived off the profits of others' toil. Merchants tried to marry into the scholar class in order to rise on the social ladder, but China did not develop an articulate bourgeoisie. At the bottom of society were actors, prostitutes, and the many beggars.

The Chinese found recreation and relaxation in many ways. All classes gambled at cards and simple numbers games. The teahouse served as the local meeting place to exchange news and gossip, and to listen to the tales of professional storytellers, who enjoyed great popularity. The affluent indulged in an alcoholic drink made from fermented and distilled rice, and both men and women liked pipes and tobacco. Everyone who could afford to went to theaters, which were a central part of Chinese culture. The actors wore happy and sad masks like their ancient Greek counterparts, and their gestures were formal and heavily stylized; the plays typically dramatized episodes from Chinese history and literature. The Chinese associated athletics, riding, and horse racing with soldiers, at best a necessary evil, and regarded the active life as the direct antithesis of the scholarly contemplation they most valued.

The first Christian missionaries in China had little impact on the bulk of the population, but among the intellectual classes their work was significant. In 1582 the Jesuit Matteo Ricci settled at Macao on the mouth of the Canton River. Like the Christian monks who had converted the Germanic tribes of early medieval Europe (page 229), Ricci sought first to convert the emperor and elite groups and then, through gradual assimilation, to win the throngs of Chinese. Ricci tried to present Christianity to the Chinese in Chinese terms. He understood the Chinese respect for learning and worked to win converts among the scholarly class. When Ricci was admitted to the Imperial City at Peking, he addressed the emperor Wan-li:

Li Ma-tou [Ricci's name transliterated into Chinese], your Majesty's servant, comes from the Far West, addressed himself to Your Majesty with respect, in order to offer gifts from his country. Your Majesty's servant comes from a far distant land which has never exchanged presents with the Middle Kingdom [the Chinese name for China, based on the belief that the Chinese empire occupied the middle of the earth and was surrounded by barbarians]. Despite the distance, fame told me of the remarkable teaching and fine institutions with which the imperial court has endowed all its peoples. I desired to

share these advantages and live out my life as one of Your Majesty's subjects, hoping in return to be of some small use.[12]

Ricci presented the emperor with two clocks, one of them decorated with dragons and eagles in the Chinese style. The emperor's growing fascination with clocks gave Ricci the opportunity to display other examples of Western technology. He instructed court scholars about astronomical equipment and the manufacture of cannons, and drew for them a map of the world—with China at its center. These inventions greatly impressed the Chinese intelligentsia. Over a century later a Jesuit wrote, "The Imperial Palace is stuffed with clocks . . . watches, carillons, repeaters, organs, spheres, and astronomical clocks of all kinds—there are more than four thousand pieces from the best masters of Paris and London."[13]

But the Christians and the Chinese did not understand one another. Because the Jesuits served the imperial court as mathematicians, astronomers, and cartographers, the Chinese emperors allowed them to remain in Peking. For the Jesuits, however, their service was only a means for converting the Chinese to Christianity. The missionaries thought that by showing the preeminence of Western science, they were demonstrating the superiority of Western religion. This was a relationship the Chinese did not acknowledge. They could not accept a religion that required total commitment and taught the existence of an absolute. Only a small number of the highly educated, convinced of a link between ancient Chinese tradition and Christianity, became Christians. Most Chinese were hostile to the Western faith. They accused Christians of corrupting Chinese morals because they forbade people to honor their ancestors—and corruption of morals translated into disturbing the public order; of destroying Chinese sanctuaries; of revering a man (Christ) who had been executed as a public criminal; and of spying on behalf of the Japanese.

The "Rites Controversy," a dispute over ritual between the Jesuits and other Roman Catholic religious orders, sparked a crisis. The Jesuits supported the celebration of the Mass in Chinese and the performance of other ceremonies in terms understandable by the Chinese. The Franciscans and other missionaries felt that the Jesuits had sold out the essentials of the

Christian faith in order to win converts. One burning issue was whether the Chinese reverence for ancestors was homage to the good the dead had done during their lives or an act of worship. The Franciscans secured the support of the Roman authorities, who considered themselves authorities on Chinese culture and decided against the Jesuits. In 1704 and again in 1742 Rome decreed that Roman ceremonial practice (that is, in Latin) was to be the law for Chinese missions. (This decision continued to govern Roman Catholic missionary activity until the Second Vatican Council in 1962.) Papal letters also forbade Chinese Christians from participating in the rites of ancestor worship. The emperor in turn banned Christianity in China, and the missionaries were forced to flee.

The Christian West and the Chinese world had a great deal to learn from each other. The Jesuits probably were "responsible for the rebirth of Chinese mathematics in the seventeenth and eighteenth centuries," and Western contributions stimulated the Chinese development of other sciences.[14] On the other hand, Europeans got the idea of building bridges suspended by chains from the Chinese. The first Western experiments in electrostatics and magnetism in the seventeenth century derived from Chinese models. Travel accounts about Chinese society and customs had a profound impact on Europeans, making them more sensitive to the beautiful diversity of peoples and manners, as the essays of Montaigne (pages 582–583) and other Western thinkers reveal.

JAPAN
(CA 1400–1800)

The Ashikaga Shogunate lasted from the middle of the fourteenth to the late sixteenth century. During this period, Japanese society experienced almost continual violence and civil war. Weak central governments could not maintain order. Throughout the islands, local strong men destroyed weak ones: around 1450, 250 *daimyos*, or lords, held power; by 1600, there were only 12 daimyos. Successful military leaders carved out large territories and governed them as independent rulers. Political and social conditions in fifteenth- and sixteenth-century Japan strongly resembled those of western Europe in the

tenth and eleventh centuries. Political power was in the hands of a small group of military leaders. Historians often use the same term—*feudalism*—to describe the Japanese and the European experience. As in medieval Europe, feudalism paved the way for the rise of a strong centralized state in seventeenth-century Japan.

FEUDALISM IN JAPAN

Feudalism played a powerful role in Japanese culture until the nineteenth century. The similarities between feudalism in Japan and in medieval Europe have fascinated scholars, as have their very significant differences. Feudalism in Europe emerged out of the fusion of Germanic and Roman social institutions, and flowered under the impact of Muslim and Viking invasions. In Japan, on the other hand, feudalism evolved in complete isolation from outside cultural forces. Japan was more secluded from alien influences than any other country of comparable cultural development. When foreign pressures finally opened up Japan in the nineteenth century, Japanese feudalism collapsed.

The two constituent elements of Japanese feudalism appeared between the eighth and the twelfth centuries: the *shoen* or land with its *shiki* or rights, and the military warrior clique. Some scholars have equated the shoen with the European manor, but the comparison needs careful qualification. A manor corresponded to one composite village, while a particular family's shoen was widely scattered. Those who held shoen possessed the shiki there—that is, the right to the income or rice produced by the land. On the other hand, just as several persons might hold rights—military, judicial, grazing—on a medieval manor, and all these rights yielding income, so several persons frequently held shiki on a Japanese estate.

The Japanese samurai warrior resembled the knight of twelfth-century France. Both were armed with expensive weapons, and both fought on horseback. Just as the knight was supposed to live according to the chivalric code (see page 369), so Japanese samurai were expected to live according to *Bushido*, a code that stressed military honor, courage, stoic acceptance of hardship, and, above all, loyalty. Disloyalty brought social disgrace, which the samurai could avoid only through *seppuku* (or *hara-kiri*), ritual suicide by slashing his belly. Samurai and knights were both highly conscious of themselves as aristocrats; but while knights fought as groups, samurai fought as individuals.

By the middle of the sixteenth century Japanese feudalism had taken on other distinctive features. As the number of shoen decreased and the powerful daimyos consolidated their territories, the practice of primogeniture became common. Instead of dividing an estate among all the lord's children, the shoen was kept intact and assigned to the eldest or ablest son. Also, only a small proportion of samurai attained the rank of daimyo and possessed a shoen; most warriors received support in rice, not in land. In this respect they resembled European knights, who were supported by cash or money fiefs. They were salaried fighters with no connection to land. Third, the nature of warfare changed in two basic ways. Daimyos employed large numbers of foot soldiers equipped with spears, along with armed cavalrymen. The countryside also saw the construction of new castles. As in medieval Europe, the typical method of warfare was to besiege a castle and wait for it to surrender. Around 1540 the introduction of the musket from Europe made infantrymen effective against mounted samurai; the use of Western cannon required more elaborately fortified castles. These military and social developments occurred during a century of turbulence and chronic disorder, out of which emerged a leader who ended the chaos and began the process of unification, laying the foundation of the modern Japanese national state.

NOBUNAGA AND NATIONAL UNIFICATION

A samurai of the lesser daimyo class, Oda Nobunaga won control of his native province of Owari in 1559. He began immediately to extend his power and made himself lord of the eastern province of Mikawa. Nobunaga defeated a powerful daimyo in 1560, and eight years later seized Kyoto, the capital city, where the emperor and his court resided. As a result, Nobunaga became the virtual ruler of central Japan.

Scholars have called the years 1568 to 1600 the period of "national unification." During this time the country underwent aggressive and dynamic change. Adopting the motto "Rule the empire by force," No-

bunaga set out to subdue all real and potential enemies of unification. With the support of a brilliant but low-born general, Toyotomi Hideyoshi, he subdued most of western Japan. In 1575 Nobunaga's use of firearms at the Battle of Nagashino led to a decisive victory that added the province of Totomi to his domain. When Hideyoshi smashed the great fortress of Odawara, eastern and northern Japan came under Nobunaga's control as well.

The great Buddhist temple-fortresses proved to be Nobunaga's biggest problem. Some of these monasteries possessed vast wealth and armed retainers, and they actively intervened in secular affairs. During the civil wars the Buddhists had supported various daimyos in their private wars, but Nobunaga would tolerate no such interference. The strategically located monastery on Mount Hiei near Kyoto had long provided sanctuary for political factions, but previous daimyos had refused to attack it because it was sacred. Nobunaga had his troops surround Mount Hiei and set fire to the thickets on the lower slopes of the mountain. As the monks and lay people fled the fire, Nobunaga's men slaughtered them by the thousands. The destruction of Japan's most powerful monastery ended Buddhist influence as a political force.

Although Nobunaga won control of most of Japan by the sword, he backed up his conquests with governmental machinery and a policy of conciliation. He gave lands and subordinate positions in the army to his defeated enemies. Trusted daimyos received complete civil jurisdiction over entire provinces. At strategic points, such as Nijo near Kyoto and Azuchi on the shore of Lake Biwa, Nobunaga built castles to serve as key administrative and defensive centers for the surrounding territories. He opened the little fishing village of Nagasaki to foreign commerce; it soon grew into the nation's largest port. He standardized the currency, eliminated customs barriers, and encouraged the development of trade and industry. In 1582, when Nobunaga was murdered by one of his vassals, his general and staunchest adherent Hideyoshi carried on his work.

The son of a peasant, Hideyoshi had risen to power by his military bootstraps: he was an exceptionally able field commander. Hideyoshi made two significant contributions to the unification and centralization of Japan. In 1582 he attacked the great fortress of Takamatsu; when direct assault failed, he had his

Hanabusa Itchō: Marketplace Perhaps the greatest cartoon artist in Japanese history, Itchō (1652–1724) worked with ink and color on paper. This elegantly simple representation of a vegetable market shows Itchō's appreciation for the activities of everyday life and helps explain his enormous contemporary popularity. *(Courtesy of the Freer Gallery of Art, Smithsonian Institution)*

troops flood the surrounding moat until the castle was forced into submission. When Takamatsu fell, so did the large province of Mori. A successful siege of the town of Kagoshima then brought the southern island of Kyushu under his domination. Hideyoshi soothed the vanquished daimyos as Nobunaga had done—with lands and military positions—but he also required them to swear allegiance and to obey him "down to the smallest particular."[15]

Having reduced his most dangerous adversaries and taken steps to control the daimyos, Hideyoshi ordered a survey of the entire country. The military power of the unified Japanese state depended on a strong agricultural basis, and Hideyoshi wanted to exploit the peasantry fully. His agents collected detailed information about the daimyos' lands, and about towns, villages, agricultural produce, and in-

dustrial output all over Japan. A sort of Japanese equivalent of the *Domesday Book* (page 390), this material enabled him to assess military quotas and taxable property. Hideyoshi's surveys tied the peasant population to the land and tightened the collection of the land tax. When Hideyoshi died in 1598, he left a strong centralized state. Brute force had created a unified Japan.

On his deathbed the old soldier had set up a council of regents to govern during the minority of his infant son. The strongest regent was Hideyoshi's longtime supporter, Tokugawa Ieyasu, who ruled vast territories around Edo, modern-day Tokyo. Ieyasu quickly eliminated the young ruler, and in 1600 at Sekigahara he smashed a coalition of daimyo defenders of the heir. This battle marked the beginning of the Tokugawa regime.

THE TOKUGAWA REGIME

Japanese children are taught that "Ieyasu ate the pie Nobunaga made and Hideyoshi baked." As the aphorism suggests, Ieyasu took over and completed the work begun by his able predecessors. He took decisive steps to solidify his dynasty and control the feudal nobility, and to maintain peace and prosperity in Japan. The Tokugawa regime that Ieyasu fashioned worked remarkably well, lasting until 1867.

Ieyasu obtained from the emperor the title of shogun, which meant that he and his heirs had the right to command everyone. Constitutionally, the emperor exercised sovereign authority; in practice, authority and power—both the legal right and the physical means—were held by the Tokugawa shogun. Ieyasu declared the emperor and his court at Kyoto "very precious and decorative, like gold and silver," and surrounded the imperial court with all the ceremonial trappings and none of the realities of power.

In a scheme reminiscent of Louis XIV (pages 594–595) and Peter the Great (page 639), Ieyasu forced the feudal lords to establish "alternate residence" at his capital city of Edo, to spend every other year there, and to leave their wives and sons there—essentially as hostages. This device had obvious advantages: the shogun could keep close tabs on the daimyos, control them through their children, and weaken them financially with the burden of maintaining two residences. Ieyasu justified this institution by invoking the Bushido code, with its emphasis on loyalty. He forbade members of the nobility to marry without his consent, thus preventing the formation of dangerous alliances. The Tokugawa shoguns also severely restricted the construction of castles—symbols, in Japan as in medieval Europe, of feudal independence. Members of the aristocratic samurai class, however, possessed the right to wear two swords, and they exercised full administrative powers within their own domains. In effect, the country was governed by martial law in peacetime. Only warriors could hold official positions in the state bureaucracy. Finally, a network of spies kept close watch on the nobility.

As in medieval Europe and early modern China, the agricultural class held a respected position because its members provided Japanese society with sustenance. Even so, farmers had to mind their betters, and they bore a disproportionate share of the taxload. According to the survey made by Hideyoshi, taxes were imposed on villages, not individuals; the tax varied between 30 and 40 percent of the rice crop.

As in Europe and China, the commercial classes occupied the lowest rungs on the social ladder because they profited from the toil of others. The peace that the Tokugawa Shogunate imposed in the seventeenth century brought a steady rise in population and prosperity. As demand for goods grew, so did the numbers of merchants. To maintain stability, the early Tokugawa shoguns froze the four social categories—imperial court nobility, samurai, peasants, and merchants. Laws rigidly prescribed what each class could and could not do. Nobles, for example, were "strictly forbidden whether by day or by night, to go sauntering through the streets or lanes in places where they have no business to be." Daimyos were prohibited from moving troops outside their frontiers, making alliances, and coining money. Designated dress and stiff rules of etiquette distinguished one class from another.[16] This kind of stratification succeeded in its purpose: it protected the Tokugawa shoguns from daimyo attack and inaugurated a long era of peace.

MAP 24.2 Tokugawa Japan Consider the cultural and political significance of the fact that Japan is an island. How did the concentration of shogunate lands affect its government of Japan?

Procession of a Daimyo to Edo The Tokugawa shogun controlled the nobility through the *sankin kotai,* or system of "alternate residence," by which a daimyo spent alternate years at the shogun's court and on his own estates. The great processions of the daimyos and their followers between Kyoto and Edo, which imposed heavy financial burdens on the daimyo, were among the remarkable pageants of the period. *(The Tokugawa Art Museum)*

To maintain dynastic stability and internal peace, Ieyasu's descendants imposed measures called *sakoku,* or the "closed country policy," which sealed Japan's borders around 1636. Japanese were forbidden to leave the country; foreigners were excluded. Shortly after the Jesuit missionary Francis Xavier landed at Kagoshima in 1549, he made many converts among the poor and even some among the daimyos. By 1600 there were 300,000 baptized Christians, most of them on the southernmost island of Kyushu where the shogun's power was weakest and the loyalty of the daimyos most doubtful (Map 24.2). In 1615 bands of Christian samurai supported Ieyasu's enemies at the fierce Battle of Osaka. In 1637 30,000 peasants in the heavily Catholic area of northern Kyushu revolted. The shoguns came to associate Christianity with domestic disorder and feudal rebellion. Accordingly, what had earlier been mild persecution became ruthless repression after 1639. Foreign priests were expelled or tortured, and thousands of Japanese Christians suffered crucifixion. The policy of sakoku remained in force for almost two centuries as a means of controlling religious organizations and securing political order. The shogunate kept Japan isolated.

The Life of the People

Two hundred years of peace is no mean achievement in the history of world societies. Moreover, profound social and economic development occurred in spite of Japan's near-total isolation. The lives of the Japanese people changed profoundly in the seventeenth and eighteenth centuries.

The Tokugawa Shogunate subdued the nobility by emasculating it politically. Stripped of power and required to spend every other year at Edo, the daimyos and samurai passed their lives pursuing pleasure. They spent frantically on fine silks, paintings, concubines, boys, the theater, and the redecoration of their castles. Around 1700 one scholar observed that the entire military class was living "as in an inn, that is consuming now and paying later."[17] Eighteenth-century Japanese novels, plays, and histories portray the samurai engrossed in tavern brawls and sexual orgies. These frivolities, plus the heavy costs of maintaining an alternate residence at Edo, traveling with their retinues, and the sophisticated pleasures of the capital gradually ruined the warrior class.

The samurai spent heavily on kabuki theater, which enjoyed enormous popularity. An art form created by townspeople, *kabuki* consisted of crude, bawdy skits dealing with love and romance or aspects of prostitution, an occupation in which the actors and actresses had usually had professional experience. Performances featured elaborate costumes, song, dance, and poetry. Because female actresses were thought to be corrupting the public morals, the Tokugawa government banned them from the stage in 1629. From that time men played all the parts. Male actors in female dress and makeup performed as seductively as possible in order to entice the burly samurai who thronged the theaters. Homosexuality, long accepted in Japan, was widely practiced among the samurai, who pursued the actors and spent profligately on them. According to one seventeenth-century writer:

"Youth's kabuki" began with beautiful youths being made to sing and dance, whereupon droll fools . . . had their hearts captivated and their souls stolen. As they rapturously gave themselves up to visiting the youths in high spirits, the early depletion of even substantial fortunes was like light snow exposed to the spring sun. How much worse it was for those whose fortunes were slight to begin with. There were many of these men who soon had run through their fortunes. . . . Even though the lineage of every one of the youths was extremely base, these beautiful youths were respected by the stupid; they flapped about like kites and owls and, going into the presence of the exalted [distinguished persons], befouled the presence; and these were scoundrels who, saying insolent things as it pleased them, ruined men and held them in contempt.[18]

Some moralists and bureaucrats periodically complained, but the Tokugawa government accepted kabuki and prostitution as necessary evils. They provided employment, gratified the tastes of samurai and townspeople, and diverted former warriors from potential criminal and political mischief.[19] How did the samurai pay for their pleasures? In the same way their European counterparts did—by fleecing the peasants and borrowing from the merchants.

According to Japanese tradition, farmers deserved respect. In practice, peasants were sometimes severely oppressed and led miserable lives. It was government policy to tax them to the level of bare subsistence, and official legislation repeatedly defined their duties. In 1649 every village in Japan received these regulations:

• *Peasants must rise early and cut grass before cultivating the fields. In the evening they are to make straw rope or straw bags, all such work to be done with great care.*
• *They must not buy tea or sake [a fermented liquor made from rice] to drink nor must their wives.*
• *Men must plant bamboo or trees round the farmhouse and must use the fallen leaves for fuel so as to save expense.*
• *Peasants are people without sense or forethought. Therefore they must not give rice to their wives and children at harvest time, but must save food for the future. They should eat millet, vegetables, and other coarse food instead of rice. Even the fallen leaves of plants should be saved as food against famine. . . . During the seasons of planting and harvesting, however, when the labor is arduous, the food taken may be a little better. . . .*
• *The husband must work in the fields, the wife must work at the loom. Both must do night work. However good-looking a wife may be, if she neglects her household duties by drinking tea or sightseeing or rambling on the hillsides, she must be divorced.*
• *Peasants must wear only cotton or hemp—no silk. They may not smoke tobacco. It is harmful to health, it takes up time, and costs money. It also creates a risk of fire.*[20]

The state demanded that peasants work continually and live frugally. The conspicuous consumption of the upper classes led them in the course of the seventeenth and eighteenth centuries to increase taxes from 30 to 40 percent of the rice crop to 50 percent. Mountains cover much of Japan, and only 20 percent of its land is arable. Although the amount of cultivated land rose from about 5 million acres in 1600 to roughly 11.5 million in 1860, the long period of peace brought a great increase in population. The merchants who bought farm produce fixed the price of rice so low that it seemed to farmers that the more they produced, the less they earned. They found release from their frustrations either in flight from the village or in revolt. After 1704, peasant rebellions were chronic. Oppressive taxation provoked 84,000 farmers in the province of Iwaki to revolt in 1739. Following widespread burning and destruction, their demands were met. In other instances the shoguns

Kabuki Scene Kabuki drama, for which elaborate sets and a revolving stage were developed, stressed realism and—as this eighteenth-century painting by Torri Kiyonobu reflects—often contained a high degree of tension, melodrama, and violence. *(Courtesy of the Freer Gallery of Art, Smithsonian Institution)*

ordered savage repression, and natural disasters added to the peasants' misery. In the 1770s fires, floods, and volcanic eruptions hit all parts of Japan. Drought and torrential rain led to terrible famines between 1783 and 1788 and again between 1832 and 1836. Oppressive taxation, bad weather, and the contempt of lords and the central government often combined to make the lot of peasants virtually unrelieved wretchedness.

This picture of the Japanese peasantry tells only part of the story. The Japanese peasantry in the Tokugawa period was not a single homogeneous class. Recent scholarship has demonstrated that peasant society was more "a pyramid of wealth and power . . . that rose from the tenant farmer at the bottom through small landholders to wealthy peasants at the top."[21] Agricultural productivity increased substantially during the Tokugawa period, and, although assessed taxes remained high, they were fixed. Peasants who improved their lands and increased their yields continued to pay the same assessed tax, but they paid proportionately less and pocketed the surplus as profit. Their social situation accordingly rose. By the early nineteenth century there existed a large class of relatively wealthy, educated, and ambitious peasant

Pleasure Quarter of Kyoto These scenes give superb information about the dress and customs of the Japanese upper class in the mid-seventeenth century. In the foreground people pace in front of elegant bordellos. In the interior garden, beautifully dressed courtesans entertain wealthy patrons. The expensive materials used—ink, colors, and gold on paper—suggest that the folding screens were made for a rich merchant. *(Museum of Fine Arts, Boston, Gift of Denman Waldo Ross)*

families. This upper stratum of village peasants resembled the middle ranks of the warrior class more than it did the peasantry.

The Tokugawa period witnessed a major transformation of agriculture, a great leap in productivity and specialization. The rural population increased, but surplus labor was drawn to other employment and to the cities; the agricultural population did not increase. In fact, Japan suffered an acute shortage of farm labor from 1720 to 1868. In some villages, industry became almost as important as agriculture. At Hirano near Osaka, for example, 61.7 percent of all arable land was sown in cotton. The peasants had a thriving industry: they ginned the cotton locally before transporting it to wholesalers in Osaka. In many rural places, as many peasants worked in the manufacture of silk or cotton or vegetable oil as in the production of rice.[22]

The urban commercial classes, scorned for benefiting from the misery of the peasants and the appetites of the samurai, theoretically occupied the bottom rung of the social ladder. Merchants had no political power but they accumulated wealth, sometimes great wealth. They also proved the possibility of social mobility, and thus the inherent weakness of the regime's system of strict social stratification. The commercial class grew in response to the phenomenal development of urban life. The seventeenth-century surplus rural population, together with underemployed samurai, desperately poor peasants, and the ambitious and adventurous, thronged to the cities. All wanted a better way of life than could be found in the dull farming villages. Japan's cities grew tremendously: Kyoto, the imperial capital of the emperor and his pleasure-loving court; Edo, the political capital, with its multitudes of government bureaucrats, daimyos in alternate residence, intellectuals, and police; and Osaka, by this time the greatest commercial city in Japan, with its huge grain exchange and commercial banks. In the eighteenth century, Edo's population of almost 1 million represented the largest demand for goods and services in the world. The Tokugawa shoguns provided order and political stability, and turned the samurai into urban consumers by denying them military opportunities. Merchants stood ready to serve them. Towns offered all kinds of luxury goods and catered to every extravagant and exotic taste. By marketing the daimyos' grain, they gave the aristocrats the cash they needed to support their rich establishments. Merchants formed guilds and banks and lent money to the samurai. Those who defaulted on their debts found themselves cut off from further credit.[23]

As the ruling samurai with their fixed stipends became increasingly poorer, the despised merchants grew steadily wealthier. By contemporary standards anywhere in the world, the Japanese "middle" class lived very well. In 1705 the shogunate confiscated the property of a merchant in Osaka "for conduct unbecoming a member of the commercial class." In fact, the confiscation was at the urging of influential daimyos and samurai who owed the merchant gigantic debts. The government seized 50 pairs of gold screens, 360 carpets, several mansions, 48 granaries and warehouses scattered around the country, and hundreds of thousands of gold pieces. Although this merchant possessed fabulous wealth, other merchants too enjoyed a rich lifestyle.[24]

In the eighteenth and early nineteenth centuries China experienced a rapid increase in both prosperity and population. On the basis of highly developed agriculture, the Ch'ing Empire supported a population of 200 million in 1762 and 374 million in 1812, compared to only 193 million in all of Europe in 1800. Ch'ing China was also geographically larger than the People's Republic of China today, encompassing some of present-day Russia. But China's political and economic systems began to deteriorate in the late eighteenth and early nineteenth centuries. The country suffered from excessive centralization, in that all local questions had to be referred to Peking. The extravagant court placed an intolerable drain on the state treasury. Graft and corruption pervaded the imperial bureaucracy, provincial administration, and the army. The population explosion led to a severe land shortage, causing tension and frequent revolts in the countryside. The massive opium trade also had a disastrous effect on Chinese society: The volume of opium smuggled by the British East India Company into China increased tenfold between 1790 and 1820. So vast was the amount of opium imported, relative to Chinese exports of tea and silk, that China suffered a highly unfavorable balance of trade. The outflow of silver severely damaged the Chinese economy and thus the Ch'ing Dynasty.

In 1800 Tokugawa Japan was reaping the rewards of two centuries of peace and social order. Steady economic growth and improved agricultural technology had swelled the population. The samurai had been transformed into peaceful city dwellers and civil bureaucrats. The wealth of the business classes grew, and the samurai, dependent on fixed agricultural rents in a time of rising standards of living, fell into debt. Although the shogunate maintained a policy of national isolation, and no foreign power influenced Japan's political or social life, Japan was not really cut off from outside cultural contacts. Through the port of Nagasaki, Western scientific ideas and some Western technology entered the country in response to the persistent interest of Japanese scholars. The Japanese readily absorbed foreign technological ideas. The Tokugawa regime formed model citizens whose discipline is apparent even today.

NOTES

1. J. Gernet, *A History of Chinese Civilization* (New York: Cambridge University Press, 1982), p. 391.
2. Ibid.
3. L. Zewen et al., *The Great Wall* (New York: McGraw-Hill, 1981), p. 140.
4. See E. L. Dreyer, *Early Ming China. A Political*

History, 1355–1435 (Stanford, Calif.: Stanford University Press, 1982), pp. 194–205.

5. R. Huang, *1587: A Year of No Significance. The Ming Dynasty in Decline* (New Haven, Conn.: Yale University Press, 1981), p. 13.

6. Gernet, *History of Chinese Civilization,* pp. 425–426.

7. J. E. Wills, Jr., "Maritime China from Wang Chih to Shih Long," in *From Ming to Ch'ing: Conquest, Region, and Continuity in Seventeenth-century China,* ed. J. D. Spence and J. E. Wills, Jr. (New Haven, Conn.: Yale University Press, 1979), pp. 203–216.

8. F. Braudel, *The Wheels of Commerce: Civilization and Capitalism, 15th–18th Century,* vol. 2, trans. S. Reynolds (New York: Harper & Row, 1982), pp. 198–199.

9. Gernet, *History of Chinese Civilization,* p. 431.

10. See Huang, *Year of No Significance,* pp. 120–129.

11. F. Wakeman, Jr., *The Fall of Imperial China* (New York: Free Press, 1975), pp. 58–64.

12. Quoted in S. Neill, *A History of Christian Missions* (New York: Penguin Books, 1977), p. 163.

13. Quoted in C. M. Cipolla, *Clocks and Culture* (New York: Norton, 1978), p. 86.

14. Gernet, *History of Chinese Civilization,* p. 458.

15. See G. B. Sansom, *A History of Japan, 1344–1615,* vol. 2 (Stanford, Calif.: Stanford University Press, 1961), chaps. 20–21.

16. Ibid., chap. 25.

17. Quoted in D. H. Shively, "Bakufu Versus Kabuki," in *Studies in the Institutional History of Early Modern Japan,* ed. J. W. Hall (Princeton, N.J.: Princeton University Press, 1970), p. 236.

18. Quoted in ibid., pp. 241–242.

19. Ibid.

20. Quoted in G. B. Sansom, *A History of Japan, 1615–1867,* vol. 3 (Stanford, Calif.: Stanford University Press, 1978), p. 99.

21. T. C. Smith, "The Japanese Village in the Seventeenth Century," in Hall, *Studies,* p. 280.

22. T. C. Smith, *The Agrarian Origins of Modern Japan* (Stanford, Calif.: Stanford University Press, 1959), pp. 78–79.

23. See W. Bingham, H. Conroy, and F. W. Ikle, *A History of Asia,* vol. 2 (Boston: Allyn and Bacon, 1967), pp. 140–142.

24. G. B. Sansom, *Japan: A Short Cultural History,* rev. ed. (New York: Appleton-Century-Crofts, 1962), p. 472.

SUGGESTED READING

In recent years a considerable number of expert treatments of the traditional cultures of East Asia have appeared, many of them in easily accessible paperback form. The best starting point for the weaknesses of Yuan rule and the early development of the Ming Dynasty in China is C. O. Hucker, *The Ming Dynasty: Its Origins and Evolving Institutions* (1978); but see also Dreyer's *Early Ming China* (listed in the Notes), which contains a valuable up-to-date bibliography. Hucker's *The Traditional Chinese State in Ming Times, 1368–1644* (1962), is a standard study written in simple, untechnical language. J. D. Spence, *Ts'ao Yin and the K'ang-hsi Emperor, Bondservant and Master* (1966), uses the life of an official in the Chinese bureaucracy to describe the era and institutional framework in which he operated. Spence and Wills, *From Ming to Ch'ing,* cited in the Notes, focuses on the transition from Ming to Ch'ing in a collection of wide-ranging essays by leading scholars.

The best one-volume survey of Japanese history and culture is E. O. Reischauer, *Japan: The Story of a Nation,* 3d ed. (1981), which combines expert knowledge with superb readability. Sansom's *Japan: A Short Cultural History* (see the Notes) is an older but still useful account. More detailed treatments of Japanese history are A. M. Craig and E. O. Reischauer, *Japan: Tradition and Transformation* (1978), and Sansom's *A History of Japan,* 3 vols. (1958–1978). For Japanese feudalism, see P. Duus, *Feudalism in Japan* (1976), and J. W. Hall and J. P. Maas, eds., *Medieval Japan: Essays in Institutional History* (1974). The sophisticated study of H. Ooms, *Tokugawa Ideology. Early Constructs, 1570–1680* (1985), describes how early Tokugawa rulers developed ideological constructs and military values to create a highly disciplined people and a stable society. M. Cooper, ed., *They Came to Japan. An Anthology of European Reports on Japan, 1543–1640* (1981), gives first European impressions of Japan and the Japanese. G. Elison and B. L. Smith, eds., *Warlords, Artists, and Commoners. Japan in the Sixteenth Century* (1987) is an excellent collection of articles by leading scholars.

The following studies are valuable for specific topics: M. Colcutt, *Five Mountains: The Zen Monastic Institution in Medieval Japan* (1980); C. R. Boxer, *The Christian Century in Japan, 1549–1650* (1967); R. P. Dore, *Education in Tokugawa Japan* (1965); and C. D. Sheldon, *The Rise of the Merchant Class in Tokugawa Japan, 1600–1868* (1958).

25

THE REVOLUTION IN WESTERN POLITICS, 1775–1815

*T*HE LAST YEARS of the eighteenth century were a time of great upheaval. A series of revolutions and revolutionary wars challenged the old order of kings and aristocrats. The ideas of freedom and equality, ideas that have not stopped shaping the world since that era, flourished and spread. The revolution began in North America in 1775. Then in 1789 France, the most influential country in Europe, became the leading revolutionary nation. It established first a constitutional monarchy, then a radical republic, and finally a new empire under Napoleon. The armies of France also joined forces with patriots and radicals abroad in an effort to establish new governments based on new principles throughout much of Europe. The world of modern domestic and international politics was born.

What caused this era of revolution? What were the ideas and objectives of the men and women who rose up violently to undo the established system? What were the gains and losses for privileged groups and for ordinary people in a generation of war and upheaval? These are the questions on which this chapter's examination of the French and American revolutions will be based.

LIBERTY AND EQUALITY

Two ideas fueled the revolutionary period in both America and Europe: liberty and equality. What did eighteenth-century politicians and other people mean by liberty and equality, and why were those ideas so radical and revolutionary in their day?

The call for liberty was first of all a call for individual human rights. Even the most enlightened monarchs customarily claimed that it was their duty to regulate what people wrote and believed. Liberals of the revolutionary era protested such controls from on high. They demanded freedom to worship according to the dictates of their consciences instead of according to the politics of their prince. They demanded the end of censorship and the right to express their beliefs freely in print and at public meetings. They demanded freedom from arbitrary laws and from judges who simply obeyed orders from the government.

These demands for basic personal freedoms, which were incorporated into the American Bill of Rights and other liberal constitutions, were very far-reaching. Indeed, eighteenth-century revolutionaries demanded more freedom than most governments today believe it is desirable to grant. The Declaration of the Rights of Man, issued at the beginning of the French Revolution, proclaimed, "Liberty consists in being able to do anything that does not harm another person." A citizen's rights had, therefore, "no limits except those which assure to the other members of society the enjoyment of these same rights." Liberals called for the freedom of the individual to develop and to create to the fullest possible extent. In the context of the aristocratic and monarchial forms of government that then dominated Europe, this was a truly radical idea.

The call for liberty was also a call for a new kind of government. The revolutionary liberals believed that the people were sovereign—that is, that the people alone had the authority to make laws limiting the individual's freedom of action. In practice, this system of government meant choosing legislators who represented the people and who were accountable to them. Moreover, liberals of the revolutionary era believed that every people—every ethnic group—had this right of self-determination and thus the right to form a free nation.

By equality, eighteenth-century liberals meant that all citizens were to have identical rights and civil liberties. Above all, the nobility had no right to special claims and privileges granted solely on the accident of birth.

Liberals did not define equality as meaning that everyone should be equal economically. Quite the contrary. As Thomas Jefferson wrote in an early draft of the American Declaration of Independence, before changing "property" to the more noble-sounding "happiness," everyone was equal in "the pursuit of property." Jefferson and other liberals certainly did not expect equal success in that pursuit. Great differences in wealth and income between rich and poor were perfectly acceptable to liberals. The essential point was that everyone should legally have an equal chance. French liberals and revolutionaries said they wanted "careers opened to talent." They wanted employment in government, in business, and in the professions to be granted on the basis of talent and ability rather than family background or legal status.

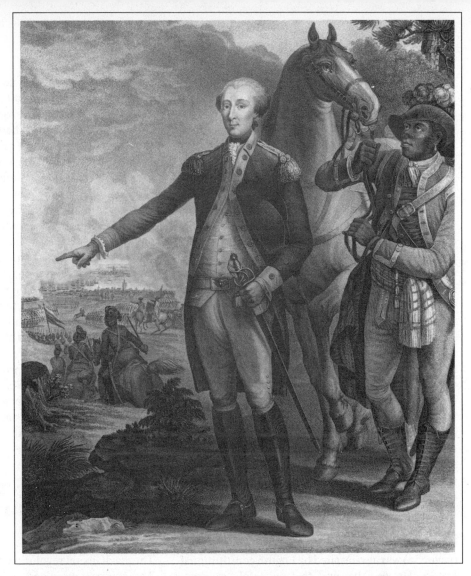

The Marquis de Lafayette was the most famous great noble to embrace the liberal revolution. Shown here directing a battle in the American Revolution, he returned to champion liberty and equality in France. For admirers he was the "hero of two worlds." *(Anne S. K. Brown Military Collection, John Hay Library, Brown University)*

Equality of opportunity was a very revolutionary idea in eighteenth-century Europe. Legal inequality between classes and groups was the rule, not the exception. Society was still legally divided into groups with special privileges, such as the nobility and the clergy, and groups with special burdens, like the peasantry. In many countries, various middle-class groups—professionals, businessmen, townspeople, and craftsmen—enjoyed privileges that allowed them to monopolize all sorts of economic activity. It was this kind of economic inequality, an inequality based on artificial legal distinctions, against which liberals protested.

THE ROOTS OF LIBERALISM

The ideas of liberty and equality—the central ideas of classical liberalism—have deep roots in Western history. The ancient Greeks and the Judeo-Christian tradition had affirmed for hundreds of years the sanctity and value of the individual human being. The Judeo-Christian tradition, reinforced by the Reformation, had long stressed personal responsibility on the part of both common folk and exalted rulers, thereby promoting the self-discipline without which liberty becomes anarchy. The hounded and persecuted Protestant radicals of the later sixteenth century had died for the revolutionary idea that individuals were entitled to their own religious beliefs.

Although the liberal creed had roots deep in the Western tradition, classical liberalism first crystallized at the end of the seventeenth century and during the Enlightenment of the eighteenth century.

Liberal ideas reflected the Enlightenment's stress on human dignity and human happiness on earth. Liberals shared the Enlightenment's general faith in science, rationality, and progress: the adoption of liberal principles meant better government and a better society for all. Almost all the writers of the Enlightenment were passionately committed to greater personal liberty. They preached religious toleration, freedom of press and speech, and fair and equal treatment before the law.

Certain English and French thinkers were mainly responsible for joining the Enlightenment's concern for personal freedom and legal equality to a theoretical justification of liberal self-government. The two most important were John Locke and the baron de Montesquieu, considered earlier. Locke (page 607) maintained that England's long political tradition rested on "the rights of Englishmen" and on representative government through Parliament. Locke admired especially the great Whig noblemen who had made the bloodless revolution of 1688, and he argued that a government that oversteps its proper functions —protecting the natural rights of life, liberty, and private property—becomes a tyranny. Montesquieu (page 656) was also inspired by English constitutional history. He, too, believed that powerful "intermediary groups"—such as the judicial nobility of which he was a proud member—offered the best defense of liberty against despotism.

THE ATTRACTION OF LIBERALISM

The belief that representative institutions could defend their liberty and interests appealed powerfully to ambitious and educated bourgeois. Yet it is important to realize that liberal ideas about individual rights and political freedom also appealed to much of the aristocracy, at least in western Europe and as formulated by Montesquieu. Representative government did not mean democracy, which liberal thinkers tended to equate with mob rule. Rather, they envisioned voting for representatives as being restricted to those who owned property, those with "a stake in society." England had shown the way. After 1688 it had combined a parliamentary system and considerable individual liberty with a restricted franchise and unquestionable aristocratic pre-eminence. In the course of the eighteenth century, many leading French nobles, led by a judicial nobility inspired by Montesquieu, as shown in Chapter 21, were increasingly eager to follow the English example.

Eighteenth-century liberalism, then, appealed not only to the middle class, but also to some aristocrats. It found broad support among the educated elite and the substantial classes in western Europe. What it lacked from the beginning was strong mass support. For comfortable liberals, the really important questions were theoretical and political. They had no need to worry about their stomachs and the price of bread. For the much more numerous laboring poor, the great questions were immediate and economic. Getting enough to eat was the crucial challenge. These differences in outlook and well-being were to lead to many misunderstandings and disappointments for both groups in the revolutionary era.

THE AMERICAN REVOLUTION, 1775–1789

The era of liberal revolution began in the New World. The thirteen mainland colonies of British North America revolted against their mother country and then succeeded in establishing a new unified government.

Americans have long debated the meaning of their revolution. Some have even questioned whether or not it was a real revolution, as opposed to a war for independence. According to some scholars, the Revolution was conservative and defensive in that its demands were for the traditional liberties of Englishmen; Americans were united against the British, but otherwise they were a satisfied people, not torn by internal conflict. Other scholars have argued that, on the contrary, the American Revolution was quite radical. It split families between patriots and Loyalists and divided the country. It achieved goals that were fully as advanced as those obtained by the French in their great revolution a few years later.

How does one reconcile these positions? Both contain large elements of truth. The American revolutionaries did believe they were demanding only the traditional rights of English men and women. But those traditional rights were liberal rights, and in the American context they had very strong democratic and popular overtones. Thus the American Revolution was fought in the name of established ideals that were still quite radical in the context of the times. And in founding a government firmly based on liberal principles, the Americans set an example that had a forceful impact on Europe and speeded up political development there.

THE ORIGINS
OF THE REVOLUTION

The American Revolution had its immediate origins in a squabble over increased taxes. The British government had fought and decisively won the Seven Years' War (page 811) on the strength of its professional army and navy. The American colonists had furnished little real aid. The high cost of the war to the British, however, had led to a doubling of the British national debt. Anticipating further expense defending its recently conquered western lands from Indian uprisings like that of Pontiac, the British government in London set about reorganizing the empire with a series of bold, largely unprecedented measures. Breaking with tradition, the British decided to maintain a large army in North America after peace was restored in 1763. Moreover, they sought to exercise strict control over their newly conquered western lands and to tax the colonies directly. In 1765 the government pushed through Parliament the Stamp Act, which levied taxes on a long list of commercial and legal documents, diplomas, pamphlets, newspapers, almanacs, dice, and playing cards. A stamp glued to each article indicated the tax had been paid.

The effort to increase taxes as part of tightening up the empire seemed perfectly reasonable to the British. Heavier stamp taxes had been collected in Great Britain for two generations, and Americans were being asked only to pay a share of their own defense. Moreover, Americans had been paying only very low local taxes. The Stamp Act would have doubled taxes to about two shillings per person. No other people in the world (except the Poles) paid so little. The British,

meanwhile, paid the world's highest taxes in about 1765—twenty-six shillings per person. It is not surprising that taxes per person in the newly independent American nation were much higher in 1785 than in 1765, when the British no longer subsidized American defense. The colonists protested the Stamp Act vigorously and violently, however, and after rioting and boycotts against British goods, Parliament reluctantly repealed the new tax.

As the fury of the Stamp Act controversy revealed, much more was involved than taxes. The key question was political. To what extent could the home government refashion the empire and reassert its power while limiting the authority of colonial legislatures and their elected representatives? Accordingly, who should represent the colonies, and who had the right to make laws for Americans? While a troubled majority of Americans searched hard for a compromise, some radicals began to proclaim that "taxation without representation is tyranny." The British government replied that Americans were represented in Parliament, albeit indirectly (like most Englishmen themselves), and that the absolute supremacy of Parliament throughout the empire could not be questioned. Many Americans felt otherwise. As John Adams put it, "A Parliament of Great Britain can have no more rights to tax the colonies than a Parliament of Paris." Thus imperial reorganization and parliamentary supremacy came to appear as grave threats to Americans' existing liberties and time-honored institutions.

Americans had long exercised a great deal of independence and gone their own way. In British North America, unlike England and Europe, no powerful established church existed, and personal freedom in questions of religion was taken for granted. The colonial assemblies made the important laws, which were seldom overturned by the home government. The right to vote was much more widespread than in England. In many parts of colonial Massachusetts, for example, as many as 95 percent of the adult males could vote.

Moreover, greater political equality was matched by greater social and economic equality. Neither a hereditary nobility nor a hereditary serf population existed, although the slavery of the Americas consigned blacks to a legally oppressed caste. Independent farmers were the largest group in the country and set much of its tone. In short, the colonial experience

The Boston Tea Party This contemporary illustration shows men disguised as Indians dumping East India Company tea into Boston's harbor. The enthusiastic crowd cheering from the wharf indicates widespread popular support. *(Library of Congress)*

had slowly formed a people who felt themselves separate and distinct from the home country. The controversies over taxation intensified those feelings of distinctiveness and separation and brought them to the fore.

In 1773 the dispute over taxes and representation flared up again. The British government had permitted the financially hard-pressed East India Company to ship its tea from China directly to its agents in the colonies, rather than through London middlemen, who then sold to independent merchants in the colonies. Thus the company secured a vital monopoly on the tea trade, and colonial merchants were suddenly excluded from a highly profitable business. The colonists were quick to protest.

In Boston, men disguised as Indians had a rowdy "tea party" and threw the company's tea into the harbor. This led to extreme measures. The so-called Coercive Acts closed the port of Boston, curtailed local elections and town meetings, and greatly expanded the royal governor's power. County conventions in Massachusetts protested vehemently and urged that the acts be "rejected as the attempts of a wicked administration to enslave America." Other colonial assemblies joined in the denunciations. In September 1774, the First Continental Congress met in Philadelphia, where the more radical members argued successfully against concessions to the Crown. Compromise was also rejected by the British Parliament, and in April 1775 fighting began at Lexington and Concord.

INDEPENDENCE

The fighting spread, and the colonists moved slowly but inevitably toward open rebellion and a declaration of independence. The uncompromising attitude of the British government and its use of German mercenaries went a long way toward dissolving long-standing loyalties to the home country and rivalries among the separate colonies. *Common Sense* (1775), a brilliant attack by the recently arrived English radical Thomas Paine (1737–1809), also mobilized public opinion in favor of independence. A runaway best seller with sales of 120,000 copies in a few months, Paine's tract ridiculed the idea of a small island ruling

The Signing of the Declaration, July 4, 1776 John Trumbull's famous painting shows the dignity and determination of America's revolutionary leaders. An extraordinarily talented group, they succeeded in rallying popular support without losing power to more radical forces in the process. *(Yale University Art Gallery)*

a great continent. In his call for freedom and republican government, Paine expressed Americans' growing sense of separateness and moral superiority.

On July 4, 1776, the Second Continental Congress adopted the Declaration of Independence. Written by Thomas Jefferson, the Declaration of Independence boldly listed the tyrannical acts committed by George III (1760–1820) and confidently proclaimed the natural rights of man and the sovereignty of the American states. Sometimes called the world's greatest political editorial, the Declaration of Independence in effect universalized the traditional rights of Englishmen and made them the rights of all mankind. It stated that "all men are created equal . . . they are endowed by their Creator with certain unalienable rights . . . among these are life, liberty, and the pursuit of happiness." No other American political document has ever caused such excitement, both at home and abroad.

Many American families remained loyal to Britain; many others divided bitterly. After the Declaration of Independence, the conflict often took the form of a civil war pitting patriot against Loyalist.

The Loyalists tended to be wealthy and politically moderate. Many patriots, too, were wealthy—individuals such as John Hancock and George Washington—but willingly allied themselves with farmers and artisans in a broad coalition. This coalition harassed the Loyalists and confiscated their property to help pay for the American war effort. The broad social base of the revolutionaries tended to make the liberal revolution democratic. State governments extended the right to vote to many more people in the course of the war and re-established themselves as republics.

On the international scene, the French sympathized with the rebels from the beginning. They wanted revenge for the humiliating defeats of the Seven Years' War. Officially neutral until 1776, they supplied the great bulk of guns and gunpowder used by the American revolutionaries, very much as neutral great powers supply weapons for "wars of national liberation" today. By 1777 French volunteers were arriving in Virginia, and a dashing young nobleman, the marquis de Lafayette (1757–1834), quickly became one of Washington's most trusted generals.

In 1778 the French government offered the Americans a formal alliance, and in 1779 and 1780 the Spanish and Dutch declared war on Britain. Catherine the Great of Russia helped organize a League of Armed Neutrality in order to protect neutral shipping rights, which Britain refused to recognize.

Thus, by 1780 Great Britain was engaged in an imperial war against most of Europe as well as the thirteen colonies. In these circumstances, and in the face of severe reverses in India, the West Indies, and at Yorktown in Virginia, a new British government decided to cut its losses. American negotiators in Paris were receptive. They feared that France wanted a treaty that would bottle up the new United States east of the Alleghenies and give British holdings west of the Alleghenies to France's ally, Spain. Thus the American negotiators ditched the French and accepted the extraordinarily favorable terms Britain offered.

By the Treaty of Paris of 1783, Britain recognized the independence of the thirteen colonies and ceded all its territory between the Appalachians and the Mississippi River to the Americans. Out of the bitter rivalries of the Old World, the Americans snatched dominion over half a continent.

FRAMING THE CONSTITUTION

The liberal program of the American Revolution was consolidated by the federal Constitution, the Bill of Rights, and the creation of a national republic. Assembling in Philadelphia in the summer of 1787, the delegates to the Constitutional Convention were determined to end the period of economic depression, social uncertainty, and very weak central government that had followed independence. The delegates decided, therefore, to grant the federal, or central, government important powers: regulation of domestic and foreign trade, the right to levy taxes, and the means to enforce its laws.

Strong rule was placed squarely in the context of representative self-government. Senators and congressmen would be the lawmaking delegates of the voters, and the president of the republic would be an elected official. The central government was to operate in Montesquieu's framework of checks and balances. The executive, legislative, and judicial branches would systematically balance each other. The power of the federal government would in turn be checked by the powers of the individual states.

When the results of the secret deliberation of the Constitutional Convention were presented to the states for ratification, a great public debate began. The opponents of the proposed constitution—the Anti-Federalists—charged that the framers of the new document had taken too much power from the individual states and made the federal government too strong. Moreover, many Anti-Federalists feared for the personal liberties and individual freedoms for which they had just fought. In order to overcome these objections, the Federalists solemnly promised to spell out these basic freedoms as soon as the new constitution was adopted. The result was the first ten amendments to the Constitution, which the first Congress passed shortly after it met in New York in March 1789. These amendments formed an effective bill of rights to safeguard the individual. Most of them—trial by jury, due process of law, right to assemble, freedom from unreasonable search—had their origins in English law and the English Bill of Rights of 1689. Others—the freedoms of speech, the press, and religion—reflected natural-law theory and the American experience.

The American Constitution and the Bill of Rights exemplified the great strengths and the limits of what came to be called "classical liberalism." Liberty meant individual freedoms and political safeguards. Liberty also meant representative government but did not necessarily mean democracy with its principle of one man, one vote.

Equality—slaves excepted—meant equality before the law, not equality of political participation or economic well-being. Indeed, economic inequality was resolutely defended by the elite who framed the Constitution. The right to own property was guaranteed by the Fifth Amendment, and if the government took private property, the owner was to receive "just compensation." The radicalism of liberal revolution in America was primarily legal and political, not economic or social.

THE REVOLUTION'S IMPACT ON EUROPE

Hundreds of books, pamphlets, and articles analyzed and romanticized the American upheaval. Thoughtful Europeans noted, first of all, its enormous long-term implications for international politics. A secret report by the Venetian ambassador to Paris in 1783 stated what many felt: "If only the union of the Provinces is preserved, it is reasonable to expect that, with the favorable effects of time, and of European arts and sciences, it will become the most formidable power in the world."[1] More generally, American independence fired the imaginations of those few aristocrats who were uneasy with their privileges and of those commoners who yearned for greater equality. Many Europeans believed that the world was advancing now and that America was leading the way. As one French writer put it in 1789: "This vast continent which the seas surround will soon change Europe and the universe."

Europeans who dreamed of a new era were fascinated by the political lessons of the American Revolution. The Americans had begun with a revolutionary defense against tyrannical oppression, and they had been victorious. They had then shown how rational beings could assemble together to exercise sovereignty and write a permanent constitution—a new social contract. All this gave greater reality to the concepts of individual liberty and representative government. It reinforced one of the primary ideas of the Enlightenment, the idea that a better world was possible.

THE FRENCH REVOLUTION, 1789–1791

No country felt the consequences of the American Revolution more directly than France. Hundreds of French officers served in America and were inspired by the experience. The most famous of these, the young and impressionable marquis de Lafayette, left home as a great aristocrat determined only to fight France's traditional foe, England. He returned with a love of liberty and firm republican convictions. French intellectuals and publicists engaged in passionate analysis of the federal Constitution, as well as the constitutions of the various states of the new United States. The American Revolution undeniably hastened upheaval in France.

Yet the French Revolution did not mirror the American example. It was more violent and more complex, more influential and more controversial, more loved and more hated. For Europeans and most of the rest of the world, it was *the* great revolution of the eighteenth century, the revolution that opened the modern era in politics.

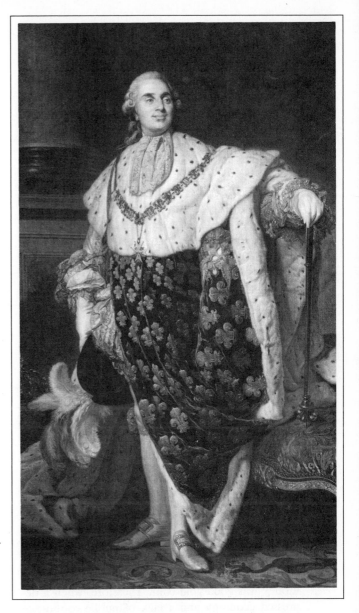

Louis XVI Idealized in this stunning portrait by Duplessis as a majestic, self-confident ruler and worthy heir of Louis XIV, Louis XVI was actually shy, indecisive, and somewhat stupid. *(Château de Versailles/Giraudon/Art Resource)*

THE BREAKDOWN OF THE OLD ORDER

Like the American Revolution, the French Revolution had its immediate origins in the financial difficulties of the government. As noted in Chapter 21, the efforts of Louis XV's ministers to raise taxes had been thwarted by the Parlement of Paris, strengthened in its opposition by widespread popular support. When renewed efforts to reform the tax system met a similar fate in 1776, the government was forced to finance all of its enormous expenditures during the American war with borrowed money. The national debt and the annual budget deficit soared. By the 1780s fully half of France's annual budget went for ever-increasing interest payments on the ever-increasing debt. Another quarter went to maintain the military, while 6 percent was absorbed by the costly and extravagant king and his court at Versailles. Less than one-fifth of the entire national budget was available for the productive functions of the state, such as transportation and general administration. It was an impossible financial situation.

One way out would have been for the government to declare partial bankruptcy, forcing its creditors to accept greatly reduced payments on the debt. The powerful Spanish monarchy had regularly repudiated large portions of its debt in earlier times, and France had done likewise, after an attempt to establish a French national bank ended in financial disaster in 1720. Yet by the 1780s the French debt was held by an army of aristocratic and bourgeois creditors, and the French monarchy, though absolute in theory, had become far too weak for such a drastic and unpopular action.

Nor could the king and his ministers, unlike modern governments, print money and create inflation to cover their deficits. Unlike England and Holland, which had far larger national debts relative to their populations, France had no central bank, no paper currency, and no means of creating credit. French money was good gold coin. Therefore, when a depressed economy and a lack of public confidence made it increasingly difficult for the government to obtain new gold loans in 1786, it had no alternative but to try to increase taxes. And since France's tax system was unfair and out of date, increased revenues were possible only through fundamental reforms. Such reforms would affect all groups in France's complex and fragmented society and opened a Pandora's box of social and political demands.

LEGAL ORDERS AND SOCIAL REALITIES

As in the Middle Ages, France's 25 million inhabitants were still legally divided into three orders or "estates"—the clergy, the nobility, and everyone else. As the nation's first estate, the clergy numbered about 100,000 and had important privileges. It owned about 10 percent of the land and paid only a "voluntary gift" to the government every five years. Moreover, the church levied a tax (the tithe) on landowners, which averaged somewhat less than 10 percent. Much of the church's income was actually drained away from local parishes by political appointees and worldly aristocrats at the top of the church hierarchy, to the intense dissatisfaction of the poor parish priests.

The second legally defined estate consisted of some 400,000 noblemen and noblewomen—the descendants of "those who fought" in the Middle Ages. The nobles owned outright about 25 percent of the land in France, and they, too, were taxed very lightly. Moreover, nobles continued to enjoy certain manorial rights, or privileges of lordship, that dated back to medieval times and allowed them to tax the peasantry for their own profit. This was done by means of exclusive rights to hunt and fish, village monopolies on baking bread and pressing grapes for wine, fees for justice, and a host of other "useful privileges." In addition, nobles had "honorific privileges," such as the right to precedence on public occasions and the right to wear a sword. These rights conspicuously proclaimed the nobility's legal superiority and exalted social position.

Everyone else was a commoner, a member of the third estate. A few commoners were rich merchants or highly successful doctors and lawyers. Many more were urban artisans and unskilled day laborers. The vast majority of the third estate consisted of the peasants and agricultural workers in the countryside. Thus the third estate was a conglomeration of vastly different social groups, united only by their shared legal status as distinct from the privileged nobility and clergy.

In discussing the long-term origins of the French Revolution, historians have long focused on growing tensions between the nobility and the comfortable members of the third estate, usually known as the bourgeoisie, or middle class. A dominant historical interpretation has held sway for at least two generations. According to this interpretation, the bourgeoisie was basically united by economic position and class interest. Aided by the gradual economic expansion of the period, the middle class grew rapidly in the eighteenth century, tripling to about 2.3 million persons, or about 8 percent of France's population. Increasing in size, wealth, culture, and self-confidence, this rising bourgeoisie became progressively exasperated by archaic "feudal" laws restraining the economy and by the growing pretensions of a reactionary nobility, which was closing ranks against middle-class needs and aspirations. As a result, the French bourgeoisie eventually rose up to lead the entire third estate in a great social revolution, a revolution that destroyed feudal privileges and established a capitalist order based on individualism and a market economy.

In recent years, a flood of new research has challenged these accepted views, and once again the French Revolution is a subject of heated scholarly debate. Above all, revisionist historians have questioned the existence of a growing social conflict between a progressive capitalistic bourgeoisie and a reactionary feudal nobility in eighteenth-century France. Instead, these historians see both bourgeoisie and nobility as being riddled with internal rivalries and highly fragmented. The great nobility, for example, was profoundly separated from the lesser nobility by differences in wealth, education, and worldview. Differences within the bourgeoisie—between wealthy financiers and local lawyers, for example—were no less profound. Rather than standing as unified blocs against each other, nobility and bourgeoisie formed two parallel social ladders, increasingly linked together at the top by wealth, marriage, and Enlightenment culture.

Revisionist historians stress in particular three developments in their reinterpretation. First, the nobility remained a fluid and relatively open order. Throughout the eighteenth century, substantial numbers of successful commoners continued to seek and obtain noble status through government service and purchase of expensive positions conferring nobility. Thus the nobility of the robe continued to attract the wealthiest members of the middle class and to permit social mobility. Second, key sections of the nobility were no less liberal than the middle class, which until revolution actually began, generally supported the judicial opposition led by the Parlement of Paris. Finally, the nobility and the bourgeoisie were not really at odds in the economic sphere. Both looked to investment in land and government service as their preferred activities, and the ideal of the merchant capitalist was to gain enough wealth to retire from trade, purchase estates, and live nobly as a large landowner. At the same time, wealthy nobles often acted as aggressive capitalists, investing especially in mining, metallurgy, and foreign trade.

The revisionists have clearly shaken the belief that the bourgeoisie and the nobility were inevitably locked in growing conflict before the Revolution. But in stressing the similarities between the two groups, especially at the top, they have also reinforced the view, long maintained by historians, that the Old Regime had ceased to correspond with social reality by the 1780s. Legally, society was still based on rigid orders inherited from the Middle Ages. In reality, France had already moved far toward being a society based on wealth and economic achievement, where an emerging elite that included both aristocratic and bourgeois notables was frustrated by a bureaucratic monarchy that had long claimed the right to absolute power.

THE FORMATION OF THE NATIONAL ASSEMBLY

The Revolution was under way by 1787, though no one could have realized what was to follow. Spurred by a depressed economy and falling tax receipts, Louis XVI's minister of finance revived old proposals to impose a general tax on all landed property, as well as provincial assemblies to help administer the tax, and he convinced the king to call an Assembly of Notables to gain support for the idea. The assembled notables, who were mainly important noblemen and high-ranking clergy, were not in favor of it. In return for their support, they demanded that control over all government spending be given to the provincial assemblies, which they expected to control. When the government refused, the nobles responded that such sweeping tax changes required the approval of the Estates General, the representative body of all three estates, which had not met since 1614.

Facing imminent bankruptcy, the king tried to reassert his authority. He dismissed the nobles and established new taxes by decree. In stirring language, the Parlement of Paris promptly declared the royal initiative null and void. The Parlement went so far as to specify some of the "fundamental laws" against which no king could transgress, such as national consent to taxation and freedom from arbitrary arrest and imprisonment. When the king tried to exile the judges, a tremendous wave of protest swept the country. Frightened investors also refused to advance more loans to the state. Finally, in July 1788, a beaten Louis XVI called for a spring session of the Estates General. Absolute monarchy was collapsing.

What would replace it? Throughout the unprecedented election campaign of 1788 and 1789, that question excited France. All across the country, clergy, nobles, and commoners came together in their respective orders to draft petitions for change and to elect their respective delegates to the Estates General. The local assemblies of the clergy showed considerable dissatisfaction with the church hierarchy, and two-thirds of the delegates were chosen from the poorer parish priests, who were commoners by birth. The nobles, already badly split by wealth and education, remained politically divided. A conservative majority was drawn from the poorer and more numerous provincial nobility, but fully a third of the nobility's representatives were liberals committed to major changes.

As for the third estate, there was great popular participation in the elections. Almost all male commoners twenty-five years or older had the right to vote. However, voting required two stages, which meant that most of the representatives finally selected by the third estate were well-educated, prosperous members of the middle class. Most of them were not businessmen, but lawyers and government officials. Social status and prestige were matters of particular concern to this economic elite. There were no delegates from the great mass of laboring poor—the peasants and the artisans.

The petitions for change from the three estates showed a surprising degree of agreement on most issues, as recent research has clearly revealed. There was general agreement that royal absolutism should give way to constitutional monarchy, in which laws and taxes would require the consent of an Estates General meeting regularly. All agreed that, in the future, individual liberties must be guaranteed by law and that the position of the parish clergy had to be improved. It was generally acknowledged that economic development required reforms, such as the abolition of internal trade barriers. The striking similarities in the grievance petitions of the clergy, nobility, and third estate reflected the broad commitment of France's elite to liberalism.

Yet an increasingly bitter quarrel undermined this consensus during the intense election campaign: *how* would the Estates General vote, and precisely *who* would lead in the political reorganization that was generally desired? The Estates General of 1614 had sat as three separate houses. Any action had required the agreement of at least two branches, a requirement that had guaranteed control by the privileged orders —the nobility and the clergy. Immediately after its victory over the king, the aristocratic Parlement of Paris ruled that the Estates General should once again sit separately, mainly out of respect for tradition but partly to enhance the nobility's political position. The ruling was quickly denounced by certain middle-class intellectuals and some liberal nobles. They demanded instead a single assembly dominated by representatives of the third estate, to ensure fundamental reforms. Reflecting a growing hostility toward aristocratic aspirations, the abbé Sieyès argued in 1789 in his famous pamphlet, *What Is the Third Estate?*, that the nobility was a tiny, overprivileged minority and that the neglected third estate constituted the true strength of the French nation. When the government agreed that the third estate should have as many delegates as the clergy and the nobility combined, but then rendered its act meaningless by upholding voting by separate order, middle-class leaders saw fresh evidence of a noble conspiracy.

In May 1789, the twelve hundred delegates of the three estates paraded in medieval pageantry through the streets of Versailles to an opening session resplendent with feudal magnificence. The estates were almost immediately deadlocked. Delegates of the third estate refused to transact any business until the king ordered the clergy and nobility to sit with them in a single body. Finally, after a six-week war of nerves, a few parish priests began to go over to the third estate, which on June 17 voted to call itself the National Assembly. On June 20, excluded from their hall because of "repairs," the delegates of the third estate moved to a large indoor tennis court. There they swore the famous Oath of the Tennis Court, pledging never to disband until they had written a new constitution.

The king's actions were then somewhat contradictory. On June 23, he made a conciliatory speech to a joint session, urging reforms, and then ordered the three estates to meet together. At the same time, he apparently followed the advice of relatives and court nobles, who urged him to dissolve the Estates General by force. The king called an army of eighteen thousand troops toward Versailles, and on July 11 he dismissed his finance minister and his other more liberal ministers. Faced with growing opposition since 1787, Louis XVI had resigned himself to bankruptcy. Now he sought to reassert his divine and historic right to rule. The middle-class delegates had done their best, but they were resigned to being disbanded at bayonet point. One third-estate delegate reassured a worried colleague: "You won't hang—you'll only have to go back home."[2]

THE REVOLT OF THE POOR AND THE OPPRESSED

While the third estate pressed for symbolic equality with the nobility and clergy in a single legislative body at Versailles, economic hardship gripped the masses of France in a tightening vise. Grain was the basis of the diet of ordinary people, and in 1788 the harvest had been extremely poor. The price of bread, which had been rising gradually since 1785, began to soar. By July 1789, the price of bread in the provinces climbed as high as eight sous per pound. In Paris, where bread was subsidized by the government in an attempt to prevent popular unrest, the price rose to four sous. The poor could scarcely afford to pay two sous per pound, for even at that price a laborer with a wife and three children had to spend half of his wages to buy the family's bread.

Harvest failure and high bread prices unleashed a classic economic depression of the preindustrial age. With food so expensive and with so much uncertainty, the demand for manufactured goods collapsed. Thousands of artisans and small traders were thrown out of work. By the end of 1789, almost half of the French people would be in need of relief. One person in eight was a pauper, living in extreme want. In Paris the situation was desperate in July 1789: perhaps 150,000 of the city's 600,000 people were without work.

Against this background of dire poverty and excited by the political crisis, the people of Paris entered decisively onto the revolutionary stage. They believed in a general, though ill-defined, way that the economic distress had human causes. They believed that they should have steady work and enough bread

to survive. Specifically, they feared that the dismissal of the king's moderate finance minister would throw them at the mercy of aristocratic landowners and grain speculators. Stories like that quoting the wealthy financier Joseph François Foulon as saying that the poor "should eat grass, like my horses," and rumors that the king's troops would sack the city began to fill the air. Angry crowds formed and passionate voices urged action. On July 13, the people began to seize arms for the defense of the city, and on July 14, several hundred of the most determined people marched to the Bastille to search for gunpowder.

An old medieval fortress with walls ten feet thick and eight great towers each a hundred feet high, the Bastille had long been used as a prison. It was guarded by eighty retired soldiers and thirty Swiss guards. The governor of the fortress-prison refused to hand over the powder, panicked, and ordered his men to fire, killing ninety-eight people attempting to enter. Cannon were brought to batter the main gate, and fighting continued until the governor of the prison surrendered. While he was being taken under guard to city hall, a band of men broke through and hacked him to death. His head and that of the mayor of Paris, who had been slow to give the crowd arms, were stuck on pikes and paraded through the streets. The next day, a committee of citizens appointed the marquis de Lafayette commander of the city's armed forces. Paris was lost to the king, who was forced to recall the finance minister and to disperse his troops. The uprising had saved the National Assembly.

As the delegates resumed their long-winded and inconclusive debates at Versailles, the people in the countryside sent them a radical and unmistakable message. All across France, peasants began to rise in spontaneous, violent, and effective insurrection against their lords, ransacking manor houses and burning feudal documents that recorded the peasants' obligations. In some areas, the nobles and bourgeoisie combined forces and organized patrols to protect their property. Yet the peasant insurrection went on. Recent enclosures were undone, old common lands were reoccupied, and the forests were seized. Taxes went unpaid. Fear of vagabonds and outlaws—the so-called Great Fear—seized the countryside and fanned the flames of rebellion. The long-suffering peasants were doing their best to free themselves from aristocratic privilege and exploitation.

Storming the Bastille This contemporary drawing conveys the fury and determination of the revolutionary crowd on July 14, 1789. This successful popular action had enormous symbolic significance, and July 14 has long been France's most important national holiday. *(Photo: Flammarion)*

Faced with chaos, yet fearful of calling on the king to restore order, some liberal nobles and middle-class delegates at Versailles responded to peasant demands with a surprise maneuver on the night of August 4, 1789. The duke of Aiguillon, one of France's greatest noble landowners, declared that

in several provinces the whole people forms a kind of league for the destruction of the manor houses, the ravaging of the lands, and especially for the seizure of the archives where the title deeds to feudal properties are kept. It seeks to throw off at last a yoke that has for many centuries weighted it down.[3]

He urged equality in taxation and the elimination of feudal dues. In the end, all the old exactions were abolished, generally without compensation: serfdom where it still existed, exclusive hunting rights for nobles, fees for justice, village monopolies, the right to make peasants work on the roads, and a host of other dues. Though a clarifying law passed a week later was less generous, the peasants ignored the "fine print." They never paid feudal dues again. Thus the French peasantry, which already owned about 30 percent of all the land, quickly achieved a great and unprecedented victory. Henceforth, the French peasants would seek mainly to consolidate their triumph.

As the Great Fear subsided, they became a force for order and stability.

A LIMITED MONARCHY

The National Assembly moved forward. On August 27, 1789, it issued the Declaration of the Rights of Man. This great liberal document had a very American flavor, and Lafayette even discussed his draft in detail with the American ambassador in Paris, Thomas Jefferson, the author of the American Declaration of Independence. According to the French declaration, "men are born and remain free and equal in rights." Mankind's natural rights are "liberty, property, security, and resistance to oppression." Also, "every man is presumed innocent until he is proven guilty." As for law, "it is an expression of the general will; all citizens have the right to concur personally or through their representatives in its formation. . . . Free expression of thoughts and opinions is one of the most precious rights of mankind: every citizen may therefore speak, write, and publish freely." In short, this clarion call of the liberal revolutionary ideal guaranteed equality before the law, representative government for a sovereign people, and individual freedom. This revolutionary credo, only two pages long, was propagandized throughout France and Europe and around the world.

Moving beyond general principles to draft a constitution proved difficult. The questions of how much power the king should retain and whether he could permanently veto legislation led to another deadlock. Once again the decisive answer came from the poor, in this instance the poor women of Paris.

To understand what happened, one must remember that the work and wages of women and children were essential in the family economy of the laboring poor. In Paris great numbers of women worked, particularly within the putting-out system in the garment industry—making lace, fancy dresses, embroidery, ribbons, bonnets, corsets, and so on. Many of these goods were beautiful luxury items, destined for an aristocratic and international clientele.[4] Immediately after the fall of the Bastille, many of France's great court nobles began to leave Versailles for foreign lands, so that a plummeting demand for luxuries intensified the general economic crisis. International markets also declined, and the church was no longer able to give its traditional grants of food and money to the poor. Unemployment and hunger increased further, and the result was another popular explosion.

On October 5, some seven thousand desperate women marched the twelve miles from Paris to Versailles to demand action. This great crowd invaded the Assembly, "armed with scythes, sticks and pikes." One coarse, tough old woman directing a large group of younger women defiantly shouted into the debate: "Who's that talking down there? Make the chatterbox shut up. That's not the point: the point is that we want bread."[5] Hers was the genuine voice of the people, essential to any understanding of the French Revolution.

The women invaded the royal apartments, slaughtered some of the royal bodyguards, and furiously searched for the despised queen, Marie Antoinette. "We are going to cut off her head, tear out her heart, fry her liver, and that won't be the end of it," they shouted, surging through the palace in a frenzy. It seems likely that only the intervention of Lafayette and the National Guard saved the royal family. But the only way to calm the disorder was for the king to go and live in Paris, as the crowd demanded.

The next day, the king, the queen, and their son left for Paris in the midst of a strange procession. The heads of two aristocrats, stuck on pikes, led the way. They were followed by the remaining members of the royal bodyguard, unarmed and surrounded and mocked by fierce men holding sabers and pikes. A mixed and victorious multitude surrounded the king's carriage, hurling crude insults at the queen. There was drinking and eating among the women. "We are bringing the baker, the baker's wife, and the baker's boy," they joyfully sang. The National Assembly followed the king to Paris. Reflecting the more radical environment, it adopted a constitution that gave the virtually imprisoned "baker" only a temporary veto in the lawmaking process. And, for a time, he and the government made sure that the masses of Paris did not lack bread.

The next two years until September 1791 saw the consolidation of the liberal Revolution. Under middle-class leadership, the National Assembly abolished the French nobility as a legal order and pushed forward with the creation of a constitutional monarchy, which Louis XVI reluctantly agreed to accept in July 1790. In the final constitution, the king remained the head of state, but all lawmaking power was placed in the hands of the National Assembly, elected by the economic upper half of French males. Eighty-three departments of approximately equal size replaced the complicated old patchwork of provinces with their many historic differences. The jumble of weights and measures that varied from province to province was reformed, leading to the introduction of the simple, rational metric system in 1793. The National Assembly promoted economic freedom. Monopolies, guilds, and workers' combinations were prohibited, and barriers to trade within France were abolished in the name of economic liberty. Thus the National Assembly applied the critical spirit of the Enlightenment to reform France's laws and institutions completely.

The Assembly also threatened nobles who had emigrated from France with the loss of their lands. It nationalized the property of the church and abolished the monasteries as useless relics of a distant past. The government used all former church property as collateral to guarantee a new paper currency, the *assignats,* and then sold these properties in an attempt to put the state's finances on a solid footing. Although the church's land was sold in large blocks, a procedure that favored nimble speculators and the rich, peasants eventually purchased much of it as it was subdivided. These purchases strengthened their attachment to the revolutionary state.

The most unfortunate aspect of the reorganization of France was that it brought the new government into conflict with the Catholic church. Many middle-class delegates to the National Assembly, imbued with the rationalism and skepticism of the eighteenth-century philosophes, harbored a deep distrust of popular piety and "superstitious religion." They were interested in the church only to the extent that they could seize its land and use the church to strengthen the new state. Thus they established a national church, with priests chosen by voters. In the face of resistance, the National Assembly required the clergy to take a loyalty oath to the new government. The clergy became just so many more employees of the state. The pope formally condemned this attempt to subjugate the church. Against such a backdrop, it is not surprising that only half the priests of France took the oath of allegiance. The result was a deep division within both the country and the clergy itself on the religious question, and confusion and hostility among French Catholics were pervasive. The attempted reorganization of the Catholic church was the revolutionary government's first important failure.

"To Versailles" This print is one of many commemorating the women's march on Versailles. Notice on the left that the fashionable lady from the well-to-do is a most reluctant revolutionary. *(Photo: Flammarion)*

WORLD WAR AND REPUBLICAN FRANCE, 1791-1799

When Louis XVI accepted the final version of the completed constitution in September 1791, a young and still obscure provincial lawyer and member of the National Assembly named Maximilien Robespierre (1758–1794) evaluated the work of two years and concluded, "The Revolution is over." Robespierre was both right and wrong. He was right in the sense that the most constructive and lasting reforms were in place. Nothing substantial in the way of liberty and equality would be gained in the next generation, though much would be lost. He was wrong in the sense that a much more radical stage lay ahead. New heroes and new ideologies were to emerge in the process of revolutionary wars and international conflict.

THE BEGINNING OF WAR

The outbreak and progress of revolution in France produced great excitement and a sharp division of opinion in Europe and the United States. Liberals and radicals such as the English scientist Joseph Priestley (1733–1804) and the American patriot Thomas Paine saw a mighty triumph of liberty over despotism. Conservative spirits like Edmund Burke (1729–1797) were deeply troubled. In 1790 Burke published *Reflections on the Revolution in France,* one of the great intellectual defenses of European conservatism. He defended inherited privileges in general and those of the English monarchy and aristocracy in particular. He predicted that unlimited reform would lead only to chaos and renewed tyranny. By 1791 fear was growing outside France that the great hopes raised by the Revolution might be tragically dashed. The moderate German writer Friedrich von Gentz was apprehensive that, if moderate and intelligent revolution failed in France, all the old evils would be ten times worse: "It would be felt that men could be happy only as slaves, and every tyrant, great or small, would use this confession to seek revenge for the fright that the awakening of the French nation had given him."[6]

The kings and nobles of Europe, who had at first welcomed the revolution in France as weakening a competing power, began to feel threatened themselves. At their courts they listened to the diatribes of great court nobles who had fled France and were urging intervention in France's affairs. When Louis XVI and Marie Antoinette were arrested and returned to Paris after trying unsuccessfully to slip out of France in June 1791, the monarchs of Austria and Prussia issued the Declaration of Pillnitz. This carefully worded statement declared their willingness to intervene in France, but only with the unanimous agreement of all the Great Powers, which they did not expect to receive. Austria and Prussia expected their threat to have a sobering effect on revolutionary France without causing war.

The crowned heads of Europe misjudged the revolutionary spirit in France. When the National Assembly had disbanded, it had sought popular support by decreeing that none of its members would be eligible for election to the new Legislative Assembly. This meant that, when the new representative body was duly elected and convened in October 1791, it had a different character. The great majority were still prosperous, well-educated, and middle class, but they were younger and less cautious than their predecessors. Loosely allied as "Jacobins," so named after their political club, the new representatives to the Assembly were passionately committed to liberal revolution.

The Jacobins increasingly lumped "useless aristocrats" and "despotic monarchs" together, and they easily whipped themselves into a patriotic fury with bombastic oratory. So the courts of Europe were attempting to incite a war of kings against France; well then, "we will incite a war of people against kings. . . . Ten million Frenchmen, kindled by the fire of liberty, armed with the sword, with reason, with eloquence would be able to change the face of the world and make the tyrants tremble on their thrones."[7] Only Robespierre and a very few others argued that people do not welcome liberation at the point of a gun. Such warnings were brushed aside. France would "rise to the full height of her mission," as one deputy urged. In April 1792, France declared war on Francis II, archduke of Austria and king of Hungary and Bohemia.

France's crusade against tyranny went poorly at first. Prussia joined Austria in the Austrian Netherlands (present-day Belgium), and French forces broke and fled at their first encounter with armies of this First Coalition. The road to Paris lay open, and it is possible that only conflict between the eastern monarchs over the division of Poland saved France from defeat.

Military reversals and Austro-Prussian threats caused a wave of patriotic fervor to sweep France. The Legislative Assembly declared the country in danger. Volunteer armies from the provinces streamed through Paris, fraternizing with the people and singing patriotic songs like the stirring "Marseillaise," later the French national anthem.

In this supercharged wartime atmosphere, rumors of treason by the king and queen spread in Paris. Once again, as in the storming of the Bastille, the common people of Paris acted decisively. On August 10, 1792, a revolutionary crowd attacked the royal palace at the Tuileries, capturing it after heavy fighting with the Swiss Guards. The king and his family fled for their lives to the nearby Legislative Assembly, which suspended the king from all his functions, imprisoned him, and called for a new National Convention to be elected by universal male suffrage. Monarchy in France was on its deathbed, mortally wounded by war and popular revolt.

THE SECOND REVOLUTION

The fall of the monarchy marked a rapid radicalization of the Revolution, which historians often call the "second revolution." Louis's imprisonment was followed by the September Massacres, which sullied the Revolution in the eyes of most of its remaining foreign supporters. Wild stories seized the city that imprisoned counter-revolutionary aristocrats and priests were plotting with the allied invaders. As a result, angry crowds invaded the prisons of Paris and summarily slaughtered half the men and women they found. In late September 1792, the new, popularly elected National Convention proclaimed France a republic. The republic adopted a new revolutionary calendar, and citizens were expected to address each other with the friendly "thou" of the people, rather than with the formal "you" of the rich and powerful.

All of the members of the National Convention were Jacobins and republicans, and the great majority continued to come from the well-educated middle class. But the Convention was increasingly divided into two well-defined, bitterly competitive groups—the Girondists and the Mountain, so called because its members, led by Danton and Robespierre, sat on the uppermost left-hand benches of the assembly hall. Many indecisive members seated in the "Plain" below floated back and forth between the rival factions.

The division was clearly apparent after the National Convention overwhelmingly convicted Louis XVI of treason. By a single vote, 361 of the 720 members of the Convention then unconditionally sentenced him to death in January 1793. Louis died with tranquil dignity on the newly invented guillotine. One of his last statements was, "I am innocent and shall die without fear. I would that my death might bring happiness to the French, and ward off the dangers which I foresee."[8]

Both the Girondists and the Mountain were determined to continue the "war against tyranny." The Prussians had been stopped at the indecisive battle of Valmy on September 20, 1792, one day before the republic was proclaimed. Republican armies then successfully invaded Savoy and captured Nice. A second army corps invaded the German Rhineland and took the city of Frankfurt. To the north, the revolutionary armies won their first major battle at Jemappes and occupied the entire Austrian Netherlands by November 1792. Everywhere they went, French armies of occupation chased the princes, "abolished feudalism," and found support among some peasants and middle-class people.

But the French armies also lived off the land, requisitioning food and supplies and plundering local treasures. The liberators looked increasingly like foreign invaders. International tensions mounted. In February 1793, the National Convention, at war with Austria and Prussia, declared war on Britain, Holland, and Spain as well. Republican France was now at war with almost all of Europe, a great war that would last almost without interruption until 1815.

As the forces of the First Coalition drove the French from the Austrian Netherlands, peasants in western France revolted against being drafted into the army. They were supported and encouraged in their resistance by devout Catholics, royalists, and foreign agents.

In Paris, the quarrelsome National Convention found itself locked in a life-and-death political struggle between the Girondists and the Mountain. The two groups were in general agreement on questions of policy. Sincere republicans, they hated privilege and wanted to temper economic liberalism with social concern. Yet personal hatreds ran deep. The Girondists feared a bloody dictatorship by the Mountain, and the Mountain was no less convinced that the more moderate Girondists would turn to conservatives and even royalists in order to retain power. With the middle-class delegates so bitterly divided, the laboring poor of Paris emerged as the decisive political factor.

The great mass of the Parisian laboring poor always constituted—along with the peasantry in the summer of 1789—the elemental force that drove the Revolution forward. It was the artisans, shopkeepers, and day laborers who had stormed the Bastille, marched on Versailles, driven the king from the Tuileries, and carried out the September Massacres. The petty traders and laboring poor were often known as the *sans-culottes,* "without breeches," because they wore trousers instead of the knee breeches of the aristocracy and the solid middle class.

Though their immediate interests were economic, by the spring of 1793 the sans-culottes were keenly interested in politics. Encouraged by the so-called angry men, such as the passionate young ex-priest and journalist Jacques Roux, the sans-culottes were demanding radical political action to guarantee them their daily bread. At first the Mountain joined the Girondists in violently rejecting these demands. But in the face of military defeat, peasant revolt, and hatred of the Girondists, the Mountain and especially Robespierre became more sympathetic. The Mountain joined with sans-culottes activists in the city government to engineer a popular uprising, which forced the Convention to arrest thirty-one Girondist deputies for treason on June 2. All power passed to the Mountain.

Robespierre and others from the Mountain joined the recently formed Committee of Public Safety, to which the Convention had given dictatorial power to deal with the national emergency. These developments in Paris triggered revolt in leading provincial cities, such as Lyons and Marseilles, where moderates denounced Paris and demanded a decentralized government. The peasant revolt spread and the republic's armies were driven back on all fronts. By July 1793, only the areas around Paris and on the eastern frontier were firmly controlled by the central government. Defeat appeared imminent.

TOTAL WAR AND THE TERROR

A year later, in July 1794, the Austrian Netherlands and the Rhineland were once again in the hands of conquering French armies, and the First Coalition was falling apart. This remarkable change of fortune was due to the revolutionary government's success in harnessing, for perhaps the first time in history, the explosive forces of a planned economy, revolutionary terror, and modern nationalism in a total war effort.

Robespierre and the Committee of Public Safety advanced with implacable resolution on several fronts in 1793 and 1794. In an effort to save revolutionary France, they collaborated with the fiercely patriotic and democratic sans-culottes. They established, as best they could, a planned economy with egalitarian social overtones. Rather than let supply and demand determine prices, the government decreed the maximum allowable prices, fixed in paper assignats, for a host of key products. Though the state was too weak to enforce all its price regulations, it did fix the price of bread in Paris at levels the poor could afford. Rationing and ration cards were introduced to make sure that the limited supplies of bread were shared fairly. Quality was also controlled. Bakers were permitted to make only the "bread of equality" —a brown bread made of a mixture of all available flours. White bread and pastries were outlawed as frivolous luxuries. The poor of Paris may not have eaten well, but they ate.

They also worked, mainly to produce arms and munitions for the war effort. Craftsmen and small manufacturers were told what to produce and when to deliver. The government nationalized many small workshops and requisitioned raw materials and grain from the peasants. Sometimes planning and control did not go beyond orders to meet the latest emergency: "Ten thousand soldiers lack shoes. You will take the shoes of all the aristocrats in Strasbourg and deliver them ready for transport to headquarters at 10 A.M. tomorrow." Failures to control and coordinate were failures of means and not of desire: seldom if ever before had a government attempted to manage an economy so thoroughly. The second revolution and the ascendancy of the sans-culottes had produced an embryonic emergency socialism, which was to have great influence on the subsequent development of socialist ideology.

While radical economic measures supplied the poor with bread and the armies with weapons, a

The Reign of Terror A man, woman, and child accused of political crimes are brought before a special revolutionary committee for trial. The Terror's iron dictatorship crushed individual rights as well as treason and opposition. *(Photo: Flammarion)*

Reign of Terror (1793–1794) was solidifying the home front. Special revolutionary courts, responsible only to Robespierre's Committee of Public Safety, tried rebels and "enemies of the nation" for political crimes. Drawing on popular sans-culottes support centered in the local Jacobin clubs, these local courts ignored normal legal procedures and judged severely. Some 40,000 French men and women were executed or died in prison. Another 300,000 suspects crowded the prisons and often brushed close to death in a revolutionary court.

Robespierre's Reign of Terror was one of the most controversial phases of the French Revolution. Most historians now believe that the Terror was not directed against any single class. Rather, it was a politi-

cal weapon directed impartially against all who might oppose the revolutionary government. For many Europeans of the time, however, the Reign of Terror represented a terrifying perversion of the generous ideals of 1789. It strengthened the belief that France had foolishly replaced a weak king with a bloody dictatorship.

The third and perhaps most decisive element in the French republic's victory over the First Coalition was its ability to continue drawing on the explosive power of patriotic dedication to a national state and a national mission. This is the essence of modern nationalism. With a common language and a common tradition, newly reinforced by the ideas of popular sovereignty and democracy, the French people were stirred by a common loyalty. The shared danger of foreign foes and internal rebels unified all classes in a heroic defense of the nation.

In such circumstances, war was no longer the gentlemanly game of the eighteenth century, but a life-and-death struggle between good and evil. Everyone had to participate in the national effort. According to a famous decree of August 23, 1793:

The young men shall go to battle and the married men shall forge arms. The women shall make tents and clothes, and shall serve in the hospitals; children shall tear rags into lint. The old men will be guided to the public places of the cities to kindle the courage of the young warriors and to preach the unity of the Republic and the hatred of kings.

Like the wars of religion, war in 1793 was a crusade; this war, though, was fought for a secular rather than a religious ideology.

As all unmarried young men were subject to the draft, the French armed forces swelled to 1 million men in fourteen armies. A force of this size was unprecedented in the history of European warfare. The soldiers were led by young, impetuous generals, who had often risen rapidly from the ranks and personified the opportunities the Revolution seemed to offer gifted sons of the people. These generals used mass attacks at bayonet point by their highly motivated forces to overwhelm the enemy. By the spring of 1794, French armies were victorious on all fronts. The republic was saved.

THE THERMIDORIAN REACTION AND THE DIRECTORY, 1794–1799

The success of the French armies led Robespierre and the Committee of Public Safety to relax the emergency economic controls, but they extended the political Reign of Terror. Their lofty goal was increasingly an ideal democratic republic, where justice would reign and there would be neither rich nor poor. Their lowly means were unrestrained despotism and the guillotine, which struck down any who might seriously question the new order. In March 1794, to the horror of many sans-culottes, Robes-

pierre's Terror wiped out many of the "angry men," led by the radical social democrat Jacques Hébert. Two weeks later, several of Robespierre's long-standing collaborators, led by the famous orator Danton, marched up the steps to the guillotine. Knowing that they might be next, a strange assortment of radicals and moderates in the Convention organized a conspiracy. They howled down Robespierre when he tried to speak to the National Convention on 9 Thermidor (July 27, 1794). On the following day, it was Robespierre's turn to be shaved by the revolutionary razor.

As Robespierre's closest supporters followed their leader, France unexpectedly experienced a thorough reaction to the despotism of the Reign of Terror. In a general way, this "Thermidorian reaction" recalled the early days of the Revolution. The respectable middle-class lawyers and professionals who had led the liberal Revolution of 1789 reasserted their authority. Drawing support from their own class, the provincial cities, and the better-off peasants, the National Convention abolished many economic controls, printed more paper currency, and let prices rise sharply. It severely restricted the local political organizations where the sans-culottes had their strength. And all the while, the wealthy bankers and newly rich speculators celebrated the sudden end of the Terror with an orgy of self-indulgence and ostentatious luxury.

The collapse of economic controls, coupled with runaway inflation, hit the working poor very hard. The gaudy extravagance of the rich wounded their pride. The sans-culottes accepted private property, but they believed passionately in small business and the right of all to earn a decent living. Increasingly disorganized after Robespierre purged their radical spokesmen, the common people of Paris finally revolted against the emerging new order in early 1795. The Convention quickly used the army to suppress these insurrections. For the first time since the fall of the Bastille, bread riots and uprisings by Parisians living on the edge of starvation were effectively put down by a government that made no concessions to the poor.

In the face of all these catastrophes, the revolutionary fervor of the laboring poor finally subsided. As far as politics was concerned, their interest and influence would remain very limited until 1830. There arose, especially from the women, a great cry for peace and

THE FRENCH REVOLUTION

May 5, 1789	Estates General convene at Versailles
June 17, 1789	Third Estate declares itself the National Assembly
June 20, 1789	Oath of the Tennis Court
July 14, 1789	Storming of the Bastille
July–August 1789	The Great Fear in the countryside
August 4, 1789	National Assembly abolishes feudal privileges
August 27, 1789	National Assembly issues Declaration of the Rights of Man
October 5, 1789	Parisian women march on Versailles and force royal family to return to Paris
November 1789	National Assembly confiscates church lands
July 1790	Civil Constitution of the Clergy establishes a national church
	Louis XVI reluctantly agrees to accept a constitutional monarchy
June 1791	Arrest of the royal family while attempting to flee France
August 1791	Declaration of Pillnitz by Austria and Prussia
April 1792	France declares war on Austria
August 1792	Parisian mob attacks palace and takes Louis XVI prisoner
September 1792	September Massacres
	National Convention declares France a republic and abolishes monarchy
January 1793	Execution of Louis XVI
February 1793	France declares war on Britain, Holland, and Spain
	Revolts in provincial cities
March 1793	Bitter struggle in the National Convention between Girondists and the Mountain
April–June 1793	Robespierre and the Mountain organize the Committee of Public Safety and arrest Girondist leaders
September 1793	Price controls to aid the sans-culottes and mobilize war effort
1793–1794	Reign of Terror in Paris and the provinces
Spring 1794	French armies victorious on all fronts
July 1794	Execution of Robespierre
	Thermidorean Reaction begins
1795–1799	The Directory
1795	End of economic controls and suppression of the sans-culottes
1797	Napolean defeats Austrian armies in Italy and returns triumphant to Paris
1798	Austria, Great Britain, and Russia form the Second Coalition against France
1799	Napoleon overthrows the Directory and seizes power

a turning toward religion. As the government looked the other way, the women brought back the Catholic church and the worship of God. In one French town, women fought with each other over which of their children should be baptized first. After six tumultuous years, the women of the poor concluded that the Revolution was a failure.

As for the middle-class members of the National Convention, they wrote yet another constitution, which they believed would guarantee their economic position and political supremacy. The mass of the population could vote only for electors, who would be men of means. Electors then elected the members of a reorganized legislative assembly, as well as key officials throughout France. The assembly also chose the five-man executive—the Directory.

The men of the Directory continued to support French military expansion abroad. War was no longer so much a crusade as a means to meet the ever-present, ever-unsolved economic problem. Large, victorious French armies reduced unemployment at home, and they were able to live off the territories they conquered and plundered.

The unprincipled action of the Directory reinforced widespread disgust with war and starvation. This general dissatisfaction revealed itself clearly in the national elections of 1797, which returned a large number of conservative and even monarchist deputies who favored peace at almost any price. Fearing for their skins, the members of the Directory used the army to nullify the elections and began to govern dictatorially. Two years later, Napoleon Bonaparte ended the Directory in a coup d'état and substituted a strong dictatorship for a weak one. Truly, the Revolution was over.

THE NAPOLEONIC ERA, 1799–1815

For almost fifteen years, from 1799 to 1814, France was in the hands of a keen-minded military dictator of exceptional ability. One of history's most fascinating leaders, Napoleon Bonaparte realized the need to put an end to civil strife in France, in order to create unity and consolidate his rule. And he did. But Napoleon saw himself as a man of destiny, and the glory

Napoleon Crossing the Alps: David Bold and commanding, with flowing cape and surging stallion, the daring young Napoleon Bonaparte leads his army across the Alps from Italy to battle the Austrians in 1797. This painting by the great Jacques-Louis David (1748–1825) is a stirring glorification of Napoleon, a brilliant exercise in mythmaking. *(The Granger Collection)*

of war and the dream of universal empire proved irresistible. For years he spiraled from victory to victory; but in the end he was destroyed by a mighty coalition united in fear of his restless ambition.

NAPOLEON'S RULE OF FRANCE

In 1799, when he seized power, young General Napoleon Bonaparte was a national hero. Born in Corsica into an impoverished noble family in 1769, Napoleon left home to become a lieutenant in the French artillery in 1785. After a brief and unsuccessful adventure fighting for Corsican independence in 1789, he returned to France as a French patriot and a dedicated revolutionary. Rising rapidly in the new army, Napoleon was placed in command of French forces in Italy and won brilliant victories there in

1796 and 1797. His next campaign, in Egypt, was a failure, but Napoleon made his way back to France before the fiasco was generally known. His reputation remained intact.

Napoleon soon learned that some prominent members of the Legislative Assembly were plotting against the Directory. The dissatisfaction of these plotters stemmed not so much from the fact that the Directory was a dictatorship as from the fact that it was a weak dictatorship. Ten years of upheaval and uncertainty had made firm rule much more appealing than liberty and popular politics to these disillusioned revolutionaries. The abbé Sieyès personified this evolution in thinking. In 1789 he had written in his famous pamphlet, *What Is the Third Estate?*, that the nobility was grossly overprivileged and that the entire people should rule the French nation. Now Sieyès's motto was "confidence from below, authority from above."

Like the other members of his group, Sieyès wanted a strong military ruler. The flamboyant thirty-year-old Napoleon was ideal. Thus the conspirators and Napoleon organized a takeover. On November 9, 1799, they ousted the directors, and the following day soldiers disbanded the Assembly at bayonet point. Napoleon was named first consul of the republic, and a new constitution consolidating his position was overwhelmingly approved in a plebiscite in December 1799. Republican appearances were maintained, but Napoleon was already the real ruler of France.

The essence of Napoleon's domestic policy was to use his great and highly personal powers to maintain order and put an end to civil strife. He did so by working out unwritten agreements with powerful groups in France, whereby these groups received favors in return for loyal service. Napoleon's bargain with the solid middle class was codified in the famous Civil Code of 1804, which reasserted two of the fundamental principles of the liberal and essentially moderate revolution of 1789: equality of all citizens before the law and absolute security of wealth and private property. Napoleon and the leading bankers of Paris established a privately owned Bank of France, which loyally served the interests of both the state and the financial oligarchy. Napoleon's defense of the economic status quo also appealed to the peasants, who had bought some of the lands confiscated

from the church and nobility. Thus Napoleon reconfirmed the gains of the peasantry and reassured the middle class, which had already lost a large number of its revolutionary illusions in the face of social upheaval.

At the same time, Napoleon accepted and strengthened the position of the French bureaucracy. Building on the solid foundations that revolutionary governments had inherited from the Old Regime, he perfected a thoroughly centralized state. A network of prefects, subprefects, and centrally appointed mayors depended on Napoleon and served him well. Nor were members of the old nobility slighted. In 1800 and again in 1802 Napoleon granted amnesty to a hundred thousand émigrés on the condition that they return to France and take a loyalty oath. Members of this returning elite soon ably occupied many high posts in the expanding centralized state. Only a thousand die-hard monarchists were exempted and remained abroad. Napoleon also created a new imperial nobility in order to reward his most talented generals and officials.

Napoleon's great skill in gaining support from important and potentially hostile groups is illustrated by his treatment of the Catholic church in France. In 1800 the French clergy was still divided into two groups: those who had taken an oath of allegiance to the revolutionary government and those in exile or hiding who had refused to do so. Personally uninterested in religion, Napoleon wanted to heal the religious division so that a united Catholic church in France could serve as a bulwark of order and social peace. After long and arduous negotiations, Napoleon and Pope Pius VII (1800–1823) signed the Concordat of 1801. The pope gained for French Catholics the precious right to practice their religion freely, but Napoleon gained the most politically. His government now nominated bishops, paid the clergy, and exerted great influence over the church in France.

The domestic reforms of Napoleon's early years were his greatest achievement. Much of his legal and administrative reorganization has survived in France to this day. More generally, Napoleon's domestic initiatives gave the great majority of French people a welcome sense of order and stability. And when Napoleon added the glory of military victory, he rekindled a spirit of national unity that would elude France throughout most of the nineteenth century.

Order and unity had their price: Napoleon's authoritarian rule. Free speech and freedom of the press —fundamental rights of the liberal revolution, enshrined in the Declaration of the Rights of Man— were continually violated. Napoleon constantly reduced the number of newspapers in Paris. By 1811 only four were left, and they were little more than organs of government propaganda. The occasional elections were a farce. Later laws prescribed harsh penalties for political offenses.

These changes in the law were part of the creation of a police state in France. Since Napoleon was usually busy making war, this task was largely left to Joseph Fouché, an unscrupulous opportunist who had earned a reputation for brutality during the Reign of Terror. As minister of police, Fouché organized a ruthlessly efficient spy system, which kept thousands of citizens under continuous police surveillance. People suspected of subversive activities were arbitrarily detained, placed under house arrest, or even consigned to insane asylums. After 1810 political suspects were held in state prisons, as they had been during the Terror. There were about 2,500 such political prisoners in 1814.

NAPOLEON'S WARS AND FOREIGN POLICY

Napoleon was above all a military man, and a great one. After coming to power in 1799, he sent peace feelers to Austria and Great Britain, the two remaining members of the Second Coalition, which had been formed against France in 1798. When these overtures were rejected, French armies led by Napoleon decisively defeated the Austrians. In the Treaty of Lunéville (1801) Austria accepted the loss of its Italian possessions, and German territory on the west bank of the Rhine was incorporated into France. Once more, as in 1797, the British were alone, and war-weary, like the French.

Still seeking to consolidate his regime domestically, Napoleon concluded the Treaty of Amiens with Great Britain in 1802. Britain agreed to return Trinidad and the Caribbean islands, which it had seized from France in 1793. The treaty said very little about Europe, though. France remained in control of Holland, the Austrian Netherlands, the west bank of the Rhine, and most of the Italian peninsula. Napoleon

was free to reshape the German states as he wished. To the dismay of British businessmen, the Treaty of Amiens did not provide for expansion of the commerce between Britain and the Continent. It was clearly a diplomatic triumph for Napoleon, and peace with honor and profit increased his popularity at home.

In 1802 Napoleon was secure but unsatisfied. Ever a romantic gambler as well as a brilliant administrator, he could not contain his power drive. Aggressively redrawing the map of Germany so as to weaken Austria and attract the secondary states of southwestern Germany toward France, Napoleon was also mainly responsible for renewed war with Great Britain. Regarding war with Britain as inevitable, he threatened British interests in the eastern Mediterranean and tried to restrict British trade with all of Europe. Britain had technically violated the Treaty of Amiens by failing to evacuate the island of Malta, but it was Napoleon's decision to renew war in May 1803. He concentrated his armies in the French ports on the Channel in the fall of 1803 and began making preparations to invade England. Yet Great Britain remained mistress of the seas. When Napoleon tried to bring his Mediterranean fleet around Gibraltar to northern France, a combined French and Spanish fleet was, after a series of mishaps, virtually annihilated by Lord Nelson at the Battle of Trafalgar on October 21, 1805. Invasion of England was henceforth impossible. Renewed fighting had its advantages, however, for the first consul used the wartime atmosphere to have himself proclaimed emperor in late 1804.

Austria, Russia, and Sweden joined with Britain to form the Third Coalition against France shortly before the Battle of Trafalgar. Actions like Napoleon's assumption of the Italian crown had convinced both Alexander I of Russia and Francis II of Austria that Napoleon was a threat to their interests and to the European balance of power. Yet the Austrians and the Russians were no match for Napoleon, who scored a brilliant victory over them at the Battle of Austerlitz in December 1805. Alexander I decided to pull back, and Austria accepted large territorial losses in return for peace as the Third Coalition collapsed.

Victorious at Austerlitz, Napoleon proceeded to reorganize the German states to his liking. In 1806 he abolished many of the tiny German states, as well as

THE NAPOLEONIC ERA

November 1799	Napoleon overthrows the Directory
December 1799	French voters overwhelmingly approve Napoleon's new constitution
1800	Napoleon founds the Bank of France
1801	France defeats Austria and acquires Italian and German territories in the Treaty of Lunéville
	Napoleon signs a concordat with the pope
1802	Treaty of Amiens with Britain
December 1804	Napoleon crowns himself emperor
October 1805	Battle of Trafalgar: Britain defeats the French and Spanish fleets
December 1805	Battle of Austerlitz: Napoleon defeats Austria and Prussia
1807	Treaties of Tilsit: Napoleon redraws the map of Europe
1810	Height of the Grand Empire
June 1812	Napoleon invades Russia with 600,000 men
Winter 1812	Disastrous retreat from Russia
March 1814	Russia, Prussia, Austria, and Britain form the Quadruple Alliance to defeat France
April 1814	Napoleon abdicates and is exiled to Elba
February–June 1815	Napoloen excapes from Elba and rules France until suffering defeat at the Battle of Waterloo

the ancient Holy Roman Empire, whose emperor had traditionally been the ruler of Austria. Napoleon established by decree a German Confederation of the Rhine, a union of fifteen German states minus Austria, Prussia, and Saxony. Naming himself "protector" of the confederation, Napoleon firmly controlled western Germany.

Napoleon's intervention in German affairs alarmed the Prussians, who had been at peace with France for more than a decade. Expecting help from his ally Russia, Frederick William III of Prussia mobilized his armies. Napoleon attacked and won two more brilliant victories in October 1806 at Jena and Auerstädt, where the Prussians were outnumbered two to one. The war with Prussia and Russia continued into the following spring, and after Napoleon's larger armies won another victory, Alexander decided to seek peace.

For several days in June 1807, the young tsar and the French emperor negotiated face to face on a raft anchored in the middle of the Niemen River. All the while, the helpless Frederick William rode back and forth on the shore, anxiously awaiting the results. As the German poet Heinrich Heine said later, Napoleon had but to whistle and Prussia would have ceased to exist. In the subsequent treaties of Tilsit, Prussia lost half of its population, while Russia accepted Napoleon's reorganization of western and central Europe. Alexander also promised to enforce Napoleon's recently decreed economic blockade against British goods and to declare war on Britain if Napoleon could not make peace on favorable terms with his island enemy.

After the victory of Austerlitz and even more after the treaties of Tilsit, Napoleon saw himself as the emperor of Europe and not just of France. The so-called Grand Empire he built had three parts. The core was an ever-expanding France, which by 1810 included Belgium, Holland, parts of northern Italy, and much German territory on the east bank of the Rhine.

Map 25.1 Napoleonic Europe in 1810

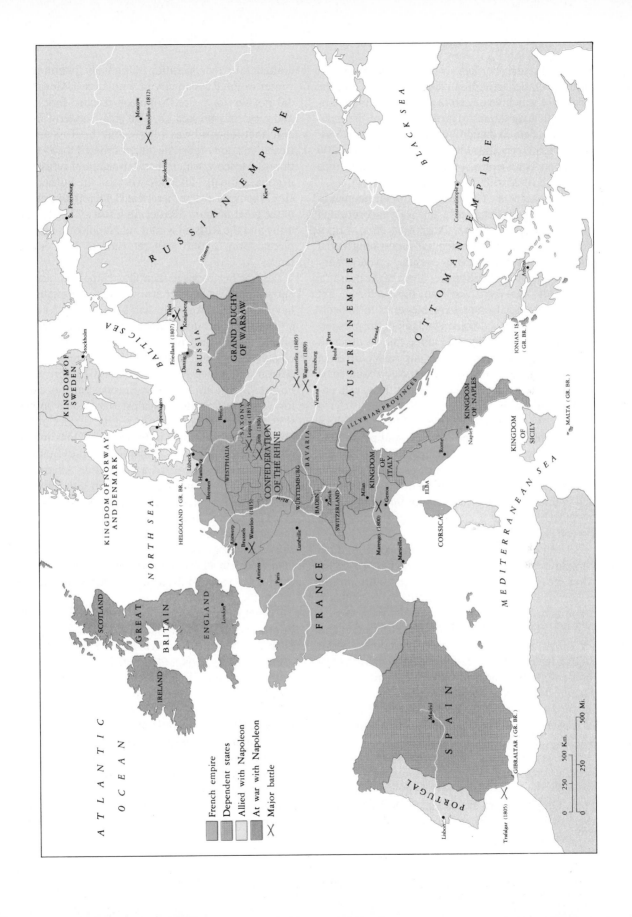

ATLANTIC OCEAN

NORTH SEA

BALTIC SEA

BLACK SEA

MEDITERRANEAN SEA

KINGDOM OF SWEDEN

KINGDOM OF NORWAY AND DENMARK

GREAT BRITAIN

SCOTLAND

IRELAND

ENGLAND

RUSSIAN EMPIRE

PRUSSIA

GRAND DUCHY OF WARSAW

AUSTRIAN EMPIRE

OTTOMAN EMPIRE

SAXONY

WESTPHALIA

CONFEDERATION OF THE RHINE

BAVARIA

WÜRTEMBURG

BADEN

SWITZERLAND

KINGDOM OF ITALY

ILLYRIAN PROVINCES

KINGDOM OF NAPLES

KINGDOM OF SICILY

FRANCE

SPAIN

PORTUGAL

CORSICA

ELBA

Moscow
Borodino (1812)
Smolensk
Kiev
St. Petersburg
Stockholm
Niemen
Tilsit
Friedland (1807)
Königsberg
Danzig
Copenhagen
Berlin
Leipzig (1813)
Jena (1806)
Lübeck
Hamburg
Bremen
Antwerp
Brussels
Waterloo (1815)
Amiens
Paris
Lunéville
Zürich
Milan
Genoa
Marengo (1800)
Marseilles
Austerlitz (1805)
Wagram (1809)
Pressburg
Vienna
Pest
Buda
Danube
Rome
Naples
Constantinople
Athens
IONIAN IS. (GR. BR.)
MALTA (GR. BR.)
HELGOLAND (GR. BR.)
Madrid
Lisbon
Trafalgar (1805)
GIBRALTAR (GR. BR.)
Rhine

French empire
Dependent states
Allied with Napoleon
At war with Napoleon
Major battle

0   250   500 Km.
0   250   500 Mi.

Beyond French borders Napoleon established a number of dependent satellite kingdoms, on the thrones of which he placed (and replaced) the members of his large family. Third, there were the independent but allied states of Austria, Prussia, and Russia. Both satellites and allies were expected after 1806 to support Napoleon's continental system and thus to cease all trade with Britain.

The impact of the Grand Empire on the peoples of Europe was considerable. In the areas incorporated into France and in the satellites (Map 25.1), Napoleon introduced many French laws, abolishing feudal dues and serfdom where French revolutionary armies had not already done so. Some of the peasants and middle class benefited from these reforms. Yet while he extended progressive measures to his cosmopolitan empire, Napoleon had to put the prosperity and special interests of France first in order to safeguard his power base. Levying heavy taxes in money and men for his armies, Napoleon came to be regarded more as a conquering tyrant than as an enlightened liberator.

The first great revolt occurred in Spain. In 1808 a coalition of Catholics, monarchists, and patriots rebelled against Napoleon's attempts to make Spain a French satellite with a Bonaparte as its king. French armies occupied Madrid, but the foes of Napoleon fled to the hills and waged uncompromising guerrilla warfare. Spain was a clear warning. Resistance to French imperialism was growing.

Yet Napoleon pushed on, determined to hold his complex and far-flung empire together. In 1810, when the Grand Empire was at its height, Britain still remained at war with France, helping the guerrillas in Spain and Portugal. The continental system, organized to exclude British goods from the Continent and force that "nation of shopkeepers" to its knees, was a failure. Instead, it was France that suffered from Britain's counterblockade, which created hard times for French artisans and the middle class. Perhaps looking for a scapegoat, Napoleon turned on Alexander I of Russia, who had been fully supporting Napoleon's war of prohibitions against British goods.

Napoleon's invasion of Russia began in June 1812 with a force that eventually numbered 600,000, probably the largest force yet assembled in a single army. Only one-third of this force was French, however; nationals of all the satellites and allies were

drafted into the operation. Originally planning to winter in the Russian city of Smolensk if Alexander did not sue for peace, Napoleon reached Smolensk and recklessly pressed on. The great Battle of Borodino that followed was a draw, and the Russians retreated in good order. Alexander ordered the evacuation of Moscow, which then burned, and refused to negotiate. Finally, after five weeks in the burned-out city, Napoleon ordered a retreat. That retreat was one of the great military disasters in history. The Russian army and the Russian winter cut Napoleon's army to pieces. Only 30,000 men returned to their homelands.

Leaving his troops to their fate, Napoleon raced to Paris to raise yet another army. Possibly he might still have saved his throne if he had been willing to accept a France reduced to its historical size—the proposal offered by Austria's foreign minister Metternich. But Napoleon refused. Austria and Prussia deserted Napoleon and joined Russia and Great Britain in the Fourth Coalition. All across Europe, patriots called for a "war of liberation" against Napoleon's oppression, and the well-disciplined regular armies of Napoleon's enemies closed in for the kill. This time the coalition held together, cemented by the Treaty of Chaumont, which created a Quadruple Alliance to last for twenty years. Less than a month later, on April 4, 1814, a defeated, abandoned Napoleon abdicated his throne. After this unconditional abdication, the victorious allies granted Napoleon the island of Elba off the coast of Italy as his own tiny state. Napoleon was even allowed to keep his imperial title, and France was required to pay him a large yearly income of 2 million francs.

The allies also agreed to the restoration of the Bourbon dynasty, in part because demonstrations led by a few dedicated French monarchists indicated some support among the French people for that course of action. The new monarch, Louis XVIII (1814–1824), tried to consolidate that support by issuing the Constitutional Charter, which accepted many of France's revolutionary changes and guaranteed civil liberties. Indeed, the charter gave France a constitutional monarchy roughly similar to that established in 1791, although far fewer people had the right to vote for representatives to the resurrected parliamentary assembly, now called the "Chamber of Deputies." Moreover, after Louis XVIII stated firmly that his government would not pay any war reparations, France was treated leniently by the allies, who agreed to meet in Vienna to work out a general peace settlement.

Yet Louis XVIII—old, ugly, and crippled by gout—totally lacked the glory and magic of Napoleon. Hearing of political unrest in France and diplomatic tensions in Vienna, Napoleon staged a daring escape from Elba in February 1815. Landing in France, he issued appeals for support and marched on Paris with a small band. French officers and soldiers who had fought so long for their emperor responded to the call. Louis XVIII fled, and once more Napoleon took command. But Napoleon's gamble was a desperate long shot, for the allies were united against him. At the end of a frantic period known as the Hundred Days, they crushed his forces at Waterloo on June 18, 1815, and imprisoned him on the rocky island of St. Helena, far off the western coast of Africa. Old Louis XVIII returned again—this time "in the baggage of the allies," as his detractors scornfully put it—and recommenced his reign. The allies now dealt more harshly with the apparently incorrigible French (see page 838). And Napoleon, doomed to suffer crude insults at the hands of sadistic English jailers on distant St. Helena, could take revenge only by writing his memoirs, skillfully nurturing the myth that he had been Europe's revolutionary liberator, a romantic hero whose lofty work had been undone by oppressive reactionaries. An era had ended.

The revolution that began in America and spread to France was a liberal revolution. Inspired by English history and some of the teachings of the Enlightenment, revolutionaries on both sides of the Atlantic sought to establish civil liberties and equality before the law within the framework of representative government. Success in America was subsequently matched by success in France. There liberal nobles and an increasingly class-conscious middle class overwhelmed declining monarchial absolutism and feudal privilege, thanks to the common people—the sans-culottes and the peasants. The government and society established by the Declaration of the Rights of Man and the French constitution of 1791 were re-markably similar to those created in America by the federal Constitution and the Bill of Rights. Thus the new political system, based on electoral competition and civil equality, came into approximate harmony with France's evolving social structure, which had become increasingly dependent on wealth and personal achievement rather than on tradition and legal privileges.

Yet the Revolution in France did not end with the liberal victory of 1789 to 1791. As Robespierre led the determined country in a total war effort against foreign foes, French revolutionaries became more democratic, radical, and violent. Their effort succeeded, but at the price of dictatorship—first by Robespierre himself and then by the Directory and Napoleon. Some historians blame the excesses of the French revolutionaries for the emergence of dictatorship, while others hold the conservative monarchs of Europe responsible. In any case, historians have often concluded that the French Revolution ended in failure.

This conclusion is highly debatable, though. After the fall of Robespierre, the solid middle class, with its liberal philosophy and Enlightenment world-view, reasserted itself. Under the Directory, it salvaged a good portion of the social and political gains that it and the peasantry had made between 1789 and 1791. In so doing, the middle-class leaders repudiated the radical social and economic measures associated with Robespierre, but they never re-established the old pattern of separate legal orders and absolute monarchy. Napoleon built on the policies of the Directory. With considerable success he sought to add the support of the old nobility and the church to that of the middle class and the peasantry. And though Napoleon sharply curtailed thought and speech, he effectively promoted the reconciliation of old and new, of centralized government and careers open to talent, of noble and bourgeois in a restructured property-owning elite. Little wonder, then, that Louis XVIII had no choice but to accept a French society solidly based on wealth and achievement. In granting representative government and civil liberties to facilitate his restoration to the throne in 1814, Louis XVIII submitted to the rest of the liberal triumph of 1789 to 1791. The core of the French Revolution had survived a generation of war and dictatorship. Old Europe would never be the same.

NOTES

1. Quoted in R. R. Palmer, *The Age of the Democratic Revolution* (Princeton, N.J.: Princeton University Press, 1959), 1.239.
2. G. Lefebvre, *The Coming of the French Revolution* (New York: Vintage Books, 1947), p. 81.
3. P. H. Beik, ed., *The French Revolution* (New York: Walker, 1970), p. 89.
4. O. Hufton, "Women in Revolution," *Past and Present* 53 (November 1971): 91–95.
5. G. Pernoud and S. Flaisser, eds., *The French Revolution* (Greenwich, Conn.: Fawcett Publications, 1960), p. 61.
6. L. Gershoy, *The Era of the French Revolution, 1789–1799* (New York: Van Nostrand, 1957), p. 150.
7. Ibid., p. 150.
8. Pernoud and Flaisser, pp. 193–194.

SUGGESTED READING

In addition to the fascinating eyewitness reports on the French Revolution in P. Beik, *The French Revolution* (1970), and G. Pernoud and S. Flaisser, eds., *The French Revolution* (1960), A. Young's *Travels in France During the Years 1787, 1788 and 1789* (1969) offers an engrossing contemporary description of France and Paris on the eve of revolution. Edmund Burke, *Reflections on the Revolution in France,* first published in 1790, is the classic conservative indictment. The intense passions the French Revolution has generated may be seen in the nineteenth-century French historians, notably the enthusiastic Jules Michelet, *History of the French Revolution;* the hostile Hippolyte Taine; and the judicious Alexis de Tocqueville, whose masterpiece, *The Old Regime and the French Revolution,* was first published in 1856. Important general studies on the entire period are R. R. Palmer, *The Age of the Democratic Revolution* (1959, 1964), which paints a comparative international picture; E. J. Hobsbawm, *The Age of Revolution, 1789–1848* (1962); C. Breunig, *The Age of Revolution and Reaction, 1789–1850* (1970); O. Connelly, *French Revolution—Napoleonic Era* (1979); and L. Dehio, *The Precarious Balance: Four Centuries of the European Power Struggle* (1962). C. Brinton's older but delightfully written *A Decade of Revolution, 1789–1799* (1934) complements his stimulating *Anatomy of Revolution* (1938, 1965), an ambitious comparative approach to revolution in England, America, France, and Russia. A. Cobban, *The Social Interpretation of the French Revolution* (1964), and F. Furet, *Interpreting the French Revolution* (1981), are exciting reassessments of many well-worn ideas, to be compared with W. Doyle, *Origins of the French Revolution* (1981); G. Lefebvre, *The Coming of the French Revolution* (1947); and N. Hampson, *A Social History of the French Revolution* (1963). G. Rudé makes the men and women of the great days of upheaval come alive in his *The Crowd in the French Revolution* (1959). R. R. Palmer studies sympathetically the leaders of the Terror in *Twelve Who Ruled* (1941). Two other particularly interesting, detailed works are C. L. R. James, *The Black Jacobins* (1938, 1980), on the black slave revolt in Haiti, and J. C. Herold, *Mistress to an Age* (1955), on the remarkable Madame de Staël. On revolution in America, E. Morgan, *The Birth of the Republic, 1763–89* (1956), and B. Bailyn, *The Ideological Origins of the American Revolution* (1967), are noteworthy. Three important recent studies on aspects of revolutionary France are D. Jordan's vivid *The King's Trial: Louis XVI vs. the French Revolution* (1979); W. Sewell, Jr.'s imaginative *Work and Revolution in France: The Language of Labor from the Old Regime to 1848* (1980); and P. Higonnet, *Class, Ideology and the Rights of Nobles During the French Revolution* (1981).

P. Geyl, *Napoleon, For and Against* (1949), is a delightful discussion of changing historical interpretations of Napoleon, which may be compared with a more recent treatment by R. Jones, *Napoleon: Man and Myth* (1977). Good biographies are J. M. Thompson, *Napoleon Bonaparte: His Rise and Fall* (1952); F. H. M. Markham, *Napoleon* (1964); and V. Cronin, *Napoleon Bonaparte* (1972). L. Bergeron, *France Under Napoleon* (1981), is an important synthesis. Wonderful novels inspired by this period include Rafael Sabatini's *Scaramouche,* a swashbuckler of revolutionary intrigue with accurate historical details; Charles Dickens's classic *Tale of Two Cities;* and Leo Tolstoy's monumental saga of Napoleon's invasion of Russia (and much more), *War and Peace.*

26

THE INDUSTRIAL REVOLUTION IN EUROPE

HILE THE REVOLUTION in France was opening a new political era, another revolution was transforming economic and social life. This was the Industrial Revolution, which began in England in the 1780s and spread after 1815 to continental Europe and then around the world. Because the Industrial Revolution was less dramatic than the French Revolution, some historians see industrial development as basically moderate and evolutionary. In the long perspective, however, it was rapid and brought about radical changes. Perhaps only the development of agriculture during Neolithic times had a similar impact and significance.

The Industrial Revolution profoundly modified much of human experience. It changed patterns of work, transformed the social class structure, and even altered the international balance of political and military power, giving added impetus to ongoing Western expansion into non-Western lands. It may quite possibly have saved Europe from the poverty of severe overpopulation and even from famine. How did this happen? How and why did drastic changes occur in industry, and how did these changes affect people and society? These are the questions this chapter will seek to answer. Chapter 28 will examine in detail the emergence of accompanying changes in urban civilization, while Chapter 30 will probe the consequences of industrialization in Europe for non-Western peoples.

THE INITIAL BREAKTHROUGH IN ENGLAND

The Industrial Revolution began in England. It was something new in history, and it was quite unplanned. With no models to copy and no idea of what to expect, England had to pioneer not only in industrial technology but also in social relations and urban living. Between 1793 and 1815, these formidable tasks were complicated by almost constant war with France. As the trailblazer in economic development, as France was in political change, England must command special attention.

Although many aspects of the Industrial Revolution continue to generate vigorous debate, most scholars agree that it grew out of a complex combination of factors. These factors came together in eighteenth-century England and initiated a decisive breakthrough, a breakthrough that many place in the 1780s—after the American war for independence and just before the French Revolution. Thus the great economic and political revolutions that have shaped the modern world occurred almost simultaneously, though they began in different countries. The Industrial Revolution was, however, a longer process. It was not complete in England until 1830 at the earliest, and it had no real impact on continental countries until after the Congress of Vienna ended the era of revolutionary wars in 1815.

In analyzing the causes of the late-eighteenth-century acceleration in the English economy, historians have paid particular attention to dramatic changes in agriculture, foreign trade, technology, energy supplies, and transportation. Though this chapter will also focus on these issues, one must first understand that England had other, less conspicuous, assets that provided favorable conditions for long-term economic development.

Relatively good government was one such asset. The monarchy and the aristocratic oligarchy, which jointly ruled the country after the constitutional settlement of 1688 (see Chapter 19), provided stable and predictable government. Neither civil strife nor invading armies threatened the peace of the realm. Thus the government let the domestic economy operate fairly freely and with few controls, encouraging personal initiative, technological change, and a free market.

A related asset was an experienced business class with very modern characteristics. This business class, which traced its origins to the High Middle Ages, eagerly sought to make profits and to accumulate capital.

England also had a large class of hired agricultural laborers, whose numbers were further increased by agricultural changes in the eighteenth century. These rural wage earners were relatively mobile—compared to village-bound peasants in France and western Germany, for example—and along with cottage workers they formed a potential labor force for capitalist entrepreneurs.

Three other assets supporting English economic growth stand out. First, unlike France and most other countries, England had an effective central bank and well-developed credit institutions. Second, although England may seem a rather small country today, it undoubtedly enjoyed the largest effective domestic market in eighteenth-century Europe. In an age when it was much cheaper to ship goods by water than by land, no part of England was more than twenty miles from navigable water. Beginning in the 1770s, a canal-building boom greatly enhanced this natural advantage (Map 26.1). Nor were there any tariffs within the country to hinder trade, as there were in France before 1789 and in politically fragmented Germany and Italy. Finally, only in Holland did the lower classes appear to live as well as in England. The ordinary English family did not have to spend almost everything it earned just to buy bread. It could spend more on other items, which added significantly to the total demand for manufactured goods. And growing demand for manufactured goods was probably the critical factor in initiating England's industrial breakthrough.

THE AGRICULTURAL REVOLUTION

According to an older generation of historians, England's industrial transformation depended on an earlier revolution in agriculture and rural life. Although scholars no longer believe that radical agricultural change was a necessary precondition for the industrial breakthrough, the general stress on the importance of agricultural improvement remains valid. A gradual but profound revolution in agricultural methods did promote accelerated economic growth, and that revolution mirrored the general economic leadership underpinning England's epoch-making industrial surge.

In essence, the Agricultural Revolution eliminated the traditional pattern of village agriculture found in northern and central Europe. It replaced the medieval open-field system (see page 362) with a new system of continuous rotation that resulted in more food for humans and their animals. The new agricultural system had profound implications, for it eliminated long-standing common rights as well as the fal-

MAP 26.1 Cottage Industry and Transportation in Eighteenth-Century England England had an unusually good system of navigable waterways even before river-linking canals made it better.

low. But whereas peasants and rural laborers checked the spread of the new system on the Continent in the eighteenth century, large landowners and powerful market forces overcame such opposition in England.

The new methods of agriculture originated in the Low Countries. The vibrant, dynamic middle-class society of seventeenth-century republican Holland was the most advanced in Europe in many areas of human endeavor, including agriculture. By 1650 intensive farming was well established throughout much of the Low Countries. Enclosed fields, continuous rotation, heavy manuring, and a wide variety of crops—all these innovations were present. Agriculture was highly specialized and commercialized. The same skills that grew turnips produced flax to be spun into linen for clothes and tulip bulbs to lighten the

Harvesting This harvest scene by Pieter Brueghel the Elder (ca 1525–1569) suggests how the relatively prosperous Low Countries might take the lead in agricultural development. Brueghel was a master at depicting everyday peasant life. *(The Nelson-Atkins Museum of Art, Kansas City, MO., Nelson Fund)*

heart with their beauty. The fat cattle of Holland, so beloved by Dutch painters, gave the most milk in Europe.

The reasons for early Dutch leadership in farming were basically threefold. First, the Low Countries were densely populated, and the Dutch were forced at an early date to seek maximum yields from their land and to increase it through the steady draining of marshes and swamps. Second, the growth of towns and cities—Amsterdam grew from 30,000 to 200,000 in its golden seventeenth century—provided Dutch peasants with good markets and encouraged each region to specialize in what it did best. Finally, there was the quality of the people. Oppressed by neither grasping nobles nor war-minded monarchs, the Dutch could develop their potential in a free and capitalistic society. The Low Countries became "the Mecca of foreign agricultural experts who came . . . to see Flemish agriculture with their own eyes, to write about it and to propagate its methods in their home lands."[1]

The English were the best students. They learned about water control from the Dutch, the world's leaders after centuries of effort in the skills of drainage. In the seventeenth century, Dutch experts made a great contribution to draining the extensive marshes, or fens, of wet and rainy England. On such new land, where traditions and common rights were not established, farmers introduced new crops and new rotations fairly easily.

Selective Breeding meant bigger livestock and more meat on English tables. This gigantic champion, one of the new improved shorthorn breed, was known as the Newbus Ox. Such great fat beasts were pictured in the press and praised by poets. *(Institute of Agricultural History and Museum of English Rural Life, University of Reading)*

Dutch experience was also important to Viscount Charles Townsend (1674–1738), one of the pioneers of English agriculture improvement. This lord from the upper reaches of the English aristocracy learned about turnips and clover while serving as English ambassador to Holland. In the 1710s, he was growing these crops in the sandy soil of his large estates in Norfolk in eastern England, already one of the most innovative agricultural areas in the country. When Lord Charles retired from politics in 1730 and returned to Norfolk, it was said that he spoke of turnips, turnips, and nothing but turnips. This led some wit to nickname his lordship "Turnip" Townsend. But Townsend had the last laugh. Draining extensively, manuring heavily, and sowing crops in regular rotation without fallowing, the farmers who leased Townsend's lands produced larger crops. They and he earned higher incomes. Those who had scoffed reconsidered. By 1740 agricultural improvement had become a craze among the English aristocracy.

Jethro Tull (1674–1741), part crank and part genius, was another important English innovator. A true son of the early Enlightenment, Tull constantly tested accepted ideas about farming in an effort to develop better methods through empirical research. He was especially enthusiastic about using horses for plowing, in preference to slower-moving oxen. He also advocated sowing seed with drilling equipment, rather than scattering it by hand. Drilling distributed seed evenly and at the proper depth. There were also improvements in livestock, inspired in part by the earlier successes of English country gentlemen in breeding ever-faster horses for the races and fox hunts that were their passions. Selective breeding of ordinary livestock was a marked improvement over the old pattern, which has been graphically described as little more than "the haphazard union of nobody's son with everybody's daughter."

By the mid-eighteenth century, English agriculture was in the process of a radical and technologically desirable transformation. The eventual result was that by 1870 English farmers produced 300 percent more food than they had produced in 1700, although the number of people working the land had increased by only 14 percent. This great surge of agricultural production provided food for England's rapidly growing urban population. It was a tremendous achievement.

To what extent was this technological progress a product of social injustice? The oldest and still widely accepted view is that the powerful ruling class, the English landowning aristocracy, enclosed the open fields and divided up the common pasture in such a way that poor people lost their small landholdings and were pushed off the land. The large landowners controlled Parliament, which made the laws. They had Parliament pass hundreds of "enclosure acts," each of which authorized the fencing of open fields in a given district and abolished common rights there. Small farmers who had little land and cottagers who had only common rights could no longer make a living. They lost position and security and had to work for a large landowner for wages or else move to town in search of work.

There is some validity to this idea, although more recent studies have shown that the harmful consequences of enclosure in the eighteenth century have often been exaggerated. As much as half of English farmland was already enclosed by 1750. A great wave of enclosure of English open fields into sheep pastures had already occurred in the sixteenth and early seventeenth centuries, in order to produce wool for the thriving textile industry. Subsequently, many open fields were enclosed fairly harmoniously by mutual agreement among all classes of landowners in English villages. Thus parliamentary enclosure, the great bulk of which occurred after 1760 and particularly during the Napoleonic wars, only completed a process that was in full swing. Nor did an army of landless farm laborers appear only in the last years of the eighteenth century. Much earlier, and certainly by 1700, there were perhaps two landless agricultural workers in England for every self-sufficient farmer.

These realities reflected the highly distinctive pattern of landownership that already existed in England by 1700. At one extreme were a few large landowners, at the other a large mass of laborers who held little land and worked for wages. In between stood small, self-sufficient farmers who owned their own land and substantial tenant farmers who rented land from the big landowners and hired wage laborers. Already in retreat by 1700, the small, independent English farmers continued to decline in the eighteenth century. They could not compete with the profit-minded, market-oriented tenant farmers.

The tenant farmers, many of whom had formerly been independent owners, were the key to mastering the new methods of farming. Well financed by the large landowners, the tenant farmers fenced fields, built drains, and improved the soil with fertilizers. Such improvements and the more intensive farming methods actually increased employment opportunities and did not force people off the land by eliminating jobs. But these opportunities were for wage laborers in a market economy that had completed the destruction of common rights and village agriculture.

THE GROWTH OF FOREIGN TRADE

In addition to leading Europe in agricultural improvement, Great Britain (formed in 1707 by the union of England and Scotland into a single kingdom) gradually became the leading maritime power. In the eighteenth century, British ships and merchants succeeded in dominating long-distance trade, particularly intercontinental trade across the Atlantic. This foreign trade stimulated the economy.

Britain's commercial leadership in the eighteenth century had its origins in the mercantilism of the seventeenth century (see page 595). European mercantilism was a system of economic regulations aimed at increasing the power of the state. What distinguished English mercantilism was the unusual idea that governmental economic regulations could and should serve the private interest of individuals and groups as well as the public needs of the state. As Josiah Child, a very wealthy brewer and director of the East India Company, put it, in the ideal economy "Profit and Power ought jointly to be considered."[2]

The seventeenth-century Navigation Acts reflected the desire of Great Britain to increase both its military power and its private wealth. The initial target of these instruments of economic warfare was the Dutch, who were far ahead of the English in shipping and foreign trade in the mid-seventeenth century. The Navigation Acts, in conjunction with three Anglo-Dutch wars between 1652 and 1674, did seriously damage the Dutch. By the later seventeenth century, the Netherlands was falling behind England in shipping, trade, and colonies. France then stood clearly as England's most serious rival in the competition for overseas empire. Rich in natural resources and endowed with a population three or four times that of England, continental Europe's leading military power was already building a powerful fleet and

The East India Dock, London This painting by Samuel Scott captures the spirit and excitement of British maritime expansion. Great sailing ships line the quay, bringing profit and romance from far-off India. London grew in population from 350,000 in 1650 to 900,000 in 1800, when it was twice as big as Paris, its nearest rival. *(Victoria & Albert Museum, London)*

a worldwide system of rigidly monopolized colonial trade. And France, aware that Great Britain coveted large parts of Spain's American empire, was determined to revitalize its Spanish ally. Thus from 1701 to 1763, Britain and France were locked in a series of wars to decide, in part, which nation would become the leading maritime power and claim a lion's share of the profits of Europe's overseas expansion (Map 26.2).

The first round was the War of the Spanish Succession (page 598), which resulted in major gains for Great Britain in the Peace of Utrecht (1713). France ceded Newfoundland, Nova Scotia, and the Hudson Bay territory to Britain. Spain was compelled to give Britain control of the lucrative West African slave trade—the so-called *asiento*—and to let Britain send one ship of merchandise into the Spanish colonies annually. In the course of the War of the Austrian

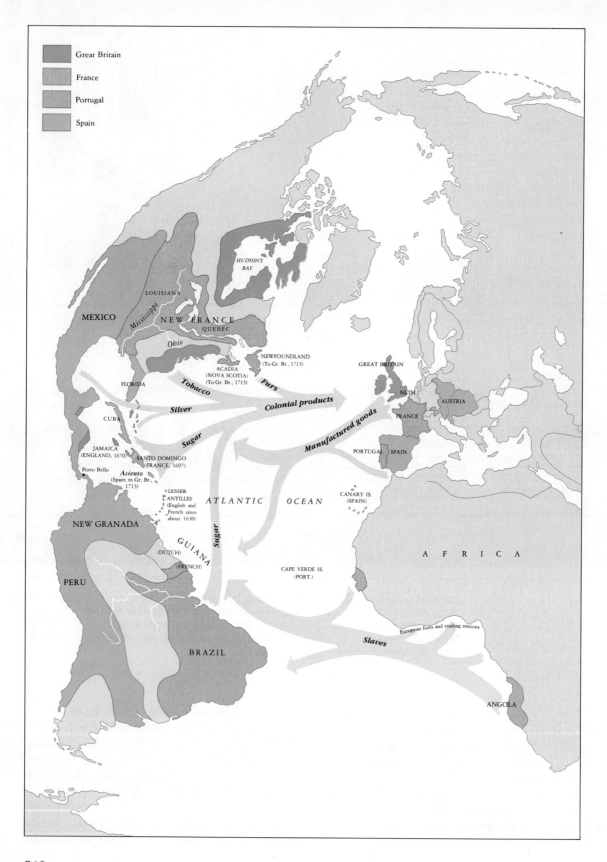

Great Britain
France
Portugal
Spain

HUDSON'S BAY

LOUISIANA

Mississippi

NEW FRANCE
QUEBEC

Ohio

MEXICO

NEWFOUNDLAND
(To Gr. Br., 1713)

ACADIA
(NOVA SCOTIA)
(To Gr. Br., 1713)

GREAT BRITAIN

FLORIDA

Tobacco

Furs

NETH.

AUSTRIA

Silver

Colonial products

FRANCE

CUBA

Sugar

Manufactured goods

JAMAICA
(ENGLAND, 1670)

SANTO DOMINGO
(FRANCE, 1697)

PORTUGAL

SPAIN

Porto Bello

Asiento
(Spain; to Gr. Br.,
1713)

LESSER
ANTILLES
(English and
French since
about 1630)

ATLANTIC   OCEAN

CANARY IS.
(SPAIN)

NEW GRANADA

GUIANA

(DUTCH)

Sugar

AFRICA

(FRENCH)

PERU

CAPE VERDE IS.
(PORT.)

European forts and trading stations

BRAZIL

Slaves

ANGOLA

Succession (1740–1748), New England colonists momentarily seized French territory in Canada.

This inconclusive stand-off helped set the stage for the Seven Years' War (1756–1763), which was the decisive round in the Franco-British competition for colonial empire. Led by William Pitt, whose grandfather had made a fortune as a trader in India, the British concentrated on using superior sea power to destroy the French fleet and choke off French commerce around the world. With the Treaty of Paris (1763), France lost all its possessions on the mainland of North America and gave up most of its holdings in India as well. By 1763, Britain had realized its goal of monopolizing a vast trade and colonial empire for its benefit.

This interconnected expansion of trade and empire marked a major step toward the Industrial Revolution, although people could not know it at the time. Since the late Middle Ages, England had successfully manufactured woolen cloth, which had provided an outstanding opportunity for profit and economic growth. By 1700 much of this cloth was exported abroad, and fully 90 percent of it was sold to Europeans. In the course of the eighteenth century, however, the states of continental Europe were trying to develop their own cottage textile industries in an effort to deal with the growth of rural poverty and population discussed in Chapter 22. Like England earlier, these states adopted protectionist, mercantilist policies. They tried, with some success, by means of tariffs and other measures to exclude competing goods from abroad, and by 1773 England was selling only about two-thirds as much woolen cloth to northern and western Europe as it had in 1700. The English economy badly needed new markets and new products in order to develop and prosper.

Protected colonial markets came to the rescue and provided a great stimulus for many branches of English manufacturing. Sales of manufactured products to the Atlantic economy—primarily the mainland colonies of North America and the West Indian sugar islands, with an important assist from West Africa and Latin America—soared from £500,000 in 1700 to £3.9 million in 1773, as may be seen in Figure

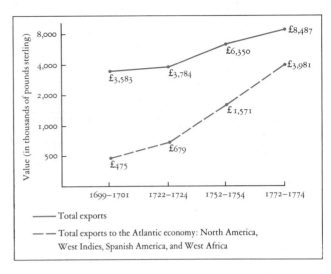

FIGURE 19.3 **Exports of English Manufactured Goods 1700–1774** While trade between England and Europe stagnated after 1700, English exports to Africa and the Americas boomed and greatly stimulated English economic development. *(Source: R. Davis, "English Foreign Trade, 1700–1774,"* Economic History Review, *2d series, 15 [1962]; 302–303)*

26.1. English exports of manufactured goods to continental Europe grew hardly at all in these years.

English exports became much more balanced and diversified. To America and Africa went large quantities of metal items—axes to frontiersmen, firearms, chains for slaveowners. There were also clocks and coaches, buttons and saddles, china and furniture, musical instruments and scientific equipment, and a host of other things. By 1750 half the nails made in England were going to the colonies. Foreign trade became the bread and butter of some industries. Thus the mercantile system formed in the seventeenth century to attack the Dutch and to win power and profit for England continued to shape trade in the eighteenth century. The English concentrated in their hands much of the demand for manufactured goods from the growing Atlantic economy. Sales to other "colonies"—Ireland and India—also rose substantially in the eighteenth century. Nor was this all. Demand from the well-integrated home market was also rising. The English were relatively well off, and their population was growing. Moreover, new methods of farming and good weather brought a period of bountiful crops and low food prices, especially before 1760. Ordinary people could buy more manufactured goods. Rising demand from home and abroad

MAP 26.2 **The Economy of the Atlantic Basin in 1701** The growth of trade encouraged both economic development and military conflict in the Atlantic Basin.

Tobacco was a key commodity in the Atlantic trade. This engraving from 1775 shows a merchant and his slaves preparing a cargo for sail. *(The British Library)*

put intense pressure on the whole system of production.

LAND AND WEALTH IN NORTH AMERICA

Britain's colonies on the North American mainland proved particularly valuable in the long run. The settlements along the Atlantic coast provided an important outlet for surplus population, so that migration abroad limited poverty in England, Scotland, and Northern Ireland. The settlers also benefited because for most of the eighteenth century they had privileged access to virtually free and unlimited land. The abundance of almost-free land also resulted in a rapid increase in the white population, which multiplied a staggering ten times between 1700 and 1774, as immigrants arrived and colonial couples raised large families. In 1774, 2.2 million whites and 330,000 blacks inhabited what would soon become the independent United States.

Rapid population growth did not reduce the settlers to poverty. On the contrary, agricultural development resulted in fairly high standards of living. It has been estimated that between 1715 and 1775 the real income of the average American was increasing about 1 percent per year per person, almost two-thirds as fast as it increased with massive industrialization between 1840 and 1959.[3] There was also an unusual degree of economic equality, by European standards. Few people were extremely rich and few were extremely poor. On the eve of the American Revolution, the *average* white man or woman in the mainland British colonies probably had the highest income and standard of living in the world.

The availability of land made labor expensive. This in turn encouraged the growth of black slavery in the southern colonies, and created a wealthy planter class with a taste for home-country luxuries.

THE FIRST FACTORIES

The pressure to produce more goods was directly related to the first decisive breakthrough of the Industrial Revolution—the creation of the world's first large factories in the English cotton textile industry. Technological innovations in the manufacture of cloth led to a whole new pattern of production and social relationships, and these trail-blazing developments deserve special consideration.

Although the putting-out system of merchant capitalism (page 684) was expanding all across Europe in the eighteenth century, this pattern of rural industry was most fully developed in England. Thus it was in England, under the pressure of growing demand, that the system's shortcomings first began to outweigh its advantages. This was especially true in the cottage textile industry after about 1760.

There was always a serious imbalance in this family enterprise: the work of four or five spinners was needed to keep one weaver steadily employed. Therefore, the wife and the husband had constantly to try to find more thread and more spinners. Widows and unmarried women—those "spinsters" who spun for their living—were recruited by the wife. Or perhaps the weaver's son went off on horseback to seek thread. The need for more thread might even lead the weaver and his wife to become small capitalist employers, putting out raw wool or cotton to other cottagers.

Deep-seated conflict between workers and employers complicated increased production. An English popular song written about 1700, called "The Clothier's Delight, or the Rich Men's Joy and The Poor Men's Sorrow," has the merchant boasting of his countless tricks used to "beat down wages":

We heapeth up riches and treasure great store
Which we get by griping and grinding the poor.
 And this is a way for to fill up our purse
 Although we do get it with many a curse.[4]

There was another problem, at least from the merchant-capitalist's point of view. Rural labor was cheap, scattered, and poorly organized. For these reasons it was hard to control. Cottage workers tended to work in spurts. After they got paid on Saturday afternoon, the men in particular tended to drink and carouse for two or three days. Indeed, Monday was called "holy Monday" because inactivity was so religiously observed. By the end of the week the weaver was probably working feverishly to make his quota. But if he did not succeed, there was little the merchant could do. When times were good and the merchant could easily sell everything produced, the weaver and his family did fairly well and were particularly inclined to loaf, to the dismay of the capitalist. Thus, in spite of its early virtues, the putting-out system in the textile industry revealed growing limitations, and the merchant-capitalist's search for more efficient methods of production intensified.

Attention focused on ways to improve spinning. Many a merchant and tinkering worker knew that a better spinning wheel promised rich rewards. Spinning of the traditional raw materials—wool and flax —proved hard to change, but cotton was different. Cotton textiles had first been imported into England from India by the East India Company, and by 1760 there was a tiny domestic industry in northern England. After many experiments over a generation, a gifted carpenter and jack-of-all-trades, James Hargreaves, invented his cotton spinning jenny about 1765. At almost the same moment a barber-turned-manufacturer, Richard Arkwright, invented (or possibly pirated) another kind of spinning machine, the

Hargreave's Spinning Jenny The loose cotton strands on the slanted bobbins passed up to the sliding carriage and then on to the spindles in back for fine spinning. By 1783 one woman could spin by hand a hundred threads at a time on an improved model. *(University of Illinois, Champaign)*

water frame. These breakthroughs produced an explosion in the infant industry. By 1790 the new machines produced ten times as much cotton yarn as had been made in 1770. By 1800 the production of cotton thread was England's most important industry.

Hargreaves's jenny was simple and inexpensive. It was also hand operated. In early models, from six to twenty-four spindles were mounted on a sliding carriage, and each spindle spun a fine, slender thread. The woman moved the carriage back and forth with one hand and turned a wheel to supply power with the other. Now it was the weaver who could not keep up with his vastly more efficient wife.

Arkwright's water frame employed a different principle. It quickly acquired a capacity of several hundred spindles and demanded much more power —water power. The water frame thus required large specialized mills, factories that employed hundreds of workers from the very beginning. The water frame could spin only coarse, strong thread, which was then put out for respinning on hand-powered cottage jennies. Around 1790 another innovation, Samuel Crompton's "mule," which combined the best aspects of the jenny and the water frame, began to require more power than the human arm could supply. Thus, all cotton spinning gradually became concentrated in factories.

The first consequences of these revolutionary developments were more beneficial than is generally believed. Cotton goods became much cheaper, and they were bought and treasured by all classes. In the past, only the wealthy could afford the comfort and cleanliness of underwear, which was called "body linen" because it was made from expensive linen cloth. Now millions of poor people, who had earlier worn nothing underneath their coarse, filthy outer garments, could afford to wear cotton slips and underpants.

The family was freed from its constant search for adequate yarn from scattered, part-time spinners, since all the thread needed could be spun in the cottage on the jenny or obtained from a nearby factory. The wages of weavers, now hard pressed to keep up with the spinners, rose markedly until about 1792. Weavers were among the best-paid workers in England. They were known to walk proudly through the streets with £5 notes stuck in their hatbands, and they dressed like the middle class.

One result of this unprecedented prosperity was that large numbers of agricultural laborers became weavers. Meanwhile, however, mechanics and capitalists were seeking to invent a power loom to save on labor costs. This Edmund Cartwright achieved in 1785. But the power looms of the factories worked poorly at first, and handloom weavers continued to receive good wages until at least 1800.

Working conditions in the early factories were less satisfactory than those of cottage weavers and spinners. But until the late 1780s, most English factories were in rural areas, where they had access to water power. These factories employed a relatively small percentage of all cotton textile workers. Since people were reluctant to work in them, factory owners often turned to children who had been abandoned by their parents and put in the care of local parishes. The parish officers often "apprenticed" such unfortunate orphans to factory owners. The parish thus saved money, and the factory owners gained workers over whom they exercised almost the authority of slave-owners. The hours were terrible, the conditions appalling. Poor children had been victimized in the past, but the nakedness of this exploitation was new and shocking.

The creation of the world's first modern factories in the English cotton textile industry in the 1770s and 1780s, which grew out of the putting-out system of cottage production, was a momentous development.

Both symbolically and in substance, the big new cotton mills marked the beginning of the Industrial Revolution in England.

ENERGY AND TRANSPORTATION

The growth of the cotton textile industry might have been stunted or cut short, however, if water from rivers and streams had remained the primary source of power for the new factories. But this did not occur. Instead, an epoch-making solution was found to the age-old problem of energy and power. It was this solution to the energy problem—a problem that has reappeared in recent times—that permitted continued rapid development in cotton textiles, the gradual generalization of the factory system, the revolution in transportation, and the triumph of the Industrial Revolution.

THE PROBLEM OF ENERGY

Human beings, like all living organisms, require energy. Adult men and women need 2,000 to 4,000 calories (units of energy) daily, simply to fuel their bodies, work, and survive. Energy comes from a variety of sources; it also takes different forms, and one form may be converted into another. Plants have been converting solar energy into caloric matter for eons. And human beings have used their toolmaking abilities to construct machines that convert one form of energy into another for their own benefit.

Prehistoric people relied on plants and plant-eating animals as their sources of energy. With the development of agriculture, early civilizations were able to increase the number of useful plants and thus the supply of energy. Some plants could be fed to domesticated animals, like the horse. Stronger than human beings, these animals converted the energy in the plants into work. In the medieval period, people began to develop water mills to grind their grain and windmills to pump water and drain swamps. In the sixteenth and seventeenth centuries, more efficient use of water and wind enabled human beings, especially Europeans, to accomplish somewhat more; intercontinental sailing ships are a prime example. Nevertheless, even into the eighteenth century, European society continued to rely for energy mainly on plants, and human beings and animals continued to perform most work. This dependence meant that Western civilization remained poor in energy and power.

Lack of power lay at the heart of the poverty that afflicted the large majority of people worldwide. The man behind the plow and the woman at the spinning wheel could employ only horsepower and human muscle in their labor. No matter how hard they worked, they could not produce very much. What people needed were new sources of energy and more power at their disposal. Then they would be able to work more efficiently, produce more, and live better.

Where was more energy to be found? Almost all energy came directly or indirectly from plants and therefore from the land: grain for people, hay for animals, and wood for heat. The land was also the principal source of raw materials needed for industrial production: wool and flax for clothing; leather for shoes; wood for housing, tools, and ironmaking. Although the land's yield could be increased, through the elimination of fallow, for example, there were definite limits to such improvements.

The shortage of energy was becoming particularly severe in England by the eighteenth century. Because of the growth of population, most of the great forests of medieval England had long ago been replaced by fields of grain and hay. Wood was in ever shorter supply; yet it remained tremendously important. In addition to serving as the primary source of heat and as a basic raw material, processed wood (charcoal) was mixed with iron ore in the blast furnace to produce pig iron. The iron industry's appetite for wood was enormous, and by 1740 the English iron industry was stagnating. Vast forests enabled Russia in the eighteenth century to become the world's leading producer of iron, much of which was exported to England. But Russia's potential for growth was limited, too, and in a few decades Russia would reach the barrier of inadequate energy that was already holding England back.

"STEAM IS AN ENGLISHMAN"

As this early energy crisis grew worse, England looked toward its abundant and widely scattered reserves of coal as an alternative to its vanishing wood. Coal was first used in England in the late Middle Ages as a source of heat. By 1640 most homes in London were heated with it, and it also provided heat for making beer, glass, soap, and other products. Coal was not used, however, to produce mechanical energy or to power machinery. It was there that coal's potential was enormous, as a simple example shows.

One pound of good bituminous coal contains about 3,500 calories of heat energy. A miner who eats 3,500 calories of food can produce about 1 horsepower-hour as he digs out 500 pounds of coal in a day, using hand tools. Even an extremely inefficient converter, which transforms only 1 percent of the heat energy in coal into mechanical energy, will produce 27 horsepower-hours of work from the 500 pounds of coal the miner cut out of the earth. Much more energy is consumed by the converter, but much more work can be done.

Early steam engines were just such inefficient converters. As more coal was produced, mines were dug deeper and deeper and were constantly filling with water. Mechanical pumps, usually powered by animals walking in circles at the surface, had to be installed. At one mine, fully five hundred horses were used in pumping. Such power was expensive and bothersome. In an attempt to overcome these disadvantages, Thomas Savery in 1698 and Thomas Newcomen in 1705 invented the first primitive steam engines.

Both engines were extremely inefficient. Both burned coal to produce steam, which was then injected into a cylinder or reservoir. In Newcomen's engine, the steam in the cylinder was cooled, creating a partial vacuum in the cylinder. This vacuum allowed the pressure of the earth's atmosphere to push the piston in the cylinder down and operate a pump. By the early 1770s, many of the Savery engines and hundreds of the Newcomen engines were operating successfully, though inefficiently, in English mines.

In the early 1760s, a gifted young Scot named James Watt (1736–1819) was drawn to a critical study of the steam engine. Watt was employed at the time by the University of Glasgow as a skilled craftsman making scientific instruments. The Scottish universities were pioneers in practical technical education, and in 1763 Watt was called on to repair a Newcomen engine being used in a physics course. After a series of observations, Watt saw why the Newcomen engine wasted so much energy: the cylinder was being heated and cooled for every single stroke of the piston. To remedy this problem, Watt added a separate condenser, where the steam could be condensed without cooling the cylinder. This splendid

The ENGINE for Raiſing Water (with a power made) by Fire

The Newcomen Engine The huge steam-filled cylinder (C) was cooled by injecting water from the tank above (G) through a pipe (M). Atmospheric pressure then pushed down the piston, raised the beam, and pumped water from the mine. *(Science Museum, London)*

invention greatly increased the efficiency of the steam engine.

To invent something in a laboratory is one thing; to make it a practical success is quite another. Watt needed skilled workers, precision parts, and capital, and the relatively advanced nature of the English economy proved essential. A partnership with a wealthy, progressive toymaker provided risk capital and a manufacturing plant. In the craft tradition of locksmiths, tinsmiths, and millwrights, Watt found skilled mechanics who could install, regulate, and repair his sophisticated engines. From ingenious manufacturers like the cannonmaker John Wilkinson, who learned to bore cylinders with a fair degree of accuracy, Watt was gradually able to purchase precision parts. This support allowed him to create an effective vacuum and regulate a complex engine. In more than twenty years of constant effort, Watt made many fur-

ther improvements. By the late 1780s, the steam engine was a practical and commercial success in England. As a nineteenth-century saying put it, "Steam is an Englishman."

The steam engine of Watt and his followers was the Industrial Revolution's most fundamental advance in technology. For the first time in history, humanity had, at least for a few generations, almost unlimited power at its disposal. For the first time, inventors and engineers could devise and implement all kinds of power equipment to aid people in their work. For the first time, abundance was at least a possibility for ordinary men and women.

The steam engine was quickly put to use in many industries in England. It made possible the production of even more coal to feed steam engines elsewhere. The steam-power plant began to replace the use of water power in the cotton-spinning mills during the 1780s, as well as in the flour, malt, and sugar mills.

Steam power promoted important breakthroughs in other industries. The English iron industry was radically transformed. The use of powerful, steam-driven bellows in blast furnaces helped ironmakers switch over rapidly from limited charcoal to unlimited coke (which is made from coal) in the smelting of pig iron after 1770. In the 1780s Henry Cort developed the puddling furnace, which allowed pig iron to be refined in turn with coke. Strong, skilled ironworkers—the puddlers—"cooked" molten pig iron in a great vat, raking off globs of refined iron for further processing. Cort also developed heavy-duty steam-powered rolling mills, which were capable of spewing out finished iron in every shape and form.

The economic consequences of these technical innovations was a great boom in the English iron industry. In 1740 annual British iron production was only 17,000 tons. With the spread of coke smelting and the first impact of Cort's inventions, production reached 68,000 tons in 1788, 125,000 tons in 1796, and 260,000 tons in 1806. In 1844 Britain produced 3 million tons of iron. This was truly phenomenal expansion. Once scarce and expensive, iron became the cheap, basic building block of the economy.

The Coming of the Railroads

Sailing ships had improved noticeably since the Age of Discovery, and the second half of the eighteenth century saw extensive construction of hard and relatively smooth roads in Europe. Yet it was passenger traffic that benefited most from this construction. Overland shipment of freight, relying solely on horsepower, was still quite limited and frightfully expensive; shippers used rivers and canals for heavy freight whenever possible. It was logical therefore that inventors would try to use steam power to improve inland transportation.

As early as 1800, an American ran a "steamer on wheels" through city streets. Other experiments followed. In the 1820s, English engineers perfected steam cars capable of carrying fourteen passengers at ten miles an hour—as fast as the mail coach. But the noisy, heavy steam automobiles frightened passing horses and damaged themselves as well as the roads with their vibrations. For the rest of the century, horses continued to reign on highways and city streets.

The coal industry had long been using plank roads and rails to move coal wagons within mines and at the surface. Rails reduced friction and allowed a horse or a human being to pull a heavier load. Thus, once a rail capable of supporting a heavy locomotive was developed in 1816, all sorts of experiments with steam engines on rails went forward. In 1825, after ten years of work, George Stephenson built an effective locomotive. In 1830 his *Rocket* sped down the track of the just-completed Liverpool and Manchester Railway at sixteen miles per hour. This was the world's first important railroad, fittingly steaming in the heart of industrial England.

The line from Liverpool to Manchester was a financial as well as a technical success, and many private companies were quickly organized to build more rail lines. These companies had to get permission for their projects from Parliament and pay for the rights of way they needed; otherwise, their freedom was great. Within twenty years, they had completed the main trunk lines of Great Britain. Other countries followed quickly with similar railway construction.

The significance of the railroad was tremendous. The railroad dramatically reduced the cost and uncertainty of shipping freight overland. This advance had many economic consequences. Previously, markets had tended to be small and local; as the barrier of high transportation costs was lowered, they became larger and even nationwide. Larger markets encouraged larger factories with more sophisticated machinery. Such factories could make goods cheaper, enabling people to pay less for them. They also tended to drive most cottage workers, many urban artisans, and other manufacturers out of business.

In all countries, the construction of railroads contributed to the growth of a class of urban workers. Cottage workers, farm laborers, and small peasants did not generally leave their jobs and homes to go directly to work in factories. However, the building of railroads created a strong demand for labor, especially unskilled labor, throughout a country. Like farm work, hard work on construction gangs was done in the open air with animals and hand tools. Many farm laborers and poor peasants, long accustomed to leaving their villages for temporary employment, went to build railroads. By the time the work was finished, life back home in the village often seemed dull and unappealing, and many men drifted to towns in search of work—with the railroad companies, in construction, in factories. By the time they

The Third-Class Carriage The French artist Honoré Daumier was fascinated by the railroad and its human significance. This great painting focuses on the peasant grandmother, absorbed in memories. The nursing mother represents love and creativity; the sleeping boy, innocence. *(The Metropolitan Museum of Art. Bequest of Mrs. H. O. Havemeyer, 1929. The H. O. Havemeyer Collection)*

sent for their wives and sweethearts to join them, they had become urban workers.

The railroad changed the outlook and values of the entire society. The last and culminating invention of the Industrial Revolution, the railroad dramatically revealed the power and increased the speed of the new age. Racing down a track at sixteen miles per hour or, by 1850, at a phenomenal fifty miles per hour was a new and awesome experience. As a noted French economist put it after a ride on the Liverpool and Manchester in 1833, "There are certain impressions that one cannot put into words!"

Some great painters, notably J. M. W. Turner (1775–1851) and Claude Monet (1840–1926), succeeded in expressing this sense of power and awe. So did the massive new train stations, the cathedrals of the industrial age. Leading railway engineers like Isambard Kingdom Brunel and Thomas Brassey, whose tunnels pierced mountains and whose bridges spanned valleys, became public idols—the astronauts of their day. Everyday speech absorbed the images of railroading. After you got up a "full head of steam," you "highballed" along. And if you didn't "go off the track," you might "toot your own whistle." The railroad fired the imagination.

BRITAIN AT MIDCENTURY

In 1851 London was the site of a famous industrial fair. This exposition was held in the newly built Crystal Palace, an architectural masterpiece made entirely of glass and iron, both of which were now cheap and abundant. For the hundreds of thousands who visited, one fact stood out. The little island of Britain—England, Wales, and Scotland—was the "workshop of the world." It alone produced two-thirds of the world's coal and more than half of its iron and cotton cloth. Britain was the first industrial nation (Map 26.3).

Britain had unlocked and developed a new source of energy. With practically unlimited power, the British economy had significantly increased its production of manufactured goods. Between 1780 and 1800, Britain doubled its production of industrial goods. Between 1801 and 1851, the gross national product (GNP) rose three and a half times at constant prices. In other words, the British increased their wealth and their national income dramatically. At the same time, the population of Great Britain boomed, growing from about 9 million in 1780 to almost 21 million in 1851.

Since the economy grew much faster than the number of people, average real income per person increased markedly. (*Real income* is the actual monetary value of people's wages after adjusting for the effects of inflation or deflation.) In fact, average real income per person in Britain just about *doubled* between 1801 and 1851, from £13 per person to £24 per person. Put very simply, and all other things being equal, the woman or man of 1851 could buy twice as much as the woman or man of 1801. Considering the poverty of the eighteenth century, poverty that all the drama and excitement of the French Revolution did little to reduce, this would appear to be a monumental achievement.

But perhaps all other things were not equal. Perhaps workers, farmers, and ordinary people did not share in the new wealth. Perhaps only the rich got richer, while the poor got poorer or made no progress. This great issue will be examined after a look at the spread of the Industrial Revolution from Britain to the Continent.

THE SPREAD OF THE INDUSTRIAL REVOLUTION

The new methods of the Industrial Revolution spread slowly at first. Whereas Britain's economy began to speed up about 1780 and had created an industrial urban society by 1850, the economies of con-

MAP 26.3 The Industrial Revolution in England, ca 1850 Industry concentrated in the rapidly growing cities of the north and the midlands, where rich coal and iron deposits were in close proximity.

tinental Europe began to follow only after 1815 and particularly after about 1830. First Belgium took up the challenge; then between about 1840 and 1860, France and the various states of Germany began developing rapidly, as did the United States. After 1870, Sweden, Russia, and Japan started to industrialize, and during the twentieth century many more countries did so.

THE CHALLENGE OF INDUSTRIALIZATION

If poverty was so widespread in Europe and if industrial development created so much more wealth per person in Great Britain, why did continental countries wait years and even decades before they followed the British example? The eighteenth century was an era of agricultural improvement, population increase, expanding foreign trade, and growing cottage industry. England led in these developments, but other countries participated in the general trend. Thus, when the pace of English industry began to accelerate in the 1780s, countries like France began to copy the new methods. English industry enjoyed clear superiority, but the Continent was not very far behind.

By 1815, however, the situation was quite different. In spite of wartime difficulties, English industry maintained the momentum of the 1780s and continued to grow and improve rapidly between 1789 and 1815. On the Continent, the political and economic upheavals that began with the French Revolution had another effect. They disrupted trade, created runaway inflation, and fostered social anxiety. War severed normal communications between England and the Continent, severely handicapping continental efforts to use new British machinery and technology. Moreover, the years from 1789 to 1815 were, even for the privileged French economy, a time of "national catastrophe"—in the graphic words of a leading French historian.[5] Thus, whatever the French Revolution and the Napoleonic era meant politically, economically and industrially they meant that France and the rest of Europe were much further behind Britain in 1815 than in 1789.

This widening gap made it more difficult for other countries to follow the British example in energy and industry after 1815. British goods were being produced very economically, and they had come to dominate world markets completely while the continental states were absorbed in war between 1792 and 1815. In addition, British technology had become so advanced and complicated that very few engineers or skilled technicians outside England understood it. Moreover, the technology of steam power had grown much more expensive. It involved large investments in the iron and coal industries and, after 1830, required the existence of railroads, which were very costly. Continental businessmen had great difficulty finding the large sums of money the new methods demanded, and there was a shortage of laborers accustomed to working in factories. Landowners and government officials were often so suspicious of the new form of industry and the changes it brought that they did little at first to encourage it. All these disadvantages slowed the spread of modern industry (Map 26.4).

After 1815, however, when continental countries began to industrialize seriously, they had at least two important advantages. First, they did not need to develop, ever so slowly and expensively, their own advanced technology. Instead, they could simply "borrow" the new methods developed in Great Britain, as well as engineers and some of the financial resources they lacked. Further, European countries like France and Russia had a second, enormously important asset that many non-Western areas lacked in the nineteenth century. They had strong independent governments, which did not fall under foreign political control. These governments could fashion economic policies to serve their own interests, as they proceeded to do. They would eventually use the power of the state to promote the growth of industry and catch up with Britain.

AGENTS OF INDUSTRIALIZATION

The British realized the great value of their technical discoveries and tried to keep their secrets to themselves. Until 1825 it was illegal for artisans and skilled mechanics to leave Britain; until 1843 the export of textile machinery and other equipment was forbidden. Many talented, ambitious workers, however, slipped out of the country illegally and introduced the new methods abroad.

One such man was William Cockerill, a Lancashire carpenter. He and his sons began building cotton-spinning equipment in French-occupied Belgium in 1799. In 1817 the most famous son, John Cockerill, began converting an old summer palace near Liège in southern Belgium. Cockerill converted the palace into a large industrial enterprise, which produced machinery, steam engines, and then railway locomotives. He also established modern ironworks and coal mines.

Cockerill's plants became an industrial nerve center, continually gathering new information and transmitting it across Europe. Many skilled British workmen came, illegally, to work for Cockerill, and some went on to found their own companies throughout Europe. Newcomers brought the latest plans and secrets, so that Cockerill could boast that, ten days after an industrial advance occurred in Britain, he knew all about it in Belgium. Thus, British technicians and skilled workers were a powerful force in the spread of early industrialization.

MAP 26.4 Continental Industrialization, ca 1850 Though continental countries were beginning to make progress by 1850, they still lagged far behind England. For example, continental railroad building was still in an early stage, whereas the English rail system was essentially complete.

Another instructive career is that of Fritz Harkort, a pioneer in the German machinery industry. Serving in England as a Prussian army officer during the Napoleonic wars, Harkort was impressed and enchanted with what he saw. He concluded that Germany had to match all these English achievements as quickly as possible. Setting up shop in an abandoned castle in the still-tranquil Ruhr Valley, Harkort felt an almost religious calling to build steam engines and become the "Watt of Germany."

Harkort's basic idea was simple, but it was extremely difficult to carry out. Lacking trained laborers, Harkort turned to England for experienced, though expensive, mechanics. He could not be choosy, and he longed for the day he could afford to replace the haughty foreigners with his fellow countrymen. Getting materials also posed a great problem, and he had to import the thick iron boilers he needed from England at great cost. German roads

were so bad that steam engines had to be built at the works, completely dismantled and shipped piece by piece to the buyer, and then reassembled by Harkort's technicians.

In spite of all these problems, Harkort built and sold engines, and he won fame and praise. His ambitious efforts also resulted in large financial losses for himself and his partners. These proved fatal, for Harkort's enterprise, like almost all the others of the day, was a private, capitalistic undertaking. It could not lose money indefinitely. In 1832, after sixteen years of activity and accomplishment, Harkort was forced out of his company by his financial backers, who cut back operations to reduce losses. His career illustrates both the great efforts of a few important business leaders to duplicate the British achievement and the difficulty of the task.

Support from the government often helped businessmen in continental countries to overcome some of their difficulties. Tariff protection was one such support. For example, after Napoleon's wars ended in 1815, France was suddenly flooded with cheaper and better English goods. The French government responded by laying high tariffs on many English imports, in order to protect the French economy. After 1815 continental governments bore the cost of building roads and canals to improve transportation, and they also bore to a significant extent the cost of building railroads.

The career of the German journalist and thinker Friedrich List (1789–1846) reflects government's greater role in the Industrial Revolution on the Continent than in England. List considered the growth of modern industry of the utmost importance because manufacturing was a primary means of increasing people's well-being and relieving their poverty. Moreover, List was a dedicated nationalist. He wrote that the "wider the gap between the backward and advanced nations becomes, the more dangerous it is to remain behind." For an agricultural nation was not only poor but weak, increasingly unable to defend itself and maintain its political independence. To promote industry was to defend the nation.

The practical policy List focused on in articles and in his *National System of Political Economy* (1841) was the tariff. He supported the formation of a customs union, or *Zollverein,* among the separate German states. Such a tariff union came into being in 1834. It allowed goods to move between the German member states without tariffs, and a single uniform tariff was erected against all other nations. List wanted a high protective tariff to encourage German industrial growth. He denounced the English doctrine of free trade as little more than England's attempt "to make the rest of the world, like the Hindus, its serfs in all industrial and commercial relations." By the 1840s List's ideas were increasingly popular in Germany and elsewhere.

Banks, like governments, also played a larger and more creative role on the Continent than in England. Previously, almost all banks in Europe had been private partnerships, which were content to deal with a few rich clients and a few big merchants. They avoided industry. In the 1830s, two important Belgian banks pioneered in a new direction. They operated as big corporations with many stockholders, large and small. Thus their financial resources were large. The banks were able to use that money to de-

velop industrial companies. They became, in short, industrial banks.

Similar banks became important in France and Germany in the 1850s. They established and developed many railroads and many companies working in heavy industry. The most famous such bank was the Crédit Mobilier of Paris, founded by Isaac and Emile Pereire, two young Jewish journalists from Bordeaux. The Crédit Mobilier advertised extensively. It used the savings of thousands of small investors, as well as the resources of big ones. The activities of the bank were far-reaching; it built railroads all over France and Europe. As Emile Pereire had said in 1835, "It is not enough to outline gigantic programs on paper. I must write my ideas on the earth."

Industrial banks like the Crédit Mobilier mobilized the savings of thousands of small investors and invested those savings in industry and transportation, particularly in the 1850s. In doing so, the directors of these banks helped their countries find the capital needed for industrialization. They also often made themselves very wealthy.

CAPITAL AND LABOR

Industrial development brought new social relations and problems between capital and labor. A new group of factory owners and industrial capitalists arose. These men strengthened the wealth and size of the middle class, which had previously been made up mainly of merchants and professional people. The nineteenth century became the golden age of the middle class. Modern industry also created a much larger group—the factory workers. For the first time, large numbers of men and women came together under one roof to work with complicated machinery for major capitalists and large companies. What was the nature of relations between these two new groups—capital and labor? Did the new industrial middle class ruthlessly exploit the workers, as Karl Marx and others have charged?

THE NEW CLASS OF FACTORY OWNERS

Early industrialists operated in a highly competitive economic system, and success and large profits were

Heavy Industry required skilled workers and large capital investments. In this illustration English dignitaries visit a plant with a new technology for making steel wheels. *(BBC Hulton/The Bettman Archive)*

by no means certain. Manufacturers, therefore, waged a constant battle to cut their production costs and stay afloat. Most profit had to go back into the business for new and better machinery. "Dragged on by the frenzy of this terrible life," according to one of his dismayed critics, the struggling manufacturer had "no time for niceties. He must conquer or die, make a fortune or drown himself."[6]

The early industrialists came from a variety of backgrounds. Many, like Harkort, were from well-established merchant families, who provided capital and contacts. Others, like Watt and Cockerill, were of modest means, especially in the early days. Artisans and skilled workmen of exceptional ability had unparalleled opportunities. The ethnic and religious groups that had been discriminated against in the traditional occupations controlled by the landed aristocracy jumped at the new chances. Quakers and Scots were tremendously important in England; Protestants and Jews dominated banking in Catholic France. Many of the industrialists were newly rich, and, not surprisingly, they were very proud and self-satisfied.

As factories grew larger, opportunities declined, at least in well-developed industries. It became considerably harder for a gifted but poor young mechanic to end up as a wealthy manufacturer. Formal education became more important as a means of advancement, and formal education at the advanced level was expensive. In England by 1830 and in France and Germany by 1860, leading industrialists were more likely to have inherited their well-established enterprises, and they were financially much more secure than their fathers and grandfathers. They were also aware of a greater gap between themselves and their workers.

THE NEW FACTORY WORKERS

The social consequences of the Industrial Revolution have long been hotly debated. Since any honest observer will see that some conditions got better and others got worse, vigorous debate is likely to continue. (Also, industry promoted rapid urbanization with its own great problems, as will be shown in Chapter 28.) Nevertheless, for workers and ordinary families, the Industrial Revolution brought a great transformation, which was, on balance, desirable. It marked a decisive step forward from the pattern of preindustrial life for the common people and the poor.

The condition of English workers in the Industrial Revolution has always generated the most controversy among historians, because England was the first country to industrialize and because the social consequences seem harshest there. Before 1850, other countries had not proceeded very far with industrialization, and almost everyone agrees that the economic conditions of European workers improved after 1850. The countries that followed England were able to benefit from English experience in social as well as technical matters. Thus the early English Industrial Revolution provides the strongest case for the harmful social consequences of modern industrial development, at least prior to 1914, and it is fitting to focus on it.

From the beginning, the Industrial Revolution in England had its critics. Among the first were the romantic poets. William Blake (1757–1827) called the early factories "satanic mills" and protested against the hard life of the London poor. William Wordsworth (1770–1850) lamented the destruction of the rural way of life and the pollution of the land and water. Doctors and reformers wrote eloquently of problems in the factories and new towns. Some handicraft workers—notably the Luddites, who attacked whole factories in northern England in 1812 and after—smashed the new machines, which they believed were putting them out of work.

Another early critic was Friedrich Engels (1820–1895), the future revolutionary and colleague of Karl Marx. After studying conditions in northern England, this young middle-class German published *The Condition of the Working Class in England* in 1844. Engels cast the problem of industrial life in class terms. "At the bar of world opinion," he wrote, "I charge the English middle classes with mass murder, wholesale robbery, and all the other crimes in the calendar."[7] Engels's charge of middle-class exploitation and increasing worker poverty was embellished by Marx and later socialists. It was extremely influential.

Meanwhile, other observers believed that conditions were improving for the working class. Andrew Ure wrote in 1835 in his study of the cotton industry that conditions in most factories were not harsh and were even quite good. Edwin Chadwick, a great and conscientious government official, well acquainted with the problems of the working class, concluded that the "whole mass of the laboring community" was increasingly able "to buy more of the necessities and minor luxuries of life."[8]

If all the contemporary indictments and all the defenses were counted up, those who thought conditions were getting worse for working people would probably be the majority. Yet it is clear that opinions differed greatly. In an attempt to go deeper into the problem, historians must look at different kinds of sources.

Statistical evidence is one such source. If working people suffered a great decline, then they must have bought less and less food, clothing, and other necessities as time went on. The purchasing power of the working person's wages must have declined drastically.

At the end of the nineteenth century, dispassionate British statisticians tried to pull together all the evidence on wages and prices and thereby measure what working-class people could or could not have bought. There were many gaps and shortcomings in the available numbers, but this approach does offer important insights.

During the period from about 1750 to 1790, when cottage industry was still dominant, the purchasing power of the average British laborer's wages seems to have risen somewhat. The workers—primarily cottage workers, artisans, and farm hands—could buy more goods, like food and clothing, over the years. Wages in industry were substantially higher than in agriculture, and all kinds of wages rose faster in the industrializing areas of the north than in the purely agricultural counties of the south. The cautious conclusion must be that from 1750 to 1790 the growth of industry made for a more abundant life for working people, in terms of material goods.

The years from 1792 to 1815, a period of constant war against revolutionary and Napoleonic France, brought very different circumstances. Wages rose, but they did not keep up with inflation. Food prices rose most, as the price of wheat approximately doubled from 1790 to 1810. The condition of the working poor declined.

Between 1815 and 1850, the purchasing power of workers' wages increased again. Money wages remained steady or fell somewhat, but prices fell more. The fullest studies show that the real wages of the average worker—agricultural and industrial—increased 25 percent between 1800 and 1825 and another 40 percent between 1825 and 1850.[9] The trend was definitely upward, but the course was erratic. Between 1820 and 1840, real wages increased by only 5 to 10 percent. However, the wages of unskilled workers in British industry were again, as before 1790, about twice as high as those of unskilled workers in British agriculture. In short, throughout the Industrial Revolution, with the exception of the wartime period, there was apparently substantial economic improvement for British workers.

This important conclusion must be qualified, though. Increased purchasing power meant more goods, but it did not necessarily mean greater happiness. Also, these figures do not say anything about how the level of unemployment may have risen, for the simple reason that there are no good unemployment statistics from this period. Furthermore, the hours in the average workweek increased; to an unknown extent, workers earned more simply because they worked more. Finally, the wartime decline was of great importance. The war years were formative years for the new factory labor force, and they colored the early experience of modern industrial life in somber tones.

Another way to consider workers' standard of living is to look at the goods they purchased. Again the evidence is somewhat contradictory. Speaking generally, workers ate somewhat more food of higher nutritional quality as the Industrial Revolution progressed, except during wartime. Diets became more varied; people ate more potatoes, dairy products, fruits, and vegetables.

Clothing improved, but housing for working people did not. In short, per capita use of specific goods supports the position that the standard of living of the working classes rose, at least moderately, during the Industrial Revolution. The rich did get richer. So did the poor to some extent, especially if they worked in industry.

CONDITIONS OF WORK

What about working conditions? Did workers earn more only at the cost of working longer and harder? Were workers exploited harshly by the new factory owners?

The first factories were cotton mills, which began functioning along rivers and streams in the 1770s. Cottage workers, accustomed to the putting-out system, were reluctant to work in factories even when they received relatively good wages, because factory work was different from what they were used to and unappealing. In the factory, workers had to keep up with the machine and follow its tempo. They had to show up every day and work long, monotonous hours. Factory workers had to adjust their daily lives to the shrill call of the factory whistle.

Cottage workers were not used to that kind of life and discipline. All members of the family worked hard and long, but in spurts, setting their own pace. They could interrupt their work when they wanted to. Women and children could break up their long hours of spinning with other tasks, and in good times the men could enjoy a long weekend of relaxation and drinking.

Also, early factories resembled English poorhouses, where totally destitute people went to live on welfare. Some poorhouses were industrial prisons, where the inmates had to work in order to receive their food and lodging. The similarity between large brick factories and large stone poorhouses increased the cottage workers' fear of factories and their hatred of factory discipline.

It was cottage workers' reluctance to work in factories that prompted the early cotton mill owners to turn to abandoned and pauper children for their labor. As noted earlier, they contracted with local officials to employ large numbers of these children, who had no say in the matter. Pauper children were often badly treated and terribly overworked in the mills, as they were when they were apprenticed as chimney sweeps, market girls, shoemakers, and so forth. In the eighteenth century, semiforced child labor seemed necessary and was socially accepted. From our modern point of view, it was cruel exploitation and a blot on the record of the new industrial system.

By 1790 the early pattern was rapidly changing. The use of pauper apprentices was in decline, and in 1802 it was forbidden by Parliament. Many more factories were being built, mainly in urban areas, where they could use steam rather than water power and attract a work force more easily than in the countryside. The need for workers was great. Indeed, people came from near and far to work in the cities, both as factory workers and as laborers, builders, and domestic servants. Yet, as they took these new jobs, working people did not simply give in to a system of labor that had formerly repelled them. Rather, they

Cotton Mill Workers Family members often worked side by side in industry. Here women and children are combing raw cotton and drawing it into loose strands called rovings, which will then be spun into fine thread. *(The Mansell Collection)*

helped modify the system by carrying over old, familiar working traditions.

For one thing, they came to the mills and the mines as family units. This was how they had worked on farms and in the putting-out system. The mill or mine owner bargained with the head of the family and paid him or her for the work of the whole family. In the cotton mills, children worked for their mothers or fathers, collecting wastes and "piecing" broken threads together. In the mines, children sorted coal and worked the ventilation equipment. Their mothers hauled coal in the narrow tunnels below the surface, while their fathers hewed with pick and shovel at the face of the seam.

The preservation of the family as an economic unit in the factories from the 1790s on made the new surroundings more tolerable, both in Great Britain and in other countries during the early stages of industrialization. Parents disciplined their children, making firm measures socially acceptable, and directed their upbringing. The presence of the whole family meant that children and adults worked the same long hours (twelve-hour shifts were normal in cotton mills in 1800). In the early years, some very young children were employed solely to keep the family together. Manufacturer Jedediah Strutt, for example, believed children should be at least ten years old to work in his mills, but he reluctantly employed seven-year-olds to satisfy their parents. Adult workers were not particularly interested in limiting the minimum working age or hours of their children, as long as they worked side by side. Only when technical changes threatened to place control and discipline in the hands of impersonal managers and foremen did they protest against inhuman conditions in the name of their children.

But some enlightened employers and social reformers in Parliament definitely felt otherwise. "In an age of rising standards of humanitarianism the few were determined to impose higher standards on the many; and were able to exploit developing means of

Girl Dragging Coal Tubs Published by reformers in Parliament in 1842, this picture shocked public opinion and contributed to the Mines Act of 1842. *(The British Library)*

mass communication to do it."[10] These reformers had important successes.

Their first major accomplishment was the Factory Act of 1833. It limited the workday for children between nine and thirteen to eight hours and that of adolescents between fourteen and eighteen to twelve hours. The law also prohibited the employment of children under nine; they were to be enrolled in the elementary schools factory owners were required to establish. Since efficiency required standardized shifts for all workers, the Factory Act shattered the pattern of whole families working together in the factory. The employment of children in factories declined rapidly. Similarly, the Mines Act of 1842 prohibited all women and boys under ten from working underground.

Ties of blood and kinship remained important in other ways in England in the formative years between about 1790 and 1840. Many manufacturers and builders hired workers not directly but through subcontractors. They paid the subcontractors on the basis of what the subcontractors and their crews produced—for smelting so many tons of pig iron or moving so much dirt or gravel for a canal or roadbed. Subcontractors in turn hired and fired their own workers, many of whom were friends and relations. The subcontractor might be as harsh as the greediest capitalist, but the relationship between subcontractor and work crew was close and personal. This kind of traditional relationship was more acceptable to workers than impersonal factory discipline. This system also provided people an easy way to find a job. Even today, a friend or relative who is a foreman is often worth a hundred formal application forms.

Ties of kinship were particularly important for newcomers, who often traveled considerable distances to find work. Many urban workers in Great Britain were from Ireland. Forced out of rural Ireland by population growth and deteriorating economic conditions from 1817 on, Irish in search of jobs could not be choosy; they took what they could get. As early as 1824, most of the workers in the Glasgow cotton mills were Irish; in 1851 one-sixth of the population of the great port of Liverpool was Irish. Even when Irish workers were not related directly by blood, they were held together by ethnic and religious ties. Like other immigrant groups elsewhere, they worked together, formed their own neighborhoods, and not only survived but thrived.

A Mature Working Class

By about 1850, the working people of urban Britain had, like British industry, gone a long way toward attaining maturity. Family employment in the factory

"Be United and Industrious" This handsome membership certificate of the "new model" Amalgamated Society of Engineers exalts the nobility of skilled labor and the labor movement. Union members are shown rejecting the call of Mars, the God of War, and accepting well-deserved honors from the Goddess of Peace. Other figures represent the strength of union solidarity, famous English inventors, and the trades of the members. *(Library of Congress)*

had given way to the employment of adults, for whom the discipline of the clock and the regularity of the machine were familiar taskmasters. Gone were violent demonstrations against industrialization. In their place were increasing acceptance of the emerging industrial system and an ongoing effort to make that system serve workers better.

In Great Britain and in other countries later on, workers slowly created a labor movement to serve their needs. In 1799, partly in panicked reaction to the French Revolution, Parliament had passed the Combination Acts outlawing unions and strikes. These acts were widely disregarded by workers. Societies of skilled factory workers organized unions, as printers, papermakers, carpenters, and other such craftsmen had long since done. The unions sought to control the number of skilled workers, limit apprenticeship to members' own children, and bargain with owners over wages. They were not afraid to strike; there was, for example, a general strike of adult cotton spinners in Manchester in 1810. In the face of widespread union activity, Parliament repealed the Combination Acts in 1824, and unions were tolerated though not fully accepted after 1825.

The next stage in the development of the British trade-union movement was the attempt to create a single large national union. This effort was led not so much by working people as by social reformers like Robert Owen (1771–1858). Owen, a self-made cotton manufacturer, had pioneered in industrial relations by combining firm discipline with concern for the health, safety, and hours of his workers. After 1815 he experimented with cooperative and socialist communities, including one at New Harmony, Indiana. Then, in 1834, Owen organized one of the largest and most visionary of the early national unions, the Grand National Consolidated Trades Union. When this and other grandiose schemes collapsed, the British labor movement moved once again after 1851 in the direction of bread-and-butter craft unions. The most famous of these "new model" unions was the Amalgamated Society of Engineers. These craft unions won real benefits for their members by fairly conservative means and thus became an accepted part of the industrial scene.

The maturity of British workers was also expressed in direct political activity in defense of their own interests. After the collapse of Owen's national trade union, a great deal of the energy of working people went into the Chartist movement, whose goal was political democracy. The key Chartist demand—that all men be given the right to vote—became the great hope of millions of aroused people. Workers were also active in campaigns to limit the workday in the factories to ten hours and to permit duty-free importation of wheat into Great Britain to secure cheap bread. Thus working people played an active role in shaping the new industrial system. Clearly, British workers were neither helpless victims nor passive beneficiaries.

THE ALTERNATIVE TO INDUSTRIALIZATION

What was the alternative to the Industrial Revolution and the new urban society? What would have been the likely course of events—the likely alternative for Europe—if industrialization had not occurred? It is impossible to know exactly, yet a look at general developments and at the case of Ireland, which did not industrialize, may shed some light on this question.

THE GROWTH OF POPULATION

The drama of industrialization must be viewed alongside the drama of rapid population growth. Europe's population began growing after 1720 (pages 682–684), leading to severe pressures on available resources and overpopulation in many areas. Large numbers of people had serious difficulty growing or buying the food they needed. There was widespread underemployment, acute poverty, and constant migration in search of work.

All these forces operated during and after the era of the French Revolution. Europe had roughly 140 million people in 1750, 188 million in 1800, and 266 million in 1850—an increase of almost 40 percent in each half-century. Overpopulation worsened between 1800 and 1850 on much of the Continent, most noticeably in Flanders, parts of Scandinavia, and southwestern Germany. One result was migration from the countryside to nearby cities and towns, where unskilled laborers were already irregularly employed and poorly paid. Another result was that growing numbers of peasants liquidated their small and inadequate landholdings and went abroad. Thus, in the early nineteenth century, particularly in the hungry 1840s, many German and Swedish settlers tried their luck and skill on prairie lands of the American Midwest.

The pressure of increasing numbers and rural poverty was most severe in Ireland. Although Ireland supplied many workers for factories in Britain, Ireland itself did not industrialize in the nineteenth century. Therefore, although Ireland was a particularly oppressed and exploited nation, its fate could have been that of much of Europe if not for the Industrial Revolution.

THE POTATO FAMINE IN IRELAND

Late eighteenth-century Ireland was a conquered country. The great mass of the population (outside the northern counties of Ulster, which were partly Presbyterian) were Irish Catholic peasants, who rented their land from a tiny minority of Church of England Protestants, many of whom lived in England (page 697). These Protestant landlords lacked the improving zeal of their English counterparts. They knew they were perched on top of a volcano that erupted periodically, but they were quite content to use their powers to grab as much as possible, as quickly as possible.

The result was that the condition of the Irish peasantry around 1800 was abominable. The typical peasant family lived in a wretched cottage made of mud and could afford neither shoes nor stockings. Hundreds of shocking accounts describe hopeless poverty. For a French traveler, Ireland was "pure misery, naked and hungry. . . . I saw the American Indian in his forests and the black slave in his chains, and I believed that I was seeing in their pitiful condition the most extreme form of human misery; but that was before I knew the lot of poor Ireland."[11] Yet in spite of these terrible conditions, population growth sped onward. The 3 million of 1725 reached 4 million in 1780 and doubled to 8 million in 1840. Between 1780 and 1840, 1.75 million men and women left Ireland for Britain and America.

The population of Ireland grew so quickly for three reasons: extensive cultivation of the potato, early marriage, and ruthless exploitation of peasants by landlords. The potato, first introduced into Ireland in the late sixteenth century, was the principal food of the Irish peasantry by the last years of the eighteenth century. The reason for dependence on the potato was originally the pressure of numbers, which forced the peasants to wring as many calories as they could out of a given piece of land. But once peasants began to live almost exclusively on potatoes, many more people could exist. A single acre of land spaded and planted with potatoes could feed a family of six for a year, whereas it would take at least two and probably four acres of grain and pasture to feed the same number. Moreover, the potato was not choosy and could thrive on boggy wastelands.

Needing only a potato patch of an acre or two for survival, Irish boys and girls married much earlier

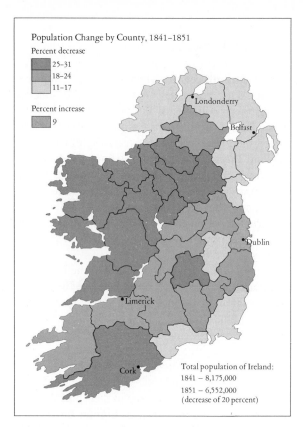

Population Change by County, 1841–1851

Percent decrease
- 25–31
- 18–24
- 11–17

Percent increase
- 9

Total population of Ireland:
1841 – 8,175,000
1851 – 6,552,000
(decrease of 20 percent)

MAP 26.5 The Irish Potato Famine Though all Ireland suffered, population losses were highest in the west were dependency on the potato was greatest.

than did their counterparts in rural England and France by the end of the eighteenth century. Setting up housekeeping was easy, for a cabin of mud and stone could be slapped together in a few days with the willing assistance of the young couple's neighbors and relatives. A mat for a bed, a chair or two, a table, and an iron pot to boil potatoes were easily acquired. To be sure, the young couple was accepting the life of extreme poverty that travelers and people of good conscience lamented. They would literally live on potatoes—ten pounds a day every day all year long for the average male—moistened with a cup of milk if they were lucky.

Nonetheless, the decision to marry early and have large families was quite reasonable, given Irish conditions. Because landlords, leased land only for short periods on uncertain terms, peasants had no incentive to make permanent improvements. Anything beyond what preserved the peasants from absolute

starvation was extorted from them. Poverty thus being inescapable in rural Ireland, it was better shared with a wife or husband. Children were a precious asset, as in many poor countries today, for there was no welfare or social security system, and an infirm or aged person's best hope of escaping starvation was a dutiful son or a loving daughter.

As the population continued to grow, conditions became increasingly precarious. The peasantry depended on a single crop, the size of which varied substantially from year to year. Potato failures cannot be detected in time to plant other crops, nor can potatoes be stored for more than a year. Furthermore, a potato economy is a subsistence economy. It lacks a well-developed network of roads and trade capable of distributing other foods in time of disaster. From 1820 on, deficiencies in the potato crop became increasingly serious. Disease in the potato crop was becoming more common, and the accompanying fever epidemics that struck the population were growing more frequent. Some great catastrophe in the near future was almost inevitable.

In 1845 and 1846 and again in 1848 and 1851, the potato crop failed in Ireland and throughout much of Europe. The general result was high food prices, widespread suffering, and social unrest. In Ireland, which was furthest down the road to rural overpopulation and dependence on a disease-prone plant, the result was unmitigated disaster—the Great Famine. Blight attacked the young plants, the leaves withered, and the tubers rotted. Widespread starvation and mass fever epidemics followed. Cannibalism occurred, although starving people generally lived on the carcasses of diseased cattle, dogs, and horses and on herbs of the field. In some places, dead people were found with grass in their mouths.

Total losses were staggering. The population of Ireland was roughly 8 million in 1845, and without the famine it would have reached 9 million in 1851 (Map 26.5). But that year, Ireland's population was only 6.5 million. Fully 1 million emigrants fled the famine between 1845 and 1851 (2 million left between 1840 and 1855), going primarily to the United States and Great Britain. Thus at least 1.5 million people died or went unborn because of the disaster. The British government's efforts at famine relief were too little and too late. Moreover, the government continued to collect its taxes, and the landlords continued to demand their rents. Tenants who could not pay were evicted

Evicting Irish Peasants, 1848 Unable to pay their rent, famine-stricken peasants are ordered from their home, which is already being torn down. Soldiers with fixed bayonets stand ready to quell any disturbance. *(Illustrated London News/Library of Congress)*

and their homes broken up or burned. Famine or no, Ireland was still the conquered jewel of foreign landowners.

The Great Famine shattered and reversed the pattern of Irish population growth. Alone among the nations of Europe, Ireland's numbers declined in the nineteenth century, to 4.4 million in 1911. Ireland remained a land of continuous out-migration. It also became a land of late marriage and widespread celibacy, as the landowning classes discouraged potato farming and converted much of the country into pasture for cattle and sheep. After great population decline and untold suffering, Ireland found a new demographic equilibrium within the framework of a poor pastoral economy.

The fate of Ireland has real relevance for an understanding of the Industrial Revolution. The rapid population growth without industrialization that occurred in Ireland between 1780 and 1845 occurred elsewhere, too—in central Russia, in western Germany, and in southern Italy, to name only three crucial regions. In these areas, there were indications of acute poverty and overpopulation, and the potato played a crucial role as it had done in Ireland. In Prussia, for example, annual potato production grew from 1 to 11 million tons from 1815 to 1860. By 1850 in some parts of Europe, bread was a luxury; workers and peasants were subsisting almost entirely on potatoes. In 1500 the average German had eaten about 200 pounds of meat a year; in 1850 his counterpart ate about 40 pounds.[12] The standard of living was declining. Other Irelands were in the making.

Population growth threatened to produce a morass of rural poverty, a demographic catastrophe, or both. In this connection, the historian T. S. Ashton once argued that the Industrial Revolution was the salvation rather than the curse of England and of the parts of Europe fortunate enough to follow England's lead. He may have overstated the case, but Ashton was surely closer to the truth than those who persist in arguing the contrary. The alternative to the revolution in energy and industry would probably have been, sooner or later, disaster.

NOTES

1. B. H. Slicher van Bath, *The Agrarian History of Western Europe, A.D. 500–1850* (New York: St. Martin's Press, 1963), p. 240.
2. Quoted in C. Wilson, *England's Apprenticeship, 1603–1763* (London: Longmans, Green, 1965), p. 169.
3. G. Taylor, "America's Growth Before 1840," *Journal of Economic History* 24 (December 1970):427–444.
4. Quoted in P. Mantoux, *The Industrial Revolution in the Eighteenth Century* (New York: Harper & Row, 1961), p. 75.
5. M. Lévy-Leboyer, *Les banques européennes et l'industrialisation dans la première moitié du XIXe siècle* (Paris: Presses Universitaires de France, 1964), p. 29.
6. J. Michelet, *The People* (Urbana: University of Illinois Press, 1973, originally published 1846), p. 64.
7. F. Engels, *The Condition of the Working Class in England,* trans. and ed., W. O. Henderson and W. H. Chaloner (Stanford, Calif.: Stanford University Press, 1968), p. xxiii.
8. Quoted in W. A. Hayek, ed., *Capitalism and the Historians* (Chicago: University of Chicago Press, 1954), p. 126.
9. P. Deane and W. A. Cole, *British Economic Growth, 1688–1959* (Cambridge, Eng.: Cambridge University Press, 1964), p. 25.
10. P. Mathias, *The First Industrial Nation: An Economic History of Britain, 1700–1914* (New York: Charles Scribner's Sons, 1969), p. 205.

11. Quoted in G. O'Brien, *The Economic History of Ireland from the Union to the Famine* (London: Longmans, Green, 1921), p. 24.
12. W. L. Langer, *Political and Social Upheaval, 1832–1852* (New York: Harper & Row, 1969), p. 188.

SUGGESTED READING

There is a vast and exciting literature on the Industrial Revolution. D. S. Landes, *The Unbound Prometheus: Technological Change and Industrial Development in Western Europe from 1750 to the Present* (1969), and S. Pollard, *Peaceful Conquest: The Industrialization of Europe* (1981), are the best general treatments of European industrial growth since 1750. P. Mathias, *The First Industrial Nation: An Economic History of Britain, 1700–1914* (1969); P. Deane, *The First Industrial Revolution* (1966); and P. Mantoux, *The Industrial Revolution in the Eighteenth Century* (1961), admirably discuss the various aspects of the English breakthrough and offer good bibliographies. J. de Vries, *The Dutch Rural Economy in the Golden Age, 1500–1700* (1974), skillfully examines the causes of early Dutch leadership in farming, and E. L. Jones, *Agriculture and Economic Growth in England, 1650–1815* (1967), shows the importance of the Agricultural Revolution for England. W. Rostow, *The Stages of Economic Growth: A Non-Communist Manifesto* (1960), is a popular, provocative study. R. Cameron brilliantly traces the spread of railroads and industry across Europe in *France and the Economic Development of Europe, 1800–1914* (1961). The recent works of A. S. Milward and S. B. Saul, *The Economic Development of Continental Europe, 1780–1870* (1973) and *The Development of the Economies of Continental Europe, 1850–1914* (1977), may be compared with J. Clapham's old-fashioned classic, *Economic Development of France and Germany* (1963). C. Kindleberger, *Economic Growth in France and Britain, 1851–1950* (1964), is a stimulating study, especially for those with some background in economics. Other important works in recent years on industrial developments are C. Tilly and E. Shorter, *Strikes in France, 1830–1848* (1974); D. Ringrose, *Transportation and Economic Stagnation in Spain, 1750–1850* (1970); L. Schofer, *The Formation of a Modern Labor Force* (1975), which focuses on the Silesian part of Germany; and W. Blackwell, *The Industrialization of Russia,* 2nd ed. (1982).

The debate between "optimists" and "pessimists" about the consequences of industrialization in England goes on. P. Taylor, ed., *The Industrial Revolution: Triumph or Disaster?* (1970), is a useful introduction to different viewpoints, while W. A. Hayek, ed., *Capitalism and the Historians* (1954), is a good collection of essays stressing positive aspects. It is also fascinating to compare Friedrich Engels's classic condemnation, *The Condition of the Working Class in England,* with Andrew Ure's optimistic defense, *The Philosophy of Manufactures,* first published in 1835 and reprinted recently. E. P. Thompson continues and enriches the Engels tradition in *The Making of the English Working Class* (1963), an exciting book rich in detail and early working-class lore. An unorthodox but moving account of a doomed group is D. Bythell, *The Handloom Weavers* (1969). F. Klingender, *Art and the Industrial Revolution,* rev. ed. (1968), is justly famous, and M. Ignatieff, *A Just Measure of Pain* (1980), is an engrossing study of prisons during English industrialization. D. S. Landes, *Revolution in Time: Clocks and the Making of the Modern World* (1983), is a brilliant integration of industrial and cultural history.

Among general studies, many of which are cited in the Suggested Reading for Chapter 27, G. S. R. Kitson Clark, *The Making of Victorian England* (1967), is particularly imaginative. A. Briggs, *Victorian People* (1955), provides an engrossing series of brief biographies. H. Ausubel discusses a major reformer in his work, *John Bright* (1966), and B. Harrison skillfully illuminates the problem of heavy drinking in *Drink and the Victorians* (1971). On poverty and politics in Ireland, K. H. Connell, *The Population of Ireland, 1750–1850* (1950), and S. Cronin, *Irish Nationalism: A History of Its Roots and Ideology* (1981), are excellent points of departure, while C. Smith, *The Great Hunger* (1962), is a moving account of the famine. The most famous contemporary novel dealing with the new industrial society is Charles Dickens's *Hard Times,* an entertaining but exaggerated story. *Mary Barton* and *North and South* by Elizabeth Gaskill are more realistic portrayals, and both are highly recommended, as is Emile Zola's *Germinal,* a grim, powerful story of love and hate during a violent strike by French coal miners.

27

IDEOLOGIES AND UPHEAVALS IN EUROPE, 1815–1850

*T*HE MOMENTOUS economic and political transformation of modern times began in the late eighteenth century with the Industrial Revolution in England and then the French Revolution. Until about 1815, these economic and political revolutions were separate, involving different countries and activities and proceeding at very different paces. The Industrial Revolution created the factory system and new groups of capitalists and industrial workers in northern England, but almost continuous warfare with France checked its spread to continental Europe. Meanwhile, England's ruling aristocracy suppressed all forms of political radicalism at home and joined with crowned heads abroad to oppose and eventually defeat revolutionary and Napoleonic France. The economic and political revolutions worked at cross-purposes and even neutralized each other.

After peace returned in 1815, the situation changed. Economic and political changes tended to fuse, reinforcing each other and bringing about what the historian Eric Hobsbawm has incisively called the "dual revolution." For instance, the growth of the industrial middle class encouraged the drive for representative government, while the demands of the French sans-culottes in 1793 and 1794 inspired many socialist thinkers. Gathering strength and threatening almost every aspect of the existing political and social framework, the dual revolution rushed on to alter completely first Europe and then the world. Much of world history in the last two centuries can be seen as the progressive unfolding of the dual revolution.

Yet three qualifications must be kept firmly in mind. In Europe in the nineteenth century, as in Asia and Africa in more recent times, the dual revolution was not some inexorable mechanical monster grinding peoples and cultures into a homogenized mass. The economic and political transformation it wrought was built on complicated histories, strong traditions, and highly diverse cultures. Radical change was eventually a constant, but the particular results varied enormously.

Nor should the strength of the old forces be underestimated. In Europe especially, the traditional elites —the monarchs, noble landowners, and bureaucrats —long proved capable of defending their privileges and even of rerouting the dual revolution to serve their interests.

Finally, the dual revolution posed a tremendous intellectual challenge. The meanings of the economic, political, and social changes that were occurring, as well as the ways they could be shaped by human action, were anything but clear. These questions fascinated observers and stimulated new ideas and ideologies.

How, then, did the political revolution, derailed by class antagonisms in France and resisted by European monarchs, break out again in the era of early industrialization? And what ideas did thinkers develop to describe and shape the transformation going on before their eyes? These are the questions this chapter will explore.

THE PEACE SETTLEMENT

The eventual triumph of revolutionary economic and political forces was by no means certain in 1814. Quite the contrary. The conservative, aristocratic monarchies with their preindustrial armies and economies (Great Britain excepted) appeared firmly in control once again. France had been decisively defeated by the off-again, on-again alliance of Russia, Prussia, Austria, and Great Britain. That alliance had been strengthened and reaffirmed in March 1814, when the allies pledged not only to defeat France but to hold it in line for twenty years thereafter. The Quadruple Alliance had then forced Napoleon to abdicate in April 1814 and restored the Bourbon dynasty to the French throne (page 798). But there were many other international questions outstanding, and the allies agreed to meet in Vienna to fashion a general peace settlement. Interrupted by Napoleon's desperate gamble during the Hundred Days, the allies concluded their negotiations at the Congress of Vienna after Napoleon's defeat at Waterloo.

Most people felt profound longing for peace. The great challenge for statesmen in 1814 was to construct a peace settlement that would last and not sow the seeds of another war. Their efforts were largely successful and contributed to a century unmarred by destructive, generalized war (Map 27.1).

Map 27.1 Europe in 1815 Europe's leaders re-established a balance of political power after the defeat of Napoleon.

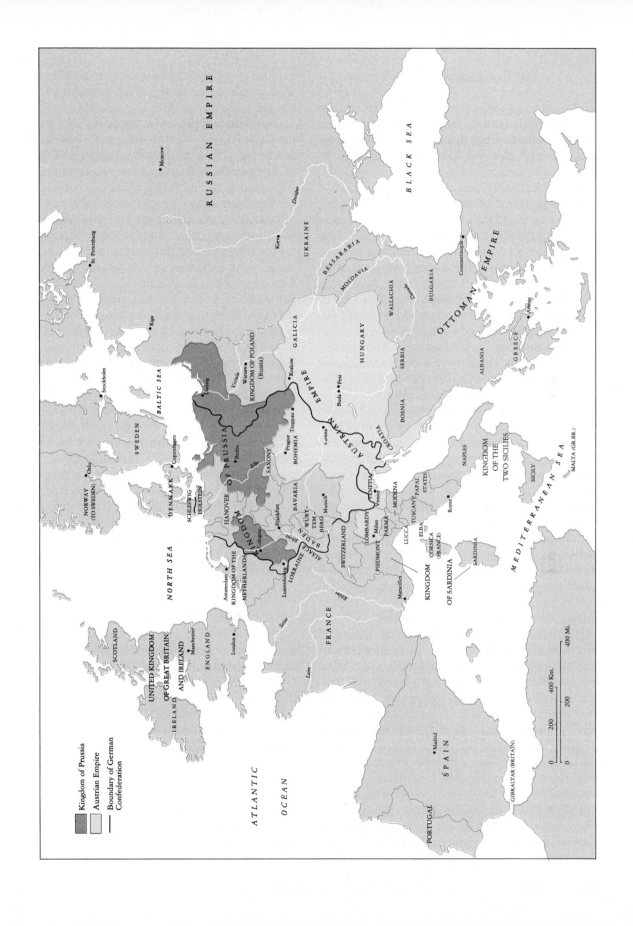

Kingdom of Prussia

Austrian Empire

Boundary of German Confederation

The Congress of Vienna

The allied powers were concerned first and foremost with the defeated enemy, France. Agreeing to the restoration of the Bourbon dynasty, the allies signed the first Peace of Paris with Louis XVIII on May 30, 1814.

The allies were quite lenient toward France. France was given the boundaries it possessed in 1792, which were larger than those of 1789. France lost only the territories it had conquered in Italy, Germany, and the Low Countries, in addition to a few colonial possessions. Although there was some sentiment for levying a fine on France to pay for the war, the allies did not press the matter when Louis XVIII stated firmly that his government would not pay any reparations. France was even allowed to keep the art treasures Napoleon's agents had looted from the museums of Europe. Thus the victorious powers did not punish harshly, and they did not foment a spirit of injustice and revenge in the defeated country.

When the four allies met together at the Congress of Vienna, assisted in a minor way by a host of delegates from the smaller European states, they also agreed to raise a number of formidable barriers against renewed French aggression. The Low Countries—Belgium and Holland—were united under an enlarged Dutch monarchy capable of opposing France more effectively. Moreover, Prussia received considerably more territory on France's eastern border, so as to stand as the "sentinel on the Rhine" against France. In these ways the Quadruple Alliance combined leniency toward France with strong defensive measures. They held out a carrot with one hand and picked up a bigger stick with the other.

In their moderation toward France the allies were motivated by self-interest and traditional ideas about the balance of power. To Metternich and Castlereagh, the foreign ministers of Austria and Great Britain, as well as their French counterpart Talleyrand, the balance of power meant an international equilibrium of political and military forces, which would preserve the freedom and independence of each of the Great Powers. Such a balance would discourage aggression by any combination of states or, worse, the domination of Europe by any single state. As they saw it, the task of the powers was thus twofold. They had to make sure that France would not dominate Europe again, and they also had to arrange international relations so that none of the victors would be tempted to strive for domination in its turn. Such a balance involved many considerations and all of Europe.

The balance of power was the mechanism used by the Great Powers—Austria, Britain, Prussia, Russia, and France—to settle their own dangerous disputes at the Congress of Vienna. There was general agreement among the victors that each of them should receive compensation in the form of territory for their successful struggle against the French. Great Britain had already won colonies and strategic outposts during the long wars, and these it retained. Metternich's Austria gave up territories in Belgium and southern Germany but expanded greatly elsewhere, taking the rich provinces of Venetia and Lombardy in northern Italy as well as its former Polish possessions and new lands on the eastern coast of the Adriatic (see Map 27.1). There was also agreement that Prussia and Russia should be compensated. But where, and to what extent? That was the ticklish question that almost led to renewed war in January 1815.

The vaguely progressive, impetuous Alexander I of Russia had already taken Finland and Bessarabia on his northern and southern borders. Yet he burned with ambition to restore the ancient kingdom of Poland, on which he expected to bestow the benefits of his rule. The Prussians were willing to go along and give up their Polish territories, provided they could swallow up the large and wealthy kingdom of Saxony, their German neighbor to the south.

These demands were too much for Castlereagh and Metternich, who feared an unbalancing of forces in central Europe. In an astonishing about-face, they turned for diplomatic support to the wily Talleyrand and the defeated France he represented. On January 3, 1815, Great Britain, Austria, and France signed a secret alliance directed against Russia and Prussia. As Castlereagh concluded somberly, it appeared that the "peace we have so dearly purchased will be of short duration."[1]

The outcome, however, was compromise rather than war. When rumors of the alliance were intentionally leaked, the threat of war caused the rulers of Russia and Prussia to moderate their demands. They accepted Metternich's proposal: Russia established a small Polish kingdom, and Prussia received two-fifths rather than all of Saxony (see Map 27.1). This compromise was very much within the framework of balance-of-power ideology and eighteenth-century diplomacy: Great Powers became greater, but not too

The Congress of Vienna While the Great Powers hammered out a peace settlement, a host of delegates from all over Europe celebrated with endless balls, receptions, and romantic intrigues. Here the "dancing congress" enjoys a glittering evening-dress ball given by the Austrian emperor and empress. *(The Bettmann Archive)*

much greater. In addition, France had been able to intervene and tip the scales in favor of the side seeking to prevent undue expansion of Russia and Prussia. In so doing France regained its Great Power status and was no longer isolated, as Talleyrand gleefully reported to Louis XVIII.

Unfortunately for France, as the final touches were being put on the peace settlement at Vienna, Napoleon suddenly reappeared on the scene. Escaping from his "comic kingdom" on the island of Elba in February 1815 and rallying his supporters for one last campaign during the Hundred Days, Napoleon was defeated at Waterloo and exiled to St. Helena. Yet the resulting peace—the second Peace of Paris—was still relatively moderate toward France. Fat old Louis XVIII was restored to his throne for a second time. France lost some territory, had to pay an indemnity

of 700 million francs, and had to support a large army of occupation for five years.

The rest of the settlement already concluded at the Congress of Vienna was left intact. The members of the Quadruple Alliance did, however, agree to meet periodically to discuss their common interests and to consider appropriate measures for the maintenance of peace in Europe. This agreement marked the beginning of the European "congress system," which lasted long into the nineteenth century and settled international crises through diplomatic conferences.

INTERVENTION AND REPRESSION

There was also a domestic political side to the re-establishment of peace. Within their own countries, the leaders of the victorious states were much less flexible. In 1815, under Metternich's leadership, Austria, Prussia, and Russia embarked on a crusade against the ideas and politics of the dual revolution. The crusade lasted until 1848.

The first step was the Holy Alliance, formed by Austria, Prussia, and Russia in September 1815. First proposed by Russia's Alexander I, the alliance proclaimed the intention of the three eastern monarchs to rule exclusively on the basis of Christian principles and to work together to maintain peace and justice on all occasions. Castlereagh refused to sign, characterizing the vague statement of principle as "a piece of sublime mysticism and nonsense." Yet it soon became a symbol of the repression of liberal and revolutionary movements all over Europe.

In 1820 revolutionaries succeeded in forcing the monarchs of Spain and the southern Italian Kingdom of the Two Sicilies to grant liberal constitutions against their wills. Metternich was horrified: revolution was rising once again. Calling a conference at Troppau in Austria, under the provisions of the Quadruple Alliance, he and Alexander I proclaimed the principle of active intervention to maintain all autocratic regimes whenever they were threatened. Austrian forces then marched into Naples and restored Ferdinand I to the throne of the Two Sicilies. The French armies of Louis XVIII likewise restored the Spanish regime—after the Congress of Troppau had rejected Alexander's offer to send his Cossacks across Europe to teach the Spanish an unforgettable lesson.

Great Britain remained aloof, arguing that intervention in the domestic politics of foreign states was not an object of British diplomacy. In particular, Great Britain opposed any attempts by the restored Spanish monarchy to reconquer its former Latin American possessions, which had gained their independence during and after the Napoleonic wars. Encouraged by the British position, the young United States proclaimed its celebrated Monroe Doctrine in 1823. This bold document declared that European powers were to keep their hands off the New World and in no way attempt to re-establish their political system there. In the United States, constitutional liberalism, an ongoing challenge to the conservatism of continental Europe, retained its cutting edge.

In the years following the crushing of liberal revolution in southern Italy in 1821 and in Spain in 1823, Metternich continued to battle against liberal political change. Sometimes he could do little, as in the case of the new Latin American republics. Nor could he undo the dynastic changes of 1830 in western Europe. Nonetheless, until 1848 Metternich's system proved quite effective in central Europe, where his power was greatest.

Metternich's policies dominated not only Austria and the Italian peninsula but the entire German Confederation, which the peace settlement of Vienna had called into being. The confederation was composed of thirty-eight independent German states, including Prussia and Austria. (The Hungarian half of the Austrian Empire was not a member.) These states met in complicated assemblies dominated by Austria, with Prussia a willing junior partner in the planning and execution of repressive measures.

It was through the German Confederation that Metternich had the infamous Carlsbad Decrees issued in 1819. The decrees required the thirty-eight German member states to root out subversive ideas in their universities and newspapers. They also established a permanent committee with spies and informers to investigate and punish any liberal or radical organizations. Metternich's ruthless imposition of repressive internal policies on the governments of central Europe contrasted with the intelligent moderation he had displayed in the general peace settlement of 1815.

METTERNICH AND CONSERVATISM

Metternich's determined defense of the status quo made him a villain in the eyes of most progressive, optimistic historians of the nineteenth century. Yet rather than denounce the man, it is more useful to try to understand him and the general conservatism he represented.

Born into the middle ranks of the landed nobility of the Rhineland, Prince Klemens von Metternich (1773–1859) was an internationally oriented aristocrat. In 1795 his splendid marriage to Eleonora von Kaunitz, granddaughter of Austria's famous statesman and heiress to vast estates, opened the door to the highest court circles and a brilliant diplomatic career. Austrian ambassador to Napoleon's court in 1806 and Austrian foreign minister from 1809 to 1848, the cosmopolitan Metternich always remained loyal to his class and jealously defended its rights and privileges to the day he died. Like most other conservatives of his time, he did so with a clear conscience.

The nobility was one of Europe's most ancient institutions, and conservatives regarded tradition as the basic source of human institutions. In their view, the proper state and society remained that of pre-1789 Europe, which rested on a judicious blend of monarchy, bureaucracy, and aristocracy.

Metternich's commitment to conservatism was coupled with a passionate hatred of liberalism. He firmly believed that liberalism, as embodied in revolutionary America and France, had been responsible for a generation of war with untold bloodshed and suffering. Liberal demands for representative government and civil liberties had unfortunately captured the imaginations of some middle-class lawyers, businessmen, and intellectuals. Metternich thought that these groups had been and still were engaged in a vast conspiracy to impose their beliefs on society and destroy the existing order. Like many conservatives then and since, Metternich blamed liberal revolutionaries for stirring up the lower classes, whom he believed to be indifferent or hostile to liberal ideas, desiring nothing more than peace and quiet.

The threat of liberalism appeared doubly dangerous to Metternich because it generally went with national aspirations. Liberals, especially liberals in central Europe, believed that each people, each national group, had a right to establish its own independent government and seek to fulfill its own destiny. The idea of national self-determination was repellent to Metternich. It not only threatened the existence of the aristocracy, it also threatened to destroy the Austrian Empire and revolutionize central Europe.

The vast Austrian Empire of the Habsburgs was a great dynastic state. Formed over centuries by war, marriage, and luck, it was made up of many peoples speaking many languages (see Map 27.2). The Germans, long the dominant element, had supported and profited by the long-term territorial expansion of Austria; yet they accounted for only a quarter of the population. The Magyars (Hungarians), a substantially smaller group, dominated the kingdom of Hungary—which was part of the Austrian Empire—though they did not account for a majority of the population even there.

The Czechs, the third major group, were concentrated in Bohemia and Moravia. There were also large numbers of Italians, Poles, and Ukrainians, as well as smaller groups of Slovenes, Croats, Serbs, Ruthenians, and Rumanians. The various Slavic peoples, together with the Italians and the Rumanians, represented a widely scattered and completely divided majority in an empire dominated by Germans and Hungarians. Different ethnic groups often lived in the same provinces and even the same villages. Thus the different parts and provinces of the empire differed in languages, customs, and institutions. They were held together primarily by their ties to the Habsburg emperor.

The multinational state Metternich served was both strong and weak. It was strong because of its large population and vast territories; it was weak because of its many and potentially dissatisfied nationalities. In these circumstances, Metternich virtually had to oppose liberalism and nationalism, for Austria was simply unable to accommodate those ideologies of the dual revolution. Other conservatives supported Austria because they could imagine no better fate for the jumble of small nationalities wedged precariously between masses of Germans and hordes of Russians in east central Europe. Castlereagh even went so far as to say that Austria was the "great hinge upon which the fate of Europe must ultimately depend." Metternich's repressive conservatism may not hold appeal for many people today, but it had understandable roots in the dilemma of a multinational state in an age of rising nationalism.

RADICAL IDEAS AND EARLY SOCIALISM

The years following the peace settlement of 1815 were years of profound intellectual activity. Intellectuals and social observers were seeking to understand the revolutionary changes that had occurred and were still taking place. These efforts led to ideas that still motivate the world.

Almost all of these basic ideas were radical. In one way or another they opposed the old, deeply felt conservatism that Metternich exemplified so well. The revived conservatism, with its stress on tradition, a hereditary monarchy, a strong and privileged landowning aristocracy, and an official church, was rejected by radicals. Instead, radicals developed and refined alternative visions—alternative ideologies—and tried to convince society to act on them. With time, they were very successful.

RUSSIA

GALICIA

POLAND

TRANSYLVANIA

RUMANIA

OTTOMAN EMPIRE

Danube

Germans
Hungarians
Italians
Rumanians
Poles
Czechs

Carpatho-Ukrainians (Ruthenians)
Serbs and Croats
Slovaks
Slovenes

Habsburg Monarchy
boundaries

Tisza

SILESIA

MORAVIA

• Prague

BOHEMIA

Vienna •

AUSTRIA

• Budapest

HUNGARY

Danube

CROATIA—SLAVONIA

BOSNIA

SERBIA

STYRIA

ILLYRIA

GERMAN

STATES

BAVARIA

TYROL

SALZBURG

CORINTHIA

VENETIA

Venice •

ADRIATIC SEA

SWITZERLAND

LOMBARDY

Po

• Milan

ITALIAN STATES

0   50   100 Km.

0   50   100 Mi.

MAP 27.2 Peoples of the Habsburg Monarchy, 1815 The old dynastic state was a patchwork of nationalities. Note the widely scattered pockets of Germans and Hungarians.

LIBERALISM

The ideas of liberalism—liberty and equality—were by no means defeated in 1815. First realized successfully in the American Revolution and then achieved in part in the French Revolution, this political and social philosophy continued to pose a radical challenge to revived conservatism. Liberalism demanded representative government as opposed to autocratic monarchy, equality before the law as opposed to legally separate classes. Liberty also continued to mean specific individual freedoms: freedom of the press, freedom of speech, freedom of assembly, and freedom from arbitrary arrest. In Europe, only France with Louis XVIII's Constitutional Charter and Great Britain with its Parliament and historic rights of English men and women had realized much but by no means all of the liberal program in 1815. Elsewhere, liberal demands were still a call for change.

Yet although "classical" liberalism still had its cutting edge, it was not as sharp a tool as it had been. This was especially true of liberal economic principles, which called for unrestricted private enterprise and no government interference in the economy. This philosophy was popularly known as the doctrine of *laissez faire.*

The idea of a free economy had first been persuasively formulated by a Scottish professor of philosophy, Adam Smith (1723–1790). Smith, whose *Inquiry into the Nature and Causes of the Wealth of Nations* (1776) founded modern economics, was highly critical of eighteenth-century mercantilism. Mercantilism, he said, meant stifling government regulations as well as unjust privileges for private monopolies and government favorites. Far preferable was free competition, which would give all citizens a fair and equal opportunity to do what they did best. Smith argued effectively that freely competitive private enterprise would result in greater income for everyone, not just the rich.

Unlike some of his contemporaries, Smith applauded the modest rise in real wages of British workers in the eighteenth century and went so far as to say, "No society can surely be flourishing and happy, of which the far greater part of the members are poor and miserable." Smith also believed that greater competition meant higher wages for workers, since manufacturers and "masters are always and everywhere in a sort of tacit, but constant and uniform, combination, not to raise the wages of laborers above their actual rate." In short, Adam Smith was a spokesman for general economic development, not narrow business interests.

In the early nineteenth century, the British economy was progressively liberalized, as old restrictions on trade and industry were relaxed or eliminated. This liberalization promoted continued rapid economic growth in the Industrial Revolution. At the same time, however, economic liberalism and laissez-faire economic thought were tending to become a doctrine serving business interests. Businessmen used the doctrine to defend their right to do exactly as they wished in their factories. Labor unions were outlawed because they supposedly restricted free competition and the individual's "right to work."

The teachings of a kindly parson, Thomas Malthus (1776–1834), helped make economic liberalism an ideology of business interests in many people's minds. In his "Essay on the Principle of Population" (1798), Malthus argued that population would always tend to grow faster than the supply of food. In Malthus's opinion, the only hope of warding off such "positive checks" to population growth as war, famine, and disease was "prudential restraint." That is, young men and women had to limit the growth of population by the old tried-and-true means of marrying late in life. But Malthus was not optimistic about this possibility. The powerful attraction of the sexes would cause most people to marry early and have many children.

The wealthy English stockbroker and economist David Ricardo (1772–1823) was even less optimistic. His depressing "iron law of wages" posited that, because of the pressure of population growth, wages would always sink to the subsistence level. That is, wages would be just high enough to keep the workers from starving. Malthus and Ricardo thought of themselves as objective social scientists. Yet their teachings were often used by industrial and middle-class interests in England, the Continent, and the United States to justify opposing any kind of government intervention to protect or improve the lot of workers: if workers were poor, it was their own fault, the result of their breeding like rabbits.

In the early nineteenth century, liberal political ideals also became more closely associated with narrow class interests. Early-nineteenth-century liberals favored representative government, but they generally wanted property qualifications attached to the right to vote. In practice, this meant limiting the vote to well-to-do aristocratic landowners, substantial businessmen, and successful members of the professions. Workers and peasants as well as the lower middle class of shopkeepers, clerks, and artisans did not own the necessary property and thus could not vote.

As liberalism became increasingly middle class after 1815, some intellectuals and foes of conservatism felt that it did not go nearly far enough. Inspired by memories of the French Revolution and the contemporary example of exuberant Jacksonian democracy in the young American republic, they called for universal voting rights, at least for males. Giving all men the vote, they felt, would allow the masses to join in government and would lead to democracy.

Many people who believed in democracy also believed in the republican form of government. They detested the power of the monarchy, the privileges of the aristocracy, and the great wealth of the upper middle class. These democrats and republicans were more radical than the liberals. Taking for granted much of the liberal program, they sought to go beyond it. Democrats and republicans were also more willing than most liberals to endorse violent upheaval to achieve goals. All of which meant that liberals and radical, democratic republicans could join forces against conservatives only up to a point.

NATIONALISM

Nationalism was a second radical idea in the years after 1815, an idea destined to have an enormous influence in the modern world. In a summation of this complex ideology, three points stand out. First, nationalism has normally evolved from a real or imagined *cultural* unity, manifesting itself especially in a common language, history, and territory. Second, nationalists have usually sought to turn this cultural unity into *political* reality, so that the territory of each people coincides with its state boundaries. It was this goal that made nationalism so potentially explosive in central and eastern Europe after 1815, when there were either too few states (Austria, Russia, and the Ottoman Empire) or too many (the Italian peninsula

and the German Confederation) and when different peoples overlapped and intermingled. Third, modern nationalism had its immediate origins in the French Revolution and the Napoleonic wars. Nationalism was effectively harnessed by the French republic during the Reign of Terror to help repel foreign foes, and all across Europe patriots tried to kindle nationalist flames in the war against Napoleon. Thus by 1815 there were already hints of nationalism's remarkable ability to spread and develop.

Between 1815 and 1850, most people who believed in nationalism also believed in either liberalism or radical, democratic republicanism. In more recent times, however, many governments have been very nationalistic without favoring liberty and democracy. Why, then, was love of liberty almost synonymous with love of nation in the early nineteenth century?

A common faith in the creativity and nobility of the people was perhaps the single most important reason for people's linking these two concepts. Liberals and especially democrats saw the people as the ultimate source of all government. The people (or some of them) elected their officials and governed themselves within a framework of personal liberty. Yet such self-government would be possible only if the people were united by common traditions and common loyalties. In practice, common loyalties rested above all on a common language. Thus liberals and nationalists agreed that a shared language forged the basic unity of a people, a unity that transcended local or provincial interests and even class differences.

Early nationalists usually believed that every nation, like every citizen, has the right to exist in freedom and to develop its character and spirit. They were confident that the independence and freedom of other nations, as in the case of other citizens within a nation, would not lessen the freedom of their own country. Rather, the symphony of nations would promote the harmony and ultimate unity of all peoples. As the French historian Jules Michelet put it in *The People* in 1846, each citizen "learns to recognize his country . . . as a note in the grand concert; through it he himself participates and loves the world." Similarly, the Italian patriot Giuseppe Mazzini believed that "in laboring according to the true principles of our country we are laboring for Humanity." Thus the liberty of the individual and the love of a free nation overlapped greatly in the early nineteenth century.

Nationalism also had a negative side. Even as they talked of serving the cause of humanity, early nationalists stressed the differences between peoples. The German pastor and philosopher Johann Herder (1744–1803) had argued that every people has its own particular spirit and genius, which it expresses through its culture and language. Yet Herder (and others after him) could not define the uniqueness of the French, German, and Slavic peoples without comparing and contrasting one people with another. Thus, even early nationalism developed a strong sense of "we" and "they."

"They" were often the enemy. The leader of the Czech cultural revival, the passionate democrat and nationalist historian Francis Palacký, is a good example of this tendency. In his histories he lauded the achievements of the Czech people, which he characterized as a long struggle against brutal German domination. To this "we-they" outlook, it was all too easy for nationalists to add two other highly volatile ingredients: a sense of national mission and a sense of national superiority. As Mazzini characteristically wrote, "Peoples never stop before they have achieved the ultimate aim of their existence, before having fulfilled their mission." Even Michelet, so alive to the aspirations of other peoples, could not help speaking in 1846 of the "superiority of France"; the principles espoused in the French Revolution had made France the "salvation of mankind."

German and Spanish nationalists had a very different opinion of France. To them the French often seemed as oppressive as the Germans seemed to the Czechs, as hateful as the Russians seemed to the Poles. The despised enemy's mission might seem as oppressive as the American national mission—as the American journalist and strident nationalist John Louis O'Sullivan sketched it in 1845 after the annexation of Texas—seemed to the Mexicans. O'Sullivan wrote that taking land from an "imbecile and distracted Mexico" was a laudable step in the "fulfillment of our manifest destiny to overspread the continent allotted by Providence for the free development of our yearly multiplying millions."[2]

Early nationalism was thus ambiguous. Its main thrust was liberal and democratic. But below the surface lurked ideas of national superiority and national mission, which could lead to aggressive crusades and counter-crusades, as had happened in the French Revolution and in the "wars of liberation" against Napoleon.

FRENCH UTOPIAN SOCIALISM

To understand the rise of socialism, one must begin with France. Despite the fact that France lagged far behind Great Britain in developing modern industry, almost all the early socialists were French. Although they differed on many specific points, these French thinkers were acutely aware that the political revolution in France and the rise of modern industry in England had begun a transformation of society. Yet they were disturbed by what they saw. Liberal practices in politics and economics appeared to be fomenting selfish individualism and splitting the community into isolated fragments. There was, they believed, an urgent need for a further reorganization of society to establish cooperation and a new sense of community. Starting from this shared outlook, individual French thinkers went in many different directions. They searched the past, analyzed existing conditions, and fashioned luxurious utopias. Yet certain ideas tied their critiques and visions together.

Early French socialists believed in economic planning. Inspired by the emergency measures of 1793 and 1794 in France, they argued that the government should rationally organize the economy and not depend on destructive competition to do the job. Early socialists also shared an intense desire to help the poor and to protect them from the rich. With passionate moral fervor they preached that the rich and the poor should be more nearly equal economically. Finally, socialists believed that most private property should be abolished and replaced by state or community ownership. Planning, greater economic equality, and state ownership of property: these were the key ideas of early French socialism and of all socialism since.

One of the most influential of these thinkers was a nobleman, Count Henri de Saint-Simon (1760–1825). A curious combination of radical thinker and successful land speculator, Saint-Simon optimistically proclaimed the tremendous possibilities of industrial development: "The age of gold is before us!" The key to progress was proper social organization. Such an arrangement of society required the "parasites"—the court, the aristocracy, lawyers, churchmen—to give way, once and for all, to the "doers"— the leading scientists, engineers, and industrialists. The doers would carefully plan the economy and guide it forward by undertaking vast public works projects and investment banks. Saint-Simon also

Fourier's Utopia The vision of a harmonious planned community freed from capitalism and selfish individualism radiates from this 1847 illustration of Fourier's principles. *(Mary Evans Picture Library)*

stressed in highly moralistic terms that every social institution ought to have as its main goal improved conditions for the poor. Saint-Simon's stress on industry and science inspired middle-class industrialists and bankers, like the Pereire brothers, founders of the Crédit Mobilier (page 822).

After 1830, the socialist critique of capitalism became sharper. Charles Fourier (1772–1837), a lonely, saintly man with a tenuous hold on reality, described a socialist utopia in lavish mathematical detail. Hating the urban wage system, Fourier envisaged self-sufficient communities of 1,620 people living communally on five thousand acres devoted to a combination of agriculture and industry. Fourier was also an early proponent of the total emancipation of women, abolition of marriage, and complete sexual freedom. Although Fourier waited in vain each day at noon in his apartment for a wealthy philanthropist to endow his visionary schemes, he was very influential. Several utopian communities were founded along the lines he prescribed, mainly in the United States.

Louis Blanc (1811–1882), a sharp-eyed, intelligent journalist, was much more practical. In his *Organization of Work* (1839), he urged workers to agitate for universal voting rights and to take control of the state peacefully. Blanc believed that the full power of the state should be directed at setting up government-backed workshops and factories to guarantee full employment. The right to work had to become as sacred as any other right. Finally, there was Pierre Joseph Proudhon (1809–1865), a self-educated printer, who wrote a pamphlet in 1840 entitled *What Is Property?* His answer was that it was nothing but theft. Property was profit that was stolen from the worker, who was the source of all wealth. Unlike most socialists, Proudhon feared the power of the state and thus was often considered an anarchist.

Thus a variety of French thinkers blazed the way with utopian socialism in the 1830s and 1840s. Their ideas were very influential, particularly in Paris, where poverty-stricken workers with a revolutionary tradition were attentive students. Yet the economic arguments of the French utopians were weak, and their specific programs usually seemed too fanciful to be taken seriously. To Karl Marx was left the task of establishing firm foundations for modern socialism.

THE BIRTH OF MARXIAN SOCIALISM

In 1848 the thirty-year-old Karl Marx (1818–1883) and the twenty-eight-year-old Friedrich Engels (1820–1895) published the *Communist Manifesto,* the Bible of socialism. The son of a Jewish lawyer who had converted to Christianity, the atheistic young Marx had studied philosophy at the University of Berlin before turning to journalism and economics. He read widely in French socialist thought and was developing his own socialist ideas by the time he was twenty-five.

Early French socialists often appealed to the middle class and the state to help the poor. Marx argued that the interests of the middle class and those of the industrial working class are inevitably opposed to each other. Indeed, according to the *Manifesto,* the "history of all previously existing society is the history of class struggles." In Marx's view, one class had always exploited the other, and with the advent of modern industry, society was split more clearly than ever before: between the middle class—the bourgeoisie—and the modern working class—the proletariat. Moreover, the bourgeoisie had reduced everything to a matter of money and "naked self-interest." "In a word, for exploitation, veiled by religious and political illusions, the bourgeoisie had substituted naked, shameless, direct brutal exploitation."

Just as the bourgeoisie had triumphed over the feudal aristocracy, Marx predicted, the proletariat was destined to conquer the bourgeoisie in a violent revolution. While a tiny minority owned the means of production and grew richer, the ever-poorer proletariat was constantly growing in size and in class consciousness. In this process, the proletariat was aided, according to Marx, by a portion of the bourgeoisie who had gone over to the proletariat and who (like Marx and Engels) "had raised themselves to the level of comprehending theoretically the historical moment." And the critical moment was very near. "Let the ruling classes tremble at a Communist revolution. The proletarians have nothing to lose but their chains. They have a world to win. WORKING MEN OF ALL COUNTRIES, UNITE!" So ends the *Communist Manifesto.*

The Marx Family In 1849 the exiled Marx settled in London. There he wrote *Capital,* the weighty exposition of his socialist theories, and worked to organize the working class. With his coauthor and financial supporter Friedrich Engels (right), Marx is shown here with his daughters, ironically a picture of middle-class respectability. *(Culver Pictures)*

In brief outline, Marx's ideas may seem to differ only slightly from the wild and improbable ideas of the utopians of his day. Yet whatever one may think of the validity of Marx's analysis, he must be taken seriously. He united sociology, economics, and all human history in a vast and imposing edifice. He synthesized in his socialism not only French utopian schemes but English classical economics and German philosophy—the major intellectual currents of his day. Moreover, after the young Marx fled to England as a penniless political refugee following the revolutions of 1848, he continued to show a rare flair for combining complex theorization with both lively popular writing and practical organizational ability. This combination of theoretical and practical skills contributed greatly to the diffusion of Marx's socialist synthesis after 1860 (Chapter 29).

Marx's debt to England was great. He was the last of the classical economists. Following David Ricardo, who had taught that labor was the source of all value, Marx went on to argue that profits were really wages stolen from the workers. Moreover, Marx incorporated Engels's charges of terrible oppression of the new class of factory workers in England; thus his doctrines seemed to be based on hard facts.

Marx's theory of historical evolution was built on the philosophy of the German Georg Hegel (1770–1831). Hegel believed that history is "ideas in motion": each age is characterized by a dominant set of ideas, which produces opposing ideas and eventually a new synthesis. The idea of being had been dominant initially, for example, and it had produced its antithesis, the idea of nonbeing. This idea in turn had resulted in the synthesis of becoming. History has, therefore, pattern and purpose.

Marx retained Hegel's view of history as a dialectic process of change but made economic relationships between classes the driving force. This dialectic explained the decline of agrarian feudalism and the rise of industrial capitalism. And Marx stressed again and again that the "bourgeoisie, historically, has played a most revolutionary part. . . . During its rule of scarcely one hundred years the bourgeoisie has created more massive and more colossal productive forces than have all preceding generations together." Here was a convincing explanation for people trying to make sense of the dual revolution. Marx's next idea, that it was now the bourgeoisie's turn to give way to the socialism of revolutionary workers, appeared to many the irrefutable capstone of a brilliant interpretation of humanity's long development. Thus Marx pulled together powerful ideas and insights to create one of the great secular religions out of the intellectual ferment of the early 1800s.

THE ROMANTIC MOVEMENT

Developing radical concepts of politics and society were accompanied by comparable changes in literature and other arts during the dual revolution. The early nineteenth century marked the acme of the romantic movement, which profoundly influenced the arts and enriched European culture immeasurably.

The romantic movement was in part a revolt against classicism and the Enlightenment. Classicism was essentially a set of artistic rules and standards that went hand in glove with the Enlightenment's belief in rationality, order, and restraint. The classicists believed that the ancient Greeks and Romans had discovered eternally valid aesthetic rules long ago and that playwrights and painters should continue to follow them. Classicists could enforce these rules in the eighteenth century because they dominated the courts and academies for which artists worked.

Forerunners of the romantic movement appeared from about 1750 on. Of these, Rousseau (see page 661) —the passionate advocate of feeling, freedom, and natural goodness—was the most influential. Romanticism then crystallized fully in the 1790s, primarily in England and Germany. The French Revolution kindled the belief that radical reconstruction was also possible in cultural and artistic life (even though many early English and German romantics became disillusioned with events in France and turned from liberalism to conservatism in politics). Romanticism gained strength until the 1840s, when realism began to challenge it seriously.

ROMANTICISM

Romanticism was characterized by a belief in emotional exuberance, unrestrained imagination, and spontaneity in both art and personal life. In Germany early romantics of the 1770s and 1780s called themselves the "Storm and Stress" (*Sturm und Drang*) group, and many romantic artists of the early nineteenth century lived lives of tremendous emotional intensity. Suicide, duels to the death, madness, and strange illnesses were not uncommon among leading romantics. Romantic artists typically led bohemian lives, wearing their hair long and uncombed in preference to powdered wigs and living in cold garrets rather than frequenting stiff drawing rooms. They rejected materialism and sought to escape to lofty spiritual heights through their art. Great individualists, the romantics believed the full development of one's unique human potential to be the supreme purpose in life. The romantics were driven by a sense of an unlimited universe and by a yearning for the unattained, the unknown, the unknowable.

Nowhere was the break with classicism more apparent than in romanticism's general conception of

Delacroix: Liberty Leading the People This great romantic painting glorifies the July Revolution in Paris in 1830. Raising high the revolutionary tricolor, Liberty unites the worker, bourgeois, and street child in a righteous crusade against privilege and oppression. *(Louvre, Paris/Giraudon/Art Resource)*

nature. Classicism was not particularly interested in nature. In the words of the eighteenth-century English author Samuel Johnson, "A blade of grass is always a blade of grass; men and women are my subjects of inquiry." Nature was portrayed by classicists as beautiful and chaste, like an eighteenth-century formal garden. The romantics, on the other hand, were enchanted by nature. Sometimes they found it awesome and tempestuous, as in Théodore Géricault's painting *The Raft of the Medusa,* which shows the survivors of a shipwreck adrift in a turbulent sea. Others saw nature as a source of spiritual inspiration. As the great English landscape artist John Constable (1776–1837) declared, "Nature is Spirit visible."

Most romantics saw the growth of modern industry as an ugly, brutal attack on their beloved na-

ture and on the human personality. They sought escape—in the unspoiled Lake District of northern England, in exotic North Africa, in an idealized Middle Ages. Yet some romantics found a vast, awesome, terribly moving power in the new industrial landscape. In ironworks and cotton mills they saw the flames of Hell and the evil genius of Satan himself. One of John Martin's last and greatest paintings, *The Great Day of His Wrath* (1850), vividly depicts the last judgment foretold in Revelation VI, "when the sun became black as sackcloth of hair, and the moon became as blood; and the stars of heaven fell unto the earth." Martin's romantic masterpiece was inspired directly by a journey through the "Black country" of the industrial Midlands in the dead of night. According to Martin's son:

The glow of the furnaces, the red blaze of light, together with the liquid fire, seemed to him truly sublime and awful. He could not imagine anything more terrible even in the regions of everlasting punishment. All he had done or attempted in ideal painting fell far short, very far short, of the fearful sublimity.[3]

Fascinated by color and diversity, the romantic imagination turned toward the study and writing of history with a passion. For romantics, history was not a minor branch of philosophy from which philosophers picked suitable examples to illustrate their teachings. History was beautiful, exciting, and important in its own right. It was the art of change over time—the key to a universe that was now perceived to be organic and dynamic, no longer mechanical and static as it had appeared to the philosophes of the eighteenth-century Enlightenment.

Historical studies supported the development of national aspirations and encouraged entire peoples to seek in the past their special destinies. This trend was especially strong in Germany and eastern Europe. As the famous English historian Lord Acton put it, the growth of historical thinking associated with the romantic movement was a most fateful step in the story of European thought.

LITERATURE

Britain was the first country where romanticism flowered fully in poetry and prose, and the British romantic writers were among the most prominent in Europe. Wordsworth, Coleridge, and Scott were all active by 1800, to be followed shortly by Byron, Shelley, and Keats. All were poets: romanticism found its distinctive voice in poetry, as the Enlightenment had in prose.

A towering leader of English romanticism, William Wordsworth (1770–1850) traveled in France after his graduation from Cambridge. There he fell passionately in love with a French woman, who bore him a daughter. He was deeply influenced by the philosophy of Rousseau and the spirit of the early French Revolution. Back in England, prevented by war and the Terror from returning to France, Wordsworth settled in the countryside with his sister Dorothy and Samuel Taylor Coleridge (1772–1834).

In 1798 the two poets published their *Lyrical Ballads,* one of the most influential literary works in the history of the English language. In defiance of classical rules, Wordsworth and Coleridge abandoned flowery poetic conventions for the language of ordinary speech, simultaneously endowing simple subjects with the loftiest majesty. This twofold rejection of classical practice was at first ignored and then harshly criticized, but by 1830 Wordsworth had triumphed.

One of the best examples of Wordsworth's romantic credo and genius is "Daffodils":

I wandered lonely as a cloud
That floats on high o'er vales and hills,
When all at once I saw a crowd,
A host, of golden daffodils;
Beside the lake, beneath the trees,
Fluttering and dancing in the breeze.

. . . .

The waves beside them danced, but they
Out-did the sparkling waves in glee:
A poet could not but be gay,
In such a jocund company:
I gazed—and gazed—but little thought
What wealth the show to me had brought:

For oft, when on my couch I lie
In vacant or in pensive mood,
They flash upon that inward eye
Which is the bliss of solitude;
And then my heart with pleasure fills,
And dances with the daffodils.

Here indeed is simplicity and love of nature in commonplace forms. Here, too, is Wordsworth's romantic conviction that nature has the power to elevate and instruct, especially when interpreted by a high-minded poetic genius. Wordsworth's conception of poetry as the "spontaneous overflow of powerful feeling recollected in tranquility" is well illustrated by the last stanza.

At first, the strength of classicism in France inhibited the growth of romanticism there. Then, between 1820 and 1850, the romantic impulse broke through in the poetry and prose of Lamartine, Alfred de Vigny, Victor Hugo, Alexander Dumas, and George Sand. Of these, Victor Hugo (1802–1885) was the greatest in both poetry and prose.

Son of a Napoleonic general, Hugo achieved an amazing range of rhythm, language, and image in his lyric poetry. His powerful novels exemplified the romantic fascination with fantastic characters, strange settings, and human emotions. The hero of Hugo's famous *Hunchback of Notre Dame* (1831) is the great cathedral's deformed bellringer, a "human gargoyle" overlooking the teeming life of fifteenth-century Paris. A great admirer of Shakespeare, whom classical critics had derided as undisciplined and excessive, Hugo also championed romanticism in drama. His play *Hernani* (1830) consciously broke all the old rules, as Hugo renounced his early conservatism and equated freedom in literature with liberty in politics and society. Hugo's political evolution was thus exactly the opposite of Wordsworth's, in whom youthful radicalism gave way to middle-aged caution. As the contrast between the two artists suggests, romanticism was a cultural movement compatible with many political beliefs.

George Sand (1804–1876), a strong-willed and gifted woman, defied the narrow conventions of her time in an unending search for self-fulfillment. After eight years of unhappy marriage in the provinces, she abandoned her dullard of a husband and took her two children to Paris to pursue a career as a writer. There she soon achieved fame and wealth, eventually writing over eighty novels on a variety of romantic and social themes. All were shot through with a typically romantic love of nature and moral idealism. George Sand's striking individualism went far beyond her flamboyant preference for men's clothing and cigars and her notorious affairs with the poet Alfred de Musset and the composer Frédéric Chopin, among others. Her semi-autobiographical novel *Lélia* was shockingly modern, delving deeply into her tortuous quest for sexual and personal freedom.

In central and eastern Europe, literary romanticism and early nationalism often reinforced each other. Seeking a unique greatness in every people, well-educated romantics plumbed their own histories and cultures. Like modern anthropologists, they turned their attention to peasant life and transcribed the folk songs, tales, and proverbs that the cosmopolitan Enlightenment had disdained. The brothers Jacob and Wilhelm Grimm were particularly successful at rescuing German fairy tales from oblivion. In the Slavic lands, romantics played a decisive role in converting spoken peasant languages into modern written languages. The greatest of all Russian poets, Alexander Pushkin (1799–1837), rejecting eighteenth-century attempts to force Russian poetry into a classical straitjacket, used his lyric genius to mold the modern literary language.

ART AND MUSIC

The greatest and most moving romantic painter in France was Eugène Delacroix (1798–1863), probably the illegitimate son of the French foreign minister Talleyrand. Delacroix was a master of dramatic, colorful scenes that stir the emotions. He was fascinated with remote and exotic subjects, whether lion hunts in Morocco or the languishing, sensuous women of a sultan's harem. Yet he was also a passionate spokesman for freedom. His masterpiece, *Liberty Leading the People,* celebrated the nobility of popular revolution in general and revolution in France in particular.

In England, the most outstanding romantic painters were J. M. W. Turner (1775–1851) and John Constable (1776–1837). Both were fascinated by nature, but their interpretations of it contrasted sharply, aptly symbolizing the tremendous emotional range of the romantic movement. Turner depicted nature's power and terror; wild storms and sinking ships were favorite subjects. Constable painted gentle Wordsworthian landscapes in which human beings are at one with their environment, the comforting countryside of unspoiled rural England (see Color Insert V).

It was in music that romanticism realized most fully and permanently its goals of free expression and emotional intensity. Whereas the composers of the eighteenth century had remained true to well-defined structures, like the classical symphony, the great romantics used a great range of forms to paint a thousand landscapes and evoke a host of powerful emotions. Romantic composers also transformed the small classical orchestra, tripling its size by adding wind instruments, percussion, and more brass and strings. The crashing chords evoking the surge of the masses in Chopin's "Revolutionary" etude, the bottomless despair of the funeral march in Beethoven's Third Symphony, the solemn majesty of a great religious event in Schumann's Rhenish Symphony—such were the modern orchestra's musical paintings that plumbed the depths of human feeling.

This range and intensity gave music and musicians much greater prestige than in the past. Music no longer simply complemented a church service or helped a nobleman digest his dinner. Music became a

Heroes of Romanticism Observed by a portrait of Byron and bust of Beethoven, Liszt plays for friends. From left to right sit Alexander Dumas, George Sand (characteristically wearing men's garb), and Marie d'Agoult, Liszt's mistress. Standing are Victor Hugo, Paganini, and Rossini. *(Bildarchiv Preussischer Kulturbesitz)*

sublime end in itself. It became for many the greatest of the arts, precisely because it achieved the most ecstatic effect and most perfectly realized the endless yearning of the soul. It was worthy of great concert halls and the most dedicated sacrifice. The composer Franz Liszt (1811–1886) vowed to do for the piano what Paganini had done for the violin, and he was lionized as the greatest pianist of his age. People swooned for Liszt as they scream for rock stars today.

Though romanticism dominated music until late in the nineteenth century, no composer ever surpassed its first great master, Ludwig van Beethoven (1770–1827). Extending and breaking open classical forms, Beethoven used contrasting themes and tones to produce dramatic conflict and inspiring resolutions. His range was tremendous; his output included symphonies, chamber music, sonatas for violin and piano, masses, an opera, and a great many songs.

At the peak of his fame, in constant demand as a composer and recognized as the leading concert pianist of his day, Beethoven began to lose his hearing. He considered suicide but eventually overcame despair: "I will take fate by the throat; it will not bend me completely to its will."[4] Beethoven continued to pour out immortal music. Among other achievements, he fully exploited for the first time the richness and beauty of the piano. Beethoven never heard much of his later work, including the unforget-

Delacroix: Massacre at Chios The Greek struggle for freedom and independence won the enthusiastic support of liberals, nationalists, and romantics. The Ottoman Turks were seen as cruel oppressors holding back the course of history, as in this powerful masterpiece by Delacroix. *(Louvre/Cliché des Musées Nationaux)*

table choral finale to the Ninth Symphony, for his last years were silent, spent in total deafness.

REFORMS AND REVOLUTIONS

While the romantic movement was developing, liberal, national, and socialist forces battered against the conservatism of 1815. In some countries, change occurred gradually and peacefully. Elsewhere, pressure built up like steam in a pressure cooker without a safety valve and eventually caused an explosion in

1848. Three important countries—Greece, Great Britain, and France—experienced variations on this basic theme.

NATIONAL LIBERATION IN GREECE

National, liberal revolution, frustrated in Italy and Spain by conservative statesmen, succeeded first after 1815 in Greece. Since the fifteenth century, the Greeks had been living under the domination of the Ottoman Turks. In spite of centuries of foreign rule, the Greeks had survived as a people, united by their language and the Greek orthodox religion. It was perfectly natural that the general growth of national aspirations and a desire for independence would inspire some Greeks in the early nineteenth century. This rising national movement led to the formation of secret societies and then to revolt in 1821, led by Alexander Ypsilanti, a Greek patriot and a general in the Russian army.

The Great Powers, particularly Metternich, were opposed to all revolution, even revolution against the Islamic Turks. They refused to back Ypsilanti and supported the Ottoman Empire. Yet for many Europeans the Greek cause became a holy one. Educated Americans and Europeans were in love with the culture of classical Greece; Russians were stirred by the piety of their Orthodox brethren. Writers and artists, moved by the romantic impulse, responded enthusiastically to the Greek struggle. The flamboyant, radical poet Lord Byron went to Greece and died there in the struggle "that Greece might still be free." Turkish atrocities toward the rebels fanned the fires of European outrage and Greek determination. One of Delacroix's romantic masterpieces memorialized the massacre at Chios, where the Turks slaughtered nearly 100,000 Greeks.

The Greeks, though often quarreling among themselves, battled on against the Turks and hoped for the eventual support of European governments. In 1827 Great Britain, France, and Russia responded to popular demands at home and directed Turkey to accept an armistice. When the Turks refused, the navies of these three powers trapped the Turkish fleet at Navarino and destroyed it. Russia then declared another of its periodic wars of expansion against the Turks. This led to the establishment of a Russian protectorate over much of present-day Rumania, which had also been under Turkish rule. Great Britain, France, and Russia finally declared Greece independent in 1830 and installed a German prince as king of the new country in 1832. In the end the Greeks had won: a small nation had gained its independence in a heroic war against a foreign empire.

LIBERAL REFORM IN GREAT BRITAIN

Eighteenth-century British society had been both flexible and remarkably stable. It was dominated by the landowning aristocracy, but that class was neither closed nor rigidly defined. Successful business and professional people could buy land and become gentlemen, while the common people had more than the usual opportunities of the preindustrial world. Basic civil rights for all were balanced by a tradition of deference to one's social superiors. Parliament was manipulated by the king and was thoroughly undemocratic. Only about 6 percent of the population could vote for representatives to Parliament, and by the 1780s there was growing interest in some kind of political reform.

But the French Revolution threw the aristocracy into a panic for a generation, making it extremely hostile to any attempts to change the status quo. The Tory party, completely controlled by the landed aristocracy, was particularly fearful of radical movements at home and abroad. Castlereagh initially worked closely with Metternich to restrain France and restore a conservative balance in central Europe. This same intense conservatism motivated the Tory government at home. After 1815, the aristocracy defended its ruling position by repressing every kind of popular protest.

The first step in this direction was the Corn Law of 1815. During a generation of war with France, the British had been unable to import food. As shortages occurred and agricultural prices skyrocketed, a great deal of marginal land had been brought under cultivation. This development had been a bonanza for the landed aristocracy, whose fat rent rolls became even fatter. Peace meant that grain could be imported again and that the price of wheat and bread would go down. To almost everyone except the aristocracy, lower prices seemed highly desirable. The aristocracy, however, rammed the Corn Law through Parliament. This law prohibited the importation of foreign grain unless the price at home rose above eighty shillings per quarter-ton—a level reached only in time of harvest disaster before 1790. Seldom has a class legislated more selfishly for its own narrow economic advantage.

The Corn Law, coming at a time of widespread unemployment and postwar adjustment, led to protests and demonstrations by urban laborers. They were supported by radical intellectuals, who campaigned for a reformed House of Commons that would serve the nation and not just the aristocracy. In 1817 the Tory government responded by temporarily suspending the traditional rights of peaceable assembly and habeas corpus. Two years later, Parliament passed the infamous Six Acts, which among other things controlled a heavily taxed press and practically

THE PRELUDE TO 1848

March 1814	Russia, Prussia, Austria, and Britain form the Quadruple Alliance to defeat France
April 1814	Napoleon abdicates
May–June 1814	Restoration of the Bourbon monarchy; Louis XVIII issues Constitutional Charter providing for civil liberties and representative government
	First Peace of Paris: allies combine leniency with defensive posture toward France
October 1814– June 1815	Congress of Vienna peace settlement: establishes balance-of-power principle and creates the German Confederation
February 1815	Napoleon escapes from Elba and marches on Paris
June 1815	Battle of Waterloo
September 1815	Austria, Prussia, and Russia form the Holy Alliance to repress liberal and revolutionary movements
November 1815	Second Peace of Paris and renewal of Quadruple Alliance: punishes France and establishes the European "congress system"
1819	Carlsbad Decrees: Metternich imposes harsh measures throughout the German Confederation
1820	Revolution in Spain and the Kingdom of the Two Sicilies
	Congress of Troppau: Metternich and Alexander I of Russia proclaim principle of intervention to maintain autocratic regimes
1821	Austria crushes liberal revolution in Naples and restores the Sicilian autocracy
	Greek revolt against the Ottoman Turks
1823	French armies restore the Spanish regime
	United States proclaims the Monroe Doctrine
1824	Reactionary Charles X succeeds Louis XVIII in France
1830	Charles X repudiates the Constitutional Charter; insurrection and collapse of government; Louis Philippe succeeds to the throne and maintains a narrowly liberal regime until 1848
	Greece wins independence from the Ottoman Empire
1832	Reform Bill expands British electorate and encourages the middle class
1839	Louis Blanc, *Organization of Work*
1840	Pierre Joseph Proudhon, *What Is Property?*
1846	Jules Michelet, *The People*
1848	Karl Marx and Friedrich Engels, *The Communist Manifesto*

eliminated all mass meetings. These acts followed an enormous but orderly protest at Saint Peter's Fields in Manchester, which had been savagely broken up by armed cavalry. Nicknamed the "Battle of Peterloo," in scornful reference to the British victory at Waterloo, this incident expressed the government's determination to repress and stand fast.

Ongoing industrial development was not only creating urban and social problems but also strengthening the upper middle classes. The new manufacturing and commercial groups insisted on a place for their new wealth alongside the landed wealth of the aristocracy in the framework of political power and social prestige. They called for certain kinds of liberal reform: reform of town government, organization of a new police force, and more rights for Catholics and dissenters. In the 1820s, a less frightened Tory government moved in the direction of better urban administration, greater economic liberalism, and civil equality for Catholics. The prohibition on imports of foreign grain was replaced by a heavy tariff. These actions encouraged the middle classes to press on for reform of Parliament, so they could have a larger say in government and perhaps repeal the revised Corn Law, that symbol of aristocratic domination.

The Whig party, though led like the Tories by great aristocrats, had by tradition been more responsive to commercial and manufacturing interests. In 1830 a Whig ministry introduced "an act to amend the representation of the people of England and Wales." Defeated, then passed by the House of Commons, this reform bill was rejected by the House of Lords. But when in 1832 the Whigs got the king to promise to create enough new peers to pass the law, the House of Lords reluctantly gave in rather than see its snug little club ruined by upstart manufacturers and plutocrats. A mighty surge of popular protest had helped the king and lords make up their minds.

The Reform Bill of 1832 had profound significance. The House of Commons had emerged as the all-important legislative body. In the future, an obstructionist House of Lords could always be brought into line by the threat of creating new peers. The new industrial areas of the country gained representation in the Commons, and many old "rotten boroughs" —electoral districts with very few voters that the landed aristocracy had bought and sold—were eliminated.

The redistribution of seats reflected the shift in population to the northern manufacturing counties and the gradual emergence of an urban society. As a result of the Reform Bill of 1832, the number of voters increased about 50 percent. Comfortable middle-class groups in the urban population, as well as some substantial farmers who leased their land, received the vote. Thus the pressures building in Great Britain were successfully—though only temporarily —released. A major reform had been achieved peacefully, without revolution or civil war. More radical reforms within the system appeared difficult but not impossible.

The principal radical program was embodied in the "People's Charter" of 1838 and the Chartist movement (page 828). Partly inspired by the economic distress of the working class, the Chartists' core demand was universal male (not female) suffrage. They saw complete political democracy and rule by the common people as the means to a good and just society. Hundreds of thousands of people signed gi-

gantic petitions calling on Parliament to grant all men the right to vote, first and most seriously in 1839, again in 1842, and yet again in 1848. Parliament rejected all three petitions. In the short run, the working poor failed with their Chartist demands, but they learned a valuable lesson in mass politics.

While calling for universal suffrage, many working-class people joined with middle-class manufacturers in the Anti-Corn Law League, founded in Manchester in 1839. Mass participation made possible a popular crusade against the tariff on imported grain and against the landed aristocracy. People were fired up by dramatic popular orators such as John Bright and Richard Cobden. These fighting liberals argued that lower food prices and more jobs in industry depended on repeal of the Corn Law. Much of the working class agreed. The climax of the movement came in 1845, when Ireland's potato crop failed and famine seemed likely in England. In 1846 the Tory prime minister Robert Peel joined with the Whigs and a minority of his own party to repeal the Corn Law. Thereafter, free trade became almost sacred doctrine in Great Britain.

The following year, the Tories passed a bill designed to help the working classes, but in a different way. This was the Ten Hours Act of 1847, which limited the workday for women and young people in factories to ten hours. Tory aristocrats continued to champion legislation regulating factory conditions. They were competing vigorously with the middle class for the support of the working class. This healthy competition between a still-vigorous aristocracy and a strong middle class was a crucial factor in Great Britain's peaceful evolution. The working classes could make temporary alliances with either competitor to better their own conditions.

THE REVOLUTION OF 1830 IN FRANCE

Louis XVIII's Constitutional Charter of 1814—theoretically a gift from the king but actually a response to political pressures—was basically a liberal constitution (page 798). The economic gains of the middle class and the prosperous peasantry were fully protected; great intellectual and artistic freedom was permitted; and a real parliament with upper and lower houses was created. Immediately after Napoleon's abortive Hundred Days, the moderate, worldly-wise king refused to bow to the wishes of diehard aristocrats like his brother Charles, who wished to sweep away all the revolutionary changes and return to a bygone age of royal absolutism and aristocratic pretension. Instead, Louis appointed as his ministers moderate royalists, who sought and obtained the support of a majority of the representatives elected to the lower Chamber of Deputies between 1816 and Louis's death in 1824.

Louis XVIII's charter was anything but democratic. Only about 100,000 of the wealthiest people out of a total population of 30 million had the right to vote for the deputies who, with the king and his ministers, made the laws of the nation. Nonetheless, the "notable people" who did vote came from very different backgrounds. There were wealthy businessmen, war profiteers, successful professionals, ex-revolutionaries, large landowners from the middle class, Bourbons, and Bonapartists.

The old aristocracy with its pre-1789 mentality was a minority within the voting population. It was this situation that Louis's younger brother and successor, Charles X (1824–1830), could not abide. Crowned in a lavish, utterly medieval, five-hour ceremony in the cathedral of Reims in 1824, Charles was a true reactionary. He wanted to re-establish the old order in France. Increasingly blocked by the opposition of the deputies, Charles finally repudiated the Constitutional Charter in an attempted coup in July 1830. He issued decrees stripping much of the wealthy middle class of its voting rights, and he censored the press. The reaction was an immediate insurrection. In "three glorious days" the government collapsed. Paris boiled with revolutionary excitement, and Charles fled. Then the upper middle class, which had fomented the revolt, skillfully seated Charles's cousin, Louis Philippe, duke of Orléans, on the vacant throne.

Louis Philippe (1830–1848) accepted the Constitutional Charter of 1814, adopted the red, white, and blue flag of the French Revolution, and admitted that he was merely the "king of the French people." In spite of such symbolic actions, the situation in France remained fundamentally unchanged. As Casimir Périer, a wealthy banker and Louis Philippe's new chief minister, bluntly told a deputy who complained when the vote was extended only from 100,000 to 170,000 citizens: "The trouble with this country is that there are too many people like you who imagine that there has been a revolution in France."[5] The

Free-Trade Optimism Appearing in *Punch* in 1846 as the Corn Law was being repealed, this cartoon looked to the future and reflected British self-confidence. Socially and economically advanced Great Britain had no need for protective tariffs. The British economy actually did boom after 1850. *(The British Library)*

wealthy "notable" elite actually tightened its control as the old aristocracy retreated to the provinces to sulk harmlessly. For the upper middle class there had been a change in dynasty, in order to protect the status quo and the narrowly liberal institutions of 1815. Republicans, democrats, social reformers, and the poor of Paris were bitterly disappointed. They had made a revolution, but it seemed for naught.

THE REVOLUTIONS OF 1848

In 1848 revolutionary political and social ideologies combined with economic crisis and the romantic impulse to produce a vast upheaval. Only the most advanced and the most backward major countries —reforming Great Britain and immobile Russia—

Daumier: The Legislative Belly Protected by freedom of the press after 1830, French radicals bitterly attacked the do-nothing government of Louis Philippe. Here Daumier savagely ridicules the corruption of the Chamber of Deputies. *(Charles Deering Collection. Courtesy of the Art Institute of Chicago)*

escaped untouched. Governments toppled; monarchs and ministers bowed or fled. National independence, liberal-democratic constitutions, and social reform: the lofty aspirations of a generation seemed at hand. Yet, in the end, the revolutions failed. Why was this so?

A DEMOCRATIC REPUBLIC IN FRANCE

The late 1840s in Europe were hard economically and tense politically. The potato famine in Ireland in 1845 had echoes on the Continent. Bad harvests jacked up food prices and caused misery and unemployment in the cities. "Prerevolutionary" outbreaks occurred all across Europe: an abortive Polish revolution in the northern part of Austria in 1846, a civil war between radicals and conservatives in Switzerland in 1847, and an armed uprising in Naples, Italy, in January 1848. Revolution was almost universally expected, but it took revolution in Paris—once again—to turn expectations into realities.

From its beginning in 1830, Louis Philippe's "bourgeois monarchy" was characterized by stubborn inaction. There was a glaring lack of social legislation, and politics was dominated by corruption and selfish special interests. The king's chief minister in the 1840s, François Guizot, was complacency personified. Guizot was especially satisfied with the electoral system. Only the rich could vote for deputies, and many of the deputies were docile government bureaucrats. It was the government's stubborn refusal to consider electoral reform that touched off popular revolt in Paris. Barricades went up on the night of February 22, 1848, and by February 24, Louis Philippe had abdicated in favor of his grandson. But the common people in arms would tolerate no more monarchy. This refusal led to the proclamation of a provisional republic, headed by a ten-man executive committee and certified by cries of approval from the revolutionary crowd.

In the flush of victory, there was much about which Parisian revolutionaries could agree. A generation of historians and journalists had praised the First French Republic, and their work had borne fruit: the revolutionaries were firmly committed to a republic as opposed to any form of constitutional monarchy, and they immediately set about drafting a constitution for France's Second Republic. Moreover, they wanted a truly popular and democratic republic, so that the healthy, life-giving forces of the common people—the peasants and the workers—could reform society with wise legislation. In practice, building such a republic meant giving the right to vote to every adult male, and this was quickly done. Revolutionary compassion and sympathy for freedom were expressed in the freeing of all slaves in French colonies, abolition of the death penalty, and the establishment of a ten-hour workday for Paris.

Yet there were profound differences within the revolutionary coalition in Paris. On the one hand there were the moderate, liberal republicans of the middle class. They viewed universal manhood suffrage as the ultimate concession to be made to popular forces and strongly opposed any further radical social measures. On the other hand were the radical republicans. Influenced by the critique of capitalism and unbridled individualism elaborated by a generation of utopian socialists, and appalled by the poverty and misery of the urban poor, the radical republicans were committed to socialism. To be sure, socialism came in many utopian shapes and sizes for the Parisian working poor and their leaders, but that did not make their commitment to it any less real. Finally, wedged in between were individuals like the poet Lamartine and the democrat Ledru-Rollin, who were neither doctrinaire socialists nor stand-pat liberals and who sought to escape an impending tragedy.

Worsening depression and rising unemployment brought these conflicting goals to the fore. Louis Blanc (page 846), who along with a worker named Albert represented the republican socialists in the provisional government, pressed for recognition of a socialist right to work. Blanc asserted that permanent government-sponsored cooperative workshops should be established for workers. Such workshops would be an alternative to capitalist employment and a decisive step toward a new social order.

The moderate republicans wanted no such thing. They were willing to provide only temporary relief. The resulting compromise set up national workshops —soon to become a vast program of pick-and-shovel public works—and established a special commission under Louis Blanc to "study the question." This satisfied no one. As bad as the national workshops were, though, they were better than nothing. An army of desperate poor from the French provinces and even from foreign countries streamed into Paris to sign up. The number enrolled in the workshops soared from 10,000 in March to 120,000 by June, and another 80,000 workers were trying unsuccessfully to become members.

While the workshops in Paris grew, the French masses went to the polls in late April. Voting in most cases for the first time, the people elected to the new Constituent Assembly about five hundred moderate republicans, three hundred monarchists, and one hundred radicals who professed various brands of socialism. One of the moderate republicans was the author of *Democracy in America*, Alexis de Tocqueville (1805–1859), who had predicted the overthrow of Louis Philippe's government. To this brilliant observer, socialism was the most characteristic aspect of the revolution in Paris.

This socialist revolution had evoked a violent reaction not only among the frightened middle and upper classes but also among the bulk of the population— the peasants. The French peasants owned land, and according to Tocqueville, "private property had become with all those who owned it a sort of bond of fraternity."[6] The countryside, Tocqueville wrote, had been seized with a universal hatred of radical Paris. Returning from Normandy to take his seat in the new Constituent Assembly, Tocqueville saw that a majority of the members were firmly committed to the republic and strongly opposed to the socialists, and he shared their sentiments.

The clash of ideologies—of liberal capitalism and socialism—became a clash of classes and arms after the elections. The new government's executive committee dropped Louis Blanc and thereafter included no representative of the Parisian working class. Fearing that their socialist hopes were about to be dashed, the workers invaded the assembly on May 15 and tried to proclaim a new revolutionary state. But the government was ready and used the middle-class National Guard to squelch this uprising. As the workshops continued to fill and grow more radical, the fearful but powerful propertied classes in the Assembly took the offensive. On June 22 the government dissolved the national workshops in Paris, giving the workers the choice of joining the army or going to workshops in the provinces.

The result was a spontaneous and violent uprising. Frustrated in their attempts to create a socialist society, masses of desperate people were now losing even their life-sustaining relief. As a voice from the crowd cried out when the famous astronomer François Arago counseled patience: "Ah, Monsieur Arago, you have never been hungry!"[7] Barricades sprang up in the narrow streets of Paris, and a terrible class war began. Working people fought with the courage of utter desperation, but the government had the army and the support of peasant France. After three terrible "June Days" and the death or injury of more than ten thousand people, the republican army under General Louis Cavaignac stood triumphant in a sea of working-class blood and hatred.

The revolution in France thus ended in spectacular failure. The February coalition of the middle and working classes had in four short months become locked in mortal combat. In place of a generous democratic republic, the Constituent Assembly completed a constitution featuring a strong executive. This allowed Louis Napoleon, nephew of Napoleon Bonaparte, to win a landslide victory in the election of December 1848. The appeal of his great name, as well as the desire of the propertied classes for order at any cost, had produced a semi-authoritarian regime.

The Austrian Empire in 1848

Throughout central Europe, news of the upheaval in France evoked feverish excitement and eventually revolution. Liberals demanded written constitutions, representative government, and greater civil liberties. When governments hesitated, popular revolts followed. Urban workers and students served as the shock troops, but they were allied with middle-class liberals and peasants. In the face of this united front, monarchs collapsed and granted almost everything. The popular revolutionary coalition, having secured great and easy victories, then broke down as it had in France. The traditional forces—the monarchy, the aristocracy, and the regular army—recovered their nerve, reasserted their authority, and took back many though not all of the concessions. Reaction was everywhere victorious.

The revolution in the Austrian Empire began in Hungary. Nationalism had been growing among Hungarians since about 1790, and in 1848 under the leadership of Louis Kossuth, the Hungarians demanded national autonomy, full civil liberties, and

universal suffrage. When the monarchy in Vienna hesitated, Viennese students and workers took to the streets on March 13 and added their own demands. Peasant disorders broke out in parts of the empire. The Habsburg emperor Ferdinand I (1835–1848) capitulated and promised reforms and a liberal constitution. Metternich fled in disguise toward London. The old order seemed to be collapsing with unbelievable rapidity.

The coalition of revolutionaries was not completely stable, though. The Austrian Empire was overwhelmingly agricultural, and serfdom still existed. On March 20, as part of its capitulation before upheaval, the monarchy abolished serfdom with its degrading forced labor and feudal services. Peasants throughout the empire felt they had won a victory reminiscent of that in France in 1789. Newly free, men and women of the land lost interest in the political and social questions agitating the cities. The government had in the peasants a potential ally of great importance, especially since, in central Europe as in France, the army was largely composed of peasants.

The coalition of March was also weakened—and ultimately destroyed—by conflicting national aspirations. In March the Hungarian revolutionary leaders pushed through an extremely liberal, almost democratic, constitution granting widespread voting rights and civil liberties and ending feudal obligations. So far, well and good. Yet the Hungarian revolutionaries were also nationalists with a mission. They wanted the ancient Crown of Saint Stephen, with its mosaic of provinces and nationalities, transformed into a unified centralized Hungarian nation. To the minority groups that formed half the population of the kingdom of Hungary—the Croats, the Serbs, and the Rumanians—such unification was completely unacceptable. Each felt entitled to political autonomy and cultural independence. The Habsburg monarchy in Vienna exploited the fears of the minority groups, and they were soon locked in armed combat with the new Hungarian government.

In a somewhat different way, Czech nationalists based in Bohemia and the city of Prague, led by the Czech historian Palacký, came into conflict with German nationalists. Like the minorities in Hungary, the Czechs saw their struggle for autonomy as a struggle against a dominant group—the Germans. Thus the national aspirations of different peoples in the Austrian Empire came into sharp conflict, a situation that the monarchy was able to exploit.

THE REVOLUTIONS OF 1848

February	Revolt in Paris against Louis Philippe's "bourgeois monarchy"; Louis Philippe abdicates; proclamation of a provisional republic
February–June	Establishment and rapid growth of government-sponsored workshops in France
March 3	Hungarians under Kossuth demand autonomy from Austrian Empire
March 13	Uprising of students and workers in Vienna; Metternich flees to London
March 19–21	Frederick William IV of Prussia is forced to salute the bodies of slain revolutionaries in Berlin and agrees to a liberal constitution and merger into a new German state
March 20	Ferdinand I of Austria abolishes serfdom and promises reforms
March 26	Workers in Berlin issue a series of socialist demands
April 22	French voters favor moderate republicans over radicals 5:1
May 15	Parisian socialist workers invade the Constitutional Assembly and unsuccessfully proclaim a new revolutionary state
May 18	Frankfurt National Assembly begins writing a new German constitution
June 17	Austrian army crushes working-class revolt in Prague
June 22–26	French government abolishes the national workshops, provoking an uprising June Days: republican army defeats rebellious Parisian working class
October	Austrian army besieges and retakes Vienna from students and working-class radicals
December	Conservatives force Ferdinand I of Austria to abdicate in favor of young Francis Joseph
	Frederick William IV disbands Prussian Constituent Assembly and grants Prussia a conservative constitution
	Louis Napoleon wins a landslide victory in French presidential elections
March 1849	Frankfurt Assembly elects Frederick William IV of Prussia emperor of the new German state; Frederick William refuses and reasserts royal authority in Prussia
June–August 1849	Habsburg and Russian forces defeat the Hungarian independence movement

Nor was this all. The urban working classes of poor artisans and day laborers were not as radical in the Austrian Empire as they were in France, but then neither were the middle class and lower middle class. Throughout Austria and the German states, where Metternich's brand of absolutism had so recently ruled supreme, the middle class wanted liberal reform, complete with constitutional monarchy, limited voting rights, and modest social measures. They wanted a central European equivalent of the English Reform Bill of 1832 and the Corn Law repeal of 1846. When the urban poor rose in arms, as they did in the Austrian cities of Vienna, Prague, and Milan and throughout the German Confederation as well, and presented their own demands for universal vot-

ing rights and socialist workshops, the prosperous middle classes recoiled in alarm. As in Paris, the union of the urban poor and the middle class was soon a mere memory, and a bad memory at that.

Finally, the conservative aristocratic forces gathered around Emperor Ferdinand I regained their nerve and reasserted their great strength. The archduchess Sophia, a conservative but intelligent and courageous Bavarian princess married to the emperor's brother, provided a rallying point. Deeply ashamed of the emperor's collapse before a "mess of students,"[8] she insisted that Ferdinand, who had no heir, abdicate in favor of her eighteen-year-old son, Francis Joseph. Powerful nobles who held high positions in the government, the army, and the church agreed completely. They organized around Sophia in a secret conspiracy to reverse and crush the revolution.

Their first breakthrough came when one of the most dedicated members of the group, Prince Alfred Windischgrätz, bombarded Prague and savagely crushed a working-class revolt there on June 17. Other Austrian officials and nobles began to lead the minority nationalities of Hungary against the revolutionary government proclaimed by the Hungarian patriots. Another Austrian army reconquered Austria's possessions in northern Italy in late July 1848. Revolution failed as miserably in Italy as everywhere else. At the end of October, the well-equipped, predominantly peasant troops of the regular Austrian army attacked the student and working-class radicals in Vienna and retook the city at the cost of more than four thousand casualties. Thus, the determination of the Austrian aristocracy and the loyalty of its army were the final ingredients in the triumph of reaction and the defeat of revolution.

Only in Hungary were the forces represented by Sophia's son Francis Joseph (1848–1916), crowned emperor of Austria immediately after his eighteenth birthday in December 1848, at first unsuccessful. Yet another determined conservative, Nicholas I of Russia (1825–1855), obligingly lent his iron hand. On June 6, 1849, 130,000 Russian troops poured into Hungary. After bitter fighting—in which the Hungarian army supported the revolutionary Hungarian government—they subdued the country. For a number of years the Habsburgs ruled Hungary as a conquered territory.

PRUSSIA AND THE FRANKFURT ASSEMBLY

The rest of the states in the German Confederation generally recapitulated the ebb and flow of developments in France and Austria. The key difference was the additional goal of unifying the thirty-eight states of the German Confederation, with the possible exception of Austria, into a single sovereign nation. Therefore events in Germany were extraordinarily complex, since they were occurring not only in the individual principalities but at the all-German level as well.

After Austria, Prussia was the largest and most influential German kingdom. Prior to 1848, the goal of middle-class Prussian liberals had been to transform absolutist Prussia into a liberal constitutional monarchy. Such a monarchy would then take the lead in merging itself and all the other German states into a liberal unified nation. The agitation following the fall of Louis Philippe encouraged Prussian liberals to press their demands. When they were not granted, the artisans and factory workers in Berlin exploded, joining temporarily with the middle-class liberals in the struggle against the monarchy. The autocratic yet paternalistic Frederick William IV (1840–1861), already displaying the instability that later became insanity, vacillated. Humiliated by the revolutionary crowd, which forced him to salute from his balcony the blood-spattered corpses of workers who had fallen in an uprising on March 18, the nearly hysterical king finally caved in. On March 21 he promised to grant Prussia a liberal constitution and to merge it into a new national German state that was to be created. He appointed two wealthy businessmen from the Rhineland—perfect representatives of moderate liberalism—to form a new government.

The situation might have stabilized at this point if the workers had not wanted much more and the Prussian aristocracy much less. On March 26, the workers issued a series of radical and vaguely socialist demands, which troubled their middle-class allies: universal voting rights, a ministry of labor, a minimum wage, and a ten-hour day. At the same time, a wild-tempered Prussian landowner and aristocrat, Otto von Bismarck, joined the conservative clique gathered around the king to urge counter-revolution. While these tensions in Prussia were growing, an elected assembly arrived in Berlin to write a constitution for the Prussian state.

To add to the complexity of the situation, a self-appointed committee of liberals from various German states successfully called for the formation of a national constituent assembly to begin writing a federal constitution for a unified German state. That body met for the first time on May 18 in Saint Paul's Church in Frankfurt. The Frankfurt National Assembly was a most curious revolutionary body. It was really a serious middle-class body whose 820 members included some 200 lawyers; 100 professors; many doctors, judges, and officials; and 140 businessmen for good measure.

Called together to write a constitution, the learned body was soon absorbed in a battle with Denmark over the provinces of Schleswig and Holstein. Juris-

Revolutionary Justice in Vienna As part of the conservative resurgence, in October 1848 the Austrian minister of war ordered up reinforcements for an army marching on Hungary. In a last defiant gesture the outraged revolutionaries in Vienna seized the minister and lynched him from a lamppost for treason. The army then reconquered the city in a week of bitter fighting. *(Mary Evans Picture Library)*

diction over them was a hopelessly complicated issue from a legal point of view. Britain's Foreign Minister Lord Palmerston once said that only three people had ever understood the Schleswig-Holstein question, and of those one had died, another had gone mad, and he himself had forgotten the answer. The provinces were inhabited primarily by Germans but were ruled by the king of Denmark, although Holstein was a member of the German Confederation. When Frederick VII, the new nationalistic king of Denmark, tried to integrate both provinces into the rest of his state, the Germans there revolted.

Hypnotized by this conflict, the National Assembly at Frankfurt debated ponderously and finally called on the Prussian army to oppose Denmark in the name of the German nation. Prussia responded and began war with Denmark. As the Schleswig-Holstein issue demonstrated, the national ideal was a crucial factor motivating the German middle classes in 1848.

Almost obsessed with the fate of Germans under Danish rule, many members of the Frankfurt Assembly also wanted to bring the German-speaking provinces of Austria into the new German state. Yet resurgent Austria resolutely opposed any division of its territory. Once this Austrian action made a "big German state" impossible, the Frankfurt Assembly completed drafting a liberal constitution. Finally, in March 1849, the Assembly elected King Frederick William of Prussia emperor of the new German national state (minus Austria and Schleswig-Holstein).

By early 1849, however, reaction had been successful almost everywhere. Frederick William reasserted his royal authority, disbanded the Prussian Constituent Assembly, and granted his subjects a limited, essentially conservative, constitution. Reasserting that he ruled by divine right, Frederick William contemptuously refused to accept the "crown from the gutter." The reluctant revolutionaries in Frankfurt had waited too long and acted too timidly.

When Frederick William, who really wanted to be emperor but only on his own authoritarian terms, tried to get the small monarchs of Germany to elect him emperor, Austria balked. Supported by Russia, Austria forced Prussia to renounce all its schemes of unification in late 1850. The German Confederation was re-established. After two turbulent years, the political map of the German states remained unchanged. Attempts to unite the Germans—first in a liberal national state and then in a conservative Prussian empire—had failed completely.

The liberal and nationalistic revolutions of 1848 were abortive. Political, economic, and social pressures that had been building since 1815 exploded dramatically, but very few revolutionary goals were realized. The moderate, nationalistic middle classes were unable to consolidate their initial victories in France or elsewhere in Europe. Instead, they drew back when artisans, factory workers, and radical socialists rose up to present their own much more revolutionary demands. This retreat facilitated the efforts of dedicated aristocrats in central Europe and made possible the crushing of Parisian workers by a coalition of solid bourgeoisie and landowning peasantry in France. A host of fears, a sea of blood, and a torrent of disillusion had drowned the lofty ideals and utopian visions of a generation. The age of romantic revolution was over.

NOTES

1. A. J. May, *The Age of Metternich, 1814–1848,* rev. ed. (New York: Holt, Rinehart & Winston, 1963), p. 11.
2. H. Kohn, *Nationalism* (New York: Van Nostrand, 1955), pp. 141–142.
3. Quoted in F. D. Klingender, *Art and the Industrial Revolution* (St. Albans, Eng.: Paladin, 1972), p. 117.
4. Quoted in F. B. Artz, *From the Renaissance to Romanticism: Trends in Style in Art, Literature, and Music, 1300–1830* (Chicago: University of Chicago Press, 1962), pp. 276, 278.
5. Quoted in G. Wright, *France in Modern Times* (Chicago: Rand McNally, 1960), p. 145.
6. A. de Tocqueville, *Recollections* (New York: Columbia University Press, 1949), p. 94.
7. M. Agulhon, *1848* (Paris: Editions du Seuil, 1973), pp. 68–69.
8. Quoted in W. L. Langer, *Political and Social Upheaval, 1832–1852* (New York: Harper & Row, 1969), p. 361.

SUGGESTED READING

All of the works cited in the Notes are highly recommended. May's is a good brief survey, while Kohn has written perceptively on nationalism in many books. Wright's *France in Modern Times* is a lively introduction to French history with stimulating biographical discussions; Langer's is a balanced synthesis with an excellent bibliography. Among general studies, C. Morazé, *The Triumph of the Middle Classes* (1968), a wide-ranging procapitalist interpretation, may be compared with E. J. Hobsbawm's flexible Marxism in *The Age of Revolution, 1789–1848* (1962). For English history, A. Brigg's socially oriented *The Making of Modern England, 1784–1867* (1967) and D. Thomson's *England in the Nineteenth Century, 1815–1914* (1951) are excellent. Restoration France is sympathetically portrayed by G. de Bertier de Sauvigny in *The Bourbon Restoration* (1967). T. Hamerow studies the social implications of the dual revolution in Germany in *Restoration, Revolution, Reaction, 1815–1871* (1966), which may be compared to H. Treitschke's bombastic, pro-Prussian *History of Germany in the Nineteenth Century* (1915–1919), a classic of nationalistic history, and L. Snyder, *Roots of German Nationalism* (1978). E. Kedourie, *Nationalism* (1960), is a stimulating critique of the new faith. H. Kissinger, *A World Restored* (1957), offers not only a provocative interpretation of the Congress of Vienna but also insights into the mind of Richard Nixon's famous secretary of state. Compare with H. Nicolson's entertaining *The Congress of Vienna* (1946). On 1848, L. B. Namier's highly critical *1848: The Revolution of the Intellectuals* (1964) and P. Robertson's *Revolutions of 1848: A Social History* (1960) are outstanding. I. Deak, *The Lawful Revolution: Louis Kossuth and the Hungarians, 1848–49* (1979), is a noteworthy study of an interesting figure.

On early socialism and Marxism, there are W. Sewell, Jr.'s *Work and Revolution in France* (1980) and E. Wilson's engrossing survey of nineteenth-century developments, *To the Finland Station* (1953), as well as G. Lichtheim's high-powered *Marxism* (1961) and his *Short History of Socialism* (1970). J. Schumpeter, *Capitalism, Socialism and Democracy* (1947), is magnificent but difficult, a real mind-stretcher. On liberalism, there is R. Heilbroner's entertaining *The Worldly Philosophers* (1967) and G. de Ruggiero's classic *History of European Liberalism* (1959). J. Barzun, *Classic, Romantic and Modern* (1961), skillfully discusses the emergence of romanticism. R. Stromberg, *An Intellectual History of Modern Europe,* 3rd ed. (1981), and F. Baumer, *Modern European Thought: Continuity and Change in Ideas, 1600–1950* (1970), are valuable surveys. The important place of religion in nineteenth-century thought is considered from different perspectives in H. McLeod, *Religion and the People of Western Europe* (1981), and O. Chadwick, *The Secularization of the European Mind in the Nineteenth Century* (1976). Two good church histories with useful bibliographies are J. Altholz, *The Churches in the Nineteenth Century* (1967), and A. Vidler, *The Church in an Age of Revolution: 1789 to the Present Day* (1961).

The thoughtful reader is strongly advised to delve into the incredibly rich writing of contemporaries. J. Bowditch and C. Ramsland, eds., *Voices of the Industrial Revolution* (1961), is an excellent starting point, with well-chosen selections from leading economic thinkers and early socialists. H. Hugo, ed., *The Romantic Reader,* is another fine anthology. Jules Michelet's compassionate masterpiece *The People,* a famous historian's anguished examination of French social divisions on the eve of 1848, draws one into the heart of the period and is highly recommended. Alexis de Tocqueville covers some of the same ground less romantically in his *Recollections,* which may be compared with Karl Marx's white-hot "instant history," *Class Struggles in France, 1848–1850* (1850). Great novels that accurately portray aspects of the times are Victor Hugo, *Les Misérables,* an exciting story of crime and passion among France's poor; Honoré de Balzac, *Cousin Bette* and *Père Goriot;* and Thomas Mann, *Buddenbrooks,* a wonderful historical novel that traces the rise and fall of a prosperous German family over three generations during the nineteenth century.

28

LIFE IN EUROPEAN URBAN SOCIETY

*T*HE ERA of intellectual and political upheaval that culminated in the revolutions of 1848 was also an era of rapid urbanization. After 1848 Western political development veered off in a novel and uncharted direction, but the growth of towns and cities rushed forward with undiminished force. Thus Western society was urban and industrial in 1900, as surely as it had been rural and agrarian in 1800. The urbanization of society was both a result of the Industrial Revolution and a reflection of its enormous impact. What was life like in the cities, and how did it change? What did the emergence of urban industrial society mean for rich and poor and in between? How did families cope with the challenges and respond to the opportunities of the developing urban civilization? Finally, what changes in science and thought inspired and gave expression to this new civilization? These are the questions this chapter will investigate.

TAMING THE CITY

The consequences of economic transformation were, from the beginning, more positive than historians have often recognized. Indeed, given the poverty and uncertainty of preindustrial life, the history of industrialization is probably better written in terms of increasing opportunities than of greater hardships. But does not this relatively optimistic view of the consequences of industrialization neglect the quality of life in urban areas? Were not the new industrial towns and cities awful places where people, especially the poor, suffered from bad housing, lack of sanitation, and a sense of hopelessness? Did not these drawbacks more than cancel out higher wages and greater opportunity?

INDUSTRY AND THE GROWTH OF CITIES

Since the Middle Ages, European cities had been centers of government, culture, and large-scale commerce. They had also been congested, dirty, and unhealthy. People were packed together almost as tightly as possible within the city limits. The typical city was a "walking city": for all but the wealthiest classes, walking was the only available form of transportation.

Infectious disease spread with deadly speed in cities, and people were always more likely to die in the city than in the countryside. In the larger towns, more people died each year than were born, on the average, and urban populations were able to maintain their numbers only because newcomers were continuously arriving from rural areas. Little could be done to improve these conditions. Given the pervasive poverty, absence of urban transportation, and lack of medical knowledge, the deadly and overcrowded conditions could only be accepted fatalistically. They were the urban equivalents of bad weather and poor crops, the price of urban excitement and opportunity.

Clearly, deplorable urban conditions did not originate with the Industrial Revolution. What the Industrial Revolution did was to reveal those conditions more nakedly than ever before. The steam engine freed industrialists from dependence on the energy of fast-flowing streams and rivers, which meant that by 1800 there was every incentive to build new factories in urban areas. Cities had better shipping facilities and thus better supplies of coal and raw materials. There were also many hands wanting work in the cities, for cities drew people like a magnet. And it was a great advantage for a manufacturer to have other factories nearby to supply his needs and buy his products. Therefore, as industry grew, there was also a rapid expansion of already overcrowded and unhealthy cities.

The challenge of the urban environment was felt first and most acutely in Great Britain. The number of people living in cities of 20,000 or more in England and Wales jumped from 1.5 million in 1801 to 6.3 million in 1851 and reached 15.6 million by 1891. Such cities accounted for 17 percent of the total English population in 1801, 35 percent as early as 1851, and fully 54 percent in 1891. Other countries duplicated the English pattern as they industrialized. An American observer was hardly exaggerating when he wrote in 1899 that "the most remarkable social phenomenon of the present century is the concentration of population in cities"[1] (Map 28.1).

In the 1820s and 1830s, people in Britain and France began to worry about the condition of their cities. In those years, the populations of a number of British cities were increasing by 40 to 70 percent each decade. Manchester, the cotton city, grew by 40 percent between 1811 and 1821, and by 47 percent between 1821 and 1831. With urban areas expanding at

MAP 28.1 European Cities of 100,000 or More, 1800 and 1900 There were more large cities in Great Britain in 1900 than in all Europe in 1800.

such previously undreamed-of rates, people's traditional fatalistic indifference to overcrowded, unsanitary urban living conditions began to give way to active concern. Something had to be done.

On one point everyone could agree: except on the outskirts, each town and city was using every scrap of land to the fullest extent. Parks and open areas were almost nonexistent. A British parliamentary committee reported in 1833 that "with a rapidly increasing population, lodged for the most part in narrow courts and confined streets, the means of occasional exercise and recreation in fresh air are every day lessened, as inclosures [of vacant areas] take place and buildings spread themselves on every side."[2] Buildings were erected on the smallest possible lots, in order to pack the maximum number of people into a given space. Narrow houses were built wall to wall, in long rows. These row houses had neither front nor back yards, and only a narrow alley in back separated one row from the next. Or buildings were built around tiny courtyards completely enclosed on all four sides. Many people lived in cellars and attics. The tiny rooms within such buildings were often overcrowded, with six or eight persons occupying a single room.

These highly concentrated urban populations lived in extremely unsanitary and unhealthy conditions. Open drains and sewers flowed alongside or down the middle of unpaved streets. Due to poor construction and an absence of running water, the sewers often filled with garbage and excrement. Toilet facilities were primitive in the extreme. In parts of Manchester, as many as two hundred people shared a single outhouse. Such privies filled up rapidly, and since they were infrequently emptied, sewage often overflowed and seeped into cellar dwellings.

The extent to which filth lay underfoot and the smell of excrement filled the air is hard to believe; yet it was abundantly documented between 1830 and 1850. One London construction engineer found, for example, that the cellars of two large houses on a major road were "full of night-soil [human excrement], to the depth of three feet, which had been permitted for years to accumulate from the overflow of the cesspools." Moreover, some courtyards in poorer neighborhoods became dunghills, collecting excrement that was sometimes sold as fertilizer. By the 1840s there was among the better-off classes a growing, shocking "realization that, to put it as mildly as possible, millions of English men, women, and children were living in shit."[3]

Who or what was responsible for these awful conditions? The crucial factors were the tremendous pressure of more people coupled with the *total* absence of public transportation. People simply had to jam themselves together if they were to be able to

A COURT FOR KING CHOLERA.

Filth and Disease This 1852 drawing from *Punch* tells volumes about the unhealthy living conditions of the urban poor. In the foreground children play with a dead rat and a woman scavenges a dungheap. Cheap rooming houses provide shelter for the frightfully overcrowded population. *(The British Library)*

walk to shops and factories. Another factor was that government in Great Britain, both local and national, was slow to provide sanitary facilities and establish adequate building codes. This slow pace was probably attributable more to a need to explore and identify what precisely should be done than to rigid middle-class opposition to government action. Certainly Great Britain had no monopoly on overcrowded and unhealthy urban conditions; many continental cities were every bit as bad.

Most responsible of all was the sad legacy of rural housing conditions in preindustrial society, combined with appalling ignorance. As the author of a recent study concludes, there "were rural slums of a horror not surpassed by the rookeries of London. . . .

The evidence shows that the decent cottage was the exception, the hovel the rule."[4] Thus housing was far down on the newcomer's list of priorities, and it is not strange that many carried the filth of the mud floor and the dung of the barnyard with them to the city.

Indeed, ordinary people generally took dirt and filth for granted, and some even prized it. As one English miner told an investigator, "I do not think it usual for the lasses [in the coal mines] to wash their bodies; my sisters never wash themselves." As for the men, "their legs and bodies are as black as your hat." When poor people were admitted to English workhouses, they often resisted the required bath. One man protested that it was "equal to robbing him of a great coat which he had had for some years."[5]

The Public Health Movement

Although cleanliness was not next to godliness in most people's eyes, it was becoming so for some reformers. The most famous of these was Edwin Chadwick, one of the commissioners charged with the administration of relief to paupers under the revised Poor Law of 1834. Chadwick was a good *Benthamite* —that is, a follower of the radical philosopher Jeremy Bentham (1748–1832). Bentham had taught that public problems ought to be dealt with on a rational, scientific basis and according to the "greatest good for the greatest number." Applying these principles, Chadwick soon saw that much more than economics was involved in the problems of poverty and the welfare budget. Indeed, he soon became convinced that disease and death actually caused poverty, simply because a sick worker was an unemployed worker and orphaned children were poor children. Most important, Chadwick believed that disease could be prevented by quite literally cleaning up the urban environment. That was his "sanitary idea."

Building on a growing number of medical and sociological studies, Chadwick collected detailed reports from local Poor Law officials on the "sanitary conditions of the laboring population." After three years of investigation, these reports and Chadwick's hard-hitting commentary were published in 1842 to wide publicity. This mass of evidence proved that disease was related to filthy environmental conditions, which were in turn caused largely by lack of drainage, sewers, and garbage collection. Putrefying, smelly excrement was no longer simply disgusting. For reformers like Chadwick, it was a threat to the entire community. It polluted the atmosphere and caused disease.

The key to the energetic action Chadwick proposed was an adequate supply of clean piped water. Such water was essential for personal hygiene, public bathhouses, street cleaning, firefighting, and industry. Chadwick correctly believed that the stinking excrement of communal outhouses could be dependably carried off by water through sewers at less than one-twentieth the cost of removing it by hand. The cheap iron pipes and tile drains of the industrial age would provide running water and sewerage for all sections of town, not just the wealthy ones. In 1848, spurred on by the cholera epidemic of 1846, Chadwick's report became the basis of Great Britain's first public health law, which created a national health board and gave cities broad authority to build modern sanitary systems.

The public health movement won dedicated supporters in the United States, France, and Germany from the 1840s on. As in Great Britain, governments accepted at least limited responsibility for the health of all citizens. Moreover, they adopted increasingly concrete programs of action, programs that broke decisively with the age-old fatalism of urban populations in the face of shockingly high mortality. Thus, despite many people's skepticism about sanitation, European cities were making real progress toward adequate water supplies and sewage systems by the 1860s and 1870s. And city dwellers were beginning to reap the reward of better health.

The Bacterial Revolution

Effective control of communicable disease required more than a clean water supply and good sewers. Victory over disease also required a great leap forward in medical knowledge and biological theory. Reformers like Chadwick were seriously handicapped by the prevailing *miasmatic theory* of disease—the belief that people contract disease when they breathe the bad odors of decay and putrefying excrement; in short, the theory that smells cause disease. The miasmatic theory was a reasonable deduction from empirical observations: cleaning up filth did produce laudable results. Yet the theory was very incomplete.

Keen observation by doctors and public health officials in the 1840s and 1850s pinpointed the role of bad drinking water in the transmission of disease and suggested that contagion was spread through filth and not caused by it. Examples of particularly horrid stenches, such as that of the sewage-glutted Thames River at London in 1858, that did not lead to widely feared epidemics also weakened the miasmatic idea. Another factor was the successful merging of anatomical and clinical approaches to medicine between 1800 and 1850, particularly at the University of Paris school of medicine. Doctors there recognized a definite connection between the symptoms of certain illnesses observed at the bedside and the diseased organs seen when the body was dissected at autopsy. Medical research began zeroing in on specific diseases in an attempt to find specific treatments.

The breakthrough was the development of the germ theory of disease by the French chemist Louis

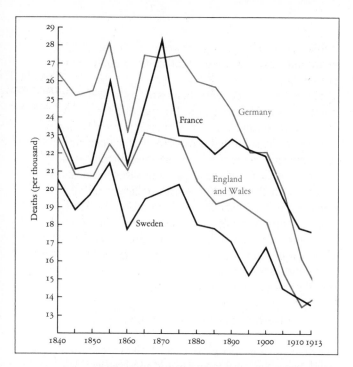

FIGURE 28.1 The Decline of Death Rates in England and Wales, Germany, France, and Sweden, 1840–1913 A rising standard of living, improvements in public health, and better medical knowledge all contributed to the dramatic decline of death rates in the nineteenth century.

Pasteur (1822–1895). After important discoveries about the structure of crystals, he turned in 1854 to the study of fermentation. For ages people had used fermentation to make bread and wine, beer and cheese, but without really understanding what was going on. And from time to time, beer and wine would mysteriously spoil for no apparent reason. As rapidly growing cities provided a vast concentrated demand, large brewers and winemakers were seeking ways to prevent spoilage and financial loss. Responding to their calls for help, Pasteur used his microscope to develop a simple test brewers could use to monitor the fermentation process and avoid spoilage. He then investigated various kinds of fermentation.

Pasteur found that fermentation depended on the growth of living organisms. Moreover, he demonstrated that the activity of these organisms could be suppressed by heating the wine or milk—by *pasteurizing* it. The breathtaking implication was that specific diseases were caused by specific living organisms—germs—and that those organisms could be controlled in people as well as in milk and wine. This

theory was confirmed in 1868. After three years of intensive research, Pasteur isolated and controlled parasitic microorganisms that were killing off the silkworms used in France's large silk industry.

By 1870 the work of Pasteur and others had demonstrated the general connection between germs and disease. When, in the middle of the 1870s, the German country doctor Robert Koch and his coworkers developed pure cultures of harmful bacteria and described their life cycles, the dam broke. Over the next twenty years, researchers—mainly Germans—identified the organisms responsible for disease after disease, often identifying several in a single year. At the same time, Pasteur and his colleagues concentrated on modifying and controlling the virulence of disease-producing germs. Building on the example of Edward Jenner's pioneering conquest of smallpox, Pasteur and his team developed a number of effective vaccines. The most famous was his vaccination for rabies in 1885, a crucial step in the development of modern immunology.

Acceptance of the germ theory brought about dramatic improvements in the deadly environment of hospitals and surgery. The English surgeon Joseph Lister (1827–1912) had noticed that patients with simple fractures were much less likely to die than those with compound fractures, in which the skin was broken and internal tissues were exposed to the air. In 1865, when Pasteur showed that the air was full of bacteria, Lister immediately grasped the connection between aerial bacteria and the problem of wound infection. He reasoned that a chemical disinfectant applied to a wound dressing would "destroy the life of the floating particles." Lister's "antiseptic principle" worked wonders. In the 1880s, German surgeons developed the practice of sterilizing not only the wound but everything—hands, instruments, clothing—that entered the operating room.

The achievements of the bacterial revolution coupled with the ever-more-sophisticated public health movement saved millions of lives, particularly after about 1890. Mortality rates began to decline dramatically in European countries (Figure 28.1), as the awful death sentences of the past—diphtheria, typhoid and typhus, cholera, yellow fever—became vanishing diseases. City dwellers benefited especially from these developments. By 1910 the likelihood of death for people of all ages in urban areas was generally no greater than in rural areas, and sometimes it was less. A great silent revolution had occurred: the

MAP 28.2 The Modernization of Paris, ca 1850–1870 Broad boulevards, large parks, and grandiose train stations transformed Paris. The cutting of the new north-south axis—known as the Saint-Michel Boulevard—was one of Haussmann's most controversial projects. It razed much of Paris's medieval core and filled the Île de la Cité with massive government buildings.

terrible ferocity of death from disease-carrying bacteria in the cities had almost been tamed.

URBAN PLANNING AND PUBLIC TRANSPORTATION

Public health was only part of the urban challenge. Overcrowding, bad housing, and lack of transportation could not be solved by sewers and better medicine; yet in these areas, too, important transformations significantly improved the quality of urban life after midcentury.

More effective urban planning was one of the keys to improvement. Earlier urban planning had declined by the early nineteenth century; after 1850 it was revived and extended. France took the lead during the rule of Napoleon III (1848–1870), who sought to stand above class conflict and promote the welfare of all his subjects through government action. He believed that rebuilding much of Paris would provide employment, improve living conditions, and testify to the power and glory of his empire. In the baron Georges Haussmann, an aggressive, impatient Alsatian whom he placed in charge of Paris, Napoleon III found an authoritarian planner capable of bulldozing both buildings and opposition. Within twenty years the city of Paris was quite literally transformed (Map 28.2).

Apartment Living in Paris This contemporary drawing shows how different social classes lived close together in European cities about 1850. Passing the middle-class family on the first (American second) floor, the economic condition of the tenants declined until one reached abject poverty in the garret. *(Bibliothèque Nationale, Paris)*

Experimenting with Steam Countless inventors sought to adapt steam engines to the demands of urban transit. Yet even the most ingenious steam locomotives, like the one above being introduced in Paris in 1876, remained undependable. And they frightened horses, which toiled on until relieved by electric motors. *(Photo: Caroline Buckler)*

The Paris of 1850 was a labyrinth of narrow, dark streets, the result of desperate overcrowding. In an area not twice the size of New York's Central Park lived more than one-third of the city's 1 million inhabitants. Terrible slum conditions and extremely high death rates were facts of life. There were few open spaces and only two public parks for the entire metropolis. Public transportation played a very small role in this enormous walking city.

Haussmann and his fellow planners proceeded on many interrelated fronts. With a bold energy that often shocked their contemporaries, they razed old buildings in order to cut broad, straight, tree-lined boulevards through the center of the city as well as in new quarters on the outskirts. These boulevards, designed in part to prevent the easy construction and defense of barricades by revolutionary crowds, also permitted traffic to flow freely. Their construction also demolished some of the worst slums. New streets stimulated the construction of better housing, especially for the middle classes. Small neighborhood parks and open spaces were created throughout the city, and two very large parks suitable for all kinds of holiday activities were developed on either side of the city. The city also improved its sewers, and a system of aqueducts more than doubled the city's supply of good fresh water.

Haussmann and Napoleon III tried to make Paris a more beautiful city, and to a large extent they succeeded. The broad, straight boulevards, such as those radiating out like the spokes of a wheel from the Arch of Triumph and those centering on the new Opera House, afforded impressive vistas. If for most people Paris remains one of the world's most beautiful and enchanting cities, it is in part because of the transformations of the Second Empire.

The rebuilding of Paris provided a new model for urban planning and stimulated modern urbanism throughout Europe, particularly after 1870. In city after city, public authorities mounted a coordinated attack on many of the interrelated problems of the urban environment. As in Paris, improvements in public health through better water supply and waste disposal often went hand in hand with new boulevard construction. Cities like Vienna and Cologne followed the Parisian example of tearing down old walled fortifications and replacing them with broad, circular boulevards on which office buildings, town halls, theaters, opera houses, and museums were erected. These ring roads and the new boulevards that radiated out from them toward the outskirts eased movement and encouraged urban expansion.

The development of mass public transportation was also of great importance in the improvement of urban living conditions. Such transportation came late, but in a powerful rush. In the 1870s, many European cities authorized private companies to operate horse-drawn streetcars, which had been developed in the United States, to carry riders along the growing number of major thoroughfares. Then, in the 1890s, occurred the real revolution: European countries adopted another American transit innovation, the electric streetcar.

Electric streetcars were cheaper, faster, more dependable, and more comfortable than their horse-drawn counterparts. Service improved dramatically. Millions of Europeans—workers, shoppers, schoolchildren—hopped on board during the workweek. And on weekends and holidays, streetcars carried millions on happy outings to parks and countryside, racetracks and music halls. The average European was using public transportation four times as often in 1910 as in 1886.[6]

Good mass transit helped greatly in the struggle for decent housing. Just as the new boulevards and horse-drawn streetcars had facilitated the middle-class move to better housing in the 1860s and 1870s, so electric streetcars gave people of modest means access to new, improved housing after 1890. The still-crowded city was able to expand and become less congested. In England in 1901, only 9 percent of the urban population was "overcrowded" in terms of the official definition of more than two persons per room. On the Continent, many city governments in the early twentieth century were building electric streetcar systems that provided transportation to new public and private housing developments in outlying areas of the city for the working classes. Poor, overcrowded housing, long one of the blackest blots on the urban landscape, was in retreat—another graphic example of the gradual taming of the urban environment.

RICH AND POOR AND IN BETWEEN

General improvements in health and in the urban environment had beneficial consequences for all kinds of people. Yet differences in living conditions among social classes remained gigantic.

SOCIAL STRUCTURE

How much had the almost-completed journey to an urban, industrialized world changed the social framework of rich and poor? The first great change was a substantial and undeniable increase in the standard of living for the average person. The real wages of British workers, for example, which had already risen substantially by 1850, almost doubled between 1850 and 1906. Similar unmistakable increases occurred in continental countries as industrial development quickened after 1850. Ordinary people took a great step forward in the centuries-old battle against poverty, reinforcing efforts to improve many aspects of human existence.

There is another side to the income coin, however, and it must be stressed as well. Greater economic rewards for the average person did *not* eliminate poverty, nor did they make the wealth and income of the rich and the poor significantly more equal. In almost every advanced country around 1900, the richest 5 percent of all households in the population received fully one-third of all national income. The richest one-fifth of households received anywhere from 50 to 60 percent of all national income, while the entire bottom four-fifths received only 40 to 50 percent. Moreover, the bottom 30 percent of households received 10 percent or less of all income. These enormous differences are illustrated in Figure 28.2.

The middle classes were smaller than they are today and accounted for only about 20 percent of the population; thus, statistics show that the upper and middle classes alone received more than one-half of all income. The poorest four-fifths—the working classes, including peasants and agricultural laborers—received less altogether than the two richest classes. Moreover, income taxes on the wealthy were light or nonexistent. Thus the gap between rich and poor remained enormous at the beginning of the twentieth century. It was probably almost as great as it had been in the age of agriculture and aristocracy, before the Industrial Revolution.

The great gap between rich and poor endured, in part, because industrial and urban development made society more diverse and less unified. By no means did society split into two sharply defined opposing classes, as Marx had predicted. Instead, economic specialization enabled society to produce more effectively and in the process created more new social groups than it destroyed. There developed an almost unlimited range of jobs, skills, and earnings; one group or subclass shaded off into another in a complex, confusing hierarchy. Thus the tiny elite of the very rich and the sizable mass of the dreadfully poor were separated from each other by many subclasses, each filled with individuals struggling to rise or at least to hold their own in the social order. In this atmosphere of competition and hierarchy, neither the middle classes nor the working classes acted as a unified force. The age-old pattern of great economic inequality remained firmly intact.

THE MIDDLE CLASSES

By the beginning of the twentieth century, the diversity and range within the urban middle class were striking. Indeed, it is more meaningful to think of a confederation of middle classes, loosely united by occupations requiring mental rather than physical skill. At the top stood the upper middle class, composed mainly of the most successful business families from banking, industry, and large-scale commerce. These families were the prime beneficiaries of modern industry and scientific progress. As the incomes of people in the upper middle class rose and as they progressively lost all traces of radicalism after the trauma of 1848, they were almost irresistibly drawn toward the aristocratic lifestyle.

As the aristocracy had long divided the year between palatial country estates and lavish town houses during "the season," so the upper middle class purchased country places or built beach houses for weekend and summer use. Private coaches and carriages, ever an expensive item in the city, were also signs of rising social status. More generally, the rich businessman and certainly his son devoted less time to business and more to "culture" and easy living than was the case in less wealthy or well-established commercial families.

The topmost reaches of the upper middle class tended to shade off into the old aristocracy to form a new upper class. This was the 5 percent of the population that received roughly one-third of the national income in European countries before 1914. Much of the aristocracy welcomed this development. Having experienced a sharp decline in its relative income in the course of industrialization, the landed aristocracy had met big business coming up the staircase and was

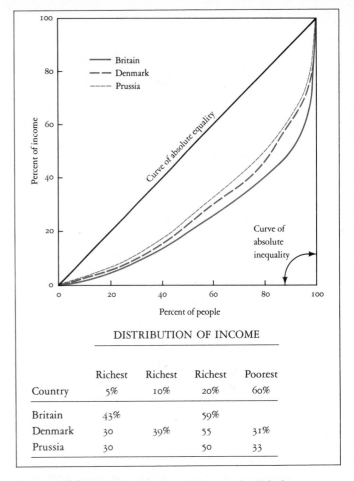

DISTRIBUTION OF INCOME

Country	Richest 5%	Richest 10%	Richest 20%	Poorest 60%
Britain	43%		59%	
Denmark	30	39%	55	31%
Prussia	30		50	33

FIGURE 28.2 The Distribution of Income in Britain, Denmark, and Prussia in 1913 The so-called Lorenz curve is useful for showing the degree of economic inequality in a given society. The closer the actual distribution of income lies to the (theoretical) curve of absolute equality, where each 20 percent of the population receives 20 percent of all income, the more incomes are nearly equal. European society was very far from any such equality before World War One. Notice that incomes in Prussia were somewhat more equal than those in Britain. *(Source: S. Kuznets,* Modern Economic Growth, *Yale University Press, New Haven, 1966, pp. 208–209)*

often delighted to trade titles, country homes, and snobbish elegance for good hard cash. Some of the best bargains were made through marriages to American heiresses. Correspondingly, wealthy aristocrats tended increasingly to exploit their agricultural and mineral resources as if they were businessmen. Bismarck was not the only proud nobleman to make a fortune distilling brandy on his estates.

Below the wealthy upper middle class were much larger, much less wealthy, and increasingly diversified middle-class groups. Here one found the moderately successful industrialists and merchants, as well as professionals in law and medicine. This was the middle middle class, solid and quite comfortable but lacking great wealth. Below them were independent shopkeepers, small traders, and tiny manufacturers —the lower middle class. Both of these traditional elements of the middle class expanded modestly in size with economic development.

Meanwhile, the traditional middle class was gaining two particularly important additions. The expansion of industry and technology created a growing demand for experts with specialized knowledge. The most valuable of the specialties became solid middle-class professions. Engineering, for example, emerged from the world of skilled labor as a full-fledged profession of great importance, considerable prestige, and many branches. Architects, chemists, accountants, and surveyors—to name only a few—first achieved professional standing in this period. They established criteria for advanced training and certification and banded together in organizations to promote and defend their interests.

Management of large public and private institutions also emerged as a kind of profession, as governments provided more services and as very large corporations like railroads came into being. Government officials and many private executives were not capitalists in the sense that they owned business enterprises. But public and private managers did have specialized knowledge and the capacity to earn a good living. And they shared most of the values of the business-owning entrepreneurs and the older professionals.

Industrialization also expanded and diversified the lower middle class. The number of independent, property-owning shopkeepers and small businessmen grew and so did the number of white-collar employees—a mixed group of traveling salesmen, bookkeepers, store managers, and clerks who staffed the offices and branch stores of large corporations. White-collar employees were propertyless and often earned no more than the better-paid skilled or semi-skilled workers did. Yet white-collar workers were fiercely committed to the middle class and to the ideal of moving up in society. In the Balkans, for example, clerks let their fingernails grow very long to distinguish themselves from people who worked with

their hands. The tie, the suit, and soft, clean hands were no less subtle marks of class distinction than wages.

Relatively well educated but without complex technical skills, many white-collar groups aimed at achieving professional standing and the accompanying middle-class status. Elementary school teachers largely succeeded in this effort. From being miserably paid part-time workers in the early nineteenth century, teachers rode the wave of mass education to respectable middle-class status and income. Nurses also rose from the lower ranks of unskilled labor to precarious middle-class standing. Dentistry was taken out of the hands of the working-class barbers and placed in the hands of highly trained (and middle-class) professionals.

In spite of their growing occupational diversity and conflicting interests, the middle classes were loosely united by a certain style of life. Food was the largest item in the household budget, for middle-class people liked to eat very well. In France and Italy, the middle classes' love of good eating meant that, even in large cities, activity ground almost to a halt between half past twelve and half past two on weekdays, as husbands and schoolchildren returned home for the midday meal. Around eight in the evening, the serious business of eating was taken up once again.

The English were equally attached to substantial meals, which they ate three times a day if income allowed. The typical English breakfast of bacon and eggs, toast and marmalade, and stewed fruits—not to mention sardines, kidneys, or fresh fish—always astonished French and German travelers, though large-breakfast enthusiasts like the Dutch and Scandinavians were less awed. The European middle classes consumed meat in abundance, and a well-off family might spend fully 10 percent of its substantial earnings on meat alone. In the 1890s, even a very prosperous English family—with an income of, say, $10,000 a year while the average working-class family earned perhaps $400 a year—spent fully a quarter of its income on food and drink.

Spending on food was also great because the dinner party was this class's favored social occasion. A wealthy family might give a lavish party for eight to twelve almost every week, while more modest households would settle for once a month. Throughout middle-class Europe, such dinners were served in the "French manner" (which the French had borrowed from the Russian aristocracy): eight or nine separate

"A Corner of the Table" With photographic precision this 1904 oil painting by the French academic artist Paul-Emile Chabas (1867–1937) skillfully idealizes the elegance and intimacy of a sumptuous dinner party. *(The Granger Collection)*

courses, from appetizers at the beginning to coffee and liqueurs at the end. An ordinary family meal normally consisted of only four courses—soup, fish, meat, and dessert.

The middle-class wife could cope with this endless procession of meals, courses, and dishes because she had both servants and money at her disposal. The middle classes were solid members of what some contemporary observers called the "servant-keeping classes." Indeed, the employment of at least one enormously helpful full-time maid to cook and clean was the best single sign that a family had crossed the vague line separating the working classes from the middle classes. The greater its income, the greater the number of servants a family employed. The all-purpose servant gave way to a cook and a maid, then to a

cook, a maid, and a boy, and so on. A prosperous English family, far up the line with $10,000 a year, in 1900 spent fully one-fourth of its income on a hierarchy of ten servants: a manservant, a cook, a kitchen maid, two housemaids, a serving maid, a governess, a gardner, a coachman, and a stable boy. Domestic servants were the second largest item in the budget of the middle classes. Thus food and servants absorbed about one-half of income at all levels of the middle classes.

Well fed and well served, the middle classes were also well housed by 1900. Many quite prosperous families rented rather than owned their homes. Apartment living, complete with tiny rooms for servants under the eaves of the top floor, was commonplace (outside Great Britain), and wealthy investors and speculative builders found good profits in middle-class housing. By 1900 the middle classes were also quite clothes-conscious. The factory, the sewing machine, and the department store had all helped to reduce the cost and expand the variety of clothing. Middle-class women were particularly attentive to the fickle dictates of fashion.

Education was another growing expense, as middle-class parents tried to provide their children with ever more crucial advanced education. The keystones of culture and leisure were books, music, and travel. The long realistic novel, the heroics of Wagner and Verdi, the diligent striving of the dutiful daughter on a piano, and the packaged tour to a foreign country were all sources of middle-class pleasure.

Finally, the middle classes were loosely united by a shared code of expected behavior and morality. This code was strict and demanding. It laid great stress on hard work, self-discipline, and personal achievement. Men and women who fell into crime or poverty were generally assumed to be responsible for their own circumstances. Traditional Christian morality was reaffirmed by this code and preached tirelessly by middle-class people who took pride in their own good conduct and regular church attendance. Drinking and gambling were denounced as vices; sexual purity and fidelity were celebrated as virtues. In short, the middle-class person was supposed to know right from wrong and was expected to act accordingly.

THE WORKING CLASSES

About four out of five people belonged to the working classes at the turn of the century. Many members of the working classes—that is, people whose livelihoods depended on physical labor and who did not employ domestic servants—were still small land-owning peasants and hired farm hands. This was especially true in eastern Europe. In western and central Europe, however, the typical worker had left the land. In Great Britain, less than 8 percent of the people worked in agriculture, while in rapidly industrializing Germany only one person in four was employed in agriculture and forestry. Even in less-industrialized France, less than half the people depended on the land in 1900.

The urban working classes were even less unified and homogeneous than the middle classes. In the first place, economic development and increased special-ization expanded the traditional range of working-class skills, earnings, and experiences. Meanwhile, the old sharp distinction between highly skilled artisans and unskilled manual workers was gradually breaking down. To be sure, highly skilled printers and masons, as well as unskilled dock workers and common laborers, continued to exist. But between these extremes there were ever-more semiskilled groups, many of which were composed of factory workers and machine tenders (see Figure 28.3).

In the second place, skilled, semiskilled, and unskilled workers had widely divergent lifestyles and cultural values, and their differences contributed to a keen sense of social status and hierarchy within the working classes. The result was great variety and limited class unity.

Highly skilled workers, who comprised about 15 percent of the working classes, were a real "labor aristocracy." By 1900 they were earning about £2 a week in Great Britain, or roughly $10 a week and $500 per year. This was only about two-thirds the income of the bottom ranks of the servant-keeping classes. But it was fully twice as much as the earnings of unskilled workers, who averaged about $5 per week, and substantially more than the earnings of semiskilled workers, who averaged perhaps $7 per week. Other European countries had a similar range of earnings.

The most "aristocratic" of the highly skilled workers were construction bosses and factory foremen, men who had risen from the ranks and were fiercely proud of their achievement. The labor aristocracy also included members of the traditional highly skilled handicraft trades that had not been mechanized or placed in factories. These included makers of scientific and musical instruments, cabinetmakers, potters, jewelers, bookbinders, engravers, and printers. This group as a whole was under constant long-term pressure. Irregularly but inexorably, factory methods were being extended to more crafts, and many skilled artisans were being replaced by lower-paid semiskilled factory workers. Traditional woodcarvers and watchmakers virtually disappeared, for example, as the making of furniture and time-pieces was taken out of the shop and put into the factory.

At the same time, a contrary movement was occurring. The labor aristocracy was consistently being enlarged by the growing need for highly skilled workers, such as shipbuilders, machine-tool makers, railway locomotive engineers, fine cotton textile spinners, and some metalworkers. Thus, the labor elite was in a state of flux as individuals and whole crafts moved in and out of it.

To maintain their precarious standing, the upper working class adopted distinctive values and strait-laced, almost puritanical, behavior. Like the middle classes, the labor aristocracy was strongly committed to the family and to economic improvement. Families in the upper working class saved money regularly, worried about their children's education, and valued good housing. Despite these similarities, which superficial observers were quick to exaggerate, skilled workers viewed themselves not as aspirants to the middle class but as the pacesetters and natural leaders of all the working classes. Well aware of the poverty and degradation not so far below them, they practiced self-discipline and stern morality.

The upper working class in general frowned on heavy drinking and sexual permissiveness. The organized temperance movement was strong in the countries of northern Europe, such as Great Britain, where a generation advocated tea as the "cup that cheers but does not inebriate." As one German labor aristocrat somberly warned, "the path to the brothel leads through the tavern" and from there quite possibly to drastic decline or total ruin for person and family.[7]

Below the labor aristocracy stood semiskilled and unskilled urban workers. The enormous complexity of this sector of the world of labor is not easily summarized. Workers in the established crafts—carpenters, bricklayers, pipefitters—stood near the top of the semiskilled hierarchy, often flirting with (or having backslid from) the labor elite. A large number of the semiskilled were factory workers, who earned highly variable but relatively good wages and whose relative importance in the labor force was increasing.

The unskilled was the larger group, made up of day laborers such as longshoremen, wagon-driving teamsters, teenagers, and every kind of "helper." Many of these people had real skills and performed valuable services, but they were unorganized and divided, united only by the common fate of meager earnings. The same lack of unity characterized street vendors and market people—self-employed workers who competed savagely with each other and with the established shopkeepers of the lower middle class.

One of the largest components of the unskilled group was domestic servants, whose numbers grew steadily in the nineteenth century. In advanced Great

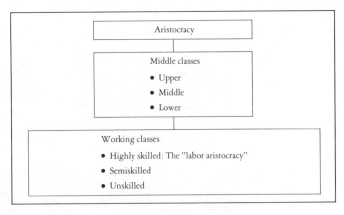

FIGURE 28.3 The Urban Social Hierarchy

Britain, for example, one out of every seven employed persons was a domestic servant in 1911. The majority were women; indeed, one out of every three girls in Britain between the ages of fifteen and twenty was a domestic servant. Throughout Europe and America, a great many female domestics in the cities were recent migrants from rural areas. As in earlier times, domestic service was still hard work at low pay with limited personal independence.

Nonetheless, domestic service had real attractions for "rough country girls" with strong hands and few specialized skills. Marriage prospects were better, or at least more varied, in the city. And though wages were low, they were higher and more regular than in hard agricultural work. Finally, as one London observer noted, young girls and other migrants were drawn to the city by "the contagion of numbers, the sense of something going on, the theaters and the music halls, the brightly lighted streets and busy crowds—all, in short, that makes the difference between the Mile End fair on a Saturday night, and a dark and muddy country lane, with no glimmer of gas and with nothing to do."[8]

Many young domestics from the countryside made a successful transition to working-class wife and mother. Yet, with an unskilled or unemployed husband and a growing family, such a woman often had to join the broad ranks of working women in the "sweated industries." These industries resembled the old putting-out and cottage industries of the eighteenth and early nineteenth centuries. The women normally worked at home, though sometimes together in some loft or garret, for tiny merchant-manufacturers. Paid by the piece and not by the hour, these women (and their young daughters), for whom

Servants Seeking Work in Moscow bargained with prospective employers (or their agents) in this special hiring yard just outside the ancient city walls. Moscow's bustling "market for servants" was open every day of the year and was busiest on Sundays. *(University of Illinois, Champaign)*

organization was impossible, earned pitiful wages and lacked any job security.

Some women did hand decorating of every conceivable kind of object; the majority, however, made clothing, especially after the advent of the sewing machine. Foot-powered sewing machines allowed the poorest wife or widow in the foulest dwelling to rival and eventually supplant the most highly skilled male tailor. By 1900 only a few such tailors lingered on in high-priced "tailor-made" shops. An army of poor women accounted for the bulk of the inexpensive "ready-made" clothes displayed on department store racks and in tiny shops. All of these considerations graphically illustrate the rise and fall of groups and individuals within the working classes.

The urban working classes sought fun and recreation, and they found it. Across the face of Europe, drinking was unquestionably the favorite leisure-time activity of working people. For many middle-

class moralists, as well as moralizing historians since, love of drink has been a curse of the modern age—a sign of social dislocation and popular suffering. Certainly, drinking was deadly serious business. One English slum dweller recalled that "drunkenness was by far the commonest cause of dispute and misery in working class homes. On account of it one saw many a decent family drift down through poverty into total want."[9]

Generally, however, heavy "problem" drinking declined by the late nineteenth century, as it became less and less socially acceptable. This decline reflected in part the firm moral leadership of the upper working class. At the same time, drinking became more public and social, especially as on-the-job drinking, an ancient custom of field laborers and urban artisans, declined. Cafés and pubs became increasingly bright, friendly places. Working-class political activities, both moderate and radical, were also

Sweated Industry About 1900 This moving photograph shows an English family making cheap toys at home for low wages. Women and children were the backbone of sweated industry, and this husband may be filling in while unemployed. *(University of Reading, Institute of Agricultural History and Museum of English Rural Life)*

concentrated in taverns and pubs. Moreover, social drinking by married couples and sweethearts became an accepted and widespread practice for the first time. This greater participation by women undoubtedly helped to civilize the world of drink and hard liquor.

The two other leisure-time passions of the working classes were sports and music halls. By the late nineteenth century there had been a great decline in "cruel sports," such as bullbaiting and cockfighting, throughout Europe. Their place was filled by modern spectator sports, of which racing and soccer were the most popular. There was a great deal of gambling on sports events, and for many a workingman the desire to decipher the racing forms was a powerful incentive toward literacy. Music halls and vaudeville theaters, the working-class counterparts of middle-class opera and classical theater, were enormously popular throughout Europe. In the words of one English

printer, "It is to the music halls that the vast body of working people look for recreation and entertainment."[10] In 1900 there were more than fifty in London alone. Music-hall audiences were thoroughly mixed, which may account for the fact that drunkenness, sexual intercourse and pregnancy before marriage, marital difficulties, and problems with mothers-in-law were favorite themes of broad jokes and bittersweet songs.

In more serious moments, religion and the Christian churches continued to provide working people with solace and meaning. The eighteenth-century vitality of popular religion in Catholic countries and the Protestant rejuvenation exemplified by German Pietism and English Methodism (pages 704–706) carried over into the nineteenth century. Indeed, many historians see the early nineteenth century as an age of religious revival. Yet historians also recognize that, by the last two or three decades of the nineteenth century, a considerable decline in both church attendance and church donations was occurring in most European countries. And it seems clear that this decline was greater for the urban working classes than for their rural counterparts or for the middle classes.

What did the decline in working-class church attendance really mean? Some have argued that it accurately reflected a general decline in faith and religious belief. Others disagree, noting correctly that most working-class families still baptized their children and considered themselves Christians. Admitting that more research is necessary, it appears that the urban working classes in Europe did become more secular and less religious in the late nineteenth and early twentieth centuries. They rarely repudiated the Christian religion, but it tended to play a diminishing role in their daily lives.

Part of the reason was that the construction of churches failed to keep up with the rapid growth of urban population, especially in new working-class neighborhoods. Thus the vibrant, materialistic urban environment undermined popular religious impulses, which were poorly served in the cities. Equally important, however, was the fact that throughout the nineteenth century both Catholic and Protestant churches were normally seen as they saw themselves —as conservative institutions defending social order and custom. Therefore, as the European working classes became more politically conscious, as the next chapter will show, they tended to see the established (or quasi-established) "territorial church" as defending what they wished to change and allied with their political opponents. Especially the men of the urban working classes developed vaguely antichurch attitudes, even though they remained neutral or positive toward religion. They tended to regard regular church attendance as "not our kind of thing"—not part of urban working-class culture.

The pattern was different in the United States. There, most churches also preached social conservatism in the nineteenth century. But because church and state had always been separated and because there was always a host of competing denominations and even different religions, working people identified churches much less with the political and social status quo. Instead, individual churches in the United States were often closely identified with an ethnic group rather than with a social class, and churches thrived, in part, as a means of asserting ethnic identity.

THE FAMILY

Urban life wrought many fundamental changes in the family. Although much is still unknown, it seems clear that by the late nineteenth century, the family had stabilized considerably after the disruption of the late eighteenth and early nineteenth centuries. The home became more important for both men and women. The role of women and attitudes toward children underwent substantial change, and adolescence emerged as a distinct stage of life. These are but a few of the transformations that affected all social classes in varying degrees.

PREMARITAL SEX AND MARRIAGE

By 1850 the preindustrial pattern of lengthy courtship and mercenary marriage was pretty well dead among the working classes. In its place, the ideal of romantic love had triumphed. Couples were ever more likely to come from different, even distant, towns and to be more nearly the same age, further indicating that romantic sentiment was replacing tradition and financial considerations.

Economic considerations in marriage long remained much more important to the middle classes than to the working classes. In France, dowries and elaborate legal marriage contracts were standard practice, and marriage was for many families life's most crucial financial transaction. A popular author advised young Frenchmen that "marriage is in general a means of increasing one's credit and one's fortune and of insuring one's success in the world."[11] This preoccupation with money led many middle-class men, in France and elsewhere, to marry late and to choose women considerably younger and less sexually experienced than themselves. These differences between husband and wife became a source of tension in many middle-class marriages.

A young woman of the middle class found her romantic life carefully supervised by her well-meaning mother, who schemed for a proper marriage and guarded her daughter's virginity like the family's credit. After marriage, middle-class morality sternly demanded fidelity.

Middle-class boys were watched, too, but not as vigilantly. By the time they reached late adolescence, they had usually attained considerable sexual experience with maids or prostitutes. With marriage a distant, uncertain possibility, it was all too easy for the young man of the middle classes to turn to the urban underworld of whoredom and sexual exploitation to satisfy his desires.

Sexual experimentation before marriage had also triumphed, as had illegitimacy. There was an "illegitimacy explosion" between 1750 and 1850 (page 688). By the 1840s, as many as one birth in three was occurring outside of wedlock in many large cities. Although poverty and economic uncertainty undoubtedly prevented many lovers from marrying, there were also many among the poor and propertyless who saw little wrong with having illegitimate offspring. As one young Bavarian woman answered happily when asked why she kept having illegitimate children: "It's O.K. to make babies. . . . The king has o.k.'d it!" [12] Thus the pattern of romantic ideals, premarital sexual activity, and widespread illegitimacy was firmly established by midcentury among the urban working classes.

It is hard to know how European couples managed sex, pregnancy, and marriage in the second half of the nineteenth century, because such questions were considered improper both in polite conversation and in public opinion polls. Yet there are many telltale clues. The rising rate of illegitimacy was reversed: more babies were born to married mothers. Some observers have argued that this shift reflected the growth of puritanism and a lessening of sexual permissiveness among the unmarried. This explanation, however, is unconvincing.

The percentage of brides who were pregnant continued to be high and showed little or no tendency to decline. In many parts of urban Europe around 1900, as many as one woman in three was going to the altar an expectant mother. Moreover, unmarried people almost certainly used the cheap condoms and diaphragms the industrial age had made available to prevent pregnancy, at least in predominantly Protestant countries.

Unmarried young people were probably engaging in just as much sexual activity as their parents and grandparents, who had created the illegitimacy explosion of 1750 to 1850. But toward the end of the nineteenth century, pregnancy usually meant marriage and the establishment of a two-parent household. This important development reflected the growing respectability of the working classes, as well as their gradual economic improvement. Skipping out was less acceptable, and marriage was less of an economic disaster. Thus the urban working-class couple became more stable, and its stability strengthened the family as an institution.

PROSTITUTION

In Paris alone, 155,000 women were registered as prostitutes between 1871 and 1903, and 750,000 others were suspected of prostitution in the same years. Men of all classes visited prostitutes, but the middle and upper classes supplied much of the motivating cash. Thus, though many middle-class men abided by the publicly professed code of stern puritanical morality, many others indulged their appetites for prostitutes and sexual promiscuity.

My Secret Life, the anonymous eleven-volume autobiography of an English sexual adventurer from the servant-keeping classes, provides a remarkable picture of such a man. Beginning at an early age with a maid, the author becomes progressively obsessed with sex and devotes his life to living his sexual fantasies. In almost every one of his innumerable encounters all across Europe, this man of wealth simply buys his pleasure. Usually meetings are arranged in a businesslike manner: regular and part-time prostitutes quote their prices; working-class girls are corrupted by hot meals and warm baths.

At one point, however, he offers a young girl a sixpence for a kiss and gets it. Learning that the pretty, unskilled working girl earns ninepence a day, he offers her the equivalent of a week's salary for a few moments of fondling. When she finally agrees, he savagely exults that *"her* want was my opportunity." [13] Later he offers more money for more gratification, and when she refuses, he tries unsuccessfully to rape her in a hackney cab.

Obviously atypical in its excesses, the encyclopedic thoroughness of *My Secret Life* does mirror accurately the dark side of sex and class in urban society. Thinking of their wives largely in terms of money and social position, the men of the comfortable classes often purchased sex and even affection from

An Awkward Encounter in Regent Street—"That girl seems to know you, George!" Prostitution was commonly known as the "great social evil" because it was so widespread. This young woman probably sold more than flowers. *(Mary Evans Picture Library)*

poor girls both before and after marriage. Moreover, the great continuing differences between rich and poor made for every kind of debauchery and sexual exploitation, including the brisk trade in poor virgins that the author of *My Secret Life* particularly relished. Brutal sexist behavior was part of life—a part the sternly moral women (and men) of the upper working class detested and tried to shield their daughters from. For many poor young women, prostitution, like domestic service, was a stage of life. Having passed through it, they went on to marry men of their own class and establish homes and families.

Kinship Ties

Within working-class homes, ties to relatives after marriage—kinship ties—were in general much stronger than superficial social observers have recognized. Most newlyweds tried to live near their parents, though not in the same house. Indeed, for many married couples in the cities, ties to mothers and fathers, uncles and aunts, became more important, and ties to nonrelated acquaintances became weaker.

People turned to their families to help in coping with sickness, unemployment, death, and old age. Although governments were generally providing more welfare services by 1900, the average couple and their children inevitably faced crises. Funerals, for example, were an economic catastrophe, requiring a sudden large outlay for special clothes, carriages, and burial services. Unexpected death or desertion could leave widows and orphans in need of financial aid or perhaps a foster home. Relatives responded to such cries, knowing full well that their time of need and repayment would undoubtedly come.

Relatives were also valuable at less tragic moments. If a couple was very poor, an aged relation often moved in to cook and mind the children so the wife could earn badly needed income outside the home. Sunday dinners and holiday visits were often shared, as was outgrown clothing and useful information. Often the members of a large family group all lived in the same neighborhood.

Women and Family Life

Industrialization and the growth of modern cities brought great changes to the lives of European women. These changes were particularly consequential for married women, and most women did marry in the nineteenth century.

The work of most wives became quite distinct and separate from that of their husbands. Husbands became wage earners in factories and offices, while wives tended to stay home and manage the household and care for the children. The preindustrial pattern among both peasants and cottage workers, in which husbands and wives worked together and divided up household duties and child rearing, declined. Only in a few occupations, such as retail trade, did married couples live where they worked and struggle together to make their mom-and-pop operations a success. Factory employment for married women also declined as the early practice of hiring entire families in the factory disappeared.

As economic conditions improved late in the nineteenth century, married women tended to work outside the home only in poor families. One old English worker recalled that the "boy wanted to get into a position that would enable him to keep a wife and family, as it was considered a thoroughly unsatisfactory state of affairs if the wife had to work to help maintain the home."[14] The ideal was a strict division of labor by sex: the wife as mother and homemaker, the husband as wage earner.

This rigid division of labor meant that married women faced great injustice if they tried to move into the man's world, the world of employment outside the home. Husbands were unsympathetic or hostile. Well-paying jobs were off limits to women, and a woman's wage was almost always less than a man's, even for the same work. No wonder some women rebelled by the second half of the nineteenth century and began the long-continuing fight for equality of the sexes and the rights of women. More generally, rigidly separate roles narrowed women's horizons and fenced in their world.

There was a brighter side to the same coin. As home and children became the wife's main concerns, her control and influence there apparently became increasingly absolute throughout Europe. Among the English working classes, it was the wife who generally determined how the family's money was spent. In many families the husband gave all his earnings to his wife to tend. She returned to him only a small allowance for carfare, beer, tobacco, and union dues. All the major domestic decisions, from the children's schooling and religious instruction to the selection of new furniture or a new apartment, were hers. In France women had even greater power in their assigned domain. One English feminist noted in 1908 that "though legally women occupy a much inferior status than men [in France], in practice they constitute the superior sex. They are the power behind the throne."[15]

Women ruled at home partly because running the urban household was a complicated and extremely demanding task. Twice-a-day food shopping, penny-pinching, economizing, and the growing crusade against dirt—not to mention child raising—were a full-time occupation. Nor were there any laborsaving appliances to help. The wife also ruled at home because a good deal of her effort was directed toward pampering her husband as he expected. In countless humble households, she saw that he had meat while she ate bread, that he relaxed by the fire while she did the dishes.

The woman's guidance of the household went hand in hand with the increased emotional importance of home and family. The home she ran was idealized as a warm shelter in a hard and impersonal urban world. By the 1820s, one observer of the comfortable middle classes in Marseilles had noted, for example, that the "family father, obliged to occupy

A Working-Class Home, 1875 Emotional ties within ordinary families grew stronger in the nineteenth century. *(Illustrated London News, LXVI, 1875. Photo courtesy of Boston Public Library)*

himself with difficult business problems during the day, can relax only when he goes home. . . . Family evenings together are for him a time of the purest and most complete happiness."[16]

In time the central place of the family spread down the social scale. For a child of the English slums in the early 1900s,

home, however poor, was the focus of all love and interests, a sure fortress against a hostile world. Songs about its beauties were ever on people's lips. "Home, sweet home," first heard in the 1870s, had become "almost a second national anthem." Few walls in lower-working-class houses lacked "mottoes"—colored strips of paper, about nine inches wide and eighteen inches in length, attesting to domestic joys: EAST, WEST, HOME'S BEST; BLESS OUR HOME; GOD IS MASTER OF THIS HOUSE; HOME IS THE NEST WHERE ALL IS BEST.[17]

By 1900 home and family were what life was all about for millions of people of all classes.

Women also developed stronger emotional ties to their husbands. Even in the comfortable classes, marriages were increasingly founded on sentiment and sexual attraction rather than on money and calculation. Affection and eroticism became more central to the couple after marriage. Gustave Droz, whose bestseller *Mr., Mrs., and Baby* went through 121 editions between 1866 and 1884, saw love within marriage as the key to human happiness. He condemned men who made marriage sound dull and practical, men who were exhausted by prostitutes and rheumatism and who wanted their young wives to be little angels. He urged women to follow their hearts and marry a man more nearly their own age:

A husband who is stately and a little bald is all right, but a young husband who loves you and who drinks out of your glass without ceremony, is better. Let him, if he ruffles your dress a little and places a kiss on your neck as he passes. Let him, if he undresses you after the ball, laughing like a fool. You have fine spiritual qualities, it is true, but your little body is not bad either and when one loves, one loves completely. Behind these follies lies happiness.[18]

Many French marriage manuals of the late 1800s stressed that women had legitimate sexual needs, such as the "right to orgasm." Perhaps the French were a bit more enlightened in these matters than other nationalities. But the rise of public socializing by couples in cafés and music halls, as well as franker affection within the family, suggest a more erotic, pleasurable intimate life for women throughout Western society. This, too, helped make the woman's role as mother and homemaker acceptable and even satisfying.

CHILD REARING

One of the most striking signs of deepening emotional ties within the family was the mother's love and concern for her tiny infants. This was a sharp break with the past. It may seem scarcely believable today that the typical mother in preindustrial Western society was very often indifferent toward her baby. This indifference—unwillingness to make real sacrifices for the welfare of the infant—was giving way among the comfortable classes by the later part of the eighteenth century, but the ordinary mother adopted new attitudes only as the nineteenth century progressed. The baby became more important, and women became better mothers.

Mothers increasingly breast-fed their infants, for example, rather than paying wet nurses to do so. Breast-feeding involved sacrifice—a temporary loss of freedom, if nothing else. Yet in an age when there was no good alternative to mother's milk, it saved lives. The surge of maternal feeling also gave rise to a wave of specialized books on child rearing and infant hygiene, such as Droz's phenomenally successful book. Droz urged fathers to get into the act and pitied those "who do not know how to roll around on the carpet, play at being a horse and a great wolf, and undress their baby."[19] Another sign, from France, of increased affection is that fewer illegitimate babies were abandoned as foundlings, especially after about 1850. Moreover, the practice of swaddling disappeared completely. Instead, ordinary mothers allowed their babies freedom of movement and delighted in their spontaneity.

The loving care lavished on infants was matched by greater concern for older children and adoles-

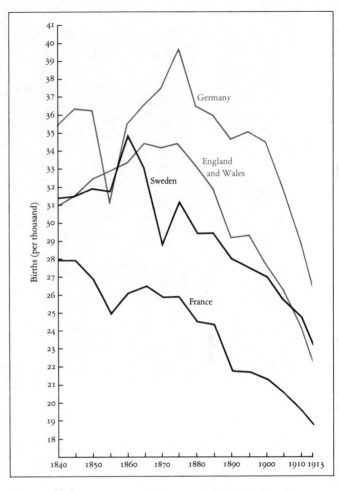

FIGURE 28.4 The Decline of Birthrates in England and Wales, France, Germany, and Sweden, 1840–1913 Women had fewer babies for a variety of reasons, including the fact that their children were increasingly less likely to die before reaching adulthood. Compare with Figure 28.2 on page 877.

cents. They, too, were wrapped in the strong emotional ties of a more intimate and protective family. For one thing, European women began to limit the number of children they bore, in order to care adequately for those they had. It was evident by the end of the century that the birthrate was declining across Europe, as Figure 28.4 shows, and it continued to do so until after World War Two. The Englishwoman who married in the 1860s, for example, had an average of about six children; her daughter marrying in the 1890s had only four; and her granddaughter marrying in the 1920s had only two or possibly three.

The most important reason for this revolutionary reduction in family size, in which the comfortable

The Drawing Room The middle-class ideal of raising cultured, educated and properly protected young women is captured in this illustration. A serious mother lovingly teaches her youngest child while the older daughters practice their genteel skills. A drawing room was a kind of nineteenth-century family room, mercifully spared the tyranny of television. *(BBC Hulton/The Bettman Archive)*

and well-educated classes took the lead, was parents' desire to improve their economic and social position and that of their children. Children were no longer an economic asset. By having fewer youngsters, parents could give those they had valuable advantages, from music lessons and summer vacations to long, expensive university educations and suitable dowries. A young German skilled worker with only one child spoke for many in his class when he said, "We want to get ahead, and our daughter should have things better than my wife and sisters did." [20] Thus, the growing tendency of couples in the late nineteenth century to use a variety of contraceptive methods—rhythm, withdrawal, and mechanical devices—certainly reflected increased concern for the welfare of children.

Indeed, many parents were probably *too* concerned about their children, unwittingly subjecting them to an emotional pressure cooker of almost unbearable intensity. The result was that many children and especially adolescents came to feel trapped and in desperate need of greater independence.

Biological and medical theories led parents to believe that their own emotional characteristics were passed on to their offspring and that they were thus directly responsible for any abnormality in a child. The moment the child was conceived was thought to be of enormous importance. "Never run the risk of conception when you are sick or over-tired or unhappy," wrote one influential American woman. "For the bodily condition of the child, its vigor and magnetic qualities, are much affected by conditions ruling this great moment." [21] So might the youthful "sexual excess" of the father curse future generations. Although this was true in the case of syphilis, which could be transmitted to unborn children, the rigid determinism of such views left little scope for the child's individual development.

Another area of excessive parental concern was the sexual behavior of the child. Masturbation was viewed with horror, for it represented an act of independence and even defiance. Diet, clothing, games, and sleeping were carefully regulated. Girls were discouraged from riding horses and bicycling because rhythmic friction simulated masturbation. Boys were dressed in trousers with shallow and widely separated pockets.

These and less blatant attempts to repress the child's sexuality were a source of unhealthy tension, often made worse by the rigid division of sexual roles within the family. It was widely believed that mother and child love each other easily, but that relations between father and child are necessarily difficult and often tragic. The father was a stranger; his world of business was far removed from the maternal world of spontaneous affection. Moreover, the father was demanding, often expecting the child to succeed where he himself had failed and making his love conditional on achievement. Little wonder that the imaginative literature of the late nineteenth century came to deal with the emotional and destructive elements of father-son relationships. In the Russian Feodor Dostoevsky's great novel *The Brothers Karamazov* (1880–1881), for example, four sons work knowingly or unknowingly to destroy their father. Later, at the murder trial, one of the brothers claims to speak for all mankind and screams out: "Who doesn't wish his father dead?"

Sigmund Freud (1856–1939), the Viennese founder of psychoanalysis, formulated the most striking analysis of the explosive dynamics of the family, particularly the middle-class family in the late nineteenth century. A physician by training, Freud began his career treating mental illness. He noted that the hysteria of his patients appeared to originate in bitter early childhood experiences, wherein the child had been obliged to repress strong feelings. When these painful experiences were recalled and reproduced under hypnosis or through the patient's free association of ideas, the patient could be brought to understand his or her unhappiness and eventually to deal with it.

One of Freud's most influential ideas concerned the Oedipal tensions resulting from the son's instinctive competition with the father for the mother's love and affection. More generally, Freud postulated that much of human behavior is motivated by unconscious emotional needs, whose nature and origins are kept from conscious awareness by various mental devices he called "defense mechanisms." Freud concluded that much unconscious psychological energy is sexual energy, which is in turn repressed and precariously controlled by rational thinking and moral rules. If Freud exaggerated the sexual and familial roots of adult behavior, that exaggeration was itself a reflection of the tremendous emotional intensity of family life in the late nineteenth century.

The working classes probably had more avenues of escape from such tensions than did the middle classes. Unlike their middle-class counterparts, who remained economically dependent on their families until a long education was finished or a proper marriage secured, working-class boys and girls went to work when they reached adolescence. Earning wages on their own, they could bargain with their parents for greater independence within the household by the time they were sixteen or seventeen. If they were unsuccessful, they could and did leave home, to live cheaply as paying lodgers in other working-class homes. Thus, the young person from the working classes broke away from the family more easily when emotional ties became oppressive. In the twentieth century, middle-class youth would follow this lead.

SCIENCE AND THOUGHT

Major changes in Western thought accompanied the emergence of urban society. Two aspects of these complex intellectual developments stand out as especially significant. Scientific knowledge expanded rapidly and came to influence the Western world-view more profoundly than it had since the Scientific Revolution and the early Enlightenment. And, between about the 1840s and the 1890s, European literature underwent a shift from soaring romanticism to tough-minded realism.

THE TRIUMPH OF SCIENCE

As the pace of scientific advance quickened and as theoretical advances resulted in great practical benefits, science exercised growing influence on human thought. The intellectual achievements of the Scientific Revolution had resulted in few such benefits, and theoretical knowledge had also played a relatively small role in the Industrial Revolution in England. But breakthroughs in industrial technology enormously stimulated basic scientific inquiry, as researchers sought to explain theoretically how such things as steam engines and blast furnaces actually worked. The result was an explosive growth of fundamental scientific discoveries from the 1830s onward. And unlike earlier periods, these theoretical discoveries were increasingly transformed into material improvements for the general population.

A perfect example of the translation of better scientific knowledge into practical human benefits was the work of Pasteur and his followers in biology and the medical sciences. Another was the development of the branch of physics known as *thermodynamics.* Building on Newton's laws of mechanics and on studies of steam engines, thermodynamics investigated the relationship between heat and mechanical energy. By midcentury, physicists had formulated the fundamental laws of thermodynamics, which were then applied to mechanical engineering, chemical processes, and many other fields. The *law of conservation of energy* held that different forms of energy—such as heat, electricity, and magnetism—could be converted but neither created nor destroyed. Nineteenth-century thermodynamics demonstrated that the physical world is governed by firm, unchanging laws.

Chemistry and electricity were two other fields characterized by extremely rapid progress. Chemists devised ways of measuring the atomic weight of different elements, and in 1869 the Russian chemist Dmitri Mendeleev (1834–1907) codified the rules of chemistry in the periodic law and the periodic table. Chemistry was subdivided into many specialized branches, such as *organic chemistry*—the study of the compounds of carbon. Applying theoretical insights gleaned from this new field, researchers in large German chemical companies discovered ways of transforming the dirty, useless coal tar that accumulated in coke ovens into beautiful, expensive synthetic dyes for the world of fashion. The basic discoveries of Michael Faraday (1791–1867) on electromagnetism in the 1830s and 1840s resulted in the first dynamo (generator) and opened the way for the subsequent development of electric motors, electric lights, and electric streetcars.

The triumph of science and technology had at least three significant consequences. First, though ordinary citizens continued to lack detailed scientific knowledge, everyday experience and innumerable popularizers impressed the importance of science on the popular mind.

As science became more prominent in popular thinking, the philosophical implications of science formulated in the Enlightenment spread to broad sections of the population. Natural processes appeared to be determined by rigid laws, leaving little room for either divine intervention or human will. Yet scientific and technical advances had also fed the Enlightenment's optimistic faith in human progress, which now appeared endless and automatic to many middle-class minds.

Finally, the methods of science acquired unrivaled prestige after 1850. For many, the union of careful experiment and abstract theory was the only reliable route to truth and objective reality. The "unscientific" intuitions of poets and the revelations of saints seemed hopelessly inferior.

SOCIAL SCIENCE AND EVOLUTION

From the 1830s onward, many thinkers tried to apply the objective methods of science to the study of society. In some ways these efforts simply perpetuated the critical thinking of the philosophes. Yet there were important differences. The new "social scientists" had access to the massive sets of numerical data that governments had begun to collect, on everything from children to crime, from population to prostitution. In response, they developed new statistical methods to analyze these facts "scientifically" and supposedly to test their theories. And the systems of the leading nineteenth-century social scientists were more unified, all-encompassing, and dogmatic than those of the philosophes. Marx was a prime example (pages 847–848).

Another extremely influential system builder was the French philosopher Auguste Comte (1798–1857). Initially a disciple of the utopian socialist Saint-Simon (page 845), Comte wrote a six-volume *System of Positive Philosophy* (1830–1842), which was largely overlooked during the romantic era. But when the political failures of 1848 completed the swing to realism, Comte's philosophy came into its own. Its influence has remained great to this day.

Comte postulated that all intellectual activity progresses through predictable stages, "the Theological, or fictitious; the Metaphysical, or abstract; and the

Scientific, or positive . . . . The first is the necessary point of departure of human understanding, and the third is the fixed and definitive state. The second is merely a transition."[22] By way of example, Comte noted that the prevailing explanation of cosmic patterns had shifted, as knowledge of astronomy developed, from the will of God (the theological) to the will of an orderly Nature (the metaphysical) to the rule of its own unchanging laws (the scientific). Later, this same intellectual progression took place in increasingly complex fields—physics, chemistry, and finally, the study of society. By applying the scientific, positivist method, Comte believed, his new discipline of sociology would soon discover the eternal laws of human relations. This colossal achievement would in turn enable expert social scientists to impose a disciplined harmony and well-being on less-enlightened citizens. Dismissing the "fictions" of traditional religions, Comte became the chief priest of the religion of science and rule by experts.

Comte's stages of knowledge exemplify the nineteenth-century fascination with the idea of evolution and dynamic development. Thinkers in many fields, like the romantic historians and "scientific" Marxists, shared and applied this basic concept. In geology, Charles Lyell (1797–1875) effectively discredited the long-standing view that the earth's surface had been formed by short-lived cataclysms, such as biblical floods and earthquakes. Instead, according to Lyell's principle of uniformitarianism, the same geological processes that are at work today slowly formed the earth's surface over an immensely long time. The evolutionary view of biological development, first proposed by the Greek Anaximander in the sixth century B.C., re-emerged in a more modern form in the work of Jean Baptiste Lamarck (1744–1829). Lamarck asserted that all forms of life had arisen through a long process of continuous adjustment to the demands of the environment.

Lamarck's work was flawed—he believed that characteristics parents acquired in the course of their lives could be inherited by their children—and was not accepted, but it helped prepare the way for Charles Darwin (1809–1882), the most influential of all nineteenth-century evolutionary thinkers. As the official naturalist on a five-year scientific cruise to Latin America and the South Pacific in 1831, Darwin carefully collected specimens of the different animal species he encountered on the voyage. Back in Eng-

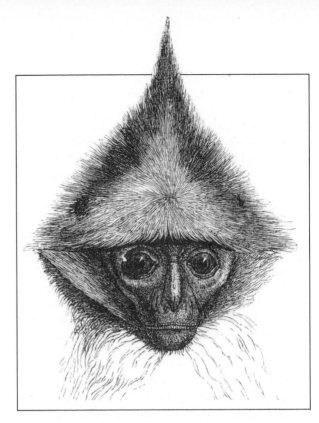

Attracting Females was an integral part of the struggle for survival, according to Darwin. He theorized that those males who were most attractive to females would have the most offspring, like this type of monkey that had developed ornamental hair with devastating sex appeal. Darwin used this illustration in *The Descent of Man* (1871). *(Library of Congress)*

land and convinced by fossil evidence and by his friend Lyell that the earth and life on it were immensely ancient, Darwin came to doubt the general belief in a special divine creation of each species of animal. Instead, he concluded, all life had gradually evolved from a common ancestral origin in an unending "struggle for survival." After long hesitation, Darwin published his research, which immediately attracted wide attention.

Darwin's great originality lay in suggesting precisely *how* biological evolution might have occurred. His theory is summarized in his title—*On the Origin of Species by the Means of Natural Selection* (1859). Decisively influenced by Malthus's gloomy theory that populations naturally grow faster than their food supplies, Darwin argued that chance differences among the members of a given species help some to survive while others die. Thus the variations that prove useful in the struggle for survival are selected naturally and gradually spread to the entire species through reproduction. Darwin did not explain why such variations occurred in the first place, and not until the early twentieth century did the study of genetics and the concept of mutation provide some answers.

As the capstone of already widespread evolutionary thinking, Darwin's theory had a powerful and many-sided influence on European thought and the European middle classes. Darwin was hailed as the great scientist par excellence, the "Newton of biology," who had revealed once again the powers of objective science. Darwin's findings also reinforced the teachings of secularists like Comte and Marx, who scornfully dismissed religious belief in favor of agnostic or atheistic materialism. In the great cities especially, religion was on the defensive. Finally, many writers applied the theory of biological evolution to human affairs. Herbert Spencer (1820–1903), an English disciple of Auguste Comte, saw the human race as driven forward to ever-greater specialization and progress by the brutal economic struggle that efficiently determined the "survival of the fittest." The poor were the ill-fated weak, the prosperous the chosen strong. Understandably, Spencer and other Social Darwinists were especially popular with the upper middle class.

REALISM IN LITERATURE

In 1868 Emile Zola (1840–1902), the giant of the realist movement in literature, defended his violently criticized first novel against charges of pornography and corruption of morals. Such accusations were meaningless, Zola claimed: he was only a purely objective scientist using "the modern method, the universal instrument of inquiry of which this age makes such ardent use to open up the future."

I chose characters completely dominated by their nerves and their blood, deprived of free-will, pushed to each action of their lives by the fatality of their flesh. . . . I have simply done on living bodies the work of analysis which surgeons perform on corpses. [23]

Zola's literary manifesto articulated the key themes of realism, which had emerged in the 1840s and continued to dominate Western culture and style until the 1890s. Realist writers believed that literature should depict life exactly as it was. Forsaking poetry for prose and the personal, emotional viewpoint of the romantics for strict, scientific objectivity, the realists simply observed and recorded—content to let the facts speak for themselves.

The major realist writers focused their extraordinary powers of observation on contemporary everyday life. Emphatically rejecting the romantic search for the exotic and the sublime, they energetically pursued the typical and the commonplace. Beginning with a dissection of the middle classes, from which most of them sprang, many realists eventually focused on the working classes, especially the urban working classes, who had been neglected in imaginative literature before this time. They put a microscope to many unexplored and taboo subjects—sex, strikes, violence, alcoholism—and hastened to report that slums and factories teemed with savage behavior. Many shocked middle-class critics denounced realism as ugly sensationalism, wrapped provocatively in pseudoscientific declarations and crude language.

The realists' claims of objectivity did not prevent the elaboration of a definite world-view. Unlike the romantics, who had gloried in individual freedom and an unlimited universe, realists such as Zola were strict determinists. Human beings, like atoms, were components of the physical world, and all human actions were caused by unalterable natural laws. Heredity and environment determined human behavior; good and evil were merely social conventions.

The realist movement began in France, where romanticism had never been completely dominant, and three of its greatest practitioners—Balzac, Flaubert, and Zola—were French. Honoré de Balzac (1799–1850) spent thirty years writing a vastly ambitious panorama of postrevolutionary French life. Known collectively as *The Human Comedy,* this series of nearly one hundred books vividly portrays more than two thousand characters from virtually all sectors of French society. Balzac pictures urban society as grasping, amoral, and brutal, characterized by a Darwinian struggle for wealth and power. In *Père Goriot* (1835), the hero, a poor student from the provinces, eventually surrenders his idealistic integrity to feverish ambition and society's all-pervasive greed.

Madame Bovary (1857), the masterpiece of Gustave Flaubert (1821–1880), is far narrower in scope than Balzac's work but unparalleled in its depth and accuracy of psychological insight. Unsuccessfully prosecuted as an outrage against public morality and religion, Flaubert's carefully crafted novel tells the ordinary, even banal, story of a frustrated middle-class housewife who has an adulterous love affair and is betrayed by her lover. Without moralizing, Flaubert portrays the provincial middle class as petty, smug, and hypocritical.

Zola was most famous for his seamy, animalistic view of working-class life. But he also wrote gripping, carefully researched stories featuring the stock exchange, the big department store, and the army, as well as urban slums and bloody coal strikes. Like many later realists, Zola sympathized with socialism, a sympathy evident in his overpowering *Germinal* (1885).

Realism quickly spread beyond France. In England, Mary Ann Evans (1819–1880), who wrote under the pen name George Eliot, brilliantly achieved a more deeply felt, less sensational kind of realism. "It is the habit of my imagination," George Eliot wrote, "to strive after as full a vision of the medium in which a character moves as one of the character itself." Her great novel *Middlemarch: A Study of Provincial Life* examines masterfully the ways in which people are shaped by their social medium as well as their own inner strivings, conflicts, and moral choices. Thomas Hardy (1840–1928) was more in the Zola tradition. His novels, such as *Tess of the D'Urbervilles* and *The Return of the Native,* depicted men and women frustrated and crushed by fate and bad luck.

The greatest Russian realist, Count Leo Tolstoy (1828–1910), combined realism in description and character development with an atypical moralizing, which came to dominate his later work. Tolstoy's greatest work was *War and Peace,* a monumental novel set against the historical background of Napoleon's invasion of Russia in 1812. Tolstoy probes deeply into the lives of a multitude of unforgettable characters, such as the ill-fated Prince Andrei; the shy, fumbling Pierre; and the enchanting, level-headed Natasha. Tolstoy goes to great pains to develop his fatalistic theory of history, which regards free will as an illusion and the achievements of even the greatest leaders as only the channeling of historical necessity. Yet Tolstoy's central message is one that most of the people discussed in this chapter would readily accept: human love, trust, and everyday family ties are life's enduring values.

George Eliot Reared in a strict religious atmosphere against which she later rebelled, Mary Ann Evans accepted scientific attitudes but never lost a strong moral sense of personal responsibility. Her first novels appeared when she was in her early forties. *(National Portrait Gallery, London)*

The Industrial Revolution had a decisive influence on the urban environment. The populations of towns and cities grew rapidly because it was economically advantageous to locate factories and offices in urban areas. This rapid growth worsened long-standing overcrowding and unhealthy living conditions and posed a frightening challenge for society. Eventually government leaders, city planners, reformers, scientists, and ordinary citizens responded. They took effective action in public health and provided themselves with other badly needed urban services. Gradually they tamed the ferocious savagery of the traditional city.

As urban civilization came to prevail, there were major changes in family life. Especially among the lower classes, family life became more stable, more loving, and less mercenary. These improvements had a price, though. Sex roles for men and women became sharply defined and rigidly separate. Women especially tended to be locked into a subordinate and stereotypic role. Nonetheless, on balance, the quality of family life improved for all family members. Better, more stable family relations reinforced the benefits for the masses of higher real wages, increased social security, political participation, and education.

While the quality of urban and family life improved, the class structure became more complex and diversified than before. Urban society featured many distinct social groups, which existed in a state of constant flux and competition. Thus, the gap between rich and poor remained enormous and really quite traditional in mature urban society, although there were countless gradations between the extremes. Large numbers of poor women in particular continued to labor as workers in sweated industries, as domestic servants, and as prostitutes in order to satisfy the demands of their masters in the servant-keeping classes. Urban society in the late nineteenth century represented a great step forward for humanity, but it remained very unequal.

Inequality was a favorite theme of realist novelists like Balzac and Zola. More generally, literary realism reflected Western society's growing faith in science, progress, and evolutionary thinking. The emergence of urban, industrial civilization accelerated the secularization of the Western world-view.

NOTES

1. A Weber, *The Growth of Cities in the Nineteenth Century* (New York: Columbia University Press, 1899), p. 1.
2. Quoted in W. Ashworth, *The Genesis of Modern British Town Planning* (London: Routledge & Kegan Paul, 1954), p. 17.
3. S. Marcus, "Reading the Illegible," in *The Victorian City: Images and Realities,* ed. H. J. Dyos and Michael Wolff (London: Routledge & Kegan Paul, 1973), 1.266.
4. E. Gauldie, *Cruel Habitations: A History of Working-Class Housing, 1780–1918* (London: George Allen & Unwin, 1974), p. 21.
5. Quoted in E. Chadwick, *Report on the Sanitary Condition of the Labouring Population of Great Britain,* ed. M. W. Flinn (Edinburgh: University of Edinburgh Press, 1965, originally published 1842), pp. 315–316.
6. J. P. McKay, *Tramways and Trolleys: The Rise of Urban Mass Transport in Europe* (Princeton, N. J.: Princeton University Press, 1976), p. 81.
7. Quoted in R. P. Neuman, "The Sexual Question and Social Democracy in Imperial Germany," *Journal of Social History* 7 (Winter 1974):276.
8. Quoted in J. A. Banks, "The Contagion of Numbers," in Dyos and Wolff, 1.112.
9. R. Roberts, *The Classic Slum: Salford Life in the First Quarter of the Century* (Manchester, Eng.: University Press, 1971), p. 95.
10. Quoted in B. Harrison, "Pubs," in Dyos and Wolff, 1.175.
11. Quoted in T. Zeldin, *France, 1848–1945* (Oxford, Eng.: Clarendon Press, 1973), 1.288.
12. Quoted in J. M. Phayer, "Lower-Class Morality: The Case of Bavaria," *Journal of Social History* 8 (Fall 1974):89.
13. Quoted in S. Marcus, *The Other Victorians: A Study of Sexuality and Pornography in Mid-Nineteenth-Century England* (New York: Basic Books, 1966), p. 142.
14. Quoted in G. S. Jones, "Working-Class Culture and Working-Class Politics in London, 1870–1900: Notes on the Remaking of a Working Class," *Journal of Social History* 7 (Summer 1974): 486.
15. Quoted in Zeldin, 1.346.
16. Quoted in Shorter, pp. 230–231.
17. Roberts, p. 35.
18. Quoted in Zeldin, 1.295.
19. Ibid., 1.328
20. Quoted in Neuman, p. 281.
21. Quoted in S. Kern, "Explosive Intimacy: Psychodynamics of the Victorian Family," *History of Childhood Quarterly* 1 (Winter 1974):439.
22. A. Comte, *The Positive Philosophy of Auguste Comte,* trans. H. Martineau (London: J. Chapman, 1853), 1. 1–2.
23. Quoted in G. J. Becker, ed., *Documents of Modern Literary Realism* (Princetown, N.J.: Princeton University Press, 1963), p. 159.

SUGGESTED READING

All of the books and articles cited in the Notes are highly recommended; each in its own way is an important contribution to social history and life in the urban society. Note that the *Journal of Social History,* which has a strong European orientation, is excellent both for its articles and for its reviews of new books. T. Zeldin, *France, 1848–1945,* 2 vols. (1973, 1977), is a pioneering social history that opens many doors, as is the ambitious synthesis by T. Hamerow, *The Birth of a New Europe: State and Society in the Nineteenth Century* (1983).

On the European city, D. Pickney, *Napoleon III and the Rebuilding of Paris* (1972), is fascinating, as are G. Masur, *Imperial Berlin* (1970), and M. Hamm, ed., *The City in Russian History* (1976). So also are N. Evenson's beautifully illustrated *Paris: A Century of Change, 1878–1978* (1979); D. Grew's authoritative *Town in the Ruhr: A Social History of Bochum, 1860–1914* (1979); and the essays in J. Merriman, ed., *French Cities in the 19th Century: Class, Power, and Urbanization* (1982). D. Olsen's scholarly *Growth of Victorian London* (1978) complements H. Mayhew's wonderful contemporary study, *London Labour and the Labouring Poor* (1861), reprinted recently. M. Crichton's realistic historical novel on organized crime, *The Great Train Robbery* (1976), is excellent. J. J. Tobias, *Urban Crime in Victorian England* (1972), is a lively, scholarly approach to declining criminal activity in the nineteenth century, with a wealth of detail. G. Rosen, *History of Public Health* (1958), is an excellent introduction to medical developments. For society as a whole, J. Burnett, *History of the Cost of Living* (1969), cleverly shows how different classes spent their money, and B. Tuchman, *The Proud Tower* (1966), draws an unforgettable portrait of people and classes before 1914. J. Laver's handsomely illustrated *Manners and Morals in the Age of Optimism, 1848–1914* (1966), investigates the urban underworld and relations between the sexes. Sexual attitudes are also examined by E. Trudgill, *Madonnas and Magdalenas: The Origin and Development of Victorian Sexual Attitudes* (1976); A. McLaren, *Sexuality and Social Order: Birth Control in Nineteenth-Century France* (1982); and J. Phayer, *Sexual Liberation and Religion in Nineteenth Century Europe* (1977).

Women are coming into their own in historical studies. In addition to the general works by Shorter, Wrigley, Stone, and Tilly and Scott cited in Chapter 22, there are a growing number of eye-opening specialized investigations. These include L. Davidoff, *The Best Circles* (1973), on upper-class society types; O. Banks, *Feminism and Family Planning in Victorian England* (1964);

and P. Branca, *Women in Europe Since 1750* (1978). L. Holcombe, *Victorian Ladies at Work* (1973), pioneers in examining middle-class women at work. M. Vicinus, ed., *Suffer and Be Still* (1972) and *A Widening Sphere* (1981), are far-ranging collections of essays on women's history, as is R. Bridenthal and C. Koonz, eds., *Becoming Visible: Women in European History* (1976). Feminism is treated perceptively in R. Evans, *The Feminists: Women's Emancipation in Europe, America, and Australia* (1979), and K. Blair, *The Clubwoman as Feminist: True Womanhood Redefined, 1868–1914* (1980). J. Gillis, *Youth and History* (1974), is a good introduction. D. Ransel, ed., *The Family in Imperial Russia* (1978), is an important work on the subject, as is J. Donzelot, *The Policing of Families* (1979), which stresses the loss of family control of all aspects of life to government agencies.

Among studies of special groups, J. Scott, *The Glass-Workers of Carmaux* (1974), is outstanding on skilled French craftsmen, and D. Lockwood, *The Blackcoated Worker* (1958), carefully examines class consciousness in the English lower middle class. Two fine studies on universities and their professors are S. Rothblatt, *Revolution of the Dons: Cambridge and Society in Victorian England* (1968), and F. Ringer, *The Decline of the German Mandarins* (1969). Servants and their employers receive excellent treatment in T. McBride, *The Domestic Revolution: The Modernization of Household Service in England and France, 1820–1920* (1976), and B. Smith, *Ladies of the Leisure Class: The Bourgeoises of Northern France in the Nineteenth Century* (1981), which may be compared with the innovative study by M. Miller, *The Bon Marché: Bourgeois Culture and the Department Store, 1869–1920* (1981).

On Darwin, M. Ruse, *The Darwinian Revolution* (1979), is a good starting point, as is G. Himmelfarb, *Darwin and the Darwinian Revolution* (1968). O. Chadwick, *The Secularization of the European Mind in the Nineteenth Century* (1976), analyzes the impact of science (and other factors) on religious belief. The masterpieces of the great realist social novelists remain one of the best and most memorable introductions to nineteenth-century culture and thought. In addition to the novels discussed in this chapter, and those cited in the Suggested Reading for Chapters 26 and 27, I. Turgenev's *Fathers and Sons* and Zola's *The Dram-Shop (L'Assommoir)* are especially recommended.

29

THE AGE OF NATIONALISM IN EUROPE, 1850–1914

*T*HE REVOLUTIONS OF 1848 closed one era and opened another. Urban industrial society began to take strong hold on the Continent, as it already had in Great Britain. Internationally, the repressive peace and diplomatic stability of Metternich's time was replaced by a period of war and rapid change. In thought and culture, soaring romanticism gave way to tough-minded realism. In the European economy, the hard years of the 1840s were followed by good times and prosperity throughout most of the 1850s and 1860s. Perhaps most important of all, European society progressively found, for better or worse, a new and effective organizing principle, capable of coping with the many-sided challenge of the dual revolution and the emerging urban civilization. That principle was nationalism—dedication to and identification with the nation-state.

The triumph of nationalism in Europe after 1850 is a development of enormous historical significance. It was by no means completely predictable. After all, nationalism had been a powerful force since at least 1789. Yet it had repeatedly failed to realize its goals, most spectacularly so in 1848. Why, then, did nationalism become in one way or another an almost universal faith in Europe between 1850 and 1914? More specifically, how did nationalism evolve so that it appealed not only to predominantly middle-class liberals but to the broad masses of society as well? These are the weighty questions this chapter will seek to answer.

NAPOLEON III IN FRANCE

Early nationalism was at least liberal and idealistic and often democratic and radical as well. The ideas of nationhood and popular sovereignty posed an awesome revolutionary threat to conservatives like Metternich. Yet, from the vantage point of the twentieth century, it is clear that nationalism wears many masks; it may be democratic and radical, as it was for Mazzini and Michelet; but it can also flourish in dictatorial states, which may be conservative, fascist, or communist. Napoleon I's France had already combined national devotion with authoritarian rule. Significantly, it was Napoleon's nephew, Louis Napo-

leon, who revived and extended this merger. It was he who showed how governments could reconcile popular and conservative forces in an authoritarian nationalism. In doing so, he provided a model for political leaders elsewhere.

THE SECOND REPUBLIC AND LOUIS NAPOLEON

The overwhelming victory of Louis Napoleon Bonaparte in the French presidential elections of December 1848 has long puzzled historians. The nephew of Napoleon I, Louis Napoleon had lived most of his life outside of France and played no part in French politics before 1848. Why did universal manhood suffrage give such an unproven nobody 5.5 million votes, while the runner-up, General Cavaignac of June Days fame, polled only 1.5 million and the other three candidates (including the poet Lamartine) received insignificant support?

The usual explanation is that, though Louis Napoleon had only his great name in common with his uncle, that was enough. According to some historians, the Napoleonic legend—a monument to the power of romanticism between 1820 and 1848—had transformed a dictator into a demigod in the minds of the unsophisticated French masses. Another explanation, popularized by Karl Marx, has stressed the fears of middle-class and peasant property owners in the face of the socialist challenge of urban workers. These classes wanted protection. They wanted a tough cop with a big stick on the beat. They found him in Louis Napoleon, who had indeed served briefly as a special constable in London at the height of the Chartist agitation.

These explanations are not wrong, but there was more to Louis Napoleon's popularity than stupidity and fear. In late 1848, Louis Napoleon had a positive "program" for France, which was to guide him throughout most of his long reign. This program had been elaborated earlier in two pamphlets, *Napoleonic Ideas* and *The Elimination of Poverty*, which Louis Napoleon had written while imprisoned for a farcical attempt to overthrow Louis Philippe's government. The pamphlets had been widely circulated prior to the presidential election.

Louis Napoleon believed that the government should represent the people and that it should also try hard to help them economically. How was this to be done? Parliaments and political parties were not the answer, according to Louis Napoleon. Politicians represented special-interest groups, particularly middle-class ones. When they ran a parliamentary government, they stirred up class hatred because they were not interested in helping the poor. This had occurred under Louis Philippe, and it was occurring again under the Second Republic. The answer was a strong, even authoritarian, national leader, like the first Napoleon, who would serve all the people, rich and poor. This leader would be linked to the people by direct democracy and universal male suffrage. Sovereignty would flow from the entire population to the leader and would not be diluted or corrupted by politicians and legislative bodies.

These political ideas went hand in hand with Louis Napoleon's vision of national unity and social progress. Unlike his uncle, who had reduced unemployment and social tensions by means of foreign wars, Louis Napoleon favored peaceful measures to relieve the awful poverty of the poor. Rather than doing nothing or providing only temporary relief, the state and its leader had a sacred duty to provide jobs and stimulate the economy. All classes would benefit by such action.

Louis Napoleon's political and social ideas were at least vaguely understood by large numbers of French peasants and workers in December 1848. To many common people he appeared to be both a strong man *and* a forward-looking champion of their interests, and that is why they voted for him.

Elected to a four-year term, President Louis Napoleon had to share power with a conservative National Assembly. With some misgivings he signed a bill to increase greatly the role of the Catholic church in primary and secondary education. In France as elsewhere in Europe after 1848, the anxious well-to-do saw religion as a bulwark against radicalism. As one leader of the church in France put it, "There is only one recipe for making those who own nothing believe in property-rights: that is to make them believe in God, who dictated the Ten Commandments and who promises eternal punishment to those who steal."[1] Very reluctantly, Louis Napoleon also signed another conservative law depriving many poor people of the right to vote. He took these conservative measures for two main reasons: he wanted the Assembly to vote funds to pay his personal debts, and he wanted it to change the constitution so he could run for a second term.

The Assembly did neither. Thus in 1851, Louis Napoleon began to organize a conspiracy with key army officers. On December 2, 1851, he illegally dismissed the Assembly and seized power in a coup d'état. There was some armed resistance in Paris and other cities, but the actions of the Assembly had left the Second Republic with few defenders. Restoring universal male suffrage, Louis Napoleon called on the French people to legalize his actions as his uncle had done. They did: 92 percent voted to make him a strong president for ten years. A year later, 97 percent agreed in a national plebiscite to make him hereditary emperor. For the third time, and by the greatest margin yet, the authoritarian Louis Napoleon was overwhelmingly elected to lead the French nation.

NAPOLEON III'S SECOND EMPIRE

Louis Napoleon—now Emperor Napoleon III—experienced both success and failure between 1852 and 1870. His greatest success was with the economy, particularly in the 1850s. His government encouraged the new investment banks and massive railroad construction that were at the heart of the Industrial Revolution on the Continent. General economic expansion was also fostered by the government's ambitious program of public works, which included the rebuilding of Paris to improve the urban environment. The profits of businessmen soared with prosperity, and the working classes did not fare poorly either. Their wages more than kept up with inflation, and jobs were much easier to find. France's economy benefited from a worldwide economic boom and other external events, such as gold discoveries in California and Australia. Yet the contribution of Napoleon III's economic policies was real all the same.

Louis Napoleon always hoped that economic progress would reduce social and political tensions. This hope was at least partially realized. Until the mid-1860s, there was little active opposition and even considerable support for his government from France's most dissatisfied group, the urban workers. Napoleon III's regulation of pawnshops and his support of credit unions and better housing for the working class were evidence of positive concern in the 1850s. In the 1860s, he granted workers the right to form unions and the right to strike—important economic rights denied by earlier governments.

Rebuilding Paris Expensive and time consuming, boulevard construction in Paris brought massive demolition, considerable slum clearance, and protests of ruin to the old city. In addition to expecting economic benefits, Napoleon III rightly believed that broad boulevards would be harder for revolutionaries to barricade than narrow twisting streets. *(The Mansell Collection)*

At first, political power remained in the hands of the emperor. He alone chose his ministers, and they had great freedom of action. At the same time, Napoleon III restricted but did not abolish the Assembly. To be sure, the French parliament in the 1850s had little power. It could not initiate legislation, and it did not control the budget. Parliamentary sessions were not open to the public, and the government permitted only a dry summary of its debates to be published. Yet the members of the Assembly were elected by universal male suffrage every six years. In each district the government put up its candidate and permitted opposition candidates, although it restricted speeches and discussions during the electoral campaigns.

Louis Napoleon and his government took the parliamentary elections very seriously. They tried to entice notable people, even those who had opposed the regime, to stand as government candidates in order to expand its base of support. Moreover, the government rewarded districts that elected government candidates. It used its officials and appointed mayors to spread the word that the election of the government's candidate was the key to roads, schools, tax rebates, and a thousand other local concerns.

In 1857 and again in 1863, Louis Napoleon's system worked well and produced overwhelming electoral victories. The poet-politician Alphonse de Lamartine was convinced that Louis Napoleon was France's greatest politician since Talleyrand, and possibly even greater than he. Yet in the course of the 1860s Napoleon III's electoral system gradually disintegrated, for several reasons. France's problems in Italy and the rising power of Prussia led to increasing criticism at home from his Catholic and nationalist supporters. With increasing effectiveness, the middle-class liberals who had always detested his dictatorship continued to denounce his rule as a disgrace to France's republican tradition.

Napoleon was always sensitive to the public mood. Public opinion, he once said, always wins the last victory. Thus in the 1860s, he progressively "liberalized" his empire. He gave the Assembly greater powers and the opposition candidates greater freedom, which they used to good advantage. In 1869 the opposition, consisting of republicans, monarchists, and liberals, polled almost 45 percent of the vote.

The following year, a sick and weary Louis Napoleon once again granted France a new constitution, which combined a basically parliamentary regime with a hereditary emperor as chief of state. In a final great plebiscite on the eve of a disastrous war with Prussia, 7.5 million Frenchmen voted in favor of the new constitution, and only 1.5 million opposed it. Napoleon III's attempt to reconcile a strong national state with universal manhood suffrage was still evolving, in a democratic direction.

NATION BUILDING IN ITALY AND GERMANY

Louis Napoleon's triumph in 1848 and his authoritarian rule in the 1850s provided the old ruling classes of Europe with a new model in politics. As the great Swiss historian Jacob Burckhardt later noted,

Louis Napoleon had risked universal suffrage for the elections, and others followed his lead. The conservative streak in the rural populations had been recognized, though no attempt had been made to assess precisely how far it might be extended from the elections to everything and everybody."[2]

To what extent was it possible that the expanding urban middle classes and even the growing working classes might, like people in rural areas, rally to a strong and essentially conservative national state?

This was one of the great political questions in the 1850s and 1860s. In central Europe, a resounding and definitive answer came with the national unification of Italy and Germany.

ITALY TO 1850

Italy had never been a united nation prior to 1860. Part of Rome's great empire in ancient times, the Italian peninsula was divided in the Middle Ages into competing city-states, which led the commercial and cultural revival of the West with amazing creativity. A battleground for great powers after 1494, Italy had been reorganized in 1815 at the Congress of Vienna. The rich northern provinces of Lombardy and Venetia were taken by Metternich's Austria. Sardinia and Piedmont were under the rule of an Italian monarch, and Tuscany with its famous capital of Florence shared north central Italy with several smaller states. Central Italy and Rome were ruled by the papacy, which had always considered an independent political existence necessary to fulfill its spiritual mission. Naples and Sicily were ruled, as they had been for almost a hundred years, by a branch of the Bourbons. Metternich was not wrong in dismissing Italy as "a geographical expression" (see Map 29.1).

Between 1815 and 1848, the goal of a unified Italian nation captured the imaginations of increasing numbers of Italians. There were three basic approaches. The first was the radical program of the idealistic patriot Mazzini, who preached a centralized democratic republic based on universal suffrage and the will of the people. The second was that of Gioberti, a Catholic priest, who called for a federation of existing states under the presidency of a progressive pope. Finally, there were those who looked for leadership toward the autocratic kingdom of Sardinia-Piedmont, much as many Germans looked toward Prussia.

The third alternative was strengthened by the failures of 1848, when Austria smashed and discredited Mazzini's republicanism. Almost by accident, Sardinia's monarch Victor Emmanuel retained the liberal constitution granted under duress in March 1848. This constitution provided for a fair degree of civil liberties and real parliamentary government, complete with elections and parliamentary control of taxes. To the Italian middle classes, Sardinia appeared to be a liberal, progressive state, ideally suited to achieve the goal of national unification. By con-

MAP 29.1 The Unification of Italy, 1859–1870 The leadership of Sardinia-Piedmont and nationalist fervor were decisive factors in the dramatic political unification of the Italian peninsula.

trast, Mazzini's brand of democratic republicanism seemed quixotic and too radical. As for the papacy, the initial cautious support by Pius IX (1846–1878) for unification had given way to fear and hostility after he was temporarily driven from Rome during the upheavals of 1848. For a long generation, the papacy would stand resolutely opposed not only to na-

tional unification but to most modern trends. In 1864, in the *Syllabus of Errors,* Pius IX strongly denounced rationalism, socialism, separation of church and state, and religious liberty, denying that "the Roman pontiff can and ought to reconcile and align himself with progress, liberalism, and modern civilization."

CAVOUR AND GARIBALDI

Sardinia had the good fortune of being led by a brilliant statesman, Count Camillo Benso di Cavour, the dominant figure in the Sardinian government from 1850 until his death in 1861. Cavour's development was an early sign of the coming tacit alliance between the aristocracy and the solid middle class throughout much of Europe. Beginning as a successful manager of his father's large landed estates in Piedmont, Cavour was also an economic liberal. He turned toward industry and made a substantial fortune in sugar mills, steamships, banks, and railroads. Economically secure, he then entered the world of politics and became chief minister in the liberalized Sardinian monarchy. Cavour's national goals were limited and realistic. Until 1859 he sought unity only for the states of northern and perhaps central Italy in a greatly expanded kingdom of Sardinia. It was not one of his goals to incorporate the papal states or the Kingdom of the Two Sicilies, with their very different cultures and governments, into an Italy of all the Italians. Cavour was a moderate nationalist.

In the 1850s Cavour worked to consolidate Sardinia as a liberal state capable of leading northern Italy. His program of highways and railroads, of civil liberties and opposition to clerical privilege, increased support for Sardinia throughout northern Italy. Yet Cavour realized that Sardinia could not drive Austria out of Lombardy and Venetia and unify northern Italy under Victor Emmanuel without the help of a powerful ally. He sought that ally in the person of Napoleon III, who sincerely believed in the general principle of nationality, as well as modest expansion for France.

In a complicated series of diplomatic maneuvers, Cavour in 1854 entered the Crimean War (page 912) against Russia, on the side of Great Britain and France, and tenaciously worked for a diplomatic alliance with Napoleon III against Austria. Finally he succeeded. In July 1858, Cavour and Napoleon III agreed orally in the utmost secrecy that if Cavour could goad Austria into attacking Sardinia, France would come to Sardinia's "defense."

For a time, Cavour feared that an international congress and a diplomatic compromise would thwart his plans. But in the end, Austria obligingly issued an ultimatum and declared war. Napoleon III came to Sardinia's defense. Then, after the victory of the combined Franco-Sardinian forces, he did a complete about-face. Nauseated by the gore of war and criticized by French Catholics for supporting the pope's declared enemy, Napoleon III abandoned Cavour. He made a compromise peace with the Austrians at Villafranca in July 1859. Sardinia would receive only Lombardy, the area around Milan. The rest of the map of Italy would remain essentially unchanged. Cavour resigned in a rage.

Yet Cavour's plans were salvaged by popular revolts and Italian nationalism. While the war against Austria had raged in the north, dedicated nationalists in central Italy had risen and driven out their rulers. Nationalist fervor seized the urban masses. Large crowds demonstrated, chanting, "Italy and Victor Emmanuel!" and singing passionately, "Foreigners, get out of Italy!" Buoyed up by this enthusiasm, the leaders of the nationalist movement in central Italy ignored the compromise peace of Villafranca and called for fusion with Sardinia. This was not at all what France and the other Great Powers wanted, but the nationalists held firm and eventually had their way. Cavour returned to power in early 1860 and worked out a diplomatic deal with Napoleon III. The people of central Italy voted overwhelmingly to join a greatly enlarged kingdom of Sardinia. Cavour had achieved his original goal of a north Italian state (see Map 29.1).

For superpatriots like Giuseppe Garibaldi (1801–1882), the job of unification was still only half done. The son of a poor sailor, Garibaldi personified the romantic, revolutionary nationalism of Mazzini and 1848. As a lad of seventeen, he had traveled to Rome and been converted to the "New Italy, the Italy of all the Italians." As he later wrote in his *Autobiography*, "The Rome that I beheld with the eyes of youthful imagination was the Rome of the future—the dominant thought of my whole life." Sentenced to death in 1834 for his part in an uprising in Genoa, Garibaldi escaped to South America. For twelve years he led a guerrilla band in Uruguay's struggle for independence. "Shipwrecked, ambushed, shot through the neck," he found in a tough young woman, Anna da Silva, a mate and companion in arms. Their first children nearly starved in the jungle while Garibaldi, clad in his long red shirt, fashioned a legend not unlike that of the Cuban Che Guevara in recent times. He returned to Italy to fight in 1848 and led a corps of volunteers against Austria in 1859. By the spring of

Garibaldi Landing in Sicily With a thousand volunteers the flamboyant Garibaldi conquered the kingdom of the Two Sicilies in 1860 and paved the way for Italian unification. *(Historical Pictures Service, Chicago)*

guerrilla leader took Palermo. Then he and his men crossed to the mainland, marched triumphantly toward Naples, and prepared to attack Rome and the pope. But the wily Cavour quickly sent Sardinian forces to occupy most of the Papal States (but not Rome) and to intercept Garibaldi.

Cavour realized that an attack on Rome would bring about war with France, and he also feared Garibaldi's popular appeal. Therefore, he immediately organized a plebiscite in the conquered territories. Despite the urging of some of his more radical supporters, the patriotic Garibaldi did not oppose Cavour, and the people of the south voted to join Sardinia. When Garibaldi and Victor Emmanuel rode through Naples to cheering crowds, they symbolically sealed the union of north and south, of monarch and people.

Cavour had succeeded. He had controlled Garibaldi and had turned popular nationalism in a conservative direction. The new kingdom of Italy, which did not include Venice until 1866 or Rome until 1870, was neither radical nor democratic. Italy was a parliamentary monarchy under Victor Emmanuel, but in accordance with the Sardinian constitution only a small minority of Italians had the right to vote. There was a definite division between the propertied classes and the common people. There was also a great social and cultural gap between the progressive, industrializing north and the stagnant, agrarian south. This gap would increase, since peasant industries in the south would not be able to survive. Italy was united politically. Other divisions remained.

GERMANY BEFORE BISMARCK

In the aftermath of 1848, while Louis Napoleon consolidated his rule and Cavour schemed, the German states were locked in a political stalemate. With Russian diplomatic support, Austria had blocked the halfhearted attempt of Frederick William IV of Prussia (1840–1861) to unify Germany "from above." This action contributed to a growing tension between Austria and Prussia, as each power sought to block the other within the reorganized German Confederation (pages 840 and 864). Stalemate also prevailed in the domestic politics of the individual states, as Austria, Prussia, and the smaller German kingdoms entered a period of reaction and immobility.

1860, Garibaldi had emerged as a powerful independent force in Italian politics.

Partly to use him and partly to get rid of him, Cavour secretly supported Garibaldi's bold plan to "liberate" Sicily. Landing in Sicily in May 1860, Garibaldi's guerrilla band of a thousand "Red Shirts" captured the imagination of the Sicilian peasantry. Outwitting the twenty-thousand-man royal army, the

At the same time, powerful economic forces were undermining the political status quo. As discussed earlier, modern industry grew rapidly in Europe throughout the 1850s. Nowhere was this growth more rapid than within the German customs union (Zollverein). Developing gradually under Prussian leadership after 1818 and founded officially in 1834 to stimulate trade and increase the revenues of member states, the customs union had not included Austria. After 1848 it became a crucial factor in the Austro-Prussian rivalry.

Tariff duties were substantially reduced so that Austria's highly protected industry could not bear to join. In retaliation, Austria tried to destroy the Zollverein by inducing the south German states to leave it, but without success. Indeed, by the end of 1853 all the German states except Austria had joined the customs union. A new Germany excluding Austria was becoming an economic reality, and the middle class and business groups were finding solid economic reasons to bolster their idealistic support of national unification. Thus economic developments helped Prussia greatly in its struggle against Austria's traditional supremacy in German affairs.

The national uprising in Italy in 1859 made a profound impression in the German states. In Prussia, great political change and war—perhaps with Austria, perhaps with France—seemed quite possible. The tough-minded William I of Prussia (1858–1888), who had replaced the unstable Frederick William IV as regent in 1858 and become king in 1861, and his top military advisers were convinced of the need for major army reforms. William I wanted to double the size of the regular army. He also wanted to reduce the importance of the reserve militia, a semipopular force created during the Napoleonic wars. William had contempt for the "dirty reservists," those "civilians in uniform," who lacked efficiency and complete obedience. By drafting every young man into the army for three years, the king and his conservative supporters hoped to promote military attitudes in daily life. Of course, reform of the army meant a bigger defense budget and higher taxes.

Prussia had emerged from 1848 with a parliament of sorts, and by 1859 the Prussian parliament was in the hands of the liberal middle class. The middle class, like the landed aristocracy, was overrepresented by the Prussian electoral system, and it wanted society to be less, not more, militaristic. Above all, middle-class representatives wanted to establish once and for all that parliament, not the king, had the ultimate political power. They also wanted to ensure that the army was responsible to the people and not a "state within a state." These demands were popular. The parliament rejected the military budget in 1862, and the liberals triumphed so completely in new elections that the conservatives "could ride to the parliament building in a single coach." King William considered abdicating in favor of his more liberal son. In the end, he called on Count Otto von Bismarck to head a ministry and defy the parliament. It was a momentous choice.

BISMARCK TAKES COMMAND

The most important figure in German history between Luther and Hitler, Otto von Bismarck (1815–1898) has been the object of enormous interest and debate. Like his contemporary Abraham Lincoln, who successfully led the North against the South in a great civil war between 1861 and 1865, Bismarck used military victory to forge a strong, unified national state.

A great hero to some, a great villain to others, Bismarck was above all a master of politics. Born into the Prussian landowning aristocracy, the young Bismarck was a wild and tempestuous student, given to duels and drinking. Proud of his Junker heritage—"my fathers have been born and have lived and died in the same rooms for centuries"—and always devoted to his Prussian sovereign, Bismarck had a strong personality and an unbounded desire for power.

Bismarck entered the civil service, which was the only socially acceptable career except the army for a Prussian aristocrat. But he soon found bureaucratic life unbearable and fled to his ancestral estate. The civil servant was like a musician in an orchestra, he said, and "I want to play the tune the way it sounds to me or not at all. . . . My pride bids me command rather than obey."[3] Yet in his drive for power, power for himself and for Prussia, Bismarck was extraordinarily flexible and pragmatic. "One must always have two irons in the fire," he once said. He kept his options open, pursuing one policy and then another as he moved with skill and cunning toward his goal.

Bismarck first honed his political skills as a diplomat. Acquiring a reputation as an ultraconservative

Otto von Bismarck A fierce political fighter with a commanding personality and a brilliant mind, Bismarck was devoted to Prussia and its king and aristocracy. Uniforms were worn by civilian officials as well as by soldiers in Prussia. *(Brown Brothers)*

in the Prussian assembly in 1848, he fought against Austria as the Prussian ambassador to the German Confederation from 1851 to 1859. Transferred next to St. Petersburg and then to Paris, Bismarck had an excellent opportunity to evaluate Alexander II and Napoleon III at close range. A blunt, expansive talker, especially after a few drinks, Bismarck's basic goal was well known in 1862—to build up Prussia's strength and consolidate Prussia's precarious Great Power status.

To achieve this goal, Bismarck was convinced that Prussia had to control completely the northern, predominantly Protestant part of the German Confederation. He saw three possible paths open before him. He might work with Austria to divide up the smaller German states lying between them. Or he might combine with foreign powers—France and Italy, or even Russia—against Austria. Or he might ally with the forces of German nationalism to defeat and expel Austria from German affairs. Each possibility was explored in many complicated diplomatic maneuvers, but in the end the last path was the one Bismarck took.

That Bismarck would join with the forces of German nationalism to increase Prussia's power seemed unlikely when he took office in 1862. Bismarck's appointment made a strong but unfavorable impression. One of the liberal middle-class members of the Prussian parliament expressed enlightened public opinion throughout Prussia and the other German states: "Bismarck, that is to say: government without budget, rule by the sword in home affairs, and war in foreign affairs. I consider him the most dangerous Minister for Prussia's liberty and happiness."[4]

Bismarck's speeches were a sensation and a scandal. Declaring that the government would rule without parliamentary consent, Bismarck lashed out at the middle-class opposition: "The great questions of the day will not be decided by speeches and resolutions—that was the blunder of 1848 and 1849—but by blood and iron." In 1863 he told the Prussian parliament, "If a compromise cannot be arrived at and a conflict arises, then the conflict becomes a question of power. Whoever has the power then acts according to his opinion." Denounced for this view that "might makes right," Bismarck and the bureaucracy went right on collecting taxes, even though the parliament refused to approve the budget, and reorganized the army. And for four years, from 1862 to 1866, the voters of Prussia continued to express their opposition by sending large liberal majorities to the parliament.

THE AUSTRO-PRUSSIAN WAR OF 1866

Opposition at home spurred the search for success abroad. The ever-knotty question of Schleswig-Holstein (page 864) provided a welcome opportunity. When the Danish king tried again, as in 1848, to bring the provinces into a centralized Danish state against the will of the German Confederation, Prussia joined Austria in a short and successful war against Denmark in 1864. Then, rather than following nationalist sentiment and allowing the conquered provinces to become another medium-sized independent state within the German Confederation, Bismarck maneuvered Austria into a tricky position. Prussia and Austria agreed to joint administration of the conquered provinces, thereby giving Bismarck a weapon he could use either to force Austria into peacefully accepting Prussian domination in northern Germany or to start a war against Austria.

Bismarck knew that a war with Austria would have to be localized war. He had to be certain that Prussian expansion did not provoke a mighty armed coalition, such as the coalition that had almost crushed Frederick the Great in the eighteenth century. Russia, the great bear to the east, was no problem. Bismarck had already gained Alexander II's gratitude by supporting Russia's repression of a Polish uprising in 1863. Napoleon III—the "sphinx without a riddle," according to Bismarck—was another matter. But Bismarck charmed him into neutrality with vague promises of more territory along the Rhine. Thus, when Austria proved unwilling to give up its historic role in German affairs, Bismarck was in a position to engage in a war of his own making.

The Austro-Prussian War of 1866 lasted only seven weeks. Utilizing railroads to mass troops and the new breechloading needle gun for maximum firepower, the reorganized Prussian army overran northern Germany and defeated Austria decisively at the battle of Königgrätz in Bohemia. Anticipating Prussia's future needs, Bismarck offered Austria realistic, even generous, peace terms. Austria paid no reparations and lost no territory to Prussia, although Venice was ceded to Italy. But the German Confederation was dissolved, and Austria agreed to withdraw from German affairs. The states north of the Main River were grouped in a new North German Confederation led by an expanded Prussia. The mainly Catholic states of the south were permitted to remain independent, while forming military alliances with Prussia. Bismarck's fundamental goal of Prussian expansion was being realized (Map 29.2).

THE TAMING OF PARLIAMENT

Bismarck had long been convinced that the old order he so ardently defended should make peace—on its own terms—with the liberal middle class and the nationalist movement. Inspired somewhat by Louis Napoleon, he realized that nationalism was not necessarily hostile to conservative, authoritarian government. Moreover, Bismarck believed that, because of the events of 1848, the German middle class could be led to prefer the reality of national unity to a long, uncertain battle for truly liberal institutions. During the constitutional struggle over army reform and parliamentary authority, he had delayed but not abandoned this goal. Thus, during the attack on Austria in 1866, he increasingly identified Prussia's fate with the "national development of Germany."

In the aftermath of victory, Bismarck fashioned a federal constitution for the new North German Confederation. Each state retained its own local government, but the king of Prussia was to be president of the confederation and the chancellor—Bismarck—

MAP 29.2 The Unification of Germany, 1866–1871 This map deserves careful study. Note how Prussian expansion, Austrian expulsion from the old German Confederation, and the creation of a new German Empire went hand in hand. Austria lost no territory but Prussia's neighbors in the north suffered grievously or simply disappeared.

was to be responsible only to the president. The federal government—William I and Bismarck—controlled the army and foreign affairs. There was also a legislature, consisting of an upper house whose delegates were appointed by the different states and a lower house. Both houses shared equally in the making of laws. Members of the lower house were elected by universal, equal manhood suffrage. With this radi-

cal innovation, Bismarck opened the door to popular participation and went over the head of the middle class directly to the people. All the while, however, ultimate power rested as securely as ever in the hands of Prussia and its king and army.

Events within Prussia itself were even more significant than those at the federal level. In the flush of victory, the ultraconservatives expected Bismarck to suspend the Prussian constitution or perhaps abolish the Prussian parliament altogether. Yet he did nothing of the sort. Instead, he held out an olive branch to the parliamentary opposition. Marshaling all his diplomatic skill, Bismarck asked the parliament to pass a special indemnity bill to approve after the fact all of the government's spending between 1862 and 1866. Most of the liberals snatched at the chance to cooperate. For four long years, they had opposed and criticized Bismarck's "illegal" measures. And what had happened? Bismarck, the king, and the army had persevered, and in the end these conservative forces had succeeded beyond the wildest dreams of the liberal middle class. In 1866 German unity was in sight, and the people were going to be allowed to participate actively in the new state. Many liberals repented their "sins" and were overjoyed that Bismarck would forgive them.

None repented more ardently or more typically than Hermann Baumgarten, a mild-mannered, thoroughly decent history professor and member of the liberal opposition. In an essay entitled "A Self Criticism of German Liberalism," he confessed in 1866:

We thought by agitation we could transform Germany. But . . . almost all the elements of our political system have been shown erroneous by the facts themselves. . . . Yet we have experienced a miracle almost without parallel. The victory of our principles would have brought us misery, whereas the defeat of our principles has brought boundless salvation. [5]

The constitutional struggle was over. The German middle class was bowing respectfully before Bismarck and the monarchial authority and aristocratic superiority he represented. They did not stand upright again in the years before 1914.

The Franco-Prussian War of 1870–1871

The rest of the story of German unification is anticlimactic. In 1867 Bismarck brought the four south German states into the customs union and established a customs parliament. But the south Germans were reluctant to go further because of their different religious and political traditions. Bismarck realized that a patriotic war with France would drive the south German states into his arms. The French oblig-

"His First Thought" This 1896 cartoon provides a brilliant commentary on German middle-class attitudes. Suddenly crippled, the man's first thought is "Disaster! Now I can no longer be an army reserve officer." Being a part-time junior officer, below the dominant aristocratic career officers, became a great middle-class status symbol. *(Photo: Caroline Buckler)*

ingly played their part. The apparent issue—whether a distant relative of Prussia's William I (and France's Napoleon III) might become king of Spain—was only a diplomatic pretext. By 1870 the French leaders of the Second Empire, alarmed by their powerful new neighbor on the Rhine, had decided on a war to teach Prussia a lesson.

As soon as war against France began in 1870, Bismarck had the wholehearted support of the south German states. With other governments standing still—Bismarck's generosity to Austria in 1866 was paying big dividends—German forces under Prussian leadership decisively defeated Louis Napoleon's armies at Sedan on September 1, 1870. Three days later, French patriots in Paris proclaimed yet another French republic and vowed to continue fighting. But after five months, in January 1871, a starving Paris surrendered, and France went on to accept Bismarck's harsh peace terms. By this time, the south German states had agreed to join a new German Empire. The victorious William I was proclaimed emperor of Germany in the Hall of Mirrors in the palace of Versailles. Europe had a nineteenth-century German "sun king." As in the 1866 constitution, the king of Prussia and his ministers had ultimate power in the new empire, and the lower house of the legislature was elected popularly by universal male suffrage.

The Franco-Prussian War of 1870 to 1871, which Europeans generally saw as a test of nations in a pitiless Darwinian struggle for existence, released an enormous surge of patriotic feeling in Germany. Bismarck's genius, the invincible Prussian army, the solidarity of king and people in a unified nation—these and similar themes were trumpeted endlessly during and after the war. The weakest of the Great Powers in 1862—after Austria, Britain, France, and Russia—Prussia fortified by the other Germans states had become the most powerful state in Europe in less than a decade. Most Germans were enormously proud, enormously relieved. And they were somewhat drunk with success, blissfully imagining themselves the fittest and best of the European species. Semi-authoritarian nationalism had triumphed. Only a few critics remained dedicated to the liberal ideal of truly responsible parliamentary government.

THE MODERNIZATION OF RUSSIA

In Russia, unlike Italy and Germany, there was no need to build a single state out of a jumble of principalities. The vast Russian Empire was a great multinational state. In the early nineteenth century, nationalism there was a subversive ideology, identified with revolution. After 1853, however, old autocratic Russia was in serious trouble. It became clear to Russia's leaders that the country had to embrace the process of modernization.

A vague and often overworked term, *modernization* is a great umbrella under which some writers place most of the major developments of the last two

hundred or even five hundred years. Yet defined narrowly—as changes that enable a country to compete effectively with the leading countries at a given time—modernization can be a useful concept. It fits Russia after the Crimean War particularly well.

THE "GREAT REFORMS"

In the 1850s Russia was a poor agrarian society. Industry was little developed, and almost 90 percent of the population lived on the land. Agricultural techniques were backward: the ancient open-field system reigned supreme. Serfdom was still the basic social institution. Bound to the lord on a hereditary basis, the peasant serf was little more than a slave. Individual serfs and serf families were regularly sold, with and without land, in the early nineteenth century. Serfs were obliged to furnish labor services or money payments as the lord saw fit. Moreover, the lord could choose freely among them for army recruits, who had to serve for twenty-five years, and he could punish a serf with deportation to Siberia whenever he wished. Sexual exploitation of female serfs by their lords was common.

Serfdom had become the great moral and political issue for the government by the 1840s, but it might still have lasted many more years had it not been for the Crimean War of 1853 to 1856. The war began as a dispute with France over who should protect certain Christian shrines in the Ottoman Empire. Because the fighting was concentrated in the Crimean peninsula in the Black Sea, Russia's transportation network of rivers and wagons failed to supply the distant Russian armies adequately. France and Great Britain, aided by Sardinia, inflicted a humiliating defeat on Russia.

The military defeat marked a turning point in Russian history. The Russian state had been built on the military, and Russia had not lost a major war for a century and a half. This defeat demonstrated that Russia had fallen behind the rapidly industrializing nations of western Europe in many areas. At the very least, Russia needed railroads, better armaments, and reorganization of the army if it was to maintain its international position. Moreover, the disastrous war had caused hardship and raised the specter of massive peasant rebellion. Reform of serfdom was imperative. And, as the new tsar, Alexander II (1855–1881), told the serf owners, it would be better if reform came from above rather than from below. Military disaster thus forced Alexander II and his ministers along the path of rapid social change and general modernization.

The first and greatest of the reforms was the freeing of the serfs in 1861. Human bondage was abolished forever, and the emancipated peasants received, on the average, about half of the land. Yet they had to pay fairly high prices for their land, and because the land was owned collectively, each peasant village was jointly responsible for the payments of all the families in the village. The government hoped that collective responsibility would strengthen the peasant village as a social unit and prevent the development of a class of landless peasants. In practice, collective ownership and responsibility made it very difficult for individual peasants to improve agricultural methods or leave their villages. Thus the effects of the reform were limited, for it did not encourage peasants to change their old habits and attitudes.

Most of the later reforms were also halfway measures. In 1864 the government established a new institution of local government, the *zemstvo*. Members of this local assembly were elected by a three-class system of towns, peasant villages, and noble landowners. A zemstvo executive council dealt with local problems. The establishment of the zemstvos marked a significant step toward popular participation, and Russian liberals hoped it would lead to a national parliament. They were soon disappointed. The local zemstvo remained subordinate to the traditional bureaucracy and the local nobility, who were heavily favored by the property-based voting system. More successful was reform of the legal system, which established independent courts and equality before the law. Education was also liberalized somewhat, and censorship was relaxed but not removed.

The Industrialization of Russia

Until the twentieth century, Russia's greatest strides toward modernization were economic rather than political. Industry and transport, both so vital to the military, were transformed in two industrial surges. The first of these came after 1860. The government encouraged and subsidized private railway companies, and construction boomed. In 1860 the empire had only about 1,250 miles of railroads; by 1880 it had about 15,500 miles. The railroads enabled agri-

"Farewell," says the triumphant German soldier on the left in this French cartoon. "No, till we meet again," replies the French soldier. "Visits must be returned." German victory and Bismarck's seizure of French territory poisoned Franco-German relations after 1871. *(Photo: Caroline Buckler)*

cultural Russia to export grain and thus earn money for further industrialization. Domestic manufacturing was stimulated, and by the end of the 1870s Russia had a sophisticated and well-developed railway-equipment industry. Industrial suburbs grew up around Moscow and St. Petersburg, and a class of modern factory workers began to take shape.

Industrial development strengthened Russia's military forces and gave rise to territorial expansion to the south and east. Imperial expansion greatly excited many ardent Russian nationalists and superpatriots, who became some of the government's most enthusiastic supporters. Industrial development also contributed mightily to the spread of Marxian thought and the transformation of the Russian revolutionary movement after 1890.

In 1881 Alexander II was assassinated by a small group of terrorists. The era of reform came to an abrupt end, for the new tsar, Alexander III (1881–1894), was a determined reactionary. Russia, and indeed all of Europe, experienced hard times economically in the 1880s. Political modernization remained

Novgorod Merchants Drinking Tea This late nineteenth-century photograph suggests how Russian businessmen were slow to abandon traditional dress and attitudes in the face of change. Stern authoritarians in the family circle and staunchly devoted to church and tsar, they were often suspicious of foreigners as well as the lawyers and journalists who claimed to speak for the nation's middle class. *(BBC Hulton/The Bettmann Archive)*

frozen until 1905, but economic modernization sped forward in the massive industrial surge of the 1890s. As it had after the Crimean War, nationalism played a decisive role. The key leader was Sergei Witte, the tough, competent minister of finance from 1892 to 1903. Early in his career, Witte found in the writings of Friedrich List (page 822) an analysis and a program for action. List had stressed the peril for Germany of remaining behind England in the 1830s and 1840s. Witte saw the same threat of industrial backwardness hindering Russia's power and greatness.

Witte moved forward on several fronts. A railroad manager by training, he believed that railroads were "a very powerful weapon . . . for the direction of the economic development of the country."[6] Therefore,

the government built railroads rapidly, doubling the network to 35,000 miles by the end of the century. The gigantic trans-Siberian line connecting Moscow with Vladivostok on the Pacific Ocean 5,000 miles away was Witte's pride, and it was largely completed during his term of office. Following List's advice, Witte raised high protective tariffs to build Russian industry, and he put the country on the gold standard of the "civilized world" in order to strengthen Russian finances.

Witte's greatest innovation, however, was to use the West to catch up with the West. He aggressively encouraged foreigners to use their abundant capital and advanced technology to build great factories in backward Russia. As he told the tsar, "The inflow of foreign capital is . . . the only way by which our industry will be able to supply our country quickly with abundant and cheap products."[7] This policy was brilliantly successful, especially in southern Russia. There, in the eastern Ukraine, foreign capitalists and their engineers built an enormous and very modern steel and coal industry almost from scratch in little more than a decade. By 1900 only the United States, Germany, and Great Britain were producing more steel than Russia. The Russian petroleum industry had even pulled up alongside that of the United States and was producing and refining half the world's output of oil.

Witte knew how to keep foreigners in line. Once a leading foreign businessman came to him and angrily demanded that the Russian government fulfill a contract it had signed and pay certain debts immediately. Witte asked to see the contract. He read it and then carefully tore it to pieces and threw it in the wastepaper basket without a word of explanation. It was just such a fiercely independent Russia that was catching up with the advanced nations of the West.

THE REVOLUTION OF 1905

Catching up partly meant vigorous territorial expansion, for this was the age of Western imperialism. By 1903 Russia had established a sphere of influence in Chinese Manchuria and was casting greedy eyes on northern Korea. When the protests of equally imperialistic Japan were ignored, the Japanese launched a surprise attack in February 1904. To the world's amazement, Russia suffered repeated losses and was forced in August 1905 to accept a humiliating defeat.

As is often the case, military disaster abroad brought political upheaval at home. The business and professional classes had long wanted to match economic with political modernization. Their minimal goal was to turn the last of Europe's absolutist monarchies into a liberal, representative regime. Factory workers, strategically concentrated in the large cities, had all the grievances of early industrialization and were organized in a radical labor movement. Peasants had gained little from the era of reforms and were suffering from poverty and overpopulation. Finally, nationalist sentiment was emerging among the empire's minorities. The politically and culturally dominant ethnic Russians were only about 45 percent of the population, and by 1900 some intellectuals among the subject nationalities were calling for

self-rule and autonomy. Separatist nationalism was strongest among the Polish and Ukrainians. With the army pinned down in Manchuria, all these currents of discontent converged in the revolution of 1905.

The beginning of the revolution pointed up the incompetence of the government. On a Sunday in January 1905, a massive demonstration of workers and their families converged peacefully on the Winter Palace in St. Petersburg to present a petition to the tsar. The workers were led by a trade unionist priest named Father Gapon, who had been secretly supported by the police as a preferable alternative to more radical unions. Carrying icons and respectfully singing "God Save the Tsar," the workers did not know Nicholas II had fled the city. Suddenly troops opened fire, killing and wounding hundreds. The "Bloody Sunday" massacre turned ordinary workers against the tsar and produced a wave of general indignation.

Outlawed political parties came out into the open, and by the summer of 1905 strikes, peasant uprisings, revolts among minority nationalities, and troop mutinies were sweeping the country. The revolutionary surge culminated in October 1905 in a great paralyzing general strike, which forced the government to capitulate. The tsar issued the October Manifesto, which granted full civil rights and promised a popularly elected Duma (parliament) with real legislative power. The manifesto split the opposition. It satisfied most moderate and liberal demands, but the Social Democrats rejected it and led a bloody workers' uprising in Moscow in December 1905. Frightened middle-class moderates helped the government repress the uprising and survive as a constitutional monarchy.

On the eve of the opening of the first Duma in May 1906, the government issued the new constitution, the Fundamental Laws. The tsar retained great powers. The Duma, elected indirectly by universal male suffrage, and a largely appointive upper house could debate and pass laws, but the tsar had an absolute veto. As in Bismarck's Germany, the emperor appointed his ministers, who did not need to command a majority in the Duma.

The disappointed, predominantly middle-class liberals, the largest group in the newly elected Duma, saw the Fundamental Laws as a great step backward. Efforts to cooperate with the tsar's ministers soon broke down. The government then dismissed the Duma, only to find that a more hostile and radical opposition was elected in 1907. After three months of deadlock, the second Duma was also dismissed. Thereupon the tsar and his reactionary advisers unilaterally rewrote the electoral law so as to increase greatly the weight of the propertied classes at the expense of workers, peasants, and national minorities.

The new law had the intended effect. With landowners assured half the seats in the Duma, the government finally secured a loyal majority in 1907 and again in 1912. Thus armed, the tough, energetic chief minister, Peter Stolypin, pushed through important agrarian reforms designed to break down collective village ownership of land and to encourage the more enterprising peasants—the so-called wager on the strong. On the eve of the First World War, Russia was partially modernized, a conservative constitutional monarchy with a peasant-based but industrializing economy.

THE RESPONSIVE NATIONAL STATE, 1871–1914

For central and western Europe, the unification of Italy and Germany by "blood and iron" marked the end of a dramatic period of nation building. After 1871 the heartland of Europe was organized in strong national states. Only on the borders of Europe—in Ireland and Russia, in Austria-Hungary and the Balkans—did subject peoples still strive for political unity and independence. Despite national differences, European domestic politics after 1871 had a common framework—the firmly established national state. The common themes within that framework were the emergence of mass politics and growing mass loyalty toward the national state.

For good reason, ordinary people—the masses of an industrializing, urbanizing society—felt increasing loyalty to their governments. More and more people could vote. By 1914 universal manhood suffrage was the rule rather than the exception. This development had as much psychological as political significance. Ordinary men were no longer denied the right to vote because they lacked wealth or education. They counted; they could influence the government to some extent. They could feel that they were becoming "part of the system."

Women began to demand the right to vote. The women's suffrage movement achieved its first success in the western United States, and by 1913 women could vote in twelve states. Europe, too, moved slowly in this direction. In 1914 Norway gave the vote to most women. Elsewhere, women like the English Emmeline Pankhurst were very militant in their demands. They heckled politicians and held public demonstrations. These efforts generally failed before 1914, but they prepared the way for the triumph of the women's suffrage movement immediately after World War One.

As the right to vote spread, politicians and parties in national parliaments represented the people more responsively. Most countries soon had many political parties. The multiparty system meant that parliamentary majorities were built on shifting coalitions, which were unstable but did give parties leverage. They could obtain benefits for their supporters. Governments increasingly passed laws to alleviate general problems and to help specific groups. Governments seemed to care, and they seemed more worthy of support.

THE GERMAN EMPIRE

Politics in Germany after 1871 reflected many of these developments. The new German Empire was a federal union of Prussia and twenty-four smaller states. Much of the everyday business of government was conducted by the separate states, but there was a strong national government with a chancellor—until 1890, Bismarck—and a popularly elected parliament, called the Reichstag. Although Bismarck refused to be bound by a parliamentary majority, he tried nonetheless to maintain such a majority. This situation gave the political parties opportunities. Until 1878 Bismarck relied mainly on the National Liberals, who had rallied to him after 1866. They supported legislation useful for further economic and legal unification of the country.

Less wisely, they backed Bismarck's attack on the Catholic church, the so-called *Kulturkampf,* or "struggle for civilization." Like Bismarck, the middle-class National Liberals were particularly alarmed by Pius IX's declaration of papal infallibility in 1870. That dogma seemed to ask German Catholics to put loyalty to their church above loyalty to their nation.

Only in Protestant Prussia did the Kulturkampf have even limited success. Catholics throughout the country generally voted for the Catholic Center party, which blocked passage of national laws hostile to the church. Finally in 1878, Bismarck abandoned his attack. Indeed, he and the Catholic Center party entered into an uneasy but mutually advantageous alliance. The reasons were largely economic.

After a worldwide financial bust in 1873, European agriculture was in an increasingly difficult position. Wheat prices plummeted as cheap grain poured in from the United States, Canada, and Russia. New lands were opening up in North America and Russia, and the combination of railroads and technical improvements in shipping cut freight rates for grain drastically. European peasants with their smaller, less efficient farms could not compete in cereal production, especially in western and southern Germany. The peasantry there was largely Catholic, and the Catholic Center party was thus converted to the cause of higher tariffs to protect the economic interests of its supporters.

The same competitive pressures caused the Protestant Junkers, who owned large estates in eastern Germany, to embrace the cause of higher tariffs. They were joined by some of the iron and steel magnates of the Prussian Rhineland and Westphalia, who had previously been for free trade. With three such influential groups lobbying energetically, Bismarck was happy to go along with a new protective tariff in 1879. In doing so, he won new supporters in parliament—the Center party of the Catholics and the Conservative party of the Prussian landowners—and he held on to most of the National Liberals.

Bismarck had been looking for a way to increase taxes and raise more money for the government. The solution was higher tariffs. Many other governments acted similarly. The 1880s and 1890s saw a widespread return to protectionism. France in particular established very high tariffs to protect agriculture and industry, peasants and manufacturers. Thus the German government and other governments responded to a major economic problem and simultaneously won greater loyalty.

At the same time, Bismarck tried to stop the growth of German socialism because he genuinely feared its revolutionary language and allegiance to a movement transcending the nation-state. In 1878, after two attempts on the life of William I by radicals

Bismarck and William II Shown here visiting Bismarck's country estate in 1888, shortly after he became emperor of Germany (and king of Prussia), the young and impetuous William II soon quarrelled with his chief minister. Determined to rule, not merely to reign, his dismissal of Bismarck in 1890 was a fatal decision. *(Bildarchiv Preussicher Kulturbesitz)*

(though not socialists), Bismarck succeeded in ramming through the Reichstag a law repressing socialists. Socialist meetings and publications were strictly controlled. The Social Democratic party was outlawed and driven underground. However, German socialists displayed a discipline and organization worthy of the Prussian army itself. Bismarck had to try another tack.

Thus Bismarck's state pioneered with social measures designed to win the support of working-class people. In 1883 he pushed through the parliament the first of several modern social security laws to help wage earners. The laws of 1883 and 1884 established national sickness and accident insurance; the law of 1889 established old-age pensions and retirement benefits. Henceforth sick, injured, and retired workers could look forward to regular weekly benefits from the state. This national social security system, paid for through compulsory contributions by wage earners and employers as well as grants from the state, was the first of its kind anywhere. It was to be fifty years before similar measures would be taken in the United States. Bismarck's social security system did not wean workers from socialism, but it did protect them from some of the uncertainties of the complex urban industrial world. This enormously significant development was a product of political competition and governmental efforts to win popular support.

Increasingly, the great issues in German domestic politics were socialism and the Marxian Social Democratic party. In 1890 the new emperor, the young, idealistic, and unstable William II (1888–1918), opposed Bismarck's attempt to renew the law outlawing the Social Democratic party. Eager to rule in his own right, as well as to earn the support of the workers, William II forced Bismarck to resign. After the "dropping of the pilot," German foreign policy changed profoundly and mostly for the worse, but the government did pass new laws to aid workers and to legalize socialist political activity.

Yet William II was no more successful than Bismarck in getting workers to renounce socialism. Indeed, socialist ideas spread rapidly, and more and more Social Democrats were elected to the parliament in the 1890s. After opposing a colonial war in German Southwest Africa in 1906 and thus suffering important losses in the general elections of 1907, the German Social Democratic party broadened its base in the years before World War One. In the elections of 1912, the party scored a great victory, becoming the largest single party in the Reichstag. The "revolutionary" socialists were, however, becoming less and less revolutionary in Germany. In the years before World War One, the strength of socialist opposition to greater military spending and imperialist expansion declined greatly. German socialists marched under the national banner.

REPUBLICAN FRANCE

In 1871 France seemed hopelessly divided once again. The patriotic republicans who proclaimed the Third Republic in Paris after the military disaster at Sedan refused to admit defeat. They defended Paris with great heroism for weeks, living off rats and zoo animals, until they were quite literally starved into submission by German armies in January 1871.

When national elections then sent a large majority of conservatives and monarchists to the National Assembly, the traumatized Parisians exploded and proclaimed the Paris Commune in March 1871. Vaguely radical, the leaders of the Commune wanted to govern Paris without interference by the conservative French countryside. The National Assembly, led by the aging politician Adolphe Thiers, would hear none of it. The Assembly ordered the French army into Paris and brutally crushed the Commune. Twenty thousand people died in the fighting. As in June 1848, it was Paris against the provinces, French against French.

Out of this tragedy France slowly formed a new national unity, achieving considerable stability before 1914. How is one to account for this? Luck played a part. Until 1875 the monarchists in the "republican" National Assembly had a majority but could not agree who should be king. The compromise Bourbon candidate refused to rule except under the white flag of his ancestors—a completely unacceptable condition. In the meantime, Thiers's slaying of the radical Commune and his other firm measures showed the fearful provinces and the middle class that the Third Republic might be moderate and socially conservative. France therefore retained the republic, though reluctantly. As President Thiers cautiously said, it was "the government which divides us least."

Another stabilizing factor was the skill and determination of the moderate republican leaders in the early years. The most famous of these was Léon Gambetta, the son of an Italian grocer, a warm, easygoing, unsuccessful lawyer turned professional politician. A master of emerging mass politics, Gambetta combined eloquence with the personal touch as he preached a republic of truly equal opportunity. Gambetta was also instrumental in establishing absolute parliamentary supremacy between 1877 and 1879, when the somewhat autocratic president Marie Edmé MacMahon was forced to resign. By 1879 the great majority of members of both the upper and the lower houses of parliament were republicans. Although these republicans were split among many parliamentary groups and later among several parties— a situation that led to constant coalition politics and the rapid turnover of ministers—the Third Republic had firm foundations after almost a decade.

The moderate republicans sought to preserve their creation by winning the hearts and minds of the next

Civil War in France When the French army invaded Paris, the Communards retaliated by placing hostages before firing squads, as this photograph reveals. The conquering army replied by summarily executing many prisoners and deporting others. Atrocities on both sides nurtured a tradition of class conflict that has often plagued modern France. *(BBC Hulton/The Bettman Archive)*

generation. Trade unions were fully legalized, and France acquired a colonial empire. More important, under the leadership of Jules Ferry, the moderate republicans of small towns and villages passed a series of laws between 1879 and 1886 establishing free compulsory elementary education for both girls and boys. At the same time, they greatly expanded the state system of public tax-supported schools. Thus France shared fully in the general expansion of public education, which served as a critical nation-building tool throughout the Western world in the late nineteenth century.

In France most elementary and much secondary education had traditionally been in the parochial schools of the Catholic church, which had long been hostile to republics and to much of secular life. Free compulsory elementary education in France became secular republican education. The pledge of allegiance and the national anthem replaced the catechism and the Ave Maria. Militant young elementary teachers carried the ideology of patriotic republicanism into every corner of France. In their classes, they sought to win the loyalty of the young citizens to the republic, so that France would never again vote en masse for dictators like the two Napoleons.

Although these educational reforms disturbed French Catholics, many of them rallied to the republic in the 1890s. The limited acceptance of the modern world by the more liberal Pope Leo XIII (1878–1903) eased tensions between church and state. Unfortunately, the Dreyfus affair changed all that.

Alfred Dreyfus, a Jewish captain in the French army, was falsely accused and convicted of treason. His family never doubted his innocence and fought unceasingly to reopen the case, enlisting the support of prominent republicans and intellectuals such as the novelist Emile Zola. In 1898 and 1899, the case split France apart. On one side was the army, which had manufactured evidence against Dreyfus, joined by anti-Semites and most of the Catholic establishment. On the other side stood the civil libertarians and most of the more radical republicans.

This battle, which eventually led to Dreyfus's being declared innocent, revived republican feeling against the church. Between 1901 and 1905, the government severed all ties between the state and the Catholic church, after centuries of close relations. The salaries of priests and bishops were no longer paid by the government, and all churches were given to local committees of lay Catholics. Catholic schools were put completely on their own financially, and in a short time they lost a third of their students. The state school system's power of indoctrination was greatly strengthened. In France, only the growing socialist movement, with its very different and thoroughly secular ideology, stood in opposition to patriotic, republican nationalism.

GREAT BRITAIN AND IRELAND

Britain in the late nineteenth century has often been seen as a shining example of peaceful and successful political evolution. Germany was stuck with a manipulated parliament that gave an irresponsible emperor too much power; France had a quarrelsome parliament that gave its presidents too little power. Great Britain, in contrast, seemed to enjoy an effective two-party parliament that skillfully guided the country from classical liberalism to full-fledged democracy with hardly a misstep.

This view of Great Britain is not so much wrong as incomplete. After the right to vote was granted to males of the solid middle class in 1832, opinion leaders and politicians wrestled long and hard with the uncertainties of a further extension of the franchise. In his famous "Essay on Liberty," published in 1859, the philosopher John Stuart Mill (1806–1873), the leading heir to the Benthamite tradition (page 871), probed the problem of how to protect the rights of individuals and minorities in the emerging age of mass electoral participation. Mill pleaded eloquently for the practical and moral value inherent in safeguarding individual differences and unpopular opin-

ions. In 1867 Benjamin Disraeli and the Conservatives extended the vote to all middle-class males and the best-paid workers. The son of a Jewish stockbroker, himself a novelist and urban dandy, the ever-fascinating Disraeli (1804–1881) was willing to risk this "leap in the dark" in order to gain new supporters. The Conservative party, he believed, needed to broaden its traditional base of aristocratic and landed support if it was to survive. After 1867 English political parties and electoral campaigns became more modern, and the "lower orders" appeared to vote as responsibly as their "betters." Hence the Third Reform Bill of 1884 gave the vote to almost every adult male.

While the House of Commons was drifting toward democracy, the House of Lords was content to slumber nobly. Between 1901 and 1910, however, that bastion of aristocratic conservatism tried to reassert itself. Acting as supreme court of the land, it ruled against labor unions in two important decisions. And after the Liberal party came to power in 1906, the Lords vetoed several measures passed by the Commons, including the so-called People's Budget. The Lords finally capitulated, as they had done in 1832, when the king threatened to create enough new peers to pass the bill.

Aristocratic conservatism yielded to popular democracy, once and for all. The result was that extensive social welfare measures, slow to come to Great Britain, were passed in a spectacular rush between 1906 and 1914. During those years, the Liberal party, inspired by the fiery Welshman David Lloyd George (1863–1945), substantially raised taxes on the rich as part of the People's Budget. This income helped the government pay for national health insurance, unemployment benefits, old-age pensions, and a host of other social measures. The state was integrating the urban masses socially as well as politically.

This record of accomplishment was only part of the story, though. On the eve of World War One, the ever-emotional, ever-unanswered question of Ireland brought Great Britain to the brink of civil war. In the 1840s, Ireland had been decimated by famine, which fueled an Irish revolutionary movement. Thereafter, the English slowly granted concessions, such as the abolition of the privileges of the Anglican church and rights for Irish peasants. The Liberal prime minister William Gladstone (1809–1898), who had proclaimed twenty years earlier that "my mission is to pacify Ireland," introduced bills to give Ireland self-government in 1886 and in 1893. They failed to pass. After two decades of relative quiet, Irish nationalists in the British Parliament saw their chance. They supported the Liberals in their battle for the People's Budget and received passage of a home-rule bill for Ireland in return.

Thus Ireland, the emerald isle, achieved self-government—but not quite, for Ireland is composed of two peoples. As much as the Irish Catholic majority in the southern counties wanted home rule, precisely that much did the Irish Protestants of the northern counties of Ulster come to oppose it. Motivated by the accumulated fears and hostilities of generations, the Protestants of Ulster refused to submerge themselves in a Catholic Ireland, just as Irish Catholics had refused to submit to a Protestant Britain.

The Ulsterites vowed to resist home rule in northern Ireland. By December 1913, they had raised 100,000 armed volunteers, and they were supported by much of English public opinion. Thus in 1914, the Liberals in the House of Lords introduced a compromise home-rule law that did not apply to the northern counties. This bill, which openly betrayed promises made to Irish nationalists, was rejected and in September the original home-rule plan was passed but simultaneously suspended for the duration of the hostilities. The momentous Irish question had been overtaken by cataclysmic world war in August 1914.

Irish developments illustrated once again the power of national feeling and national movements in the nineteenth century. Moreover, they were proof that European states, which traced their development far back in history, could not elicit greater loyalty unless they could capture and control that elemental current of national feeling. Thus, though Great Britain had much going for it—power, Parliament, prosperity—none of these availed in the face of the conflicting nationalisms espoused by Catholics and Protestants in Northern Ireland. Similarly, progressive Sweden was powerless to stop the growth of the Norwegian national movement, which culminated in Norway breaking away from Sweden and becoming a fully independent nation in 1905. One can also see how hopeless was the cause of the Ottoman Empire in Europe in the later nineteenth century. The Ottoman Empire was an old dynastic state without ethnic or linguistic unity. It was only a matter of time before the Serbs, Bulgarians, and Rumanians would break away to form their own independent nation-states, and they did (pages 1007–1008).

THE AUSTRO-HUNGARIAN EMPIRE

The dilemma of conflicting nationalisms in Ireland also helps one appreciate how desperate the situation in the Austro-Hungarian Empire had become by the early twentieth century. In 1849 Magyar nationalism had driven Hungarian patriots to declare an independent Hungarian republic, which was savagely crushed by Russian and Austrian armies (pages 860–862). Throughout the 1850s, Hungary was ruled as a conquered territory, and Emperor Francis Joseph and his bureaucracy tried hard to centralize the state and germanize the language and culture of the different nationalities.

Then, in the wake of defeat by Prussia in 1866, a weakened Austria was forced to strike a compromise and establish the so-called dual monarchy. The empire was divided in two and the nationalistic Magyars gained virtual independence for Hungary. Henceforth each half of the empire agreed to deal with its own "barbarians"—its own minorities—as it saw fit. The two states were joined only by a shared monarch and common ministries for finance, defense, and foreign affairs. After 1867 the disintegrating force of competing nationalisms continued unabated, for both Austria and Hungary had several "Irelands" within their borders.

In Austria, ethnic Germans were only one-third of the population, and by the late 1890s many Germans saw their traditional dominance threatened by Czechs, Poles, and other Slavs. A particularly emotional and divisive issue in the Austrian parliament was the language used in government and elementary education at the local level. From 1900 to 1914, the parliament was so divided that ministries generally could not obtain a majority and ruled instead by decree. Efforts by both conservatives and socialists to defuse national antagonisms by stressing economic issues cutting across ethnic lines—which led to the introduction of universal male suffrage in 1907— proved largely unsuccessful.

One aspect of such national antagonisms was anti-Semitism, which was particularly virulent in Austria. The Jewish populations of Austrian cities grew very rapidly after Jews obtained full legal equality in 1867, reaching 10 percent of the population of Vienna by 1900. Many Jewish businessmen were quite successful in banking and retail trade, while Jewish artists, intellectuals, and scientists, like the world-famous Sigmund Freud, played a major role in making

1851	Louis Napoleon dismisses French National Assembly in coup d'état
1852–1870	Second Empire in France
1853–1856	Crimean War
1859	Mill, *Essay on Liberty*
1859–1870	Unification of Italy
1861	Abolition of serfdom in Russia
1862–1890	Bismarck's reign of power in German affairs
1864–1871	First Socialist International
1866	Prussia wins decisive victory in Austro-Prussian War
1866–1871	Unification of the German Empire
1867	Magyar nobility increases its power by restoring the constitution of 1848 in Hungary, thereby further dividing the Austro-Hungarian Empire
	Marx, *Capital*
	Second Reform Bill passed by British Parliament
1870–1871	Prussia wins decisive victory in Franco-Prussian War; William I proclaimed emperor of a united Germany
1871	Paris Commune
1871–1914	Third Republic in France
1878	Suppression of Social Democrats in Germany
1881	Assassination of Tsar Alexander II
1883–1889	Enactment of social security laws in Germany
1884	Third Reform Bill passed by British Parliament
1889–1914	Second Socialist International
1890	Repeal of anti-Social Democrat law in Germany
1892–1903	Witte directs modernization of Russian economy
1904–1905	Japan wins decisive victory in Russo-Japanese War
1905	Revolution in Russia: Tsar Nicholas II forced to issue the October Manifesto promising a popularly elected Duma
1906–1914	Liberal reform in Great Britain
1907–1912	Stolypin's agrarian reforms in Russia
1912	German Social Democratic party becomes largest party in the German Reichstag
1914	Irish Home Rule bill passed by British Parliament but immediately suspended with outbreak of First World War

Vienna a leading center of European culture and modern thought. When extremists charged the Jews with controlling the economy and corrupting German culture with alien ideas and ultramodern art, anxious Germans of all classes tended to listen. The popular mayor of Vienna from 1897 to 1910, Dr. Karl Lueger, combined anti-Semitic rhetoric with calls for "Christian socialism" and municipal ownership of basic services. Lueger appealed especially to the German lower middle class—and to an unsuccessful young artist named Adolf Hitler.

In Hungary, the Magyar nobility in 1867 restored the constitution of 1848 and used it to dominate both the Magyar peasantry and the minority populations until 1914. Only the wealthiest one-fourth of adult males had the right to vote, making the parliament the creature of the Magyar elite. Laws promoting use of the Magyar (Hungarian) language in schools and government were rammed through and bitterly resented, especially by the Croatians and Rumanians. While Magyar extremists campaigned loudly for total separation from Austria, the radical leaders of the subject nationalities dreamed in turn of independence from Hungary. Unlike most major countries, which harnessed nationalism to strengthen the state after 1871, the Austro-Hungarian Empire was progressively weakened and destroyed by it.

MARXISM AND THE SOCIALIST MOVEMENT

Nationalism served, for better or worse, as a new unifying principle. But what about socialism? Did the rapid growth of socialist parties, which were generally Marxian parties, dedicated to an international proletarian revolution, mean that national states had failed to gain the support of workers? Certainly, many prosperous and conservative citizens were greatly troubled by the socialist movement. And many historians have portrayed the years before 1914 as a time of increasing conflict between revolutionary socialism on the one hand and a nationalist alliance between conservative aristocracy and the prosperous middle class on the other. This question requires close examination.

THE SOCIALIST INTERNATIONAL

The growth of socialist parties after 1871 was phenomenal. Neither Bismarck's antisocialist laws nor his extensive social security system checked the growth of the German Social Democratic party, which espoused the Marxian ideology. By 1912 it had attracted millions of followers and was the largest party in the parliament. Socialist parties also grew in other countries, though nowhere else with quite such success. In 1883 Russian exiles in Switzerland founded a Russian Social Democratic party, which grew rapidly in the 1890s and thereafter, despite internal disputes. In France, various socialist parties re-

emerged in the 1880s after the carnage of the Commune. Most of them were finally unified in a single, increasingly powerful Marxian party, called the French Section of the Workers International, in 1905. Belgium and Austria-Hungary also had strong socialist parties of the Marxian persuasion.

As the name of the French party suggests, Marxian socialist parties were eventually linked together in an international organization. As early as 1848, Marx had laid out his intellectual system in the *Communist Manifesto* (pages 847–848). He had declared that "the working men have no country," and he had urged proletarians of all nations to unite against their governments. Joining the flood of radicals and republicans who fled continental Europe for England and America after the revolutions of 1848, Marx settled in London. Poor and depressed, he lived on his meager earnings as a journalist and on the gifts of his friend Engels. Marx never stopped thinking of revolution. Digging deeply into economics and history, he concluded that revolution follows economic crisis and tried to prove it in *Critique of Political Economy* (1859) and his greatest theoretical work, *Capital* (1867).

The bookish Marx also excelled as a practical organizer. In 1864 he played an important role in founding the First International of socialists—the International Working Men's Association. In the following years, he battled successfully to control the organization and used its annual meetings as a means of spreading his realistic, "scientific" doctrines of inevitable socialist revolution. Then Marx enthusiastically embraced the passionate, vaguely radical patriotism of the Paris Commune and its terrible conflict with the French National Assembly as a giant step toward socialist revolution. This impetuous action frightened many of his early supporters, especially the more moderate British labor leaders. The First International collapsed.

Yet international proletarian solidarity remained an important objective for Marxists. In 1889, as the individual parties in different countries grew stronger, socialist leaders came together to form the Second International, which lasted until 1914. Although the International was only a federation of various national socialist parties, it had great psychological impact. Every three years, delegates from the different parties met to interpret Marxian doctrines and plan coordinated action. May 1—May Day—

Socialist Clubs helped spread Marxian doctrines among the working classes. There workers (and intellectuals) from different backgrounds debated the fine points and developed a sense of solidarity. *(Historical Pictures Service, Chicago)*

was declared an annual international one-day strike, a day of marches and demonstrations. A permanent executive for the International was established. Many feared and many others rejoiced in the growing power of socialism and the Second International.

Unions and Revisionism

Was socialism really radical and revolutionary in these years? On the whole, it was not. Indeed, as socialist parties grew and attracted large numbers of members, they looked more and more toward gradual change and steady improvement for the working class, less and less toward revolution. The mainstream of European socialists became militantly moderate; that is, they increasingly combined radical rhetoric with sober action.

Workers themselves were progressively less inclined to follow radical programs. There were several reasons for this. As workers gained the right to vote and to participate politically in the nation-state, their attention focused more on elections than on revolutions. And as workers won real, tangible benefits, this furthered the process. Workers were not immune to patriotic education and indoctrination during military service, however ardently socialist intellectuals might wish the contrary. Nor were workers a unified social group, as demonstrated in Chapter 28.

Perhaps most important of all, workers' standard of living rose substantially after 1850 as the promise of the Industrial Revolution was at least partially realized. In Great Britain, for example, workers could buy almost twice as much with their wages in 1906 as in 1850, and most of the increase came after 1870.

Workers experienced similar increases in most continental countries after 1850, though much less strikingly in late-developing Russia. Improvement in the standard of living was much more than merely a matter of higher wages. The quality of life improved dramatically in urban areas. For all these reasons, workers tended more and more to become militantly moderate: they demanded gains, but they were less likely to take to the barricades in pursuit of them.

The growth of labor unions reinforced this trend toward moderation. In the early stages of industrialization, modern unions were generally prohibited by law. A famous law of the French Revolution had declared all guilds and unions illegal in the name of "liberty" in 1791. In Great Britain, attempts by workers to unite were considered criminal conspiracies after 1799. Other countries had similar laws, and these obviously hampered union development. In France, for example, about two hundred workers were imprisoned each year between 1825 and 1847 for taking part in illegal combinations. Unions were considered subversive bodies, only to be hounded and crushed.

From this sad position workers struggled to escape. Great Britain led the way in 1824 and 1825, when unions won the right to exist but (generally) not the right to strike. After the collapse of Robert Owen's attempt to form one big union in the 1830s (page 828), new and more practical kinds of unions appeared. Limited primarily to highly skilled workers such as machinists and carpenters, the "new model unions" avoided both radical politics and costly strikes. Instead, their sober, respectable leaders concentrated on winning better wages and hours for their members through collective bargaining and compromise. This approach helped pave the way to full acceptance in Britain in the 1870s, when unions won the right to strike without being held legally liable for the financial damage inflicted on employers. After 1890 unions for unskilled workers developed, and between 1901 and 1906, the legal position of British unions was further strengthened.

Germany was the most industrialized, socialized, and unionized continental country by 1914. German unions were not granted important rights until 1869, and until the antisocialist law was repealed in 1890, they were frequently harassed by the government as socialist fronts. Nor were socialist leaders particularly interested in union activity, believing as they did in the iron law of low wages and the need for political

revolution. The result was that, as late as 1895, there were only about 270,000 union members in a male industrial work force of nearly 8 million. Then, with German industrialization still storming ahead and almost all legal harassment eliminated, union membership skyrocketed to roughly 3 million in 1912.

This great expansion both reflected and influenced the changing character of German unions. Increasingly, unions in Germany focused on concrete bread-and-butter issues—wages, hours, working conditions—rather than on instilling pure socialist doctrine. Genuine collective bargaining, long opposed by socialist intellectuals as a "sellout," was officially recognized as desirable by the German Trade Union Congress in 1899. When employers proved unwilling to bargain, a series of strikes forced them to change.

Between 1906 and 1913, successful collective bargaining was gaining a prominent place in German industrial relations. In 1913 alone, over ten thousand collective bargaining agreements affecting 1.25 million workers were signed. Further gradual improvement, not revolution, was becoming the primary objective of the German trade union movement.

The German trade unions and their leaders were —in fact, if not in name—thoroughgoing revisionists. *Revisionism*—that most awful of sins in the eyes of militant Marxists in the twentieth century—was an effort by various socialists to update Marxian doctrines to reflect the realities of the time. Thus the socialist Edward Bernstein argued in 1899 in his *Evolutionary Socialism* that Marx's predictions of ever-greater poverty for workers and ever-greater concentration of wealth in ever-fewer hands had been proven false. Therefore, Bernstein suggested, socialists should reform their doctrines and tactics. They should combine with other progressive forces to win gradual evolutionary gains for workers through legislation, unions, and further economic development. These views were formally denounced as heresy by the German Social Democratic party and later by the entire Second International. Nevertheless, the revisionist, gradualist approach continued to gain the tacit acceptance of many German socialists, particularly in the trade unions.

Moderation found followers elsewhere. In France, the great humanist and socialist leader Jean Jaurès formally repudiated revisionist doctrines in order to establish a unified socialist party, but he remained at heart a gradualist. Questions of revolutionary versus gradualist policies split Russian Marxists.

Socialist parties before 1914 had clear-cut national characteristics. Russians and socialists in the Austro-Hungarian Empire tended to be the most radical. The German party talked revolution and practiced reformism, greatly influenced by its enormous trade union movement. The French party talked revolution and tried to practice it, unrestrained by a trade union movement that was both very weak and very radical. In England, the socialist but non-Marxian Labour party, reflecting the well-established union movement, was formally committed to gradual reform. In Spain and Italy, Marxian socialism was very weak. There anarchism, seeking to smash the state rather than the bourgeoisie, dominated radical thought and action.

In short, socialist policies and doctrines varied from country to country. Socialism itself was to a large extent "nationalized" behind the imposing façade of international unity. This helps explain why, when war came in 1914, socialist leaders almost without exception supported their governments.

———————————

From the mid-nineteenth century on, Western society became nationalistic as well as urban and industrial. Nation-states and strong-minded national leaders gradually enlisted widespread support and gave men and women a sense of belonging. Even socialism became increasingly national in orientation, gathering strength as a champion of working-class interests in domestic politics. Yet, while nationalism served to unite peoples, it also drove them apart. Though most obvious in Austria-Hungary and Ireland, this was in a real sense true for all of Western civilization. For the universal national faith, which reduced social tensions within states, promoted a bitter, almost Darwinian competition between states and thus ominously threatened the progress and unity it had helped to build.

NOTES

———————————

1. Quoted in G. Wright, *France in Modern Times* (Chicago: Rand McNally, 1960), p. 179.
2. J. Burckhardt, *Reflections on History* (London: G. Allen & Unwin, 1943), p. 165.
3. Quoted in O. Pflanze, *Bismarck and the Development of Germany: The Period of Unification, 1815–1871* (Princeton, N.J.: Princeton University Press, 1963), p. 60.
4. Quoted in E. Eyck, *Bismarck and the German Empire* (New York: W. W. Norton, 1964), p. 59.
5. Quoted in H. Kohn, *The Mind of Germany: The Education of a Nation* (New York: Charles Scribner's Sons & Macmillan, 1960), pp. 156–161.
6. Quoted in T. von Laue, *Sergei Witte and the Industrialization of Russia* (New York: Columbia University Press, 1963), p. 78.
7. Quoted in J. P. McKay, *Pioneers for Profit: Foreign Entrepreneurship and Russian Industrialization, 1885–1913* (Chicago: University of Chicago Press, 1970), p. 11.

SUGGESTED READING

———————————

In addition to the general works mentioned in the Suggested Reading for Chapter 27, which treat the entire nineteenth century, G. Craig, *Germany, 1866–1945* (1980), and B. Moore, *Social Origins of Dictatorship and Democracy* (1966), are outstanding.

Among specialized works of high quality, R. Williams, *Gaslight and Shadows* (1957), brings the world of Napoleon III vibrantly alive, while Karl Marx's *The Eighteenth Brumaire of Louis Napoleon* is a famous denunciation of the coup d'état. The engaging collective biography by R. Shattuck, *The Banquet Years* (1968), captures the spirit of artistic and intellectual Paris at the end of the century. E. Weber, *Peasants into Frenchmen* (1976), stresses the role of education and modern communications in the transformation of rural France after 1870. E. Thomas, *The Women Incendiaries* (1966), examines radical women in the Paris Commune. G. Chapman, *The Dreyfus Case: A Reassessment* (1955), and D. Johnson, *France and the Dreyfus Affair* (1967), are careful examinations of the famous case. In *Jean Barois,* Nobel Prize winner R. M. Du Gard accurately recreates in novel form the Dreyfus affair, and Emile Zola's novel *The Debacle* treats the Franco-Prussian War realistically.

D. M. Smith has written widely on Italy, and his *Garibaldi* (1956) and *Italy: A Modern History,* rev. ed. (1969), are recommended. P. Schroeder, *Austria, Great Britain and the Crimean War* (1972), is an outstanding and highly original diplomatic study. In addition to the important studies on Bismarck and Germany by Pflanze, Eyck, and Kohn cited in the Notes, F. Stern, *Gold and Iron* (1977), is a fascinating examination of relations between Bismarck and his financial adviser, the Jewish banker Bleichröder. G. Iggers, *The German Conception of History* (1968); K. D. Barkin, *The Controversy over German Industrialization, 1890–1902* (1970); and E. Spencer, *Management and Labor in Imperial Germany: Ruhr Industrialists as Employers* (1984), are valuable in-depth investigations. H. Glasser, ed., *The German Mind in the Nineteenth Century* (1981), is an outstanding anthology, as is P. Mendès-Flohr, *The Jew in the Modern World: A Documentary History* (1980). C. Schorske, *Fin de Siècle Vienna: Politics and Culture* (1980), and P. Gay, *Freud, Jews, and Other Germans* (1978), are brilliant on aspects of modern culture. R. Kann, *The Multinational Empire*, 2 vols. (1950, 1964), probes the intricacies of the nationality problem in Austria-Hungary, while S. Stavrianos has written extensively on southeastern Europe, including *The Balkans, 1815–1914* (1963).

In addition to the studies on Russian industrial development by von Laue and McKay cited in the Notes, W. Blackwell, *The Industrialization of Russia*, 2nd. ed. (1982), and A. Rieber, *Merchants and Entrepreneurs in Imperial Russia* (1982), are recommended. Among fine studies on Russian social development and modernization, T. Emmons, *The Russian Landed Gentry and the Peasant Emancipation of 1861* (1968); R. Zelnik, *Labor and Society in Tsarist Russia, 1855–1870* (1971); R. Johnson, *Peasant and Proletarian: The Working Class*

of Moscow at the End of the Nineteenth Century (1979); and H. Troyat, *Daily Life in Russia Under the Last Tsar* (1962), are particularly noteworthy. W. E. Mosse, *Alexander II and the Modernization of Russia* (1958), provides a good discussion of midcentury reforms, while C. Black, ed., *The Transformation of Russian Society* (1960), offers a collection of essays on Russian modernization. I. Turgenev's great novel *Fathers and Sons* probes the age-old conflict of generations as well as nineteenth-century Russian revolutionary thought.

G. Dangerfield, *The Strange Death of Liberal England* (1961), brilliantly examines social tensions in Ireland as well as Englishwomen's struggle for the vote before 1914. W. Arnstein convincingly shows how the Victorian aristocracy survived and even flourished in nineteenth-century Britain in F. Jaher, ed., *The Rich, the Well-Born, and the Powerful* (1973), an interesting collection of essays on social elites in history. The theme of aristocratic strength and survival is expanded in A. Mayer's provocative *Persistence of the Old Regime: Europe to the Great War* (1981).

On late-nineteenth-century socialism, C. Schorske, *German Social Democracy, 1905–1917* (1955), is a modern classic. V. Lidtke, *The Outlawed Party* (1966), ably treats the German socialists between 1878 and 1890. H. Goldberg, *The Life of Jean Jaurès* (1962), is a sympathetic account of the great French socialist leader. P. Stearns, who has written several books on European labor history, considers radical labor leaders in *Revolutionary Syndicalism and French Labor* (1971). M. Hanagan, *The Logic of Solidarity* (1980), examines workers in three French towns between 1870 and 1914.

30

THE WEST AND THE WORLD

WHILE INDUSTRIALIZATION and nationalism were transforming urban life and Western society, Western society itself was reshaping the world. At the peak of its power and pride, the West entered the third and most dynamic phase of the aggressive expansion that began with the Crusades and continued with the great discoveries and the rise of seaborne colonial empires. An ever-growing stream of products, people, and ideas flowed out of Europe in the nineteenth century. Hardly any corner of the globe was left untouched. The most spectacular manifestations of Western expansion came in the late nineteenth century, when the leading European nations established or enlarged their far-flung political empires. The political annexation of territory in the 1880s—the "new imperialism," as it is often called by historians—was the capstone of a profound underlying economic and technological process. How and why did this many-sided, epoch-making expansion occur in the nineteenth century, and what were some of its consequences for the West and the rest of the world? These are the questions that this chapter will examine.

INDUSTRIALIZATION AND THE WORLD ECONOMY

The Industrial Revolution created, first in Great Britain and then in continental Europe and North America, a growing and tremendously dynamic economic system. In the course of the nineteenth century, that system was extended across the face of the earth. Some of this extension into non-Western areas was peaceful and beneficial for all concerned, for the West had many products and techniques the rest of the world desired. If peaceful methods failed, however, Europeans did not stand on ceremony. They used their superior military power to force non-Western nations to open their doors to Western economic interests. In general, Westerners fashioned the global economic system so that the largest share of the ever-increasing gains from trade, technology, and migration flowed to the West and its propertied classes.

The Industrial Revolution in Europe marked a momentous turning point in world history. Indeed, it is only by placing Europe's economic breakthrough in a world perspective that one can truly appreciate its revolutionary implications and consequences.

From a world perspective, the ultimate significance of the Industrial Revolution was that it allowed those regions of the globe that industrialized in the nineteenth century to increase their wealth and power enormously in comparison to those that did not. As a result, a gap between the industrializing regions—mainly Europe and North America—and the nonindustrializing ones—mainly Africa, Asia, and Latin America—opened up and grew steadily throughout the nineteenth century. Moreover, this pattern of uneven global development became institutionalized, or built into the structure of the world economy. Thus we evolved a "lopsided world," a world of rich lands and poor.

Historians have long been aware of this gap, but it is only recently that historical economists have begun to chart its long-term evolution with some precision. Their findings are extremely revealing, although one must understand that they contain a margin of error and other limitations as well. The findings of one such study are summarized in Figure 30.1. This figure compares the long-term evolution of average income per person in today's "developed" (or industrialized) regions—defined as western and eastern Europe, North America, and Japan—with that found in the "Third World"—a term that is now widely used by international organizations and by scholars to group Africa, Asia, and Latin America into a single unit. To get these individual income figures, researchers estimate a country's gross national product (GNP) at different points in time, convert those estimates to some common currency, and divide by the total population.

Figure 30.1 highlights three main points. First, in 1750 the average standard of living was no higher in Europe as a whole than the rest of the world. In 1750 Europe was still a poor agricultural society. Moreover, the average per person income in the wealthiest western European country (Great Britain) was less than twice that in the poorest non-Western (or eastern European) land. By 1970, however, the average person in the wealthiest countries had an income fully twenty-five times as great as that received by the average person in the poorest countries of Africa and Asia.

Second, it was industrialization that opened the gap in average wealth and well-being between countries and regions. One sees that Great Britain had jumped well above the European average by 1830, when the first industrial nation was well in advance of its continental competitors. One also sees how Great Britain's lead gradually narrowed, as other European countries and the United States industrialized in the course of the nineteenth century.

Finally, income per person stagnated in the Third World before 1913, in striking contrast to the industrializing regions. Only after 1945, in the era of political independence and decolonialization, did Third World countries finally make some real economic progress, beginning in their turn the critical process of industrialization.

The rise of these enormous income disparities, which are poignant indicators of equal disparities in food and clothing, health and education, life expectancy and general material well-being, has generated a great deal of debate. One school of interpretation stresses that the West used science, technology, capitalist organization, and even its critical world-view to create its wealth and greater physical well-being. Another school argues that the West used its political and economic power to steal much of its riches, continuing in the nineteenth (and twentieth) century the rapacious colonialism born of the era of expansion.

These issues are complex, and there are few simple answers. As noted in Chapter 26, the wealth-creating potential of technological improvement and more intensive capitalist organization was indeed great. At the same time, those breakthroughs rested, in part, on Great Britain having already used political force to dominate world trade and the Atlantic economy for its own great advantage. Great Britain and the other Western powers continued to tilt the expanding world economy in their favor in the nineteenth century. Wealth—unprecedented wealth—was indeed created, but the lion's share of that new wealth flowed to the West and its propertied classes.

Trade and Foreign Investment

Commerce between nations has always been a powerful stimulus to economic development. Never was this more true than in the nineteenth century, when

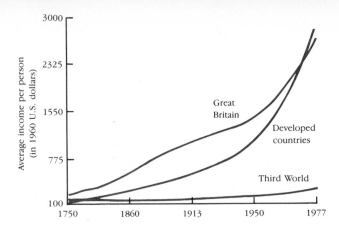

Note: The Third World includes Africa, Asia, Latin America, and Oceania. Developed countries include all European countries, Canada, the United States, and Japan.

Figure 30.1 The Growth of Average Income per Person in the Third World, Developed Countries, and Great Britain, 1750–1970, in 1960 U.S. dollars and prices. *(Source: P. Bairoch and M. Lévy-Leboyer, eds.,* Disparities in Economic Development Since the Industrial Revolution. *New York: St. Martin's Press, 1981, pp. 7–8, 10)*

world trade grew prodigiously. World trade grew modestly until about 1840, and then it took off. After a slowdown in the last years of the century, another surge lasted until World War One. In 1913 the value of world trade was roughly $38 billion, or about *twenty-five* times what it had been in 1800. (This amount actually understates the growth, since average prices of both manufactured goods and raw materials were lower in 1913 than in 1800.) In a general way, the enormous increase in international commerce summed up the growth of an interlocking world economy, centered in and directed by Europe.

Great Britain played a key role in using trade to tie the world together economically. In 1815 Britain already had a colonial empire, for India, Canada, Australia, and other scattered areas remained British possessions after American independence. The technological breakthroughs of the Industrial Revolution allowed Britain to manufacture cotton textiles, iron, and other goods more cheaply and to far outstrip domestic demand for such products. Thus British manufacturers sought export markets, first in Europe and then around the world.

Take the case of cotton textiles. By 1820 Britain was exporting half of its production. Europe bought half of these cotton-textile exports, while India bought only 6 percent. Then, as European nations and the United States exercised sovereignty to erect protective tariff barriers and promote domestic industry, British cotton-textile manufacturers aggressively sought and found other foreign markets in non-Western areas. By 1850 India bought 25 percent and Europe only 16 percent of a much larger total. As a British colony, India could not raise tariffs to protect its ancient cotton-textile industry, and thousands of Indian weavers lost their livelihoods.

After the repeal of the Corn Laws in 1846 (page 856), Britain also became the world's single best market. The decisive argument in the battle against tariffs on imported grain had been, "We must give, if we mean honestly to receive, and buy as well as sell." Until 1914 Britain thus remained the world's emporium, where not only agricultural products and raw materials but also manufactured goods entered freely. Free access to the enormous market of Britain stimulated the development of mines and plantations in many non-Western areas.

The growth of trade was facilitated by the conquest of distance. The earliest railroad construction occurred in Europe (including Russia) and in America north of the Rio Grande; other parts of the globe saw the building of rail lines after 1860. By 1920 more than one-quarter of the world's railroads were in Latin America, Asia, Africa, and Australia. Wherever railroads were built, they drastically reduced transportation costs, opened new economic opportunities, and called forth new skills and attitudes. Moreover, in the areas of massive European settlement—North America and Australia—they were built in advance of the population and provided a means of settling the land.

The power of steam revolutionized transportation by sea as well as by land. In 1807 inhabitants of the Hudson Valley in New York saw the "Devil on the way to Albany in a saw-mill," as Robert Fulton's steamship *Clermont* traveled 150 miles upstream in thirty-two hours. Steam power, long used to drive paddle-wheelers on rivers, particularly in Russia and North America, finally began to supplant sails on the oceans of the world in the late 1860s. Lighter, stronger, cheap steel replaced iron, which had replaced wood. Screw propellers superseded paddle wheels, while mighty compound steam engines cut fuel consumption by half. Passenger and freight rates tumbled, and the intercontinental shipment of low-priced raw materials became feasible. In addition to the large passenger liners and freighters of the great shipping companies, there were innumerable independent tramp steamers searching endlessly for cargo around the world.

An account of an actual voyage by a typical tramp freighter will highlight nineteenth-century developments in global trade. The ship left England in 1910, carrying rails and general freight to western Australia. From there, it carried lumber to Melbourne in southeastern Australia, where it took on harvester combines for Argentina. In Buenos Aires it loaded wheat for Calcutta, and in Calcutta it took on jute for New York. From New York it carried a variety of industrial products to Australia, before returning to England with lead, wool, and wheat after a voyage of approximately 72,000 miles to six continents in seventeen months.

The revolution in land and sea transportation helped European pioneers to open up vast new territories and to produce agricultural products and raw materials there for sale in Europe. Moreover, the development of refrigerated railway cars and, from the 1880s, refrigerator ships enabled first Argentina and then the United States, Australia, and New Zealand to ship mountains of chilled or frozen beef and mutton to European (mainly British) consumers. From Asia, Africa, and Latin America came not only the traditional tropical products—spices, tea, sugar, coffee—but new raw materials for industry, such as jute, rubber, cotton, and coconut oil.

Intercontinental trade was enormously facilitated by the Suez and Panama canals. Of great importance, too, was large and continuous investment in modern port facilities, which made loading and unloading cheaper, faster, and more dependable. Finally, transoceanic telegraph cables inaugurated rapid communications among the financial centers of the world. While a British tramp freighter steamed from Calcutta to New York, a broker in London was arranging, by telegram, for it to carry an American cargo to Australia. World commodity prices were also instantaneously conveyed by the same network of communications.

The growth of trade and the conquest of distance encouraged the expanding European economy to make massive foreign investments. Beginning about 1840, European capitalists started to invest large sums in foreign lands. They did not stop until the

The Opening of the Suez Canal in 1869 revolutionized communications between Europe and Asia. This drawing shows opening-day ceremonies. *(BBC Hulton/The Bettmann Archive)*

outbreak of World War One in 1914. By that year, Europeans had invested more than $40 billion abroad. Great Britain, France, and Germany were the principal investing countries, although by 1913 the United States was emerging as a substantial foreign investor. The sums involved were enormous (Map 30.1). In the decade before 1914, Great Britain was investing 7 percent of its annual national income abroad, or slightly more than it was investing in its entire domestic economy. The great gap between rich and poor within Europe meant that the wealthy and moderately well-to-do could and did send great sums abroad in search of interest and dividends.

Most of the capital exported did not go to European colonies or protectorates in Asia and Africa. About three-quarters of total European investment went to other European countries, the United States and Canada, Australia and New Zealand, and Latin America. This was because Europe found its most profitable opportunities for investment in construction of the railroads, ports, and utilities that were necessary to settle and develop those almost-vacant lands. By loaning money for a railroad in Argentina or in Canada's prairie provinces, for example, Europeans not only collected interest but also enabled white settlers to buy European rails and locomotives, developed sources of cheap wheat, and opened still more territory for European settlement. Much of this investment—such as in American railroads, fully a third of whose capital in 1890 was European, or in Russian railroads, which drew heavily on loans from France—was peaceful and mutually beneficial. The victims were native American Indians and Australian aborigines, who were decimated by the diseases, liquor, and weapons of an aggressively expanding Western society.

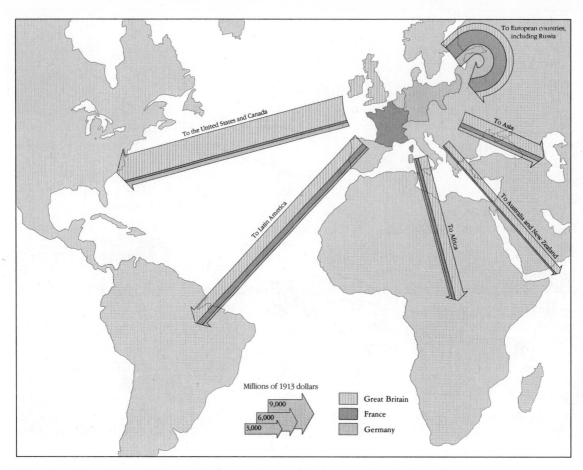

To European countries, including Russia

To the United States and Canada

To Asia

To Latin America

To Africa

To Australia and New Zealand

Millions of 1913 dollars

9,000
6,000
3,000

Great Britain
France
Germany

MAP 30.1 European Investment to 1914 Foreign investment grew rapidly after 1850, and Britain, France, and Germany were the major investing nations. As shown, most European investment was not directed to the area seized by the "new imperialism."

THE OPENING OF CHINA AND JAPAN

Europe's relatively peaceful development of robust offshoots in sparsely populated North America, Australia, and much of Latin America absorbed huge quantities of goods, investments, and migrants. From a Western point of view, that was perhaps the most important aspect of Europe's global thrust. Yet Europe's economic and cultural penetration of old, densely populated civilizations was also profoundly significant for the non-European peoples affected by it. With such civilizations Europeans also increased their trade and profit. Moreover, as had been the case ever since Vasco da Gama and the Spanish conquistadors, the expanding Western society was prepared to use force to attain its desires, if necessary. This was

what happened in China and Japan, two crucial examples of the general pattern of intrusion into non-Western lands.

Traditional Chinese civilization was self-sufficient. For centuries China had sent more to Europe in the way of goods and inventions than it received, and this was still the case in the eighteenth century. Europeans and the English in particular had developed a taste for Chinese tea, but they had to pay for it with hard silver since China was supremely uninterested in European wares. Trade with Europe was carefully regulated by the Chinese imperial government—the Manchu Dynasty—which was more interested in isolating and controlling the strange "sea barbarians" than in pursuing commercial exchange. The imperial government refused to establish diplomatic relations with the "inferior" European states, and it required all foreign merchants to live in the southern city of Canton and to buy and sell only from the local merchant monopoly. Practices considered harmful to Chinese interests, such as the sale of opium and the export of silver from China, were strictly forbidden.

For years the little community of foreign merchants in Canton had to accept the Chinese system. By the 1820s, however, the dominant group, the British, was flexing its muscles. Moreover, in the smoking of opium—that "destructive and ensnaring vice" denounced by Chinese decrees—they had found something the Chinese really wanted. Grown legally in British-occupied India, opium was smuggled into China by means of fast ships and bribed officials. The more this rich trade developed, the greedier British merchants became and the more they resented the patriotic attempts of the Chinese government to stem the tide of drug addiction. By 1836 the aggressive goal of the British merchants in Canton was an independent British colony in China and "safe and unrestricted liberty" in trade. They pressured the British government to take decisive action and enlisted the support of British manufacturers with visions of vast Chinese markets to be opened.

At the same time, the Manchu government decided that the opium trade had to be stamped out. It was ruining the people and stripping the empire of its silver, which was going to British merchants to pay for the opium. The government began to prosecute Chinese drug dealers vigorously and in 1839 sent special envoy Lin Tse-hsü to Canton. Lin Tse-hsü ordered the foreign merchants to obey China's laws, "for our great unified Manchu Empire regards itself as responsible for the habits and morals of its subjects and cannot rest content to see any of them become victims of a deadly poison."[1] The British merchants refused and were expelled, whereupon war soon broke out.

Using troops from India and in control of the seas, the British occupied several coastal cities and forced China to surrender. In the Treaty of Nanking in 1842, the imperial government was forced to cede the island of Hong Kong to Britain, pay an indemnity of $100 million, and open up four large cities to foreign trade with low tariffs.

Thereafter the opium trade flourished, and Hong Kong developed rapidly as an Anglo-Chinese enclave. China continued to nurture illusions of superiority and isolation, however, and refused to accept foreign diplomats to Peking, the imperial capital. Finally, there was a second round of foreign attack between 1856 and 1860, culminating in the occupation of Peking by seventeen thousand British and French troops and the intentional burning of the emperor's summer palace. Another round of harsh treaties gave European merchants and missionaries greater privileges and protection. Thus did Europeans use military aggression to blow a hole in the wall of Chinese seclusion. Blasting away at Chinese sovereignty as well, they forced the Chinese to accept trade and investment on unfavorable terms for the foreseeable future.

China's neighbor, Japan, had its own highly distinctive civilization and even less use for Westerners. European traders and missionaries first arrived in Japan in the sixteenth century. By 1640 Japan had reacted quite negatively to their presence. The government decided to seal off the country from all European influences, in order to preserve its traditional culture and society. It ruthlessly persecuted Japanese Christians and expelled all but a few Dutch merchants, who were virtually imprisoned in a single port and rigidly controlled. When American and British whaling ships began to appear off Japanese coasts almost two hundred years later, the policy of exclusion was still in effect. An order of 1825 commanded Japanese officials to "drive away foreign vessels without second thought."[2]

Japan's unbending isolation seemed hostile and barbaric to the West, particularly to the United States. It complicated the practical problems of shipwrecked American sailors and provisioning of whaling ships and China traders sailing in the eastern Pacific. It also thwarted the hope of trade and profit. Also, Americans shared the self-confidence and dynamism of expanding Western society. They had taken California from Mexico in 1848, and Americans felt destined to play a great role in the Pacific. It seemed, therefore, the United States' duty to force the Japanese to share their ports and behave like a "civilized" nation.

After several unsuccessful American attempts to establish commercial relations with Japan, Commodore Matthew Perry steamed into Edo (now Tokyo) Bay in 1853 and demanded diplomatic negotiations

East Meets West This painting gives a Japanese view of the first audience of the American Consul and his staff with the shogun, Japan's hereditary military governor, in 1859. The Americans appear strange and ill at ease. *(Gemini Smith, Inc. La Jolla CA, © Bradley Smith)*

with the emperor. Japan entered a grave crisis. Some Japanese warriors urged resistance, but senior officials realized how defenseless their cities were against naval bombardment. Shocked and humiliated, they reluctantly signed a treaty with the United States that opened two ports and permitted trade. Over the next five years, more treaties spelled out the rights and privileges of the Western nations and their merchants in Japan. Japan was "opened." What the British had done in China with war, the Americans had done in Japan with the threat of war.

WESTERN PENETRATION OF EGYPT

Egypt's experience illustrates not only the explosive power of the expanding European economy and society but also their seductive appeal for modernizing elites in non-Western lands. Of great importance in African and Middle Eastern history, the ancient land of the pharaohs had since 525 B.C. been ruled by a succession of foreigners, most recently by the Ottoman Turks. In 1798 French armies under young General Napoleon Bonaparte invaded the Egyptian part of the Ottoman Empire and occupied the territory for three years. Into the power vacuum left by the French withdrawal stepped an extraordinary Albanian-born Ottoman general, Muhammad Ali (1769–1849).

First appointed governor of Egypt by the Ottoman sultan, Muhammad Ali soon disposed of his political rivals and set out to build his own state on the strength of a large, powerful army organized along European lines. He drafted for the first time the illiterate, despised peasant masses of Egypt, and he hired French and Italian army officers to train these raw recruits and their Ottoman officers. By the time of his death, Muhammad Ali had established a strong and virtually independent Egyptian state, to be ruled by his family on a hereditary basis within the Ottoman Empire.

ART: A MIRROR OF SOCIETIES

Art reveals the interests and values of societies and frequently gives intimate and unique glimpses of how people actually lived. In portraits and statues, whether of gods, ghanas, saints, samurai, maharanas, or merchants, it preserves the memory and fame of men and women who shaped societies. In paintings, drawings, and carvings it also shows how people worked, played, relaxed, suffered, and triumphed. Art, therefore, is extremely useful to the historian, especially for distant periods and remote cultures where written records are scarce or hard to understand.

Art also manifests the changes and continuity of societies; as values changed, so did major artistic themes. In the eighteenth century some European artists recalled the Renaissance by choosing to focus on aristocratic lifestyles and interests. Painters like Fragonard (overleaf) developed the rococo style, whose elements reflected the elegant refinement of Enlightenment culture. The ro-

mantic artists of the eighteenth and nineteenth centuries, however, rejected materialism and, driven by a sense of an unlimited universe, sought to reach new levels of spiritual understanding through their art. The romantic movement testified to a turbulent Europe caught up in revolutionary change. For painters such as John Constable (also represented here), nature replaced rationalism as the proper source of inspiration.

Art shows the changes and continuity of life and the impact of societies and cultures on one another. The graceful Mughal painting below combines Indian, Persian, Turkish, and Arabic elements, a fusion that reflects the cosmopolitan nature of eighteenth-century India. Typical of the best works of the Mughal period, which rested solidly on the Hindu caste system, this formalized scene of a spring festival portrays a court activity. (By courtesy of the Board of Trustees of the Victoria & Albert Museum.)

The Swing *(left)* Jean-Honoré Fragonard (1732–1806). The sophistication and frivolity of the eighteenth-century French salon radiate from this delicately naughty work by Fragonard, a brilliant colorist in perfect harmony with the elitist taste of his age. An aging bishop swings a coy beauty, who "accidentally" loses her shoe, allowing her lover an enraptured peek under her petticoat. *(The Wallace Collection)*

The Haywain *(above)* John Constable (1776–1837). Even as the Industrial Revolution was transforming the land, the beauties of the English countryside found their loftiest celebration in the landscapes of John Constable. In sharp contrast to Joseph Turner, England's other great romantic painter, Constable revealed a nature that was peculiarly harmonious, well maintained, and rich in spiritual values. The first artist of importance to paint outdoors, he strongly influenced young French painters like Delacroix. *(Reproduced by courtesy of the Trustees, The National Gallery, London)*

Japanese Tea Ceremony This delicate painting by the Japanese master Kitagawa Toshi-kata (ca 1890) shows women preparing a tea ceremony, a custom that provides deep insights into the Japanese character. Gracious but ritualized with strict rules of dress and behavior, the ceremonial serving of tea to honored guests displays the highly prized values of courtesy, loyalty, and self-discipline. The elegant simplicity of traditional Japanese interiors is also apparent. *(E. T. Archive)*

Summer in Peking Wang Da Quang (ca 1900). A popular quarter of the Chinese capital in the early twentieth century bustles with energy in this animated scene. Traditional pushcarts and rickshaws coexist with a fancy carriage and a Western bicycle as children play their games and shoppers go about their business. Despite all the activity and hard work, a certain tranquility seems to reign. *(E. T. Archive)*

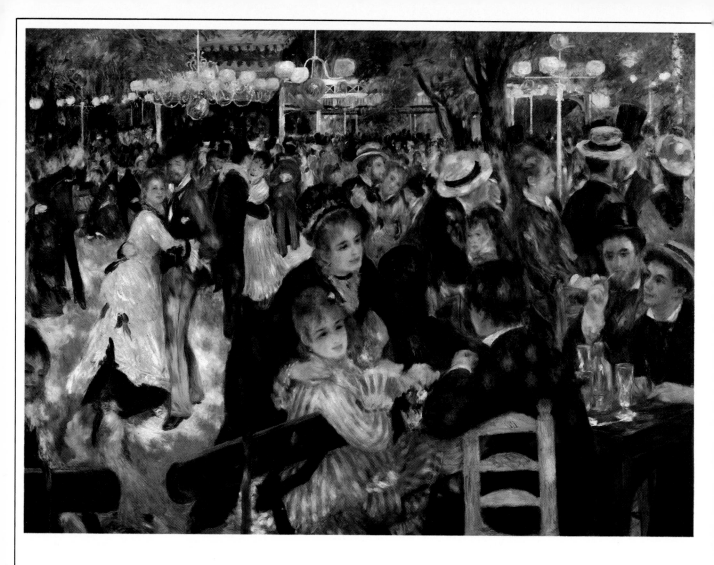

Le Moulin de la Galette à Montmartre Auguste Renoir (1841–1919). The painters of the French impressionist school generally affirmed the beauty and value of modern life, reflecting western Europe's nineteenth-century faith in science, progress, and democracy. In this 1876 masterpiece, the joyous Renoir has transformed a popular outdoor dance hall of the urban masses into an enchanted fairyland. Impressionist painters applied colors directly to the canvas without first mixing them, a revolutionary technique that let the eye participate (by itself "mixing" the colors) in this ultimate form of optical realism. *(Cliché des Musées Nationaux-Paris)*

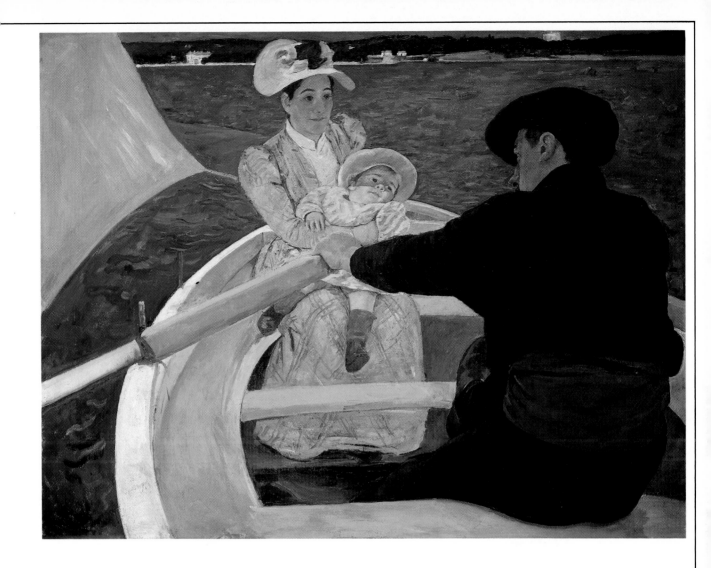

The Boating Party Mary Cassatt (1844–1926). Born into a wealthy business family in the United States, Mary Cassatt moved to Paris, where she painted mothers and their children with a sensitivity unequaled in recent times. Here she captures with tender realism an attentive mother and her squirming child on a hot afternoon outing. Cassatt helped many French impressionists by successfully encouraging American collectors to buy their paintings. *(National Gallery of Art, Washington, Chester Dale Collection)*

Young Girl from a Carved Sceptre *(below, left)* As this nineteenth-century wooden figurine from the Belgian Congo (modern Zaire) suggests, African colonies were not passive objects of European conquest. Many native rulers used diplomacy and trade leverage to increase their own power; warfare, though rendered unsuccessful by European technological superiority, was also widespread. *(Private collection/Werner Forman Archive)*

Helmet Mask of Kuba Tribe *(below, right)* The Kuba, a Bantu-speaking people who settled in the Congo region, believed their king ruled by divine appointment. Symbolic of his authority is this ferocious mask made of cloth, shells, beads and hemp. *(Lee Boltin)*

Muhammad Ali's policies of modernization attracted large numbers of Europeans to the banks of the Nile. As one Arab sheik of the Ottoman Empire remarked in the 1830s, "Englishmen are like ants; if one finds a bit of meat, hundreds follow."[3] The port city of Alexandria had more than fifty thousand Europeans by 1864, most of them Italians, Greeks, French, and English. Europeans served not only as army officers but also as engineers, doctors, high government officials, and policemen. Others found their "meat" in trade, finance, and shipping.

To pay for a modern army as well as for European services and manufactured goods, Muhammad Ali encouraged the development of commercial agriculture geared to the European market. This development had profound implications. Egyptian peasants had been poor but largely self-sufficient, growing food for their own consumption on state-owned lands allotted to them by tradition. Faced with the possibility of export agriculture, high-ranking officials and members of Muhammad Ali's family began carving large private landholdings out of the state domain. The new landlords made the peasants their tenants and forced them to grow cash crops for European markets. Borrowing money from European lenders at high rates and still making good profits, Egyptian landowners "modernized" agriculture, but to the detriment of peasant well-being.

These trends continued under Muhammad Ali's grandson Ismail, who in 1863 began his sixteen-year rule as Egypt's *khedive,* or "prince." Educated at France's leading military academy, Ismail was a westernizing autocrat. He dreamed of using European technology and capital to accelerate Egyptian modernization and build a vast empire in northwest Africa. The large irrigation networks he promoted caused a further growth of large estates and commercial agriculture. Cotton production and exports to Europe boomed. Ismail also borrowed large sums to install modern communications, and with his support the Suez Canal was completed by a French company in 1869. The Arabic of the masses rather than the Turkish of the conquerors became the official language, and young Egyptians educated in Europe helped spread new skills and new ideas in the bureaucracy. Cairo acquired modern boulevards, Western hotels, and an opera house. As Ismail proudly declared: "My country is no longer in Africa, we now form part of Europe."[4]

Yet Ismail was too impatient and too reckless. His projects were enormously expensive, and the sale of his stock in the Suez Canal to the British government did not relieve the situation. By 1876 Egypt owed foreign bondholders a colossal $450 million and could not pay the interest on its debt. Rather than let Egypt go bankrupt and repudiate its loans, as had some Latin American countries and U.S. state governments in the early nineteenth century, the governments of France and Great Britain intervened politically to protect the European bankers who held the Egyptian bonds. They forced Ismail to appoint French and British commissioners to oversee Egyptian finances, in order that the Egyptian debt would be paid in full. This was a momentous decision. It implied direct European political control and was a sharp break with the previous pattern of trade and investment. Throughout most of the nineteenth century, Europeans had used naked military might and political force primarily to make sure that non-Western lands would accept European trade and investment. Now Europeans were going to determine the state budget and effectively rule Egypt.

Foreign financial control evoked a violent nationalistic reaction among Egyptian religious leaders, young intellectuals, and army officers. In 1879, under the leadership of Colonel Ahmed Arabi, they formed the Egyptian Nationalist party. Continuing diplomatic pressure, which forced Ismail to abdicate in favor of his weak son Tewfiq (1879–1892), resulted in bloody anti-European riots in Alexandria in 1882. A number of Europeans were killed, and Tewfiq and his court had to flee to British ships for safety. When the British fleet bombarded Alexandria, more riots swept the country, and Colonel Arabi declared that "an irreconcilable war existed between the Egyptians and the English." But a British expeditionary force decimated Arabi's forces and occupied all of Egypt.

The British said their occupation was temporary, but British armies remained in Egypt until 1956. They maintained the façade of the khedive's government as an autonomous province of the Ottoman Empire, but the khedive was a mere puppet. The able British consul general Evelyn Baring, later Lord Cromer, ruled the country after 1883. Once a vocal opponent of involvement in Egypt, Baring was an authoritarian reformer who had come to believe that "without European interference and initiative reform is impossible here." Baring's rule did result in

British Influence in Egypt was pervasive after 1882. In this unusual photograph from 1890, Scottish soldiers swarm over the ancient and mysterious Great Sphinx like school children on an outing. *(BBC Hulton/The Bettmann Archive)*

better conditions for peasants and tax reforms, while foreign bondholders tranquilly clipped their coupons and Egyptian nationalists nursed their injured pride.

In Egypt, Baring and the British provided a new model for European expansion in densely populated lands. Such expansion was based on military force, political domination, and a self-justifying ideology of beneficial reform. This model was to flourish until 1914. Thus did Europe's Industrial Revolution lead to tremendous political as well as economic expansion throughout the world.

THE GREAT MIGRATION

Before considering European political empires, it is well to realize that a poignant human drama was part of the West's global expansion: literally millions of people picked up stakes and left their ancestral lands in the course of history's greatest migration. To mil-

lions of ordinary people, for whom the opening of China and the interest on the Egyptian debt had not the slightest significance, this great movement was the central experience in the saga of Western expansion. It was, in part, because of this great migration that the West's impact on the world in the nineteenth century was so powerful and many-sided.

THE PRESSURE OF POPULATION

In the early eighteenth century, the growth of European population entered its third and decisive stage, which continued unabated until the twentieth century. Birthrates eventually declined in the nineteenth century, but so did death rates, mainly because of the rising standard of living and secondarily because of the medical revolution. Thus the population of Europe (including Asiatic Russia) more than doubled, from approximately 188 million in 1800 to roughly 432 million in 1900.

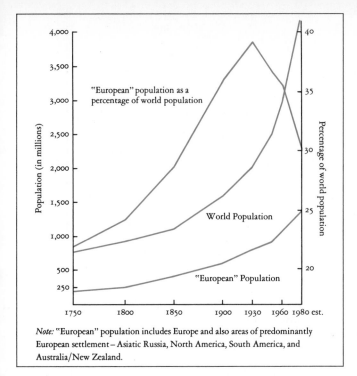

FIGURE 30.2 The Increase of European and World Populations, 1750–1980 *(Sources: W. Woodruff,* Impact of Western Man: A Study of Europe's Role in the World Economy. *St. Martin's Press, New York, 1967, p. 103; United Nations,* Statistical Yearbook, 1982, *1985, pp. 2–3.)*

FIGURE 30.3 Emigration from Europe by Decades, 1851–1940 *(Source: W. Woodruff,* Impact of Western Man: A Study of Europe's Role in the World Economy. *St. Martin's Press, New York, 1967, pp. 106–107 and references cited therein.)*

These figures actually understate Europe's population explosion, for between 1815 and 1932 more than 60 million people left Europe. These migrants went primarily to the "areas of European settlement"—North and South America, Australia, New Zealand, and Siberia—where they contributed to a rapid growth of numbers. The population of North America (the United States and Canada) alone grew from 6 million to 81 million between 1800 and 1900 because of continuous immigration and the high fertility rates of North American women. Since population grew more slowly in Africa and Asia than in Europe, as Figure 30.2 shows, Europeans and people of European origin jumped from about 22 percent of the world's total to about 38 percent on the eve of World War One.

The growing number of Europeans provided further impetus for Western expansion. It was a driving force behind emigration. As in the eighteenth century, the rapid increase in numbers put pressure on the land and led to land hunger and relative overpopulation in area after area. In most countries, migration increased twenty years after a rapid growth in population, as many children of the baby boom grew up, saw little available land and few opportunities, and migrated. This pattern was especially prevalent when rapid population increase predated extensive industrial development, which offered the best long-term hope of creating jobs within the country and reducing poverty. Thus millions of country folk went abroad, as well as to nearby cities, in search of work and economic opportunity.

Before looking at the people who migrated, let us consider three facts. First, the number of men and women who left Europe increased steadily until World War One. As Figure 30.3 shows, more than 11 million left in the first decade of the twentieth century, over five times the number departing in the 1850s. The outflow of migrants was clearly an enduring characteristic of European society for the entire period.

Second, different countries had very different patterns of movement. As Figure 30.3 also shows, people left Britain and Ireland (which are not distinguished in the British figures) in large numbers from the 1840s on. This emigration reflected not only rural

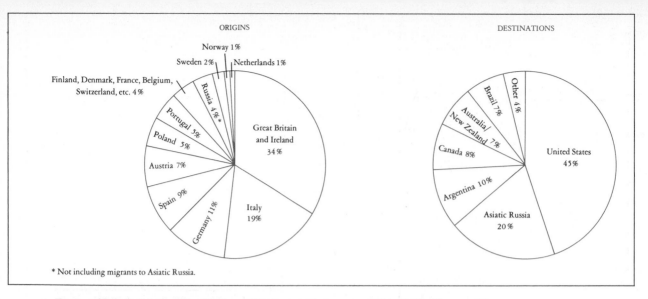

FIGURE 30.4 Origin and Destination of European Emigrants, 1851–1960 *(Source: W. Woodruff,* Impact of Western Man: A Study of Europe's Role in the World Economy. *St. Martin's Press, New York, 1967, pp. 108–109 and references cited therein.)*

poverty but also the movement of skilled, industrial technicians and the preferences shown to British migrants in the British Empire. Ultimately, about one-third of all European migrants between 1840 and 1920 came from the British Isles. German migration was quite different. It grew irregularly after about 1830, reaching a first peak in the early 1850s and another in the early 1880s. Thereafter it declined rapidly, for Germany's rapid industrialization was providing adequate jobs at home. This pattern contrasted sharply with that of Italy. More and more Italians left the country right up to 1914, reflecting severe problems in Italian villages and relatively slow industrial growth. In sum, migration patterns mirrored social and economic conditions in the various European countries and provinces.

Third, although the United States absorbed the largest number of European migrants, only slightly less than half went to the United States. Asiatic Russia, Canada, Argentina, Brazil, and Australia also attracted large numbers, as Figure 30.4 shows. Moreover, migrants accounted for a larger proportion of the total population in Argentina, Brazil, and Canada than in the United States. Between 1900 and 1910, for example, new arrivals represented 3 percent of Argentina's population each year, as opposed to only 1 percent for the United States. The common American assumption that European migration meant migration to the United States is quite inaccurate.

EUROPEAN MIGRANTS

What kind of people left Europe, and what were their reasons for doing so? Most were poor people from rural areas, though seldom from the poorest classes. Indeed, the European migrant was most often a small peasant landowner or a village craftsman, whose traditional way of life was threatened by too little land, estate agriculture, and cheap, factory-made goods. German peasants who left the Rhineland and southwestern Germany between 1830 and 1854, for example, felt trapped by what Friedrich List (page 822) called the "dwarf economy," with its tiny landholdings and declining craft industries. Selling out and moving to buy much cheaper land in the American Midwest became a common response.

Determined to maintain or improve their status, migrants were a great asset to the countries that received them. This was doubly so because the vast majority were young and very often unmarried. Fully two-thirds of those admitted to the United States were under thirty-one years of age, and 90 percent were under forty. They came in the prime of life and were ready to work hard in the new land, at least for a time.

Many Europeans, especially by the end of the nineteenth century, were truly migrants as opposed to immigrants—that is, they returned home after some time abroad. One in two migrants to Argentina, and probably one in three to the United States, eventually returned to their native land. The likelihood of repatriation varied greatly by nationality. Seven out of eight people who migrated from the Balkans to the United States in the late nineteenth century returned to their countries. At the other extreme, only one person in ten from Ireland and only one in twenty among eastern European Jews returned to the country of origin.

Once again, the possibility of buying land in the old country was of central importance. Land in Ireland (as well as in England and Scotland) was tightly held by large, often absentee landowners, and little land was available for purchase. In Russia, Jews were left in relative peace until the assassination of Alexander II by non-Jewish terrorists in 1881 brought a new tsar and an official policy of pogroms and savage discrimination. Russia's 5 million Jews were already confined to the market towns and small cities of the so-called Pale of Settlement, where they worked as artisans and petty traders. Most land was held by

non-Jews. When, therefore, Russian Jewish artisans began in the 1880s to escape both factory competition and oppression by migrating—a migration that eventually totaled 2 million people—it was basically a once-and-for-all departure. Non-Jewish migrants from Russia, who constituted a majority of those leaving the tsar's empire after 1905, had access to land and thus returned much more frequently to their peasant villages in central Russia, Poland, and the Ukraine.

The mass movement of Italians illustrates many of the characteristics of European migration. As late as the 1880s, three in every four Italians depended on agriculture. With the influx of cheap North American wheat, the long-standing problems of the Italian village became more acute. And since industry was not advancing fast enough to provide jobs for the rapidly growing population, many Italians began to leave their country for economic reasons. Most Italian migrants were not landless laborers from areas

Cheap Land in distant North America was an irresistible magnet for millions of Europeans. *The Modern Ship of the Plains* by Rufus Zogbaum portrays with sympathy the long journey by rail to the farming frontier in the 1880s. *(Library of Congress)*

dominated by large estates; such people tended to stay in Italy and turned increasingly toward radical politics. Instead, most were small landowning peasants, whose standard of living was falling because of rural overpopulation and agricultural depression. Migration provided them both an escape valve and a possible source of income to buy more land.

Many Italians went to the United States, but before 1900 more went to Argentina and Brazil. Indeed, two out of three migrants to those two developing countries came from Italy. Other Italians migrated to other European countries. France was a favorite destination. In 1911 the Italian-born population of France was roughly a third as large as that in the United States.

Ties of family and friendship played a crucial role in the movement of peoples. There are many examples of people from a given province or village settling together in rural enclaves or tight-knit urban neighborhoods thousands of miles away. Very often a strong individual—a businessman, a religious leader —would blaze the way and others would follow.

Many landless young European men and women were spurred to leave by a spirit of revolt and independence. In Sweden and in Norway, in Jewish Russia and in Italy, these young people felt frustrated by the small privileged classes, who often controlled both church and government and resisted demands for change and greater opportunity. Many a young Norwegian seconded the passionate cry of their national poet, Bjørnson: "Forth will I! Forth! I will be crushed and consumed if I stay."[5]

Many young Jews wholeheartedly agreed with a spokesman of Kiev's Jewish community in 1882, who declared, "Our human dignity is being trampled upon, our wives and daughters are being dishonored, we are looted and pillaged: either we get decent human rights or else let us go wherever our eyes may lead us."[6] Thus, for many, migration was a radical way to "get out from under." Migration slowed down when the people won basic political and social reforms, such as the right to vote and social security.

ASIAN MIGRANTS

Not all migration was from Europe. A substantial number of Chinese, Japanese, Indians, and Filipinos —to name only four key groups—responded to rural hardship with temporary or permanent migration. At least 3 million Asians (as opposed to more than 60 million Europeans) moved abroad before 1920. Most went as indentured laborers to work under incredibly difficult conditions on the plantations or in the gold-fields of Latin America, southern Asia, Africa, California, Hawaii, and Australia. White estate owners very often used Asians to replace or supplement blacks after the suppression of the slave trade.

In the 1840s, for example, there was a strong demand for field hands in Cuba, and the Spanish government actively recruited Chinese laborers. They came under eight-year contracts, were paid about twenty-five cents a day, and were fed potatoes and salted beef. Between 1853 and 1873, when such migration was stopped, more than 130,000 Chinese laborers went to Cuba. The majority spent their lives as virtual slaves. The great landlords of Peru also brought in more than 100,000 workers from China in the nineteenth century, and there were similar movements of Asians elsewhere.

Such migration from Asia would undoubtedly have grown to much greater proportions if planters and mine owners in search of cheap labor had had their way. But they did not. Asians fled the plantations and goldfields as soon as possible, seeking greater opportunities in trade and towns. There they came into conflict with other brown-skinned peoples —such as in Malaya and East Africa—and with white settlers in areas of European settlement.

These settlers demanded a halt to Asian migration. One Australian brutally summed up the typical view: "The Chinaman knows nothing about Caucasian civilization.... In fact, a Chinaman is a mere dumb animal... and could never be anything else. It would be less objectionable to drive a flock of sheep to the poll than to allow Chinamen to vote. The sheep at all events would be harmless."[7] By the 1880s Americans and Australians were building "great white walls"— discriminatory laws designed to keep Asians out. Thus a final, crucial factor in the migrations before 1914 was the general policy of "whites only" in the rich open lands of possible permanent settlement. This, too, was part of Western dominance in the increasingly lopsided world. Largely successful in monopolizing the best overseas opportunities, Europeans and people of European ancestry reaped the main benefits from the great migration. By 1913 people in Australia, Canada, and the United States all had higher average incomes than people in Great Britain, still Europe's wealthiest nation.

WESTERN IMPERIALISM

The expansion of Western society reached its apex between about 1880 and 1914. In those years, the leading European nations not only continued to send massive streams of migrants, money, and manufactured goods around the world, but also rushed to create or enlarge vast *political* empires abroad. This political empire building contrasted sharply with the economic penetration of non-Western territories between 1816 and 1880, which had left a China or a Japan "opened" to European economic interests but still politically independent. By contrast, the empires of the late nineteenth century recalled the old European colonial empires of the seventeenth and eighteenth centuries and led contemporaries to speak of the new imperialism.

Characterized by a frantic rush to plant the flag over as many people and as much territory as possible, the new imperialism had momentous consequences. It resulted in new tensions among competing European states, and it led to wars and rumors of war with non-European powers. The new imperialism was aimed primarily at Africa and Asia. It put millions of black, brown, and tan peoples directly under the rule of whites. How and why did whites come to rule these peoples?

THE SCRAMBLE FOR AFRICA

The most spectacular manifestation of the new imperialism was the seizure of Africa, which broke sharply with previous patterns and fascinated contemporary Europeans and Americans.

As late as 1880, European nations controlled only 10 percent of the African continent, and their possessions were hardly increasing. The French had begun conquering Algeria in 1830, and within fifty years substantial numbers of French, Italian, and Spanish colonists had settled among the overwhelming Arab majority.

At the other end of the continent, in southern Africa, the British had taken possession of the Dutch settlements at Cape Town during the wars with Napoleon I. This takeover had led disgruntled Dutch cattlemen and farmers in 1835 to make their so-

The Chinese Exclusion Act This vicious cartoon from a San Francisco newspaper celebrates American anti-migration laws. Americans and Europeans generally shared the same attitudes regarding the non-Western world. *(Photo: Caroline Buckler)*

called Great Trek into the interior, where they fought the Zulu and Xhosa peoples for land. After 1853, while British colonies like Canada and Australia were beginning to evolve toward self-government, the Boers, or Afrikaners (as the descendants of the Dutch in the Cape Colony were beginning to call themselves), proclaimed their political independence and defended it against British armies. By 1880 Afrikaner and British settlers, who detested each other, had wrested control of much of the southern tip of Africa from the Zulu, Xhosa, and other African peoples.

European trading posts and forts dating back to the Age of Discovery and the slave trade dotted the coast of West Africa. The Portuguese proudly but ineffectively held their old possessions in Angola and Mozambique. Elsewhere, over the great mass of the continent, Europeans did not rule.

Between 1880 and 1900, the situation changed drastically. Britain, France, Germany, and Italy scrambled for African possessions as if their lives depended on it. By 1900 nearly the whole continent had been carved up and placed under European rule: only Ethiopia in northeast Africa and Liberia on the west African coast remained independent. Even the Afrikaner settler republics of southern Africa were conquered by the British in the bloody Boer War (1899–1902). In the years before 1914, the European powers tightened their control and established colonial governments to rule their gigantic empires (Map 30.2).

In the complexity of the European seizure of Africa, certain events and individuals stand out. Of enormous importance was the British occupation of Egypt, which established the new model of formal political control. There was also the role of Leopold II of Belgium (1865–1909), an energetic, strong-willed monarch with a lust for distant territory. "The sea bathes our coast, the world lies before us," he had exclaimed in 1861. "Steam and electricity have annihilated distance, and all the non-appropriated lands on the surface of the globe can become the field of our operations and of our success."[8] By 1876 Leopold was focusing on central Africa. Subsequently he formed a financial syndicate under his personal control to send H. M. Stanley, a sensation-seeking journalist and part-time explorer, to the Congo basin. Stanley established trading stations, signed "treaties" with African chiefs, and planted Leopold's flag. Leopold's actions alarmed the French, who quickly sent out an expedition under Pierre de Brazza. In 1880 de Brazza signed a treaty of protection with the chief of the large Teke tribe and began to establish a French protectorate on the north bank of the Congo River.

Leopold's buccaneering intrusion into the Congo area raised the question of the political fate of black Africa—Africa south of the Sahara. By the time the British successfully invaded and occupied Egypt, the richest and most developed land in Africa in 1882, Europe had caught "African fever." There was a gold-rush mentality, and the race for territory was on.

To lay down some basic rules for this new and dangerous game of imperialist competition, Jules Ferry of France and Bismarck of Germany arranged an international conference on Africa in Berlin in 1884 and 1885. The conference established the principle that European claims to African territory had to rest on "effective occupation" in order to be recognized by other states. This principle was very important. It meant that Europeans would push relentlessly into interior regions from all sides and that no single European power would be able to claim the entire continent. The conference recognized Leopold's personal rule over a neutral Congo Free State and declared all of the Congo basin a free-trade zone. The conference also agreed to work to stop slavery and the slave trade in Africa.

The Berlin conference coincided with Germany's sudden emergence as an imperial power. Prior to about 1880, Bismarck, like many European leaders at the time, had seen little value in colonies. Colonies

MAP 30.2 The Partition of Africa European nations carved up Africa after 1880 and built vast political empires.

reminded him, he said, of a poor but proud nobleman who wore a fur coat when he could not afford a shirt underneath. Then, in 1884 and 1885, as political agitation for expansion increased, Bismarck did an abrupt about-face, and Germany established protectorates over a number of small African kingdoms and tribes in Togo, Cameroon, South West Africa, and later in East Africa.

In acquiring colonies, Bismarck cooperated against the British with France's Jules Ferry, who was as ardent for empire as he was for education. With Bismarck's tacit approval, the French pressed vigorously southward from Algeria, eastward from their old forts on the Senegal coast, and northward from de Brazza's newly formed protectorate on the Congo River. The object of these three thrusts was Lake Chad, a malaria-infested swamp on the edge of the Sahara.

Meanwhile, the British began enlarging their west African enclaves and impatiently pushing northward from the Cape Colony and westward from Zanzibar. Their thrust southward from Egypt was blocked in the Sudan by fiercely independent Muslims, who massacred a British force at Khartoum in 1885.

A decade later, another British force under General Horatio H. Kitchener moved cautiously and more successfully up the Nile River, building a railroad to supply arms and reinforcements as it went. Finally, in 1898, these British troops met their foe at Omdurman, where Muslim tribesmen charged time and time again only to be cut down by the recently invented machine gun. For one smug participant, the young British officer Winston Churchill, it was "like a pantomime scene" in a play. "These extraordinary foreign figures . . . march up one by one from the darkness of Barbarism to the footlights of civilization . . . and their conquerors, taking their possessions, forget even their names. Nor will history record such trash." For another more somber English observer, "It was not a battle but an execution. The bodies were not in heaps . . . but they spread evenly over acres and acres."[9] In the end, eleven thousand fanatical Muslim tribesmen lay dead, while only twenty-eight Britons had been killed.

MEDITERRANEAN SEA

TANGIER
MADEIRA IS.
(PORTUGAL)
Algiers
Casablanca
TUNISIA
MOROCCO
Tripoli
Cyrene
IFNI
Cairo
CANARY IS.
(SPAIN)
ALGERIA
LIBYA
RIO DE ORO
EGYPT
ARABIA

SAHARA
Nile
RED SEA

FRENCH WEST AFRICA
Khartoum
ERITREA
GAMBIA
L. Chad
Adowa
PORTUGUESE
GUINEA
ANGLO-EGYPTIAN
SUDAN
FRENCH SOMALILAND
SIERRA LEONE
NIGERIA
Fashoda
Blue Nile
BRITISH
SOMALILAND
LIBERIA
IVORY
COAST
GOLD
COAST
ETHIOPIA
White Nile
TOGOLAND
CAMEROONS
ITALIAN SOMALILAND
RIO MUNI
EQUATORIAL AFRICA
Ubangi
UGANDA
BRITISH
EAST AFRICA
FRENCH
Congo
L. Victoria Nyanza
BELGIAN CONGO
CABINDA
L. Tanganyika
Mombasa
GERMAN
EAST AFRICA
ZANZIBAR (GR.BR.)

ATLANTIC OCEAN
INDIAN
OCEAN

L. Nyasa
ANGOLA

RHODESIA
NYASALAND
Zambesi
MADAGASCAR
MOZAMBIQUE
GERMAN
SOUTHWEST
AFRICA
BECHUANALAND
TRANSVAAL
ORANGE
FREE STATE
SWAZILAND
UNION OF
SOUTH AFRICA
BASUTOLAND
Capetown
NATAL

ARAB STATES
Egypt
SAHARA
SUDANESE EMPIRES
Ashanti
Ibo
Kikuyu
SWAHILI LANGUAGE
BANTU PEOPLES

AFRICA IN 1878
Bushmen
Hottentots

British   Portuguese
French   Belgian
German   Spanish
Italian   Independent African states

0   400   800 Km.
0   400   800 Mi.

945

Continuing up the Nile after the battle of Omdurman, Kitchener's armies found that a small French force had already occupied the village of Fashoda. Locked in imperial competition ever since Britain had occupied Egypt, France had tried to beat the British to one of Africa's last unclaimed areas—the upper reaches of the Nile. The result was a serious diplomatic crisis, and even the threat of war. Eventually, wracked by the Dreyfus affair (see page 919) and unwilling to fight, France backed down and withdrew its forces.

The reconquest of the Sudan exemplifies the general process of empire building in Africa. The fate of the Muslim force at Omdurman was eventually inflicted on all native peoples who resisted European rule: they were blown away by vastly superior military force. But however much the European powers squabbled for territory and privilege around the world, they always had the sense to stop short of actually fighting each other for it. Imperial ambitions were not worth a great European war.

IMPERIALISM IN ASIA

Although the sudden division of Africa was more spectacular, Europeans also extended their political control in Asia. In 1815 the Dutch ruled little more than the island of Java in the East Indies. Thereafter they gradually brought almost all of the three-thousand-mile archipelago under their political authority, though—in good imperialist fashion—they had to share some of the spoils with Britain and Germany. In the critical decade of the 1880s, the French under the leadership of Jules Ferry took Indochina. India, Japan, and China also experienced a profound imperialist impact (Map 30.3).

Two other great imperialist powers, Russia and the United States, also acquired rich territories in Asia. Russia, whose history since the later Middle Ages has been marked by almost continuous expansion, moved steadily forward on two fronts throughout the nineteenth century. Russians conquered Muslim areas to the south in the Caucasus and in central Asia and also proceeded to nibble greedily on China's provinces in the Far East, especially in the 1890s.

The United States great conquest was the Philippines, taken from Spain in 1898 after the Spanish-American War. When it quickly became clear that the United States had no intention of granting inde-

MAP 30.3 Asia in 1914 India remained under British rule while China precariously preserved its political independence.

pendence, Philippine patriots rose in revolt and were suppressed only after long, bitter fighting. (Not until 1933 was a timetable for independence established.) Some Americans protested the taking of the Philippines, but to no avail. Thus another great Western power joined the imperialist ranks in Asia.

CAUSES OF THE NEW IMPERIALISM

Many factors contributed to the late nineteenth-century rush for territory and empire, which was in turn one aspect of Western society's generalized expansion in the age of industry and nationalism. Little wonder that controversies have raged over interpretation of the new imperialism, especially since authors of every persuasion have often exaggerated particular aspects in an attempt to prove their own theories. Yet despite complexity and controversy, basic causes are clearly identifiable.

Economic motives played an important role in the extension of political empires, especially the British Empire. By the late 1870s, France, Germany, and the United States were industrializing rapidly behind rising tariff barriers. Great Britain was losing its early lead and facing increasingly tough competition in foreign markets. In this new economic situation, Britain came to value old possessions, such as India and Canada, more highly. The days when a leading free-trader like Richard Cobden could denounce the "bloodstained fetish of Empire" and statesman Benjamin Disraeli could call colonies a "millstone round our necks" came to an abrupt end. When continental powers began to grab any and all unclaimed territory in the 1880s, the British followed suit immediately. They feared that France and Germany would seal off their empires with high tariffs and restrictions and that future economic opportunities would be lost forever.

Actually, the overall economic gains of the new imperialism proved limited before 1914. The new colonies were simply too poor to buy many manufactured goods, and they offered few immediately profitable investments. Nonetheless, even the poorest, most barren desert was jealously prized, and no territory was ever abandoned. Colonies became im-

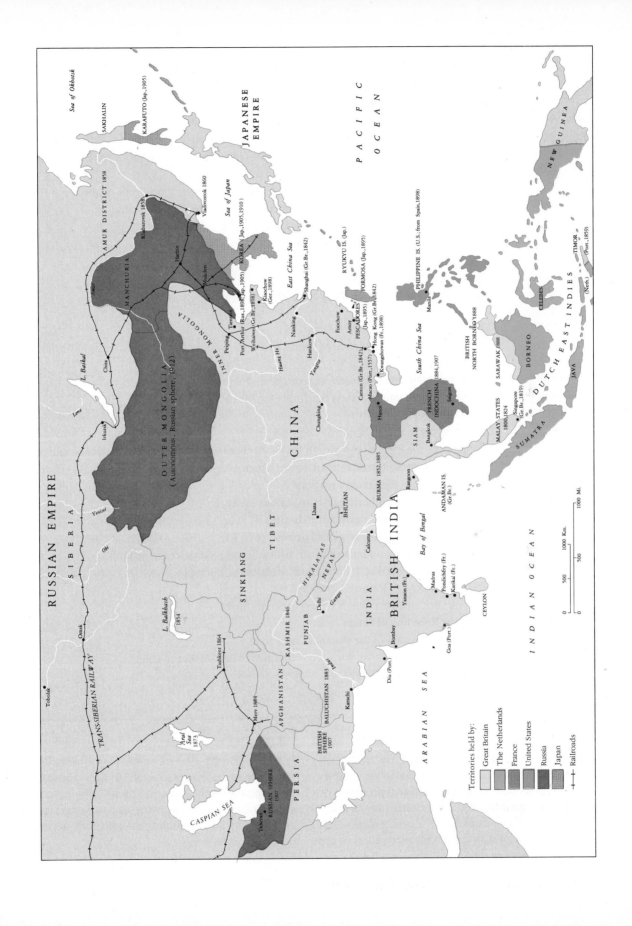

Sea of Okhotsk

SAKHALIN

KARAFUTO (Jap.,1905)

RUSSIAN EMPIRE

SIBERIA

AMUR DISTRICT 1858

Khabarovsk 1858

Vladivostok 1860

JAPANESE EMPIRE

PACIFIC OCEAN

NEW GUINEA

Sea of Japan

Harbin

MANCHURIA

Mukden

KOREA (Jap.,1905,1910)

Chita

L. Baikal

INNER MONGOLIA

Peiping Tientsin

Port Arthur (Rus.,1898; Jap.,1905)
Weihaiwei (Gr.Br.,1898)

East China Sea

Kiaochow (Ger.,1898)

Lena

OUTER MONGOLIA
(Autonomous, Russian sphere, 1912)

Shanghai (Gr.Br.,1842)

RYUKYU IS. (Jap.)

FORMOSA (Jap.,1895)

Irkutsk

Nanking

Hankow

Huang Ho

Foochow

Amoy

PESCADORES (Jap.,1895)

PHILIPPINE IS. (U.S.,from Spain,1898)

Manila

Yenisei

Yangtze

Chungking

CHINA

Canton (Gr.Br.,1842)
Macao (Port.,1557)

Hong Kong (Gr.Br.,1842)
Kwangchowan (Fr.,1898)

South China Sea

BRITISH NORTH BORNEO 1888

SARAWAK 1888

BORNEO

DUTCH EAST INDIES

TIMOR
(Port.,1859)

(Neth.)

CELEBES

Obi

SINKIANG

TIBET

Lhasa

BHUTAN

HIMALAYAS

NEPAL

Hanoi

FRENCH INDOCHINA
1884,1907

Saigon

SIAM

Bangkok

MALAY STATES
1800,1824

Singapore (Gr.Br.,1819)

SUMATRA

JAVA

L. Balkhash
1854

Omsk

KASHMIR 1846

PUNJAB

Delhi

Ganges

BURMA 1852,1885

Rangoon

Calcutta

ANDAMAN IS.
(Gr.Br.)

Bay of Bengal

INDIAN OCEAN

1000 Mi.

Tashkent 1864

AFGHANISTAN

BALUCHISTAN 1883

Kabul

Karachi

INDIA

BRITISH INDIA

Madras
Pondichery (Fr.)
Yanaon (Fr.)
Karikal (Fr.)

CEYLON

1000 Km.

500

500

TRANS-SIBERIAN RAILWAY

Merv 1884

BRITISH SPHERE
1907

Aral Sea
1873

Bombay

Goa (Port.)

Diu (Port.)

ARABIAN SEA

0
0

Tobolsk

CASPIAN SEA

RUSSIAN SPHERE
1907

PERSIA

Teheran

Territories held by:

Great Britain

The Netherlands

France

United States

Russia

Japan

Railroads

THE SPREAD OF WESTERN IMPERIALISM

1800–1913	World trade increases 25-fold
1816–1880	European economic penetration of non-Western countries
1835	Great Trek: Boers proclaim independence from Great Britain in the South African hinterland
1840s	European capitalists begin large-scale foreign investment
1842	Treaty of Nanking: Manchu government of China cedes Hong Kong to Great Britain
1846	Repeal of Corn Laws: Great Britain declares its strong support of free trade
1848	British defeat of last independent native state in India
1853	Perry's arrival in Tokyo: Japan opened to European influence
1857–1858	Great Rebellion in India
1858–1863	Anti-foreign reaction in Japan
1867	Meiji Restoration in Japan: adoption of Western reforms
1869	Completion of Suez Canal
1871	Abolition of feudal domains in Japan
1876	Ismail, khedive of Egypt, appoints British and French commissioners to oversee government finances
1880	Establishment of French protectorate on the northern bank of the Congo
1880–1900	European powers intensify their "scramble for Africa"
1882	British occupation of Egypt
1883	Formation of the Indian National Congress
1884–1885	International conference on Africa in Berlin: European powers require "effective occupation"; Germany acquires protectorates in Togo, Cameroon, South West Africa, and East Africa; Belgium acquires the Congo Free State
1890	Establishment of an authoritarian constitution in Japan
1893	France completes its acquisition of Indochina
1894	Sino-Japanese War: Japan acquires Formosa
1898	Battle of Omdurman: under Kitchener, British forces reconquer the Sudan
	Spanish-American War: United States acquires the Philippines
	"Hundred Days of Reform" in China
1899–1902	Boer War: British defeat Dutch settlers in South Africa
1900–1903	The Boxer Rebellion in China
1903	American occupation of the Panama Canal zone
1904–1905	Russo-Japanese War: Japan wins protectorate over Port Arthur in China
1910	Japanese annexation of Korea
1912	Fall of Manchu dynasty in China

portant for political and diplomatic reasons. Each leading country saw colonies as crucial to national security, military power, and international prestige. For instance, safeguarding the Suez Canal played a key role in the British occupation of Egypt, and protecting Egypt in turn led to the bloody reconquest of the Sudan. National security was a major factor in the United States decision to establish firm control over the Panama Canal Zone in 1903. Far-flung possessions guaranteed ever-growing navies the safe havens and the dependable coaling stations they needed in time of crisis or war.

Many people were convinced that colonies were essential to great nations. "There has never been a great power without great colonies," wrote one French publicist in 1877. "Every virile people has established colonial power," echoed the famous nationalist historian of Germany, Heinrich von Treitschke. "All great nations in the fullness of their strength have desired to set their mark upon barbarian lands and those who fail to participate in this great rivalry will play a pitiable role in time to come."[10]

Treitschke's harsh statement reflects not only the increasing aggressiveness of European nationalism after Bismarck's wars of German unification but also Social Darwinian theories of brutal competition between races. As one prominent English economist argued, the "strongest nation has always been conquering the weaker . . . and the strongest tend to be best." Thus European nations, which were seen as racially distinct parts of the dominant white race, had to seize colonies to show they were strong and virile. Moreover, since racial struggle was nature's inescapable law, the conquest of inferior peoples was just. "The path of progress is strewn with the wreck . . . of inferior races," wrote one professor in 1900. "Yet these dead peoples are, in very truth, the stepping stones on which mankind has risen to the higher intellectual and deeper emotional life of today."[11] Social Darwinism and racial doctrines fostered imperial expansion.

Finally, certain special-interest groups in each country were powerful agents of expansion. Shipping companies wanted lucrative subsidies and promoters wanted mining concessions. White settlers on dangerous, turbulent frontiers constantly demanded more land and greater protection. Missionaries and humanitarians wanted to spread religion and stop the slave trade. Explorers and adventurers sought knowledge and excitement. Military men and colonial officials, whose role has often been overlooked by writers on imperialism, foresaw rapid advancement and high-paid positions in growing empires. The actions of such groups and the determined individuals who led them thrust the course of empire forward.

Western society did not rest the case for empire solely on naked conquest and a Darwinian racial struggle, or on power politics and the need for naval bases on every ocean. In order to satisfy their consciences and answer their critics, imperialists developed additional arguments.

A favorite idea was that Europeans could and should "civilize" more primitive nonwhites. According to this view, nonwhites would eventually receive the benefits of modern economies, cities, advanced medicine, and higher standards of living. In time, they might be ready for self-government and Western democracy. Thus the French spoke of their sacred "civilizing mission." Rudyard Kipling (1865–1936), who wrote masterfully of Anglo-Indian life and was perhaps the most influential writer of the 1890s, exhorted Europeans to unselfish service in distant lands:

Take up the White Man's Burden—
    Send forth the best ye breed—
Go bind your sons to exile
    To serve your captives' need,
To wait in heavy harness,
    On fluttered folk and wild—
Your new-caught, sullen peoples
    Half-devil and half-child.[12]

Many Americans accepted the ideology of the white man's burden. It was an important factor in the decision to rule rather than liberate the Philippines after the Spanish-American War. Like their European counterparts, these Americans sincerely believed that their civilization had reached unprecedented height and that they had unique benefits to bestow on all "less-advanced" peoples. Another argument was that imperial government protected natives from tribal warfare as well as cruder forms of exploitation by white settlers and businessmen.

Peace and stability under European control also permitted the spread of Christianity. In Africa, Catholic and Protestant missionaries competed with Islam south of the Sahara, seeking converts and building schools to spread the Gospel. Many Africans' first real contact with whites was in mission schools. As late as 1942, for example, 97 percent of Nigeria's student population was in mission schools. Some peoples, like the Ibos in Nigeria, became highly christianized.

Such occasional successes in black Africa contrasted with the general failure of missionary efforts in India, China, and the Islamic world. There, Christians often preached in vain to peoples with ancient, complex religious beliefs. Yet the number of Christian believers around the world did increase substan-

"The Administration of Justice" In this 1895 illustration from a popular magazine, a Belgian official, flanked by native soldiers, settles a tribal dispute in the Congo State. This flattering view of Europe's "civilizing mission" suggests how imperial rule rested on more than just brute force. *(BBC Hulton/The Bettmann Archive)*

tially in the nineteenth century, and missionary groups kept trying. Unfortunately, "many missionaries had drunk at the well of European racism," and this probably prevented them from doing better.[13]

CRITICS OF IMPERIALISM

The expansion of empire aroused sharp, even bitter, critics. A forceful attack was delivered in 1902, after the unpopular Boer War, by the radical English economist J. A. Hobson (1858–1940) in his *Imperialism,* a work that influenced Lenin and others. Hobson contended that the rush to acquire colonies was due to the economic needs of unregulated capitalism, particularly the need of the rich to find outlets for

their surplus capital. Yet, Hobson argued, imperial possessions do not pay off economically for the country as a whole. Only unscrupulous special-interest groups profit from them, at the expense of both the European taxpayer and the natives. Moreover, the quest for empire diverts attention from domestic reform and closing the gap between rich and poor. These and similar arguments were not very persuasive. Most people then (and now) believed that imperialism was economically profitable for the homeland, and a broad and genuine enthusiasm for empire developed among the masses.

Hobson and many other critics struck home, however, with their moral condemnation of whites imperiously ruling nonwhites. They rebelled against crude Social Darwinian thought. "O Evolution, what crimes are committed in thy name!" cried one foe. Another sardonically coined a new beatitude: "Blessed are the strong, for they shall prey on the weak."[14] Kipling and his kind were lampooned as racist bullies, whose rule rested on brutality, racial contempt, and the Maxim machine gun. Henri Labouchère, a member of Parliament and prominent spokesman for this position, mocked Kipling's famous poem:

Pile on the Brown Man's burden!
And if ye rouse his hate,
Meet his old-fashioned reasons
With Maxims up to date,
With shells and Dum-Dum bullets
A hundred times plain
The Brown Man's loss must never
Imply the White Man's gain.[15]

In *Heart of Darkness,* the Polish-born novelist Joseph Conrad (1857–1924) castigated the "pure selfishness" of Europeans in "civilizing" Africa; the main character, once a liberal scholar, turns into a savage brute.

Critics charged Europeans with applying a degrading double standard and failing to live up to their own noble ideals. At home, Europeans had won or were winning representative government, individual liberties, and a certain equality of opportunity. In their empires, Europeans imposed military dictatorships on Africans and Asians, forced them to work involuntarily, almost like slaves, and discriminated against them shamelessly. Only by renouncing imperialism, its critics insisted, and giving captive peoples the freedoms Western society had struggled for since the French Revolution, would Europeans be worthy of their traditions. Europeans who denounced the imperialist tide provided colonial peoples with a Western ideology of liberation.

RESPONSES TO WESTERN IMPERIALISM

To peoples in Africa and Asia, Western expansion represented a profoundly disruptive assault. Everywhere it threatened traditional ruling classes, tradi-

tional economies, and traditional ways of life. Christian missionaries and European secular ideologies challenged established beliefs and values. Non-Western peoples experienced a crisis of identity, a crisis made all the more painful by the power and arrogance of the white intruders.

The initial response of African and Asian rulers was to try to drive the unwelcome foreigners away. This was the case in China, Japan, and the upper Sudan, as we have seen. Violent antiforeign reactions exploded elsewhere again and again, but the superior military technology of the industrializing West almost invariably prevailed. Beaten in battle, many Africans and Asians concentrated on preserving their cultural traditions at all costs. Others found themselves forced to reconsider their initial hostility. Some (like Ismail of Egypt) concluded that the West was indeed superior in some ways and that it was therefore necessary to reform their societies and copy European achievements. Thus it is possible to think of responses to the Western impact as a spectrum, with "traditionalists" at one end, "westernizers" or "modernizers" at the other, and many shades of opinion in between. Both before and after European domination, the struggle among these groups was often intense. With time, however, the modernizers tended to gain the upper hand.

When the power of both the traditionalists and the modernizers was thoroughly shattered by superior force, the great majority of Asians and Africans accepted imperial rule. Political participation in non-Western lands was historically limited to small elites, and the masses were used to doing what their rulers told them. In these circumstances Europeans, clothed in power and convinced of their righteousness, governed smoothly and effectively. They received considerable support from both traditionalists —local chiefs, landowners, religious leaders—and modernizers—the Western-educated professional classes and civil servants.

Nevertheless, imperial rule was in many ways a hollow shell built on sand. Support for European rule among the conforming and accepting millions was shallow and weak. Thus the conforming masses followed with greater or lesser enthusiasm a few determined personalities who came to oppose the Europeans. Such leaders always arose, both when Europeans ruled directly and when they manipulated native governments, for at least two basic reasons.

Senegalese Scouts, 1913 Europeans recruited large numbers of native soldiers to expand and enforce their rule in Africa and Asia. Senegalese scouts were the pride of the French army in black Africa. *(Roger-Viollet)*

First, the nonconformists—the eventual anti-imperialist leaders—developed a burning desire for human dignity. They came to feel that such dignity was incompatible with foreign rule with its smirks and smiles, its paternalism and condescension. Second, potential leaders found in the Western world the ideologies and justification for their protest. They discovered liberalism with its credo of civil liberty and political self-determination. They echoed the demands of anti-imperialists in Europe and America that the West live up to its own ideals.

More important, they found themselves attracted to modern nationalism, which asserted that every people had the right to control its own destiny. After 1917 anti-imperialist revolt would find another weapon in Lenin's version of Marxian socialism. Thus the anti-imperialist search for dignity drew strength from Western culture, as is apparent in the development of three major Asian countries—India, Japan, and China.

EMPIRE IN INDIA

India was the jewel of the British Empire, and no colonial area experienced a more profound British impact. Unlike Japan and China, which maintained a real or precarious independence, and unlike African territories, which were annexed by Europeans only at the end of the nineteenth century, India was ruled more or less absolutely by Britain for a very long time.

Arriving in India on the heels of the Portuguese in the seventeenth century, the British East India Company had conquered the last independent native state by 1848. The last "traditional" response to European rule—the attempt by the established ruling classes to drive the white man out by military force—was broken in India in 1857 and 1858. Those were the years of the Great Rebellion (which the British called a "mutiny"), when an insurrection by Muslim and Hindu mercenaries in the British army spread throughout northern and central India before it was finally crushed, primarily by loyal native troops from southern India. Thereafter Britain ruled India directly. India illustrates, therefore, for better and for worse, what generations of European domination might produce.

After 1858 India was ruled by the British Parliament in London and administered by a tiny, all-white civil service in India. In 1900 this elite consisted of fewer than 3,500 top officials, for a population of 300 million. The white elite, backed by white officers and native troops, was competent and maintained reasonably good authoritarian rule. Yet it practiced strict job discrimination and social segregation, and most of its members quite frankly considered the jumble of Indian peoples and castes to be racially inferior. As Lord Kitchener, one of the most distinguished top military commanders of India, stated:

It is this consciousness of the inherent superiority of the European which has won for us India. However well educated and clever a native may be, and however brave he may prove himself, I believe that no rank we can bestow on him would cause him to be considered an equal of the British officer. [16]

When, for example, the British Parliament in 1883 was considering a major bill to allow Indian judges to try white Europeans in India, the British community rose in protest and defeated the measure. The idea that they might be judged by Indians was inconceivable to Europeans, for it was clear to the Europeans that the empire in India rested squarely on racial inequality.

In spite of (perhaps even because of) their strong feelings of racial and cultural superiority, the British acted energetically and introduced many desirable changes to India. Realizing that they needed well-educated Indians to serve as skilled subordinates in the government and army, the British established a modern system of progressive secondary education, in which all instruction was in English. Thus, through education and government service the British offered some Indians excellent opportunities for both economic and social advancement. High-caste Hindus were particularly quick to respond and emerged as skillful intermediaries between the British rulers and the Indian people—a new elite profoundly influenced by Western thought and culture.

The British in India This photo suggests not only the incredible power and luxury of the British ruling class in India but its confidence and self-satisfaction as well. As one British viceroy said: "We are all British gentlemen engaged in the magnificent work of governing an inferior race." *(BBC Hulton/The Bettmann Archive)*

This new bureaucratic elite played a crucial role in modern economic development, which was a second result of British rule. Irrigation projects for agriculture, the world's third largest railroad network for good communications, and large tea and jute plantations geared to the needs of the British economy were all developed. Unfortunately, the lot of the Indian masses improved little, for the increase in agricultural production was quite literally eaten up by population increase, and the unlimited importation of European manufactured goods led to a decline in the handicraft industry.

Finally, with a well-educated, English-speaking Indian bureaucracy and modern communications, the British created a unified, powerful state. They placed under the same general system of law and administration the different Hindu and Muslim peoples and the vanquished kingdoms of the entire subcontinent —groups that had fought each other for centuries during the Middle Ages and had been repeatedly conquered by Muslim and Mongol invaders. It was as if Europe, with its many states and varieties of

Christianity, had been conquered and united in a single great empire.

In spite of these achievements, the decisive reaction to European rule was the rise of nationalism among the Indian elite. No matter how anglicized and necessary a member of the educated classes became, he or she could never become the white ruler's equal. The top jobs, the best clubs, the modern hotels, and even certain railroad compartments were sealed off to brown-skinned men and women. The peasant masses might accept such inequality as the latest version of age-old oppression, but the well-educated, English-speaking elite eventually could not. For the elite, racial discrimination meant not only injured pride but bitter injustice. It flagrantly contradicted those cherished Western concepts of human rights and equality. Moreover, it was based on dictatorship, no matter how benign.

By 1885, when educated Indians came together to found the predominantly Hindu Indian National Congress, demands were increasing for the equality and self-government Britain enjoyed and had already granted white-settler colonies, such as Canada and Australia. By 1907, emboldened in part by Japan's success (see the next section), the radicals in the Indian National Congress were calling for complete independence. Even the moderates were demanding home rule for India through an elected parliament. Although there were sharp divisions between Hindus and Muslims, Indians were finding an answer to the foreign challenge. The common heritage of British rule and Western ideals, along with the reform and revitalization of the Hindu religion, had created a genuine movement for national independence.

THE EXAMPLE OF JAPAN

When Commodore Perry arrived in Japan in 1853 with his crude but effective gunboat diplomacy, Japan was a complex feudal society. At the top stood a figurehead emperor, but for more than two hundred years, real power had been in the hands of a hereditary military governor, the *shogun*. With the help of a warrior nobility known as *samurai*, the shogun governed a country of hardworking, productive peasants and city dwellers. Often poor and restless, the intensely proud samurai were deeply humiliated by the sudden American intrusion and the unequal treaties with Western countries. When foreign diplomats and merchants began to settle in Yokohama,

radical samurai reacted with a wave of antiforeign terrorism and antigovernment assassinations between 1858 and 1863. The imperialist response was swift and unambiguous. An allied fleet of American, British, Dutch, and French warships demolished key forts, which further weakened the power and prestige of the shogun's government. Then, in 1867, a coalition led by patriotic samurai seized control of the government with hardly any bloodshed and restored the political power of the emperor. This was the Meiji Restoration, a great turning point in Japanese development.

The immediate, all-important goal of the new government was to meet the foreign threat. The battle cry of the Meiji reformers was "enrich the state and strengthen the armed forces." Yet how was this to be done? In an about-face that was one of history's most remarkable chapters, the young but well-trained, idealistic but flexible leaders of Meiji Japan dropped their antiforeign attacks. Convinced that Western civilization was indeed superior in its military and industrial aspects, they initiated from above a series of measures to reform Japan along modern lines. They were convinced that "Japan must be reborn with America its mother and France its father."[17] In the broadest sense, the Meiji leaders tried to harness the power inherent in Europe's dual revolution, in order to protect their country and catch up with the West.

In 1871 the new leaders abolished the old feudal structure of aristocratic, decentralized government and formed a strong unified state. Following the example of the French Revolution, they dismantled the four-class legal system and declared social equality. They decreed freedom of movement in a country where traveling abroad had been a most serious crime. They created a free, competitive, government-stimulated economy. Japan began to build railroads and modern factories. Thus the new generation adopted many principles of a free, liberal society; and, as in Europe, such freedom resulted in a tremendously creative release of human energy.

Yet the overriding concern of Japan's political leadership was always a powerful state, and to achieve this, more than liberalism was borrowed from the West. A powerful modern navy was created, and the army was completely reorganized along French and German lines, with three-year military service for all males and a professional officer corps. This army of draftees effectively put down disturbances in the countryside, and in 1877 it was used to

MAP 30.4 The Expansion and Modernization of Japan, 1868–1914 Japan was
uniquely successful among Asian states in responding to the challenge of Western imperialism before 1914. Japan made great progress in building a modern economy and in
creating a political empire byond the home islands.

crush a major rebellion by feudal elements protesting
the loss of their privileges. Japan also borrowed rapidly and adopted skillfully the West's science and
modern technology, particularly in industry, medicine, and education. Many Japanese were encouraged to study abroad, and the government paid large
salaries to attract foreign experts. These experts were
always carefully controlled, though, and replaced by
trained Japanese as soon as possible.

By 1890, when the new state was firmly established, the wholesale borrowing of the early restoration had given way to more selective emphasis on
those things foreign that were in keeping with Japanese tradition. Following the model of the German
Empire, Japan established an authoritarian constitution and rejected democracy. The power of the emperor and his ministers was vast, that of the legislature limited.

横濱名所之内
野毛の眺望

永林筆

彫辰政

左甚五
イセモ
板

The Modernization of Japan Soon after it reluctantly opened its doors to foreigners, Japan built its first railroad, sketched here by a native artist. *(Historical Pictures Service, Chicago)*

Japan successfully copied the imperialism of Western society. Expansion not only proved that Japan was strong, it also cemented the nation together in a great mission. Having "opened" Korea with the gunboat diplomacy of imperialism in 1876, Japan decisively defeated China in a war over Korea in 1894 and took Formosa. In the next years, Japan competed aggressively with the leading European powers for influence and territory in China, particularly Manchuria. There Japanese and Russian imperialism met and collided. In 1904 Japan attacked Russia without warning, and after a bloody war, Japan emerged with a valuable foothold in China, Russia's former protectorate over Port Arthur (see Map 30.4). By 1910, when it annexed Korea, Japan was a major

imperial power, continuously expanding its influence in China in spite of sharp protests from its distant Pacific neighbor, the United States.

Japan became the first non-Western country to use an ancient love of country to transform itself and thereby meet the many-sided challenge of Western expansion. Moreover, Japan demonstrated convincingly that a modern Asian nation could defeat and humble a great Western power. Many Chinese nationalists were fascinated by Japan's achievement. A group of patriots in French-ruled southern Vietnam sent Vietnamese students to Japan to learn the island empire's secret of success. Japan provided patriots in Asia and Africa with an inspiring example of national recovery and liberation.

TOWARD REVOLUTION IN CHINA

In 1860 the two-hundred-year-old Manchu Dynasty in China appeared on the verge of collapse. Efforts to repel the foreigner had failed, and rebellion and chaos wracked the country. Yet the government drew on its traditional strengths and made a surprising comeback that lasted more than thirty years.

Two factors were crucial in this reversal. First, the traditional ruling groups temporarily produced new and effective leadership. Loyal scholar-statesmen and generals quelled disturbances like the great Tai Ping rebellion. A truly remarkable woman, the empress dowager Tzu Hsi, governed in the name of her young son and combined shrewd insight with vigorous action to revitalize the bureaucracy.

Second, destructive foreign aggression lessened, for the Europeans had obtained their primary goal of advantageous commercial and diplomatic relations. Indeed, some Europeans even contributed to the dynasty's recovery. A talented Irishman effectively reorganized China's customs office and increased the government tax receipts, while a sympathetic American diplomat represented China in foreign lands and helped strengthen the central government. Such efforts dovetailed with the dynasty's efforts to adopt some aspects of Western government and technology while maintaining traditional Chinese values and beliefs.

The parallel movement toward domestic reform and limited cooperation with the West collapsed under the blows of Japanese imperialism. The Sino-Japanese war of 1894–1895 and the subsequent

The Hatred of Foreigners burns in the eyes of this Chinese prisoner condemned to death for murdering foreign missionaries in the aftermath of the Sino-Japanese war. Both his face and crime foretell the fury of the Boxer Rebellion. *(BBC Hulton/The Bettmann Archive)*

harsh peace treaty revealed China's helplessness in the face of aggression, triggering a rush for foreign concessions and protectorates in China. At its high point in 1898, it appeared that the European powers might actually divide China among themselves, as they had recently divided Africa. Probably only the jealousy each nation felt toward its imperial competitors saved China from partition, although the United States Open Door policy, which opposed formal annexation of Chinese territory, may have helped tip the balance. In any event, the tempo and impact of foreign penetration greatly accelerated after 1894.

So, too, did the intensity and radicalism of the Chinese reaction. Like the men of the Meiji Restoration, some modernizers saw salvation in Western institutions. In 1898 the government launched a desperate "hundred days of reform" in an attempt to meet the foreign challenge. More radical reformers like the revolutionary Sun Yat-sen (1866–1925), who came from the peasantry and was educated in Hawaii by Christian missionaries, sought to overthrow the dynasty altogether and establish a republic.

On the other side, some traditionalists turned back toward ancient practices, political conservatism, and fanatical hatred of the "foreign devils." "Protect the country, destroy the foreigner" was their simple motto. Such conservative, antiforeign patriots had often clashed with foreign missionaries, whom they charged with undermining reverence for ancestors and thereby threatening the Chinese family and the entire society. In the agony of defeat and unwanted reforms, secret societies like the Boxers rebelled. In northeastern China, more than two hundred foreign missionaries and several thousand Chinese Christians were killed. Once again, the imperialist response was swift and harsh. Peking was occupied and plundered by foreign armies. A heavy indemnity was imposed.

The years after the Boxer Rebellion (1900–1903) were even more troubled. Anarchy and foreign influence spread, as the power and prestige of the Manchu Dynasty declined still further. Antiforeign, antigovernment revolutionary groups agitated and plotted. Finally, in 1912, a spontaneous uprising toppled the

Manchu Dynasty. After thousands of years of emperors and empires, a loose coalition of revolutionaries proclaimed a Western-style republic and called for an elected parliament. The transformation of China under the impact of expanding Western society entered a new phase, and the end was not in sight.

In the nineteenth century the industrializing West entered the third and most dynamic phase of its centuries-old expansion into non-Western lands. In so doing, Western nations profitably subordinated those lands to their economic interests, sent forth millions of emigrants, and established political influence in Asia and vast political empires in Africa. The reasons for this culminating surge were many, but the economic thrust of robust industrial capitalism, an ever-growing lead in technology, and the competitive pressures of European nationalism were particularly important.

Western expansion had far-reaching consequences. For the first time in human history, the world became in many ways a single unit. Moreover, European expansion diffused the ideas and techniques of a highly developed civilization. Yet the West imposed inequality in commercial relations, and it relied on force to conquer and rule. It treated non-Western peoples as racial inferiors. Thus non-Western elites, often armed with Western doctrines, gradually responded to the Western challenge. They launched a national, anti-imperialist struggle for dignity, genuine independence, and modernization. This struggle would emerge as a central drama of world history after the great European civil war of 1914 to 1918, which reduced the West's technological advantage and shattered its self-confidence and complacent moral superiority.

NOTES

1. Quoted in A. Waley, *The Opium War Through Chinese Eyes* (New York: Macmillan, 1958), p. 29.
2. Quoted in J. W. Hall, *Japan, from Prehistory to Modern Times* (New York: Delacorte Press, 1970), p. 250.

3. Quoted in R. Hallett, *Africa to 1875* (Ann Arbor: University of Michigan Press, 1970), p. 109.
4. Quoted in the Earl of Cromer, *Modern Egypt* (London: 1911), p. 48.
5. Quoted in T. Blegen, *Norwegian Migration to America* (Northfield, Minn.: Norwegian-American Historical Association, 1940), 2.468.
6. Quoted in I. Howe, *World of Our Fathers* (New York: Harcourt Brace Jovanovich, 1976), p. 25.
7. Quoted in C. A. Price, *The Great White Walls Are Built: Restrictive Immigration to North America and Australia, 1836–1888* (Canberra: Australian National University Press, 1974), p. 175.
8. Quoted in W. L. Langer, *European Alliances and Alignments, 1871–1890* (New York: Vintage Books, 1931), p. 290.
9. Quoted in J. Ellis, *The Social History of the Machine Gun* (New York: Pantheon Books, 1975), pp. 86, 101.
10. Quoted in G. H. Nadel and P. Curtis, eds., *Imperialism and Colonialism* (New York: Macmillan, 1964), p. 94.
11. Quoted in W. L. Langer, *The Diplomacy of Imperialism,* 2d ed. (New York: Knopf, 1951), pp. 86, 88.
12. Rudyard Kipling, *The Five Nations* (London: 1903), quoted by the permission of Mrs. George Bambridge, Methuen & Company, and Doubleday & Company, Inc.
13. E. H. Berman, "African Responses to Christian Mission Education," *African Studies Review* 17:3 (1974): 530.
14. Quoted in Langer, *Diplomacy of Imperialism,* p. 88.
15. Quoted in Ellis, pp. 99–100.
16. Quoted in K. M. Panikkar, *Asia and Western Dominance* (London: George Allen & Unwin, 1959), p. 116.
17. Quoted in Hall, p. 289.

SUGGESTED READING

General surveys of European expansion in a broad perspective include R. Betts, *Europe Overseas* (1968); A. Thornton, *Imperialism in the 20th Century* (1977); T. Smith, *The Patterns of Imperialism* (1981); and W. Woodruff, *Impact of Western Man* (1967), which has an extensive bibliography. D. K. Fieldhouse has also written two fine surveys, *Economics and Empire, 1830–*

1914 (1970) and *Colonialism, 1870–1945* (1981). G. Barraclough, *An Introduction to Contemporary History* (1964), argues powerfully that Western imperialism and the non-Western reaction to it have been crucial in world history since about 1890. J. A. Hobson's classic *Imperialism* (1902) is readily available, and the Marxist-Leninist case is effectively presented in V. G. Kieran, *Marxism and Imperialism* (1975). Two excellent anthologies on the problem of European expansion are G. Nadel and P. Curtis, eds., *Imperialism and Colonialism* (1964), and H. Wright, ed., *The "New Imperialism,"* rev. ed. (1975).

Britain's leading position in European imperialism is examined in a lively way by B. Porter, *The Lion's Share* (1976); J. Morris, *Pax Britannica* (1968); and D. Judd, *The Victorian Empire* (1970), a stunning pictorial history. B. Semmel has written widely on the intellectual foundations of English expansion, as in *The Rise of Free Trade Imperialism* (1970). J. Gallagher and R. Robinson, *Africa and the Victorians: The Climax of Imperialism* (1961), is an influential reassessment. H. Brunschwig, *French Colonialism, 1871–1914* (1966), and W. Baumgart, *Imperialism: The Idea and Reality of British and French Colonial Expansion* (1982), are well-balanced studies. A. Moorehead, *The White Nile* (1971), tells the fascinating story of the European exploration of the mysterious upper Nile. Volumes 5 and 6 of K. Latourette, *History of the Expansion of Christianity,* 7 vols. (1937–1945), examine the powerful impulse for missionary work in non-European areas. D. Headrick stresses Western technological superiority in *Tools of Empire* (1981).

G. Perry, *The Middle East: Fourteen Islamic Centuries* (1983), concisely surveys nineteenth-century developments and provides up-to-date bibliographies. B. Lewis, *The Middle East and the West* (1963), is a penetrating analysis of the impact of Western ideas on Middle Eastern thought. Hallett, cited in the Notes, and R. July, *A History of the African People* (1970), contain excellent introductions to Africa in the age of imperialism. J. D. Fage, *A History of Africa* (1978), is also recommended. Basil Davidson, *The African Genius: An Introduction to African Social and Cultural History* (1969), imaginatively looks at Western expansion from an Afri-

can point of view. A classic study of that same expansion from an Indian viewpoint is found in K. M. Panikkar, *Asia and Western Dominance: A Survey of the Vasco da Gama Epoch of Asian History* (1959). S. Wolpert, *A New History of India,* 2d ed. (1982), incorporates recent scholarship in a wide-ranging study that is highly recommended. On Africa and India, see also the Suggested Reading for Chapters 23 and 33.

A. Waley, cited in the Notes, has written extensively and well on China. Valuable surveys of Chinese history include I. Hsü, *The Rise of Modern China,* 2d ed. (1975), and K. Latourette, *The Chinese: Their History and Culture,* rev. ed. (1964). Both have many suggestions for further reading. The most comprehensive scholarly work is the multivolume series edited by J. Fairbank and D. Twitchett, *The Cambridge History of China.* In addition to Hall, cited in the Notes, E. Reischauer's topical survey, *Japan: The Story of a Nation* (1981), is recommended. Also recommended are G. Akita, *Foundations of Constitutional Government in Modern Japan, 1868–1900* (1967), and Y. Fukuzawa, *Autobiography* (1966), the personal account of a leading intellectual who witnessed the emergence of modern Japan.

Two unusual and provocative studies on personal relations between European rulers and non-European subjects are D. Mannoni, *Prospero and Caliban: The Psychology of Colonialization* (1964), and F. Fanon, *The Wretched of the Earth* (1965), a bitter attack on white racism by a black psychologist active in the Algerian revolution. The recent Indian work by A. Nandy, *The Intimate Enemy: Loss and Recovery of Self Under Colonialism* (1983), is another stimulating psychological study, as is K. Ballhatchet, *Race, Sex and Class Under the Raj* (1980). Novels also bring the psychological and human dimensions of imperialism alive. H. Rider Haggard, *King Solomon's Mines,* portrays the powerful appeal of adventure in exotic lands, while Rudyard Kipling, the greatest writer of European expansion, is at his stirring best in *Kim* and *Soldiers Three.* Joseph Conrad unforgettably probes European motives in *Heart of Darkness,* while André Gide, *The Immoralist,* closely examines European moral corruption in North Africa.

31

THE WESTERN HEMISPHERE IN THE NINETEENTH CENTURY

*I*N THE WESTERN hemisphere, as in Europe, the nineteenth century was a period of nation building. It was also an era of geographic expansion and dynamic industrial and commercial growth. The century witnessed unparalleled waves of migration from Europe and Asia to the Americas. The millions of immigrants who braved the oceans populated and built the new nations; they also linked the Western Hemisphere with the rest of the globe. The countries of North and South America became highly diverse ethnically and culturally. One aspect of this pluralism was racial differences, and the issue of race created serious tensions throughout the hemisphere. In the United States it helped to bring on the Civil War, which jeopardized the existence of the Union itself. In the late nineteenth and early twentieth century European immigration directly affected the ways with which the United States and the Latin American nations coped with racial situations.

At the end of the eighteenth century, the several countries of South America and Canada remained colonies, whose European mother countries looked upon the democratic experiment of the infant United States with suspicion and scorn. By 1914 the Latin American states and Canada were enjoying political independence and playing a crucial role in the world economy. The United States had achieved the stature of a colossus, upon which the Old World depended in the First World War. How had this transformation come about? Why and how did the Spanish colonies of Latin America shake off European domination and develop into national states? What role did the concept of manifest destiny play in the evolution of the United States? How did slavery affect the black family in the United States? How did the Americas absorb new peoples and what was their social impact? This chapter will address these questions.

LATIN AMERICA, 1800–1929

In 1800 the Spanish Empire in the Western Hemisphere stretched from the headwaters of the Mississippi River in present-day Minnesota to the tip of Cape Horn in the Antarctic. The Spanish crown claimed 7 million square miles, roughly one-third of the entire hemisphere. According to the Kentucky statesman Henry Clay, "Within this vast region, we behold the most sublime and interesting objects of creation: the loftiest mountains, the most majestic rivers in the world; the richest mines of precious metals, the choicest productions of the earth."[1] Spain believed that this great wealth existed for its benefit, and Spanish policies fostered bitterness and the desire for independence in the colonies.

Between 1806 and 1825 the Spanish colonies in Latin America were convulsed by upheavals that ultimately resulted in their separation from Spain. Some scholars regard these insurrections as wars of revolution; others call them wars of independence; still others consider them civil wars. All three characterizations contain elements of truth. The Latin American wars were revolutions in the sense that the colonists revolted against the domination of Spain and fought for direct self-government. They were wars of independence in that the colonies sought economic liberation and management of their own commercial affairs. They were civil wars in the sense that social and racial groups fought one another. The Creoles—people of Spanish descent born in America—resented the economic and political dominance of the *peninsulares,* as natives of Spain or Portugal were called. Peninsulares controlled the rich export-import trade, inter-colonial trade, and the mining industries. At the same time *mestizos* of mixed Spanish and Indian background and *mulattoes* of mixed Spanish and African heritage sought an end to their systematic subordination.

Between 1850 and the worldwide depression of 1929, the countries of Latin America developed into national states. The predominant factors in this evolution were the heritage of colonial exploitation, a "neocolonial" economic structure, massive immigration from Europe and Asia, and the resulting fusion of Amerindian, Caucasian, African, and Asian peoples. The Latin American societies that emerged in the twentieth century can best be understood against this background.

THE ORIGINS OF THE REVOLUTIONS

Because of regional, geographic, and racial diversities, the Latin American movements for independence took different forms in different places. Everywhere, however, they grew out of recent colonial economic grievances. By the late seventeenth century the Spanish colonies had achieved a high degree of economic diversity and independence. The mercantilist imperialism of the days of Cortés and Pizarro (see Chapter 18), which held that the colonies existed for Spain's financial benefit and should be economically dependent on Spain, had faded away. The colonies had become agriculturally and commercially self-sufficient producers of foodstuffs, wine, textiles, and consumer goods. What was not produced domestically was secured through trade between colonies. Despite formidable geographic obstacles, a healthy intercolonial trade had developed independent of Spain.

In Peru, for example, domestic agriculture supported the large mining settlements, and the colony did not have to import food. Craft workshops owned by the state or by private individuals produced consumer goods for the working class; what was not manufactured locally was bought from Mexico and transported by the Peruvian merchant marine. By 1700 Mexico and Peru were sending shrinking percentages of their revenues to Spain and retaining more for public works, defense, and administration. The colonies lived for themselves and not for Spain.

The reforms of the Spanish Bourbons radically reversed this economic independence. Spain's humiliating defeat in the War of the Spanish Succession prompted demands for sweeping reform of all its institutions, including colonial policies and practices (page 598). To improve administrative efficiency, the enlightened monarch Charles III (1759–1788) carved the region of modern Colombia, Venezuela, and Ecuador out of the vast viceroyalty of Peru; it became the new viceroyalty of New Granada with its capital at Bogotá. The Crown also created the viceroyalty of Rio de la Plata (present-day Argentina) with its capital at Buenos Aires (Map 31.1). Far more momentous was Charles III's radical overhaul of colonial trade policies, to enable Spain to compete with Great Britain and Holland in the great eighteenth-century struggle for empire. The Spanish crown intended that the colonies serve as sources of raw materials and as markets for Spanish manufactured goods. Charles III's free trade policies cut duties drastically for Spanish merchants. All Iberian ports, no longer just Cadiz, were allowed to trade with the colonies. In America these actions stimulated production of crops in demand in Europe: coffee in Venezuela; sugar in Cuba and throughout the Caribbean; hides, leather, and salted beef in the Rio de la Plata. In Mexico and Peru, production of silver climbed steadily in the last quarter of the century. The volume of Spain's trade with the colonies soared, possibly as much as 700 percent between 1778 and 1788.[2]

Colonial manufacturing, which had been growing steadily, suffered severely. Better-made and cheaper European goods drove colonial goods out of the marketplace. Colonial textiles, chinaware, and wine, for example, could not compete with cheap Spanish products. For one thing, American free laborers were paid more than European workers in the eighteenth century; this helps explain the great numbers of immigrants to the colonies. Also, intercolonial transportation costs were higher than transatlantic costs: in Buenos Aires, for example, Spanish wines were actually cheaper than locally produced Mendoza wine.

In the Rio de la Plata region, heavy export taxes and light import duties shattered the wine industry. When the wine merchants complained of "tyrannical taxes" and asked an end to the import of Spanish wines, the imperial government rejected their appeal. Geographic obstacles also hampered Latin American economic development. Mountains, deserts, jungles, and inadequate natural harbors frustrated colonial efforts to promote economic integration.

Having made the colonies dependent on essential Spanish goods, however, Spain found that it could not keep the sea routes open. After 1789 the French Revolution and Napoleonic wars isolated Spain from Latin America. Foreign traders, especially from the United States, swarmed into Spanish-American ports. In 1796 the Madrid government lifted the restrictions against neutrals trading with the colonies, thus acknowledging Spain's inability to supply the colonies with needed goods and markets.[3] All these difficulties spelled disaster for colonial trade and industry.

At the end of the eighteenth century colonists also complained bitterly that only peninsulares were appointed to the *audiencias*—the colonies' highest judicial bodies, which also served as councils to the viceroys—and other positions in the colonial governments, to the exclusion of Creoles. According to the nineteenth-century Mexican statesman and historian Lucas Alamán (1792–1853),

this preference shown to Spaniards in political offices and ecclesiastical benefices has been the principal cause of the rivalry between the two classes; add to this the fact that Europeans possessed great wealth, which although it may have been the just reward of effort and industry,

Disputed by England,
Spain, and Russia

Effective frontier of
Spanish settlement

COAHUILA

VICEROYALTY
OF NEW SPAIN

BAJIO LEÓN

Mexico City
Veracruz

Guatemala

Havana

CUBA

HAITI/SAINT DOMINIQUE

JAMAICA

PUERTO RICO

CARIBBEAN SEA

ATLANTIC

OCEAN

Caracas

Bogotá

VICEROYALTY OF
NEW GRANADA

GUIANA

Amazon

Sucre

ANDES

VICEROYALTY
OF PERU

Lima

PACIFIC

OCEAN

VICEROYALTY OF BRAZIL

Bahia

MOUNTAINS

Rio de Janeiro

São Paulo

Paraná

VICEROYALTY OF
RIO DE LA PLATA

Santiago

Montevideo

Buenos Aires

AUDIENCIA
OF CHILE

0   1000 Km.

0   1000 Mi.

FALKLAND /MALVINAS ISLANDS

Map 31.1 Latin America Before Independence Consider the factors that led to the boundaries of the various Spanish and Portuguese colonies in North and South America.

excited the envy of Americans and was considered as so much usurpation from them; consider that for all these reasons the Spaniards had obtained a decided preponderance over those born in the country; and it will not be difficult to explain the increasing jealousy and rivalry between the two groups which culminated in hatred and enmity.[4]

In the late seventeenth and early eighteenth centuries, large numbers of Creoles had been appointed to government positions, including the audiencias. Then, beginning in 1751, the Crown drastically reduced appointments of Creoles. The upper levels of colonial bureaucracies became overwhelmingly Spanish. Between 1730 and 1750, fully 53 percent of appointees to the audiencias had been Creoles; from 1751 to 1775, only 13 percent were Creoles.[5] This change in imperial policy provoked American outrage. From the perspective of the Creole elite of Spanish America, the world seemed "upside down."[6] Creoles hungered for political office and resented their successful Spanish rivals.

Madrid's tax reforms aggravated discontent. In the 1770s and 1780s the Spanish crown needed income to finance imperial defense. Colonial ports had to be fortified and standing armies built. Like Great Britain, Spain believed its Latin American colonies should bear some of the costs of their own defense. Accordingly, Madrid raised the prices of tobacco and liquor and increased the *alcabala* (a sales tax of Arabic origin) on many items. Improved governmental administration made tax collection more efficient. Creole business and agricultural interests resented the Crown's monopoly of the tobacco industry and opposed new taxes.

Like the thirteen North American colonies a decade earlier, the Latin American protest movements claimed that the colonies were being taxed unconstitutionally. However, where the merchants of Boston and Philadelphia had protested taxation without representation, the Spanish colonies had no tradition of legislative approval of taxes. Creole mercantile leaders argued instead that the constitutional system was being violated when taxes were imposed without

consultation. They asserted that relations between imperial authorities and colonial interests stayed on an even keel through consultation and compromise; when the Crown imposed taxes without consultation, therefore, it violated ancient constitutional practice.

North American ships calling at Spanish-American ports had introduced the subversive writings of Thomas Paine and Thomas Jefferson. The imperial government recognized the potential danger of the North American example: although Spain had joined France on the side of the rebel colonies against Great Britain during the American Revolution, the Madrid government refused in 1783 to grant diplomatic recognition to the new United States. For decades the ideas of Voltaire, Rousseau, and Montesquieu also trickled into Latin America. In 1794 the Colombian Antonio Nariño translated and published the French *Declaration of the Rights of Man and the Citizen.* Although Spanish authorities sentenced him to ten years in an African prison, Nariño lived to become the father of Colombian independence. By 1800 the Creole elite throughout Latin America was familiar with liberal Enlightenment political thought.[7]

RACE IN THE COLONIAL PERIOD

The Creoles assumed the "rights of man" to be limited to themselves; they had no thought of sharing such rights with the Indian and black masses. The racial complexion of Latin American societies is perhaps the most complicated in the world. Few European women emigrated to the colonies; thus Spanish males had relations with Indian and African women. African men deprived of black women sought Indian women. The result was a population composed of every possible combination of Indian, Spanish, and African blood. Spanish theories of racial purity rejected people of mixed blood, and particularly those of African descent. A person's social status depended on the degree of European blood he or she possessed or appeared to possess. Peninsulares and Creoles reinforced their privileged status by showing contempt for the nonwhite. As the great nineteenth-century German scientist Alexander von Humboldt put it, having spent five years traveling throughout South America, "Any white person, although he rides his horse barefoot, imagines himself to be of the nobility of the country."[8] Coupled with the Spaniard's aristocratic disdain for manual labor, a three-hundred-year

Diamond Mining in Brazil The discovery of gold and diamonds in Brazil in the seventeenth century increased the demand for slave labor. The English geologist John Mawe made this dramatic engraving of slaves washing for diamonds in the early nineteenth century. *(Courtesy, Oliveira Lima Library, The Catholic University of America. Photo: Paul McKane, OSB)*

had Indian majorities; the regions that became Argentina and Chile had European majorities. As the Indians declined in the seventeenth century, the Spanish grabbed up Indian lands for wheat, corn, cattle, and sheep raising. Indians and black slaves toiled in the silver and gold mines of Mexico, Colombia, and Peru, the wheat fields of Chile, the humid, mosquito-ridden cane brakes of Mexico and the Caribbean, the diamond mines and the coffee and sugar plantations of Brazil.

Nevertheless, nonwhites did experience some social mobility in the colonial period, certainly more than in North America. In Mexico, decreasing reliance on slaves in the economic system led to a great increase in manumissions. Once freed, however, Negroes immediately became subject to the payment of tribute, as were the Indians. Freedmen also incurred the obligation of military service. A few mulattoes rose in the army, some as high as the rank of colonel; the army and the Church seem to have offered the greatest opportunities for social mobility. Many black slaves gained their freedom by fleeing to the jungles or mountains, where they established self-governing communities. Around 1800 Venezuela counted 24,000 fugitive slaves in a total population of 87,000.

Conditions varied, but many Indians were still subject to the *mita* and *repartimiento*. The mita, a system of forced labor requiring that all adult Indian males work for part of each year in the silver mines, was thinly disguised slave labor; the silver mines were deathtraps. The law of repartimiento required Indians to buy goods solely from the local *corregidores*, the officials who collected taxes. The new taxes of the 1770s and 1780s fell particularly heavily on the Indians. When Indian opposition to these taxes and to oppressive conditions exploded into violence, Creoles organized the protest movements and assumed leadership of them.

THE COMUNERO REVOLUTION

In Peru in November 1779 the wealthy, well-educated mestizo Tupac Amaru, a descendant of the Inca kings, captured, tried, and executed the local corregidor. Tupac Amaru and his mostly Indian followers demanded the abolition of the alcabala and the mita, and replacement of the corregidores with Indian governors. Proclaiming himself liberator of

tradition had instilled in the minds of Latin Americans the notion that dark skin and manual labor went together. Owners of mines, plantations, and factories had a vested interest in keeping blacks and Indians in a servile position. A pervasive racism and discrimination characterized all the Latin American colonies.

In spite of the catastrophes that had befallen them in the sixteenth and seventeenth centuries, Indians still constituted the majority of the population of Latin America at the end of the colonial period. Demographers estimate that Indians accounted for between three-fifths and three-fourths of the total population. The colonies that became Peru and Bolivia the people, Tupac Amaru waged a war of blood and fire against the Spanish governors. Violence swept the Peruvian highlands. Thousands lost their lives and a vast amount of private property was destroyed. Poor communication among the rebel forces and the superior organization of the imperial armies enabled the Spanish to crush the revolt. Tupac Amaru, his family, and his captains were captured and savagely executed. Frightened colonial administrators did, however, grant some reforms. The Crown repealed the repartimiento, reduced the mita, and replaced the corregidores with a lighter system of intendants. The condition of the Indians temporarily improved.

News of the rebellion of Tupac Amaru trickled northward, where it helped stimulate revolution in New Granada. Disorders occurred first at Socorro in modern Colombia (Map 31.2). Throughout the eighteenth century Socorro had prospered. Sugar cane, corn, and cattle flourished on its exceptionally fertile soil. Large cotton crops stimulated the production of textiles, mostly in a primitive cottage industry worked by women. Socorro's location on the Suarez River made it an agricultural and manufacturing center and an entrepôt for trade with the hinterland. Hardworking Spanish immigrants had prospered and often intermarried with the Indians, creating a sizable mestizo population. When the viceroy published new taxes on tobacco and liquor and reorganized the alcabala, riots broke out in Socorro in March 1781 and spread to other towns. Representatives of peasants and artisan groups from many towns elected a *comun,* or central committee, to lead the insurrection. Each town elected its local comun and the captain of its militia. Known as the Comunero Revolution, the insurrection in New Granada enjoyed broad-based support and good organization, and appeared far more threatening to governmental authorities than had the uprising in Peru.

An Indian peasant army commanded by Creole captains marched on Bogotá. Government officials, lacking adequate military resources, sent a commission to play for time by negotiating with the comuneros. On June 4 the commission agreed to the rebels' terms: reduction of the alcabala and of the Indians' forced tribute, abolition of the new taxes on tobacco, and preference for Creoles over peninsulares in governmental positions. The joyful Indian army disbanded and went home. What they did not know was that the commission had already secretly disclaimed

the agreement with the rebels on the grounds that it had been taken by force. Having succeeded in dispersing the Indians, the government at Bogotá won over the Creole leaders with promises of pardons and then moved in reserve troops who captured large numbers of rebels. When the last rebel holdout—that of José Antonio Galan—had been captured, the kangaroo court that tried him condemned Galan

to be taken out of jail, dragged and taken to the place of execution where he will be hung until dead, that his head be removed from his dead body, that the rest of his body be quartered, that his torso be committed to flames for which purpose a fire shall be lit in front of the platform. His head shall be sent to Guaduas, the scene of his scandalous insults, his right arm shall be displayed in the main square of Socorro, his left arm shall be displayed in the square of San Gil, his right leg shall be displayed in Charala his birthplace, and his left leg in the parish of Mogotes. All his descendants shall be declared infamous, all his property shall be confiscated by the royal treasury, his home shall be burnt, and the ground salted, so that in this fashion his infamous name may be forgotten.[9]

Thus ended the revolt of the comuneros in New Granada. The comuneros failed to win self-rule, but they forced the authorities to act in accordance with the spirit of the "unwritten constitution," whose guiding principle was consultation and compromise. Although the authorities used Galan's execution as a stick to kill social revolution, over the next twenty years they extended the carrot of governmental concern to promote colonial prosperity.

INDEPENDENCE

Napoleon Bonaparte lit the fuse of the Latin American powder keg. In 1808, as part of his effort to rule Europe, Napoleon deposed the Spanish king Ferdinand VII and placed his own brother on the Spanish throne (page 798). In Latin America the Creoles seized the opportunity: since everything in Spanish America was done in the name of the king, the Creoles argued that the removal of the legitimate king shifted sovereignty to the people—that is, themselves. The small, wealthy Creole aristocracy used the removal of the Spanish king as justification for their seizure of political power and their preservation of that power.

UNITED STATES

ATLANTIC

OCEAN

MEXICO
Mexico City • • Veracruz

Havana •
CUBA
JAMAICA
BR. HONDURAS
Guatemala •
GUATEMALA
HONDURAS
NICARAGUA
COSTA RICA
PANAMA

DOMINICAN REP.
HAITI
PUERTO RICO
CARIBBEAN SEA

Caracas •
VENEZUELA
BR. GUIANA
DUTCH GUIANA
FR. GUIANA

• Bogota
COLOMBIA

Quito •
ECUADOR

Amazon

B R A Z I L

PERU
Lima •

• Bahia

La Paz •
• BOLIVIA

MINAS GERAIS

PACIFIC

OCEAN

PARAGUAY

SÃO PAULO
São Paulo •
RIO DE JANEIRO
Rio de Janeiro •

Parana

RIO GRANDE
DO SUL

Valpariso •
CHILE
• Santiago
Buenos Aires •
ARGENTINA
Bahia Blanca •

URUGUAY
Montevideo •

PATAGONIA

Independent nations

Colonial possessions

FALKLAND/MALVINAS ISLANDS

0   1000 Km.

0   1000 Mi.

968

MAP 31.2 Latin America in 1830 What geographical factors have led to the relative political power of the United States and the Latin American nations?

Simón Bolívar (1783–1830) His success in defeating Spanish armies earned him the title, "the Liberator." President of Greater Colombia, Bolívar organized the government of Peru, created Bolivia, and dreamt of a United Spanish America. He is respected as the greatest Latin American hero. *(Courtesy of the Organization of American States)*

Thus began the war for independence. An able scholar has described it as

a prolonged, confused, and in many ways contradictory movement. In Mexico it began as a popular social movement [and] ended many years later as a conservative uprising against a liberal Spanish constitution. In Venezuela it came to be a war unto the death; in other places it was a war between a small [Creole] minority and the Spanish authorities. It was not an organized movement with a central revolutionary directorate. It had no Continental Congress. . . . If there was no central direction, no centrally recognized leadership, likewise there was no formally accepted political doctrine.[10]

The Creoles who led the various movements for independence did not intend a radical redistribution of property or reconstruction of society; they merely rejected the authority of the Spanish crown.

In the final battle . . . the soldiers on the field came from Venezuela, Colombia, Ecuador, Peru, Argentina, and Chile, and among the officers there were Frenchmen and .Englishmen who had opposed each other in the Napoleonic Wars. It was a continental, if not an international, army. The war stopped but did not officially end. There was no treaty of peace. There was no recognition of the new states. There was no definite agreement as to the form of government or even as to national boundaries. . . . In Latin America each separate area went its own way. Central America broke away from Mexico and then splintered into five separate nations. Uruguay, Paraguay, and Bolivia separated themselves from Argentina, Chile from Peru, and Bolívar's attempt to federate the state of Gran Colombia (Venezuela, Colombia, and Ecuador) with Peru and Bolivia under a centralized government broke down.[11]

Simón Bolívar (1783–1830), the great hero of the movement for independence, is considered the Spanish-American George Washington. A very able general, Bolívar's victories over the royalist armies won him the presidency of Greater Colombia in 1819. Bolívar dreamt of a continental union, and in 1826 he summoned a conference of South American republics at Panama. The meeting achieved little. Bolívar organized the government of Bolivia and became the head of the new state of Peru. The territories of Greater Colombia splintered apart, however, and a sadly disillusioned Bolívar went into exile, saying, "America is ungovernable. Those who served the revolution plowed the seas." The failure of pan-

Street Scene in Rio de Janeiro Soldiers, planter-aristocrats, merchants, slaves, friars, and carriages thronged the cobblestone streets of the capital of Brazil. *(Department of Rare Books, Cornell University Library)*

Americanism isolated individual countries, prevented collective action, and later paved the way for the political and economic intrusion of the United States and other powers.

Portuguese Brazil's quest for independence was unique: Brazil won its independence without violent upheaval. When Napoleon's troops entered Portugal, King John VI and the royal family fled to Brazil and made Rio de Janeiro the capital of the Portuguese empire. The new government immediately lifted the old mercantilist restrictions and opened Brazilian ports to the ships of all friendly nations. Under popular pressure, John's son, Pedro I, proclaimed Brazil's independence in 1822 and published a constitution. Pedro's administration was wracked by factional disputes between Portuguese courtiers and Brazilian Creoles, a separatist movement in the Rio Grande do Sul region, and provincial revolts. His successor, Pedro II (1831–1889), restored order and laid the foundations of the modern Brazilian state. His reign witnessed the expansion of the coffee industry, the beginnings of the rubber industry, and massive immigration.

THE CONSEQUENCES OF INDEPENDENCE

The wars of independence ended around 1825. What effects did they have on South American societies? How were South American countries governed in the nineteenth century? What factors worked against the development of modern nations? Because the movements for independence differed in character and course in different regions and countries, generalizations about Mexico, the Caribbean islands, and South America are likely to be misleading. Significant changes did occur, however, throughout South America.

The newly independent nations did not achieve immediate political stability when the wars of independence ended. The Spanish crown had served as a unifying symbol, and its disappearance left a power vacuum. Civil disorder typically followed. The Creole leaders of the revolutions had no experience in government, and the wars had left a legacy of military, not civilian, leadership. Throughout the continent, idealistic but impractical leaders proclaimed republics—independent states governed by an assembly of representatives of the electorate. In practice, the generals ruled. In Argentina, for example, Juan Manuel de Rosas (1835–1852) assumed power amid widespread public disorder and ruled as dictator. In Mexico, liberals declared a federal republic, but incessant civil strife led to the rise of the dictator Antonia Lopez de Santa Anna in the mid-nineteenth century. Likewise in Venezuela, strongmen, dictators, and petty aristocratic oligarchs governed from 1830 to 1892. Some countries suffered constant revolutions: in the course of the century Bolivia had sixty and Venezuela fifty-two. The rule of force prevailed almost everywhere. Enlightened dictatorship was the typical form of government.

The wars of liberation disrupted the economic life of most Latin American countries. The prosperity many areas had achieved toward the end of the colonial period was destroyed. Mexico and Venezuela in particular lost large percentages of their populations and suffered great destruction of farm land and animals. Even countries that saw relatively little violence, such as Chile and New Granada, experienced a weakening of economic life. Armies were frequently recruited by force, and when the men were demobilized many did not return home. The consequent population dislocation hurt agriculture and mining. Guerrilla warfare disrupted trade and communications; forced loans and the seizure of private property for military use ruined many people. In the 1820s Peru's economy staggered under the burden of supporting large armies. Isolated territories such as Paraguay and much of Central America suffered little damage, but most countries gained independence at the price of serious economic problems.

Brazil and Cuba, which had very large slave populations, did not free them until long after independence. Elsewhere, however, independence accelerated the abolition of slavery. The destruction of agriculture in countries such as Mexico and Venezuela caused the collapse of the plantation system, and fugitive slaves could not be recaptured. Also, both the royalists and the patriot generals Bolívar and San Martín offered slaves freedom in exchange for military service. The result was that slaves constituted a large part of the military forces, perhaps a third of San Martín's army. Finally, most of the new independent states adopted republican constitutions declaring the legal equality of all men. For Indians and blacks, however, these noble words were meaningless, since the revolution brought about no redistribution of property. Nor could ancient racist attitudes be eliminated by the stroke of a pen.

Although the edifice of racism persisted in the nineteenth century, Latin America experienced much more assimilation and offered Negroes greater economic and social mobility than did the United States. As a direct result of their heroic military service in the wars of independence, a substantial number of Negroes improved their social status. Some even attained the political heights: the Mexican revolutionary Vicente Guerrero, who served as president of his country in 1829; Antonio Guzmán, who governed Venezuela as a benevolent dictator (1870–1888); and Ramón Castilla, whose term as president of Peru (1845–1851, 1855–1862) witnessed the strengthening of state financing.

What accounts for the relative racial permeability of Latin America in comparison with the system of severe segregation in the United States? As the Dutch scholar Hoetink points out, Latin American countries evolved a three-tiered socioracial structure, in contrast to the two-tiered racial edifice in the United States. Legally and socially, Latin American societies classified people as white, colored, or black, and marriages between whites and light-skinned colored people were commonly accepted. Legislative discrimination against colored people proved unenforceable. Thus light skin allowed for gradual assimilation into the middle and upper social echelons. In the United States, by contrast, anyone who was not "pure" white was classified as black.

Hoetink explains the problem partly in terms of the large population of poor whites in the United States. "Nowhere, but in the North American mainland, did the number of extremely poor whites always exceed the number of slaves. Nowhere, but in the [U.S.] South, were special police forces predominantly manned by poor whites."[12] Also, Latin American elites' perception of "whiteness" and of physical beauty seems to have been broader than that of the white majority in the United States.

The advantages of assimilation did not, and do not, apply to dark-skinned people in Latin America. While substantial numbers of light-skinned colored people rose economically and socially, the great mass of dark-skinned blacks continued to experience all the consequences of systematic and insistent racism.

NEOCOLONIALISM

The leaders of the Latin American revolutions had hoped that their nations, once independent, would attract European and North American investment. Instead, political instability and the preoccupation of European and North American financiers with industrial expansion in their own countries discouraged investment. The advent of stable dictatorships, however, eventually paved the way for real economic growth. After 1870 capital began to flow south and across the Atlantic. In Mexico, North American capital supported the production of hemp (used in the United States for grain harvesting), sugar, bananas, and rubber, frequently on American-owned plantations. British and American interests backed the development of Mexican tin, copper, and gold mining; oil drilling leaped forward, and by 1911 Mexico had taken third place among the world's oil producers. British financiers built Argentina's railroads, meat-packing industry, and utilities. British businessmen in Chile developed the copper and nitrate industries (nitrate is used in the production of pharmaceuticals and fertilizers); by 1890 the British controlled 70 percent of the nitrate industry. Likewise in Brazil, foreign capital—mainly British—flowed into coffee, cotton, and sugar production and manufacturing. In 1889 Brazil produced 56 percent of the world's coffee; by 1904 that figure had risen to 76 percent. When massive overproduction of coffee led to a sharp drop in prices in 1906, a commission of British, American, German, and French bankers rescued the Brazilian government from near disaster.

Thus, the economic development of Latin America at the end of the nineteenth century was purchased at the high price of a new, economic form of domination. Foreign investors acquired control of the railroads, mineral resources, and banking, and they made heavy inroads into real estate. British investments led all others, but beginning in 1898 the United States flexed its imperialistic muscles and sent gunboats and troops to defend its dollars in the Caribbean and Central America. By the turn of the century the Latin American nations were active participants in the international economic order, but foreigners controlled most of their industries.

Another distinctive feature of the neocolonial order was the cultivation of one crop. Each country's economy revolved around only one or two products: sugar in Cuba, nitrates and copper in Chile, meat in Argentina, coffee in Brazil. A sharp drop in the world market demand for a product could destroy the industry and with it the nation's economic structure. The outbreak of the First World War in 1914 drastically reduced exports of Latin American raw materials and imports of European manufactured goods, provoking general economic crisis.[13]

Throughout the eighteenth century the Spanish-owned *haciendas*—large landed estates—and plantations had continued to expand to meet the needs of commercial agriculture: wheat for the cities, corn for the Indians' consumption, sugar for export to Europe and North America. By means of purchase, forced removal of Indians, and outright seizure, the Spanish continued to take Indian land, as they had in the seventeenth century. Some land was acquired merely to eliminate Indian competition by depriving them of their fields, which were then left fallow.

The late nineteenth century witnessed ever greater concentrations of land in ever fewer hands. In places like the Valley of Mexico, a few large haciendas controlled all the land. Under the dictatorship of General Porfirio Díaz, the Mexican government in 1883 passed a law allowing real estate companies (controlled by Díaz's political cronies) to survey public and "vacant" lands and to retain one-third of the land they surveyed. An 1894 law provided that land could be declared vacant if legal title to it could not be produced. Since few Indians could come up with deeds to the land their ancestors had worked for centuries, the door swung open to wholesale expropriation of small landowners and entire villages. Shrewd speculators tricked illiterate Indians into selling their lands for trifling sums. Thousands of litigants immobilized the courts. Indians who dared armed resistance were crushed by government troops and carried off to virtual slave labor. Vast stretches of land came into the hands of private individuals—in one case, 12 million acres. According to one authority, "the government had divested itself of an area roughly equal to that of California or equal to the combined totals of Ohio, Indiana, Illinois, and half of Kentucky; . . . nearly one-fifth of the total land area

Mexico Today, Mexico Tomorrow In this detail from a huge mural cycle completed for the National Palace of Mexico City, the naturalist painter Diego Rivera (1886–1957), in the style of traditional Mexican folk art, celebrates the triumph of creative labor in farming, mining, and industry, and denounces the evils of capitalism. A member of the Mexican Communist party, Rivera condemned through his art what he considered the oppression of both communism and fascism. *(Rapelye/Art Resource)*

of Mexico."[14] The Indians, stripped of their lands, represented a ready labor supply. They were mercilessly exploited. Debt peonage became common practice: landowners paid their laborers not in cash but in vouchers, redeemable only at the company store, whose high prices and tricky bookkeeping kept the peons permanently in debt.

Some scholars maintain that the owners of these huge estates hardly exploited their land at all, letting it lie fallow until it rose in value or attracted American investors. The lack of cultivation, they assert, kept the prices of corn and other crops artificially high. Where the land was cultivated, landowners used antiquated machinery and old-fashioned methods of irrigation and fertilization. The owners themselves, supported by rents, passed indolent lives in extravagant luxury in Mexico City and other cities.

Recent scholars deny all this. They argue that the haciendas were in fact efficient capitalistic enterprises whose owners sought to maximize profits on invested capital. The Sanchez Navarro family of northwestern Mexico, for instance, engaged in a wide variety of agricultural and commercial pursuits, exploiting their lands and resources as fully as possible. The Sanchez Navarros controlled 800,000 acres in 1821, and continued to acquire chunks of land; ultimately their *latifundio*—an estate of two or more haciendas—was about the size of West Virginia. Along with vast cattle ranches and sheep runs containing as many as 250,000 sheep, the Sanchez Navarros cultivated maize, wheat, and cotton. They invested heavily and profitably in silver mining and manufacturing, and lent sizable sums at high interest. Although they brutally exploited their peons and practiced debt

Latin America, CA 1760–1900

1764–1780	Charles III of Spain's administrative and economic reforms
1781	Communero revolution in New Granada
1810–1825	Latin American wars of independence against Spain
1822	Proclamation by Portugal of Brazil's independence
1826	Call by Simón Bolívar for Panama Conference on Latin American union
1825–ca 1870	Political instability in most Latin American nations
ca 1870–1919	Latin American neocolonialism
1876–1911	Porfirio Diaz' control of Mexico
1888	Emancipation of slaves in Brazil; final abolition of slavery in Western Hemisphere
1880–1914	Massive immigration from Europe and Asia to Latin America
1898	Spanish American War; end of Spanish control over Cuba; transfer of Puerto Rico to United States

peonage, the Sanchez Navarros lived very modestly on their own estates rather than luxuriating in the capital. A final determination of whether the Sanchez Navarros were unique or representative of a type of magnate prevalent in the agricultural and business communities of nineteenth-century Mexico[15] must await further investigation.

The Impact of Immigration

In 1852 the Argentine political philosopher Juan Bautista Alberdi published a book, *Bases and Points of Departure for Argentine Political Organization,* arguing that "to govern is to populate." Alberdi meant that the development of his country—and, by extension, all of Latin America—depended on immigration. Argentina actually had an adequate labor supply, but it was unevenly distributed throughout the country. Moreover, Alberdi maintained, the Indians and blacks lacked basic skills and it would take too long to train them. Therefore he pressed for massive immigration from the "advanced" countries of northern Europe and the United States. Alberdi's ideas won immediate acceptance and were even incorporated into the Argentine constitution, which declared that "the Federal government will encour-

age European immigration." Other Latin American countries adopted similar policies promoting immigration.[16]

European needs coincided perfectly with those of Latin America (pages 938–940). After 1880, Ireland, Great Britain, Germany, Italy, Spain, and the central European nations experienced greater population growth than their labor markets could absorb. Meanwhile the growing industries of Europe needed South American raw materials and markets for their finished goods, and South American countries wanted European markets for their minerals, coffee, sugar, beef, and manufactured goods. Italian, Spanish, and Portuguese peoples poured into Latin America, and immigration linked the two hemispheres.

Immigration led to rapid urbanization, which meant Europeanization and industrialization. By 1900, Buenos Aires and Rio de Janeiro had populations of more than 500,000 people; Mexico City, Montevideo, Santiago de Chile, and Havana also experienced spectacular growth. Portuguese, Italian, French, Chinese, and Japanese immigrants gave an international flavor to the cities, and a more vigorous tempo replaced the somnolent Spanish atmosphere.

By 1914 Buenos Aires had emerged as one of the most cosmopolitan cities in the world. In less than half a century, the population of the city and its province had grown from 500,000 to 3.6 million. Argentina's political capital, the city housed all its governmental bureaucracies and agencies. The meat-packing, food-processing, flour-milling, and wool industries concentrated in Buenos Aires; half of all overseas tonnage passed through the city, which was also the heart of the nation's railroad network. The University of Buenos Aires was the intellectual hub of the nation. The elegant shops near the Plaza de Mayo catered to the expensive tastes of the elite upper classes, who constituted about 5 percent of the population.

Meanwhile the thousands of immigrants who toiled twelve hours a day, six days a week, on the docks and construction sites and in the meat-packing plants crowded into the city's *conventillos,* or tenements:

The one-room dwelling . . . served a family with two to five children or a group of four or five single men. At the door to each room stood a pile of wooden boxes. One generally held a basin for washing; another a charcoal brazier on which to cook the daily watery stew, or puchero; *and garbage accumulated in a third. Two or three iron cots, a pine table, a few wooden chairs, an old trunk, perhaps a sewing machine, and more boxes completed the furnishings. Light came from the open door and one window, from an oil or gas lamp, or occasionally from a bare electric light bulb. On the once-whitewashed walls were tacked pictures of popular heroes, generals, or kings torn from magazines, an image of the Madonna and a couple of saints, perhaps a faded photograph of family members in Europe. The women often eked out miserable incomes by taking in laundry and washing and drying it in the patios. Others ironed or sewed on a piece-work basis. Some men worked here: in one corner a shoemaker might ply his trade, in another a man might bend over a small table repairing watches.*[17]

Immigrants dreamed of rapid economic success in the New World, and there was in fact plenty of upward social mobility. The first generation almost always did manual labor, but its sons often advanced to upper blue-collar or white-collar jobs. The rare Genoese or Neapolitan immigrant whose labor and thrift made his son a millionaire quickly learned the meaning of assimilation: the son typically assumed the dress, style, and values of the Spanish elite. Hispanic attitudes toward class, manual labor, and egali-

Domestic Scenes in Mid-nineteenth-century Rio The servants, lace table cloth, and fancy dress of the mistress imply that this is a well-to-do household. The meal, consisting of meat, bread, fruit, and wine, seems to be eaten on imported china. *(Courtesy, Oliveira Lima Library, The Catholic University of America. Photo: Paul McKane, OSB)*

tarianism prevailed, and the new immigrant rich imitated the Spanish nobility.[18]

Europeans gave an enormous boost to the development of industry and commerce. Italian and Spanish settlers in Argentina stimulated the expansion of the cattle industry and the development of the wheat and shoe industries. In Brazil, English investments facilitated the growth of the iron industry and the railroads. Swiss immigrants built the cheese business, Italians gained a leading role in the coffee industry, and the Japanese pioneered the development of the cotton industry. In Peru, the British controlled railroad construction, Italians became influential in banking and the restaurant business, while the French dominated jewelry, dressmaking, and pharmaceutical ventures. The arrival of millions of migrants changed the entire commercial structure of South America.

Immigration also promoted further ethnic integration. The vast majority of migrants were unmarried males; seven out of ten people who landed in Argentina between 1857 and 1924 were single males between thirteen and forty years old. Those who stayed often sought out Indian or other lower-class women. This kind of assimilation also occurred in Brazil, Mexico, Peru, and other South American countries. Male settlers from eastern Europe and women of all nationalities preferred to marry within their own ethnic groups. But men greatly outnumbered women, and a man who chose to marry usually had to marry an Indian.[19] Immigration, then, furthered racial mixture of Europeans, Asians, and native South Americans.

For Latin America's sizable black population, immigration proved a calamity. Slavery had been technically abolished in Spanish America after independence and in Portuguese Brazil by 1888, but the economic and social status of the Negro population had scarcely changed. Accustomed to working the rural coffee plantations and the mines, blacks sometimes had little preparation for urban living. Many ex-slaves had skills, even for factory work, but racism explains the greater presence of immigrants in factories. In 1893, 71.2 percent of the working population of Sao Paulo was foreign-born. Anxious to adapt to America and to climb the economic ladder, immigrants quickly learned the ancient racial prejudices. Negro women usually found work as domestics, but employers excluded black males from good jobs. Racial prejudice kept the vast bulk of the South American black population in a wretched socioeconomic position until the Second World War.

After independence, the social structure of most Latin American countries remained basically unchanged. Republican constitutions declared all men (but not women) equal under the law, but everywhere—except perhaps in Venezuela—an aristocratic white agrarian class exercised wealth and power. European ideas, such as utopian socialism, entered Latin American ports and stimulated mild intellectual ferment, but made only a slight impact on social change before the twentieth century. Social

structure, capital, and market and labor conditions determined economic growth. In the United States, by contrast, a dynamic commercial and capitalistic elite held economic and political power at the turn of the century. As Great Britain and the United States came to hold neocolonial control over the Latin American economy, the ruling aristocracy gradually became receptive to capitalistic values and ideals. European styles of dress became highly popular because they signified social status. Modernization in industry and commerce, however, came only in the twentieth century.

THE UNITED STATES, 1789–1929

The victory of the North American colonies and the founding of the United States seemed to validate the Enlightenment idea that a better life on earth was possible (pages 653–660). Americans carried over into the nineteenth and twentieth centuries an unbounded optimism about the future. The vastness of the land and its untapped resources reinforced that faith. The young nation, confident of its "manifest destiny," pushed relentlessly across the continent. Westward movement, however, threatened to extend black slavery, which generated increasing disagreement between the industrialized North and the agricultural South. The ensuing Civil War cost more lives than any other war the nation was to fight. Union victory did not resolve the racial issue that had caused the war, but it did preserve the federal system and American confidence in the future.

The years between 1865 and 1917 witnessed the building of a new industrialized nation. Massive waves of immigrants pursued the frontier to its end, provided the labor to exploit the country's huge mineral resources, turned small provincial towns into sophisticated centers of ethnic and cultural diversity, and built the railroads that tied the country together. However, the American economy absorbed immigrants faster than American society did. The ideology of manifest destiny lived on after the frontier closed, and considerably affected United States-Latin American relations. In the First World War, American aid and American troops were the deciding factor in the Allied victory. After the war, "normalcy" and the façade of prosperity supported a persistent optimism. Only the Great Depression, beginning in 1929 and bringing enormous unemployment and terrible social problems, shook Americans' confidence in their potential and their future.

MANIFEST DESTINY

In an 1845 issue of the *United States Magazine and Democratic Review,* editor John L. O'Sullivan boldly declared that foreign powers were trying to prevent American annexation of Texas in order to impede "the fulfillment of our manifest destiny to overspread the continent allotted by Providence for the free development of our yearly multiplying millions." O'Sullivan was articulating a sentiment prevalent in the United States since early in its history: that God had foreordained the nation to cover the entire continent. After a large-circulation newspaper picked up the phrase "manifest destiny," it was used on the floor of Congress and soon entered the language as a catchword for and justification of expansion. The concept of manifest destiny played an important role in some basic developments in American history: the settlement of peoples of diverse nationalities, the issue of slavery, the conflict over whether the United States was to remain agrarian or become a commercial and industrial society.

When George Washington took the presidential oath of office on Wall Street in 1789, fewer than 4 million people inhabited the thirteen states on the eastern seaboard. By the time Abraham Lincoln became the sixteenth president in 1861, the United States was as large as it is today, excepting Alaska and Hawaii, and had 31 million inhabitants. During the colonial period, pioneers had pushed westward to the Appalachian Mountains. After independence, westward movement accelerated. The eastern states claimed all the land from the Atlantic to the Mississippi River, but two forces blocked immediate expansion. The Indians, trying to save their lands, allied with the British in Canada to prevent further American encroachment. However, the federal government, with an almost empty treasury, wanted revenue from land sales. In 1794 special commissioner John Jay concluded a treaty whereby Britain agreed to evacuate border forts in the Northwest Territory, which meant the end of British support for the Indians. A similar treaty with Spain paved the way for southeastern expansion (Map 31.3).

Events in Europe and the Caribbean led to a massive increase in American territory. In 1800 Spain ceded the Louisiana Territory—the land between the Mississippi and the Rocky Mountains—to France. Napoleon intended to use the Louisiana Territory to make France an imperial power in America, but a black revolution on the island of Hispaniola (present-day Haiti and Santa Domingo) upset his plans. Under Toussaint L'Ouverture, Haiti's 500,000 slaves revolted against their 40,000 white owners. Napoleon quickly dispatched troops with orders to crush the revolt, seize New Orleans, and take possession of the Louisiana Territory. President Thomas Jefferson, alarmed at the prospect of a French army on U.S. territory, ordered the American minister in Paris, Robert Livingston, to negotiate to buy the Louisiana Territory.

When yellow fever and Haitian bullets carried off most of the French troops, Napoleon relinquished his grandiose plans. He was planning war with Great Britain and realized that France's weak sea power could not prevent Britain from taking Louisiana. The day Napoleon opened hostilities with England, his foreign minister Talleyrand casually asked Livingston, "What would you give us for the whole of Louisiana?" The astonished American proposed $4 million. "Too low!" said Talleyrand. "Reflect and see me tomorrow." Less than three weeks later the deed of sale was signed. The United States paid only $12 million for millions of acres of some of the world's richest farm land; the Louisiana Purchase has proved to be the greatest bargain in U.S. history.

Scarcely was the ink dry on the treaty when pressure rose in the western sections of the United States for war with England: western settlers wanted further expansion. Repeated British attacks on American vessels on the high seas and British interference in American trade provided diplomatic justification for war. In fact, the "war hawks" believed a war with Britain would yield Canada, permanently end Indian troubles, and open up vast forest land for additional expansion. The Treaty of Ghent (1814) ended the conflict; ultimately the boundary situation prior to 1812 prevailed.

Peace launched the "Great Migration" as settlers poured into the Northwest and the Gulf Plains. Congress sold land in lots of 160 acres at $2 an acre; only $80 was needed as down payment, enabling even the poorest person to buy a farm. Irish and German immigrants rapidly put the black earth of Indiana and Illinois under cultivation; pioneers of American stock planted cotton in the lush delta of the Gulf

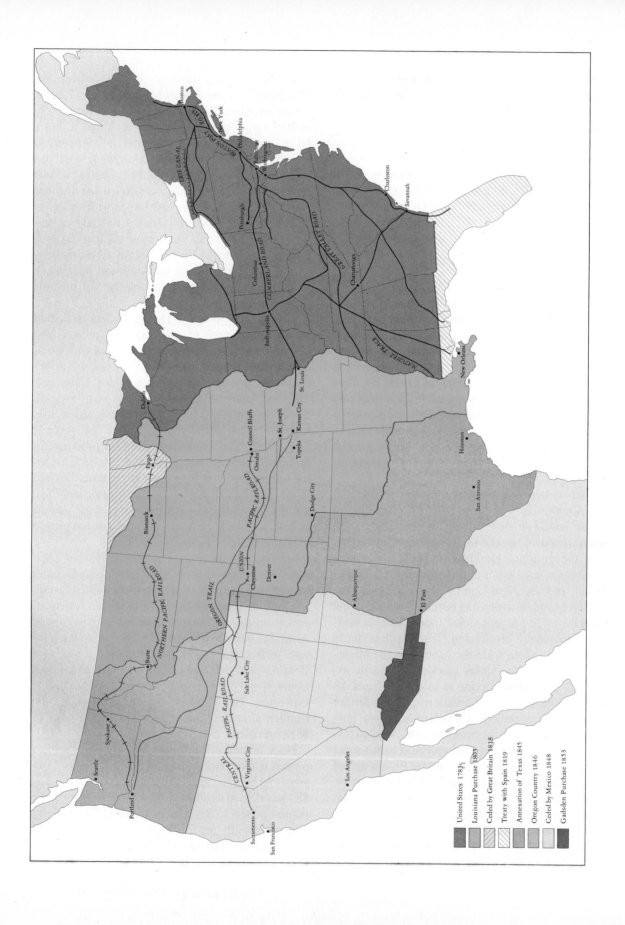

United States 1783
Louisiana Purchase 1803
Ceded by Great Britain 1818
Treaty with Spain 1819
Annexation of Texas 1845
Oregon Country 1846
Ceded by Mexico 1848
Gadsden Purchase 1853

ERIE CANAL
BOSTON POST ROAD
CUMBERLAND ROAD
GREAT VALLEY ROAD
NATCHEZ TRACE
UNION PACIFIC RAILROAD
NORTHERN PACIFIC RAILROAD
CENTRAL PACIFIC RAILROAD
OREGON TRAIL

Boston
New York
Philadelphia
Baltimore
Washington
Pittsburgh
Columbus
Charleston
Savannah
Chattanooga
Indianapolis
New Orleans
St. Louis
Duluth
St. Joseph
Kansas City
Council Bluffs
Omaha
Topeka
Houston
Dodge City
Fargo
San Antonio
Bismarck
Denver
Cheyenne
Albuquerque
El Paso
Butte
Salt Lake City
Spokane
Seattle
Virginia City
Los Angeles
Portland
Sacramento
San Francisco

MAP 31.3 **Territorial Growth of the United States** The Cumberland Road between Cumberland, Maryland and—by 1833—Columbus, Ohio, and the Erie Canal, which linked New York City and the Great Lakes region, carried thousands of easterners and immigrants to the Old Northwest and the frontier beyond. Transcontinental railroads subsequently made all the difference.

Plains; Scandinavian and German settlers found the softly rolling hills of the Wisconsin country ideal for cattle herds. As a popular song of the era ran, "Ioway, Ioway, that's where the tall corn grows."

Meanwhile Spain, preoccupied with South American rebellions, sold the Florida territory to the federal government. Beginning in 1821 settlers poured into the Mexican territory of Texas, whose soil proved excellent for the production of cotton and sugar. Contemptuous of the dictatorial and incompetent government of the Mexican President Santa Anna, Texans seceded from Mexico and proclaimed an independent republic in 1836. Southern politicians, fearing that Texas would become a refuge for fugitive slaves, pressured President Tyler to admit Texas to the Union. A joint resolution of Congress, hastily signed by Tyler, did so in 1845.

The absorption of Texas's 267,339 square miles (France, by comparison, covers 211,200 square miles) whetted American appetites for the rest of the old Spanish Empire in North America. Some expansionists even dreamed of Cuba and Central America. President Polk tried to buy California from Mexico, but Mexicans harbored a grudge over the annexation of Texas and refused to do business. Exploiting Mexico's political instability, Polk goaded Mexico into war. When a cavalry skirmish in disputed border territory led to several American deaths, Polk announced to Congress, "The cup of forbearance has been exhausted. After reiterated menaces, Mexico has passed the boundary of the United States, has invaded our territory and shed American blood on American soil." Congress obligingly responded that "by act of the Republic of Mexico, a state of war exists between that Government and the United states." Texas and the Mississippi valley states, eager for more slave territory, rushed 49,000 soldiers "to revel in the halls of Montezuma." Mexico suffered total defeat. In the Treaty of Guadalupe Hidalgo (1848), Mexico surrendered its claims to Texas, yielded New Mexico and California, and recognized the Rio Grande as the international border. A treaty with Great Britain in 1846 had already recognized the American settlement in the Oregon territory. The continent had been acquired. The nation's "manifest destiny" was fulfilled.

THE FATE OF THE INDIANS

But what of the millions of Indians—the only native Americans—who inhabited this vast territory? As the dean of American historians, Samuel Eliot Morison, recounts, "An American journalist who had spent several years in India, and whose small children had come to love the Indians, came home in 1958. Shortly thereafter he found the boys crying as they watched a TV 'Western' because, as one moaned, 'They're killing Indians!' Papa had to explain that these were not Indians of India but Red Indians, and that to kill them was part of the American Way of Life."[20] And so it was.

While the Indians faithfully observed their treaties with the United States, "white pioneers in the Northwest committed the most wanton and cruel murders of them, for which it was almost impossible to obtain a conviction from a pioneer jury."[21] Government officials frequently manipulated the Indians by gathering a few chiefs, plying them with cheap whiskey, and then inducing them to hand over their tribes' hunting grounds. By this method William Henry Harrison, superintendent of the Indians of the Northwest Territory and a future president, got the native Americans to part with 48 million acres. He had the full backing of President Jefferson.

The policy of pushing the Indians westward across the Mississippi, which President Monroe's administration had adopted early in the century, accelerated during Andrew Jackson's presidency (1829–1837). Thousands of Delaware, Shawnee, and Wyandot, tricked into moving from the Northwest Territory to reservations west of Missouri, died of cholera and measles during the journey. The survivors found themselves hopelessly in debt for supplies and farming equipment. The state of Georgia, meanwhile, was nibbling away at Cherokee lands, which were theoretically protected by treaty with the United States government. Then gold was discovered on the Cherokee lands, and a gold rush occurred. A Vermont missionary, the Reverend Samuel C. Worcester, carried the Indians' case to the Supreme Court. When Chief Jus-

Sioux Camp in South Dakota The Sioux were a nomadic people who lived in harmony with the natural environment. Once they moved from a place, the abandoned landscape looked almost undisturbed. This photograph, taken in 1891, shows a scene characteristic of their camps. *(Library of Congress)*

tice John Marshall ruled that the laws of Georgia had no force within the Cherokee territory—which meant that white settlers and gold rustlers had to leave—President Jackson retorted, "John Marshall has made his decision. Now let him enforce it." The Creek, Cherokee, and other tribes were rounded up, expelled, and sent beyond the western boundaries of Missouri and Arkansas; they were guaranteed complete possession of their new reservations "as long as grass grows and water runs."[22] The shameful price of westward expansion was the dislocation and extermination of millions of native Americans (Map 31.4).

BLACK SLAVERY IN THE SOUTH

Since the first black slaves landed in the Virginia colony in 1619, slavery and race relations have posed a serious dilemma for the American majority. A powerful array of moral, legal, political, and sociological arguments have characterized slavery as a great evil, an irrational and peculiar institution, a violation of the central principle of the Declaration of Independence that all men are created equal. Eighteenth- and nineteenth-century Americans, however, could not decide whether the ringing words of the Declaration applied to blacks. As one scholar recently posed the question,

How did the slave-holding class, which was molded by the same forces that shaped the nation, which fought America's wars and helped inspire its Revolution, a class which boasted of its patriotism, its devotion to freedom, its adherence to the major tenets of liberalism—how did such a class justify its continuing commitment to slavery and remain so steadfast in that commitment that it willingly separated from the Union it had helped to create? In short, how could the slaveholders' ideology prove so malleable as to reinforce simultaneously their devotion to black slavery and to democratic freedom? It is here, in the triumph of the slaveholders' liberalism, that the legacy of slavery becomes a truly American dilemma.[23]

MAP 31.4 Indian Cession of Lands to the United States Forced removal of the Creek, Cherokee, and Chickasaw Indians led to the deaths of thousands on the famous Trail of Tears to reservations in Oklahoma, and to the destruction of their cultures.

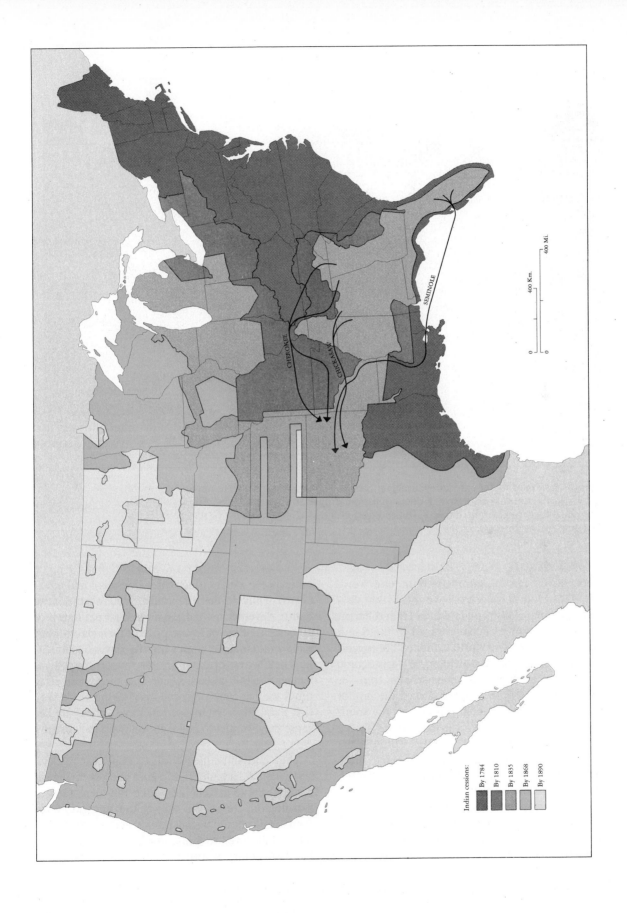

SEMINOLE

CHEROKEE

CHICKASAW

Indian cessions:

By 1784
By 1810
By 1835
By 1868
By 1890

400 Km.
400 Mi.
0
0

Making Bricks Because they are more durable than stone and resistant to high temperatures, bricks have always been in high demand for building in the United States. Black workers like these in Georgia in the 1870s produced millions. *(Courtesy of the Georgia Department of Archives and History)*

The answer can be summarized in one word: profit. A long line of historians have argued that slavery was not financially productive, and that different social and economic values prevailed in the South than in the North. The North exhibited "bourgeois capitalist" values, the South embraced "aristocratic anticapitalist" values. As one scholar put it, "Whereas in the North people followed the lure of business and money for their own sake, in the South specific forms of property carried the badges of honor, prestige, and power."[24] In other words, slaveowners cared about profits, but they cared more about the social prestige and political power that the slaveowner enjoyed in the Old South. But this was not so. The economic historians Fogel and Engerman have convincingly demonstrated that southern planters were not indolent aristocrats but "hard, calculating businessmen who priced their slaves, and

other assets, with as much shrewdness as could be expected of any northern capitalist."[25] Across the entire South, slaveowners realized an annual net return of 10 percent of the purchase price of their slaves, both male and female. A man with fifty slaves had an annual net income of about $7,500 (roughly the equivalent of $75,000 today), which was more than sixty times the per capita income in 1860; he was a very rich man. Planters engaged in slave agriculture because they wanted to make a profit, and they usually did so.

They and subsequently all of American society, however, paid a high price in guilt and psychological conflict. Some slaveholders, like President George Washington, found the subject too uncomfortable even to talk about: "I shall frankly declare to you that I do not like even to think, much less talk of it."[26] In the half-century before the Civil War, most slaveowners were deeply religious. On the one hand, they taught their children to get rich by the accumulation of land and slaves; on the other hand, they taught that God would punish the greedy with eternal damnation. Slaveholders justified slavery by dismissing blacks as inferior, but religion preached that in the eyes of God black and white were equal and would ultimately be judged on that basis. This posed a terrible psychological contradiction that few could resolve. Some slaveowners felt completely trapped by the system. As one master wrote, "I cannot just take them up and sell them though that would be clearly the best I could do for myself. I cannot free them. I cannot keep them with comfort. . . . What would I not give to be freed from responsibility for these poor creatures." Perhaps even more than men, women of the planter class felt troubled by slavery. The South Carolina aristocrat Mary Boykin Chesnut confided to her diary in 1861,

I wonder if it be a sin to think slavery a curse to any land. Sumner [the Massachusetts senator and abolitionist who bitterly denounced slavery in the U.S. Senate] said not one word of this hated institution which is not true. Men and women are punished when their masters and mistresses are brutes and not when they do wrong. . . . God forgive us, but ours is a monstrous system and wrong and iniquity. Perhaps the rest of the world is as bad—this only I see. Like the patriarchs of old our men live all in one house with their wives and their concubines, and the mulattoes one sees in every family exactly resemble the white children—and every lady tells you who is the father of all the mulatto children in everybody's household, but those in her own she seems to think drop from the clouds, or pretends so to think. . . . my disgust sometimes is boiling over. . . . Thank God for my countrywomen— alas for the men! No worse than men everywhere but the lower their mistresses, the more degraded they must be.[27]

Mary Chesnut believed that most white women of the South were abolitionists in their hearts, and fiery ones too. Though Mary Chesnut enjoyed the attentions and services of her slaves, when Lincoln issued the Emancipation Proclamation she welcomed it with "an unholy joy."[28]

WESTWARD EXPANSION AND CIVIL WAR

Cotton was king in the mid-nineteenth century, and cotton carried slavery westward. It was westward ex-

pansion, not moral outrage, that brought the controversy over slavery to a head. As Congress created new territories, the question of whether slavery would be extended arose again and again (Map 31.5). For years elaborate compromises were worked out, but the North increasingly feared that the South was intent on controlling the nation. The South feared that free territories would harbor fugitive slaves. Issues of sectional political power became more and more heated.

In the 1850s the question of the further expansion of slavery agitated the nation. Perhaps no statesman better summarized the dilemma than Lincoln in a speech in 1854:

When they [southern proponents of expansion] remind us of their constitutional rights, I acknowledge them, not grudgingly, but fully, and fairly; and I would give them any legislation for the reclaiming of their fugitives, which should not, in its stringency, be more likely to carry a free man into slavery, than our ordinary criminal laws are to hang an innocent one. . . . But all this, to my judgment, furnishes no more excuse for permitting slavery to go into our own free territory, than it would for reviving the African slave trade by law.

Slavery is founded in the selfishness of man's nature —opposition to it, in his love of justice. These principles are in eternal antagonism; and when brought into collision so fiercely, as slavery extension brings them, shocks, and throes, and convulsions must ceaselessly follow.[29]

Accepting the Republican party nomination for a seat in the U.S. Senate in 1858, Lincoln predicted the tragic events ahead:

A house divided against itself cannot stand.
I believe this government cannot endure, permanently half slave and half free.
I do not expect the Union to be dissolved—I do not expect the house to fall—but I do expect it will cease to be divided.
It will become all one thing, or all the other.
Either the opponents of slavery will arrest the further spread of it, and place it where the public mind shall rest in the belief that it is in the course of ultimate extinction; or its advocates will push it forward, till it shall become alike lawful in all the States, old as well as new—North as well as South.[30]

In this and every other speech Lincoln made between 1854 and his election to the presidency in 1860, he

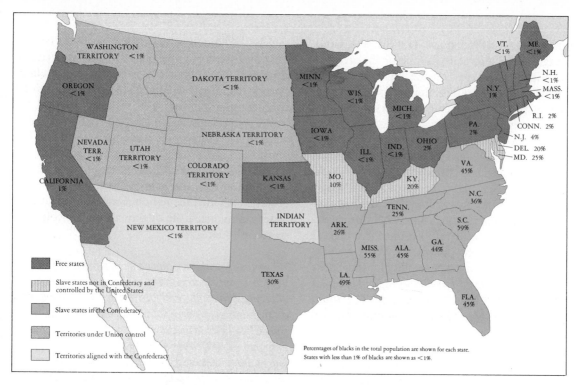

Map 31.5 Slavery in the United States, 1860 The Confederacy waged an heroic struggle, but the North's industrial might and the waves of immigrants who fought in the Union army decided the war. Note the slave populations of such states as South Carolina and Mississippi and consider how they influenced the later social and economic history of those regions.

argued against slavery less on moral or legal grounds than in terms of free labor's self-interest. If slavery continued to expand, Lincoln insisted, it would become a nationwide institution. He appealed to both immigrants and native-born whites when he declared that slavery should be excluded from new territories so that they could be "an outlet for free white people everywhere, the world over—in which Hans, and Baptiste, and Patrick, and all other men from all the world, may find new homes and better their condition in life."[31] Free white workers, in other words, could not compete in the labor market against blacks. Therefore the territories should be kept open. To protest Lincoln's victory in the election of 1860, South Carolina seceded from the Union in December 1860. Ten southern states soon followed South Carolina's example and formed the Confederacy with its capital at Richmond, Virginia.

When the Civil War began in 1861, Lincoln fought it to preserve the Union and to maintain the free labor system; the abolition of slavery was a secondary outcome, which he in fact tried to avoid. When a general in the field declared the slaves of South Carolina and Georgia free, Lincoln overruled the order. He wanted to bring the seceding states back into the Union with their institutions intact. To many people it seemed absurd to fight the Confederacy, which depended upon slavery to wage the war, without abolishing slavery. As one historian has put it, Lincoln wanted "to conduct the war for the preservation of the *status quo,* which had produced the war."[32] Only when the war dragged on and the slaughter had become frightful on both sides, only when it appeared that Great Britain might recognize the Confederacy, and when it had been proved obvious that the southern war effort benefited considerably from slave labor—only then did Lincoln, reluctantly, resolve on emancipation. The Emancipation Proclamation, which became effective on January 1, 1863, expressed no moral indignation. It freed slaves only in those states and areas in rebellion against the United States—the very places it was least effective; it preserved slavery in states loyal to the United States or under military jurisdiction. As the London *Spectator* sneered, "The principle is not that a human being cannot justly own another, but that he cannot own him unless he is loyal to the United States."[33] The Emancipation Proclamation nevertheless spelled the doom of North American slavery. It transformed the war from a political struggle to preserve the Union into a moral crusade for the liberty of all Americans.

European and English liberals greeted the announcement with great joy. A gathering of working people in Manchester, England, wrote President Lincoln:

The erasure of that foul blot upon civilization and Christianity—chattel slavery—during your Presidency will cause the name of Abraham Lincoln to be honoured and revered by posterity. Accept our high admiration of your firmness in upholding the proclamation of freedom.[34]

As Lincoln acknowledged, this statement reflects enormous charity, because the Civil War deeply affected Manchester working people. In fact, it had a worldwide impact socially and economically.

Because the English and continental textile industries relied on raw American cotton, the Confederacy sought European help. In 1861, however, England had a 50 percent oversupply of fiber and cotton cloth; a huge crop, 23 billion pounds, shipped before the Union blockade, filled British warehouses. Cotton brokers in Manchester and Liverpool sold their stock at huge profits. By 1862, however, the English picture had changed. Deprived of cotton, the mills of Lancashire closed. Tens of thousands of workers were thrown out of work and starved. Many emigrated to the United States. Between 1862 and 1864, efforts to alleviate the terrible suffering severely taxed the resources of the British government. The depression forced English manufacturers to search for new markets, and the Civil War stimulated cotton production in Egypt, India, and Brazil. The demands of English industry for Egyptian and Indian cotton played a significant role in the expansion of the English merchant marine fleet. Although England initially opposed construction of the Suez Canal, it later became a major shareholder; Suez was the swiftest route to Indian cotton.

The war also had important political consequences in Europe. In 1861 British and European opinion had divided along class lines. The upper classes sympathized with the American South, while the commercial classes and working people sided with the North. The English people interpreted the northern victory as a triumph for the democratic experiment over aristocratic oligarchy. The Union success proved that popular government worked. Thus, the United States gave a powerful stimulus to those in Britain and elsewhere who supported the cause of political democracy. When parliaments debated the extension of suffrage, the American example was frequently cited.

Military historians describe the American Civil War as the first modern war. "It was the first conflict in which the massive productive capacities of the Industrial Revolution were placed at the disposal of the miliary machine. It witnessed the first prominent use of mass production of goods to sustain mass armies, mass transportation on railroads, and telegraphic communication between different theaters and on the battlefield. It saw also the first use of such devices of the future as armored warships, breech-loading and repeating rifles, rifled artillery, land and sea mines, submarines, balloons, precursors of the machine gun, and trench warfare. . . . In its material manifestations alone, in its application of the resources of technology to the business of killing, the Civil War presaged the later world wars."[35]

In April 1865, the Confederate general Robert E. Lee surrendered his army at Appomattox Court House in Virginia, ending the costliest and bloodiest war Americans had ever fought. Lincoln had called for "malice toward none and charity for all" in his second inaugural address in 1864, and planned a generous policy toward the defeated South. The bullet that killed him brought on a different kind of reconstruction, the central figure in which was the Negro.

During Reconstruction (1865–1877), the vanquished South adjusted to a new social and economic order without slavery, and the eleven Confederate states rejoined the Union. Congress and the nation debated the political and social status of the Negro in the reconstructed South. For former slaves, Reconstruction represented the opportunity to exercise their new freedom, but southerners detested the very notion of social equality and northerners were ambivalent on the subject. In practical terms, Reconstruction meant the reunion of black families separated before emancipation. Blacks wanted land to farm but, lacking cash, they soon accepted the sharecropping system: farmers paid landowners about half of the year's crops at harvest time in return for a cabin, food, mules, seed, and tools the rest of the year. Believing that education was the key to economic advancement, blacks flocked to country schools and to colleges supported by northern religious groups. Although the Fifteenth Amendment forbade states to deny anyone the vote "on account of race, color, or previous condition of servitude," whites used violence, terror, and, between 1880 and 1920, so-called Jim Crow laws to prevent blacks from voting and to enforce rigid racial segregation. Lacking strong northern support, blacks did not gain legal equality or suffrage in many parts of the old Confederacy until the 1960s.

THE BLACK FAMILY

What impact did slavery have on the black family? Able scholars, both black and white, have long maintained that the enslavement of Africans in the eighteenth century led to the deterioration of the black family as a social unit in the nineteenth and twentieth centuries. As two authorities put it, "The most rudimentary type of family organization was not permitted to survive, to say nothing of the extensions of the family. The mother-child family, with the father either unknown, absent, or, if present, incapable of wielding influence, was the only type of family that could survive."[36] However, Herbert G. Gutman's authoritative *The Black Family in Slavery and Freedom, 1750–1925* has demonstrated that such theories are not supported by fact. In spite of the destructive effects of slavery, Afro-Americans established strong family units.

Most slave couples had long marriages. A study of the entire adult slave population of North Carolina in 1860 has shown that 25 percent of slave marriages lasted between ten and nineteen years, 20 percent lasted at least twenty years, and almost 10 percent endured thirty years or more. Most slave women spent their entire adult lives in settled unions with the same husband. In 1864–1865 Union Army officers who recorded slave marriages were deeply impressed by their durability. As one white soldier wrote, "It is not pretended that all marriages that have taken place were well advised, or will be happy, or faithfully observed. When marriages among whites shall all prove so, without exception, it will be time to look for such a happy state among blacks. . . . Marriage is not treated as a light matter."[37] Planters encouraged slave

marriages, because, as one owner put it, "marriage adds to the comfort, happiness, and health of those entering upon it, besides insuring a greater increase." Large slave families advanced owners' economic interests, and planters rewarded slave women who had many children.[38]

Forcible separation due to the sale of one partner proved the greatest threat to the permanence of slave marriages. In spite of illiteracy, separated spouses tried to remain in touch with one another. Once slavery had been abolished, separated couples went to enormous lengths to reunite their families. Evidence from all parts of the South reveals that this was the common pattern.

Women often had to resist the attentions of the slaveowners themselves; in addition, owners not infrequently supplied slave women with black men who had reputations for sexual prowess. Slave women, however, made choices: they tried to select their own husbands, rejecting—up to the point of risking being sold—mates chosen by their owners.

Historians of medicine know little about the birth-control methods used by slave couples. Considerable information survives, however, about abortion. In 1860 a Tennessee physician reported that slave women tried to abort by "medicine," "violent exercise," and other means. Cotton plants were "habitually and effectively resorted to by slaves of the South for producing abortion."[39]

Typically, slave women had their first child around the age of nineteen. The continual labor shortage in the South led slaveowners to encourage slaves to produce children rapidly. Owners urged slave women to begin bearing children as teenagers and to have more children rapidly thereafter. On the Good Hope plantation in South Carolina, for example, 80 percent of slave couples had at least four children. Almost all women had all their children by one husband, and most children grew to their teens in households with both parents present. Although premarital intercourse was common among slaves—though not as common as among young American adults during the 1970s—the weight of the evidence shows that women rarely engaged in extramarital sexual activity.

Settled slave marriages provided models for growing children, which allowed them to pass a strong tradition of marital and kin obligations from generation to generation. The pattern of stable black marriages lasted well into the present century. Research on black households in New York City in 1925 shows

The Hoggard Family, Jersey City, New Jersey, 1928 The black church exercised a powerful social influence in the black community, and—as this family portrait suggests—the minister expected good behavior, especially of his own children. The Hoggard children later became government officials, social workers, a college professor, a bishop. *(Courtesy, Philip Hoggard)*

that 85 percent were headed by two parents.[40] The period since the Great Depression of 1929 has witnessed a general decline in the stability of American families, both white and black. Shifting values throughout American society, such as changed sexual attitudes and an enormous increase in the divorce rate, have increased the proportion of black families headed by one parent. In recent decades, the 1980 census shows, the difference between black and white wages has narrowed, but total household income has remained highly divergent because many more black households depended on the income of a single parent. The decline in family stability has proved an obstacle to black economic advancement.

INDUSTRIALIZATION AND IMMIGRATION

After the Civil War the United States underwent a gigantic industrial boom based on exploitation of the country's natural resources. The federal government turned over vast amounts of land and mineral resources to industry for development. In particular, the railroads—the foundation of industrial expansion—received 130 million acres. By 1900 the American railroad system was 193,000 miles long, connected every part of the nation, and represented 40 percent of the railroad mileage of the entire world. Immigrant workers built it.

The late nineteenth and early twentieth centuries witnessed the immigration of unprecedented numbers of Europeans and Asians to the United States (see page 940). Between 1860 and 1900, 14 million immigrants came, and during the peak years between 1900 and 1914, another 14 million passed through the customs inspection at Ellis Island in New York City. All sought a better life and higher standard of living. The immigrants' ambitions precisely matched the labor needs of the times. Chinese, Scandinavian, and Irish immigrants laid 30,000 miles of railroad tracks between 1867 and 1873, and another

The Irish Vote As Irish immigrants arrived in torrential waves in the 1880s and 1890s, American politicians began to recognize the potential of the Irish vote. Here a British cartoonist viciously caricatures both leading politicians, kowtowing, and the "Irish Vote." *(Puck, American Heritage Collection)*

73,000 miles in the 1880s. Poles, Hungarians, Bohemians, and Italians poured into the coal and iron mines of western Pennsylvania and Appalachia. The steel magnate Andrew Carnegie recruited southern and eastern European immigrants for his smoking mills around Pittsburgh, Cleveland, and Gary, Indiana. The Carnegie Steel Corporation (later USX), worked almost entirely by Slavs and Italians, produced one-third of the world's total annual steel supply in 1900. John D. Rockefeller, whose Standard Oil Company earned tens of billions of dollars, employed thousands of Czechs, Poles, and other Slavs in his oil fields around the country. Lithuanians, Poles, Croats, Scandinavians, Irish, and Negroes entered the Chicago stockyards and built the meat-packing industry. Irish immigrants continued to operate the spinning frames and knitting machines of New England's textile mills. Industrial America developed on the sweat and brawn—the cheap labor—of its immigrant millions.

As industrial expansion transformed the eastern half of the United States, settlers conquered the trans-Mississippi West. Thousands of land-hungry farmers moved westward, where land was still only $1.25 an acre. In the final third of the nineteenth century, the last pioneers acquired 430 million acres and put 225 million of them under cultivation.

The West also held precious metals. The discovery of gold and silver in California, Colorado, Arizona, Montana, and on the reservations of the Sioux Indians of South Dakota precipitated huge rushes. Even before 1900, miners had extracted $1.24 billion in gold and $901 million in silver from western mines. Some miners left the West as soon as they had made their piles, but others settled down to farm and help their territories toward statehood. By 1912 the West had been won and the last frontier closed.

In the entire movement westward, women shared with men the long and dangerous journey, and then the dawn-to-dusk backbreaking work of carving a homestead out of the wilderness. Generally speaking, the frontier blurred sex roles: women commonly did the same agricultural work as men.[41] In addition, it fell to women to "make a home" out of crude log cabins without windows or doors or tarpaper shacks with mud floors, if they were lucky; more frequently, settlers lacked even a roof over their heads. One "gently reared" bride of seventeen took one look at her mud roof and dirt floor and indignantly announced, "My father had a much better house for his hogs!" Lacking cookstoves, they had to prepare food over open fireplaces, using all kinds of substitutes for ingredients easily available back East. Before they could wash clothes, women had to make soap out of lye and carefully saved household ashes.

Considered the carriers of "high culture," women organized such educational, religious, musical, and recreational activities as frontier society possessed. Frontierswomen also had to defend their homes against prairie fires and Indian attacks. These burdens were accompanied by frequent pregnancies, and women often gave birth without medical help or even the support of other women. Frontier women often used such contraceptive devices as spermicides, condoms, and, after 1864, vaginal diaphragms and abortifacients. Even so, frontier women had large families; the death rate for infants and young children ran as high as 30 percent in the mid-nineteenth century.

As in South America, immigration led to rapid urbanization. In 1790 only 5.1 percent of Americans had lived in centers of 2,500 or more people. By 1860 this figure had risen to 19.9 percent, and by 1900 almost 40 percent lived in cities. The overwhelming majority of the southern and eastern Europeans who came to North America at the turn of the century became urban industrial workers, their entire existence framed by the factory and the tenement. Newly uprooted from rural Europe, Italians, Greeks, Croats, Hungarians, Czechs, Poles, Russians, and Jews contrasted sharply with urban surroundings and with each other. Older residents saw only "a sea of strange faces, babbling in alien tongues and framed by freakish clothes. Walking through these multitudes now was really like a voyage round the globe."[42]

Between 1880 and 1920 industrial production soared. New inventions such as the steam engine, the dynamo (generator), and the electric light were given industrial and agricultural applications. Transcontinental railroads and technological innovations like the sewing machine and the assembly line made large-scale production more economical. Large factories replaced small ones, because only large factories could buy large machines, operate them at full capacity, and take advantage of railroad discount rates. In the automobile industry, for example, Henry Ford of Detroit set up assembly lines where each worker, instead of assembling an entire car, performed only one task in the flow of automobile construction. In 1910 Ford sold 10,000 cars; in 1914, a year after he inaugurated the first moving assembly line, he sold 248,000 cars. Such developments changed the face of American society. Sewing machines made cheap, varied, mass-produced clothing available to city people in department stores and to country people through mail-order catalogues. The automobile increased opportunities for travel, general mobility, and change.

By the 1890s factory managers were stressing industrial efficiency and the importance of time. Management engineers wanted to produce more at lower cost, which meant reducing labor costs by eliminating unnecessary workers. As the quantity rather than the quality of goods produced became the measure of acceptable work, workers' skills were less valued. As assembly-line workers increasingly performed only monotonous and time-determined work, in effect they became interchangeable parts of the machines they operated.

Despite accelerated production, and perhaps because of overproduction, the national economy experienced repeated cycles of boom and bust in the late nineteenth century. Serious depressions in 1873, 1884, and 1893 slashed prices and threw many people out of work. Leading industrialists responded by establishing larger corporations and trusts. Trusts granted control of their stock to a board of trustees, which then managed the operation of all the companies the trust owned. The legalization of trusts led to huge conglomerates, such as John D. Rockefeller's Standard Oil Company, which as a result of the merger of several smaller oil companies controlled 84 percent of the nation's oil in 1898. Standard Oil also controlled most American pipelines and was involved in natural gas production. Standard Oil monopolized the oil industry, J. P. Morgan's United States Steel the iron and steel industries, and Swift & Co. of Chicago the meat-processing industry.

Industrialization led to the creation of a vast class of salaried workers who depended totally on their employers for work. Corporate managers, however,

New York's Lower East Side For the thousands of East European Jews who fled the shtetls (rural communities) of Russia and Poland, American cities were their first experience of urban life. Besides the frightful squalor of the tenements, the noise, size of buildings, and rush of daily existence were terrifying experiences. Fierce determination backed by centuries of social endurance gave them the moral power to persevere. *(Library of Congress)*

were always preoccupied with cutting labor costs. Thus employers paid workers piecemeal for the number of articles produced, to encourage the use of the new machines; managers hired more women and children and paid them much less than men. Most women worked in the textile industry; some earned as little as $1.56 for seventy hours work, while men received $7 to $9 for the same work. And employers reduced wages, forcing workers to toil longer and harder to maintain the same incomes. Because owners fought in legislatures and courts against the

installation of safety devices, working conditions in mines and mills were frightful. In 1913, even after some safety measures had been taken, 25,000 people died in industrial accidents, and between 1900 and 1917, 72,000 railroad worker deaths occurred. Workers responded with strikes, violence, and, gradually, unionization.

Urbanization brought serious problems. In *How the Other Half Lives* (1890), a newspaper reporter and recent immigrant from Denmark, Jacob Riis, drew national attention to what he called "the foul core of New York's slums." His phrase "the other half" soon became a synonym for the urban poor. Riis estimated that 300,000 people inhabited a single square mile on New York's Lower East Side. Overcrowding, poor sanitation, and lack of health services caused frequent epidemics. The blight of slums increased crime, prostitution, alcoholism, and other drug-related addictions. Riis attacked the vicious economic exploitation of the immigrant poor and the dangers to our political system:

The slum complaint had been chronic in all ages, but the great changes which the nineteenth century saw, the new industry, political freedom, brought on an acute attack which put that very freedom in jeopardy. Too many of us had supposed that, built as our commonwealth was on universal suffrage, it would be proof against the complaints that harassed older states; but in fact it turned out that there was extra hazard in that. Having solemnly resolved that all men are created equal and have certain inalienable rights, among them life, liberty, and the pursuit of happiness, we shut our eyes and waited for the formula to work. . . . When after a hundred years, we opened our eyes. . . . Our country had grown great and rich; through our ports was poured food for the millions of Europe. But in the back streets multitudes huddled in ignorance and want. . . . Political freedom we had won; but the problem of helpless poverty, grown vast with the added offscourings of the Old World, mocked us, unsolved. Liberty at sixty cents a day set presently its stamp upon the government of our cities, and it became the scandal and the peril of our political system.[43]

New York City was not unique; slums and the social problems resulting from them existed in all large American cities. Reformers fought for slum clearance, but public apathy and vested economic interests delayed massive urban renewal until after the Second World War. In spite of all these industrial and urban difficulties, immigrants continued to come: the United States offered opportunity, upward social mobility, and a better life.

European and Asian immigrants aroused nativist sentiments—that is, intense hostility to their foreign and "un-American" looks, behavior, and loyalties on the part of native-born Americans. Some of this antagonism sprang from the deep-rooted Anglo-Saxon racism of many Americans. Some grew out of old Protestant suspicion of Roman Catholicism, the faith of most of the new arrivals. A great deal of the dislike of the foreign-born sprang from fear of economic competition. To most Americans, the Chinese with their exotic looks and willingness to work for very little seemed the most dangerous. Increasingly violent agitation against Orientals led to race riots in California and finally culminated in the Chinese Exclusion Act of 1882, which denied Chinese laborers entrance to the country.

Immigrants from Europe seized on white racism as a way of improving themselves in the job market: they could compensate for their immigrant status by claiming superiority to ex-slaves and their descendants. The arrival of thousands of Irish immigrants in the 1850s, followed by millions of Italians and Slavs in the period 1880 to 1914, aggravated an already bad situation. What the German scientist Alexander von Humboldt wrote about the attitude of peninsulares toward Creoles in Latin America in the early nineteenth century—"the lowest , least educated, and uncultivated European believes himself superior to the white born in the New World"[44]—precisely applies to the outlook of Irish, Italian, or Slavic immigrants to the United States at the turn of this century if one merely substitutes *black* for *white*. In the eyes of all ethnic groups, the social status of blacks remained the lowest while that of immigrants rose. As the United States underwent expansion and industrialization in the course of the nineteenth century, blacks remained the worst off *because of* immigration.[45]

In the 1890s the nation experienced a severe economic depression. Faced with overproduction, the rich and politically powerful owners of mines, mills, and factories fought the organization of labor unions, laid off thousands, slashed wages, and ruthlessly exploited their workers. Workers in turn feared that immigrant labor would drive salaries lower. The frustrations provoked by pitifully low salaries in "good times," by unemployment during the depression, and by all the unresolved problems of industrial urban society boiled over into savage attacks on the foreign-born. One of the bloodiest incidents occurred in western Pennsylvania in 1897, when about 150 unarmed Polish and Hungarian coal miners tried to persuade others to join their walkout. The mine owners convinced the local sheriff that the strike was illegal. As the strikers approached, the sheriff panicked and ordered his deputies to shoot. Twenty-one immigrants died and forty were wounded. The sheriff

Harlem Hellfighters Returning to New York in 1919 aboard the U.S.S. *Stockholm*, these black men of the famed U.S. 369th Division had fought in the bloody battle of the Meuse-Argonne during the First World War. The French government awarded 150 of them the coveted Croix de Guerre. *(Springer/Bettmann Film Archive)*

subsequently explained that the miners were only "infuriated foreigners . . . like wild beasts." Local people agreed that if the strikers had been American-born, no blood would have been shed.[46]

Pressures to restrict immigration varied with economic conditions: it slackened in times of relative prosperity and increased in periods of recession. After the First World War, labor leaders lobbied Congress for restrictions because they feared losing the wage gains achieved during the war. Some intellectuals argued that immigrants from southern and eastern Europe, with their unfamiliar cultural traditions, threatened to destroy American society. Italians were feared because of possible Cosa Nostra connections; eastern Europeans were thought to have communist connections. In the 1920s Congress responded with

laws that set severe quotas—2 percent of resident nationals as of the 1890 census—on immigration from southern and eastern Europe. The Japanese were completely excluded. These racist laws remained on the books until 1965.

CANADA: FROM COLONY TO NATION

In 1608 the French explorer Samuel de Champlain (1567–1635) sailed down the St. Lawrence River and established a trading post on the site of present-day Quebec. Thus began the permanent colony of New

France. The fur-trading monopolies subsequently granted to Champlain by the French crown attracted settlers, and Jesuit missionaries to the Indians further increased the French population. The British, however, vigorously challenged French control of the lucrative fur trade, and the long mid-eighteenth century global struggle for empire between the British and the French, known in North America as the "French and Indian Wars" because of Indian border warfare, tested French control (see Chapter 19). In 1759, on the Plains of Abraham, a field north of the city of Quebec, the English under General James Wolfe defeated the French under General Louis Montcalm. This battle ended the French Empire in North America; by the Treaty of Paris of 1763, France ceded Canada to Great Britain.

For the French Canadians, who then numbered about 90,000, the British conquest was a tragedy and the central event in their history. British governors replaced the French; English-speaking merchants from Britain and the thirteen American colonies to the south took over the colony's economic affairs. The Roman Catholic church remained, and until about 1960 played a powerful role in the political and cultural, as well as religious, life of French Canadians. Most of the French Canadians engaged in agriculture, though a small merchant class sold furs and imported manufactured goods.

Intending to establish a permanent administration for Canada, in 1774 the British Parliament passed the Quebec Act. This law granted religious freedom to French Canadians and recognized French law in civil matters, but it denied Canadians a legislative assembly, a traditional feature of British colonial government. Parliament held that French Canadians had no experience in elective institutions; moreover, the example of the assemblies of the thirteen American colonies, which were then demanding more political power than the British wanted to grant, discouraged the establishment of a Canadian counterpart. Therefore, Parliament placed power in the hands of an appointed governor and an appointed council; the latter, however, was composed of French Canadians as well as English-speaking members. English Canadian businessmen protested that they were being denied a basic right of Englishmen—representation.

During the American Revolution, about 40,000 Americans demonstrated their loyalty to Great Britain and its empire by emigrating to Canada. These "Loyalists" not only altered the French-English ratio in the population; they pressed for a representative assembly, and English Canadians strongly concurred. In 1791 Parliament responded with the Constitution Act, which divided the province of Quebec at the Ottawa River into Lower Canada (present-day Quebec, predominantly French and Catholic) and Upper Canada (present-day Ontario, primarily English and Protestant). The Act also provided for an elective assembly in each of the two provinces. Because the assemblies' decisions could be vetoed by an appointed upper house or by the governor and his council, general discontent continued. Finally, in 1837, disputes over control of revenue, the judiciary, and the established churches erupted into open rebellion in both Upper and Lower Canada. The British government, fearful of a repetition of the American events of 1776, decided on a full investigation and appointed Lord Durham, a prominent liberal reformer, to make recommendations for reform.

THE AGE OF CONFEDERATION, 1841–1867

Lord Durham published his *Report on the Affairs of British North America,* later called the "Magna Carta" of British colonial administration, in 1839. He proposed the union of Upper and Lower Canada and the establishment in Canada of "responsible government," meaning that Canadians should manage their own local affairs through ministries responsible to their legislatures. The imperial government in London was to retain control over trade, foreign affairs, public lands, and the colonial constitution. Accordingly, Parliament in 1840 passed the Union Act, which united Ontario and Quebec under one government composed of a governor, an appointed legislative council, and an elective assembly in which the two provinces had equal representation. When Lord Durham's son-in-law, Lord Elgin, was appointed governor in 1847, he made it clear that his cabinet (council) would be chosen from the party with the majority in the elected assembly; and, following the British model, the cabinet had to retain the support of that majority in order to stay in office.

The idea of a union or confederation of all the Canadian provinces persisted in the 1860s. During the American Civil War, English-American relations were severely strained, and "Canada found herself in the centre of the storm. The resulting fear of American aggression was a powerful factor in bringing con-federation to completion."[47] Parliament's passage of the British North America Act in 1867 brought the Canadian constitution to its modern form. By the Act the traditional British parliamentary system was adapted to the needs of the new North American na-tion. The provinces of New Brunswick and Nova Scotia joined Ontario and Quebec to form the Do-minion of Canada. A governor-general, who repre-sented the British crown and fulfilled ceremonial functions, governed through the Dominion cabinet, which, like the British cabinet, was composed of members selected from the lower house of the legisla-ture, to which it was responsible.

In the new federal system legislative power rested in a parliament of two houses: a Senate, whose mem-bers were appointed for life by the governor-general, and a House of Commons, representatives elected by adult males. (Canadian women won the right to vote in national elections in 1917, shortly before women in the United States and Great Britain.) In theory, the two houses had equal power, though money bills had to originate in the House of Commons; in practice, the Senate came to serve only as a deliberative check on hasty legislation and as a means of rewarding elder statesmen for their party services. The Dominion cabinet received complete jurisdiction over internal affairs, while Britain retained control over foreign policy. (In 1931 the British Statute of Westminster of-ficially recognized Canadian autonomy in foreign af-fairs.) The constitution of 1982 abolished the power of the London Parliament to amend Canada's consti-tution and ended all appeals from the provinces to London. Because Quebec did not sign the 1982 docu-ment, however, federal-provincial relationships re-main under study.

Believing that the American system of the division of powers between the states and the federal govern-ment left the states too strong and helped to bring on the Civil War, the framers of the Canadian constitu-tion intended to create a powerful central govern-ment. Provincial legislatures, therefore, were as-signed powers explicitly stated and applicable only to local conditions. With the implementation of the British North America Act, Canada attained "responsible government," John A. Macdonald (1815–1891), the strongest advocate of confedera-tion, became the Dominion's first prime minister.

EXPANSION AND DEVELOPMENT

The expansion and development of Canada after 1867 bears some striking similarities to that of the United States. Macdonald vigorously pushed Can-ada's "manifest destiny" to absorb all the northern part of the continent. In 1869 his government pur-chased for $1,500,000 the vast Northwest Territories of the Hudson Bay Company. From this territory the province of Manitoba emerged to become part of the Dominion in 1870. Fearful that the sparsely settled colony of British Columbia would join the United States, Macdonald lured British Columbia into the confederation with a subsidy to pay its debts and the promise of a transcontinental railroad to be com-pleted between 1873 and 1883. Likewise, the debt-ridden little maritime province of Prince Edward Island was drawn into confederation with a large sub-sidy. In five short years, between 1868 and 1873, through Macdonald's imagination and drive, Cana-dian sovereignty stretched from coast to coast.

Only one thing could tie the vast continent to-gether—railroads. Determined that a transcontinen-tal railroad was essential to Canada's survival as a na-tion, Macdonald declared that "until this great work is completed our Dominion is little more than a 'geo-graphical expression.' We have as much interest in British Columbia as in Australia, and no more. The railroad, once finished, we become a great united country with a large interprovincial trade and a com-mon interest."[48] On November 7, 1885, Macdonald received a telegram announcing that the first train from Montreal in Quebec was approaching the Pa-cific; traveling at 24 miles per hour, the coast-to-coast running time was a little over five days. The comple-tion of the railroad led to the formation of two new prairie provinces, Alberta and Saskatchewan, which in 1905 entered the Dominion. (Only in 1949 did the island of Newfoundland renounce colonial status and join the Dominion.) The Canadian Pacific Rail-road represents Macdonald's greatest achievement.

Macdonald's hopes for large numbers of immi-grants to people the thinly populated country did not immediately materialize. Between 1897 and 1912, however, 961,000 entered Canada from the British Isles, 594,000 from Europe, and 784,000 from the United States. Some immigrants went to work in the urban factories of Hamilton, Toronto, and Montreal.

Prospectors in the Klondike The discovery of gold in 1896 in the Canadian Klondike (in the Yukon Territory just east of the Alaskan border) drew thousands, including these hardy women prospectors. *(Library of Congress)*

Most immigrants from continental Europe—Poles, Germans, Scandinavians, and Russians—flooded the Midwestern plains and soon transformed the prairies into one of the world's greatest grain-growing regions. Because of Canada's small population, most of which in the early twentieth century was concentrated in Ontario and Quebec, the assimilation of the immigrants to the older English-Canadian culture occurred more slowly than in the "melting pot" of the United States. French Canadians remained the largest minority in the population. Distinctively different in language, law, and religion, and fiercely proud of their culture, they resisted assimilation. Since the 1950s, the immigration of Italians and

Hungarians (following the Hungarian Revolution of 1956; see Chapter 37) has contributed to the evolution of a more cosmopolitan culture.

Supported by population growth, Canada experienced an agricultural and industrial boom between 1891 and 1914. In those years wheat production rocketed from 2 million bushels per year to 150 million bushels. The discovery of gold, silver, copper, and nickel in northern Ontario led to the full exploitation of those mineral resources. British Columbia, Ontario, and Quebec produced large quantities of wood pulp, much of it sold to the United States. Canada's great rivers were harnessed to supply hydroelectric power for industrial and domestic use. Meanwhile, the government erected tariffs to protect Canadian industry, established a national civil service, and built a sound banking system.

Canada's powerful support of the Allied cause in the First World War demonstrated its full maturity as a nation. In 1914 the British government still controlled the foreign policy of all parts of the Empire; when Britain declared war on Germany, Canada unhesitatingly followed. More than 600,000 Canadian soldiers served with distinction in the army, some of them in the bloodiest battles in France; the 60,661 killed represent a higher loss than that of the more populous United States. Canadian grain and foodstuffs supplied much of the food of the Allied troops, while Canadian metals were in high demand for the production of guns and shells. Canadian resentment, therefore, over lack of voice in the formulation of Allied war policies proved understandable. In 1917 the British government established the Imperial War Cabinet, a body composed of the chief British ministers and the prime ministers of the Dominions to set policy. In 1918 Canada demanded and received—over the initial opposition of Britain, France, and the United States—the right to participate in the Versailles Peace Conference and in the League of Nations. Canada had become a respected and independent nation.

In the later years of the nineteenth century, industrialization, expansion, and the assimilation of foreign peoples preoccupied the nations of the Western Hemisphere. Political instability slowed the development of most Latin American countries. A few reformers sought closer relations between North and South America, but little of significance was accomplished. In 1889, for example, a Pan-American Conference in Washington rejected a proposal to settle disputes among nations by arbitration.

A revolt in Cuba against incompetent Spanish administration had more far-reaching consequences. The American "yellow press" luridly described the horrors of the concentration camps where the Spanish incarcerated the rebels. When the battleship *Maine* was mysteriously blown up in Havana harbor, inflamed public opinion swept the United States into war. The Spanish-American War of 1898—the

"splendid little war," as Secretary of State John Hay called it—lasted just ten weeks and resulted in the United States acquiring Cuba and the Philippine Islands. Denying any imperialistic ambitions in the Philippines, President William McKinley declared that the United States wanted only "to take them all and educate the Filipinos and uplift and civilize and Christianize them." McKinley, like most Americans, did not know that the Filipinos had an old and sophisticated culture and had been Christians for three centuries.

The notion of manifest destiny had swept the United States into the Caribbean and across the Pacific. Between 1900 and 1929 the United States intervened in Latin American affairs whenever it felt its economic interests were threatened. Americans secured control of the Panama Canal on their own terms, and in 1912 and 1926 U.S. Marines intervened in Nicaragua to bolster conservative governments. The result has been a bitter legacy of anti-American feeling throughout Latin America. Only with the launching of President Franklin D. Roosevelt's Good Neighbor Policy did relations between the two halves of the hemisphere begin to improve.

NOTES

1. Quoted in William Spence Robertson, *Rise of the Spanish American Republics* (New York: The Free Press, 1965), p. 19.
2. See Benjamin Keen and Mark Wasserman, *A Short History of Latin America* (Boston: Houghton Mifflin, 1980), pp. 109–115.
3. John Lynch, *The Spanish-American Revolutions, 1808–1826* (New York: Norton, 1973), pp. 13–14; Keen and Wasserman, pp. 145–146.
4. Quoted in Lynch, p. 18.
5. Mark Burkholder and D. S. Chandler, *From Impotence to Authority: The Spanish Crown and the American Audiencias, 1687–1808* (Columbia, Mo.: University of Missouri Press, 1977), p. 145.
6. Ibid., p. 141.
7. Keen and Wasserman, p. 146.
8. Quoted in J. L. Phelan, *The People and the King. The Communero Revolution in Columbia, 1781* (Madison, Wis.: University of Wisconsin Press, 1978), p. 62; see also Leslie B. Rout, *The African*

Experience in Spanish America (New York: Cambridge University Press, 1977), p. 165.

9. Quoted in Phelan, pp. 206–207.

10. Frank Tannenbaum, *Ten Keys to Latin America* (New York: Random House, 1962), pp. 69–71.

11. Ibid.

12. H. Hoetink, *Slavery and Race Relations in the Americas* (New York: Harper & Row, 1973), p. 14.

13. Keen and Wasserman, pp. 201–204.

14. Ibid., p. 207.

15. See Charles H. Harris, *A Mexican Family Empire: The Latifundio of the Sanchez Navarros, 1765–1867* (Austin: University of Texas Press, 1975), passim.

16. Nicolas Sanchez-Albornoz, *The Population of Latin America: A History,* trans. W. A. R. Richardson (Berkeley: University of California Press, 1974), pp. 151–152.

17. James R. Scobie, "Buenos Aires as a Commercial-Bureaucratic City, 1880–1910: Characteristics of a City's Orientation," *American Historical Review* 77: 4 (October 1972): 1046.

18. Ibid., p. 1064.

19. See Magnus Morner, ed., *Race and Class in Latin America. Part II: Immigration, Stratification, and Race Relations* (New York: Columbia University Press, 1971), pp 73–122; Sanchez-Albornoz, pp. 160–167.

20. Samuel Eliot Morison, *The Oxford History of the American People* (New York: Oxford University Press, 1965), p. 445.

21. Ibid., pp. 380–381.

22. Ibid., pp. 446–452.

23. James Oakes, *The Ruling Race: A History of American Slaveholders* (New York: Alfred A. Knopf, 1982), pp. x–xi.

24. Quoted in Robert William Fogel and Stanley L. Engerman, *Time on the Cross: The Economics of American Negro Slavery* (Boston: Little, Brown, 1974), p. 64.

25. Ibid., p. 73.

26. Quoted in Oakes, p. 120.

27. C. Vann Woodward, ed., *Mary Chesnut's Civil War* (New Haven: Yale University Press, 1981), p. 29.

28. Ibid., pp. xlix–l.

29. Roy P. Basler, ed., *The Collected Works of Abraham Lincoln,* Vol. II (New Brunswick, N.J.: Rutgers University Press, 1953), pp. 255–256, 271.

30. Ibid., pp. 461–462.

31. Quoted in Richard Hofstadter, *The American Political Tradition* (New York: Random House, 1948), p. 114.

32. T. Harry Williams, quoted in Hofstadter, pp. 128–129.

33. Quoted in Hofstadter, p. 132.

34. Quoted in Morison, p. 654.

35. T. Harry Williams, *The History of American Wars: From Colonial Times to World War I* (New York: Alfred A. Knopf, 1981), p. 202.

36. Quoted in Herbert G. Gutman, *The Black Family in Slavery and Freedom, 1750–1925* (New York: Random House, 1977), p. xvii.

37. Ibid., pp. 14–16, 21–22.

38. Quoted in Fogel and Engerman, p. 84.

39. Ibid., pp. 81–82.

40. Gutman, p. xix.

41. Sandra L. Myres, *Westering Women and the Frontier Experience, 1800–1915* (Albuquerque: University of New Mexico Press, 1982), Chaps. 6 and 7.

42. Gunther Barth, *City People: The Rise of Modern City Culture in the Nineteenth Century* (New York: Oxford University Press, 1980), p. 15.

43. Quoted in Daniel Boorstin, ed., *An American Primer* (New York: New American Library, 1966), pp. 667–668.

44. Quoted in Lynch, p. 18.

45. Hoetink, pp. 18.

46. Quoted in John Higham, *Strangers in the Land: Patterns of American Nativism, 1860–1925* (New York: Atheneum, 1971), pp. 89–90.

47. Quoted in R. Cook, *Canada: A Modern Study* (Toronto: Clarke, Irwin & Co., 1971), p. 89.

48. Quoted in Cook, p. 127.

SUGGESTED READING

Perhaps the best introduction to the independence movements in Latin America is John Lynch, *The Spanish-American Revolutions* (1973), which is soundly researched and includes a good bibliography. The most useful biographies of Simón Bolívar are those of Gerhard Masur, *Simón Bolívar,* 2nd ed. (1969), and J. J. Johnson and D. M. Ladd, *Simón Bolívar and Spanish American Independence, 1783–1830* (1968), which contains good selections of Bolívar's writings. J. C. J. Metford, *San Martín the Liberator* (1950), is a good short life of that revolutionary. For Brazil, see K. R. Maxwell, *Conflicts and Conspiracies: Brazil and Portugal, 1750–1808* (1973), and A. J. R. Russell-Wood, ed., *From Colony to Nation: Essays in the Independence of Brazil* (1975). A. P. Whitaker, *The United States and the Independence of Latin America, 1800–1830* (1941), remains the standard study of the role of the United States.

Jan Bazant, *A Concise History of Mexico* (1978), is a good starting point for the study of Mexican history, but M. C. Meyer and W. L. Sherman, *The Course of Mexican History* (1979), is the most thorough treatment. Tulio Halperin-Donghi, *The Aftermath of Revolution in Latin America* (1973), and C. C. Griffin, "Economic and Social Aspects of the Era of Spanish-American Independence," *Hispanic American Historical Review* 29 (1949), provide important interpretations of the consequences of the revolutions.

The following studies offer good treatments of society and politics in Latin America in the nineteenth century: Richard Graham and P. H. Smith, eds., *New Approaches to Latin American History* (1974); Ralph Roeder, *Juarez and His Mexico,* 2 vols. (1947), perhaps the best available work in English; H. S. Ferns, *Argentina* (1969); Jay Kinsbruner, *Chile: A Historical Interpretation* (1973); A. J. Bauer, *Chilean Rural Society from the Spanish Conquest to 1930* (1975); E. B. Burns, *A History of Brazil* (1970); Robert Conrad, *The Destruction of Brazilian Slavery, 1850–1888* (1973); and R. B. Toplin, *The Abolition of Slavery in Brazil* (1972).

For social and economic developments and the triumph of neocolonialism, the following titles are useful: Robert Cortes Conde, *The First Stages of Modernization in Spanish America* (1967); Jan Bazant, *A Concise History of Mexico from Hidalgo to Cardenas, 1805–1940* (1978); R. Knowlton, *Church Property and the Mexican Reform, 1856–1910* (1976); R. D. Anderson, *Outcasts in Their Own Land: Mexican Industrial Workers, 1906–1911* (1976); James Scobie, *Argentina: A City and a Nation,* 2nd ed. (1971); M. J. Mamalakis, *The Growth and Structure of the Chilean Economy from Independence to Allende* (1976), which provides an excellent economic overview; Andre Gunder Frank, *Capitalism and Underdevelopment in Latin America: Historical Studies of Chile and Brazil* (1969); David Rock, *Politics in Argentina, 1890–1930: The Rise and Fall of Radicalism* (1975); Richard Graham, *Britain and the Onset of Modernization in Brazil, 1850–1914* (1968).

The major themes in United States history have been extensively treated by many able scholars, and students will have no difficulty finding a wealth of material. James MacGregor Burns, *The Vineyard of Liberty* (1982), traces the origins and development of American society, politics, and culture, emphasizing the growth of liberty, from the 1780s to 1863; this work is a classic achievement. The standard study of manifest destiny remains Frederick Merk, *Manifest Destiny and Mission in American History: A Reinterpretation* (1963), but see also K. Jack Bauer, *The Mexican-American War, 1846–1848* (1976). In *The Only Land They Knew: The Tragic Story of the American Indians in the Old South* (1981), J. Leitch Wright recounts the interaction of native Americans, Africans, and Europeans in the American South. On slavery, see Stanley M. Elkins, *Slavery: A Problem in American Institutional and Intellectual Life,* 3d rev. ed. (1976), a great achievement, which includes a good comparison of slavery in the United States and Latin America and a fine bibliographical essay. Eugene D. Genovese, *Roll, Jordan, Roll: The World the Slaves Made* (1974), is a comprehensive Marxist treatment of plantation slavery, stressing the paternalism of the planter class. For the origins and development of racial attitudes in both North and South America, see Winthrop D. Jordan, *White Over Black: American Attitudes Toward the Negro, 1550–1812* (1969).

On the black family, see, in addition to Gutman's book cited in the Notes, the following studies: August Meier and Elliott M. Rudwick, *From Plantation to Ghetto: An Interpretive History of American Negroes* (1968); E. Franklin Frazier, *Black Bourgeoisie,* 15th ed. (1975); Benjamin Quarles, *The Negro in the Making of America* (1974); and Gerda Lerner, ed., *Black Women in White America: A Documentary History* (1973).

The literature on the Civil War and Reconstruction is mammoth, and the following titles treat important aspects of it: David Donald, ed., *Why the North Won the Civil War* (1977); John Hope Franklin, *Reconstruction* (1965); Harold M. Hyman, *A More Perfect Union* (1973); and James McPherson, *The Abolitionist Legacy* (1975).

Thomas C. Cochrane, *Business in American Life* (1977); Alfred D. Chandler, *Strategy and Structure: Chapters in the History of American Industrial Enterprise* (1966); Harold C. Livesay, *Andrew Carnegie and the Rise of Big Business* (1975); and David F. Hawkes, *John D.: The Founding Father of the Rockefellers* (1980) are fine studies of industrialism and corporate growth in the late nineteenth century.

On the lives of Jews and other immigrants in American cities, see Irving Howe's brilliant achievement, *World of Our Fathers* (1976), which is splendidly illustrated and contains a good bibliography.

For developments in Canada, see, in addition to the highly readable sketch by R. Cook cited in the Notes, K. McNaught, *The Pelican History of Canada* (1976), a sound survey that emphasizes those cultural traits that are distinctly Canadian. For the Age of Confederation, J. M. S. Careless, *The Union of the Canadas, 1841–1857* (1967), offers a solid treatment by a distinguished scholar, while D. G. Creighton, *John A. Macdonald,* two volumes (1952, 1955), is probably the best study of the great Prime Minister. The critical years of expansion and development are discussed in the full accounts of R. C. Brown and G. R. Cook, *Canada, 1896–1921* (1974), and R. Graham, *Canada, 1922–1939* (1979).

THE GREAT BREAK:
WAR AND REVOLUTION

*I*N THE SUMMER OF 1914 the nations of Europe went willingly to war. They believed they had no other choice. Moreover, both peoples and governments confidently expected a short war leading to a decisive victory. Such a war, they believed, would "clear the air," and European society would go on as before.

These expectations were almost totally mistaken. The First World War was long, indecisive, and tremendously destructive. To the shell-shocked generation of survivors, it was known simply as the Great War: the war of unprecedented scope and intensity. From today's perspective it is clear that the First World War marked a great break in the course of Western historical development since the French and Industrial revolutions. A noted British political scientist has gone so far as to say that even in victorious and relatively fortunate Great Britain, the First World War was *the* great turning point in government and society, "as in everything else in modern British history. . . . There's a much greater difference between the Britain of 1914 and, say, 1920, than between the Britain of 1920 and today."[1]

This is a strong statement, but it contains much truth, for all of Europe as well as for Britain. It suggests three questions this chapter will try to answer. What caused the Great War? How and why did war and revolution have such enormous and destructive consequences? And where in the trauma and bloodshed were formed elements of today's world, many of which people now accept and even cherish?

THE FIRST WORLD WAR

The First World War was so long and destructive because it involved all the Great Powers and because it quickly degenerated into a senseless military stalemate. Like two evenly matched boxers in a championship bout, each side tried to wear down its opponent. There was no referee to call a draw, only the blind hammering of a life-or-death struggle.

THE BISMARCKIAN SYSTEM OF ALLIANCES

The Franco-Prussian War and the foundation of the German Empire opened a new era in international relations. France was decisively defeated in 1871 and forced to pay a large war indemnity and give up Alsace-Lorraine. In ten short years, from 1862 to 1871, Bismarck had made Prussia-Germany—traditionally the weakest of the Great Powers—the most powerful nation in Europe (pages 907–909). Had Bismarck been a Napoleon I or a Hitler, for whom no gain was ever sufficient, continued expansion would no doubt sooner or later have raised a powerful coalition against the new German Empire. Yet he was not. As Bismarck never tired of repeating after 1871, Germany was a "satisfied" power. Germany had no territorial ambitions and only wanted peace in Europe.

But how was peace to be preserved? The most serious threat to peace came from the east, from Austria-Hungary and from Russia. Those two enormous multinational empires had many conflicting interests, particularly in the Balkans, where the Ottoman Empire—the "sick man of Europe"—was ebbing fast. There was a real threat that Germany might be dragged into a great war between the two rival empires. Bismarck's solution was a system of alliances (Figure 32.1) to restrain both Russia and Austria-Hungary, to prevent conflict between them, and to isolate a hostile France.

A first step was the creation in 1873 of the conservative Three Emperors' League, which linked the monarchs of Austria-Hungary, Germany, and Russia in an alliance against radical movements. In 1877 and 1878, when Russia's victories over the Ottoman Empire threatened the balance of Austrian and Russian interests in the Balkans and the balance of British and Russian interests in the Middle East, Bismarck played the role of sincere peacemaker. At the Congress of Berlin in 1878, he saw that Austria obtained the right to "occupy and administer" the Ottoman provinces of Bosnia and Herzegovina to counterbalance Russian gains, while independent Balkan states were also carved from the disintegrating Ottoman Empire.

Bismarck's balancing efforts at the Congress of Berlin infuriated Russian nationalists, which led Bismarck to conclude a defensive military alliance with Austria against Russia in 1879. Motivated by tensions with France, Italy joined Germany and Austria in 1882, thereby forming the Triple Alliance.

Bismarck continued to work for peace in eastern Europe, seeking to neutralize tensions between Aus-

The Congress of Berlin, 1878 With the Austrian representative on his right and with other participants looking on, Bismarck the mediator symbolically seals the hard-won agreement by shaking hands with the chief Russian negotiator. The Great Powers often relied on such special conferences to settle their international disputes. *(The Bettmann Archive)*

tria-Hungary and Russia. In 1881 he capitalized on their mutual fears and cajoled them both into a secret alliance with Germany. This Alliance of the Three Emperors lasted until 1887. It established the principle of cooperation among all three powers in any further division of the Ottoman Empire, while each state pledged friendly neutrality in case one of the three found itself at war with a fourth power (except the Ottoman Empire).

Bismarck also maintained good relations with Britain and Italy, while cooperating with France in Africa but keeping France isolated in Europe. In 1887 Russia declined to renew the Alliance of the Three Emperors because of new tensions in the Balkans. Bismarck craftily substituted a Russian-German Reinsurance Treaty, by which both states promised neutrality if the other were attacked.

Bismarck's accomplishments in foreign policy after 1871 were great. For almost a generation, he

maintained German leadership in international affairs, and he worked successfully for peace by managing conflicts and by restraining Austria-Hungary and Russia with defensive alliances.

THE RIVAL BLOCS

In 1890 the young, impetuous emperor William II dismissed Bismarck, in part because of the chancellor's friendly policy toward Russia since the 1870s. William then adamantly refused to renew the Russian-German Reinsurance Treaty, in spite of Russian willingness to do so. This fateful departure in foreign affairs prompted long-isolated republican France to court absolutist Russia, offering loans, arms, and friendship. In both countries there were enthusiastic public demonstrations, and in St. Petersburg the autocratic Alexander III stood bareheaded on a French battleship while a band played the "Marseillaise," the

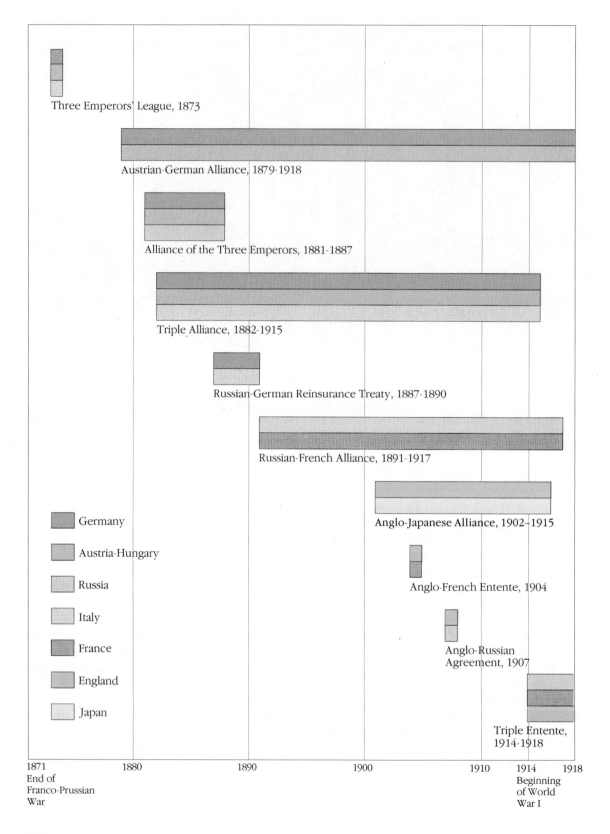

Three Emperors' League, 1873

Austrian-German Alliance, 1879-1918

Alliance of the Three Emperors, 1881-1887

Triple Alliance, 1882-1915

Russian-German Reinsurance Treaty, 1887-1890

Russian-French Alliance, 1891-1917

Anglo-Japanese Alliance, 1902–1915

Anglo-French Entente, 1904

Anglo-Russian
Agreement, 1907

Triple Entente,
1914-1918

Germany

Austria-Hungary

Russia

Italy

France

England

Japan

1871
End of
Franco-Prussian
War

1880

1890

1900

1910

1914
Beginning
of World
War I

1918

FIGURE 32.1 The Alliance System After 1871 Bismarck's subtle diplomacy maintained reasonably good relations among the eastern monarchies—Germany, Russia, and Austria-Hungary—and kept France isolated. The situation changed dramatically in 1891, when the Russian-French Alliance divided the Great Powers into two fairly equal military blocs.

hymn of the Revolution. A preliminary agreement between the two countries was reached in 1891, and in early 1894 France and Russia became military allies. This alliance (Figure 32.1) was to remain in effect as long as the Triple Alliance of Austria, Germany, and Italy: continental Europe was dangerously divided into two rival blocs.

The policy of Great Britain became increasingly crucial. Long content with "splendid isolation" and no permanent alliances, Britain after 1891 was the only uncommitted Great Power. Could Britain afford to remain isolated, or would it feel compelled to take sides? Alliance with France or Russia certainly seemed highly unlikely. With its vast and rapidly expanding empire, Britain was often in serious conflict with these countries around the world in the heyday of imperialism.

Britain also squabbled with Germany, but many Germans and some Britons still believed that their statesmen would eventually formalize the "natural alliance" they felt already united the advanced, racially related Germanic and Anglo-Saxon peoples. Alas, such an understanding never materialized. Instead, the generally good relations that had prevailed between Prussia and Great Britain ever since the mid-eighteenth century, and certainly under Bismarck, gave way to a bitter Anglo-German rivalry.

There were several reasons for this tragic development. The hard-fought Boer War (1899–1902) between the British and the tiny Dutch republics of South Africa had a major impact on British policy. British statesmen saw that Britain was overextended around the world. The Boer War also brought into the open widespread anti-British feeling, as editorial writers in many nations denounced the latest manifestation of British imperialism. There was even talk of Germany, Austria, France, and Russia forming a grand alliance against the bloated but insatiable British Empire. Therefore British statesmen prudently set about shoring up their exposed position with alliance and agreements.

Britain improved its often-strained relations with the United States and in 1902 concluded a formal alliance with Japan (Figure 32.1). Britain then responded favorably to the advances of France's skillful foreign minister, Théophile Delcassé, who wanted better relations with Britain and was willing to accept British rule in Egypt in return for British support of French plans to dominate Morocco. The resulting Anglo-French Entente of 1904 (Figure 32.1) settled all outstanding colonial disputes between Britain and France.

Frustrated by Britain's turn toward France in 1904, Germany decided to test the strength of the entente and drive Britain and France apart. First Germany threatened and bullied France into dismissing Delcassé. However, rather than accept the typical territorial payoff of imperial competition—a slice of French jungle in Africa or a port in Morocco—in return for French primacy in Morocco, the Germans foolishly rattled their swords in 1905. They insisted on an international conference on the whole Moroccan question without presenting precise or reasonable demands. Germany's crude bullying forced France and Britain closer together, and Germany left the Algeciras Conference of 1906 empty-handed and isolated (except for Austria-Hungary).

The result of the Moroccan crisis and the Algeciras Conference was something of a diplomatic revolution. Britain, France, Russia, and even the United States began to see Germany as a potential threat, which might seek to dominate all Europe. At the same time, German leaders began to see sinister plots to "encircle" Germany and block its development as a world power. In 1907 Russia, battered by the disastrous war with Japan and the revolution of 1905, agreed to settle its quarrels with Great Britain in Persia and central Asia with a special Anglo-Russian Agreement (Figure 32.1). As a result of that agreement, Germany's blustering paranoia increased and so did Britain's thinly disguised hostility.

Germany's decision to add a large, enormously expensive fleet of big-gun battleships to its already expanding navy also heightened tensions after 1907. German nationalists, led by the all-too-persuasive Admiral Tirpitz, saw a large navy as the legitimate mark of a great world power. But British leaders like Lloyd George saw it as a detestable military challenge, which forced them to spend the People's Budget on battleships rather than on social welfare. As

German Warships Under Full Steam As this impressive row of ships on maneuvers in 1911 suggests, Germany did succeed in building a large modern navy. But Britain was equally determined to maintain its naval superiority, and the spiraling arms race helped poison relations between the two countries. *(Süddeutscher Verlag)*

Germany's rapid industrial growth allowed it to overcome Britain's early lead, economic rivalry also contributed to distrust and hostility between the two nations. Unscrupulous journalists and special-interest groups in both countries portrayed healthy competition in foreign trade and investment as a form of economic welfare.

Many educated shapers of public opinion and ordinary people in Britain and Germany were increasingly locked in a fateful "love-hate" relationship between the two countries. Proud nationalists in both countries simultaneously admired and feared the power and accomplishments of their nearly equal rival. In 1909 the mass-circulation London *Daily Mail* hysterically informed its readers in a series of reports that "Germany is deliberately preparing to destroy the British Empire."[2] By then, Britain was

psychologically, if not officially, in the Franco-Russian camp. The leading nations of Europe were divided into two hostile blocs, both ill prepared to deal with upheaval on Europe's southeastern frontier.

THE OUTBREAK OF WAR

In the early years of this century, war in the Balkans was as inevitable as anything can be in human history. The reason was simple: nationalism was destroying the Ottoman Empire and threatening to break up the Austro-Hungarian Empire. The only questions were what kinds of wars would occur and where they would lead.

Greece had long before led the struggle for national liberation, winning its independence in 1832. In 1875 widespread nationalist rebellion in the Ottoman Empire had resulted in Turkish repression, Russian intervention, and Great Power tensions. Bismarck had helped resolve this crisis at the 1878 Congress of Berlin, which worked out the partial division of Turkish possessions in Europe. Austria-Hungary obtained the right to "occupy and administer" Bosnia and Herzegovina. Serbia and Rumania won independence, and a part of Bulgaria won local autonomy. The Ottoman Empire retained important Balkan holdings, for Austria-Hungary and Russia each feared the other's domination of totally independent states in the area (see Map 32.1).

After 1878 the siren call of imperialism lured European energies, particularly Russian energies, away from the Balkans. This division helped preserve the fragile balance of interests in southeastern Europe. By 1903, however, Balkan nationalism was on the rise once again. Serbia led the way, becoming openly hostile toward both Austria-Hungary and the Ottoman Empire. The Serbs, a Slavic people, looked to Slavic Russia for support of their national aspirations. To block Serbian expansion and to take advantage of Russia's weakness after the revolution of 1905, Austria in 1908 formally annexed Bosnia and Herzegovina with their predominantly Serbian populations. The kingdom of Serbia erupted in rage but could do nothing without Russian support.

Then in 1912, in the First Balkan War, Serbia turned southward. With Greece and Bulgaria it took Macedonia from the Ottoman Empire and then quarreled with its ally Bulgaria over the spoils of victory—a dispute that led in 1913 to the Second Balkan War. Austria intervened in 1913 and forced Serbia to give up Albania. After centuries, nationalism had finally destroyed the Ottoman Empire in Europe. This sudden but long-awaited event elated the Balkan nationalists and dismayed the leaders of multinational Austria-Hungary. The former hoped and the latter feared that Austria might be next to be broken apart.

Within this tense context, Archduke Francis Ferdinand, heir to the Austrian and Hungarian thrones, and his wife Sophie were assassinated by Bosnian revolutionaries on June 28, 1914, during a state visit to the Bosnian capital of Sarajevo. The assassins were closely connected to the ultranationalist Serbian society The Black Hand. This revolutionary group was secretly supported by members of the Serbian government and was dedicated to uniting all Serbians in a single state. Although the leaders of Austria-Hun-

MAP 32.1 The Balkans After the Congress of Berlin, 1878 The Ottoman Empire suffered large territorial losses but remained a power in the Balkans.

gary did not and could not know all the details of Serbia's involvement in the assassination plot, they concluded after some hesitation that Serbia had to be severely punished once and for all. After a month of maneuvering, Austria-Hungary presented Serbia with an unconditional ultimatum, on July 23.

The Serbian government had just forty-eight hours in which to agree to cease all subversion in Austria and all anti-Austrian propaganda in Serbia. Moreover, a thorough investigation of all aspects of the assassination at Sarajevo was to be undertaken in Serbia by a joint commission of Serbian and Austrian officials. These demands amounted to control of the Serbian state. When Serbia replied moderately but evasively, Austria began to mobilize and then declared war on Serbia on July 28. Thus a desperate multinational Austria-Hungary deliberately chose war in a last-ditch attempt to stem the rising tide of

MAP 32.2 The Balkans in 1914 Ethnic boundaries did not follow political boundaries, and Serbian national aspirations threatened Austria-Hungary.

hostile nationalism. The "Third Balkan War" had begun (Map 32.2).

Of prime importance in Austria-Hungary's fateful decision was Germany's unconditional support. Emperor William II and his chancellor, Theobald von Bethmann-Hollweg, gave Austria-Hungary a "blank check" and urged aggressive measures in early July, even though they realized that war between Austria and Russia was the most probable result. They knew Russian pan-Slavs saw Russia not only as the protector, but also as the eventual liberator, of southern Slavs. As one pan-Slav had said much earlier, "Austria can hold her part of the Slavonian mass as long as Turkey holds hers and vice versa."[3] At the very least a resurgent Russia could not stand by, as in the Bosnian crisis, and simply watch the Serbs be crushed. Yet Bethmann-Hollweg apparently hoped that while Russia (and therefore France) would go to war, Great Britain would remain neutral, unwilling to fight for "Russian aggression" in the distant Balkans. After

all, Britain had reached only "friendly understandings" with France and Russia on colonial questions and had no alliance with either power.

In fact, the diplomatic situation was already out of control. Military plans and timetables began to dictate policy. Russia, a vast country, would require much longer to mobilize its armies than Germany and Austria-Hungary. On July 28, as Austrian armies bombarded Belgrade, Tsar Nicholas II ordered a partial mobilization against Austria-Hungary. Almost immediately he found that this was impossible. All the complicated mobilization plans of the Russian general staff had assumed a war with both Austria *and* Germany: Russia could not mobilize against one without mobilizing against the other. On July 29, therefore, Russia ordered full mobilization and in effect declared general war.

The same tragic subordination of political considerations to military strategy descended on Germany. The German general staff had also thought only in terms of a two-front war. Their plan for war called for knocking out France first with a lightning attack through neutral Belgium before turning on Russia.

Thus, on August 2, 1914, General Helmuth von Moltke, "acting under a dictate of self-preservation," demanded that Belgium permit German armies to pass through its territory. Belgium, whose neutrality was solemnly guaranteed by all the great states including Prussia, refused. Germany attacked. Thus Germany's terrible, politically disastrous response to a war in the Balkans was an all-out invasion of France by way of the plains of neutral Belgium on August 3. In the face of this act of aggression, Great Britain declared war on Germany the following day. The First World War had begun.

REFLECTIONS ON THE ORIGINS OF THE WAR

Although few events in history have aroused such interest and controversy as the coming of the First World War, the question of immediate causes and responsibilities can be answered with considerable certainty. Austria-Hungary deliberately started the "Third Balkan War." A war for the right to survive was Austria-Hungary's desperate, if understandable, response to the aggressive, yet understandable, revolutionary drive of Serbian nationalists to unify their people in a single state. In spite of Russian intervention in the quarrel, it is clear from the beginning of the crisis that Germany not only pushed and goaded Austria-Hungary but was also responsible for turning a little war into the Great War by means of its sledge-hammer attack on Belgium and France.

After Bismarck's resignation in 1890, German leaders lost control of the international system. They felt increasingly that Germany's status as a world power was declining while that of Britain, France, Russia, and the United States was growing. Indeed, the powers of what officially became in August 1914 the Triple Entente—Great Britain, France, and Russia—were checking Germany's vague but real aspirations, as well as working to strangle Austria-Hungary, Germany's only real ally. Germany's aggression in 1914 reflected the failure of all European statesmen, not just German leaders, to incorporate Bismarck's mighty empire permanently and peacefully into the international system.

There were other underlying causes. The new overseas expansion—imperialism—did not play a direct role, since the European powers always settled their colonial conflicts peacefully. Yet the easy imperialist victories did contribute to a general European overconfidence and reinforced national rivalries. In this respect it was influential.

The triumph of nationalism was a crucial underlying precondition of the Great War. Nationalism was at the heart of the Balkan wars, in the form of Serbian aspirations and the grandiose pan-German versus pan-Slavic racism of some fanatics. Nationalism drove the spiraling arms race. More generally, as shown in Chapter 29, the aristocracy and middle classes arrived at nationalistic compromises, while ordinary people looked toward increasingly responsive states for psychological and material well-being.

Broad popular commitment to "my country right or wrong" weakened groups that thought in terms of international communities and consequences. Thus the big international bankers, who were frightened by the prospect of war in July 1914, and the extreme-left socialists, who believed that the enemy was at home and not abroad, were equally out of step with national feeling.

Finally, the wealthy governing classes underestimated the risk of war in 1914. They had forgotten that great wars and great social revolutions very often go together in history. Metternich's alliance of conservative forces in support of international peace and the domestic status quo had become only a distant memory.

THE FIRST BATTLE OF THE MARNE

When the Germans invaded Belgium in August 1914, they and everyone else believed that the war would be short, for urban society rested on the food and raw materials of the world economy: "The boys will be home by Christmas." The Belgian army heroically defended its homeland, however, and fell back in good order to join a rapidly landed British army corps near the Franco-Belgian border. This action complicated Germany's plan of concentrating its armies on the right wing and boldly capturing Paris in a vast encircling movement. By the end of August dead-tired German soldiers were advancing along an enormous front in the scorching summer heat. The neatly designed prewar plan to surround Paris from the north and west had been thrown into confusion.

French armies totaling 1 million, reinforced by more than 100,000 British troops, had retreated in orderly fashion before Germany's 1.5 million men in the field. Under the leadership of the steel-nerved General Joseph Joffre, the French attacked a gap in the German line at the Battle of the Marne on September 6. For three days, France threw everything into the attack. At one point, the French government desperately requisitioned all the taxis of Paris to rush reserves to the troops at the front. Finally, the Germans fell back. Paris and France had been miraculously saved.

STALEMATE AND SLAUGHTER

The attempts of French and British armies to turn the German retreat into a rout were unsuccessful, and so were moves by both sides to outflank each other in northern France. As a result, both sides began to dig trenches to protect themselves from machine gun fire. By November 1914, an unbroken line of trenches extended from the Belgian ports through northern France past the fortress of Verdun and on to the Swiss frontier.

In the face of this unexpected stalemate, slaughter on the western front began in earnest. The defenders on both sides dug in behind rows of trenches, mines, and barbed wire. For days and even weeks ceaseless shelling by heavy artillery supposedly "softened up" the enemy in a given area (and also signaled the coming attack). Then young draftees and their junior officers went "over the top" of the trenches in frontal attacks on the enemy's line.

Preparing the Attack The great offenses of the First World War required the mobilization of men and material on an unprecedented scale. This photo shows American troops moving up. *(U.S. Army Signal Corps)*

The cost in lives was staggering, the gains in territory minuscule. The massive French and British offensives during 1915 never gained more than three miles of blood-soaked earth from the enemy. In the Battle of the Somme in the summer of 1916, the British and French gained an insignificant 125 square miles at the cost of 600,000 dead or wounded, while the Germans lost half a million men. That same year, the unsuccessful German campaign against Verdun cost 700,000 lives on both sides.

Terrible 1917 saw General Robert Nivelle's French army almost destroyed in a grand spring attack at Champagne, while at Passchendaele in the fall, the British traded 400,000 casualties for fifty square miles of Belgian Flanders. The hero of Erich Maria Remarque's great novel *All Quiet on the Western Front* (1929) describes one such attack:

We see men living with their skulls blown open; we see soldiers run with their two feet cut off. . . . Still the little piece of convulsed earth in which we lie is held. We have yielded no more than a few hundred yards of it as a prize to the enemy. But on every yard there lies a dead man.

Such was war on the western front.

The war of the trenches shattered an entire generation of young men. Millions who could have provided political creativity and leadership after the war were forever missing. Moreover, those who lived through the holocaust were maimed, shell-shocked, embittered, and profoundly disillusioned. The young soldiers went to war believing in the world of their leaders and elders, the pre-1914 world of order, progress, and patriotism. Then, in Remarque's words, the "first bombardment showed us our mistake, and

The Aftermath of Total War The extent of carnage, the emotional damage, and the physical destruction were equally unprecedented. Once great cathedrals standing in ruin symbolized the disaster. *(UPI/Bettmann Newsphotos)*

under it the world as they had taught it to us broke in pieces." For many, the sacrifice and comradeship of the battlefield became life's crucial experience, an experience that "soft" civilians could never understand. A chasm opened up between veterans and civilians, making the difficult postwar reconstruction all the more difficult.

THE WIDENING WAR

On the eastern front, slaughter did not degenerate into suicidal trench warfare. With the outbreak of the war, the "Russian steamroller" immediately moved into eastern Germany. Very badly damaged by the Germans under Generals Paul von Hindenburg and Erich Ludendorff at the battles of Tannenberg and the Masurian Lakes in August and September 1914,

Russia never threatened Germany again. On the Austrian front, enormous armies seesawed back and forth, suffering enormous losses. Austro-Hungarian armies were repulsed twice by little Serbia in bitter fighting. But with the help of German forces, they reversed the Russian advances of 1914 and forced the Russians to retreat deep into their own territory in the eastern campaign of 1915. A staggering 2.5 million Russians were killed, wounded, or taken prisoner that year.

These changing tides of victory and defeat brought neutral countries into the war (Map 32.3). Italy, a member of the Triple Alliance since 1882, had declared its neutrality in 1914 on the grounds that Austria had launched a war of aggression. Then, in May 1915, Italy joined the Triple Entente of Great Britain, France, and Russia in return for promises of Austrian territory. Bulgaria allied with Austria and Germany, now known as the Central Powers, in September 1915 in order to settle old scores with Serbia.

The entry of Italy and Bulgaria in 1915 was part of a general widening of the war. The Balkans, with the exception of Greece, came to be occupied by the Central Powers, and British forces were badly defeated in 1915 trying to take the Dardanelles from Turkey, Germany's ally. More successful was the entente's attempt to incite Arab nationalists against their Turkish overlords. An enigmatic British colonel, soon known to millions as Lawrence of Arabia, aroused the Arab princes to revolt in early 1917. In 1918 British armies from Egypt smashed the Ottoman Empire once and for all. In their Middle East campaign, the British drew on forces from Australia, New Zealand, and India. Contrary to German hopes, the colonial subjects of the British (and French) did not revolt but loyally supported their foreign masters. Instead, the European war extended around the globe as Great Britain, France, and Japan seized Germany's colonies.

A crucial development in the expanding conflict came in April 1917, when the United States declared war on Germany. American intervention grew out of the war at sea, sympathy for the entente, and the increasing desperation of total war. At the beginning of the war, Britain and France had established a total naval blockade to strangle the Central Powers and prevent deliveries of food and raw materials from overseas. No neutral ship was permitted to sail to Germany with any cargo. The blockade annoyed Americans, but effective propaganda over German atrocities in occupied Belgium and lush profits from selling war supplies to Britain and France blunted American indignation.

Moreover, in early 1915 Germany launched a counter-blockade using the murderously effective submarine, a new weapon that violated traditional niceties of fair warning under international law. In May 1915, after sinking about ninety ships in the British war zone, a German submarine sank the British passenger liner *Lusitania,* which was also carrying arms and munitions. More than a thousand lives, among them 139 Americans, were lost. President Woodrow Wilson protested vigorously, forcing Germany to relax its submarine warfare for almost two years; the alternative was almost certain war.

Early in 1917, the German military command—confident that improved submarines could starve its

MAP 32.3 **The First World War in Europe** The trench war on the western front was concentrated in Belgium and northern France, while the war in the east encompassed an enormous territory.

island enemy, Britain, into submission before the United States could come to its rescue—resumed unrestricted submarine warfare. Like the invasion of Belgium, this was a reckless gamble. British shipping losses reached staggering proportions, though by late 1917 naval strategists came up with the inevitable effective response: the convoy system for safe transatlantic shipping. In the meantime, the embattled President Wilson had told a sympathetic Congress and people that the "German submarine warfare against commerce is a warfare against mankind." Thus the last uncommitted great nation, as fresh and enthusiastic as Europe had been in 1914, entered the world war in April 1917, almost three years after it began. Eventually the United States was to tip the balance in favor of Great Britain and France.

THE HOME FRONT

The widening Great War had significant economic, social, and political repercussions for the people on the home front. The people behind the lines were tremendously involved in the titanic struggle. War's impact on them was no less massive than on the men crouched in the trenches.

MOBILIZING FOR TOTAL WAR

In August 1914 most people greeted the outbreak of hostilities enthusiastically. In every country, the masses believed that their nation was in the right and defending itself from aggression. With the exception of a few extreme left-wingers, even socialists supported the war. Tough standby plans to imprison socialist leaders and break general strikes protesting the war proved quite unnecessary in 1914. Everywhere the patriotic support of the masses and the working class contributed to national unity and an energetic war effort.

By mid-October generals and politicians began to realize that more than patriotism would be needed to

Triple Entente and its Allies

Central Powers

Neutral nations

Farthest German-Austrian advance

Major battle

ATLANTIC OCEAN

IRELAND

GREAT BRITAIN

London

FRANCE

Paris

NORTH SEA

NETHERLANDS

BELGIUM

NORWAY

DENMARK

Jutland 1916

British blockade line

SWEDEN

BALTIC SEA

FINLAND

Helsinki

St. Petersburg

Riga

GERMANY

Berlin

Rhine

SWITZERLAND

Tannenberg 1914

Masurian Lakes 1914

Warsaw

Brest-Litovsk

POLAND

GALICIA

Vienna

AUSTRIA-HUNGARY

ITALY

Rome

Caporetto 1917

Danube

Sarajevo

MONTENEGRO

SERBIA

ALBANIA

GREECE

MEDITERRANEAN SEA

Treaty of Brest-Litovsk, March 1918

Moscow

R U S S I A

Kiev

Armistice line, Dec. 1917

RUMANIA

Bucharest

BULGARIA

Dardanelles

Gallipoli 1915

Constantinople

BLACK SEA

OTTOMAN EMPIRE

200   400 Km.

100   200   300 Mi.

NETHERLANDS

Antwerp

Brussels

BELGIUM

Ghent

Ostend

FLANDERS

Passchendaele

Ypres

Calais

Dover

ENGLISH CHANNEL

Arras

Amiens

Somme

Compiègne

Château-Thierry

Paris

Seine

FRANCE

St. Quentin

Aisne

Reims

Châlons-sur-Marne

Marne

Sedan

ARGONNE FOREST

Verdun

ARDENNES

Meuse

Liège

Aix-la-Chapelle

Cologne

Rhine

Ruhr

GERMANY

Coblenz

Moselle

LUXEMBOURG

Saar

LORRAINE

Nancy

Épinal

Strasbourg

ALSACE

Mulhouse

Basel

Front at beginning of 1915

German offensive, Summer 1918

Armistice line, November 1918

Germany, 1914

German offensive, 1914

Farthest German advance, September 1914

50   100 Km.

50   100 Mi.

win the war, whose end was not in sight. Each country experienced a relentless, desperate demand for men and weapons. Countless shortages quickly developed. In each country economic life and organization had to change and change fast to keep the war machine from sputtering to a stop. And change they did.

In each country a government of national unity began to plan and control economic and social life in order to wage "total war." Free-market capitalism was abandoned, at least "for the duration." Instead, government planning boards established priorities and decided what was to be produced and consumed. Rationing, price and wage controls, and even restrictions on workers' freedom of movement were imposed by government. Only through such regimentation could a country make the greatest possible military effort. Thus, though there were national variations, the great nations all moved toward planned economies commanded by the established political leadership.

The economy of total war blurred the old distinction between soldiers on the battlefield and civilians at home. The war was a war of whole peoples and entire populations, and the loser would be the society that cracked first. Interestingly enough, the ability of governments to manage and control highly complicated economies strengthened the cause of socialism. With the First World War, socialism became for the first time a realistic economic blueprint rather than a utopian program.

Germany illustrates the general trend. It also went furthest in developing a planned economy to wage total war. As soon as war began, Walter Rathenau, the talented, foresighted Jewish industrialist in charge of Germany's largest electrical company, convinced the government to set up a War Raw Materials Board to ration and distribute raw materials. Under Rathenau's direction, every useful material from foreign oil to barnyard manure was inventoried and rationed. Moreover, the board launched spectacularly successful attempts to produce substitutes, such as synthetic rubber and synthetic nitrates, which were essential to the German war machine.

Food was also rationed in accordance with physical need. Men and women doing hard manual work were given extra rations. During the last two years of the war, only children and expectant mothers received milk rations. At the same time, Germany failed to tax the war profits of private firms heavily enough. This contributed to massive deficit financing, inflation, the growth of a black market, and the eventual re-emergence of class conflict.

Following the terrible battles of Verdun and the Somme in 1916, the military leaders Hindenburg and Ludendorff became the real rulers of Germany, and they decreed the ultimate mobilization for total war. Germany, said Hindenburg, could win only "if all the treasures of our soil that agriculture and industry can produce are used exclusively for the conduct of War. . . . All other considerations must come second."[4] This goal, they believed, required that every German man, woman, and child be drafted into the service of the war. Thus, in December 1916, the military leaders rammed through the parliament the Auxiliary Service Law, which required all males between seventeen and sixty to work only at jobs considered critical to the war effort.

Although women and children were not specifically mentioned, this forced-labor law was also aimed at them. Many women already worked in war factories, mines, and steel mills, where they labored like men at the heaviest and most dangerous jobs. With the passage of the Auxiliary Service Law, many more women followed. Children were organized by their teachers into garbage brigades to collect every scrap of useful materials: grease strained from dishwater, coffee grounds, waste paper, tin cans, metal door knockers, bottles, rags, hair, bones, and so forth, as well as acorns, chestnuts, pinecones, and rotting leaves. Potatoes gave way to turnips, and people averaged little more than a thousand calories a day. Thus in Germany total war led to the establishment of history's first "totalitarian" society, and war production increased while some people literally starved to death.

Great Britain mobilized for total war less rapidly and less completely than Germany, for it could import materials from its empire and from the United States. By 1915, however, a serious shortage of shells led to the establishment of a Ministry of Munitions under David Lloyd George. The ministry organized private industry to produce for the war, controlled profits, allocated labor, fixed wage rates, and settled labor disputes. By December 1916, when Lloyd George became prime minister, the British economy was largely planned and regulated. More than two hundred factories and 90 percent of all imports were

Waging Total War A British war plant strains to meet the insatiable demand for trench-smashing heavy artillery shells. Quite typically, many of these defense workers are women. *(By courtesy of the Trustees of the Imperial War Museum)*

bought and allocated directly by the state. Subsequently, even food was strictly rationed, while war production continued to soar. Great Britain had followed successfully in Germany's footsteps.

The Social Impact

The social impact of total war was no less profound than the economic, though again there were important national variations. The millions of men at the front and the insatiable needs of the military created a tremendous demand for workers. Jobs were available for everyone. This situation had seldom if ever been seen before 1914, when unemployment and poverty had been facts of urban life. The exceptional demand for labor brought about momentous changes.

One such change was greater power and prestige for labor unions. Having proved their loyalty in August 1914, labor unions became an indispensable partner of government and private industry in the planned war economy. Unions cooperated with war governments on work rules, wages, and production schedules in return for real participation in important decisions. This entry of labor leaders and unions into policy-making councils paralleled the entry of socialist leaders into the war governments.

The role of women changed dramatically. In every country, large numbers of women left home and domestic service to work in industry, transportation, and offices. By 1917 women formed fully 43 percent of the labor force in Russia. Moreover, women became highly visible—not only as munitions workers but as bank tellers, mail carriers, even policewomen.

At first, the male-dominated unions were hostile to women moving into new occupations, believing that their presence would lower wages and change work rules. But government pressure and the principle of equal pay for equal work (at least until the end of the war) overcame these objections. Women also served as nurses and doctors at the front. In general, the war

Wartime Propaganda was skillful and effective. The poster on the left spurred men to volunteer bravely for military service before the draft was introduced in Britain in 1916. The grim warrior on the right calls on French men and women at home to unite as firmly as the soldiers at the front against defeatist plots in 1918. *(The Trustees of the Imperial War Museum)*

greatly expanded the range of women's activities and changed attitudes toward them. As a direct result of their many-sided war effort, Britain, Germany, and Austria granted women the right to vote immediately after the war. Women also showed a growing spirit of independence during the war, as they started to bob their hair, shorten their skirts, and smoke in public.

War also promoted greater social equality, blurring class distinctions and lessening the gap between rich and poor. This blurring was most apparent in Great Britain, where wartime hardship was never extreme. In fact, the bottom third of the population generally lived *better* than ever before, for the poorest gained most from the severe shortage of labor. The English writer Robert Roberts recalled how his parents' tiny grocery store in the slums of Manchester thrived as

never before during the war, when people who had scrimped to buy bread and soup bones were able to afford fancy cakes and thick steaks. In continental countries greater equality was reflected in full employment, rationing according to physical needs, and a sharing of hardships. There, too, society became more uniform and more egalitarian, in spite of some war profiteering.

Finally, death itself had no respect for traditional social distinctions. It savagely decimated the young aristocratic officers who led the charge, and it fell heavily on the mass of drafted peasants and unskilled workers who followed. Yet death often spared the aristocrats of labor, the skilled workers and foremen. Their lives were too valuable to squander at the front, for they were needed to train and direct the newly re-

The Fruits of War This photo shows how, in desperation, the people of Vienna decimated the city's beloved forest to get a little firewood to heat their homes. Economic collapse weighed heavily on all classes. *(Osterreichische Nationalbibliothek, Bild-Archiv)*

cruited women and older unskilled men laboring valiantly in war plants at home.

GROWING POLITICAL TENSIONS

During the first two years of war, most soldiers and civilians supported their governments. Even in Austria-Hungary—the most vulnerable of the belligerents, with its competing nationalities—loyalty to the state and monarchy remained astonishingly strong through 1916. Belief in a just cause, patriotic nationalism, the planned economy, and a sharing of burdens united peoples behind their various national leaders. Furthermore, each government did its best to control public opinion to bolster morale. Newspapers, letters, and public addresses were rigorously censored. Good news was overstated; bad news was repressed or distorted.

Each government used both crude and subtle propaganda to maintain popular support. German propaganda hysterically pictured black soldiers from France's African empire raping German women, while German atrocities in Belgium and elsewhere were ceaselessly recounted and exaggerated by the French and British. Patriotic posters and slogans, slanted news, and biased editorials inflamed national hatreds and helped sustain superhuman efforts.

By the spring of 1916, however, people were beginning to crack under the strain of total war. In April 1916, Irish nationalists in Dublin tried to take advantage of this situation and rose up against British rule in their great Easter Rebellion. A week of bitter fighting passed before the rebels were crushed and their leaders executed. Strikes and protest marches over inadequate food began to flare up on every home front. Soldiers' morale began to decline. Italian troops mutinied. Numerous French units refused to fight after General Nivelle's disastrous offensive of May 1917. A rising tide of war-weariness and defeatism also swept France's civilian population before Georges Clemenceau emerged as a ruthless and effective wartime leader in November 1917. Clemenceau established a virtual dictatorship, pouncing on strikers and jailing without trial journalists and politicians who dared to suggest a compromise peace with Germany.

The strains were worse for the Central Powers. In October 1916, the chief minister of Austria was assassinated by a young socialist crying, "Down with Absolutism! We want peace!"[5] The following month, when the feeble old Emperor Francis Joseph died sixty-eight years after his mother Sophia had pushed him onto the throne in 1848 (page 862), a symbol of unity disappeared. In spite of absolute censorship, political dissatisfaction and conflicts among nationalities grew. In April 1917, Austria's chief minister summed up the situation in the gloomiest possible terms. The country and army were exhausted. Another winter of war would bring revolution and disintegration, he predicted. The allied blockade kept tightening; people were starving.

The strain of total war and the Auxiliary Service Law was also evident in Germany. In the winter of 1916 to 1917, Germany's military position appeared increasingly desperate. Stalemates and losses in the west were matched by temporary Russian advances in the east: hence the military's insistence on the all-or-nothing gamble of unrestricted submarine warfare when the entente refused in December 1916 to consider peace on terms that were favorable to the Central Powers.

Also, the national political unity of the first two years of war was collapsing as the social conflict of prewar Germany re-emerged. A growing minority of socialists in the parliament began to vote against war credits, calling for a compromise "peace without annexations or reparations." In July 1917, a coalition of socialists and Catholics passed a resolution in the parliament to that effect. Such a peace was unthinkable for conservatives and military leaders. So also was the surge in revolutionary agitation and strikes by war-weary workers that occurred in early 1917. When the bread ration was further reduced in April, more than 200,000 workers struck and demonstrated for a week in Berlin, returning to work only under the threat of prison and military discipline. Thus militaristic Germany, like its ally Austria-Hungary (and its enemy France), was beginning to crack in 1917. Yet it was Russia that collapsed first and saved the Central Powers, for a time.

THE RUSSIAN REVOLUTION

The Russian Revolution of 1917 was one of modern history's most momentous events. Directly related to the growing tensions of World War One, its significance went far beyond the wartime agonies of a single European nation. The Russian Revolution opened a new era. For some it was Marx's socialist vision come true; for others, it was the triumph of dictatorship. To all, it presented a radically new prototype of state and society.

THE FALL OF IMPERIAL RUSSIA

Like its allies and its enemies, Russia embraced war with patriotic enthusiasm in 1914. At the Winter Palace, while throngs of people knelt and sang "God Save the Tsar," Tsar Nicholas II (1894–1917) repeated the oath Alexander I had made in 1812 and vowed never to make peace as long as the enemy stood on Russian soil. Russia's lower house, the Duma, voted war credits. Conservatives anticipated expansion in the Balkans, while liberals and most socialists believed alliance with Britain and France would bring democratic reforms. For a moment, Russia was united.

Soon, however, the strains of war began to take their toll. The unprecedented artillery barrages used up Russia's supplies of shells and ammunition, and better-equipped German armies inflicted terrible losses. For a time in 1915, substantial members of Russian soldiers were sent to the front without rifles; they were told to find their arms among the dead. There were 2 million Russian casualties in 1915 alone. Morale declined among soldiers and civilians. Nonetheless, Russia's battered peasant army did not collapse but continued to fight courageously until early 1917.

Under the shock of defeat, Russia moved toward full mobilization on the home front. The Duma and organs of local government took the lead, setting up special committees to coordinate defense, industry, transportation, and agriculture. These efforts improved the military situation, and Russian factories produced more than twice as many shells in 1916 as in 1915. Yet there were many failures, and Russia mobilized less effectively for total war than the other warring nations.

The great problem was leadership. Under the constitution resulting from the revolution of 1905 (pages 915–916), the tsar had retained complete control over the bureaucracy and the army. Legislation proposed by the Duma, which was weighted in favor of the wealthy and conservative classes, was subject to the tsar's veto. Moreover, Nicholas II fervently wished to maintain the sacred inheritance of supreme royal power, which with the Orthodox church was for him the key to Russia's greatness. A kindly, slightly stupid man, Nicholas failed to form a close partnership with his citizens in order to fight the war more effectively. He relied instead on the old bureaucratic apparatus, distrusting the moderate Duma, rejecting popular involvement, and resisting calls to share power.

As a result the Duma, the educated middle classes, and the masses became increasingly critical of the tsar's leadership. Following Nicholas's belated dismissal of the incompetent minister of war, demands for more democratic and responsive government exploded in the Duma in the summer of 1915. In September, parties ranging from conservative to moderate socialist formed the Progressive Bloc, which called for a completely new government responsible to the Duma instead of the tsar. In answer, Nicholas temporarily adjourned the Duma and announced that he was traveling to the front in order to lead and rally Russia's armies.

His departure was a fatal turning point. With the tsar in the field with the troops, control of the government was taken over by the hysterical empress, Tsarina Alexandra, and a debauched adventurer, the monk Rasputin. A minor German princess and granddaughter of England's Queen Victoria, Nicholas's wife was a devoted mother with a sick child, a strong-willed woman with a hatred of parliaments. Having constantly urged her husband to rule absolutely, Alexandra tried to do so herself in his absence. She seated and unseated the top ministers. Her most trusted adviser was "our Friend Grigori," an uneducated Siberian preacher who was appropriately nicknamed Rasputin—the "Degenerate."

Rasputin began his career with a sect noted for mixing sexual orgies with religious ecstasies, and his influence rested on mysterious healing powers. Alexis, Alexandra's fifth child and heir to the throne, suffered from a rare disease, hemophilia. The tiniest cut meant uncontrollable bleeding, terrible pain, and

Family Portrait With husband Nicholas II standing behind, the beautiful but tense Alexandra shows one of her daughters, who could not inherit the Russian throne, to her grandmother, Queen Victoria of England, and Victoria's son, the future Edward VII. European monarchs were closely related by blood and breeding before 1914. *(Nicholas A. de Basily Collection, Hoover Institution)*

possible death. Medical science could do nothing. Only Rasputin could miraculously stop the bleeding, perhaps through hypnosis. The empress's faith in Rasputin was limitless. "Believe more in our Friend," she wrote her husband in 1916. "He lives for you and Russia." In this atmosphere of unreality, the government slid steadily toward revolution.

In a desperate attempt to right the situation and end unfounded rumors that Rasputin was the empress's lover, three members of the high aristocracy murdered Rasputin in December 1916. The empress went into semipermanent shock, her mind haunted by the dead man's prophecy: "If I die or you desert me, in six months you will lose your son and your throne."[6] Food shortages in the cities worsened, morale declined. On March 8, women in Petrograd (formerly St. Petersburg) calling for bread started riots, which spontaneously spread to the factories and throughout the city. From the front the tsar ordered the troops to restore order, but discipline broke down and the soldiers joined the revolutionary crowd. The Duma responded by declaring a provisional government on March 12, 1917. Three days later, Nicholas abdicated without protest.

THE PROVISIONAL GOVERNMENT

The March revolution was the result of an unplanned uprising of hungry, angry people in the capital, but it was joyfully accepted throughout the country. The patriotic upper and middle classes rejoiced at the prospect of a more determined and effective war effort, while workers happily anticipated better wages and more food. All classes and political parties called for liberty and democracy. They were not disappointed. As Lenin said, Russia became the freest country in the world. After generations of arbitrary authoritarianism, the provisional government quickly established equality before the law; freedom of religion, speech, and assembly; the right of unions to organize and strike; and the rest of the classic liberal program.

Yet both the liberal and moderate socialist leaders of the provisional government rejected social revolution. The reorganized government formed in May 1917, which included the fiery agrarian socialist Alexander Kerensky, refused to confiscate large landholdings and give them to peasants, fearing that such drastic action in the countryside would only complete the disintegration of Russia's peasant army. For the patriotic Kerensky, as for other moderate socialists, the continuation of war was still the all-important national duty. There would be plenty of time for land reform later, and thus all the government's efforts were directed toward a last offensive in July. Human suffering and war-weariness grew, sapping the limited strength of the provisional government.

From its first day, the provisional government had to share power with a formidable rival—the Petrograd Soviet (or council) of Workers' and Soldiers' Deputies. Modeled on the revolutionary soviets of 1905, the Petrograd Soviet was a huge, fluctuating mass meeting of two to three thousand workers, soldiers, and socialist intellectuals. Seeing itself as a true grass-roots revolutionary democracy, this counter- or half-government suspiciously watched the provi-

sional government and issued its own radical orders, further weakening the provisional government. The most famous of these orders was Army Order No. 1, issued to all Russian military forces as the provisional government was forming.

Order No. 1 stripped officers of their authority and placed power in the hands of elected committees of common soldiers. Designed primarily to protect the revolution from some counter-revolutionary Bonaparte on horseback, Army Order No. 1 instead led to a total collapse of army discipline. Many an officer was hanged for his sins. Meanwhile, following the foolhardy summer offensive, masses of peasant soldiers began "voting with their feet," to use Lenin's graphic phrase. That is, they began returning to their villages to help their families get a share of the land, land that peasants were simply seizing as they settled old scores in a great agrarian upheaval. All across the country, liberty was turning into anarchy in the summer of 1917. It was an unparalleled opportunity for the most radical and most talented of Russia's many socialist leaders, Vladimir Ilyich Lenin (1870–1924).

LENIN AND THE BOLSHEVIK REVOLUTION

From his youth, Lenin's whole life was dedicated to the cause of revolution. Born into the middle class, the seventeen-year-old Lenin became an implacable enemy of imperial Russia when his older brother was executed for plotting to kill the tsar in 1887. As a law student he began searching for a revolutionary faith. He found it in Marxian socialism, which began to win converts among radical intellectuals as industrialization surged forward in Russia in the 1890s. Exiled to Siberia for three years because of socialist agitation, Lenin studied Marxist doctrines with religious intensity. After his release, he joined fellow believers in western Europe. There he lived for seventeen years and developed his own revolutionary interpretations of the body of Marxian thought.

Three interrelated ideas were central for Lenin. First, turning to the early fire-breathing Marx of 1848 and the *Communist Manifesto* for inspiration, Lenin stressed that capitalism could be destroyed only by violent revolution. He tirelessly denounced all revisionist theories of a peaceful evolution to socialism as betraying Marx's message of unending class conflict. Lenin's second, more original, idea was that, under certain conditions, a socialist revolution was possible even in a relatively backward country like Russia.

Mass Demonstrations in Petrograd in June 1917 showed a surge of working-class support for the Bolsheviks. In this photo a few banners of the Mensheviks and other moderate socialists are drowned in a sea of Bolshevik slogans. *(Sovfoto)*

Though capitalism was not fully developed there and the industrial working class was small, the peasants were poor and thus potential revolutionaries.

Lenin believed that at a given moment revolution was determined more by human leadership than by vast historical laws. Thus Lenin's third basic idea: the necessity of a highly disciplined workers' party, strictly controlled by a dedicated elite of intellectuals and full-time revolutionaries like Lenin himself. Unlike ordinary workers and trade union officials, this elite would never be seduced by short-term gains. It would not stop until revolution brought it to power.

Lenin's theories and methods did not go unchallenged by other Russian Marxists. At the meetings of the Russian Social Democratic Labor party in London in 1903, matters came to a head. Lenin demanded a small, disciplined, elitist party, while his opponents wanted a more democratic party with mass membership. The Russian party of Marxian socialism promptly split into two rival factions. Lenin's camp was called *Bolsheviks,* or "Majority group"; his opponents were *Mensheviks,* or "Minority group." Lenin's majority did not last, but Lenin did not care. He kept the fine-sounding name Bolshevik and developed the party he wanted: tough, disciplined, revolutionary.

Unlike most socialists, Lenin did not rally round the national flag in 1914. Observing events from neutral Switzerland, he saw the war as a product of imperialistic rivalries and a marvelous opportunity for class war and socialist upheaval. The March revolution was, Lenin felt, a step in that direction. Since propaganda and internal subversion were accepted weapons of total war, the German government graciously provided the impatient Lenin, his wife, and about twenty trusted colleagues with safe passage across Germany and back into Russia in April 1917. The Germans hoped that Lenin would undermine the sagging war effort of the world's freest society. They were not disappointed.

Arriving triumphantly at Petrograd's Finland Station on April 3, Lenin attacked at once. To the great astonishment of the local Bolsheviks, he rejected all cooperation with the "bourgeois" provisional government of the liberals and moderate socialists. His slogans were radical in the extreme: "All power to the Soviets." "All land to the peasants." "Stop the war now." Never a slave to Marxist determinism, the brilliant but not unduly intellectual Lenin was a superb tactician. The moment was now.

Yet Lenin almost overplayed his hand. An attempt by the Bolsheviks to seize power in July collapsed, and Lenin fled and went into hiding. He was charged with being a German agent, and indeed he and the Bolsheviks were getting money from Germany.[7] But no matter. Intrigue between Kerensky, who became prime minister in July, and his commander in chief General Lavr Kornilov, a popular war hero "with the heart of a lion and the brains of a sheep," resulted in Kornilov leading a feeble attack against the provisional government in September. In the face of this rightist "counter-revolutionary" threat, the Bolsheviks were rearmed and redeemed. Kornilov's forces disintegrated, but Kerensky lost all credit with the army, the only force that might have saved him and democratic government in Russia.

Trotsky and the Seizure of Power

Throughout the summer, the Bolsheviks had appealed very effectively to the workers and soldiers of Petrograd, markedly increasing their popular support. Party membership had soared from 50,000 to 240,000 and in October the Bolsheviks gained a fragile majority in the Petrograd Soviet. Moreover, Lenin had found a strong right arm—Leon Trotsky, the second most important person in the Russian Revolution.

A spellbinding revolutionary orator and independent radical Marxist, Trotsky (1877–1940) supported Lenin wholeheartedly in 1917. It was he who brilliantly executed the Bolshevik seizure of power. Painting a vivid but untruthful picture of German and counter-revolutionary plots, Trotsky first convinced the Petrograd Soviet to form a special Military-Revolutionary Committee in October and make him its leader. Military power in the capital passed into Bolshevik hands. Trotsky's second master stroke was to insist that the Bolsheviks reduce opposition to their coup by taking power in the name, not of the Bolsheviks, but of the more popular and democratic soviets, which were meeting in Petrograd from all over Russia in early November. On the night of November 6, militants from Trotsky's committee joined with trusty Bolshevik soldiers to seize government buildings and pounce on members of the provisional government. Then on to the congress of soviets! There a Bolshevik majority—roughly 390 of 650 turbulent delegates—declared that all power had passed to the soviets and named Lenin head of the new government.

The Bolsheviks came to power for three key reasons. First, by late 1917 democracy had given way to anarchy: power was there for those who would take it. Second, in Lenin and Trotsky the Bolsheviks had an utterly determined and truly superior leadership, which both the tsarist government and the provisional government lacked. Third, in 1917 the Bolsheviks succeeded in appealing to many soldiers and urban workers, people who were exhausted by war and eager for socialism. With time, many workers would become bitterly disappointed, but for the moment they had good reason to believe they had won what they wanted.

Dictatorship and Civil War

History is full of short-lived coups and unsuccessful revolutions. The truly monumental accomplishment of Lenin, Trotsky, and the rest of the Bolsheviks was not taking power but keeping it. In the next four years, the Bolsheviks went on to conquer the chaos they had helped to create, and they began to build their kind of socialist society. How was this done?

Lenin had the genius to profit from developments over which he and the Bolsheviks had no control. Since summer, a peasant revolution had been sweeping across Russia, as the tillers of the soil invaded and divided among themselves the great and not-so-great estates of the landlords and the church. Peasant sei-

Vladimir Lenin Dramatically displaying both his burning determination and his skill as a revolutionary orator, Lenin addresses the victorious May Day celebration of 1918 in Moscow's Red Square. *(Culver Pictures)*

zure of the land—a Russian 1789—was not very Marxist, but it was quite unstoppable in 1917. Thus Lenin's first law, which supposedly gave land to the peasants, actually merely approved what peasants were already doing. Urban workers' great demand in November was direct control of individual factories by local workers' committees. This, too, Lenin ratified with a decree in November.

Unlike many of his colleagues, Lenin acknowledged that Russia had lost the war with Germany, that the Russian army had ceased to exist, and that the only realistic goal was peace at any price. The price was very high. Germany demanded in December 1917 that the Soviet government give up all its western territories. These areas were inhabited by Poles, Finns, Lithuanians, and other non-Russians—all those peoples who had been conquered by the tsars over three centuries and put into the "prison-house of nationalities," as Lenin had earlier called the Russian Empire.

At first, Lenin's fellow Bolsheviks would not accept such great territorial losses. But when German armies resumed their unopposed march into Russia in February 1918, Lenin had his way in a very close vote in the Central Committee of the party. "Not even his greatest enemy can deny that at this moment Lenin towered like a giant over his Bolshevik colleagues."[8] A third of old Russia's population was sliced away by the German meat ax in the Treaty of Brest-Litovsk in March 1918. With peace, Lenin had escaped the certain disaster of continued war and could uncompromisingly pursue his goal of absolute political power for the Bolsheviks—now renamed Communists—within Russia.

In November 1917, the Bolsheviks had proclaimed their regime only a "provisional workers' and peasants' government," promising that a freely elected Constituent Assembly would draw up a new constitution. But the freest elections in Russia's history—both before and after 1917—produced a stunning

THE RUSSIAN REVOLUTION

1914	Russia enthusiastically enters the First World War
1915	Two million Russian casualties
	Progressive Bloc calls for a new government responsible to the Duma rather than to the tsar
	Tsar Nicholas adjourns the Duma and departs for the front; control of the government falls to Alexandra and Rasputin
December 1916	Murder of Rasputin
March 8, 1917	Bread riots in Petrograd (St. Petersburg)
March 12, 1917	Duma declares a provisional government
March 15, 1917	Tsar Nicholas abdicates without protest
April 3, 1917	Lenin returns from exile and denounces the provisional government
May 1917	Reorganized provisional government, including Kerensky, continues the war
	Petrograd Soviet issues Army Order no. 1, granting military power to committees of common soldiers
Summer 1917	Agrarian upheavals: peasants seize estates, peasant soldiers desert the army to participate
October 1917	Bolsheviks gain a majority in the Petrograd Soviet
November 6, 1917	Bolsheviks seize power; Lenin heads the new "provisional workers' and peasants' government"
November 1917	Lenin ratifies peasant seizure of land and worker control of factories; all banks nationalized
January 1918	Lenin permanently disbands the Constituent Assembly
February 1918	Lenin convinces the Bolshevik Central Committee to accept a humiliating peace with Germany in order to pursue the revolution
March 1918	Treaty of Brest-Litovsk: Russia loses one-third of its population
	Trotsky as war commissar begins to rebuild the Russian army
	Government moves from Petrograd to Moscow
1918–1920	Great Civil War
Summer 1918	Eighteen competing regional governments; White armies oppose the Bolshevik revolution
1919	White armies on the offensive but divided politically; they receive little benefit from Allied intervention
1920	Lenin and Red armies victorious, retaking Belorussia and the Ukraine

setback for the Bolsheviks, who won less than one-fourth of the elected delegates. The Socialist Revolutionaries—the peasants' party—had a clear majority. The Constituent Assembly met for only one day, on January 18, 1918. It was then permanently disbanded by Bolshevik soldiers acting under Lenin's orders. Thus, even before the peace with Germany, Lenin was forming a one-party government.

The dissolution of the democratically elected Constituent Assembly helped feed the flames of civil war. People who had risen up for self-rule in November saw that once again they were getting dictatorship from the capital. For the next three years, "Long live the [democratic] soviets; down with the Bolsheviks" was to be a popular slogan. The officers of the old army took the lead in organizing the so-called White opposition to the Bolsheviks in southern Russia and the Ukraine, in Siberia, and to the west of Petrograd. The Whites came from many social groups and were united only by their hatred of the Bolsheviks—the Reds.

By the summer of 1918, fully eighteen self-proclaimed regional governments—several of which represented minority nationalities—competed with Lenin's Bolsheviks in Moscow. By the end of the year, White armies were on the attack. In October 1919, it appeared they might triumph, as they closed in on Lenin's government from three sides. Yet they did not. By the spring of 1920, the White armies had been almost completely defeated, and the Bolshevik Red Army had retaken Belorussia and the Ukraine. The following year, the Communists also reconquered the independent nationalist governments of the Caucasus. The civil war was over; Lenin had won.

Lenin and the Bolsheviks won for several reasons. Strategically, they controlled the center, while the Whites were always on the fringes and disunited. Moreover, the poorly defined political program of the Whites was vaguely conservative, and it did not unite all the foes of the Bolsheviks under a progressive, democratic banner. Most important, the Communists quickly developed a better army, an army for which the divided Whites were no match.

Once again, Trotsky's leadership was decisive. The Bolsheviks had preached democracy in the army and elected officers in 1917. But beginning in March 1918, Trotsky as war commissar re-established the draft and drastic discipline for the newly formed Red Army. Soldiers deserting or disobeying an order were summarily shot. Moreover, Trotsky made effective use of former tsarist army officers, who were actively recruited and given unprecedented powers of discipline over their troops. In short, Trotsky formed a disciplined and effective fighting force.

The Bolsheviks also mobilized the home front. Establishing "war communism"—the application of the total war concept to a civil conflict—they seized grain from peasants, introduced rationing, nationalized all banks and industry, and required everyone to work. These measures served to maintain labor discipline and to keep the Red Army supplied.

"Revolutionary terror" also contributed to the Communist victory. The old tsarist secret police was re-established as the Cheka, which hunted down and executed thousands of real or supposed foes, like the tsar's family and other "class enemies." Moreover, people were shot or threatened with being shot for minor nonpolitical failures. The Cheka sowed fear, and fear silenced opposition.

Finally, foreign military intervention in the civil war ended up helping the Communists. After Lenin made peace with Germany, the Allies (the Americans, British, and Japanese) sent troops to Archangel and Vladivostok to prevent war materiel they had sent the provisional government from being captured by the Germans. After the Soviet government nationalized all foreign-owned factories without compensation and refused to pay all of Russia's foreign debts, Western governments and particularly France began to support White armies. Yet these efforts were small and halfhearted. In 1919 Western peoples were sick of war, and few Western politicians believed in a military crusade against the Bolsheviks. Thus Allied intervention in the civil war did not aid the Whites effectively, though it did permit the Communists to appeal to the patriotic nationalism of ethnic Russians, which was particularly strong among former tsarist army officers. Allied intervention was both too little and too much.

The Russian Revolution and the Bolshevik triumph was, then, one of the reasons why the First World War was such a great turning point in modern history. A radically new government, based on socialism and one-party dictatorship, came to power in a great European state, maintained power, and encouraged worldwide revolution. Although half-hearted constitutional monarchy in Russia was undoubtedly headed for some kind of political crisis

The Fall of Monarchy Entitled simply "November 1918," this eloquent drawing from a popular German magazine shows the crowns of Europe scattered like driftwood after the final wave of war and revolution. *(Photo: Caroline Buckler)*

before 1914, it is hard to imagine the triumph of the most radical proponents of change and reform except in a situation of total collapse. That was precisely what happened to Russia in the First World War.

THE PEACE SETTLEMENT

In 1918 the guns of world war finally fell silent. After winning great concessions from Lenin in the Treaty of Brest-Litovsk in March 1918, the Germans launched their last major attack against France. Yet this offensive failed like those before it. With breathtaking rapidity, the United States, Great Britain, and

France decisively defeated Germany militarily. Then, as civil war spread in Russia and as chaos engulfed much of eastern Europe, the victorious Western Allies came together in Paris to establish a lasting peace.

Expectations were high; optimism was almost unlimited. The Allies labored intensively and soon worked out terms for peace with Germany and for the creation of the peace-keeping League of Nations. Nevertheless, the hopes of peoples and politicians were soon disappointed, for the peace settlement of 1919 turned out to be a terrible failure. Rather than creating conditions for peace, it sowed the seeds of another war. Surely this was the ultimate tragedy of the Great War, a war that left 10 million dead and another 20 million wounded. How did it happen? Why was the peace settlement unsuccessful?

THE END OF THE WAR

In early 1917, the strain of total war was showing everywhere. After the Russian Revolution in March, there were major strikes in Germany. In July a coalition of moderates passed a "peace resolution" in the German parliament, calling for peace without territorial annexations. To counter this moderation born of war-weariness, the German military established a virtual dictatorship and aggressively exploited the collapse of Russian armies after the Bolshevik Revolution. Victory in the east having quieted German moderates, General Ludendorff and company fell on France once more in the great spring offensive of 1918. For a time, German armies pushed forward, coming within thirty-five miles of Paris. But Ludendorff's exhausted, overextended forces never broke through. They were decisively stopped in July at the second Battle of the Marne, where 140,000 fresh American soldiers saw action. Adding 2 million men in arms to the war effort by August, the late but massive American intervention decisively tipped the scales in favor of Allied victory.

By September, British, French, and American armies were advancing steadily on all fronts, and a panicky General Ludendorff realized that Germany had lost the war. Yet he insolently insisted that moderate politicians shoulder the shame of defeat, and on October 4, the emperor formed a new, more liberal German government to sue for peace. As negotiations over an armistice dragged on, an angry and frustrated German people finally rose up. On November 3, sailors in Kiel mutinied, and throughout northern Germany, soldiers and workers began to establish revolutionary councils on the Russian soviet model. The same day, Austria-Hungary surrendered to the Allies and began breaking apart. Revolution broke out in Germany, and masses of workers demonstrated for peace in Berlin. With army discipline collapsing, the emperor was forced to abdicate and fled to Holland. Socialist leaders in Berlin proclaimed a German republic on November 9 and simultaneously agreed to tough Allied terms of surrender. The armistice went into effect November 11, 1918. The war was over.

REVOLUTION IN GERMANY

Military defeat brought political revolution to Germany and Austria-Hungary, as it had to Russia. In Austria-Hungary, the revolution was primarily nationalistic and republican in character. Having started the war to preserve an antinationalist dynastic state, the Habsburg Empire had perished in the attempt. In its place, independent Austrian, Hungarian, and Czechoslovakian republics were proclaimed, while a greatly expanded Serbian monarchy united the south Slavs and took the name of Yugoslavia. The prospect of firmly establishing the new national states overrode class considerations for most people in east central Europe.

The German Revolution of November 1918 resembled the Russian Revolution of March 1917. In both cases, a genuine popular uprising toppled an authoritarian monarchy and established a liberal provisional republic. In both countries, liberals and moderate socialists took control of the central government, while workers' and soldiers' councils formed a counter-government. In Germany, however, the moderate socialists won and the Lenin-like radical revolutionaries in the councils lost. In communist terms, the liberal, republican revolution in Germany in 1918 was only half a revolution: a bourgeois political revolution without a communist second installment. It was Russia without Lenin's Bolshevik triumph.

There were several reasons for the German outcome. The great majority of Marxian socialist leaders in the Social Democratic party were, as before the war, really pink and not red. They wanted to establish real political democracy and civil liberties, and they favored the gradual elimination of capitalism. They were also German nationalists, appalled by the prospect of civil war and revolutionary terror. Moreover, there was much less popular support among workers and soldiers for the extreme radicals than in Russia. Nor did the German peasantry, which already had most of the land, at least in western Germany, provide the elemental force that has driven all great modern revolutions, from the French to the Chinese.

Of crucial importance also was the fact that the moderate German Social Democrats, unlike Kerensky and company, accepted defeat and ended the war the day they took power. This act ended the decline in morale among soldiers and prevented the regular army with its conservative officer corps from disintegrating. When radicals, headed by Karl Liebknecht and Rosa Luxemburg and their supporters in the councils, tried to seize control of the government in Berlin in January, the moderate socialists called on the army to crush the uprising. Liebknecht and Luxemburg were arrested and then brutally murdered by army leaders, which caused the radicals in the Social Democratic party to break away in anger and form a pro-Lenin German Communist party shortly thereafter. Finally, even if the moderate socialists had followed Liebknecht and Luxemburg on the Leninist path, it is very unlikely they would have succeeded. Civil war in Germany would certainly have followed, and the Allies, who were already occupying western Germany according to the terms of the armistice, would have marched on to Berlin and ruled Germany directly. Historians have often been unduly hard on Germany's moderate socialists.

THE TREATY OF VERSAILLES

The peace conference opened in Paris in January 1919 with seventy delegates representing twenty-seven victorious nations. There were great expectations. A young British diplomat later wrote that the victors "were convinced that they would never commit the blunders and iniquities of the Congress of Vienna [of 1815]." Then the "misguided, reactionary, pathetic aristocrats" had cynically shuffled populations; now "we believed in nationalism, we believed in the self-determination of peoples." Indeed, "we were journeying to Paris . . . to found a new

The Treaty of Versailles was signed in the magnificent Hall of Mirrors, part of the vast palace that Louis XIV had built to celebrate his glory. The Allies did not allow Germany to participate in the negotiation of the treaty. *(National Archives, Washington)*

order in Europe. We were preparing not Peace only, but Eternal Peace."[9] The general optimism and idealism had been greatly strengthened by President Wilson's January 1918 peace proposal, the Fourteen Points, which stressed national self-determination and the rights of small countries.

The real powers at the conference were the United States, Great Britain, and France, for Germany was not allowed to participate, and Russia was locked in civil war and did not attend. Italy was considered part of the Big Four, but its role was quite secondary. Almost immediately the three great allies began to quarrel. President Wilson, who was wildly cheered by European crowds as the spokesman for a new idealistic and democratic international cooperation, was al-

most obsessed with creating a League of Nations. Wilson insisted that this question come first, for he passionately believed that only a permanent international organization could protect member states from aggression and avert future wars. Wilson had his way, although Lloyd George of Great Britain and especially Clemenceau of France were unenthusiastic. They were primarily concerned with punishing Germany.

Playing on British nationalism, Lloyd George had already won a smashing electoral victory in December on the popular platform of making Germany pay for the war. "We shall," he promised, "squeeze the orange until the pips squeak." Personally inclined to make a somewhat moderate peace with Germany,

Lloyd George was to a considerable extent a captive of demands for a total victory worthy of the sacrifices of total war against a totally depraved enemy. As Rudyard Kipling summed up the general British feeling at the end of the war, the Germans were "a people with the heart of beasts."[10]

France's Georges Clemenceau, "the Tiger" who had broken wartime defeatism and led his country to victory, wholeheartedly agreed. Like most French people, Clemenceau wanted old-fashioned revenge. He also wanted lasting security for France. This, he believed, required the creation of a buffer state between France and Germany, the permanent demilitarization of Germany, and vast German reparations. He feared that sooner or later Germany with its 60 million people would attack France with its 40 million, unless the Germans were permanently weakened. Moreover, France had no English Channel (or Atlantic Ocean) as a reassuring barrier against German aggression. Wilson, supported by Lloyd George, would hear none of it. Clemenceau's demands seemed vindictive, violating morality and the principle of national self-determination. By April the conference was deadlocked on the German question, and Wilson packed his bags to go home.

Clemenceau's obsession with security reflected his anxiety about France's long-term weakness. In the end, convinced that France should not break with its allies because France could not afford to face Germany alone in the future, he agreed to a compromise. He gave up the French demand for a Rhineland buffer state in return for a formal defensive alliance with the United States and Great Britain. Under the terms of this alliance, both Wilson and Lloyd George promised that their countries would come to France's aid in the event of a German attack. Thus Clemenceau appeared to win his goal of French security, as Wilson had won his of a permanent international organization. The Allies moved quickly to finish the peace settlement, believing that necessary adjustments would later be possible within the dual framework of a strong Western alliance and the League of Nations (Map 32.4).

The Treaty of Versailles between the Allies and Germany was the key to the settlement, and the terms were not unreasonable as a first step toward reestablishing international order. Germany's colonies were given to France, Britain, and Japan as League of Nations mandates. Germany's territorial losses within Europe were minor, thanks to Wilson. Alsace-Lorraine was returned to France. Parts of Germany inhabited primarily by Poles were ceded to the new Polish state, in keeping with the principle of national self-determination. Predominantly German Danzig was also placed within the Polish tariff lines, but as a self-governing city under League of Nations protection. Germany had to limit its army to 100,000 men and agree to build no military fortifications in the Rhineland.

More harshly, the Allies declared that Germany (with Austria) was responsible for the war and had therefore to pay reparations equal to all civilian damages caused by the war. This unfortunate and much-criticized clause expressed inescapable popular demands for German blood, but the actual figure was not set and there was the clear possibility that reparations might be set at a reasonable level in the future, when tempers had cooled.

When presented with the treaty, the German government protested vigorously. But there was no alternative, especially in that Germany was still starving because the Allies had not yet lifted their naval blockade. On June 28, 1919, German representatives of the ruling moderate Social Democrats and the Catholic party signed the treaty in the Sun King's Hall of Mirrors at Versailles, where Bismarck's empire had been joyously proclaimed almost fifty years before.

Separate peace treaties were concluded with the other defeated powers—Austria, Hungary, Bulgaria, and Turkey. For the most part, these treaties merely ratified the existing situation in east central Europe following the breakup of the Austro-Hungarian Empire. Like Austria, Hungary was a particularly big loser, as its "captive" nationalities (and some interspersed Hungarians) were ceded to Rumania, Czechoslovakia, Poland, and Yugoslavia. Italy got some Austrian territory. The Turkish Empire was broken up. France received Lebanon and Syria, while Britain took Iraq and Palestine, which was to include a Jewish national homeland first promised by Britain in 1917. Officially League of Nations mandates, these acquisitions of the Western powers were one of the more imperialistic elements of the peace settlement. Another was mandating Germany's holdings in China to Japan. The age of Western imperialism lived on. National self-determination remained a reality only for Europeans and their offspring.

MAP 32.4 Shattered Empires and Territorial Changes After World War One The Great War brought tremendous changes in eastern Europe. New nations were established, and a dangerous power vacuum was created between Germany and Soviet Russia.

AMERICAN REJECTION OF THE VERSAILLES TREATY

The rapidly concluded peace settlement of early 1919 was not perfect, but within the context of war-shattered Europe it was an acceptable beginning. The principle of national self-determination, which had played such a large role in starting the war, was ac-cepted and served as an organizing framework. Germany had been punished but not dismembered. A new world organization complemented a traditional defensive alliance of satisfied powers. The serious remaining problems could be worked out in the future. Moreover, Allied leaders had seen speed as essential for another reason: they detested Lenin and feared that his Bolshevik Revolution might spread. They realized that their best answer to Lenin's unending calls for worldwide upheaval was peace and tranquillity for war-weary peoples.

There were, however, two great interrelated obstacles to such peace: Germany and the United States. Plagued by communist uprisings, reactionary plots, and popular disillusionment with losing the war at the last minute, Germany's moderate socialists and their liberal and Catholic supporters faced an enormous challenge. Like French republicans after 1871, they needed time (and luck) if they were to establish firmly a peaceful and democratic republic. Progress in this direction required understanding yet firm treatment of Germany by the victorious Western Allies, and particularly by the United States.

However, the United States Senate and, to a lesser extent, the American people rejected Wilson's handiwork. Republican senators led by Henry Cabot Lodge refused to ratify the Treaty of Versailles without changes in the articles creating the League of Nations. The key issue was the league's power—more apparent than real—to require member states to take collective action against aggression.

Lodge and others believed that this requirement gave away Congress's constitutional right to declare war. No doubt Wilson would have been wise to accept some reservations. But, in failing health, Wilson with narrow-minded self-righteousness rejected all attempts at compromise. He instructed loyal Democratic senators to vote against any reservations whatsoever to the Treaty of Versailles. In doing so, Wilson assured that the treaty was never ratified by the United States in any form and that the United States never joined the League of Nations. Moreover, the Senate refused to ratify Wilson's defensive alliance with France and Great Britain. America turned its back on Europe.

Perhaps understandable in the light of American traditions and the volatility of mass politics, the Wilson-Lodge fiasco and the newfound gospel of isolationism nevertheless represented a tragic and cowardly renunciation of America's responsibility. Using America's action as an excuse, Great Britain, too, refused to ratify its defensive alliance with France. Bitterly betrayed by its allies, France stood alone. Very shortly, France was to take actions against Germany that would feed the fires of German resentment and seriously undermine democratic forces in the new republic. The great hopes of early 1919 were turning to ashes by the end of the year.

The Western alliance had collapsed, and a grandiose plan for permanent peace had given way to a fragile truce. For this and for what came later, the United States must share a large part of the guilt.

Why did World War One have such revolutionary consequences? Why was it such a great break with the past? World War One was, first of all, a war of committed peoples. In France, Britain, and Germany in particular, governments drew on genuine popular support. This support reflected not only the diplomatic origins of the war but also the way western European society had been effectively unified under the nationalist banner in the later nineteenth century. The relentlessness of total war helps explain why so many died, why so many were crippled physically and psychologically, and why Western civilization would in so many ways never be the same again. More concretely, the war swept away monarchs and multinational empires. National self-determination apparently triumphed, not only in Austria-Hungary but in much of Russia's western borderlands as well. Except in Ireland and parts of Soviet Russia, the revolutionary dream of national unity, born of the French Revolution, had finally come true.

Two other revolutions were products of the war. In Russia, the Bolsheviks established a radical regime, smashed existing capitalist institutions, and stayed in power with a new kind of authoritarian rule. Whether the new Russian regime was truly Marxian or socialist was questionable, but it indisputably posed a powerful, ongoing revolutionary challenge in Europe and Europe's colonial empires.

More subtle, but quite universal in its impact, was an administrative revolution. This revolution, born of the need to mobilize entire societies and economies for total war, greatly increased the power of government. And after the guns grew still, government planning and wholesale involvement in economic and social life did not disappear in Europe. Liberal market capitalism and a well-integrated world economy were among the many casualties of the administrative revolution, and greater social equality was everywhere one of its results. Thus, even in European countries where a communist takeover never came close to occurring, society still experienced a great revolution.

Finally, the "war to end war" did not bring peace but only a fragile truce: in the West the Allies failed to maintain their wartime solidarity. Germany remained unrepentant and would soon have more grievances to nurse. Moreover, the victory of national self-determination in eastern Europe created a power vacuum between a still-powerful Germany and a potentially mighty communist Russia. A vast area lay open to military aggression from two sides.

NOTES

1. M. Beloff, *U.S. News & World Report,* March 8, 1976, p. 53.
2. Quoted in J. Remak, *The Origins of World War I* (New York: Holt, Rinehart & Winston, 1967), p. 84.
3. Quoted in W. E. Mosse, *Alexander II and the Modernization of Russia* (New York: Collier Books, 1962), pp. 125–126.
4. Quoted in F. P. Chambers, *The War Behind the War, 1914–1918* (London: Faber & Faber, 1939), p. 168.
5. Quoted in R. O. Paxton, *Europe in the Twentieth Century* (New York: Harcourt Brace Jovanovich, 1975), p. 109.
6. Quoted in Chambers, pp. 302, 304.
7. A. B. Ulam, *The Bolsheviks* (New York: Collier Books, 1968), p. 349.
8. Ibid., p. 405.
9. H. Nicolson, *Peacemaking 1919* (New York: Grosset & Dunlap Universal Library, 1965), pp. 8, 31–32.
10. Ibid., p. 24.

SUGGESTED READING

O. Hale, *The Great Illusion, 1900–1914* (1971), is a thorough account of the prewar era. Both J. Remak, *The Origins of World War I* (1967), and L. Lafore, *The Long Fuse* (1971), are highly recommended studies of the causes of the First World War. A. J. P. Taylor, *The Struggle for Mastery in Europe, 1848–1919* (1954), is an outstanding survey of diplomatic developments with an exhaustive bibliography. V. Steiner, *Britain and the Origins of the First World War* (1978), and G. Kennan, *The Decline of Bismarck's European Order: Franco-Russian Relations, 1875–1890* (1979), are also major contributions. K. Jarausch's *The Enigmatic Chancellor* (1973) is an important recent study on Bethmann-Hollweg and German policy in 1914. C. Falls, *The Great War* (1961), is the best brief introduction to military aspects of the war. B. Tuchman, *The Guns of August* (1962), is a marvelous account of the dramatic first month of the war and the beginning of military stalemate. A. J. P. Taylor, *The First World War* (1963), is a strikingly illustrated history of the war, and A. Horne, *The Price of Glory: Verdun 1916* (1979), is a moving account of the famous siege. J. Ellis, *Eye-Deep in Hell* (1976), is a vivid account of trench warfare.

F. L. Carsten, *War Against War* (1982), considers radical movements in Britain and Germany. The best single volume on the home fronts is still F. Chambers, *The War Behind the War, 1914–1918* (1939). Chambers drew heavily on the many fine books on the social and economic impact of the war in different countries published by the Carnegie Endowment for International Peace under the general editorship of J. T. Shotwell. A. Marwick, *The Deluge* (1970), is a lively account of war and society in Britain, while G. Feldman, *Army, Industry, and Labor in Germany, 1914–1918* (1966), shows the impact of total war and military dictatorship on Germany. Two excellent collections of essays, J. Roth, ed., *World War I* (1967), and R. Albrecht-Carrié, ed., *The Meaning of the First World War* (1965), deftly probe the enormous consequences of the war for people and society. The debate over Germany's guilt and aggression, which has been reopened in recent years, may be best approached through G. Feldman, ed., *German Imperialism, 1914–1918* (1972), and A. Hillgruber, *Germany and the Two World Wars* (1981). M. Fainsod, *International Socialism and the World War* (1935), ably discusses the splits between radical and moderate socialists during the conflict. In addition to Erich Maria Remarque's great novel *All Quiet on the Western Front,* Henri Barbusse, *Under Fire* (1917), and Jules Romains, *Verdun* (1939), are highly recommended for their fictional yet realistic recreations of the war. P. Fussell, *The Great War and Modern Memory* (1975), probes all the powerful literature inspired by the war.

A. Ulam's *The Bolsheviks* (1968), which focuses on Lenin, is a masterful introduction to the Russian Revolution, as is B. Wolfe, *Three Who Made a Revolution* (1955), a collective biography of Lenin, Trotsky, and Stalin. R. Conquest, *V. I. Lenin* (1972), is a good short biography. Leon Trotsky himself wrote the colorful and exciting *History of the Russian Revolution* (1932), which may be compared with the classic eyewitness account of the young, pro-Bolshevik American John Reed, *Ten Days That Shook the World* (1919). R. Daniels, *Red October* (1969), provides a clear account of the Bolshevik seizure of power, and R. Pipes, *The Formation of the Soviet Union* (1968), is recommended for its excellent treatment of the nationality problem during the revolution. A. Wildman, *The End of the Russian Imperial Army* (1980), is a fine account of the soldiers' revolt, and G. Leggett, *The Cheka: Lenin's Secret Police* (1981), shows revolutionary terror in action. Boris Pasternak's justly celebrated *Doctor Zhivago* is a great historical novel of the revolutionary era. R. Massie, *Nicholas and Alexandra* (1971), is a moving popular biography of Russia's last royal family and the terrible health problem of the heir to the throne. H. Nicolson, *Peacemaking 1919* (1965), captures the spirit of the Versailles settlement. T. Bailey, *Woodrow Wilson and the Lost Peace* (1963), and W. Widenor, *Henry Cabot Lodge and the Search for an American Foreign Policy* (1981), are also highly recommended. A. Mayer provocatively stresses the influence of domestic social tensions and widespread fear of further communist revolt in *The Politics and Diplomacy of Peacemaking* (1969).

PERIOD (CA 1700–1920)	AFRICA AND THE MIDDLE EAST	THE AMERICAS	
1700	Approximately 11,000,000 slaves shipped from Africa, ca 1450–1850 Dutch found Cape Colony, 1657 Rise of the Ashanti, West Africa, ca 1700 Decline of the Safavid Empire under Nadir Shah, 1737–1747	Spain's defeat in War of the Spanish Succession, 1701–1714, prompts trade reform, leading to colonial dependence on Spanish goods, 18th century	
1750	Sultan Selim III establishes first diplomatic relations between Ottoman Empire and Europe, introduces administrative and military reforms, 1761–1808 British seize Cape Town, 1795 Napoleon's campaign in Egypt, 1798	"French and Indian wars," 1756–1763 Quebec Act, 1774 American Revolution, 1775–1783 Comunero revolution, New Granada, 1781	
1800	Muhammad Ali founds dynasty in Egypt, 1805–1848 Slavery abolished in British Empire, 1807 Peak year of African transatlantic slave trade, 1820 European capitalists begin large-scale investment in Africa, 1840s	Latin American wars of independence from Spain, 1806–1825 Brazil wins independence from Portugal, 1822 Monroe Doctrine, 1823 Political instability in most Latin American countries, 1825–1870 Mexican War, 1846–1848	
1850	Crimean War, 1853–1856 Suez Canal opens, 1869 Europeans intensify "scramble for Africa," 1880–1900 Battle of Omdurman, 1898 Boer War, 1899–1902	American Civil War, 1861–1865 British North America Act, 1867 Porfirio Diaz controls Mexico, 1876–1911 U.S. practices "dollar diplomacy" in Latin America, 1890–1920s Spanish-American War, 1898; U.S. gains Philippines	
1900	Union of South Africa formed, 1910 French annex Morocco, 1912 Ottoman Empire enters World War One on Germany's side Treaty of Sèvres dissolves Ottoman Empire, 1919; Mustafa Kemal mounts nationalist struggle in Turkey	Massive immigration from Europe and Asia to the Americas, 1880–1914 Mexican Revolution, 1910 Panama Canal opens, 1914 U.S. enters World War One, 1917 Mexico adopts constitution, 1917	

	EAST ASIA	INDIA AND SOUTHEAST ASIA	EUROPE
	Tokugawa Regime in Japan, characterized by political stability and economic growth, 1600–1867 Manchus establish Ch'ing Dynasty, 1644–1911 Height of Ch'ing Dynasty under Emperor Ch'ien-lung, 1736–1799	Mughal power contested by Hindus and Muslims, 18th century Persian invaders defeat Mughal army, loot Delhi, 1739 French and British fight for control of India, 1740–1763	Growth of absolutism in central and eastern Europe, ca 1680–1790 The Enlightenment, ca 1680–1800 Development of Cabinet system in England, 1714–1742 Height of land enclosure in England, ca 1760–1810
	Maximum extent of Ch'ing Empire, 1759	Battle of Plassey, 1757 Treaty of Paris, 1763; French colonies ceded to Britain East India Act, 1784 British conquer Ceylon, 1796	Englishman James Watt produces first steam engine, 1769 Louis XVI of France, 1774–1792 Outbreak of French Revolution, 1789 National Convention declares France a republic, 1792
	Java War, 1825–1830 Anglo-Chinese Opium War, 1839–1842 Treaty of Nanking, 1842: Manchus surrender Hong Kong to British	British found Singapore, 1819 British defeat last independent native state in India, 1848	Napoleonic Empire, 1804–1814 Congress of Vienna, 1814–1815 European economic penetration of non-Western countries, ca 1816–1880 Greece wins independence from Ottoman Empire, 1829 Revolutions in France, Prussia, Italy, and Austria, 1848–1849
	Taiping Rebellion, 1850–1864 Perry's arrival opens Japan to Europe, 1853 Meiji Restoration in Japan, 1867 Adoption of constitution in Japan, 1890 Sino-Japanese War, 1894–1895 "Hundred Days of Reform" in China, 1898	Great Rebellion in India, 1857–1858 French seize Saigon, 1859 Indian National Congress formed, 1885 French acquire Indochina, 1893	Second and Third Empires in France, 1852–1914 Unification of Italy, 1859–1870 Otto von Bismarck's reign of power in German affairs, 1862–1890 Franco-Prussian War, 1870–1871; foundation of the German Empire Parliamentary Reform Bill, Great Britain, 1867 Second Socialist International, 1889–1914
	Boxer Rebellion in China, 1900–1903 Russian-Japanese War, 1904–1905 Chinese Revolution; fall of Ch'ing Dynasty, 1911 Chinese Republic, 1912–1949	Muslim League formed, 1906 Radicals make first calls for Indian independence, 1907 Amritsar Massacre in India, 1919 Intensification of Indian nationalism, 1919–1947	Revolution in Russia; Tsar Nicholas II forced to issue October Manifesto, 1905 Triple Entente (Britain, Russia, France), 1914–1918 World War One, 1914–1918 Treaty of Versailles, 1919

33

NATIONALISM IN ASIA, 1914–1939

*F*ROM ASIA'S PERSPECTIVE the First World War was a European civil war. As a result it decisively shattered the united front of Western imperialism and convulsed prewar relationships in Asia. Most crucially, the war speeded up the development of modern nationalism in Asia. As discussed in Chapter 30, the nationalist gospel of anti-imperialist political freedom and racial equality had already won converts among Asia's westernized, educated elites before 1914. In the 1920s and 1930s it increasingly won the souls of the masses. As in Europe in the nineteenth century, nationalism became a mass movement with potentially awesome power.

There were at least three reasons for the upsurge of nationalism in Asia. First and foremost, nationalism provided the most effective means of organizing the anti-imperialist resistance to direct foreign rule and to indirect Western domination. Second, nationalism called for fundamental changes and challenged old political practices and beliefs. Therefore, modernizers used it as a weapon in their ongoing contest for influence and power with conservative traditionalists. Modernizers also used nationalism as a conduit to spread other values they espoused, like industrialization, or the European secular world-view with its faith in science, critical thinking, and progress. Third, nationalism spread because it gave both leaders and followers a vision of a shining future for a rejuvenated people. Thus nationalism provided an ideology to ennoble the sacrifices that the struggle would require.

The spread of nationalism also had its dark side. As in Europe (page 844), nationalists in Asia developed a strong sense of "we" and "they." The "they" were often the enemy—the oppressor. White-skinned European imperialists were just such a " they," and nationalist feeling generated the power to destroy European empires and successfully challenge even more widespread foreign economic domination. But, as in Europe, nationalism in Asia also stimulated bitter conflicts and even wars between peoples, in two different ways. First, it stimulated conflicts between relatively homogeneous peoples in large states, rallying, for example, Chinese against Japanese and vice versa. Second, nationalism often heightened tensions between ethnic (or religious) groups *within* states, especially states with a variety of peoples. Like the old

Austrian or Russian empires before 1914, such states had been formed largely by authoritarian rulers and their armies and bureaucracies. When such rigid rule declined or snapped, increasingly self-conscious and nationalistic peoples might easily quarrel, seeking to divide the existing state or to dominate the enemy "they" within its borders.

Although modern nationalism has everywhere exhibited certain shared characteristics, it has never been monolithic. Nowhere was this truer than in Asia, where the new and often narrow ideology of nationalism was grafted onto old, rich, and complex civilizations. Between the world wars each Asian country developed its own distinct national movement, rooted in its unique culture and particular historical experience. Each people created its own national reawakening, which renovated thought and culture as well as politics and economics.

How did modern nationalism—the dominant force in most of the world in the twentieth century—develop in Asia between the First and Second World Wars? How did national movements arise in different countries, and how did some of these parallel movements come into brutal conflict? These are the questions this chapter will seek to answer.

THE FIRST WORLD WAR AND WESTERN IMPERIALISM

Every Asian national movement shared in a burning desire for genuine freedom from foreign imperialism. The First World War had a profound effect on these aspirations by altering relations between Asia and Europe.

As a distinguished Indian historian has written, "the Great War of 1914–1918 was from the Asian point of view a civil war within the European community of nations."[1] For four years Asians watched the haughty bearers of the white man's burden vilifying and destroying each other. Far from standing united and supremely self-confident in an apparently unbeatable imperialistic phalanx, the Western nations were clawing at each other in total disarray. The impact of this spectacle was enormous. Japan's defeat of imperial Russia in 1904 (page 915) had shown that an Asian power could beat a European great power; now for the first time Asians saw the entire West as divided and vulnerable.

Few Asians particularly cared who won the vicious family quarrel in distant Europe. But the Europeans, particularly the British and the French, were driven by the harsh logic of total war to draft their colonial subjects into the conflict. The British and French uprooted hundreds of thousands of Asians and Africans to fight the Germans and Turks. This too had major consequences. An Indian or Vietnamese soldier who fought in France and came in contact there with democratic and republican ideas was likely to be less willing to accept foreign rule when he returned home.

The British and the French also made rash promises to gain the support of colonial peoples during the war. Thus British leaders were promising Jewish nationalists in Europe a homeland in Palestine even as they promised Arab nationalists independence from the Ottoman Empire. To counteract popular unrest in India due to inflation and heavy taxation, the British in 1917 were forced to announce a new policy of self-governing institutions. After the war, afflicted with second thoughts, the colonial powers found that the nationalist genie they had released refused to slip meekly back into the bottle.

The idealistic war aims of President Wilson also raised the hopes of peoples under colonial rule. In January 1918 Wilson proposed to make peace on the basis of his Fourteen Points (page 1028), whose key idea was national self-determination for the peoples of Europe and of the Ottoman Empire. Wilson also proposed that in all colonial questions "the interests of native populations be given equal weight with the desires of European governments." Wilson's program seemed to call for national self-rule, the rights of weak nations, and international justice. This subversive, even revolutionary, message was spread around the world by American propagandists in 1918 and 1919. It had enormous appeal for educated Asians, fueling their hopes of freedom and dignity.

Military service and Wilsonian self-determination also fired the hopes of some Africans and some visionary American black supporters of African freedom. But World War One had less impact on European imperialism in black Africa—Africa south of the Sahara—than in Asia and the Arab world. Because the European conquest of Africa was not completed until 1900, Africans outside of certain coastal areas had not experienced foreign domination long enough for nationalist movements to develop. Moreover, European rulers customarily grouped many tribes and peoples into a single administrative unit, and such ethnic diversity slowed the development of a common national loyalty. For black Africa, as will be discussed in Chapter 37, the Great Depression and World War Two were to prove much more influential in the growth of nationalist movements.

Once the Allies had won the war, they tried to shift gears and re-establish or increase their political and economic domination in Asia and Africa. Although fatally weakened, in retrospect, Western imperialism remained very much alive in 1918. First of all, President Wilson was no revolutionary. At the Versailles Peace Conference he proved willing to compromise on colonial questions in order to achieve some of his European goals and the creation of the League of Nations. Also, Allied statesmen and ordinary French and British citizens quite rightly believed that their colonial empires had contributed to their ultimate victory over the Central Powers. They were in no mood to give up such valuable possessions voluntarily. Third, the victors remained convinced of the superiority of their civilization. They believed that their rule was best for colonial peoples. A few "discontented" Asian or African intellectuals might agitate for self-rule; but Europeans in general, and colonial officials in particular, believed that the humble masses were grateful for the law and order brought by the white man's administration. If pressed, Europeans said that such administration was preparing colonial subjects for eventual self-rule, but only in the distant future.

The compromise at Versailles between Wilson's vague, moralistic idealism and the European preoccupation with "good administration" was the establishment of a system of League of Nations mandates over Germany's former colonies and the old Ottoman Empire. Article 22 of the League of Nations Covenant, which was part of the Treaty of Versailles, assigned territories "inhabited by peoples incapable of governing themselves" to various "developed nations." "The well-being and development of such peoples" was declared "a sacred trust of civilization." A Permanent Mandates Commission was created to oversee the developed nations' fulfillment of their international responsibility; most of the members of the Permanent Mandates Commission came from

Delegates to the Peace Conference of 1919 Standing in the foreground is Prince Faisal, third son of King Hussein of Hejaz and frustrated spokesman for the Arab cause at Versailles. The British officer T. E. Lawrence—popularly known as Lawrence of Arabia— is second from the right in the middle row. *(Imperial War Museum)*

European countries with colonies. Thus the League elaborated a new principle, development toward the eventual goal of self-government, but left its implementation to the colonial powers themselves.

The mandates system clearly demonstrated that Europe was determined to maintain its imperial rule. It is no wonder that Asian patriots were bitterly disappointed after the First World War. They saw France, Great Britain, and other nations—industrialized Japan was the only Asian state to obtain mandates—grabbing Germany's colonies as spoils of war and creating more colonial protectorates in the old Ottoman Empire. Yet Asian patriots were not about to give up. They preached the nationalist creed and

struggled to build mass movements capable of achieving independence.

In this struggle they were encouraged and sometimes inspired by Soviet communism. Immediately after the October Revolution, Lenin and his fellow Bolsheviks declared that the Asian peoples conquered by the tsars, now inhabitants of the Soviet Union, were complete equals of the Russians with a right to their own development. (In actuality this hardly happened, but the propaganda was effective nonetheless.) The Communists also denounced European (and American) imperialism and pledged to support revolutionary movements in all colonial countries, even when they were primarily movements of national independence led by "middle-class" intellectuals instead of revolutionary workers. Foreign political and economic exploitation was the immediate enemy, they said, and socialist revolution could wait until after Western imperialism had been defeated.

The example, ideology, and support of Russian Communists exerted a powerful influence in the 1920s and 1930s, particularly in China and French Indochina. Middle-class nationalists were strengthened in their battle with foreign rule, and the ranks of communist nationalists also swelled. A nationalistic young Vietnamese, who had pled the cause of Vietnamese independence unsuccessfully at the Versailles Peace Conference, described his feelings when he read Lenin's statement on national self-determination for colonial peoples, adopted by the Communist Third International in 1920:

These resolutions filled me with great emotion, enthusiasm, and faith. They helped me see the problem clearly. My joy was so great I began to cry. Alone in my room I wrote the following words, as if I were addressing a great crowd: "My dear compatriots, so miserable and oppressed, here is what we need. Here is the path to our liberation."[2]

The young nationalist was Ho Chi Minh (1890–1969), who was to fight a lifetime to create an independent, communist Vietnam.

Yet the appeal of nationalism in Asia was not confined to territories under direct European rule, like French Indochina and League of Nations mandates. The extraordinary growth of international trade after 1850 had drawn millions of peasants and shopkeepers throughout Asia into the Western-dominated world economy, disrupting local markets and often creating hostility toward European businessmen. Moreover, Europe and the United States had forced even the most solid Asian states, China and Japan, to accept unequal treaties and humiliating limitations on their sovereignty. Thus the nationalist promise of genuine independence and true equality with the West appealed as powerfully in old but weak states like China as in colonial territories like British India.

Finally, as in Russia after the Crimean War or in Japan after the Meiji Restoration, the nationalist creed went hand in hand with acceptance of modernization by the educated elites. Modernization promised changes that would enable old societies to compete effectively with the world's leading nations.

THE MIDDLE EAST

The most flagrant attempt to expand the scope of Western imperialism occurred in the Middle East, where the British and the French sought to replace the defunct Ottoman Empire with their own rule. Arab, Turkish, and Iranian nationalists, as well as Jewish nationalists arriving from Europe, reacted violently. Their struggles to win dignity and independence sometimes brought nationalists into sharp conflict with each other, most notably in Palestine.

THE ARAB REVOLT

The Ottoman Empire, which had long been subject to European pressure and had adopted European military and educational reforms in the 1820s and 1830s, became increasingly weak and autocratic in the late nineteenth century. The combination of declining international stature and domestic tyranny eventually led to an upsurge of revolutionary activity among idealistic exiles and nationalistic young army officers, who wanted to seize power and save the Ottoman state. These fervent patriots, the so-called Young Turks, succeeded in the revolution of 1908, and subsequently they were determined to hold the vast multi-ethnic empire together. Defeated by Bulgaria, Serbia, and Greece in the Balkan War of 1912, stripped of practically all territory in Europe, the Young Turks redoubled their efforts in Asia. The most important of their Asian possessions were Syria —consisting of modern-day Lebanon, Syria, Israel, and Jordan—and Iraq; the Ottoman Turks claimed the Arabian peninsula but exercised only a loose control there.

For centuries the largely Arabic populations of Syria and Iraq had been tied to their Ottoman rulers by their common faith in Islam (though there were Christian Arabs as well). Yet beneath the surface, ethnic and linguistic tensions simmered between Turks and Arabs, who were as different as Chinese and Japanese or French and Germans. As early as 1883, a Frenchman who had traveled widely in the Arab provinces reported:

Everywhere I came upon the same abiding and universal sentiment: hatred of the Turks. The notion of concerted action to throw off the detested yoke is gradually shaping itself. . . . An Arab movement,newly-risen, is looming in the distance; a race hitherto downtrodden will presently claim its due place in the destinies of Islam.[3]

The actions of the Young Turks after 1908 made the "Arab movement" a reality. Although some Turkish reformers argued for an Ottoman liberalism that would give equal political rights to all ethnic and religious groups within the empire, the majority successfully insisted on a narrow Turkish nationalism. They further centralized the Ottoman Empire, and extended the sway of the Turkish language, culture, and race. In 1909 the Turkish government brutally slaughtered thousands of Armenian Christians, a prelude to the criminal destruction of more than a million Armenians during the fighting with Russia in World War One. Meanwhile the Arab revolt gathered strength. By 1914 the great majority of Arab leaders believed that armed conflict with their Turkish masters was inevitable.

When the Young Turks made the fatal decision in 1914 to side with Germany, which had helped reform Ottoman armies before the war, Arab leaders suddenly found an unexpected ally in Great Britain. The foremost Arab leader was Hussein Ibn-Ali (1856–1931), a direct descendant of the prophet Muhammad through the house of Quraysh. As the *sharif,* or chief magistrate of Mecca, the most holy city in the Muslim world, Hussein governed much of the territory along the Red Sea, known as the Hejaz. Basically anti-Turkish, Hussein refused to second the Turkish sultan's call for a holy war against the Triple Entente. His refusal pleased the British, who feared that such calls would trigger a Muslim revolt in India.

In 1915 Hussein managed to win vague British commitments to Arab independence, and the next year he revolted against the Turks, proclaiming himself king of the Arabs. Hussein joined forces with the British under T. E. Lawrence, who in 1917 led Arab tribesmen and Indian soldiers in a highly successful guerrilla war against the Turks on the Arabian peninsula. In September 1918, British armies and their Arab allies smashed into Syria. This last great offensive culminated in the triumphal entry of Hussein's son Faisal into Damascus. There was wild Arab rejoicing, and many patriots expected independence to rise from the dust of the Ottoman collapse.

Within two years, however, many Arab nationalists felt bitterly betrayed by Great Britain and its allies. The issues involved are complex, controversial, and highly emotional, but it is undeniable that this bitterness left an enduring legacy of hatred toward the West. When Britain and France set about implementing secret wartime treaties to divide and rule the old Ottoman Empire, Arab nationalists felt betrayed. In the secret Sykes-Picot Agreement of 1916, Britain and France had agreed that France would receive modern-day Lebanon, Syria, and much of southern Turkey, and Britain would receive Palestine, Jordan, and Iraq. These treaties, drawn up to reinforce Allied determination to fight on, contradicted British (and Wilsonian) promises concerning Arab independence after the war.

A related source of Arab bitterness was Britain's wartime commitment to a Jewish homeland in Palestine. The famous Balfour Declaration of November 1917 declared:

His Majesty's Government views with favor the establishment in Palestine of a National Home for the Jewish People, and will use their best endeavors to facilitate the achievement of this object, it being clearly understood that nothing shall be done which may prejudice the civil and religious rights of existing non-Jewish communities in Palestine, or the rights and political status enjoyed by Jews in any other country.

As careful reading reveals, the Balfour Declaration made contradictory promises to European Jews and Middle Eastern Arabs, and it has been a subject of passionate debate ever since. Some British Cabinet members apparently believed such a declaration would appeal to German, Austrian, and American Jews and thus help the British war effort; others sincerely supported the Zionist vision of a Jewish homeland, which they believed would also help maintain British control of the Suez Canal. In any event, Arabs were dismayed. In 1914 Jews accounted for about 11 percent of the predominantly Arab population of the Ottoman province of Palestine. A "Jewish national home" seemed to the Arabs to imply some kind of Jewish state incompatible with majority rule. Also, a state founded on religious and ethnic exclusivity was out of keeping with both Islamic and Ottoman tradition, which had historically been more tolerant of religious diversity and minorities than had the Christian monarchs or nation-states in Europe.

Despite strong French objections, Hussein's son Faisal was allowed to attend the Paris Peace Conference; but the Allies made clear that he represented only the Kingdom of Hejaz, not all Arabs. Faisal invoked Wilson's idea of self-determination, but despite Wilson's lukewarm support his effort came to nothing. Faisal was forced to accept Franco-British demands regarding the mandate system and the Balfour Declaration. On his return to Syria, Faisal's followers repudiated his compromise. In March 1920 they met as the Syrian National Congress and proclaimed Syrian independence with Faisal as king. A similar congress declared Iraq an independent kingdom.

Western reaction was swift and decisive. France and Britain convened the League of Nations to approve the mandates they wanted. Then a French army stationed in Lebanon attacked Syria, taking Damascus in July 1920. Faisal fled and the French took over. Meanwhile the British put down an uprising in Iraq with bloody fighting and established military rule there. Western imperialism appeared to have replaced Turkish rule in the Middle East (Map 33.1).

THE TURKISH REVOLUTION

In November 1918 the Allied fleet entered Constantinople (modern Istanbul), the Ottoman capital. A young English official vividly described the strange and pathetic situation he encountered:

I found the Ottoman Empire utterly smashed, her vast territories stripped into pieces, and her conquered populations blinded and bewildered by their sudden release. The Turks were worn out, dead-tired, and without bitterness awaited their fate. . . . The debris of the old order waited to be constructed into a new system.[4]

The Allies' "new system" was blatant imperialism, and it proved harsher for the Turks than for the Arabs. A treaty forced on the helpless sultan dismembered Turkey and reduced it to a puppet state. Not only did Great Britain and France occupy parts of Turkey; Italy and Greece claimed their shares as well. There was a sizable Greek minority in western Turkey, and Greek nationalists cherished the "Great Idea" of incorporating this territory into a modern Greek empire modeled on long-dead Christian Byzantium. In 1919 a Greek army carried by British

ships landed on the Turkish coast at Smyrna. The sultan ordered his exhausted troops not to resist, and Greek armies advanced into the interior. Turkey seemed finished.

But Turkey produced a great leader and revived to become an inspiration to the entire Middle East. Mustafa Kemal (1881–1938), the father of modern Turkey, was a military man. The son of a petty government official and sympathetic to the Young Turk movement, Kemal distinguished himself in World War One by directing the successful defense of the Dardanelles against British attack, the only great Turkish victory of the war. Back in Istanbul after the armistice, Mustafa Kemal watched with anguish the Allies' aggression and the sultan's cowardice. In early 1919 he moved to central Turkey and began working to unify the Turkish resistance.

The sultan, bowing to Allied pressure, initially denounced Kemal, but the cause of national liberation proved more powerful. The catalyst was the Greek invasion and attempted annexation of much of western Turkey. One young woman who was to play a major role in the Turkish revolution described feelings she shared with countless others:

After I learned about the details of the Smyrna occupation [by Greek armies], I hardly opened my mouth on any subject except when it concerned the sacred struggle. . . . I suddenly ceased to exist as an individual. I worked, wrote and lived as a unit of that magnificent national madness.[5]

Refusing to acknowledge the Allied dismemberment of their country, the Turks battled on through 1920 despite staggering defeats. The next year the Greeks, egged on by the British, advanced almost to Ankara, the nationalist stronghold in central Anatolia. There Mustafa Kemal's forces took the offensive and won a great victory. The Greeks and their British allies sued for peace. After long negotiations, the resulting Treaty of Lausanne (1923) abolished the hated Capitulations, imposed by European powers in the nineteenth century to give their citizens special privileges in the Ottoman Empire, and recognized the territorial integrity of a truly independent Turkey; Turkey lost only its former Arab provinces.

Mustafa Kemal, a nationalist without religious faith, believed that Turkey should modernize and secularize along Western lines. His first moves were political. Drawing on his great prestige as a war hero,

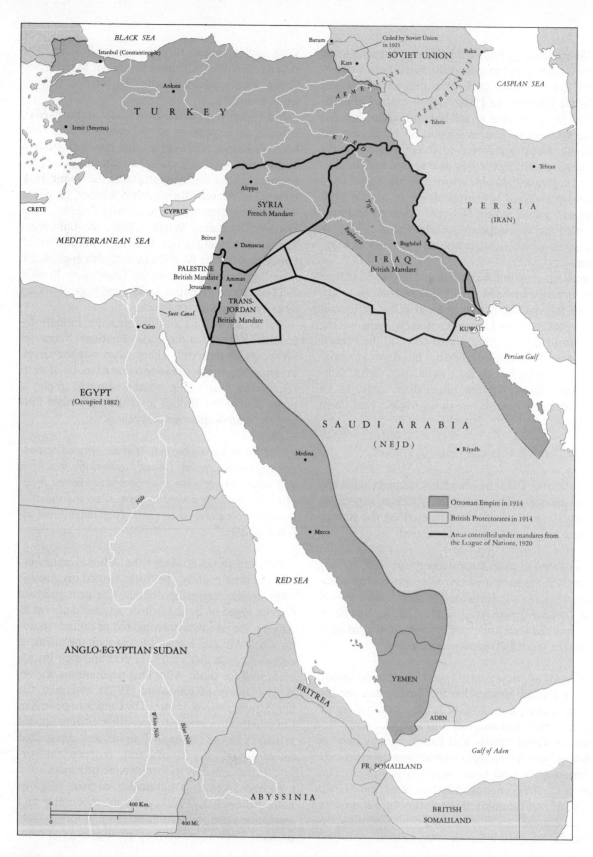

BLACK SEA

Istanbul (Constantinople)

Batum

Ceded by Soviet Union
in 1921

SOVIET UNION

Baku

Kars

CASPIAN SEA

Ankara

A R M E N I A N S

TURKEY

A Z E R B A I J A N I S

Tabriz

Izmir (Smyrna)

K U R D S

Tehran

CRETE

CYPRUS

Aleppo

SYRIA
French Mandate

P E R S I A

(IRAN)

MEDITERRANEAN SEA

Beirut

Damascus

Tigris

Euphrates

Baghdad

I R A Q
British Mandate

PALESTINE
British Mandate

Amman

Jerusalem

TRANS-
JORDAN
British Mandate

Suez Canal

KUWAIT

Cairo

Persian Gulf

EGYPT
(Occupied 1882)

SAUDI ARABIA

(N E J D)

Medina

Riyadh

Nile

RED SEA

Mecca

Ottoman Empire in 1914

British Protectorates in 1914

Areas controlled under mandates from
the League of Nations, 1920

ANGLO-EGYPTIAN SUDAN

White Nile

Blue Nile

ERITREA

YEMEN

ADEN

Gulf of Aden

FR. SOMALILAND

ABYSSINIA

BRITISH
SOMALILAND

0   400 Km.

0   400 Mi.

Kemal called on the somewhat reluctant National Assembly to depose the sultan and establish a republic. He had himself elected president and moved the capital from cosmopolitan Istanbul to Ankara in the Turkish heartland. Kemal savagely crushed the demands for independence of ethnic minorities like the Armenians and the Kurds, but realistically abandoned all thought of winning back lost Arab territories. He focused instead on internal affairs, creating a one-party system—partly inspired by the Bolshevik example—to work his will.

The most radical of Kemal's changes pertained to religion and culture. For centuries, most of the intellectual and social activities of believers had been sternly regulated by Islamic religious authorities, in keeping with the Sacred Law. Profoundly influenced by the example of western Europe, Mustafa Kemal set out, like the philosophes of the Enlightenment, to restrict the place of religion and religious leaders in daily affairs. Like Russia's Peter the Great, he employed dictatorial measures rather than reason to reach his goal. Kemal and his followers simply decreed a revolutionary separation of church and state. Religious courts were abolished, replaced by a completely new legal system based on European law codes. Religious schools gave way to state schools that taught such secular subjects as science, mathematics, and social sciences.

To dramatize the break with the past, Mustafa Kemal struck down many entrenched patterns of behavior. Women, traditionally secluded and dominated by males in Islamic society, received the right to vote. Marriage was now governed by civil law on a European model, rather than the Islamic code. Women were allowed to seek divorces, and no longer could a wealthy man take a second, third, or fourth wife, as under Islamic law. Men were forbidden to

Mustafa Kemal explains his radical reform of the written language. Impeccably elegant European dress symbolizes Kemal's conception of a modernized Turkey. *(Historical Pictures Service, Chicago)*

wear the tall red fez as headgear; government employees were ordered to wear business suits and felt hats, erasing the visible differences between Muslims and "infidel" Europeans. The old Arabic script was replaced with a new Turkish alphabet, based on Roman letters, that made the written language closer to the spoken vernacular. This revolutionary change isolated Turks from their historical heritage and literature, as the radical reformers probably hoped. The simpler, more phonetic alphabet also facilitated massive government efforts to spread basic literacy after 1928. Finally, in 1935, family names on the European model were introduced. The National Assembly granted Mustafa Kemal the surname Atatürk, which means "father of the Turks."

By the time of his death in 1938, Atatürk and his supporters had consolidated their pioneering revolution. Government-sponsored industrialization was fostering urban growth and new attitudes. Turks no longer considered business and science beneath their

MAP 33.1 The Partition of the Ottoman Empire, 1914–1923 The decline of the mighty Ottoman Empire had begun in 1699, when the Habsburgs conquered Hungary, and it had accelerated after 1805, when Egypt became virtually independent. By 1914 the Ottoman Turks had been pushed out of the Balkans and their Arab provinces were on the edge of revolt; that revolt erupted in World War One and contributed greatly to Ottoman defeat. When the Allies then attempted to implement their plans, including independence for the Armenian people, Mustafa Kemal arose to forge in battle the modern Turkish state.

dignity. Poverty persisted in rural areas, as did some religious discontent among devout Muslims, which caused Turkish governments after World War Two to modify some of Atatürk's most radical reforms in a conservative direction. But like the Japanese after the Meiji Restoration, the Turkish people had rallied around the nationalist banner to repulse European imperialism and were building a modern secular nation-state.

IRAN AND AFGHANISTAN

In Persia, renamed Iran in 1935, brutal efforts to build a unified modern nation ultimately proved less successful than in Turkey.

The late nineteenth century had been a sorry period in Iran's long and sometimes glorious history. Iran was subject to extreme foreign pressure, the Russians pressing relentlessly from the north and the British pushing upward from India and the Persian Gulf. Like China in a similar predicament at the same time, Iran managed to play the Great Powers against each other to maintain a precarious independence. However, the spectacle of the shah granting economic privileges to foreigners alienated native merchants. At the same time an inspired religious leader, Jamal al-Din al-Afghani, preached governmental reform as a means of reviving Islamic civilization. In 1906 a nationalistic coalition of merchants, religious leaders, and intellectuals revolted. The despotic shah was forced to grant a constitution and establish a national assembly, the Majlis. Nationalist hopes ran high.

Yet the Iranian revolution of 1906 was doomed to failure, largely because of European imperialism. Without consulting Iran, Britain and Russia in 1907 simply divided the country into spheres of influence. Britain's sphere ran along the Persian Gulf; the Russian sphere encompassed the whole northern half of Iran. Thereafter Russia intervened constantly. It blocked reforms, occupied cities, and completely dominated the country by 1912. When Russian power temporarily collapsed in the Bolshevik Revolution, British armies rushed into the power vacuum. By bribing corrupt Iranians liberally, Great Britain secured a 1919 agreement installing British "advisers" in every department of the government.

This blatant attempt to make Iran a British satellite was a key event in the development of Iranian nationalism. It aroused the national spirit. The Majlis refused to ratify the treaty, which confirmed Iranians' worst suspicions about Britain and the West. More important, in 1921 this reaction against the British brought to power a military dictator, Reza Shah, who proclaimed himself shah in 1925 and ruled until 1941.

Inspired throughout his reign by the example of Turkey's Mustafa Kemal, the patriotic, religiously indifferent Reza Shah had three basic goals: to build a modern nation, to free Iran from foreign domination, and to rule with an iron fist. The challenge was enormous. Iran was a vast, backward country of deserts, mountain barriers, and rudimentary communications. Most of the rural population was poor and illiterate, and there were sizable ethnic minorities with their own aspirations among the Persian majority. Furthermore, Iran's powerful religious leaders hated Western (Christian) domination, but were no less opposed to a more secular, less Islamic society.

To realize his vision of a strong Iran, the energetic shah created a modern army, built railroads, and encouraged commerce and industry. He won control over the ethnic minorities, like the Kurds in the north and the Arab tribesmen on the border with Iraq. He withdrew many of the privileges granted to foreigners and raised taxes on the powerful Anglo-Persian Oil Company. Yet Reza Shah was ultimately less successful than Atatürk. Because the European-educated elite was smaller than in Turkey, the idea of re-creating Persian greatness on the basis of a secularized society attracted fewer determined supporters. Many powerful religious leaders turned against him. Reza Shah became increasingly brutal, greedy, and tyrannical, murdering his enemies and lining his pockets. His support of Hitler's Nazi Germany also exposed Iran's tenuous and fragile independence to international conflicts.

Afghanistan, meanwhile, was nominally independent in the nineteenth century, but the British imposed political restrictions and constantly meddled in the country. In 1919 the new violently anti-British amir Ammanullah declared a holy war on the British government in India and won complete independence for the first time. Ammanullah then decreed revolutionary reforms designed to hurl his primitive country into the twentieth century. The result was tribal and religious revolt, civil war, and retreat from reform. Islam remained both religion and law. A powerful but primitive patriotism had enabled Afghanistan to win political freedom from the West,

Tel-Aviv, 1923 Founded by Jews in 1909 as a modern suburb for the old port of Jaffa, Tel-Aviv grew moderately at first, as this photo suggests. But the city's population surged in the 1930s after Hitler came to power and many European Jews sought refuge in Palestine. *(BBC Hulton/The Bettmann Archive)*

but modest efforts to build a modern society met little success.

THE ARAB STATES AND PALESTINE

The establishment of French and British mandates at the point of a gun forced Arab nationalists to seek independence by gradual means after 1920. Arab nationalists were indirectly aided by Western taxpayers, who wanted cheap empires—that is, peaceful ones. The result was that Arabs won considerable control over local affairs in the mandated states, except Palestine, though they remained European satellites in international and economic affairs.

The wily British chose Faisal, whom the French had so recently deposed in Syria, as king of Iraq. Faisal obligingly signed an alliance giving British advisers broad behind-the-scenes control. Faisal (1921–1933) proved an excellent ruler, gaining the support of his people and encouraging moderate reforms. In 1932 he secured Iraqi independence at the price of a long-term military alliance with Great Britain.

Egypt, occupied by Great Britain ever since 1882 (page 937) and a British protectorate since 1914, pursued a similar path. Following intense nationalist agitation after the war, Great Britain in 1922 proclaimed Egypt formally independent but continued to occupy the country militarily. In 1936, the British agreed to a treaty restricting their troops to the Suez Canal Zone.

The French were less compromising in Syria. They practiced a policy of divide-and-rule, carving out a second mandate in Lebanon and generally playing off ethnic and religious minorities against each other. Lebanon eventually became a republic, dominated by the Christian majority and under French protection. Arab nationalists in Syria finally won promises of Syrian independence in 1936 in return for a treaty of friendship with France.

In short, the Arab states freed themselves from Western mandates but not from Western influence. Foreign companies' seizure of control over the newly discovered oil fields also helped to convince radical nationalists that genuine independence had not yet

THE MIDDLE EAST, 1914–1939

1914	Ottoman Empire enters First World War on Germany's side
1916	Allies agree secretly to partition Ottoman Empire
1916–1917	Arab revolt against Turkish rule grows
November 1917	Balfour Declaration pledges British support for a Jewish homeland in Palestine
October 1918	Arabs and British triumph as Ottoman Empire collapses
1919	Treaty of Versailles divides old Ottoman Empire into League of Nations mandates
1919	Mustafa Kemal mounts nationalist struggle against foreign occupation
1920	Faisal proclaimed king of Syria but quickly deposed by the French, who establish their mandate in Syria
Early 1920s	Tide of Jewish immigration surges into British mandate of Palestine
1923	Treaty of Lausanne recognizes independent Turkey; Mustafa Kemal begins to secularize Turkish society
1925	Reza Shah takes power in Iran and rules to 1941
1932	Iraq gains political independence in return for long-term military alliance with Great Britain
1936	Syrian nationalists sign treaty of friendship with France in return for promises of independence
late 1930s	Tensions mount between Arabs and Jews in Palestine

been achieved. The struggle against the West had to continue.

Relations between the Arabs and the West were complicated by the tense situation in the British mandate of Palestine, which deteriorated in the interwar years. Both Arabs and Jews denounced the British, who tried unsuccessfully to compromise with both sides, but the anger of Arab nationalists was aimed primarily at Jewish settlers. The key issue was Jewish migration from Europe to Palestine. A small Jewish community had survived in Palestine ever since the destruction of Jerusalem and the dispersal of the Jews in Roman times. But Jewish nationalism, known as Zionism, was a recent phenomenon of European origin. The Dreyfus affair (page 919) and anti-Jewish riots in Russia had convinced a cultured Austrian journalist named Theodore Herzl that even nonreligious Jews would never be fully accepted in Europe. Only the re-creation of a Jewish state in Pal-

estine could guarantee Jews dignity and security. Under Herzl's leadership, the Zionist movement encouraged Jews from all over the world to settle in the Palestine region on lands purchased by Jewish philanthropists, with the approval of the relatively tolerant Ottoman rulers. Some Jewish idealists from Russia and central Europe were attracted to Palestine by the Zionist vision, but until 1921 the great majority of Jewish emigrants preferred the United States.

After World War One the situation changed radically. An isolationist United States drastically limited immigration from eastern Europe, where war and revolution had caused chaos and kindled anti-Semitism. Moreover, the British began honoring the Balfour Declaration despite Arab protests. Thus the number of Jewish immigrants to Palestine from turbulent interwar Europe grew rapidly. The first surge came in the early 1920s, the second in the 1930s when German (and Polish) persecution created a mass of Jewish refugees. By 1939 the Jewish population of Palestine had increased almost fivefold over 1914, and accounted for about 30 percent of all inhabitants.

Jewish settlers in Palestine faced formidable economic and political difficulties. Much of the land purchased by the Jewish National Fund was productive. But the sellers of such land were frequently wealthy absentee Arab landowners, the kind who had profited from the rise of commercial agriculture in Egypt and other parts of the Ottoman Empire and who had little interest in the welfare of their Arab tenants (page 937). When the new Jewish owners subsequently replaced those age-old tenants with Jewish settlers, Arab farmers and intellectuals burned with a sense of injustice. Moreover, most Jewish immigrants came from urban backgrounds and preferred to establish new cities like Tel Aviv or to live in existing towns, where they competed with the Arabs. Thus the land issue combined with economic and cultural friction in the towns to harden Arab protest into Arab hatred, and serious anti-Jewish riots and even massacres ensued. The British gradually responded to Arab pressure and tried to slow down Jewish immigration. This satisfied neither Jews nor Arabs, and by 1938 the two communities were engaged in an undeclared civil war. When, on the eve of World War Two, the frustrated British proposed an independent Palestine whose Jewish population would be permanently limited to one-third of the total, felt Zionists themselves in grave danger.

In the face of adversity, Jewish settlers from many different countries gradually succeeded in forging a cohesive community. Hebrew, which for centuries had been used only in religious worship, was revived as a living language to bind a people together. Despite its slow beginnings, rural development achieved often spectacular results. The key unit of agricultural organization was the kibbutz, a collective farm on which each member shared equally in the work, rewards, and defense of the farm. Men and women labored side by side; a nursery cared for the children and a common dining hall served meals. Some cooperative farms turned arid grazing land into citrus groves and irrigated gardens. An egalitarian socialist ideology also characterized industry, which grew rapidly and was owned largely by the Jewish trade unions. By 1939 a new but old nation was emerging in the Middle East.

TOWARD SELF-RULE IN INDIA

The national movement in British India grew out of two interconnected cultures, Hindu and Muslim, which came to see themselves as fundamentally different in rising to challenge British rule. Nowhere has the power of modern nationalism, both to unify and to divide, been more strikingly demonstrated than in India.

PROMISES AND REPRESSION, 1914–1919

Indian nationalism had emerged in the late nineteenth century (page 954), and when World War One began the British feared revolt. Instead, somewhat like Europe's equally mistrusted socialist workers, Indians loyally supported the war effort. About 1.2 million Indian soldiers and laborers volunteered for duty and served in Europe, Africa, and the Middle East. The British government in India and the native Indian princes sent large supplies of food, money, and ammunition. In return, the British opened more good government jobs to Indians and made other minor concessions.

As the war in distant Europe ground on, however, inflation, high taxes, food shortages, and a terrible influenza epidemic created widespread suffering and discontent. The prewar nationalist movement revived, stronger than ever, and the moderate and radical wings of the Indian National Congress joined forces. Moreover, in 1916 the Hindus leading the Congress party hammered out an alliance with India's Muslim League. Founded in 1906 to uphold Muslim interests, the league had grown out of fears that under British rule the once-dominant Muslim minority had fallen behind the Hindu majority, especially in the Western education necessary for good jobs in the government. The important 1916 alliance, known as the Lucknow Pact, forged a powerful united front and called for putting India on equal footing with self-governing white dominions like Canada, Australia, and New Zealand.

The British response was contradictory. On the one hand, the secretary of state for India made the unprecedented announcement in August 1917 that British policy in India called for the "gradual development of self-governing institutions and the pro-

An Indian Prince entertained British officers in 1907. India's native princes often lived in fabulous luxury, but the British always held the real power. *(The Bettmann Archive/ BBC Hulton)*

gressive realization of responsible government." The means of achieving this great step forward was spelled out in late 1919 in the Government of India Act, which established a dual administration, part Indian and elected, part British and authoritarian. Such noncontroversial activities as agriculture, health, and education were transferred to Indian officials, accountable to elected provincial assemblies. More sensitive matters like taxes, police, and prisons remained solely in British hands.

The positive impact of this reform, so typical of the British tradition of gradual political change, was seriously undermined by old-fashioned repression. Despite the unanimous opposition of the elected Indian members, the British in 1919 rammed the Rowlatt Acts through India's Imperial Legislative Council. These acts indefinitely extended wartime "emergency measures" designed to curb unrest and root out "conspiracy." The result was a wave of rioting across India.

In these tense conditions an unsuspecting crowd of some ten thousand gathered to celebrate a Hindu religious festival in an enclosed square in Amritsar, a city in the northern province of Punjab. The local English commander, General Dyer, had, unknown to the crowd, banned all public meetings that very day. Dyer marched his native Gurkha troops onto the field and, without warning, ordered them to fire. The soldiers kept firing into the unarmed mass at pointblank range until the ammunition ran out. A total of 1,650 rounds were fired, killing 379 and wounding 1,137; nine of every ten rounds claimed a victim. The Amritsar Massacre shattered wartime hopes in a frenzy of postwar reaction. India stood on the verge of more violence and repression, and, sooner or later, terrorism and guerrilla war. That India took a different path to national liberation was due largely to Mohandas "Mahatma" Gandhi, the most fascinating and influential Indian since Ashoka.

HINDU SOCIETY AND MAHATMA GANDHI

By the time of Gandhi's birth in 1869, the Indian subcontinent was firmly controlled by the British. Part of the country was directly ruled by British (and subordinate Indian) officials, ultimately answerable to the British Parliament in London. These areas included Bengal and its teeming capital of Calcutta in eastern India, Bombay and its hinterland in western India, the Punjab in the northwest, and Madras on the southeast coast. Meanwhile, the so-called protected states were more sheltered from European ideas and the world economy. Many of the old ways remained intact. The native prince—usually known as the maharaja—remained the titular ruler, though he was bound to the British by unequal treaties and had to accept the "advice" of the British resident assigned to his court.

It was in just such a tiny backwater protected state that Gandhi grew up. His father was a member of the merchant caste; *gandhi* means "grocer" in the Gujarati language. But the Indian caste system has always been more flexible and dynamic than unsympathetic Westerners have wanted to believe. For six generations the heads of Gandhi's family had served as hereditary prime ministers in various minuscule realms on the Kathiawar peninsula, north of Bombay on the Arabian Sea.

The extended (or joint) family, which had for generations been the most important unit of Indian society, powerfully influenced young Gandhi. Gandhi's father was the well-to-do head of the clan, which included five brothers and their wives, children, and children's children. The big three-story ancestral home swarmed with relatives—a whole community crowded into the labyrinth of tiny rooms and spilled out into the open courtyards. There the entire extended family celebrated holidays and Hindu festivals. There the prime minister routinely entertained a score of dinner guests each day. In such a communal atmosphere, patience, kindness, and a good-natured love of people were essential virtues; the aggressive, solitary individualism so prized in Europe and America would have threatened group harmony. So it was for Gandhi.

In the Hindu family the woman is subordinate but respected. She is "worshipped as a mother, venerated as a wife, loved as a sister, but not much regarded as a woman. Woman as woman is the handmaid of man; her duty is to worship her husband, to bear and rear his children."[6] Every Hindu girl married young, often before puberty; her husband was chosen by her parents. The young bride moved into her father-in-law's house, where, according to one famous Indian nationalist, it was "the common rule for intercourse to take place on that very night when she has the first menstruation. . . . This custom has been practiced for at least 2500 years."[7]

Marriage was a sacrament that could not be dissolved by divorce or even by death. Widows were forbidden by custom to remarry and, until the British abolished the practice in 1829, a dutiful wife from a high-ranking caste was expected to throw herself on her husband's funeral pyre and join him immediately in the world beyond. More generally, a woman's fate was linked to that of the family, in which she was the trusted guardian of orthodox Hindu values.

Gandhi's mother was the ideal Hindu housewife. Married as a young illiterate girl to a forty-two-year-old man whose first wives had died without male children, Putali Ba bore three boys and a girl. According to Gandhi, his ever-cheerful mother was "the first to rise and the last to go to bed . . . and she never made any distinction between her own children and other children in the family."[8] Very devoted but undogmatic in religious matters, Putali Ba fasted regularly and exercised a strong influence on her precocious son. Gandhi was married at thirteen to a local girl who became his lifelong companion.

After his father's death, Gandhi decided to study law in England. No member of his subcaste had ever done so and the local elders declared Gandhi an outcaste, claiming Hindu practices were impossible in alien England. Gandhi disagreed. To win over his wife and anxious mother, he swore that he would not touch meat, women, or wine in the foreign land. Gandhi kept his word and became a zealous vegetarian, refusing even to eat eggs because they were potential living creatures. After passing the English bar, he returned to India. But his practice in Bombay failed, and in 1893 he decided to try his luck as a lawyer for wealthy Indian merchants in South Africa. It was a momentous decision.

THE ROOTS OF MILITANT NONVIOLENCE

Soon after arriving in South Africa, the elegant young lawyer in Western dress took a business trip by train. A white man entered Gandhi's first-class compartment, took one look, and called the conductor. Gandhi was ordered to ride in the baggage car. When he protested, a policeman threw him off the train. Years later Gandhi recalled this experience as a critical turning point in his life. He had refused to bow to naked racial injustice.

As Gandhi's law practice flourished, he began to examine the plight of Indians in South Africa. After the British abolished black slavery in the empire, plantation owners in South Africa and elsewhere had developed a "new system of slavery"[9]: they imported desperately poor Indians as indentured laborers on five-year renewable contracts. When some thrifty, hardworking Indians completed their terms and remained in South Africa as free persons and economic competitors, the Dutch and British settlers passed brutally discriminatory laws. The law books called Indians "semi-barbarous Asiatics," and some towns even prohibited Indians from walking on the sidewalks. Poor Indians had to work on white-owned plantations or return to India; rich Indians lost the vote. Gandhi undertook the legal defense of his countrymen, infuriating the whites, and in 1896 a hysterical mob almost lynched the "coolie lawyer."

Meanwhile Gandhi was searching for a spiritual theory of social action. Identifying with South Africa's black majority as well as his own countrymen, he meditated on the Hindu pursuit of spiritual strength through fasting, sexual abstinence, devotion to duty, and reincarnation. He also studied Christian teachings. Gradually Gandhi developed and articulated a weapon for the weak that he called *Satyagraha*. *Satya* in Hindu means spiritual truth, which equals love; *agraha* is strength or force. Gandhi conceived of Satyagraha, loosely translated as "Soul Force," as a means of striving for truth and social justice through love, suffering, and conversion of the oppressor. Its tactic is courageous nonviolent resistance. Satyagraha owed a good deal to the Christian Gospels, for Christ's call to "love your enemies" touched Gandhi to the core.

As the undisputed leader of South Africa's Indians before the First World War, Gandhi put his philosophy into action. When the white government of South Africa severely restricted Asian immigration and internal freedom of movement, he led a campaign of mass resistance. Thousands of Indian men and women marched across forbidden borders and peacefully withstood beatings, arrest, and imprisonment.

The struggle was hard and the odds long, but Gandhi never wavered. He remarked to a friend at the time, "Men say I am a saint losing myself in politics. The fact is I am a politician trying my hardest to be a saint."[10] In 1914, South Africa's exasperated whites agreed to many of the Indians' demands. A law was passed abolishing discriminatory taxes on Indian traders, recognizing the legality of non-Christian marriages, and permitting continued immigration of free Indians. Satyagraha—militant nonviolence in pursuit of social justice—had proved itself a powerful force in Gandhi's hands.

GANDHI LEADS THE WAY

In 1915 Gandhi returned to India. His reputation had preceded him: the masses hailed him as a "Mahatma," or "Great Soul"—a Hindu title of veneration for a man of great knowledge and humanity—and the name stuck. Feeling his way into Indian affairs, Gandhi crisscrossed India on third-class trains dressed in peasant garb, listening to common folk and talking to Congress party leaders. Moved by the wretched misery of the very poor, he led some sharecroppers against British landowners and organized a strike of textile workers in his native Gujarat. But it was the aftermath of the Amritsar Massacre that catapulted Gandhi to leadership of the national movement in India.

Drawing on his South African experience, Gandhi in 1920 launched a national campaign of nonviolent resistance to British rule. Denouncing British injustice, he urged his countrymen to boycott British goods, jobs, and honors. He returned medals he had won in South Africa and told peasants not to pay taxes or buy heavily taxed liquor. Gandhi electrified the people.

The result was nothing less than a revolution in Indian politics. The nationalist movement had previously touched only the tiny prosperous Western-educated elite. Now both the illiterate masses of village India and the educated classes heard a voice that seemed to be in harmony with their profoundest values. Even Gandhi's renunciation of sex—with his wife's consent—accorded with a popular Hindu belief attributing special power to those who do not squander their life force in sexual intercourse. Gandhi's call for militant nonviolence was particularly appealing to the masses of Hindus who were not members of the warrior caste or the so-called military races, and who were traditionally passive and nonviolent. The British had regarded ordinary Hindus as cowards. Gandhi told them they could be courageous, and even morally superior:

Formerly, when people wanted to fight with one another, they measured between them their bodily strength; now it is possible to take away thousands of lives by one man working behind a gun from a hill. . . .

What do you think? Wherein is courage required—in blowing others to pieces from behind a cannon, or with a smiling face to approach a cannon and be blown to pieces? Who is the true warrior—he who keeps death always as a bosom-friend, or he who controls the death of others? Believe me that a man devoid of courage and manhood can never be a passive resister.[11]

Gandhi made Congress into a mass political party, welcoming members from every ethnic group and cooperating closely with the Muslim minority.

In 1922, some Indian resisters turned to violence. A mob murdered twenty-two policemen and savage riots broke out. Gandhi abruptly called off his campaign. Arrested for fomenting rebellion, Gandhi told the British judge that he had committed "a Himalayan blunder to believe that India had accepted nonviolence."[12] Released from prison after two years, Gandhi set up a commune, established a national newspaper, and set out to reform Indian society and improve the lot of the poor. He welcomed the outcaste untouchables into his fellowship. He worked to help child widows, promote cottage industry, and end the use of alcohol. For Gandhi, moral improvement, social progress, and the national movement always went hand in hand.

The resistance campaign of 1920–1922 left the British severely shaken. Although moderate Indians had participated effectively in the system of dual government, the commission the British formed in 1927 to consider further steps toward self-rule included no Indian members. Indian resentment was intense. In 1929, the radical nationalists, led by the able and aristocratic Jawaharlal Nehru, pushed through the National Congress a resolution calling for virtual independence within a year. The British predictably stiffened, and Indian radicals talked of a bloody showdown.

In this tense situation Gandhi masterfully reasserted his leadership. He took a hard line toward the British, to satisfy the extremists, but controlled them by insisting on nonviolent methods. He then organized another massive resistance campaign, this time against the hated salt tax, which affected every Indian family. Gandhi himself led 50,000 people in a spec-

Mohandas "Mahatma" Gandhi A profoundly original thinker, Gandhi also preserved a common touch that endeared him to millions of ordinary Indians. *(Historical Pictures Service, Chicago)*

tacular march to the sea to make salt without paying a tax, in defiance of the law. A Western journalist described their reception:

Suddenly, at a word of command, scores of native policemen rushed upon the advancing marchers and rained blows on their heads. . . . No one of the marchers even raised an arm to fend off the blows. They went down like ten-pins. From where I stood I heard the whack of the clubs on unprotected skulls. . . . Those struck down fell sprawling, unconscious or writhing with fractured skulls or broken shoulders. . . . The survivors, without breaking ranks, silently and doggedly marched on until struck down.[13]

Over the next few months 60,000 protesters went to jail, but this time there was very little rioting. Finally,

The March to the Sea Gandhi repeatedly used nonviolent resistance to challenge British rule and mobilize the Indian masses. Here he leads a phalanx of determined protesters in his famous march to the sea in 1929. *(BBC Hulton/The Bettmann Archive)*

in 1931, the frustrated, unnerved British released Gandhi from jail and sat down to negotiate with him, as an equal, over self-rule for India. There were many complications, including the determined opposition of diehard imperialists like Winston Churchill. But in 1935 the negotiations resulted in a new constitution, which greatly strengthened India's parliamentary representative institutions. It was virtually a blueprint for independence.

Gandhi inspired people far beyond India's borders. Martin Luther King was later to be deeply influenced by his tactic and philosophy of nonviolent social action. Gandhi did much to transform the elitist nationalism of Indian intellectuals into a mighty mass movement with social as well as political concerns. Above all, Gandhi nurtured national identity and self-respect. As Nehru summed it up, Gandhi "instilled courage and manhood in India's people; . . . courage is the one sure foundation of character, he had said; without courage there is no morality, no religion, no love."[14]

Despite his best efforts, Gandhi failed to heal the widening split between Hindus and Muslims. The development of an Indian nationalism based largely on Hindu symbols and customs increasingly disturbed the Muslim minority. Tempers mounted and atrocities were committed on both sides. By the late 1930s the leaders of the Muslim League were calling for the creation of a Muslim nation in British India, a "Pakistan" or "land of the pure." As in Palestine, the rise of conflicting nationalisms in India was to lead to tragedy after World War Two.

TURMOIL IN EAST ASIA

Nationalism and modernization were well developed in Japan by 1914, due to the efforts of the Meiji reformers. Not only was Japan capable of competing politically and economically with the world's leading nations, but it had already begun building its own empire and proclaiming its special mission in Asia. China lagged far behind, but after 1912 the pace of nationalist development there began to quicken.

The Chinese nationalist movement managed to win a large measure of political independence from the imperialist West and promoted extensive modernization in the 1920s. These achievements were soon tragically undermined by internal conflict and war with an expanding Japan. Nationalism also flourished elsewhere in Asia, scoring a major victory in the Philippine Islands.

THE RISE OF NATIONALIST CHINA

The revolution of 1911–1912 that overthrew the Manchu Dynasty (page 957) opened an era of unprecedented change for Chinese society. Before the revolution, many progressive Chinese had realized that fundamental technological and political reforms were necessary to save the Chinese state and to meet the many-sided Western challenge. Most had hoped, however, to preserve the traditional core of Chinese civilization and culture. The fall of the two-thousand-year-old dynastic system shattered such hopes once and for all. If the emperor himself was no longer sacred, what was? Everything was open to question and to alteration.

The central figure in the revolution was a crafty old military man, Yüan Shih-k'ai. Called out of retirement to save the dynasty, Yüan betrayed the Manchus and convinced the revolutionaries that he was a Chinese Bismarck who could unite the country peacefully and prevent foreign intervention. Once elected president of the republic, however, Yüan concentrated on building his own power. He quarreled with parliament and with Sun Yat-sen (page 957), the inspiring revolutionary leader who had built the Kuomintang, or Nationalist party. Once again Yüan was a betrayer. In 1914, he used military force to dissolve China's parliament and ruled as a dictator. China's first modern revolution had failed.

The extent of the failure became apparent only after Yüan's death in 1916. The central government in Peking disintegrated. For more than a decade power resided in a multitude of local military leaders, the so-called warlords. Most warlords were men of strong, flamboyant personality, capable of building armies by preying on the peasantry and of winning legal recognition from Peking. None of them proved able to establish either a new dynasty or a modern state. Their wars, taxes, and corruption created only terrible suffering.

Foreign imperialism intensified the agony of warlordism. Although China declared its neutrality in 1914, Japan aggressively seized Germany's holdings on the Shantung peninsula and forced China in 1915 to accept Japanese control of Shantung and southern Manchuria. Japan's expansion angered China's growing middle class and enraged its young patriots. On May 4, 1919, five thousand students in Peking exploded against the decision of the Versailles Peace Conference to leave the Shantung peninsula in Japanese hands. This famous incident launched the "May Fourth Movement," which opposed both foreign domination and warlord government.

The May Fourth Movement and the anti-imperialism of Bolshevik Russia renewed the hopes of Chinese nationalists. Struggling for a foothold in southern China, Sun Yat-sen decided in 1923 to ally his Nationalist party with the (Third) Communist International and the newly formed Chinese Communist party. The result was the first of many "national liberation fronts," in keeping with Lenin's blueprint for (temporarily) uniting all anticonservative, anti-imperialist forces in a common revolutionary struggle. Sun reorganized the Nationalist party along Bolshevik lines, in an effort to develop a disciplined party apparatus and a well-indoctrinated party army.

Sun was no Communist. In his *Three Principles of the People,* elaborating on the official party ideology —nationalism, democracy, and people's livelihood —nationalism remained of prime importance:

For the most part the four hundred million people of China can be spoken of as completely Han Chinese. With common habits and customs, we are completely of one race. But in the world today what position do we occupy? Compared to the other peoples of the world we have the greatest population and our civilization is four thousand years old; we should be advancing in the front rank with the nations of Europe and America. But the

Chinese people have only family and clan solidarity, they do not have national spirit. Therefore even though we have four hundred million people gathered together in one China, in reality they are just a heap of loose sand. Today we are the poorest and weakest nation in the world, and occupy the lowest position in international affairs. Other men are the carving knife and serving dish; we are the fish and the meat. Our position at this time is most perilous. If we do not earnestly espouse nationalism and weld together our four hundred million people into a strong nation, there is a danger of China's being lost and our people being destroyed. If we wish to avert this catastrophe, we must espouse nationalism and bring this national spirit to the salvation of the country.[15]

Democracy had a less exalted meaning. Sun equated it with firm rule by the Nationalists, who would promote the people's livelihood through land reform and welfare measures. Sun was in some ways a traditional Chinese rebel and reformer, who wanted to reestablish order and protect the peasants.

Sun's plan was to use the Nationalist party's revolutionary army to crush the warlords and reunite China under a strong central government. When Sun unexpectedly died in 1925, this task was assumed by Chiang Kai-shek (1887–1975), the young Japanese-educated director of the party's army training school. In 1926 and 1927, Chiang led enthusiastic Nationalist armies in a highly successful attack on warlord governments in central and northern China. Preceded by teams of party propagandists, the well-disciplined Nationalist armies were welcomed by the people. In a series of complicated moves, the Nationalists consolidated their rule in 1928 and established a new capital at Nanking in central China. Foreign states recognized the Nanking government, and superficial observers believed China to be truly reunified.

In fact, national unification was only skin-deep. China remained a vast agricultural country plagued by foreign concessions, regional differences, and a lack of modern communications. Moreover, Japan was opposed to a strong China, which could challenge Japan's stranglehold on Manchuria. Finally, the uneasy alliance between the Nationalist party and the Chinese Communist party had turned into a bitter, deadly rivalry. Justifiably fearful of Communist subversion of the Nationalist government and encouraged by his military success and by wealthy Chinese capitalists, Chiang decided in April 1927 to liquidate his left-wing "allies" in a bloody purge. Secret

agents raided Communist cells without warning, and soldiers gunned down suspects on sight. Chinese Communists went into hiding and vowed revenge.

CHINA'S INTELLECTUAL REVOLUTION

Nationalism was the most powerful idea in China between 1911 and 1929, but it was only one aspect of a highly complex intellectual revolution that hammered at traditional Chinese thought and practice, advocated cultural renaissance, and led China into the modern world. Two other currents in that intellectual revolution, generally known as the New Culture Movement, were particularly significant.

The New Culture Movement was founded by young Western-oriented intellectuals in Peking during the May Fourth era. These intellectuals fiercely attacked China's ancient Confucian ethics, which subordinated subjects to rulers, sons to fathers, and wives to husbands. Confucius lived in a distant feudal age, they said; his teachings were totally inappropriate to modern life. In such widely read magazines as *New Youth* and *New Tide,* the modernists provocatively advocated new and anti-Confucian virtues—individualism, democratic equality, and the critical scientific method. They also promoted the use of simple, understandable written language, a language freed from classical scholarship and literary conventions, as a means to clear thinking and mass education. China, they said, needed a whole new culture, a racially different world-view.

The most influential of these intellectuals championing liberalism was Hu Shih (1891–1962). Educated on a scholarship in the United States, Hu had studied with the educational philosopher John Dewey, whose thoroughly American pragmatism stressed compromise and practical problem solving. A master at tearing down old beliefs, the mature Hu Shih envisioned a vague and uninspiring future. The liberation and reconstruction of China was possible, he said, but it would have to occur gradually, "bit by bit, drop by drop." Hu personified the limitations of the Western liberal tradition in China.

The other major current growing out of the New Culture Movement was Marxian socialism. It too was Western in origin, "scientific" in approach, and materialist in its denial of religious belief and Confucian family ethics. But while liberalism and individualism reflected the bewildering range of Western thought since the Enlightenment, Marxian socialism

Civil War in China Chiang Kai-shek's move to purge his Communist allies in 1927 marked the beginning of a long bitter conflict. Here dead combatants lie on a main street in Canton, where in December 1927 a Communist uprising established an independent commune that was soon crushed. *(BBC Hulton/The Bettmann Archive)*

offered Chinese intellectuals the certainty of a single all-encompassing creed. As one young Communist exclaimed:

I am now able to impose order on all the ideas which I could not reconcile; I have found the key to all the problems which appeared to me self-contradictory and insoluble.[16]

Marxism was undeniably Western, and therefore modern. But it also provided a means of criticizing Western dominance, which salved Chinese pride: China's pitiful weakness was due precisely to rapacious *foreign* capitalistic imperialism. Also Marxism, as modified by Lenin and applied by the Bolsheviks, seemed to get results. For Chinese believers, it promised salvation soon. Finally, Chinese Communists could and did interpret Marxism-Leninism so as to appeal to China's masses—the peasants.

Mao Tse-tung (1893–1976) in particular quickly recognized the enormous revolutionary potential of the Chinese peasantry, impoverished and oppressed by parasitic landlords. Himself a member of a prosperous, hardworking peasant family, Mao converted to Marxian socialism in 1918 while working as an assistant librarian at Peking University and began his revolutionary career as an urban labor organizer. But when in 1925 protest strikes by Chinese textile workers against their Japanese employers unexpectedly spread from the big coastal cities to rural China, Mao reconsidered the peasants. Investigating the rapid growth of radical peasant associations in Hunan province, Mao argued passionately in a famous 1927 report that

the force of the peasantry is like that of the raging winds and driving rain. It is rapidly increasing in violence. No force can stand in its way. The peasantry will tear apart all nets which bind it and hasten along the road to liberation. They will bury beneath them all forces of imperialism, militarism, corrupt officialdom, village bosses and evil gentry. Every revolutionary party, every revolutionary comrade will be subjected to their scrutiny and be accepted or rejected by them.[17]

Mao Tse-tung Marxian theorist and champion of peasant revolution, Mao emerged as one of history's greatest guerrilla warriors. This photo shows him leading a small armed band across rugged terrain in northern Shensi province, moving quickly to strike the enemy, melt away, and strike again. *(Eastfoto)*

The task of Communists was to harness the peasant hurricane and use its elemental force to destroy the existing order and take power. Mao's first experiment in peasant revolt—the Autumn Harvest Uprising of September 1927—was no more successful than the abortive insurrections of urban workers launched by his more orthodox comrades. But Mao learned quickly. He advocated equal distribution of land and broke up his forces into small guerrilla groups. After 1928 he and his supporters built up a self-governing Communist soviet, centered at Juichin in southeastern China, and dug in against Nationalist attacks.

The Changing Chinese Family

Confucian reverence for the family and family ties helped stabilize traditional Chinese society and gave life its meaning for many generations. The Confucian principle of subordination suffused family life— subordination of the individual to the group, the young to the old, the wife to the husband. Given in marriage by her parents at an early age, the wife owed unquestioning obedience to her husband and mother-in-law. Wealthy husbands customarily took additional wives or purchased concubines from poor families, but for women divorce and running away were both unthinkable. Women of all ages were commonly sold, and they lacked all property rights.

A Daughter of Han, a rare autobiography of a Chinese woman, as told to an American friend, offers an unforgettable glimpse of Chinese family life. Born in 1867 to poor parents in a northern city, Lao T'ai T'ai lived it all. Her foot-binding was delayed to age nine, "since I loved so much to run and play." When the bandages were finally drawn tight, "my feet hurt so much that for two years I had to crawl on my knees."[18] Her arranged marriage at fourteen was a disaster: her husband was a drug addict—"in those days everyone took opium to some extent"—who grabbed everything to pay for his habit. "There was no freedom then for women," and she endured her situation until her husband sold their four-year-old daughter to buy opium. Taking her remaining baby daughter, Lao T'ai T'ai fled. She became a beggar, a cook in wealthy households, and a peddler of luxury goods to wealthy cooped-up women.

The two unshakable values that buoyed her were a tough, fatalistic acceptance—"Only fortune that comes of itself will come. There is no use to seek for it"—and devotion to the family. Lao T'ai T'ai eventually returned home to her husband, who was "good" in those years, "but I did not miss him when he died. I had my [newborn] son and I was happy. My house was established. . . . Truly all my life I spent thinking of my family." Her devotion was reciprocated by her son and granddaughter, who cared for her well in old age.

Lao T'ai T'ai's remarkable life history encompasses both old and new Chinese attitudes toward the family. Her son moved to the city, prospered, and had only one wife. Her granddaughter eventually became a college teacher, and anti-Japanese patriot, and a determined foe of arranged marriages, admirably personifying the trend toward greater freedom and equality for Chinese women after 1911. Footbinding was outlawed and died out unlamented. Marriage for love became increasingly common, and unprecedented educational and economic opportunities opened up for women. Polygamy declined. In the short space of three generations, rising nationalism and the intellectual revolution had accomplished monumental changes in Chinese family life.

FROM LIBERALISM TO ULTRANATIONALISM IN JAPAN

The efforts of Japan's Meiji reformers (page 954) to build a powerful nationalistic state and resist Western imperialism were spectacularly successful and deeply impressive to their fellow Asians. The Japanese, alone among non-Western peoples, had mastered modern industrial technology by 1910 and fought victorious wars against both China and Russia. World War One brought more triumphs. Japan easily seized Germany's Asian holdings and held onto most of them as League of Nations mandates. The Japanese economy expanded enormously. Profits soared as Japan won new markets that wartime Europe could no longer supply.

In the early 1920s Japan seemed to make further progress on all fronts. Most nationalists believed Japan had a semidivine mission to enlighten and protect Asia, but some were convinced they could achieve their goal peacefully. In 1922, Japan signed a naval arms limitation treaty with the Western powers and returned some of its control over the Shantung peninsula to China. These conciliatory moves reduced tensions in East Asia. At home, Japan seemed headed toward genuine democracy. The electorate expanded twelvefold between 1918 and 1925 as all males over twenty-five won the vote. Two-party competition was intense, and cabinet ministers were made responsible to the lower house. Japanese living standards were the highest in Asia. Literacy was universal.

But Japan's remarkable rise was accompanied by serious problems. First, Japan had a rapidly growing population and scarce natural resources. As early as the 1920s Japan was exporting manufactured goods in order to pay for imports of food and essential raw materials. Deeply enmeshed in world trade, Japan was vulnerable to every boom and bust. These conditions reinforced the widespread belief that colonies and foreign expansion were matters of life and death for Japan.

Also, rapid industrial development had created an imbalanced "dualistic" economy. The modern sector consisted of a handful of giant conglomerate firms, the so-called *zaibatsu*, or "financial combine." A zaibatsu firm like Mitsubishi employed thousands of workers and owned banks, mines, steel mills, cotton factories, shipyards, and trading companies, all of which sold to one another. The zaibatsu firms had enormous economic power and dominated the other sector of the economy, which consisted of an unorganized multitude of peasant farmers and craftsmen. The result was financial oligarchy, corruption of government officials, and a weak middle class.

Third, behind the façade of party politics the old and new elites—the emperor, high government officials, big businessmen, and military leaders—were jockeying savagely for the real power. Cohesive leadership, which had played such an important role in Japan's modernization by the Meiji reformers, had ceased to exist.

By far the most serious challenge to peaceful progress, however, was fanatical nationalism. As in Europe, ultranationalism first emerged in Japan in the late nineteenth century but did not flower fully until World War One and the 1930s. Though often vague,

Little Samurai Proud to wear the battle dress of Japan's feudal warriors, a group of boys imitate their leader in a patriotic procession on Empire Day in 1934. The values of Japanese nationalism are being passed to the next generation. *(UPI/Bettmann Newsphotos)*

Japan's ultranationalists shared several fundamental beliefs.

First, the ultranationalists were violently anti-Western. They rejected democracy, big business, and Marxist socialism, which they blamed for destroying the older, superior Japanese practices they wanted to restore. Reviving old myths, they stressed the emperor's godlike qualities and the samurai warrior's code of honor and obedience. Despising party politics, they assassinated moderate leaders and plotted armed uprisings to achieve their goals. Above all, the ultranationalists preached foreign expansion. Like Western imperialists with their "white man's bur-

den," the Japanese ultranationalists thought theirs was a noble mission. "Asia for the Asians" was their self-satisfied rallying cry. As the famous ultranationalist Kita Ikki wrote in 1923:

Our seven hundred million brothers in China and India have no other path to independence than that offered by our guidance and protection. . . . The noble Greece of Asian culture must complete her national reorganization on the basis of her own national polity. At the same time, let her lift the virtuous banner of an Asian league and take the leadership in a world federation which must come.[19]

1911–1912	Revolution in China overthrows Manchu dynasty and establishes republic
1915	Japan seizes German holdings in China and expands into southern Manchuria
May 4, 1919	Demonstration by Chinese students against Versailles peace conference and Japan sparks broad nationalist movement
1920s	New Cultural Movement challenges traditional Chinese values
1922	Japan signs naval agreement with Western powers
1923	Sun Yat-sen allies the Nationalist Party with Chinese Communists
	Kita Ikki advocates ultranationalism in Japan
1925–1928	Chiang Kai-shek, leader of the Nationalist Party, attacks warlord government and seeks to unify China
1927	Chiang Kai-shek purges his Communist allies
	Mao Tse-tung recognizes the revolutionary potential of the Chinese peasantry
1930–1934	Nationalists campaign continually against the Chinese Communists
1931	Mukden Incident leads to Japanese occupation of Manchuria
1932	Japan proclaims Manchuria an independent state
1934	Mao Tse-tung leads Communists on Long March to new base in northwestern China
	The Philippines gain self-governing commonwealth status from United States
1936	Japan allies with Germany in anti-Communist pact
1937	Japanese militarists launch general attack on China

The ultranationalists were noisy and violent in the 1920s, but it took the Great Depression to tip the scales decisively in their favor. The worldwide depression hit Japan like a tidal wave in 1930. Exports and wages collapsed; unemployment and raw suffering soared. Starving peasants ate the bark off trees and sold their daughters to brothels. The ultranationalists blamed the system, and people listened.

JAPAN AGAINST CHINA

Among those who listened with particular care were young Japanese army officers in Manchuria. This underpopulated, resource-rich province of northeastern China, controlled by the Japanese army since its victory over Russia in 1905, seemed a particularly valuable asset in the depression. And many junior officers in Manchuria came from the peasantry and

were distressed by the stories of rural suffering they heard from home. They also knew that the budget and prestige of the Japanese army had declined in the prosperous 1920s.

Most worrisome of all to the young officers was the rise of Chinese nationalism. This new political force challenged the control that Japan exercised over Manchuria through Chinese warlord puppets. In response, junior officers in Manchuria, in cooperation with top generals in Tokyo, secretly manufactured an excuse for aggression in late 1931. They blew up some tracks on a Japanese-owned railroad near the city of Mukden and then quickly occupied all of Manchuria in "self-defense."

In 1932 Japan proclaimed Manchuria an independent state with a Manchu puppet as emperor. When the League of Nations condemned its aggression in Manchuria, Japan resigned in protest. Politics

Shanghai Victory March, 1937 Japanese troops enter China's largest city as local Japanese civilians joyfully welcome their arrival. The "STOP" on the pavement reflects the fact that most of Shanghai had been under British (and European) rule since the mid-nineteenth century. *(BBC Hulton/The Bettmann Archive)*

in Japan became increasingly chaotic. The army, though it reported directly to the emperor, was clearly an independent force subject to no outside control.

For China, the Japanese conquest of Manchuria was disastrous. After unifying most of China in 1928, the Nationalist government had won from the Western powers the right to set tariffs and other marks of sovereignty. The government had also begun to expand higher education, build railroads, and improve the banking system. Japanese aggression in Manchuria drew attention away from these modernizing efforts, which in any event had been none too vigorous. The Nationalist government promoted a massive boycott of Japanese goods, but lost all interest in social reform.

Above all, the Nationalist government after 1931 completely neglected land reform and the grinding poverty of the Chinese peasant. As in many poor agricultural societies, Chinese peasants paid roughly half of their crops to their landlords as rent. Ownership of land was very unequal. One careful study estimated that fully half the land was owned by a mere 4 percent of the families, usually absentee landlords

living in cities. Poor peasants and farm laborers—70 percent of the rural population—owned only one sixth of the land.

Peasants were heavily in debt and chronically underfed. Eggs and meat accounted for only 2 percent of the food poor and middle peasants consumed. One contemporary Chinese economist spelled out the revolutionary implications: "It seems clear that the land problem in China today is as acute as that of eighteenth-century France or nineteenth-century Russia."[20] Mao Tse-tung certainly agreed.

Having abandoned land reform, partly because they themselves were often landowners, the Nation-

MAP 33.2 The Chinese Communist Movement and the War with Japan, 1927–1938 After urban uprisings ordered by Stalin failed in 1927, Mao Tse-tung succeeded in forming a self-governing Communist soviet in mountainous southern China. Relentless Nationalist attacks between 1930 and 1934 finally forced the Long March to Yenan, where the Communists were well-positioned for guerrilla war against the Japanese.

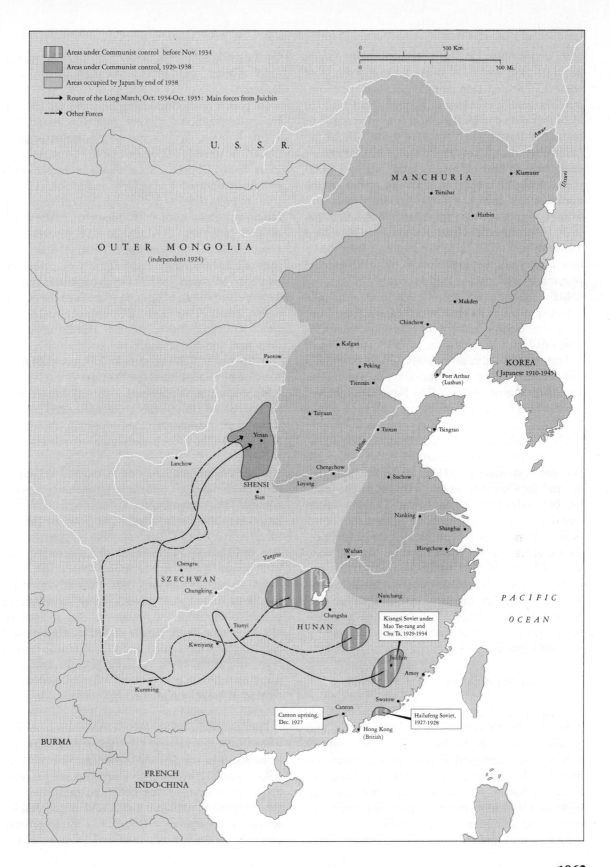

Areas under Communist control before Nov. 1934

Areas under Communist control, 1929-1938

Areas occupied by Japan by end of 1938

Route of the Long March, Oct. 1934-Oct. 1935: Main forces from Juichin

Other Forces

0   500 Km.

0   500 Mi.

U. S. S. R.

MANCHURIA

Amur

Ussuri

Kiamusze

Tsitsihar

Harbin

OUTER MONGOLIA
(independent 1924)

Mukden

Chinchow

Kalgan

Paotow

Peking

KOREA
(Japanese 1910-1945)

Tientsin

Port Arthur
(Lushun)

Taiyuan

Lanchow

Yenan

Tsinan

Tsingtao

SHENSI

Chengchow

Sian

Loyang

Suchow

Nanking

Shanghai

Chengtu

Yangtze

Wuhan

Hangchow

SZECHWAN

Chungking

Nanchang

PACIFIC

Changsha

OCEAN

Tsunyi

HUNAN

Kiangsi Soviet under
Mao Tse-tung and
Chu Ta, 1929-1934

Kweiyang

Juichin

Amoy

Kunming

Swatow

Canton uprising,
Dec. 1927

Canton

Hailufeng Soviet,
1927-1928

BURMA

Hong Kong
(British)

FRENCH
INDO-CHINA

alists under Chiang Kai-shek devoted their energies between 1930 and 1934 to five great campaigns of encirclement and extermination against the Communists' rural power base in southeastern China. In 1934 they closed in for the kill, only to miss again. In one of the most incredible sagas of modern times, the main Communist army broke out of the Nationalist encirclement, beat off attacks, and marched 6,000 miles in twelve months to a remote region on the northwestern border. Of the 300,000 men and women who began the Long March, only about 20- to 30,000 reached the final destination. There Mao Tse-tung built up his forces once again, established a new territorial base, and won the support of local peasants by undertaking land reform.

Mao Tse-tung and his Communists gradually emerged as the more determined nationalists. Once again, the decisive factor in the eyes of ordinary Chinese was Japanese aggression. In 1937, the Japanese military and the ultranationalists were in command and decided to use a minor incident near Peking as a pretext for a general attack. The Nationalist government, which had just formed a united front with the Communists in response to the demands of Chinese patriots, fought hard but could not halt the Japanese.

By late 1938, Japanese armies occupied sizable portions of coastal China (Map 33.2). The Nationalists and the Communists had retreated to the interior, both refusing to accept defeat. The determination of the Communist guerrillas equaled that of the Nationalists, and their political skill proved superior. As Europe (and the United States) edged toward World War Two in 1939, the undeclared war between China and Japan bogged down in a savage stalemate. The bloody clash on the Asian mainland was providing a spectacular example of conflicting nationalisms, convulsing China, and preparing the way for eventual Communist victory.

SOUTHEAST ASIA AND THE PHILIPPINES

The tide of nationalism was also rising in Southeast Asia. Like their counterparts in India, China, and Japan, nationalists in Southeast Asia urgently wanted genuine political independence and freedom from foreign rule. At the same time, nationalism in Southeast Asia was part of a broader movement toward modernization and cultural renaissance. Yet even as the grandiose concepts of nationalism and modernization spread across national borders, linking the world more closely together, they were grafted onto distinct and ancient civilizations by local leaders.

In both French Indochina and the Dutch East Indies, local nationalists were inspired by events elsewhere in Asia. Japan's rise to the status of great power, the struggle of Gandhi and the Congress party in India, and China's unification under the Nationalists all encouraged Vietnamese and Indonesian patriots to press their own demands. In both cases they ran up against an imperialist stone wall. In the words of one historian, "Indochina was governed by Frenchmen for Frenchmen, and the great liberal slogans of liberty, equality, and fraternity were not considered to be export goods for overseas dominions."[21] This uncompromising attitude stimulated the growth of an equally stubborn Communist opposition, which emerged despite ruthless repression as the dominant anti-French force.

In the East Indies—modern Indonesia—the Dutch made some concessions after the First World War, establishing a people's council with very limited lawmaking power. But in the 1930s the Dutch cracked down hard, jailing all the important nationalist leaders. Like the French, the Dutch were determined to hold on.

In the Philippines, however, an old and well-established nationalist movement achieved success. As in colonial Latin America, the Spanish had been indefatigable missionaries in the Philippines. By the late nineteenth century 80 percent of the Filipino population was Catholic. Filipinos shared a common cultural heritage as well as a common racial origin. Education, especially for girls, was quite advanced for Southeast Asia, and in 1843 a higher percentage of people could read in the Philippines than in Spain itself. Economic development helped to create a westernized elite, who turned first to reform and then to revolution in the 1890s. As in Egypt or Turkey, long-standing intimate contact with Western civilization created a strong nationalist movement at an early date.

Filipino nationalists were bitterly disappointed when the United States, having taken the Philippines from Spain in the Spanish-American War of 1898, failed to fulfill the universal Filipino desire for independence. The Americans convinced themselves that the Philippines were not ready and might well be seized by Germany or Britain. As an imperialist power in the Philippines, the United States behaved

Filipino Cadets Dressed in smart uniforms modeled after those of their West Point counterparts in the United States, these future officers of the Philippine army march with flawless precision. They are passing the reviewing stand in a 1937 parade celebrating American promises of political independence for the Philippines. *(UPI/Bettmann Newsphotos)*

somewhat better than average. Education was encouraged, as was capitalistic economic development. A popularly elected legislature was given real powers. In 1919 President Wilson even promised complete independence, though subsequent Republican administrators saw it as a distant goal.

In spite of relatively enlightened American rule, demands for independence grew. One important contributing factor was American racial attitudes. Americans treated Filipinos as inferiors and introduced segregationist practices borrowed from the American South. American racism made passionate nationalists of many Filipinos.

However, it was the Great Depression that had the most radical impact on the Philippines. As the United States collapsed economically, the Philippines suddenly appeared to be a liability rather than an asset. American farm groups lobbied for protection from cheap Filipino sugar, and labor unions demanded an end to Filipino immigration to protect jobs. In 1934 Congress made the Philippines a self-governing commonwealth, with independence scheduled in ten years. Sugar imports were reduced and immigration was limited to only 50 Filipinos per year.

The United States retention of its military bases in the Philippines was denounced by some Filipino nationalists. Others were less sure. Japan was fighting in China and expanding economically into the Philippines and throughout Southeast Asia. By 1939, the greatest threat to Filipino independence appeared to come from Asia itself.

—————

The Asian revolt against the West began before World War One. But only after 1914 did Asian nationalist movements broaden their bases and become capable of challenging Western domination effectively. These mass movements sought human dignity as well as political freedom. Generally speaking, Asian nationalists favored modernization, and adopted Western techniques and ideas even as they rejected Western rule. Everywhere Asian nationalists had to fight long and hard, though their struggle gained momentum from the relative decline of European power and confidence, the encouragement of the Soviet Union, and American calls for self-determination.

Asia's nationalist movements arose out of separate historical experiences and distinct cultures. In this chapter we have seen considerable diversity on the common theme of nationalism in Turkey, the Arab world, India, China, Japan, and the Philippines. This diversity helps explain why Asian peoples also became defensive in their relations with each other while rising against Western rule. As earlier in Europe, Asian nationalists developed a strong sense of "we" and "they"; "they" included other Asians as well as Europeans. Nationalism meant freedom, modernization, and cultural renaissance, but it nonetheless proved a mixed blessing.

NOTES

—————

1. K. M. Panikkar, *Asia and Western Dominance: A Survey of the Vasco da Gama Epoch of Asian History* (London: George Allen and Unwin, 1959), p. 197.

2. Quoted in Henri Grimal, *La Décolonisation, 1919–1965* (Paris: Armand Colin, 1965), p. 100.

3. Quoted in Peter Mansfield, *The Ottoman Empire and Its Successors* (New York: St. Martin's Press, 1973), p. 18.

4. Harold Armstrong, *Turkey in Travail: The Birth of a New Nation* (London: John Lane, 1925), p. 75.

5. Quoted in Lord Kinross, *Atatürk: A Biography of Mustafa Kemal, Father of Modern Turkey* (New York: William Morrow, 1965), p. 181.

6. Percival Spear, *India, Pakistan, and the West,* 3d ed. (Oxford: Oxford University Press, 1958), p. 67.

7. Quoted in Erik Erikson, *Gandhi's Truth: On the Origins of Militant Nonviolence* (New York: W. W. Norton, 1969), p. 225.

8. Ibid., p. 105.

9. Hugh Tinker, *A New System of Slavery: The Export of Indian Labour Overseas, 1830–1920* (London: Oxford University Press, 1974).

10. Quoted in Louis Fischer, *Gandhi: His Life and Message for the World* (New York: New American Library, 1954), p. 35.

11. Quoted in Erikson, p. 225.

12. Quoted in Woodbridge Bingham, Hilary Conroy, and Frank Iklé, *A History of Asia,* 2d ed. (Boston: Allyn and Bacon, 1974), 1:447.

13. Webb Miller, *I Found No Peace: The Journal of a Foreign Correspondent* (New York: Simon and Schuster, 1936), p. 193.

14. Quoted in Lloyd Rudolph and Susanne Rudolph, *The Modernity of Tradition: Political Development in India* (Chicago: University of Chicago Press, 1967), p. 248.

15. Quoted in William Theodore deBary, Wing-tsit Chan, and Burton Watson, *Sources of Chinese Tradition* (New York: Columbia University Press, 1964), pp. 768–769.

16. Quoted in John F. Fairbank, Edwin O. Reischauer, and Albert M. Craig, *East Asia: Tradition and Transformation* (Boston: Houghton Mifflin, 1973), p. 774.

17. Quoted in Benjamin I. Schwartz, *Chinese Communism and the Rise of Mao* (Cambridge, Mass.: Harvard University Press, 1951), p. 74.

18. Ida Pruitt, *A Daughter of Han: The Autobiography of a Chinese Working Woman* (New Haven: Yale University Press, 1945), p. 22. Other quotations are taken, in order, from pages 83, 71, 182, 166, and 235.

19. Quoted in William Theodore deBary, Ryusaku Tsunoda, and Donald Keene, *Sources of Japanese Tradition* (New York: Columbia University Press, 1958), 2:269.
20. Quoted in Olga Lang, *Chinese Family and Society* (New Haven: Yale University Press, 1946), p. 70.
21. Bingham, Conroy, and Iklé, 2:480.

SUGGESTED READING

All of the works cited in the Notes are highly recommended. Two important general studies of nationalism and independence movements are H. Kohn, *The Age of Nationalism: The First Era of Global History* (1962), and R. Emerson, *From Empire to Nation: The Rise to Self-Assertion of Asian and African Peoples* (1960). These may be compared with the provocative works of E. Kedourie, *Nationalism in Asia and Africa* (1970) and *England and the Middle East: The Destruction of the Ottoman Empire, 1914–1921* (1956), and a justly famous global history of the twentieth century by G. Barraclough, *An Introduction to Contemporary History* (1975). Two fine studies of the Middle East are G. Lenczowski, *The Middle East in World Affairs,* 4th ed. (1980), and S. N. Fisher, *The Middle East: A History,* 3d ed. (1979), both of which have detailed bibliographies. On Turkey, in addition to Lord Kinross's *Atatürk* (1965), see B. Lewis, *The Emergence of Modern Turkey* (1961), and D. Kushner, *The Rise of Turkish Nationalism, 1876–1908* (1977). Peter Mansfield, *The Arab World: A Comprehensive History* (1976), and S. G. Haim, ed., *Arab Nationalism: An Anthology* (1964), provide engaging general coverage and important source materials. W. Lacqueur, *A History of Zionism* (1972), and A. Eban, *My People* (1968), discuss the Jewish homeland in Palestine. The Arab viewpoint is presented by G. Antonius, *The Arab Awakening: The Story of the Arab National Movement* (1946). R. Cottam, *Nationalism in Iran,* rev. ed. (1979), complements the classic study of D. Wilbur, *Iran: Past and Present,* 9th ed. (1981).

The historical literature on modern India is very rich. S. Wolpert, *A New History of India,* 2d ed. (1982), is an excellent introduction, with up-to-date scholarship and detailed suggestions for further reading. Also see the handsomely illustrated volume by F. Watson, *A Concise History of India* (1975). In addition to the biographies of Gandhi by Erikson and Fischer cited in the Notes, J. Brown, *Gandhi's Rise to Power: Indian Politics, 1915–1922* (1972), and L. Gordon, *Bengal: The Nationalist Movement, 1876–1970* (1974), are major studies. Developments in the Muslim community are considered by P. Hardy, *The Muslims of British India* (1972); B. Metcalf, *Islamic Revival in British India: Deoband, 1860–1900* (1982); and F. Robinson, *Atlas of the Islamic World Since 1500* (1982), a beautifully illustrated recent survey encompassing far more than India.

Studies of China in the twentieth century are also very numerous. I. Hsü, *The Rise of Modern China,* 2d ed. (1975), is a comprehensive study with extensive bibliographies, which may be supplemented by the same author's *Readings in Chinese History* (1971), and the documentary collection of F. Schurmann and O. Schell, eds., *Republican China: Nationalism, War and the Rise of Communism, 1911—1949* (1967). J. Spence, *The Gate of Heavenly Peace: The Chinese and Their Revolution, 1895–1980* (1981), skillfully focuses on leading literary figures. T. Chow, *The May Fourth Movement: Intellectual Revolution in Modern China* (1960), examines a critical time period. Other important studies of China in this period include R. Hofheinz, Jr., *The Broken Wave: The Chinese Communist Peasant Movement, 1922–1928* (1977); S. Schram, *Mao Tse-tung* (1966); H. Schriffrin, *Sun Yat-sen and the Origins of the Chinese Revolution* (1970); and L. Eastman, *The Abortive Revolution: China Under Nationalist Rule, 1927–1937* (1974). P. Ebrey, ed., *Chinese Civilization and Society: A Sourcebook* (1981), complements the classic studies of the Chinese family by Lang and Pruitt, which may be compared with M. J. Levy, *The Family Revolution in Modern China* (1949). E. Reischauer, *Japan: The Story of a Nation,* rev. ed. (1970), and P. Duus, *The Rise of Modern Japan* (1976), are excellent interpretations of the recent history of the island nation. W. Lockwood, *The Economic Development of Japan, 1868–1938* (1954), and R. Storry, *The Double Patriots: A Story of Japanese Nationalism* (1973), are valuable specialized works. Two edited collections, J. Morley, *The China Quagmire* (1983), and R. Myers and M. Peattie, *The Japanese Colonial Expansion, 1895–1945* (1984), probe Japan's imperial expansion. For Southeast Asia, see D. G. E. Hall, *A History of South-east Asia,* 4th ed. (1981), J. Pluvier, *South-East Asia from Colonialism to Independence* (1974); and the Suggested Reading for Chapter 37.

34

THE AGE OF ANXIETY
IN THE WEST

HEN ALLIED DIPLOMATS met in Paris in early 1919 with their optimistic plans for building a lasting peace, most people looked forward to happier times. They hoped that life would return to normal. They hoped that once again life would make sense in the familiar prewar terms of peace, prosperity, and progress. These hopes were in vain. The Great Break—the First World War and the Russian Revolution—had mangled too many things beyond repair. Life would no longer fit neatly into the old molds.

Instead, great numbers of men and women felt themselves increasingly adrift in a strange, uncertain, and uncontrollable world. They saw themselves living in an age of anxiety, an age of continuous crisis, which lasted until at least the early 1950s. In almost every area of human experience, people went searching for ways to put meaning back into life. What did the doubts and searching mean for Western thought, art, and culture? How did political leaders try to reestablish real peace and prosperity between 1919 and 1939? And why did they fail? These are questions this chapter will explore.

UNCERTAINTY IN MODERN THOUGHT

A complex revolution in thought and ideas was under way before the First World War, but only small, unusual groups were aware of it. After the war, new and upsetting ideas began to spread through the entire population. Western society began to question and even abandon many cherished values and beliefs that had guided it since the eighteenth-century Enlightenment and the nineteenth-century triumph of industrial development, scientific advances, and evolutionary thought.

Before 1914 most people still believed in progress, reason, and the rights of the individual. Progress was a daily reality, apparent in the rising standard of living, the taming of the city, and the steady increase in popular education. Such developments also encouraged the comforting belief in the logical universe of Newtonian physics, as well as faith in the ability of a rational human mind to understand that universe through intellectual investigation. And just as there

were laws of science, so were there laws of society that rational human beings could discover and then wisely act on. Finally, the rights of the individual were not just taken for granted, they were actually increasing. Well-established rights were gradually spreading to women and workers, and new "social rights" like old-age pensions were emerging. In short, before World War One, most Europeans had a moderately optimistic world-view, with good reason.

From the 1880s on, however, a small band of serious thinkers and creative writers began to attack these well-worn optimistic ideas. These critics rejected the general faith in progress and the power of the rational human mind. One of the most influential of them was the German philosopher Friedrich Nietzsche (1844–1900).

Nietzsche believed that Western civilization had lost its creativity and decayed into mediocrity. Christianity's "slave morality" had glorified weakness and humility. Furthermore, human beings in the West had overstressed rational thinking at the expense of passion and emotion. Nietzsche viewed the pillars of conventional morality—reason, democracy, progress, respectability—as outworn social and psychological constructs whose influence was suffocating creativity. The only hope of revival was for a few superior individuals to free themselves from the humdrum thinking of the masses and embrace life passionately. Such individuals would become true heroes, supermen capable of leading the dumb herd of inferior men and women. Nietzsche also condemned both political democracy and greater social equality.

The growing dissatisfaction with established ideas before 1914 was apparent in other thinkers. In the 1890s, the French philosophy professor Henri Bergson (1859–1941) convinced many young people through his writing that immediate experience and intuition are as important as rational and scientific thinking for understanding reality. Indeed, according to Bergson, a religious experience or a mystical poem is often more accessible to human comprehension than a scientific law or a mathematical equation.

Another thinker who agreed about the limits of rational thinking was the French socialist Georges Sorel (1847–1922). Sorel frankly characterized Marxian socialism as an inspiring but unprovable religion rather than a rational scientific truth. Socialism would come to power, he believed, through a great, violent strike of all working people, which would miraculously shatter capitalist society. Sorel rejected democracy and believed that the masses of the new socialist society would have to be tightly controlled by a small revolutionary elite.

In the years after 1918, a growing chorus of thinkers, creative writers, and scientists echoed and enlarged on the themes first expressed by the small band of critics between 1880 and 1914. Many prophets of doom bore witness to the decline and decay of Western civilization. The experience of history's most destructive war suggested to many that human beings certainly were a pack of violent, irrational animals quite capable of tearing the individual and his or her rights to shreds. There was growing pessimism and a general crisis of the mind. People did not know what to think. This disorientation was particularly acute in the 1930s, when the rapid rise of harsh dictatorships and the Great Depression transformed old certainties into bitter illusions.

No one expressed this state of uncertainty better than the French poet and critic Paul Valéry (1871–1945) in the early 1920s. Speaking of the "crisis of the mind," Valéry noted that Europe was looking at its future with dark foreboding:

The storm has died away, and still we are restless, uneasy, as if the storm were about to break. Almost all the affairs of men remain in a terrible uncertainty. We think of what has disappeared, and we are almost destroyed by what has been destroyed; we do not know what will be born, and we fear the future, not without reason. . . . Doubt and disorder are in us and with us. There is no thinking man, however shrewd or learned he may be, who can hope to dominate this anxiety, to escape from this impression of darkness. [1]

In the midst of economic, political, and social disruptions Valéry saw the "cruelly injured mind," besieged by doubts and suffering from anxieties. This was the general intellectual crisis of the twentieth century, which touched almost every field of thought. The implications of new discoveries and ideas in physics, psychology, philosophy, and literature played a central role in this crisis, disturbing "thinking people" everywhere.

PHYSICS AND PSYCHOLOGY

Ever since the Scientific Revolution of the seventeenth century, scientific advances and their implications have greatly influenced the beliefs of thinking

"The War, as I Saw It" This was the title of a series of grotesque drawings that appeared in 1920 in *Simplicissimus,* Germany's leading satirical magazine. Nothing shows better the terrible impact of World War One than this profoundly disturbing example of expressionist art. *(Photo: Caroline Buckler)*

people. By the late nineteenth century, science was one of the main pillars supporting Western society's optimistic and rationalistic view of the world. The Darwinian concept of evolution had been accepted and assimilated in most intellectual circles. Progressive minds believed that science, unlike religion and philosophical speculation, was based on hard facts and controlled experiments. Science seemed to have achieved an unerring and almost completed picture of reality. Unchanging natural laws seemed to determine physical processes and permit useful solutions to more and more problems. All this was comforting, especially to people who were no longer committed to traditional religious beliefs. And all this was challenged by the new physics.

An important first step toward the new physics was the discovery at the end of the century that atoms

Freud's Consulting Room in Vienna Freud developed his theories as a therapist while treating mental disorders. He sat in the armchair on the left. His patients lay on the couch and gazed away from him, in part because Freud could not bear being watched all day long. *(Photograph by Edmund Engelman)*

were not like hard, permanent little billiard balls. They were actually composed of many far smaller, fast-moving particles, such as electrons and protons. The Polish-born physicist Marie Curie (1867–1934) and her French husband discovered that radium constantly emits subatomic particles and thus does not have a constant atomic weight. Building on this and other work in radiation, the German physicist Max Planck (1858–1947) showed in 1900 that subatomic energy is emitted in uneven little spurts, which Planck called "quanta," and not in a steady stream as previously believed. Planck's discovery called into question the old sharp distinction between matter and energy. The old view of atoms as the stable, basic building blocks of nature, with a different kind of unbreakable atom for each of the ninety-two chemical elements, was badly shaken.

In 1905 the German-born Jewish genius Albert Einstein (1879–1955) went further than the Curies and Planck in challenging Newtonian physics. His famous theory of special relativity postulated that time and space are not absolute. The closed framework of Newtonian physics was quite limited com-

pared to that of Einsteinian physics, which unified an apparently infinite universe with the incredibly small, fast-moving subatomic world. Moreover, Einstein's theory stated clearly that matter and energy are interchangeable and that all matter contains enormous levels of potential energy.

The 1920s opened the "heroic age of physics," in the apt words of one of its leading pioneers, Ernest Rutherford (1871–1937). Breakthrough followed breakthrough. In 1919 Rutherford showed that the atom could be split. By 1944 seven subatomic particles had been identified, of which the most important was the neutron. The neutron's capacity to pass through other atoms allowed for even more intense experimental bombardment of matter, leading to chain reactions of unbelievable force. This was the road to the atomic bomb.

Although few nonscientists understood the revolution in physics, the implications of the new theories and discoveries, as presented by newspapers and popular writers, were disturbing to millions of men and women in the 1920s and 1930s. The new universe was strange and troubling. It lacked any absolute objective reality. Everything was "relative," that is, dependent on the observer's frame of reference. Moreover, the universe was uncertain and undetermined, without stable building blocks. Instead of Newton's dependable, rational laws, there seemed to be only tendencies and probabilities in an extraordinarily complex and uncertain universe. And that universe, described by abstract mathematical symbols, seemed to have little to do with human experience and human problems.

With physics presenting an uncertain universe so unrelated to ordinary human experience, questions regarding the power and potential of the human mind assumed special significance. The findings and speculations of the leading psychologist, Sigmund Freud (page 891), were particularly disturbing.

Before Freud, poets and mystics had probed the unconscious and irrational aspects of human behavior. But most professional, "scientific" psychologists assumed that a single, unified conscious mind processed sense experiences in a rational and logical way. Human behavior in turn was the result of rational calculation—of "thinking"—by the conscious mind. Basing his insights on the analysis of dreams and of hysteria, Freud developed a very different view of the human psyche beginning in the late 1880s.

According to Freud, human behavior is basically irrational. The key to understanding the mind is the primitive irrational unconscious, which he called the id. The unconscious is driven by sexual, aggressive, and pleasure-seeking desires and is locked in a constant battle with the other parts of the mind: the rationalizing conscious (the ego), which mediates what a person *can* do, and ingrained moral values (the superego), which tell what a person *should* do. Human behavior is a product of fragile compromise between instinctual drives and the controls of rational thinking and moral values. Since the instinctual drives are extremely powerful, the ever-present danger for individuals and whole societies is that unacknowledged drives will overwhelm the control mechanisms in a violent, distorted way. Yet Freud also agreed with Nietzsche that the mechanisms of rational thinking and traditional moral values can be too strong. They can repress sexual desires too effectively, crippling individuals and entire peoples with guilt and neurotic fears.

Freudian psychology and clinical psychiatry had become an international movement by 1910, but only after 1918 did they receive popular attention,

especially in the Protestant countries of northern Europe and in the United States. Many opponents and even some enthusiasts interpreted Freud as saying that the first requirement for mental health is an uninhibited sex life. Thus, after the First World War, the popular interpretation of Freud reflected and encouraged growing sexual experimentation, particularly among middle-class women. For more serious students, the psychology of Freud and his followers drastically undermined the old, easy optimism about the rational and progressive nature of the human mind.

PHILOSOPHY: LOGICAL EMPIRICISM AND EXISTENTIALISM

The intellectual crisis of the twentieth century was fully reflected in philosophy, but in two very different ways. In English-speaking countries, the main development was the acceptance of logical empiricism (or logical positivism) in university circles. In continental countries, where esoteric and remote logical empiricism has never won many converts, the primary development in philosophy was existentialism.

Logical empiricism was truly revolutionary. It quite simply rejected most of the concerns of traditional philosophy, from the existence of God to the meaning of happiness, as nonsense and hot air. This outlook began primarily with the Austrian philosopher Ludwig Wittgenstein (1889–1951), who later emigrated to England, where he trained numerous disciples.

Wittgenstein argued in his pugnacious *Tractatus Logico-Philosophicus (Essay on Logical Philosophy)* in 1922 that philosophy is only the logical clarification of thoughts, and therefore the study of language, which expresses thoughts. The great philosophical issues of the ages—God, freedom, morality, and so on—are quite literally senseless, a great waste of time, for statements about them can neither be tested by scientific experiments nor demonstrated by the logic of mathematics. Logical empiricism, which has remained dominant in England and the United States to this day, drastically reduced the scope of philosophical inquiry. Anxious people could find few if any answers in this direction.

Highly diverse and even contradictory, existential thinkers were loosely united in a courageous search for moral values in a world of terror and uncertainty. Theirs were true voices of the age of anxiety.

Most existential thinkers in the twentieth century have been atheists. Like Nietzsche, who had already proclaimed that "God is dead," they did not believe a supreme being had established humanity's fundamental nature and given life its meaning. In the words of the famous French existentialist Jean-Paul Sartre (1905–1980), human beings simply exist: "They turn up, appear on the scene." Only after they "turn up" do they seek to define themselves. Honest human beings are terribly alone, for there is no God to help them. They are hounded by despair and the meaninglessness of life. The crisis of the existential thinker epitomized the modern intellectual crisis—the shattering of traditional beliefs in God, reason, and progress.

Existentialists did recognize that human beings, unless they kill themselves, must act. Indeed, in the words of Sartre, "man is condemned to be free." There is, therefore, the possibility—indeed, the necessity—of giving meaning to life through actions, of defining oneself through choices. To do so, individuals must become "engaged" and choose their own actions courageously, consistently, and in full awareness of their inescapable responsibility for their own behavior. In the end, existentialists argued, human beings can overcome the absurdity that existentialists saw in life.

Modern existentialism developed first in Germany in the 1920s, but it was in France during the years immediately after World War Two that existentialism came of age. The terrible conditions of the war reinforced the existential view of life and the existential approach to it. On the one hand, the armies of the German dictator Hitler had conquered most of Europe and unleashed a hideous reign of barbarism. On the other, men and women had more than ever to define themselves by their actions. Specifically, each individual had to choose whether to join the Resistance against Hitler or to accept and even abet tyranny. The writings of the leading French existentialists offered a powerful answer to profound moral issues and the contemporary crisis.

The Revival of Christianity

Christianity and religion in general had been on the defensive in intellectual circles since the Enlightenment, especially during the late nineteenth century. The loss of faith in human reason and in continual progress now led to a renewed interest in the Chris-

tian view of the world in the twentieth century. A number of thinkers and theologians began to revitalize the fundamentals of Christianity, especially after World War One. They had a powerful impact on society. Sometimes described as Christian existentialists because they shared the loneliness and despair of atheistic existentialists, they revived the tradition of Saint Augustine. They stressed human beings' sinful nature, the need for faith, and the mystery of God's forgiveness.

This development was a break with the late nineteenth century. In the years before 1914, some theologians, especially Protestant theologians, had felt the need to interpret Christian doctrine and the Bible so that they did not seem to contradict science, evolution, and common sense. Christ was therefore seen primarily as the greatest moral teacher, and the "supernatural" aspects of his divinity were strenuously played down. In short, some modern theologians were embarrassed by the miraculous, unscientific aspects of Christianity and turned away from them.

The revival of fundamental Christian belief after World War One was fed by rediscovery of the work of the nineteenth-century Danish religious philosopher Søren Kierkegaard (1813–1855), whose ideas became extremely influential. Kierkegaard had rejected formalistic religion and denounced the worldliness of the Danish Lutheran church. He had eventually resolved his personal anguish over his imperfect nature by making a total religious commitment to a remote and majestic God.

Similar ideas were brilliantly developed by the Swiss Protestant theologian Karl Barth (1886–1968), whose many influential writings after 1920 sought to re-create the religious intensity of the Reformation. For Barth, the basic fact about human beings is that they are imperfect, sinful creatures, whose reason and will are hopelessly flawed. Religious truth is therefore made known to human beings only through God's grace. People have to accept God's word and the supernatural revelation of Jesus Christ with awe, trust, and obedience. Lowly mortals should not expect to "reason out" God and his ways.

Among Catholics, the leading existential Christian thinker was Gabriel Marcel (1889–1973). Born into a cultivated French family, where his atheistic father was "gratefully aware of all that . . . art owed to Catholicism but regarded Catholic thought itself as obsolete and tainted with absurd superstitions,"[2] Marcel found in the Catholic church an answer to what he called the postwar "broken world." Catholicism and religious belief provided the hope, humanity, honesty, and piety for which he hungered.

Religion became much more relevant and meaningful to thinking people after 1914, and many other illustrious individuals turned to religion between about 1920 and 1950. The poets T. S. Eliot and W. H. Auden, the novelists Evelyn Waugh and Aldous Huxley, the historian Arnold Toynbee, the Oxford professor C. S. Lewis, the psychoanalyst Karl Stern, and the physicist Max Planck were all either converted to religion or attracted to it for the first time. Religion, often of a despairing, existential variety, was one meaningful answer to terror and anxiety. As another famous Roman Catholic convert, English novelist Graham Greene, wrote: "One began to believe in heaven because one believed in hell."[3]

TWENTIETH-CENTURY LITERATURE

Literature articulated the general intellectual climate of pessimism, relativism, and alienation. Novelists developed new techniques to express new realities. The great nineteenth-century novelists had typically written as all-knowing narrators, describing realistic characters and their relationship to an understandable if sometimes harsh society. In the twentieth century, most major writers adopted the limited, often confused viewpoint of a single individual. Like Freud, these novelists focused their attention on the complexity and irrationality of the human mind, where feelings and memories are forever scrambled.

Serious novelists often favored the "stream-of-consciousness" technique to explore the psyche. In *Jacob's Room* (1922), Virginia Woolf (1882–1941) turned the novel into a series of internal monologues, in which ideas and emotions from different periods of time bubble up as randomly as from a patient on a psychoanalyst's couch. The most famous stream-of-consciousness novel—and surely the most disturbing novel of its generation—was *Ulysses,* which the Irish novelist James Joyce (1882–1941) published in 1922. Into *Ulysses's* account of an ordinary day in the life of an ordinary man, Joyce weaves an extended ironic parallel between his hero's aimless wanderings through the streets and pubs of Dublin and the adventures of Homer's hero Ulysses on his way home from Troy. Abandoning conventional grammar and blending foreign words, puns, bits of knowledge, and scraps of memory together in bewildering confusion,

Virginia Woolf grew up in a famous literary family to become a leading member of England's intellectual aristocracy. Her novels captured sensations like impressionist paintings, and her home attracted a circle of artists and writers known as the Bloomsbury Group. *(BBC Hulton/The Bettmann Archive)*

the language of *Ulysses* is intended to mirror modern life itself: a gigantic riddle waiting to be unraveled.

As creative writers turned their attention from society to the individual and from realism to psychological relativity, they rejected the idea of progress. Some even described "anti-utopias," nightmare visions of things to come. In 1918 an obscure German high school teacher named Oswald Spengler (1880–1936) published *Decline of the West,* which quickly became an international sensation. According to Spengler, every culture experiences a life cycle of growth and decline. Western civilization, in Spengler's opinion, was in its old age, and death was approaching in the form of conquest by the yellow race. T. S. Eliot (1888–1965), in his famous poem *The Waste Land* (1922), depicted a world of growing desolation, although after his conversion to Anglo-Catholicism in 1927, Eliot came to hope cautiously for humanity's salvation. No such hope appeared in

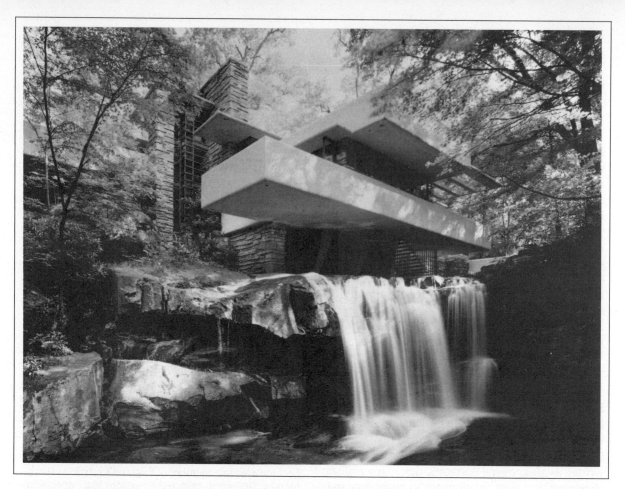

Frank Lloyd Wright: The "Falling Water" House Often considered Wright's masterpiece, Falling Water combines modern architectural concepts with close attention to a spectacular site. Anchored to a high rock ledge by means of reinforced concrete, the house soars out over a cascading waterfall at Bear Run in western Pennsylvania. Built in 1937 for a Pittsburgh businessman, Falling Water is now open to the public and attracts 70,000 visitors each year. *(Western Pennsylvania Conservancy/Art Resource)*

the work of Franz Kafka (1883–1924), whose novels *The Trial* and *The Castle,* as well as several of his greatest short stories, portray helpless individuals crushed by inexplicably hostile forces. The German-Jewish Kafka died young, at forty-one, and so did not see his nightmares materialize in the Nazi state.

MODERN ART AND MUSIC

Throughout the twentieth century, there has been considerable unity in the arts. The "modernism" of the immediate prewar years and the 1920s is still strikingly modern. Manifestations of modernism in art, architecture, and music have of course been highly varied, just as in physics, psychology, and philosophy; yet there are resemblances, for artists, scientists, and original thinkers partake of the same culture. Creative artists rejected old forms and old values. Modernism in art and music meant constant experimentation and a search for new kinds of expression. And though many people find the modern visions of the arts strange, disturbing, and even ugly, the twentieth century, so dismal in many respects, will probably stand as one of Western civilization's great artistic eras.

ARCHITECTURE AND DESIGN

Modernism in the arts was loosely unified by a revolution in architecture. The architectural revolution not only gave the other arts striking new settings, it intended nothing less than to transform the physical framework of the urban society according to a new principle: functionalism. Buildings, like industrial products, should be useful and "functional": that is, they should serve, as well as possible, the purpose for which they were made. Thus, architects and designers had to work with engineers, town planners, and even sanitation experts. Moreover, they had to throw away useless ornamentation and find beauty and aesthetic pleasure in the clean lines of practical constructions and efficient machinery.

The United States, with its rapid urban growth and lack of rigid building traditions, pioneered in the new architecture. In the 1890s, the Chicago school of architects, led by Louis H. Sullivan (1856–1924), used cheap steel, reinforced concrete, and electric elevators to build skyscrapers and office buildings which still retained striking exterior decoration. In the first decade of the twentieth century, Sullivan's student Frank Lloyd Wright (1869–1959) built a series of radically new and truly modern houses featuring low lines, open interiors, and mass-produced building materials. Europeans were inspired by these efforts and by such other American examples of functional construction as the massive, unadorned grain elevators of the Midwest.

Around 1905, when the first really modern buildings were going up in Europe, architectural leadership shifted to the German-speaking countries and remained there until Hitler took power in 1933. In 1911 the twenty-eight-year-old Walter Gropius (1883–1969) broke sharply with the past in his design of the Fagus shoe factory at Alfeld, Germany. A clean, light, elegant building of glass and iron, Gropius's new factory represented a jump right into the middle of the century.

After the First World War, the new German republic gave Gropius the authority to merge the schools of fine and applied arts at Weimar into a single, interdisciplinary school, the Bauhaus. In spite of intense criticism from conservative politicians and university professors, the Bauhaus brought together many leading modern architects, artists, designers, and theatrical innovators, who worked as an effective, inspired team. Throwing out traditional teaching methods, they combined the study of fine art, such as painting and sculpture, with the study of applied art in the crafts of printing, weaving, and furniture making. Throughout the 1920s, the Bauhaus, with its stress on functionalism and good design for everyday life, attracted enthusiastic students from all over the world. It had a great and continuing impact.

Another leader in the modern or "international" style was Ludwig Mies van der Rohe (1886–1969), who followed Gropius as director of the Bauhaus in 1930 and emigrated to the United States in 1937. His classic Lake Shore Apartments in Chicago, built between 1948 and 1951, symbolize the triumph of steel-frame and glass-wall modern architecture, which had grown out of Sullivan's skyscrapers and German functionalism in the great building boom after the Second World War.

MODERN PAINTING

Modern painting grew out of a revolt against French impressionism (see Color Insert V). The impressionism of Monet, Renoir, and Pissarro was, in part, a kind of "superrealism." Leaving exact copying of objects to photography, these artists sought to capture the momentary overall feeling, or impression, of light falling on a real-life scene before their eyes. By 1890, when impressionism was finally established, a few artists known as post-impressionists, or expressionists, were already striking out in new directions. After 1905 art took on an abstract, nonrepresentational character, which it has generally retained to the present.

Though individualistic in their styles, post-impressionists were united in their desire to know and depict worlds other than the visible world of fact. Like the early nineteenth-century romantics, they wanted to portray unseen, inner worlds of emotion and imagination. Like modern novelists, they wanted to express a complicated psychological view of reality as well as an overwhelming emotional intensity. In *The Starry Night* (1889), for example, the great Dutch expressionist Vincent van Gogh (1853–1890) painted the vision of his mind's eye. Flaming cypress trees, exploding stars, and a cometlike Milky Way swirl together in one great cosmic rhythm.

Fascination with form, as opposed to light, was characteristic of post-impressionism and expressionism (see Color Insert VI). Paul Cézanne (1839–1906), who had a profound influence on twentieth-century painting, was particularly committed to form and ordered design. He told a young painter, "You must see in nature the cylinder, the sphere, and the cone."[4] As Cézanne's later work became increasingly abstract

Picasso: Guernica In this rich, complex work a shrieking woman falls from a burning house on the far right. On the left a woman holds a dead child, while toward the center are fragments of a warrior and a screaming horse pierced by a spear. Picasso has used only the mournful colors of black, white, and gray. *(Pablo Picasso, Guernica [1937, May–early June]. Oil on canvas. © ARS, NY/SPADEM 1987)*

and nonrepresentational, it also moved away from the traditional three-dimensional perspective toward the two-dimensional plane, which has characterized so much of modern art. The expressionism of a group of painters led by Henri Matisse (1869–1954) was so extreme that an exhibition of their work in Paris in 1905 prompted shocked critics to call them *les fauves* —"the wild beasts." Matisse and his followers were primarily concerned not with real objects, but with the arrangement of color, line, and form as an end in itself.

In 1907 a young Spaniard in Paris, Pablo Picasso (1881–1973), founded another movement—cubism. Cubism concentrated on a complex geometry of zig-zagging lines and sharp-angled, overlapping planes. About three years later came the ultimate stage in the development of abstract, nonrepresentational art. Artists such as the Russian-born Wassily Kandinsky (1866–1944) turned away from nature completely. "The observer," said Kandinsky, "must learn to look at [my] pictures . . . as form and color combinations . . . as a representation of *mood* and not as a representation of *objects*."[5] On the eve of the First World War,

extreme expressionism and abstract painting were developing rapidly and had become international.

In the 1920s and 1930s, the artistic movements of the prewar years were extended and consolidated. The most notable new developments were dadaism and surrealism. Dadaism attacked all accepted standards of art and behavior, delighting in outrageous conduct. Its name, from the French word *dada,* meaning "hobbyhorse," is deliberately nonsensical. A famous example of dadaism was a reproduction of Leonardo da Vinci's *Mona Lisa* in which the famous woman with the mysterious smile sports a mustache and is ridiculed with an obscene inscription. After 1924 many dadaists were attracted to surrealism, which became very influential in art in the late 1920s and 1930s. Surrealism was inspired to a great extent by Freudian psychology. Surrealists painted a fantastic world of wild dreams and complex symbols, where watches melted and giant metronomes beat time in precisely drawn but impossible alien landscapes.

Refusing to depict ordinary visual reality, surrealist painters made powerful statements about the age of anxiety. Picasso's twenty-six-foot-long mural *Guernica* (1937) masterfully unites several powerful strands in twentieth-century art. Inspired by the Spanish Civil War, the painting commemorates the bombing of the ancient Spanish town of Guernica by fascist planes, an attack that took the lives of a thousand people—one out of every eight inhabitants—in a single night of terror. Combining the free distortion of expressionism, the overlapping planes of cubism, and the surrealist fascination with grotesque subject matter, *Guernica* is what Picasso meant it to be: an unforgettable attack on "brutality and darkness."

MODERN MUSIC

Developments in modern music were strikingly parallel to those in painting. Composers, too, were attracted by the emotional intensity of expressionism. The ballet *The Rite of Spring* by Igor Stravinsky (1882–1971) practically caused a riot when it was first performed in Paris in 1913 by Sergei Diaghilev's famous Russian dance company. The combination of pulsating, barbaric rhythms from the orchestra pit and an earthy representation of lovemaking by the dancers on the stage seemed a shocking, almost pornographic enactment of a primitive fertility rite.

After the experience of the First World War, when irrationality and violence seemed to pervade the human experience, expressionism in opera and ballet flourished. One of the most famous and powerful examples is the opera *Wozzeck* by Alban Berg (1885–1935), first performed in Berlin in 1925. Blending a half-sung, half-spoken kind of dialogue with harsh, atonal music, *Wozzeck* is a gruesome tale of a soldier driven by Kafka-like inner terrors and vague suspicions of unfaithfulness to murder his mistress.

Some composers turned their backs on long-established musical conventions. As abstract painters arranged lines and color but did not draw identifiable objects, so modern composers arranged sounds without creating recognizable harmonies. Led by the Viennese composer Arnold Schönberg (1874–1951), they abandoned traditional harmony and tonality. The musical notes in a given piece were no longer united and organized by a key; instead they were related only by an abstract, mathematical pattern, or "tone row," which could be detected only by a highly trained eye studying the musical score. Accustomed to the harmonies of classical and romantic music, audiences generally resisted modern atonal music. Only after the Second World War did it begin to win acceptance.

MOVIES AND RADIO

Until after World War Two at the earliest, these revolutionary changes in art and music appealed mainly to a minority of "highbrows" and not to the general public. That public was primarily and enthusiastically wrapped up in movies and radio. The long-declining traditional arts and amusements of people in villages and small towns almost vanished, replaced by standardized, commercial entertainment.

Moving pictures were first shown as a popular novelty in naughty peepshows—"What the Butler Saw"—and penny arcades in the 1890s, especially in Paris. The first movie houses date from an experiment in Los Angeles in 1902. They quickly attracted large audiences and led to the production of short, silent action films like the eight-minute *The Great Train Robbery* of 1903. American directors and businessmen then set up "movie factories," at first in the New York area and after 1910 in Los Angeles. These factories churned out two short films each week. On the eve of the First World War full-length feature films were suggesting the screen's vast possibilities.

During the First World War the United States became the dominant force in the rapidly expanding silent-film industry. In the 1920s, Mack Sennett (1884–1960) and his zany Keystone Cops specialized in short, slapstick comedies noted for frantic automobile chases, custard-pie battles, and gorgeous bathing beauties. Screen stars such as Mary Pickford and Lillian Gish, Douglas Fairbanks and Rudolph Valentino became household names, with their own "fan clubs." Yet Charlie Chaplin (1889–1978), a funny little Englishman working in Hollywood, was unquestionably the king of the "silver screen" in the 1920s. In his enormously popular role as a lonely tramp, complete with baggy trousers, battered derby, and an awkward, shuffling walk, Chaplin symbolized the "gay spirit of laughter in a cruel, crazy world."[6]

The early 1920s was also the great age of German films. Protected and developed during the war, the large German studios excelled in bizarre expressionist dramas. Unfortunately, their period of creativity was short-lived. By 1926 American money was drawing the leading German talents to Hollywood and

Matinee Idols Dark and handsome, Italian-born Rudolph Valentino, shown here in the stirring *Four Horsemen of the Apocalypse,* was Hollywood's original "Latin lover." Fresh and winsome, Canadian-born Mary Pickford was affectionately known as "America's Sweetheart." Starring in sentimental romances like *Poor Little Rich Girl,* she reigned over Hollywood with her husband Douglas Fairbanks. *(Picture Collection, The Branch Libraries, The New York Public Library)*

consolidating America's international domination. Film making was big business, and European theater owners were forced to book whole blocks of American films to get the few pictures they really wanted. This system put European producers at a great disadvantage until "talkies" permitted a revival of national film industries in the 1930s, particularly in France.

Whether foreign or domestic, motion pictures became the main entertainment of the masses until after the Second World War. In Great Britain one in every four adults went to the movies twice a week in the late 1930s, and two in five went once a week. Continental countries had similar figures. The greatest appeal of motion pictures was that they offered ordinary people a temporary escape from the hard realities of everyday life. For an hour or two the moviegoer could flee the world of international tensions, uncertainty, unemployment, and personal frustrations. The appeal of escapist entertainment was especially strong during the Great Depression. Millions flocked to musical comedies featuring glittering stars such as Ginger Rogers and Fred Astaire and to the fanciful cartoons of Mickey Mouse.

Radio became possible with the transatlantic "wireless" in 1901 and the development of the vacuum tube in 1904, which permitted the transmission of speech and music. But only after 1920 did every major country establish national broadcasting networks. In the United States, such networks were privately owned and financed by advertising. In Great Britain, Parliament set up an independent, high-minded public corporation, the British Broadcasting Corporation (BBC), which was supported by licensing fees. Elsewhere in Europe, the typical pattern for broadcasting networks was direct control by the government.

Whatever the institutional framework, radio became popular and influential. By the late 1930s, more than three out of every four households in both democratic Great Britain and dictatorial Germany had at least one cheap, mass-produced radio. Other European countries were not far behind.

Radio in unscrupulous hands was particularly well suited for political propaganda. Dictators like Mussolini and Hitler controlled the airwaves and could reach enormous national audiences with their frequent, dramatic speeches. In democratic countries, politicians such as President Franklin Roosevelt and Prime Minister Stanley Baldwin effectively used informal "fireside chats" to bolster their support.

Motion pictures also became powerful tools of indoctrination, especially in countries with dictatorial regimes. Lenin himself encouraged the development of Soviet film making, believing that the new medium was essential to the social and ideological transformation of the country. Beginning in the mid-1920s, a series of epic films, the most famous of which were directed by Sergei Eisenstein (1898–1948), brilliantly dramatized the Communist view of Russian history.

In Germany, Hitler turned to a young and immensely talented woman film maker, Leni Riefenstahl (b. 1902), for a masterpiece of documentary propaganda, *The Triumph of the Will,* based on the Nazi party rally at Nuremberg in 1934. Riefenstahl combined stunning aerial photography, joyful crowds welcoming Hitler, and mass processions of young Nazi fanatics. Her film was a brilliant and all-too-powerful documentary of Germany's "Nazi rebirth." The new media of mass culture were clearly potentially dangerous instruments of political manipulation.

THE SEARCH FOR PEACE AND POLITICAL STABILITY

The Versailles settlement had established a shaky truce, not a solid peace. Within the general context of intellectual crisis and revolutionary artistic experimentation, politicians and statesmen struggled to create a stable international order.

The pursuit of real and lasting peace proved difficult. Germany hated the Treaty of Versailles; France was fearful and isolated. Britain was undependable, and the United States had turned its back on European problems. Eastern Europe was in ferment, and no one could predict the future of communist Russia. Moreover, the international economic situation was poor and greatly complicated by war debts and disrupted patterns of trade. Yet for a time, from 1925 to late 1929, it appeared that peace and stability were within reach. When the subsequent collapse of the 1930s mocked these hopes, the disillusionment of liberals in the democracies was intensified.

GERMANY AND THE WESTERN POWERS

Germany was the key to lasting peace. Only under the pressure of the Allies' naval blockade and threat to extend their military occupation from the Rhineland to the rest of the country had Germany's new republican government signed the Treaty of Versailles in June 1919. To Germans of all political parties, the treaty represented a harsh, dictated peace, to be revised or repudiated as soon as possible. The treaty had neither broken nor reduced Germany, which was potentially still the strongest country in Europe. Thus the treaty had fallen between two stools: too harsh for a peace of reconciliation, too soft for a peace of conquest.

Moreover, with ominous implications for the future, France and Great Britain did not see eye to eye on Germany. By the end of 1919, France wanted to stress the harsh elements in the Treaty of Versailles. Most of the war in the west had been fought on French soil, and much of rich, industrialized, northern France had been devastated. The expected costs of reconstruction were staggering; like Great Britain, France had also borrowed large sums from the United States during the war, which had to be repaid.

Thus French politicians believed that massive reparations from Germany were a vital economic necessity. Moreover, if the Germans had to suffer to make the payments, the French would not be overly concerned. Having compromised with President Wilson only to be betrayed by America's failure to ratify the treaty, many French leaders saw strict implementation of all provisions of the Treaty of Versailles as France's last best hope. Large reparation payments could hold Germany down indefinitely, and France would realize its goal of security.

The British soon felt differently. Prewar Germany had been Great Britain's second-best market in the entire world, and after the war a healthy, prosperous Germany appeared to be essential to the British economy. Indeed, many English people agreed with the analysis of the young English economist John Maynard Keynes (1883–1946), who eloquently denounced the Treaty of Versailles in his famous *Economic Consequences of the Peace* (1919). According to Keynes's interpretation, astronomical reparations and harsh economic measures would indeed reduce Germany to the position of an impoverished second-rate power, but such impoverishment would increase economic hardship in all countries. Only a complete revision of the foolish treaty could save Germany—and Europe. Keynes's attack exploded like a bombshell and became very influential. It stirred deep guilt feelings about Germany in the English-speaking world, feelings that often paralyzed English and American leaders in their relations with Germany and its leaders between the First and Second World Wars.

The British were also suspicious of France's army —momentarily the largest in Europe—and France's foreign policy. Ever since 1890, France had looked to Russia as a powerful ally against Germany. But with Russia hostile and socialist, and with Britain and the United States unwilling to make any firm commitments, France turned to the newly formed states of eastern Europe for diplomatic support. In 1921 France signed a mutual defense pact with Poland and associated itself closely with the so-called Little Entente, an alliance that joined Czechoslovakia, Rumania, and Yugoslavia against defeated and bitter Hungary. The British and the French were also on cool terms because of conflicts relating to their League of Nations mandates in the Middle East.

While French and British leaders drifted in different directions, the Allied reparations commission completed its work. In April 1921, it announced that Germany had to pay the enormous sum of 132 billion gold marks ($33 billion), payable in annual installments of 2.5 billion gold marks. Facing possible occupation of more of its territory, the young German republic made its first payment in 1921. Then in 1922, wracked by rapid inflation and political assassinations, and motivated by hostility and arrogance as well, the Weimar Republic announced its inability to pay more. It proposed a moratorium on reparations for three years, with the clear implication that thereafter reparations would either be drastically reduced or eliminated entirely.

The British were willing to accept this offer, but the French were not. Led by their tough-minded, legalistic prime minister, Raymond Poincaré, they decided they either had to call Germany's bluff or see the entire peace settlement dissolve to France's great disadvantage. So, despite strong British protests, France and its ally Belgium decided to pursue a firm policy. In early January 1923, French and Belgian armies began to occupy the Ruhr district, the heartland of industrial Germany, creating the most serious international crisis of the 1920s.

THE OCCUPATION OF THE RUHR

The strategy of Poincaré and his French supporters was simple. Since Germany would not pay reparations in hard currency or gold, France and Belgium would collect reparations in kind—coal, steel, and machinery. If forcible collection proved impossible, France would use occupation to paralyze Germany and force it to accept the Treaty of Versailles.

Strengthened by a wave of patriotism, the German government ordered the people of the Ruhr to stop working and start resisting—passively—the French occupation. The coal mines and steel mills of the Ruhr grew silent, leaving 10 percent of Germany's total population in need of relief. The French answer to passive resistance was to seal off not only the Ruhr but the entire Rhineland from the rest of Germany, permitting only enough food to prevent starvation. They also revived plans for a separate state in the Rhineland.

By the summer of 1923, France and Germany were engaged in a great test of wills. As the German government had anticipated, French armies could not collect reparations from striking workers at gunpoint. But French occupation was indeed paralyzing

The Fruits of Germany's Inflation In the end, currency had value only as waste paper. Here bank notes are being purchased by the bail for paper mills, along with old rags *(Lumpen)* and bones *(Knochen)*. *(Archiv für Kunst u. Geschichte/Katherine Young)*

Germany and its economy, for the Ruhr district normally produced 80 percent of Germany's steel and coal. Moreover, the occupation of the Ruhr turned rapid German inflation into runaway inflation. Faced with the need to support the striking Ruhr workers and their employers, the German government began to print money to pay its bills. Prices soared. People went to the store with a big bag of paper money; they returned home with a handful of groceries. German money rapidly lost all value, and so did anything else with a stated fixed value.

Runaway inflation brought about a social revolution. The accumulated savings of many retired and middle-class people were wiped out. The old middle-class virtues of thrift, caution, and self-reliance were cruelly mocked by catastrophic inflation. People told themselves that nothing had real value any more, not even money. The German middle and lower middle classes felt cheated and burned with resentment. Many hated and blamed the Western governments, their own government, big business, the Jews, the workers, the Communists for their misfortune. They

were psychologically prepared to follow radical leaders in a moment of crisis.

In August 1923, as the mark fell and political unrest grew throughout Germany, Gustav Stresemann assumed leadership of the government. Stresemann adopted a compromising attitude. He called off passive resistance in the Ruhr and in October agreed in principle to pay reparations, but asked for a re-examination of Germany's ability to pay. Poincaré accepted. His hard line was becoming increasingly unpopular with French citizens, and it was hated in Britain and the United States. Moreover, occupation was dreadfully expensive, and France's own currency was beginning to lose value on foreign exchange markets.

More generally, in both Germany and France power was finally passing to the moderates, who realized that continued confrontation was a destructive, no-win situation. Thus, after five long years of hostility and tension culminating in a kind of undeclared war in the Ruhr in 1923, Germany and France decided to give compromise and cooperation a try. The

British, and even the Americans, were willing to help. The first step was a reasonable compromise on the reparations question.

HOPE IN FOREIGN AFFAIRS, 1924–1929

The reparations commission appointed an international committee of financial experts headed by an American banker, Charles G. Dawes, to re-examine reparations from a broad perspective. The committee made a series of recommendations known as the Dawes Plan (1924), which was accepted by France, Germany, and Britain. German reparations were reduced and placed on a sliding scale, like an income tax, whereby yearly payments depended on the level of German economic prosperity. The Dawes Plan also recommended large loans to Germany, loans that could come only from the United States. These loans were to help Stresemann's government put its new currency on a firm basis and promote German recovery. In short, Germany would get private loans from the United States and pay reparations to France and Britain, thus enabling those countries to repay the large sums they owed the United States.

This circular flow of international payments was complicated and risky. For a time, though, it worked. The German republic experienced a spectacular economic recovery. By 1929 Germany's wealth and income were 50 percent greater than in 1913. With prosperity and large, continuous inflows of American capital, Germany easily paid about $1.3 billion in reparations in 1927 and 1928, enabling France and Britain to pay the United States. In 1929 the Young Plan, named after an American businessman, further reduced German reparations and formalized the link between German reparations and French-British debts to the United States. In this way the Americans, who did not have armies but who did have money, belatedly played a part in the general economic settlement, which though far from ideal facilitated the worldwide recovery of the late 1920s.

The economic settlement was matched by a political settlement. In 1925 the leaders of Europe signed a number of agreements at Locarno, Switzerland. Stresemann, who guided German's foreign policy until his death in 1929, had suggested a treaty with France's conciliatory Aristide Briand, who had returned to office in 1924 after French voters rejected the bellicose Poincaré. By this treaty Germany and France solemnly pledged to accept their common border, and both Britain and Italy agreed to fight either country if it invaded the other. Stresemann also agreed to settle boundary disputes with Poland and Czechoslovakia by peaceful means, and France promised those countries military aid if they were attacked by Germany. For their efforts Stresemann and Briand shared the Nobel Peace Prize in 1926. The effect of the treaties of Locarno was far-reaching. For several years, a "spirit of Locarno" gave Europeans a sense of growing security in international affairs.

Hopes were strengthened by other developments. In 1926 Germany joined the League of Nations, where Stresemann continued his "peace offensive." In 1928 fifteen countries signed the Kellogg-Briand Pact, which "condemned and renounced war as an instrument of national policy." The signing states agreed to settle international disputes peacefully. The pact grew out of a suggestion by Briand that France and the United States renounce the possibility of war between their two countries. Briand was gently and subtly trying to draw the United States back into involvement with Europe. When Secretary of State Frank B. Kellogg proposed a multinational pact, Briand appeared close to success. Thus the cautious optimism of the late 1920s also rested on the hope that the United States would accept its responsibilities as a great world power and consequently contribute to European stability.

HOPE IN DEMOCRATIC GOVERNMENT

Domestic politics also offered reason to hope. During the occupation of the Ruhr and the great inflation, republican government in Germany had appeared on the verge of collapse. In 1923 Communists momentarily entered provincial governments, and in November an obscure nobody named Adolf Hitler leaped on a table in a beer hall in Munich and proclaimed a "national socialist revolution." But Hitler's plot was poorly organized and easily crushed, and Hitler was sentenced to prison, where he outlined his theories and program in his book *Mein Kampf* (*My Struggle*). Throughout the 1920s, Hitler's National Socialist party attracted support only from a few fanatical anti-Semites, ultranationalists, and disgruntled ex-servicemen. In 1928 his party had an insignificant twelve seats in the national parliament. Indeed, after 1923 democracy seemed to take root in Weimar Germany. A new currency was established, and the economy boomed.

The moderate businessmen who tended to dominate the various German coalition governments were convinced that economic prosperity demanded good relations with the Western powers, and they supported parliamentary government at home. Stresemann himself was a man of this class, and he was the key figure in every government until his death in 1929. Elections were held regularly, and republican democracy appeared to have growing support among a majority of the German people.

There were, however, sharp political divisions in the country. Many unrepentant nationalists and monarchists populated the right and the army. Germany's Communists were noisy and active on the left. The Communists, directed from Moscow, reserved their greatest hatred and sharpest barbs for their cousins the Social Democrats, whom they endlessly accused of betraying the revolution. The working classes were divided politically, but most supported the nonrevolutionary but socialist Social Democrats.

The situation in France had numerous similarities to that in Germany. Communists and Socialists battled for the support of the workers. After 1924 the democratically elected government rested mainly in the hands of coalitions of moderates, and business interests were well represented. France's great accomplishment was rapid rebuilding of its war-torn northern region. The expense of this undertaking led, however, to a large deficit and substantial inflation. By early 1926, the franc had fallen to 10 percent of its prewar value, causing a severe crisis. Poincaré was recalled to office, while Briand remained minister for foreign affairs. The Poincaré government proceeded to slash spending and raise taxes, restoring confidence in the economy. The franc was "saved," stabilized at about one-fifth of its prewar value. Good times prevailed until 1930.

Despite its political shortcomings, France attracted artists and writers from all over the world in the 1920s. Much of the intellectual and artistic ferment of the times flourished in Paris. More generally, France appealed to foreigners and the French as a harmonious combination of small businesses and family farms, of bold innovation and solid traditions.

Britain, too, faced challenges after 1920. The wartime trend toward greater social equality continued, however, helping to maintain social harmony. The great problem was unemployment. Many of Britain's best markets had been lost during the war. In June

An American in Paris The young Josephine Baker suddenly became a star when she brought an exotic African eroticism to French music halls in 1925. American blacks and Africans had a powerful impact on entertainment in Europe in the 1920s and 1930s. *(BBC Hulton/ The Bettmann Archive)*

1921, almost 2.2 million people—23 percent of the labor force—were out of work, and throughout the 1920s unemployment hovered around 12 percent. Yet the state provided unemployment benefits of equal size to all those without jobs and supplemented those payments with subsidized housing, medical aid, and increased old-age pensions. These and other measures kept living standards from seriously declining, defused class tensions, and pointed the way toward the welfare state Britain established after World War Two.

Relative social harmony was accompanied by the rise of the Labour party as a determined champion of the working classes and of greater social equality. Committed to the kind of moderate, "revisionist" socialism that had emerged before World War One (pages 924–926), the Labour party replaced the Liberal party as the main opposition to the Conservatives. The new prominence of the Labour party reflected the decline of old liberal ideals of competitive capitalism, limited government control, and individual responsibility. In 1924 and 1929, the Labour party under Ramsay MacDonald governed the country with the support of the smaller Liberal party. Yet Labour moved toward socialism gradually and democratically, so that the middle classes were not overly frightened as the working classes won new benefits.

The Conservatives under Stanley Baldwin showed the same compromising spirit on social issues. The last line of Baldwin's greatest speech in March 1925 summarized his international and domestic programs: "Give us peace in our time, O Lord." Thus, in spite of such conflicts as the 1926 strike by hard-pressed coal miners, which ended in an unsuccessful general strike, social unrest in Britain was limited in the 1920s and in the 1930s as well. In 1922 Britain granted southern, Catholic Ireland full autonomy after a bitter guerrilla war, thus removing another source of prewar friction. In summary, developments in both international relations and in the domestic politics of the leading democracies gave cause for cautious optimism in the late 1920s.

THE GREAT DEPRESSION, 1929–1939

Like the Great War, the Great Depression must be spelled with capital letters. Economic depression was nothing new. Depressions occurred throughout the nineteenth century with predictable regularity, as they recur in the form of recessions and slumps to this day. What was new about this depression was its severity and duration. It struck with ever-greater intensity from 1929 to 1933, and recovery was uneven and slow. Moreover, the Great Depression was truly global in scope.

The social and political consequences of prolonged economic collapse were enormous all around the world. Subsequent military expansion in Japan has already been described (see page 1061), and subsequent chapters will examine a similarly powerful impact on Latin America and Africa. In Europe and the United States, the depression shattered the fragile optimism of political leaders in the late 1920s. Mass unemployment made insecurity a reality for millions of ordinary people, who had paid little attention to the intellectual crisis or to new directions in art and ideas. In desperation, people looked for leaders who would "do something." They were willing to support radical attempts to deal with the crisis by both democratic leaders and dictators.

THE ECONOMIC CRISIS

There is no agreement among historians and economists about why the Great Depression was so deep and lasted so long. Thus, it is best to trace the course of the great collapse before trying to identify what caused it.

Though economic activity was already declining moderately in many countries by early 1929, the crash of the stock market in the United States in October of that year really started the Great Depression. The American stock market boom, which had seen stock prices double between early 1928 and September 1929, was built on borrowed money. Many wealthy investors, speculators, and people of modest means had bought stocks by paying only a small fraction of the total purchase price and borrowing the remainder from their stockbrokers. Such buying "on margin" was extremely dangerous. When prices started falling, the hard-pressed margin buyers either had to put up more money, which was often impossible, or sell their shares to pay off their brokers. Thus thousands of people started selling all at once. The result was a financial panic. Countless investors and speculators were wiped out in a matter of days or weeks.

The general economic consequences were swift and severe. Stripped of their wealth and confidence, battered investors and their fellow citizens started buying fewer goods. Production began to slow down, and unemployment began to rise. Soon the entire American economy was caught in a vicious, spiraling decline.

The financial panic in the United States triggered a worldwide financial crisis, and that crisis resulted in a drastic decline in production in country after country. Throughout the 1920s American bankers and investors had lent large amounts of capital not only to Germany but to many countries. Many of these loans were short term, and once panic broke, New York

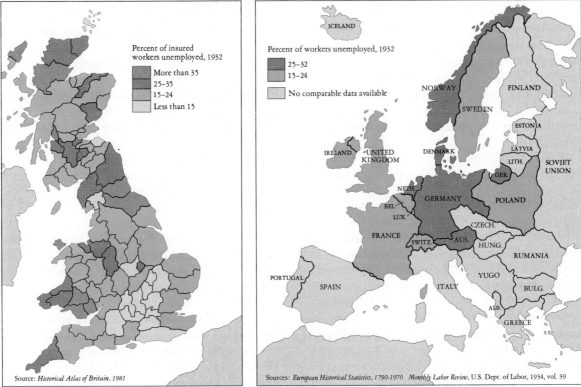

MAP 34.1 The Great Depression in the United States, Britain, and Europe National and regional differences were substantial. Germany, industrial northern Britain, and the American Middle West were particularly hard-hit.

bankers began recalling them. Gold reserves thus began to flow out of European countries, particularly Germany and Austria, toward the United States. It became very hard for European businessmen to borrow money, and the panicky public began to withdraw its savings from the banks. These banking problems eventually led to the crash of the largest bank in Austria in 1931 and then to general financial chaos. The recall of private loans by American bankers also accelerated the collapse in world prices, as businessmen around the world dumped industrial goods and agricultural commodities in a frantic attempt to get cash to pay what they owed.

The financial crisis led to a general crisis of production: between 1929 and 1933, world output of goods fell by an estimated 38 percent. As this happened, each country turned inward and tried to go it alone. In 1931, for example, Britain went off the gold standard, refusing to convert bank notes into gold, and reduced the value of its money. Britain's goal was to make its goods cheaper and therefore more salable in the world market. But because more than twenty nations, including the United States in 1934, also went off the gold standard, no country gained a real advantage. Similarly, country after country followed the example of the United States when it raised protective tariffs to their highest levels ever in 1930 and tried to seal off shrinking national markets for American producers only. Within this context of fragmented and destructive economic nationalism, recovery finally began in 1933.

Although opinions differ, two factors probably best explain the relentless slide to the bottom from 1929 to early 1933. First, the international economy lacked a leadership able to maintain stability when the crisis came. Specifically, as a noted American economic historian concludes, the seriously weakened British, the traditional leaders of the world economy, "couldn't and the United States wouldn't" stabilize the international economic system in 1929.[7] The United States, which had momentarily played a positive role after the occupation of the Ruhr, cut back its international lending and erected high tariffs.

The second factor was poor national economic policy in almost every country. Governments generally cut their budgets and reduced spending when they should have run large deficits in an attempt to stimulate their economies. Since World War Two, such a "counter-cyclical policy," advocated by John Maynard Keynes, has become a well-established weapon against depression. But in the 1930s Keynes's prescription was generally regarded with horror by orthodox economists.

MASS UNEMPLOYMENT

The need for large-scale government spending was tied to mass unemployment. As the financial crisis led to cuts in production, workers lost their jobs and had little money to buy goods. This led to still more cuts in production and still more unemployment, until millions were out of work. In Britain, unemployment had averaged 12 percent in the 1920s; between 1930 and 1935, it averaged more than 18 percent. Far worse was the case of the United States, where unemployment had averaged only 5 percent in the 1920s. In 1932 unemployment soared to about *one-third* of the entire labor force: 14 million people were out of work (Map 34.1). Only by pumping new money into the economy could the government increase demand and break the vicious cycle of decline.

Along with its economic effects, mass unemployment posed a great social problem that mere numbers cannot adequately express. Millions of people lost their spirit and dignity in an apparently hopeless search for work. Homes and ways of life were disrupted in millions of personal tragedies. Young people postponed marriages they could not afford, and birthrates fell sharply. There was an increase in suicide and mental illness. Poverty or the threat of poverty became a grinding reality. In 1932 the workers of Manchester, England, appealed to their city officials—a typical appeal echoed throughout the Western world:

We tell you that thousands of people . . . are in desperate straits. We tell you that men, women, and children are going hungry. . . . We tell you that great numbers are being rendered distraught through the stress and worry of trying to exist without work. . . .

If you do not do this—if you do not provide useful work for the unemployed—what, we ask, is your alternative? Do not imagine that this colossal tragedy of unemployment is going on endlessly without some fateful catastrophe. Hungry men are angry men.[8]

Mass unemployment was a terrible time bomb preparing to explode.

THE NEW DEAL IN THE UNITED STATES

Of all the major industrial countries, only Germany was harder hit by the Great Depression, or reacted more radically to it, than the United States. Depression was so traumatic in the United States because the 1920s had been a period of complacent prosperity. The Great Depression and the response to it was a major turning point in American history.

President Herbert Hoover and his administration initially reacted to the stock market crash and economic decline with dogged optimism and limited action. In May 1930, Hoover told a group of business and farm leaders that the worst was over and recovery would be rapid. When, however, the full force of the financial crisis struck Europe in the summer of 1931 and boomeranged back to the United States, people's worst fears became reality. Banks failed; unemployment soared. In 1932 industrial production fell to about 50 percent of its level in 1929. In these tragic circumstances Franklin Delano Roosevelt, an inspiring wheelchair aristocrat previously crippled by polio, won a landslide electoral victory with grand but vague promises of a "New Deal for the forgotten man."

Roosevelt's basic goal was to reform capitalism in order to preserve it. In his words, "A frank examination of the profit system in the spring of 1933 showed it to be in collapse; but substantially everybody in the United States, in public office and out of public office, from the very rich to the very poor, was as determined as was my Administration to save it."[9] Roosevelt rejected socialism and government ownership of industry in 1933. To right the situation, he chose forceful government intervention in the economy.

In this choice, Roosevelt and his advisers were greatly influenced by American experience in World War One. During the wartime emergency, the American economy had been thoroughly planned and regulated. Roosevelt and his "brain trust" of advisers adopted similar policies to restore prosperity and reduce social inequality. Roosevelt was flexible, pragmatic, and willing to experiment. Government intervention and experimentation were combined in some of the New Deal's most significant measures.

The most ambitious attempt to control and plan the economy was the National Recovery Administration (NRA), established by Congress right after

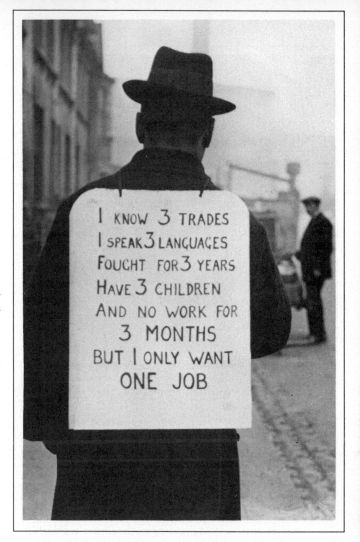

Middle-Class Unemployment An English office worker's unusual sandwich board poignantly summarizes the bitter despair of the unemployed in the 1930s. *(BBC Hulton/The Bettmann Archive)*

Roosevelt took office. The key idea behind the NRA was to reduce competition and fix prices and wages for everyone's benefit. This goal required government, business, and labor to hammer out detailed regulations for each industry. Along with this kind of national planning in the private sector of the economy, the government believed it could sponsor enough public works projects to assure recovery. Because the NRA broke with the cherished American tradition of free competition and aroused conflicts among businessmen, consumers, and bureaucrats, it did not work well. By the time the NRA was declared unconstitutional in 1935, Roosevelt and the New

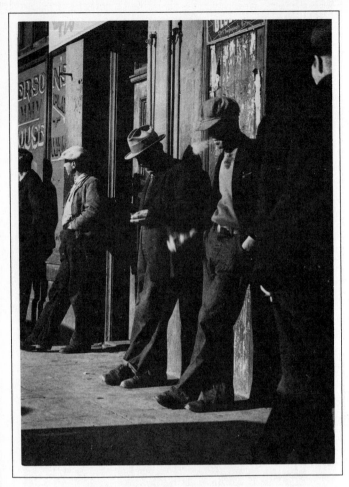

San Francisco, 1934 Standing on the corner, waiting for something to do: this classic photograph by Dorothea Lange captures the frustration and waste of unemployment in the Depression years. *(Courtesy of the Dorothea Lange Collection. The City of Oakland, The Oakland Museum, 1987)*

labor force worked for the WPA at some point in the 1930s. To this day thousands of public buildings, bridges, and highways built by the WPA stand as monuments to energetic government efforts to provide people with meaningful work. The WPA was enormously popular in a nation long schooled in self-reliance and the work ethic. The hope of a job with the government helped check the threat of social revolution in the United States.

Other social measures aimed in the same direction. Following the path blazed by Germany's Bismarck in the 1880s, the U.S. government in 1935 established a national social security system, with old-age pensions and unemployment benefits, to protect many workers against some of life's uncertainties. The National Labor Relations Act of 1935 gave union organizers the green light by declaring collective bargaining to be the policy of the United States. Following some bitter strikes, such as the sit-down strike at General Motors in early 1937, union membership more than doubled, from 4 million in 1935 to 9 million in 1940. In general, between 1935 and 1938 government rulings and social reforms chipped away at the privileges of the wealthy and tried to help ordinary people.

Yet, despite its undeniable accomplishments in social reform, the New Deal was only partly successful as a response to the Great Depression. At the height of the recovery, in May 1937, 7 million workers were still unemployed. The economic situation then worsened seriously in the recession of 1937 and 1938. Production fell sharply, and although unemployment never again reached the 15 million mark of 1933, it hit 11 million in 1938 and was still a staggering 10 million when war broke out in Europe in September 1939.

The New Deal never did pull the United States out of the depression. This failure frustrated Americans then, and it is still puzzling today. Perhaps, as some have claimed, Roosevelt should have used his enormous popularity and prestige in 1933 to nationalize the banks, the railroads, and some heavy industry, so that national economic planning could have been successful. On the other hand, Roosevelt's sharp attack on big business and the wealthy after 1935 had popular appeal but also damaged business confidence and made the great capitalists uncooperative. Given the low level of profit and the underutilization of many factories, however, it is questionable whether business would have behaved much differently even if the New Deal had catered to it.

Deal were already moving away from government efforts to plan and control the entire economy.

Instead, Roosevelt and his advisers attacked the key problem of mass unemployment directly. The federal government accepted the responsibility of employing directly as many people as financially possible, something Hoover had consistently rejected. Thus, when it became clear in late 1933 that the initial program of public works was too small, new agencies were created to undertake a vast range of projects.

The most famous of these was the Works Progress Administration (WPA), set up in 1935. At its peak in late 1938, this government agency employed more than 3 million individuals. One-fifth of the entire

Finally, it is often argued that the New Deal did not put enough money into the economy through deficit financing. Like his predecessors in the White House, Roosevelt was attached to the ideal of the balanced budget. His largest deficit was only $4.4 billion in 1936. Compare this figure with deficits of $21.5 billion in 1942 and $57.4 billion in 1943, when the nation was prosperously engaged in total war and unemployment had vanished. By 1945 many economists concluded that the New Deal's deficit-financed public works had been too small a step in the right direction. These Keynesian views were to be very influential in economic policy in Europe and America after the Second World War.

THE SCANDINAVIAN RESPONSE TO DEPRESSION

Of all the Western democracies, the Scandinavian countries under Socialist leadership responded most successfully to the challenge of the Great Depression. Having grown steadily in the late nineteenth century, Socialists became the largest political party in Sweden and then in Norway after the First World War. In the 1920s they passed important social reform legislation for both peasants and workers, gained practical administrative experience, and developed a unique kind of socialism. Flexible and nonrevolutionary, Scandinavian socialism grew out of a strong tradition of cooperative community action. Even before 1900, Scandinavian agricultural cooperatives had shown how individual peasant families could join together for everyone's benefit. Labor leaders and capitalists were also inclined to work together.

When the economic crisis struck in 1929, Socialist governments in Scandinavia built on this pattern of cooperative social action. Sweden in particular pioneered in the use of large-scale deficits to finance public works and thereby maintain production and employment. Scandinavian governments also increased social welfare benefits, from old-age pensions and unemployment insurance to subsidized housing and maternity allowances. All this spending required a large bureaucracy and high taxes, first on the rich and then on practically everyone. Yet both private and cooperative enterprise thrived, as did democracy. Some observers saw Scandinavia's welfare socialism as an appealing "middle way" between sick capitalism and cruel communism or fascism.

RECOVERY AND REFORM IN BRITAIN AND FRANCE

In Britain, MacDonald's Labour government and then, after 1931, the Conservative-dominated coalition government followed orthodox economic theory. The budget was balanced, but unemployed workers received barely enough welfare to live. Despite government lethargy, the economy recovered considerably after 1932. By 1937 total production was about 20 percent higher than in 1929. In fact, for Britain the years after 1932 were actually somewhat better than the 1920s had been, quite the opposite of the situation in the United States and France.

This good, but by no means brilliant, performance reflected the gradual reorientation of the British economy. After going off the gold standard in 1931 and establishing protective tariffs in 1932, Britain concentrated increasingly on the national rather than the international market. The old export industries of the Industrial Revolution, such as textiles and coal, continued to decline, but the new industries like automobiles and electrical appliances grew in response to British home demand. Moreover, low interest rates encouraged a housing boom. By the end of the decade there were highly visible differences between the old, depressed industrial areas of the north and the new, growing areas of the south. These developments encouraged Britain to look inward and avoid unpleasant foreign questions.

Because France was relatively less industrialized and more isolated from the world economy, the Great Depression came late. But once the depression hit France, it stayed and stayed. Decline was steady until 1935, and the short-lived recovery never brought production or employment back up to pre-depression levels. Economic stagnation both reflected and heightened an ongoing political crisis. There was no stability in government. As before 1914, the French parliament was made up of many political parties, which could never cooperate for very long. In 1933, for example, five coalition cabinets formed and fell in rapid succession.

The French lost the underlying unity that had made governmental instability bearable before 1914. Fascist-type organizations agitated against parliamentary democracy and looked to Mussolini's Italy and Hitler's Germany for inspiration. In February 1934, French fascists and semifascists rioted and threatened to overturn the republic. At the same time the Communist party and many workers opposed to the existing system were looking to Stalin's Russia for guidance. The vital center of moderate republicanism was sapped from both sides.

Frightened by the growing strength of the Fascists at home and abroad, the Communists, the Socialists, and the Radicals formed an alliance—the Popular Front—for the national elections of May 1936. Their clear victory reflected the trend toward polarization. The number of Communists in the parliament jumped dramatically from 10 to 72, while the Socialists, led by Léon Blum, became the strongest party in France with 146 seats. The really quite moderate Radicals slipped badly, and the conservatives lost ground to the semifascists.

In the next few months, Blum's Popular Front government made the first and only real attempt to deal with the social and economic problems of the 1930s in France. Inspired by Roosevelt's New Deal, the Popular Front encouraged the union movement and launched a far-reaching program of social reform, complete with paid vacations and a forty-hour workweek. Popular with workers and the lower middle class, these measures were quickly sabotaged by rapid inflation and cries of revolution from fascists and frightened conservatives. Wealthy people sneaked their money out of the country, labor unrest grew, and France entered a severe financial crisis. Blum was forced to announce a "breathing spell" in social reform.

The fires of political dissension were also fanned by civil war in Spain. The Communists demanded that France support the Spanish republicans, while many French conservatives would gladly have joined Hitler and Mussolini in aiding the attack of Spanish fascists. Extremism grew, and France itself was within sight of civil war. Blum was forced to resign in June 1937, and the Popular Front quickly collapsed. An anxious and divided France drifted aimlessly once again, preoccupied by Hitler and German rearmament.

———————

After the First World War, Western society entered a complex and difficult era—truly an age of anxiety. Intellectual life underwent a crisis marked by pessimism, uncertainty, and fascination with irrational forces. Rejection of old forms and ceaseless experimentation characterized art and music, while motion pictures and radio provided a new, standardized entertainment for the masses. Intellectual and artistic developments that had been confined to small avant-garde groups before 1914 gained wider currency along with the insecure state of mind they expressed.

Politics and economics were similarly disrupted. In the 1920s, statesmen groped to create an enduring peace and rebuild the prewar prosperity, and for a brief period late in the decade, they even seemed to have succeeded. Then the Great Depression shattered the fragile stability. Uncertainty returned with redoubled force in the 1930s. The international economy collapsed, and unemployment struck millions. The democracies turned inward as they sought to cope with massive domestic problems and widespread disillusionment. Generally speaking, they were not very successful. The old liberal ideals of individual rights and responsibilities, elected government, and economic freedom seemed ineffective to many, even when they managed to survive. And in many countries they were abandoned completely.

NOTES

1. P. Valéry, *Variety,* trans. Malcolm Cowley (New York: Harcourt, Brace, 1927), pp. 27–28.
2. G. Marcel, as quoted by S. Hughes, *The Obstructed Path: French Social Thought in the Years of Desperation, 1930–1960* (New York: Harper & Row, 1967), p. 82.
3. G. Greene, *Another Mexico* (New York: Viking Press, 1939), p. 3.
4. Quoted in A. H. Barr, Jr., *What Is Modern Painting?,* 9th ed. (New York: Museum of Modern Art, 1966), p. 27.
5. Ibid., p. 25.
6. R. Graves and A. Hodge, *The Long Week End: A Social History of Great Britain, 1918–1939* (New York: Macmillan, 1941), p. 131.
7. C. P. Kindleberger, *The World in Depression, 1929–1939* (Berkeley: University of California Press, 1973), p. 292.
8. Quoted in S. B. Clough et al., eds., *Economic History of Europe: Twentieth Century* (New York: Harper & Row, 1968), pp. 243–245.
9. Quoted in D. Dillard, *Economic Development of the North Atlantic Community* (Englewood Cliffs, N.J.: Prentice-Hall, 1967), p. 591.

SUGGESTED READING

Among general works, R. Sontag, *A Broken World, 1919–1939* (1971), and E. Wiskema, *Europe of the Dictators, 1919–1945* (1966), are particularly recommended. The former has an excellent bibliography. A. Bullock, ed., *The Twentieth Century* (1971), is a lavish visual feast combined with penetrating essays on major developments since 1900. Two excellent accounts of contemporary history—one with a liberal and the other with a conservative point of view—are R. Paxton, *Europe in the Twentieth Century* (1975), and P. Johnson, *Modern Times: The World from the Twenties to the Eighties* (1983). Crucial changes in thought before and after World War One are discussed in three rewarding intellectual histories: G. Masur, *Prophets of Yesterday* (1961); H. S. Hughes, *Consciousness and Society* (1956); and M. Biddiss, *Age of the Masses: Ideas and Society Since 1870* (1977). R. Stromberg, *European Intellectual History Since 1789,* 4th ed. (1986), and F. Baumer, *Modern European Thought: Continuity and Change in Ideas, 1600–1950* (1970), are recommended general surveys.

J. Rewald, *The History of Impressionism,* rev. ed. (1961) and *Post-Impressionism* (1956), are excellent, as are the works of A. H. Barr, Jr., cited in the Notes. P. Collaer, *A History of Modern Music* (1961), and H. R. Hitchcock, *Architecture: 19th and 20th Centuries* (1958), are good introductions, while T. Wolfe, *From Bauhaus to My House* (1981), is a lively critique of modern architecture. L. Barnett, *The Universe and Dr. Einstein* (1952), is a fascinating study of the new physics. P. Rieff, *Freud* (1956), and M. White, ed., *The Age of Analysis* (1955), open up basic questions of twentieth-century psychology and philosophy. P. Gay, *Weimar Culture* (1970), is a brilliant exploration of the many-sided artistic renaissance in Germany in the 1920s. M. Marrus, ed., *Emergence of Leisure* (1974), is a pioneering inquiry into an important aspect of mass culture. H.

Daniels-Rops, *A Fight for God,* 2 vols. (1966), is a sympathetic history of the Catholic church between 1870 and 1939.

C. Maier, *Recasting Bourgeois Europe* (1975), is an ambitious comparative study of social classes and conflicts in France, Germany, and Italy after World War One. R. Wohl, *The Generation of 1914* (1979); R. Kuisel, *Capital and State in Modern France: Renovation and Economic Management* (1982); and W. McDougall, *France's Rhineland Diplomacy, 1914–1924* (1978), are three more important studies on aspects of the postwar challenge. M. Childs, *Sweden: The Middle Way* (1961), applauds Sweden's efforts at social reform. W. Neuman, *The Balance of Power in the Interwar Years, 1919–1939* (1968), perceptively examines international politics after the Locarno treaties of 1925. In addition to the contemporary works discussed in the text, the crisis of the interwar period comes alive in R. Crossman, ed., *The God That Failed* (1950), in which famous Western writers tell why they were attracted to and later repelled by communism; Ortega y Gassett's renowned *The Revolt of the Masses* (1932); and F. A. Hayek's *The Road to Serfdom* (1944), a famous warning of the dangers to democratic freedoms.

In addition to C. Kindleberger's excellent study of the Great Depression cited in the Notes, there is J. Galbraith's very lively and understandable account of the stock market collapse, *The Great Crash* (1955). J. Garraty, *Unemployment in History* (1978), is noteworthy, though novels best portray the human tragedy of economic decline. W. Holtby, *South Riding* (1936), and W. Greenwood, *Love on the Dole* (1933), are moving stories of the Great Depression in England; H. Fallada, *Little Man, What Now?* (1932), is the classic counterpart for Germany. Also highly recommended as commentaries on English life between the wars are R. Graves, *Goodbye to All That,* rev. ed. (1957), and G. Orwell, *The Road to Wigan Pier* (1972). Among French novelists, André Gide painstakingly examines the French middle class and its values in *The Counterfeiters,* while Albert Camus, the greatest of the existential novelists, is at his unforgettable best in *The Stranger* and *The Plague.*

35

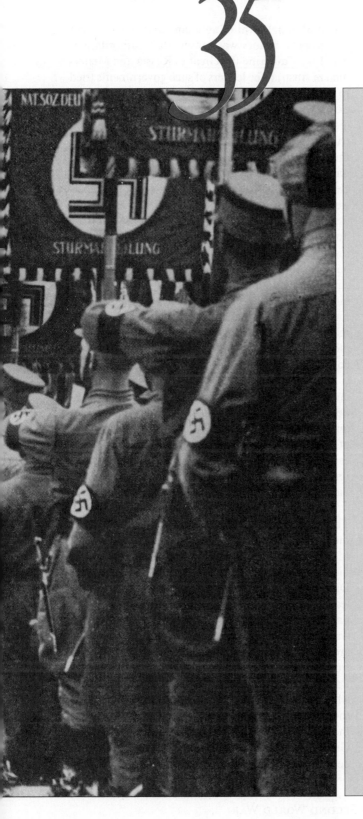

DICTATORSHIPS AND THE SECOND WORLD WAR

*T*HE ERA OF ANXIETY and economic depression was also a time of growing strength for political dictatorship. Popularly elected governments and basic civil liberties declined drastically in Europe. On the eve of the Second World War, liberal democratic government survived only in Great Britain, France, the Low Countries, the Scandinavian nations, and neutral Switzerland. Elsewhere in Europe, various kinds of "strong men" ruled. Dictatorship seemed the wave of the future. Thus the decline in liberal political institutions and the intellectual crisis were related elements in the general crisis of European civilization.

The era of dictatorship is a highly disturbing chapter in the history of Western civilization. The key development was not simply the resurgence of dictatorship but the rise of a new kind of tyranny—the modern totalitarian state. Modern totalitarianism reached its fullest realization in Communist Russia and Nazi Germany in the 1930s. Stalin and Hitler mobilized their peoples for enormous undertakings and ruled with unprecedented severity.

Today we want to believe that the era of totalitarian dictatorship was a terrible accident, that Stalin's slave labor camps and Hitler's gas chambers "can't happen again." But one cannot be sure: it was all very recent and very powerful. What was the nature of the twentieth-century totalitarian state? How did totalitarianism affect ordinary people, and why did it lead to another world war? These are the questions this chapter will seek to answer.

AUTHORITARIAN AND TOTALITARIAN STATES

The modern totalitarian state differed from the old-fashioned authoritarian state. Completely rejecting liberal values and drawing on the experience of total war, the totalitarian state exercised much greater control over the masses and mobilized them for constant action. The nature of this control may be examined through a general comparison of the old and new forms of dictatorship, before entering the strange worlds of Stalin's Russia and Hitler's Germany.

CONSERVATIVE AUTHORITARIANISM

The traditional form of antidemocratic government in European history was conservative authoritarianism. Like Catherine the Great in Russia and Metternich in Austria, the leaders of such governments tried to prevent major changes that would undermine the existing social order. To do so, they relied on obedient bureaucracies, vigilant police departments, and trustworthy armies. Popular participation in government was forbidden or else severely limited to such natural allies as landlords, bureaucrats, and high church officials. Liberals, democrats, and socialists were persecuted as radicals, often jailed or exiled.

Yet old-fashioned authoritarian governments were limited in their power and in their objectives. Lacking modern technology and communications, they had not the power to control many aspects of their subjects' lives. Nor did they wish to do so. Preoccupied with the goal of mere survival, these governments' demands were largely limited to taxes, army recruits, and passive acceptance. As long as the people did not try to change the system, they often had considerable personal independence.

After the First World War, this kind of authoritarian government revived, especially in the less-developed eastern part of Europe. There, the parliamentary regimes that had been founded on the wreckage of empires in 1918 fell one by one. By early 1938 only economically and socially advanced Czechoslovakia remained true to liberal political ideals. Conservative dictators also took over in Spain and Portugal.

There were several reasons for this development. These lands lacked a strong tradition of self-government, with its necessary restraint and compromise. Moreover, many of these new states were torn by ethnic conflicts that threatened their very existence. Dictatorship appealed to nationalists and military leaders as a way to repress such tensions and preserve national unity. Large landowners and the church were still powerful forces in these largely agrarian areas, and they often looked to dictators to save them from progressive land reform or communist agrarian upheaval. So did some members of the middle class, which was small and weak in eastern Europe. Finally, though some kind of democracy managed to stagger through the 1920s in Austria, Bulgaria, Rumania, Greece, Estonia, and Latvia, the Great Depression delivered the final blow to those countries in 1936.

Nazi Mass Rally, 1936 This picture captures the spirit of modern totalitarianism. The uniformed members of the Nazi party have willingly merged themselves into a single force and await the command of the godlike leader. *(Wide World Photos)*

Although some of the authoritarian regimes adopted certain Hitlerian and fascist characteristics in the 1930s, their general aims were not totalitarian. They were concerned more with maintaining the status quo than with forcing society into rapid change or war. This tradition lives on today, especially in some of the military dictatorships in Latin America.

Hungary was a good example of conservative authoritarianism. In the chaos of collapse in 1919, Béla Kun formed a Lenin-like government, but communism in Hungary was soon crushed by foreign troops, large landowners, and hostile peasants. Thereafter, a combination of great and medium-sized landowners instituted a semi-authoritarian regime, which main-

tained the status quo in the 1920s. Hungary had a parliament, but elections were carefully controlled. The peasants did not have the right to vote, and an upper house representing the landed aristocracy was re-established. There was no land reform, no major social change. In the 1930s, the Hungarian government remained conservative and nationalistic. Increasingly, it was opposed by a Nazi-like fascist movement, the Arrow Cross, which demanded radical reform and totalitarian measures.

Another example of conservative authoritarianism was newly independent Poland, where democratic government was overturned in 1926 when General Joseph Pilsudski established a military dictatorship.

Poland was torn by bitter party politics and sandwiched between Russia and Germany. Pilsudski silenced opposition and tried to build a strong state. His principal supporters were the army, major industrialists, and dedicated nationalists.

In Yugoslavia, King Alexander (1921–1934) proclaimed a centralized dictatorship in 1929 to prevent ethnic rivalries among Serbs, Croats, and Slovenes from tearing the country apart. An old-style authoritarian, Alexander crushed democracy, jailed separatists, and ruled through the bureaucracy.

Another example of conservative authoritarianism was Portugal, at the westernmost end of the European peninsula. Constantly shaken by military coups and uprisings after a republican revolution in 1910, very poor and backward Portugal finally got a strong dictator in Antonio de Oliveira Salazar in 1932. A devout Catholic, Salazar gave the church the strongest possible position in the country, while controlling the press and outlawing most political activity. Yet there was no attempt to mobilize the masses or to accomplish great projects. The traditional society was firmly maintained, and that was enough.

MODERN TOTALITARIANISM

Although both are dictatorships, modern totalitarianism and conservative authoritarianism differ. They may be thought of as two distinct types of political organization that in practice sometimes share certain elements.

Modern totalitarianism burst on the scene with the revolutionary total war effort of 1914 to 1918. The war called forth a tendency to subordinate all institutions and all classes to one supreme objective: victory. Nothing, absolutely nothing, had equal value. People were called to make ever-greater sacrifices, and their personal freedom was constantly reduced by ever-greater government control. As the outstanding French thinker Elie Halévy put it in 1936, the varieties of modern totalitarian tyranny—fascism, nazism, and communism—may be thought of as "feuding brothers" with a common father, the nature of modern war.[1]

The crucial experience of World War One was carried further by Lenin and the Bolsheviks during the Russian civil war. Lenin showed how a dedicated minority could make a total effort and achieve victory over a less-determined majority. Lenin also demonstrated how institutions and human rights might be subordinated to the needs of a single group—the Communist party—and its leader, Lenin. Thus Lenin provided a model for single-party dictatorship, and he inspired imitators.

Building on its immediate origins in World War One and the Russian civil war, modern totalitarianism reached maturity in the 1930s in Stalinist Russia and Nazi Germany. Both had several fundamental characteristics of modern totalitarianism.

Armed with modern technology and communications, the true totalitarian state began as a dictatorship exercising complete political power, but it did not stop there. Increasingly, the state took over and tried to control just as completely the economic, social, intellectual, and cultural aspects of life. Although such unlimited control could not be fully realized, the individual's freedom of action was greatly reduced. Deviation from the norm even in art or family behavior could become a crime. In theory, nothing was politically neutral, nothing was outside the scope of the state.

This grandiose vision of total state control broke decisively not only with conservative authoritarianism but also with nineteenth-century liberalism and democracy. Indeed, totalitarianism was a radical revolt against liberalism. Liberalism sought to limit the power of the state and protect the sacred rights of the individual. Moreover, liberals stood for rationality, harmony, peaceful progress, and a strong middle class. All of that disgusted totalitarians as sentimental slop. They believed in will power, preached conflict, and worshiped violence. They believed that the individual was infinitely less valuable than the state and that there were no lasting rights, only temporary rewards for loyal and effective service. Only a single powerful leader and a single party, both unrestrained by law or tradition, determined the destiny of the totalitarian state.

Unlike old-fashioned authoritarianism, modern totalitarianism was based not on an elite but on the masses. As in the First World War, the totalitarian state sought and sometimes won the support and even the love of ordinary people. Modern totalitarianism built on politically alert masses, on people who had already become engaged in the political process, most notably through commitment to nationalism and socialism. Its character as a mass movement gave totalitarianism much of its elemental force.

The final shared characteristic of real totalitarian states was their boundless dynamism. The totalitarian society was a fully mobilized society, a society moving toward some goal. It was never content merely to survive, like an old-fashioned military dictatorship or a decaying democracy. Paradoxically, totalitarian regimes never reached their goals. Or, more precisely, as soon as one goal was achieved at the cost of enormous sacrifice, another arose at the leader's command to take its place. Thus totalitarianism was in the end a *permanent* revolution, an *unfinished* revolution, in which rapid, profound change imposed from on high went on forever.

TOTALITARIANISM OF THE LEFT AND THE RIGHT

The two most-developed totalitarian states—Stalin's Communist Russia and Hitler's Nazi Germany—shared all the central characteristics of totalitarianism. But although those regimes may seem more alike than not, there were at least two major differences between them.

Communism as practiced in Soviet Russia grew out of Marxian socialism. Nazism in Germany grew out of extreme nationalism and racism. This distinction meant that private property and the middle class received very different treatment in the two states. In Soviet Russia, the socialist program of the radical left was realized: all large holdings of private property were taken over by the state, and the middle class lost its wealth and status. In Germany, big landowners and industrialists on the conservative right were sharply criticized but managed to maintain their private wealth. This difference in property and class relations has led some scholars to speak of "totalitarianism of the left"—Stalinist Russia—and "totalitarianism of the right"—Nazi Germany.

More important were the differing possibilities for regeneration. Socialism, with its concern for social justice and human progress, is linked to the living core of Western civilization and the Judeo-Christian tradition. Stalin's communism was an ugly perversion of socialism, but even in its darkest moments it had the potential for reforming itself and creating a more humane society. Nazism, however, had no such potential. Based on the claptrap phobias of anticapitalism, anti-Semitism, and racism, its elements could be found in many a European city before the First World War. Totally negative and devoid of even perverted truth, it promised only destruction and never rebirth.

Vicious Anti-Semitism was visible in all European countries before World War One. This 1898 French cartoon shows the Jewish banker Rothschild worshiping gold and exploiting the whole world. Jews were also denounced as revolutionary socialists intent upon destroying private property and the middle class. *(Historical Pictures Service, Chicago)*

STALIN'S RUSSIA

Lenin established the basic outlines of a modern totalitarian dictatorship in Russia after the Bolshevik Revolution and during the civil war. Joseph Stalin (1879–1953) finished the job. A master of political infighting, Stalin cautiously consolidated his power and eliminated his enemies in the mid-1920s. Then in 1928, as undisputed leader of the ruling Communist party, he launched the first five-year plan—the "revolution from above," as he so aptly termed it.

The five-year plans were extremely ambitious. Often incorrectly considered a mere set of economic measures to speed up Soviet Russia's industrial development, the five-year plans actually marked the beginning of a renewed attempt to mobilize and transform Soviet society along socialist lines. The goal was to create a new way of life and to generate new attitudes and new loyalties. The means Stalin and the small Communist party elite chose were constant propaganda, enormous sacrifice, and unlimited violence and state control. Thus the Soviet Union in the 1930s became a dynamic, totalitarian state.

FROM LENIN TO STALIN

By spring 1921, Lenin and the Bolsheviks had won the civil war, but they ruled a shattered and devastated land. Many farms were in ruins, and food supplies were exhausted. In southern Russia, drought combined with the ravages of war to produce the worst famine in generations. By 1920, according to the government, from 50 to 90 percent of the population in seventeen provinces was starving. Industrial production also broke down completely. In 1921, for example, output of steel and cotton textiles was only about 4 percent of what it had been in 1913. The revolutionary Trotsky later wrote that the "collapse of the productive forces surpassed anything of the kind history had ever seen. The country, and the government with it, were at the very edge of the abyss."[2] The Bolsheviks had destroyed the economy as well as their foes.

In the face of economic disintegration and rioting by peasants and workers, as well as an open rebellion by previously pro-Bolshevik sailors at Kronstadt, which had to be quelled with machine guns, the tough but ever-flexible Lenin changed course. In March 1921, he announced the New Economic Policy (NEP), which re-established limited economic freedom in an attempt to rebuild agriculture and industry. During the civil war, the Communists had simply seized grain without payment. Lenin in 1921 substituted a grain tax on the country's peasant producers, who were permitted to sell their surpluses in free markets. Peasants were also encouraged to buy as many goods as they could afford from private traders and small handicraft manufacturers, both of whom were allowed to reappear. Heavy industry, railroads, and banks, however, remained nationalized. Thus NEP saw only a limited restoration of capitalism.

Lenin's New Economic Policy was shrewd and successful, from two points of view. Politically, it was a necessary but temporary compromise with Russia's overwhelming peasant majority. Flushed with victory after their revolutionary gains of 1917, the peasants would have fought to hold onto their land. With fond hopes of immediate worldwide revolution fading by 1921, Lenin realized that his government was not strong enough to take it from them. As he had accepted Germany's harsh terms at Brest-Litovsk in 1918 (page 1023), Lenin made a deal with the only force capable of overturning his government.

Economically, NEP brought rapid recovery. In 1926 industrial output surpassed the level of 1913, and Russian peasants were producing almost as much grain as before the war. Counting shorter hours and increased social benefits, workers were living somewhat better than they had in the past.

As the economy recovered and the government somewhat relaxed its censorship and repression, an intense struggle for power began in the inner circles of the Communist party, for Lenin had left no chosen successor when he died in 1924. The principal contenders were the stolid Stalin and the flamboyant Trotsky.

The son of a shoemaker, Joseph Dzhugashvili—later known as Stalin—studied for the priesthood but was expelled from his theological seminary, probably for rude rebelliousness. By 1903 he had joined the Bolsheviks. In the years before the First World War, he engaged in many revolutionary activities in the Transcaucasian area of southern Russia, including a daring bank robbery to get money for the Bolsheviks. This raid gained Lenin's attention and approval. Ethnically a Georgian and not a Russian, Stalin in his early writings focused on the oppression of minority peoples in the Russian Empire. Stalin was a good organizer but a poor speaker and writer, with no experience outside of Russia.

Leon Trotsky, a great and inspiring leader who had planned the 1917 takeover (see page 1022) and then created the victorious Red Army, appeared to have all the advantages. Yet it was Stalin who succeeded Lenin. Stalin won because he was more effective at gaining the all-important support of the party, the only genuine source of power in the one-party state. Rising to general secretary of the party's Central Committee just before Lenin's first stroke in 1922, Stalin used his office to win friends and allies with jobs and promises. Stalin also won recognition as commissar of nationalities, a key position in which he governed many of Russia's minorities.

The "practical" Stalin also won because he appeared better able than the brilliant Trotsky to relate Marxist teaching to Russian realities in the 1920s. First, as commissar of nationalities, he built on Lenin's idea of granting minority groups a certain degree of freedom in culture and language while maintaining rigorous political control through carefully selected local Communists. Stalin could loudly

Lenin and Stalin in 1922 Lenin re-established limited economic freedom throughout Russia in 1921, but he ran the country and the Communist party in an increasingly authoritarian way. Stalin carried the process much further and eventually built a regime based on harsh dictatorship. *(Sovfoto)*

claim, therefore, to have found a way to solve the ancient problem of ethnic demands for independence in the multinational state. And of course he did.

Second, Stalin developed a theory of "socialism in one country," which was more appealing to the majority of Communists than Trotsky's doctrine of "permanent revolution." Stalin argued that Russia had the ability to build socialism on its own. Trotsky maintained that socialism in Russia could succeed only if revolution occurred quickly throughout Europe. To many Communists, Trotsky's views seemed to sell Russia short and to promise risky conflicts with capitalist countries by recklessly encouraging revolutionary movements around the world. Stalin's

willingness to break with NEP and push socialism at home appealed to young militants. In short, Stalin's theory of socialism in one country provided many in the party with a glimmer of hope in the midst of the capitalist-appearing NEP.

With cunning skill Stalin gradually achieved absolute power between 1922 and 1927. First he allied with Trotsky's personal enemies to crush Trotsky, who was expelled from the Soviet Union in 1929 and eventually was murdered in Mexico in 1940, undoubtedly on Stalin's order. Stalin then aligned with the moderates, who wanted to go slow at home, to suppress Trotsky's radical followers. Finally, having defeated all the radicals, he turned against his allies, the moderates, and destroyed them as well. Stalin's final triumph came at the Party Congress of December 1927, which condemned all "deviation from the general party line" formulated by Stalin. The dictator was then ready to launch his "revolution from above"—the real Russian revolution for millions of ordinary citizens.

The Five-year Plans

The Party Congress of 1927, which ratified Stalin's seizure of power, marked the end of the New Economic Policy and the beginning of the era of socialist five-year plans. The first five-year plan had staggering economic objectives. In just five years, total industrial output was to increase by 250 percent. Heavy industry, the preferred sector, was to grow even faster; steel production, for example, was to jump almost 300 percent. Agricultural production was slated to increase by 150 percent, and one-fifth of Russia's peasants were scheduled to give up their private plots and join socialist collective farms. In spite of warnings from moderate Communists that these goals were unrealistic, Stalin raised them higher as the plan got under way. By 1930 a whirlwind of economic and social change was sweeping the country.

Stalin unleashed his "second revolution" for a variety of interrelated reasons. There were, first of all, ideological considerations. Like Lenin, Stalin and his militant supporters were deeply committed to socialism as they understood it. Since the country had recovered economically and their rule was secure, they burned to stamp out NEP's private traders, independent artisans, and few well-to-do peasants. Purely economic motivations were also important. Although the economy had recovered, it seemed to have stalled in 1927 and 1928. A new socialist offensive seemed necessary if industry and agriculture were to grow rapidly.

Political considerations were most important. Internationally, there was the old problem, remaining from prerevolutionary times, of catching up with the advanced and presumably hostile capitalist nations of the West. As Stalin said in 1931, when he pressed for ever-greater speed and sacrifice: "We are fifty or a hundred years behind the advanced countries. We must make good this distance in ten years. Either we do it, or we shall go under."[3]

Domestically, there was what Communist writers of the 1920s called the "cursed problem"—the problem of the Russian peasants. For centuries, Russian peasants had wanted to own the land, and finally they had it. Sooner or later, the Communists reasoned, the peasants would become conservative little capitalists and pose a threat to the regime. Therefore, Stalin decided on a preventive war against the peasantry, in order to bring it under absolute state control.

That war was collectivization—the forcible consolidation of individual peasant farms into large, state-controlled enterprises. Beginning in 1929, peasants all over the Soviet Union were ordered to give up their land and animals and to become members of collective farms, although they continued to live in their own homes. As for the *kulaks,* the better-off peasants, Stalin instructed party workers to "liquidate them as a class." Stripped of their land and livestock, the kulaks were generally not even permitted to join the collective farms. Many starved or were deported to forced-labor camps for "re-education."

Since almost all peasants were in fact poor, the term *kulak* soon meant any peasant who opposed the new system. Whole villages were often attacked. One conscience-stricken colonel in the secret police confessed to a foreign journalist: "I am an old Bolshevik. I worked in the underground against the Tsar and then I fought in the Civil War. Did I do all that in order that I should now surround villages with machineguns and order my men to fire indiscriminately into crowds of peasants? Oh, no, no!"[4]

Forced collectivization of the peasants led to economic and human disaster. Large numbers of peasants slaughtered their animals and burned their crops in sullen, hopeless protest. Between 1929 and 1933, the number of horses, cattle, sheep, and goats in the Soviet Union fell by at least half. Nor were the state-controlled collective farms more productive. The output of grain barely increased between 1928 and 1938, when it was almost identical to that of 1913. Communist economists had expected collectivized agriculture to pay for new factories. Instead, the state had to invest heavily in agriculture, building thousands of tractors to replace slaughtered draft horses. Collectivized agriculture was unable to make any substantial financial contribution to Soviet industrial development in the first five-year plan. The human dimension of the tragedy was shocking. Collectivization created man-made famine in 1932 and 1933, and many perished. Indeed, Stalin confided to Churchill at Yalta in 1945 that 10 million people had died in the course of collectivization.

Yet collectivization was a political victory of sorts. By the end of 1932, fully 60 percent of Russian peasant families had been herded onto collective farms; by 1938, 93 percent. Regimented and indoctrinated as employees of an all-powerful state, the peasants were no longer even a potential political threat to Stalin and the Communist party. Moreover, the state was assured of grain for bread for urban workers, who were much more important politically than the peasants. Collective farmers had to meet their grain quotas first and worry about feeding themselves second. Many collectivized peasants drew much of their own food from tiny, grudgingly tolerated garden plots that they worked in their off hours. No wonder some peasants joked, with that grim humor peculiar to the totalitarian society, that the initials then used by the Communist party actually stood for "The Second Serfdom, That of the Bolsheviks."

The industrial side of the five-year plans was more successful—indeed, quite spectacular. The output of industry doubled in the first five-year plan and doubled again in the second. Soviet industry produced about four times as much in 1937 as it had in 1928. No other major country had ever achieved such rapid industrial growth. Heavy industry led the way; consumer industry grew quite slowly. Steel production— a near-obsession with Stalin, whose name fittingly meant "man of steel" in Russian—increased roughly 500 percent between 1928 and 1937. A new heavy industrial complex was built almost from scratch in western Siberia. Industrial growth also went hand in hand with urban development. Cities rose where nomadic tribes had grazed their flocks. More than 25 million people migrated to cities during the 1930s.

The great industrialization drive, concentrated between 1928 and 1937, was an awe-inspiring achievement purchased at enormous sacrifice. The sudden creation of dozens of new factories required a great increase in investment and a sharp decrease in consumption. Few nations had ever invested more than one-sixth of their yearly net national income. Soviet planners decreed that more than one-third of net income go for investment. This meant that only two-thirds of everything being produced could be consumed by the people *and* the increasingly voracious military. The money was collected from the people by means of heavy, hidden sales taxes.

There was, therefore, no improvement in the average standard of living. Indeed, the most careful studies show that the average nonfarm wage apparently

purchased only about *half* as many goods in 1932 as in 1928. After 1932 real wages rose slowly, so that in 1937 workers could buy about 60 percent of what they had bought in 1928. Thus rapid industrial development went with an unprecedented decline in the standard of living for ordinary people.

Two other factors contributed importantly to rapid industrialization: firm labor discipline and foreign engineers. Between 1930 and 1932, trade unions lost most of their power. The government could assign workers to any job anywhere in the country, and individuals could not move without the permission of the police. When factory managers needed more hands, they called on their counterparts on the collective farms, who sent them millions of "unneeded" peasants over the years.

Foreign engineers were hired to plan and construct many of the new factories. Highly skilled American engineers, hungry for work in the depression years, were particularly important until newly trained Soviet experts began to replace them after 1932. The gigantic mills of the new Siberian steel industry were modeled on America's best. Those modern mills were eloquent testimony to the ability of Stalin's planners to harness even the skill and technology of capitalist countries to promote the surge of socialist industry.

LIFE IN STALINIST SOCIETY

The aim of Stalin's five-year plans was to create a new kind of society and human personality, as well as a strong industrial economy and a powerful army. Stalin and his helpers were good Marxian economic determinists. Once everything was owned by the state, they believed, a socialist society and a new kind of human being would inevitably emerge. They were by no means totally successful, but they did build a new society, whose outlines exist to this day. For the people, life in Stalinist society held both good and bad.

The most frightening aspect of Stalinist society was brutal, unrestrained police terrorism. First directed primarily against the peasants after 1929, terror was increasingly turned on leading Communists, powerful administrators, and ordinary people for no apparent reason. As one Soviet woman later recalled: "We all trembled because there was no way of getting out of it. Even a Communist himself can be caught. To avoid trouble became an exception."[5] A climate of fear fell on the land.

In the early 1930s, the top members of the party and government were Stalin's obedient servants, but there was some grumbling in the party. At a small gathering in November 1932, even Stalin's wife complained bitterly about the misery of the people. Stalin showered her with insults, and she died that same night, apparently by her own hand. In late 1934 Stalin's number-two man, Sergei Kirov, was suddenly and mysteriously murdered. Although Stalin himself probably ordered Kirov's murder, he used the incident to launch a reign of terror.

In August 1936 sixteen prominent old Bolsheviks confessed to all manner of plots against Stalin in spectacular public trials in Moscow. Then, in 1937, lesser party officials and newer henchmen were arrested. In addition to party members, union officials, managers, intellectuals, army officers, and countless ordinary citizens were struck down. Local units of the secret police were even ordered to arrest a certain percentage of the people in their district. In all, at least 8 million people were probably arrested, and millions never returned from prisons and forced-labor camps.

Stalin's mass purges were truly baffling, and many explanations have been given for them. Possibly Stalin believed that the old Communists, like the peasants under NEP, were a potential threat to be wiped out in a preventive attack. Yet why did leading Communists willingly confess to crimes they could not possibly have committed? Their lives had been devoted to the party and the socialist revolution. In the words of the German novelist Arthur Koestler, they probably confessed "in order to do a last service to the Party," the party they loved even when it was wrong. Some of them were subjected to torture and brainwashing. It has been argued that the purges indicate that Stalin was sadistic or insane, for his bloodbath greatly weakened the government and the army. Others see the terror as an aspect of the fully developed totalitarian state, which must by its nature always be fighting real or imaginary enemies. At the least, the mass purges were a message to the people: no one was secure. Everyone had to serve the party and its leader with redoubled devotion.

Another aspect of life in the 1930s was constant propaganda and indoctrination. Party activists lectured workers in factories and peasants on collective farms, while newspapers, films, and radio broadcasts endlessly recounted socialist achievements and capitalist plots. Art and literature became highly political. Whereas the 1920s had seen considerable experimentation in modern art and theater, the intellectual elite were ordered by Stalin to become "engineers of human minds." Writers and artists who could effectively combine genuine creativity and political propaganda became the darlings of the regime. They often lived better than top members of the political elite. It became increasingly important for the successful writer and artist to glorify Russian nationalism. Russian history was rewritten so that early tsars like Ivan the Terrible and Peter the Great became worthy forerunners of the greatest Russian leader of all—Stalin.

Stalin seldom appeared in public, but his presence was everywhere—in portraits, statues, books, and quotations from his "sacred" writings. Although the government persecuted religion and turned churches into "museums of atheism," the state had both an earthly religion and a high priest—Marxian socialism and Joseph Stalin.

Life was hard in Stalin's Soviet Russia. The standard of living declined substantially in the 1930s. The masses of people lived primarily on black bread and wore old, shabby clothing. There were constant shortages in the stores, although very heavily taxed vodka was always readily available. A shortage of housing was a particularly serious problem. Millions were moving into the cities, but the government built few new apartments. In 1940 there were approximately 4 people per room in every urban dwelling, as opposed to 2.7 per room in 1926. A relatively lucky family received one room for all its members and shared both a kitchen and a toilet with others on the floor. Less fortunate workers, kulaks, and class enemies built scrap-lumber shacks or underground dugouts in shantytowns.

Life was hard, but by no means hopeless. Idealism and ideology had real appeal for many Russians, who saw themselves heroically building the world's first socialist society while capitalism crumbled in the West. This optimistic belief in the future of Soviet Russia also attracted many disillusioned Western liberals to communism in the 1930s.

On a more practical level, Soviet workers did receive some important social benefits, such as old-age pensions, free medical services, free education, and day-care centers for children. Unemployment was almost unknown. Finally, there was the possibility of personal advancement.

Adult Education Illiteracy, especially among women, was a serious problem after the Russian Revolution. This early photo shows how adults successfully learned to read and write throughout the Soviet Union. *(Sovfoto/Eastfoto)*

The keys to improving one's position were specialized skills and technical education. Rapid industrialization required massive numbers of trained experts, such as skilled workers, engineers, and plant managers. Thus the state provided tremendous incentives to those who could serve its needs. It paid the mass of unskilled workers and collective farmers very low wages, but it dangled high salaries and many special privileges before its growing technical and managerial elite. This elite joined with the political and artistic elites in a new upper class, whose members were rich, powerful, and insecure, especially during the purges. Yet the possible gains of moving up outweighed the risks. Millions struggled bravely in universities, institutes, and night schools for the all-important specialized education. One young man summed it up: "In Soviet Russia there is no capital except education. If a person does not want to become a collective farmer or just a cleaning woman, the only means you have to get something is through education."[6]

WOMEN IN SOVIET RUSSIA

Women's lives were radically altered by Stalinist society. Marxists had traditionally believed that both capitalism and the middle-class husband exploited women. The Russian Revolution of 1917 immediately proclaimed complete equality of rights for women. In the 1920s, divorce and abortion were made very easy, and women were urged to work outside the home and liberate themselves sexually. A prominent and influential Bolshevik feminist, Alexandra Kollontai, went so far as to declare that the sexual act had no more significance than "drinking a glass of water." This observation drew a sharp rebuke from the rather prudish Lenin, who said that "no sane man would lie down to drink from a puddle in the gutter or even drink from a dirty glass."[7] After Stalin came to power, sexual and familial liberation was played down, and the most lasting changes for women involved work and education.

The changes were truly revolutionary. Young women were constantly told that they must be fully equal with men, that they could and should do anything men could do. Russian peasant women had long experienced the equality of backbreaking physical labor in the countryside, and they continued to enjoy that equality on collective farms. With the advent of the five-year plans, millions of women also began to toil in factories and on heavy construction, building dams, roads, and steel mills in summer heat and winter frost. Yet most of the opportunities open to men through education were also open to women. Determined women pursued their studies and entered the ranks of the better-paid specialists in industry and science. Medicine practically became a woman's profession. By 1950, 75 percent of all doctors in Soviet Russia were women.

Thus Stalinist society gave women great opportunities but demanded great sacrifices as well. The vast majority of women simply *had* to work outside the home. Wages were so low that it was almost impossible for a family or couple to live only on the husband's earnings. Moreover, the full-time working woman had a heavy burden of household tasks in her off hours, for most Soviet men in the 1930s still considered the home and the children the woman's responsibility. Finally, rapid change and economic hardship led to many broken families, creating further physical and mental strains for women. In any event, the often-neglected human resource of women was ruthlessly mobilized in Stalinist society. This, too, was an aspect of the Soviet totalitarian state.

MUSSOLINI'S ITALY

Before turning to Hitler's Germany, it is necessary to look briefly at Mussolini's role in Italy. Like all the other emerging dictators, Mussolini hated liberalism, and he destroyed it in Italy. But that was not all. Mussolini and his supporters were the first to call themselves *Fascists,* revolutionaries determined to create a certain kind of totalitarian state. As Mussolini's famous slogan of 1926 put it: "Everything in the state, nothing outside the state, nothing against the state." But Mussolini in power, unlike Stalin and Hitler, did not in fact create a real totalitarian state. His dictatorship was rather an instructive hybrid, a halfway house between conservative authoritarianism and modern totalitarianism.

The Seizure of Power

Before the First World War, Italy was a liberal state moving gradually toward democracy. But there were serious problems. Much of the Italian population was still poor, and class differences were extreme. Many peasants were more attached to their villages and local interests than to the national state. Moreover, the papacy and many devout Catholics, as well as the socialists, were strongly opposed to the heirs of Cavour and Garibaldi, middle-class lawyers and politicians who ran the country largely for their own benefit. Church-state relations were often tense.

The war worsened the political situation. Having fought on the side of the Allies almost exclusively for purposes of territorial expansion, Italian nationalists were bitterly disappointed with Italy's modest gains at Versailles. Workers and peasants also felt cheated: to win their support during the war, the government had promised social and land reform, which it did not deliver after the war.

Encouraged by the Russian Revolution of 1917, radical workers and peasants began occupying factories and seizing land in 1920. These actions scared and radicalized the property-owning classes. The Italian middle classes were already in an ugly mood, having suffered from inflation during the war. Moreover, after the war, the pope lifted his ban on participation by Catholics in Italian politics, and a strong Catholic party quickly emerged. Thus by 1922 almost all the major groups in Italian society were opposed—though for different reasons—to the liberal parliamentary government.

Into these cross-currents of unrest and frustration stepped the blustering, bullying Benito Mussolini (1883–1945). Son of a village schoolteacher and a poor blacksmith, Mussolini began his political career as a Socialist leader and radical newspaper editor be-

Mussolini loved to swagger and bluster. Here he strikes a theatrical pose while reviewing his troops in Rome. *(BBC Hulton/The Bettmann Archive)*

fore World War One. In 1914, powerfully influenced by antiliberal cults of violent action, the young Mussolini urged that Italy join the Allies, for which he was expelled from the Italian Socialist party by its antiwar majority. Later Mussolini fought at the front and was wounded in 1917. Returning home, he began organizing other bitter veterans into a band of *Fascists*—from the Italian word for a "union of forces."

At first, Mussolini's program was a radical combination of nationalist and socialist demands, including territorial expansion, benefits for workers, and land reform for peasants. As such, it competed with the better-organized Socialist party and failed to get off the ground. When Mussolini saw that his violent verbal assaults on the rival Socialists won him growing support from the frightened middle class, he shifted gears in 1920. In thought and action, Mussolini was a striking example of the turbulence of the age of anxiety.

Mussolini and his growing private army of Black Shirts began to grow violent. Typically, a band of Fascist toughs would roar off in trucks at night and swoop down on a few isolated Socialist organizers, beating them up and force-feeding them almost deadly doses of castor oil. Few people were killed, but Socialist newspapers, union halls, and local Socialist party headquarters were destroyed. Mussolini's toughs pushed Communists and Socialists out of the city governments of northern Italy.

Mussolini, a skillful politician, refused to become a puppet of frightened conservatives and capitalists. He allowed his followers to convince themselves that they were not just opposing the "reds," but making a real revolution of their own. Many believed that they were not only destroying parliamentary government, but forming a strong, dynamic movement that would help the little people against the established interests.

With the government breaking down in 1922, largely because of the chaos created by his direct-action bands, Mussolini stepped forward as the savior of order and property. Striking a conservative note in his speeches and gaining the sympathetic neutrality of army leaders, Mussolini demanded the resignation of the existing government and his own appointment by the king. In October 1922, to force matters a large group of Fascists marched on Rome to threaten the king and force him to call on Mussolini. The threat worked. Victor Emmanuel III (1900–1946), who had no love for the old liberal politicians, asked Mussolini to form a new cabinet. Thus, after widespread violence and a threat of armed uprising, Mussolini seized power "legally." He was immediately granted dictatorial authority for one year by the king and the parliament.

THE REGIME IN ACTION

Mussolini became dictator on the strength of Italians' rejection of parliamentary government, coupled with fears of Russian-style revolution. Yet what he intended to do with his power was by no means clear until 1924. Some of his dedicated supporters pressed for a "second revolution." Mussolini's ministers, however, included old Conservatives, Moderates, and even two reform-minded Socialists. A new electoral law was passed giving two-thirds of the representatives in the parliament to the party that won the most votes, which allowed the Fascists and their allies to win an overwhelming majority in 1924. Shortly thereafter, five of Mussolini's Fascist thugs kidnaped and murdered Giacomo Matteotti, the young leader of the Socialists in the parliament. In the face of this outrage, the opposition demanded that Mussolini's armed squads be dissolved and all violence be banned.

Although he may or may not have ordered Matteotti's murder, Mussolini stood at the crossroads of a severe political crisis. After some hesitation, he charged forward. Declaring his desire to "make the nation Fascist," he imposed a series of repressive measures. Freedom of the press was abolished, elections were fixed, and the government ruled by decree. Mussolini arrested his political opponents, disbanded all independent labor unions, and put dedicated Fascists in control of Italy's schools. Moreover, he created a Fascist youth movement, Fascist labor unions, and many other Fascist organizations. By the end of 1926, Italy was a one-party dictatorship under Mussolini's unquestioned leadership.

Yet Mussolini did not complete the establishment of a modern totalitarian state. His Fascist party never became all-powerful. It never destroyed the old power structure, as the Communists did in Soviet Russia, or succeeded in dominating it, as the Nazis did in Germany. Membership in the Fascist party was more a sign of an Italian's respectability than a commitment to radical change. Interested primarily in personal power, Mussolini was content to compromise with the old conservative classes that controlled the army, the economy, and the state. He never tried to purge these classes or even move very vigorously against them. He controlled and propagandized labor, but left big business to regulate itself, profitably and securely. There was no land reform.

Mussolini also came to draw on the support of the Catholic church. In the Lateran Agreement of 1929, he recognized the Vatican as a tiny independent state, and he agreed to give the church heavy financial support. The pope expressed his satisfaction and urged Italians to support Mussolini's government.

Nothing better illustrates Mussolini's unwillingness to harness everyone and everything for dynamic action than his treatment of women. He abolished divorce and told women to stay at home and produce children. To promote that goal, he decreed a special tax on bachelors in 1934. In 1938 women were limited by law to a maximum of 10 percent of the better-paying jobs in industry and government. Italian women, as women, appear not to have changed their status in any important way under Fascist rule.

It is also noteworthy that Mussolini's government did not persecute Jews until late in the Second World War, when Italy was under Nazi control. Nor did Mussolini establish a truly ruthless police state. Only twenty-three political prisoners were condemned to death between 1926 and 1944. In spite of much pompous posing by the chauvinist leader and in spite of mass meetings, salutes, and a certain copying of Hitler's aggression in foreign policy after 1933, Mussolini's Italy—though undemocratic—was never really totalitarian.

HITLER'S GERMANY

The most frightening totalitarian state was Nazi Germany. A product of Hitler's evil genius as well as of Germany's social and political situation and the general attack on liberalism and rationality in the age of anxiety, Nazi Germany emerged rapidly after Hitler came to power in 1933. The Nazis quickly smashed or took over most independent organizations, mobilized the economy, and began brutally persecuting the Jewish population. From the start, all major decisions were in the hands of the aggressive dictator, Adolf Hitler.

THE ROOTS OF NAZISM

Nazism grew out of many complex developments, of which the most influential were extreme nationalism and racism. These two ideas captured the mind of the young Hitler, and it was he who dominated Nazism for as long as it lasted.

Born the fourth child of a successful Austrian customs official and an indulgent mother, Adolf Hitler (1889–1945) spent his childhood happily in small towns in Austria. A good student in grade school, Hitler did poorly on reaching high school and dropped out at age fourteen after the death of his father. After four years of unfocused loafing, Hitler finally left for Vienna to become an artist. Denied admission to the Imperial Academy of Fine Arts because he lacked talent, the dejected Hitler stayed on in Vienna. There he lived a comfortable, lazy life on his generous orphan's pension and found most of the perverted beliefs that guided his life.

In Vienna Hitler soaked up extreme German nationalism, which was particularly strong there. Austro-German nationalists, as if to compensate for their declining position in the Austro-Hungarian Empire, believed Germans to be a superior people and the natural rulers of central Europe. They often advocated union with Germany and violent expulsion of "inferior" peoples as the means of maintaining German domination of the Austro-Hungarian Empire.

Hitler was deeply impressed by Vienna's mayor, Karl Lueger, whom he called the "mightiest mayor of all times." Lueger claimed to be a "Christian socialist." With the help of the Catholic trade unions, he had succeeded in winning the support of the little people of Vienna for an attack on capitalism and liberalism, which he held responsible for un-Christian behavior and excessive individualism. A master of mass politics in the urban world, Lueger showed Hitler the enormous potential of anticapitalist and antiliberal propaganda.

From Lueger and others, Hitler eagerly absorbed virulent anti-Semitism, racism, and hatred of Slavs. He was particularly inspired by the racist ravings of an ex-monk named Lanz von Liebenfels. Preaching the crudest, most exaggerated distortions of the Darwinian theory of survival, Liebenfels stressed the su-

Adolf Hitler A lonely, unsuccessful misfit before 1914, Hitler found his mission during World War One and its aftermath. He emerged as a spellbinding speaker and a master of the politics of hate and violence. *(UPI/Bettmann Newsphotos)*

periority of Germanic races, the inevitability of racial conflict, and the inferiority of the Jews. Liebenfels even anticipated the breeding and extermination policies of the Nazi state. He claimed that the master race had to multiply its numbers by means of polygamy and breeding stations, while it systematically sterilized and liquidated inferior races. Anti-Semitism and racism became Hitler's most passionate convictions, his explanation for everything. He believed inferior races—the Slavs and the Jews in particular—were responsible for Austria's woes. The Jews, he claimed, directed an international conspiracy of finance capitalism and Marxian socialism against German culture, German unity, and the German race. Hitler's belief was totally irrational, but he never doubted it.

Although he moved to Munich in 1913 to avoid being drafted into the Austrian army, the lonely Hitler greeted the outbreak of the First World War as a salvation. He later wrote in his autobiography, *Mein Kampf,* that, "overcome by passionate enthusiasm, I fell to my knees and thanked heaven out of an overflowing heart." The struggle and discipline of war gave life meaning, and Hitler served bravely as a dispatch carrier on the western front.

When Germany was suddenly defeated in 1918, Hitler's world was shattered. Not only was he a fanatical nationalist, but war was his reason for living. Convinced that Jews and Marxists had "stabbed Germany in the back," he vowed to fight on. And in the bitterness and uncertainty of postwar Germany, his wild speeches began to attract attention.

In late 1919 Hitler joined a tiny extremist group in Munich called the German Workers' party. In addition to denouncing Jews, Marxists, and democrats, the German Workers' party promised unity under a uniquely German "national socialism," which would abolish the injustices of capitalism and create a mighty "people's community." By 1921 Hitler had gained absolute control of this small but growing party. Moreover, Hitler was already a master of mass propaganda and political showmanship. Party members sported badges and uniforms, gave victory salutes, and marched like robots through the streets of Munich. But Hitler's most effective tool was the mass rally, a kind of political revival meeting. Songs, slogans, and demonstrations built up the tension until Hitler finally arrived. He then often worked his audience into a frenzy with wild, demagogic attacks on the Versailles treaty, the Jews, the war profiteers, and Germany's Weimar Republic.

Party membership multiplied tenfold after early 1922. In late 1923, when the Weimar Republic seemed on the verge of collapse, Hitler decided on an armed uprising in Munich. Inspired by Mussolini's recent easy victory, Hitler had found an ally in General Ludendorff of First World War fame. After Hitler had overthrown the Bavarian government, Ludendorff was supposed to march on Berlin with Hitler's support. The plot was poorly organized, however, and it was crushed by the police, backed up by the army, in less than a day. Hitler was arrested, tried, and sentenced to five years in prison. He had failed for the moment. But Nazism had been born, and it did not die.

HITLER'S ROAD TO POWER

At his trial, Hitler violently denounced the Weimar Republic and skillfully presented his own program. In doing so he gained enormous publicity and atten-

tion. Moreover, he learned from his unsuccessful revolt. Hitler concluded that he had to undermine rather than overthrow the government, that he had to use its tolerant democratic framework to intimidate the opposition and come to power through electoral competition. He forced his more violent supporters to accept his new strategy. Finally, Hitler used his brief prison term—he was released in less than a year —to dictate *Mein Kampf.* There he expounded on his basic themes—"race," with the stress on anti-Semitism; "living space," with a sweeping vision of war and conquered territory; and the leader-dictator (*Führer*) with unlimited, arbitrary power. Hitler's followers had their bible.

In the years of prosperity and relative stability between 1924 and 1929, Hitler concentrated on building his National Socialist German Workers' party, or Nazi party. By 1928 the party had a hundred thousand highly disciplined members under Hitler's absolute control. To appeal to the middle class, Hitler de-emphasized the anticapitalist elements of national socialism and vowed to fight Bolshevism.

The Nazis were still a small splinter group in 1928, when they received only 2.6 percent of the vote in the general elections and twelve Nazis won seats in the parliament. There the Nazi deputies pursued the legal strategy of using democracy to destroy democracy. As Hitler's talented future minister of propaganda, Joseph Goebbels (1897–1945), explained in 1928 in the party newspaper: "We become Reichstag deputies in order to paralyze the spirit of Weimar with its own aid. . . . We come as enemies! As the wolf breaks into the sheepfold, so we come."[8]

In 1929 the Great Depression began striking down economic prosperity, one of the barriers that had kept the wolf at bay. Unemployment jumped from 1.3 million in 1929 to 5 million in 1930; that year Germany had almost as many unemployed as all the other countries of Europe combined. Industrial production fell by one-half between 1929 and 1932. By the end of 1932, an incredible 43 percent of the labor force was unemployed. No factor contributed more to Hitler's success than the economic crisis. Never very interested in economics before, Hitler began promising German voters economic as well as political and military salvation.

Hitler focused his promises on the middle and lower middle class—small businessmen, office workers, artisans, and peasants. Already disillu-

"Hitler, Our Last Hope" So reads the very effective Nazi campaign poster, which is attracting attention with its gaunt and haggard faces. By 1932 almost half of all Germans, like these in Berlin, had come to agree. *(Bildarchiv Preussischer Kulturbesitz)*

sioned by the great inflation of 1923, these people were seized by panic as bankruptcies increased, unemployment soared, and the dreaded Communists made dramatic election gains. The middle and lower middle classes deserted the Conservative and Moderate parties for the Nazis in great numbers.

The Nazis also appealed strongly to German youth. Indeed, in some ways the Nazi movement was a mass movement of young Germans. Hitler himself was only forty in 1929, and he and most of his top aides were much younger than other leading German politicians. "National Socialism is the organized will

of the youth," proclaimed the official Nazi slogan, and the battle cry of Gregor Strasser, a leading Nazi organizer, was, "Make way, you old ones."[9] In 1931 almost 40 percent of Nazi party members were under thirty, compared to 20 percent of Social Democrats. Two-thirds of Nazi members were under forty. National recovery, exciting and rapid change, and personal advancement: these were the appeals of Nazism to millions of German youths.

In the election of 1930, the Nazis won 6.5 million votes and 107 seats, which made them second in strength only to the Social Democrats, the moderate

The Mobilization of Young People was a prime objective of the Nazi leadership. Here boys in a Nazi youth group, some of whom are only children, are disciplined and conditioned to devote themselves to the regime. *(BBC Hulton/The Bettmann Archive)*

socialists. The economic situation continued to deteriorate, and Hitler kept promising recovery. In 1932 the Nazi vote leaped to 14.5 million, and the Nazis became the largest party in the Reichstag.

Another reason Hitler came to power was the breakdown of democratic government as early as May 1930. Unable to gain support of a majority in the Reichstag, Chancellor (chief minister) Heinrich Brüning convinced the president, the aging war hero General Hindenburg, to authorize rule by decree. The Weimar Republic's constitution permitted such rule in emergency situations, but the rather authoritarian, self-righteous Brüning intended to use it indefinitely. Moreover, Brüning was determined to overcome the economic crisis by cutting back government spending and ruthlessly forcing down prices and wages. Brüning's ultraorthodox policies not only intensified the economic collapse in Germany, they also convinced the lower middle classes that the country's republican leaders were stupid and corrupt. These classes were pleased rather than dismayed by Hitler's attacks on the republican system. After President Hindenburg forced Brüning to resign in May 1932, the new government headed by Franz von Papen continued to rule by decree.

The continuation of the struggle between the Social Democrats and Communists, right up until the moment Hitler took power, was another aspect of the breakdown of democratic government. The Communists foolishly refused to cooperate with the Social Democrats, even though the two parties together outnumbered the Nazis in the Reichstag, even after the elections of 1932. German Communists (and the complacent Stalin) were blinded by their ideology and their hatred of the Socialists. They were certain that Hitler's rise represented the last agonies of monopoly capitalism and that a Communist revolution would quickly follow his taking power. The Socialist leaders pleaded, even at the Russian embassy, for at least a temporary alliance with the Communists to block Hitler, but to no avail.

Finally, there was Hitler's skill as a politician. A master of mass propaganda and psychology, he had written in *Mein Kampf* that the masses were the "driving force of the most important changes in this world" and were themselves driven by hysterical fanaticism and not by knowledge. To arouse such hysterical fanaticism, he believed that all propaganda had to be limited to a few simple, endlessly repeated slogans. Thus, in the terrible economic and political crisis, he harangued vast audiences with passionate, irrational oratory. Men moaned and women cried, seized by emotion. And many uncertain individuals, surrounded by thousands of entranced listeners, found security and a sense of belonging.

At the same time, Hitler excelled at dirty, backroom politics. That, in fact, brought him to power. In 1932 he cleverly succeeded in gaining the support of key people in the army and big business. These people thought they could use Hitler for their own advantage, to get increased military spending, fat contracts, and tough measures against workers. Conservative and nationalistic politicians like Papen thought similarly. They thus accepted Hitler's demand to join the government only if he became chancellor. There would be only two other National Socialists and nine solid Conservatives as ministers, and in such a coalition government, they reasoned, Hitler could be used and controlled. On January 30, 1933, Hitler was legally appointed chancellor by President Hindenburg.

The Nazi State and Society

Hitler moved rapidly and skillfully to establish an unshakable dictatorship. His first step was to continue using terror and threats to gain more power while maintaining legal appearances. He immediately called for new elections and applied the enormous power of the government to restrict his opponents. In the midst of a violent electoral campaign, the Reichstag building was partly destroyed by fire. Although the Nazis themselves may have set the fire, Hitler screamed that the Communist party was responsible. On the strength of this accusation, he convinced President Hindenburg to sign dictatorial emergency acts that practically abolished freedom of speech and assembly, in addition to most personal liberties.

When the Nazis won only 44 percent of the vote in the elections, Hitler immediately outlawed the Communist party and arrested its parliamentary representatives. Then, on March 23, 1933, the Nazis pushed through the Reichstag the so-called Enabling Act, which gave Hitler absolute dictatorial power for four years. Only the Social Democrats voted against this bill, for Hitler had blackmailed the Center party by threatening to attack the Catholic church.

Armed with the Enabling Act, Hitler and the Nazis moved to smash or control all independent organiza-

tions. Meanwhile, Hitler and his propagandists constantly proclaimed that their revolution was legal and constitutional. This stress on legality, coupled with the divide-and-conquer technique, disarmed the opposition until it was too late for effective resistance.

The systematic subjugation of independent organizations and the creation of a totalitarian state had massive repercussions. The Social Democrat and Center parties were soon dissolved, and Germany became a one-party state. Only the Nazi party was legal. Elections were farces. The Reichstag was jokingly referred to as the most expensive glee club in the country, for its only function was to sing hymns of praise to the Führer. Hitler and the Nazis took over the government bureaucracy intact, installing many Nazis in top positions. At the same time, they created a series of overlapping Nazi party organizations, responsible solely to Hitler. Thus Hitler had both an established bureaucracy for normal business and a private, personal "party government" for special duties.

In the economic sphere, strikes were forbidden and labor unions were abolished, replaced by a Nazi Labor Front. Professional people—doctors and lawyers, teachers and engineers—also saw their previously independent organizations swallowed up in Nazi associations. Nor did the Nazis neglect cultural and intellectual life. Publishing houses were put under Nazi control, and universities and writers were quickly brought into line. Democratic, socialist, and Jewish literature was put on ever-growing blacklists. Passionate students and pitiful professors burned forbidden books in public squares. Modern art and architecture were ruthlessly prohibited. Life became violently anti-intellectual. As Hitler's cynical minister of propaganda, Joseph Goebbels, put it: "When I hear the word 'culture' I reach for my gun."[10] By 1934 a totalitarian state characterized by frightening dynamism and obedience to Hitler was already largely in place.

By 1934 only the army retained independence, and Hitler moved brutally and skillfully to establish his control there, too. He realized that the army, as well as big business, was suspicious of the Nazi storm troopers (the SA), the quasi-military band of 3 million toughs in brown shirts who had fought Communists and beaten up Jews before the Nazis took power. These unruly storm troopers expected top positions in the army and even talked of a "second revolution" against capitalism. Needing the support of the army and big business, Hitler decided that the SA leaders had to be eliminated. On the night of June 30, 1934, he struck.

Hitler's elite personal guard—the SS—arrested and shot without trial roughly a thousand SA leaders and assorted political enemies. While his propagandists spread lies about SA conspiracies, the army leaders and President Hindenburg responded to the purge with congratulatory telegrams. Shortly thereafter, the army leaders swore a binding oath of "unquestioning obedience . . . to the Leader of the German State and People, Adolf Hitler." The purge of the SA was another decisive step toward unlimited totalitarian terror. The SS, the elite guard that had loyally murdered the SA leaders, grew rapidly. Under its methodical, inhuman leader, Heinrich Himmler (1900–1945), the SS joined with the political police, the Gestapo, to expand its network of special courts and concentration camps. Nobody was safe.

From the beginning, the Jews were a special object of Nazi persecution. By the end of 1934, most Jewish lawyers, doctors, professors, civil servants, and musicians had lost their jobs and right to practice their professions. In 1935 the infamous Nuremberg Laws classified as Jewish anyone having one or more Jewish grandparents and deprived Jews of all rights of citizenship. By 1938 roughly one-quarter of Germany's half-million Jews had emigrated, sacrificing almost all their property in order to leave Germany.

Following the assassination of a German diplomat in Paris by a young Jewish boy trying desperately to strike out at persecution, the attack on the Jews accelerated. A well-organized wave of violence destroyed homes, synagogues, and businesses, after which German Jews were rounded up and made to pay for the damage. It became very difficult for Jews to leave Germany. Some Germans privately opposed these outrages, but most went along or looked the other way. Although this lack of response partly reflected the individual's helplessness in the totalitarian state, it was also a sign of the strong popular support Hitler's government enjoyed.

HITLER'S POPULARITY

Hitler had promised the masses economic recovery —"work and bread"—and he delivered. Breaking with Brüning's do-nothing policies, Hitler immediately launched a large public works program to pull Germany out of the depression. Work began on superhighways, offices, gigantic sports stadia, and public housing. In 1936, as Germany rearmed rapidly, government spending began to concentrate on the military. The result was that unemployment dropped steadily, from 6 million in January 1933 to about 1 million in late 1936. By 1938 there was a shortage of workers, and women eventually took many jobs previously denied them by the antifeminist Nazis. Thus everyone had work, and between 1932 and 1938 the standard of living for the average employed worker rose more than 20 percent. The profits of business also increased. For millions of people, economic recovery was tangible, daily evidence that the dynamism of Nazi rule was more than show.

For the masses of ordinary German citizens, who were not Jews, Slavs, gypsies, Jehovah's Witnesses, or Communists, Hitler's government meant greater equality and exceptional opportunities. It must be remembered that in 1933 the position of the traditional German elites—the landed aristocracy, the wealthy capitalists, and the well-educated professional classes —was still very strong. Barriers between classes were generally high. Hitler's rule introduced vast changes in this pattern. For example, stiff educational requirements, which favored the well-to-do, were greatly relaxed. The new Nazi elite was composed largely of young and poorly educated dropouts, rootless lower-middle-class people like Hitler, who rose to the top with breathtaking speed.

More generally, the Nazis, like the Russian Communists, tolerated privilege and wealth only as long as they served the needs of the party. Big business was constantly ordered around, to the point that "probably never in peacetime has an ostensibly capitalist economy been directed as non- and even anti-capitalistically as the German economy between 1933 and 1939."[11] Hitler brought about a kind of social revolution, which was enthusiastically embraced by millions of modest middle- and lower-middle-class people and even by many workers.

Hitler's extreme nationalism, which had helped him gain power, continued to appeal to Germans after 1933. Ever since the wars against Napoleon, many Germans had believed in a special mission for a superior German nation. The successes of Bismarck had furthered such feelings, and near-victory in World War One made nationalists eager for renewed expansion in the 1920s. Thus, when a great German empire seemed within reach under Hitler,

EVENTS LEADING TO WORLD WAR TWO

1919	Treaty of Versailles
	J. M. Keynes, *Economic Consequences of the Peace*
1919–1920	U.S. Senate rejects the Treaty of Versailles
1921	Germany is billed $35 billion in reparations
1922	Mussolini seizes power in Italy
	Germany proposes a moratorium on reparations
January 1923	France and Belgium occupy the Ruhr
	Germany orders passive resistance to the occupation
October 1923	Stresemann agrees to reparations with re-examination of Germany's ability to pay
1924	Dawes Plan: German reparations reduced and put on a sliding scale; large U.S. loans to Germany recommended to promote German recovery; occupation of the Ruhr ends
	Adolf Hitler, *Mein Kampf*
1924–1929	Spectacular German economic recovery; circular flow of international funds enables sizable reparations payments
1925	Treaties of Locarno promote European security and stability
1926	Germany joins the League of Nations
1928	Kellogg-Briand Pact renounces war as an instrument of international affairs
1929	Young Plan further reduces German reparations
	Crash of U.S. stock market
1929–1933	Depths of the Great Depression
1931	Japan invades Manchuria
1932	Nazis become the largest party in the Reichstag
January 1933	Hitler appointed chancellor
March 1933	Reichstag passes the Enabling Act, granting Hitler absolute dictatorial power
October 1933	Germany withdraws from the League of Nations
July 1934	Nazis murder Austrian chancellor
March 1935	Hitler announces German rearmament
June 1935	Anglo-German naval agreement
October 1935	Mussolini invades Ethiopia and receives Hitler's support
1935	Nuremburg Laws deprive Jews of all rights of citizenship
March 1936	German armies move unopposed into the demilitarized Rhineland
July 1936	Outbreak of civil war in Spain
1937	Japan invades China
	Rome-Berlin Axis
March 1938	Germany annexes Austria
September 1938	Munich Conference: Britain and France agree to German seizure of the Sudetenland from Czechoslovakia
March 1939	Germany occupies the rest of Czechoslovakia; the end of appeasement in Britain
August 1939	Russo-German nonaggression pact
September 1, 1939	Germany invades Poland
September 3, 1939	Britain and France declare war on Germany

the majority of the population was delighted and praised the Führer's actions.

By no means all Germans supported Hitler, however, and a number of German groups actively resisted him after 1933. Tens of thousands of political enemies were imprisoned, and thousands were executed. Opponents of the Nazis pursued different goals, and under totalitarian conditions they were never unified, which helps account for their ultimate lack of success. In the first years of Hitler's rule, the principal resisters were the Communists and the Social Democrats in the trade unions. But the expansion of the SS system of terror after 1935 smashed most of these leftists. A second group of opponents arose in the Catholic and Protestant churches. However, their efforts were directed primarily at preserving genuine religious life, not at overthrowing Hitler. Finally, in 1938 (and again in 1942–1944), some high-ranking army officers, who feared the consequences of Hitler's reckless aggression, plotted against him, unsuccessfully.

NAZI EXPANSION AND THE SECOND WORLD WAR

Although economic recovery and increased opportunities for social advancement won Hitler support, they were only by-products of Nazi totalitarianism. The guiding concepts of Nazism remained space and race—the territorial expansion of the superior German race. As Germany regained its economic strength and as independent organizations were brought under control, Hitler formed alliances with other dictators and began expanding. German expansion was facilitated by the uncertain, divided, pacific Western democracies, which tried to buy off Hitler to avoid war. Yet war was inevitable, in both the West and the East, for Hitler's ambitions were essentially unlimited. On both war fronts the Nazi soldiers scored enormous successes until late 1942, forming a horrifyingly vast empire of destruction.

AGGRESSION AND APPEASEMENT, 1933–1939

Hitler's tactics in international politics after 1933 strikingly resembled those he used in domestic politics between 1924 and 1933. When Hitler was weak, he righteously proclaimed that he intended to overturn the "unjust system" established by the treaties of Versailles and Locarno—but only by legal means. As he grew stronger, and as other leaders showed their willingness to compromise, he increased his demands and finally began attacking his independent neighbors (Map 35.1).

Hitler realized that his aggressive policies had to be carefully camouflaged at first, for Germany's army was limited by the Treaty of Versailles to only a hundred thousand men. As he told a group of army commanders in February 1933, the early stages of his policy of "conquest of new living space in the East and its ruthless Germanization" had serious dangers. If France had real leaders, Hitler said, "it will not give us time but attack us, presumably with its eastern satellites."[12] Thus Hitler loudly proclaimed his peaceful intentions to all the world. Nevertheless, he felt strong enough to walk out of a sixty-nation disarmament conference and withdraw from the League of Nations in October 1933. Stresemann's policy of peaceful cooperation was dead; the Nazi determination to rearm was out in the open.

Following this action, which met with widespread approval at home, Hitler moved to incorporate independent Austria into a Greater Germany. Austrian Nazis climaxed an attempted overthrow by murdering the Austrian chancellor in July 1934. They were unable to take power, however, because a worried Mussolini, who had initially greeted Hitler as a fascist little brother, massed his troops on the Brenner Pass and threatened to fight. When, in March 1935, Hitler established a general military draft and declared the "unequal" disarmament clauses of the Treaty of Versailles null and void, other countries appeared to understand the danger. With France taking the lead, Italy and Great Britain protested strongly and warned against future aggressive actions.

Yet the emerging united front against Hitler quickly collapsed. Britain adopted a policy of appeasement, granting Hitler everything he could reasonably want (and more) in order to avoid war. The first step was an Anglo-German naval agreement in June 1935, which broke Germany's isolation. The second step came in March 1936, when Hitler suddenly marched his armies into the demilitarized Rhineland, brazenly violating the treaties of Versailles and Locarno. This was the last good chance to stop the Nazis, for Hitler had ordered his troops to retreat if France resisted militarily. But an uncertain

MAP 35.1 The Growth of Nazi Germany, 1933–1939 Until March 1939, Hitler brought ethnic Germans into the Nazi state; then he turned on the Slavic peoples he had always hated.

France would not move without British support, and the occupation of German soil by German armies seemed right and just to Britain. Its strategic position greatly improved, Germany had handed France a tremendous psychological defeat.

British appeasement, which practically dictated French policy, lasted far into 1939. It was motivated by British feelings of guilt toward Germany and the pacifism of a population still horrified by the memory of the First World War. Like many Germans, British statesmen seriously underestimated Hitler. They believed that they could use him to stop Russian communism. A leading member of Britain's government personally told Hitler in November 1937 that it was his conviction that Hitler "not only had accomplished great things in Germany itself, but that through the total destruction of Communism in his own country . . . Germany rightly had to be considered as a Western bulwark against Communism."[13] Such rigid anticommunist feelings made an alliance between the Western powers and Stalin against Hitler very unlikely.

As Britain and France opted for appeasement and Russia watched all developments suspiciously, Hitler found powerful allies. In 1935 the bombastic Mussolini decided that imperial expansion was needed to revitalize fascism. From Italian colonies on the east coast of Africa he attacked the independent African kingdom of Ethiopia. The Western powers and the League of Nations piously condemned Italian aggression, which angered Mussolini, without saving Ethiopia from defeat. Hitler, who had secretly supplied Ethiopia with arms to heat up the conflict, supported Italy energetically and thereby overcame Mussolini's lingering doubts about the Nazis. The result was an agreement on close cooperation in 1936 between Italy and Germany, the so-called Rome-Berlin Axis. Japan, which had been expanding into Manchuria since 1931, soon joined the alliance between Italy and Germany.

At the same time, Germany and Italy intervened in the long, complicated Spanish Civil War, where their support eventually helped General Francisco Franco's fascist movement defeat republican Spain. Spain's only official aid came from Soviet Russia, for public opinion in Britain and especially in France was hopelessly divided on the Spanish question.

By late 1937, as he was proclaiming his peaceful intentions to the British and their gullible prime minister, Neville Chamberlain, Hitler told his generals his real plans. His "unshakable decision" was to crush Austria and Czechoslovakia at the earliest possible moment, as the first step in his long-contemplated drive to the east for "living space." By threatening Austria with invasion, Hitler forced the Austrian chancellor in March 1938 to put local Nazis in control of the government. The next day, German armies moved in unopposed, and Austria became two more provinces of Greater Germany (Map 35.1).

Simultaneously, Hitler began demanding that the pro-Nazi, German-speaking minority of western Czechoslovakia—the Sudetenland—be turned over to Germany. Yet democratic Czechoslovakia was prepared to defend itself. Moreover, France had been Czechoslovakia's ally since 1924; and if France

fought, Soviet Russia was pledged to help. As war appeared inevitable—for Hitler had already told the leader of the Sudeten Germans that "we must always ask so much we cannot be satisfied"—appeasement triumphed again. In September 1938, Chamberlain flew to Germany three times in fourteen days. In these negotiations, to which Russia was deliberately not invited, Chamberlain and the French agreed with Hitler that the Sudetenland should be ceded to Germany immediately. Returning to London from the Munich Conference, Chamberlain told cheering crowds that he had secured "peace with honor . . . peace for our time." Sold out by the Western powers, Czechoslovakia gave in.

Confirmed once again in his opinion of the Western democracies as weak and racially degenerate, Hitler accelerated his aggression. In a shocking violation of his solemn assurances that the Sudetenland was his last territorial demand, Hitler's armies occupied the Czech lands in March 1939, while Slovakia became a puppet state. The effect on Western public opinion was electrifying. For the first time, there was no possible rationale of self-determination for Nazi aggression, since Hitler was seizing Czechs and Slovaks as captive peoples. Thus, when Hitler used the question of German minorities in Danzig as a pretext to smash Poland, a suddenly militant Chamberlain declared that Britain and France would fight if Hitler attacked his eastern neighbor. Hitler did not take these warnings seriously, and he pressed on.

In an about-face that stunned the world, Hitler offered and Stalin signed a ten-year Russo-German nonaggression pact in August 1939, whereby each dictator promised to remain neutral if the other became involved in war. Even more startling was the attached secret protocol, which ruthlessly divided eastern Europe into German and Russian zones, "in the event of a political territorial reorganization." Although this top-secret protocol sealing the destruction of Poland and the Baltic States became known only after the war, the nonaggression pact itself was enough to make Britain and France cry treachery, for they too had been negotiating with Stalin. But Stalin had remained distrustful of Western intentions. Moreover, Britain and France had offered him military risk without gain, while Hitler had offered territorial gain without risk. For Hitler, everything was set. He told his generals on the day of the nonaggression pact: "My only fear is that at the last moment some dirty dog will come up with a mediation plan." On September 1, 1939, German armies and warplanes smashed into Poland from three sides. Two days later, finally true to their word, Britain and France declared war on Germany. The Second World War had begun.

HITLER'S EMPIRE, 1939–1942

Using planes, tanks, and trucks in the first example of the *Blitzkrieg,* or "lightning war," Hitler's armies crushed Poland in four weeks. While Soviet Russia quickly took its part of the booty—the eastern half of Poland and the Baltic States of Lithuania, Estonia, and Latvia—French and British armies dug in in the west. They expected another war of attrition and economic blockade.

In spring 1940, the lightning war struck again. After quickly occupying Denmark, Norway, and Holland, German motorized columns broke through southern Belgium, split the Franco-British forces, and trapped the entire British army on the beaches of Dunkirk. By heroic efforts the British managed to withdraw their troops but not their equipment to England.

France was taken by the Nazis. The aging marshal Henri-Philippe Pétain formed a new French government—the so-called Vichy government—to accept defeat, and German armies occupied most of France. By July 1940, Hitler ruled practically all of western continental Europe; Italy was an ally and the Soviet Union a friendly neutral. Only Britain, led by the uncompromising Winston Churchill (1874–1965), remained unconquered. Churchill proved to be one of history's greatest wartime leaders, rallying his fellow citizens with stirring speeches, infectious confidence, and bulldog determination.

Germany sought to gain control of the air, the necessary first step for an amphibious invasion of Britain. In the Battle of Britain, up to a thousand German planes attacked British airfields and key factories in a single day, dueling with British defenders high in the skies. Losses were heavy on both sides. Then in September Hitler angrily and foolishly changed his strategy, turning from military objectives to indiscriminate bombing of British cities in an attempt to break British morale. British factories increased production of their excellent fighter planes; antiaircraft defense improved with the help of radar;

and the heavily bombed people of London defiantly dug in. In September–October 1940, Britain was beating Germany 3 to 1 in the air war. There was no possibility of immediate German invasion of Britain.

In these circumstances, the most reasonable German strategy would have been to attack Britain through the eastern Mediterranean, taking Egypt and the Suez Canal and pinching off Britain's supply of oil. Moreover, Mussolini's early defeats in Greece had drawn Hitler into the Balkans, where Germany quickly conquered Greece and Yugoslavia while forcing Hungary, Rumania, and Bulgaria into alliances with Germany by April 1941. This reinforced the logic of a thrust into the eastern Mediterranean. But Hitler was not a reasonable person. His lifetime obsession with a vast eastern European empire for the master race irrationally dictated policy. By late 1940, he had already decided on his next move, and in June 1941, German armies suddenly attacked the Soviet Union along a vast front. With Britain still unconquered, Hitler's decision was a wild, irrational gamble, epitomizing the violent, unlimited ambitions of modern totalitarianism.

Faithfully fulfilling all his obligations under the Nazi-Soviet Pact and even ignoring warnings of impending invasion, Stalin was caught off guard. Nazi armies moved like lightning across the Russian steppe. By October 1941, Leningrad was practically surrounded, Moscow besieged, and most of the Ukraine conquered; yet the Russians did not collapse. When a severe winter struck German armies in summer uniforms, the invaders were stopped.

While Hitler's armies dramatically expanded the war in Europe, his Japanese allies did the same in Asia. Engaged in a general but undeclared war against China since 1937, Japan's rulers had increasingly come into diplomatic conflict with the Pacific Basin's other great power, the United States. When the Japanese occupied French Indochina in July 1941, the United States retaliated by cutting off sales of vital rubber, scrap iron, oil, and aviation fuel, which were essential for Japan's war effort in China. Thus Japan's military leaders decided to attack European colonies in Southeast Asia in order to gain control of vital war materials, especially oil from the rich fields of the Dutch East Indies. Convinced that such aggression would inevitably bring war with the United States and determined to cripple the American response in advance, Japan attacked the U.S.

naval base at Pearl Harbor in Hawaii on December 7, 1941. Hitler immediately declared war on the United States, even though his treaty obligations with Japan did not require him to initiate this course of action.

As Japanese forces advanced swiftly into Southeast Asia after the crippling surprise attack on Pearl Harbor, Hitler and his European allies continued the two-front war against the Soviet Union and Great Britain. Not until late 1942 did the Nazis suffer their first major defeats (see Chapter 36). In the meantime, Hitler ruled a vast European empire stretching from the outskirts of Moscow to the English Channel. Hitler and the top Nazi leadership began building their "New Order," and they continued their efforts until their final collapse in 1945. In doing so, they showed what Nazi victory would have meant.

Hitler's New Order was based firmly on the guiding principle of Nazi totalitarianism: racial imperialism. Within this New Order, the Nordic peoples—the Dutch, Norwegians, and Danes—received preferential treatment, for they were racially related to the Germans. The French, an "inferior" Latin

Prelude to Murder This photo captures the terrible inhumanity of Nazi racism. Frightened and bewildered families from the soon-to-be destroyed Warsaw ghetto are being forced out of their homes by German soldiers for deportation to concentration camps. There they face murder in the gas chambers. *(Roger-Viollet)*

people, occupied the middle position. They were heavily taxed to support the Nazi war effort, but were tolerated as a race. Once Nazi reverses began to mount in late 1942, however, all the occupied peoples of western and northern Europe were exploited with increasing intensity. Material shortages and both mental and physical suffering afflicted millions.

Slavs in the conquered territories to the east were treated with harsh hatred as "subhumans." At the height of his success in 1941 to 1942, Hitler painted for his intimate circle the fantastic details of a vast eastern colonial empire, where the Poles, Ukrainians, and Russians would be enslaved and forced to die out, while Germanic peasants resettled their abandoned lands. Himmler and the elite corps of SS volunteers struggled loyally, sometimes against the German army, to implement part of this general program even before victory was secured. In parts of Poland, the SS arrested and evacuated Polish peasants to create a German "mass settlement space." Polish workers and Russian prisoners of war were transported to Germany, where they did most of the heavy labor and were systematically worked to death. The conditions of Russian slave labor in Germany were so harsh that four out of five Russian prisoners did not survive the war.

Finally, Jews were condemned to extermination, along with gypsies, Jehovah's Witnesses, and captured Communists. By 1939 German Jews had lost all their civil rights, and after the fall of Warsaw the Nazis began deporting them to Poland. There they and Jews from all over Europe were concentrated in ghettos, compelled to wear the Jewish star, and turned into slave laborers. But by 1941, Himmler's SS was carrying out the "final solution of the Jewish question"—the murder of every single Jew. All over Hitler's empire, Jews were arrested, packed like cattle onto freight trains, and dispatched to extermination camps.

There the victims were taken by force or deception to "shower rooms," which were actually gas chambers. These gas chambers, first perfected in the quiet, efficient execution of 70,000 mentally ill Germans between 1938 and 1941, permitted rapid, hideous, and thoroughly bureaucratized mass murder. For fifteen to twenty minutes there came the terrible screams and gasping sobs of men, women, and children choking to death on poison gas. Then, only silence. Special camp workers quickly tore the victims'

gold teeth from their jaws and cut off their hair for use as chair stuffings. The bodies were then cremated, or sometimes boiled for oil to make soap, while the bones were crushed to produce fertilizers. At Auschwitz, the most infamous of the Nazi death factories, as many as 12,000 human beings were slaughtered each day. On the turbulent Russian front, the SS death squads forced the Jewish population to dig giant pits, which became mass graves as the victims were lined up on the edge and cut down by machine guns. The extermination of the European Jews was the ultimate monstrosity of Nazi racism and racial imperialism. By 1945, 6 million Jews had been murdered in cold blood.

———

The tremendous practical and spiritual maladies of the age of anxiety led in many lands to the rise of dictatorships. Many of these dictatorships were variations on conservative authoritarianism, but there was also a fateful innovation—the modern totalitarian regime, most fully developed in Communist Russia and Nazi Germany. The totalitarian regimes utterly rejected the liberalism of the nineteenth century. Inspired by the lessons of total war and Lenin's one-party rule, they tried to subordinate everything to the state. Although some areas of life escaped them, state control increased to a staggering degree. The totalitarian regimes trampled on basic human rights with unrestrained brutality and police terror. Moreover, they were armed with the weapons of modern technology, rendering opposition almost impossible.

Both Communist Russia and Nazi Germany tried to gain the *willing* support of their populations. Monopolizing the means of expression and communication, they claimed to represent the masses and to be building new, more equal societies. Many people believed them. Both regimes also won enthusiastic supporters by offering tough, ruthless people from modest backgrounds enormous rewards for loyal and effective service. Thus these totalitarian dictatorships rested on considerable genuine popular support, as well as on police terror. This combination gave them their awesome power and dynamism. That dynamism was, however, channeled in quite different directions. Stalin and the Communist party aimed at building their kind of socialism and the new socialist personality at home. Hitler and the Nazi elite aimed at unlimited territorial and racial aggression on behalf of a master race; domestic recovery was only a means to that end. Unlimited aggression made war inevitable, first with the Western democracies and then with Germany's totalitarian neighbor. It plunged Europe into the ultimate nightmare.

NOTES

1. E. Halévy, *The Era of Tyrannies* (Garden City, N.Y.: Doubleday, 1965), pp. 265–316, esp. p. 300.
2. Quoted in P. C. Roberts, " 'War Communism': A Reexamination," *Slavic Review* 29 (June 1970): 257.
3. Quoted in A. G. Mazour, *Soviet Economic Development: Operation Outstrip, 1921–1965* (Princeton, N.J.: Van Nostrand, 1967), p. 130.
4. Quoted in I. Deutscher, *Stalin: A Political Biography,* 2d ed. (New York: Oxford University Press, 1967), p. 325.
5. Quoted in H. K. Geiger, *The Family in Soviet Russia* (Cambridge, Mass.: Harvard University Press, 1968), p. 123.
6. Ibid., p. 156.
7. Quoted in B. Rosenthal, "Women in the Russian Revolution and After," in *Becoming Visible: Women in European History,* eds., R. Bridenthal and C. Koonz (Boston: Houghton Mifflin, 1976), p. 383.
8. Quoted in K. D. Bracher, in T. Eschenburg et al., *The Path to Dictatorship, 1918–1933* (Garden City, N.Y.: Doubleday, 1966), p. 117.
9. Quoted in K. D. Bracher, *The German Dictatorship: The Origins, Structure and Effects of National Socialism* (New York: Praeger, 1970), pp. 146–147.
10. Quoted in R. Stromberg, *An Intellectual History of Modern Europe* (New York: Appleton-Century-Crofts, 1966), p. 393.
11. D. Schoenbaum, *Hitler's Social Revolution: Class and Status in Nazi Germany, 1933–1939* (Garden City, N.Y.: Doubleday, 1967), p. 114.
12. Quoted in Bracher, *German Dictatorship,* p. 289.
13. Ibid., p. 306.

SUGGESTED READING

The historical literature on totalitarian dictatorships is rich and fascinating. H. Arendt, *The Origins of Totalitarianism* (1951), is a challenging interpretation. E. Weber, *Varieties of Fascism* (1964), stresses the radical social aspirations of fascist movements all across Europe. F. L. Carsten, *The Rise of Fascism,* rev. ed. (1982), and W. Laqueur, ed., *Fascism* (1976), are also recommended.

Richard Stites, *The Women's Liberation Movement in Russia: Feminism, Nihilism, and Bolshevism, 1860–1930* (1978); S. Fitzpatrick, *Cultural Revolution in Russia, 1928–1931* (1978); K. Geiger, *The Family in Soviet Russia* (1968); and I. Deutscher, *Stalin: A Political Biography* (1967), are all highly recommended, as is Deutscher's sympathetic three-volume study of Trotsky. S. Cohen, *Bukharin and the Bolshevik Revolution* (1973), examines the leading spokesman of moderate communism, who was destroyed by Stalin. R. Conquest, *The Great Terror* (1968), is an excellent account of Stalin's purges of the 1930s. A. Solzhenitsyn, *The Gulag Archipelago* (1964), passionately condemns Soviet police terror, which Solzhenitsyn tracks back to Lenin. A. Koestler, *Darkness at Noon* (1956), is a famous fictional account of Stalin's trials of the Old Bolsheviks. R. Medvedev, *Let History Judge* (1972), is a penetrating and highly recommended history of Stalinism by a Russian dissident. Three other remarkable books are J. Scott, *Behind the Urals* (1942, 1973), an eyewitness account of an American steelworker in Russia in the 1930s; S. Alliluyeva, *Twenty Letters to a Friend* (1967), the amazing reflections of Stalin's daughter, who has twice chosen to live in the United States; and M. Fainsod, *Smolensk Under Soviet Rule* (1958), a unique study based on Communist records captured first by the Germans and then by the Americans.

E. R. Tannebaum, *The Fascist Experience* (1972), is an excellent study of Italian culture and society under Mussolini. I. Silone, *Bread and Wine* (1937), is a moving novel by a famous opponent of dictatorship in Italy. Two excellent books on Spain are H. Thomas, *The Spanish Civil War* (1961), and E. Malefakis, *Agrarian Reform and Peasant Revolution in Spain* (1970). In the area of foreign relations, G. Kennan, *Russia and the West Under Lenin and Stalin* (1961), is justly famous, while A. L. Rowse, *Appeasement* (1961), powerfully denounces the policies of the appeasers. R. Paxton, *Vichy*

France (1973), tells a controversial story extremely well, and J. Lukac, *The Last European War* (1976), skillfully —and infuriatingly—argues that victory by Hitler could have saved Europe from both Russian and American domination.

On Germany, F. Stern, *The Politics of Cultural Despair* (1963), and G. Mosse, *The Crisis of German Ideology* (1964), are excellent complementary studies on the origins of Nazism. The best single work on Hitler's Germany is K. Bracher, *The German Dictatorship: The Origins, Structure and Effects of National Socialism* (1970), while W. Shirer, *The Rise and Fall of the Third Reich* (1960), is the best-selling account of an American journalist who experienced Nazi Germany firsthand. J. Fest, *Hitler* (1974), and A. Bullock, *Hitler* (1953), are engrossing biographies of the Führer. In addition to *Mein Kampf, Hitler's Secret Conversations, 1941–1944* (1953) reveals the dictator's wild dreams and beliefs. Among countless special studies, E. Kogon, *The Theory and Practice of Hell* (1958), is a chilling examination of the concentration camps; M. Mayer, *They Thought They Were Free* (1955), probes the minds of ten ordinary Nazis and why they believed Hitler was their liberator; and A. Speer, *Inside the Third Reich* (1970), contains the fascinating recollections of Hitler's wizard of the armaments industry. G. Mosse, *Toward the Final Solution* (1978), is a powerful history of European racism, and L. Dawidowicz, *The War Against the Jews, 1933–1945* (1975), is a superb account of the Holocaust. Jørgen Haestrup, *Europe Ablaze* (1978), is a monumental account of wartime resistance movements throughout Europe, and *The Diary of Anne Frank* is a remarkable personal account of a young Jewish girl in hiding during the Nazi occupation of Holland.

36

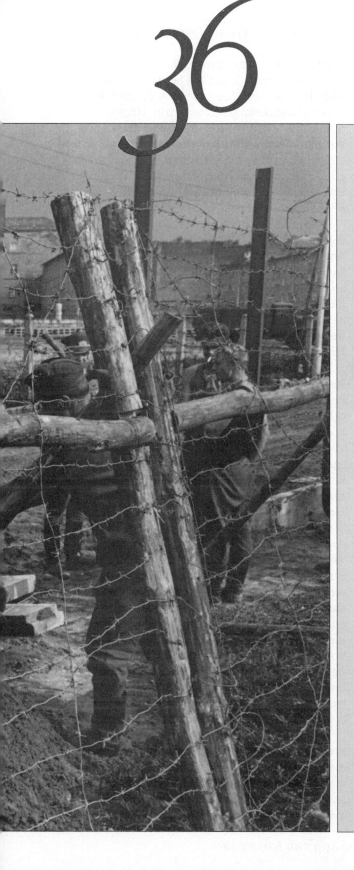

THE RECOVERY OF EUROPE AND THE AMERICAS

*I*N 1942, when Hitler's empire stretched across Europe and the Nazi "New Order" was taking shape, Western civilization was in danger of dying. A terrible, triumphant barbarism was striking at the hard-won accomplishments and uneven progress of many generations. From this low point, European society staged a truly astonishing recovery.

The Nazis and their allies were utterly defeated. Battered western Europe then experienced a great renaissance in the postwar years. The western hemisphere, with its strong European heritage, also made exemplary progress. Soviet Russia eventually became more humane and less totalitarian. Yet there was also a tragic setback. The Grand Alliance against Hitler gave way to an apparently endless cold war, in which conflict between East and West threatened world peace and troubled domestic politics.

How and why did Western society recover from the depths of despair in one of the most extraordinary periods of rebirth in its long history? What were the causes of the cold war, the most disappointing development of the postwar era? These are some of the more important questions this chapter will seek to answer.

ALLIED VICTORY AND THE COLD WAR, 1942–1950

The recovery of Western society depended on the defeat of the Nazis and their Italian, Balkan, and Japanese allies. On this point the twenty-six allied nations, led by Britain, the United States, and Soviet Russia, were firmly agreed. The Grand Alliance—to use Winston Churchill's favorite term—functioned quite effectively in military terms to achieve this overwhelming objective. By the summer of 1943, the tide of battle had turned, and Allied victory was only a matter of time.

Yet victory was flawed. The Allies could not cooperate politically when it came to peacemaking. Motivated by different goals and hounded by misunderstandings, the United States and Soviet Russia soon found themselves at loggerheads. By the end of 1947, Europe was rigidly divided. It was West versus East in the cold war.

Chance, rather than choice, brought together the anti-Axis coalition. Stalin had been cooperating fully with Hitler between August 1939 and June 1941, and only the Japanese attack on Pearl Harbor in December 1941 and Hitler's immediate declaration of war had overwhelmed powerful isolationism in the United States. The Allies' first task was to try to overcome their mutual suspicions and build an unshakable alliance on the quicksand of accident. By means of two interrelated policies they succeeded.

First, President Roosevelt accepted Churchill's contention that the United States should concentrate first on defeating Hitler. Only after victory in Europe would the United States turn toward the Pacific for an all-out attack on Japan, the lesser threat. Therefore, the United States promised and sent large amounts of military aid to Britain and Russia. America's policy of "Europe first" helped solidify the anti-Hitler coalition.

Second, within the European framework, the Americans and the British put immediate military needs first. They consistently postponed tough political questions relating to the eventual peace settlement. Thus, in December 1941 and again in May 1942, Stalin asked the United States and Britain to agree to Russia's moving its western border of 1938 farther west at the expense of Poland, in effect ratifying the gains Stalin had made from his deal with Hitler in 1939.

Stalin's request ran counter to the moralistic Anglo-American Atlantic Charter of August 1941. In good Wilsonian fashion, the Atlantic Charter had called for peace without territorial expansion or secret agreements, and free elections and self-determination for all liberated nations. Stalin thus received only a military alliance and no postwar commitments in 1942. Yet the United States and Britain did not try to take advantage of Russia's precarious position in 1942, promising an invasion of continental Europe as soon as possible. They feared that hard bargaining would anger Stalin and encourage him to consider making a separate peace with Hitler.

To encourage mutual trust, the Allies adopted the principle of the "unconditional surrender" of Germany and Japan. The policy of unconditional surrender cemented the Grand Alliance, denying Hitler any hope of dividing his foes. Equally important, it meant that Russian and Anglo-American armies would almost certainly come together to divide all of Germany, and all of Europe, among themselves.

The military resources of the Grand Alliance were awesome. The strengths of the United States were its mighty industry, its large population, and its national unity. Even before Pearl Harbor, President Roosevelt had called America the "arsenal of democracy" and given military aid to Britain and Russia. Now the United States geared up rapidly for all-out war production and drew heavily on a generally cooperative Latin America for resources. It not only equipped its own armies but eventually gave its allies about $50 billion of arms and equipment. Britain received by far the most, but about one-fifth of the total went to Russia in the form of badly needed trucks, planes, and munitions.

Too strong to lose and too weak to win when it stood alone, Britain, too, continued to make a great contribution. The British economy was totally and effectively mobilized, and the sharing of burdens through rationing and heavy taxes on war profits maintained social harmony. By early 1943, the Americans and the British combined small aircraft carriers with radar-guided bombers to rid the Atlantic of German submarines. Britain, the impregnable floating fortress, became a gigantic front-line staging area for the decisive blow to the heart of Germany.

As for Soviet Russia, so great was its strength that it might well have defeated Germany without Western help. In the face of the German advance, whole factories and populations were successfully evacuated to eastern Russia and Siberia. There, war production was reorganized and expanded, and the Red Army was increasingly well supplied. The Red Army was also well led, for a new generation of talented military leaders quickly arose to replace those so recently purged. Most important of all, Stalin drew on the massive support and heroic determination of the Soviet people. Broad-based Russian nationalism, as opposed to narrow Communist ideology, became the powerful unifying force in what was appropriately called the "Great Patriotic War of the Fatherland."

Finally, the United States, Britain, and Soviet Russia were not alone. They had the resources of much of the world at their command. And, to a greater or lesser extent, they were aided by a growing resistance movement against the Nazis throughout Europe, even in Germany. Thus, although Ukrainian peasants often welcomed the Germans as liberators, the barbaric occupation policies of the Nazis quickly

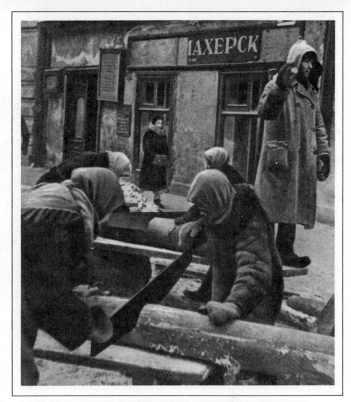

The Siege of Leningrad lasted almost three years, but the Russians heroically defended their city, which was never taken. These women are sawing poles for anti-tank defenses beside a bomb-battered building on what was once Leningrad's most stylish thoroughfare. *(Sovfoto)*

drove them to join and support behind-the-lines guerrilla forces. More generally, after Russia was invaded in June 1941, Communists throughout Europe took the lead in the underground resistance, joined by a growing number of patriots and Christians. Anti-Nazi leaders from occupied countries established governments-in-exile in London, like that of the "Free French" under the intensely proud General Charles De Gaulle. These governments gathered valuable secret information from resistance fighters and even organized armies to help defeat Hitler.

THE TIDE OF BATTLE

Barely halted at the gates of Moscow and Leningrad in 1941, the Germans renewed their Russian offensive in July 1942. This time they drove toward the southern city of Stalingrad, in an attempt to cripple communications and seize the crucial oil fields of Baku. Reaching Stalingrad, the Germans slowly oc-

B-17 Pilots These American women are returning from a training flight in their Flying Fortress, nicknamed "Pistol Packin' Mama." Women pilots ferried the planes for the U.S. Air Corps in support missions during the second World War. *(U.S. Air Force Photo)*

cupied most of the ruined city in a month of incredibly savage house-to-house fighting.

Then, in November 1942, Soviet armies counterattacked. They rolled over Rumanian and Italian troops to the north and south of Stalingrad, quickly closing the trap and surrounding the entire German Sixth Army of 300,000 men. The surrounded Germans were systematically destroyed, until by the end of January 1943 only 123,000 soldiers were left to surrender. Hitler, who had refused to allow a retreat, had suffered a catastrophic defeat. In the summer of 1943, the larger, better-equipped Soviet armies took the offensive and began moving forward (Map 36.1).

In late 1942 the tide also turned in the Pacific and North Africa. By early summer 1942, Japan had established a great empire in east Asia (Map 36.2). Unlike the Nazis, the Japanese made clever appeals to local nationalists, who hated European imperial domination and preferred Japan's so-called Greater Asian Co-Prosperity Sphere.

Then, in the Battle of the Coral Sea in May 1942, Allied naval and air power stopped the Japanese ad-

vance and also relieved Australia from the threat of invasion. This victory was followed by the Battle of Midway Island, in which American pilots sank all four of the attacking Japanese aircraft carriers and established American naval superiority in the Pacific. In August 1942, American marines attacked Guadalcanal in the Solomon Islands. Badly hampered by the policy of "Europe first"—only 15 percent of Allied resources were going to fight the war in the Pacific in early 1943—the Americans, under General Douglas MacArthur and Admiral Chester Nimitz, and the Australians nevertheless began "island hopping" toward Japan. Japanese forces were on the defensive.

In North Africa, the war had been seesawing back and forth since 1940. In May 1942, combined German and Italian armies, under the brilliant General

MAP 36.1 World War Two in Europe The map shows the extent of Hitler's empire at its height, before the battle of Stalingrad in late 1942, and the subsequent advances of the Allies until Germany surrendered on May 7, 1945.

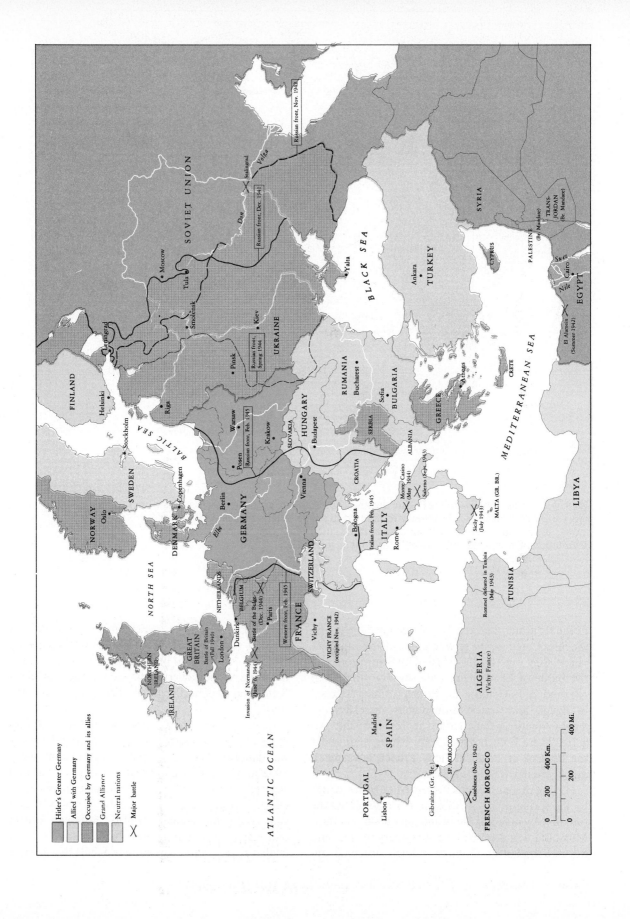

SOVIET UNION

Russian front, Nov. 1942

Volga

Stalingrad

Russian front, Dec. 1941

Don

Moscow

Tula

Smolensk

Archangel

Kiev

UKRAINE

Russian front,
Spring 1944

Pinsk

BLACK SEA

Yalta

TURKEY

Ankara

SYRIA

TRANS-
JORDAN
(Br. Mandate)

PALESTINE
(Br. Mandate)

CYPRUS

Suez

Cairo

Nile

EGYPT

El Alamein
(Summer 1942)

FINLAND

Helsinki

BALTIC SEA

Riga

Warsaw

Russian front, Feb. 1945

Krakow

SLOVAKIA

HUNGARY

Budapest

RUMANIA

Bucharest

BULGARIA

Sofia

SERBIA

ALBANIA

GREECE

Athens

CRETE

MEDITERRANEAN SEA

LIBYA

SWEDEN

Stockholm

Posen

Vienna

CROATIA

NORWAY

Oslo

DENMARK

Copenhagen

Elbe

Berlin

GERMANY

SWITZERLAND

Bologna

Italian front, Feb. 1945

ITALY

Rome

Monte Casino
(May 1944)

Salerno (Sept. 1943)

Sicily
(July 1943)

MALTA (GR. BR.)

NORTH SEA

NORTHERN
IRELAND

GREAT
BRITAIN

Battle of Britain
(Fall 1940)

London

IRELAND

Dunkirk

NETHERLANDS

BELGIUM

Battle of the Bulge
(Dec. 1944)

Paris

Western front, Feb. 1945

FRANCE

Vichy

VICHY FRANCE
(occupied Nov. 1942)

Invasion of Normandy
June 6, 1944

ATLANTIC OCEAN

Rommel defeated in Tunisia
(May 1943)

TUNISIA

ALGERIA
(Vichy France)

PORTUGAL

Lisbon

SPAIN

Madrid

Gibraltar (Gr. Br.)

SP. MOROCCO

Casablanca (Nov. 1942)

FRENCH MOROCCO

Hitler's Greater Germany

Allied with Germany

Occupied by Germany and its allies

Grand Alliance

Neutral nations

Major battle

0   200   400 Km.
0   200   400 Mi.

MAP 36.2 World War Two in the Pacific Japanese forces also overran an enormous territory in 1942, which the Allies slowly recaptured in a long bitter struggle. As this map shows, Japan still held a large Asian empire in August 1945, when the unprecedented devastation of atomic warfare suddenly forced it to surrender.

Erwin Rommel, attacked British-occupied Egypt and the Suez Canal for the second time. After a rapid advance, they were finally defeated by British forces at the Battle of El Alamein, only seventy miles from Alexandria. In October, the British counter-attacked in Egypt, and almost immediately thereafter, an Anglo-American force landed in Morocco and Algeria. These French possessions, which were under the control of Pétain's Vichy French goverment, quickly went over to the Allies.

Having driven the Axis powers from North Africa by the spring of 1943, Allied forces maintained the initiative by invading Sicily and then mainland Italy. Mussolini was deposed by a war-weary people, and the new Italian government publicly accepted un-

conditional surrender in September 1943. Italy, it seemed, was liberated. Yet Mussolini was rescued by German commandos in a daring raid and put at the head of a puppet government. German armies seized Rome and all of northern Italy. Fighting continued in Italy.

Indeed, bitter fighting continued in Europe for almost two years. Germany, less fully mobilized for war than Britain in 1941, applied itself to total war in 1942 and enlisted millions of prisoners of war and slave laborers from all across occupied Europe in that effort. Between early 1942 and July 1944, German war production actually tripled. Although British and American bombing raids killed many German civilians, they were surprisingly ineffective from a military point of view. Also, German resistance against Hitler failed. After an unsuccessful attempt on Hitler's life in July 1944, thousands of Germans were brutally liquidated by SS fanatics. Terrorized at home and frightened by the prospect of unconditional surrender, the Germans fought on with suicidal stoicism.

On June 6, 1944, American and British forces under General Dwight Eisenhower landed on the beaches of Normandy in history's greatest naval invasion. In a hundred dramatic days, more than 2 million men and almost a half-million vehicles pushed inland and broke through German lines. Rejecting proposals to strike straight at Berlin in a massive attack, Eisenhower moved forward cautiously on a broad front. Not until March 1945 did American troops cross the Rhine and enter Germany.

The Russians, who had been advancing steadily since July 1943, reached the outskirts of Warsaw by August 1944. For the next six months they moved southward into Rumania, Hungary, and Yugoslavia. In January 1945, Red armies again moved westward through Poland, and on April 26 they met American forces on the Elbe River. The Allies had closed their vise on Nazi Germany and overrun Europe. As Soviet forces fought their way into Berlin, Hitler committed suicide in his bunker, and on May 7 German commanders capitulated.

Three months later the United States dropped atomic bombs on Hiroshima and Nagasaki. Mass bombing of cities and civilians, one of the terrible new practices of World War Two, had ended in the final nightmare—unprecedented human destruction in a single blinding flash. The Japanese surrendered. The Second World War, which had claimed the lives of more than 50 million soldiers and civilians, was over.

THE ORIGINS OF THE COLD WAR

Total victory was not followed by genuine peace. The most powerful allies—Soviet Russia and the United States—began to quarrel as soon as the unifying threat of Nazi Germany disappeared. Though the hostility between the eastern and western superpowers was a tragic disappointment for millions of people, it was not really surprising. It grew sadly but logically out of military developments, wartime agreements, and long-standing political and ideological differences.

The conference Stalin, Roosevelt, and Churchill had held in the Iranian capital of Teheran in November 1943 was of crucial importance in determining subsequent events. There, the Big Three had jovially reaffirmed their determination to crush Germany and searched for the appropriate military strategy. Churchill, fearful of the military dangers of a direct attack and anxious to protect Britain's political interests in the eastern Mediterranean, argued that American and British forces should follow up their North African and Italian campaigns with an indirect attack on Germany through the Balkans. Roosevelt, however, agreed with Stalin that an American-British frontal assault through France would be better. This agreement was part of Roosevelt's general effort to meet Stalin's wartime demands whenever possible, and it had momentous political implications. It meant that the Russian and the American-British armies would come together in defeated Germany along a north-south line and that only Russian troops would liberate eastern Europe. Thus the basic shape of postwar Europe was already emerging. Real differences over questions like Poland were carefully ignored.

When the Big Three met again at Yalta on the Black Sea in southern Russia in February 1945, rapidly advancing Soviet armies were within one hundred miles of Berlin. The Red Army had occupied not only Poland but also Bulgaria, Rumania, Hungary, part of Yugoslavia, and much of Czechoslovakia. The temporarily stalled American-British forces had yet to cross the Rhine into Germany. Moreover, the United States was far from defeating Japan. Indeed, it was believed that the invasion and occupation of Japan would cost a million American casualties—an estimate that led to the subsequent decision to drop atomic bombs in order to save American lives. In short, Russia's position was strong and America's weak.

There was little the increasingly sick and apprehensive Roosevelt could do but double his bet on Stalin's peaceful intentions. It was agreed at Yalta that Germany would be divided into zones of occupation and would pay heavy reparations to the Soviet Union. At American insistence, Stalin agreed to declare war on Japan after Germany was defeated. He also agreed to join the proposed United Nations, which the Americans believed would help preserve peace after the war; it was founded in April 1945 in San Francisco. For Poland and eastern Europe, the

The Big Three In 1945 a triumphant Winston Churchill, ailing Franklin Roosevelt, and determined Joseph Stalin met at Yalta in southern Russia to plan for peace. Cooperation soon gave way to bitter hostility. *(National Archives, Washington)*

Big Three struggled to reach an ambiguous compromise at Yalta: east European governments were to be freely elected but pro-Russian. As Churchill put it at the time, "The Poles will have their future in their own hands, with the single limitation that they must honestly follow in harmony with their allies, a policy friendly to Russia."[1]

The Yalta compromise over eastern Europe broke down almost immediately. Even before the Yalta Conference, Bulgaria and Poland were in the hands of Communists, who arrived home in the baggage of the Red Army. Minor concessions to non-Communist groups thereafter did not change this situation. Elsewhere in eastern Europe, pro-Russian "coalition" governments of several parties were formed, but the key ministerial posts were reserved for Moscow-trained Communists.

At the postwar Potsdam Conference of July 1945, the long-ignored differences over eastern Europe fi-

nally surged to the fore. The compromising Roosevelt had died and been succeeded by the more determined President Harry Truman, who demanded immediate free elections throughout eastern Europe. Stalin refused pointblank. "A freely elected government in any of these East European countries would be anti-Soviet," he admitted simply, "and that we cannot allow."[2]

Here, then, is the key to the much-debated origins of the cold war. American ideals, pumped up by the crusade against Hitler, and American politics, heavily influenced by millions of voters from eastern Europe, demanded free elections in Soviet-occupied eastern Europe. On the other hand, Stalin, who had lived through two enormously destructive German invasions, wanted absolute military security from Germany and its potential Eastern allies, once and for all. Suspicious by nature, he believed that only Communist states could truly be devoted allies, and

The Berlin Air Lift Standing in the rubble of their bombed-out city, a German crowd in the American sector awaits the arrival of a U.S. transport plane flying in over the Soviet blockade in 1948. The crisis over Berlin was a dramatic indication of growing tensions among the Allies, which resulted in the division of Europe into two hostile camps. *(Walter Sanders,* Life © *Time Inc.)*

he feared that free elections would result in hostile governments on his western border. Since Stalin's armies had already occupied eastern Europe, he was bound to have his way.

WEST VERSUS EAST

The American response to Stalin's exaggerated conception of security was to "get tough." In May 1945, Truman abruptly cut off all aid to Russia. In October, he declared that the United States would never recognize any government established by force against the free will of its people. In March 1946, former British Prime Minister Churchill ominously informed an American audience that an "iron curtain" had fallen across the continent, dividing Germany and all of Europe into two antagonistic camps. Soon emotional, moralistic denunciations of Stalin and Communist Russia re-emerged as part of American politi-

cal life. Yet the United States also responded to the popular desire to "bring the boys home" and demobilized with incredible speed. When the war against Japan ended in September 1945, there were 12 million Americans in the armed forces; by 1947 there were only 1.5 million, as opposed to 6 million for Soviet Russia. "Getting tough" really meant "talking tough."

Stalin's agents quickly reheated the "ideological struggle against capitalist imperialism." Moreover, the large, well-organized Communist parties of France and Italy obediently started to uncover American plots to take over Europe and aggressively challenged their own governments with violent criticisms and large strikes. The Soviet Union also put pressure on Iran and Turkey, and while Greek Communists battled Greek royalists, another bitter civil war raged in China. By the spring of 1947, it appeared to many Americans that Stalin was determined to export communism by subversion to western Europe and Asia.

The American response to this challenge was the Truman Doctrine, which was aimed at "containing" communism to areas already occupied by the Red Army. To begin, Truman asked Congress for military aid to Greece and Turkey. Then in June, Secretary of State George C. Marshall offered Europe economic aid—the "Marshall Plan"—to help it rebuild.

Stalin refused Marshall Plan assistance for all of eastern Europe. He purged the last remaining non-Communist elements from the coalition governments of eastern Europe and established Soviet-style, one-party Communist dictatorships. The seizure of power in Czechoslovakia in February 1948 was particularly brutal and antidemocratic, and it greatly strengthened Western fears of limitless Communist expansion, beginning with Germany. Thus, when Stalin blocked all traffic through the Soviet zone of Germany to the former capital of Berlin, which had also been divided into sectors at the end of the war by the occupying powers, the Western allies responded firmly but not provocatively. Hundreds of planes began flying over the Russian roadblocks around the clock. After 324 days, the Russians backed down: containment seemed to work. In 1949, therefore, the United States formed an anti-Soviet military alliance of western governments, the North Atlantic Treaty Organization (NATO); in response, Stalin tightened his hold on his satellites, later united in the Warsaw Pact. Europe was divided into two hostile blocs.

In late 1949, the Communists triumphed in China, frightening and infuriating many Americans, who saw an all-powerful worldwide Communist conspiracy extending even into the upper reaches of the American government. When the Russian-backed Communist forces of northern Korea invaded southern Korea in 1950, President Truman's response was swift. American-led United Nations armies intervened. The cold war had spread around the world and become very hot.

It seems clear that the rapid descent from victorious Grand Alliance to bitter cold war was intimately connected with the tragic fate of eastern Europe. When the eastern European power vacuum after 1932 had lured Nazi racist imperialism, the appeasing Western democracies had quite mistakenly done nothing. They had, however, had one telling insight: how, they had asked themselves, could they unite with Stalin to stop Hitler without giving Stalin great gains on his western borders? After Hitler's invasion of Soviet Russia, the Western powers preferred to ignore this question and hope for the best. But when Stalin later began to seize the spoils of victory, a helpless but moralistic United States refused to cooperate and professed outrage. The worsening quarrel over eastern Europe then exploded into a global confrontation, which became institutionalized and lasts to this day despite intermittent periods of relaxation.

THE WESTERN EUROPEAN RENAISSANCE

As the cold war divided Europe into two blocs, the future appeared bleak on both sides of the iron curtain. Economic conditions were the worst in generations, and millions of people lived on the verge of starvation. Politically, Europe was weak and divided, a battleground for cold war ambitions. Moreover, long-cherished European empires were crumbling in the face of Asian and African nationalism. Yet Europe recovered, and the Western nations led the way. In less than a generation, western Europe achieved unprecedented economic prosperity and regained much of its traditional prominence in world affairs. It was an amazing rebirth—a true renaissance.

THE POSTWAR CHALLENGE

After the war, economic conditions in western Europe were terrible. Simply finding enough to eat was a real problem. Runaway inflation and black markets testified to severe shortages and hardship. Rationing of bread had to be introduced in Britain in 1946 for the first time. Both France and Italy produced only about half as much in 1946 as before the war. Many people believed that Europe was quite simply finished. The prominent British historian Arnold Toynbee felt that, at best, western Europeans might seek to civilize the crude but all-powerful Americans, somewhat as the ancient Greeks had civilized their Roman conquerors.

Suffering was most intense in defeated Germany. The major territorial change of the war had moved Soviet Russia's border far to the west. Poland was in turn compensated for this loss to Russia with land

Berlin Digs Out What was once a great newspaper building stands as a ghostly gutted-out shell in this altogether typical postwar scene from 1945. But the previously impassable street has been partially cleared of rubble and traffic has begun to move again. In the midst of ruins life refuses to die. *(U.S. Army Signal Corps)*

taken from Germany (Map 36.3). To solidify these boundary changes, 13 million people were driven from their homes in eastern Germany (and other eastern countries) and forced to resettle in a greatly reduced Germany. The Russians were also seizing factories and equipment as reparations, even tearing up railroad tracks and sending the rails to the Soviet Union. The command "Come here, woman," from a Russian soldier was the sound of terror, the prelude to many a rape.

In 1945 and 1946, conditions were not much better in the Western zones, for the Western allies also treated the German population with great severity at first. By February 1946, the average daily diet of a German in the Ruhr had been reduced to two slices of bread, a pat of margarine, a spoonful of porridge, and two small potatoes. Countless Germans sold many of their possessions to American soldiers to buy food. By the spring of 1947, refugee-clogged, hungry, prostrate Germany was on the verge of total collapse and threatening to drag down the rest of Europe.

Yet western Europe was not finished. The Nazi occupation and the war had discredited old ideas, and people were willing to change and experiment in hopes of building a new and better Europe. New groups and new leaders were coming to the fore to guide these aspirations. Progressive Catholics and revitalized Catholic political parties—the Christian Democrats—were particularly influential.

In Italy the Christian Democrats emerged as the leading party in the first postwar elections in 1946, and in early 1948 they won an absolute majority in the parliament in a landslide victory. Their very able leader was Alcide De Gasperi, a courageous antifascist and former Vatican librarian, firmly committed to political democracy, economic reconstruction, and moderate social reform. In France, too, the Catholic party provided some of the best postwar leaders, like Robert Schuman. This was particularly

MAP 36.3 **Europe After World War Two** Both the Soviet Union and Poland took land from Germany, which the Allies partitioned into occupation zones. Those zones subsequently formed the basis of the East and the West German states, as the Iron Curtain fell to divide both Germany and Europe.

true after January 1946, when General De Gaulle, the inspiring wartime leader of the Free French, resigned after having re-established the free and democratic Fourth Republic. As Germany was partitioned by the cold war, a radically purified Federal Republic of Germany found new and able leadership among its Catholics. In 1949 Konrad Adenauer, the former mayor of Cologne and a long-time anti-Nazi, began his long, highly successful democratic rule; the Christian Democrats became West Germany's majority party for a generation. In providing effective leadership for their respective countries, the Christian Democrats were inspired and united by a common

Christian and European heritage. They steadfastly rejected totalitarianism and narrow nationalism and placed their faith in democracy and cooperation.

The Socialists and the Communists, active in the resistance against Hitler, also emerged from the war with increased power and prestige, especially in France and Italy. They, too, provided fresh leadership and pushed for social change and economic reform with considerable success. Thus, in the immediate postwar years, welfare measures such as family allowances, health insurance, and increased public housing were enacted throughout much of Europe. In Italy social benefits from the state came to equal a large part of the average worker's wages. In France large banks, insurance companies, public utilities, coal mines, and the Renault auto company were nationalized by the government. Britain followed the same trend. The voters threw out Churchill and the Conservatives in 1945, and the socialist Labour party under Clement Attlee moved toward establishment of the "welfare state." Many industries were nationalized, and the government provided each citizen with free medical service and taxed the middle and upper classes heavily. Thus, all across Europe, social reform complemented political transformation, providing solid foundations for a great European renaissance.

The United States also provided strong and creative leadership. Frightened by fears of Soviet expansion, the United States provided western Europe with both massive economic aid and ongoing military protection. Economic aid was channeled through the Marshall Plan, which required that the participating countries coordinate their efforts for maximum effectiveness and which led to the establishment of the Organization of European Economic Cooperation (OEEC). Military protection was provided through NATO, established as a regional alliance for self-defense and featuring American troops stationed permanently in Europe as well as the American nuclear umbrella. Thus the United States assumed its international responsibilities after the Second World War, exercising the leadership it had shunned in the tragic years after 1919.

ECONOMIC "MIRACLES"

As Marshall Plan aid poured in, the battered economies of western Europe began to turn the corner in 1948. Impoverished West Germany led the way with a spectacular advance. Other countries were not far behind. The outbreak of the Korean War in 1950 further stimulated economic activity, and Europe entered a period of rapid, sustained economic progress that lasted into the late 1960s. By 1963 western Europe was producing more than two-and-one-half times as much as it had before the war. Never before had the European economy grown so fast. For politicians and economists, for workers and business leaders, it was a time of astonishing, loudly proclaimed economic "miracles."

There were many reasons for western Europe's brilliant economic performance. American aid helped overcome critical shortages quickly. Moreover, the coordinated distribution of American aid accompanied a resurgence of economic liberalism with its healthy competition and an international division of labor.

As in most of the world, economic growth became a basic objective of all western European governments, for leaders and voters were determined to avoid a return to the dangerous and demoralizing stagnation of the 1930s. Governments generally accepted Keynesian economics (see page 1088) and sought to stimulate their economies, and some also adopted a number of imaginative strategies. Those in Germany and France were particularly successful and influential.

Under Minister of Economy Ludwig Erhard, a roly-poly, cigar-smoking ex-professor, postwar West Germany broke decisively with the totally regulated, straitjacketed Nazi economy. Erhard bet on the free-market economy, while maintaining the extensive social welfare network inherited from the Hitler era. He and his teachers believed not only that capitalism was more efficient but also that political and social freedom could thrive only if there were real economic freedom. Erhard's first step was to reform the currency and abolish rationing and price controls in 1948. He boldly declared, "The only ration coupon is the Mark."[3] At first, profits jumped sharply, prompting businessmen to quickly employ more people and produce more. By the late 1950s, Germany had a prospering economy and full employment, a strong currency and stable prices. Germany's success aroused renewed respect for free-market capitalism and encouraged freer trade among other European nations.

In France the major innovation was a new kind of planning. Under the guidance of Jean Monnet, an economic pragmatist and apostle of European unity, a planning commission set ambitious but flexible goals for the French economy. It used Marshall aid money and the nationalized banks to funnel money into key industries, several of which were state owned. At the same time, the planning commission and the French bureaucracy encouraged private enterprise to "think big." The often-cautious French business community responded, investing heavily in new equipment and modern factories. Thus France combined flexible planning and a "mixed" state and private economy to achieve the most rapid economic development in its long history in the 1950s and 1960s.

Other factors also contributed to western Europe's economic boom. In most countries after the war, there were large numbers of men and women ready to work hard for low wages and the hope of a better future. Germany had millions of impoverished refugees, while France and Italy still had millions of poor peasants. Expanding industries in those countries thus had a great asset to draw on.

In 1945 impoverished Europe was still rich in the sense that it had the human skills of an advanced industrial society. Skilled workers, engineers, managers, and professionals knew what could and should be done, and they did it.

Many consumer products had been invented or perfected since the late 1920s, but few Europeans had been able to buy them during the depression and war. In 1945 the electric refrigerator, the washing machine, and the automobile were rare luxuries. There was, therefore, a great potential demand, which the economic system moved to satisfy.

Finally, ever since 1919 the nations of Europe had suffered from high tariffs and small national markets, which made for small and therefore inefficient factories. In the postwar era European countries junked many of these economic barriers and gradually created a large unified market—the Common Market. This action, which stimulated the economy, was part of the postwar search for a new European unity.

TOWARD EUROPEAN UNITY

Western Europe's political recovery was spectacular. Republics were re-established in France, West Germany, and Italy. Constitutional monarchs were restored in Belgium, Holland, and Norway. These democratic governments took root once again and thrived. The middle-of-the-road parties—primarily the Christian Democrats and the Socialists—dominated and provided continuing leadership. National self-determination was accompanied by civil liberties and great individual freedom. All of this was itself an extraordinary achievement.

Even more remarkable was the still-unfinished, still-continuing movement toward a united Europe. The Christian Democrats with their shared Catholic heritage were particularly committed to "building Europe," and other groups shared their dedication. Many Europeans believed that narrow, exaggerated nationalism had been a fundamental cause of both world wars, and that only through unity could Euro-

MAP 36.4 European Alliance Systems After the Cold War divided Europe into two hostile military alliances, six Western European countries formed the Common Market in 1957. The Common Market grew later to include most of Western Europe, while the Communist states organized their own economic association—COMECON.

pean conflict be avoided in the future. Many western Europeans also realized how very weak their countries were in comparison with the United States and the Soviet Union, the two superpowers that had divided Europe from outside and made it into a cold war battleground. Thus, the cold war encouraged some visionaries to seek a new "European nation," a superpower capable of controlling western Europe's destiny and reasserting its influence in world affairs.

The close cooperation among European states required by the Marshall Plan led to the creation of both the OEEC and the Council of Europe in 1948. European federalists hoped that the Council of Europe would quickly evolve into a true European parliament with sovereign rights, but this did not happen. Britain, with its empire and its "special relationship" with the United States, consistently opposed giving any real political power—any sovereignty—to the council. Many old-fashioned continental nationalists and Communists felt similarly. The Council of Europe became little more than a multinational debating society.

Frustrated in the direct political approach, European federalists turned toward economics. As one of them explained, "Politics and economics are closely related. Let us try, then, for progress in economic matters. Let us suppress those obstacles of an economic nature which divide and compartmentalize the nations of Europe."[4] In this they were quite successful.

Two far-seeing French statesmen, the planner Jean Monnet and Foreign Minister Robert Schuman, courageously took the lead in 1950. The Schuman Plan called for a special international organization to control and integrate all European steel and coal production. West Germany, Italy, Belgium, the Netherlands, and Luxembourg accepted the French idea in 1952; the British would have none of it. The immediate economic goal—a single competitive market without national tariffs or quotas—was rapidly realized. By 1958 coal and steel moved freely among the

French President De Gaulle and his wife bid farewell to President and Mrs. Kennedy at the presidential palace in Paris in 1961. A proud statesman who never forgot the snubs received from his American and British allies during the war, De Gaulle challenged American leadership in Western Europe. *(Wide World Photos)*

six nations of the European Coal and Steel Community. The more far-reaching political goal was to bind the six member nations so closely together economically that war among them would become unthinkable and virtually impossible. This brilliant strategy did much to reduce tragic old rivalries, particularly that of France and Germany, which practically disappeared in the postwar era.

The coal and steel community was so successful that it encouraged further technical and economic cooperation among "the Six." In 1957 the same six nations formed Euratom to pursue joint research in atomic energy; they also signed the Treaty of Rome, which created the European Economic Community, generally known as the Common Market (Map 36.4). The first goal of the treaty was gradual reduction of all tariffs among the Six to create a large free trade area. Others were the free movement of capital and labor and common economic policies and institutions.

An epoch-making stride toward unity, the Common Market was a tremendous economic success. Tariffs were rapidly reduced, and a single market almost as large as that of the United States was created. Many medium-sized American companies rushed to Europe, for a single modern factory had a vast potential market of 170 million customers.

The development of the Common Market fired imaginations and encouraged hopes of rapid progress toward political as well as economic union. In the 1960s, however, these hopes were frustrated by a resurgence of more traditional nationalism. Once again, France took the lead. Mired in a bitter colonial war in Algeria, the country turned in 1958 to General De Gaulle, who established the Fifth French Republic and ruled as its president until 1969. A towering giant both literally and figuratively, De Gaulle was the last of the bigger-than-life wartime leaders. A complex man who aroused a strong and sometimes negative response, especially in the United States, De Gaulle was at heart a romantic nationalist dedicated to reasserting France's greatness and glory. Once he had resolved the Algerian conflict, he labored to recreate a powerful, truly independent France, which would lead and even dictate to the other Common Market states.

De Gaulle personified the political resurgence of the leading nations of western Europe, as well as declining fears of the Soviet Union in the 1960s. Viewing the United States as the main threat to genuine French (and European) independence, he withdrew all French military forces from the "American-controlled" NATO command, which had to move from Paris to Brussels. De Gaulle tried to create financial difficulties for the United States by demanding gold for the American dollars France had accumulated. France also developed its own nuclear weapons. Within the Common Market, De Gaulle in 1963 and again in 1967 vetoed the application of the pro-American British, who were having second thoughts and wanted to join. More generally, he refused to permit the scheduled advent of majority rule within the Common Market, and he forced his partners to accept many of his views. Thus, throughout the 1960s the Common Market thrived economically, but it did not transcend deep-seated nationalism and remained a union of nation-states.

DECOLONIZATION

The postwar era saw the total collapse of European political empires. Between 1947 and 1962 almost every colonial territory gained formal independence. Europe's long expansion, which had begun with the Age of Discovery and crested at the beginning of the twentieth century, was dramatically reversed. Future generations will almost certainly see this rolling back of Western expansion as one of world history's truly great turning points (Map 36.5).

The most basic cause of imperial collapse—what Europeans called "decolonization"—was the rising demand of Asian and African peoples for national self-determination, racial equality, and personal dignity. This demand spread from intellectuals to the masses in virtually every colonial territory after the First World War. As a result, colonial empires had already been shaken by 1939, preparing the way for the eventual triumph of independence movements (see Chapter 37). Yet decolonization also involved the imperial powers, and looking at the process from their perspective helps explain why independence came so quickly and why a kind of neocolonialism subsequently took its place in some areas.

European empires had been based on an enormous power differential between the rulers and the ruled, a difference that had declined almost to the vanishing point by 1945. Not only was western Europe poor and battered immediately after the war, but Japan had demonstrated that whites were not invincible. With its political power and moral authority in tatters, Europe's main choice was either to submit to decolonization gracefully or to enter into risky wars of reconquest.

Most Europeans regarded their empires very differently after 1945 than before 1914, or even before 1939. Empire had rested on self-confidence and a sense of righteousness; Europeans had believed their superiority to be not only technical and military but spiritual and moral as well. The horrors of the Second World War and the near-destruction of Western civilization destroyed such complacent arrogance and gave opponents of imperialism the upper hand in Europe. After 1945 most Europeans were willing to let go of their colonies more or less voluntarily and to concentrate on rebuilding at home.

Indian independence played a key role in decolonization. When the Labour party came to power in Great Britain in 1945, it was determined to leave India. British socialists had always opposed imperialism, and the heavy cost of governing India had become an intolerable burden. Empire in India ended in 1947, and most Asian colonies achieved independence shortly thereafter. Although the French obstinately tried to re-establish colonial rule in Indochina, they were defeated in 1954, and two independent Vietnamese states came into being. The French also fought a long, dirty war to keep Algeria French, but Algeria won its independence in 1962 (see Map 36.5).

In much of Africa south of the Sahara, decolonization proceeded much more smoothly. Beginning in 1957, Britain's colonies achieved independence with little or no bloodshed and then entered a very loose association with Britain as members of the British Commonwealth of nations. In 1958 the clever De Gaulle offered the leaders of French black Africa the choice of a total break with France or immediate independence within a kind of French commonwealth. All but one of the new states chose association with France. African leaders did so because they identified with French culture and because they wanted aid from France. The French, buoyed up by economic growth and political recovery, were eager to help—provided their former colonies would accept close ties with France on French terms. As in the past, the French and their Common Market partners, who helped foot the bill, saw themselves as continuing their civilizing mission in black Africa. More importantly, they saw in Africa markets for their industrial goods, raw materials for their factories, outlets for profitable investment, and good temporary jobs for their engineers and teachers. The British acted somewhat similarly, especially after they finally joined the Common Market in 1973.

As a result, western European countries actually managed to increase their economic and cultural ties with their former African colonies in the 1960s and 1970s. Above all, they used the lure of special trading privileges with the Common Market and heavy investment in French and English-language education to enhance a powerful Western presence in the new Africa states. This situation led a variety of leaders and scholars to charge that western Europe, supported by the United States, had imposed a system of neocolonialism on its former colonies, a system designed to perpetuate Western economic domination indefinitely. More generally, these critics charged that the West had used its resurgent economic power to undermine the promise of political independence and maintain a neocolonial dependence, thereby extending to Africa (and much of Asia) the kind of subordination that has plagued Latin America since the political revolutions of the early nineteenth century (see Chapter 31). At the very least, enduring aid and influence in black Africa testified to Europe's renewed political power and its major role in international economic relations.

POLITICAL TRENDS SINCE 1968

Events in the late 1960s and 1970s suggested that the period of unprecedented postwar recovery was over and that a new era had begun. In 1968, a mini-revolution in France signaled the re-emergence of serious social and political conflict in western Europe after a generation of relative peace. The upheaval in France began when radical students occupied university buildings in Paris and appealed to France's industrial workers for support. Rank-and-file workers ignored the advice of their cautious union officials, and a spontaneous general strike spread across France in May 1968. It seemed certain that President De Gaulle's Fifth Republic would collapse. Yet De Gaulle stiffened. After securing the firm support of French army commanders in West Germany, he moved troops to Paris and called for new elections. Thoroughly frightened and fearful of an eventual Communist takeover, the masses of France voted for a return to law and order. De Gaulle and his party scored the biggest electoral victory in modern French history, and the mini-revolution fell apart.

Yet the proud De Gaulle and the old-fashioned national political revival he represented had been cruelly mocked. In 1969, De Gaulle resigned over a minor issue, and within a year he was dead. For much of the older generation in France, and indeed throughout western Europe, the student revolution of 1968 signaled the end of illusions. Twenty years of almost uninterrupted social and economic progress had unexpectedly brought renewed conflict and uncertainty.

The reappearance of serious economic problems in the 1970s had long-term significance for Europeans. These economic problems intertwined with a series of global issues that affected every country in the postcolonial world, and the social consequences for industrialized countries were profound. Economic

MAP 36.5 **The New States in Africa and Asia** India led the way to political independence as European empires passed away.

troubles also brought their share of political challenges. Anxious observers, recalling the disastrous political consequences of the Great Depression, worried that the Common Market and steps toward European unity would be destroyed by economic nationalism.

Yet the Common Market did not disintegrate in the face of severe economic dislocation. Indeed, it continued to exert a powerful attraction on nonmembers. In 1973, Denmark and Iceland, in addition to Britain, finally joined; Greece, Portugal, and Spain applied for membership in 1977. The negotiations were long and difficult, especially for Spain. Spain was a big low-cost producer of wine, olive oil, and fresh fruit, which French and Italian farmers feared would now come flooding into Common Market countries and drive them out of business. In the end, subsidies to injured farmers and special transition rules for agricultural products achieved a characteristic Common Market compromise. Greece joined in 1981, and Portugal and Spain in 1986.

Although a United States of Europe remained far in the future, the nations of the Common Market also cooperated more closely after De Gaulle's death in many international undertakings and negotiations. The Common Market decided in 1977, for example, to go ahead with plans for a nuclear breeder reactor to produce electric power, and it tried to develop a common policy on peace in the Middle East, terrorism, and economic negotiations with Third World countries. The movement toward European unity stayed alive.

Democracy also remained strong in Europe, unlike much of the world in the early 1970s, and it even expanded its sway. Both Spain and Portugal scrapped their aging dictatorships in 1974 and committed themselves to building democratic governments, which were usually led by moderate socialists. Greece also turned from military to parliamentary rule. There was also an uneven trend toward a more liberal Western communism and toward Communist participation in west European governments. The large Communist parties of France, Italy, and Spain openly criticized the Soviet Union for its inattention to human rights, and all three claimed to be stalwart

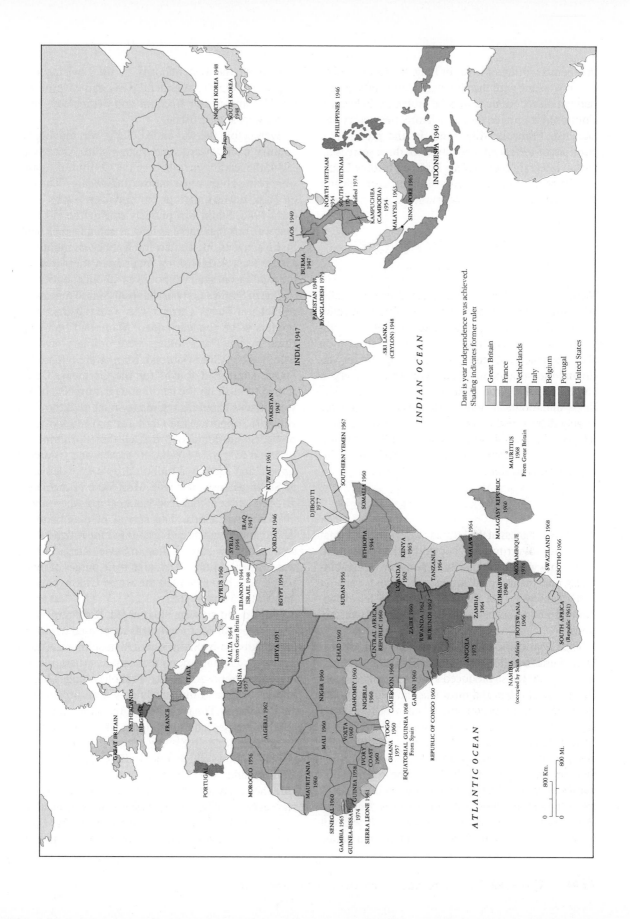

NORTH KOREA 1948
SOUTH KOREA 1948
From Japan

PHILIPPINES 1946

INDONESIA 1949

NORTH VIETNAM 1954
SOUTH VIETNAM 1954
Unified 1974
KAMPUCHEA (CAMBODIA) 1954
MALAYSIA 1963
SINGAPORE 1965

LAOS 1949

BURMA 1947

PAKISTAN 1947
BANGLADESH 1973

INDIA 1947

SRI LANKA (CEYLON) 1948

PAKISTAN 1947

INDIAN OCEAN

Date is year independence was achieved.
Shading indicates former ruler

Great Britain
France
Netherlands
Italy
Belgium
Portugal
United States

SOUTHERN YEMEN 1967

KUWAIT 1961

MAURITIUS 1968
From Great Britain

DJIBOUTI 1977

SOMALIA 1960

MALAGASY REPUBLIC 1960

IRAQ 1947

SYRIA 1944

JORDAN 1946

ETHIOPIA 1944

KENYA 1963

MALAWI 1964

MOZAMBIQUE 1974

SWAZILAND 1968

LESOTHO 1966

CYPRUS 1960
LEBANON 1944
ISRAEL 1948

EGYPT 1954

SUDAN 1956

UGANDA 1962
TANZANIA 1964

ZAMBIA 1964
ZIMBABWE 1980

MALTA 1964
From Great Britain

LIBYA 1951

CHAD 1960

CENTRAL AFRICAN REPUBLIC 1960

ZAIRE 1960
RWANDA 1962
BURUNDI 1962

ANGOLA 1975

BOTSWANA 1966

SOUTH AFRICA (Republic 1961)

TUNISIA 1957

NIGER 1960

DAHOMEY 1960

CAMEROON 1960

GABON 1960

NAMIBIA (occupied by South Africa)

ITALY

ALGERIA 1962

MALI 1960

VOLTA 1960

NIGERIA 1960

TOGO 1960

EQUATORIAL GUINEA 1968
From Spain

REPUBLIC OF CONGO 1960

GREAT BRITAIN
NETHERLANDS
BELGIUM
FRANCE

MOROCCO 1956

MAURITANIA 1960

IVORY COAST 1960

GHANA 1957

PORTUGAL

SENEGAL 1960
GAMBIA 1965
GUINEA-BISSAU 1974
GUINEA 1958
SIERRA LEONE 1961

ATLANTIC OCEAN

0   800 Km.
0   800 Mi.

democrats worthy of trust. In Italy, the Communists began working with the Christian Democrats in parliament on economic and social problems. In France, Communists entered the cabinet after the victory of a Socialist, François Mitterrand, in the presidential elections of 1981, and they stayed for three years. The partial integration of western Europe's leading Communist parties into the political mainstream clearly strengthened democratic government.

SOVIET EASTERN EUROPE

While western Europe surged ahead economically, regaining political independence as American influence gradually waned, eastern Europe followed a different path. Soviet Russia first tightened its grip on the "liberated" nations of eastern Europe under Stalin and then refused to let go. Economic recovery in eastern Europe proceeded, therefore, along Soviet lines, and political and social developments were largely determined by changes in the Soviet Union. Thus one must look primarily at Soviet Russia to understand the achievements and failures of eastern European peoples after the Second World War.

STALIN'S LAST YEARS

The unwillingness of the United States to accept what Stalin did to territories occupied by the triumphant Red Army was at least partly responsible for the outbreak and institutionalization of the cold war. Yet Americans were not the only ones who felt disappointed and even betrayed by Stalin's postwar actions.

The Great Patriotic War of the Fatherland had fostered Russian nationalism and a relaxation of totalitarian terror. It also produced a rare but real unity between Soviet rulers and most Russian people. When an American correspondent asked a distinguished sixty-year-old Jewish scientist, who had decided to leave Russia for Israel in 1972, what had been the best period in Russian history, he received a startling answer: the Second World War. The scientist explained: "At that time we all felt closer to our government than at any other time in our lives. It was not *their* country then, but *our* country. . . . It was not *their* war, but *our* war"[5] Having made such a heroic

war effort, the vast majority of the Soviet people hoped in 1945 that a grateful party and government would grant greater freedom and democracy. Such hopes were soon crushed.

Even before the war ended, Stalin was moving his country back toward rigid dictatorship. As early as 1944, the leading members of the Communist party were being given a new motivating slogan: "The war on Fascism ends, the war on capitalism begins."[6] By early 1946, Stalin was publicly singing the old tune that war was inevitable as long as capitalism existed. Stalin's invention of a new foreign foe was mainly an excuse for re-establishing totalitarian measures, for the totalitarian state cannot live without enemies.

One of Stalin's first postwar goals was to repress the millions of Soviet citizens who were outside Soviet borders when the war ended. Many had been captured by the Nazis; others were ordinary civilians who had been living abroad. Many were opposed to Stalin; some had fought for the Germans. Determined to hush up the fact that large numbers of Soviet citizens hated his regime so much that they had willingly supported the Germans and refused to go home, Stalin demanded that all these "traitors" be returned to him. At Yalta, Roosevelt and Churchill agreed, and roughly 2 million people were delivered to Stalin against their will. Most were immediately arrested and sent to forced-labor camps, where about 50 percent perished. The revival of many forced-labor camps, which had accounted for roughly one-sixth of all new construction in Soviet Russia before, was further stimulated by large-scale purges of many people who had never left the Soviet Union, particularly in 1945 and 1946.

Culture and art were also purged. Rigid anti-Western ideological conformity was reimposed in violent campaigns led by Stalin's trusted henchman, Andrei Zhdanov. Zhdanov denounced many artists, including the composers Sergei Prokofiev and Dimitri Shostakovich and the outstanding film director Sergei Eisenstein. The great poet Anna Akhmatova was condemned as "a harlot and nun who mixes harlotry and prayer" and, like many others, driven out of the writers' union, which practically ensured that her work would not be published. In 1949 Stalin launched a savage verbal attack on Soviet Jews, who were accused of being pro-Western and antisocialist.

In the political realm, Stalin reasserted the Communist party's complete control of the government and his absolute mastery of the party. Five-year plans were reintroduced to cope with the enormous task of economic reconstruction. Once again, heavy and military industry were given top priority, and consumer goods, housing, and still-collectivized agriculture were neglected. Everyday life was very hard: in 1952 the wages of ordinary people still bought 25 to 40 percent *less* than in 1928. In short, it was the 1930s all over again in Soviet Russia, although police terror was less intense.

Stalin's prime postwar innovation was to export the Stalinist system to the countries of eastern Europe. The Communist parties of eastern Europe had established one-party states by 1948, thanks to the help of the Red Army and the Russian secret police. Rigid ideological indoctrination, attacks on religion, and a lack of civil liberties were soon facts of life. Industry was nationalized, and the middle class was stripped of its possessions. Economic life was then faithfully recast in the Stalinist mold. Forced industrialization, with five-year plans and a stress on heavy industry, lurched forward without regard for human costs. For the sake of ideological uniformity, agriculture had to be collectivized; this process went much faster in Bulgaria and Czechoslovakia than in Hungary and Poland.

Only Josip Tito (1892–1980), the popular resistance leader and Communist chief of Yugoslavia, was able to resist Russian domination successfully. Tito openly broke with Stalin in 1948, and since there was no Russian army in Yugoslavia, he got away with it. Tito's successful proclamation of Communist independence led the infuriated and humiliated Stalin to purge the Communist parties of eastern Europe. Popular Communist leaders who, like Tito, had led the resistance against Germany, were made to star in reruns of the great show trials of the 1930s. Thus did history repeat itself as Stalin sought to create absolutely obedient instruments of domination in eastern Europe.

REFORM AND DE-STALINIZATION

In 1953 the aging Stalin finally died, and a new era slowly began in Soviet eastern Europe. Even as they struggled for power, Stalin's heirs realized that change and reform were necessary. There was, first of all, widespread fear and hatred of Stalin's political terrorism, which had struck both high and low with its endless purges and unjust arrests. Even Stalin's secret-police chief, Lavrenti Beria, publicly favored a relaxation of controls in an unsuccessful attempt to seize power. Beria was arrested and shot, after which the power of the secret police was curbed and many of its infamous forced-labor camps were gradually closed. Change was also necessary for economic reasons. Agriculture was in bad shape, and shortages of consumer goods were discouraging hard work and initiative. Finally, Stalin's aggressive foreign policy had led directly to an ongoing American commitment to western Europe and a strong Western alliance. Soviet Russia was isolated and contained.

On the question of just how much change should be permitted, the Communist leadership was badly split. The conservatives, led by Stalin's long-time foreign minister, the stone-faced Vyacheslav Molotov, wanted to make as few changes as possible. The reformers, led by Nikita Khrushchev, argued for major innovations. Khrushchev (1894–1971), who had joined the party as an uneducated coal miner in 1918 at twenty-four and had risen steadily to a high-level position in the 1930s, was emerging as the new ruler by 1955.

To strengthen his position and that of his fellow reformers within the party, Khrushchev launched an all-out attack on Stalin and his crimes at a closed session of the Twentieth Party Congress in 1956. In gory detail he described to the startled Communist delegates how Stalin had tortured and murdered thousands of loyal Communists, how he had trusted Hitler completely and bungled the country's defense, and how he had "supported the glorification of his own person with all conceivable methods." For hours Soviet Russia's top leader delivered an attack whose content would previously have been dismissed as "anti-Communist hysteria" in many circles throughout the Western world.

Khrushchev's "secret speech" was read to Communist party meetings throughout the country and strengthened the reform movement. The liberalization—or "de-Stalinization," as it was called in the West—of Soviet Russia was genuine. The Communist party jealously maintained its monopoly on political power, but Khrushchev shook it up and brought in new blood. The economy was made more responsive to the needs of the people, as some resources were shifted from heavy industry and the

Lenin Avenue, Volgograd Devastated Stalingrad was completely rebuilt and then renamed Volgograd as part of Khrushchev's de-Stalinization campaign. Seen here are the massive apartment blocks, the gigantic boulevard, and the stress on public transportation as opposed to private automobiles, which are all quite characteristic of Soviet urban style. *(Sovfoto/Eastfoto)*

military toward consumer goods and agriculture. Stalinist controls over workers were relaxed. Russia's very low standard of living finally began to improve and continued to rise throughout the 1960s. By 1970 Soviet citizens were able to buy twice as much food, three times as much clothing, and twelve times as many appliances as in 1950.

De-Stalinization created great ferment among writers and intellectuals, who hungered for cultural freedom. The poet Boris Pasternak (1890–1960), who survived the Stalinist years by turning his talents to translating Shakespeare, finished his great novel *Doctor Zhivago* in 1956. Published in the West but not in Russia, *Doctor Zhivago* is both a literary masterpiece and a powerful challenge to communism. It tells the story of a prerevolutionary intellectual who rejects the violence and brutality of the revolution of 1917 and the Stalinist years. Even as he is destroyed, he triumphs because of his humanity and Christian spirit. Pasternak was forced by Khrushchev himself to refuse the Nobel Prize in 1958—but he was not shot. Other talented writers followed Pasternak's lead, and courageous editors let the sparks fly.

The writer Alexander Solzhenitsyn (b. 1918) created a sensation when his *One Day in the Life of Ivan Denisovich* was published in Russia in 1962. Solzhenitsyn's novel portrays in grim detail life in a Stalinist concentration camp—a life to which Solzhenitsyn himself had been unjustly condemned—and is a damning indictment of the Stalinist past.

Khrushchev also de-Stalinized Soviet foreign policy. "Peaceful coexistence" with capitalism was possible, he argued, and great wars were not inevitable. Khrushchev made positive concessions, meeting with U.S. President Dwight Eisenhower at the first summit meeting since Potsdam and agreeing in 1955 to real independence for a neutral Austria after ten long years of Allied occupation. Thus there was considerable relaxation of cold war tensions between 1955 and 1957. At the same time, Khrushchev began wooing the new nations of Asia and Africa—even if they were not Communist—with promises and aid.

De-Stalinization stimulated rebelliousness in the eastern European satellites. Having suffered in silence under Stalin, Communist reformers and the masses were quickly emboldened to seek much greater liberty and national independence. Poland took the lead in March 1956: riots there resulted in the release of more than nine thousand political prisoners, including the previously purged Wladyslaw Gomulka. Taking charge of the government, Gomulka skillfully managed to win greater autonomy for Poland while calming anti-Russian feeling.

Hungary experienced a real and very tragic revolution. Led by students and workers—the classic urban revolutionaries—the people of Budapest installed a liberal Communist reformer as their new chief in October 1956. Soviet troops were forced to leave the country. One-party rule was abolished, and the new government promised free elections, freedom of expression, and massive social changes. Worst of all from the Russian point of view, the new government declared Hungarian neutrality and renounced Hungary's military alliance with Moscow. As in 1849, the Russian answer was to invade Hungary with a large army and to crush, once again, a national, democratic revolution.

Fighting was bitter until the end, for the Hungarians hoped that the Unied States would fulfill its earlier propaganda promises and come to their aid. When this did not occur because of American unwillingness to risk a general war, the people of eastern Europe realized that their only hope was to strive for small domestic gains while following Russia obediently in foreign affairs. This cautious approach produced some results. In Poland, for example, the peasants were not collectivized, and Catholics were allowed to practice their faith. Thus eastern Europe profited, however modestly, from Khrushchev's policy of de-Stalinization and could hope for still greater freedom in the future.

FROM BREZHNEV TO GORBACHEV

By late 1962, Khrushchev had created strong opposition to his policies in party circles and within two years he had fallen in a bloodless palace revolution. Under Leonid Brezhnev (1906–1982), Soviet Russia began a period of limited "re-Stalinization." The basic reason for this development was that Khrushchev's Communist colleagues saw de-Stalinization as a dangerous, two-sided threat. How could Khrushchev denounce the dead dictator without eventually denouncing and perhaps even arresting his still-powerful henchmen? In a heated secret debate in 1957, when the conservatives had tried without success to depose the menacing reformer, Khrushchev had pointed at two of Stalin's most devoted followers, Molotov and Kaganovich, and exclaimed: "Your hands are stained with the blood of our party leaders and of innumerable innocent Bolsheviks!" "So are yours!" Molotov and Kaganovich shouted back at him. "Yes, so are mine," Khrushchev replied. "I admit this. But during the purges I was merely carrying out your order. . . . I was not responsible. You were."[7] Moreover, the widening campaign of de-Stalinization posed a clear threat to the dictatorial authority of the party. It was producing growing, perhaps uncontrollable, criticism of the whole Communist system. The party had to tighten up while there was still time. It was clear that Khrushchev had to go.

Another reason for conservative opposition was Khrushchev's foreign policy. Although he scored some diplomatic victories, notably with Egypt and India, Khrushchev's policy toward the West was highly erratic and ultimately unsuccessful. In 1958 he order the Western allies to evacuate West Berlin within six months, which led only to a reaffirmation of allied unity and to Khrushchev's backing down. Then in 1961, as relations with Communist China deteriorated dramatically, Khrushchev ordered the East Germans to build a wall between East and West Berlin, thereby sealing off West Berlin in clear violation of existing access agreements between the Great Powers. The recently elected U.S. president, John F. Kennedy, acquiesced. Emboldened and seeing a chance to change the balance of military power decisively, Khrushchev ordered missiles with nuclear warheads installed in Fidel Castro's Communist Cuba in 1962. President Kennedy countered with a naval blockade of Cuba, and after a tense diplomatic crisis, Khrushchev was forced to remove the Russian missiles in return for American pledges not to disturb Castro's regime. Khrushchev looked like a bumbling buffoon; his influence, already slipping, declined rapidly after the Cuban fiasco.

After Brezhnev and his supporters took over in 1964, they started talking cautiously of Stalin's "good points" and ignoring his crimes. Their praise of the whole Stalinist era, with its rapid industrialization and wartime victories, informed Soviet citizens that no fundamental break with the past had occurred at home. Russian leaders also launched a massive arms buildup, determined never to suffer Khrushchev's humiliation in the face of American nuclear superiority. And they began building the large navy and air force necessary for intervention in faraway places, like Cuba, around the globe. Yet Brezhnev and company proceeded cautiously in the mid-1960s.

In the wake of Khrushchev's reforms, the 1960s brought modest liberalization and more consumer goods to eastern Europe, as well as somewhat greater national autonomy, especially in Poland and Rumania. In January 1968, the reform elements in the Czechoslovak Communist party gained a majority and voted out the long-time Stalinist leader in favor of Alexander Dubček (b. 1921). The new government launched a series of major economic and political reforms that fascinated observers around the world.

Educated in Moscow, Dubček was a dedicated Communist. But he and his allies believed that they could reconcile genuine socialism with personal freedom and internal party democracy. Thus local decision making by trade unions, managers, and consumers replaced rigid bureaucratic planning. Censorship was relaxed, and the reform program proved enormously popular.

Although Dubček remembered the lesson of the Hungarian revolution and constantly proclaimed his loyalty to the Warsaw Pact of Communist states, the determination of the Czech reformers to build "socialism with a human face" frightened hard-line Communists. These fears were particularly strong in Poland and East Germany, where the leaders knew full well that they lacked popular support. Moreover, the Soviet Union feared that a liberalized Czechoslovakia would eventually be drawn to neutralism or even to the democratic West. Thus the East bloc countries launched a concerted campaign of intimidation against the Czech leaders, and in August 1968, 500,000 Russian and allied eastern European troops suddenly occupied Czechoslovakia. The Czechs made no attempt to resist militarily, and the arrested Czech leaders were flown to Moscow, where they surrendered to Soviet demands. Gradually but inexorably, the reform program was abandoned and its supporters removed from office. Thus the Czechoslovak experiment in humanizing communism and making it serve the needs of ordinary citizens failed.

Shortly after the Czechoslovak invasion, Brezhnev declared the so-called Brezhnev Doctrine, according to which Soviet Russia and its allies had the right to intervene in any socialist country whenever they saw the need. The occupation of Czechoslovakia and the ensuing Brezhnev Doctrine raised a storm of protest, but it did not seriously alter ongoing Western efforts to secure better relations with the East bloc countries. The reason was simple. The West considered Czechoslovakia to be part of Russia's sphere of influence, for better or worse. Thus Stalin's empire remained solidly in place, and it seemed that change in eastern Europe could only continue to follow developments in the Soviet Union for years to come.

The 1968 invasion of Czechoslovakia was the crucial event of the Brezhnev era, which really lasted beyond the aging leader's death in 1982, until the emergence in 1985 of Mikhail Gorbachev. The invasion demonstrated unmistakably the intense conservatism of Russia's ruling elite and its determination to maintain the status quo in the Soviet bloc. Thus intervention in Czechoslovakia also brought further re-Stalinization of Soviet Russia, though with collective rather than personal dictatorship and without uncontrolled terror. This compromise seemed to suit the leaders and most of the people. Whether Westerners liked it or not, Soviet Russia appeared quite stable in the 1970s and early 1980s.

A gradually rising standard of living for ordinary people contributed greatly to stability. By 1974 two-thirds of the nation's families had television sets, almost 60 percent had sewing and washing machines, and about half had some kind of refrigerator. The economic crisis of the 1970s markedly slowed the rate of improvement, but long-suffering Soviet consumers compared the present with the recent past and not with conditions abroad. The enduring differences between the life of the elite and the life of ordinary people also reinforced the system. Ambitious individuals still had tremendous incentive to do as the state wished, in order to gain access to special, well-stocked stores, attend special schools, and travel abroad.

Another source of stability was that ordinary Russians remained more intensely nationalistic than almost any other people in the world. The party leaders successfully identified themselves with this patriotism, stressing their role in saving the motherland during the Second World War and protecting it now from foreign foes, including eastern European "counter-revolutionaries." Ordinary Russians took enormous pride in their country's military power, and young men accepted an inescapable three-year hitch in the army without question.

The End of Reform In August 1968 Soviet tanks rumbled into Prague to extinguish Czechoslovakian efforts to build a humane socialism. Here people watch the massive invasion from the sidewalks, knowing full well the suicidal danger of armed resistance. *(PP/Magnum)*

The weight of history also contributed to the preservation of the status quo. For centuries, the tsars were uncompromising absolutists, who taught their subjects that undivided and hence unquestioned authority was essential for the good of the state. Moreover, the politically dominant Great Russians constitute only half of the total Soviet population. As their action in Czechoslovakia showed, the Great Russian leaders feared that greater freedom and open political competition might result in demands for autonomy and even independence, not only by eastern European nationalities, but by non-Russian nationalities within the Soviet Union itself. Thus Western-style liberalism and democracy appeared as alien and divisive political philosophies that would undermine Russia's power and achievements.

The strength of the government was expressed in the re-Stalinization of culture and art. Free expression and open protest disappeared. The slightest acts of open nonconformity and protest were severely punished, but with sophisticated, cunning methods. Most frequently, dissidents were blacklisted and thus rendered unable to find a decent job, since the government was the only employer. This fate was enough to keep most in line. More determined but unrenowned protesters were quietly imprisoned in jails or mental institutions. Celebrated nonconformists such as Solzhenitsyn were permanently expelled from the country. Thus the worst aspects of Stalin's totalitarianism were eliminated, but a self-perpetuating Communist elite maintained its monopoly of power.

Superpower Summit, 1985 At their Geneva meeting U.S. President Reagan and Soviet leader Gorbachev vigorously debated arms control and the many issues that separated their governments. Smiling frequently for the press and locked in an intense campaign for public support, especially in western Europe, they agreed only to meet again. *(Wide World Photos)*

That elite seemed secure through the early 1980s. The long-established system of administrative controls continued to stretch downward from the central ministries and state committees to provincial cities, and from there to factories, neighborhoods, and villages. At each level of this massive state bureaucracy, the overlapping hierarchy of the Communist party, with its 17.5 million members, continued to watch over all decisions and manipulate every aspect of national life. Organized opposition was simply impossible, and the average Soviet citizen left politics to the bosses.

Yet the massive state and party bureaucracy was a mixed blessing. It discouraged economic efficiency and personal initiative as well as political dissent and intellectual innovation. It safeguarded the elite, but it also promoted apathy in the masses. Therefore, when the ailing Brezhnev finally died in 1982, his immedi-

ate successor, Yuri Andropov, tried to invigorate the system. Relatively little came of these efforts, but they set the stage for the emergence in March 1985 of Mikhail Gorbachev, the most vigorous Soviet leader in a generation.

The fifty-four-year-old Gorbachev was smart, charming, and tough. As long-time Soviet foreign minister Andrei Gromyko reportedly said, "This man has a nice smile, but he has got iron teeth."[8] Gorbachev attacked corruption and incompetence in the upper reaches of the bureaucracy and launched a strong campaign against alcoholism and drunkenness, which were also deadly scourges of Soviet society. He seemed determined to use tough measures to make both the elite and the masses "shape up," so that the economy would perform better while the Communist party as a whole maintained firm control. The outcome of all these initiatives was uncertain in early 1987, but Mikhail Gorbachev seemed firmly in command and a leader to be reckoned with.

THE WESTERN HEMISPHERE

One way to think of what historians used to call the New World is as a vigorous offshoot of Western civilization, an offshoot that has gradually developed its own characteristics while retaining European roots. From this perspective, one can see many illuminating parallels and divergences in the histories of Europe and the Americas. So it was after the Second World War. The western hemisphere experienced a many-faceted postwar recovery, somewhat similar to that of Europe, though it began earlier, especially in Latin America.

POSTWAR PROSPERITY IN THE UNITED STATES

The Second World War cured the depression in the United States and brought about the greatest boom in American history. Unemployment practically vanished and personal income doubled as the well-being of Americans increased dramatically. Despite fears that peace would bring renewed depression, conversion to a peacetime economy went smoothly. The U.S. economy then proceeded to advance fairly steadily for a long generation.

Prosperity helps explain why postwar domestic politics consisted largely of modest adjustments to the status quo until the 1960s. Truman's upset victory in 1948 demonstrated that Americans had no interest in undoing Roosevelt's social and economic reforms. The Congress proceeded to increase social security benefits, subsidize middle- and lower-class housing, and raise the minimum wage. These and other liberal measures consolidated the New Deal. In 1952 the Republican party and the voters turned to General Eisenhower, a national hero and self-described moderate.

The federal government's only major new undertaking during the "Eisenhower years" was the interstate highway system, a suitable symbol of the basic satisfaction of the vast majority. Some Americans feared that the United States was becoming a "blocked society," obsessed with stability and incapable of wholesome change. This feeling contributed

in 1960 to the election of the young, attractive John F. Kennedy, who promised to "get the country moving again." President Kennedy captured the popular imagination, revitalized the old Roosevelt coalition, and modestly expanded existing liberal legislation before he was struck down by an assassin's bullet in 1963.

THE CIVIL RIGHTS REVOLUTION

Belatedly and reluctantly, complacent postwar America experienced a genuine social revolution: after a long struggle, blacks (and their white supporters) threw off a deeply entrenched system of segregation, discrimination, and repression. This movement of civil rights advanced on several fronts. Eloquent lawyers from the National Association for the Advancement of Colored People (NAACP) challenged school segregation in the courts and in 1954 won a landmark decision in the Supreme Court that "separate educational facilities are inherently unequal." Blacks effectively challenged institutionalized inequality with bus boycotts, sit-ins, and demonstrations. As Martin Luther King Jr. told the white power structure, "We will not hate you, but we will not obey your evil laws."[9]

Blacks also used their growing political power in key northern states to gain the support of the liberal wing of the Democratic party. All these efforts culminated after the liberal landslide that elected Lyndon Johnson in 1964. The Civil Rights Act of 1964 categorically prohibited discrimination in public services and on the job. In the follow-up Voting Rights Act of 1965, the federal government firmly guaranteed all blacks the right to vote. By the 1970s, substantial numbers of blacks had been elected to public and private office throughout the southern states, proof positive that dramatic changes had occurred in American race relations.

Blacks enthusiastically supported the accompanying surge of new social legislation in the mid-1960s. President Johnson solemnly declared "unconditional war on poverty." Congress and the administration created a host of antipoverty projects, such as the domestic peace corps, free preschools for slum children, and community-action programs. Although these programs were directed to all poor Americans —the majority of whom are white—they were also intended to extend greater equality for blacks to the

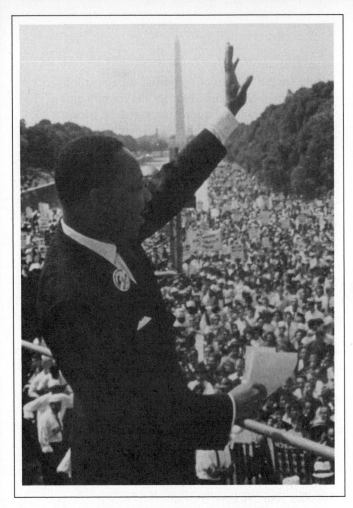

The March on Washington in August 1963 marked a dramatic climax in the civil rights struggle. More than 200,000 people gathered at the Lincoln Memorial to hear the young Martin Luther King deliver his greatest address, his "I have a dream" speech. *(UPI/Bettmann Newsphotos)*

realm of economics. More generally, the United States promoted in the mid-1960s the kind of fundamental social reform that western Europe had embraced immediately after World War Two. The United States became more of a welfare state, as government spending for social benefits rose dramatically and approached European levels.

THE VIETNAM TRAUMA AND BEYOND

President Johnson wanted to go down in history as a master reformer and a healer of old wounds. Instead he opened new ones with the Vietnam War.

American involvement in Vietnam had its origins in the cold war and the ideology of containment (page 1134). From the late 1940s on, most Americans and their leaders viewed the world in terms of a constant struggle to stop the spread of communism, although they were not prepared to try to roll back communism where it already existed. As Europe began to revive and China established a Communist government in 1949, efforts to contain communism shifted to Asia. The bloody Korean War (1950–1953) ended in stalemate, but the United States did succeed in preventing a Communist government in South Korea. After the defeat of the French in Indochina in 1954, the Eisenhower administration refused to sign the Geneva accords that temporarily divided the country into two zones pending national unification by means of free elections. President Eisenhower then proceeded to acquiesce in the refusal of the anti-Communist South Vietnamese government to accept the verdict of elections and provided it with military aid. President Kennedy greatly increased the number of American "military advisers" to 16,000 and had the existing South Vietnamese leader deposed in 1963 when he refused to follow American directives.

After successfully portraying his opponent, Barry Goldwater, as a trigger-happy extremist in a nuclear age and resoundingly winning the 1964 election on a peace platform, President Johnson proceeded to expand the American role in the Vietnam conflict. As Johnson explained to his ambassador in Saigon, "I am not going to lose Vietnam. I am not going to be the President who saw Southeast Asia go the way China went."[10] American strategy was to "escalate" the war sufficiently to break the will of the North Vietnamese and their southern allies, without resorting to "overkill' that might risk war with the entire Communist bloc. Thus the South received massive military aid, American forces in South Vietnam gradually grew to a half-million men, and the United States bombed North Vietnam with ever-greater intensity. But there was no invasion of the North, nor were essential seaborne military supplies from the Soviet Union ever disrupted. In the end, the strategy of limited war backfired. It was the Americans themselves who grew weary and the American leadership that cracked.

The undeclared war in Vietnam, fought nightly on American television, eventually divided the nation. Initial support was strong, but by 1967 a growing number of critics denounced the war as an immoral and unsuccessful intrusion into a complex and dis-

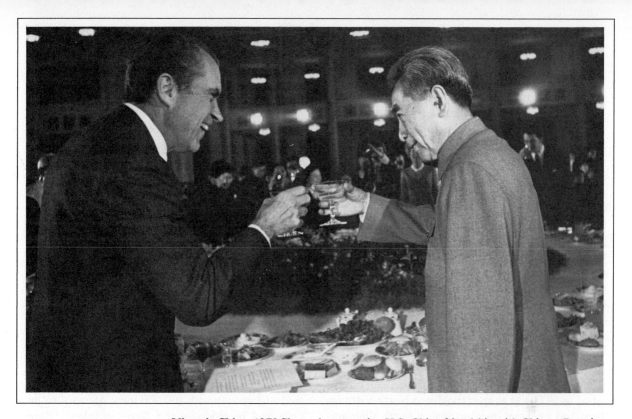

Nixon in China, 1972 Shown here toasting U.S.-China friendship with Chinese Premier Chou En-lai in Peking in February 1972, President Nixon took advantage of Chinese fears of the Soviet Union to establish good relations with Asia's Communist giant. Arriving after twenty-five years of mutual hostility, reconciliation with China was Nixon's finest achievement. *(UPI/Bettmann Newsphotos)*

tant civil war. There were major protests, often led by college students. Criticism reached a crescendo after the Vietcong "Tet Offensive" in January 1968. This, the Communists' first major attack with conventional weapons on major cities, failed militarily. But the attack did show that, despite the massive influx of American hardware and personnel, the Communist forces in South Vietnam were no closer to being eradicated than in 1965. U.S. critics of the Vietnam War interpreted the bloody battle as a decisive American defeat, clear proof that a Vietcong victory was inevitable. America's leaders now lost all heart. After an ambiguous defeat in the New Hampshire primary, President Johnson called for negotiations with North Vietnam and announced that he would not stand for re-election.

Elected by a razor-slim margin in 1968, President Richard Nixon sought to gradually disengage America from Vietnam and the accompanying national crisis. He restated the long-standing American objective of containment in Vietnam, of aiding the "South

Vietnamese people to determine their own political future without outside interference."[11] Using American military power more effectively, while simultaneously pursuing peace talks with the North Vietnamese, Nixon cut American forces in Vietnam from 550,000 to 24,000 in four years. The cost of the war dropped from $25 billion a year under Johnson to $3 billion under Nixon. Moreover, President Nixon launched a daring flank attack in diplomacy. He journeyed to China in 1971 and reached a spectacular if limited reconciliation with Communist China, which took advantage of China's growing fears of the Soviet Union and undermined North Vietnam's position. In January 1973, fortified by the overwhelming endorsement of the people in his 1972 electoral triumph, President Nixon and Secretary of State Henry Kissinger finally reached a peace agreement with North Vietnam. The agreement allowed remaining American forces to complete their withdrawal, while the United States reserved the right to resume bombing if the accords were broken. South

Vietnamese forces seemed to hold their own, and the storm of crisis in the United States seemed past.

Instead, the country reaped the Watergate whirlwind. Like some other recent American presidents, Nixon authorized spying activities that went beyond the law. Going further than his predecessors, Nixon authorized special units to use various illegal means to stop the leaking of government secrets to the press. One such group broke into the Democratic party headquarters in Washington's Watergate complex in June 1972 and was promptly arrested. Eventually, the media and the machinery of congressional investigation turned the break-in and later efforts to hush up the bungled job into a great moral issue. In 1974 a beleaguered Nixon was forced to resign in disgrace.

The consequences of renewed political crisis during the Watergate affair were profound. First, it resulted in a major shift of power away from the presidency toward Congress, especially in foreign affairs. Therefore, as American aid to South Vietnam diminished in 1973 and as an emboldened North Vietnam launched a general invasion against South Vietnamese armies in early 1974, first President Nixon and then President Gerald Ford stood by because Congress refused to permit any American response. After more than thirty-five years of battle, the Vietnamese Communists unified their country in 1975 as a totalitarian state—a second consequence of the U.S. crisis. Third, the belated fall of South Vietnam in the wake of Watergate shook America's postwar pride and confidence. Generally interpreted as a disastrous American military defeat, the Vietnam aftermath left the United States divided and uncertain about its proper role in world affairs. The long-dominant belief in containment was seriously damaged, but no alternative concept generated general support in the 1970s.

One possibility was the policy of *détente,* or progressive relaxation of cold war tensions. Nixon's phased withdrawal from Vietnam was part of détente, which reached its apogee when all European nations (except isolationist Albania), the United States, and Canada signed the Final Act of the Helsinki Conference in 1975. Thirty-five nations agreed that Europe's existing political frontiers could not be changed by force, and they solemnly accepted numerous provisions guaranteeing the human rights and political freedoms of their citizens. The Final Act was a compromise embodying Western concerns for human rights and Soviet preoccupations with military control of eastern Europe. Optimists saw a bright new day breaking in international relations.

These hopes gradually faded in the later 1970s. The Soviet Union and its allies ignored the human rights provisions of the Helsinki agreement. Moreover, East-West political competition remained very much alive outside Europe. Many Americans became convinced that the Soviet Union was taking advantage of détente, steadily building up its military might and pushing for political gains in Africa, Asia, and Latin America.

But it was in Afghanistan that Soviet action seemed most contrary to the spirit of détente. The Soviet Union had long been interested in its Islamic neighbor, and in April 1978, a pro-Soviet coup established a Marxist regime there. This new government soon made itself unpopular, and rebellion spread through the countryside. To preserve Communist rule, the Soviet Union in December 1979 suddenly airlifted crack troops to Kabul, the capital, and occupied Afghanistan with 100,000 men. Alarmed by the scale and precision of the Soviet invasion, many Americans feared that the oil-rich states of the Persian Gulf would be next, and they looked again to military might to contain Communist expansion.

The U.S. military buildup launched by Jimmy Carter in his last years in office was accelerated by President Ronald Reagan, who was swept into office in 1980 by the wave of patriotism following an agonizing hostage crisis in Iran. The new American leadership was convinced that the military balance had tipped in favor of the Soviet Union. Increasing defense spending rapidly, the Reagan administration concentrated especially on nuclear arms and an expanded navy as keys to a resurgence of American power. The Reagan administration also supported guerrilla forces seeking to topple pro-Marxist governments in Angola and Nicaragua. But to do so, the administration had to repeatedly promise Congress and the public that American troops would never be sent to "fight another Vietnam." The lessons of Vietnam contained the containment of communism in the 1980s.

ECONOMIC NATIONALISM IN LATIN AMERICA

Although the countries of Latin America share a Spanish-Portuguese heritage, their striking differences make it difficult to generalize meaningfully about modern Latin American history. Yet a growing economic nationalism seems unmistakable. As the early nineteenth century saw Spanish and Portuguese colonies win wars of political independence, recent history has been an ongoing quest for genuine economic independence through local control and industrialization.

To understand the rise of economic nationalism, one must remember that Latin American countries developed as producers of foodstuffs and raw materials, which were exported to Europe and the United States in return for manufactured goods and capital investment. This exchange brought considerable economic development, but there was a heavy price to pay. Neocolonialism (pages 972–974) settled on Latin America, which became very dependent on foreign markets, products, and investments. Industry did not develop and large landowners tied to the world market profited most from economic development, further enhancing their social and political power.

The old international division of labor was finally destroyed by the Great Depression. Prices and exports of Latin American commodities collapsed as Europe and the United States drastically reduced their purchases and raised tariffs to protect domestic procedures. With foreign sales plummeting, Latin American countries could not buy industrial goods abroad. Latin America suffered the full force of the global economic crisis.

The result in the larger, more important Latin American countries was a profound shift in the direction of economic nationalism after 1930. The more popularly based governments worked to reduce foreign influence and gain control of their own economies and natural resources. They energetically promoted national industry by means of high tariffs, government grants, and even state enterprise. They favored the lower middle and urban working classes with social benefits and higher wages in order to increase their purchasing power and gain their support. These efforts at recovery were fairly successful. By the late 1940s, the factories of Argentina, Brazil, and Chile could generally satisfy domestic consumer demand for the products of light industry. In the 1950s, some countries began moving into heavy industry. Economic nationalism and the rise of industry are particularly striking in the two largest and most influential countries, Mexico and Brazil, which together account for half the population of Latin America.

MEXICO. Overthrowing the elitist, upper-class rule of the tyrant Porfirio Díaz, the spasmodic, often-chaotic Mexican Revolution of 1910 culminated in 1917 in a new constitution. This radical nationalistic document called for universal suffrage, massive land reform, benefits for labor, and strict control of foreign capital. Actual progress was quite modest until 1934, when a charismatic young Indian from a poor family, Lázaro Cárdenas, became president and dramatically revived the languishing revolution. Under Cárdenas, many large estates were divided up among small farmers or returned undivided to Indian communities.

Meanwhile, state-supported Mexican businessmen built many small factories to meet domestic needs. The government also championed the cause of industrial workers. In 1938, when Mexican workers became locked in a bitter dispute with British and American oil companies, Cárdenas nationalized the petroleum industry—to the astonishment of a world unaccustomed to such actions. Finally, the 1930s saw the flowering of a distinctive Mexican culture, which proudly embraced its long-despised Indian past and gloried in the modern national revolution.

In 1940 the official, semiauthoritarian party that has governed Mexico continuously since the revolution selected the first of a series of more moderate presidents. These presidents used the full power of the state to promote industrialization through a judicious mixture of public, private, and even foreign enterprise. The Mexican economy grew rapidly, at about 6 percent per year from the early 1940s to the late 1960s, but the upper and middle classes reaped the lion's share of the benefits.

BRAZIL. After the fall of Brazil's monarchy in 1889 (page 970), politics was largely dominated by the coffee barons and by regional rivalries. These rivalries and deteriorating economic conditions allowed a military revolt led by Getulio Vargas, governor of one of Brazil's larger states, to seize control of the federal government in 1930. Vargas, who proved to be a consummate politician, fragmented the opposition and established a mild dictatorship that lasted until 1945. Vargas's rule was generally popular, combining as it did effective economic nationalism and moderate social reform.

Vargas decisively tipped the balance of political power away from the Brazilian states to the ever-expanding federal government, which became a truly

José Clemente Orozco (1883–1949) was one of the great and committed painters of the Mexican Revolution. Orozco believed that art should reflect the "new order of things" and inspire the common people—the workers and the peasants. This vibrant central mural in the National Palace in Mexico City, one of Orozco's many great wall paintings, depicts a brutal Spanish conquest and a liberating revolution. *(Reproduction authorized by The Instituto Nacional de Bellas Artes)*

national government for the first time. Vargas and his allies also set out to industrialize Brazil and gain economic independence. While the national coffee board used mountains of surplus coffee beans to fire railroad locomotives, the government supported Brazilian manufacturers with high tariffs, generous loans, and labor peace. This probusiness policy did not prevent new social legislation: workers received shorter hours, pensions, health and accident insurance, paid vacations, and other benefits. Finally, Vargas shrewdly upheld the nationalist cause in his relations with the giant to the north. Brazil was modernizing rapidly.

Modernization continued for the next fifteen years. The economy boomed. Presidential politics were re-established, while the military kept a watchful eye for extremism among the civilian politicians. Economic nationalism was especially vigorous under the flamboyant President Kubitschek (1956–1960). The government borrowed heavily from international bankers to promote industry and built the new capital of Brasília in the midst of a wilderness. Kubitschek's slogan was "Fifty Years' Progress in Five," and he meant it.

The Brazilian and Mexican formula of national economic development, varying degrees of electoral competition, and social reform was shared by some other Latin American countries, notably Argentina and Chile. By the late 1950s, optimism was widespread, if cautious. Economic and social progress seemed to promise less violent, more democratic politics. These expectations were shaken, however, by the Cuban Revolution.

THE CUBAN REVOLUTION

Although many aspects of the Cuban Revolution are obscured by controversy, certain background conditions are clear. First, after achieving independence in 1898, Cuba was for many years virtually an American protectorate. The Cuban constitution gave the United States the legal right to intervene in Cuban affairs, a right that was frequently exercised until Roosevelt renounced it in 1934. Second, and partly because the American army had often been the real power, Cuba's political institutions were weak and its politicians were extraordinarily corrupt. Under the strongman Fulgencio Batista, an opportunistic ex-sergeant who controlled the government almost continually from 1933 to 1958, graft and outright looting

were a way of life. Third, Cuba was one of Latin America's most prosperous and advanced countries by the 1950s, but its sugar-and-tourist economy was dependent on the United States. Finally, the enormous differences between rich and poor in Cuba were typical of Latin America. But Cuba also had a strong Communist party, which was highly unusual.

Fidel Castro, a magnetic leader with the gift of oratory, managed to unify anti-Batista elements in a revolutionary front. When Castro's guerrilla forces triumphed in late 1958, the new government's goals were unclear. Castro had promised a "real" revolution but had always laughed at charges that he was a Communist. As the regime consolidated its power in 1959 and 1960, it became increasingly clear that "real" meant "Communist" in Castro's mind. Wealthy Cubans, who owned three-quarters of the sugar industry and many profitable businesses, fled to Miami. Soon the middle class began to follow.

Meanwhile, relations with the Eisenhower administration deteriorated rapidly. Thus, in April 1961, newly elected President Kennedy went ahead with a pre-existing CIA plan to use Cuban exiles to topple Castro. But the Kennedy administration abandoned the exiles as soon as they were put ashore at the Bay of Pigs, and the exiles were quickly captured.

The Bay of Pigs invasion—a triumph for Castro and a humiliating fiasco for the United States—had significant consequences. It freed Castro to build his version of a communist society, and he did. Political life in Cuba featured "anti-imperialism," an alliance with the Soviet bloc, the dictatorship of the party, and a Castro cult. Revolutionary enthusiasm was genuine among party activists, much of Cuba's youth, and some of the masses some of the time. Prisons and emigration silenced opposition. The economy was characterized by state ownership, collective farms, and Soviet trade and aid. Early efforts to industrialize ran aground, and sugar production continued to dominate the economy. Socially, the regime pursued equality and the creation of a new socialist personality. In short, revolutionary totalitarianism came to the Americas.

The failure of the United States to derail Castro probably encouraged Khrushchev to start putting nuclear missiles in Cuba, leading directly to the most serious East-West crisis since the Korean War. The Soviets backed down (page 1147), but Castro's survival had major consequences for Latin America. Above all, it heightened both hopes and fears that similar revolutions could spread throughout the region. Leftists were emboldened to try guerrilla warfare and conservatives became more rigid and suspicious of calls for change. Social tensions and class conflicts, muffled by a generation of economic nationalism, reappeared on the horizon.

In the United States, fear of communism aroused heightened cold war-style interest in Latin America. Using the Organization of American States to isolate Cuba, the United States in 1961 pledged $10 billion in aid over ten years to a new hemispheric "Alliance for Progress." The Alliance was intended to promote long-term economic development and social reform, which American liberals typically assumed would immunize Latin America from the Cuban disease.

AUTHORITARIANISM AND DEMOCRACY IN LATIN AMERICA

U.S. aid contributed modestly to continued Latin American economic development in the 1960s, although population growth canceled out two-thirds of the increase on a per capita basis. Democratic social reforms—the other half of the Alliance for Progress formula—proceeded slowly, however. Instead, the era following the Cuban Revolution saw the rise of extremism and a new kind of conservative authoritarianism. By the late 1970s, only four Latin American countries—Costa Rica, Venezuela, Colombia, and Mexico—retained some measure of democratic government. Brazil, Argentina, and Chile represented the general trend.

Influential Brazil led the way. Intense political competition in the early 1960s prompted President João Goulart to swing to the left to gain fresh support. Castroism appeared to spread in the impoverished northeast, and mass meetings of leftists were answered by huge demonstrations of conservatives. Meanwhile Goulart called for radical change, proposing that the great landed estates be broken up and that Brazil's many illiterates receive the right to vote. When Goulart and his followers appeared ready to use force to implement their program, army leaders took over in 1964. The right-wing military government banned political parties and ruled by decree. Industrialization and urbanization proceeded rapidly under military rule, but the gap between rich and poor widened as well.

In Argentina, the military had intervened in 1955 to oust the dictatorial populist and economic nationalist Juan Perón, but it had restored elected government. Then, worried by a Peronist revival and heartened by the Brazilian example, the army took control in 1966 and again in 1976 after a brief civilian interlude. Each military takeover was followed by an escalation of repression, and culturally and economically advanced Argentina became a brutal military dictatorship.

If events in Argentina were discouraging, Chile was tragic. Chile has a population of predominantly European origin and a long tradition of democracy and moderate reform. Thus when Salvador Allende, a doctor and the Marxist head of a coalition of Communists, Socialists, and Radicals, won a plurality of 36 percent of the vote in fair elections in 1970, he was duly elected president by the Congress. Allende completed the nationalization of the American-owned copper companies—the great majority of Chileans had already embraced economic nationalism—and proceeded to socialize private industry, accelerate the breakup of landed estates, and radicalize the poor.

Marxism in action evoked a powerful backlash in Chile. The middle class fought back, and by 1973 Chile seemed headed for civil war. Then, with widespread conservative support and U.S. backing, the traditionally impartial army struck in a well-organized coup. Allende died, probably murdered, and thousands of his supporters were arrested, or worse. As in Argentina, the military imposed a harsh despotism.

The revival of antidemocratic authoritarianism in Latin America challenged not only the Marxist and socialist program but most liberal and moderate reform as well. Instructed by the Cuban experience, the upper and middle classes had no intention of playing dead: if dictatorship was necessary to protect privilege and property, so be it. Thus military governments, supported by Washington and U.S. big business, effectively defended private capital and halted or reversed radical change.

Yet some observers saw in the new military governments something more than the traditional weakness of Latin American democracy and cold war fears of communism. They noted that military takeovers grew out of intense crises that threatened national unity as well as the upper classes. In such circumstances, the politically conscious officer corps saw the military as the only institution capable of preventing chaos. Moreover, the new authoritarians were determined modernizers. Eager to catch up with the more

Facing the Crisis Heavily guarded, Chilean president Salvador Allende greets the crowd gathered on August 22, 1973 in front of the Presidential Palace. Within months he was dead, likely murdered by a member of the military *junta* that deposed him. *(Sygma)*

advanced countries, they were often deeply committed to nationalism, industrialization, technology, and some modest social progress. They even promised free elections sometime in the future.

That time came in the 1980s, when a democratic wave gained momentum throughout Latin America. In South America the three Andean nations—Peru, Bolivia, and Ecuador—led the way with the re-establishment of elected governments, which were all committed in varying degrees to genuine social reform. In Argentina, the military government gradually lost almost all popular support because of its "dirty war" against its own citizens, in which it imprisoned, tortured, and murdered thousands whom it arbitrarily accused of opposing the regime. In 1982, in a desperate gamble to rally the people around the nationalist flag, Argentina's military rulers sent nine thousand troops to seize the Falkland (or Malvinas)

Islands from Great Britain. But the British, led by the "iron lady," Prime Minister Margaret Thatcher, retook the islands in a brief war, routing Argentina's poorly led troops and forcing its humiliated generals to schedule national elections. Elected by an overwhelming majority in 1983, President Raúl Alfonsín prosecuted former military rulers for their crimes, reformed the currency, and appeared to lay solid foundations for liberty and political democracy.

In 1985, the Brazilian military also turned over power to an elected government, thereby completing a peaceful transition begun in the late 1970s. Relatively successful in its industrialization effort, Brazil's military had proved unable (or unwilling) to improve the social and economic position of the masses. After twenty-one years of rule, and with even Brazil's richest families calling for reforms to forestall social upheaval, the military leaders were ready to let civilian politicians have a try, at least temporarily. Only in Paraguay and Chile did harsh military dictatorship continue. As Latin America entered the second half of the 1980s with 94 percent of its population living under civilian and constitutional regimes, an optimist could hope that momentous political recovery was under way.

In Central America the situation was more ambiguous. In 1979, a broad coalition of liberals, socialists, and Marxist revolutionaries drove long-time dictator Anastasio Somoza from power in Nicaragua. The Somoza family had relied on solid U.S. support in its four-decade dictatorship, and the new Sandinista government viewed the United States as an oppressive imperialist power. The new leaders wanted genuine political and economic independence from the United States, as well as throughgoing land reform, some state ownership of industry, and friendly ties with Communist countries. These policies infuriated the Reagan administration, which claimed that Nicaragua was establishing a Communist dictatorship intent on spreading revolution throughout the region, most notably to neighboring El Salvador. For six years the Reagan administration tried everything short of sending American soldiers to overturn the Sandinista government, but without success. The cold war came to Central America.

The recovery of Europe and the Americas during and after World War Two is one of the most remarkable chapters in the long, uneven course of Western civilization. Although the dangerous tensions of the cold war frustrated fond hopes for a truly peaceful international order, the transition from imperialism to decolonization proceeded rapidly, surprisingly smoothly, and without serious damage to western Europe. Instead, genuine political democracy gained unprecedented strength in the West, and economic progress quickened the pace of ongoing social and cultural transformation. Thus the tremendous promise inherent in Western society's fateful embrace of the "dual revolution," which had begun in France and England in the late eighteenth century and which had momentarily halted during the agonies of the Great Depression and the horrors of Nazi totalitarianism, was largely if perhaps only temporarily realized in the shining achievements of the postwar era.

NOTES

1. Quoted in N. Graebner, *Cold War Diplomacy, 1945–1960* (Princeton, N.J.: Van Nostrand, 1962), p. 17.
2. Ibid.
3. Quoted in J. Hennessy, *Economic "Miracles"* (London: André Deutsch, 1964), p. 5.
4. P. Van Zeeland, in *European Integration,* ed. C. G. Haines (Baltimore: Johns Hopkins Press, 1957), p. xi.
5. Quoted in H. Smith, *The Russians* (New York: Quadrangle/New York Times, 1976), p. 303.
6. Quoted in D. Treadgold, *Twentieth Century Russia,* 5th ed. (Boston: Houghton Mifflin, 1981), p. 442.
7. Quoted in I. Deutscher, in *Soviet Society,* eds., A. Inkeles and K. Geiger (Boston: Houghton Mifflin, 1961), p. 41.
8. Quoted in *Time,* January 6, 1986, p. 66.
9. Quoted in S. E. Morison et al., *A Concise History of the American Republic* (New York: Oxford University Press, 1977), p. 697.
10. *Ibid.,* p. 735.
11. Richard Nixon, *Public Papers, 1969* (Washington, D.C.: U.S. Government Printing Office, 1971), p. 371.

SUGGESTED READING

G. Wright, *The Ordeal of Total War, 1939–1945* (1968), is the best comprehensive study of World War Two, while B. H. Liddell Hart, *The History of the Second World War* (1971), is a good overview of military developments. Three dramatic studies of special aspects of the war are A. Dallin, *German Rule in Russia, 1941–1945* (1957), which analyzes the effects of Nazi occupation policies on the Soviet population; L. Collins and D. La Pierre, *Is Paris Burning?* (1965), a best-selling account of the liberation of Paris and Hitler's plans to destroy the city; and J. Toland, *The Last 100 Days* (1966), a lively account of the end of the war. Great leaders and matchless stylists, Winston Churchill and Charles De Gaulle have both written histories of the war in the form of memoirs. Other interesting memoirs are those of Harry Truman (1958); Dwight Eisenhower, *Crusade in Europe* (1948); and Dean Acheson, *Present at the Creation* (1969), a beautifully written defense of American

ART: A MIRROR OF SOCIETIES

Art reveals the interests and values of societies and frequently gives intimate and unique glimpses of how people actually lived. In portraits and statues, whether of gods, ghanas, saints, samurai, maharanas, or merchants, it preserves the memory and fame of men and women who shaped societies. In paintings, drawings, and carvings it also shows how people worked, played, relaxed, suffered, and triumphed. Art, therefore, is extremely useful to the historian, especially for distant periods and remote cultures where written records are scarce or hard to understand.

Art also manifests the changes and continuity of societies; as values changed, so did major artistic themes. Latin American and African artists of the nineteenth and twentieth centuries emphasized nationalist themes in their work, turning against Western styles and techniques. The artifacts shown in Plate VI-3 are purposefully anachronistic in their intent to preserve the essence of African civilization. Similarly, in opposition to foreign control, a genuine folk culture, reflected in *Haitian Landscape* (overleaf), throve in rural pockets throughout South America.

The revolutions that established independent states in Latin America fostered a faith in progress and democracy that Europeans no longer shared. Artists of the twentieth century in Europe anticipated and then gave poignant expression to the anxieties and terrors that have plagued modern times. Some continued the impressionists' experimentation with abstract design, a process that found its ultimate expression in cubism. The cubist works of artists like Picasso reflect the distorted and multiple viewpoints of a society that lacked nineteenth-century certitudes. Others such as Gustave Klimt (also represented here) retreated from realistic depiction by conveying their ideas and emotions indirectly through symbols. Still other artists participated in the movement known as expressionism, which emphasized the subjective portrayal of inner experience. In *The Dance of Life,* below, Edvard Munch, a leading proponent of expressionism, tries to show the whole range of human emotions at once. Solitary figures struggling fitfully with terror and uncertainty—a favorite twentieth-century theme—dominate Munch's work. (Nasjonalgalleriet, Oslo.)

Haitian Landscape *(detail) (below)* Jean-Gilles (b. 1943). The folk art of Latin America has achieved wide popularity in recent times. The oil paintings of the young Haitian Joseph Jean-Gilles convey a special joy with their fresh, unaffected view of the world. In this outstanding example hundreds of multicolored trees dot the green landscape as farmers cultivate the fields below. *(Museum of Modern Art of Latin America, Washington)*

Multiple-Mask Headdress *(right, below)* This ornate, purposefully anachronistic headdress is the work of the great Nigerian carver, Ochai of Otobi (d. 1949). A committed nationalist, Ochai specialized in carvings that preserved Africa's rich heritage. *(Department of Antiquities, Lagos, Nigeria/Werner Forman Archive)*

Old Man with Medicine Horn *(right, above)* This sculpture from Kenya, composed of stone indigenous to the area, is another example of African artists' efforts to reclaim their precolonial past. Such a man as this, empowered by his medicine horn to heal, held a revered role in the tribal social order that preceded foreign domination. *(African Heritage Collection, Nairobi, Kenya/Werner Forman Archive)*

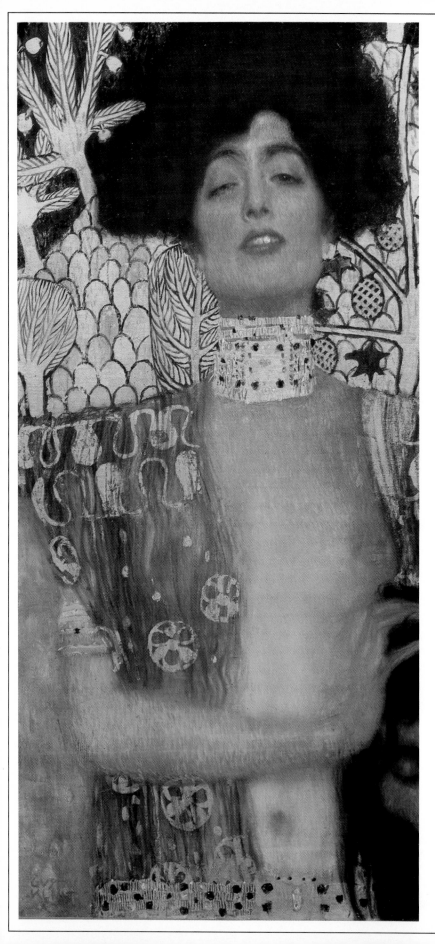

Judith I *(left)* Gustave Klimt (1862–1918). Men (and women) were firm believers in the elemental power of female seduction at the beginning of this century. This 1901 painting by a leading Viennese symbolist retells the biblical story of Judith, who slept with a Babylonian general for many nights in order to cut off his head and save her people. The symbolists' fascination with exotic sensations harkened back to romanticism. *(Osterreichische Galerie, Vienna)*

The Three Dancers *(right)* Pablo Picasso (1881–1973). A child prodigy, Picasso turned from realism to the fractured, shifting, multiple point of view known as cubism. With this immensely influential innovation Picasso shattered the continuity of composition that had prevailed since the Renaissance, and merged time and space in the relativity of an Einsteinian world. In this 1925 painting Picasso mourns in rage a friend's death through the frenzied contortions and cruciform image of the dancers. *(Tate Gallery, London/©ARS, NY/SPADEM 1987)*

Water Splashing Festival—Song of Life *(left)* Yuan Yunshen, Lian Weiyun, and Fei Zheng (1979). Chinese artists created dozens of huge murals for the decoration of the Capital International Airport in Beijing. Though reflecting the techniques of Western as well as traditional Chinese painting, the murals were received as an overwhelming and distinctly Chinese achievement. In this detail, Dai nationalists celebrate, with appropriately fluid gestures, their Water Splashing Festival. *(Eastfoto)*

Zapatistas *(below)* José Clemente Orozco (1931). "It is better to die on your feet than to live on your knees," rebel leader Emiliano Zapata told the peasants who fought with him in the Mexican Revolution. The strength and unity of the "Zapatistas" are evoked through the symmetrical composition and use of color in this painting by Orozco, one of Mexico's foremost artists. *(Collection, The Museum of Modern Art, New York. Given anonymously. Oil on canvas, 45 × 55'')*

Christmas Night *(left)* Henri Matisse (1869–1954). In his youth Matisse led avant-garde artists who delighted in breaking with tradition and shocking the public. This joyous design for a church stained-glass window, however, glows with cultural continuity and the spiritual peace of the artist's last years. Its beauty inspired by that of medieval masterpieces (see insert II), Matisse's stained-glass window proclaims the good tidings of Christmas to our time. *(Collection, The Museum of Modern Art, New York. 1952. Gouache on cut-and-pasted paper, 10′7″ × 53½″.)*

foreign policy in the early cold war. W. A. Williams, *The Tragedy of American Diplomacy* (1962), and W. La Feber, *America, Russia, and the Cold War* (1967), claim, on the contrary, that the United States was primarily responsible for the conflict with the Soviet Union. Two other important studies focusing on American policy are J. Gaddis, *The United States and the Origins of the Cold War* (1972), and D. Yergin, *Shattered Peace: The Origins of the Cold War and the National Security Council* (1977). A. Fontaine, a French journalist, provides a balanced general approach in his *History of the Cold War,* 2 vols. (1968). V. Mastny's thorough investigation of Stalin's war aims, *Russia's Road to the Cold War* (1979), is highly recommended.

R. Mayne, *The Recovery of Europe, 1945–1973,* rev. ed. (1973), and N. Luxenburg, *Europe Since World War II,* rev. ed. (1979), are recommended general surveys, as are two important works: W. Laqueur, *Europe Since Hitler,* rev. ed. (1982), and P. Johnson, *Modern Times: The World from the Twenties to the Eighties* (1983). T. White, *Fire in the Ashes* (1953), is a vivid view of European resurgence and Marshall Plan aid by an outstanding journalist. D. Swann, *The Economics of the Common Market,* 5th ed. (1984), carries developments into the 1980s. L. Barzini, *The Europeans* (1983), draws engaging group portraits of the different European peoples today and is strongly recommended. Postwar economic and technological developments are carefully analyzed by D. S. Landes, *The Unbound Prometheus: Technological Change and Industrial Development in Western Europe from 1750 to the Present* (1969). A. Shonfield, *Modern Capitalism* (1965), provides an engaging, optimistic assessment of the growing importance of government investment and planning in European economic life. F. R. Willis, *France, Germany, and the New Europe, 1945–1967* (1968), is useful for postwar European diplomacy. Three outstanding works on France are J. Ardagh, *The New French Revolution* (1969), which puts the momentous social changes since 1945 in human terms; G. Wright, *Rural Revolution in France: The Peasantry in the Twentieth Century* (1964); and D. L. Hanley et al., eds., *France: Politics and Society Since 1945* (1979). R. Dahrendorf, *Society and Democracy in Germany* (1971), and H. S. Hughes, *The United States and Italy* (1968), are excellent introductions to recent German and Italian history. A. Marwick, *British Society Since 1945* (1982), and A. H. Halsey, *Change in British Society,* 2d ed. (1981), are good on postwar developments.

H. Seton-Watson, *The East European Revolution* (1965), is a good history of the communization of eastern Europe, and S. Fischer-Galati, ed., *Eastern Europe in the Sixties* (1963), discusses major developments. P. Zinner, *National Communism and Popular Revolt in Eastern Europe* (1956) and *Revolution in Hungary* (1962), are excellent on the tragic events of 1956. Among the many books to come out of the Czechoslovak experience in 1968, three are particularly recommended: H. Schwartz, *Prague's 200 Days: The Struggle for Democracy in Czechoslovakia* (1969); I. Svitak, *The Czechoslovak Experiment, 1968–1969* (1971); and Z. Zeman, *Prague Spring* (1969). T. Ash, *The Polish Revolution: Solidarity* (1983), is the best book on the subject and is highly recommended. Z. Brzezinski, *The Soviet Bloc: Unity and Conflict* (1967), is a major inquiry. W. Connor, *Socialism, Politics and Equality: Hierarchy and Change in Eastern Europe and the USSR* (1979), and J. Hough and M. Fainsod, *How the Soviet Union Is Governed* (1978), are important general studies. A. Amalrik, *Will the Soviet Union Survive Until 1984?* (1970), is a fascinating interpretation of recent Soviet history and politics by a Russian who paid for his criticism with prison and exile. A. Lee, *Russian Journal* (1981), and H. Smith, *The Russians* (1976), are excellent journalistic yet comprehensive reports by perceptive American observers.

R. von Albertini, *Decolonialization* (1971), is a good history of the decline and fall of European empires. Two excellent general studies on Latin America are J. E. Fagg, *Latin America: A General History,* 3d ed. (1977), and R. J. Shafer, *A History of Latin America* (1978). Both contain detailed suggestions for further reading. E. Burns, *A History of Brazil* (1970); M. Meyer and W. Sherman, *The Course of Mexican History* (1979); and B. Loveman, *Chile: The Legacy of Hispanic Capitalism* (1979), are recommended studies of developments in three leading nations. W. La Feber, *Inevitable Revolutions: The United States in Central America* (1983), is an important, quite critical assessment of U.S. support of neocolonial patterns in Central America.

37

ASIA AND AFRICA IN THE CONTEMPORARY WORLD

HEN FUTURE HISTORIANS look back at our era, they are likely to be particularly struck by the epoch-making resurgence of Asia and Africa after World War Two. They will try to explain the astonishingly rapid rise of new or radically reorganized Asian and African countries and their increasingly prominent role in world affairs. That is also what this chapter will try to do, though time has only partially winnowed the facts and still provides a very imperfect perspective. This chapter and Chapter 39 also will examine how emerging nation-states are facing up to their enormous economic, social, and cultural challenges, whose solutions are proving more elusive than political strength and independence.

THE RESURGENCE OF EAST ASIA

In 1945 the two great powers of East Asia lay exhausted and devastated. Japanese aggression had sown extreme misery in China and reaped an atomic whirlwind at Hiroshima and Nagasaki. The future looked bleak. Yet both nations recovered even more spectacularly than western Europe. In the course of recovery the two countries, closely linked since the 1890s, went their separate ways. As China under Mao Tse-tung (Mao Zedong) transformed itself into a strong, self-confident communist state, Japan under American occupation turned from military expansion to democracy and extraordinarily successful economic development. Not until the 1970s would the reborn giants move somewhat closer together.

THE COMMUNIST VICTORY IN CHINA

There were many reasons for the triumph of communism in China. As a noted historian has forcefully argued, however, "Japanese aggression was . . . the most important single factor in Mao's rise to power."[1] When Japanese armies advanced rapidly in 1938 (page 1064), Chiang Kai-shek's Nationalist government moved its capital to Chungking, deep in the Chinese interior. The Japanese then occupied a swath of territory five hundred miles wide in northern and central China, and the war settled into stalemate in 1939. These wartime conditions enabled the

Communists, aided by their uneasy "united front" alliance with the Nationalists, to build up their strength in guerrilla bases in the countryside behind Japanese lines. Mao Tse-tung, at the peak of his creative powers, avoided pitched battles and concentrated on winning peasant support and forming a broad anti-Japanese coalition. By reducing rents, enticing intellectuals, and spreading propaganda, Mao and the Communists emerged in peasant eyes as the true patriots, the genuine nationalists. And the promise of radical redistribution of the land strongly reinforced their appeal to poor peasants and landless laborers.

Meanwhile, the long war with Japan was exhausting the established government and its supporters. American generals were never satisfied with China's war effort, but in fact fully half of Japan's overseas armies were pinned down in China in 1945. Chiang Kai-shek's Nationalists had mobilized 14 million men, and a staggering 3 million Chinese soldiers had been killed or wounded. The war created massive Chinese deficits and runaway inflation, hurting morale and ruining lives.

When Japan suddenly collapsed in August 1945, Communists and Nationalists both rushed to seize evacuated territory. Heavy fighting broke out in Manchuria. The United States, which had steadfastly supported the Nationalists during World War Two, tried unsuccessfully to work out a political compromise, but civil war resumed in earnest in April 1946. At first Chiang Kai-shek's more numerous Nationalists had the upper hand. Soon the better-led, more determined Communists rallied, and by 1948 the demoralized Nationalist forces were disintegrating. In 1949 Chiang Kai-shek and 1 million mainland Chinese fled to the island of Taiwan, and Mao Tse-tung proclaimed the People's Republic of China.

Within three years the Communists had already succeeded in consolidating their rule. The Communist government seized the holdings of landlords and rich peasants—10 percent of the farm population owned 70 to 80 percent of the land—and distributed it to 300 million poor peasants and landless laborers. This revolutionary land reform was extremely popular. Although the Chinese Communists soon began pushing the development of socialist collectives, they did so less brutally than had the Russians in the 1930s and retained genuine support in the countryside. The gradualness of collectivization reflects Mao's cautious, step-by-step consolidation of power.

Meanwhile the Communists were dealing harshly with their foes. Mao admitted in 1957 that 800,000 "class enemies" had been summarily liquidated between 1949 and 1954; the true figure is probably much higher. By means of mass arrests, forced-labor camps, and, more generally, re-education through relentless propaganda and self-criticism sessions, all visible opposition from the old ruling groups was destroyed.

Finally, Mao and the Communists reunited China's 550 million inhabitants in a strong centralized state. They laid claim on a new "mandate of Heaven" and demonstrated that China was once again a great power. This was the real significance of China's Korean intervention. In 1950, when the American-led United Nations forces crossed the 38th parallel and appeared to threaten China's industrial base in Manchuria, the Chinese attacked, advanced swiftly, and fought the Americans to a bloody standstill on the Korean peninsula. This struggle against "American imperialism" mobilized the masses, and military success increased Chinese self-confidence.

MAO'S CHINA

Asserting Chinese power and prestige in the armed conflict with the United States, Mao and the party looked to the Soviet Union for inspiration in the early 1950s. Mao and Stalin established close working relations, and the Chinese followed the Russian lead in world affairs. Alongside the gradual collectivization of agriculture, China adopted a typical Soviet five-year plan to develop large factories and heavy industry rapidly. Many Chinese plants were built by Russian specialists; Soviet economic aid was also considerable. The first five-year plan was successful, as were associated efforts to redirect higher education away from the liberal arts toward science and engineering. People remained very poor, but undeniable economic growth followed on the Communists' social revolution.

A People's Court tries a case as local villagers follow the proceedings intently. The man on his knees is accused of selling a young girl living in his household, an old practice that has become a serious crime in revolutionary China. *(Popperfoto)*

Chinese Red Guards line up before a giant picture of Mao Tse-tung in about 1967. They are waving the "Little Red Book," which contains a collection of Mao's slogans and teachings. *(Wide World Photos)*

In the cultural and intellectual realms too, the Chinese followed the example of Soviet totalitarianism. Basic civil and political rights, which had been seriously curtailed by the Nationalists, were simply abolished. Temples and churches were closed; all religion was persecuted. Freedom of the press died, and the government went to incredible lengths to control information. As in the Soviet Union, ordinary telephone books were kept under lock and key. The big new buildings that arose looked "made in Moscow." A Soviet-style puritanism took hold; to the astonishment of "old China hands," the Communists quickly eradicated the long-standing scourges of prostitution and drug abuse, which they had long regarded as humiliating marks of exploitation and national decline. More generally, the Communists enthusiastically promoted Soviet-Marxian ideas concerning women and the family. Full equality and freedom from housework and child care became primary goals. Work in fields and factories was hailed as a proud badge of women's liberation rather than a shameful sign of poverty. It became rather easy for a woman to get a divorce, although premarital chastity remained the accepted norm.

By the mid-1950s, Communist China seemed to be firmly set on the Marxist-Leninist course of development previously perfected in Soviet Russia. There was even a brief interlude in 1957, shortly after Khrushchev launched de-Stalinization in Russia (pages 1145–1147), when Mao called on Chinese intellectuals to cultivate "One Hundred Flowers" of free and even critical opinion. Like his Soviet counterparts, Mao soon decided that the "flowers" he had nurtured were weeds and cut them down as he re-established uniformity of thought.

In 1958, however, Communist China began to go its own way. Mao had always stressed revolutionary free will and peasant equality. Now he proclaimed a spectacular acceleration of development, a "Great Leap Forward" in which soaring industrial growth was to be based on small-scale backyard workshops run by peasants living in gigantic self-contained communes. Creating an authentic new socialist personality was a second goal: commune members ate in common dining halls, nurseries cared for children, and fire-eating crusaders preached the evils of family ties.

The intended great leap past the Russians to socialist utopia—true communism—was an economic disaster in the countryside, for frantic efforts with primitive technology often resulted only in chaos. By 1960, only China's efficient rationing system was preventing starvation. But when Khrushchev criticized Chinese policy, Mao reacted angrily and relations between the communist giants deteriorated rapidly. Mao condemned Khrushchev and the Russians as detestable "modern revisionists"—capitalists and cowards unwilling to risk a world war that would bring communist revolution in the United States. The Russians abruptly cut off economic aid and withdrew their scientists who were helping China build an atomic bomb. A mood of mutual fear and hatred appeared to develop in both countries in the 1960s, as the communist world split apart.

Mao lost influence in the party after the fiasco of the Great Leap Forward and the Sino-Soviet split, but in 1965 the old revolutionary staged a dramatic comeback. Apprehensive that China was becoming bureaucratic, capitalistic, and "revisionist" like Soviet Russia, Mao launched what he called the "Great Proletarian Cultural Revolution." Its objective was to purge the party of time-serving bureaucrats and to recapture the revolutionary fervor and social equality of the Long March and his guerrilla struggle. The army and the nation's young people, especially students, responded enthusiastically. Encouraged by Mao to organize themselves into radical cadres called Red Guards, young people denounced their teachers and practiced rebellion in the name of revolution. As one Red Guard manifesto, "Long Live the Revolutionary Rebel Spirit of the Proletariat," exulted:

Revolution is rebellion, and rebellion is the soul of Mao Tse-tung's thought. Daring to think, to speak, to act, to break through, and to make revolution—in a word, daring to rebel—is the most fundamental and most precious quality of proletarian revolutionaries; it is fundamental to the Party spirit of the Party of the proletariat! . . .

You say we are too arrogant? "Arrogant" is just what we want to be. Chairman Mao says, "And those in high positions we counted as no more than the dust." We are bent on striking down not only the reactionaries in our school, but the reactionaries all over the world. Revolutionaries take it as their task to transform the world. How can we not be "arrogant"?[2]

The Red Guards also sought to forge a new socialist spirit by purging China of all traces of "feudal" and "bourgeois" culture and thought. Some ancient monuments and works of art were destroyed in the process. Party officials, professors, and intellectuals were exiled to remote villages to purify themselves with the heavy labor of the peasant masses and to rekindle a burning devotion to the semidivine Chairman Mao. The Red Guards attracted enormous worldwide attention: many observers were appalled, but China's young revolutionaries inspired radical admirers around the world and served as an extreme model for the student rebellions of the late 1960s.

DENG'S "SECOND REVOLUTION"

Mao and the Red Guards succeeded in mobilizing the masses, shaking up the party, and creating greater social equality. But the Cultural Revolution also created growing chaos and a general crisis of confidence, especially in the cities. Intellectuals, technicians, and purged party officials saw themselves as victims of senseless persecution. Fighting back, they launched a counterattack on the radicals and regained much of their influence by 1969. This shift, coupled with actual fighting between China and Russia on the northern border in 1969 and not-so-secret Russian talk of atomic attack, opened the door to a limited but long-

lasting reconciliation between China and the United States in 1971.

The moderates were led by Deng Xiao-ping (b. 1904), a long-time member of the Communist elite who had been branded a dangerous agent of capitalism during the Cultural Revolution. After Mao's death in 1976, Deng and his supporters initiated a series of major reforms, embodied in the ongoing campaign of the Four Modernizations—agriculture, industry, science and technology, and national defense. The campaign to modernize has already had a profound effect on China's people, and Deng was probably not exaggerating when he proudly called it China's "second revolution."

China's 800 million peasants experienced the greatest and most beneficial change from this "second revolution"—a fact that at first glance may seem surprising. The support of the peasantry had played a major role in the Communist victory; after 1949, land reform and rationing undoubtedly improved the diet of poor peasants. Subsequently, literacy campaigns taught rural people how to read, while "barefoot doctors"—local peasants trained to do simple diagnosis and treatment—brought modern medicine to the countryside. The Communists also promoted handicraft industries to provide rural employment. Nevertheless, rigid collectivized agriculture had failed to provide either the peasants or the country with adequate food, as Chinese documents published in the last ten years make clear. Levels of agricultural production and per capita food consumption were no higher in the mid-1970s than the mid-1950s, and only slightly higher than in 1937, before the war with Japan.

Determined to prevent a return to Maoist extremism as well as to modernize the economy, Deng and the reformers looked to the peasants as natural allies. Their answer to the stalemate in agricultural production was to let China's peasants farm the land in small family units rather than in large collectives. Peasants were encouraged to produce what they could produce best and to sell their surpluses on free markets. "Dare to be rich"—that became the official new message for the rural masses. Peasants responded enthusiastically. Working hard to increase their incomes and live better, Chinese peasants increased food production by more than 50 percent in just six years after 1978. As a result of this outstanding achievement, both rural and urban Chinese finally gained enough calories and protein for normal

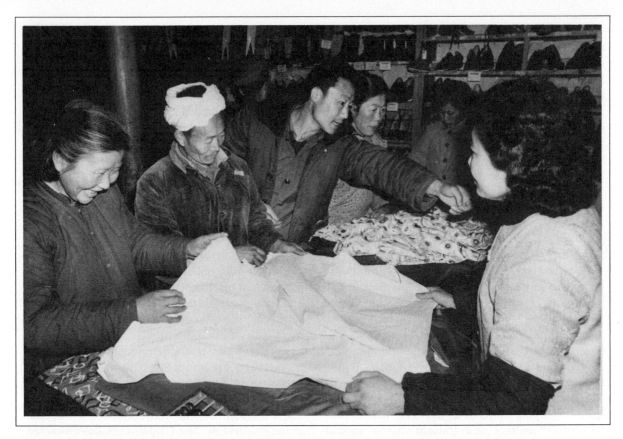

China's Peasants benefitted the most from Deng's reforms and the subsequent economic progress. Still clad in the blue cotton jackets of the Maoist era, these peasants are purchasing more expensive synthetic fabrics, which they will sew into brightly colored dresses and fancy shirts. *(Camera Press)*

life and growth, although the grain-dominated diet remained monotonous.

The successful use of free markets and family responsibility in agriculture convinced some foreign observers that China really was going capitalist. Certainly China's leaders were flexible and willing to experiment, stating repeatedly that the teachings of Marx and Lenin could not solve all China's problems. Private enterprise was also permitted in cities. Snack shops, beauty parlors, and a host of small businesses sprang up, along with rock music and a rage for English lessons. Signs of liberalization abounded.

Yet the extent of change must not be exaggerated. Industry remained largely state-owned and centrally planned; only 3 percent of the urban work force was employed by private enterprise in 1986. Cultural change and the media were still under strict party control. Above all, the Communist party zealously preserved its monopoly of political power and its dictatorial rule. For example, the party maintained decrees stating that families must have no more than one child in order to limit China's population growth. Yet in a country where sons traditionally supported their aged parents while daughters supported only their husbands' families, this drastic measure led to considerable forced abortion and female infanticide. Such arbitrary government action helps explain why at the end of 1986 thousands of Chinese university students staged massive demonstrations, calling for democracy and personal liberties. The government responded temperately, but it banned all demonstrations nonetheless. Like so many leading Chinese in modern times, Deng and his circle were most interested in making China strong, and they still saw authoritarian rule as the means to that goal.

JAPAN'S AMERICAN REVOLUTION

After Japan's surrender in August 1945, American occupation forces began landing in the Tokyo-Yokohama area. Riding through what had been the very heart of industrial Japan, the combat-hardened veterans saw an eerie sight. Where mighty mills and factories had once hummed with activity, only smokestacks and giant steel safes remained standing amid miles of rubble and debris. The empty landscape manifested Japan's state of mind as it lay helpless before its conqueror.

Japan, like Nazi Germany, was formally occupied by all the Allies, but real power resided in American hands. The commander was General Douglas MacArthur, the five-star hero of the Pacific, who with his advisers exercised almost absolute authority.

MacArthur and the Americans had a revolutionary plan for defeated Japan. Convinced that militaristic, antidemocratic forces were responsible for Japanese aggression and had to be destroyed, they introduced radical reforms designed to make Japan a free, democratic society along American lines. The Americans believed in their mission and in the obvious superiority of their civilization; the exhausted, demoralized Japanese, who had feared a worse fate, accepted passively. Long-suppressed liberal leaders emerged to offer crucial support and help carry the reforms forward.

Japan's sweeping American revolution began with "demilitarization" and a systematic purge. Twenty-five top government leaders and army officers were tried and convicted as war criminals by a special international tribunal; other courts sentenced hundreds to death and sent thousands to prison. Over 220,000 politicians, businessmen, and army officers were declared ineligible for office.

Many Americans wanted to try Emperor Hirohito as a war criminal, but MacArthur hesitated in the face of strong Japanese opposition. When the emperor voluntarily renounced his divinity—according to legend, the founder of the ancient imperial dynasty was the grandson of the sun goddess—and courageously assumed the shame of defeat on behalf of all his people, MacArthur wisely decided to let him reign as a useful figurehead. According to the American-dictated constitution of 1946, the emperor was "the symbol of the State and of the people with whom resides sovereign power."

The new constitution made the government fully responsible to the Diet, whose members were popularly elected by all adults. A bill of rights granted basic civil liberties and freed all political prisoners, including Communists. The constitution also abolished forever all Japanese armed forces. Japan's resurrected liberals enthusiastically supported this American move to destroy militarism.

The American occupation left Japan's powerful bureaucracy largely intact and used it to implement the fundamental social and economic reforms that were rammed through the Japanese Diet. Many had a New Deal flavor. The occupation promoted the Japanese labor movement, and the number of union workers increased fifteenfold in three years. The occupation also introduced American-style antitrust laws. The gigantic zaibatsu firms (page 1059) were broken up into many separate companies in order to encourage competition and economic democracy. The American reformers proudly "emancipated" Japanese women, granting them equality before the law. And, of lasting significance, Japan's educational system was restructured along American lines, insofar as local authorities gained greater control over local schools and access to higher education was democratized.

The occupation also imposed truly revolutionary land reform. MacArthur, often portrayed in the United States as a rigid conservative, pressured the Japanese Diet into buying up all the land owned by absentee landlords and selling it to peasants on very generous terms. This reform strengthened the small, independent peasant, who became a staunch defender of postwar democracy.

The United States efforts to remake Japan in its own image were powerful but short-lived. By 1948, when the United States began to look at the world through a cold war lens, occupation policy shifted gears. The Japanese later referred to this about-face as "the reverse course." As China went decisively communist, American leaders began to see Japan as a potential ally, not an object of social reform. The American command began purging left-wingers and rehabilitating prewar nationalists, many of whom joined the Democratic Liberal party, which became increasingly conservative and emerged as the dominant political organization in postwar Japan. Efforts to break up the zaibatsu monopolies and encourage labor unions were quietly dropped. The United

States ended the occupation in 1952. By the treaty terms, Japan regained independence and the United States retained its vast military complex in Japan. In actuality, Japan became a military protectorate, a special ally shielded, and restricted, by America's nuclear capability.

"JAPAN, INC."

Restricted to satellite status in world politics, the Japanese people applied their exceptional creative powers to rebuilding their country. Japan's economic recovery, like Germany's, proceeded painfully slowly immediately after the war. Beginning with the Korean War, however, the economy took off and rose with spectacular speed for a whole generation. Between 1950 and 1970 the real growth rate of Japan's economy—adjusted for inflation—averaged a breathtaking 10 percent a year—almost three times that of the United States. When the occupation officially ended in 1952, Japan produced only about one-third as much as France or Great Britain; by the 1970s it already produced as much as France and Great Britain combined. Even after the Arab oil shock of 1973, the petroleum-poor Japanese did considerably better than most other peoples. In 1986 average per capita income in Japan exceeded that in the United States for the first time. As recently as 1965, the average Japanese had earned only a quarter of the average American's income.

Japan's emergence as an economic superpower fascinated some outsiders and troubled others. While Asians and Africans looked to Japan for the secrets of successful modernization, Americans and Europeans whipped up recipes for copying Japanese success. Some of Japan's Asian neighbors again feared Japanese exploitation. And in the 1970s and 1980s, some Americans and Europeans bitterly accused "Japan Inc." of an unholly alliance between government and business. Industries and workers hurt by Japanese "unfair competition" called on their governments for aggressive countermeasures.

Many of the ingredients in western Europe's recovery also operated in Japan. American aid, cheap labor, and freer international trade all helped spark the process. As in western Europe, the government concentrated its energies on economic development. Japanese businessmen recognized the opportunity to replace their bombed-out plants with the latest, most efficient technology.

Japan's astonishing economic surge also seems to have had deep roots in Japanese history, culture, and national character. Restricted by geography to mountainous islands, Japan was for centuries safely isolated from invaders. By the time American and European pressure forced open its gates in the mid-nineteenth century, Japan was politically unified and culturally homogeneous. Agriculture, education, and material well-being were advanced even by European standards. Moreover, Japanese society put the needs of the group before those of the individual. When the Meiji reformers redefined Japan's primary task as catching up with the West, they had the support of a sophisticated and disciplined people. Japan's modernization, even including a full share of aggressive imperialism, had been extremely rapid.

By the end of the American occupation, this tight-knit, group-centered society had reassessed its future and worked out a new national consensus. Japan's new task was to build its economy and compete efficiently in world markets. Improved living standards emerged as a related goal after the initial successes of the 1950s. The ambitious "double-your-income" target for the 1960s was ultimately surpassed by 50 percent.

Government and big business shared leading roles in the drama of economic growth. As during the Meiji Restoration (page 954), capable, respected bureaucrats directed and aided the efforts of cooperative business leaders. The government decided which industries were important, then made loans and encouraged mergers to create powerful firms in those industries. The antitrust policy introduced by the American occupation, based on the very un-Japanese values of individualism and unrestrained competition, was scrapped.

Big business was valued and respected because it served the national goal and mirrored Japanese society. Big companies, and to a lesser extent small ones, traditionally hired workers for life immediately after they finished school. Employees were never fired and seldom laid off, and in return they were loyal and obedient. To an extent difficult for a Westerner to imagine, the business firm in Japan was a big, well-disciplined family. The workday began with the company song; employees' social lives also revolved around the company. Wages were based on age. (Discrimination against women remained severe: wages and job security were strikingly inferior.) Most unions were moderate, agreeable company unions. The social and economic distance between salaried managers and workers was slight and often breached. Efficiency, quality, and quantity were the watchwords. Management was quick to retrain employees, secure in the knowledge that they would not take their valuable new skills elsewhere. These factors, not "unfair competition," were most important in accounting for Japan's economic success.

Japanese society, with its inescapable stress on cooperation and compromise, has proved well-adapted to the challenges of modern industrial urban civilization. For example, Japan alone among industrial nations has experienced a marked decrease in crime over the last generation. In the 1970s and 1980s the Japanese addressed themselves effectively to such previously neglected problems as serious industrial pollution and energy resources. Highly dependent on imported resources and foreign sales, Japan groped for a new role in world politics. Closer relations with China, increased loans to Southeast Asia, and tough trade negotiations with the United States were all features of that ongoing effort.

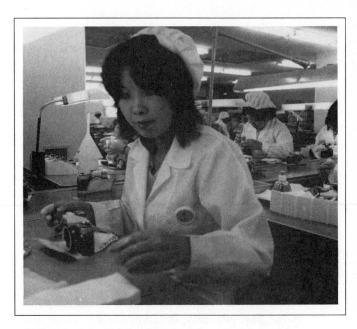

"Made in Japan" Disciplined, educated, and attentive to details, this young woman at the Minolta camera works is assembling a world-famous product. She epitomizes the high-quality labor force that has given Japanese goods a reputation for excellence. *(Rupert Harrison/Camera Press)*

NEW NATIONS IN SOUTH ASIA AND THE MUSLIM WORLD

South Asia and the Muslim world have transformed themselves no less spectacularly than China and Japan. The national independence movements, which had been powerful mass campaigns since the 1930s, triumphed decisively over weakened and demoralized European imperialism after World War Two. Between 1947 and 1962, as decolonization gathered almost irresistible strength, virtually every colonial territory won its political freedom. The complete reversal of the long process of European expansion was a turning point in world history.

The new nations of South Asia and the revitalized states of the Muslim world exhibited many variations on the dominant themes of national renaissance and modernization, especially as the struggle for political independence receded into the past.

INDEPENDENCE ON THE INDIAN SUBCONTINENT

As discussed in Chapter 33, Mahatma Gandhi and the Indian Congress party developed the philosophy of militant nonviolence to oppose British rule of India after World War One and to lessen oppression of the Indian poor by the Indian rich (pages 1051–1054). By 1929 Gandhi had succeeded in transforming the Congress party from a narrow, middle-class party into a mass independence movement. Gradually and grudgingly, Britain's rulers introduced reforms culminating in limited self-government in 1937.

World War Two accelerated the drive toward independence, but also pointed it in a new direction. Humiliated that Great Britain had declared war against Germany on India's behalf without consulting them, Congress party leaders resigned their posts in the Indian government and demanded self-rule as the immediate price of political cooperation. In 1942, when Gandhi called on the British to "Quit India," threatening another civil disobedience campaign, he and the other Congress leaders were quickly arrested and jailed for the virtual duration of the war. As a result, India's wartime support for hard-pressed Britain was substantial but not always enthusiastic. Meanwhile the Congress party's prime political rival skillfully seized the opportunity to increase its influence.

That rival was the Muslim League, led by the brilliant, elegant English-educated lawyer Muhammad Ali Jinnah (1876–1948). Jinnah and the other leaders of the Muslim League feared Hindu domination of an independent Indian state led by the Congress party. Asserting in nationalist terms the right of Muslim areas to separate from the Hindu majority, Jinnah described the Muslims of India as

a nation of a hundred million, and what is more, we are a nation with our distinct culture and civilization, language, literature, arts, and architecture . . . laws and moral codes, customs and special aptitudes and ambitions. In short, we have our own distinctive outlook on life and of life.[3]

As Jinnah told 100,000 listeners at the Muslim League's Lahore Conference in March 1940, "If the British Government is really in earnest and sincere to secure the peace and happiness of the people of the subcontinent, the only course open to us all is to allow the major nations separate homelands by dividing India into autonomous national states."[4]

The Muslim League's insistence on the division of India appalled Gandhi. He regarded Jinnah's two-nation theory as simply untrue, and as promising the victory of hate over love. Gandhi's argument was most accurate when applied to the Bengali Muslims of northeastern India's Ganges River basin, whose language, dress, racial appearance, food, and social customs were virtually identical to those of Bengali Hindus; only in religion did they differ. The passionate debate between Jinnah and Gandhi continued unabated during the war, as millions argued whether India was one nation or two. By 1945 the subcontinent was intellectually and emotionally divided, though still momentarily held together by British rule.

When Britain's Labour government agreed to speedy independence for India after 1945, conflicting Hindu and Muslim nationalisms and religious hatred became the obstacles, leading to murderous clashes between the two communities in 1946. In a last attempt to preserve the subcontinent's political unity, the British proposed a federal constitution providing for extensive provincial—and thus religious and cultural—autonomy. When after some hesitation Jinnah and the Muslim League would accept nothing less than an independent Pakistan, India's last viceroy—war hero Lord Louis Mountbatten (1900–1979), Queen Victoria's great-grandson—proposed partition. Both sides accepted. At the stroke of midnight on August 14, 1947, one-fifth of humanity gained political independence. As the sumptuous, horse-drawn coach of the last viceroy pulled away from the final ceremony, endless cries of "Long live Mountbatten!" rose from the gigantic crowds—ringing testimony to India's residue of good feeling toward its vanquished conquerors and their splendidly peaceful departure.

Yet independence through partition was to bring tragedy. In the weeks after independence, communal strife exploded into an orgy of massacres and mass expulsions. Perhaps 100,000 Hindus and Muslims were slaughtered, and an estimated 5 million refugees from both communities fled in opposite directions to escape being hacked to death by frenzied mobs.

This wave of violence was a bitter potion for Congress leaders, who were completely powerless to stop it. "What is there to celebrate?" exclaimed Gandhi. "I see nothing but rivers of blood."[5] In January 1948, announcing yet another fast to protest Hindu persecution of Muslims in the Indian capital of New Delhi and to restore "heart friendship" between the two communities, Gandhi was gunned down by a Hindu fanatic. As the Mahatma's death tragically testifies, the constructive and liberating forces of modern nationalism have frequently deteriorated into blind hatred.

After the ordeal of independence, relations between India and Pakistan—both members of the British Commonwealth—remained tense. Fighting over the disputed area of Kashmir continued until 1949 and broke out again in 1965–1966 and 1971. Mutual hostility remains deeply ingrained to this day (Map 37.1).

PAKISTAN. Like many newly independent states, Pakistan eventually adopted an authoritarian government in 1958. Unlike most, Pakistan failed to preserve its exceptionally fragile unity, which proved to be the unworkable dream of its Muslim League leaders.

Pakistan's western and eastern provinces were separated by more than a thousand miles of Indian territory, and by language, ethnic background, and social custom. They shared only the Muslim faith that had temporarily brought them together against the Hindus. The Bengalis of East Pakistan constituted a majority of the total population, but were neglected by the central government, which remained in the hands of West Pakistan's elite after Jinnah's death. In essence, East Pakistan remained a colony—of West Pakistan.

Tensions gradually came to a head in the late 1960s. Bengali leaders calling for virtual independence were charged with treason, and martial law was proclaimed in East Pakistan. In 1971 the Bengalis revolted. Despite savage repression—10 million Muslim Bengalis fled temporarily to India, which provided some military aid—the Bengalis won their independence as the new nation of Bangladesh. The world's eighth most populous country, Bangladesh remains one of its poorest.

INDIA. India was ruled for a generation after 1947 by Jawaharlal Nehru (1889–1964) and the Congress party, which introduced major social reforms. Hindu women and even young girls were granted legal equality, which included the right to vote, to seek a divorce, and to marry outside their caste. The constitution also abolished the untouchable caste and established "ex-untouchable" quotas for university scholarships and government jobs in an effort to compensate for centuries of the most profound discrimination. In practice, attitudes toward women and untouchables evolved slowly—especially in the villages, where 85 percent of the people lived.

The Congress leadership tried with modest success to develop the country economically by means of democratic socialism. But population growth ate up much of the increase in output, and intense poverty remained the lot of most people. Poverty also encouraged widespread corruption within the bureaucracy. The population continued to grow relentlessly about 2.4 percent per year, a rate capable of doubling India's already enormous multitude in just thirty years. Halfhearted governmental efforts to promote birth control met with indifference or hostility.

The Congress party maintained a moralizing neutrality in the cold war and sought to group the newly independent states into a "third force" of "non-

Muslims Seeking Sanctuary Independence and partition brought a wave of bloodshed that sent millions fleeing for their lives. Here Muslims living in New Delhi stream into an old fort that has been converted into a refugee camp. Most will go on to Pakistan in armed convoys. *(Popperfoto)*

aligned" nations. This effort culminated in the Afro-Asian Conference in Bandung, Indonesia, in 1955.

Nehru's daughter, Indira Gandhi (1917–1984), became prime minister in 1966. Mrs. Gandhi (whose deceased husband was no relation to Mahatma Gandhi) dominated Indian political life for a generation with a skillful combination of charm, tact, and toughness. As it became clear that population growth was frustrating efforts to improve living standards, Mrs. Gandhi's government stepped up measures to promote family planning. Bus posters featuring smiling youngsters proclaimed that "A Happy Family Is a Small Family," and doctors and nurses promoted

MAP 37.1 The Partition of British India, 1947 Violence and fighting were most intense where there were large Hindu and Muslim minorities—in Kashmir, Punjab, and Bengal. The tragic result, which has occurred repeatedly throughout the world in the twentieth century, was a forced exchange of populations and greater homogeneity on both sides of the border.

loop rings for women, and condoms and surgical vasectomy for men. Although vasectomy is the most effective form of contraception, since it does not require continual conscientiousness, most Indian males rejected it for both psychological and religious reasons. As a doctor in a market town explained to a Western journalist:

They have mostly heard of family planning around here by now, but they are afraid. They are afraid that the ster-

On the Campaign Trail Prime Minister Indira Gandhi gives the traditional Hindu sign of blessing as she travels through rural India, accompanied by crowds of jogging well-wishers. Indian elections have been colorful, and even those born into the political elite, like the late Prime Minister, must know how to mix with the masses. *(Stern/Black Star)*

ilizing operation will destroy their male power and make them docile, like castrated animals. Mostly, they are afraid of interfering with God's will.[6]

In the face of such reluctance—and in an effort to clamp down on widespread corruption at all levels of government—Mrs. Gandhi in 1975 subverted parliamentary democracy and proclaimed a state of emergency. Attacking dishonest officials, black marketeers, and tax evaders, she also threw the weight of the government behind a heavy-handed, semitotalitarian campaign of mass sterilization to reduce population growth. In some areas, poor men with very large families were rounded up and made to accept a few cents' payment to submit to a simple, almost painless irreversible vasectomy. Everywhere the pressure was intense, and seven million men were sterilized in 1976.

Many Indian and foreign observers believed that Mrs. Gandhi's emergency measures marked the end of the parliamentary democracy and Western liberties introduced in the last phase of British rule. But Mrs. Gandhi—true to the British tradition—called for free elections, in which she suffered a spectacular defeat, largely because of the vastly unpopular sterilization campaign and her subversion of democracy. But her successors fell to fighting among themselves, and in 1980 Mrs. Gandhi won an equally stunning electoral victory. Her defeat and re-election undoubtedly strengthened India's democratic tradition.

1945	Japan surrenders
	Civil war begins in China
1946	Japan receives democratic constitution
	The Philippines gain independence
1947	Communal strife follows independence for India and Pakistan
1948	Civil war between Arabs and Jews in Palestine
1949	Korean War begins
	Mao Tse-tung (Mao Zedong) proclaims the People's Republic of China
	Indonesia under Sukarno wins independence from the Dutch
1950	China enters Korean War
	Japan begins long period of rapid economic growth
1951	Iran tries unsuccessfully to nationalize the Anglo-Iranian Oil Company
1952	American occupation of Japan officially ends
1954	Vietnamese nationalists defeat the French at Dien Bien Phu
1955	First Afro-Asian Conference of non-aligned nations meets at Bandung, Indonesia
1958	Mao Tse-tung announces the Great Leap Forward
1960	Open split between China and the Soviet Union emerges
1965	The Great Proletarian Cultural Revolution begins in China
	Growing American involvement in the Vietnamese civil war
1966	Indira Gandhi becomes Prime Minister of India
1971	President Nixon's visit to China signals improved Sino-American relations
1975	War in Vietnam ends with Communist victory
1976	China pursues modernization after Mao's death
1979	Revolution topples the shah of Iran

Mrs. Gandhi's last years in office were plagued by another old political problem, one that cost her her life. Democratic India remained a patchwork of religions, languages, and peoples. This enduring diversity threatened to divide the country along ethnic or religious lines, as conflicting national aspirations had earlier torn British India into two and then three different states. Several peoples developed a strong ethnic consciousness and made political demands, most notably the 15 million Sikhs of the Punjab in northern India.

The Sikhs had their own religion—a blend of Islam and Hinduism—and a distinctive culture, including a warrior tradition and the wearing of elegantly

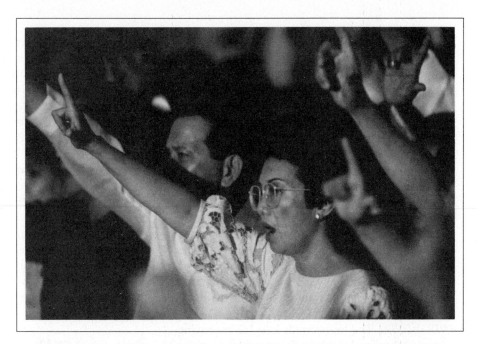

The New Filipino Leader Shown here after being sworn in as the new president of the Philippines, Corazon Aquino enjoyed tremendous popular support. For millions of Filipinos she was simply "Cory"—their trusted friend. *(Steven McCurry/Magnum)*

coiled turbans. Industrious and cohesive, most Sikhs wanted greater autonomy for the Punjab. By 1984, some radicals were fighting for an independent homeland—a Sikh national state. In retaliation, Mrs. Gandhi tightened control in the Punjab and ordered the army to storm the Sikhs' sacred Golden Temple at Amritsar. Six hundred died in the assault. Five months later, two of Mrs. Gandhi's Sikh bodyguards —she prided herself on their loyalty—cut her down with machine-gun fire in her own garden. Violence followed as Hindu mobs slaughtered over a thousand Sikhs throughout India. Elected prime minister by a landslide sympathy vote, Indira's son, the forty-year-old Rajiv Gandhi, showed considerable skill at effecting a reconciliation with a large majority of the Sikh population. But a lot of blood had flowed, and ethnic conflict promised more challenges to Indian unity.

SOUTHEAST ASIA

Indian independence fixed the pattern of Britain's policies in its smaller Asian possessions.

SRI LANKA AND MALAYA. Sri Lanka (Ceylon) quickly and smoothly gained independence in 1948. Malaya, however, encountered serious problems not unlike those of British India. The native Malays, an Islamic agricultural people, feared and disliked the Chinese, who had come to Malaya as poor migrant workers in the nineteenth century and stayed on to dominate the urban economy. The Malays having pressured the British into giving them the dominant voice in the federation, local Chinese Communists launched an all-out guerrilla war. They were eventually defeated by the British and the Malays, and Malaya became self-governing in 1957 and independent in 1961. Yet two peoples soon meant two nations. In 1965, the largely Chinese city of Singapore was pushed out of the Malayan-dominated Federation of Malaysia. Ethnic tension continued to erupt periodically in Malaya, which still retained a large Chinese minority. The independent city-state of Singapore prospered on the hard work and inventiveness of its largely Chinese population.

THE PHILIPPINE ISLANDS. The Philippine Islands had suffered enormous destruction in World War Two. The United States extended economic aid while retaining its large military bases, and then followed through on its earlier promises by granting the Philippines independence in 1946. As in Malaya, Communist guerrillas tried unsuccessfully to seize power. The Philippines pursued American-style two-party competition until 1965, when President Ferdinand Marcos (b. 1917) subverted the constitution and ruled as a dictator. Abolishing martial law in 1981 but retaining most of his power, Marcos faced growing opposition as the economy crumbled and land-hungry Communist guerrillas made striking gains in the countryside. Led by a courageous Corazon Aquino (b. 1933), whose politician husband had been murdered, probably by Marcos supporters, the opposition won a spectacular electoral victory in 1986 and forced Marcos to take refuge in Hawaii. After negotiating a cease-fire with the Communist rebels, President Aquino and the Filipino people faced a tremendous challenge of reconciliation and genuine reform. A tiny elite dominated the country, and the gap between rich and poor remained huge.

INDONESIA. The Netherlands East Indies, having successfully resisted stubborn Dutch efforts at reconquest, emerged as independent Indonesia under the nationalist leader Achmed Sukarno (1901–1970) in 1949. The populous new nation encompassed a variety of peoples, islands, and religions (Islam was predominant). Beginning in 1957, Sukarno tried to forge unity by means of his so-called guided democracy, which rejected parliamentary democracy as politically divisive and claimed to replicate at the national level the traditional deliberation and consensus of the Indonesian village. For a time it seemed that the authoritarian, anti-Western Sukarno was under the sway of the well-organized Indonesian Communists, who murdered and mutilated the seven leading army generals they kidnaped as part of an unsuccessful uprising in 1965. The army immediately retaliated, systematically slaughtering a half-million or more Indonesian Communists, radicals, and non-Communist Chinese. Sukarno was forced to resign, and Muslim generals ruled thereafter without any pretense of democracy.

VIETNAM, LAOS, AND CAMBODIA. The most bitterly destructive fighting occurred in French Indochina. The French tried to reimpose imperial rule there after the Communist and nationalist guerrilla leader Ho Chi Minh (1890–1969) declared an independent republic in 1945. In spite of considerable aid from the Americans, the French were decisively defeated in 1954 in the battle of Dien Bien Phu. At the subsequent international peace conference, French

Indochina gained independence. Laos and Cambodia became separate states; Vietnam was "temporarily" divided into two hostile sections at the 17th parallel pending elections to select a single unified government within two years.

The elections were never held and the civil war that soon broke out between the two Vietnamese governments, one Communist and one anti-Communist, became a very hot cold war conflict in the 1960s. The United States, as discussed earlier, invested tremendous military effort but fought its Vietnam War as a deeply divided country (pages 1152–1154). The tough, dedicated Communists eventually proved victorious in 1975. Thus events in Vietnam roughly recapitulated those in China, but in a long, drawn-out fashion: after a bitter civil war exacerbated by cold war hatreds, the Communists succeeded in creating a unified Marxist nation.

THE MUSLIM WORLD

Throughout the vast arc of predominantly Islamic lands that stretches from Indonesia in Southeast Asia to Senegal in West Africa, change and bewildering internal conflict prevailed after 1945. Everywhere, however, nationalism remained the predominant political force. Although anti-Western and hospitable to radical social reform, nationalism in the Muslim world remained consistently true to Islam and generally anti-Communist. Cold war conflicts and enormous oil resources enhanced the region's global standing.

In the Arab countries of North Africa and the Middle East, with their shared but highly differentiated language and culture, nationalism wore two faces. The practical, down-to-earth side occupied itself with nation building within the particular states that supplanted former League of Nations mandates and European colonies. The idealistic, unrealized side focused on the pan-Arab dream, the dream of uniting all Arabs to recapture ancient glory and smash their enemies. Although this dream foundered on the intense regional, ideological, and personal rivalries within the Arab world, it did contribute to political and economic alliances like the Arab League (Map 37.2).

PALESTINE AND ISRAEL. Arab nationlists were already loosely united before World War Two in their opposition to the colonial powers and to Jewish mi-

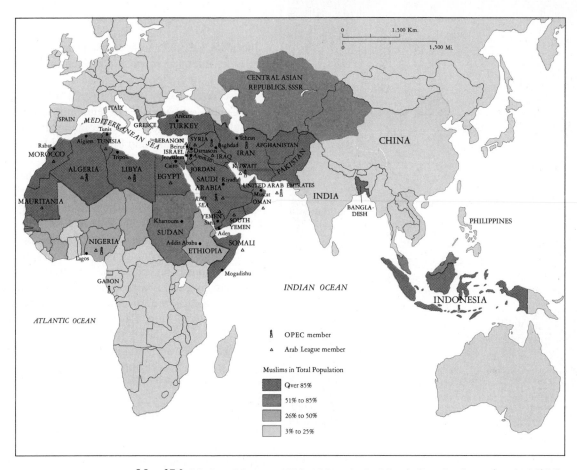

MAP 37.2 **Modern Islam, ca 1980** Although the Islamic heartland remains the Middle East and North Africa, Islam is growing steadily in black Africa and is the faith of heavily populated Indonesia. Compare Maps 10.1 and 10.2.

gration to Palestine. After the French gave up their League of Nations mandates in Syria and Lebanon in 1945, having been forced by popular uprisings and British-American pressure to follow the British example, attention focused even more sharply on British-mandated Palestine. The situation was volatile. The Jews' demand that the British permit all survivors of Hitler's death camps to settle in Palestine was strenuously opposed by the Palestinian Arabs and the seven independent states of the newly founded Arab League. Murder and terrorism flourished, nurtured by bitterly conflicting Arab and Jewish nationalisms.

The British—their occupation policies in Palestine condemned by Arabs and Jews, by Russians and Americans—announced in 1947 their intention to withdraw from Palestine in 1948. Initiating a pattern that was to become familiar, the insoluble problem was dumped in the lap of the United Nations. In November 1947 the United Nations General Assembly passed a nonbinding resolution supporting a plan to partition Palestine into two separate states—one Arab and one Jewish. The Jews accepted but the Arabs rejected partition of Palestine, and by early 1948 an undeclared civil war raged in Palestine. The departing British looked on impartially. When the British mandate officially ended on May 14, 1948, the Jews proclaimed the state of Israel. The Arab countries immediately launched an all-out attack on the new Jewish state. Fighting for their lives, the Israelis drove off the invaders and conquered more territory; 900,000 Arab refugees fled or were expelled from old Palestine. This war left an enormous legacy of Arab bitterness toward Israel and its political allies, Great Britain and the United States.

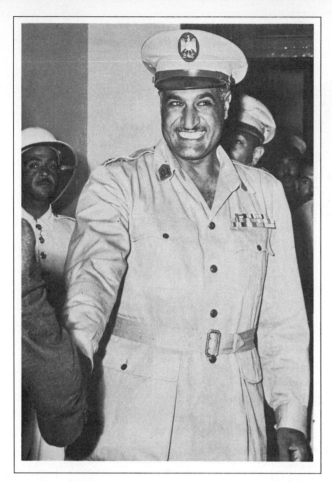

Gamal Abdel Nasser Egypt's charismatic leader and pan-Arab visionary flashes his famous smile during an army parade in Cairo in 1955. *(The Bettmann Archive)*

EGYPT. The humiliation of defeat triggered a nationalist revolution in Egypt, where a young army colonel named Gamal Abdel Nasser (1918–1970) drove out the corrupt and pro-Western king Farouk in 1952. A gifted politician and the unchallenged leader of the largest Arab state, Nasser enjoyed a powerful influence in the Middle East and throughout Asia and Africa. Perhaps his most successful and widely imitated move was radical land reform: large estates along the Nile were nationalized and divided up among peasants, without accompanying violence or drastic declines in production. Nasser, who preached the gospel of neutralism in the cold war and jailed Egyptian Communists, turned for aid to the Soviet Union to demonstrate Egypt's independence. Relations with Israel and the West worsened, and in 1956 Secretary of State John Foster Dulles abruptly canceled a U.S. offer to finance a giant new dam on the Nile, intended to promote economic development.

Nasser retaliated by immediately nationalizing the Suez Canal Company, the last remaining symbol and real substance of European power in the Middle East. Infuriated, the British and French joined forces with the Israelis and successfully invaded Egypt. This was to be the dying gasp of imperial power. Then the Americans, suddenly moralistic, reversed course and joined with the Russians—who were at that very moment crushing the Hungarian revolution—to force the British, French, and Israelis to withdraw from Egypt. This great victory for Nasser encouraged anti-Western radicalism, hopes of pan-Arab political unity, and a vague "Arab socialism." In Iraq radicals overthrew a pro-Western moderate government. In the aftermath of Suez, Egypt merged—temporarily—with Syria.

Yet the Arab world remained deeply divided. The only shared goals were opposition to Israel—war recurred in 1967 and in 1973—and support for the right of Palestinian refugees to return to their homeland. In late 1977, after more than a generation of bitter Arab-Israeli conflict, President Anwar Sadat of Egypt tried another tack: a stunningly unexpected official visit to Israel, where his meeting with Israeli Prime Minister Menachim Begin was watched on television by millions around the world. Sadat's visit led to direct negotiations between Israel and Egypt and a historic if limited peace settlement effectively mediated by U.S. President Jimmy Carter. Sadat's brave initiative was denounced as treason by other Arab leaders, who continued to support the uncompromisingly nationalist Palestine Liberation Organization against Israel.

After Sadat was assassinated by Islamic fundamentalists in 1981, Egypt's relations with the Begin government deteriorated badly over the question of ever-increasing Israeli settlement on the West Bank—the area west of the Jordan River inhabited by Palestinian Arabs but taken by Israel from Jordan during the 1967 Six-Day War and occupied by Israel ever since. Yet Egypt quietly stood by when Israeli troops occupied southern Lebanon in 1982 in an attempt to destroy the Palestine Liberation Organization. Israel's subsequent withdrawal from Lebanon helped preserve the still fragile peace between the former enemies (Map 37.3).

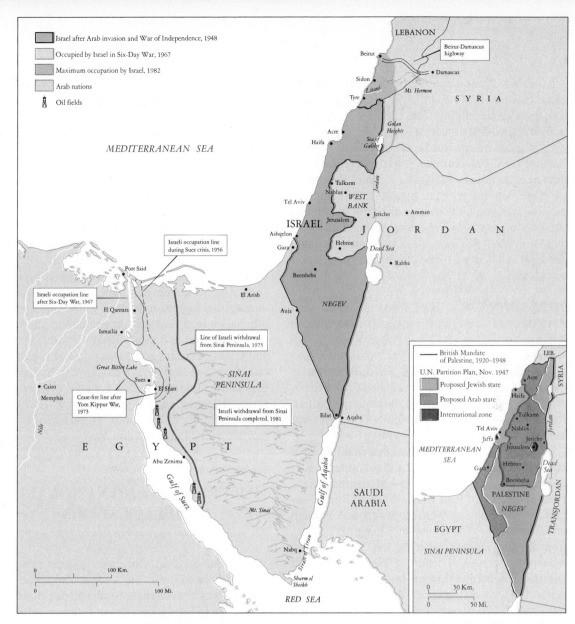

MAP 37.3 Palestine, Israel, and the Middle East, 1947–1983 Since the British mandate expired on May 14, 1948, there have been five major wars and innumerable armed clashes on what was formerly Palestine. After winning the War of Independence in 1948, Israel achieved spectacular victories in 1967 in the Six Day War, occupying the Sinai Peninsula, the Golan Heights, and the West Bank. The Yom Kippur War of 1973 eventually led to the Israeli evacuation of the Sinai and peace with Egypt, but there has been no agreement on the West Bank.

ALGERIA. In the French colony of Algeria, meanwhile, Arab nationalism was emboldened by Nasser's triumph—and by the defeat of the French in Indochina. Neighboring Tunisia and Morocco, both more recently colonized, had won independence from France in 1956. But Algeria's large European popula-tion—1 million French-speaking Europeans lived among 8 million Muslims—considered Algeria home, and an integral part of France. When nationalism stirred Algerian Muslims to revolt, they found themselves confronting a solid bloc of European settlers determined to defend their privileged position.

It was this determination that made the ensuing Algerian war so bitter and bloody. In 1958 a military coup in Algeria, resulting from the fears of the European settlers that a disillusioned, anticolonial majority of French voters would sell them out, brought General De Gaulle back to power in France. Contrary to expectations, De Gaulle accepted the principle of self-determination for Algeria in 1959, and in a national referendum the vast majority of the French population agreed. In 1962, after more than a century of French conquest, Algeria became an independent Arab state. The European population quickly fled.

TURKEY AND IRAN. Developments in the non-Arab states of Turkey and Iran testify to the diverse forms nationalism took in the Muslim world. Turkey remained basically true to Atatürk's vision of a thoroughly modernized, secularized, Europeanized state (page 1045). Islam played a less influential role in daily life and thought there than in other Middle Eastern countries, and Turkey also joined NATO to protect itself from possible Russian aggression.

Iran tried again to follow Turkey's example, as it had before 1939 (see page 1046). Once again, its success was limited. The new shah—Muhammad Reza Pahlavi, the son of Reza Shah—angered Iranian nationalists by courting Western powers and Western oil companies in the course of freeing his country from Russian influence after the war. The shah subsequently accepted the effort of the Iranian Majlis and the fiery Prime Minister Muhammad Mossaddeq in 1951 to nationalize the British-owned Anglo-Iranian Oil Company, until an effective Western boycott of Iranian oil plunged the economy into chaos. Refusing to compromise or be dismissed, Mossaddeq forced the shah to flee to Europe in 1953. But Mossaddeq's victory was short-lived, for the shah was quickly restored to his throne by loyal army officers and with the help of the American CIA. The shah set out to build a powerful modern nation to ensure his rule. Iran's gigantic oil revenues provided the necessary cash. The shah undermined the power bases of the traditional politicians—big landowners and religious leaders—by means of land reform, secular education, and increased power for the central government. Modernization surged forward, but at the price of ancient values, widespread corruption, and harsh dictatorship. The result was a violent reac-

tion against secular values, an Islamic revolution in 1978 led by religious leaders grouped around the spellbinding Ayatollah Ruholla Khomeini. After the shah fled in 1979, radicals seized fifty-two American diplomats and imprisoned them for a year as they battled successfully to consolidate their power.

Iran's radical Islamic republic frightened its neighbors. Iraq, especially, feared that Iran—a nation of Shi'ite Muslims (pages 265–266)—would succeed in getting Iraq's Shi'ite majority to revolt against its Sunnite leaders. Thus in September 1980, Iraq launched a surprise attack, expecting its well-equipped armies to rout an increasingly chaotic Iran. Instead, as the student of history might well have predicted, Iraqi aggression galvanized the Iranian revolutionaries in a fanatical determination to defend their homeland and punish Iraq's leaders. Iranians and Iraqis—Persians and Arabs—locked together in one of the bloodiest wars in modern times, a combat that killed hundreds of thousands of soldiers. The savage stalemate was still grinding on in 1987, awesome testimony to the combined power of Islamic radicalism and Iranian nationalism.

IMPERIALISM AND NATIONALISM IN BLACK AFRICA

Most of sub-Saharan Africa won political independence fairly rapidly after the Second World War. Only Portugal's old but relatively underdeveloped African territories and white-dominated southern Africa remained beyond the reach of African nationalists by 1964. The rise of independent states in black Africa —a decisive development in world history—resulted directly from both a reaction against Western imperialism and the growth of African nationalism.

THE IMPERIAL SYSTEM, 1900–1930

European traders had been in constant contact with Africa's coastal regions ever since the Age of Discovery. In the nineteenth century, as trade in so-called "legitimate products" like peanuts and palm oil increasingly supplanted "illegitimate" traffic in human beings, European influence continued to grow. Then came the political onslaught. After 1880 the Great

District Officer on Tour For many Africans, imperialism meant the local colonial official, who might be a vicious, petty tyrant or a relatively enlightened administrator. This humorous wood carving by Thomas Ona grows out of the rich satirical tradition upheld by the Yoruba of western Nigeria. *(Berta Bascom/Lowie Museum of Anthropology, University of California, Berkeley)*

Powers scrambled for territory and pushed into the interior, using overwhelming military force to mow down or intimidate African opposition and establish firm rule (pages 943–946). By 1900, most of black Africa had been conquered—or, as Europeans preferred to say, "pacified"—and a system of imperial administration was taking shape.

Gradually but relentlessly, this imperial system transformed Africa. Generally speaking, its effect was to weaken or shatter the traditional social order and challenge accepted values. Yet this generalization must be qualified. For one thing, sub-Saharan Africa consisted of an astonishing diversity of peoples and cultures prior to the European invasion. There were, for example, over eight hundred distinct languages and literally thousands of independent political units, ranging all the way from tiny kinship groups to large and powerful kingdoms like Ashanti of central Ghana and Ethiopia. The effects of imperialism varied accordingly.

Furthermore, the European powers themselves took rather different approaches to colonial rule. The British, for example, tended to exercise indirect rule through existing chiefs. The French believed in direct rule by appointed officials, both black and white. Finally, the number of white settlers varied greatly from region to region, which had important consequences. With these qualifications in mind, how did imperial systems generally operate in black Africa?

The self-proclaimed political goal of the French and the British—the principal foreign powers in black Africa—was to provide "good government" for their African subjects, especially after 1919. Good government meant, above all, law and order. It meant maintaining a small army and building up an African police force to put down rebellion, suppress tribal warfare, and protect life and property. More broadly, good government required a modern bureaucracy capable of taxing and governing the population. Since many African leaders and their peoples realistically chose not to resist the invader's superior force, and most others stopped fighting after experiencing crushing military defeat, the goal of law and order was widely achieved. This was a great source of satisfaction to colonial officials; it strengthened their self-confidence and convinced them that they were serving the common people, who were assumed to want only peace and security.

Colonial governments demonstrated much less interest in providing basic social services. Expenditures on education, public health, hospitals, and other social services increased after the First World War, but still remained small. Europeans feared the political implications of mass education, and typically relied instead on the modest efforts of state-subsidized mission schools. Moreover, they tried to make even their poorest colonies pay for themselves. This meant that salaries for government workers normally absorbed nearly all tax revenues.

Economically, the imperialist goal was to draw the vast untapped interior of the continent into the rapidly expanding world economy on terms that were favorable for the dominant Europeans. Thus, as they completed their sometimes bloody conquest, the Europeans acted in black Africa as they had in Asia, North Africa, and Latin America. The key was railroads, from coastal trading centers to outposts hundreds of miles into the interior. Cheap, dependable transportation facilitated easy shipment of raw materials out and manufactured goods in. Most African railroads were built after 1900; 5,200 miles were in operation by 1926, when attention turned to road building for trucks. Railroads and roads had two other important outcomes: troops could be moved quickly to put down any local unrest. And many African peasants began to earn wages for the first time.

Efforts to force Africa into the world economy on European terms went hand in hand with the advent of plantations and mines. The Europeans often imposed head taxes, payable in money or labor, to compel Africans to work for their white overlords. No aspect of imperialism was more disruptive and more despised by Africans than forced labor, widespread until about 1920. In some regions, however, particularly in West Africa, African peasants responded freely to the new economic opportunities by voluntarily shifting to export crops on their own farms. Overall, the result was increased production geared to the world market and a gradual decline in both traditional self-sufficient farming and nomadic herding.

In sum, the imposition of bureaucratic Western rule and the gradual growth of a world-oriented cash economy between 1900 and 1930 had a revolutionary impact on large parts of Africa. The experiences of two very different African countries will dramatically illustrate variations on the general pattern.

GHANA AND KENYA

Present-day Ghana, which takes its name from one of West Africa's most famous early kingdoms, had a fairly complex economy well before British armies smashed the powerful Ashanti kingdom in 1873 and established a Crown colony they called the Gold Coast. Precolonial local trade was vigorous and varied, though occasionally disrupted by war and hindered by poor transportation, especially in the rainy season.

It was into this sophisticated economy that the British introduced production of cocoa beans for the world's chocolate bars. Output rose spectacularly, from a few hundred tons in the 1890s to 305,000 tons in 1936. British imperialists loved to brag about the railroads to the interior, but recent studies clearly show that independent peasants and energetic African businesspeople—many of the traders were women—were mainly responsible for the spectacular success of cocoa-bean production. Creative African entrepreneurs even went so far as to build their own roads, and they sometimes reaped big profits; in the boom of 1920, "motor cars were purchased right and left, champagne flowed freely, and expensive cigars scented the air."[7] As neighboring West African territories followed the Gold Coast's lead, West Africa took its place in the world economy.

The Gold Coast also showed the way politically and culturally. The westernized elite—relatively prosperous and well-educated lawyers, professionals, and journalists—and businesspeople took full advantage of opportunities provided by the fairly enlightened colonial regime. The black elite was the main presence in the limited local elections permitted by the British, for few permanent white settlers had ventured to hot and densely populated West Africa.

Across the continent in the British East African colony of Kenya, events unfolded differently. The East African peoples were more self-sufficient, less numerous, and less advanced commercially and politically. Once the British had built a strategic railroad

A West African Market West Africa experienced considerable economic development in the 1920s, much of it due to the imaginative efforts of enterprising African traders and peasants. These women are local traders on the Gold Coast. *(Popperfoto)*

from the coast across Kenya to Uganda, foreigners from Great Britain and India moved in to exploit the situation. Indian settlers became shopkeepers, clerks, and laborers in the towns. The British settlers, an amalgam of greedy adventurers and rich aristocrats, shared a common dream: to turn the cool, beautiful, and fertile Kenya highlands into a "white man's country" like Southern Rhodesia or the Union of South Africa. They dismissed the local population of peasant farmers as "barbarians," fit only to toil as cheap labor on their large estates and plantations. By 1929, two thousand white settlers, connected to the coast by a network of railroads, were producing a variety of crops for export.

The white settlers in Kenya manipulated the colonial government for their own interests and imposed rigorous segregation on the black (and Indian) population. Kenya's Africans thus experienced much

harsher colonial rule than their fellow Africans in the Gold Coast.

THE GROWTH OF AFRICAN NATIONALISM

Western intrusion was the critical factor in the development of African nationalism, as it had been in Asia and the Middle East. Yet two things were different about Africa. Because the imperial system and Western education did not solidify in Africa until after 1900, national movements did not come of age there until after 1945. And too, Africa's multiplicity of ethnic groups, coupled with imperial boundaries that often bore no resemblance to existing ethnic boundaries, greatly complicated the development of political —as distinct from cultural—nationalism. Was a modern national state to be based on ethnic tribal loyalties (as it had been in France and Germany, in

China and Japan)? Was it to be founded on an all-African union of all black peoples? Or would such a state have to be built on the multitribal territories arbitrarily carved out by competing European empires? Only after 1945 did a tentative answer emerge.

A few educated West Africans in British colonies had articulated a kind of black nationalism before 1914. But the first real impetus came from the United States and the British West Indies. American blacks struggling energetically for racial justice and black self-confidence early in the twentieth century took a keen interest in their African origins and in the common problems of all black people. Their influence on educated Africans was great.

Of the many persons who participated in this "black nationalism" and in the "Renaissance" of American black literature in the 1920s, the most renowned was W. E. B. Du Bois (1868–1963). The first black to receive a Ph.D. from Harvard, this brilliant writer and historian was poignantly aware of his African origins and of the psychological pressures of Western culture. As Du Bois wrote in 1903 in *The Souls of Black Folk*:

It is a peculiar sensation, this double consciousness, this sense of always looking at one's self through the eyes of others, of measuring one's soul by the tape of a world that looks on in amused contempt and pity. One ever feels his two-ness—an American, a Negro: two souls, two thoughts, two unreconciled strivings, two warrings ideals in one dark body, whose dogged strength alone keeps it from being torn asunder.[8]

Stirred by President Wilson's promises of self-determination, Du Bois organized pan-African congresses in Paris during the Versailles Peace Conference and in Brussels in 1921. The goals of pan-Africanists (that is, "all-Africanists") were solidarity among blacks everywhere and, eventually, a vast self-governing union of all African peoples.

The European powers were hostile, of course, but so was the tiny minority of educated blacks in the French Empire. As the influential Blaise Daigne, a black politician elected to the French parliament by the privileged African "citizens" of Senegal, told Du Bois:

We Frenchmen of Africa wish to remain French, for France has given us every liberty and accepted us with-

out reservation along with her European children. None of us aspire to see French Africa delivered exclusively to the Africans as is demanded, though without any authority, by the American Negroes.[9]

More authoritarian than the British but less racist, French imperialists aimed to create a tiny elite of loyal "black Frenchmen" who would link the uneducated African masses to their white rulers. They were sometimes quite successful.

But educated French and British Africans experienced a strong surge of pride and cultural nationalism in the 1920s and 1930s, ignited in part by American and West Indian blacks. The Senegalese poet and political leader Léopold Senghor (b. 1906) is an outstanding example.

Senghor, a gifted interpreter of Catholicism and of the French language in his native Senegal, discovered his African heritage in the cafés and lecture halls of Paris. He and other black and white students and intellectuals marveled at the accomplishments of American blacks in art, literature, African history, and anthropology. They listened to black musicians —jazz swept Europe by storm—and concluded that

in music American Negroes have acquired since the War a place which one can call pre-eminent; for they have impressed the entire world with their vibrating or melancholy rhythms.[10]

Senghor and his circle formulated and articulated the rich idea of *négritude,* or blackness. By blackness they meant racial pride, self-confidence, and joy in black creativity and the black spirit. The powerful cultural nationalism that grew out of the cross-fertilization of African intellectuals and blacks from the United States and the West Indies was an unexpected by-product of European imperialism.

Black consciousness also emerged in the British colonies between the world wars—especially in West Africa, which remained more advanced than East and Central Africa. The westernized elite pressed for more equal access to government jobs, modest steps toward self-government, and an end to humiliating discrimination. This elite began to claim the right to speak for ordinary Africans and to denounce the government-supported chiefs as Uncle Toms. Yet the great majority of well-educated British and French Africans remained moderate in their demands. They wanted to join the white man's club, not to tear it down.

The Great Depression was the decisive turning point in the development of African nationalism. For the first time unemployment was widespread among educated Africans, who continued to increase in number as job openings in government and the big foreign trading companies remained stable or even declined. Hostility toward well-paid white officials rose sharply. The Western-educated elite became more vocal and more political in its call for change. Some real radicals appeared.

Educated Africans ventured into new activities, often out of necessity. Especially in the towns, they supplied the leadership for many new organizations, including not only political parties and trade unions but also social clubs, native churches, and agricultural cooperatives. Radical journalists published uncompromising attacks on colonial governments in easy-to-read mass-circulation newspapers. The most spectacular of these journalists was the Nigerian Nnamdi Azikiwe, who had attended black colleges in the United States and learned his trade on an Afro-American weekly in Baltimore. The popular, flamboyant "Zik" was demanding independence for Nigeria as early as the late 1930s.

The Great Depression also produced extreme economic hardship and profound discontent among the African masses. African peasants and small business-people who had been drawn into world trade, and sometimes profited from booms, now felt the agony of decade-long bust. Urban workers, many of whom were disaffiliated from their rural tribal origins, experienced a similar fate. In some areas the result was unprecedented mass protest.

The Gold Coast "cocoa holdups" of 1930–1931 and 1937–1938 are the most famous example. Cocoa completely dominated the Gold Coast's economy. As prices plummeted and cash incomes collapsed after 1929, cocoa farmers refused to sell their beans to the big British firms that fixed prices and monopolized the export trade. Instead, the farmers organized cooperatives to cut back production and sell their crops directly to European and American chocolate manufacturers. Small African traders and traditional tribal leaders largely supported the movement, which succeeded in mobilizing much of the population against the foreign companies. Many Africans saw the economic conflict in racial terms. The holdups were only partially successful, but they did force the government to establish an independent cocoa marketing board. They also demonstrated that mass organization and mass protest had come to advanced West Africa. Powerful mass-based movements for national independence could not be far behind.

ACHIEVING INDEPENDENCE WITH NEW LEADERS

The repercussions of the Second World War in black Africa greatly accelerated the changes begun in the 1930s. Mines and plantations strained to meet wartime demands. Towns mushroomed into cities, whose tin-can housing, inflation, and shortages of consumer goods created discontent and hardship. Africans had such eye-opening experiences as the curious spectacle of the British denouncing the racism of the Germans. Many African soldiers who served in India were powerfully impressed by Indian nationalism.

The attitudes of Western imperialists also changed. Both the British and the French acknowledged the need for rapid social and economic improvement in their colonies; both began sending money and aid on a large scale for the first time. The French funneled more money into their west African colonies between 1947 and 1957 than during the entire previous half-century. The principle of self-government was written into the United Nations charter and was now fully supported by Great Britain's postwar Labour government. As one top British official stated in 1948:

The central purpose of British colonial policy is simple. It is to guide the colonial territories to responsible government within the commonwealth in conditions that ensure to the people concerned both a fair standard of living and freedom from oppression from any quarter.[11]

Thus the key question for Great Britain's various African colonies was their rate of progress toward self-government. As usual the British, like the French, were in no rush. But a new breed of African leader was emerging, first in the British and then in the French colonies. Impatient and insistent, figures like Nkrumah, Azikiwe, and Touré were determined to gain political independence as soon as possible. These authentic spokesmen for modern African na-

Nationalism in Black Africa

1919	Du Bois organizes first pan-African congress
1920s	Cultural nationalism grows among Africa's educated elites
1929	Great Depression brings economic hardship and discontent
1930–1931	Farmers in the Gold Coast organize first "cocoa hold-ups"
1939–1945	World War Two accelerates political and economic change
1951	Nkrumah and Convention People's Party win national elections
1957	Nkrumah leads Ghana—former Gold Coast—to independence
1958	De Gaulle offers commonwealth status to France's African territories; Guinea alone chooses independence
1960	Mali and Nigeria become independent states
1966	Ghana's Nkrumah deposed in military coup
1967	Eastern Region secedes from Nigeria to form state of Biafra
1975	Nigeria's military rulers permit elected civilian government
1980	Blacks rule Zimbabwe—formerly southern Rhodesia—after long civil war with white settlers
1983	South Africa's whites maintain racial segregation and discrimination

tionalism were remarkably successful: by 1964 almost all of West, East, and Central Africa had achieved statehood, usually without much bloodshed. Only the uncompromising Portuguese and the white settlers of southern Africa remained impervious to nationalist demands.

The new postwar African leaders shared common characteristics. They formed an elite by virtue of advanced European (or American) education and they had been profoundly influenced by Western thought. But compared to the interwar generation of educated Africans, they were more radical and humbler in social origin. Among them were former schoolteachers, union leaders, government clerks, and unemployed students, as well as lawyers and prize-winning poets.

Furthermore, the postwar African leaders expressed their nationalism in terms of the existing territorial governments. They accepted prevailing boundaries to avoid border disputes and to facilitate building unified modern states. Sometimes traditional tribal chiefs became their worst political ene-

mies. Skillfully, the new leaders channeled postwar hope and discontent into support for mass political parties. These new parties in turn organized gigantic protests, and eventually came to power by winning elections held by the colonial government to choose its successor.

Ghana Shows the Way

Perhaps the most charismatic of this fascinating generation of African leaders was Kwame Nkrumah (1909–1972), under whose leadership the Gold Coast —which he rechristened Ghana—became the first independent African state to emerge from colonialism. Having begun his career as a schoolteacher in the Gold Coast, Nkrumah spent ten years studying in the United States, where he was deeply influenced by European socialists and by the Jamaican-born black leader Marcus Garvey. Garvey, convinced that blacks could never win justice in countries with white majorities, had organized a massive "Back to Africa" movement in the 1920s. He also preached "Africa for the Africans," advocating independence. Nkrumah returned to the Gold Coast immediately after the war and entered politics.

The time was ripe. Economic discontent erupted in rioting in February 1948; angry crowds looted European and Lebanese stores. The British, embarking on their new course, invited African proposals for constitutional reform. These proposals became the basis of the new constitution, which gave more power to Africans within the framework of (eventual) parliamentary democracy.

Meanwhile Nkrumah was building a radical mass party appealing particularly to modern elements—urban toughs, ex-servicemen, market women, union members, and cocoa farmers. Nkrumah and his party injected the joy and enthusiasm of religious revivals into their rallies and propaganda: "Self-Government Now" was their credo, secular salvation the promise.

Rejecting halfway measures—"We prefer self-government with danger to servitude in tranquillity"—Nkrumah and his Convention People's party staged strikes and riots. Arrested, the "Deliverer of Ghana" campaigned from jail and saw his party win a smashing victory in the national elections of 1951. Called from prison to head the transitional government, Nkrumah and his nationalist party continued to win victories in free elections, defeating both westernized moderates and more traditional "tribal" rivals. By 1957 Nkrumah had achieved worldwide fame and influence as Ghana became the first African state to emerge from colonial control.

After Ghana's breakthrough, independence for other African colonies followed with breathtaking speed. As in Algeria, the main problem was the permanent white settlers, as distinguished from the colonial officials. Wherever white settlers were at all numerous, as in Kenya, they sought to preserve their privileged position. This white hope was fed by a substantial influx of white settlers after 1945, especially in Central Africa. Yet only in Southern Rhodesia were whites numerous enough to prevail long. Southern Rhodesian whites declared independence illegally in 1965 and held out for more than a decade until black nationalists won a long guerrilla war and renamed the country Zimbabwe. In Zambia (formerly Northern Rhodesia) and East Africa, white settlers simply lacked the numbers to challenge black nationalists or the British colonial office for long.

Kwame Nkrumah This flamboyant radical leader built a mass movement to gain political independence, though he failed to create a pan-African political union. *(UPI/ Bettmann Newsphotos)*

FRENCH-SPEAKING REGIONS

Decolonization took a somewhat different course in French-speaking Africa. As already discussed (pages 1181–1182), France tried desperately after 1945 to hold on to Indochina and Algeria. Thus, although France upped its financial and technical aid to its African colonies, independence remained a dirty word until De Gaulle came to power in 1958. Seeking to head off radical nationalists, and with the crucial support of moderate black leaders, De Gaulle divided the federations of French West Africa and French

Equatorial Africa into thirteen separate governments, thus creating a "French commonwealth." Plebiscites were called in each territory to ratify the new arrangement. The ballot was worded so that an affirmative vote meant continued ties with France; a *no* vote signified immediate independence and a complete break with France.

De Gaulle's gamble was shrewd. The educated black elite—as personified by the poet Senghor, who now led the government of Senegal—loved France and dreaded a sudden divorce. They also wanted continued French aid. France, in keeping with its ideology of assimilation, had given the vote to the educated elite in its colonies after World War Two, and about forty Africans held seats in the French parliament after 1946. Some of these impressive African politicians exercised real power and influence in metropolitan France. The Ivory Coast's Félix Houphouët-Boigny, for instance, served for a time as France's minister of health. For both cultural and practical reasons, therefore, French Africa's leaders tended to be moderate and in no rush for independence.

Yet political nationalism was not totally submerged. In Guinea, an inspiring young radical named Sekou Touré (1922–1984) led his people in overwhelming rejection of the new constitution in 1958. Touré had risen to prominence as a labor leader in his country's rapidly expanding mining industry; he had close ties with France's Communist-dominated trade unions and was inspired by Ghana's Nkrumah. Touré laid it out to De Gaulle, face to face:

We have to tell you bluntly, Mr. President, what the demands of the people are. . . . We have one prime and essential need: our dignity. But there is no dignity without freedom. . . . We prefer freedom in poverty to opulence in slavery.[12]

De Gaulle punished Guinea as best he could. French officials and equipment were withdrawn, literally overnight, down to the last man and pencil. Guinea's total collapse was widely predicted—and devoutly hoped for in France. Yet Guinea's new government survived. Following Guinea's lead, Mali asked for independence in 1960. The other French territories quickly followed suit, though the new states retained very close ties with France.

Belgium tried belatedly to imitate De Gaulle in its enormous Congo colony, but without success. Long-

MAP 37.4 Nationalism and Independence in West Africa Most of West Africa achieved independence by 1960. Borders inherited from the colonial era were generally accepted, although the Ibo people tried unsuccessfully to break away from Nigeria in the bitter Nigerian Civil (Biafran) War.

time practitioners of extreme paternalism coupled with harsh, selfish rule, the Belgians had discouraged the development of an educated elite. In 1959, therefore, when following wild riots they suddenly decided to grant independence, the fabric of government simply broke down. Independence was soon followed by violent tribal conflict, civil war, and foreign intervention. The Belgian Congo was the great exception to black Africa's generally peaceful and successful transition to independence between 1957 and 1964 (Map 37.4).

BLACK AFRICA SINCE 1960

The ease with which most of black Africa achieved independence stimulated buoyant optimism in the early 1960s. While Europeans congratulated themselves on having fulfilled their "civilizing mission," Africans and sympathetic Americans anticipated even more rapid progress.

Twenty years later the outlook was different. In most former colonies, democratic government and civil liberties had given way to one-party rule or military dictatorship. Even where dictatorship did not prevail or was overturned, political conduct in Africa often seemed to slip into reverse gear. In many countries it was routine for the winners in a political power struggle to imprison, exile, or murder the losers. Corruption was widespread; politicians, army officers, and even lowly government clerks used their positions to line their pockets and reward their relatives. Meanwhile the challenge of constructive economic and social development, which will be examined in Chapter 39, sometimes appeared overwhelming.

Some European and American observers, surveying these conditions, went so far as to write off Africa as a lost cause. Such a dismissal betrayed a limited vision and a serious lack of historical perspective. Given the scope of their challenges, the new African

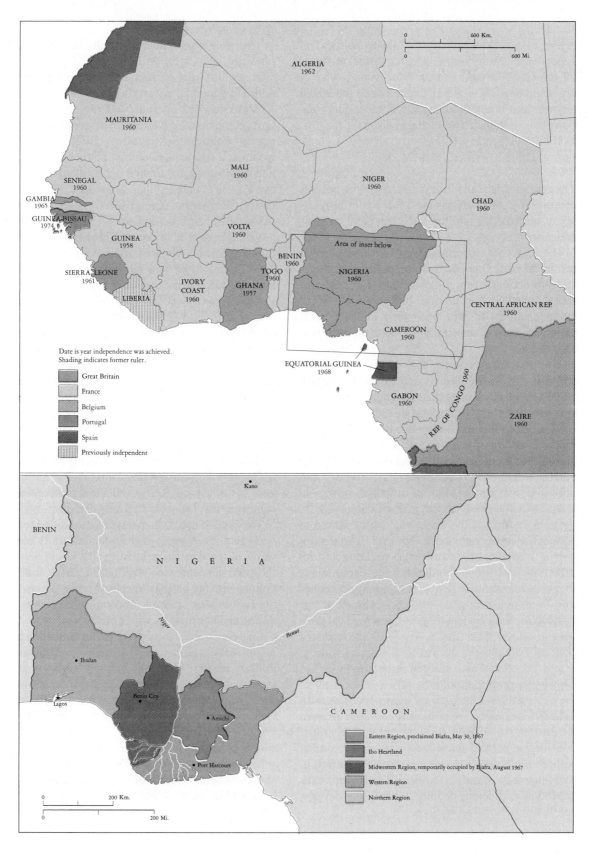

ALGERIA
1962

MAURITANIA
1960

MALI
1960

NIGER
1960

CHAD
1960

SENEGAL
1960

GAMBIA
1965

GUINEA-BISSAU
1974

GUINEA
1958

VOLTA
1960

SIERRA LEONE
1961

IVORY
COAST
1960

LIBERIA

TOGO
1960

GHANA
1957

BENIN
1960

NIGERIA
1960

Area of inset below

CENTRAL AFRICAN REP.
1960

CAMEROON
1960

Date is year independence was achieved.
Shading indicates former ruler.

Great Britain
France
Belgium
Portugal
Spain
Previously independent

EQUATORIAL GUINEA
1968

GABON
1960

REP. OF CONGO 1960

ZAIRE
1960

Kano

BENIN

N I G E R I A

Niger

Benue

Ibadan

Lagos

Benin City

Amichi

CAMEROON

Port Harcourt

Eastern Region, proclaimed Biafra, May 30, 1967
Ibo Heartland
Midwestern Region, temporarily occupied by Biafra, August 1967
Western Region
Northern Region

0   200 Km.

0   200 Mi.

0   600 Km.

0   600 Mi.

countries did rather well after achieving political independence. Nationalism, first harnessed to throw off imperialism, served to promote some degree of unity and ongoing modernization. Fragile states held together and began to emerge as viable modern nation-states with their own distinct personalities.

BUILDING NATIONAL UNITY

The course of African history after independence was complex and often confusing. Yet the common legacy of imperialism resulted in certain basic patterns and problems.

The legacy of imperialism in Africa was by no means all bad. One positive outcome was the creation of about forty well-defined states. These new states inherited functioning bureaucracies, some elected political leaders, and some modern infrastructure—that is, transportation, schools, hospitals, and the like.

The new African states also inherited relatively modern, diversified social structures. Traditional tribal and religious rulers had generally lost out to a dynamic westernized elite, whose moderate and radical wings faithfully reproduced the twentieth-century political spectrum. Each new state also had the beginnings of an industrial working class (as well as a volatile urban poor population). Each country also inherited the cornerstone of imperial power—a tough, well-equipped army to maintain order.

Other features of the imperialist legacy served to torment independent Africa, however. The disruption of traditional life caused real suffering and resulted in fantastic postindependence expectations that could not be met. The prevailing export economies were weak, lopsided, and concentrated in foreign hands. Technical, managerial, and medical skills were in acutely short supply. Above all, the legacy of political boundaries imposed by foreigners without regard to ethnic and cultural groupings weighed heavily on postindependence Africa. Almost all of the new states encompassed a variety of peoples, with different languages, religions, and cultures. In such circumstances, building up the central government and forging a truly unified country could conflict with ethnic loyalties. As in the Austrian Empire in the nineteenth century or in British India before independence, different peoples might easily develop conflicting national aspirations.

The multiethnic character of the new states had a powerful impact on African political development after 1960. Great Britain and France had granted Africa democratic government in the belief that, if Africans insisted on independence, they might as well get the best. Yet Western-style democracy served poorly. Political parties often coalesced along regional and ethnic lines, so that political competition encouraged regional and ethnic conflict. Many African leaders concluded that democracy threatened to destroy the existing states, which they deemed essential for social and economic progress, in spite of their less-than-perfect boundaries. These leaders imposed tough measures to hold their countries together. Thus free elections and representative governments often gave way to dictators and one-party rule.

After Ghana won its independence, for instance, Nkrumah jailed without trial his main opponents—chiefs, lawyers, and intellectuals—and outlawed opposition parties. Embracing the totalitarian model, Nkrumah worked to build a dynamic "revolutionary" one-party state. Nkrumah's personality, his calls for African unity, and his bitter attacks on "Western imperialists" aroused both strong support and growing opposition. By the mid-1960s Nkrumah's grandiose economic projects had almost bankrupted Ghana, and in 1966 the army suddenly seized power while Nkrumah was visiting China. Across the continent in East Africa, Kenya and Tanzania likewise became one-party states with strong leaders.

The French-speaking countries also shifted toward one-party government to promote state unity and develop distinctive characteristics that could serve as the basis for statewide nationalism. Mali followed Guinea into fire-eating radicalism, while Senegal and the Ivory Coast stressed moderation and close economic and cultural ties with France.

Like Nkrumah, many of the politicians at the helm of one-party states were eventually overthrown by military leaders. "The man on horseback" became a familiar figure in postindependence Africa. Between 1952, when Egypt's King Farouk was overthrown by Colonel Nasser, and 1968, Africa experienced at least seventy attempted military takeovers, twenty of which succeeded. The trend continued after 1968 with important coups in Ethiopia, Liberia, Uganda, and elsewhere. The rise of would-be Napoleons was lamented by many Western liberals and African intellectuals, who often failed to note that military rule was also widespread in Latin America, Asia, and the Near East.

As elsewhere, military rule in Africa was by nature authoritarian and undemocratic. Sometimes it placed a terrible burden on Africans; in Uganda, for instance, a brutal ex-sergeant named Idi Amin (b. 1925?) seized power, packed the army with his tribal supporters, and terrorized the population for a decade. Yet military government often had redeeming qualities. Generally speaking, African military leaders managed to hold their countries together, and they worked to build existing states into viable nations. In the former Belgian Congo in the early 1960s, and in Ethiopia in the late 1970s, military governments successfully defeated separatist movements.

Equally important, military regimes were deeply committed to social and economic modernization. Drawing on a well-educated, well-organized, and highly motivated elite, they sometimes accomplished a good deal. Finally, African military leaders often believed in the ultimate goal of free, representative civilian government, which they sometimes restored after surmounting a grave national crisis. It was a question of priorities: unity came first, democracy second.

Nigeria, Africa's Giant

The history of Nigeria illustrated just how difficult nation building could be when state and ethnic boundaries were at odds with each other. Nigeria was a name coined by the British to designate their conquests in the Niger River basin. The peoples of Nigeria encompassed many ancient kingdoms and hundreds of smaller groupings. The northern region was part of a great open plain, devoted to grazing and intensive farming; the much smaller southern region was a combination of coastal swamp and inland forest belt. Generally speaking, the peoples of the north were Muslims, while most southerners were Christians or animists. The south was dominated by two very different peoples: in the west the proud Yorubas, with a military tradition and strong, well-defined kingdom, and in the east the Ibos, with a tradition of business enterprise and independent villages.

Modern Nigeria came into being in 1914, when the British arbitrarily consolidated the northern and southern territories for administrative convenience. One British governor described Nigeria in 1920 as a:

collection of self-contained and mutually independent Native States, separated from one another, as many of them are, by differences of history and traditions, and by ethnological, racial, tribal, political, and religious barriers.

Such a land, the governor believed, could never be welded into a single homogeneous nation.

In spite of its internal divisions, Nigeria had spawned a powerful independence movement by 1945. The British responded receptively, and Nigeria entered into a period of intense but peaceful negotiation. In 1954, the third constitution in seven years set up the framework within which independence was achieved in 1960.

The key constitutional question was the relationship between the central government and the various regions. Some Nigerians, like the fiery Ibo journalist Azikiwe, wanted a strong centralized state; but the Yorubas in the west and the Muslim Hausa-Fulani leaders in the north wanted real power concentrated at the regional level. Ultimately Nigeria adopted a federal system, whereby the national government at Lagos shared power with three regional or state governments in the north, west, and east. Each region had a dominant tribe and a corresponding political party. The parties were expected to cooperate in the national parliament, and the rights of minorities were protected by law.

With a population of 55 million in 1963, "Africa's Giant" towered over the other new African nations. But after independence, Nigerians' bright hopes gradually dimmed. Ethnic rivalries made for political tensions. In 1964, minorities in the Western Region began forming their own Mid-West Region in an attempt to escape Yoruba domination. Tribal battles ensued, and in 1965 law and order broke down completely in the Western Region. At this point a group of young army officers seized power in the capital city of Lagos, executing leading politicians and all officers above the rank of major. In an attempt to end the national crisis, the new military council imposed martial law and abolished the regional governments.

At first the young officers were popular, for the murdered politicians had been widely considered weak, corrupt, and too pro-Western. However, most of the new military leaders were Ibos. The Muslim northerners had long distrusted the hardworking and clannish Ibos, who under the British had come to

Mobilizing in Biafra A Biafran officer, himself only nine years old, drills a column of fresh recruits in 1969 during the Nigerian civil war. The boy soldiers were used for spying and sabotage, as Biafra struggled desperately against encirclement and starvation to win its independence. *(Pictorial Parade)*

dominate business and the professions throughout Nigeria. Every northern town had its Ibo "strangers' district." When the Ibo-led military council proclaimed a highly centralized dictatorship, angry mobs in northern cities went wild. Thousand of Ibos were brutally massacred, and the panic-stricken survivors fled to their Ibo homeland. When a group of northern officers then seized the national government in a counter-coup, the traumatized Ibos revolted. Like the American South in the Civil War, the Eastern Region seceded from Nigeria in 1967 and proclaimed itself the independent state of Biafra.

The war in Biafra lasted three long years. The Ibos fought with heroic determination, believing that political independence was their only refuge from genocide. Heavily outnumbered, the Ibos were gradually surrounded. Hundreds of thousands, perhaps millions, starved to death as Biafra became another name for monumental human tragedy.

But Nigeria, like Abraham Lincoln's Union, endured. The civil war entered the history books of the victors as the War for Nigerian Unity, not the War for Biafran Independence. Whatever its name, the conflict in Nigeria showed the world that Africa's "artificial" boundaries and states were remarkably durable.

Having preserved the state in the 1960s, Nigeria's military focused on building a nation in the 1970s. While the federal government held the real power, the country was divided into nineteen small, manageable states to handle local and cultural matters. The defeated Ibos were generously pardoned, not slaughtered, and Iboland was rebuilt with federal money. Modernizing investments of this kind were made possible by soaring oil revenues; Nigeria became the world's seventh-largest oil producer. In 1979, after thirteen years of military rule, Nigeria's army leaders were confident enough to relinquish power to an elected civilian government. With 80 million people, Nigeria became the world's fourth-largest democracy.

Yet history repeated itself. Four years later the army again seized control, arresting the civilian politicians at the head of Nigeria's Second Republic. Once again, the coup was popular, for the politicians had mismanaged the economy and lined their pockets with bribes and kickbacks. But the military rulers soon imposed a harsh dictatorship that violated human rights as badly as the greedy politicians had abused the public trust. Any citizen could be described a security risk and imprisoned indefinitely without trial. Most ominously, the military dictatorship was dominated by Hausa-Fulani Muslims, and these northerners practiced a tribal favoritism that threatened to reignite the regional and ethnic tensions that were never far beneath the surface. Thus a group of reforming officers engineered another coup in 1985, promising more liberty and less favoritism. Nigeria appeared headed for years of military rule, but the generals appeared ready to respect basic rights as they held the country together.

The Struggle in Southern Africa

After the great rush toward political independence, decolonization stalled. Meanwhile southern Africa remained under white rule, largely due to the numerical strength and determination of its white settlers. In Portuguese Angola and Mozambique, the white population actually increased from 70,000 to 380,000 between 1940 and the mid-1960s as white settlers established large coffee farms using forced native labor.

As economic exploitation grew, so did resentment. Nationalist liberation movements arose to wage unrelenting guerrilla warfare. After a coup overturning the long-established dictatorship in Portugal, the guerrillas managed to take control in Angola and Mozambique in 1975. Shortly thereafter, a coalition of nationalist groups also won in Zimbabwe after a long war of liberation.

This second round of decolonization in black Africa was bloodier than the first. The third round, now in progress in South Africa, promises to be worse yet. The racial conflict in the white-ruled Republic of South Africa can be traced back in history—to the seventeenth-century Dutch settlers, complex rivalries between black tribes, settler wars of extermination and enslavement in the eighteenth and nine-

teenth centuries, and the surging British imperialism that resulted in the Boer War (page 943). Although the British finally conquered the inland Afrikaner republics, they had to compromise to avoid a long guerrilla war. Specifically, the British agreed to grant all of South Africa self-government as soon as possible and to let its government decide which nonwhites, if any, should vote. It was to be a tragic compromise.

Defeated on the battlefield, the embittered Afrikaners elaborated a potently racist nationalism. Between 1910—when South Africa became basically a self-governing dominion, like Canada and Australia—and 1948, the Afrikaners gradually won political power from their English-speaking settler rivals. Since their decisive electoral victory in 1948, Afrikaner nationalists have spoken increasingly for a large majority of South African whites, who support the political leadership with varying degrees of enthusiasm.

The goals of Afrikaner nationalism in the twentieth century have been remarkably consistent: white supremacy and racial segregation. In 1913, the new South African legislature passed the Native Land Act, which limited black ownership of land to native reserves encompassing a mere one-seventh of the country. Poor, overpopulated, and too small to feed themselves, the reserves served as a pool of cheap, temporary black labor for white farms, gold mines, and factories. A black worker—typically a young black man without a family—could leave the reserve only with special permission. In the eyes of the law, he was only a temporary migrant, who could be returned at will by his employer or the government. Thus so-called "pass laws" required every black outside the reserves to carry at all times an up-to-date pass approved by the white police. The native reserves system, combining racial segregation and indirect forced labor, formed the foundation of white supremacy in South Africa.

After 1948, successive Afrikaner governments wove the somewhat haphazard early racist measures into an authoritarian fabric of racial discrimination and inequality. This system was officially known as *apartheid,* meaning "separation" or "segregation." The population was dogmatically divided into four legally unequal racial groups—whites, blacks, Asians, and racially mixed Coloureds. Afrikaner propagandists claimed to serve the interests of all racial groups by preserving separate cultures and racial pu-

MAP 37.5 The Republic of South Africa and Apartheid, ca 1960 Despite the repressive apartheid laws, many blacks have managed to leave the reserves for South Africa's growing cities, where most Indians and coloureds already live.

rity; marriage and sexual relations between races became criminal offenses. Most observers saw apartheid as a way of maintaining the lavish privileges of the white minority, who account for only one-sixth of the total population.

South Africa's cities grew rapidly after 1940, in conjunction with its emergence as the most highly industrialized country in Africa. Good jobs were reserved for whites. The whites lived in luxurious modern central cities; the blacks were restricted to outlying townships plagued by poverty, crime, and white policemen. In spite of everything, these cities have produced a vibrant urban black culture, largely distinct from that of the tribal reserves. As a black journalist in Johannesburg explained in 1966:

I am supposed to be a Pondo, but I don't even know the language of that tribe. . . . I am just not a tribesman, whether I like it or not. I am, inescapably, a part of the

city slums, the factory machines and our beloved she-beens [illegal bars.][14]

South Africa's harsh white supremacy has elicited many black nationalist protests since the 1920s. Black nationalists began as moderates, seeking gradual reforms. By the 1950s and early 1960s, blacks—and their Coloured, white, and Asian allies—were staging large-scale peaceful protests. These experiments in militant nonviolence were crushed by police and the army (Map 37.5).

By the late 1970s, the white government had apparently destroyed the black moderates. Operating out of sympathetic black states to the north, the main black nationalist organization—the African National Congress, or ANC—turned increasingly to armed struggle. South Africa struck back hard. It used its awesome economic and military strength to support separatist movements that destabilized its neighbors, and it forced Marxist Mozambique in particular to curtail the ANC's guerrilla activities. Fortified by these successes, South Africa's white leaders launched in 1984 a program of "reforms"—changes designed to ensure continued white domination by means of a few strategic concessions.

The main reform was constitutional. The government set up a new parliament, with one house for the 5 million whites and, for the first time, two much less powerful houses for the 3 million Coloureds and the 1 million South Africans of Asian descent. But no provision was made for any representation of the country's 22 million blacks, on the grounds that they were citizens of the tribal reserves, relabeled in recent years as black homelands. The government also made cosmetic adjustments to apartheid, permitting marriage between races, for example. But the hated pass laws were replaced only by a new identity card, which still controlled black movement and settlement.

The government's self-serving reforms provoked black indignation and triggered a massive reaction. In the segregated townships surrounding white cities,

young black militants took to the streets, attacking especially black civil servants and policemen as traitorous agents of white oppression. White security forces, armed with tear gas, whips, and guns, clashed repeatedly with black protesters, who turned funerals for fallen comrades into mass demonstrations. Foreign governments and opinion leaders urged fundamental changes that would move South Africa toward universal suffrage and black majority rule.

Instead, the white government defiantly dug in. In 1985, it imposed a state of emergency, which gave the police and army virtually unlimited powers to put down protest. In late 1986, the government imposed equally unlimited press censorship. White South Africans had long prided themselves on the superiority of their civilization, a civilization that gave them basic freedoms and parliamentary democracy even though it excluded blacks. Now their hard-line government was taking a gigantic step toward dictatorship for all, regardless of race. Such a dictatorship promised to silence white critics, intensify repression of blacks, and increase bloodshed.

Soweto, 1976 Police patrol a street in the sprawling black township near Johannesburg after two days of massive anti-government riots. With a population today of 1.2 million blacks, Soweto remains the focus of the struggle against the white minority government. *(Popperfoto)*

This chapter has examined the remarkable resurgence of Asian and African peoples after World War Two, which will almost certainly stand as a decisive turning point in world history. It has examined how the long-developing nationalist movement in China culminated in a social revolution led by the Communists, who went on to pursue innovative and fiercely independent policies that redeemed China as a great power in world affairs. Meanwhile Japan, defeated, demilitarized, and democratized, took a completely different path to the rank of economic superpower in a no less spectacular renaissance. Elsewhere—in India, Indonesia, and the Philippines—Asian peoples won their freedom and self-confidently charted independent courses. The Muslim world was also rejuvenated, most notably in Egypt under Nasser. In black Africa, a generation of nationalist leaders guided colonial territories to self-rule so successfully that by the middle 1960s only the Soviet Union still retained a large colonial empire.

The resurgence and political self-assertion of Asian and African peoples in revitalized or developing nation-states did not proceed without conflict. Serious regional and ethnic confrontations erupted, notably between Hindus and Muslims in India and between Arabs and Israelis in the Middle East. Moreover, the vestiges of Western colonialism and cold war struggles resulted in atypical but highly destructive conflicts in Algeria, Vietnam, and Zimbabwe. The revitalized peoples of Asia and Africa continue to face tremendous economic and social challenges, as will be discussed in Chapter 39. These challenges must be met if the emerging nations are to realize fully the promise of self-assertion and independence.

NOTES

1. Stuart Schram, *Mao Tse-tung* (New York: Simon and Schuster, 1966), p. 151.
2. Quoted in P. B. Ebrey, ed., *Chinese Civilization and Society: A Source Book* (New York: The Free Press, 1981), p. 393.
3. Quoted in Woodbridge Bingham, Hilary Conroy, and Frank Iklé, *A History of Asia,* 2d ed. (Boston: Allyn and Bacon, 1974), 2.459.

4. Quoted in Stanley Wolpert, *A New History of India,* 2d ed. (New York: Oxford University Press, 1982), p. 330.
5. Quoted in Krishan Bhata, *The Ordeal of Nationhood: A Social Study of India Since Independence, 1947–1970* (New York: Atheneum, 1971), p. 9.
6. Bernard D. Nossiter, *Soft State: A Newspaperman's Chronicle of India* (New York: Harper and Row, 1970), p. 52.
7. Quoted in G. B. Kay, ed., *The Political Economy of Colonialism in Ghana: A Collection of Documents and Statistics* (Cambridge, Eng.: Cambridge University Press, 1972), p. 48.
8. W. E. B. Du Bois, *The Souls of Black Folk* (Chicago: A. C. McClung, 1903), p. 3.
9. Quoted in Robert W. July, *A History of the African People,* 3d ed. (New York: Charles Scribner's Sons, 1980), pp. 519–520.
10. Quoted in Jacques Louis Hymans, *Léopold Sédar Senghor: An Intellectual Biography* (Edinburgh: University of Edinburgh Press, 1971), p. 58.
11. Quoted in L. H. Gann and Peter Duignan, *Colonialism in Africa* (Cambridge, Eng.: Cambridge University Press, 1970), 2. 512.
12. Quoted in Robin Hallett, *Africa Since 1875: A Modern History* (Ann Arbor: University of Michigan Press, 1974), pp. 378–379.
13. Ibid., p. 345.
14. Ibid., p. 657.

SUGGESTED READING

Many of the works mentioned in the Suggested Reading for Chapter 33 are also valuable for considering postwar developments in Asia and the Middle East. Three other important studies on developments in China are C. Johnson, *Peasant Nationalism and Communist Power: The Emergence of Revolutionary China, 1937–1945* (1962); C. K. Yang, *The Chinese Family in the Communist Revolution* (1959); and W. L. Parish and M. K. Whyte, *Village and Family in Contemporary China* (1978). M. Meisner, *Mao's China: A History of the People's Republic* (1977), is an excellent comprehensive study, and C. P. FitzGerald, *Communism Takes China: How the Revolution Went Red* (1971), is a lively, illustrated account by a scholar who spent many years in China. Very recent developments are ably analyzed by I.

Hsü, *China Without Mao: The Search for a New Order* (1983). F. Butterfield, *China, Alive in a Bitter Sea* (1982), is a journalist's perceptive eyewitness account, while R. Lardy, *Agriculture in China's Economic Development* (1983), carefully examines the poor performance that led to Deng's reforms.

K. Kawai, *Japan's American Interlude* (1960), and R. P. Dore, *Land Reform in Japan* (1959), consider key problems of occupation policy. Three excellent and thought-provoking studies of contemporary Japanese society are E. Reischauer, *The Japanese* (1977); F. Gibney, *Japan, the Fragile Superpower* (1977); and E. Vogel, *Japan as Number One: Lessons for America* (1979). G. Bernstein, *Haruko's World: A Japanese Farm Woman and Her Community* (1983), probes changing patterns of rural life. Akira Iriye, *The Cold War in Asia: A Historical Introduction* (1974), and M. Schaller, *The United States and China in the Twentieth Century* (1979), analyze international conflicts in the postwar Pacific Basin.

F. G. Hutchins, *India's Revolution: Gandhi and the Quit India Movement* (1973), is an excellent account of wartime developments in India, which may be compared with J. Nehru, *An Autobiography* (1962), the appealing testimony of a principal architect of Indian freedom. F. Frankel, *India's Political Economy, 1947–1977* (1978), intelligently discusses the economic policies of independent India. There is a good biography of Indira Gandhi by D. Moraes (1980). For Southeast Asia there are solid general accounts by C. Dubois, *Social Forces in Southeast Asia* (1967), and R. N. Kearney, *Politics and Modernization in South and Southeast Asia* (1974). C. Cooper, *The Lost Crusade: America in Vietnam* (1972), and F. FitzGerald, *Fire in the Lake* (1973), probe the tragic war in Vietnam. Two valuable works on other Asian countries are B. Dahm, *Sukarno and the Struggle for Indonesian Independence* (1969), and T. Friend, *Between Two Empires: The Ordeal of the Philippines,*

1929–1946 (1965). Recommended studies of the Middle East and Israel include a cultural investigation by R. Patai, *The Arab Mind* (1973); W. R. Polk's penetrating examination, *The United States and the Arab World,* 3d ed. (1975); and an excellent biography of Israel's inspiring leader during its war for independence by A. Avi-Hai, *Ben Gurion, State Builder* (1974).

The studies by July and Hallett cited in the Notes are outstanding interpretations of modern Africa's rich and complex history. Both have extensive bibliographies. Important works on the colonial era include R. W. July, *The Origins of Modern African Thought* (1967); J. A. Langley, *Pan-Africanism and Nationalism in West Africa, 1900–1945: A Study in Ideology and Social Classes* (1973); R. O. Collins, *Problems in the History of Colonial Africa, 1860–1960* (1970); T. Hodgkin, *Nationalism in Colonial Africa* (1957); and the monumental investigation edited by L. H. Gann and P. Duignan, *Colonialism in Africa, 1870–1960,* 5 vols. (1969–1975). W. E. B. Du Bois, *The World and Africa* (1947), and J. Kenyatta, *Facing Mount Kenya* (1953), are powerful comments on African nationalism by the distinguished American black thinker and Kenya's foremost revolutionary and political leader. A Hopkins, *An Economic History of West Africa* (1973), is a pioneering synthesis. C. Dewey and A. Hopkins, eds., *The Imperial Impact: Studies in the Economic History of Africa and India* (1978), is an innovative comparative study. R. Olaniyan, ed., *African History and Culture* (1982), is a valuable recent collection. Major works on specific countries include M. Crowder, *The Story of Nigeria,* 4th ed. (1978); P. Hill, *Migrant Cocoa Farmers in Ghana* (1963); and R. W. Johnson, *How Long Will South Africa Survive?* (1977). I Wallerstein, *Africa, the Politics of Independence* (1961), and P. C. Lloyd, *Africa in Social Change* (1972), are useful studies on the contemporary era. F. Willett, *African Art* (1971), is a good introduction.

38

LIFE IN INDUSTRIALIZED NATIONS

WHILE EUROPE staged its remarkable political and economic recovery from the Nazi nightmare, the patterns of everyday life and the structure of Western society were changing no less rapidly and remarkably. Major inventions and new technologies—the atomic bomb, television, computers, jet planes, and contraceptive pills, to name only a few—profoundly affected human existence. Important groups in society formulated new attitudes and demands, which were reflected in such diverse phenomena as the ever-expanding role of government and the women's movement. Rapid social change was clearly a fact of life in the Western world.

It is by no means easy to make sense out of all these changes. Many "revolutions" and "crises" proved to be merely passing fads, sensationally ballyhooed by the media one day and forgotten the next. Some genuinely critical developments, such as those involving social classes and the family, are complex and contradictory, making it hard to understand what has really been happening, much less explain why. This is certainly the case with the economy, where the vivid contrast between the postwar boom and the serious problems of recent years has bewildered even the experts. In short, we are so close to what has been happening that we lack vital perspective. It becomes, therefore, difficult to interpret intelligently the life we all think we know best—the life of our own times. As Voltaire once said, "The man who ventures to write contemporary history must expect to be attacked both for everything he has said and everything he has not said."[1]

Yet the historian must take a stand. How did Western society and everyday life change in the postwar years, and why? What did these changes mean to people? Why did economic problems return to plague the industrialized nations from the early 1970s onward, and what were the social consequences? This chapter will seek to answer these questions.

SCIENCE AND TECHNOLOGY

Ever since the Scientific Revolution of the seventeenth century and the Industrial Revolution at the end of the eighteenth century, scientific and technical developments have powerfully influenced attitudes,

society, and everyday life. Never was this influence stronger than after about 1940. Fantastic pipe dreams of science fiction a brief century ago became realities. Submarines passed under the North Pole, and astronauts walked on the moon. Millions of people around the world simultaneously watched a historic event on television. The list of wonders seemed endless.

The reason science and technology proved so productive and influential was that, for the first time in history, they were effectively joined together on a massive scale. This union of "pure theoretical" science with "applied" science or "practical" technology had already made possible striking achievements in the late nineteenth century in some select fields, most notably organic chemistry, electricity, and preventive medicine. Generally, however, the separation of science and technology still predominated in the late 1930s. Most scientists were university professors, who left the creation of better machines and new products to job-trained technicians and a few engineers. During World War Two, however, scientists and technicians joined forces. They focused on difficult but highly practical military problems and achieved some spectacular breakthroughs. After the war, this close and successful cooperation continued.

The consequences of the new, intimate link between science and technology were enormous. Seventeenth-century propagandists for science, such as Francis Bacon, had predicted that scientific knowledge of nature would give human beings the power to control the physical world and thus create material abundance. The successful union of science and technology did spur rapid economic growth after 1945, making this prediction finally come true for the large majority of people in the industrialized nations. Yet the unprecedented capacity to alter the physical world also produced many unexpected and unwanted side effects, from acid rain to nuclear accidents. By the late 1960s, concern about such undesirable side effects gave rise to the somber realization that the power to alter nature was a two-edged sword, which had to be wielded with great care and responsibility.

THE STIMULUS OF WORLD WAR TWO

Just before the outbreak of World War Two, a young Irish scientist and Communist named John Desmond Bernal wrote a book entitled *The Social Function of Science.* Bernal argued that the central government should be the source of funds for scientific research and that these funds should be granted on the basis of the expected social and political benefits. Most scientists were horrified by Bernal's proposals. They were committed to designing their own research and relatively inexpensive experiments without regard for their immediate usefulness.

The Second World War changed this pattern. Pure science lost its impractical innocence. Most leading university scientists went to work on top-secret projects to help their governments fight the war. Take the momentous development of radar by British scientists.

Before the war, a group of experts calculated that the detection of enemy aircraft by radio waves was theoretically possible, and by 1939 the British had succeeded in installing a very primitive radar system along the English coast. Immediately after the outbreak of war with Germany, the British military enlisted leading academic scientists in an all-out effort to improve the radar system. The basic problem was developing a high-powered transmitter capable of sending beams of very short wavelengths, which could then bounce off an approaching plane so that it could be detected by a receiver on the ground. In the summer of 1940, British physicists dramatically solved this problem, and the radically improved radar system played a key role in Britain's victory in the battle for air supremacy in the fall of 1940. During the war, many different types of radar were developed—for fighter planes, for bombers, for detection of submarines.

After 1945, war-born microwave technology generated endless applications, especially in telecommunications. Microwave transmission very conveniently carried long-distance telephone conversations, television programs, and messages via satellites.

The air war also greatly stimulated the development of jet aircraft. The challenge was to build a new kind of engine—a jet engine—capable of burning the low-grade "leftovers" of petroleum refining, thereby helping to overcome the desperate shortage of aviation fuel. The task proved extremely difficult, and only toward the end of the war did fast, high-flying jet fighters become a reality. Quickly adopted for military purposes, jet airplanes contributed to the enormous expansion of commercial aviation in the postwar years.

Lord Rutherford The great British physicist Ernest Rutherford split the atom in 1919 with a small device he could hold in his hands. Here he is seen with a colleague in Cambridge University's renowned Cavendish Laboratory in 1932, when pure science was still relatively small-scale and unconcerned with practical applications. *(Cavendish Laboratory, University of Cambridge)*

Atomic Weapons were the ultimate in state-directed scientific research. In this awesome photo the mushroom cloud of an American atomic bomb rises over the Pacific island of Bikini. *(Joint Army Navy Task Force)*

The problems of air defense also spurred further research on electronic computers, which had barely come into existence before 1939. Computers calculated the complex mathematical relationships between fast-moving planes and antiaircraft shells, to increase the likelihood of a hit.

Wartime needs led to many other major technical breakthroughs. Germany had little oil and was almost completely cut off from foreign supplies. But Germany's scientists and engineers found ways to turn coal into gasoline so that the German war machine did not sputter to a halt.

The most spectacular result of directed scientific research during the war was the atomic bomb. In August 1939, Albert Einstein wrote to President Franklin Roosevelt, stating that recent work in physics suggested that

it may become possible to set up a nuclear chain reaction in a large mass of uranium, by which vast amounts of power and large quantities of new radium-like elements would be generated. . . . This new phenomenon would also lead to the construction of bombs, and it is conceivable—though much less certain—that extremely powerful bombs of a new type may thus be constructed.[2]

This letter and ongoing experiments by nuclear physicists led to the top-secret Manhattan Project and the decision to build the atomic bomb.

The American government spared no expense to turn a theoretical possibility into a practical reality. A mammoth crash program went forward in several universities and special laboratories. The most important of these was the newly created laboratory at Los Alamos in New Mexico, at which was assembled a team of brilliant American and European scientists for the sole purpose of designing and building the ultimate weapon. After three years of intensive effort, the first atomic bomb was successfully tested in July 1945. In August 1945, two bombs were dropped on Hiroshima and Nagasaki, ending the war with Japan.

The atomic bomb showed the world both the awesome power and the heavy moral responsibilities of modern science and its high priests. As one troubled scientist exclaimed while he watched the first mushroom cloud rise: "We are all sons-of-bitches now!"[3]

THE RISE OF BIG SCIENCE

The spectacular results of government-directed research during World War Two inspired a new model for science—"Big Science." By combining theoretical work with sophisticated engineering in a large organization, Big Science could attack extremely difficult problems. Enthusiasts assumed that almost any conceivable technical goal might be attained and that solutions would lead to better products for consumers and better weapons for the military.

Science became so "big" largely because its equipment grew ever more complex and expensive. Many advances depended directly on better instruments, as in atomic physics, perhaps the most prestigious and influential area of modern science. When Ernest Rutherford first "split the atom" in 1919, his equipment cost only a few dollars. In the 1930s, the price of an accelerator, or "atom smasher," reached $10,000, and the accelerators used in high-energy experiments while the atomic bomb was being built were in the $100,000 range. By 1960, however, when the western European nations pooled their resources in the European Council for Nuclear Research (CERN) to build an accelerator outside of Geneva—an accelerator with power in billions rather than millions of electron volts—the cost had jumped to $30 million. These big accelerators did an amazingly good job of prying atoms apart, but new answers produced new questions, and sophisticated observations demanded ever more powerful and ever more costly accelerators in the postwar years.

Astronomers followed physicists in the ways of Big Science. Their new eye was the radio telescope, which picked up radio emissions rather than light. In the 1960s the largest of these costly radio telescopes sat atop a mountain and had a bowl a thousand feet wide to focus the radio signals from space. Even ordinary science became big and expensive by historical standards. The least costly laboratory capable of doing useful research in either pure or applied science required around $200,000 a year in the 1960s.

Populous, victorious, and wealthy, the United States took the lead in Big Science after World War Two. Between 1945 and 1965, spending on scientific research and development in the United States grew five times as fast as the national income. While large American corporations maintained impressive research laboratories, fully three-quarters of all funds spent on scientific research and development in the United States was coming from the government by 1965. It was generally accepted that government should finance science heavily. Similar conditions prevailed in the Soviet Union.

The Apollo Program Astronauts Neil Armstrong, Michael Collins, and Edwin Aldrin, Jr. took off from Florida on July 16, 1969 in the Apollo II spacecraft. Astronaut Armstrong was the first man to set foot on the moon, four days later, on July 20. His footprint in the lunar dust brought to reality another fantasy of science fiction. The astronauts splashed down in the Pacific Ocean, and recovery was made by the U.S.S. *Hornet* on July 24. *(National Aeronautics and Space Administration)*

One reason for the similarity was that science was not demobilized in either country after the war. Indeed, scientists remained a critical part of every major military establishment, and a large portion of all scientific research continued to go for "defense." Jet bombers gave way to rockets, battleships were overtaken by submarines with nuclear warheads, and spy planes were replaced with spy satellites. All such new weapons demanded breakthroughs no less remarkable than those of radar and the first atomic bomb, and all propelled Big Science forward.

Sophisticated science, lavish government spending, and military needs all came together in the space race of the 1960s—the most sensational example of Big Science in action after the creation of the atomic bomb. In 1957 the Russians used long-range rockets developed in their nuclear weapons program to put a satellite in orbit. In 1961 they sent the world's first cosmonaut circling the globe. Breaking with President Eisenhower's opposition to an expensive space program, President Kennedy made an all-out U.S. commitment to catch up with the Russians and land a manned spacecraft on the moon "before the decade was out." Harnessing pure science, applied technology, and up to $5 billion a year, the Apollo Program achieved its ambitious objective in 1969. Four more moon landings followed by 1972.

The United States attracted many of Europe's best scientists during the 1950s and 1960s, and some thoughtful Europeans lamented this "brain drain." They warned that Europe was falling hopelessly behind the United States in science and technology. The only hope was to copy American patterns of research before the United States achieved an absolute stranglehold on the vital dynamic sectors of the world economy.

In fact, European countries were beginning to pool their efforts in big projects like the *Concorde* supersonic passenger airliner and the peaceful uses of atomic energy. Thus European countries created their own Big Science, and by 1974 they were in the process of achieving equality with the United States in many fields of scientific endeavor (Figure 38.1).

THE LIFE OF SCIENTISTS AND TECHNOLOGISTS

The rise of Big Science and of close ties between science and technology greatly altered the lives of scientists. The scientific community grew much larger than ever before. There were about four times as many scientists in 1975 as in 1945, just as there were a *million times* as many scientists as there were in 1670. Scientists, technologists, engineers, and medical specialists counted in modern society, in part because there were so many of them.

A high degree of specialization accompanied the growth in the number of scientists. With close to a hundred thousand scientific journals being published by the 1970s, no one could possibly master a broad field like physics or medicine. Instead, a field like physics was constantly dividing and subdividing into new specialties and subdisciplines. The fifty or one hundred men and women who were truly abreast of the latest developments in a highly specialized field formed an international "invisible college," cooperating and competing as they kept the problems of the subdiscipline under constant attack. Specialization undoubtedly increased the rates at which both basic knowledge was acquired and practical applications were made.

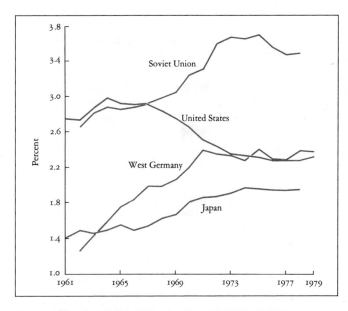

FIGURE 38.1 Research and Development Expenditures as a Percentage of GNP in the United States, Soviet Union, West Germany, and Japan, 1961–1979 While the United States spent less of its national income on research and development after the early 1960s, European nations and Japan spent more. This helped Europe and Japan narrow or even close the technological gap that had existed after the end of World War Two. *(Source: Data Resources, Inc.)*

Highly specialized modern scientists and technologists normally had to work as members of a team. The problems and equipment of Big Science were simply too complicated and expensive for a person to work effectively as an individual researcher. The collaborative "team" character of much of modern scientific research completely changed the work and lifestyle of modern scientists. A great laboratory assembled hundreds or even thousands of people—scientists, technicians, and every kind of support personnel. A great deal of modern science and technology went on, therefore, in large, well-defined bureaucratic organizations. The individual was very often a small cog in a great machine, a member of a scientific army.

The advent of large-scale scientific bureaucracies led to the emergence of science managers and research administrators. Such managers generally had scientific backgrounds, but their main tasks were scheduling research, managing people, and seeking money from politicians or large corporations.

Many science managers were government bureaucrats who doled out funds and assessed research results as well as the impact of specific technologies. Was the *Concorde* supersonic jet too noisy to land in New York City? Did saccharin cause cancer, and should it be banned? The list of potentially undesirable side effects of technological advance was endless. More generally, the growth of the scientific bureaucracy suggested how scientists and technical thinking permeated the entire society.

Two other changes in the lives of scientists should be noted briefly. First, there was the difficulty of appraising an individual's contribution to a collaborative team effort. Who deserved the real credit (or blame) for a paper coauthored by a group of twenty-five researchers? Second, modern science became highly, even brutally, competitive. This competitiveness is well depicted in Nobel Prize winner James Watson's fascinating book *The Double Helix,* which tells how in 1953 Watson and an Englishman, Francis Crick, discovered the structure of DNA, the molecule of heredity. A brash young American Ph.D. in his twenties, Watson seemed almost obsessed by the idea that some other research team would find the solution first and thereby deprive him of the fame and fortune he desperately wanted. With so many thousands of like-minded researchers in the industrialized countries of the world, scientific and technical knowledge rushed forward in the postwar era.

TOWARD A NEW SOCIETY

The prodigious expansion of science and technology greatly affected the peoples of the Western world. By creating new products and vastly improved methods of manufacturing and farming, it fueled rapid economic growth and rising standards of living. Moreover, especially in Europe, scientific and technological progress, combined with economic prosperity, went a long way toward creating a whole new society after World War Two.

This new society was given many catchy titles. Some called it the "technocratic society," a society of highly trained specialists and experts. For others, fascinated by the great increase in personal wealth, it was the "affluent society" or the "consumer society." For those struck by the profusion of government-provided social services, it was simply the "welfare state." For still others, it was the "permissive society," where established codes of conduct no longer prevailed. In fact, Western society in the postwar years was all of these: technocratic, affluent, welfare-oriented, and permissive. These characteristics reflected changes in the class structure and indicated substantial social progress.

THE CHANGING CLASS STRUCTURE

After 1945 European society became more mobile and more democratic. Old class barriers relaxed, and class distinctions became fuzzier.

Changes in the structure of the middle class were particularly influential in the general drift toward a less rigid class structure. The model for the middle class in the nineteenth and early twentieth centuries was the independent, self-employed individual who owned a business or practiced a liberal profession like law or medicine. Many businesses and professional partnerships were tightly held family firms, and strong family ties were often the keys to property and standing within the middle class.

This traditional pattern, which first changed in the United States and the Soviet Union (for very different reasons) before the Second World War, declined drastically in western Europe after 1945. A new breed of salaried managers rose to replace traditional property owners as the leaders of the middle class. Ability to serve the needs of a large organization, which usually depended on special expertise, largely replaced inherited property and family connections in determining an individual's social position in the middle class. Social mobility, both upward and downward, increased. At the same time, the middle class grew massively and became harder to define.

There were various reasons for these developments. First, rapid industrial and technological expansion created in large corporations and government agencies a powerful demand for technologists and managers capable of responding effectively to an ever more complicated world. Second, the old propertied middle class lost control of many family-owned businesses. Even very wealthy families had to call on the general investing public for capital. Many small businesses (including family farms) simply passed out of existence, and their ex-owners joined the ranks of salaried employees. Finally, the wave of

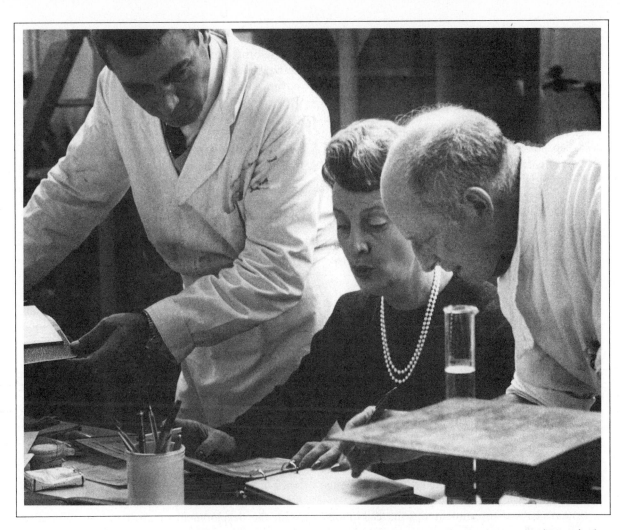

A Modern Manager Despite considerable discrimination, women were increasingly found in the expanding middle class of salaried experts after World War Two, working in business, science, and technology. *(Niépce-Rapho)*

nationalization in western and eastern Europe after the Second World War automatically replaced capitalist owners with salaried managers and civil servants in state-owned companies.

Representing the model for a new middle class of salaried specialists, top managers and ranking civil servants were well paid and highly trained. They were also pragmatic and realistic, concerned primarily with efficiency and practical solutions to concrete problems. Generally, they were not very interested in the old ideological debates about capitalism and socialism, confidently assuming that their skills were indispensable in either system.

Indeed, the new middle class of experts and salaried managers was a growing international class, whose members shared characteristics that crossed national boundaries. Everywhere successful managers and technocrats passed on the opportunity for all-important advanced education to their children, but only in rare instances could they pass on the positions they had attained. Thus the new middle class, which was based largely on education and specialized skills, was more open and insecure than the old propertied middle class.

The structure of the traditional lower classes also became more flexible and open. There was a mass exodus from the countryside. Peasants, one of the most traditional and least mobile groups in European society, declined by more than 50 percent in almost every European country after 1945. Meanwhile, because of rapid technological change, the industrial working class ceased to expand, stabilizing at slightly less than one-half of the labor force in wealthy advanced countries. Job opportunities for white-collar and service employees, however, expanded rapidly. Such employees bore a greater resemblance to the new middle class of salaried specialists than to industrial workers, who were themselves better educated and more specialized. Developments within the lower classes contributed, therefore, to the breakdown of rigid social divisions.

SOCIAL SECURITY REFORMS AND RISING AFFLUENCE

While the demands of modern technology and big bureaucracies helped break down rigid class divisions, European governments, with their new and revitalized political leadership, reduced class tensions with a series of social security reforms. Many of these reforms simply strengthened social security measures first pioneered in Bismarck's Germany before World War One. Unemployment and sickness benefits were increased and extended, as were retirement benefits and old-age pensions. Other programs were new.

Britain's Labour government took the lead immediately after the Second World War in establishing a comprehensive national health system; other European governments followed the British example. Depending on the system, patients either received completely free medical care or paid only a very small portion of the total cost.

Most countries also introduced family allowances —direct government grants to parents to help them raise their children. Lower-paid workers generally received the largest allowances, which helped many poor families make ends meet. Most European governments also gave maternity grants and built inexpensive public housing for low-income families and individuals. Other social welfare programs ranged from cash bonuses for getting married to subsidized vacations for housewives.

The expansion of social security services after World War Two did not provide for every human need "from cradle to grave," as early advocates of the welfare state hoped and as critics feared. But these so-

cial reforms did provide a humane floor of well-being, below which few individuals could fall in the advanced countries of northern and western Europe. Reforms and social benefits were expensive, and they were paid for in part by higher taxes on the rich. Thus extensive welfare measures leveled society both by raising the floor and by lowering the ceiling.

The rising standard of living and the spread of standardized, mass-produced consumer goods also worked to level Western society. A hundred years ago, food and drink cost roughly two-thirds of the average family's income in western and northern Europe; by the mid-1960s, they took only about one-third to two-fifths of that family's income. Consumption of traditional staples like bread and potatoes actually declined after 1945 as rising incomes enabled people to eat more meat, fish, and dairy products. The long-elusive goal of adequate and good food was very widely attained in industrialized countries.

The phenomenal expansion of the automobile industry exemplified most strikingly the emergence of the consumer society. In the United States, automobile ownership was commonplace far down the social scale by the mid-1920s, whereas only the rich could generally afford cars in Europe before the Second World War. In 1948 there were only 5 million cars in western Europe, and most ordinary people dreamed at most of stepping up from a bicycle to a motorcycle. With the development of cheaper, mass-produced cars, this situation changed rapidly. By 1957 the number of cars had increased to 15 million, and automobiles had become a standard item of middle-class consumption. By 1965 the number of cars in western Europe had tripled again to 44 million, and car ownership had come well within the range of better-paid workers.

Europeans took great pleasure in the products of the "gadget revolution" as well. Like Americans, Europeans filled their houses and apartments with washing machines, vacuum cleaners, refrigerators, dishwashers, radios, TVs, and stereos. The purchase of such consumer goods was greatly facilitated by installment purchasing, which allowed people to buy on credit. Before World War Two, Europeans had rarely bought "on time." But with the expansion of social security safeguards, reducing the need to accumulate savings for hard times, ordinary people were increasingly willing to take on debt. This change had far-reaching consequences.

Household appliances became necessities for most families. Middle-class women had to do much of their own housework, for young girls avoided domestic service like the plague. Moreover, more women than ever before worked outside the home, and they needed machines to help do household chores as quickly as possible. The power tools of "do-it-yourself" work also became something of a necessity, for few dependable artisans were available for household repairs.

Leisure and recreation occupied an important place in consumer societies. Indeed, leisure became big business. In addition to ever-popular soccer matches and horse races, movies, and a growing addiction to television, individuals had at their disposal a vast range of commercialized hobbies, most of which could soak up a lot of cash. Interest in "culture," as measured by attendance at concerts and exhibitions, also increased. Even so, the commercialization of leisure through standardized manufactured products was striking.

The most astonishing leisure-time development in the consumer society was the blossoming of mass travel and tourism. Before the Second World War, most people had neither the time nor the money to travel for pleasure. But with month-long paid vacations required by law in most European countries, and widespread automobile ownership, beaches and ski resorts came within the reach of the middle class and many workers. At certain times of the year, hordes of Europeans surged to the sea or the mountains, and woe to the traveler who had not made arrangements well in advance. By the late 1960s packaged tours with cheap group flights and bargain hotel accommodations had made even distant lands easily accessible. A French company, the Club Méditerranée, grew rich building imitation Tahitian paradises around the world. At Swedish nudist colonies on secluded West African beaches, secretaries and salesmen from Stockholm fleetingly worshiped the sun in the middle of the long northern winter. Truly, consumerism had come of age.

RENEWED DISCONTENT AND THE STUDENT REVOLT

For twenty years after 1945, Europeans were largely preoccupied with the possibilities of economic progress and consumerism. The more democratic class structure also helped to reduce social tension, and ideological conflict went out of style. In the late 1960s, however, sharp criticism and social conflicts re-emerged. Radical students in particular rejected the materialism of their parents and claimed that the new society was repressive and badly flawed. These criticisms and the movements they sparked reflected some real problems of youth, education, and a society of specialists.

In contrast to the United States, high school and university educations in Europe were limited for centuries to a small elite. That elite consisted mainly of young men and women from the well-to-do classes, along with a sprinkling of scholarship students from humble origins. Whereas 22 percent of the American population was going on to some form of higher education in 1950, only 3 to 4 percent of west European youths were doing so. Moreover, European education was still directed toward traditional fields: literature, law, medicine, and pure science. Its basic goal was to pass on culture and pure science to an elite, and with the exception of law and medicine, applied training for specialists was not considered very important.

After World War Two, public education in western Europe began to change dramatically. Enrollments exploded. By 1960 there were at least three times as many students going to some kind of university as there had been before the war, and the number continued to rise sharply until the 1970s. European universities opened their doors to more students from the lower middle and lower classes, and in response to the prodigious expansion of science and technology, the curriculum gradually changed. All sorts of new, "practical" fields—from computer science to business administration—appeared alongside the earlier liberal arts and sciences.

The rapid expansion of higher education created problems as well as opportunities for students. Classes were badly overcrowded, and there was little contact with professors. Competition for grades became intense. Moreover, although more "practical" areas of study were added, they were added less quickly than many students wanted. Thus many students felt that they were not getting the kind of education they needed for the modern world and that basic university reforms were absolutely necessary. The emergence of a distinctive "youth culture" also brought students into conflict with those symbols of the older generation and parental authority—professors and school officials.

Student Protest in Paris These rock-throwing students in the Latin Quarter of Paris are trying to force educational reforms, or even to topple De Gaulle's government. Throughout May 1968 students clashed repeatedly with France's tough riot police in bloody street fighting. *(Bruno Barbey/Magnum Photos, Inc.)*

These tensions within the exploding university population came to a head in the late 1960s and early 1970s. Following in the footsteps of their American counterparts, who pioneered with large-scale student protests in the mid-1960s, European university students rose to challenge their university administrations and even their governments. The most far-reaching of these revolts occurred in France in 1968, and it almost brought down De Gaulle's government (page 1142).

The student protest of the 1960s, which peaked in 1968 but echoed into the 1970s, was due to more than overcrowded classrooms and outdated courses. It reflected a rebirth of romantic revolutionary idealism, which repudiated the quest for ever more consumer goods as stupid and destructive. Student radicalism was also related to the Vietnam War, which led many students in Europe and America to convince themselves that Western civilization was immoral and imperialistic. Finally, the students of the late 1960s were a completely new generation: they had never known anything but prosperity and tranquillity, and they had grown bored with both.

The student revolt was also motivated by new perceptions about the new society of highly trained experts. Some reflective young people feared that universities would soon do nothing but turn out docile technocrats to stock large organizations and to serve "the establishment." Others saw the class of highly trained specialists they expected to enter as the new exploited class in society. The remedy to this situation, both groups believed, was "participation"—the democratization of decision making *within* large, specialized bureaucratic organizations. Only in this way would such organizations serve real human needs and not merely exploit the individual and the environment. Thus the student radicals tried to answer a vital question: how was the complex new society of specialized experts to be made humane and responsive?

WOMEN AND THE FAMILY

The growing emancipation of women in Europe and North America was unquestionably one of the most important developments after the Second World War. This development gathered speed in the 1960s and reached a climax in the mid-1970s. Women demanded and won new rights. Having shared fully in the postwar education revolution, women were better educated than ever before. They took advantage of the need for trained experts in a more fluid society and moved into areas of employment formerly closed to them. Married women in particular became much more likely to work outside the home. Women no longer had to fatalistically accept childbearing and childrearing, for if they wished they could use modern techniques of contraception to control the number and spacing of their offspring. In short, women became more equal and independent, less confined and stereotyped. A major transformation was in process.

The changing position of women altered the modern family. Since the emancipation of women is still incomplete, it is impossible to say for certain whether some major revolution has occurred within the family. Nevertheless, as women today consolidate and expand the breakthroughs of the 1960s and early 1970s, it seems clear that the family has experienced some fundamental reorientations at the very least. This becomes apparent if we examine women's traditional role in the home and then women's new roles outside the home in the postwar era.

MARRIAGE AND MOTHERHOOD

Before the Industrial Revolution, most men and women married late, and substantial numbers never married at all. Once a woman was married, though, she normally bore several children, of whom a third to a half would not survive to adulthood. Moreover, many women died in childbirth. With the growth of industry and urban society, people began to marry earlier, and fewer remained unmarried. As industrial development led to higher incomes and better diets, more children survived to adulthood, and population grew rapidly in the nineteenth century. By the late nineteenth century, contraception within marriage was spreading.

In the twentieth century, and especially after World War Two, these trends continued. In the postwar era, women continued to marry earlier. Moreover, more than nine out of ten women were marrying at least once, usually in their early twenties. Marriage was never more in vogue than in the generation after the Second World War, and perhaps never before had young couples expected so much emotional satisfaction from matrimony.

After marrying early, the typical woman in Europe, the United States, and Canada had her children quickly. Whereas women in the more distant past very often had children as long as they were fertile, women in Europe and North America were having about 80 percent of their children before they were thirty. As for family size, the "baby boom" that lasted several years after 1945 made for fairly rapid population growth of 1 to 1.5 percent per year in many European countries. In the 1960s, however, the long-term decline in birthrates resumed. Surveys began to reveal that most women believed that two instead of three children were ideal.

Women must have 2.1 children on the average if total population is to remain constant over the long term. Indeed, the number of births fell so sharply in the 1960s that total population practically stopped growing in many European countries. By the mid-1970s, total numbers were actually declining in Austria, East Germany, West Germany, and Luxembourg. The United States followed the same trend; the birthrate declined from 25 per thousand in 1957 to 15 per thousand in 1973. Since the American death rate remained practically unchanged, the rate of population growth from natural increase (that is, excluding immigration) dropped by two-thirds, from 1.5 percent to .6 percent per year between the 1950s and the 1970s. The population of Africa, Latin America, and parts of Asia was still growing very rapidly from natural increase, but that was certainly not true for most industrialized nations.

The culmination of the trends toward early, almost universal marriage and small family size in wealthy societies had revolutionary implications for women. An examination of these implications suggests why the emancipation of women—sooner or later—was almost assuredly built into the structure of modern life.

The main point is that motherhood occupied a much smaller portion of a woman's life than at the beginning of this century. The average woman's life expectancy at birth increased from about fifty years in 1900 to about seventy-five years in 1970. At the same time, women were increasingly compressing childbearing into the decade between their twentieth and thirtieth birthdays. When the youngest child trooped off to kindergarten, the average mother still had more than forty years of life in front of her.

This was a momentous change. Throughout history, most married women had been defined to a considerable extent as mothers. Motherhood was very demanding: pregnancy followed pregnancy, and there were many children to nurse, guide, and bury. Now, however, the years devoted to having babies and caring for young children represented a relatively short phase in most women's total life span. Perhaps a good deal of the frustration that many women felt in the 1960s and 1970s was due to the fact that their traditional role as mothers no longer absorbed the energies of a lifetime, and new roles in the male-dominated world outside the family opened up slowly.

A related revolutionary change for women was that the age-old biological link between sexual intercourse and motherhood was severed. As is well known, beginning in the early 1960s many women chose to gain effective control over pregnancy with oral contraceptives and intrauterine devices. They no longer relied on undependable males and their undependable methods. Less well known are certain physiological facts, which help explain why many women in the advanced countries elected to practice birth control at some point in their lives.

Women in the postwar era were capable of having children for many more years than their forebears. The age of menarche—the age at which girls begin to menstruate and become fertile—had dropped from about seventeen years in the early nineteenth century to about thirteen years by the 1970s. At the same time, the age at onset of menopause rose from about thirty-six to about fifty. These physiological changes

over time are poorly understood, but they were apparently due to better diets and living standards, which also substantially increased people's height and size. In any event, many modern women chose to separate their sexual lives from their increased reproductive power. In doing so, these women became free to pursue sensual pleasure for its own sake. The consequences of this revolutionary development will continue to work themselves out for a long time.

WOMEN AT WORK

For centuries before the Industrial Revolution, ordinary women were highly productive members of society. Young women labored to accumulate a dowry, and married women worked hard on farms and in home industries while bearing and caring for their large families. With the growth of modern industry, young women continued to work as wage earners. But once a poor woman married, she typically stopped working in a factory or a shop, struggling instead to earn money at home by practicing some low-paid craft as she looked after her children. In the middle classes, it was a rare and tough-minded woman who worked outside the home for wages, although charity work was socially acceptable.

Since the beginning of the twentieth century and especially after World War Two, the situation has changed dramatically once again. Opportunities for women of modest means to earn cash income within the home practically disappeared. Moreover, motherhood took less time, so that the full-time mother-housewife had less economic value for families. Thus the reduction of home-centered work and child care resulted in a sharp rise across Europe and North America in the number of married women who were full-time wage earners.

In Communist countries, the trend went the furthest. In the Soviet Union, most married women worked outside the home; there women accounted for almost half of all employed persons in the postwar era. In non-Communist western Europe and North America there was a good deal of variety, but the percentage of married women who worked rose sharply in all countries, from a range of roughly 20 to 25 percent in 1950 to a range of 35 to 60 percent in the 1970s. This rise was particularly dramatic in the United States, where married women were twice as likely to be employed in 1979 as they were in 1952.

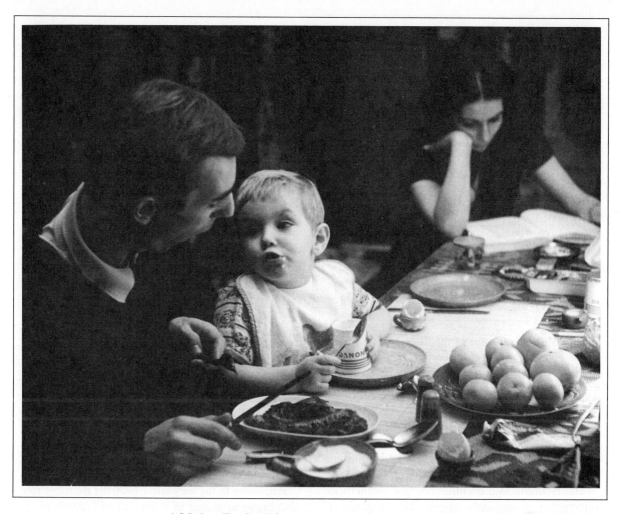

A Modern Family This scene sums up some important changes taking place within the family in the postwar era. The young father feeds and talks with the baby, while the student-mother concentrates on the education essential for successful employment. *(Niépce-Rapho)*

The dramatic growth of employment among married women was a powerful force in the drive for women's equality and emancipation. Take the critical matter of widespread discrimination between men and women in pay, occupation, and advancement. The young unmarried woman of a hundred years ago generally accepted such injustices. She thought of them as temporary nuisances and looked forward to marriage and motherhood for fulfillment. In the postwar era, a married wage earner in her thirties developed a totally different perspective. Employment became a permanent condition, and sexism and discrimination quickly became increasingly

loathsome and evoked that sense of injustice that drives revolutions and reforms. The "movement" spread, winning converts among the young and newly awakened.

Rising employment for married women was a factor in the decline of the birthrate (Figure 38.2). Women who worked had significantly fewer children than women of the same age who did not. Moreover, survey research showed that young women who had worked and intended to work again revised downward the number of children they expected to have after the first lovable but time-consuming baby was born. The multiple demands of job, motherhood,

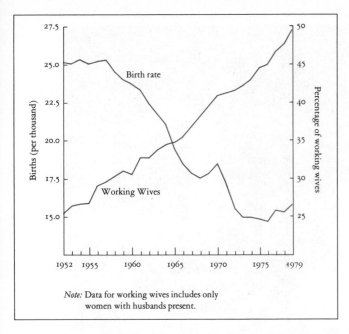

FIGURE 38.2 The Decline of the Birthrate and the Increase of Working Wives in the United States, 1952–1979 The challenge of working away from home encouraged American wives to prefer fewer children and helped to lower the birthrate.

and marriage simply became more manageable with fewer children.

The birthrate also declined because motherhood interrupted a woman's career. The majority of women in Western countries preferred or were forced to accept—interpretations varied—staying at home for a minimum of two or three years while their children were small. The longer the break in employment, the more a woman's career suffered.

Because most Western countries did little to help women in the problem of re-employment after their children were a little older, some women came to advocate the pattern of career and family typically found in Communist eastern Europe. There, women were usually employed continuously until they retired. A woman received as her right up to three months of maternity leave to care for her newborn infant and recover her strength. Then she returned to her job, leaving her baby in the care of a state-run nursery or, more frequently, a retired relative or neighbor. By the 1970s some western European countries were beginning to provide well-defined maternity leaves as part of their social security systems. The United States lagged far behind in this area.

What the increasing numbers of career-minded women with independent, self-assertive spirits meant for marriage and relations between the sexes was by no means clear. As already noted, marriage remained an almost universal experience. Moreover, the decline of informal village and neighborhood socializing with the advent of the automobile and suburban living made most wives and husbands more dependent than ever on their mates (and their children) for their emotional needs. Husbands were also getting the message that the old rule of leaving the dishes and diapers exclusively to wives needed rewriting, especially in two-income families. In short, the nuclear family showed great strength, adapting itself once again to changing values and changing conditions.

At the same time, contrary trends clearly emerged in the late 1960s, which carried over strongly into the 1970s and 1980s. Everywhere the divorce rate kept moving up: it doubled in the United States between 1970 and 1980, for example. Studies of marriage consistently showed that working women were considerably more likely to get divorced than nonworking women. The independent working woman could more easily afford to leave if dissatisfied, while the no-income career housewife was more nearly locked into her situation.

Beginning in the very late 1960s, the marriage rate also began to plunge in a number of Western countries, and it continued to decline throughout the 1970s before stabilizing in the 1980s. Both women and men married progressively later, and those who never married grew as a portion of the population. As the number of singles grew, there was also a considerable increase in the number of unmarried couples living together, reminiscent of patterns among the European working classes in the early days of industrialization. Some observers argued that young women and men were only postponing marriage because of serious economic problems (see the next section). Others contended that marriage, after its long rise, was finally in retreat in the face of growing careerism and acceptance of new, less structured relations between (and within) the sexes. More fundamentally, falling birthrates, more married women in the workplace, later marriage, and increased divorce (and remarriage) rates were all related to the growing emancipation of women. They were all part of a complicated constellation of striking changes, which strongly suggested that a major break with the past had taken place in marriage patterns and family relationships in industrialized nations.

ECONOMIC TROUBLES IN RECENT TIMES

This chapter has focused thus far on fundamental changes that accompanied the political recovery and economic expansion discussed in Chapter 36. To summarize, it has been argued that science combined with technology, often under government direction, to promote not only economic expansion but also a more fluid, less antagonistic class structure, in which specialized education was the high road to advancement. Within the prosperous, increasingly technocratic society, women asserted themselves. Beginning in the 1960s, they moved increasingly into the labor market and gave birth to fewer children, developments that have continued to this day with far-reaching consequences. Since science and technology, as well as salaried managers and their bureaucratic organizations, show no sign of becoming less important, it might be argued that this portrait of life in the industrialized nations is complete. Yet such an argument would be mistaken, for recent economic developments have altered the perspective and put the portrait in a different light.

As discussed in Chapter 36, the reconstruction of Western society after World War Two marched hand in hand with an astonishing postwar economic advance. That advance was unparalleled in its rapidity and consistency, but it came to an abrupt halt in the early 1970s. Old, almost forgotten problems like high unemployment, expensive energy, and international monetary instability suddenly re-emerged. Moreover, the apparent cause of these problems, and hence any quick solutions, lay in the hands of nonindustrialized, oil-exporting countries, countries over which western Europe and the United States could no longer exercise control. The industrialized nations, so long accustomed to savoring the lion's share of the benefits derived from the world economy, were confounded. Throughout the Western world the general mood changed from optimism to pessimism as a new and uncertain era unfolded.

MONEY AND OIL

Two factors loom large in the sudden transition from almost automatic postwar growth to serious economic difficulties in the 1970s and 1980s. The first was the collapse of the postwar monetary system in 1971. The second was the energy crisis with its skyrocketing oil prices.

During the Second World War, British and American statesmen were convinced that international financial disorder after 1918 had contributed mightily to economic problems, the Great Depression, and renewed global warfare. They were determined not to repeat their mistakes, and in the Bretton Woods Agreement of 1944, they laid the foundations for a new international monetary system, which proved instrumental in the unprecedented postwar boom.

The new system, operating through the World Bank and the International Monetary Fund, was based on the American dollar, which was supposed to be "as good as gold" because foreign governments could always exchange dollars for gold at $35 an ounce. The United States proceeded to make needed dollars readily available to the rest of the world, so readily that by early 1971 it had only $11 billion in gold left, and foreigners had accumulated 50 billion American dollars. The result was a classic, long-overdue "run on the bank" in 1971, as foreigners panicked and raced to buy gold with their dollars. President Richard Nixon was forced to stop the sale of American gold. The price of gold then soared on free markets, and the value of the dollar declined. Moreover, fixed rates of exchange were abandoned, and all major currencies began to fluctuate rapidly against each other. Great uncertainty replaced postwar predictability in international finance, which also complicated trade and foreign investment.

Even more serious was the dramatic reversal in the price and availability of energy. As described in Chapter 26, coal-fired steam engines broke the bottleneck of chronically inadequate energy in the late eighteenth-century economy, making possible the Industrial Revolution and improved living standards in the nineteenth century. In the twentieth century, petroleum proved its worth, and the great postwar boom was fueled by cheap oil, especially in western

Europe and Japan. Cheap oil from the Middle East permitted energy-intensive industries—automobiles, chemicals, and electric power—to expand rapidly and lead other sectors of the economy forward. More generally, cheap oil and cheap energy encouraged businesses to invest massively in machinery and improved technology. This investment enabled workers to produce more and allowed a steady rise in the standard of living without much inflation.

In the 1950s and 1960s, the main oil-exporting countries, grouped together after 1960 in the Arab-dominated Organization of Petroleum Exporting Countries (OPEC), had watched the Western oil companies keep prices low to win profitable new markets and serve the needs of the industrialized nations. The Egyptian leader Nasser argued that Arab countries should push oil prices up to further increase their revenues and also to strike at Israel and its Western allies. But Egypt lacked oil and Nasser failed. Colonel Moammar Khadafy of Libya proved more successful. He won important concessions from Western nations and oil companies in the early 1970s, and his example activated OPEC's members, both Arab and non-Arab. In 1971 OPEC for the first time presented a united front against the oil companies and obtained a solid price increase. The stage was set for the revolution in energy prices during the fourth Arab-Israeli war in October 1973.

The war began on the solemn sabbath celebration of Yom Kippur, or the Day of Atonement, the holiest day in the Jewish calendar. Egypt and Syria launched a surprise attack on an unsuspecting Israel, breaking through defense positions and destroying a large part of the Israeli air force. In response to urgent pleas, the United States airlifted $2.2 billion of its most sophisticated weapons to Israel, which accepted a cease-fire after its successful counterattack had encircled much of the Egyptian army. Surprisingly, the Yom Kippur War eventually led to peace between Egypt and Israel. Egypt's initial military victories greatly enhanced the power and prestige of General Anwar Sadat, Nasser's successor. This advantage enabled the realistic Sadat to achieve in 1979 the negotiated settlement with Israel that he had long desired (page 1180).

In the first days of the war, the Arab (and non-Arab) oil producers in OPEC placed an embargo on oil shipments to the United States and the Netherlands, in retaliation for their support of Israel. They also cut production and raised prices by 70 percent, ostensibly to prevent Europe from sharing oil with the United States. In reality, greed and a desire for revenge against the West took over: a second increase in December, after the cease-fire, meant that crude oil prices quadrupled in less than a year. It was widely realized that OPEC's sudden action would injure the industrialized nations, although some Asians and Africans believed that OPEC's initiative was a necessary first step toward global economic justice. In any event, the world's industrialized powers did nothing. The Soviet Union was a great oil exporter and benefited directly, while a cautious western Europe looked to the United States for leadership. But the United States was immobilized, its attention absorbed by the Watergate crisis (see page 1154). Thus governments, companies, and individuals were left to deal piecemeal and manage as best they could with the so-called oil shock—a "shock" that was really an earthquake.

INFLATION, DEBT, AND UNEMPLOYMENT

Coming close on the heels of upheaval in the international monetary system, the price revolution in energy sources plunged the world into its worst economic decline since the 1930s. The energy-intensive industries that had driven the economy up in the 1950s and 1960s now dragged it down in the mid-1970s. Yet, while industrial output fell, soaring energy costs sent prices surging. "Stagflation"—the unexpected combination of economic stagnation and rapid inflation—appeared, to bedevil the public and baffle economists. Unemployment rose, while productivity and living standards declined.

But no cycle lasts forever, and by 1976 a modest recovery was in progress. People were learning to save energy, turning down thermostats and buying smaller cars. Optimists argued that the challenge of redesigning lifestyles to cope with expensive energy actually represented a great opportunity.

Iran's Islamic revolution in 1978 and 1979 (page 1182) confounded these hopes, at least in the short run. Iranian oil production collapsed, OPEC again doubled the price of crude oil, and the industrialized countries succumbed to the second oil shock. Once again, unemployment and inflation rose very dramatically. Renewed recovery began in 1982, driven by a reversal in oil prices, falling interest rates, and

The Egyptian-Israeli Peace Treaty of 1979 is celebrated by the men who made it possible, Egypt's President Anwar al-Sadat, U.S. President Jimmy Carter, and Israeli Prime Minister Menachem Begin. Egypt recognized Israel's right to exist and established normal diplomatic relations, while Israel agreed to withdraw from Egyptian territory occupied in the Six-Day War of 1967. *(National Archives and Records Administration)*

large U.S. trade and budget deficits. But the recovery was very uneven. In the summer of 1985, the unemployment rate in western Europe rose to its highest levels since the Great Depression. Fully 19 million people were unemployed. The recovery was also fragile, since oil prices would probably rise again, and the oversized American deficits promised grave problems sooner or later.

Many means were devised in the 1970s to measure the troubled economy, but perhaps none was more telling than the "misery index." First used with considerable effect by candidate Jimmy Carter in the 1976 U.S. presidential debates, the misery index combined rates of inflation and unemployment in a single, powerfully emotional number. Figure 38.3 presents a comparison of misery indexes for the United States and the Common Market countries between 1970 and 1985. As may be seen, "misery" increased on both sides of the Atlantic, but the increase was substantially greater in western Europe. This helps explain why these hard times—often referred to by Europeans simply as "the crisis"—probably had an even greater psychological impact on Europeans than on Americans.

Nor was the Soviet bloc spared. Both the Soviet Union and the satellite states of its eastern European empire did less and less well: annual rates of economic growth fell from 6 to 7 percent in the late

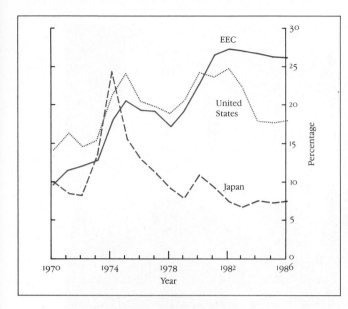

FIGURE 38.3 The Misery Index, 1970–1985 Combining rates of unemployment and inflation provided a simple but effective measure of economic hardship. This particular index represents the sum of two times the unemployment rate plus the inflation rate, reflecting the widespread belief that joblessness causes more suffering than higher prices. EEC = European Economic Community, or Common Market countries. *(Source: OECD data, as given in* The Economist, *June 15, 1985, p. 69.)*

1960s to 2 to 3 percent in 1980. This performance was no worse than that of most Western countries, but it mocked the long-standing propaganda boast to "catch and surpass the capitalistic West," which was quietly dropped in favor of less amusing slogans.

The revolution in energy prices had major consequences for economic and political relations between East bloc members. Eastern Europe is generally poor in energy resources, especially petroleum, whereas the Soviet Union has enormous gas deposits and is the world's largest oil producer. Thus the explosion of oil prices greatly increased the economic leverage of the Soviet Union over eastern Europe, and it strengthened trade ties within COMECON, the economic "club" formed by the Soviet Union and its allies. The Russians supplied more desperately needed oil and raw materials, and they took in return the pick of eastern European manufacturers. Eastern European hopes of closer commercial (and cultural) ties with their Western neighbors necessarily faded.

Debts and deficits piled up quickly in the industrialized nations in the 1970s and 1980s. In the first place, the price hikes of 1973 and 1979 required a massive global transfer of wealth to the OPEC countries from both rich and poor nations. Like individual consumers suddenly faced with a financial emergency, countries scrambled to borrow to pay their greatly increased fuel bills. Governments went on a borrowing binge to maintain social welfare services as their economies declined and tax receipts fell. Even in West Germany, justly famous for its commitment to low inflation and sound money, interest on the national debt consumed one-quarter of all government spending in 1981.

Western consumers also joined the race for ever-higher levels of debt. Borrowing to buy before prices rose seemed smart in the 1970s, and that attitude carried over into the 1980s. Like burgeoning government debt, a record-high level of consumer debt was a two-edged sword. It sustained current economic activity but quite possibly posed serious repayment problems, an appropriately ambiguous reflection of the troubled economy.

SOME SOCIAL CONSEQUENCES

The most pervasive consequences of recent economic stagnation were probably psychological and attitudinal. Optimism gave way to pessimism; romantic utopianism yielded to sober realism. This drastic change in mood—a complete surprise only to those who had never studied history—affected states, institutions, and individuals in countless ways.

To be sure, there were heartbreaking human tragedies—lost jobs, bankruptcies, and mental breakdowns. But, on the whole, the welfare system fashioned in the postwar years held firm and prevented mass suffering and degradation. Extended benefits for the unemployed, pensions for the aged, free medical care for the needy, surplus food and special allowances for parents with children—all these and a host of lesser supports did their part. The responsive, socially concerned national state undoubtedly contributed to the preservation of political stability and democracy in the face of economic difficulties, difficulties that might have brought revolution and dictatorship in earlier times.

The energetic response of governments to social needs helps explain the sharp increase in total gov-

"The New Poor" Economic crisis and prolonged unemployment in the early 1980s reduced many from modest affluence to harsh poverty, creating a class of new poor. This photo captures that human tragedy. After two years of unemployment, this homeless French office worker must sleep each night in a makeshift shelter for the destitute. *(Dennis Stock/Magnum)*

ernment spending in most countries during the 1970s and 1980s. In 1982 western European governments spent an average of more than one-half of gross national income, as compared to only 37 percent fifteen years earlier. In the United States, the combined share of federal, state, and local government expenditures rose from 31 to 35 percent in the same years. The role of government in everyday life became even more important.

In all countries, people were much more willing to see their governments increase spending than raise taxes. This imbalance contributed to the rapid growth of budget deficits, national debts, and inflation discussed earlier. By the late 1970s, a powerful

reaction to government's ever-increasing role set in, and Western governments were gradually forced to introduce austerity measures to slow the seemingly inexorable growth of public spending and the welfare state. The partially successful efforts of Margaret Thatcher in Britain and Ronald Reagan in the United States to limit the growth of social programs absorbed the attention of the English-speaking world, but François Mitterrand of France was the temporary exception who proved the general rule. After his election as president in 1981, Mitterrand led his Socialist party and Communist allies on a vast program of nationalization and public investment designed to spend France out of economic stagnation. By 1983 this attempt had clearly failed. Mitterrand's Socialist government was then compelled to impose a wide variety of austerity measures fully worthy of Reagan and Thatcher, until elections in 1986 brought a conservative coalition to power by a narrow margin.

When governments were eventually forced to restrain spending, Big Science was often singled out for cuts, unless its ties to the military were very direct. The problems of CERN were a good example. Formed to pool western European efforts in high-energy particle physics, CERN succeeded admirably in stealing the lead from the United States in this exciting but esoteric and uncommercial field. But the costs had become so enormous—$400 million for construction of the latest electron-smashing accelerator—that some governments, such as Great Britain's, found themselves budgeting 10 percent of all their spending for scientific research on particle physics alone. In the 1980s, CERN was increasingly attacked as an extravagant misallocation of scarce resources at a time when new fields, such as computers and genetic research, were bursting with scientific opportunities that offered mouth-watering commercial applications. More generally, tighter funding for Big Science accelerated the ongoing computer revolution. That revolution thrived on the diffusion of unprecedented computational and informational capacity to small research groups and private businesses, which were both cause and effect of the revolution itself.

Individuals felt the impact of austerity even earlier, for unlike governments, they could not pay their bills by printing money and going ever further into debt. The energy crisis forced them to re-examine not only their fuel bills but the whole pattern of self-indulgent materialism in the postwar era as well. The result was a leaner, tougher lifestyle, featuring more attention to nutrition and a passion for exercise. Correspondingly, there was less blind reliance on medical science for good health and a growing awareness that individuals must accept a large portion of the responsibility for illness and disease. More people began to realize that they could substantially increase their life spans simply by eating regular meals, sleeping seven or eight hours each night, exercising two or three times a week, maintaining moderate weight, forgoing smoking, and using alcohol only in moderation. A forty-five-year-old American male who practiced three or fewer of these habits could expect to live to be sixty-seven; one who adhered to five or six could expect to live eleven more years, to age seventy-eight.

Yet it was the very real threat of unemployment that probably had the most profound impact. A good job promised pride and well-being, while the most generous unemployment benefits only prevented catastrophe. The increased focus on jobs continued the 1960s trend of more married women working. It also encouraged both men and women to postpone marriage until they had put their careers on a firm foundation, so that the age of marriage rose sharply for both sexes in many Western countries.

Indeed, the employment question seemed to shape the outlook of a whole generation. The students of the 1980s were serious, practical, and often conservative. As one young woman at a French university told a reporter in 1985, "Jobs are the big worry now, so everyone wants to learn something practical."[4] In France, as elsewhere, it was an astonishing shift from the romantic visions and political activism of the late 1960s and eloquent testimony to the impact of tough times.

Major social changes accompanied political recovery and economic expansion in the industrialized nations after World War Two. Science combined with technology to produce dazzling triumphs that helped drive the consumer society. The class structure became less rigid, partly because education replaced inherited property as the critical factor in job selection and economic success. Women struck off in new directions, asserting themselves and redefining their objectives.

All of these developments continue to the present day, but the return of difficult economic conditions has modified substantially the emphasis. Above all, perhaps, people in the industrialized nations have experienced the full effect of living in an interdependent world. They have learned that the ever-rising prosperity they took for granted in the 1960s depends on a global economic system, a system that many non-Westerners deem unjust and exploitative. The future of the industrialized world is now understood to be inextricably intertwined with the lives and actions of non-Western peoples, which form the subject of the final two chapters.

NOTES

1. Quoted in W. Laqueur, *Europe Since Hitler* (Baltimore: Penguin Books, 1972), p. 9.
2. Quoted in J. Ziman, *The Force of Knowledge: The Scientific Dimension of Society* (Cambridge, Eng.: Cambridge University Press, 1976), p. 128.
3. Quoted in S. Toulmin, *The Twentieth Century: A Promethean Age,* ed. A. Bullock (London: Thames & Hudson, 1971), p. 294.
4. *Wall Street Journal,* June 25, 1985, p. 1.

SUGGESTED READING

J. Ziman, *The Force of Knowledge: The Scientific Dimension of Society* (1976), which has an excellent bibliography, is a penetrating look at science by a leading physicist. C. P. Snow, *The Two Cultures and the Scientific Revolution,* rev. ed. (1963), explores the gap between scientists and nonscientists in a widely discussed book. A. Toffler, *Future Shock* (1970), is an interesting but exaggerated best-seller, which claims that many contemporary psychological problems are due to overly rapid technical and scientific development. J. Ellul, *The Technological Society* (1964), is also highly critical of technical progress, while D. S. Landes, *The Unbound Prometheus: Technological Change and Industrial Development in Western Europe from 1750 to the Present* (1969), remains enthusiastic. Two more stimulating works on technology are J. J. Servan-Schreiber, *The World Challenge* (1981), and H. Jacoby, *The Bureaucratization of the World* (1973).

In addition to studies cited in the Suggested Reading for Chapter 36, A. Simpson, *The New Europeans* (1968), is a good guide to contemporary Western society. Two engaging books on recent intellectual developments are J. Barzun, *The House of Intellect* (1959), and R. Stromberg, *After Everything: Western Intellectual History Since 1945* (1970). L. Wylie, *Village in the Vauclause,* rev. ed. (1964), and P. J. Hélias, *The Horse of Pride* (1980), provide fascinating pictures of life in the French village. A. Kriegel, *The French Communists* (1972) and *Eurocommunism* (1978), are also recommended. A. Touraine, *The May Movement* (1971), is sympathetic toward the French student revolt, while the noted sociologist R. Aron, *The Elusive Revolution* (1969), is highly critical. F. Zweig, *The Worker in an Affluent Society* (1961), probes family life and economic circumstances in the British working class on the basis of extensive interviews. R. E. Tyrrell, ed., *The Future That Doesn't Work* (1977), is a polemical but absorbing attack on British socialism. W. Hollstein, *Europe in the Making* (1973), is a fervent plea to integrate Europe by a former top official of the Common Market. The magazines *Encounter, Commentary,* and *The Economist* often carry interesting articles on major social and political trends, as do *Time* and *Newsweek.*

E. Sullerot, *Women, Society and Change* (1971), is an outstanding introduction to women's evolving role. R. Patia, ed., *Women in the Modern World* (1967), compares women's situations in many countries. Two other influential books on women and their new awareness are S. de Beauvoir, *The Second Sex* (1962), and B. Friedan, *The Feminine Mystique* (1963). These may be compared with C. Lasch, *Haven in a Heartless World* (1977), and A. Cherlin, *Marriage, Divorce, Remarriage* (1981), which interpret changes in the American family.

Among innumerable works on recent economic developments, L. Thurow, *The Zero-Sum Society* (1981), is an interesting example of early 1980s pessimism in the United States, and it may be compared with the engaging and informative work by J. Eatwell, *Whatever Happened to Britain? The Economics of Decline* (1982). W. Rowtow, *The World Economy: History and Prospect* (1977), is a massive scholarly tome by a perennial optimist, and P. Hawkins, *The Next Economy* (1983), contains intelligent insights that merit consideration by the ordinary citizen.

LIFE IN THE THIRD WORLD

EVERYDAY LIFE in the emerging nations of Asia and Africa changed dramatically after World War Two, as their peoples struggled to build effective nation-states. Some of the changes paralleled the experiences of Europe and North America: science and modern technology altered people's lives in countless ways, and industrialization efforts to raise the standard of living profoundly affected family life and relations among social classes. Yet most observers stressed the differences in development between the emerging nations and the industrialized world. Life remained very hard in the new nations, which shared—along with the older states of Latin America—widespread poverty and a heritage of foreign domination. Moreover, many discerned a widening economic gap between the industrialized nations of North America and Europe, including the Communist countries of eastern Europe on the one hand and the emerging nations on the other. Some writers even argued that the gap between North and South—that is, between rich nations and poor nations—had replaced the East-West cold war and its immediate aftermath as mankind's most explosive division.

Chapter 37 described a little of the awe-inspiring diversity of cultures and peoples in Asia, Africa, and Latin America. This chapter will concentrate on shared problems of development and everyday life in the vast geographical expanse known collectively as the Third World. Three key questions will guide the investigation. How have the emerging nations of the Third World sought to escape from poverty, and what have been the results of their efforts? What has caused the prodigious growth of Third World cities, and what does their growth mean for their inhabitants? Finally, how did Third World thinkers and artists interpret the modern world and the experiences of their peoples before, during, and after foreign domination?

ECONOMIC AND SOCIAL CHALLENGES IN THE THIRD WORLD

Alongside the tough postindependence task of preserving political unity and building cohesive nation-states, the emerging countries of the Third World faced the enormous challenges of poverty, malnutrition, and disease. These scourges weighed especially heavily on rural people, who depended on agriculture for survival and accounted for most of the Third World's population. Stirred by nationalism and the struggle for political freedom, peasants and landless laborers wanted the brighter future their leaders had promised them.

Most Third World leaders and their advisers in the 1950s and 1960s saw rapid industrialization and "modernization" as the answer to rural poverty and disease. Industrialization and modernization also kindled popular enthusiasm and thus served nation building, which in turn promised economic self-sufficiency and genuine independence. For these reasons, the leaders and peoples of the Third World in the 1950s and 1960s set themselves the massive task of building modern factories, roads, and public health services like those of Europe and North America. Their considerable success fueled rapid economic progress.

Yet social problems, complicated by surging population growth, almost dwarfed the accomplishment. Disappointments multiplied. By and large, the poorest rural people in the poorest countries gained the least from industrialization, and industrial expansion provided jobs for only a small segment even of the urban population. By the late 1960s, widespread dissatisfaction with policies of all-out industrialization prompted a greater emphasis on rural development. The serious economic downturn of the 1970s reinforced this trend. More generally, different approaches proliferated from the late 1960s onward, as Third World nations responded to their common challenge in different ways.

DEFINING THE THIRD WORLD AND ITS POVERTY

Before considering the problems of the Third World, let us ask whether Africa, Asia, and Latin America can be validly and usefully lumped together as a single entity. Some experts prefer to speak of "the emerging nations" or "the less developed countries"—deliberately vague terms suggesting a spectrum of conditions ranging from near-hopeless poverty to moderate well-being. Others add a Fourth and even a Fifth World in order to distinguish among the less developed nations. Still, these countries do

An Indian Family walking barefoot across the countryside captures the human dimension of Third World poverty. Quite possibly they are landless laborers, searching for work, and carrying all their meager belongings. *(Harmit Singh/Black Star)*

share important characteristics that make it valid—with reservations—to speak of them jointly.

First, the countries of the Third World have virtually all experienced political and/or economic domination, nationalist reaction, and a struggle for independence or autonomy. This shared past has given rise to a common consciousness and a widespread feeling of having been oppressed and victimized in their relations with Europe and North America. This outlook has been nurtured by a variety of nationalists, Marxists, and anti-imperialist intellectuals, who have argued forcibly that the Third World's problems are the result of past and present exploitation by the wealthy capitalist nations. Precisely because of their shared sense of past injustice, many influential Latin Americans identify with the Third World, despite their countries' greater affluence. Indeed, the term *Third World* first widely used by Latin American intellectuals in the late 1950s, who picked up the term from a French scholar who likened the peoples of Africa, Asia, and Latin America to the equally diverse but no less oppressed and humiliated French third estate before the revolution of 1789. Later the term came into global use as a handy way of distinguishing Africa, Asia, and Latin America from the "first" and "second" worlds, the capitalist and Communist industrialized nations.

Second, a large majority of men and women in Third World countries still live in the countryside and depend on agriculture for a living. Agricultural goods and raw materials are still the primary exports. In Europe, North America, and Japan, by contrast, people live mainly in cities, depending chiefly on industry and urban services for employment.

Finally, the agricultural countries of Asia, Africa, and most of Latin America are united by awareness of their common poverty. By no means everyone in the Third World is poor; some people are quite wealthy. The average standard of living, however, is low, especially compared with that of people in the wealthy industrial nations, and massive poverty remains ever present.

It is easy to lose sight of the true dimensions of poverty in the Third World in a fog of economic statistics. In the 1950s and 1960s the United Nations and the emerging nations began collecting national income statistics; dividing those estimates by total population yields a nation's average per capita income. These figures received enormous attention because they were stunningly low compared to those of wealthy nations. In 1960, for example, average annual income per person in all of Africa and Southeast Asia was about $100. In North America it was $2,500—twenty-five times more. Journalists, politicians, and scholars often concluded that Third World people were unspeakably poor and verging on mass starvation.

Such comparisons exaggerated the economic gap between the North and the South. They made a hard, sometimes desperate situation seem utterly hopeless. For example, average income per person in the United States in 1973 was about $5,000; in India it was about $100. Yet the average American was not necessarily fifty times better off than the average Indian. As an English and an Indian economist jointly pointed out, "Merely to survive, to be able to buy enough basic food, clothing and shelter in the United States would cost over $1,000 while $100 would suffice for these in India, so that someone with $1,000 in America may be worse off than someone in India with $100."[1] Basic necessities cost considerably less in poor countries than in rich countries.

Reliance on national income statistics also promotes distorted comparisons because the statistics on poor countries are less complete and tend to leave out many wage-earning activities. Furthermore, fewer economic activities involve money transactions in poor countries than in rich ones, and only wage-earning work shows up consistently in national income statistics. In industrialized countries, only housewives do not receive money wages and thus do not show up in income statistics; there are many such "housewife" groups in the Third World.

A deeper understanding arises from considering Third World poverty in human terms, as did the postwar generation of nationalist leaders. Poverty meant, above all, not having enough to eat. Hunger and malnutrition were harsh facts of life for millions. In the poorest countries, like India, Ethiopia, and Bolivia, the average adult ate fewer than 2,000 calories a day —only 85 percent of the minimal requirement. Although many poor countries fared better, none but Argentina could match the 3,000 or more calories consumed in the more fortunate North. Even Third World people who consumed enough calories often suffered from the effects of unbalanced high-starch diets and inadequate protein. Severe protein deficiency stunts the brain as well as the body, and many of the poorest children grew up mentally retarded.

Poor housing—crowded, often damp, and exposed to the elements—contributed significantly to the less developed world's high incidence of chronic ill health. So too did malnutrition, scanty education, and lack of such fundamentals of modern public health as adequate and safe water, sewage disposal, immunizations, prenatal care, and control of communicable diseases. Infant mortality was savage, and chronic illness weakened and demoralized many adults, making them unfit for the hard labor their lives required.

Generally speaking, health status in Asia and Latin America has been better than in the new states of tropical Africa. As one authority described the situation in the early 1960s:

In the African social drama, sickness has a strong claim to being archvillain. . . . In tropical Africa, most men, women, and children are habitually unwell. Many are unwell from the day of their birth to the day of their death. . . . Most of the sick are sick of more than one disease.[2]

The populations of poor countries were also overwhelmingly concentrated in the countryside, as small farmers and landless laborers. Rural people were often unable to read or write, and they lacked steady employment. Even with hard work, simple tools limited productivity. Basic services like safe running water were uncommon: village women around the world spent much of each day carrying water and

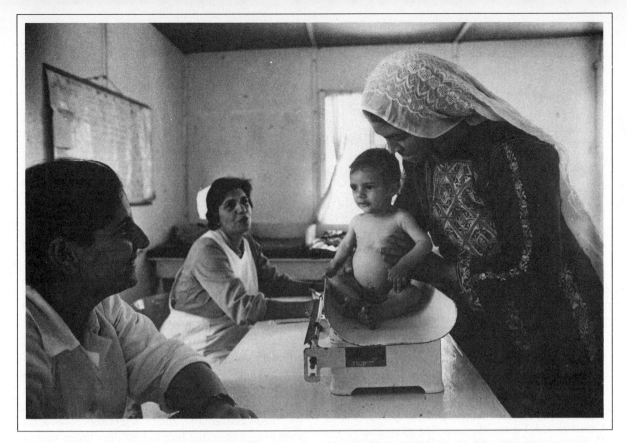

Modern Health Care In this UN clinic for Palestinian refugees in Jordan, a baby receives the professional care that dramatically reduces infant mortality. *(Owen Franken/ Stock, Boston)*

searching for firewood or dung to use as fuel, as they must still do in many countries.

Mass poverty represented an awesome challenge to the postwar leaders of the newly emerging nations. Having raised peoples' hopes in the struggle for independence, they had to start delivering on their promises if they were to maintain trust and stay in power. A strong commitment to modern economic and social development, already present in parts of Latin America in the 1930s, took hold in Asia and Africa in the postwar era.

THE MEDICAL REVOLUTION AND THE POPULATION EXPLOSION

The most thoroughgoing success the Third World achieved after the Second World War was its spectacular, ongoing medical revolution. Immediately after winning independence, the governments of emerging nations began adapting modern methods of immu-

nology and public health. These methods were often simple, inexpensive, and extremely effective. One famous measure involved spraying with DDT in Southeast Asia, in order to control mosquitoes bearing malaria, one of the deadliest and most debilitating of tropical diseases. In Sri Lanka (formerly Ceylon), DDT spraying halved the yearly toll of deaths in the very first postwar decade—at a modest cost of $2 per person. According to the UN's World Health Organization, which helped provide medical expertise to the new states, deaths from smallpox, cholera, and plague declined by more than 95 percent worldwide between 1951 and 1966.

Asian and African countries also increased the small numbers of hospitals, doctors, and nurses they had inherited from the colonial past. Large African cities' biggest, most modern, and most beautiful buildings were often their hospitals. Sophisticated medical facilities became symbols of the commitment to a better life.

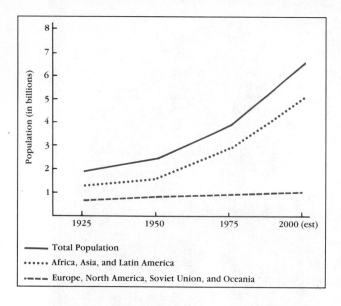

FIGURE 39.1 The Increase of World Population, 1925–2000 Since the first quarter of the twentieth century Africa, Asia, and Latin America—the Third World—has been growing much more rapidly than industrialized Europe, North America, and the Soviet Union. Compare with Figure 30.2 for a long-term perspective. *(Source: United Nations,* Concise Report on the World Population Situation in 1970–1975 and Its Long-Range Implications, *New York, 1974, p. 59.)*

Some critics maintained that expensive medical technology was an indulgence their countries could not afford, for they were ill-suited to the pressing health problems of the bulk of the population. Such criticism prompted a greater emphasis on medical services in the countryside in more recent years. Local people have been successfully trained as paramedics to staff rural outpatient clinics offering medical treatment, health education, and pre- and postnatal care to the neglected rural masses. Most paramedics are women: many health problems involve childbirth and infancy, and villagers the world over consider it improper for a male to examine a woman's body.

The medical revolution significantly lowered death rates and lengthened life expectancy in the Third World. In particular, children became increasingly likely to survive their early years, though infant mortality remained far higher than in rich countries. By 1980 the average inhabitant of the Third World could expect at birth to live about 54 years; life expectancy varied from 40 to 64 years depending on the country. In developed countries, by contrast, life expectancy at birth averaged 71 years.

A much less favorable consequence of the medical revolution was accelerated population growth. Rapid decline in the death rate was not immediately accompanied by a similar decline in the birthrate; women generally continued to bear five to seven children, as their mothers and grandmothers had. The combined populations of Asia, Africa, and Latin America, which had grown relatively modestly from 1925 to 1950, increased between 1950 and 1975 from 1,750 million to 3,000 million, as Figure 39.1 shows (see also Map 39.1). Barring gigantic natural or manmade catastrophe, the population of the three continents is expected to surge to about 5,200 million in the year 2000—an unprecedented explosion.

The population explosion in turn aroused fears of approaching famine and starvation. Thomas Malthus's gloomy late-eighteenth-century conclusion that population always tends to grow faster than food supply (see page 843) was revived and updated by "neo-Malthusian" social scientists. Such fears were exaggerated, but they did produce uneasiness in the Third World, whose leaders saw that their countries had to run fast just to maintain their already low standards of living. Some governments began pushing family planning and birth control to slow the growth of population.

These measures were not very successful in the 1950s and 1960s. In many countries, Islamic and Catholic religious teachings were hostile to birth control. Moreover, widespread cultural attitudes dictated that a real man keeps his wife pregnant. There were also solid economic reasons for preferring large families: farmers need plenty of children as cheap labor at planting and harvest times. And since sons and daughters were the only social security system, a prudent couple wanted several children because some would surely die young.

THE RACE TO INDUSTRIALIZE, 1950–1970

Many key Third World leaders, pressed on by their European, American, and Soviet advisers, were convinced throughout the 1950s and most of the 1960s that all-out industrialization was the only answer to

MAP 39.1 World Population Density

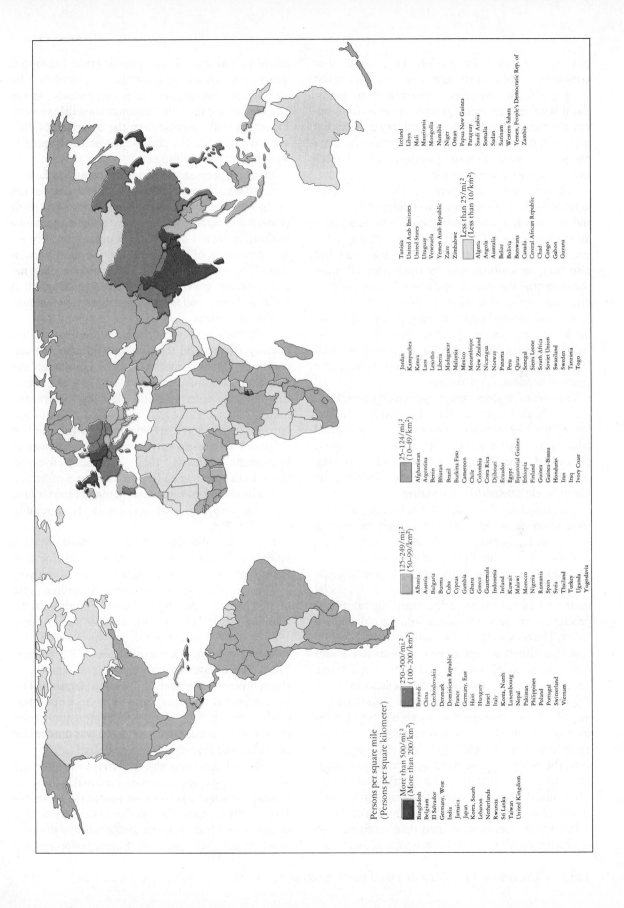

Persons per square mile
(Persons per square kilometer)

More than 500/mi.² (More than 200/km²)
Bangladesh, Belgium, El Salvador, Germany, West, India, Jamaica, Japan, Korea, South, Lebanon, Netherlands, Rwanda, Sri Lanka, Taiwan, United Kingdom

250–500/mi.² (100–200/km²)
Burundi, China, Czechoslovakia, Denmark, Dominican Republic, France, Germany, East, Ghana, Haiti, Hungary, Israel, Italy, Korea, North, Luxembourg, Nepal, Pakistan, Philippines, Poland, Portugal, Switzerland, Vietnam

125–249/mi.² (50–99/km²)
Albania, Austria, Bulgaria, Burma, Cuba, Cyprus, Gambia, Greece, Guatemala, Indonesia, Ireland, Kuwait, Malawi, Morocco, Nigeria, Rumania, Spain, Syria, Thailand, Turkey, Uganda, Yugoslavia

25–124/mi.² (10–49/km²)
Afghanistan, Argentina, Benin, Bhutan, Brazil, Burkina Faso, Cameroon, Chile, Colombia, Costa Rica, Djibouti, Ecuador, Egypt, Equatorial Guinea, Ethiopia, Finland, Guinea, Guinea-Bissau, Honduras, Iran, Iraq, Ivory Coast, Jordan, Kampuchea, Kenya, Laos, Lesotho, Liberia, Madagascar, Malaysia, Mexico, Mozambique, New Zealand, Nicaragua, Norway, Panama, Peru, Qatar, Senegal, Sierra Leone, South Africa, Soviet Union, Swaziland, Sweden, Tanzania, Togo, Tunisia, United Arab Emirates, United States, Uruguay, Venezuela, Yemen Arab Republic, Zaire, Zimbabwe

Less than 25/mi.² (Less than 10/km²)
Algeria, Angola, Australia, Belize, Bolivia, Botswana, Canada, Central African Republic, Chad, Congo, Gabon, Guyana, Iceland, Libya, Mali, Mauritania, Mongolia, Namibia, Niger, Oman, Papua New Guinea, Paraguay, Saudi Arabia, Somalia, Sudan, Surinam, Western Sahara, Yemen, People's Democratic Rep. of, Zambia

poverty and population growth. The masses, they concluded, were poor because they were imprisoned in a primitive, inefficient agricultural economy. Farm families' tiny holdings were too small for modern machinery. Big landowners exhibited more, but still limited, promise. Only modern factory industry appeared capable of creating wealth quickly enough to outrace the growth of numbers.

The two-century experience of the West, Japan, and the Soviet Union seemed to validate this faith in industrialization. Economic history became a popular subject among Third World elites. It taught the encouraging lesson that the wealthy countries had also been agricultural and "underdeveloped" until the Industrial Revolution had lifted them out of poverty, one by one. According to this view, the uneven progress of industrialization was primarily responsible for the great income gap that existed between the rich countries of North America and Europe (including the Soviet Union) and the poor countries of the postindependent Third World.

Theories of modernization, particularly popular in the 1960s, also assumed that all countries were following the path already taken by the industrialized nations, and that it was the task of the elite to speed the trip. Marxism, with its industrial and urban bias, preached a similar gospel. These ideas reinforced the Third World's desire to industrialize.

Nationalist leaders believed that successful industrialization required state action and enterprise. Many were impressed by socialism in general and Stalin's forced industrialization in particular, which they saw as having won the Soviet Union international power and prominence, whatever its social costs. In Asia and Africa, furthermore, capitalists and private enterprise were equated with the old colonial rulers. The reasoning was practical as well as ideological: in addition to high-paying administrative jobs for political allies, modern industry meant ports, roads, schools and hospitals, as well as factories. Only the state could afford such expensive investments— as, indeed, the colonial governments had begun to realize in the twilight years of colonial rule. With the exception of the People's Republic of China, however, the new governments recognized private property and tolerated native (and foreign) businessmen. The "mixed economy"—part socialist, part capitalist—became the general rule in the Third World.

Political leaders concentrated state investment in big, highly visible projects that proclaimed their inde-

pendence and stimulated national pride. Enormous dams for irrigation and hydroelectric power were favored undertakings. Nasser's stupendous Aswan Dam harnessed the Nile, demonstrating that modern Egyptians could surpass even the pyramids of their ancient ancestors. The gigantic state-owned steel mill was another favorite project.

These big projects testified to the prevailing faith in expensive advanced technology and modernization along European lines. Nationalist leaders and their economic experts generally believed that rapid industrialization would depend on squeezing money for investment out of agriculture and the farm population. They measured overall success by how fast national income grew, and they tended to assume that social problems and income distribution would take care of themselves.

India, the world's most populous non-Communist country, exemplified the general trends. After independence, Gandhi's special brand of nationalism was redirected toward economic and social rebirth through state enterprise and planning. Nehru and many Congress Party leaders believed that unregulated capitalism and free trade under British rule had deepened Indian poverty. Considering themselves democratic socialists, they introduced five-year plans, built state-owned factories and steel mills, and raised tariffs to protect Indian manufacturers. Quite typically, they neglected agriculture, land reform, and village life.

The Third World's first great industrialization drive was in many ways a success. Industry grew faster than ever before, though from an admittedly low base in Africa and most of Asia. According to the United Nations, industry in the non-Communist developing nations grew 6.5 percent per year between 1950 and 1976. Because this growth exceeded the average annual population increase of 2.5 percent, Third World industrial production per capita grew about 4 percent per year for a long generation. This was very solid industrial growth by historical standards: it matched the fastest rates of industrialization in the United States before 1914 and was double that of Britain and France in the same years.

Industrial expansion also stimulated the other sectors of Third World economies. National income per capita grew about 2 percent per year in the 1950s and 1960s. This pace was far superior to the very modest increases that had occurred under colonial domination between 1900 and 1950. Future historians may

Building the Aswan Dam Financed and engineered by the Soviet Union, the massive high dam at Aswan was Nasser's dream for Egypt's economic future. Here an army of workers lay the stones that will harness the Nile for irrigation and hydroelectric power. *(Popperfoto)*

well see the era after political emancipation as the era of industrial revolution in Asia and Africa.

This was certainly the case for a few small Asian countries that downgraded government control and emphasized private enterprise and the export of manufactured goods. South Korea, Taiwan, the city-state of Singapore, and the British colony of Hong Kong were genuine "economic miracles," industrializing rapidly and remarkably improving the living standards of ordinary people.

South Korea and Taiwan were typical underdeveloped countries after World War Two—poor, small, agricultural, densely populated, and lacking in natural resources. They had also suffered from Japanese imperialism. How did these countries manage to make good?

Radical land reform drew the mass of small farmers into a competitive market economy, which proved an excellent school of self-reliance and initiative. As in Japan, pro-business governments cooperated with capitalists and helped keep wages low. Large-scale American aid also helped, as did almost free access to the large American market. And like Japan, both countries succeeded in preserving the fundamentals of traditional Chinese and Korean culture even as they accepted and mastered Western technology. Tough nationalist leaders maintained political stability at the expense of genuine political democracy.

Nevertheless, disillusionment with the Third World's relatively rapid industrialization was spreading by the late 1960s. In the first place, the experience of a few small states like South Korea and Taiwan was quite exceptional. The countries of Asia, Africa, and Latin America did not as a whole match the "miraculous" concurrent advances of western Europe and Japan: the great economic gap between the rich and the poor nations continued to widen.

Also, most Third World leaders had genuinely believed that rapid industrial development would help the rural masses. Yet careful studies showed that the main beneficiaries of industrialization were businessmen, bureaucrats, skilled workers, and urban professionals. Peasants and agricultural laborers gained little or nothing. In fast-growing, dynamic Mexico, for instance, it was estimated that about 40 percent of the population was completely excluded from the benefits of industrialization. Moreover, the very poorest countries, such as India and Indonesia in Asia, and Ethiopia and the Sudan in Africa, were growing most slowly in per capita terms. The industrialization prescription appeared least effective where poverty was most intense. The economic dislocations of the 1970s and 1980s accentuated this trend, visiting particularly devastating effects on the poorest countries.

Perhaps most seriously, industrialization was failing to provide the sheer number of jobs needed for the sons and daughters of the population explosion. Statisticians estimated that the growth of Third World manufacturing between 1950 and 1970 provided jobs for only about one-fifth of the 200 million young men and women who entered the exploding labor force in the same period. Most new enterprises employed advanced technology that required few workers. One person on a bulldozer could do the job of hundreds with shovels. For the foreseeable future, most Third World people would have to remain on the farm or work in traditional handicrafts and service occupations. All-out modern industrialization had failed as a panacea.

Agriculture and Village Life

The limitations of industrial development forced Third World governments to take a renewed interest in rural people and village life from the late 1960s onward. At best, this attention meant giving agriculture its due and coordinating rural development with industrialization and urbanization. At worst, it fostered a resigned "second-best" approach to the unrelenting economic and social challenge, especially in the very poorest countries. The optimistic vision of living standards approaching those of the wealthy North gave way to the pessimistic conclusion that it was possible to ease only slightly the great hardships of the rural masses.

Nationalist elites had neglected agriculture in the 1950s for various reasons. They regarded an agricultural economy as a mark of colonial servitude, which they were symbolically repudiating by embracing industrialization. They wanted to squeeze agriculture and peasant producers in order to provide capital for industry. Thus governments often established artificially low food prices, which also subsidized their volatile urban supporters at the expense of the farmers. In addition, the obstacles to more productive farming seemed overwhelming to unsympathetic urban elites and condescending foreign experts: farms were too small and fragmented for mechanization, peasants were too stubborn and ignorant to change their ways, and so on. Little wonder that only big farmers and some plantations received much government support.

More to the point, most honest observers were convinced that improved farm performance required land reform. Wherever large estates and absentee landlords predominated—large parts of Asia and most of Latin America, excluding Mexico, though not in black Africa—poor peasants who had to rent land and landless laborers simply lacked the incentive to work harder. Any increased profits from larger crops went mainly to the absentee landowners.

Yet ever since the French Revolution, genuine land reform has been a profoundly radical measure, frequently bringing violence and civil war. Powerful landowners and their allies have generally succeeded in blocking or subverting redistribution of land to benefit the poor. Land reform, unlike industrialization, has generally been too hot for most politicians to handle.

Third World governments also neglected agriculture because feeding the masses was deceptively easy in the 1950s and early 1960s. Very poor countries received food from the United States at give-away prices, as part of a U.S. effort to dispose of its enormous grain surpluses and help American farmers. The countries of Asia, Africa, and Latin America, which had collectively produced more grain than they had consumed before 1939, began importing ever increasing quantities after 1945 as their populations soared. Crops might fail, but starvation seemed a thing of the past. When India was urged to build up its food reserves in 1965, one top Indian official expressed a widespread attitude: "Why should we bother? Our reserves are the wheat fields of Kansas."[3]

In the short run, the Indian official was right. In 1966 and again in 1967, when the monsoon failed to deliver its life-giving rains to the Indo-Pakistan subcontinent and famine gripped the land, the United States gave India one-fifth of its wheat crop. More than 60 million Indians lived exclusively on American grain. The effort required a food armada of six hundred ships, the largest fleet assembled since the Normandy invasion of 1944. The famine was ultimately contained, and instead of millions of deaths there were only a few thousand.

This close brush with mass starvation sent a shiver down the world's spine. Complacency dissolved in the Third World; prophecies of disaster multiplied in wealthy nations. Paul Ehrlich, an American scientist, envisioned a grisly future in his polemical 1968 bestseller *The Population Bomb:*

The battle to feed all of humanity is over. In the 1970s the world will undergo famines—hundreds of millions of people are going to starve to death in spite of any crash programs embarked upon now. At this stage nothing can prevent a substantial increase in the world death rate.[4]

Other Western commentators outdid each other with nightmare visions. One portrayed the earth as a crowded lifeboat in a sea of hungry poor, who would have to drown in order not to swamp the lifeboat. Another version compared truly poor countries like Bangladesh, Egypt, and Haiti to hopelessly wounded soldiers on a gory battlefield. Such victims were best left to die, so that scarce resources could be concentrated on the "walking wounded" who might yet be saved. Such crude and brutal Social Darwinism made it easy for Third World intellectuals to believe the worst about the rich industrialized nations and their economies.

Yet there was another face, a technological face, to the European and American interest in the Third World's food supply. Plant scientists and agricultural research stations had already set out to develop new hybrid seeds genetically engineered to suit the growing conditions of tropical agriculture. Their model

Plantation Agriculture These women in Haiti are sorting coffee beans, which are being dried on the roof of a building. Like many Third World countries, Haiti has needed to export a plantation product in order to buy food from abroad to feed its population. *(Fritz Henle/ Photo Researchers)*

was extraordinarily productive hybrid corn developed for the American Midwest in the 1940s. The first breakthrough came in Mexico in the 1950s, when an American-led team developed new high-yielding dwarf wheats. These varieties enabled farmers to double their yields from one year to the next, though they demanded greater amounts of fertilizer and water for irrigation. Mexican wheat production soared.

Thus began the transformation of Third World agriculture—the so-called Green Revolution. In the 1960s an American-backed team of scientists in the Philippines turned their attention to rice, the Asian staff of life; they quickly developed a "miracle rice." The new hybrid also required more fertilizer and water, but yielded more and grew much faster. It permitted the revolutionary advent of year-round farming on irrigated land, making possible two, three, or

Old and New With a fetish statue designed to frighten off evil spirits standing by, the proud owner of a two-acre plot in southern India shows a visiting expert his crop of miracle rice. As this picture suggests, the acceptance of modern technology does not necessarily require the repudiation of cultural traditions. *(Marc and Evelyne Bernheim/ Woodfin Camp)*

even four crops a year. The brutal tropical sun of the hot dry season became an agricultural blessing for the first time. Asian scientists, financed by their governments, developed similar hybrids to meet local conditions. Increases in grain production were rapid and dramatic in some Asian countries. In gigantic India, for example, farmers upped production more than 60 percent in fifteen years. By 1980, thousands of new grain bins dotted the countryside, symbols of the agricultural revolution in India and the country's newfound ability to feed all its people. Communist China followed with its own highly successful version of the Green Revolution under Deng Xiao-ping.

The Green Revolution offered new hope to the Third World, but it too was no cure-all. At first it seemed that most of its benefits flowed to the big landowners and substantial peasant farmers, who could afford the necessary investments in irrigation

and fertilizer. Recent experience in China and other Asian countries has shown, however, that even peasant families with tiny farms can gain substantially. The new techniques of year-round cropping require more work, but they enable the peasant family to squeeze more food out of its precious land. For any family lucky enough to have even three acres, the ongoing Green Revolution has been a godsend. Yet the technical revolution has shared relatively few of its benefits with the poorest classes—landless laborers, tenant farmers, and tiny landholders. Lacking even the two or three acres necessary to feed themselves with intensive effort, the very poorest groups have gained only slightly more regular employment from the Green Revolution's demand for more labor.

After early breakthroughs in Mexico, the Green Revolution's greatest successes occurred not in Latin America but in Asia, most notably in countries with broad-based peasant ownership of land. Countries with large numbers of landless peasants and insecure tenant farmers, such as Pakistan and the Philippines, experienced less improvement than countries like South Korea and Taiwan, where land is generally peasant-owned. This helps to explain why the Green Revolution failed to spread from Mexico throughout Latin America: as long as 3 or 4 percent of the rural population owns 60 to 80 percent of the land, which is the case in many Latin American countries, the Green Revolution will probably remain stillborn.

The same fatal equation has prevailed in Asian countries like Bangladesh. There an elite tenth of the population owns half the land, and the poorest half owns nothing at all. People eat less today than fifteen years ago, yet land reform remains a political and social minefield. As one member of a big (fifty-acre) landowning family in Bangladesh told an American reporter in 1981: "They talk of removing property markers. It cannot happen. I will kill you if you move my property markers one inch."[5]

The Green Revolution, like the medical revolution and industrialization, represented a large but uneven step forward for the Third World. Most unfortunately, black Africa benefited little from the new agricultural techniques, even though land reform was a serious problem only in white-ruled South Africa. Poor transportation, inadequate storage facilities, and low government-imposed agricultural prices had to bear much of the blame. Also, the climatic conditions of black Africa encouraged continued adherence to dry farming and root crops, whereas the Green Revolution has been almost synonymous with intensive irrigation and grain production. Throughout the Third World, therefore, relatively few of its benefits have flowed to the poorest groups—black Africans and the landless peasants of Asia and Latin America. These poor, who lacked political influence and had no clear idea what needed to be done, increasingly longed to escape from ill-paid, irregular work in somebody else's fields. For many of the bravest and most enterprising, life in a nearby town or city seemed a way out.

THE GROWTH OF CITIES

Life in the less developed countries is marked by violent contrasts, and it is in urban areas that such contrasts are most striking. Shiny airports, international hotels and massive government buildings are built next to tar-paper slums. Like their northern counterparts, these rapidly growing cities are monuments to political independence and industrial development. Unfortunately, they are also testimonials to increasing populations, limited opportunities in the countryside, and neocolonial influence. Runaway urban growth has become a distinctive feature of the Third World.

URBANIZATION IN THE THIRD WORLD

The cities of the Third World expanded at an astonishing pace after World War Two. Many doubled and some even tripled in size in a single decade. The Algerian city of Algiers jumped from 300,000 to 900,000 between 1950 and 1960; Accra in Ghana, Lima in Peru, and Nairobi in Kenya grew just as fast. Thus the less developed countries have become far more thoroughly urbanized in recent times than most people realize. In Latin America, three out of four people already live in towns and cities; in Asia and Africa, as Table 39.1 shows, one in four lives in an urban area.

This urban explosion was so rapid that by 1980 at least half of the planet's city dwellers lived in the cities of the Third World. This represented a tremendous change in a short period. As recently as 1920, three out of every four of the world's urban inhabitants were concentrated in Europe and North America.

In most Third World countries the largest cities grew fastest. Gigantic "super cities" of 2 to 10 million persons arose. The capital typically emerged as the all-powerful urban center, encompassing all the important elite groups and dwarfing smaller cities as well as villages. Mexico City, for example, grew from 3 million to 9 million people between 1950 and 1970, and it will probably have 30 million in the year 2000. The pattern of a dominant megapolis has continued to spread from Latin America to Africa and Asia (though not to Asia's giants, China and India).

In the truly poor countries of Africa and Asia, moreover, the process of urbanization is still in the early stages. However populous the cities, the countryside still holds most of the people. If present trends continue, a city like Jakarta, the capital of Indonesia, will have 20 million people by the end of this century. Calcutta could be much larger. In the year 2000, the world will have 25 megapolises with more than 10

Table 39.1 Urban Population as a Percentage of Total Population in the World and in Eight Major Areas, 1925–2025

Area	1925	1950	1975	2000 (est.)	2025 (est.)
World total	21	28	39	50	63
North America	54	64	77	86	93
Europe	48	55	67	79	88
USSR	18	39	61	76	87
East Asia	10	15	30	46	63
Latin America	25	41	60	74	85
Africa	8	13	24	37	54
South Asia	9	15	23	35	51
Oceania	54	65	71	77	87

Little more than one-fifth of the world's population was urban in 1925. The urban proportion in the world total now exceeds two-fifths and, according to United Nations experts, it may attain one-half by the century's end and two-thirds about 2025. The most rapid urban growth will come in the Third World, where the move to cities is still in its early stages. Thus in the next fifty years the urban populations of Europe and North America may grow by another two-thirds, while those of the Soviet Union and Oceania may double. But the urban population of East Asia may grow more than threefold, that of Latin America fourfold, South Asia sixfold and Africa eightfold. *(Source: United Nations,* Concise Report on the World Population Situation in 1970–1975 and Its Long-Range Implications, *New York, 1974, p. 63.)*

million people—and 20 of them will be in the Third World, according to World Bank estimates. Such growth poses enormous questions for the future.

This urban explosion was due, first of all, to the general growth of population in the Third World. Urban residents gained greatly from the medical revolution, but they only gradually began to reduce the size of their families. At the same time, the pressure of numbers in the countryside encouraged millions to set out for the nearest city. More than half of all urban growth has been due to rural migration.

Even more than in Europe and North America in the nineteenth century, great cities became the undisputed centers of industry in the less developed countries. Half of all the industrial jobs in Mexico were concentrated in Mexico City in 1980. The same kind of extreme concentration of industry occurred in many Third World countries. Yet careful study leads scholars to play down industrialization as a cause of urban explosion. In the words of a leading authority:

After about 1930 a new phenomenon which might be termed "urbanization without industrialization" began to appear in the Third World. This phenomenon very rapidly acquired an inflationary character and in the early 1960s began to present most serious problems of urban employment and underemployment.[6]

In short, urban population grew much faster than industrial employment. It was a lucky migrant who found a real factory job.

Nevertheless, newcomers continued to stream to the cities. Many were pushed: they simply lacked enough land to survive. The big landowners found it more profitable to produce export crops, like sugar or coffee, for wealthy industrialized countries, and their increasingly mechanized operations provided few jobs. The push factor was particularly strong in Latin America, where the neocolonial pattern of large landowners and foreign companies exporting food and raw materials to the industrialized nations worked against peasant agriculture. More generally, much migration was seasonal or temporary. Many a young person left home for the city to work in construction or serve as a maid, planning to return shortly with a modest nest egg. Higher wages and steadier work in the city also strongly influenced most decisions to migrate.

Yet the magnetic attraction of Third World cities was more than economic. Their attraction rested on the services and opportunities they offered, as well as changing attitudes and the urge to escape from the traditional restraints of village life. Most of the modern hospitals, secondary schools, and transportation systems in less developed countries were in the cities. So were most banks, libraries, movie houses, and basic conveniences. Safe piped water and processed food were rare in rural areas, for instance, and village women by necessity spent much of their time carrying water and grinding grain.

The city held a special appeal for rural people who had been exposed to the seductive influence of modern education. In Africa, it was said, "the number of people who are prepared to go back to the land after more than three or four years in the classroom is infinitesimal."[7] One survey in the Ivory Coast found two out of three rural high school graduates planning to move to the city; only one in ten of the illiterates expressed the same intention. Africa was not unique in this. For the young and the ambitious, the allure of the city was the excitement and opportunity of modern life. The village took on the curse of boredom and failure.

OVERCROWDING AND SHANTYTOWNS

Rapid population growth placed great pressure on already inadequate urban social services, and in many Third World cities the quality of life deteriorated. In addition to running water, many people lacked paved streets, electricity, and police and fire protection. As in the early days of England's industrial revolution, sanitation was minimal in poor sections of town. Outdoor toilets were shared by many. Raw sewage often ran in streets and streams.

Faced with a rising human tide, government officials and their well-to-do urban allies sometimes tried to restrict internal migration to preserve the cities. Particularly in Africa, politicians talked of sending newcomers "back to the land" in order to reduce urban unemployment, crime rates, congestion, and environmental decline. In Africa as elsewhere, these antimigration efforts proved unsuccessful, and frustrated officials often threw up their hands in despair.

Surging population growth had particularly severe consequences for housing. As in western Europe in the early nineteenth century, overcrowding reached

Shacks and Skyscrapers This striking view of Rio de Janeiro, Brazil, from a hillside shantytown has many counterparts in the Third World. Makeshift dwellings coexist with luxurious high-rise apartments, and the urban landscape expands rapidly as newcomers pour into the city from rural areas. *(P. Villiers LeMoy/Camera Press)*

staggering proportions in a great many Third World cities. Old buildings were often divided and redivided until population density reached the absolute saturation point. Take, for example, this vivid description of an older inner-city area, Singapore's Chinatown, in the late 1950s:

Chinatown ... consists almost entirely of two or three story shop-houses. These shop-houses, originally in-

tended to house one or two families, have been divided by a maze of interior partitions into cubicles, the majority of which are without windows and in permanent semi-darkness. Most of these cubicles are about the size of two double beds, placed side by side. In one such cubicle— dark, confined, unsanitary, and without comfort—may live a family of seven or more persons. Many of them sleep on the floor, often under the bed. Their possessions are in boxes, placed on shelves to leave the floor free for sleeping. Their food . . . is kept in tiny cupboards, which hang from the rafters. Their clothes hang on the walls, or from racks.[8]

Makeshift squatter settlements were another manifestation of the urban housing problem. These shantytowns sprang up continuously, almost overnight, on the worst possible urban land. Mudflats, garbage dumps, railroad sidings, steep hills on the outskirts, even polluted waterfronts—these were the dismal sites that squatters claimed. Typically, a group of urban poor "invaded" unoccupied land and quickly threw up tents or huts. Often beaten off by the police, they invaded again and again until the authorities gave up and a new squatter beachhead had been secured.

Squatter shantytowns grew much faster than more conventional urban areas in most Third World cities. In the giant Brazilian city of Rio de Janeiro, for example, the population of the shantytowns grew four times faster than the rest of the city in the 1950s and 1960s. As a result, the Third World's squatter settlements came to house up to two-fifths of the urban population. The proportion was particularly high in Asia. Such settlements occasionally mushroomed in American mining towns and in Europe, but never to the extent of Latin America, Asia, and Africa. The Third World created a new urban form.

The meaning of squatter housing has been hotly debated. For a long time the "pessimists" stressed the miseries of squatter settlements—the lack of the most basic services, the pitiful one-room shacks, the hopelessness of disoriented migrants in a strange environment, the revolutionary discontent. More recently, detailed case studies have presented a more "optimistic" interpretation, stressing the vitality of the settlements and the resourcefulness of their inhabitants. Shantytowns appeared to be real neighborhoods, whose residents often shared common ethnic origins and kinship ties.

Moreover, the shantytowns themselves evolved, most notably in Latin America, where they have existed longest. Their poor but enterprising inhabitants relied on self-help to improve their living conditions. With much sweat labor and a little hard-earned cash, a family replaced its mud walls with concrete blocks and gradually built a real home. Or the community pressured the city to install a central water pump or build a school. Low-paid office workers in search of cheap housing sometimes moved in and continued the upgrading process.

Few members of squatter communities were particularly attracted to revolutionary doctrines, despite widespread fears (and hopes) to the contrary. Making a living and holding the family together were challenges enough. Indeed, one close observer described squatters' beliefs as closely resembling those of the classic small businessman:

These beliefs can be summed up in the familiar and accepted maxims: Work hard, save your money, trust only family members (and them not too much), outwit the state, vote conservatively if possible, but always in your own economic self-interest; educate your children for their future and as old-age insurance for yourself.[9]

Thus the optimists counseled politicians to abandon their hostility to squatter settlements and help them to help themselves. The rush to the city cannot be stopped, they said. However bad life in the city was, it appeared desirable to the millions of rural people who "voted with their feet." Since hard-pressed Third World governments could provide only a fraction of the urban masses with subsidized housing, they had to support the creativity of the "spontaneous settlement." However squalid such settlements appeared, they were preferable to sleeping on sidewalks.

RICH AND POOR

Massive inequality continued, with few exceptions, to be the reality of life in less developed countries after they achieved political independence. Rich and poor were separated by a monumental gap, a gap that could be measured, to some extent, as Third World governments began gathering better statistical information (Figure 39.2). In about 1970 in most developing countries, the top 10 percent of all households re-

	Richest 10%	Richest 20%	Poorest 60%	Poorest 20%
Third World average (15 countries)	38%	55%	25%	4%
Brazil	51%	67%	16%	2%
India	35%	49%	32%	7%
United States	28%[a]	41%	35%	5%

[a]Estimate; the richest 5% received 16% of income.

———— Third World (average of 15 countries)

– – – Brazil

• • • • India

–•–•– United States

FIGURE 39.2 The Distribution of Income in the Third World, Brazil, India, and the United States, ca 1970 The Lorenz curve is useful for showing the degree of economic inequality in a given country. The closer the actual distribution lies to the (theoretical) curve of absolute equality, the more nearly equal are incomes. In general, Third World countries have a high degree of income inequality, as great as that in Europe before 1914 (see Figure 28.2). However, a few Third World countries, notably Taiwan and South Korea, are as equitable as the United States. Also, the United States is somewhat more equitable than most non-Communist industrialized countries (but almost identical to Canada, Great Britain, Israel, and Japan). France and West Germany are very similar to India, for example. The Communist countries appear most equitable in such comparisons, although their official data omit the tremendously valuable nonmonetary privileges of the ruling elites. *(Sources: M. Todaro,* Economic Development in the Third World, *2nd ed., [New York: Longman, 1981], p. 128 and references cited therein; U.S. Department of Commerce,* Historical Statistics of the United States: Colonial Times to 1970, *[Washington, D.C.: GPO, 1975], Part I, p. 291.)*

ceived more than one-third of all national income; the top 20 percent took from 50 to 60 percent. At the other end of the scale, the poorest 60 percent received only a fifth to at most a third of all income; the poorest fifth got less than 5 percent. This meant that the average household in the top fifth of the population received about *fifteen times* as much monetary income as the average household in the bottom fifth.

Such differences have been the rule in human history. If we compare Figure 39.2 with Figure 28.2 on page 877, it is clear that the situation in the Third World has strongly resembled that of Europe prior to World War One, before the movement toward greater equality accelerated sharply. It is noteworthy that the usual distinctions between rightist and leftist govern-

ments in the Third World, or between capitalist and socialist economies, has had limited significance where shares of income are concerned. In the 1970s, income inequality was almost as pronounced in Mexico with its progressive, even revolutionary, tradition, as in Brazil with its rightist military rule. The fast-growing, market-oriented countries of Taiwan and South Korea exhibited substantially greater equality than moderately socialist India.

Differences in wealth and well-being were most pronounced in the towns and cities of the Third World. Few rich or even middle-class people lived in the countryside. Urban squatters may have been better off than landless rural laborers, but they were light-years away from the luxury of the urban elite.

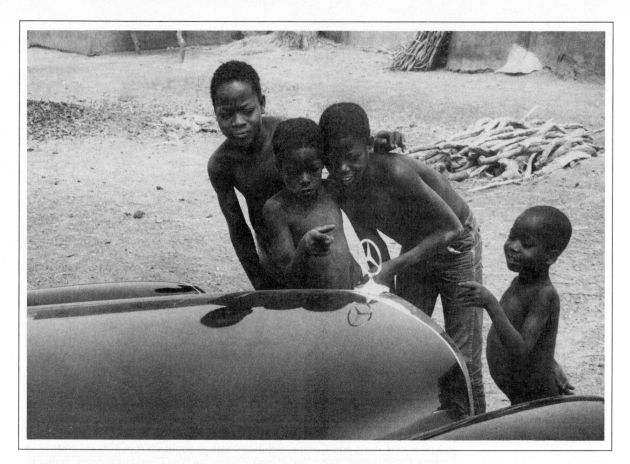

A Sleek Automobile fascinates four boys in an African village. The most ambitious youngster may already dream of acquiring power and wealth in the city. *(Marc and Evelyne Bernheim/Woodfin Camp)*

Consider housing. In the sober words of one careful observer, "The contrast between the opulent housing enjoyed by the tiny minority of the rich and the conditions under which the vast majority of the urban poor must live is extreme."[10] In Asia and Africa, the rich often moved into the luxurious sections previously reserved for colonial administrators and white businessmen. Particularly in Latin America, upper- and upper-middle-class people built fine mansions in exclusive suburbs, where they lived behind high walls, with many servants, protected from intruders by armed guards and fierce dogs.

A lifestyle in the "modern" mold was almost the byword of the Third World's urban elite. From French perfume and Scotch whiskey to electronic games and the latest rock music, imported luxuries became the unmistakable signs of wealth and privilege. In Swahili-speaking East Africa, the common

folk called them *wa Benzi*—"those who ride in a Mercedes-Benz." Even in relatively egalitarian China, the urban masses saved to buy bicycles while government officials rode in chauffeur-driven state-owned limousines. The automobile became the ultimate symbol of the urban elite.

Education also distinguished the wealthy from the masses. Young people from the elite often studied abroad, at leading European and North American universities, or monopolized openings in local universities. While absorbing the latest knowledge in a prestigious field like civil engineering or economics, they also absorbed foreign customs and values. They mastered the fluent English or French that is indispensable for many top-paying jobs, especially with international agencies and giant multinational corporations. Thus Third World elites often had more in common with the power brokers of the industrialized nations than with their own people. Willing tools of neocolonial penetration, they became "white men with black faces," as one angry critic put it.

The middle classes of the Third World remained quite small relative to the total population. White-collar workers and government bureaucrats joined the traditional ranks of merchants and professionals in the urban middle class. Their salaries, though modest, were wonderfully secure and usually carried valuable fringe benefits. Unlike recent migrants and the rural poor, white-collar workers often received ration cards entitling them to cheap subsidized food.

An unexpected component of the urban middle classes was the modern factory proletariat, a privileged segment of the population in many poor countries. Few in number because sophisticated machines require few workers, relative to agriculture or traditional crafts, they received high wages for their skilled work. On the Caribbean island of Jamaica in the late 1960s, for example, aluminum workers in big, modern American-owned plants earned $60–65 a week. Meanwhile cane cutters on sugar plantations earned $3 a week, and many laborers on small farms only a dollar a week. Little wonder that modern factory workers tended to be self-satisfied in the Third World.

The great majority, the urban poor, earned precarious livings in the modern traditional "bazaar economy" of petty trades and unskilled labor. Regular salaried jobs were rare and highly prized, and a complex world of tiny, unregulated businesses and service occupations predominated.

As in industrializing Europe a century ago, irregular armies of peddlers and pushcart operators hawked their wares and squeezed a living from commerce. West African market women, with their colorful dresses and overflowing baskets, provided a classic example of this pattern. Sweatshops and home-based workers manufactured cheap goods for popular consumption. Maids, prostitutes, small-time crooks, and unemployed ex-students sold all kinds of services. This old-yet-new bazaar economy showed no signs of dying out in the 1980s. Indeed, it continued to grow prodigiously as migrants streamed to the cities, as modern industry provided few jobs, and as the wide gap between rich and poor persisted.

MIGRATION AND THE FAMILY

Large-scale urban migration had a massive impact on traditional family patterns in the Third World.

Particularly in Africa and Asia, the great majority of migrants to the city were young men, married and unmarried. Women tended to stay in the villages, creating a sexual imbalance in both places. There were several reasons for this pattern. Much of the movement to cities (and mines) remained temporary or seasonal. At least at first, young men left home to earn hard cash to bring back to their villages. Moreover, the cities were expensive and prospects there were uncertain. Only after a man secured a genuine foothold did he become married or call for his wife and children.

Kinship and village ties helped ease the rigors of temporary migration. Often a young man could go to the city rather easily because his family had close ties with friends and relatives there. Many city neighborhoods were urban versions of their residents' original villages. Networks of friendship and mutual aid helped young men (and some women, especially brides) move back and forth without being overwhelmed.

For rural women, the consequences of male out-migration were mixed. Asian and African women had long been treated as subordinates, if not inferiors, by their fathers and husbands. Rather suddenly, such women found themselves heads of households, faced with managing the farm, feeding the children, and running their own lives. In the east African country of Kenya, for instance, one-third of all rural households were headed by women in the late 1970s.

African and Asian village women had to become unprecedentedly self-reliant and independent. The real beginnings of more equal rights and opportunities, of women's liberation, became readily visible in Africa and Asia. But the price was high and progress uneven. Rural women often had only their children to help in the endless, backbreaking labor. And their husbands, when they returned, often expected their wives to revert to the old subordination.

In economically more advanced Latin America, the pattern of migration has been different. Whole families have migrated, very often to squatter settlements, much more commonly than in Asia and Africa. These families frequently belonged to the class of landless laborers, which was generally larger in Latin America than in Africa or even Asia. Migration was also more likely to be once-and-for-all. Another difference was that single women have been as likely as single men to move to the city. The situation in Mexico in the late 1970s was typical:

They [women] leave the village seeking employment, often as domestic servants. When they do not find work in the cities, they have few alternatives. If they are young, they frequently turn to prostitution; if not, they often resort to begging in the streets. Homeless peasant women, often carrying small children, roam every quarter of Mexico City.[11]

Some women also left to escape the narrow, male-dominated villages. Even so, urban migration in Latin America seemed to have had less impact on traditional family patterns and on women's attitudes than in Asia and Africa. This helps explain why the women's movement lagged behind in Latin America.

MASS CULTURE AND CONTEMPORARY THOUGHT

Ideas and beliefs continued to change dramatically in the Third World after independence. Education fostered new attitudes, while mass communications relentlessly spread the sounds and viewpoints of modern life. Third World intellectuals, in their search for the meanings of their countries' experiences, articulated a wide spectrum of independent opinion in keeping with growing national diversity.

EDUCATION AND MASS COMMUNICATIONS

In their efforts to modernize and better their societies, Third World leaders became increasingly convinced of the critical importance of education. They realized that "human capital"—skilled and educated workers, managers, and citizens—played a critical role in the development process.

Faith in education and "book learning" spread surprisingly rapidly to the Third World's masses, for whom education principally meant jobs. Asked how their lives differed from their mothers' and grandmothers', poor and often illiterate peasant women in several countries in the late 1970s testified to the need for an education, along with the need to earn money and have fewer children. A young African woman in Kenya was quite typical of Third World women when she explained it this way.

My mother has eleven children. She is my father's only wife. She works in the fields and grows the food we eat. She plants cabbage, spinach, and corn. She works very hard, but with so many children it is difficult to get enough food or money. All of my brothers and sisters go to school. One is already a teacher. . . .

My life is very different from my mother's. . . . Women have to get an education. Then if you get a large family and don't know how to feed it, you can find work and get some cash. That's what I will teach my children: "Get an education first."[12]

As this voice suggests, young people in the Third World headed for schools and universities in unprecedented numbers. To be sure, general averages obscure wide variations by country, region, and social class. Rural people everywhere spent fewer years in school. Latin America, in keeping with its higher incomes and greater urbanization, had the highest percentage of students in all age groups, followed by Asia and then by Africa. There still remained, however, a wide education gap with the rich countries, where more than 90 percent of both sexes attended school through age seventeen (Map 39.2).

Moreover, the quality of education in the Third World was often mediocre. African and Asian universities tended to retain the old colonial values, stressing law and liberal arts at the expense of technical and vocational training. As a result, many poor countries found themselves with large numbers of unemployed or underemployed liberal-arts graduates. These "generalists" competed for scarce jobs in the already bloated government bureaucracies while less prestigious technical jobs went begging.

A related problem was the Third World's "brain drain": many gifted students in vital fields like engineering and medicine ended up pursuing their careers in the rich countries of the developed world, which needed their talents far less than their native lands. In the early 1980s, as many Indian-trained doctors practiced abroad, mainly in advanced countries, as served India's entire rural population of 480

MAP 39.2 World Literacy Rates (1983–1984) In recent years Third World countries have made considerable progress toward achieving basic literacy, as this map suggests. Definitions of literacy vary widely, however, from being able to fill out a simple form to merely having attended school.

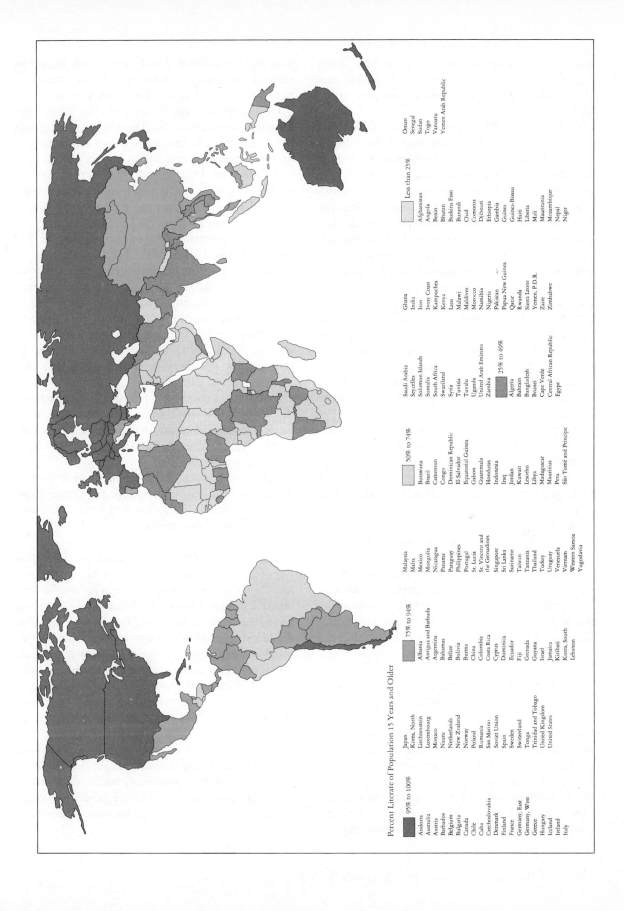

Percent Literate of Population 15 Years and Older

million. The threat represented by the brain drain helped explain why the Third World's professional elite received high salaries even in very poor countries.

By the early 1980s, many observers believed that the education drive, like its forerunner, the industrialization drive, had served the rural masses poorly. It sometimes seemed that its greatest beneficiaries were schoolteachers, who profited from the elite status provided by a permanent government job. Instruction was often impractical and mind-numbing. The children of farmers generally learned little about agriculture, animal raising, or practical mechanics. Instead, students often memorized passages from ancient literary works and religious texts, and spewed back cut-and-dried answers. No wonder children stayed away from school in droves. Village schools succeeded best at identifying the exceptional pupils, who were then siphoned off to the city for further study and lost forever to the village.

Whatever its shortcomings, formal education spread hand in hand with another influential agent of popular instruction: mass communications. The transistor radio penetrated the most isolated hamlets of the Third World. Governments universally embraced radio broadcasting as a means of power, propaganda, and education. Relentlessly, the transistor propagated the outlook and attitudes of urban elites and in the process challenged old values.

Moreover, the second communications revolution —the visual one—is now in the process of reaching rural people everywhere. Television is bringing the whole planet into the bars and meetinghouses of the world's villages. Judging from experience elsewhere —in remote French villages, in Eskimo communities above the Arctic Circle—television will have a profound, even revolutionary impact. For one thing, the lure of the city seems certain to grow.

INTERPRETING THE EXPERIENCES OF THE EMERGING WORLD

Popular education and mass communications compounded the influence of the Third World's writers and thinkers, its purveyors of explanations. Some intellectuals meekly obeyed their employers, whether the Ministry of Information or a large newspaper. Others simply embellished or reiterated some received ideology like Marxism or free-market capitalism. But some Third World intellectuals led in the search for meanings and direction that has accompanied rapid social change and economic struggle.

Having come of age during and after the struggle for political emancipation, Third World intellectuals have been centrally preoccupied with achieving genuine independence and freedom from outside control. Thus some Third World writers argued that real independence required a total break with the former colonial powers and a total rejection of Western values. This was the message of Frantz Fanon (1925–1961) in his powerful study of colonial peoples, *The Wretched of the Earth.*

Fanon, a French-trained black psychiatrist from the Caribbean island of Martinique, was assigned to a hospital in Algeria during the bloody war for Algerian independence. He quickly came to sympathize with the guerrillas and probed deeply into the psychology of colonial revolt. According to Fanon, decolonization was always a violent and totally consuming process, whereby one "species" of men, the colonizers, was completely replaced by an absolutely different species—the colonized, the wretched of the earth. During decolonization the colonized masses mock colonial values, "insult them, and vomit them up," in a psychic purge.

Fanon was convinced that the battle for formal independence was only the first step. The former imperialists and their local collaborators—the "white men with black faces"—remain the enemy:

The mobilization of the masses, when it arises out of the war of liberation, introduces into each man's consciousness the ideas of a common cause, of a national destiny, and of a collective history. In the same way the second phase, that of the building-up of the nation, is helped on by the existence of this cement which has been mixed with blood and anger. . . . During the colonial period the people are called upon to fight against oppression; after national liberation, they are called upon to fight against poverty, illiteracy, and underdevelopment. The struggle, they say, goes on. The people realize that life is an unending contest.

. . . The apotheosis of independence is transformed into the curse of independence, and the colonial power through its immense resources of coercion condemns the young nation to regression. In plain words, the colonial power says: "Since you want independence, take it and starve."

Mass Communications An enterprising merchant in West Africa uses television to attract a crowd to a tiny shop in Dakar, Senegal. Only the man passing on the right, suggestively clad in the traditional dress of the Muslim believer, appears oblivious to the siren call of the modern age. *(Philip Jon Bailey/Stock, Boston)*

. . . We are not blinded by the moral reparation of national independence; nor are we fed by it. The wealth of the imperial countries is our wealth too. . . . Europe is literally the creation of the Third World. The wealth which smothers her is that which was stolen from the underdeveloped peoples.[13]

For Fanon, independence and national solidarity went hand in hand with outrage at the misdeeds and moral posturings of the former colonial powers. Fanon's passionate, angry work became a sacred text for radicals worried about the ravages of imperialism.

Some more recent writers looked beyond wholesale rejection of the industrialized powers. They too were "anti-imperialist," but they saw colonial domination as only one chapter in the life of their people.

Many of these writers were cultural nationalists, who applied their talents to celebrating the rich histories and cultures of their people. At the same time, they did not hesitate to criticize their own leaders and fellow citizens, with whom they often disagreed.

The Nigerian writer Chinua Achebe (b. 1930) rendered these themes with acute insight and vivid specificity in his short, moving novels. Achebe wrote in English rather than his native Ibo tongue, but he wrote primarily for Africans, seeking to restore his people's self-confidence by reinterpreting the past. For Achebe, the "writer in a new nation" had first to dispose of the "fundamental theme":

This theme—quite simply—is that the African people did not hear of culture for the first time from Europeans;

On Location Third World countries responded to the overthrow of foreign domination with a renewed interest in their own cultures. Here director Marcela Fernandez Volante is shown shooting a film set in Mexico. *(Courtesy of John Mosier)*

that their societies were not mindless but frequently had a philosophy of great depth and volume and beauty, that they had poetry and above all, they had dignity. It is this dignity that many African peoples all but lost in the colonial period, and it is this that they must now regain. The worst thing that can happen to any people is the loss of their dignity and self-respect. The writer's duty is to help them regain it by showing what happened to them, what they lost.[14]

In *Things Fall Apart,* Achebe achieves his goal by bringing vividly to life the men and women of an Ibo village at the beginning of the twentieth century, with all their virtues and frailties. The hero, Okonkwo, is a mighty wrestler and hardworking, prosperous farmer, but he is stern and easily angered. Enraged at the failure of his people to reject newcomers, and especially at the white missionaries who convert his

son to Christianity and provoke the slaying of the sacred python, Okonkwo kills a colonial messenger. When his act fails to spark a tribal revolt, he commits suicide. Okonkwo is destroyed by the general breakdown of tribal authority and his own intransigent recklessness. Woven into the story are the proverbs and wisdom of a sophisticated people and the beauty of a vanishing world.

In later novels, especially *A Man of the People,* Achebe portrays the postindependence disillusionment of many Third World intellectuals. The villain is Chief the Honorable Nanga, a politician with the popular touch. This "man of the people" lives in luxury, takes bribes to build expensive apartment buildings for foreigners, and flimflams the voters with celebrations and empty words. The hero, an idealistic young schoolteacher, tries to unseat Chief Nanga, with disastrous results. Beaten and hospitalized, the hero broods that the people "had become even more cynical than their leaders and were apathetic into the bargain."[15] Achebe's harsh but considered judgment reflected trends in many Third World nations in the 1960s and 1970s: the rulers seemed increasingly corrupted by Western luxury and estranged from the rural masses, while the idealistic intellectuals could only gnash their teeth in frustration.

The celebrated novelist V. S. Naipaul, born in Trinidad in 1932 of Indian parents, has also castigated Third World governments for corruption, ineptitude, and self-deception. Another of Naipaul's recurring themes is the poignant loneliness and homelessness of uprooted people. In *The Mimic Men,* the blacks and whites, the Hindus and Chinese who populate the tiny Caribbean islands are all aliens, thrown together by "shipwreck." As one of the characters says:

It was my hope [in writing] to give expression to the restlessness, the deep disorder, which the great exploration, the overthrow in three continents of established social organizations, the unnatural bringing together of peoples who could achieve fulfillment only within the security of their own societies and the landscapes hymned by their ancestors . . . has brought about. The empires of our time were short-lived, but they altered the world for ever; their passing away is their least significant feature. It was my hope to sketch a subject which, fifty years hence, a great historian might pursue. . . . But this work will not now be written by me; I am too much a victim of that restlessness which was to have been my subject.[16]

Naipaul and Achebe, like many other talented Third World writers and intellectuals, probed Third World experiences in pursuit of understanding and identity. This same searching went on in other creative fields, from art and dance to architecture and social science, and seemed to reflect the intellectual maturity of genuine independence.

As Third World leaders and peoples threw off foreign domination after 1945 and reasserted themselves in new or revitalized states, they turned increasingly inward to attack poverty and limited economic development. The collective response was an unparalleled

medical revolution and the Third World's first great industrialization drive. Long-neglected agriculture also made progress, and some countries experienced a veritable Green Revolution. Moreover, rapid urbanization, expanding educational opportunities, and greater rights for women were striking evidence of modernization and fundamental human progress. The achievement was great.

Yet so was the challenge, and results fell far short of aspirations. Deep and enduring rural poverty, overcrowded cities, enormous class differences, and the sharp criticisms of leading Third World writers mocked early hopes of quick solutions. Since the late 1960s there has been growing dissatisfaction and frustration in Third World nations. And, as the final chapter will examine, the belief has grown that the Third World can meet the challenge only by reordering the entire global system and dissolving the unequal ties that bind it to the rich nations.

NOTES

1. A. MacBean and V. N. Balasubramanyam, *Meeting the Third World Challenge* (New York: St. Martin's, 1976), p. 27.
2. P. J. McEwan and R. B. Sutcliffe, eds., *Modern Africa* (New York: Thomas Y. Crowell, 1965), p. 349.
3. Quoted in L. R. Brown, *Seeds of Change: The Green Revolution and Development in the 1970s* (New York: Praeger, 1970), p. 16.
4. P. Ehrlich, *The Population Bomb* (New York: Ballantine, 1968), p. 11.
5. *Wall Street Journal,* April 16, 1981, p. 17.
6. P. Bairoch, *The Economic Development of the Third World Since 1900* (London: Methuen, 1975), p. 144.
7. R. Dumont, *False Start in Africa* (London: Deutsch, 1966), p. 88.
8. B. Kaye, *Upper Nankin Street, Singapore: A Sociological Study of Households Living in a Densely Populated Area* (Singapore: University of Malaya Press, 1960), p. 2.
9. W. Mangin, "Latin American Squatter Settlements," *Latin American Research Review* 2 (1967): 84–85.

10. D. J. Dwyer, *People and Housing in Third World Cities: Perspectives on the Problem of Spontaneous Settlements* (London: Longman, 1975), p. 24.

11. P. Hudson, *Third World Women Speak Out: Interviews in Six Countries on Change, Development, and Basic Needs* (New York: Praeger, 1979), p. 11.

12. Ibid., p. 22.

13. F. Fanon, *The Wretched of the Earth* (New York: Grove Press, 1968), pp. 43, 93–94, 97, 102.

14. C. Achebe, *Morning Yet on Creation Day* (London: Heinemann, 1975), p. 81.

15. C. Achebe, *A Man of the People* (London: Heinemann, 1966), p. 161.

16. V. S. Naipaul, *The Mimic Men* (New York: Macmillan, 1967), p. 38.

SUGGESTED READING

P. Bairoch, *The Economic Development of the Third World Since 1900* (1975), is a valuable historical study. A. B. Mountjoy, ed., *The Third World: Problems and Perspectives* (1978), and A. MacBean and V. N. Balasubramanyam, *Meeting the Third World Challenge* (1976), are reliable, even-handed introductions to contemporary trends and policies. R. Gamer, *The Developing Nations: A Comparative Perspective,* 2d ed. (1986), is a stimulating synthesis. Two excellent recent works from a truly Third World perspective are especially recommended: E. Hermassi, *The Third World Reassessed* (1980), and M. ul-Haq, *The Poverty Curtain: Choices for the Third World* (1976). The many clear and compelling works of B. Ward, notably *The Rich Nations and the Poor Nations* (1962) and *The Lopsided World* (1968), movingly convey the hopes and frustrations of sympathetic Western economists in the 1960s. Equally renowned are studies by the Swedish socialist G. Myrdal: *Asian Drama: An Inquiry Into the Poverty of Nations,* 3 vols. (1968) and *The Challenge of World Poverty: A World Anti-Poverty Program in Outline* (1970). Valuable introductions to world agriculture and population are found in various works by L. R. Brown, notably *Seeds of Change: The Green Revolution and Development in the 1970s* (1970) and *In the Human Interest: A Strategy to Stabilize World Population* (1974). R. King, *Land Reform: A World Survey* (1977), is a useful introduction to key problems.

Two valuable studies on African questions are K. Patterson, *History and Disease in Africa: An Introductory Survey and Case Studies* (1978), and P. Lloyd, ed., *The New Elites of Tropical Africa* (1966). C. Turnbull, *The Lonely African* (1962), provides intimate portraits of Africans caught up in decolonization and rapid social change. Critical aspects of contemporary Indian economic development are carefully considered by M. Franda, *India's Rural Development: An Assessment of Alternatives* (1980), and A. G. Noble and A. K. Dutt, eds., *Indian Urbanization and Planning: Vehicles of Modernization* (1977). China's economic and social problems are skillfully placed in a broad and somewhat somber perspective by two Chinese-speaking journalists, F. Butterfield, *China: Alive in the Bitter Sea* (1982), and R. Bernstein, *From the Center of the Earth: The Search for the Truth About China* (1982).

For the prodigious growth of Third World cities, J. Abu-Lughod and R. Hay, Jr., eds., *Third World Urbanization* (1977), and the lively studies of D. J. Dwyer, *People and Housing in Third World Cities: Perspectives on the Problem of Spontaneous Settlements* (1975) and *The City in the Third World* (1974), are highly recommended. Similarly recommended is a fascinating investigation of enduring urban-rural differences by M. Lipton, *Why Poor People Stay Poor: Urban Bias in World Development* (1977), which may be complemented by C. Elliott, *Patterns of Poverty in the Third World: A Study of Social and Economic Stratification* (1975).

A good introduction to changes within families is P. Hudson, *Third World Women Speak Out: Interviews in Six Countries on Change, Development, and Basic Needs* (1979), a truly remarkable study. Other useful works on Third World women and the changes they are experiencing include L. Iglitzen and R. Ross, *Women in the World: A Comparative Study* (1976); A. de Souza, *Women in Contemporary India and South Asia* (1980); N. J. Hafkin and E. Bay, eds., *Women in Africa* (1977); J. Ginat, *Women in Muslim Rural Society: Status and Role in Family and Community* (1982); and M. Wolf, *Revolution Postponed: Women in Contemporary China* (1985); K. Kakar, *The Inner World: A Psychoanalytic Study of Childhood and Society in India* (1978), is a fascinating interpretation of Indian dependence on family and personal relations, which is provocatively compared with the compulsive individualism of Western society.

The reader is especially encouraged to enter into the contemporary Third World with the aid of the gifted writers discussed in this chapter. F. Fanon, *The Wretched of the Earth* (1968), is a particularly strong indictment of colonialism from the 1960s. The wide-ranging work of Chinua Achebe illuminates the proud search for a viable past in his classic novel of precolonial Africa, *Things Fall Apart* (1959), and the disillusionment with unprincipled postindependence leaders in *A Man of the People* (1966). G. Moore and U. Beier, eds., *Modern Poetry from Africa* (1963), is a recommended anthology. In addition to his rich and introspective novels like *The Mimic Men* (1967), V. S. Naipaul has reported extensively on life in Third World countries. His *India: A Wounded Civilization* (1978), impressions gleaned from a trip to his family's land of origin, and *A Bend in the River* (1980), an investigation of the high price postcolonial Africa is paying for modernization, are especially original and thought-provoking. Finally, L. Heng and J. Shapiro, *Son of the Revolution* (1983), brilliantly captures the drama of Mao's China through the turbulent real-life story of a young Red Guard.

PERIOD (CA 1920–1980)	AFRICA AND THE MIDDLE EAST	THE AMERICAS	
1920	French depose Faisal, establish mandate in Syria, 1920 Cultural nationalism in Africa, 1920s Treaty of Lausanne recognizes Turkish Republic, 1923 Reza Shah leads Iran, 1925–1941	U.S. "consumer revolution," 1920s Stock market crash in U.S.; Great Depression begins, 1929	
1930	African farmers organize first "cocoa hold-ups," 1930–1931 Iraq gains independence, 1932 Syrian-French friendship treaty, 1936	Revolutions in six South American countries, 1930 U.S. inaugurates Good Neighbor Policy with Latin America, 1933 New Deal under U.S. President Franklin D. Roosevelt, 1933	
1940	Civil war between Arabs and Jews in Palestine; state of Israel is created, 1948 Apartheid system in South Africa, 1948 to present Libya gains independence, 1949	Surprise attack by Japan on Pearl Harbor; U.S. enters World War Two, 1941 Paris Peace Conference; U.N. established, 1945 Marshall Plan, 1947 Péron regime in Argentina, 1946–1953	
1950	Egypt declared a republic; Nasser named premier, 1954 Morocco, Tunisia, Sudan, and Ghana gain independence, 1956–1957 French-British Suez invasion, 1956	Fidel Castro takes power in Cuba, 1959	
1960	French maintain powerful presence in Africa, ca 1960–1980 Mali, Nigeria, and the Congo gain independence, 1960 Biafra declares independence from Nigeria, 1967 Arab-Israeli Six-Day War, 1967	Cuban Missile Crisis, 1962 Military dictatorship in Brazil, 1964–1985 U.S. escalates war in Vietnam, 1964 Separatist movement in Quebec, 1967 to present	
1970	"Yom Kippur War," 1973 Mozambique and Angola gain independence, 1975 Ayatollah Khomeini seizes power in Iran, 1979 Camp David Accords, 1979 U.S. Embassy held in Teheran, 1979–1981	SALT treaties, 1972, 1979 Military dictatorship in Chile, 1973 to present U.S. Watergate scandal, 1974 Panama Canal treaties, 1977 Revolutions in Nicaragua and El Salvador, 1979	

EAST ASIA	INDIA AND SOUTHEAST ASIA	EUROPE
New Cultural Movement in China, 1920s Kita Ikki advocates ultranationalism in Japan, 1923 Chiang Kai-shek unites China, 1928	Mohandas "Mahatma" Gandhi launches nonviolent resistance campaign, 1920	Mussolini seizes power in Italy, 1922 Spectacular German economic recovery under Dawes Plan, 1924–1929 Stalin takes power in U.S.S.R., 1927 Treaties of Locarno, 1925 Depths of Great Depression, 1929–1933
Japan invades Manchuria, 1931 Manchuria gains independence, 1932 Mao Tse-tung's Long March, 1934 Sino-Japanese War, 1937–1945	Mahatma Gandhi's Salt March, 1930 Japanese conquer empire in southeast Asia, 1939–1942	Hitler gains dictatorial power, 1933 Civil war in Spain, 1936–1939 Germany invades Poland; Britain and France declare war on Germany, 1939 World War Two, 1939–1945
U.S. drops atomic bombs on Hiroshima and Nagasaki, 1945 Chinese civil war, 1945–1949 Mao Tse-tung proclaims People's Republic of China, 1949	Philippines gain independence, 1946 Vietnam War, French phase, 1947–1954 India (Hindu) and Pakistan (Muslim) gain independence, 1947; violent clashes continue	Yalta Conference, 1945 NATO alliance, 1949 Soviet Union and Red China sign 30-year alliance treaty, 1949
Korean War, 1950–1953 Japan begins long period of rapid economic growth, 1950 Mao Tse-tung announces Great Leap Forward, 1958	Vietnamese nationalists defeat French at Dien Bien Phu; Vietnam divided, 1954 Islamic Republic of Pakistan declared, 1956	Death of Stalin, 1953 Warsaw Pact, 1955 Revolution in Hungary crushed by Soviets, 1956 Creation of the Common Market, 1957
Sino-Soviet split becomes apparent, 1960 Great Proletarian Cultural Revolution in China, 1965–1969	Vietnam War, American phase, 1963–1975 Indira Gandhi Prime Minister of India, 1966–1977, 1980–1984	Construction of Berlin Wall, 1961 Soviet invasion of Czechoslovakia, 1968 German Chancellor Willy Brandt's Ostpolitik, 1969–1973
Communist victory in Vietnam War, 1975 China pursues modernization after Mao Tse-tung's death, 1976 Sino-Japanese friendship treaty, 1978	India-Pakistan war, 1971 Republic of Bangladesh, 1972 Vietnam-Cambodia war, 1978–1979 Chinese invade Vietnam, 1979	Fall of Polish government of Gomulka, 1970 Détente reaches apogee in Helsinki Agreement, 1975 Soviet invasion of Afghanistan, 1979

40

ONE SMALL PLANET

HE IDEA OF VISITORS from elsewhere in the universe has kindled the modern imagination. Motorists swear they have seen unidentified flying objects; the alchemy of imagination even lands Captain Kirk and the crew of the *Enterprise* on our earth in our era. A best-selling author spins preposterous theories about "ancient astronauts" who landed on earth and built everything from the pyramids at Giza to the temples of the Aztecs. It is as if we earthlings, believers in the power of technology but weighed down by apparently insoluble human conflicts, yearn for some superior intelligence to decipher our little world and set it straight while there is still time.

Yet perhaps our yearning for enlightened interstellar visitors can be put to good use. We can imagine how superior intelligences, easily able to grasp our world and its complex history, would view the planet and its talented but quarrelsome human race. Surely interstellar observers would take a genuinely global perspective, free from our customary biases of creed and nation. If we try to do the same, perhaps we too can gain insight into our world's ongoing development.

From a global perspective, three questions might seem particularly important. How is the planet organized politically? How does the human race use its resources to meet its material needs? What key ideas guide its behavior as our planet moves toward an uncertain future?

WORLD POLITICS

Although many earthlings are deeply impressed by our recent scientific and technological achievements, highly advanced space travelers might well be less so. They might instead be astonished that accelerated technological achievement has not been matched by any corresponding change in the way the human race governs—or fails to govern—itself. Sovereign nation-states still reign supreme, as assertive and as competitive as ever, and now reinforced by ever more destructive weapons. The embryonic growth of an effective global political organization, of a government that could protect the world's nations from themselves, seems permanently arrested. The tension

generated by powerful, warlike states in a fragile and interdependent world is one of the most striking— and dangerous— characteristics of this small planet.

NATION-STATES AND THE UNITED NATIONS

The rise of the nation-state and the global triumph of nationalism has been a grand theme of modern world history. The independent territorial nation-state— despite the ongoing problem of separatist ethnic groups—is clearly the fundamental principle of political organization in our times. Yet, from a global perspective we must surely question what we take for granted. Has the nation-state system, with its apparently inevitable conflicts, become a threat to life on the planet?

Some have thought so. It is one of history's ironies that nationalism has been widely condemned, especially in Europe, just as it has triumphed decisively in world politics. In *Mankind and Mother Earth* (1976), his last work, the renowned British historian Arnold Toynbee (1889–1975) poignantly expressed the post-1914 disillusionment of many European and American intellectuals. At the time of his birth, Toynbee wrote, his middle-class countrymen "supposed Earthly Paradise was just around the corner." They also assumed that the national state was "the natural, normal, rightful political unit."

Toynbee's generation of Europeans, however, lived through an era of "self-inflicted tribulation," war and genocide, largely due to their "explosive, subversive" faith in national self-determination. Toynbee borrowed a term from the ancient Greeks to explain that the spread of the western European political idea of the national state, first to eastern Europe and then to Asia and Africa, has created a fatal discrepancy—

the discrepancy between the political partition of the Oikoumenê [the habitat of the human race] into local sovereign states and the global unification of the Oikoumenê on technological and economic planes. This misfit is the crux of mankind's present plight. Some form of global government is now needed for keeping the peace . . . and for reestablishing the balance between Man and the rest of the biosphere.[1]

Similar views prevail among a small but articulate group of intellectuals and political scientists. Thus we should probably take the "unrealistic" question of world government seriously. Let us look more closely than usual at the United Nations for signs of the emergence of a global authority transcending sovereign states.

When the United Nations was founded in San Francisco in 1945, the United States was the driving force behind its creation. President Roosevelt and Democrats in the Wilsonian tradition believed that the failure of the United States to join the League of Nations had contributed tragically to the breakdown of "collective security" in the 1930s. A resurrected League would, they believed, facilitate Allied cooperation in the postwar era.

It was to be the prime purpose of the new organization "to maintain international peace and security." Primary responsibility for this awesome task was assigned to the twelve-nation Security Council. According to the UN charter, the Security Council had the authority to examine any international conflict, impose economic and political penalties on an aggressor, and even "take such action by air, sea, or land forces as may be necessary to restore international peace and security." In short, the Security Council had the power to police the world.

Yet this theoretical power was severely restricted in practice. China, Great Britain, France, the Soviet Union, and the United States were all made permanent members of the Security Council, and all five had to agree on any peace-keeping action. The veto power of the Big Five has been subsequently criticized for preventing the United Nations from ever regulating its most powerful members. But that was precisely the point: none of the Big Five, and certainly not the United States, was willing to surrender sovereign power to a potential world government.

Indeed, the United Nations has affirmed and reinforced the primacy of the national state in world politics. The charter directed the United Nations to pursue "friendly relations between nations based on the principle of equal rights and self-determination of peoples." Every "peace-loving" state was eligible to join and to participate in the General Assembly, the UN's other main body. Founded with 50 members, the General Assembly reached 159 members in 1986. Each state, whatever its size, had one voice and one vote on all resolutions. However, such resolutions became binding on states only if all five of the Security Council's permanent members agreed—a rare

event on major issues. The General Assembly was a world debating society for nation-states, not a law-making body.

The third express purpose of the United Nations testified to the expanded scope of governmental tasks since the late nineteenth century, as well as to global interdependence. According to its charter, the United Nations was "to achieve international cooperation in solving international problems of an economic, social, cultural, or humanitarian character, and in promoting and encouraging respect for human rights and for fundamental freedom for all without distinction as to race, sex, language, or religion." This open-ended assignment was the province of a Social and Economic Council, whose eighteen members were elected periodically by the General Assembly. The council also worked with such specialized affiliated agencies as the World Health Organization in Geneva and the Food and Agriculture Organization in Rome.

The scope of its original purposes helps explain the United Nations evolution. Fond hopes of effective Allied cooperation in the Security Council soon faded as cold war rhetoric and vetoes by the badly outnumbered Soviet Union began to paralyze that body. The Security Council proved somewhat more successful at quieting bloody conflicts between smaller states where the interests of the superpowers were not directly involved, such as the dispute between India and Pakistan over Kashmir, and that between Greece and Turkey over Cyprus. In 1960, it even sent military forces to re-establish order in the former Belgian Congo. This ambitious undertaking, criticized from all sides, marked the high point of Security Council peace-keeping.

With the Security Council often deadlocked, the rapidly changing General Assembly claimed ever greater authority. As decolonization picked up speed and the number of member states more than doubled, a nonaligned anticolonial "Afro-Asian bloc" emerged. Reinforced by sympathetic Latin American countries, the bloc succeeded in organizing a coherent "Third World majority" in the General Assembly by the mid-1960s. This majority concentrated on economic and social issues, passing many fiery and fine-sounding resolutions often directed against the former colonial powers, the United States, Israel, imperialist Portugal, and racist South Africa.

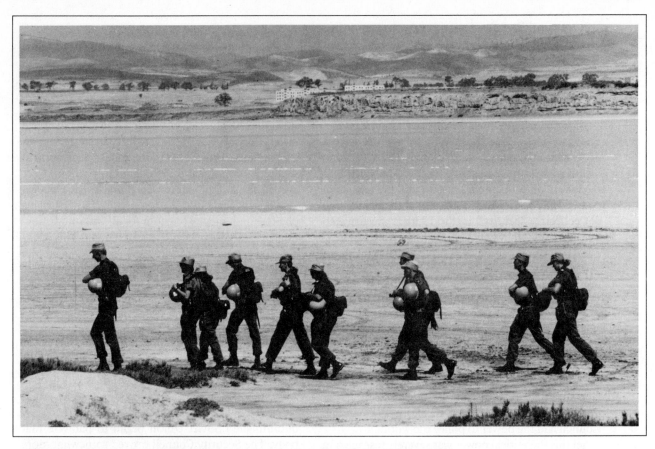

United Nations Peacekeeping Force in Cyprus Men and women of the Swedish Infantry Batallion in Cyprus move out on a military exercise in 1980. The eight-nation U.N. force in Cyprus was created by the U.N. Security Council in 1964, in an attempt to prevent fighting between the Greek and Turkish communities of the island republic. *(United Nations/J. K. Isaac)*

The long-term significance of these developments at the United Nations is by no means clear. The Third World majority, predominantly composed of small and poor countries, clearly mistook the illusion of power at the United Nations for the substance of power in world affairs. By the 1970s, many of its resolutions were simply ignored. Meanwhile, critical international issues such as the Arab-Israel conflict were increasingly resolved by resort to traditional diplomacy or war. In the mid-1980s, the United Nations experienced a serious financial crisis as the United States and other Western countries cut their contributions in order to retaliate against UN policies they opposed.

Nor did the United Nations generate much popular support around the world. Most people continued to identify with their national states, which may even provide adults with a psychological substitute for the family bonds that nurtured them in childhood. Thus nation-states have continued to weave the powerful social bonds necessary for group action. As two American political scientists put it, "The nation-state may all too seldom speak the voice of reason. But it remains the only serious alternative to chaos."[2]

And yet the United Nations has also proved to be a remarkably hardy institution. Particularly significant was the Third World majority's successful expansion of the scope of its economic, social, and cultural mission. By the early 1980s, an alphabet soup of UN committees, specialized agencies, and affiliated international organizations were studying and promoting health, labor, agriculture, industrial development, and world trade, not to mention disarmament, control of narcotics, and preservation of the great whales. These UN agencies and affiliated organizations derived their initial authority from treaties and agreements between sovereign states, but once in operation they took on a life of their own.

Staffed by a talented international bureaucracy, UN agencies worked tenaciously to consolidate their power and to serve their main constituency, the Third World majority. Without directly challenging national sovereignty, they exerted a steady pressure for more "international cooperation" in dealing with specific global issues. Partly because there were few alternatives, the world's nations sometimes went along. Thus sharp-eyed observers detected a gradual, many-sided enlargement of UN involvement in planetary affairs. And although this development appeared stalled in the 1980s, it is not impossible that early steps toward some kind of world government have already been taken.

COMPLEXITY AND VIOLENCE

In between territorial nation-states and international organizations that concentrate on specific problems there stretches a vast middle ground of alliances, blocs, partnerships, and ongoing conflicts and rivalries. It is difficult to make sense of this tangle of associations, and by the early 1980s some observers feared that the precarious world order was simply disintegrating.

One thing was clear: East-West competition was still very much alive. The mutual hostility of the two bloc leaders, the United States and the Soviet Union, again reached cold war intensity in the 1980s (see page 1154). Even so, it was clear that neither bloc was as solid as it had been a generation earlier. China had long since broken with the Soviet Union and become an independent regional power. Poland tried to follow suit in 1980–1981; its attempt failed, but demonstrated that there were real tensions within the Warsaw Pact and COMECON, the military and economic arms of the East bloc. As for the West, serious differences on military matters surfaced within NATO (which France had long since quit), and economic quarrels recurred between the Common Market and the United States. Both bloc superpowers were apparently being restrained by their allies.

One of the most striking global developments of recent times was the increasingly "multipolar" na-

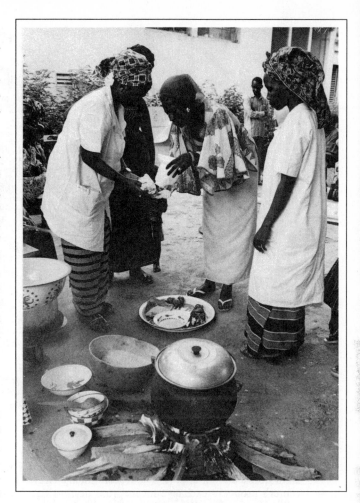

Learning About Nutrition The United Nations expert in the center is showing women with hospitalized children in Mali how to prepare meals providing maximum nourishment. *(United Nations/Ray Witlin)*

ture of world politics. Regional conflict and a fluid, complicated jockeying for regional influence were the keynotes. While the two superpowers were working to control their allies and competing for global power and influence, a number of increasingly assertive "middle powers" were arising around the world. These middle powers strove to be capable of leading or dominating their neighbors and of standing up to the world's superpowers on regional questions. The rise of middle powers reflected the fact that most of the world's countries are small and weak, with fewer than 20 million people. Only a few have the large populations, natural resources, and industrial base necessary for real power on a regional or global scale.

Colombian Drug Raid On March 10, 1984, police seized 13.8 tons of cocaine estimated to be worth $1.2 billion at a refining center in southern Colombia. Guarded by the Communist guerrilla group, the Revolutionary Armed Forces, the center included ten laboratories and an airport. The Revolutionary Armed Forces took 10 percent of the center's profits in exchange for its protection—a figure translating roughly into $3.3 million per month. *(Parga-Tiempo/Sygma)*

Latin America presented two striking examples. Brazil, with more than 100 million people, vast territory and resources, and one of the world's more rapidly industrializing economies, emerged rather suddenly as South America's dominant nation-state. Even more striking was the rapid rise of Mexico, with its population of over 74 million, its substantial industrial base, oil wealth, and proud nationalism. Although the world recession of the early 1980s hit hard, Mexico clearly saw itself as the natural leader of the Spanish-speaking Americas. As a major regional power, it challenged the long-dominant influence of the United States in the tiny states of Central America.

Strong regional powers like France and West Germany had re-emerged in western Europe by the early 1960s. Resurgent Nigeria was unquestionably the leading power in sub-Saharan Africa; heavily populated Egypt and much smaller Israel were also regional powerhouses. Iran sought under the shah to dominate the Persian Gulf, and it continued to do so since the Iranian revolution in its bitter war with Iraq. China, India, and Japan were of course all leading regional powers; several other Asian countries, notably Indonesia, Vietnam, Pakistan, and the Philippines, were determined to join them.

A high degree of competition and violent conflict characterized the emerging multipolar political system. Conflict in Europe has remained mainly verbal, but in Africa, Asia, and Central America blood flowed freely. Of the 145 wars that occurred worldwide between 1945 and 1979, 117 were in the Third World. Like Germany in the Thirty Years' War, some countries were literally torn apart. Lebanon, long considered the most advanced state in the Arab world, was practically destroyed by endless war, civil conflict, and foreign occupation. Cambodia (Kampuchea), invaded by American armies in 1970, then ravaged by the ultra-savage Pol Pot regime and finally occupied by Vietnamese armies, was another terrible tragedy.

The ongoing plague of local wars and civil conflicts caused great suffering. Millions of refugees, like Vietnam's "boat people," fled for their lives. The war for independence in Bangladesh temporarily created over 10 million refugees, who fled into India toward Calcutta. Hungry, homeless people overwhelmed the Indian relief centers, sleeping in trees, huddling in the rain, starving to death. After the Soviet invasion of Afghanistan, fully *one-tenth* of that country's population — 1.7 million people — fled. In 1981, the United Nations commission for emergency relief counted 10 million refugees in Asia and Africa. It was an appalling commentary on organized violence in our time.

THE ARMS RACE AND NUCLEAR PROLIFERATION

Regional competition and local hot wars brought military questions once again to the forefront of world attention. Indeed, nearly every country in the world joined the superpowers in the ever-intensifying arms race. In garrison states like Israel, South Africa, and Vietnam, defense expenditures assumed truly fantastic proportions. Unified Vietnam, having defeated the Americans and fought the Chinese to a standstill, emerged as a modern-day Prussia or Sparta. In the early 1980s, Vietnam was spending half its national income on the military; its standing army of a million men was the world's third largest, after Russia and China, and one of the best. Vietnam, with its population of 54 million, will be a major Asian power for the foreseeable future. In both India and Brazil, there developed a widespread belief that heavy defense spending was a key to economic development.

The most ominous aspect of the global arms race was the threat of nuclear proliferation. For a generation after 1945, nuclear weapons were concentrated mainly in the hands of the two superpowers, who learned a grudging respect for each other. More recently, however, nuclear weapons have begun to spread, perhaps like wildfire. Some experts believe

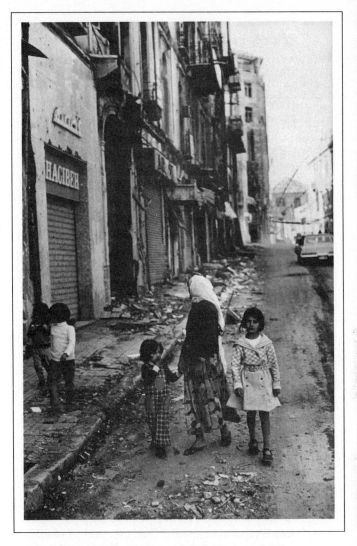

Battered Beirut A mother walks with her children through war-ravaged Beirut. Looking back, does she see the street as it once was, a bustling thoroughfare in a capital renowned for its elegance and sophistication? Beirut's dramatic decline testifies to the evil power of violence and civil war. *(David Lomax/Camera Press)*

that as many as twenty countries may have their own atomic bombs in a few brief years. How has this frightening situation arisen?

Having let the atomic genie out of the bottle at Hiroshima and Nagasaki in 1945, a deeply troubled United States immediately proposed that it be recaptured through effective international control of all atomic weapons. As American representative Bernard Baruch told the first meeting of the United Nations Atomic Energy Commission in 1946:

We are here to make a choice between the quick and the dead. . . . We must elect World Peace or World Destruction. . . . [Therefore] the United States proposes the creation of an International Atomic Development Authority, to which should be entrusted all phases of the development and use of atomic energy. . . .

The Soviets, suspicious that the United States was really trying to preserve its atomic monopoly through its proposal for international control and inspection, rejected the American idea and continued their crash program to catch up with the United States. The Soviet Union exploded its first atomic bomb in 1949. As the cold war raged on in the 1950s, the two superpowers pressed forward with nuclear development. The United States exploded its first hydrogen bomb in 1952; within ten months the Soviet Union did the same. Further American, Soviet, and then British tests aroused intense worldwide concern about nuclear fallout. There was well-founded fear that radioactive fallout entering the food chain would cause leukemia, bone cancer, and genetic damage. Concerned scientists called for an international agreement to stop all testing of atomic bombs. Partly in response to worldwide public pressure, the United States, the Soviet Union, and Great Britain agreed in 1958 to stop testing for three years. In 1963 these three powers signed an agreement, later signed by more than one hundred countries, banning nuclear tests in the atmosphere. A second step toward control was the 1968 Treaty on the Non-Proliferation of Nuclear Weapons, designed to halt their spread to other states. It seemed that the nuclear arms race might yet be reversed.

Unfortunately, this outcome did not come to pass. France and China, seeing themselves as great world powers, simply disregarded the test ban and refused to sign the nonproliferation treaty. By 1968, they too had hydrogen bombs. In 1974, India exploded an atomic device, reversing its previous commitment to nuclear arms limitations.

India's reversal was partly due to the failure of the Soviet Union and the United States to abide by the terms of the 1968 treaty on nuclear nonproliferation. According to the terms of the treaty, the nuclear powers agreed "to pursue negotiations in good faith on effective measures relating to cessation of the nuclear arms race at an early date and to nuclear disarmament, and on a treaty on general and complete disarmament under strict and effective international

control." The nonnuclear states, which had seen serious efforts at disarmament by the superpowers as their payoff for promising not to go nuclear, had offered a whole series of proposals ranging from a complete test ban to a freeze or reduction on nuclear weapons before agreeing to sign the treaty.

In fact, the nuclear arms race between the Soviet Union and the United States surged ahead after 1968. According to American officials, the United States was capable in 1974 of dropping 36 bombs on each of the 218 Soviet cities with populations of 100,000 or more. The Soviet Union had 11 nuclear weapons for each American city of comparable size. The much-discussed SALT talks confined themselves to limiting the *rate* at which the Soviet Union and the United States produced more nuclear warheads. After 1980, when the second Strategic Arms Limitation Treaty failed to be ratified by the United States Senate, the superpowers appeared once again to be locked into a nuclear arms race.

Partly out of fear for their own security, many near-nuclear powers appeared poised to "go nuclear" in the 1980s (Map 40.1). The worldwide energy crisis of the 1970s had played a part: peaceful use of the atom to generate electric power had created as a byproduct large quantities of plutonium, the raw material for bombs. Ominously, some countries were beginning to regard nuclear bombs as just another weapon in the struggle for power and survival.

India, for instance, developed its atomic capability out of fear of China, which had manhandled India in a savage border war in 1962. India's nuclear blast in 1974 in turn frightened Pakistan, which regarded India as a bitter enemy after 1947 and which lost Bangladesh because of Indian armies. Pakistan's President Bhutto was reported to have said that Pakistan must have the bomb even if its people had to eat grass. In the 1980s, Pakistan was clearly on the verge of producing nuclear weapons. It was also widely believed that both Israel and South Africa had arsenals of nuclear bombs. Israel's apparent nuclear superiority was of course profoundly distasteful to the Arabs. Hence Iraq pushed hard, with help from France, to

MAP 40.1 The Use of Nuclear Power in the 1980s One major consequence of the growing use of nuclear power to generate electricity is that many countries have developed the expertise necessary to make nuclear weapons should they so choose.

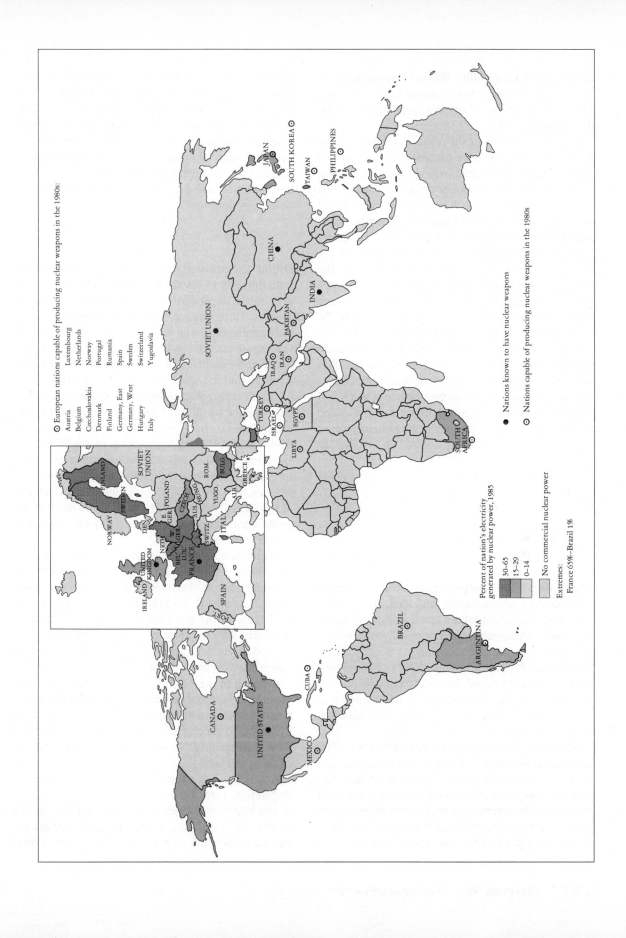

European nations capable of producing nuclear weapons in the 1980s:

Austria	Luxembourg
Belgium	Netherlands
Czechoslovakia	Norway
Denmark	Portugal
Finland	Rumania
Germany, East	Spain
Germany, West	Sweden
Hungary	Switzerland
Italy	Yugoslavia

● Nations known to have nuclear weapons

⊙ Nations capable of producing nuclear weapons in the 1980s

Percent of nation's electricity generated by nuclear power, 1985

- 30–65
- 15–29
- 0–14

No commercial nuclear power

Extremes:

France 65%–Brazil 1%

develop nuclear capability. When Israel suddenly attacked, destroying the Iraqi nuclear reactor, in June 1981, the dangers of nuclear proliferation were driven home to all.

If there are twenty or thirty nuclear powers in the early 1990s, as some have predicted, and if regional conflicts remain so intense, will not some nation use the dreadful weapons sooner or later? And if so, is there not a danger that such a nuclear war will spread to the superpowers? And what about nuclear terrorism and blackmail? In a world full of nuclear weapons and nuclear potential, might desperate political groups, like the most radical elements of the Palestine Liberation Organization and the Irish Republican Army, steal bombs and threaten to use them? Mere airplane hijackings might seem like the good old days. And if the gap between rich and poor nations continues to widen, might not desperate states, or even regions, resort to nuclear blackmail to gain their demands? None of these ominous possibilities has yet come to pass in the 1980s, but in a world of bitter national rivalries they make the hardheaded observer grimly apprehensive. Is the human race, as one expert on nuclear arms warns, "an endangered species"?[3]

GLOBAL INTERDEPENDENCE

Alongside political competition and the arms race, a contradictory phenomenon unfolded: as Toynbee suggested, the nations of our small world became increasingly interdependent economically and technologically. Even the great continental states with the largest land masses and populations and the richest natural resources found they could not depend only on themselves. The United States required foreign oil and the Soviet Union needed foreign grain. All countries and peoples had need of each other.

Mutual dependence in economic affairs was often interpreted as a hopeful sign for the human race. Dependence promoted peaceful cooperation and limited the scope of violence. Yet the existing framework of global interdependence also came under intense attack. The poor countries of the South—the Third World—charged that the North continued to receive far more than its rightful share from existing economic relationships, relationships forged to the South's disadvantage in the era of European expansion and political domination. The South demanded a new international economic order. Critics also saw strong evidence of neocolonialism in the growing importance of the North's huge global business corporations—the so-called multinationals—in world economic development.

PRESSURE ON VITAL RESOURCES

During the postwar economic boom, which lasted until the early 1970s, the nations of the world became ever more dependent on each other for vital resources. Yet resources seemed abundant, and rapid industrialization was a worldwide article of faith. Only those alarmed by the population explosion predicted grave shortages, and they spoke almost exclusively about food shortages in the Third World.

The situation changed suddenly in the early 1970s. Fear that the world was running out of resources was widely voiced. In a famous study aptly titled *The Limits to Growth* (1972), a group of American and European scholars argued that unlimited growth is impossible on a finite planet. By the early twenty-first century, they predicted, the ever increasing demands of too many people and factories would exhaust the world's mineral resources and destroy the fragile biosphere with pollution.

Meanwhile Japan was importing 99 percent of its petroleum, western Europe 96 percent. When the Organization of Petroleum Exporting Countries (OPEC) increased the price of crude oil *fourfold* in 1973 (page 1218), there was panic in many industrial countries. Skyrocketing prices and shortages of oil seemed to confirm grim predictions that the world was exhausting its vital resources.

In much of the Third World, the pressure to grow more food for more people led to piecemeal destruction of forests and increased soil erosion. Much of the Third World suffered from what has been called "the other energy crisis"—severe lack of firewood for cooking and heat.

A striking case is the southern edge of the Sahara. Population growth caused the hard-pressed peoples of this region to overgraze the land and denude the forests. As a result, the sterile sand of the Sahara advanced southward as much as thirty miles a year along a 3,000-mile front. Thus land available for cultivation decreased, leaving Africa all the more exposed to terrible droughts in the 1980s. Crops shriveled up and famine stalked the land. Yet an interdependent world mobilized, and international relief prevented mass starvation.

A recognition of interdependence was also reinforced by a common dependence on the air and the sea. Just as radioactive fallout has no respect for national boundaries, so pollution may sully the whole globe. Deadly chemicals, including mercury, lead, and arsenic, accumulated in the biosphere. Some feared that pollution of the oceans would lead to the contamination of its fish, one of the world's main sources of protein. Others, worried that the oceans had been overfished, feared that the significant decline in worldwide fish catch in the 1970s indicated abuse of the sea, the common heritage of mankind.

Of all the long-term pressures on global resources, the growth of population was probably the most serious. Here recent experience offered some room for cautious optimism. Population growth in the industrialized countries slowed markedly or even stopped (page 1215). Of much greater importance from a global perspective, the world's poor women began to bear fewer children. Small countries like Barbados, Chile, Costa Rica, South Korea, Taiwan, Tunisia, and the British colony of Hong Kong led the way. Between 1970 and 1975, China had history's fastest five-year decline in the birthrate; it fell from 32 births per thousand people to only 19 births per thousand and stayed level thereafter.

There were several reasons why the birthrate began to decline in many Third World countries. Fewer babies were dying of disease or malnutrition, which meant that fewer births were necessary to guarantee surviving children. As had happened earlier in the industrialized nations (page 1213), better living conditions, urbanization, and more education all encouraged women to have fewer children. No wonder that the most rapidly industrializing countries, like Taiwan or South Korea, led the way in birthrate declines. State-run birth control programs proved most successful in China. The Pill, borrowed from the West but manufactured locally, was widely used in conjunction with heavy financial penalties for those couples exceeding the birth quota, increasingly fixed at one child per couple. As in most Communist countries, abortion was free and on demand.

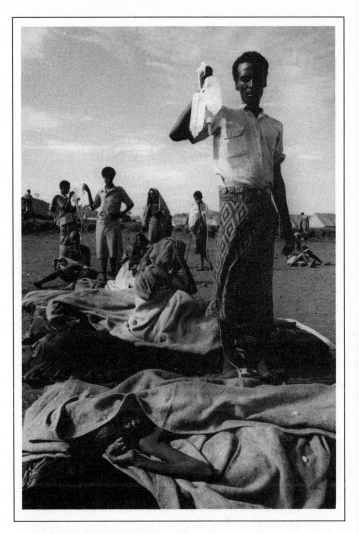

Famine Relief in Ethiopia, 1985 Famine killed more than a million people in the East African country of Ethiopia and sent great numbers fleeing in search of food. These doctors are giving emergency blood transfusions to famine victims outside an overcrowded hospital tent in one relief camp. *(Sebastiao Salgado/Magnum)*

Elsewhere—in Africa, the Muslim world, and North and South America—contraception and abortion remained controversial in the 1970s and 1980s. This helps explain why birthrates and population growth have remained much higher in Africa and South America than in Asia in recent years. In 1985, Africa led the world with a population growth of 3.2 percent per year—enough to double the continent's numbers in only twenty-two years.

Indira Gandhi's fiasco with compulsory sterilization (page 1174) suggests that, barring catastrophe, worldwide population growth will decline only gradually, as a result of billions of private decisions supplemented by government policies. This means that world population will continue to grow for a long time, as the Third World's current huge population of young adults form their own families. Thus the world's population—5 billion in 1987—will probably not stabilize until the mid-twenty-first century at the earliest, when it will have reached 10 to 12 billion people. Such continued growth will put tremendous pressure on global resources.

Yet gloom is not the only possible perspective. Even with 11 billion people, the earth would be less densely populated than Europe is today, and only one fourth as densely populated as small, prosperous countries like Belgium and the Netherlands, which largely feed themselves. Such countries, often overlooked in world politics, are promising models for life on a crowded planet. Moreover, the human race has exhibited considerable skill throughout its history at finding new resources and inventing new technologies. A striking example was the way that conservation, alternative energy sources, and world recession in the early 1980s at least temporarily belied gloomy prophecies about dwindling energy resources. An optimist could conclude that, at least from a quantitative and technical point of view, the adequacy of resources is a serious but by no means insoluble problem.

North-South Relations

The real key to adequate resources is probably global cooperation. Will the world's peoples work together, or will they eventually fight over resources like wild dogs over meat?

Since the late 1960s there has been dissatisfaction in Asia, Africa, and Latin America not only with the fruits of their industrialization drive but also with the world's economic system. Scholars imbued with a Third World perspective and spokesmen for the United Nations majority have declared that the international system is unjust and in need of radical change.

A brilliant Pakistani, World Bank official, and member of the international bureaucratic elite sympathetically articulated this position:

The vastly unequal relationship between the rich and the poor nations is fast becoming the central issue of our time. The poor nations are beginning to question the basic premises of an international order which leads to ever-widening disparities between the rich and the poor countries and to a persistent denial of equality of opportunity to many poor nations. They are, in fact, arguing that in international order—just as much as within national orders—all distribution of benefits, credit, services, and decision-making becomes warped in favor of a privileged minority and that this situation cannot be changed except through fundamental institutional reforms.[4]

The subsequent Third World demand for a "new international economic order" had many causes, both distant and immediate. Critics of imperialism like J. A. Hobson (page 950) and Third World writers on decolonization like Franz Fanon (page 1246) had long charged that the colonial powers grew rich exploiting Asia, Africa, and Latin America. Beginning in the 1950s, a number of writers, many of them Latin American Marxists, breathed new life into these ideas with their "theory of dependency." The poverty and so-called underdevelopment of the South, they argued, was not the starting point but the deliberate and permanent result of exploitation by the capitalist industrialized nations in the modern era. Third World countries produced cheap raw materials for wealthy, industrialized countries and were conditioned to buy their expensive manufactured goods. As in the case of Latin America since the nineteenth century, the industrialized nations perpetuated this neocolonial pattern after Third World countries gained political independence. Thus the prevailing economic interdependence was the unequal, unjust interdependence of dominant and subordinate, of master and peon. Declining economic aid, smug pronouncements about the overpopulation of the Third World, and the natural resentment of the poor toward the rich also fostered calls for radical restructuring of the international order.

It was the fabulously successful OPEC oil coup of 1973–1974 that ignited Third World hopes of actually achieving a new system of economic interdependence. From the industrialized North's point of view, OPEC's action in quadrupling the price of oil was a brutal attack. It brought an end to the postwar economic boom and created serious social problems.

An OPEC Meeting Begins As this picture suggests, the Organization of Petroleum Exporting Countries (OPEC) took on many aspects of an international political alliance, through which ministers of member states met periodically to fix the price of world trade's most vital commodity. The OPEC alliance rode high in the 1970s as the industrialized nations failed to make a concerted response. *(Wide World Photos)*

From a global perspective, however, the sudden price rise brought a massive global transfer of wealth unprecedented since the looting of Mexico and Peru by the Spanish conquistadors. Perhaps 2 percent of all the income of the rich nations was suddenly forwarded to the OPEC countries.

Third World critics of dependence and neocolonialism were euphoric. For years the developed countries had gradually reduced their economic aid. They had never seriously tried to meet the goal suggested by the UN General Assembly of earmarking 1 percent of their income each year for foreign aid. Yet OPEC's success showed that radical change was possible. In 1974, a special session of the General Assembly rammed through two landmark resolutions calling for a "new international economic order" and a "program of action" to attain it.

Among the specific demands were firm control by each country of its own natural resources, higher and more stable prices for raw materials, and equal tariff treatment for manufacturing goods from the Third World. These demands were subject to "collective bargaining," but the Third World vigorously insisted on new terms. As one sympathetic scholar observed:

There has taken place a unionization of the Third World that has marked a profound shift in international relations. It looks as if the confrontation between unions and employers that stirred capitalist societies in the nineteenth century is being reenacted, but this time on a world scale between developed and developing nations. The question this time is whether the new nations command as many assets and opportunities as did the laboring classes of capitalist nations.[5]

That profound question remained unanswered in the 1980s. The developing countries did negotiate some victories, notably a Common Fund under UN auspices to support the prices of raw materials and a limited scaling down of their enormous debts to the industrial nations. But the North, deeply troubled by inflation and its own economic problems, proved a very tough bargainer when it came to basic changes.

For example, in the late 1970s the South laid great hopes on a long, complicated conference to formulate a new Law of the Sea. The proposed new law was based on the principle that the world's oceans are "a common heritage of mankind" and should be exploited only for the benefit of all nations. In practice, this was to mean that a UN-sponsored authority would regulate and tax use of the sea and that a global organization would even mine it. Some countries and business firms were reluctant to accept such an infringement of their economic sovereignty and scope of action. The United States withdrew from the negotiations in 1981, and in 1982 the Reagan administration and several other developed nations refused to sign the final draft of the new Law of the Sea.

Increasingly frustrated in their desire to fashion a new international economic order quickly, some Third World leaders predicted more confrontation and perhaps military conflict between North and South. Some alarmists predicted that the northern industrial nations would eventually find themselves locked in a life-and-death struggle with the poor countries of Africa, Asia, and Latin America.

In considering these ominous predictions, an impartial observer is initially struck by the great gap between the richest and poorest nations. As discussed throughout this book, that gap was built on the coercive power of Western imperialism as well as on the wealth-creating achievements of continuous technological improvement since the Industrial Revolution. In the face of bitter poverty, unbalanced economies, and local elites that often cater to Western interests, Third World peoples have reason for anger.

Yet close examination of our small planet hardly suggests two sharply defined economic camps, a

MAP 40.2 Estimated World Per Capita Income in the Early 1980s

"North" and a "South." Rather, there are several distinct classes of nations in terms of wealth and income, as may be seen in Map 40.2. The Communist countries of eastern Europe form something of a middle-income group, as do the major oil-exporting states, which still lag behind the wealthier countries of western Europe and North America. Latin America is much better off than sub-Saharan Africa, having a number of middle-range countries to match their counterparts in highly diverse Asia.

When one adds global differences in culture, religion, politics, and historical development, the supposed clear-cut split between the rich North and the poor South breaks down further. Moreover, the solidarity of the Third World is fragile, resting largely on the ideas of some Third World intellectuals and their supporters. As one writer put it,

in the advocacy of growth and equalization at the international level ... Third World states have astonished everybody, their enemies and their friends alike, for no one has ever believed that such a diverse congress of countries, separated by geography, geopolitics, cultural traditions, size, ideology, and a host of other factors, could ever manage to build a cohesive alliance."[6]

The oil cartel's achievement rested in large part on regional Arab solidarity, for example, and it has proved impossible to duplicate its success with less vital raw materials and more complicated issues.

Thus continuing global collective bargaining seems more likely than international class (and race) war. The poorer nations will press to reduce international economic differences through taxation and redistribution measures. And because global interdependence is a reality, they will gradually win concessions, as has occurred domestically for the working classes in the wealthy nations since the later nineteenth century.

The international debt crisis suggests that this global bargaining is already occurring. The economic dislocations of the 1970s and early 1980s exacerbated the problems of many Third World countries, especially those that had to import the oil they needed. Growing unemployment, unbalanced budgets, and

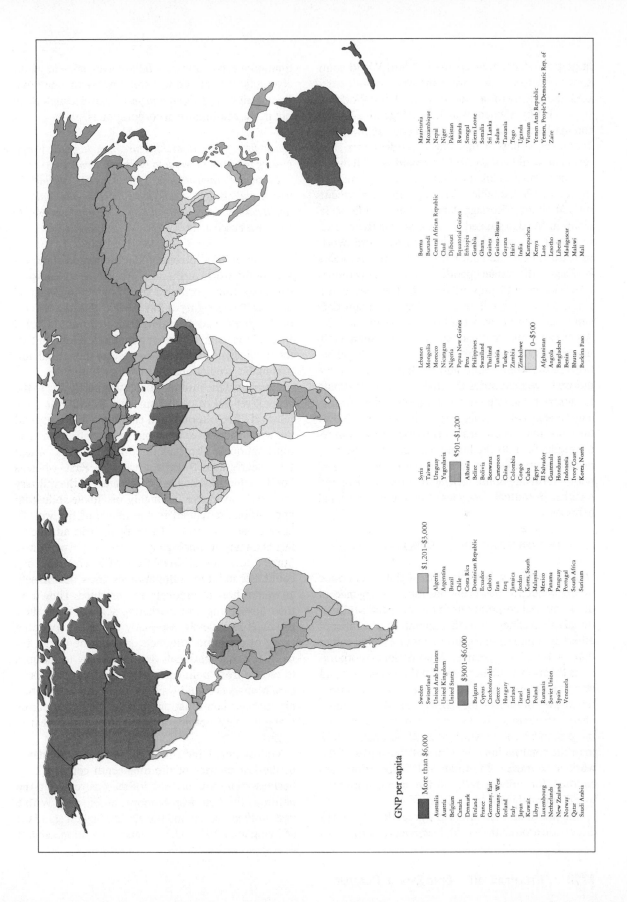

GNP per capita

large trade deficits forced many Third World countries to borrow rapidly from the wealthy industrialized nations. By the middle of 1982, Third World nations—led by Mexico, Brazil, and Argentina—owed foreign banks and governments about $600 billion. Moreover, much of this staggering debt was short term and could not possibly be repaid as it fell due.

When Mexico closed its foreign exchange markets in August 1982, unable to keep up with the payments on $80 billion of foreign debts, default and financial chaos in Mexico seemed at hand. Yet the Reagan administration, consistently opposed to Third World calls for a new international system, quickly organized a gigantic rescue operation to pump new money into Mexico and prevent default. The reason was simple: Mexico's failure to service its foreign debt would cripple or even bankrupt some of the large American banks that had lent it money. Such a failure promised to touch off such massive debt repudiations in the Third World and corporate losses in the industrialized countries that the whole world would be plunged into depression and even social turmoil. Thus a series of ongoing negotiations began all over the globe to reduce Third World debts, stretch out repayments far into the future, and grant desperately needed new loans. Lenders and borrowers, rich and poor, North and South realized that they were bound together in mutual dependence by the international debt crisis.

THE MULTINATIONAL CORPORATIONS

One of the most striking features of global economic interdependence has been the rapid emergence of multinational corporations in recent years. Multinationals are business firms that operate in a number of different countries and tend to adopt a global rather than national perspective. Multinational corporations themselves are not new, but their great size and importance are. By 1971, the ten largest multinational corporations—the IBMs, the Royal Dutch Shell Petroleums, the General Motors—each sold more than $3 billion worth of goods annually, more than the total national incomes of four-fifths of the world's countries. Multinational corporations accounted for fully a fifth of the non-Communist world's annual income.

The multinationals aroused a great deal of heated discussion around the world. Defenders saw the mul-

tinational corporations as building an efficient world economic system and transcending narrow national boundaries. As a top manager of Royal Dutch Shell put it, the multinational corporation is:

a new form of social architecture, matching the world-girding potential inherent in modern technology. . . .

In an age when modern technology has shrunk the world, and brought us all closer together, the multinational corporation and the nation state must get used to living with each other.[7]

Critics worried precisely that the nation-state was getting the worst of the new arrangement. Provocative book titles portrayed the "Frightening Angels" holding "Sovereignty at Bay," while building "Invisible Empires" and extending their nefarious "Global Reach." As usual whenever a major development attracts widespread attention, exaggerations and unreasonable predictions abounded on both sides.

The rise of the multinationals was partly due to the general revival of capitalism after World War Two, relatively free international economic relations, and the worldwide drive for rapid industrialization. The multinationals also had three major assets, which they clearly used to their advantage. First, whereas "pure" scientific knowledge unrelated to the military was freely available, its highly profitable industrial applications remained in the hands of the world's largest business firms. These firms held advanced, fast-changing technology as a kind of property and hurried to make profitable use of it wherever they could. Second, the multinationals knew how to sell, as well as how to innovate and produce. They used their advertising and marketing skills to push their products relentlessly, especially the ever expanding range of consumer products, around the world. Finally, the multinationals developed new techniques to escape from political controls and national policies. Managers found ways to treat the world as one big market, coordinating complex activities across many political boundaries so as to reap the greatest profits.

Multinational industrial corporations originated in the last quarter of the nineteenth century. U.S. businessmen took the lead, for reasons rooted in the nature of the American economy and society. With a vast, unified market and the world's highest standard of living after 1918, U.S. businessmen pioneered in the mass production of standardized consumer goods. Many of the most famous examples — such as kerosene (John D. Rockefeller and Standard Oil), sewing machines (Singer), and farm machinery (Cyrus McCormick and International Harvester) — date from the 1880s, and others, like the cheap automobile (Henry Ford), the mass retailer (Sears), and standardized food (Coca-Cola, Wrigley's chewing gum) were thriving by 1914.

Having developed mass-marketing techniques as well as new products, the biggest, most monopolistic American corporations quickly expanded abroad. They created wholly owned subsidiaries to produce and sell American-style consumer goods in foreign lands before 1914, and they continued to do so between the world wars. With ever more products and the attractions of the European Common Market, there followed a mighty surge of American investment in Europe after 1945. Nor were other parts of the world neglected by the giant American manufacturing firms: there was continued multinational investment in raw-material production in Latin America (particularly copper, sugar, and bananas) as well as the Middle East and Africa (primarily oil and gold). By 1967, American corporations — mainly the largest, most familiar household names — had sunk $60 billion into their foreign operations (Figure 40.1).

A few European companies, notably the German chemical and electrical firms, also became multinationals before 1900. Others emerged in the twentieth century. By the 1970s these European multinationals were in hot pursuit. Some, like Volkswagen, pushed directly into the American heartland. Big Japanese firms like Sony also rushed to go multinational in the 1960s and 1970s. While American investment was heavily concentrated in Europe and Canada, Japanese firms turned primarily to Asia for raw materials and cheap, high-quality labor. By the 1970s Japanese subsidiaries in Taiwan, Thailand, Hong Kong, and Malaysia were pouring out a torrent of transistor radios, televisions, cameras, and pocket calculators. Fearful of a growing protectionist reaction in their largest foreign market, the United States, where unemployed autoworkers symbolically demolished a Japanese automobile with sledgehammers in 1979, many Japanese firms followed Sony's example and began manufacturing in the United States. The emergence of European and Japanese multinational

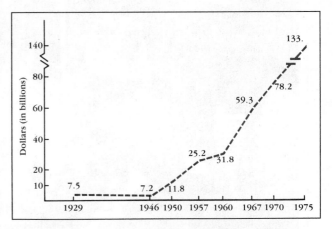

FIGURE 40.1 Total Investment by American Corporations in Foreign Subsidiaries (*Source:U.S. Department of Commerce.* Survey of Current Business)

corporations alongside their American forerunners marked the coming of age of global business in an interdependent world.

The impact of multinational corporations was heatedly debated, especially in Third World countries. From an economic point of view, the results were mixed. Above all, the giant firms provided advanced technology; but such technology was expensive and often inappropriate for poor countries with widespread unemployment.

The social consequences were also quite striking. In brief, the multinationals helped spread the products and values of consumer society to the elites of the Third World. Thus they helped to create islands of Western wealth, management, and consumer culture around the world. In doing so, the multinational corporations often turned to Third World business leaders for their managers, frequently after buying up their companies with offers that local manufacturers dared not refuse. Critics saw this as an integral part of the process of neocolonialism, whereby local elites abandoned the national interest and made themselves willing tools of continued foreign domination.

Global corporations also used aggressive techniques of modern marketing to sell products that are not always well suited to Third World conditions. For example, Third World mothers were urged to abandon "old-fashioned, primitive" breast-feeding (which was, ironically, making a strong comeback in

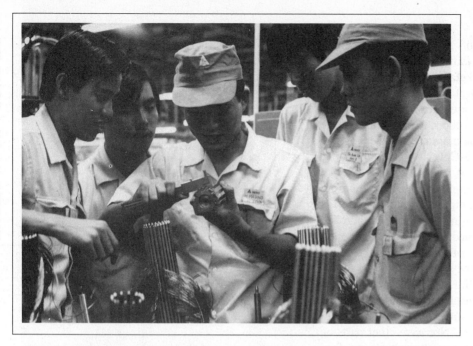

Japanese Multinationals have been playing an increasingly important role in East Asia's regional economy. In this 1973 photo Japanese engineers (wearing caps) show Chinese workers how to wind motors for refrigerator compressors at a new Japanese plant in Singapore. *(Paolo Koch/Rapho/Photo Researchers)*

rich countries) and to buy powdered milk formulas for their babies. Yet, because mothers frequently used unsanitary bottles and contaminated water, and diluted the expensive formula to make it last longer, this "advance" tragically resulted in more infant deaths. On this and many other issues, the multinationals came into sharp conflict with host countries.

Far from acting helpless in such conflicts, poor countries sometimes proved capable of exercising their sovereign rights over the foreign multinationals. Following earlier trends, many foreign mining companies, like the fabulously profitable U.S. oil companies in the Middle East, were simply nationalized. More importantly, Third World governments began to learn how to make foreign manufacturing companies conform to some of their plans and desires. Multinationals had to share ownership with local investors, hire more local managers, provide technology on better terms, and accept a variety of controls. Governments learned to play Americans, Europeans, and Japanese off against each other. Frustrated by such treatment, one American managing director in Malaysia pounded his desk in 1979 and

sputtered, "This little country and her little people need help, but they must be reasonable, otherwise we will get out of here." A Japanese manager in the same country expressed a more cooperative view: "We came here as guests, and our nation is small and needs natural resources, as well as foreign trade and investment to survive."[8] A growing proliferation of multinationals opened up new opportunities for Third World countries that wanted to use these powerful foreign corporations without being dominated by them.

PATTERNS OF THOUGHT

The renowned economist John Maynard Keynes often said that we live by our ideas and by very little else. True or not, a global perspective surely requires keen attention to patterns of collective thinking. As Keynes saw, we need to be aware of the ideas that are shaping the uncertain destiny of this small, politically fragmented, economically interdependent planet.

To be sure, human thought can be baffling in its rich profusion. Nevertheless, three distinct patterns on a global scale can be identified: the enduring strength of the modern world's secular ideologies, a vigorous revival of the world's great religions, and a search for mystical experience. The human race lives by these ideas in the late twentieth century.

SECULAR IDEOLOGIES

A good deal has been said in this book about the modern world's great secular ideologies. Almost all of these bodies of ideas, including liberalism, nationalism, and Marxian socialism, as well as faith in scientific and technical progress, industrialism, and democratic republicanism, took form in Europe between the eighteenth-century Enlightenment and the revolutions of 1848. These ideologies continued to evolve with the coming of mass society in the late nineteenth century and were carried by imperialism to the highly diverse societies of Asia and Africa. There they won converts among the local elites, who eventually conquered their imperialist masters in the twentieth century. European ideologies became worldwide ideologies, gradually outgrowing their early, specifically European character.

All this can be seen as an aspect of global interdependence. The world has come to live, in part, by shared ideas. These ideas have continued to develop in a complex global dialogue, and champions of competing views now arise from all regions. This has certainly been true of nationalist ideology and also of Marxism. Europe, the birthplace of Marxism, has made few original intellectual contributions to Marxism since Stalin transformed it into a totalitarian ideology of forced industrialization. Since 1945, it has been Marxists from the Third World who have injected new meanings into the old ideology, notably Mao's brand of peasant-based revolution and the Marxist theory of Third World dependency. Leftist intellectuals in Europe cheered and said "me too."

It has been primarily as critics that Europeans have contributed to world Marxism. Yugoslavs have been particularly influential. After breaking with Stalin in 1948, they revived and expanded the ideas of Stalin's vanquished rival, Leon Trotsky. Trotsky had claimed that Stalin perverted socialism by introducing "state capitalism" and reactionary bureaucratic dictatorship. According to the influential Yugoslav Milovan Djilas (b. 1911) Lenin's dedicated elite of full-time revolutionaries became Stalin's ruthless bureaucrats, "a new class' unprecedented in history. Djilas's powerful impact stemmed from his mastery of the Marxian dialectic:

The social origin of the new class lies in the proletariat just as the aristocracy arose in peasant society, and the bourgeoisie in a commercial and artisians' society. . . .

Former sons of the working class are the most steadfast members of the new class. It has always been the fate of slaves to provide for their masters the most clever and gifted representatives. In this case a new exploiting and governing class is born from the exploited class. . . .

The communists are . . . a new class.

As in other owning classes, the proof that it is a special class lies in its ownership and in its special relations to other classes. In the same way, the class to which a member belongs is indicated by the material and other privileges which ownership brings him.

As defined by Roman law, property constitutes the use, enjoyment, and disposition of material goods. The communist political bureaucracy uses, enjoys, and disposes of nationalized property.[9]

Non-Marxian criticism of communism also continued to develop, as in Jean François Revel's provocative *The Totalitarian Temptation* (1977). According to Revel, the application of the Marxist-Leninist-Maoist model, which was adopted by many countries not strictly belonging to the Communist camp, brought about phony revolution. Under the guise of supposedly progressive socialism, it built reactionary totalitarian states of the Stalinist variety.

Old-fashioned, long-battered liberalism and democracy, which people like Revel greatly prefer, has also survived as a global ideology. In every Communist country small, persecuted "human rights movements" have bravely demanded the basic liberties first set into law in the American and French revolutions. And there have always been a few African and Asian intellectuals, often in exile, calling for similar rights even in the most authoritarian states.

Of the bewildering array of alternatives to dominant secular creeds, three seem particularly noteworthy. The physicist Andrei Sakharov (b. 1921), the father of the Russian atomic bomb, who in the 1960s became a fearless leader of the human rights movement in the Soviet Union, was an eloquent spokes-

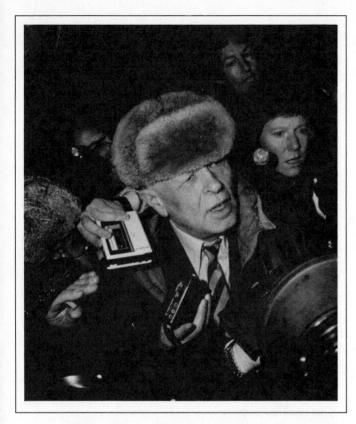

Sakharov Returns Exiled to the provincial city of Gorki for seven hard years, Sakharov was allowed to return to Moscow in December 1986. Met by a mob of journalists, the Soviet dissident leader vowed to continue the fight for freedom and human rights. *(Jasmin/Gamma-Liaison)*

man for what might be called the "convergence school." According to Sakharov, humanity's best hope lay in the accelerated convergence of liberal capitalism and dictatorial communism on some middle ground of welfare capitalism and democratic socialism, like that which flourishes so successfully in the small, close-knit societies of Scandinavia, Iceland, and New Zealand. This outlook waxes and wanes in influence. But it has deep historical roots in modern society and does not die. Meanwhile internationalists like the historian Toynbee advocated some form of world government. Many internationalists were social scientists, who characteristically believed in theoretical abstractions and technical solutions to human problems.

Finally, there has been a many-sided global reaction to the dominant faith in industrialization, con-

sumerism, and unrestrained "modernization." The disillusionment of the Third World has been matched by open resistance in the developed countries. The student revolt of the 1960s, with its vague ideology of participation, coincided with widespread nostalgia for simple, close-knit rural societies. The great Russian novelist Solzhenitsyn, caught up in the vanishing-resources doctrine of the 1970s, called on Soviet leaders to renounce Western technology and return to the earth:

Herein lies Russia's hope for winning time and winning salvation: In our vast northeastern spaces, which over four centuries our sluggishness has prevented us from mutilating by our mistakes, we can build anew: not the senseless, voracious civilization of "progress"—no; we can set up a stable economy without pain or delay and settle people there for the first time according to the needs and principles of that economy. These spaces allow us to hope that we shall not destroy Russia in the general crisis of Western civilization.[10]

Communes sprang up in the United States and Europe in the 1960s, and there were many advocates, like E. F. Schumacher in *Small Is Beautiful* (1973), of alternative technologies—like solar-heated houses to conserve nonrenewable oil—and lifestyles. Africa and Asia increasingly stressed "appropriate technologies," tailored to village life rather than borrowed from large-scale urban industrialized society—such as small, rugged, three-wheeled mechanical carts suited to existing country lanes, rather than large trucks requiring expensive modern highways, elaborate maintenance facilities, and large amounts of imported fuel.

Perhaps the most striking aspect of the worldwide reappraisal of industrialization was the heretical revival of Jean-Jacques Rousseau's belief in the superiority of the simple, frugal "noble savage." As Robert Heilbroner poignantly put it in 1974, in his otherwise gloomy *An Inquiry into the Human Prospect:*

One element [of hope] . . . is our knowledge that some human societies have existed for millennia, and that others can probably exist for future millennia, in a continuous rhythm of birth and coming of age and death, without pressing toward those dangerous ecological limits, or engendering those dangerous social tensions, that threaten present-day "advanced" societies. In our

Pope John Paul II The man of peace and good will arrives in Warsaw in 1983 for a second pilgrimage to his homeland. John Paul drew vast and enthusiastic crowds, demonstrating their opposition to an oppressive system as well as their deep-rooted Christian faith. *(Jean-Claude Francolon/Alain Mingam/Chip Hires/François Lochon/Gamma-Liaison)*

discovery of "primitive" cultures, living out their timeless histories, we may have found the single most important object lesson for future man.[11]

RELIGIOUS BELIEF: CHRISTIANITY AND ISLAM

The reaction to industrialism and consumerism was part of a broader religious response to the primacy of secular ideologies in general. The revival of Christianity among intellectuals after World War One (pages 1074–1075) was matched in the 1970s and early 1980s by a surge of popular, often fundamentalist, Christianity in many countries. Judaism and Islam also experienced resurgence, and Buddhism and Hinduism stopped losing ground. The continuing importance of religion in contemporary human thought—an importance that has often escaped those fascinated by secular ideology and secular history—must impress the unbiased observer.

Pope John Paul II (1978–   ) exemplified several aspects of the worldwide Christian revival. A jet-age global evangelist, John Paul journeyed to Africa, Asia, and North and South America, inspiring enthusiastic multitudes with his warm sincerity and unfailing popular touch. John Paul's melding of a liberal social gospel with conservatism in doctrinal matters also seemed to reflect the spirit of the age. Thus the pope boldly urged a more equitable distribution of wealth in plutocratic Brazil and more civil liberties in Marcos's authoritarian Philippines, while reaffirming the church's long-standing opposition to mechanical contraception and women in the priesthood. Many of Christianity's most rapidly growing Protestant churches also espoused theological fundamentalism, based on a literal reading of the Bible.

Ayatollah Khomeini The apostle of Islamic regeneration and the unwavering critic of the Shah returns in triumph to Teheran from exile in February 1979. The Shah had visions of making Iran a major military power, but all his military might crumbled before the emotional appeal of Islamic revolution. *(Black Star/Sipa Press-Setboun)*

It was also emblematic that the "Polish Pope" came from an officially atheist Communist country. Yet after thirty-five years of Communist rule, Poland was more intensely Catholic than ever before. Lech Walesa, the courageous leader of Poland's trade union Solidarity, has said that he could never become a Communist precisely because he is a devout Roman Catholic. Poland illustrated the enduring strength of spiritual life in the face of materialistic culture and secular ideologies, of which communism is only the most openly hostile.

The attempted assassination of the pope in 1981 by a mysterious Turkish terrorist, who was possibly connected with the Russian KGB, in an effort to undermine the Catholic church in Poland also dramatized the appeal of religious thinking. In a frightening, violent world, faith and prayer offer comfort and courage.

Islam, the religion of one-seventh of the earth's people, has also experienced a powerful resurgence in the 1970s and 1980s. Like orthodox Christianity, Islam had been challenged by the self-confident secular ideologies of the West since the early nineteenth century. And although the acids of modern thought did not eat as deeply as in Europe and North America, they etched a seductive alternative to Islam. Moderate Muslim intellectuals advocated religious reforms; radicals wanted drastic surgery. The most famous and successful of the radicals was the twentieth-century Turkish nationalist Kemal Atatürk (pages 1043–1046), who reflected and accelerated the impact of secularism on the Muslim world.

The generation of Muslim intellectual and political leaders born in the interwar years, who reached maturity after World War Two, agreed that Islam required at least some modernizing. They accepted the attractively simple Muslim creed, "There is no god but Allah and Muhammad is his prophet," but they did not think that the laws of the Qur'an should be taken literally. The prohibition on lending money at interest, the social inferiority of women, even cutting off the hands of thieves and public beheading of murderers, had made sense for the Arabian peninsula in the Middle Ages. But such practices did not suit the modern age. Islam had to adapt.

These views were still common among educated elites in the 1970s, and they remained dominant in Turkey and probably in Egypt. Yet throughout much of the Middle East they have had to bow before a revival of intense Islamic fundamentalism, the critical development of the last decade. Like some of their Christian counterparts, orthodox Muslim believers wanted to return to unalterable fundamentals. In taking the Qur'an literally, they demanded that the modern world adapt to the prophet's teachings, not vice versa. And because the masses remained deeply religious and distrustful of change, Islamic fundamentalism aroused a heartfelt popular response.

Iran provided a spectacular manifestation of resurgent Islamic fundamentalism at the end of the 1970s. Iran's religious leaders, notably the charismatic Ayatollah Khomeini, catalyzed intense popular dissatisfaction with the shah's all-out industrialization and heavy-handed religious reform into a successful revolution. An "Islamic Republic" was declared, to govern according to the sacred laws of the Qur'an. State and church were to become one. The holy men and their followers were absolutely serious: they sanctioned the stoning to death of prostitutes and adulterers, and proposed revising the legal code along strictly Qur'anic lines.

Iran's fundamentalism was exceptionally rigid and antimodern, partly because the country adhered to the minority Shi'ite version of Islam. But there has existed a similar movement in every Muslim country. Even where the fundamentalists are unlikely to take power, as in Indonesia or Pakistan, and where they are coopted and neutralized, as in Saudi Arabia, they have revitalized the Muslim faith. Islamic religious thought remains vigorous and continues to win converts, especially in black Africa.

SEARCHING FOR MYSTICAL EXPERIENCE

Alongside secular ideologies and a revival of organized religion, the third strong current of intellectual attraction has consisted of an enormous variety of religious sects, cults, and spiritual yearnings. Some of these new outpourings welled up within one or another of the great organized religions; many more did not. Though widely divergent, these movements seemed to share a common urge toward nonrational experiences, such as meditation, spiritual mysteries, and direct communication with supernatural forces.

Not that this is new. So-called "primitive" peoples have always embraced myths, visions, and continuous revelation. So too have the world's great religions, especially those of the ancient East—Taoism, Hinduism, and the Zen form of Buddhism. What is new is the receptiveness of many people in the rationalistic, scientific industrialized countries (and their disciples, the Third World elite) to ancient modes of mystical experience. Some of this interest stems from the doubt about the power of the rational human mind that blossomed after World War One. By the 1960s, it had struck deep roots in the mass culture of Europe and North America.

In this sense, the late twentieth century is reminiscent of the initial encounter of West and East in the Hellenistic Age. Then, the rationalistic, humanistic Greeks encountered the eastern mystery religions and were profoundly influenced by them. Now, various strains of mystical thought again appeared from the East and from "primitive" peoples. It could be said that the non-Western world was providing intellectual repayment for the powerful secular ideologies it had borrowed in the nineteenth century.

Reflecting on this ongoing encounter, the American social scientist Robert Heilbroner was not alone in suggesting startling implications for the future:

It is therefore possible that a post-industrial society would also turn in the direction of many preindustrial societies—toward the exploration of inner states of experience rather than the outer world of fact and material accomplishment. Tradition and ritual, the pillars of life in virtually all societies other than those of an industrial character, would probably once again assert their ancient claims as the guide to and solace for life.[12]

Some observers see the onrush of science and technology as actually reinforcing the search for spiritual experience. Electronic communications demolish time and distance; information itself is becoming the new global environment. According to the philosopher William Thompson:

East and West "Hare Krishna!" So chant these American disciples of the Hare Krishna sect as they dance and beg their way down New York's Fifth Avenue. Krishna is an especially popular Hindu god, and each stage of his life is the object of religious devotion. *(Eugene Gordon/Photo Researchers)*

Culture is full of many surprises, because culture is full of the play of opposites. And so there will be scientists and mystics in the New Age. . . . To look at the American counterculture today, one would guess . . . that the East was about to engulf the West. But [in fact] . . . America is swallowing up and absorbing the traditional Eastern techniques of transformation, because only these are strong enough to humanize its technology. In the days before planetization, when civilization was split between East and West, there were basically two cultural directions. The Westerner went outward to level forests, conquer nations, and walk on the moon; the Easterner went inward and away from the physical into the astral and causal planes. Now . . . we can glimpse the beginnings of a new level of religious experience, neither Eastern nor Western, but planetary.[13]

Many people have doubts about the significance of such views. But it is just possible that the upsurge of mysticism and religious searching will exert a growing influence in the coming era, especially if disorder and economic difficulties continue to undermine the old secular faith in endless progress.

———————

Whatever does or does not happen, the study of world history puts the future in perspective. Future developments on this small planet will surely build on the many-layered foundations hammered out in the past. Moreover, the study of world history, of mighty struggles and fearsome challenges, of shining achievements and tragic failures, imparts a strong sense of life's essence: the process of change over time. Again and again we have seen how peoples and societies evolve, influenced by such things as ideas, human passions, and material conditions. Armed with the ability to think historically, students of history are prepared to comprehend this inexorable process of change in their own lifetimes, as the world races forward toward an uncertain destiny.

NOTES

1. A. Toynbee, *Mankind and Mother Earth* (New York: Oxford University Press, 1976), pp. 576–577.
2. D. Calleo and B. Rowland, *America and the World Political Economy* (Bloomington: Indiana University Press, 1973), p. 191.
3. W. Epstein, *The Last Chance: Nuclear Proliferation and Arms Control* (New York: Free Press, 1976), p. 274.
4. M. ul-Haq, *The Poverty Curtain: Choices for the Third World* (New York: Columbia University Press, 1976), p. 152.
5. E. Hermassi, *The Third World Reassessed* (Berkeley: University of California Press, 1980), p. 76.
6. Ibid., p. 185.
7. Quoted in H. Stephenson, *The Coming Clash: The Impact of Multinational Corporations on National States* (New York: Saturday Review Press, 1973), p. 60.
8. Quoted in A. R. Negandhi, *The Functioning of the Multinational Corporation: A Global Comparative Study* (New York: Pergamon Press, 1980), p. 142.
9. M. Djilas, *The New Class* (New York: Praeger, 1957), pp. 41–42, 44.
10. A. I. Solzhenitsyn, *Letter to the Soviet Leaders* (New York: Harper and Row, 1974), p. 33.
11. R. L. Heilbroner, *An Inquiry into the Human Prospect* (New York: Norton, 1974), p. 141.
12. Ibid., p. 140.
13. W. I. Thompson, *Evil and World Order* (New York: Harper and Row, 1980), p. 53.

SUGGESTED READING

Many of the books cited in the Suggested Reading for Chapters 38 and 39 pertain to the themes of this chapter. Three helpful and stimulating studies on global politics from different viewpoints are R. Barnet, *The Lean Years: The Politics of the Age of Scarcity* (1980); F. M. Lappé and J. Collins, *Food First: Beyond the Myth of Scarcity* (1977); and S. Hoffman, *Primacy or World Order: American Foreign Policy Since the Cold War* (1978). An excellent if ominous introduction to international negotiations for the control of nuclear arms is W. Epstein, *The Last Chance: Nuclear Proliferation and Arms Control* (1976). Two clear and judicious recent studies on the evolving nuclear policies of the two great superpowers, by relatively impartial British scholars, are D. Holloway, *The Soviet Union and the Arms Race* (1983), and L. Freedman, *The Evolution of Nuclear Strategy* (1982), a history of American thinking about nuclear weapons and nuclear war. J. Hackett, *The Third World War, August 1985* (1978), is a gripping but all too optimistic best-selling account of limited nuclear war by a retired British general, writing "in consultation with NATO experts."

M. ul Haq, *The Poverty Curtain: Choices for the Third World* (1976), is an excellent presentation of Third World demands for a new economic order. This position is expanded in J. Tinbergen and A. J. Dolman, eds., *RIO, Reshaping the International Order: A Report to the Club of Rome* (1977), and *North-South: A Program for Survival* (1980), a report calling for increased help for the South by the blue-ribbon Independent Commission on International Development Issues, under the chairmanship of Willy Brandt. Such views do not go unchallenged, and P. T. Bauer, *Equality, The Third World, and Economic Delusion* (1981), is a vigorous defense of the industrialized nations and their wealth. J. K. Galbraith, the witty economist and former U.S. ambassador to India, argues simply and effectively that poor countries have important lessons to teach rich countries in *The Voice of the Poor* (1983). Common problems and aspirations are also the focus of E. Laszlo et al., *Goals for Mankind* (1977). The important study by R. Ayres, *Banking on the Poor: The World Bank and World Poverty* (1983), shows how this international financial organization has emerged as a standard-bearer for the poorest countries. *The World Development Report,* which the World Bank publishes annually, is an outstanding source of information about current trends. Valuable studies on multinational corporations and global indebtedness include L. Solomon, *Multinational Corporations and the Emerging World Order* (1978); A. R. Negandhi, *The Functioning of the Multinational Corporation: A Global Comparative Study* (1980); R. Barnet and R. Muller, *Global Reach: The Power of the Multinational Corporations* (1975); and A. Sampson, *The Money Lenders: The People and Politics of the World Banking Crisis* (1983).

Contemporary thought is so rich and diverse that any selection must be highly arbitrary. Among works not mentioned elsewhere, E. Banfield, *The Unheavenly City Revisited* (1974), is a provocative and influential reassessment of urban problems and solutions in the United States. D. H. Meadows and D. L. Meadows, *The Limits of Growth* (1974), argue that the world will soon exhaust its natural resources. E. F. Schumacher, *Small Is Beautiful: Economics as if People Mattered* (1973), advocates conservation and a scaling down of technology to avoid disaster. R. M. Pirsig, *Zen and the Art of Motorcycle Maintenance: An Inquiry into Values* (1976), is a stimulating exploration of the tie between modern technology and personal development.

T. R. Gurr, *Why Men Rebel* (1970), skillfully reworks the idea that revolutions occur when rising expectations are frustrated. M. Djilas, *The New Class* (1957), criticizes the ruling Communist bureaucracies from a Marxist point of view, while J. Revel, *The Totalitarian Temptation* (1977), claims that many Western intellectuals have been seduced into seeing Communist dictatorships as progressive socialist societies. A. Sakharov, *Progress, Coexistence, and Intellectual Freedom,* rev. ed. (1970), soberly assesses the prospects for improved relations between the Soviet Union and the United States.

The Islamic revival may be approached through the sympathetic work of E. Gellner, *Muslim Society* (1981); the reservations of V. S. Naipaul, *Among the Believers: An Islamic Journey* (1981); H. Algar, ed., *Islam and Revolution: Writings and Declarations of Iman Khomeini* (1982); and J. Stempel, *Inside the Iranian Revolution* (1981). Muslim writers address issues in the Islamic world in J. Donohue and J. Esposito, eds., *Islam in Transition: Muslim Perspectives* (1982).

Studies of the future are so numerous that M. Marien, *Societal Directions and Alternatives: A Critical Guide to the Literature* (1977), is a useful aid with its annotated bibliography. The many future-oriented works of the members of the Hudson Institute usually combine optimism and conservatism, as in H. Kahn et al., *The Next Two Hundred Years* (1976), and H. Kahn, *The Coming Boom* (1982). J. Lorraine, *Global Signposts to the 21st Century* (1979), and R. L. Heilbroner, *An Inquiry into the Human Prospect* (1974), are especially recommended as stimulating and intelligent studies. L. Stavrianos, *The Promise of the Coming Dark Age* (1976), is especially suited to those with cataclysmic dispositions.

CHAPTER OPENER CREDITS

NOTES ON THE ILLUSTRATIONS

CHAPTER OPENER CREDITS

NOTES ON THE ILLUSTRATIONS

Page 546   Engagement near Isle of Wight in 1588, Spanish fleet on the left, English on the right. In left foreground a Spanish vessel is exchanging shots with two English vessels to the right.

Page 549   World chart by Vesconte Maggiolo, 1511, showing North America as a promontory of Asia.

Page 565   Long the site of a royal residence and hunting lodge, Fontainebleau was expanded and transformed by Francis I in 1530–1540. Il Rosso (Giovanni Battista de'Rossi, 1494–1540), Florentine painter; Francesco Primaticcio, Italian painter and architect (1504–1570); and Sebastiano Serlio, Italian architect and writer on art (1475–1554) were called by Francis I from Italy to build and decorate the palace. The gallery of Francis I set a fashion in decoration imitated throughout Europe.

Page 695 *Famille de paysans,* ca 1640, by Louis Le Nain (1593–1648), French painter. The original can be seen in the Louvre.

Page 700 Engraving, 1746.

Page 713 Primitive African bronze plaque: King mounted with attendants. Metalwork of the 16th–17th centuries, from Benin, Nigeria; 19½ by 16½ inches. From the Metropolitan Museum of Art.

Page 714 Wooden rice ladle of the Dan peoples, Liberia and Ivory Coast.

Page 716 The colony of Capetown, South Africa, as it appeared when first taken by the English under Admiral Elphinstone and General Clarke, September 16, 1795.

Page 718 Pieter van der Aa, *View of Loango.* Plate 47 from Galérie Agréable du Monde (Vol. 60–67).

Page 723 Steel helmet with inlaid gold, rubies, and turquoise, originating from the Ottoman Empire during the rule of Sultan Suleyman I (1520–1566), renowned legislator, statesman, poet, and patron of the arts. Height 11 1/16 inches, depth 9¼ inches. Topkapi Sarayi Muzesi, Istanbul.

Page 724 *Lady Gazing at the Reflection in a Pool from Arifi's Rawzat ul-Ushaq.* (The Garden of Lovers.) Opaque watercolor on paper, Turkey, Ottoman, ca 1560–1575. From the Edward Binney 3rd Collection of Turkish Art at the Harvard University Art Museums.

Page 730 *A Magnanimous Vizier.* Opaque watercolor on paper, attributed to Manohar. From the Divan of Anvari, dated 1588, 14 by 8 cm.

Page 731 *Heavenly Joys Come to Earth.* Opaque watercolor on paper, attributed to Khem Karan. From the Divan of Anvari, India, Mughal; 13.8 by 7.5 cm.

Page 732 Bichitr, *Jahangir Preferring a Sufi Shaikh to Kings.* Indian, Mughal, ca 1615–1618; 10 by 7⅛ inches.

Page 733 The Taj Mahal is the mausoleum in memory of Arjumand Banu Begum, called Mumtaz Mahal ("chosen one of the palace"), of which Taj Mahal is a corruption. She died in 1631. The building was begun in 1632, after plans were submitted by a council of architects. Credit for the final design is given to Usted Isa, who was either Turkish or Persian. Workmen and materials came from all over India and Central Asia. The mausoleum itself was completed by 1643, although the whole complex—consisting of the mausoleum, central garden square, mosque, and service buildings surrounded by a red sandstone wall— took much longer.

Page 747 Detail of Chinese silk scroll: *Going up the River at the Spring Festival.* Sung Dynasty.

Page 755 Chinese (?Ming) painting: *Children Playing in a Garden.* Silk fan in an album; 10 by 10⅝ inches.

Page 757 Tai Chin (1388–1462), *Fishermen on an Autumn River.* Ming, mid-15th century. Paper makimono; 18⅛ by 291⅜ inches.

Page 761 Marketplace. Detail from a Japanese screen by Hanabusa Itchō, *Pastimes and Occupations of the Twelve Months.* Edo period, Ukiyoe school. Ink and color on paper; 11 5/16 by 342 inches.

Page 762 Odagiri Shunko, *The Procession of a Daimyo to Edo.* Edo period, 19th century. Hand scroll, ink and colors on paper; 28.9 by 2,588.2 cm. Feudal lords, or daimyos, maintained two households, one in their native domain and another in the capital city of Edo. A shogunal decree obliged them to spend alternate years at their Edo residence. Every year approximately 265 daimyos made the round trip journey between their own provinces and the capital.

Page 766 Scenes from the Pleasure Quarters of Kyoto, one of a pair of six-panel folding screens of the Edo period, mid-17th century. Ink, colors, and gold on paper; each panel 104.5 by 45.5 cm.

Page 770 Jacques-Louis David (French, 1748–1825), *The Tennis Court Oath.*

Page 777 John Trumbull (American, 1756–1843), *The Declaration of Independence.* Oil on canvas, 1786; 21⅛ by 31⅛ inches.

Page 779 This portrait of Louis XVI by Joseph-Siffrein Duplessis, French portrait painter (1725–1802), hangs in the Marie Antoinette Gallery at Versailles.

Page 784 This drawing by Persin de Prieur, "Premier assaut contre La Bastille," can be seen in the Musée Carnavalet, Paris.

Page 790 "Un Comité révolutionnaire sous la Terreur," after Alexandre Evariste Fragonard (1780–1850), French historical painter.

Page 793 Jacques-Louis David (French, 1748–1825), *Napoleon Crossing the Alps.* Oil on canvas.

Page 802 Fritz the giant steam hammer at the Krupp steelworks in Germany, photographed on September 16, 1861.

Page 806 Peter Brueghel, the younger (1564–1637), *Harvesting Scene.* Oil on panel; 23⅛ by 17¼ inches. William Rockhill Nelson Gallery of Art, Atkins Museum of Fine Arts, K. C. Nelson Fund.

Page 807 Painting by Thomas Weaver, engraved by William Ward and published July 21, 1812. Mezzotint; 23 7/10 by 17 4/5 inches.

Page 809 Samuel Scott (English, 1702–1772), *Old East India Quay, London,* Victoria and Albert Museum. Samuel Scott was the most distinguished native English topographical view painter in the eighteenth century. Such painting was popularized in England by Canaletto during his residence there from 1746–1755.

Page 812 Frontispiece from a map of "the most Inhabited part of Virginia containing the whole province of Maryland with part of Pennsylvania, New Jersey and North Carolina drawn by Joshua Fry and Peter Jefferson in 1775," in Thomas Jeffrey's *America Atlas,* 1776, in The British Library.

Page 813 James Hargreaves (d. 1778), English inventor, weaver, and mechanic, invented the spinning jenny about 1765.

Page 816 Engraving by Henry Beighton, 1717, of the atmospheric steam engine invented about 1705 by Thomas Newcomen, English blacksmith (1663–1729).

Page 818 Honoré Daumier (1808–1879), *The Third-Class Carriage.* Oil on canvas. Daumier was both a caricaturist and a serious painter.

Page 823 Royal visit to steelworks in Crewe, Cheshire: the tire-expanding machine, February 1866.

Page 827 From *Parliamentary Papers,* 1842, vol. XV.

Page 834 "Proclamation of the Roman Republic," 1848 lithograph by Bertarelli, Milan.

Page 839 Yohann Hochle, *Ball in the Winter Riding School,* 1815.

Page 847 Left to right: K. Marx, F. Engels (rear), with Marx's daughters: Jenny, Eleanor, and Laura, photographed in the 1860s.

Page 849 Eugene Delacroix (1798–1863), French painter and leader of the Romantic school.

Page 852 *Liszt am Klavier,* 1840, by Josef Danhauser, German painter (1805–1845).

Page 853 Eugene Delacroix (French, 1798–1863), *Les Massacres de Scio.* Louvre. This dramatic interpretation of a contemporary event scandalized Paris Salon visitors in 1824.

Page 857 From *Punch,* 1846. The humorous weekly *Punch*—founded in 1841 by the British journalist and sociologist Henry Mayhew (1812–1887) and others—is the most famous of its kind. Its cartoons and caricatures became a powerful vehicle of political and social comment.

Page 858 *The Legislative Belly,* lithograph by Honoré Daumier (1808–1879).

Page 866 Paul Gustav Doré (French illustrator and painter, 1833–1883), *Over London by Rail* from his *London,* published in 1872.

Page 870 "The Court for King Cholera," cartoon from *Punch,* XXIII (1852), 139.

Page 874 Cross-section of a Parisian house, about 1850, from Edmund Texier, *Tableauade Paris,* Paris, 1852, vol. I, p. 65.

Page 875 Opening of steam-propelled tramways by the locomotive *Harding* in Paris between the railroad stations of Montparnasse and Austerlitz. From *L'Illustration,* August 19, 1876.

Page 879 *Un Coin de Table,* 1904, by Paul-Émile Chabas (French painter, 1869–1937). Oil on canvas.

Page 882 Market for servants, situated just outside the ancient boundary wall (the Kitai Yard) of Moscow and open every day of the year, Sundays being the busiest. From *The Illustrated London News,* November 1, 1850, p. 458. England had no fully illustrated newspaper until the first number of the weekly *Illustrated London News* appeared on May 14, 1842, with 16 printed pages and 32 woodcuts.

Page 895 Sir Frederick William Burton (Irish watercolorist, 1816–1900), portrait of George Eliot (Mary Anne Cross), 1865.

Page 898 From *Album of Photographic Views, 1890–1899, for the Construction of the Novoselitsa Branches of the Southwestern Railway in the Ukraine.*

Page 902 Demolition of part of the Latin Quarter in 1860. Engraving from a drawing by Félix Thorigny.

Page 914 Merchants of Nijni-Novgorod drinking tea. From *L'Illustration,* August 29, 1905.

Page 919 Assassination of 62 hostages in Haxo Road, Belville, France, by the Communards, 1872.

Page 928 Sir Benjamin Stone's photograph of a steamer on the Aswan Dam in 1907. Giant statues of Ramses II guard the ancient Egyptian rock temples he built at Abu Simbel. These were preserved at vast expense when the Aswan Dam was rebuilt in the 1960s and its rising water level threatened to flood them.

Page 957 Min-Chiang-Chek, prisoner number 7, was condemned to death for murdering missionaries at Kucheng. *The Graphic,* November 23, 1895.

Page 980 "Villa of Brule—The Great Hostile Indian Camp." Pine Ridge, S.D., 1891, by John C. H. Grabill. Sioux camp.

Page 982 Macon slave workers made bricks by the thousands to build the Confederate States Armory and Central Ordnance Laboratory. When this photograph was taken in the 1870s, the work had changed very little, but the pay was better.

Page 988   *Puck* was founded in 1876. It provided a forum for new artists working in a lithographic style with clever analogies and caricature. The political cartoons contained literary references reminiscent of *Punch*.

Page 1003   *The Congress at Berlin 1878* by Anton von Werner (1843–1915), German painter of portraits and historical subjects.

Page 1047   Jewish settlement near Jaffa, July 1923.

Page 1054   Gandhi on the Salt March, 1930.

Page 1057   "Anti-Reds" wrest Canton from the Communists, with over 3,000 casualties. This January 1928 photo shows the dead strewn in the principal streets of Canton.

Page 1062   Japanese "Victory March" in Shanghai, December 1937.

Page 1065   Philippine "West Pointers" on parade: Cadets of the Baguio Military Academy march in a parade to celebrate the second anniversary of the Philippine Commonwealth.

Page 1068   Berlin family living in railway boxcar after World War I.

Page 1072   Edmund Engelmann took this and other photographs secretly in May 1938 while Freud's apartment was under surveillance by the Gestapo. His chance for survival was about 50 percent. When leaving Vienna it was too dangerous for him to take the negatives, so he left them with an acquaintance. After the war this acquaintance had died, and Engelmann recovered these unique photographs only with great difficulty.

Page 1076   Frank Lloyd Wright (American architect, 1869–1959), Falling Water, Bear Run, Pennsylvania—perhaps the greatest modern house in America, 1936. The largely self-taught Wright was an exponent of what he called "organic architecture": the idea that a building should blend in with its setting and be harmonious with nature.

Page 1078   *Guernica,* 1937, by Pablo Picasso, Spanish painter and sculptor (1881–1973). The original oil on canvas, 11 feet, 5½ inches by 25 feet, 5¾ inches, is in the Museo del Prado, Madrid.

Page 1080   Mary Pickford (1893–1979) photographed by Hartsook in 1918. Rudolph Valentino (1895–1926) as he appeared in *Four Horsemen of the Apocalypse* (1921).

Page 1090   Scene in San Francisco in 1934, photographed by Dorothea Lange.

Page 1097   100,000 Nazi Storm Troopers gathered in the Luitpodarena in Nuremberg, Germany, to hear Adolf Hitler on Brown Shirt Day at the Nazi Party convention, September 20, 1936.

Page 1099   French caricature by C. Leavdre, 1898.

Page 1124   East German troops supervising construction workers at the Berlin Wall, photographed from West Berlin.

Page 1135   The *Deutscher Verlag* building in Berlin after impassable street had been cleared of rubble, photographed on July 6, 1945.

Page 1156   Muro Central in the Palacio Nacional, Mexico City, painted 1929–1935 by José Clemente Orozco (1883–1949), Mexican painter of the modernist school.

Page 1159   President Allende makes his way through the crowd to his office in the Presidential Palace, August 22, 1973.

Page 1200   Demonstrators link arms across Boulevard St. Michel on Left Bank during Paris riots of May 1968.

Page 1204   First atomic bomb test at Bikini Atoll, in photograph released July 26, 1946.

Page 1206   Astronaut Edwin E. Aldrin, Jr., leaving the lunar module. Apollo II was launched in Florida on July 16, 1969. Astronauts Neil A. Armstrong and Aldrin landed on the moon on July 20 while Michael Collins circled in the main spacecraft until rejoined by the others on July 21. The astronauts returned to Earth on July 24, when they were picked up in the Pacific Ocean.

Page 1212   Students in the Boulevard Saint Michel in Paris protesting the closing of the suburban Nanterre University, photographed on May 3, 1968.

Page 1260   On March 10, 1984, the Colombian narcotics police seized 13.8 tons of cocaine—estimated to be worth 1.2 billion dollars—at a refining center located in the jungle of Caqueta Province in southern Colombia. This was reported to be the largest haul ever made by authorities anywhere in the world.

INDEX

Automobile industry, 1210
Auxiliary Service Law (Germany), 1014, 1018
Aztecs, conquest of, 556–557

Ba, Putali, 1051
Babur (Bah-burr), Mughal ruler, 710, 728, 734
Baby boom, 1213
Bach, Johann Sebastian, 635
Bacon, Francis, 650–652, 653, 1202
Bacterial revolution, 871–873
Badshah, 728, 730
Baldwin, Stanley, 1081, 1086
Balfour Declaration, 1042, 1043, 1048
Balkans, nationalism in, 1007
Balkan wars, 1007, 1008
Balzac, Honoré de, 894
Banking: Bank of Amsterdam, 610; Bank of France, establishment of, 794; industrialization and, 822; Great Depression and, 1088
Baring, Evelyn (Lord Cromer), 937–938
Baroque culture, absolutism and, 634–639
Barroes, historian, 734
Barth, Karl, 1074
Baruch, Bernard, 1261
Bases and Points of Departure for Argentine Political Organizations (Alberdi), 974
Bastille, French Revolution and, 783
Batista, Fulgencio, 1157
"Battle of Peterloo," 855
Bauhaus school of architecture, 1077
Baumgarten, Hermann, 911
Bayle, Pierre, 655, 666
Bay of Pigs invasion, 1157
Beethoven, Ludwig van, 851, 852–853
Begin, Menachem, 1180
Belgian Congo, decolonization of, 1190
Belgium: German attack on, 1008; occupation of Ruhr by, 1082
Benin, 712–713, 717
Bentham, Jeremy, 871
Benthamites, 871
Berg, Alban, 1079
Bergson, Henri, 1070
Beria, Lavrenti, 1145
Berlin, Congress of, 1002, 1007
Berlin Wall, 1147
Bernal, John Desmond, 1202–1203
Bernstein, Edward, 925
Bethmann-Hollweg, Theobald von, 1008
Bhutto (Bu'-tow), Zulfikar ali, 1262
Biafra, war in, 1194
Bible: Dutch translations of, 567; King James version of, 583, 584
Big Five, 1257
Big Science, 1205–1207, 1222
Big Three, 1131–1132
Bight of Benin, slave trade and, 717
Bill of Rights (England), 607

Bill of Rights (United States), 778
Birth control: in 18th-century Europe, 687–688; slavery and, 986; in American west, 989; in India, 1173, 1175; modern use of, 1214, 1265–1266
Birthrate: in 18th-century Europe, 681; declining, in 19th century, 889–890; modern, 1213–1214, 1215–1216
Bismarck, Otto von, 862, 944; growth of German socialism and, 916–918, 923; World War I and, 1002–1003, 1009, 1114
Bjørnson (Be-yorn'-son), Martinius, 942
Black consciousness, African, 1186–1187
Black Death, 616, 682
Black Family in Slavery and Freedom, 1750–1925, The (Gutman), 986
Black Hand, The, 1007
Blacks: origin of attitudes toward, 581–582; in Latin America, 971, 976; American Civil War and, 985–987; in United States, 1151–1152; in South Africa, 1195–1197
Black Shirts, 1107
Blake, William, 824
Blanc, Louis, 846, 859
Blitzkrieg, 1119
Blood, Council of, 568
Bloody Sunday massacre, 915
Blum, Léon, 1092
Boers (Afrikaners), 943, 1195–1196
Boer War, 1005
Bohemia: Thirty Years' War and, 572–573; in Habsburg Empire, 620
Bologna, Concordat of, 564–565
Bolshevik Revolution, 1020–1022
Bonaparte, Louis Napoleon. *See* Napoleon III
Bonaparte, Napoleon. *See* Napoleon I
Book of Various Experiences (Polo), 554
Books, in Mughal Empire, 731–732
Borla, 558
Bossuet (Bo-su-ay), Jacques-Bénigne, 593
Boston Tea Party, 776
Bourbons: succession of, 564 (chart); restoration of, 798
Bourgeoisie: French Revolution and, 780–781; Marxian socialism and, 847–848
Bourse, 553
Boxer Rebellion, 957
Boyars, 628
Brahe (Bray'-e), Tycho, 646
Brain drain, 1244, 1246
Brandenburg, in Habsburg Empire, 622, 623
Brassey, Thomas, 818
Brazil, 1260; Portuguese government of, 560; slave trade and, 717–720; quest for independence, 970; foreign investment in, 972, 975; economic nationalism in, 1155, 1157; democracy in, 1158, 1159–1160
Brazza, Pierre de, 944
Breast-feeding, in 19th-century European cities, 889
Brest-Litovsk, Treaty of, 1023, 1026
Bretton Woods Agreement, 1217
Brezhnev, Leonid, 1147–1148
Brezhnev Doctrine, 1148

Kornilov, Lavr, 1022
Kossuth, Louis, 860
Kubitschek, 1157
Kulaks, 1102
Kulturkampf, 916–917
Kun, Béla, 1097
Kuomintang, 1055
Kuprili, Muhammad, 727

Labouchère (Lab-u-sher'), Henri, 951
Labour party (England), 1085–1086, 1137, 1141
Lafayette, marquis de, 777, 779, 783, 785
Laissez-faire doctrine, 843
Lake Shore Apartments, 1077
Lamarck, Jean Baptiste, 893
Lamartine, Alphonse de, 850, 859, 900, 902
Landownership: in Middle Ages, 617; in 18th-century
    Europe, 678; in feudal Japan, 760; French Revolution
    and, 786; Agricultural Revolution and, 807; in Latin
    America, 972–973
Languages: French, 594; of Eastern Orthodox Church, 626;
    of Egypt, 937; in Turkey, 1045
Laos, independence of, 1178
Lao T'ai T'ai (Low' Tie' Tie'), 1058–1059
La Plata, 560
La Salle, 596
Las Casas, Bartolomé de, 559, 580
Lateran Agreement, 1108
Latifundia, 973
Latin America: independence in, 957, 968 (map), 959–972;
    in 19th century, 962–963, 964 (map), 965–976; origins
    of revolutions in, 962–963, 965; race in colonial period
    and, 965–966; Comunero Revolution in, 966–967;
    neocolonialism in, 972–974; from 1760–1900, 974
    (chart); impact of immigration on, 974–976;
    nationalism in, 1154–1157; authoritarianism and
    democracy in, 1158–1160; migration in, 1243–1244;
    powers in, 1260
Laud, William, 604–605
Lausanne, Treaty of, 1043
Law: under Catherine the Great, 667; Islamic, 733; Bushido,
    759, 762; of Qur'an, 1277
Law of the Sea, 1268
Lawrence, T. E. (Lawrence of Arabia), 1012, 1042
League of Armed Neutrality, 778
League of Augsburg, 598
League of Nations, 1026, 1029, 1039–1040; Wilson's at-
    tempt to create, 1028; creation of, 1031; French attack
    on Syria and, 1043; German entrance into, 1084; Ger-
    man withdrawal from, 1116
Learning. See Education
Ledru-Rollin, Alexandre-Auguste, 859
Lee, Robert E., 985
Legazpi, Miguel Lopez de, 561
Legislative Assembly (France), 788
Lélia (Sand), 851
Lenin: Bolshevik Revolution and, 1020–1026; influence on
    Asia, 1040, 1041, 1055, 1057; modern totalitarianism
    and, 1098–1102, 1106, 1273

Leo XIII, pope, 919
Leopold I, Holy Roman emperor, 636
Leopold II, Holy Roman emperor, 671
Leopold II, king of Belgium, 944
Lerma, duke of, 600
Lescot, Pierre, 564
Les fauves, 1078
Lespinasse, Julie de, 663
Le Vau, Louis, 594
Lewis, C. S., 1075
Liberalism, 1273; roots of, 773–774; attraction of, 774;
    Metternich's hatred of, 841; early socialism and, 843–
    844; totalitarianism and, 1098
Liberal party (England), 1086
Liberty: concept of, 772–774; American, 778
Liberty Leading the People (Delacroix), 851
Liebenfels, Lanz von, 1109
Liebknecht (Lep'-knekt), Karl, 1027
Lincoln, Abraham, 907, 977, 983–985
Lin Tse-hsü, 935
List, Friedrich, 822, 914, 940
Lister, Joseph, 872
Liszt, Franz, 852
Literacy: in 18th-century Europe, 693; Chinese, in Ming and
    Ch'ing dynasties, 756
Literature: Elizabethan and Jacobean, 583–585; of Mughal
    Empire, 731–732; Chinese, in Ch'ing Dynasty, 754;
    romantic, 850–851; realism in, 894–896; of 20th cen-
    tury, 1075–1076; de-Stalinization and, 1146
Little Entente, 1082
Liu Chin, 748
Liu Pang (Lie-u Pang), 744
Living standard. See Standard of living
Livingston, Robert, 977
Lloyd George, David, 920, 1005, 1014, 1028–1029
Locke, John, 607–608, 655–656, 661, 774
Lodge, Henry Cabot, 1029
Logical empiricism, 1073
London Daily Mail, 1006
London Foundling Hospital, 691
Long March, 1064
Long Parliament, 605
Lords, House of. See House of Lords
Louis XIII, king of France, 573, 591, 592, 593
Louis XIV (the Sun King): reign of, 592–599, 609, 636, 736;
    religion and, 606, 607; absolutism and, 611, 620–624,
    634, 668, 669; Enlightenment and, 654–656
Louis XV, king of France, 668–670, 703, 779–780
Louis XVI, king of France, 670, 781–783, 785, 787–788
Louis XVIII, king of France, 798–799, 838, 839, 856–857
Louisiana Purchase, 977
Louis Napoleon. See Napoleon III
Louis Philippe, king of France, 857, 858, 901
Low Countries. See Belgium; Netherlands
Loyalists (Canada), 993
Loyalists (colonial North America), 777
Loyola, Ignatius, 568
Lucknow Pact, 1049
Luddites, 824

Osman, Anatolian ruler, 723
O'Sullivan, John Louis, 845, 977
Othello (Shakespeare), 583–584
Ottoman Empire: French invasion of, 936; World War I and, 1002; nationalism and, 1006–1007; smashed by Britain, 1012; breakup of, 1029; Arab revolt and, 1041–1043
Ottoman Turks: Austria and, 619–621; kingdoms from 1450–1800, 710; in Ethiopia, 715; empire of, 723–727, 725 (map)
Oviedo (O-vya-tho), Gonzalo Fernández de, 554
Owen, Robert, 828, 925

Pacification, 568
Pahlavi, Muhammad Reza (Pah'-lah-vee, Mu-ham'-mad Rayza), 1182
Paine, Thomas, 776–777, 787, 965
Pakistan, 1172–1173; nuclear weapons and, 1262
Palaces, baroque, 636–637
Palacky, Francis, 845, 860
Palestine: Jewish homeland in, 1042, 1048–1049, 1179; independence of, 1178–1179
Palestine Liberation Organization, 1180
Palmerston, Lord, 864
Panama Canal, 932; United States' control of, 948
Panipat, Battle of, 734
Pankhurst, Emmeline, 916
Papacy: Concordat of Bologna and, 564–565; rule of central Italy and Rome, 903; opposition to unification of Italy, 904
Papen, Franz von, 1112
Paris: Treaty of, 736, 778, 811, 993; Peace of, 838, 839; rebuilding of, 873, 875
Paris Commune, 918, 923
Paris Peace Conference, 1043
Parlement of Paris: absolutism and, 668–670; French Revolution and, 780–782
Parliament (Canada), 994
Parliament (England), 605, 607–609; Long, 605; development of, 605, 607–609; American representation in, 775; British rule of India and, 953; Canadian administration and, 993. *See also* House of Commons (England); House of Lords (England)
Parliament (France): creation of, 856; Communists in, 1092
Parliament (North German Confederation), 909–911
Party Congress (Russia), 1102
Pashas, 726
Pass laws, 1195, 1197
Pasternak, Boris, 1146
Pasteur, Louis, 871–872, 892
Pasteurization, 872
Peace of Augsburg, 571–572
Pearl harbor, Japanese attack on, 1119–1120
Peasants: in eastern Europe, 616–619; building of St. Petersburg and, 638–639; in Habsburg Empire, 670–671; in 18th-century Europe, 680–681; Chinese, under Hung Wu, 746, 747; Japanese, under Tokugawa Shogunate, 764–766; Irish, around 1800, 828; in Austrian Empire, 860; Egyptian, 937; Russian, revolu-

tion of, 1022–1023; Chinese, 1057–1058, 1062, 1167; Russian, 1102–1103; technology and, 1210
Pedro I, king of Portugal, 970
Pedro II, king of Portugal, 970
Peel, Robert, 856
Peking, 749
Peninsulares, 962, 963, 965, 967
Penn, William, 606
People, The (Michelet), 844
People's Budget (England), 920, 921, 1005
People's Charter, 856
People's Republic of China, 1164. *See also* China
Père Goriot (Balzac), 894
Pereire, Emile, 822
Pereire, Isaac, 822
Pericles (Shakespeare), 583
Pèrier (Par-ya), Casimir, 857
Permanent Mandates Commission, 1039–1040
Perón, Juan, 1158
Perry, Matthew, 935–936
Perry, Oliver Hazard, 954
Persian Empire: Safavid, 727–728; imperialism in, 1046
Persian Letters, The (Montesquieu), 656
Peru: under Spanish rule, 560; silver from, 600; agriculture in, 963; Comunero Revolution in, 966–967; foreign investment in, 975–976
Pétain (Pay'-tan), Henri-Philippe, 1119, 1130
Peter I (the Great), tsar of Russia, 1045, 1104; palace of, 594; as absolutist monarch, 626; reforms of, 631–634; growth of St. Petersburg and, 637–639; hereditary succession and, 666
Peter III, tsar of Russia, 665, 666
Petrograd Soviet, 1020, 1022
Pharmacists, in 18th-century Europe, 698
Philip II, Holy Roman Emperor, 563, 568–571, 572
Philip II, king of Spain, 560, 568, 600, 609
Philip III, king of Spain, 600
Philip IV, king of Spain, 600, 602
Philip V (of Anjou), king of Spain, 598
Philippines: nationalism in, 1064–1066; independence of, 1177–1178
Philosophes, 656–660
Philosophical Dictionary (Voltaire), 658
Philosophy, modern, 1073–1074
Physicians, in 18th-century Europe, 698
Physics: Newtonian, 649; modern, 1071–1073
Picasso, Pablo, 1078, 1079
Piccolomini, Aeneas Silvius (Pius II), 723
Pickford, Mary, 1079
Pietism, 883
Pillnitz, Declaration of, 787
Pilsudski, Joseph, 1097–1098
Pinel, Philippe, 699–700
Pissarro, Camille, 1077
Pitt, William, 811
Pius II, pope, 723
Pius IV, pope, 577
Pius VII, pope, 794
Pius IX, pope, 904, 916

Pizarro, Francisco, 553, 557, 558, 559

Plague. *See* Black Death

Plain, in French National Convention, 788–789

Planck, Max, 1072, 1075

Plessis, Armand Jean du. *See* Richelieu, cardinal

Poetry, romantic, 850–851

Poincaré (Pwan-ca-re'), Raymond, 1082, 1083, 1084, 1085

Poitiers, Diana de, 564

Poland: partitioning of, 668, 669 (map); authoritarianism in, 1097–1098; rebellion of, 1147; revival of Christianity in, 1276

Police: secret, Chinese, 748; in Stalinist Russia, 1103

Politics, international, 1256–1264

Politiques, 567

Polk, James Knox, 979

Pollution, global, 1265

Polo, Marco, 554

Popes. *See* Papacy; specific pope

Popular Front, 1092

Population: of Americas, Spanish conquests and, 558–559; Spanish, 560; in 18th-century Europe, 681–684; Chinese, about 1550, 745–746; Chinese, in Ch'ing Dynasty, 754; Chinese, in 18th and 19th centuries, 767; of North America, 812; Industrial Revolution and, 829; of Ireland, 829–830; Malthus's treatise on, 843; great migration and, 938–942; in Third World, 1229–1230; world resources and, 1265

Population Bomb, The (Ehrlich), 1235

Portugal: imperialism of, 550–551; colonial administration of, 560; trade of, 561; in Africa, 715, 716; slave trade and, 717–720; authoritarianism in, 1098

Post-Impressionism, 1077–1078

Potato famine, in Ireland, 828–832

Potsdam Conference, 1132

Poverty, in Third World, 1228. *See also* Income; Standard of living

Pragmatic Sanction, 620, 664

Pragmatic Sanction of Bourges, 564

Prague, defenestration of, 572

Premarital sex: in 18th-century Europe, 687–688; in 19th-century European cities, 884–885; slavery and, 986

Presbyterian Church, Laud's attempt to impose prayer book on, 605

Prester John, 550

Priestley, Joseph, 787

Priests. *See* Clergy; Monks; Papacy

Prokofiev (Pro-kof'-yef), Sergei, 1144

Propaganda: World War I and, 1017; Russian, 1104; under Hitler, 1112–1113

Prostitution, in 19th-century European cities, 885–886

Protectorate, of Cromwell, 605

Protestantism: in France, 566; in Netherlands, 568–570; Thirty Years' War and, 571–576, 575 (map); in England, 604; required, for English monarch, 607; 18th-century revival of, 704–706; liberalism and, 773–774; Irish, 921

Protestant Union, 572

Proudhon (Pru-don'), Pierre Joseph, 846

Prussia: in 17th century, 621–623, 622 (map); absolutism consolidated in, 623–625; defense against Maria There-

sa, 664–666; education in, 693; in Austro-French war, 787–788; Napoleon's defeat of, 796; Congress of Vienna and, 838–839; in Holy Alliance, 840; Frankfurt Assembly and, 862–864; in 1859, 907; in Austro-Prussian War of 1866, 909, 910 (map); in Franco-Prussian War of 1870–1871, 911–912

Psychology, modern, 1073

Ptolemy, Claudius, 645

Public health movement, 871

Pugachev, Emelian, 667–668

Puritans, 570, 604

Pushkin, Alexander, 851

Putting-out system: in 18th-century Europe, 684–685; expansion of, 812–813

Pyrenees, Treaty of, 601

Quadruple Alliance, 798, 836, 838, 839, 840

Quebec, division of, 993

Quebec Act, 993

Quinto, 560

Qutb-ud-din (Kut-bud-den'), sultan of Delhi, 728

Racism: American, origins of, 581–582; imperialism and, 949, 951, 954; in American colonies, 965–966; in Latin America, 971, 976; Nazism and, 1109–1110; civil rights movement and, 1151–1152

Radar, 1203

Radical party (France), 1092

Radio, 1081, 1246

Radio telescope, 1205

Raft of the Medusa, The (Géricault), 849

Railroads: development in England, 817–818; in Russia, 913, 914; trade and world economy and, 932; in United States, 987; in Canada, 994; in Africa, 1184

Rakoczy (Ra-kot'-see), Francis, prince of Hungary, 621

Rasputin, Grigori, 1019

Rastrelli, Bartolomeo, 639

Rathenau (Ra'-te-nau), Walter, 1014

Rat, Black Death and, 683

Razin, Stenka, 631, 668

Reagan, Ronald, 1154, 1160, 1221, 1270

Realist movement, literature and, 894–896

Reconstruction, following American Civil War, 985–986

Recreation: Chinese, in Ming and Ch'ing dynasties, 758; of working classes, 883; technology and, 1211

Red Army, Russian, 1025

Red Fort, 732

Red Guards, 1167

Red Shirts, 906

Red Turbans, 744

Reflections on the Revolution in France (Burke), 787

Reforestation, in China, 745

Reformation: Protestant, 702; in France, 566

Reform Bill of 1832, 856

Reichstag, under Hitler, 1113

Reign of Terror, 790, 791, 844

Religion: Dutch toleration and, 609–610; science and, 652–653; Enlightenment and, 655; in 18th-century Europe, 701–706; of Mughal Empire, 729–730, 733; syncretic,

730; in Ming and Ch'ing China, 758–759; of working classes, 883–884; in India, 1172–1173, 1176–1177; in global thought, 1275–1277. *See also* Christianity; Clergy; Protestantism; Roman Catholic Church; specific religion

Remarque (Re-mark'), Erich Maria, 1010–1011

Renaissance, in France, 564

Renoir, Pierre Auguste, 1077

Repartimiento, 966, 967

Repatriation, of immigrants, 940–941

Report on the Affairs of British North America (Durham), 993

Republicans, French, 788–789

Resources, global interdependence and, 1264–1266

Restitution, Edict of, 573

Return of the Native, The (Hardy), 895

Revel, Jean François, 1273

Revisionism, 925

Revolutionary era, Western, 772–779; liberty and equality and, 772–774; American Revolution and, 774–779; French Revolution and, 779–786, 792 (chart) ; world war and republican France, 787–793; Napoleonic era and, 793–799, 796 (chart), 797; of 1848, prelude to, 855 (chart); of 1848, 857–864

Reza (Ray'-za) Shah, 1046, 1182

Ricardo, David, 843, 848

Ricci, Matteo, 751, 758

Rice: Chinese economy and, 744; miracle, 1235–1236

Richard II (Shakespeare), 583

Richard III (Shakespeare), 583

Richelieu (Re-shel-yu'), cardinal, 573, 574, 591–593, 597

Riefenstahl, Leni, 1081

Riis, Jacob, 990–991

Rio de Janiero, 974, 1240

Rio de la Plata, 963

Rite of Spring, The (Stravinsky), 1079

Rites Controversy, 758–759

Roads: in United States, 1151; in Africa, 1184

Roberts, Robert, 1016

Robespierre (Robes'-pi-ehr), Maximilien, 787, 788, 789, 791, 799

Robot (unpaid labor), 620

Rockefeller, John D., 988, 989, 1271

Roe, Sir Thomas, 734

Rogers, Ginger, 1080

Roman Catholic Church: French Calvinist conflict with, 566–567; English, attempt to restore, 570; Thirty Years' War and, 571–576, 575 (map); support by James I and Charles I, 604–605; English fear of restoration of, 605, 606–607; hostility toward science, 653; schools associated with, 693; 18th-century piety of, 703–704; missionaries of, in China, 758–759; missionaries of, in Japan, 764; conflict with French government, 786; French, under Napoleon, 794; Bismarck's attack on, 916–917; Irish, 921; in Canada, 993

Romantic movement, 848–853

Rome, Treaty of, 1140

Rome-Berlin Axis, 1118

Rommel, Erwin, 1128–1130

Roosevelt, Franklin Delano, 1151, 1257; Good Neighbor Policy of, 996; fireside chats, 1081; Great Depression and, 1089–1091; New Deal under, 1089–1091, 1092; in World War II, 1126, 1127; origins of Cold War and, 1131–1132; at Yalta, 1144; development of atomic bomb and, 1205

Rosas, Juan Manuel de, 971

Rotten boroughs, 856

Rousseau (Ru-so'), Jean-Jacques, 661, 693, 848, 850, 965, 1274

Roux (Ru), Jacques, 789

Rowlatt Acts, 1050

Royal African Company, 581

Royal Society of London, 650

Rubens, Peter Paul, 634, 635

Ruhr, occupation of, 1082–1084

Ruirik, Slavic chieftain, 626, 628

Rumanians, 860

Russia: development of, 625–634, 627 (map); Vikings and Kievan principality, 626, 628; Mongols and rise of Moscow, 628–629; tsar and people to 1689, 629–631; reforms of Peter the Great, 631–634; Catherine as empress of, 666–668; imperialism of, 668, 669 (map); Napoleon's defeat of, 796; Napoleon's invasion of, 798; Congress of Vienna and, 838–839; in Holy Alliance, 840; reforms in, 912–913; modernization of, 912–916; imperialism of, 913, 946; industrialization of, 913–915; revolution of 1905 in, 915–916; Jewish migration from, 941; World War I and, 1002; French support of, 1003, 1005; declaration of war with Austria and Germany, 1008; in World War I, 1011; totalitarianism in, 1099; under Stalin, 1099–1106; German attack on, 1119; following World War II, 1127; German offensive against, 1127–1128; in World War II, 1131

Russian-German Reinsurance Treaty, 1003

Russian Revolution, 1018–1026, 1024 (chart); fall of imperial Russia and, 1018–1020; provisional government and, 1020; Lenin and Bolshevik Revolution, 1020–1022; Trotsky and seizure of power, 1022; dictatorship and civil war, 1022–1026; women's rights and, 1105

Rutherford, Ernest, 1072, 1205

Sadat, Anwar, 1180, 1218

Safavid (Sah-fah-vid) Empire, 710, 727–728

Sahara, energy crisis in, 1264–1265

St. Augustine of Hippo, 577

St. Bartholomew's Day massacre, 567

St. Lawrence of the Escorial, 570; monastery of, 570

Saint-Médard, church of, 566

St. Petersburg, growth of, 637–639

Saint-Simon, Claude Henri de, 845–846, 892

Saint-Simon, Louis de Rouvroy, 594, 599, 668

St. Vincent de Paul, 691

Sait, 733

Sakharov, Andrei, 1273–1274

Sakoku, 764

Salazar, Antonio de Oliveira, 1098

Salons, of Enlightenment, 661

Samurais, 759–760, 762, 954

Unions: British, in 18th century, 828; socialism and, 924–926; in United States, 991–992, 1090; World War I and, 1015–1016

United Nations, 1256–1259; Soviet Union joins, 1131; partition of Palestine and, 1179

United Provinces of the Netherlands, 569–570, 570 (map), 576, 609–610

United States: Japanese isolation and, 935–936; European migrants and, 940; conquest of Philippines, 946; westward expansion and civil war in, 976, 983–986; in 19th century, 976–977, 978 (map), 979–992; manifest destiny and, 977, 979; fate of Indians in, 979–980, 981 (map); slavery in, 980, 982–985, 984 (map); black family in, 986–987; industrialization and immigration in, 987–992; entry into World War I, 1012; rejection of Treaty of Versailles, 1030–1031; occupation of Philippines, 1064–1066; architecture in, 1077; movie industry of, 1079; Great Depression in, 1086, 1088, 1089–1091; following World War II, 1127, 1137; cold war and, 1131–1133, 1259, 1262; postwar prosperity in, 1151; civil rights movement in, 1151–1152; Vietnam War and, 1152–1154, 1178; Japanese occupation by, 1169; Big Science in, 1205; space race and, 1206–1207

United States Magazine and Democratic Review (O'Sullivan, ed.), 977

United States Steel, 989

Universities: medieval, scientific revolution and, 650; Scottish, 815; student revolts and, 1211–1213; in Third World, 1244

University of Paris, 871

Urban VIII, pope, 649

Urbanization. *See* Cities

Ure, Andrew, 824

Utrecht, Peace of, 598, 809

Utrecht, Union of, 569, 609

Vaccines, 872

Valentino, Rudolph, 1079

Valéry, Paul, 1071

Valmy, battle of, 788

van Gogh, Vincent, 1077

Vargas, Getulio, 1155, 1157

Verdun (Vair-dun), Battle of, 1014

Versailles, Louis XIV's court at, 594

Versailles, Treaty of, 1027–1029, 1030 (map); American rejection of, 1030–1031; Germany and, 1081–1082; German army and, 1116

Versailles Peace Conference, 1039, 1055, 1186

Viceroy, 560

Vichy government, 1119

Victor Emmanuel I, king of Sardinia, 903, 906

Victor Emmanuel III, king of Italy, 1108

Victoria, queen of England, 1172

Vienna, Congress of, 836, 838–839, 903

Vietnam: Chinese domination of, 750–751; establishment of, 1141; independence of, 1178

Vietnam War, 1152–1154, 1178

Vigny (Ven-ye), Alfred de, 850

Vikings, 548–550; Kievan principality and, 626, 628

Villafranca, Peace of, 905

Vinci, Leonardo da, 564, 1078

Virocha, 558

Vitalism, 699

Voltaire (François Marie Arouet), 656–659, 661, 663, 666, 672, 965, 1202

Vondel, Joost van den, 610

Voting rights. *See* Suffrage

Voting Rights Act, 1151

Wa Benzi, 1242

Wages, iron law of, 843

Wałesa, Lech, 1276

Walpole, Sir Robert, 609

Wang Chih, 748

Wang Zhen, 750

Wan-li (Wahn-lee), emperor, 750, 751, 752, 754, 758

War and Peace (Tolstoy), 895

War Communism, 1025

Warfare: gunpowder and, 563; civil, in Netherlands, 568–569; under Louis XIV, 597–599; in 18th-century Europe, 682; in feudal Japan, 760; mobilization for, 1012, 1014; among Third World countries, 1260–1261

War of the Austrian Succession, 664, 669, 809, 811

War of the Spanish Succession, 598, 610–611, 809, 963

War of the Three Henrys, 567

War Raw Materials Board (Germany), 1014

Warsaw Pact, 1148

Washington, George, 777, 969, 977, 982

Waste Land, The (Eliot), 1075

Watergate affair, 1154

Waterloo, Battle of, 799, 839

Watson, James, 1208

Watt, James, 815–816, 823

Waugh (Wo), Evelyn, 1075

Wealth: exploration as quest for, 554–556; global inequality in, 930–931

Weapons: exploration and, 556; of American Civil War, 985; nuclear, 1131, 1205, 1261–1262, 1263 (map), 1264

Wei Chung-hsien, 748, 751–752

Weimar Republic, 1082, 1084; Hitler's denunciation of, 1110; constitution of, 1112

Wellesley, Richard, 737

Wesley, John, 692, 704–706

Wesley, Susannah, 692

West African Forest Region, 710, 711 (map)

West Germany, economy of, 1137

West Indies, Columbus's voyages to, 551

Westphalia, Peace of, 563, 574, 576, 609

Wet-nursing, in 18th-century Europe, 690, 691

What Is Property? (Proudhon), 846

What Is the Third Estate? (Sieyès), 782, 794

Whig party (England), 856

White Mountain, Battle of the, 620

Whites (Russia), 1025

Wilkinson, John, 816

William (the Silent), stadholder of the Netherlands, 570, 609

William I, king of Prussia, 907, 910, 911, 912

William II (of Orange), king of England, 568, 569, 598, 607